PISA 2009 Results: Learning to Learn

STUDENT ENGAGEMENT, STRATEGIES AND PRACTICES

(VOLUME III)

OECD

This work is published on the responsibility of the Secretary-General of the OECD. The opinions expressed and arguments employed herein do not necessarily reflect the official views of the Organisation or of the governments of its member countries.

Please cite this publication as:
OECD (2010), PISA 2009 Results: Learning to Learn – Student Engagement, Strategies and Practices (Volume III)
http://dx.doi.org/10.1787/9789264083943-en

ISBN 978-92-64-09147-4 (print)
ISBN 978-92-64-08394-3 (PDF)

The statistical data for Israel are supplied by and under the responsibility of the relevant Israeli authorities. The use of such data by the OECD is without prejudice to the status of the Golan Heights, East Jerusalem and Israeli settlements in the West Bank under the terms of international law.

Photo credits:
Getty Images © Ariel Skelley
Getty Images © Geostock
Getty Images © Jack Hollingsworth
Stocklib Image Bank © Yuri Arcurs

Corrigenda to OECD publications may be found on line at: www.oecd.org/publishing/corrigenda.
PISA™, OECD/PISA™ and the PISA logo are trademaks of the Organisation for Economic Co-operation and Development (OECD). All use of OECD trademarks is prohibited without written permission from the OECD.

Foreword

One of the ultimate goals of policy makers is to enable citizens to take advantage of a globalised world economy. This is leading them to focus on the improvement of education policies, ensuring the quality of service provision, a more equitable distribution of learning opportunities and stronger incentives for greater efficiency in schooling.

Such policies hinge on reliable information on how well education systems prepare students for life. Most countries monitor students' learning and the performance of schools. But in a global economy, the yardstick for success is no longer improvement by national standards alone, but how education systems perform internationally. The OECD has taken up that challenge by developing PISA, the Programme for International Student Assessment, which evaluates the quality, equity and efficiency of school systems in some 70 countries that, together, make up nine-tenths of the world economy. PISA represents a commitment by governments to monitor the outcomes of education systems regularly within an internationally agreed framework and it provides a basis for international collaboration in defining and implementing educational policies.

The results from the PISA 2009 assessment reveal wide differences in educational outcomes, both within and across countries. The education systems that have been able to secure strong and equitable learning outcomes, and to mobilise rapid improvements, show others what is possible to achieve. Naturally, GDP per capita influences educational success, but this only explains 6% of the differences in average student performance. The other 94% reflect the potential for public policy to make a difference. The stunning success of Shanghai-China, which tops every league table in this assessment by a clear margin, shows what can be achieved with moderate economic resources in a diverse social context. In mathematics, more than a quarter of Shanghai-China's 15-year-olds can conceptualise, generalise, and creatively use information based on their own investigations and modelling of complex problem situations. They can apply insight and understanding and develop new approaches and strategies when addressing novel situations. In the OECD area, just 3% of students reach this level of performance.

While better educational outcomes are a strong predictor of economic growth, wealth and spending on education alone are no guarantee for better educational outcomes. Overall, PISA shows that an image of a world divided neatly into rich and well-educated countries and poor and badly-educated countries is out of date.

This finding represents both a warning and an opportunity. It is a warning to advanced economies that they cannot take for granted that they will forever have "human capital" superior to that in other parts of the world. At a time of intensified global competition, they will need to work hard to maintain a knowledge and skill base that keeps up with changing demands.

PISA underlines, in particular, the need for many advanced countries to tackle educational underperformance so that as many members of their future workforces as possible are equipped with at least the baseline competencies that enable them to participate in social and economic development. Otherwise, the high social and economic cost of poor educational performance in advanced economies risks becoming a significant drag on economic development. At the same time, the findings show that poor skills are not an inevitable consequence of low national income – an important outcome for countries that need to achieve more with less.

But PISA also shows that there is no reason for despair. Countries from a variety of starting points have shown the potential to raise the quality of educational outcomes substantially. Korea's average performance was already high in 2000, but Korean policy makers were concerned that only a narrow elite achieved levels of excellence in PISA. Within less than a decade, Korea was able to double the share of students demonstrating excellence in reading literacy. A major overhaul of Poland's school system helped to dramatically reduce performance variability among schools, reduce the share of poorly performing students and raise overall performance by the equivalent of more than half a school year. Germany was jolted into action when PISA 2000 revealed a below-average performance and large social disparities in results, and has been able to make progress on both fronts. Israel, Italy and Portugal have moved closer to the OECD average and Brazil, Chile, Mexico and Turkey are among the countries with impressive gains from very low levels of performance.

But the greatest value of PISA lies in inspiring national efforts to help students to learn better, teachers to teach better, and school systems to become more effective.

A closer look at high-performing and rapidly improving education systems shows that these systems have many commonalities that transcend differences in their history, culture and economic evolution.

First, while most nations declare their commitment to education, the test comes when these commitments are weighed against others. How do they pay teachers compared to the way they pay other highly-skilled workers? How are education credentials weighed against other qualifications when people are being considered for jobs? Would you want your child to be a teacher? How much attention do the media pay to schools and schooling? Which matters more, a community's standing in the sports leagues or its standing in the student academic achievement league tables? Are parents more likely to encourage their children to study longer and harder or to spend more time with their friends or in sports activities?

In the most successful education systems, the political and social leaders have persuaded their citizens to make the choices needed to show that they value education more than other things. But placing a high value on education will get a country only so far if the teachers, parents and citizens of that country believe that only some subset of the nation's children can or need to achieve world class standards. This report shows clearly that education systems built around the belief that students have different pre-ordained professional destinies to be met with different expectations in different school types tend to be fraught with large social disparities. In contrast, the best-performing education systems embrace the diversity in students' capacities, interests and social background with individualised approaches to learning.

Second, high-performing education systems stand out with clear and ambitious standards that are shared across the system, focus on the acquisition of complex, higher-order thinking skills, and are aligned with high stakes gateways and instructional systems. In these education systems, everyone knows what is required to get a given qualification, in terms both of the content studied and the level of performance that has to be demonstrated to earn it. Students cannot go on to the next stage of their life – be it work or further education – unless they show that they are qualified to do so. They know what they have to do to realise their dream and they put in the work that is needed to achieve it.

Third, the quality of an education system cannot exceed the quality of its teachers and principals, since student learning is ultimately the product of what goes on in classrooms. Corporations, professional partnerships and national governments all know that they have to pay attention to how the pool from which they recruit is established; how they recruit; the kind of initial training their recruits receive before they present themselves for employment; how they mentor new recruits and induct them into their service; what kind of continuing training they get; how their compensation is structured; how they reward their best performers and how they improve the performance of those who are struggling; and how they provide opportunities for the best performers to acquire more status and responsibility. Many of the world's best-performing education systems have moved from bureaucratic "command and control" environments towards school systems in which the people at the frontline have much more control of the way resources are used, people are deployed, the work is organised and the way in which the work gets done. They provide considerable discretion to school heads and school faculties in determining how resources are allocated, a factor which the report shows to be closely related to school performance when combined with effective accountability systems. And they provide an environment in which teachers work together to frame what they believe to be good practice, conduct field-based research to confirm or disprove the approaches they develop, and then assess their colleagues by the degree to which they use practices proven effective in their classrooms.

Last but not least, the most impressive outcome of world-class education systems is perhaps that they deliver high-quality learning consistently across the entire education system, such that every student benefits from excellent learning opportunities. To achieve this, they invest educational resources where they can make the greatest difference, they attract the most talented teachers into the most challenging classrooms, and they establish effective spending choices that prioritise the quality of teachers.

These are, of course, not independently conceived and executed policies. They need to be aligned across all aspects of the system, they need to be coherent over sustained periods of time, and they need to be consistently implemented. The path of reform can be fraught with political and practical obstacles. Moving away from administrative and bureaucratic control toward professional norms of control can be counterproductive if a nation does not yet have teachers and schools with the capacity to implement these policies and practices. Pushing authority down to lower levels can be as problematic if there is not agreement on what the students need to know and should be able to do. Recruiting high-quality teachers is not of much use if those who are recruited are so frustrated by what they perceive to be a mindless system of initial teacher education that they will not participate in it and turn to another profession. Thus a country's success in making these transitions depends greatly on the degree to which it is successful in creating and executing plans that, at any given time, produce the maximum coherence in the system.

These are daunting challenges and thus devising effective education policies will become ever more difficult as schools need to prepare students to deal with more rapid change than ever before, for jobs that have not yet been created, to use technologies that have not yet been invented and to solve economic and social challenges that we do not yet know will arise. But those school systems that do well today, as well as those that have shown rapid improvement, demonstrate that it can be done. The world is indifferent to tradition and past reputations, unforgiving of frailty and complacency and ignorant of custom or practice. Success will go to those individuals and countries that are swift to adapt, slow to complain and open to change. The task of governments will be to ensure that countries rise to this challenge. The OECD will continue to support their efforts.

***

This report is the product of a collaborative effort between the countries participating in PISA, the experts and institutions working within the framework of the PISA Consortium, and the OECD Secretariat. The report was drafted by Andreas Schleicher, Francesca Borgonovi, Michael Davidson, Miyako Ikeda, Maciej Jakubowski, Guillermo Montt, Sophie Vayssettes and Pablo Zoido of the OECD Directorate for Education, with advice as well as analytical and editorial support from Marilyn Achiron, Simone Bloem, Marika Boiron, Henry Braun, Nihad Bunar, Niccolina Clements, Jude Cosgrove, John Cresswell, Aletta Grisay, Donald Hirsch, David Kaplan, Henry Levin, Juliette Mendelovitz, Christian Monseur, Soojin Park, Pasi Reinikainen, Mebrak Tareke, Elisabeth Villoutreix and Allan Wigfield. Volume II also draws on the analytic work undertaken by Jaap Scheerens and Douglas Willms in the context of PISA 2000. Administrative support was provided by Juliet Evans and Diana Morales.

The PISA assessment instruments and the data underlying the report were prepared by the PISA Consortium, under the direction of Raymond Adams at the Australian Council for Educational Research (ACER) and Henk Moelands from the Dutch National Institute for Educational Measurement (CITO). The expert group that guided the preparation of the reading assessment framework and instruments was chaired by Irwin Kirsch.

The development of the report was steered by the PISA Governing Board, which is chaired by Lorna Bertrand (United Kingdom), with Beno Csapo (Hungary), Daniel McGrath (United States) and Ryo Watanabe (Japan) as vice chairs. Annex C of the volumes lists the members of the various PISA bodies, as well as the individual experts and consultants who have contributed to this report and to PISA in general.

Angel Gurría
OECD Secretary-General

Table of Contents

This book has...

StatLinkS

**A service that delivers Excel® files
from the printed page!**

Look for the *StatLinks* at the bottom left-hand corner of the tables or graphs in this book.
To download the matching Excel® spreadsheet, just type the link into your Internet browser,
starting with the ***http://dx.doi.org*** prefix.
If you're reading the PDF e-book edition, and your PC is connected to the Internet, simply
click on the link. You'll find *StatLinks* appearing in more OECD books.

BOXES

FIGURES

TABLES

Executive Summary

PISA results show that mastering strategies that assist learning, such as methods to remember and understand or summarise texts and reading widely, are essential if students are to become proficient readers. Practicing reading by reading for enjoyment is most closely associated with better outcomes when it is accompanied by high levels of critical thinking and strategic learning. Across OECD countries, students who have low levels of awareness about which strategies are most effective for understanding, remembering and summarising information are less proficient readers than those who have high levels of awareness about these strategies, regardless of their reading habits.

In all countries, students who enjoy reading the most perform significantly better than students who enjoy reading the least. There has been considerable debate as to what type of reading may be most effective in fostering reading skills and improving reading performance. The results from PISA suggest that, although students who read fiction are more likely to achieve high scores, it is students who read a wide variety of material who perform particularly well in reading. Compared with not reading for enjoyment at all, reading fiction for enjoyment appears to be positively associated with higher scores in the PISA 2009 reading assessment, while reading comic books is associated with little improvement in reading proficiency in some countries, and with lower overall reading performance in other countries. Also, students who are extensively engaged in online reading activities, such as reading e-mails, chatting on line, reading news online, using an on line dictionary or encyclopaedia, participating in online group discussions and searching for information online, are generally more proficient readers than students who do little online reading.

On average across OECD countries, 37% of students – and 45% or more in Austria, the Netherlands, and Luxembourg – report that they do not read for enjoyment at all.
In all but a few countries, students who use appropriate strategies to understand and remember what they read, such as underlining important parts of the texts or discussing what they read with other people, perform at least 73 points higher in the PISA assessment – that is, one full proficiency level or nearly two full school years – than students who use these strategies the least. In Belgium, Switzerland and Austria, the quarter of students who use these strategies the most score an average of 110 points higher than the quarter of students who use them the least. That translates into a difference of roughly one-and-a-half proficiency levels or nearly three years of formal schooling.

In all countries, boys are not only less likely than girls to say that they read for enjoyment, they also have different reading habits when they do read for pleasure.
Most boys and girls in the countries that took part in PISA 2009 sit side by side in the same classrooms and work with similar teachers. Yet, PISA reveals that in OECD countries, boys are on average 39 points behind girls in reading, the equivalent of an average year of schooling. PISA suggests that differences in how boys and girls approach learning and how engaged they are in reading account for most of the gap in reading performance between boys and girls, so much so that this gap could be predicted to shrink by 14 points if boys approached learning as positively as girls, and by over 20 points if they were as engaged in reading as girls. This does not mean that if boys' engagement and awareness of learning strategies rose by this amount, the increase would automatically translate into respective performance gains, since PISA does not measure causation. But the fact that most of the gender gap can be explained by boys being less engaged, and less engaged students having lower performance, is a good reason to look hard for more effective ways of increasing boys' interest in reading at school or at home.

PISA reveals that, although girls have higher mean reading performance, enjoy reading more and are more aware of effective strategies to summarise information than boys, the differences within genders are far greater than those between the genders. Moreover, the size of the gender gap varies considerably across countries, suggesting that boys and girls do not have inherently different interests and academic strengths, but that these are mostly acquired and socially induced. The large gender gap in reading is not a mystery: it can be attributed to differences that have been identified in the attitudes and behaviours of boys and girls.

Girls are more likely than boys to be frequent readers of fiction, and are also more likely than boys to read magazines. However, over 65% of boys regularly read newspapers for enjoyment and only 59% of girls do so. Although relatively few students say that they read comic books regularly, on average across OECD countries, 27% of boys read comic books several times a month or several times a week, while only 18% of girls do so.

High-performing countries are also those whose students generally know how to summarise information.
Across OECD countries, the difference in reading performance between those students who know the most about which strategies are best for summarising information and those who know the least is 107 score points. And students who say that they begin the learning process by figuring out what they need to learn, then ensure that they understand what they read, figure out which concepts they have not fully grasped, try to remember the most important points in a text and look for additional clarifying information when they do not understand something they have read, tend to perform better on the PISA reading scale than those who do not.

While factors such as predisposition, temperament, peer pressure and socialisation may contribute to boys having less interest in reading than girls, boys could be encouraged to enjoy reading more and to read more for enjoyment.
PISA results suggest that boys would be predicted to catch up with girls in reading performance if they had higher levels of motivation to read and used effective learning strategies. In Finland, for example, if boys were equally aware as girls of the most effective ways of summarising complex information in their reading, their scores in the PISA assessment would be predicted to be 23 points higher. Similarly, in most of the countries that participated in PISA 2009, if the most socio-economically disadvantaged students had the same levels of awareness about these strategies as their most advantaged peers, their reading performance would be predicted to be at least 15 points higher.

Across OECD countries, if socio-economically disadvantaged students were as aware of effective strategies to summarise information as advantaged students, the performance gap between the two groups of students could be 20% narrower. The poor reading proficiency seen among socio-economically disadvantaged boys is of particular concern because, without the ability to read well enough to participate fully in society, these students and their future families will have fewer opportunities to escape a cycle of poverty and deprivation. On average in the OECD area, socio-economically disadvantaged boys would be predicted to perform 28 points higher in reading if they had the same level of awareness of effective summarising strategies as socio-economically advantaged girls and 35 points higher if they enjoyed reading as much as socio-economically advantaged girls.

In recent years, the gender gap in reading engagement has widened, as well as the gender gap in reading performance.
Changing students' attitudes and behaviours may be inherently more difficult than providing equal access to high quality teachers and schools, two of the factors that explain the low performance of socio-economically disadvantaged students – an area where PISA shows that over the past decade, some countries have achieved significant progress.

The following table provides selected results from the volume.

- The first column shows students' mean reading scores.
- The second column shows the percentage of students who reported high levels of awareness about effective learning strategies and who regularly read a wide range of materials, including fiction and non-fiction books or at least magazines and newspapers, for enjoyment (considered 'wide and deep' or 'narrow and deep' readers).
- The third column shows the score point differences in reading between boys and girls, with negative numbers indicating an advantage for boys and positive numbers indicating an advantage for girls.
- The fourth column shows gender differences in the percentage of 'wide and deep' or 'narrow and deep' readers.
- The fifth column shows the portion of the gender gap that would be predicted to be closed if boys had the same level of enjoyment of reading as girls.
- The sixth column shows the score point difference between the top and bottom quarters of the socio-economic distribution of students.

- The seventh column shows the differences in the share of students who are 'wide and deep' or 'narrow and deep' readers between the top and bottom quarters of the socio-economic distribution of students. Larger numbers indicate a higher share of 'wide and deep' or 'narrow and deep' readers among socio-economically advantaged students.

- The last column shows the portion of the socio-economic gap in reading performance that would be predicted to be closed if socio-economically disadvantaged students had the same level of awareness of effective reading strategies (here, summarising strategies) as socio-economically advantaged students.

Values that are larger than the OECD average are shown in light blue; while values that are smaller than the OECD average are shown in medium blue and values that are not statistically different from the OECD average are shown in dark blue.

■ Table III.A ■

COMPARING THE CONTRIBUTION OF STUDENTS' ENGAGEMENT IN READING AND APPROACHES TO LEARNING TO READING PERFORMANCE AND EQUITY

Statistically significantly **above** the OECD average
Not statistically significantly different from the OECD average
Statistically significantly **below** the OECD average

	Mean Reading Score	Percentage of "wide and deep" and "narrow and deep readers"	Difference in reading performance (G – B)	Difference in the percentage of girls and boys that can be considered "wide and deep" and "narrow and deep" readers (G – B)	Proportion of the overall gender gap that could be closed if boys enjoyed reading as much as girls	Socio-economic differences in reading performance (top – bottom quarter of ESCS)	Socio-economic differences in the percentage of students that are "wide and deep" and "narrow and deep" (top – bottom quarter of ESCS)	Proportion of the socio-economic gap that could be closed if socio-economically disadvantaged students had values on the index of summarising as socio-economically advantaged students
	Mean Score	%	Dif.	Dif.	%	Dif.	Dif.	%
OECD average	493	45	39	11	61	89	17	20
OECD								
Korea	539	35	35	5	30	70	32	27
Finland	536	60	55	20	64	62	17	27
Canada	524	37	34	14	86	68	15	13
New Zealand	521	37	46	11	63	102	14	20
Japan	520	54	39	6	33	73	18	25
Australia	515	35	37	9	76	91	16	22
Netherlands	508	34	24	9	102	83	23	23
Belgium	506	46	27	3	81	116	23	27
Norway	503	56	47	14	52	70	17	22
Estonia	501	61	44	14	65	60	12	17
Switzerland	501	54	39	11	76	94	22	24
Poland	500	50	50	20	49	88	17	20
Iceland	500	49	44	20	58	62	12	18
United States	500	30	25	7	95	105	12	14
Sweden	497	43	46	16	68	91	19	18
Germany	497	41	40	0	80	105	21	23
Ireland	496	45	39	14	48	86	5	15
France	496	46	40	1	54	110	20	21
Denmark	495	48	29	8	75	80	21	20
United Kingdom	494	40	25	10	90	91	11	19
Hungary	494	52	38	15	65	118	20	20
Portugal	489	43	38	9	61	87	17	24
Italy	486	39	46	7	56	85	15	20
Slovenia	483	45	55	16	42	87	15	20
Greece	483	34	47	1	54	90	18	13
Spain	481	38	29	6	73	83	22	15
Czech Republic	478	47	48	14	59	84	12	23
Slovak Republic	477	52	51	16	35	87	13	18
Israel	474	36	42	17	44	102	14	19
Luxembourg	472	50	39	8	70	114	16	19
Austria	470	50	41	10	70	102	20	23
Turkey	464	38	43	12	25	92	16	11
Chile	449	37	22	17	57	91	19	15
Mexico	425	36	25	6	27	82	16	17
Partners								
Shanghai-China	556	59	40	5	31	74	21	11
Hong Kong-China	533	41	33	7	44	46	15	14
Singapore	526	59	31	11	81	98	19	17
Liechtenstein	499	49	32	14	76	62	25	34
Chinese Taipei	495	44	37	6	53	76	24	17
Macao-China	487	44	34	11	38	25	18	23
Latvia	484	45	47	20	52	63	16	19
Croatia	476	53	51	19	40	74	17	19
Lithuania	468	53	59	21	47	83	20	17
Dubai (UAE)	459	56	51	10	38	102	15	19
Russian Federation	459	46	45	16	43	78	9	16
Serbia	442	43	39	16	37	67	18	24
Bulgaria	429	42	61	20	27	132	22	16
Uruguay	426	35	42	15	30	116	15	20
Romania	424	44	43	13	23	85	16	17
Thailand	421	40	38	12	22	63	15	8
Trinidad and Tobago	416	49	58	19	26	92	10	19
Colombia	413	46	9	10	41	89	12	19
Brazil	412	37	29	14	34	83	13	16
Montenegro	408	42	53	8	30	80	18	15
Jordan	405	34	57	14	12	66	12	9
Tunisia	404	45	31	11	0	63	12	4
Indonesia	402	43	37	11	8	45	18	13
Argentina	398	40	37	14	24	122	15	15
Kazakhstan	390	46	43	13	-1	84	12	12
Albania	385	50	62	17	38	77	15	10
Qatar	372	42	50	8	23	56	9	14
Panama	371	37	33	13	10	108	10	13
Peru	370	50	22	9	19	129	20	14
Azerbaijan	362	32	24	6	21	50	12	4
Kyrgyzstan	314	34	53	7	10	94	18	14

Countries are ranked by their mean reading score.
Source: OECD, *PISA 2009 Database.*
StatLink ⟐ http://dx.doi.org/10.1787/888932360309

Introduction to PISA

THE PISA SURVEYS

Are students well prepared to meet the challenges of the future? Can they analyse, reason and communicate their ideas effectively? Have they found the kinds of interests they can pursue throughout their lives as productive members of the economy and society? The OECD Programme for International Student Assessment (PISA) seeks to answer these questions through its triennial surveys of key competencies of 15-year-old students in OECD member countries and partner countries/economies. Together, the group of countries participating in PISA represents nearly 90% of the world economy.[1]

PISA assesses the extent to which students near the end of compulsory education have acquired some of the knowledge and skills that are essential for full participation in modern societies, with a focus on reading, mathematics and science.

PISA has now completed its fourth round of surveys. Following the detailed assessment of each of PISA's three main subjects – reading, mathematics and science – in 2000, 2003 and 2006, the 2009 survey marks the beginning of a new round with a return to a focus on reading, but in ways that reflect the extent to which reading has changed since 2000, including the prevalence of digital texts.

PISA 2009 offers the most comprehensive and rigorous international measurement of student reading skills to date. It assesses not only reading knowledge and skills, but also students' attitudes and their learning strategies in reading. PISA 2009 updates the assessment of student performance in mathematics and science as well.

The assessment focuses on young people's ability to use their knowledge and skills to meet real-life challenges. This orientation reflects a change in the goals and objectives of curricula themselves, which are increasingly concerned with what students can do with what they learn at school and not merely with whether they have mastered specific curricular content.

PISA's unique features include its:

- Policy orientation, which connects data on student learning outcomes with data on students' characteristics and on key factors shaping their learning in and out of school in order to draw attention to differences in performance patterns and identify the characteristics of students, schools and education systems that have high performance standards.
- Innovative concept of "literacy", which refers to the capacity of students to apply knowledge and skills in key subject areas and to analyse, reason and communicate effectively as they pose, interpret and solve problems in a variety of situations.
- Relevance to lifelong learning, which does not limit PISA to assessing students' competencies in school subjects, but also asks them to report on their own motivations to learn, their beliefs about themselves and their learning strategies.
- Regularity, which enables countries to monitor their progress in meeting key learning objectives.
- Breadth of geographical coverage and collaborative nature, which, in PISA 2009, encompasses the 34 OECD member countries and 41 partner countries and economies.[2]

The relevance of the knowledge and skills measured by PISA is confirmed by studies tracking young people in the years after they have been assessed by PISA. Longitudinal studies in Australia, Canada and Switzerland display a strong relationship between performance in reading on the PISA assessment at age 15 and future educational attainment and success in the labour market (see Volume I Chapter 2).[3]

The frameworks for assessing reading, mathematics and science in 2009 are described in detail in *PISA 2009 Assessment Framework: Key Competencies in Reading, Mathematics and Science* (OECD, 2009).

Decisions about the scope and nature of the PISA assessments and the background information to be collected are made by leading experts in participating countries. Governments guide these decisions based on shared, policy-driven interests. Considerable efforts and resources are devoted to achieving cultural and linguistic breadth and balance in the assessment materials. Stringent quality-assurance mechanisms are applied in designing the test, in translation, sampling and data collection. As a result, PISA findings are valid and highly reliable.

Policy makers around the world use PISA findings to gauge the knowledge and skills of students in their own country in comparison with those in other countries. PISA reveals what is possible in education by showing what students in the highest performing countries can do in reading, mathematics and science. PISA is also used to gauge the pace of educational progress by allowing policy makers to assess to what extent performance changes observed nationally are in line with performance changes observed elsewhere. In a growing number of countries, PISA is also used to set policy targets against measurable goals achieved by other systems, to initiate research and peer-learning designed to identify policy levers and to reform trajectories for improving education. While PISA cannot identify cause-and-effect relationships between inputs, processes and educational outcomes, it can highlight key features in which education systems are similar and different, sharing those findings with educators, policy makers and the general public.

THE FIRST REPORT FROM THE 2009 ASSESSMENT

This volume is the third of six volumes that provide the first international report on results from the PISA 2009 assessment. It explores the information gathered on students' levels of engagement in reading activities and attitudes towards reading and learning and describes 15-year-olds' motivations, engagement and learning strategies.

The other volumes cover the following issues:

- Volume I, *What Students Know and Can Do: Student Performance in Reading, Mathematics and Science*, summarises the performance of students in PISA 2009, starting with a focus on reading, and then reporting on mathematics and science performance. It provides the results in the context of how performance is defined, measured and reported, and then examines what students are able to do in reading. After a summary of reading performance, it examines the ways in which this performance varies on subscales representing three aspects of reading. It then breaks down results by different formats of reading texts and considers gender differences in reading, both generally and for different reading aspects and text formats. Any comparison of the outcomes of education systems needs to take into consideration countries' social and economic circumstances and the resources they devote to education. To address this, the volume also interprets the results within countries' economic and social contexts. The chapter concludes with a description of student results in mathematics and science.

- Volume II, *Overcoming Social Background: Equity in Learning Opportunities and Outcomes,* starts by closely examining the performance variation shown in Volume I, particularly the extent to which the overall variation in student performance relates to differences in results achieved by different schools. The volume then looks at how factors such as socio-economic background and immigrant status affect student and school performance, and the role that education policy can play in moderating the impact of these factors.

- Volume IV, *What Makes a School Successful? Resources, Policies and Practices,* explores the relationships between student-, school- and system-level characteristics, and educational quality and equity. It explores what schools and school policies can do to raise overall student performance and, at the same time, moderate the impact of socio-economic background on student performance, with the aim of promoting a more equitable distribution of learning opportunities.

- Volume V, *Learning Trends: Changes in Student Performance Since 2000,* provides an overview of trends in student performance in reading, mathematics and science from PISA 2000 to PISA 2009. It shows educational outcomes over time and tracks changes in factors related to student and school performance, such as student background and school characteristics and practices.

- Volume VI, *Students On Line: Reading and Using Digital Information* explains how PISA measures and reports student performance in digital reading and analyses what students in the 20 countries participating in this assessment are able to do.

All data tables referred to in the analysis are included at the end of the respective volume. A Reader's Guide is also provided in each volume to aid in interpreting the tables and figures accompanying the report.

Technical annexes that describe the construction of the questionnaire indices, sampling issues, quality assurance procedures and the process followed for developing the assessment instruments, and information about reliability of coding are posted on the OECD PISA website (*www.pisa.oecd.org*). Many of the issues covered in the technical annexes are elaborated in greater detail in the *PISA 2009 Technical Report* (OECD, forthcoming).

THE PISA STUDENT POPULATION

In order to ensure the comparability of results across countries, PISA devoted a great deal of attention to assessing comparable target populations. Differences between countries in the nature and extent of pre-primary education and care, in the age of entry to formal schooling, and in the structure of the education system do not allow school grade levels to be defined so that they are internationally comparable. Valid international comparisons of educational performance, therefore, need to define their populations with reference to a target age. PISA covers students who are aged between 15 years 3 months and 16 years 2 months at the time of the assessment and who have completed at least 6 years of formal schooling, regardless of the type of institution in which they are enrolled, whether they are in full-time or part-time education, whether they attend academic or vocational programmes, and whether they attend public or private schools or foreign schools within the country. (For an operational definition of this target population, see the *PISA 2009 Technical Report* [OECD, forthcoming].) The use of this age in PISA, across countries and over time, allows the performance of students to be compared in a consistent manner before they complete compulsory education.

As a result, this report can make statements about the knowledge and skills of individuals born in the same year who are still at school at 15 years of age, despite having had different educational experiences, both in and outside school.

Stringent technical standards were established to define the national target populations and to identify permissible exclusions from this definition (for more information, see the PISA website *www.pisa.oecd.org*). The overall exclusion rate within a country was required to be below 5% to ensure that, under reasonable assumptions, any distortions in national mean scores would remain within plus or minus 5 score points, i.e. typically within the order of magnitude of two standard errors of sampling (see Box I.1.2). Exclusion could take place either through schools that participated or students who participated within schools. There are several reasons why a school or a student could be excluded from PISA. Schools might be excluded because they are situated in remote regions and are inaccessible or because they are very small, or because of organisational or operational factors that precluded participation. Students might be excluded because of intellectual disability or limited proficiency in the language of the test.

In 29 out of 65 countries participating in PISA 2009, the percentage of school-level exclusions amounted to less than 1%; it was less than 5% in all countries. When the exclusion of students who met the internationally established exclusion criteria is also taken into account, the exclusion rates increase slightly. However, the overall exclusion rate remains below 2% in 32 participating countries, below 5% in 60 participating countries, and below 7% in all countries except Luxembourg (7.2%) and Denmark (8.6%). In 15 out of 34 OECD countries, the percentage of school-level exclusions amounted to less than 1% and was less than 5% in all countries. When student exclusions within schools are also taken into account, there were 9 OECD countries below 2% and 25 countries below 5%. Restrictions on the level of exclusions in PISA 2009 are described in Annex A2.

The specific sample design and size for each country aimed to maximise sampling efficiency for student-level estimates. In OECD countries, sample sizes ranged from 4 410 students in Iceland to 38 250 students in Mexico. Countries with large samples have often implemented PISA both at national and regional/state levels (*e.g.* Australia, Belgium, Canada, Italy, Mexico, Spain, Switzerland and the United Kingdom). This selection of samples was monitored internationally and adhered to rigorous standards for the participation rate, both among schools selected by the international contractor and among students within these schools, to ensure that the PISA results reflect the skills of the 15-year-old students in participating countries. Countries were also required to administer the test to students in identical ways to ensure that students receive the same information prior to and during the test (for details, see Annex A4).

Box III.A **Key features of PISA 2009**

Content

- The main focus of PISA 2009 was reading. The survey also updated performance assessments in mathematics and science. PISA considers students' knowledge in these areas not in isolation, but in relation to their ability to reflect on their knowledge and experience and to apply them to real-world issues. The emphasis is on mastering processes, understanding concepts and functioning in various contexts within each assessment area.

- For the first time, the PISA 2009 survey also assessed 15-year-old students' ability to read, understand and apply digital texts.

Methods

- Around 470 000 students completed the assessment in 2009, representing about 26 million 15-year-olds in the schools of the 65 participating countries and economies. Some 50 000 students took part in a second round of this assessment in 2010, representing about 2 million 15-year-olds from 10 additional partner countries and economies.

- Each participating student spent two hours carrying out pencil-and-paper tasks in reading, mathematics and science. In 20 countries, students were given additional questions via computer to assess their capacity to read digital texts.

- The assessment included tasks requiring students to construct their own answers as well as multiple-choice questions. The latter were typically organised in units based on a written passage or graphic, much like the kind of texts or figures that students might encounter in real life.

- Students also answered a questionnaire that took about 30 minutes to complete. This questionnaire focused on their background, learning habits, attitudes towards reading, and their involvement and motivation.

- School principals completed a questionnaire about their school that included demographic characteristics and an assessment of the quality of the learning environment at school.

Outcomes

PISA 2009 results provide:

- a profile of knowledge and skills among 15-year-olds in 2009, consisting of a detailed profile for reading and an update for mathematics and science;

- contextual indicators relating performance results to student and school characteristics;

- an assessment of students' engagement in reading activities, and their knowledge and use of different learning strategies;

- a knowledge base for policy research and analysis; and

- trend data on changes in student knowledge and skills in reading, mathematics, science, changes in student attitudes and socio-economic indicators, and in the impact of some indicators on performance results.

Future assessments

- The PISA 2012 survey will return to mathematics as the major assessment area, PISA 2015 will focus on science. Thereafter, PISA will turn to another cycle beginning with reading again.

- Future tests will place greater emphasis on assessing students' capacity to read and understand digital texts and solve problems presented in a digital format, reflecting the importance of information and computer technologies in modern societies.

■ Figure III.A ■
A map of PISA countries and economies

OECD countries

Australia	Japan
Austria	Korea
Belgium	Luxembourg
Canada	Mexico
Chile	Netherlands
Czech Republic	New Zealand
Denmark	Norway
Estonia	Poland
Finland	Portugal
France	Slovak Republic
Germany	Slovenia
Greece	Spain
Hungary	Sweden
Iceland	Switzerland
Ireland	Turkey
Israel	United Kingdom
Italy	United States

Partner countries and economies in PISA 2009

Albania	Mauritius*
Argentina	Miranda-Venezuela*
Azerbaijan	Montenegro
Brazil	Netherlands-Antilles*
Bulgaria	Panama
Colombia	Peru
Costa Rica*	Qatar
Croatia	Romania
Georgia*	Russian Federation
Himachal Pradesh-India*	Serbia
Hong Kong-China	Shanghai-China
Indonesia	Singapore
Jordan	Tamil Nadu-India*
Kazakhstan	Chinese Taipei
Kyrgyzstan	Thailand
Latvia	Trinidad and Tobago
Liechtenstein	Tunisia
Lithuania	Uruguay
Macao-China	United Arab Emirates*
Malaysia*	Viet Nam*
Malta*	

Partners countries in previous PISA surveys

Dominican Republic
Macedonia
Moldova

* These partner countries and economies carried out the assessment in 2010 instead of 2009.

Notes

1. The GDP of countries that participated in PISA 2009 represents 87% of the 2007 world GDP. Some of the entities represented in this report are referred to as partner economies. This is because they are not strictly national entities.

2. Thirty-one partner countries and economies originally participated in the PISA 2009 assessment and ten additional partner countries and economies took part in a second round of the assessment.

3. Marks, G.N (2007); Bertschy, K., M.A. Cattaneo and S.C. Wolter (2009); OECD (2010a).

Reader's Guide

Data underlying the figures

The data referred to in this volume are presented in Annex B and, in greater detail, on the PISA website (*www.pisa.oecd.org*).

Five symbols are used to denote missing data:

a   The category does not apply in the country concerned. Data are therefore missing.

c   There are too few observations or no observation to provide reliable estimates (*i.e.* there are fewer than 30 students or less than five schools with valid data).

m   Data are not available. These data were not submitted by the country or were collected but subsequently removed from the publication for technical reasons.

w   Data have been withdrawn or have not been collected at the request of the country concerned.

x   Data are included in another category or column of the table.

Country coverage

This publication features data on 65 countries and economies, including all 34 OECD countries and 31 partner countries and economies (see Figure IV.A). The data from another ten partner countries were collected one year later and will be published in 2011.

The statistical data for Israel are supplied by and under the responsibility of the relevant Israeli authorities. The use of such data by the OECD is without prejudice to the status of the Golan Heights, East Jerusalem and Israeli settlements in the West Bank under the terms of international law.

Calculating international averages

An OECD average was calculated for most indicators presented in this report. The OECD average corresponds to the arithmetic mean of the respective country estimates.

Readers should, therefore, keep in mind that the term "OECD average" refers to the OECD countries included in the respective comparisons.

Rounding figures

Because of rounding, some figures in tables may not exactly add up to the totals. Totals, differences and averages are always calculated on the basis of exact numbers and are rounded only after calculation.

All standard errors in this publication have been rounded to one or two decimal places. Where the value 0.00 is shown, this does not imply that the standard error is zero, but that it is smaller than 0.005.

Reporting student data

The report uses "15-year-olds" as shorthand for the PISA target population. PISA covers students who are aged between 15 years 3 months and 16 years 2 months at the time of assessment and who have completed at least 6 years of formal schooling, regardless of the type of institution in which they are enrolled and of whether they are in full-time or part-time education, of whether they attend academic or vocational programmes, and of whether they attend public or private schools or foreign schools within the country.

Reporting school data

The principals of the schools in which students were assessed provided information on their schools' characteristics by completing a school questionnaire. Where responses from school principals are presented in this publication, they are weighted so that they are proportionate to the number of 15-year-olds enrolled in the school.

Focusing on statistically significant differences

This volume discusses only statistically significant differences or changes. These are denoted in darker colours in figures and in bold font in tables. See Annex A3 for further information.

Abbreviations used in this report

ESCS PISA index of economic, social and cultural status

GDP Gross domestic product

ISCED International Standard Classification of Education

PPP Purchasing power parity

S.D. Standard deviation

S.E. Standard error

Further documentation

For further information on the PISA assessment instruments and the methods used in PISA, see the *PISA 2009 Technical Report* (OECD, forthcoming) and the PISA website (*www.pisa.oecd.org*).

This report uses the OECD's StatLinks service. Below each table and chart is a url leading to a corresponding Excel workbook containing the underlying data. These urls are stable and will remain unchanged over time. In addition, readers of the e-books will be able to click directly on these links and the workbook will open in a separate window, if their Internet browser is open and running.

Effective Learners, Proficient Readers

This chapter examines how engaging in reading activities and approaching learning positively relates to reading proficiency. More specifically, it looks at how much students enjoy reading, how much time they spend reading for enjoyment, and what they read for enjoyment. The chapter also examines the extent to which 15-year-olds have "learned how to learn" as indicated by their knowledge and use of specific learning strategies, such as understanding, remembering and summarising. Students' reading and learning habits are then related to their reading performance.

The ability to transmit information in written form as well as orally is one of humankind's greatest assets. Sharing information across time and space without being limited by the strength of one's voice, the size of a venue or the accuracy of memory has been fundamental to human progress. And yet, learning how to read and write requires effort, because it cannot be achieved without mastering a collection of complex skills. As Pinker notes (1995), "Children are wired for sound, but print is an optional accessory that must be painstakingly bolted on".

The brain is biologically primed to acquire language, but writing and reading are relatively recent achievements in human history. As such, exposure to written material does not automatically trigger a set of biological processes that lead to reading proficiency and writing (OECD, 2007a). Becoming a proficient reader is a goal that requires practice and dedication. More than ever, reading is key to acquiring knowledge, and mastery of reading is a precondition for individuals' success in all domains of life (for example, Cunningham and Stanovich, 1998; Smith, Mikulecky, Kibby and Dreher, 2000). The pervasiveness of information technology means that reading proficiency is becoming even more crucial. New media are continually emerging and redefining what it means to be an avid reader and how to teach and learn reading. With information overload becoming a growing problem, people must also learn how to manage a constant flow of information and identify material relevant to their needs.

Reading was the main focus of the PISA 2009 assessment. The PISA assessment was developed to accommodate a wide and deep conception of reading literacy, one that aims to encompass the range of situations in which people read, the different forms in which written text is presented, and the variety of approaches that readers bring to texts. These approaches range from the functional and finite, such as finding a particular piece of practical information, to the more expansive: reading to learn and understand other ways of doing, thinking and being (Volume I, *What Students Know and Can Do*, for a detailed description of the PISA approach to assessing student reading performance).

This chapter examines how engaging in reading activities and approaching learning relates to reading proficiency. The analyses seek to offer pointers on what parents, teachers and school administrators can do to help students become proficient and engaged readers. Figure III.1.1 and Figure III.1.2 illustrate how PISA measures reading habits and approaches to learning. Students who are highly engaged in a wide range of reading activities and who adopt particular strategies to aid them in their learning are more likely than other students to be effective learners and to perform well at school (Guthrie & Wigfield, 2000; Guthrie, Wigfield, & You, in press). Research also shows a strong link between the incidence and intensity of reading practices, reading motivation and reading proficiency among adults (OECD and Statistics Canada, 2000).

■ Figure III.1.1 ■
How does PISA define "engagement in reading activities"?

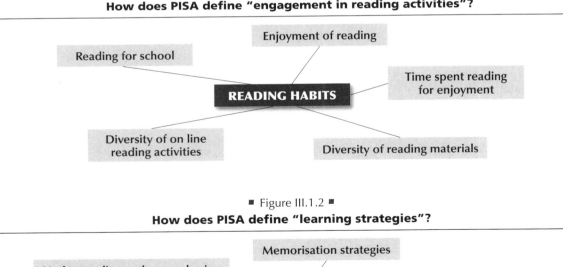

■ Figure III.1.2 ■
How does PISA define "learning strategies"?

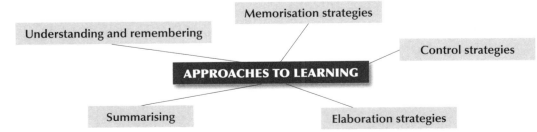

Results emerging from this volume suggest that students who read for enjoyment, who self-direct their learning (*i.e.* use control strategies) and particularly students who enjoy reading and who know what they should do when they have to understand, remember and summarise complex information, are students who perform well in the PISA reading assessment. Failure to succeed in academic work at school may result in student disaffection, low levels of practice and failure to develop effective learning strategies (OECD, 2001; Skinner *et al.,* 2009). As Box III.1.1 suggests, PISA cannot determine causal relationships among engagement in reading activities, learning strategies and reading achievement. What PISA can do, however, is indicate the cumulative strength of such relationships among students approaching the end of compulsory education.

Box III.1.1 **A cycle of engagement in reading activities, learning strategies and reading performance**

Students who are highly engaged in diverse reading activities and who are aware of what strategies work best for reading and understanding texts perform better in the PISA reading assessment. However, this finding cannot be interpreted as direct evidence of a causal relationship between being engaged in reading, adopting effective learning strategies and achieving high levels of reading proficiency. Evidence presented in this chapter rather reflects the cumulative observed association between how engaged students are, the learning strategies they adopt and how well they do.

What does cumulative association mean? Studies in education and applied psychology suggest that reading proficiency is the result of multiple developmental cumulative cycles (Aunola, et al., 2002 for a review). Attitudes towards reading and learning, motivation, engagement in reading activities and reading proficiency are mutually reinforcing. Positive reinforcement operates at two levels. The first reflects the fact that the future depends on the past. Past engagement matters for current and future engagement and past reading performance is also a very good predictor of future reading performance (Fredericks, Blumenfeld, and Paris, 2004; Stanovich, 2004). This suggests that a student's past reading activities will influence his or her future reading activities. Similarly, how effectively the student applied learning strategies in the past is one of the factors that determine how well he or she will apply learning strategies in the future.

The second level indicates that associations among engagement, learning strategies and performance are circular. Engaging in reading activities, adopting effective learning strategies and being a proficient reader are mutually dependent: as students read more they become better readers; and when they read well and expect good performance in reading, they tend to read more and enjoy reading (Nurmi, *et al.,* 2003).

The graph below illustrates how results on associations between how engaged in reading activities students are, the learning strategies they adopt and how well they read should be interpreted in the context of the two levels of reinforcement.

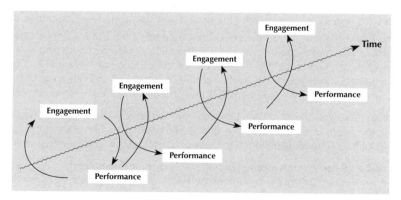

The evidence that emerges from PISA on the positive interplay between engagement in reading activities, the adoption of particular learning strategies and reading performance suggests that preparing students to read well and promoting a passion for reading and effective learning does not necessarily involve trade-offs. Students who are highly engaged and are effective learners are most likely to be proficient readers and proficient readers are also those students that are most engaged and interested in reading.

HOW PISA 2009 EXAMINES ENGAGEMENT IN READING AND APPROACHES TO LEARNING

Most children come to school willing to learn. International surveys of primary school-age children generally reveal high levels of interest in and positive attitudes towards reading, mathematics and science among these students (see Mullis et al, 2007). How can schools foster and strengthen this predisposition and ensure that young adults leave school with the motivation and capacity to continue learning throughout life? Schools can influence students' attitudes towards learning as much by fostering motivation as by imparting knowledge and skills. In fact, many adults with little interest in learning blame their lack of motivation on bad experiences at school in their early years (McKenna, Kear, Ellsworth, 1995). Motivation, engagement and the use of effective learning strategies can be regarded as important outcomes in their own right, as they can affect students' quality of life during their adolescence, and can influence their decision to pursue further education or their capacity to seize labour market opportunities.

This volume looks at how engagement in reading activities and approaches to learning relate to reading performance and analyses the degree to which engagement in reading and approaches to learning could have potential compensatory effects. The volume not only describes the strong positive link that exists between engagement in reading, approaches to learning and reading performance, but illustrates that boys and socio-economically disadvantaged students have lower levels of engagement and approach learning less effectively than girls and socio-economically advantaged students. Chapter 2 of this volume maps countries according to the extent to which their students, in general, and some groups of students in particular, are engaged in reading activities and know about and use learning strategies in their studies. By so doing, Chapter 2 identifies the relationship that 15-year-olds in participating countries and economies have with reading and learning. Chapter 3 suggests that a large part of the gap in reading performance between boys and girls and socio-economically disadvantaged and advantaged students could be closed if they had similar reading and learning habits.

Box III.1.2 **The association between reading habits, approaches to learning and reading performance**

Results presented in the chapter on the relationship between reading performance and students' reading habits and approaches to learning can be used to answer two main policy issues:

How strong is the association between reading performance and reading habits and approaches to learning? Two indicators can be used to answer this question: the slope and the inter-quartile range.

The slope represents the score point difference that is associated with a change of one unit in reading habits and approaches to learning. This indicator measures how powerful the association is.

- If this number is low, no differences are observed in the reading performance of students with different reading habits and approaches to learning. Students whose reading habits and approaches to learning are similar to those of the average student in the OECD area (index value of 0) have a reading performance that is similar to the reading performance of students who are one standard deviation above the average students in the OECD area with respect to their reading habits and approaches to learning (index value of 1).

- If this number is high and positive, large differences are observed in the reading performance of students with different reading habits and approaches to learning. Students whose reading habits and approaches to learning are similar to those of the average student in the OECD area (index value of 0) have a reading performance that is lower than the reading performance of students who are one standard deviation above the average students in the OECD area with respect to their reading habits and approaches to learning (index value of 1).

The inter-quartile range represents the difference between the students with the highest and those with the lowest reading habits and approaches to learning (*i.e.* those in the top and bottom quartiles of these indicators). This indicator shows how severe inequalities in reading performance between "enthusiastic and unenthusiastic readers" are.

Are reading habits and approaches to learning good predictors of performance?
The proportion of the variation in student performance that is accounted for by engaging in reading and approaches to learning, or "explained variance", helps to answer this question by identifying the proportion of the observed variation in student performance that can be attributed to reading habits and approaches to learning.

- If this number is low, knowing the reading habits of students or how they approach their learning tells very little about their reading performance.

- If this number is high, by knowing the reading habits of students or how they approach their learning one can predict students' reading performance relatively well.

Box III.1.3 **Interpreting PISA indices**

Comparing countries that are above or below the OECD average on each of the indices of reading engagement and learning strategies:

Indices used to characterise students' engagement in reading activities and awareness and use of learning strategies were constructed so that the average OECD student would have an index value of zero and about two-thirds of the OECD student population would be between the values of -1 and 1 (*i.e.* the index has a standard deviation of 1). Negative values on the index, therefore, do not imply that students responded negatively to the underlying question. Rather, students with negative scores are students who responded less positively than the average response across OECD countries. Likewise, students with positive scores are students who responded more positively than the average student in the OECD area (Annex A1 for a detailed description of how indices were constructed).

Most of the indicators of engagement-in-reading activities and approaches to learning are based on students' self-reports. Such measures can thus suffer from a degree of measurement error because students are asked to assess their level of engagement in reading activities and their use of different learning strategies retrospectively. Apart from potential measurement error, cultural differences in attitudes towards self-enhancement can influence country-level results in engagement-in-reading activities and the use of learning strategies (Bempechat, *et al.,* 2002). The literature consistently shows that response biases, such as social desirability, acquiescence and extreme response choice, are more common in countries with low GDP than in more affluent countries, as they are, within countries, among individuals with lower socio-economic background and less education.

As in the first PISA cycle, many of the self-reported indicators of engagement in reading and approaches to learning and reading are strongly and positively associated with reading performance within countries, but show a weak or negative association with performance at the country level. This may be due to different response biases across countries or the fact that country-level differences in reading performance are due to many factors that go beyond levels of engagement in reading activities and approaches to learning, and that are negatively associated with reading performance and positively associated with engagement in reading and approaches to learning.

PISA 2009 used two indicators aimed at assessing the extent to which students are aware of effective strategies to understand, remember and summarise information. These measures suffer less from self-reported biases because they gauge whether students agree with education experts on what strategies work best to achieve certain goals (Annex A1 for a detailed description of how these indices were constructed). Analyses presented in this volume confirm that these indicators are strongly associated with reading performance both within and across countries. This evidence is in line with previous studies that attempt to measure the influence of self-reported bias in country-level attitudinal scales in previous PISA cycles (Lie and Turmo, 2005), and suggests that self-reported biases may be at least partially responsible for observed cross-country differences in self-reported engagement-in-reading activities and approaches to learning.

Caution is advised when comparing levels of engagement and the use of different learning strategies across countries because students in different countries may not always mean the same thing when answering questions. The *PISA 2009 Technical Report* (OECD, forthcoming) contains a detailed description of all the steps that were taken in PISA 2009 to ensure the highest possible level of cross-country comparability and to assess the validity of cross-country comparisons based on the indices featured in the report.[1]

ENGAGEMENT IN READING ACTIVITIES AND READING PERFORMANCE

This section examines the relationship between engagement in reading activities and reading performance, focusing on three aspects of how students engage in reading activities:

- how much students enjoy reading;
- how much time students spend reading for enjoyment; and
- what students read for enjoyment.

Are students who enjoy reading better readers?

Being interested in and enjoying a particular subject affects both the degree and the continuity of engagement in learning and the depth of understanding achieved, an effect that research has shown to operate largely independently of students' general motivation to learn.

In all countries – except Kazakhstan – students who enjoy reading the most perform significantly better than students who enjoy reading the least. Figure III.1.3 (Table III.1.1) shows the share of the variation in student reading performance that can be explained by a change in one unit in the *index of enjoyment of reading* and variations in performance on the reading scale across different groups of students. Enjoying or being interested in reading has been found to be associated with high levels of reading proficiency and the use of deep-level reading strategies (Schiefele, 2009). This is a useful measure of the strength in the relationship between students who reported enjoying reading and their reading performance. For each country, four groups of students were identified according to the extent to which they enjoy reading (top quarter, second quarter, third quarter and bottom quarter), as they reported in the PISA questionnaire. For each country, Figure III.1.3 displays the length of the line connecting the reading score of the group of students who enjoy reading the most and the group of students who enjoy reading the least – in other words, the performance gap between the top and the bottom groups. Countries are ranked according to the share of the variation in reading performance that is associated with a one unit change in the enjoyment of reading index; thus, countries on the upper part of Figure III.1.3 are those where a large share of variation in student performance can be explained by how much students reported enjoying reading, while countries where a relatively small share of this variation can be explained by how much students reported enjoying reading are in the lower part of Figure III.1.3.

What is meant by a difference of, say, 70 points between the scores of two different groups of students? What does such a difference translate into? Box III.1.4 can be used to visualise the different ways in which a given difference in PISA score points can be used and thought of.

Box III.1.4 **Interpreting differences in PISA scores: how large a gap?**

In PISA 2009, student performance in reading is described through seven proficiency levels (Levels 1b, 1a, 2, 3, 4, 5 and 6). A difference of about 73 score points represents one proficiency level on the PISA reading scale. This can be considered a comparatively large difference in student performance. For example, as described in Volume I, *What Students Know and Can Do*, and the PISA 2009 assessment framework, students proficient at Level 3 on the overall reading literacy scale are capable of completing moderately complex reading tasks, such as locating multiple pieces of information, making links between different parts of a text, and relating the text to familiar knowledge. Meanwhile, students proficient at Level 2 on the reading literacy scale are able to locate information that meets several conditions, to make comparisons or contrasts around a single feature, to work out what a well-defined part of a text means, even when the information is not prominent, and to make connections between the text and personal experience.

For the 32 OECD countries in which a sizeable number of 15-year-olds in the PISA samples were enrolled in at least two different grade levels, the difference between students in the two grades implies that one school year corresponds to an average of 39 score points on the PISA reading scale (Table A1.2).

The difference in performance on the reading scale between the countries with the highest and lowest mean performance is 242 score points, and the performance gap between the countries with the fifth highest and the fifth lowest mean performance is 154 score points.

In relation to the overall distribution of students on the PISA reading scale, one hundred points represent one standard deviation, which means that two-thirds of the OECD student population has scores within 100 points of the OECD mean.

Across OECD countries, 18% of student variation in reading performance can be explained by differences in how much students reported enjoying reading. The explained variation in reading performance is higher than 20 percentage points in 16 OECD countries and one partner economy. In Australia, New Zealand, France, Ireland, Sweden, Finland, Iceland, the United Kingdom, Switzerland, Austria, Norway, the Czech Republic, Germany, Luxembourg and Belgium, and the partner country Singapore, the quarter of students who enjoy reading the most can perform reading tasks that are more than 1.5 proficiency levels higher than students who enjoy reading the least.

The difference between the top and the bottom quarters on the *index of enjoyment of reading* shows what large inequalities in reading performance there are between enthusiastic and unenthusiastic readers in all countries. Table III.1.1 also shows the score point difference that is associated with a change in one unit in the *index of enjoyment of reading*.[2] On average across OECD countries, a difference of one unit on the *index of enjoyment of reading* corresponds to 40 points on the PISA reading scale, or the equivalent of an average school year's progress.

■ Figure III.1.3 ■
Relationship between enjoying reading and performance in reading

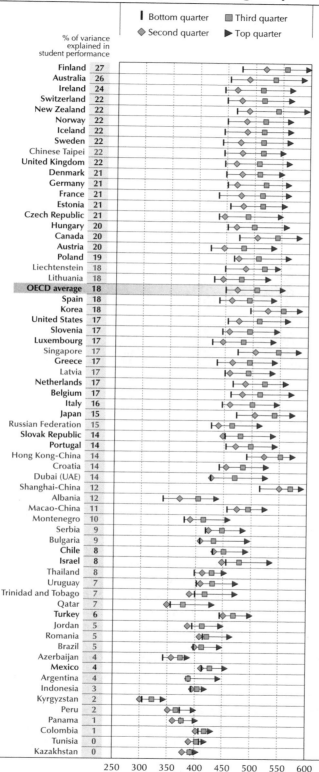

Countries are ranked in descending order of the percentage of explained variance in student performance.
Source: OECD, *PISA 2009 Database,* Table III.1.1.
StatLink ⟨⟩ http://dx.doi.org/10.1787/888932360176

Figure III.1.4 (Table III.1.2) shows a strong association between how much students enjoy reading and how well they perform in the PISA reading assessment. It places students who have lower-than-average levels of enjoyment of reading across the proficiency levels, detailed in Volume I, *What Students Know and Can Do*, and represents two sample countries, Finland and Japan, where the relationship between enjoyment of reading activities and reading performance is markedly different. In the context of Figure III.1.4, students with low levels of enjoyment of reading are those whose values on the *index of enjoyment in reading* are below the average for their country.

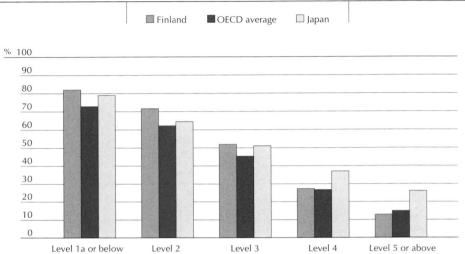

■ Figure III.1.4 ■
How proficient in reading are students who don't enjoy reading?

Note: This figure shows the proportion of students with below average levels of enjoyment of reading (compared to the average student in the country), by proficiency level on the reading scale.
Source: OECD, *PISA 2009 Database*, Table III.1.2.
StatLink 🔗 http://dx.doi.org/10.1787/888932360176

In the absence of an association between enjoyment of reading and reading performance, students with average or below-average levels of enjoyment would make up 50% of students in each proficiency level. On average though, students who do not enjoy reading tend to be vastly over-represented in proficiency Levels 1b, 1a, 2 and 3 and are under-represented in Levels 4, 5 and 6. The distribution of students who have lower-than-average levels of enjoyment of reading across the seven proficiency levels is not uniform across countries. In Israel, Belgium, Japan, Portugal, the United States and the Slovak Republic, and in the partner countries and economies Qatar, Brazil, Shanghai-China, Macao-China, Hong Kong-China and Dubai (UAE), the gradient is very gentle, suggesting a weak association between enjoyment of reading and reading performance, while in Australia, the Czech Republic, Estonia and Finland, and the partner economy Chinese Taipei, the gradient is relatively steep.

The association between time spent reading for enjoyment and reading performance

Time spent reading for enjoyment measures how frequently and for how long students read. The amount of time students spend reading for enjoyment provides an indicator of their interest in reading. The frequency of reading is strongly related to reading comprehension (Baker & Wigfield, 1999; Cipielewski & Stanovich, 1992). Stanovich (1986) describes a circular association, the so-called Matthew effect, between reading practices and achievement. Better readers tend to read more because they are more motivated to read, which, in turn, leads to improved vocabulary and comprehension skills.

PISA 2009 asked students how much time they usually spend reading for enjoyment. Students could choose from "I do not read for enjoyment", "I read for up to 30 minutes a day", "I read for more than 30 minutes but less than 60 minutes a day", "I read for between 1 and 2 hours a day" and "I read for more than 2 hours a day".

■ Figure III.1.5 ■

Relationship between time spent reading for enjoyment and performance in reading

○ Do not read for enjoyment
□ Up to 30 minutes a day
◆ More than 30 minutes to less than 60 minutes a day
▌ One to two hours a day
▶ More than two hours a day

Score point difference between students who read up to 30 minutes a day and students who don't read for enjoyment

Country	Score point difference
Iceland	66
Liechtenstein	64
Shanghai-China	63
Belgium	63
France	62
Switzerland	60
Sweden	60
Norway	58
Austria	57
Netherlands	57
Luxembourg	56
Australia	55
Germany	55
Chinese Taipei	55
Finland	54
Slovenia	53
New Zealand	52
Canada	49
Czech Republic	48
Ireland	48
United States	47
United Kingdom	47
Estonia	45
OECD average	44
Japan	44
Singapore	42
Slovak Republic	41
Italy	40
Denmark	39
Hungary	37
Lithuania	36
Croatia	35
Poland	35
Hong Kong-China	34
Korea	32
Portugal	32
Spain	31
Greece	29
Serbia	29
Macao-China	27
Thailand	26
Russian Federation	25
Dubai (UAE)	24
Turkey	24
Latvia	24
Israel	23
Bulgaria	23
Uruguay	22
Montenegro	22
Kyrgyzstan	15
Qatar	14
Chile	12
Romania	12
Jordan	10
Indonesia	10
Brazil	7
Azerbaijan	4
Argentina	4
Albania	4
Mexico	-1
Trinidad and Tobago	-2
Kazakhstan	-2
Panama	-4
Colombia	-5
Tunisia	-11
Peru	-13

250   300   350   400   450   500   550   600
Mean score

Countries are ranked in descending order of the score point difference.
Source: OECD, *PISA 2009 Database*, Table III.1.3.

StatLink ᵐˢᵖ http://dx.doi.org/10.1787/888932360176

Students who read for enjoyment tend to be more proficient readers than students who do not read for enjoyment in all PISA participating countries. Figure III.1.5 (Table III.1.3) shows the average score in the PISA 2009 reading assessment for five groups of students in each country: students who do not read for enjoyment; students who read for up to 30 minutes per day; students who spend between half an hour and one hour daily reading for enjoyment; students who spend between one and two hours; and a group of extremely dedicated readers who reported spending more than two hours per day reading for enjoyment. Countries are ranked by the length of the line connecting the average score of the group of students who read for less than 30 minutes a day for enjoyment and the group of students who do not read for enjoyment.

On average across OECD countries, over one-third of students – and 40% or more in Austria, the Netherlands, Luxembourg, Switzerland, Belgium, Japan, the Czech Republic, the United States, Ireland, Germany, the Slovak Republic, Norway and in the partner countries Liechtenstein and Argentina – reported that they did not read for enjoyment at all.[3] The average performance for these students on the reading scale, 460 points, is well below the average for the OECD as a whole. Another one-third of students across OECD countries read for 30 minutes or less per day. Their mean performance, 504 points, is in line with the OECD average of 493 points. A further 17% of students across OECD countries read for between half-an-hour and one hour per day, with performance levels of 527 points. Students who reported reading for longer, between one and two hours per day, or assiduous readers, who read for enjoyment for more than two hours daily, score 532 and 527 points, respectively (Table III.1.3).

In more than two-thirds of countries that participated in PISA, the score point difference associated with at least some daily reading for enjoyment is far greater than the score point difference associated with increasing amounts of time spent reading. The gap in performance between students who read for enjoyment for 30 minutes or less per day and students who do not read for enjoyment is more than 30 points in 36 countries; in Iceland, Belgium, France, the partner country Liechtenstein and the partner economy Shanghai-China, it is above 60 points. However, the performance gap between students who read for enjoyment between 30 minutes and one hour and students who read 30 minutes or less is above 30 points in only eight countries: Australia, Ireland, New Zealand, Germany, the Czech Republic, and the partner countries and economy Bulgaria, Qatar and Dubai (UAE). In no country is the performance gap between students who read for enjoyment between one and two hours per day and students who read between half-an-hour and one hour per day more than 20 points.

Figure III.1.5 indicates that, in most countries, the score point difference between students who spend less than 30 minutes per day reading for enjoyment and students who spend no time reading for enjoyment is greater than the score point difference between students who spend half an hour to an hour reading for enjoyment and students who spend less than 30 minutes. In general, the score point difference between different groups of students decreases as students spend more time reading for enjoyment. This may mean that the returns on the time students spend reading for enjoyment decrease as time invested by students increases or, alternatively, that poor readers need more time to read a text. Of course, it is not just how long students spend reading, but also the types of materials and their levels of complexity that are relevant. This is considered in the next section.

Results presented in Figure III.1.5 indicate that reading for enjoyment is associated with reading proficiency. The low reading performance among students who do not read for enjoyment calls for education systems to encourage reading both in and outside of school. The existence of a threshold effect and in how fast students of different abilities are able to access written information means that the focus should remain on encouraging students to read daily for enjoyment rather than on how much time they spend reading.

The association between the material students read and reading performance

There has been considerable debate as to which type of reading may be most effective in fostering reading skills and improving reading performance. The results from PISA suggest that, although the students who reported reading fiction are more likely to have higher scores in the 2009 PISA reading assessment, it is the students who read a wide variety of materials who perform particularly well in reading. Table III.1.6 illustrates that in all countries except for Turkey and the partner country Kazakhstan, these students perform better on the PISA reading scale than students who show less diverse reading patterns.

PISA 2009 offers a valuable opportunity to explore the association between what students report reading in their free time and reading performance and although it cannot establish causal relations, it offers a glimpse of how proficient in reading students who read different materials are. PISA 2009 asked students to indicate how often they read magazines, comic books, fiction (novels, narratives, stories), non-fiction and newspapers, *because they want to.* Students could indicate that they read each material "Never or almost never", "A few times a year", "About once a month", "Several times a month" and "Several times a week".

Table III.1.6 shows how students who reported reading fiction and non-fiction books regularly, *i.e.* several times a month or several times a week, are particularly likely to perform well in the PISA reading assessment. Findings emerging from analyses of the association between what students reported reading for enjoyment and their reading performance are in line with evidence suggesting that some reading materials may nurture reading proficiency more than others (Smith, 1996; OECD 2002). More specifically, reading long and complex texts, such as fiction and non-fiction books, appears to be particularly associated with how well both students and adults read.

Figure III.1.6 presents the reading performance of students who report reading regularly, either several times a month or several times a week, and for their enjoyment, different types of material: magazines, comic books, fiction (novels, narratives, stories), non-fiction, and newspapers.[4] Compared to someone who reports not reading fiction for enjoyment, reading fiction for a student's own enjoyment appears to be positively associated with higher performance in the PISA 2009 reading assessment, while reading comic books is associated with little improvement in reading proficiency in some countries, and with lower overall reading performance in other countries (Table III.1.24).

Students who reported reading fiction for their own enjoyment several times a month or several times a week are more proficient readers than students who do not read fiction, or who reported reading fiction only occasionally in all countries except Mexico and the partner countries Colombia, Jordan, Tunisia, Peru, Kazakhstan, Brazil, Argentina and Panama (Table III.1.24).[5] The performance difference is 36 points or more – or half a proficiency level – in as many as 36 countries and 73 points or more – or one proficiency level – in five countries: Sweden, Australia, Luxembourg, Austria and Finland. Fifteen-year-olds who reported reading non-fiction for their own enjoyment at least several times a month generally have higher reading scores than students who do not. The score point difference associated with reading non-fiction, however, appears to be lower than the score point difference observed for fiction: it is higher than 50 points only in Spain and the partner country Croatia. In 14 countries, no difference could be observed; but in Turkey and in the partner countries Kazakhstan and Peru, reading non-fiction books is negatively associated with reading performance.

Reading magazines and newspapers for enjoyment on a regular basis is also associated with higher reading scores, although, as in the case of non-fiction books, the score point difference between reading these materials frequently and not reading or reading them only sporadically is lower than in the case of fiction. For example, the score point difference between students who reported reading newspapers several times a month or several times a week and students who reported not reading newspapers or reading them once a month or less is 35 points or more only in Iceland, Israel and Sweden and the partner country Peru. Similarly, the score point difference between students who read magazines several times a month or several times a week and students who do not read magazines or read them once a month or less is above 35 points only in six countries: the Netherlands, Hungary, Finland, the Slovak Republic and the partner countries Bulgaria and Montenegro.

Reading comic books, on the other hand, is generally associated with low levels of reading. proficiency. Students who reported reading comics several times a month or several times a week have lower reading scores than students who reported not reading comic books in 33 countries. The difference in performance between students who reported reading and students who reported not reading comic books is very negative – 30 points or more – in Estonia and the partner countries Kazakhstan, the Russian Federation and Bulgaria. In 14 countries – Belgium, Norway, Italy, Iceland, Switzerland, France, the Netherlands, Denmark, Sweden, Finland and the partner countries and economy Jordan, Thailand, Indonesia and Macao-China – students who reported reading comics regularly achieve higher scores than students who reported not reading comic books regularly. The causal nature of this relationship cannot be established by PISA. It may well be that students with lower performance levels find comic books, with a lighter reading load, more accessible.

Students who reported reading fiction and who may also have reported reading other material, except for comic books, were the students who achieved the highest scores in the reading scale: on average, over 100 points more than students who read nothing in Iceland, Austria, Sweden, Switzerland, Finland, the Slovak Republic, France, Luxembourg and the partner country and economy Bulgaria and Dubai (UAE) (Figure III.1.7 and Table III.1.9). On average, students across the OECD who reported reading fiction and any other material regularly, but not comic books, have a reading score of 538 points in the reading assessment. In most countries, these students have reading scores that place them more than one proficiency level above students who do not read any material regularly.

■ Figure III.1.6 [Part 1/2] ■

Relationship between the types of materials students read and performance in reading

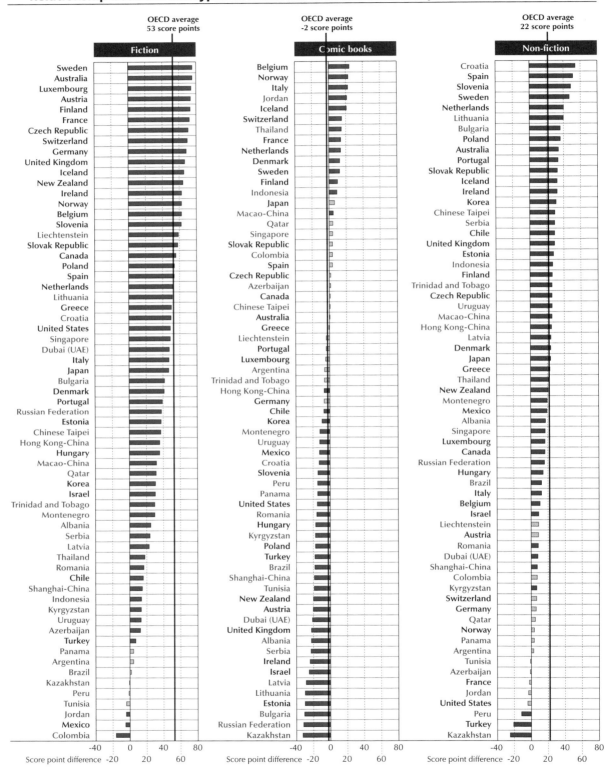

Note: Score point differences that are statistically significant are marked in a darker tone.
Countries are ranked in ascending order of the score point differences.
Source: OECD, *PISA 2009 Database,* Table III.1.24.
StatLink ⚓ http://dx.doi.org/10.1787/888932360176

■ Figure III.1.6 [Part 2/2] ■
Relationship between the types of materials students read and performance in reading

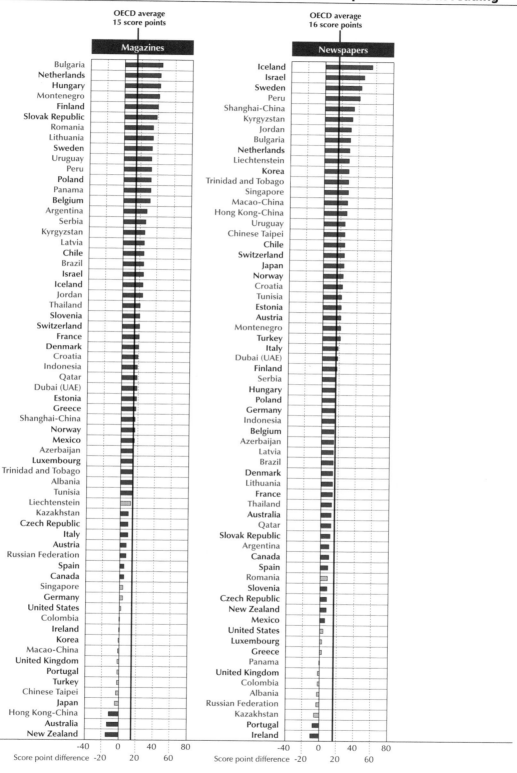

Note: Score point differences that are statistically significant are marked in a darker tone.
Countries are ranked in ascending order of the score point differences.
Source: OECD, *PISA 2009 Database,* Table III.1.24.

StatLink ᴹˢᴾ http://dx.doi.org/10.1787/888932360176

■ Figure III.1.7 ■

Performance on the reading scale of students who read different materials

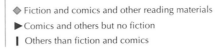

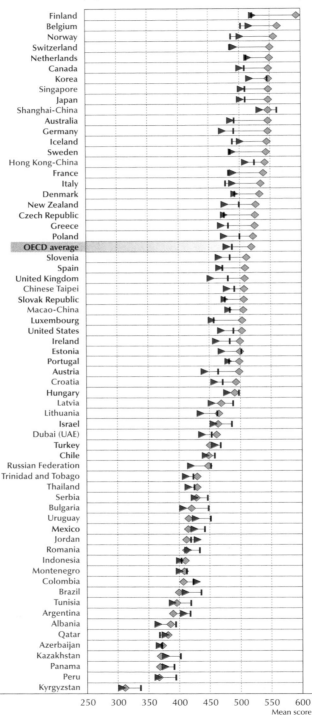

Note: Liechtenstein does not feature in this figure, because of small sample size issues.

Countries are ranked in descending order of the mean performance of students who read fiction, comics and other reading materials.

Source: OECD, *PISA 2009 Database,* Table III.1.9.

StatLink ᴹˢᴾ http://dx.doi.org/10.1787/888932360176

Students in Israel, Turkey and Mexico, and in the partner countries Colombia, Serbia, Latvia, Romania, Tunisia, Panama, Kyrgyzstan, Peru, Bulgaria, Argentina, Kazakhstan Uruguay and Brazil who reported reading fiction and comic books and who may also read other materials, such as magazines, newspapers and non-fiction regularly, score at least 15 score points lower on the reading scale than students who only read magazines, newspapers and non-fiction. This variation is not due to different patterns of reading comic books among boys and girls. Indeed, in several countries, boys and girls who reported reading comic books and who may also read magazines, newspapers and non-fiction, have lower scores than when they reported reading only magazines, newspapers and non-fiction. The reading performance of boys who reported reading fiction, comic books and who may also read other material is lower than the reading performance of boys who reported reading only magazines, newspapers and non-fiction in 26 countries. This suggests that in the vast majority of countries, comic books are not associated with better reading performance, even when they may help inspire students who are less engaged and motivated to read, such as boys, to try other reading material, such as fiction.

In most countries, proficient readers are not only those students who enjoy reading and who read for enjoyment regularly, but they are also those students who are versatile readers. Students who are familiar with several written codes and practice reading a variety of styles appear to master reading better than students who are more restricted in their reading habits. Figure III.1.8 appears to contradict commonly held beliefs about how what one reads influences reading proficiency. While it is true that regularly reading some materials, such as fiction, is associated with better reading proficiency (Figure III.1.6), reading other materials, such as newspapers and magazines, does so too if it complements other types of texts.

For each country, four groups of students were identified on the basis of them reporting the extent to which they read a diversity of materials (top quarter, second quarter, third quarter and bottom quarter). Countries on the upper part of Figure III.1.8 are those where the diversity of material read explains a large share of the variance in reading performance among students in each country.

Figure III.1.8 (Table III.1.10) also suggests that the association between the variety of reading material and reading proficiency is generally large: the gap between the group of students with the most varied reading patterns and the group with the least varied reading patterns corresponds to one PISA proficiency level or more in Sweden, Iceland, the Netherlands, Finland, Belgium, France and Switzerland, and is still 36 points or more – half a proficiency level – in 42 countries.

Diversity of reading materials explains a very high share – 10% or more – of the overall variance in reading performance in Finland, Sweden, the Netherlands and Iceland (Figure III.1.8). Table III.1.10 also reports the score point difference that is associated with a change in one unit in the *index of diversity of reading materials*. The score point difference represents the average difference in PISA scores that two students can expect to have when one student has reading patterns that are similar to those of the average student in the OECD area (index value of 0) and the other reads a greater variety of reading materials than five out of six students in the OECD area (index value of 1). On average across OECD countries, a difference of one unit on the *index of diversity of reading materials* corresponds to 22 points on the PISA reading scale. In Finland, Sweden, France and Iceland however, a difference of one unit on the *index of diversity of reading materials* corresponds to more than 30 points.

Students with relatively undiversified reading patterns[6] are over-represented among students who are only able to perform at Levels 1b, 1a, 2 and 3 and under-represented at the higher proficiency Levels 4, 5 and 6 (Table III.1.11). As Table III.1.11 suggests, the link between diversity of reading materials and reading proficiency is particularly marked in the Netherlands, Finland and Sweden.

Online reading and reading performance of print texts

Students' engagement in reading is also indicated by the diversity of the material that students read online and by the amount of time they spend accessing online material. Online reading is becoming increasingly popular among many adolescents (Mills, 2010). Students who are extensively engaged in these activities, such as reading e-mails, chatting on line, reading news on line, using an online dictionary or encyclopaedia, participating in online group discussions and searching for information online, either because they access several types of online material or because they access online material regularly, are generally more proficient readers than students who do little online reading.

■ Figure III.1.8 ■
Relationship between diversity in reading habits and performance in reading

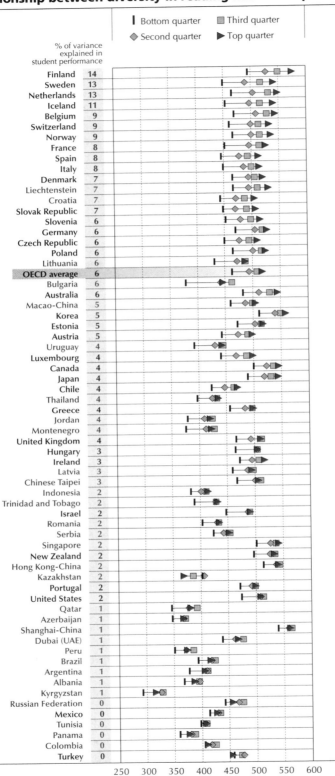

Countries are ranked in descending order of the percentage of explained variance in student performance.
Source: OECD, *PISA 2009 Database,* Table III.1.10.
StatLink ᐧᐧᐧᔕ http://dx.doi.org/10.1787/888932360176

■ Figure III.1.9 ■

Relationship between reading on line and performance in reading

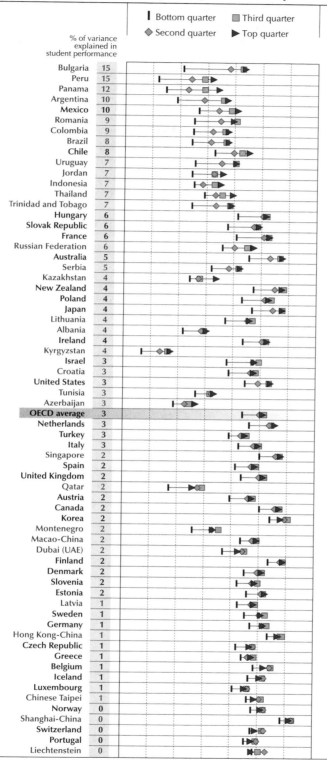

Legend: | Bottom quarter ◆ Second quarter ■ Third quarter ► Top quarter

% of variance explained in student performance

Country	%
Bulgaria	15
Peru	15
Panama	12
Argentina	10
Mexico	10
Romania	9
Colombia	9
Brazil	8
Chile	8
Uruguay	7
Jordan	7
Indonesia	7
Thailand	7
Trinidad and Tobago	7
Hungary	6
Slovak Republic	6
France	6
Russian Federation	6
Australia	5
Serbia	5
Kazakhstan	4
New Zealand	4
Poland	4
Japan	4
Lithuania	4
Albania	4
Ireland	4
Kyrgyzstan	4
Israel	3
Croatia	3
United States	3
Tunisia	3
Azerbaijan	3
OECD average	3
Netherlands	3
Turkey	3
Italy	3
Singapore	2
Spain	2
United Kingdom	2
Qatar	2
Austria	2
Canada	2
Korea	2
Montenegro	2
Macao-China	2
Dubai (UAE)	2
Finland	2
Denmark	2
Slovenia	2
Estonia	2
Latvia	1
Sweden	1
Germany	1
Hong Kong-China	1
Czech Republic	1
Greece	1
Belgium	1
Iceland	1
Luxembourg	1
Chinese Taipei	1
Norway	0
Shanghai-China	0
Switzerland	0
Portugal	0
Liechtenstein	0

250 300 350 400 450 500 550 600
Mean score

Countries are ranked in descending order of the percentage of explained variance in student performance.
Source: OECD, *PISA 2009 Database,* Table III.1.12.
StatLink ᵃᵢˢ┐ http://dx.doi.org/10.1787/888932360176

Volume VI of this report, *Students On Line: Reading and Using Digital Information* explains how PISA measures and reports student performance in digital reading and analyses what students participating in this assessment can do. However, PISA 2009 also examined the extent to which students are engaged in online reading activities for enjoyment by asking students how often they were involved in the following activities: reading emails; chatting on line; reading online news; using an online dictionary or encyclopaedia (*e.g.* <Wikipedia®>); searching online information to learn about a particular topic; taking part in online group discussions or forums; and searching for practical information online (*e.g.* schedules, events, tips, recipes). Students could indicate that they read each material "never or almost never", "several times a month", "several times a week" or "several times a day". Students could also indicate that they did not know what the activity was.

Figure III.1.9 (Table III.1.12) illustrates that, in 45 countries, the extent to which students reported reading online explains less than 5% of the student variation in reading performance and that in general, the difference in the reading performance of students who reported being the most engaged in reading activities and the group that reports being the least engaged in each country is smaller than the gap observed for differences in how much students reported enjoying reading or the time students allocate to reading for enjoyment.

Reading online is associated with better reading performance in all PISA participating countries and economies, excluding Liechtenstein. Although the score point difference that is associated with online reading is quantitatively small, results presented in Figure III.1.9 disprove commonly held beliefs that students who engage too much in online reading are poorer readers of print texts. In all the countries that participated in PISA 2009, the score point difference that is associated with a one unit difference in the *index of online reading activities* is lower than 30 points; but it is at least 20 points in Australia, France, New Zealand, Hungary, the Slovak Republic, the Netherlands, Ireland and the partner countries Bulgaria, Argentina and Uruguay.

APPROACHES TO LEARNING AND READING PERFORMANCE

Countries vary widely in the extent to which different learning strategies are used by students in general and by some particular groups of students. Within the OECD countries, girls are more knowledgeable than boys about effective ways to understand, remember and summarise texts. Girls also use memorisation and control strategies more than boys, while boys rely more than girls on elaboration strategies. Students from socio-economically advantaged backgrounds know more about and report using learning strategies more than students from socio-economically disadvantaged backgrounds, although memorisation strategies are used to the same extent by students from all socio-economic backgrounds (Chapter 2 of this volume for a detailed description of whether students in general, and some groups of students in particular, have high levels of engagement in reading activities and know how to approach their learning effectively).

This section examines the relationship between awareness and the use of learning strategies and reading performance. The learning strategies examined in the context of PISA 2009 are:

- awareness of the most effective strategies to understand and remember information;
- awareness of the most effective strategies to summarise information;
- use of control strategies;
- use of memorisation strategies; and
- use of elaboration strategies.

The association between strategies to understand and remember information and reading performance

PISA 2009 assessed the extent to which students were aware that doing things like "after reading the text, I discuss its content with other people", "I underline important parts of the text" and "I summarise the text in my own words" were effective strategies to understand and remember information, while doing things like "I concentrate on the parts of the text that are easy to understand", "I quickly read through the text twice" and "I read the text aloud to another person" were less effective strategies. In order to determine the relative effectiveness of different strategies, PISA 2009 consulted reading experts in participating countries. Student awareness of what strategies were effective was then established by comparing the rating of students with those of the experts. Annex A1 describes in detail how the index was constructed.

Across the OECD countries, an increase of one unit on the *index of understanding and remembering information* is associated with a performance difference of 35 points or more in 25 countries. The relationship appears to be particularly strong in the case of Belgium and Switzerland. Most of these countries perform above the OECD average in the PISA 2009 reading assessment. The association between the extent to which students are aware of appropriate strategies to understand and remember information and how well they read is strongest in countries where students generally read the best. Figure III.10 (Tables I.2.3 and III.1.14) illustrates how countries in which the average student is aware that "discussing the content of a text they just read with other people", "underlining important parts of a text and summarising the text in their own words" are effective strategies to understand and remember information are also the countries where students tend to perform better in the PISA reading assessment.

■ Figure III.1.10 ■

Association between awareness of effective strategies to understand and remember information and performance in reading

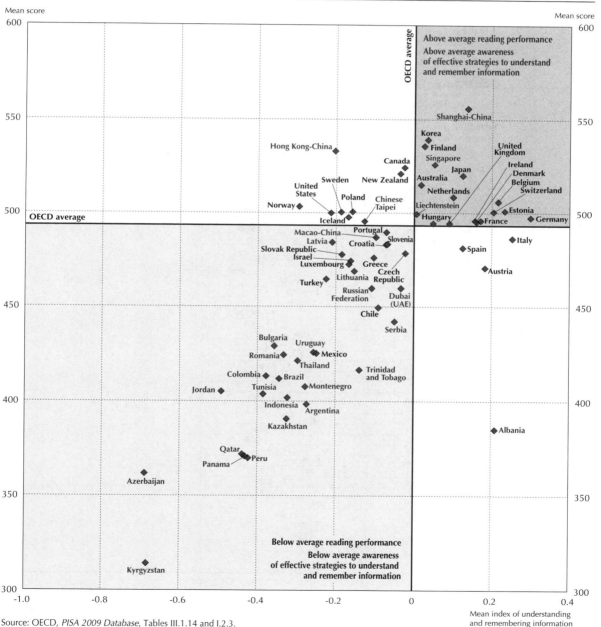

Source: OECD, *PISA 2009 Database*, Tables III.1.14 and I.2.3.
StatLink ᔆᔆᔆ http://dx.doi.org/10.1787/888932360176

■ Figure III.1.11 ■

How students' awareness of effective strategies to understand and remember information relates to their reading performance

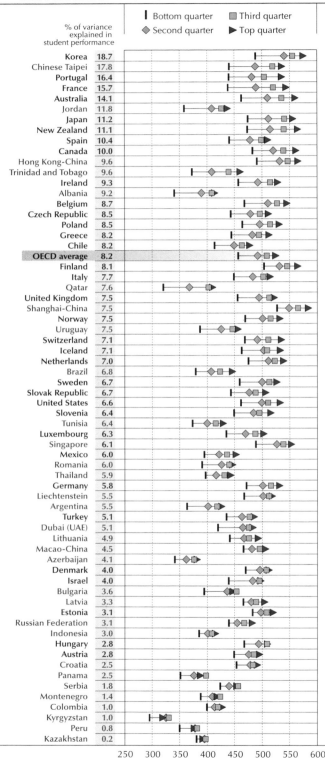

Countries are ranked in descending order of the percentage of explained variance in student performance.

Source: OECD, *PISA 2009 Database,* Table III.1.14.

StatLink ⛬ http://dx.doi.org/10.1787/888932360176

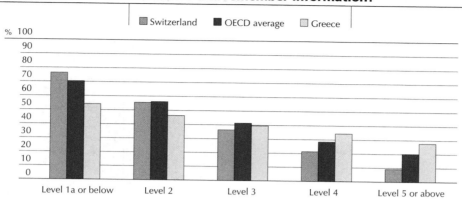

■ Figure III.1.12 ■
How proficient in reading are students who are not aware of effective strategies to understand and remember information?

Note: This figure shows the proportion of students with below average levels of enjoyment of reading (compared to the average student in the country), by proficiency level on the reading scale.
Source: OECD, *PISA 2009 Database*, Table III.1.15.
StatLink http://dx.doi.org/10.1787/888932360176

Within each country, these students tend to perform better on the PISA reading scale than those who do not (Figures III.1.11 and III.1.12, and Tables III.1.14 and III.1.15). In Switzerland, Belgium, Germany, the Netherlands and the partner country Liechtenstein, over 20% of the overall variation in student reading performance can be explained by differences in students' level of awareness of effective strategies to understand and remember information. In all but 10 countries, over 10% of the overall variation in student reading performance can be explained by differences in students' level of awareness of effective strategies to understand and remember information. In all countries except for Greece, Turkey, Canada and the partner countries and economies Azerbaijan, Tunisia, Macao-China, Jordan, Indonesia, Thailand and Shanghai-China, students who use appropriate strategies to understand and remember information the most perform 70 points or more higher – or one full proficiency level – in the PISA reading assessment than students who use them the least. The association is most marked in Belgium, Switzerland, Austria, Luxembourg, Germany and the partner countries and economy Liechtenstein, Dubai (UAE) and Trinidad and Tobago. In these countries, the quarter of students who use appropriate understanding and remembering strategies for learning the most are, on average, more than 105 points, or one-and-a-half proficiency levels, ahead of the quarter of students who use them the least. These results do not only hold within countries, they are also mirrored in the performance patterns across countries. At the OECD average level, the difference between the top and bottom quarters is 90 points.

The association between strategies to summarise information and reading performance

PISA 2009 assessed the extent to which students were aware that doing things like "I carefully check whether the most important facts in the text are represented in the summary" and "I read through the text, underlining the most important sentences. Then I write them in my own words as a summary" are the most effective strategies, that "I write a summary. Then I check that each paragraph is covered in the summary, because the content of each paragraph should be included" and "before writing the summary, I read the text as many times as possible" are moderately effective, while "I try to copy out accurately as many sentences as possible" is the least effective strategy to summarise information. Annex A1 describes in detail how the index on strategies to understand and remember information was constructed.

Figure III.1.13 (Tables III.1.16 and I.2.3) shows that high-performing countries are also those where students generally know how to summarise information. Countries where students have a better understanding that doing things like checking whether the most important facts in the text are represented in the summary, underlining the most important sentences and then rewriting them in a reworded format are useful ways to summarise information, while copying accurately as many sentences as possible is not particularly useful, are countries where students are generally more proficient readers. The positive relationship between the awareness of effective summarising strategies and reading performance is also clearly evident within OECD countries. Across these countries, an increase of one unit on the *index of summarising* is associated with a performance difference of 42 points on the PISA reading scale and a difference of 35 points or more in as many as 48 countries.

■ Figure III.1.13 ■

Association between awareness of effective strategies to summarise information and performance in reading

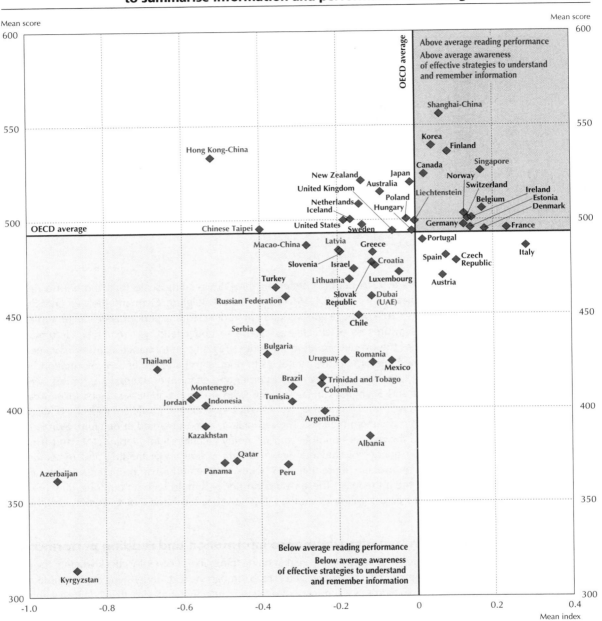

Source: OECD, *PISA 2009 Database,* Tables III.1.16 and I.2.3.
StatLink http://dx.doi.org/10.1787/888932360176

Within countries, students who are aware of what strategies are effective for summarising information tend to achieve higher scores than students who are not aware of these strategies. Across OECD countries, the difference in reading performance between those students who know the most about which strategies are best for summarising information and those who know the least is 107 points. Figure III.1.14 (Table III.1.16) indicates that the average difference in reading performance between the top and the bottom quarters of students in terms of their awareness of the relative effectiveness of different strategies to summarise a text is below 50 points only in the partner countries Azerbaijan and Thailand, and is as much as 120 points in the OECD countries Belgium, Japan, Switzerland, Luxembourg, New Zealand, Austria and the Czech Republic.

■ Figure III.1.14 ■

How students' awareness of effective strategies to summarise information relates to their reading performance

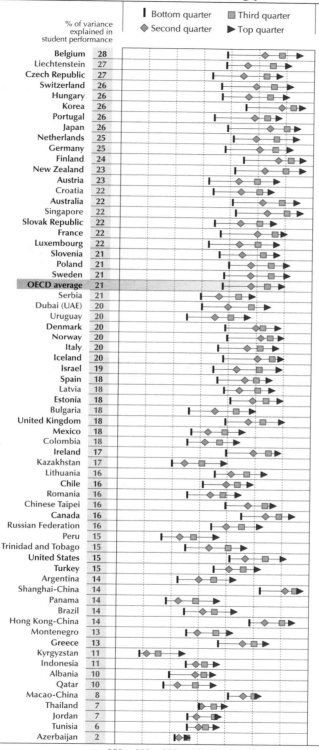

| | Bottom quarter | Third quarter |
| Second quarter | Top quarter |

% of variance explained in student performance

Belgium	28
Liechtenstein	27
Czech Republic	27
Switzerland	26
Hungary	26
Korea	26
Portugal	26
Japan	26
Netherlands	25
Germany	25
Finland	24
New Zealand	23
Austria	23
Croatia	22
Australia	22
Singapore	22
Slovak Republic	22
France	22
Luxembourg	22
Slovenia	21
Poland	21
Sweden	21
OECD average	21
Serbia	21
Dubai (UAE)	20
Uruguay	20
Denmark	20
Norway	20
Italy	20
Iceland	20
Israel	19
Spain	18
Latvia	18
Estonia	18
Bulgaria	18
United Kingdom	18
Mexico	18
Colombia	18
Ireland	17
Kazakhstan	17
Lithuania	16
Chile	16
Romania	16
Chinese Taipei	16
Canada	16
Russian Federation	16
Peru	15
Trinidad and Tobago	15
United States	15
Turkey	15
Argentina	14
Shanghai-China	14
Panama	14
Brazil	14
Hong Kong-China	14
Montenegro	13
Greece	13
Kyrgyzstan	11
Indonesia	11
Albania	10
Qatar	10
Macao-China	8
Thailand	7
Jordan	7
Tunisia	6
Azerbaijan	2

250 300 350 400 450 500 550 600
Mean score

Countries are ranked in descending order of the percentage of explained variance in student performance.
Source: OECD, *PISA 2009 Database,* Table III.1.16.

StatLink ▄▄▄■ http://dx.doi.org/10.1787/888932360176

The association between the use of memorisation, elaboration and control strategies and reading performance

Self-regulated learning – measured by PISA through students' use of control strategies – is consistently associated with higher performance in the PISA reading assessment. Within each country, students who reported beginning the learning process by figuring out what they needed to learn, who ensured that they understood what they read, tried to figure out which concepts they had not fully grasped, attempted to remember the most important points in a text and sought additional clarifying information when they did not understand something they had read, tended to perform better on the PISA reading scale than those who do not. The association is most marked in France, Australia, Portugal and New Zealand, among OECD countries, and in the partner economy Chinese Taipei, where the quarter of students who use these strategies for learning the most are, on average, 90 points or more ahead of the quarter who use them least (Figure III.1.16 and Table III.1.18). Only in the partner countries Kazakhstan, Kyrgyzstan, Peru, Colombia, Indonesia, Montenegro and Serbia is the performance gap between students who reported using control strategies the most and those who reported using them the least lower than 35 points. At the OECD average level, the difference between the top and bottom quarters is 68 points.

■ Figure III.1.15 ■

How PISA 2009 assesses students' use of learning strategies

MEMORISATION STRATEGIES

Memorisation strategies refer to the memorisation of texts and contents in all their details and repeated reading.

Items of the index of memorisation strategies:
- When I study, I try to memorise everything that is covered in the text
- When I study, I try to memorise as many details as possible
- When I study, I read the text so many times that I can recite it
- When I study, I read the text over and over again

ELABORATION STRATEGIES

Elaboration strategies refer to the transfer of new information to prior knowledge, out-of-school context and personal experiences.

Items of the index of elaboration strategies:
- When I study, I try to relate new information to prior knowledge acquired in other subjects
- When I study, I figure out how the information might be useful outside school
- When I study, I try to understand the material better by relating it to my own experiences
- When I study, I figure out how the text information fits in with what happens in real life

CONTROL STRATEGIES

Control strategies mean to formulate control questions about the purpose of a task or a text and its main concepts. It also means to self-supervise current study activities, particularly whether the reading material was understood.

Items of the index of control strategies:
- When I study, I start by figuring out what exactly I need to learn
- When I study, I check if I understand what I have read
- When I study, I try to figure out which concepts I still haven't really understood
- When I study, I make sure that I remember the most important points in the text
- When I study and I don't understand something, I look for additional information to clarify this

Figure III.16 (Table III.1.18) suggests that, on average across OECD countries, 8% of the variation in students' reading performance can be explained by the extent to which they reported using control strategies. In Korea, Portugal, France, Australia, Japan, New Zealand, Spain, Canada and the partner country and economy Chinese Taipei and Jordan, more than 10% of this variation can be explained by differences in how much students reported using self-regulated learning strategies; in 15 partner countries and economies and five OECD countries, less than 5% of the variation can be so explained.

Control strategies are essential for effective self-regulation of learning because they help students adapt their learning to the particular task at hand. Schools may need to focus on allowing students to manage and control their learning in order to help them develop effective strategies, not only to support their learning at school but also to provide them with the tools to manage their learning later in life.

■ Figure III.1.16 ■

Relationship between the use of control strategies and performance in reading

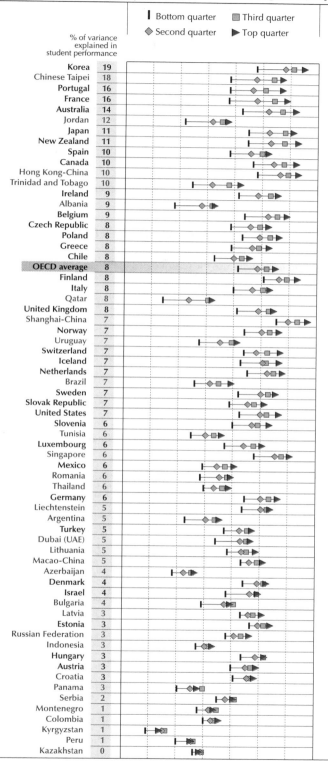

| | Bottom quarter | Third quarter |
| | Second quarter | Top quarter |

Countries are ranked in descending order of the percentage of explained variance in student performance.

Source: OECD, *PISA 2009 Database,* Table III.1.18.

StatLink ⫶⫶⫶⫶ http://dx.doi.org/10.1787/888932360176

Memorisation strategies, such as reading material aloud several times and learning key terms, are important in many tasks, but they commonly lead only to verbatim repetitions of information. Students who rely heavily on memorisation strategies tend to store information as it is, with little further processing. Memorisation strategies are useful when all a learner is asked to do is store information and retrieve it as originally presented. Since research suggests that memorisation strategies do not lead to deep understanding, they do not help develop students' skills to extrapolate the underlying meaning and message of stored information so that new material can be integrated with prior knowledge accumulated on/from diverse contexts (Tables III.1.20 and III.1.21).

Elaboration strategies, such as exploring how the material relates to things one has learned in other contexts, or asking how the information might be applied in other situations, can be used to reach the goal of deep understanding. Elaboration strategies reflect the extent to which students are prepared to use the knowledge acquired at school outside of school. Schools and education systems that ensure that students can use effective elaboration strategies can help equip them for the challenges of an ever-changing world by fostering their ability to become lifelong learners (Tables III.1.22 and III.1.23).

Figure III.17 (Table III.1.20) suggests that in some countries, reading performance relates positively to the use of memorisation strategies, while in other countries, the use of memorisation strategies is associated with lower reading performance. Figure III.17 shows a positive score point difference, in as many as 27 countries, between students who reported using memorisation strategies more frequently than the OECD average and those who use those strategies to the same extent as the OECD average. In 13 countries, students who use memorisation strategies more frequently than the OECD average and those who use those strategies to the same extent as the OECD average perform equally well in reading. In as many as 25 countries, students who use memorisation strategies more are poorer readers than those who are closer to the OECD average in memorisation use strategies.

■ Figure III.1.17 ■
Relationship between the use of memorisation strategies and student performance in reading

The association between the use of memorisation strategies and reading performance is…

Positive			Neither positive nor negative			Negative		
	Score point change per unit of the index of memorisation	S.E.		Score point change per unit of the index of memorisation	S.E.		Score point change per unit of the index of memorisation	S.E.
Thailand	24.8	(1.62)	Hungary	3.3	(2.50)	Netherlands	-21.9	(1.76)
Korea	24.6	(2.47)	New Zealand	3.1	(2.00)	Dubai (UAE)	-20.5	(1.61)
Jordan	20.8	(1.50)	Finland	2.9	(1.68)	Peru	-18.7	(2.31)
Chinese Taipei	20.7	(1.56)	Qatar	1.9	(1.15)	Slovak Republic	-18.1	(2.26)
Albania	13.1	(3.34)	United Kingdom	1.2	(1.59)	Slovenia	-15.9	(1.75)
Kyrgyzstan	12.9	(1.90)	Mexico	-0.1	(0.83)	Turkey	-15.1	(2.03)
Trinidad and Tobago	12.1	(2.03)	Iceland	-1.0	(1.90)	Serbia	-14.7	(1.70)
Brazil	12.1	(1.30)	Tunisia	-1.3	(2.02)	Montenegro	-14.5	(1.86)
Indonesia	11.2	(2.16)	Croatia	-1.4	(1.81)	Singapore	-14.1	(1.42)
France	11.0	(2.68)	Uruguay	-1.4	(1.65)	Belgium	-12.4	(1.46)
Sweden	10.3	(1.97)	Portugal	-2.7	(1.50)	Colombia	-11.5	(2.00)
Luxembourg	10.2	(1.72)	Latvia	-3.0	(2.27)	Italy	-10.1	(1.27)
Australia	9.7	(1.17)	Liechtenstein	-5.5	(7.14)	Denmark	-9.5	(2.01)
Macao-China	9.2	(1.38)				Kazakhstan	-9.0	(2.29)
Hong Kong-China	8.2	(1.77)				Austria	-8.9	(2.00)
Azerbaijan	7.6	(1.68)				Lithuania	-8.4	(2.38)
Poland	7.2	(1.89)				Russian Federation	-7.5	(2.30)
Ireland	7.0	(2.35)				Panama	-6.9	(2.69)
Romania	6.8	(2.01)				Estonia	-6.7	(2.23)
Japan	6.5	(1.82)				Czech Republic	-6.4	(1.55)
Greece	5.3	(1.87)				Switzerland	-5.8	(1.56)
Chile	5.2	(1.79)				Argentina	-5.7	(2.09)
Shanghai-China	4.9	(1.80)				Israel	-5.6	(1.94)
Bulgaria	4.7	(2.04)				Germany	-5.1	(1.78)
Spain	4.2	(1.35)				United States	-4.4	(1.59)
Norway	3.8	(1.53)						
Canada	3.3	(0.99)						

Source: OECD, *PISA 2009 Database*, Table III.1.20.
StatLink ⟲🇸🇵 http://dx.doi.org/10.1787/888932360176

Frequent use of elaboration strategies tends to be positively associated with reading performance: the difference in performance between students who use elaboration strategies the most and students who use them the least is, on average, 14 points across OECD countries. However, the score point difference varies greatly across countries: the top quarter of students are at least 35 points, or half a proficiency level, ahead of the bottom quarter of students in Korea, Japan, Portugal, Norway and the partner country and economies Chinese Taipei, Jordan and Macao-China (Figure III.1.18 and Table IIII.1.22).

■ Figure III.1.18 ■
Relationship between the use of elaboration strategies and performance in reading

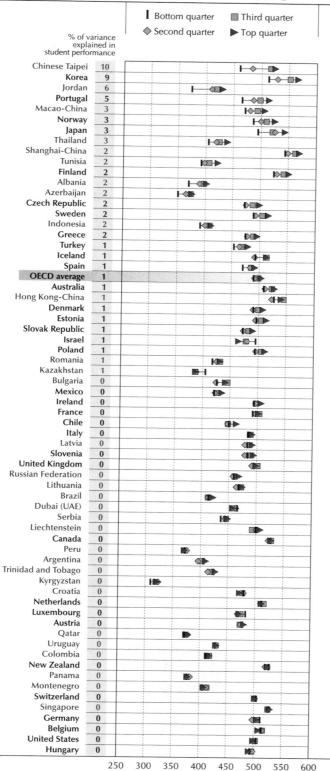

Countries are ranked in descending order of the percentage of explained variance in student performance.
Source: OECD, *PISA 2009 Database,* Table III.2.22.
StatLink ᴍᴤᴘ http://dx.doi.org/10.1787/888932360176

Overall, the data suggest that learning strategies that are most closely related to student reading performance are: strategies to understand and remember information, strategies to summarise information and control strategies. Reported use of elaboration strategies, and particularly memorisation strategies, are associated with improved reading performance in some countries but not in others.

DO OBSERVED ASSOCIATIONS MIRROR THE DEMOGRAPHIC AND SOCIO-ECONOMIC BACKGROUND OF STUDENTS?

Not all students reported being equally engaged in reading activities and using memorisation, elaboration and control strategies to the same extent, nor are they equally aware of the most effective strategies to understand, remember and summarise information. Students also vary considerably in their average performance in the PISA 2009 reading assessment. Volume I, *What Students Know and Can Do*, illustrates how girls generally outperform boys, while Volume II, *Overcoming Social Background*, shows how socio-economically advantaged students are, on average, more proficient readers than students from socio-economically disadvantaged backgrounds. Therefore, the kind of associations presented in the previous sections could mirror not just engagement in reading and the use of appropriate learning strategies but also the socio-economic background of students.

Results presented in Tables III.1.24, III.1.25 and III.1.26 illustrate the extent to which different levels of engagement, use and knowledge of learning strategies are associated with reading performance when adjusting for gender, socio-economic background, students' immigrant status and whether they speak the same language at home as the language in which the PISA assessment was administered.

Overall, results on the relationship between reading performance and higher levels of enjoyment of reading, greater diversity of reading activities, greater use of memorisation, elaboration and control strategies, and greater awareness of the most effective strategies to understand, remember and summarise information do not change substantially when accounting for the socio-economic background of students. In some countries and for some indices, however, accounting for the socio-economic background of students makes a significant difference. For example in the the partner countries and economy Albania, Dubai (UAE) and Bulgaria, the difference between the observed relationship between enjoyment of reading and performance and the relationship that emerges after accounting for the socio-economic background of students exceeds 15 score points on the reading scale.

What do high-performing readers look like?

This section builds on evidence of the strong association between reading performance and what students read for enjoyment, and identifies six profiles of readers based on whether they read comic books, magazines, newspapers, fiction and non-fiction books for enjoyment – as an indicator of how "wide" their reading habits are – as well as on their awareness of effective learning strategies to understand, remember and summarise information – as indicators of how "deep" their reading and learning is. Figure III.1.19 illustrates how the reading process can be characterised along the width and depth dimensions.

■ Figure III.1.19 ■
How the reading process can be characterised

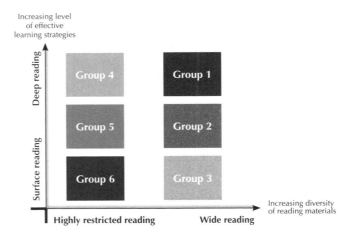

■ Figure III.1.20 ■
Profiles of readers

	Does not read any material regularly	Reads magazines and newspapers regularly	Reads all material regularly
High levels of effective learning strategies	Deep and highly restricted readers	Deep and narrow readers	Deep and wide readers
Low levels of effective learning strategies	Surface and highly restricted readers	Surface and narrow readers	Surface and wide readers

Results presented in previous sections of this chapter indicated that countries differ considerably with respect to whether, how much and what students read for enjoyment, and to what extent students know and use effective learning strategies. This section uses Latent Profile Analysis (Annex A5) to group students into the six profiles shown in Figure III.1.20 and determines whether proficient readers share common characteristics in all PISA participating countries.

- **Group 1 – Deep and wide readers:** Students who have high levels of awareness about effective learning strategies and who read all sorts of materials, including fiction and non-fiction books for enjoyment, can be considered as "deep and wide readers". The average index value of "remembering and understanding" among students in this group is 0.2, and the average of the index value of "summarising" is 0.6. Over 99% of students in this group read fiction at least several times a month and 53% reported reading non-fiction at least several times per month. Students in this group are those who have high levels of awareness about the most effective strategies to understand, remember and summarise information, but who also read all types of materials regularly. An estimated 19% of students across OECD countries are in this group (Table III.1.27).

- **Group 2 – Deep and narrow readers:** Students in this group are those who have as high levels of awareness about the most effective strategies to understand, remember and summarise information as students in Group 1, but who also read magazines and newspapers regularly: 85% read magazines and 83% read newspapers at least several times per month. They reported rarely reading comic books, fiction and non-fiction books. Across OECD countries, 25% of students are in Group 2 (Table III.1.27).

- **Group 3 – Deep and highly restricted readers:** Students in this group are those who are aware of effective learning strategies, but who do not read any material often. The average of the "remembering and understanding" index is 0.2, and the average of the "summarising" index is 0.6. The only type of material they read frequently is newspapers (37%). A small percentage (26%) frequently reads magazines or comics (12%) or fiction (17%), and an even smaller percentage (6%) reported reading non-fiction. Across OECD countries, 29% of students belong to Group 3 (Table III.1.27).

- **Group 4 – Surface and wide readers:** Students in this group are those who have low levels of awareness of effective strategies to understand, summarise and remember information, but who read all types of materials regularly. The average index value of "remembering and understanding" among students in this group is -0.7, and the average of index value of "summarising" is -1.5. Almost all students in Group 4 read fiction at least several times per month, and 53% of students in Group 4 read non-fiction books regularly. Across OECD countries, 5% of students are in Group 4 (Table III.1.27).

- **Group 5 – Surface and narrow readers:** Students in this group are those who have little awareness of effective strategies to understand, remember and summarise information (the level of their awareness about effective learning strategies is similar to that of students in Group 4), but who generally read magazines and newspapers for enjoyment regularly (85% read magazines and 83% read newspapers several times per month) and who are also likely to read non-fiction books: about 15% of students in Group 5 reported reading non-fiction books at least several times per month. Across OECD countries, 10% of students are in Group 5 (Table III.1.27).

- **Group 6 – Surface and highly restricted readers:** Students in this group are those who have low levels of awareness about effective learning strategies and who spend little time reading any type of printed material for enjoyment, especially fiction and non-fiction books. The only type of material these students read frequently is newspapers: 37% reported reading newspapers at least several times per month. Only 17% of students in this group read fiction at least several times a month, and only 6% read non-fiction books regularly – and these are the types of reading materials that are most strongly associated with reading proficiency. Across OECD countries, 13% of students belong to Group 6 (Table III.1.27).

■ Figure III.1.21 ■
Share of students by reader profile

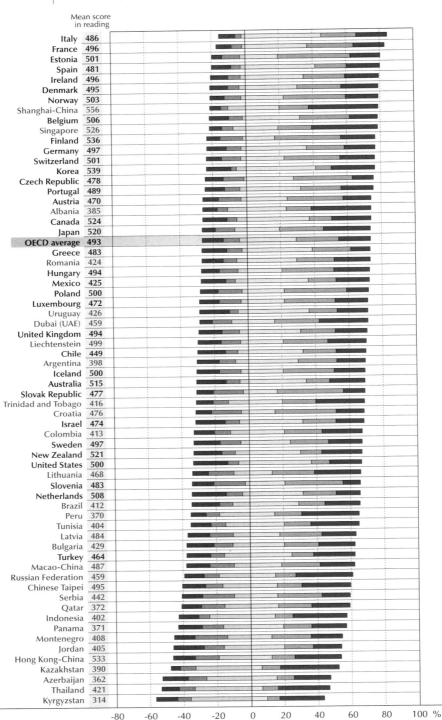

Countries are ranked in descending order of the percentage of students in G1, G2 and G3.
Source: OECD, *PISA 2009 Database*, Tables I.2.3 and III.1.27.
StatLink ⟐⟐⟐ http://dx.doi.org/10.1787/888932360176

What students read and how "wide" their reading habits are may be less indicative of better reading performance than *how* they read or how "deeply" they can read. Practicing reading by reading for enjoyment is most effective when it is accompanied by high levels of critical thinking and strategic learning. Across OECD countries, students who have low levels of awareness about which strategies are most effective for understanding, remembering and summarising information are less proficient readers than those who have high levels of awareness about these strategies, regardless of the students' reading patterns. Students in Groups 1, 2 and 3 are, in fact, more proficient readers, on average, than students in Groups 4, 5 and 6 (Figure III.1.22 and Table III.1.28).

■ Figure III.1.22 ■
How different kinds of readers perform in reading

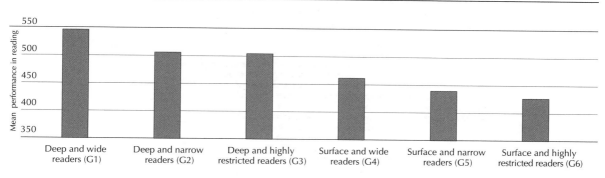

Source: OECD, *PISA 2009 Database,* Table III.1.28.
StatLink ▤▤▤ http://dx.doi.org/10.1787/888932360176

Students in Group 1 achieve an average of 546 points in the reading assessment. These are students who have high levels of awareness about effective learning strategies and who regularly read all types of materials, including fiction and non-fiction books: they are "wide and deep readers". The improved reading performance that is associated with high levels of knowledge about effective learning strategies is notable in OECD countries in general, but particularly in Iceland, Australia, Finland, the Netherlands, Japan, Slovenia, Sweden, Belgium, Norway, Spain, the Slovak Republic, the Czech Republic, Austria, France and Switzerland, and in the partner country and economy Dubai (UAE) and Bulgaria. Students in Groups 2 and 3, who have high levels of knowledge about learning strategies and who either do not read for enjoyment regularly (Group 3) or read magazines and newspapers regularly (Group 2) attain almost the same score (506 and 504 points, respectively). Students who have low levels of awareness of learning strategies but read diverse materials regularly, *i.e.* those in Group 4, have an average score of 462. Students in Group 5 who have low levels of knowledge about learning strategies but who read magazines and newspapers regularly, achieve marginally higher scores (440). Students in Group 6 (low levels of knowledge about learning strategies and low levels of reading for enjoyment) are the least capable readers. Students in this group achieve 427 points in the PISA reading assessment on average across OECD countries (Table III.1.28).

Figure III.1.23 illustrates how many countries with high overall performance in the PISA 2009 reading assessment are countries where many students can be classified in Groups 1 and 2. For example, in Finland, almost 60% of students belong to Group 1 or Group 2 and 21% belong to either Group 5 or Group 6. Conversely, many of the countries with below-average performance in the 2009 PISA reading assessment have high shares of students in Groups 5 and 6 and few students in Groups 1 and 2. For example, in the partner country Jordan, 30% of students belong to Group 5 or Group 6 and only 34% belong to Groups 1 or 2.

■ Figure III.1.23 ■

Country-level performance in reading and the prevalence of different profiles of readers

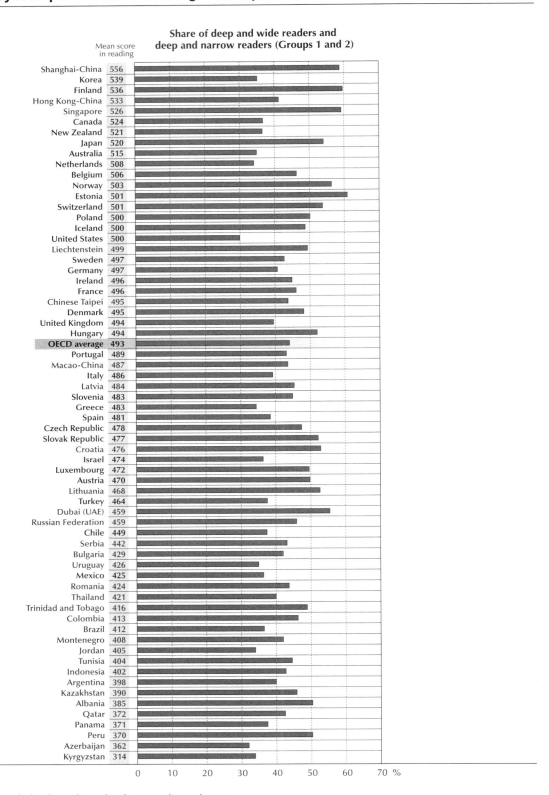

Share of deep and wide readers and
deep and narrow readers (Groups 1 and 2)

Mean score
in reading

Country	Mean score
Shanghai-China	556
Korea	539
Finland	536
Hong Kong-China	533
Singapore	526
Canada	524
New Zealand	521
Japan	520
Australia	515
Netherlands	508
Belgium	506
Norway	503
Estonia	501
Switzerland	501
Poland	500
Iceland	500
United States	500
Liechtenstein	499
Sweden	497
Germany	497
Ireland	496
France	496
Chinese Taipei	495
Denmark	495
United Kingdom	494
Hungary	494
OECD average	493
Portugal	489
Macao-China	487
Italy	486
Latvia	484
Slovenia	483
Greece	483
Spain	481
Czech Republic	478
Slovak Republic	477
Croatia	476
Israel	474
Luxembourg	472
Austria	470
Lithuania	468
Turkey	464
Dubai (UAE)	459
Russian Federation	459
Chile	449
Serbia	442
Bulgaria	429
Uruguay	426
Mexico	425
Romania	424
Thailand	421
Trinidad and Tobago	416
Colombia	413
Brazil	412
Montenegro	408
Jordan	405
Tunisia	404
Indonesia	402
Argentina	398
Kazakhstan	390
Albania	385
Qatar	372
Panama	371
Peru	370
Azerbaijan	362
Kyrgyzstan	314

0   10   20   30   40   50   60   70 %

Countries are ranked in descending order of mean reading performance.
Source: OECD, *PISA 2009 Database,* Tables III.1.27 and I.2.3.
StatLink ᴍᴤᴸ http://dx.doi.org/10.1787/888932360176

Notes

1. In PISA 2009, several tests were conducted to determine whether the use of country-specific item parameters improved cross-country comparability of indices. For example, simulation studies indicated that using country-specific item parameters in regression models did not lead to improvements in the comparability of indices across countries. During the estimation procedure, an index of differential item functioning (DIF) across countries is produced that can be used to gauge the amount of DIF for each item across countries. If necessary, the impact of DIF on items can then be tackled using country-specific item parameters. However, simulation studies have shown that introducing country-specific item parameters for DIF items has a negligible impact on the regression coefficients in a two-level regression (students within countries) of background variables (with and without country-specific items) on cognitive scores in reading, math and science.

2. The score point difference represents the average difference in PISA scores that students can expect to have when one student enjoys reading to the same degree as the average student in the OECD area (index value of 0) and the other enjoys reading more than five out of six students in the OECD area do (index value of 1).

3. The scale had the response categories "I do not read for enjoyment", "30 minutes or less each day", "more than 30 minutes to less than 60 minutes each day", "1 to 2 hours each day" and "more than 2 hours each day".

4. Results show the difference in reading performance between students who do not read any material and students who read a particular material, adjusting for other materials a student may also report reading on a regular basis.

5. Results show the difference in reading performance between students who do not read any material and students who read a particular material, adjusting for other materials a student may also report reading on a regular basis.

6. These are students who have values on the *index of diversity of reading activities* that are below the average value for students in their country.

2

The Reading
and Learning Habits
of 15-Year-Olds

Students' reading and learning habits not only affect their performance in school, but can influence how they live their lives after their school careers. Based on students' own reports, this chapter examines country differences in how much students read for enjoyment, what they read, and how much they enjoy reading. It also discusses students' knowledge and use of effective learning strategies.

Chapter 1 shows that students who reported being highly engaged in reading activities and those who approach learning positively are more proficient readers than students who reported not being engaged in reading activities and having less positive approaches to learning.

This chapter explores to what extent countries differ in how much their students reported reading for enjoyment, in what they reported reading and in how much they reported enjoying reading, as well as whether students have "learned how to learn" by favouring and adopting effective learning strategies.

The reading and learning habits students develop as youngsters not only affect their current reading performance, but are also important outcomes in their own right and can shape students' future lifestyles and practices.

PROFILES OF READERS

The six groups into which Chapter 1 classified students, depending on their characteristics as learners, provide the starting point for the analysis presented in this chapter.

- **Group 1 – Deep and Wide Readers:** High levels of awareness of effective strategies to understand, remember and summarise information, and regular reading of all materials (Table III.1.27). Across OECD countries, 19% of students belong to Group 1.

- **Group 2 – Deep and Narrow Readers:** High levels of awareness of effective strategies to understand, remember and summarise information, and regularly reading of magazines and newspapers (Table III.1.27). Across OECD countries, 25% of students belong to Group 2.

- **Group 3 – Deep and Highly Restricted Readers:** High levels of awareness of effective strategies to understand, remember and summarise information, and very limited reading practices (Table III.1.27). Across OECD countries, 29% of students belong to Group 3.

- **Group 4 – Surface and Wide Readers:** Low levels of awareness of effective strategies to understand, remember and summarise information, and very limited reading practices (Table III.1.27). Across OECD countries, 5% of students belong to Group 4.

- **Group 5 – Surface and Narrow Readers:** Low levels of awareness of effective strategies to understand, remember and summarise information, and regular reading of magazines and newspapers (Table III.1.27). Across OECD countries, 10% of students belong to Group 5.

- **Group 6 – Surface and Highly Restricted Readers:** Low levels of awareness of effective strategies to understand, remember and summarise information, and very limited reading practices (Table III.1.27). Across OECD countries, 13% of students belong to Group 6.

Countries vary widely in the proportion of their students who fall into each of the six groups: more than 30% of 15-year-olds in the partner countries and economies Kazakhstan, the Russian Federation, Albania, Singapore, Shanghai-China, Indonesia, Peru and Thailand belong to Group 1, while in Slovenia, Greece, the Czech Republic, the Slovak Republic, Poland and the Netherlands, less than 15% of students read regularly and have high levels of awareness about effective strategies to understand, remember and summarise information. In the partner countries and economy Albania, Shanghai-China and Singapore there is a particularly high prevalence of "Group 1 students" and a particularly low prevalence of "Group 6 students". These are countries and economies where most students read a variety of materials frequently and critically, and where few students do not read any materials for enjoyment regularly and show low levels of awareness about effective learning strategies. In contrast, in Jordan, 18% of students belong to Group 6 and 17% of students belong to Group 1. Few students in Jordan read a variety of materials frequently and critically, while many other students there do not read for enjoyment regularly and are unaware of effective learning strategies.

The difference in the share of boys and girls who approach their learning positively and who read a wide variety of texts for enjoyment, in other words, students who are "deep and wide" readers, is, on average, approximately 11 percentage points across OECD countries (Table III.1.29). The gender gap in the share of "deep and wide" readers is relatively small – less than 10 percentage points – in France, Japan, Korea and the partner countries Montenegro, Colombia, Jordan, Qatar, Kyrgyzstan and Azerbaijan, while it is above 20 percentage points in Finland and the partner countries Lithuania and Albania. Boys are under-represented among students who are "deep and wide" readers in all the PISA participating countries and economies; and they are over-represented among students who read very little and who are not aware of effective learning strategies, *i.e.* "narrow and surface" readers.

■ Figure III.2.1 ■

Share of boys and girls who are either deep and wide readers or deep and narrow readers

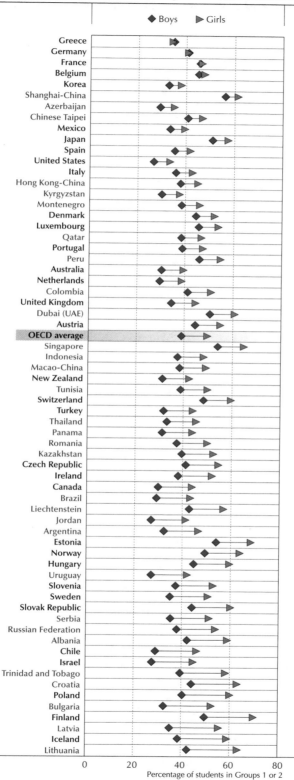

Countries are ranked in ascending order of the percentage difference of girls and boys in Groups 1 or 2.
Source: OECD, *PISA 2009 Database*, Table III.1.29.
StatLink ᴹˢᴾ http://dx.doi.org/10.1787/888932360195

■ Figure III.2.2 ■

Share of socio-economically advantaged and disadvantaged students who are either deep and wide readers or deep and narrow readers

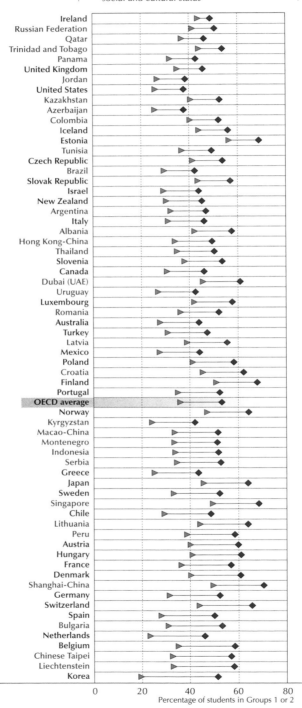

◆ Top quarter of the PISA index of economic, social and cultural status

▶ Bottom quarter of the PISA index of economic, social and cultural status

Percentage of students in Groups 1 or 2

Countries are ranked in ascending order of the percentage difference of students in Groups 1 or 2 in the top and bottom quarter of the PISA index of economic, social and cultural status.
Source: OECD, *PISA 2009 Database,* Table III.1.30.
StatLink ᴹˢᴸ http://dx.doi.org/10.1787/888932360195

The over-representation of boys among Group 6 readers is less than five percentage points in 14 countries and economies, while it is greater than 10 percentage points in Canada, Sweden, Poland, Israel, Iceland and Australia and the partner countries Serbia, the Russian Federation, Brazil, Bulgaria and Latvia (the OECD average is 8%).

Similarly, Figure III.2.2 shows that the difference in the share of "deep and wide" readers from a socio-economically disadvantaged or advantaged background is about 13 percentage points on average across the OECD countries. In 14 OECD countries and five partner countries and economies, the difference in the share of "deep and wide readers" between socio-economically advantaged and disadvantaged students is greater than 15 percentage points. Only in the partner countries Colombia, Argentina, Tunisia, Trinidad and Tobago and Jordan is there no observed difference in the share of socio-economically advantaged and disadvantaged students who belong to Group 1. Socio-economically advantaged students, on the other hand, are particularly over-represented among "deep and wide" readers in Korea and the partner countries Singapore and Liechtenstein. In all these countries, the difference in the share of socio-economically advantaged and disadvantaged students who belong to Group 1 is 20 percentage points or more. A similar picture emerges when examining whether different socio-economic groups are over- or under-represented among "surface and narrow" readers: on average in the OECD area, the difference between the share of socio-economically advantaged and disadvantaged students who belong to Group 6 is 10 percentage points. In Korea, Belgium and the partner country Uruguay, the under-representation of socio-economically advantaged students among Group 6 readers is 15 percentage points or more (Table III.1.30).

THE READING HABITS OF 15-YEAR-OLD STUDENTS

How often do students read for enjoyment?

Cross-country differences in whether, and for how long, students reported reading for enjoyment may be due to differences in the extent to which various traditions and cultures value reading, in the opportunities students have to read outside of school, the extent to which students find reading an enjoyable activity and the materials students can access in their free time. Given the fact that reading habits are self-reported by participating students, such differences could also stem partly from how much students in different countries over- or under-report their reading habits (Box III.1.3 for a detailed description of difficulties in interpreting cross-country differences in self-reported reading habits).[1]

On average across OECD countries, 37% of students reported that they did not read for enjoyment; in Austria and the partner country Liechtenstein, more than half of the 15-year-olds reported not reading for enjoyment at all. In contrast, more than 90% of students in the partner countries and economy Kazakhstan, Albania, Shanghai-China and Thailand said that they read for enjoyment (Figure III.2.3). Another 30% of students across the OECD area reported reading for 30 minutes or less per day, 17% read for more than 30 minutes but less than one hour per day, 11% read for between one and two hours per day, and fewer than 5% read for more than two hours daily (Table III.1.3). Greece is the only OECD country where more than 10% of students read for enjoyment for longer than two hours on a daily basis.

Girls read more for enjoyment than boys in all countries and economies, except for Korea. Figure III.2.4 (Table III.1.4) shows that the frequency of reading for enjoyment is 21 percentage points higher for girls than for boys, on average across the OECD countries. In Italy, Canada, the Czech Republic, Finland, Germany, Portugal, Slovenia, Poland, Estonia, the Netherlands and the partner countries Uruguay, Latvia and Lithuania, the difference in the number of girls and boys who read for enjoyment is 25 percentage points or larger. In Korea, boys and girls are equally likely to read for enjoyment, and gender differences in reading for enjoyment are also relatively small in Japan and the partner countries and economies Kazakhstan, Azerbaijan, Peru, Shanghai-China, Jordan, Kyrgyzstan, Hong Kong-China, Indonesia, Albania and Thailand. The gender gap in whether boys and girls read for enjoyment is widening: as Figure III.2.5 shows, between 2000 and 2009, both boys and girls lost interest in reading, but the decrease in the number of boys reading for enjoyment was greater than that in the number of girls (Chapter 5 in Volume V, *Learning Trends: Changes in Student Performance since 2000,* for a detailed description of changes in reading habits between 2000 and 2009).

■ Figure III.2.3 ■
Percentage of students who read for enjoyment

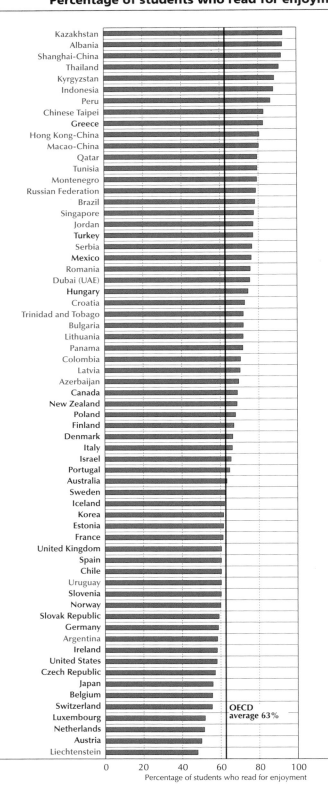

Percentage of students who read for enjoyment

Countries are ranked in descending order of the percentage of students who read for enjoyment.
Source: OECD, *PISA 2009 Database,* Table III.1.4.
StatLink http://dx.doi.org/10.1787/888932360195

■ Figure III.2.4 ■
Percentage of boys and girls who read for enjoyment

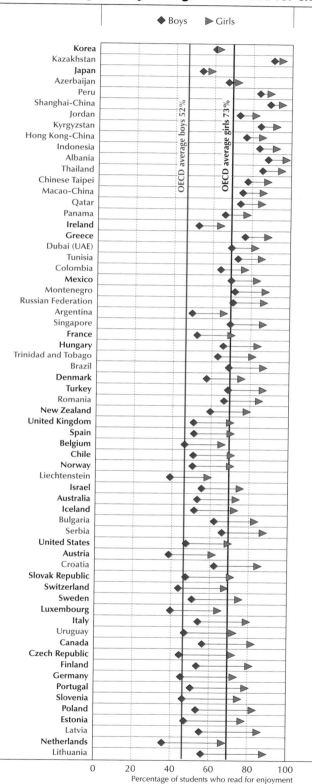

◆ Boys   ▶ Girls

Countries are ranked in ascending order of the difference of boys and girls who read for enjoyment.
Source: OECD, *PISA 2009 Database*, Table III.1.4.
StatLink ᐃᔐ http://dx.doi.org/10.1787/888932360195

■ Figure III.2.5 ■

Change in the percentage of boys and girls who read for enjoyment between 2000 and 2009

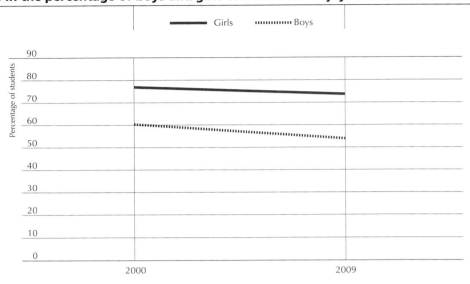

Note: OECD average for 26 countries in 2000 and 2009.
Source: OECD, *PISA 2009 Database,* Table V.5.1.
StatLink ᵐ𝔰┹ http://dx.doi.org/10.1787/888932360195

On average across OECD countries, 72% of socio-economically advantaged students – students in the top quarter of the *PISA index of economic, social and cultural status* in the country of assessment – reported reading for enjoyment daily while only 56% of disadvantaged students reported doing the same. In general, the difference in whether socio-economically advantaged and disadvantaged students read for enjoyment is greater among OECD countries than among partner countries and economies. In eleven OECD countries – Ireland, Germany, France, Belgium, Luxembourg, Australia, Switzerland, Korea, Estonia, Austria and Luxembourg – the difference in the share of socio-economically advantaged and disadvantaged students who read for enjoyment is more than 20 percentage points (Table III.1.5).

Figures III.2.7, III.2.8 and III.2.9 relate country-level differences in the share of students who reported reading for enjoyment to the activities in which students engage both in and outside school. Differences in what students do while at school, in the length of the school day, homework requirements and other out-of-school activities may, in fact, limit students' opportunities to read for enjoyment.

PISA 2009 does not contain sufficient information to map countries and economies precisely on the basis of how much time students spend in school, doing homework and in different out-of-school activities. Figures III.2.7, III.2.8 and III.2.9, however, show that countries and economies in which large numbers of students do not read for enjoyment are not necessarily those where students spend more time in regular school lessons on the language of instruction, science and mathematics; but that participation in remedial and enrichment courses may at least partially crowd-out students' reading for enjoyment. When students engage in remedial and enrichment courses, reading for enjoyment may be one of the entertainment activities that students are willing to forgo (Volume IV, *What Makes a School Successful?,* for a detailed description of between- and within-country variations in the time students spend in regular lessons at school and in after-school lessons).

In general, countries and economies where large numbers of students reported participating in literature courses and in school activities that are aimed at interpreting literary texts are also those where large numbers of students reported reading for enjoyment in PISA 2009. Figure III.2.10 and Figure III.2.11 indicate that school activities do not dampen, but rather foster students' interest in reading and motivation to read in their free time.

■ Figure III.2.6 ■
Percentage of students who read for enjoyment, by socio-economic background

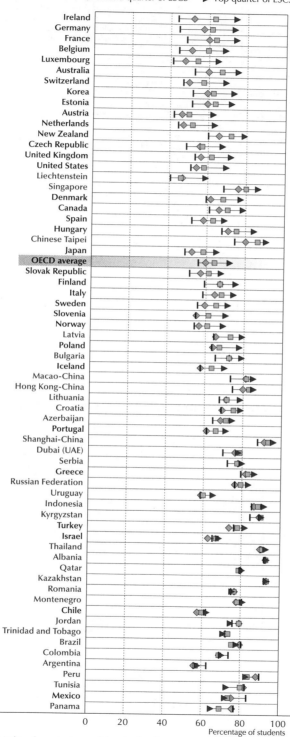

Note: ESCS refers to the PISA index of economics, social and cultural status.
Countries are ranked in descending order of the difference between the percentage of students who read for enjoyment in the top and bottom quarter of ESCS.
Source: OECD, *PISA 2009 Database,* Table III.1.5.
StatLink ᴍᴤᴸ http://dx.doi.org/10.1787/888932360195

■ Figure III.2.7 ■

Does time spent in regular lessons at school crowd-out reading for enjoyment?

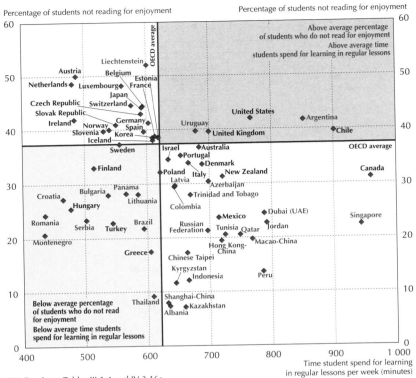

Source: OECD, *PISA 2009 Database,* Tables III.1.4 and IV.3.16a.
StatLink ⌐■⬚┗ http://dx.doi.org/10.1787/888932360195

■ Figure III.2.8 ■

Does participation in remedial lessons crowd-out reading for enjoyment?

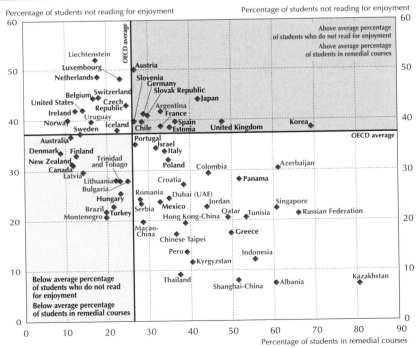

Source: OECD, *PISA 2009 Database,* Tables III.1.4 and IV.3.17a.
StatLink ⌐■⬚┗ http://dx.doi.org/10.1787/888932360195

■ Figure III.2.9 ■

Does participation in enrichment lessons crowd-out reading for enjoyment?

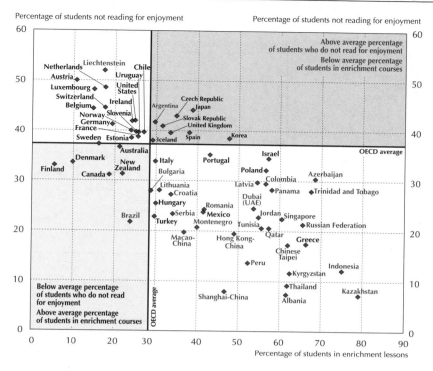

Source: OECD, *PISA 2009 Database,* Tables III.1.4 and IV.3.17a.
StatLink ᗰᕲᔿ http://dx.doi.org/10.1787/888932360195

■ Figure III.2.10 ■

Do education systems which value promoting the interpretation of literary texts at school have a larger number of students who read for enjoyment?

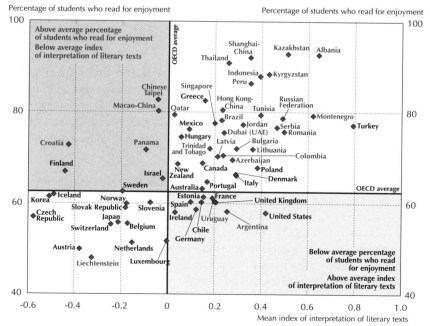

Source: OECD, *PISA 2009 Database,* Tables III.1.4 and III.2.3.
StatLink ᗰᕲᔿ http://dx.doi.org/10.1787/888932360195

■ Figure III.2.11 ■

Do education systems which value traditional literature courses have a larger number of students who read for enjoyment?

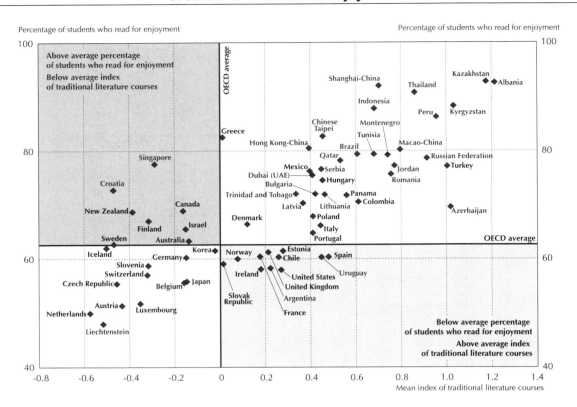

Source: OECD, *PISA 2009 Database,* Tables III.1.4 and III.2.5.
StatLink ⬛ http://dx.doi.org/10.1787/888932360195

What do students read for enjoyment?

Printed materials

Figure III.2.12 illustrates the share of students in OECD countries who reported reading regularly, either "several times a month" or "several times a week", and for their enjoyment, magazines, comic books, fiction (novels, narratives and stories), non-fiction or newspapers. On average across OECD countries, more than six in ten students reported reading magazines and newspapers regularly. About three in ten students, however, reported reading fiction regularly in OECD countries, while only about two in ten read comic books or non-fiction regularly (Table III.2.7).

Students in different countries reported similar tastes in what they liked to read. Magazines and newspapers were the materials students reported reading the most in almost all countries, while comic books and fiction were the materials that students reported they were least likely to read regularly in almost all countries (Figure III.2.12). Notable exceptions are found in two OECD countries. While students in Japan and, to a lesser extent, students in Finland, reported reading magazines and newspapers in line with students in the other OECD countries, these students were marginally less likely than students in the other OECD countries to read non-fiction, were more likely to read fiction and were especially likely to read comic books. The shares of students who reported reading magazines, fiction and non-fiction books regularly was in line with the average, but very few students in the United States reported reading newspapers and comic books regularly. Large shares of students in Korea reported reading fiction either several times a month or several times a week, while comparatively few of them read magazines regularly.

■ Figure III.2.12 [Part 1/2] ■
What students read for enjoyment

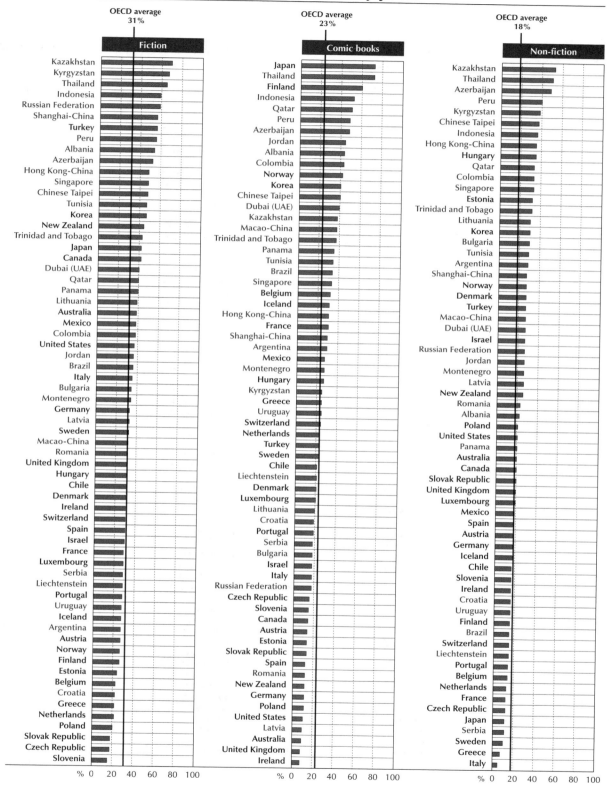

Countries are ranked in descending order of the percentage of students on the items of the index of diversity of reading materials.
Source: OECD, *PISA 2009 Database*, Table III.2.7.
StatLink ⟨ms⟩ http://dx.doi.org/10.1787/888932360195

■ Figure III.2.12 [Part 2/2] ■
What students read for enjoyment

Countries are ranked in descending order of the percentage of students on the items of the index of diversity of reading materials.
Source: OECD, *PISA 2009 Database*, Table III.2.7.
StatLink ᴍ𝔰ᴸ http://dx.doi.org/10.1787/888932360195

Although magazines and newspapers are the most common material students read for enjoyment, results presented in Volume V, *Learning Trends*, suggest that, on average across OECD countries, the share of students who read magazines and newspapers either several times a month or several times a week has declined sharply. Figure III.2.13 shows that, across the OECD countries that participated in both PISA 2000 and PISA 2009, the number of students reading newspapers has decreased by five percentage points, the number of students reading magazines has decreased by ten percentage points, while the number of students who reported reading fiction regularly has increased by three percentage points (Volume V, Chapter 5 for a detailed description of trends in reading patterns).

■ Figure III.2.13 ■
Change in what students read for enjoyment between 2000 and 2009, OECD average

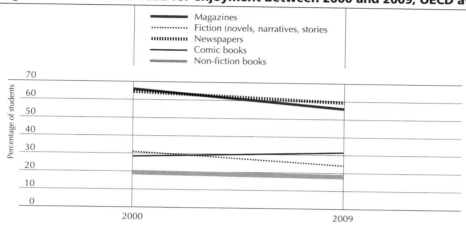

Note: OECD average for 26 countries in 2000 and 2009.
Source: OECD, *PISA 2009 Database*, Table V.5.6.
StatLink ᴍᴩ http://dx.doi.org/10.1787/888932360195

Boys are not only less likely than girls to report reading for enjoyment in almost all countries – with the exception of Korea (Figure III.2.14 and Table III.1.4), they also have different reading patterns. On average across OECD countries, 66% of boys read newspapers for enjoyment regularly, while only 59% of girls do so. Although reading comic books regularly is much less common, on average in OECD countries, boys are 33% more likely than girls to read comic books several times a month or several times a week (27% for boys and 18% for girls). On the other hand, girls are more likely than boys to be frequent readers of fiction in every participating country (Figure III.2.14 and Table III.2.8), and in almost all countries, girls are more likely than boys to read magazines (65% for girls and 51% for boys).

■ Figure III. 2.14 ■
What boys and girls read for enjoyment, OECD average
Percentage of boys and girls who reported that they read the following materials because they want to "several times a month" or "several times a week"

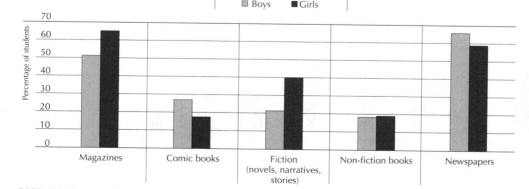

Source: OECD, *PISA 2009 Database*, Table III.2.8.
StatLink ᴍᴩ http://dx.doi.org/10.1787/888932360195

Table III.1.10 shows the extent to which students in different participating countries can be considered to be diversified readers, that is, whether they read a wide variety of reading materials for their own enjoyment. The *index of diversity of reading materials*, set to have a mean of 0 and a standard deviation of 1 across OECD countries, suggests that within OECD countries, students in Turkey, Finland, Japan, Norway, Estonia and Hungary tend to read a variety of materials, while students in Greece, the Netherlands and the United States are more likely to favour particular materials over others when reading for enjoyment.

Online reading activities

On average across OECD countries, the most common type of online reading activity reported by students is chatting on line, with almost three-quarters of students reporting that they engaged in this activity at least several times a week. This is followed by reading e-mails (64%) and searching online information (51%). In virtually all countries, chatting online is the most common form of online reading activity, and where it is not – such as in Korea, Mexico and Turkey – searching for online information is the most common. Japan is a notable exception: in Japan, reading e-mails is by far the most frequent form of online reading activity (Table III.2.9).

Results presented in Table III.2.10 suggest that in most countries, boys and girls do not differ, or differ only marginally, in how much they use the Internet for reading for enjoyment. However, boys and girls appear to use the Internet for different purposes: Figure III.2.15 and Table III.2.10 show that girls are more likely than boys to use the Internet to communicate, while boys are more likely than girls to surf the Internet for information and to read the news.

■ Figure III.2.15 ■
What boys and girls read on line, OECD average
Percentage of boys and girls who reported that they were involved in the following online reading activities "several times a week" or "several times a day"

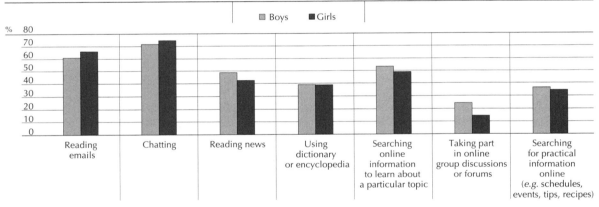

Source: OECD, *PISA 2009 Database,* Table III.2.10.
StatLink ⌨ http://dx.doi.org/10.1787/888932360195

■ Figure III.2.16 ■
What students enjoy about reading, OECD average

Source: OECD, *PISA 2009 Database,* Table III.2.11.
StatLink ⌨ http://dx.doi.org/10.1787/888932360195

■ Figure III.2.17 ■

To what extent do students who read for enjoyment enjoy reading

Legend:
◆ Average index of enjoyment of reading
● Students who do not read for enjoyment
▶ Students who read for enjoyment

Average index of enjoyment of reading		Students who do not read for enjoyment		Students who read for enjoyment		Difference between students who do not and students who read for enjoyment		Country
Mean Index	S.E.	Mean Index	S.E.	Mean Index	S.E.	Dif.	S.E.	
-0.13	(0.03)	-0.97	(0.03)	0.71	(0.03)	-1.68	(0.05)	Austria
0.07	(0.02)	-0.90	(0.03)	0.76	(0.02)	-1.66	(0.03)	Germany
-0.04	(0.02)	-0.92	(0.02)	0.67	(0.02)	-1.59	(0.03)	Switzerland
-0.20	(0.05)	-0.96	(0.05)	0.60	(0.07)	-1.56	(0.08)	Liechtenstein
0.13	(0.01)	-0.91	(0.01)	0.62	(0.02)	-1.53	(0.02)	Canada
0.00	(0.02)	-0.96	(0.01)	0.55	(0.03)	-1.50	(0.03)	Australia
-0.16	(0.02)	-0.90	(0.02)	0.55	(0.02)	-1.46	(0.03)	Luxembourg
0.05	(0.02)	-0.87	(0.03)	0.50	(0.02)	-1.37	(0.04)	Finland
0.01	(0.03)	-0.83	(0.03)	0.52	(0.05)	-1.35	(0.03)	France
-0.20	(0.02)	-0.94	(0.02)	0.41	(0.01)	-1.34	(0.02)	Belgium
0.13	(0.02)	-0.79	(0.02)	0.55	(0.02)	-1.34	(0.02)	New Zealand
-0.04	(0.03)	-0.81	(0.02)	0.53	(0.02)	-1.34	(0.02)	United States
-0.08	(0.02)	-0.84	(0.03)	0.48	(0.02)	-1.32	(0.04)	Ireland
0.20	(0.02)	-0.53	(0.03)	0.77	(0.03)	-1.29	(0.05)	Japan
-0.06	(0.02)	-0.86	(0.02)	0.43	(0.02)	-1.29	(0.03)	Iceland
-0.11	(0.02)	-0.91	(0.03)	0.38	(0.02)	-1.29	(0.02)	Sweden
0.06	(0.02)	-0.86	(0.02)	0.42	(0.02)	-1.28	(0.03)	Lithuania
-0.19	(0.02)	-0.94	(0.03)	0.34	(0.04)	-1.28	(0.03)	Norway
-0.32	(0.03)	-0.97	(0.02)	0.30	(0.03)	-1.27	(0.02)	Netherlands
0.06	(0.01)	-0.77	(0.01)	0.49	(0.02)	-1.26	(0.02)	Italy
-0.12	(0.02)	-0.87	(0.02)	0.38	(0.02)	-1.26	(0.03)	United Kingdom
0.06	(0.02)	-0.77	(0.03)	0.47	(0.04)	-1.24	(0.03)	Israel
0.00	(0.00)	-0.76	(0.00)	0.47	(0.00)	-1.23	(0.01)	OECD average
0.02	(0.03)	-0.81	(0.03)	0.41	(0.03)	-1.21	(0.05)	Poland
-0.01	(0.01)	-0.73	(0.01)	0.46	(0.01)	-1.19	(0.02)	Spain
0.21	(0.02)	-0.54	(0.02)	0.62	(0.02)	-1.16	(0.02)	Portugal
0.29	(0.01)	-0.61	(0.03)	0.53	(0.03)	-1.14	(0.02)	Singapore
-0.20	(0.01)	-0.87	(0.02)	0.25	(0.02)	-1.12	(0.04)	Slovenia
-0.13	(0.02)	-0.76	(0.01)	0.34	(0.02)	-1.10	(0.02)	Czech Republic
-0.03	(0.02)	-0.70	(0.02)	0.38	(0.02)	-1.09	(0.02)	Estonia
-0.09	(0.02)	-0.80	(0.02)	0.28	(0.02)	-1.07	(0.03)	Denmark
0.14	(0.02)	-0.67	(0.02)	0.40	(0.04)	-1.07	(0.05)	Hungary
0.28	(0.02)	-0.53	(0.03)	0.54	(0.02)	-1.07	(0.02)	Dubai (UAE)
0.39	(0.02)	-0.46	(0.03)	0.58	(0.02)	-1.04	(0.04)	Chinese Taipei
-0.13	(0.02)	-0.84	(0.02)	0.14	(0.02)	-0.99	(0.03)	Croatia
0.21	(0.01)	-0.57	(0.03)	0.41	(0.02)	-0.99	(0.03)	Montenegro
-0.02	(0.03)	-0.72	(0.02)	0.26	(0.04)	-0.98	(0.04)	Bulgaria
-0.14	(0.02)	-0.72	(0.02)	0.25	(0.02)	-0.98	(0.02)	Uruguay
-0.04	(0.02)	-0.70	(0.02)	0.24	(0.02)	-0.94	(0.04)	Latvia
0.21	(0.01)	-0.47	(0.02)	0.47	(0.02)	-0.94	(0.02)	Trinidad and Tobago
0.37	(0.02)	-0.36	(0.05)	0.58	(0.02)	-0.93	(0.04)	Tunisia
0.32	(0.01)	-0.41	(0.02)	0.51	(0.02)	-0.93	(0.03)	Hong Kong-China
-0.10	(0.02)	-0.64	(0.02)	0.27	(0.02)	-0.91	(0.03)	Slovak Republic
0.27	(0.01)	-0.43	(0.02)	0.47	(0.01)	-0.90	(0.02)	Brazil
0.67	(0.02)	-0.15	(0.04)	0.74	(0.01)	-0.89	(0.04)	Albania
0.07	(0.02)	-0.65	(0.03)	0.23	(0.03)	-0.88	(0.05)	Greece
0.13	(0.02)	-0.42	(0.02)	0.46	(0.03)	-0.88	(0.04)	Korea
0.04	(0.02)	-0.62	(0.03)	0.25	(0.03)	-0.88	(0.03)	Serbia
0.57	(0.01)	-0.23	(0.05)	0.64	(0.01)	-0.86	(0.05)	Shanghai-China
0.20	(0.01)	-0.47	(0.02)	0.37	(0.01)	-0.85	(0.02)	Qatar
0.14	(0.01)	-0.48	(0.01)	0.34	(0.01)	-0.82	(0.02)	Mexico
-0.06	(0.01)	-0.55	(0.02)	0.27	(0.03)	-0.82	(0.03)	Chile
0.10	(0.02)	-0.49	(0.02)	0.30	(0.03)	-0.79	(0.03)	Romania
0.08	(0.01)	-0.55	(0.02)	0.23	(0.01)	-0.79	(0.02)	Macao-China
0.54	(0.02)	-0.17	(0.04)	0.60	(0.02)	-0.78	(0.05)	Kazakhstan
0.07	(0.01)	-0.52	(0.03)	0.24	(0.02)	-0.75	(0.04)	Russian Federation
-0.16	(0.02)	-0.58	(0.03)	0.14	(0.02)	-0.73	(0.04)	Argentina
0.64	(0.02)	0.09	(0.03)	0.80	(0.02)	-0.70	(0.04)	Turkey
0.37	(0.02)	-0.16	(0.02)	0.54	(0.02)	-0.70	(0.04)	Jordan
0.18	(0.02)	-0.32	(0.06)	0.38	(0.04)	-0.70	(0.08)	Panama
0.14	(0.02)	-0.34	(0.05)	0.30	(0.07)	-0.64	(0.03)	Colombia
0.35	(0.01)	-0.16	(0.03)	0.44	(0.02)	-0.61	(0.03)	Peru
0.54	(0.01)	-0.01	(0.04)	0.59	(0.01)	-0.60	(0.04)	Thailand
0.39	(0.01)	0.03	(0.04)	0.42	(0.03)	-0.39	(0.03)	Kyrgyzstan
0.43	(0.01)	0.16	(0.05)	0.48	(0.01)	-0.32	(0.05)	Indonesia
0.39	(0.01)	0.23	(0.02)	0.47	(0.02)	-0.23	(0.03)	Azerbaijan

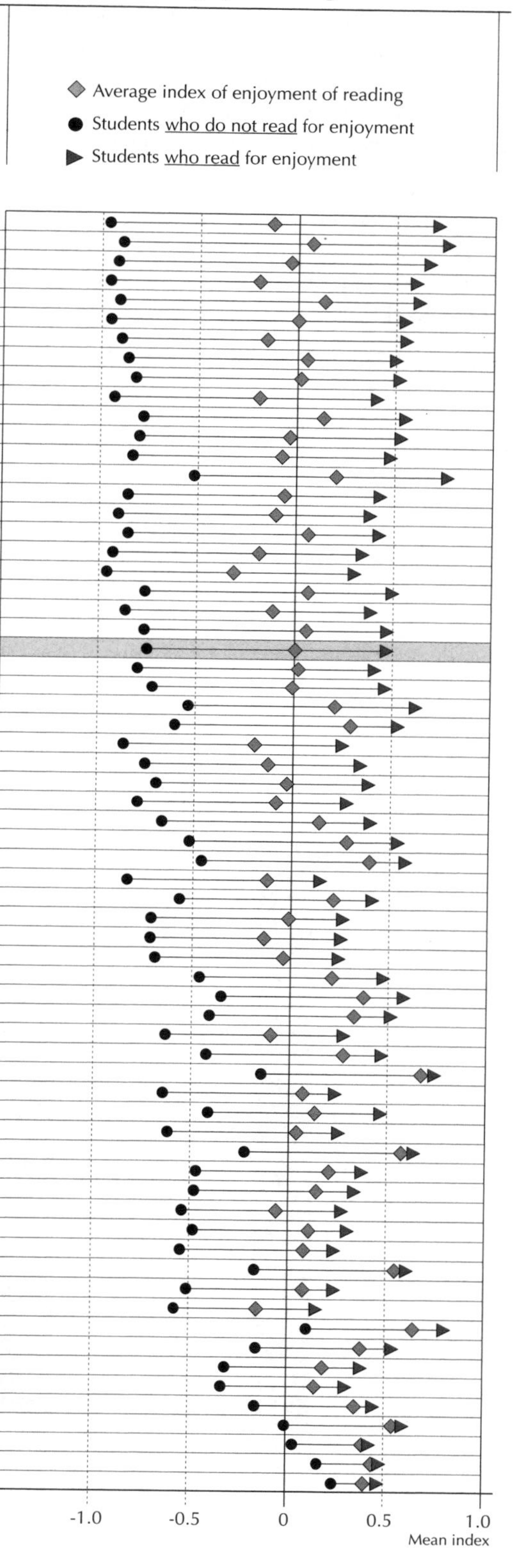

Note: All mean index differences between students who do not and students who read for enjoyment are statistically significant.
Countries are ranked in descending order of the mean index differences between students who do not and students who read for enjoyment.
Source: OECD, *PISA 2009 Database.*
StatLink ⟐⟐⟐ http://dx.doi.org/10.1787/888932360195

How much do students enjoy reading?

Being interested in and enjoying particular subjects, or being intrinsically motivated, can affect both the degree and the continuity shown by a student's engagement in learning and the depth of understanding achieved. Research has shown this effect to operate largely independently of students' general motivation to learn. For example, a student who is interested in reading may or may not show a high level of general learning motivation and vice versa. Hence, an analysis of the pattern of students' interest in reading is important because it may reveal strengths and weaknesses in the attempts made by education systems to promote a greater desire to read among different sub-groups of students.

On average across OECD countries, relatively large proportions of students reported negative attitudes towards reading beyond the essential. For instance, 46% of students agreed or strongly agreed that they read only to obtain the information they need, 41% reported that they read only if they have to, 24% reported that reading is a waste of time and only one-third of students agreed or strongly agreed that reading was one of their favourite hobbies (Table III.2.11).

Figure III.2.3 and Table III.1.3 show how countries vary with respect to how many of their students read for enjoyment and how much time they spend doing so. Students who do not read for enjoyment are those who generally do not enjoy reading. Figure III.2.17 shows that students who do not read for enjoyment are less likely to enjoy reading – as indicated by their values on a composite *index of enjoyment of reading*[2] than students who read for enjoyment.

Figure III.2.18 and Table III.1.1 illustrate how girls enjoy reading more than boys in all the countries that participated in PISA. In 37 countries, the difference in the average value of the *index of enjoyment of reading* of girls and boys is greater than half a standard deviation. Girls enjoy reading more than boys the most in Finland, Germany, Canada, Austria, Switzerland and the partner country Lithuania, where gender differences in the *index of enjoyment of reading* are greater than 0.8 of a standard deviation.

■ Figure III.2.18 ■
Disparities in enjoyment of reading, OECD average

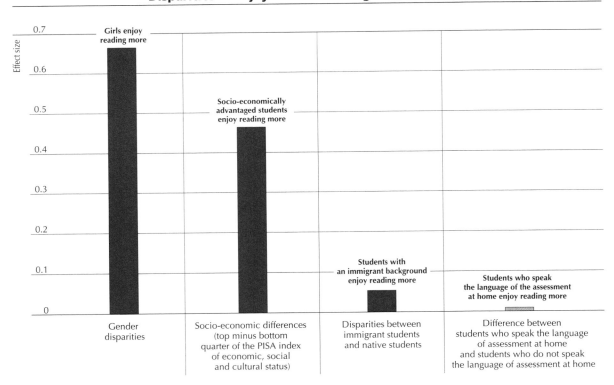

Note: Effect sizes that are statistically significant are marked in a darker tone.
Source: OECD, *PISA 2009 Database,* Tables III.2.12, III.2.13, III.2.14 and III.2.15.
StatLink ⤢ http://dx.doi.org/10.1787/888932360195

Table III.2.16 illustrates that in most countries, differences in average levels of enjoyment of reading between socio-economically advantaged and disadvantaged students[3] are not as large as gender differences: only in Australia, Belgium, Denmark, France, Ireland, Japan, Korea, the United Kingdom and the partner country and economies Shanghai-China, Singapore and Chinese Taipei, is the difference in average levels of enjoyment of reading between socio-economically advantaged and disadvantaged students greater than the difference in the level of enjoyment of reading between boys and girls. Differences between students without an immigrant background and students with an immigrant background are generally small, as are differences between students who speak the same language at home as the language in which the PISA assessment was conducted and those who do not (Tables III.2.14 and III.2.15).

APPROACHES TO LEARNING

Students do not passively receive and process information; they are active participants in the learning process, constructing meaning in ways shaped by their own prior knowledge and experiences as well as by features of the text (Goldman & Rakestraw, 2000; Kintsch, 2004). Students with a well-developed ability to manage their own learning can choose appropriate learning goals, use their existing knowledge and skills to direct their learning, and select learning strategies appropriate to the task at hand (Zimmerman & Clearly, 2009). These skills are increasingly not only recognised as important determining factors of academic achievement, but as necessary for lifelong learning (Boekaerts, 2009; Ryan & Deci, 2009).

An effective learner not only practices assiduously and enjoys practicing, but also processes information efficiently (Hacker, 2004). This requires, in part, the ability to relate new material to existing knowledge and to determine how knowledge can be applied in the real world. A good understanding of which strategies are effective in promoting learning strengthens students' capacity to organise their own learning and to be ready for lifelong learning. Good learners can apply an arsenal of learning strategies in a flexible manner. Students who have problems learning on their own often have no access to strategies to help them learn, or they fail to select a strategy that is appropriate to the task at hand.

Awareness of effective strategies to understand and remember information

PISA 2009 asked students to report the extent to which they are aware that doing things like "after reading the text, I discuss its content with other people", "I underline important parts of the text" and "I summarise the text in my own words" are effective strategies to understand and remember information, while doing things like "I concentrate on the parts of the text that are easy to understand", "I quickly read through the text twice" and "I read the text aloud to another person" are less effective strategies.[4]

Figure III.2.19 shows how countries differ in the extent to which their students are aware of effective strategies to understand and summarise information. For each country, it shows the country-level mean index value – *index of understanding and remembering* is standardised to have a mean of 0 and standard deviation of 1 across the OECD countries – and the difference in the average index value for the students who know the most and least about these strategies. Among OECD countries, students are most knowledgeable about effective strategies to understand and remember information in Germany, Italy, Estonia, Belgium and Switzerland, while students are least knowledgeable about these strategies in Norway, Mexico, Turkey and the United States (Table III.1.14).

Greece, Italy, Japan and Ireland are the OECD countries where the difference between students who are the most knowledgeable about effective strategies to understand and remember information (the top quarter of the *index of understanding and remembering*) and the least knowledgeable students (the bottom quarter of the *index of understanding and remembering*) is smallest, while Portugal, Luxembourg, Sweden, Chile and Iceland are the OECD countries where the difference between the top and the bottom quarters is largest (Figure III.2.19).

On average, girls have greater levels of awareness of effective strategies to understand and remember information than boys. The difference in the average index value between boys and girls in the OECD area is 0.27 and it is higher than 0.4 in Finland, Iceland and the partner country Liechtenstein. There are no gender differences in the partner countries Panama, Azerbaijan, Peru and Colombia, and gender differences are smaller than 0.1 in Mexico and the partner countries Argentina, Tunisia, Singapore and Qatar (Table III.1.14). On average across OECD countries, socio-economically advantaged students have a greater awareness of effective strategies to understand and remember information than disadvantaged students (Table III.2.13). Socio-economic differences in awareness of effective strategies to understand and remember information are smallest in Greece and the partner countries and economies Azerbaijan, Tunisia, Hong Kong-China, Shanghai-China and Macao-China. These differences are more than half a standard deviation in Switzerland, Belgium, Germany, Austria, Chile, Denmark, Australia and the partner countries Uruguay, Colombia, Kyrgyzstan, Bulgaria, Panama and Liechtenstein.

■ Figure III.2.19 ■

To what extent are students aware of effective strategies to understand and remember information?

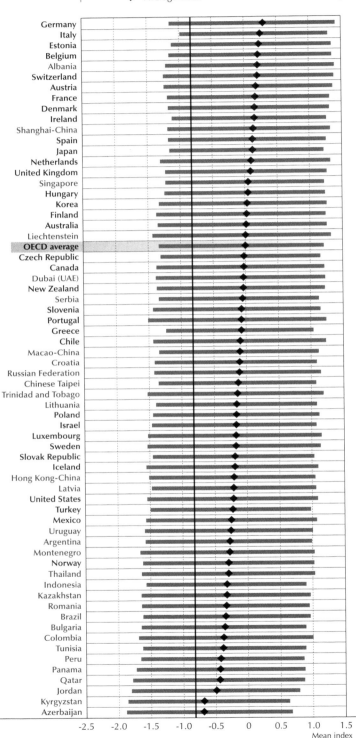

Countries are ranked in descending order of the average index of understanding and remembering.
Source: OECD, *PISA 2009 Database,* Table III.1.14.

StatLink ⧉ http://dx.doi.org/10.1787/888932360195

In five countries, students with an immigrant background have greater levels of awareness of effective strategies to understand and remember information, on average, than students without an immigrant background. In the partner country and economy Dubai (UAE) and Kyrgyzstan, the average level of awareness of these strategies among students with an immigrant background is almost half a standard deviation higher than among students without such a background. In 18 countries, students without an immigrant background have higher levels of awareness of effective strategies to understand and remember information than students with an immigrant background.

Awareness of effective strategies to summarise information

PISA 2009 assessed the extent to which students were aware of effective learning strategies. For example, did students know that when they agreed with the statements "I carefully check whether the most important facts in the text are represented in the summary" and "I read through the text, underlining the most important sentences. Then I write them in my own words as a summary" that they recognised that these are the most effective strategies? Did they know that when they agreed with the statements "I write a summary. Then I check that each paragraph is covered in the summary, because the content of each paragraph should be included" and "before writing the summary, I read the text as many times as possible" that these were moderately effective strategies? And when they reported that "I try to copy out accurately as many sentences as possible", did they know that this was the least effective way to summarise information?[5]

Students in Italy and France are particularly knowledgeable about effective strategies to summarise information while, among OECD countries, students in Turkey, Slovenia, the United States and Iceland are the least knowledgeable. Figure III.2.20 indicates that the difference between the least knowledgeable students – those in the bottom quarter of the *index of summarising* – and the most knowledgeable students – those in the top quarter of the *index of summarising* – is smallest in Italy and Spain (Figure III.2.20 and Table III.1.16) and largest in Sweden and the partner country and economy Hong Kong-China and Qatar.

The difference in the average level of awareness of effective strategies to summarise information between boys and girls corresponds to 0.4 of a standard deviation or more in 14 countries and it is greatest in Finland, Iceland and the partner country Liechtenstein, where it is greater than half a standard deviation (Table III.1.16). Socio-economic differences in awareness of these strategies are relatively large: the difference between socio-economically advantaged and disadvantaged students in awareness of these strategies is half a standard deviation or more in 10 OECD countries and in 8 partner countries and economies, and it is above 0.6 in Belgium, Hungary and the partner countries Uruguay and Peru (Table III.2.16). In 21 countries, students without an immigrant background show greater levels of awareness of effective summarising strategies, while in Australia and the partner economy Dubai (UAE), students with an immigrant background show greater levels of awareness. In 31 countries, students who speak the language of assessment at home show higher levels of awareness of these strategies than students who do not, while the opposite is true in six countries.

On average across OECD countries, those where students know which strategies are effective for understanding and remembering information are also countries where students know which strategies are useful for summarising information (the correlation between the two indicators is 0.69 across OECD countries). For example, in Ireland, Denmark, Switzerland, Belgium, France, Germany and Italy, students generally have high levels of awareness about effective strategies to understand, remember and summarise information. In contrast, students in Iceland, the United States and Turkey have relatively low levels of awareness about these strategies.

Use of memorisation, elaboration and control strategies

PISA 2009 assessed both students' self-reported use of memorisation strategies and students' self-reported awareness of which strategies are most effective for remembering information. While the two indices appear to be closely linked, in fact they measure very different ways in which students store information. The *index of understanding and remembering* clarifies the extent to which students can store information, integrate it into a prior knowledge base and elaborate on it so that it can be applied to novel situations. The *index of memorisation strategies* examines how often students use memorisation techniques in which new information is stored in the memory with little or no further processing.[6]

PISA 2009 asked students to report whether they use memorisation, elaboration and control strategies "almost never", "sometimes", "often" or "almost always". On the basis of their responses, three indices were created. As shown in Figure III.1.15, the *index of memorisation strategies* measures the extent to which students try to memorise new material in order to be able to recite it, and how far they practise by reading the material over and over again.

■ Figure III.2.20 ■
To what extent are students aware of effective strategies to summarise information?

Countries are ranked in descending order of the average index of summarising.
Source: OECD, *PISA 2009 Database,* Table III.1.16.
StatLink ██▆▆▆ http://dx.doi.org/10.1787/888932360195

■ Figure III.2.21 ■
Socio-economic disparities in the use of control strategies

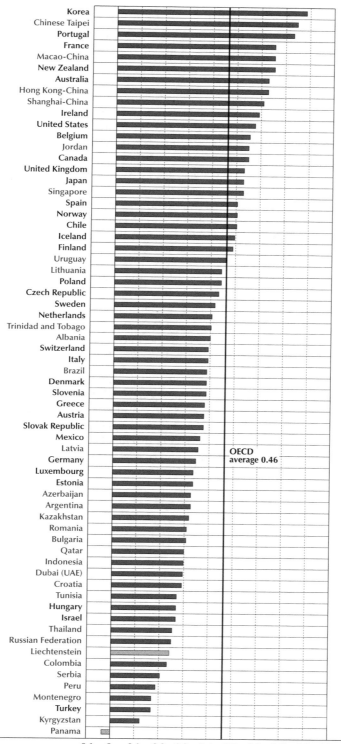

Note: Effect sizes that are statistically significant are marked in a darker tone.
Countries are ranked in descending order of the effect of socio-economic background on the use of control strategies.
Source: OECD, *PISA 2009 Database*, Table III.2.13.

StatLink ⌦ http://dx.doi.org/10.1787/888932360195

The *index of elaboration strategies* measures whether students try to understand the material better by relating it to things they already know, whether they try to relate new material to things learned in other subjects, or whether they try to determine how the information might be useful in the real world. The *index of control strategies* defines control strategies as the plans students say they use to ensure that they reach their learning goals. These involve determining what they have already learned and working out what they still need to learn. The *index of control strategies* measures whether students know which concepts they have not understood from their reading, whether they check to be certain that they remember the most important points from the text they have read, and whether they look for additional information to clarify what they do not understand.

Girls generally reported making greater use of both memorisation and especially control strategies than boys (Table III.2.12). On the other hand, boys tended to report making greater use of elaboration strategies, although gender differences are generally small (effect size below 0.2), and in as many as eight OECD countries and 12 partner countries and economies, girls are just as likely as boys to use elaboration strategies. While boys and girls tended to report similar levels of use of memorisation, elaboration and control strategies, socio-economic disparities in the reported use of learning strategies are relatively large. Panama is the only country where socio-economically advantaged students are not more likely than disadvantaged students – as identified by the top and the bottom quarters of the *PISA index of economic, social and cultural status* – to use control strategies. The difference in the reported use of control strategies between advantaged and disadvantaged students is 0.46 on average across OECD countries. It is less than 0.2 only in Turkey and the partner countries Peru, Montenegro and Kyrgyzstan, while it is 0.78 in Korea (Figure III.2.21 and Table III.2.13).

Countries differ widely in the extent to which students reported using memorisation, elaboration and control strategies (Tables III.1.18, III.1.19 and III.1.20). Among OECD countries, the use of memorisation strategies is particularly pronounced in Hungary, followed by Austria and Poland, while students in Japan reported using memorisation strategies relatively rarely. Students in Japan reported using all three learning strategies - memorisation, elaboration and control - to a lesser degree, on average, than students in the other OECD countries. Elaboration strategies are widely used in Turkey and Portugal, while the use of control strategies is not very widespread in Japan, Norway and Finland.

Countries where students consistently reported using one strategy were also those where students generally reported using other strategies regularly. Among OECD countries, the correlation between memorisation and elaboration strategies is 0.41, between memorisation and control strategies is 0.55, and between elaboration and control strategies is 0.55. Despite this strong association in the use of different learning strategies, some countries show very different patterns. In Italy, for example, the use of control strategies is relatively common, but the use of both memorisation and elaboration strategies is relatively rare.

Notes

1. A detailed description of how the *index of enjoyment of reading* was constructed can be found in Annex A1.

2. A detailed description of how the *index of enjoyment of reading* was constructed can be found in Annex A1.

3. Students with values in the bottom quarter of the *PISA index of economic, social and cultural status* in the country of assessment are considered socio-economically disadvantaged and students with values in the top quarter of the index are considered socio-economically advantaged.

4. A detailed description of how the *index of understanding and remembering* was constructed can be found in Annex A1.

5. A detailed description of how the *index of summarising* was constructed can be found in Annex A1.

6. A detailed description of how the *index of understanding and remembering* are the *index of memorisation strategies* were constructed can be found in Annex A1.

3

Tackling Gender and Socio-Economic Inequalities in Reading

Girls outperform boys in reading in all countries assessed by PISA. This chapter discusses the extent to which reading and learning habits relate to these performance differences between boys and girls, and between socio-economic groups. It then examines whether those habits that are associated with better reading performance could be more widely encouraged among boys and among students from disadvantaged backgrounds to help minimise differences in reading proficiency. The chapter also highlights underachievement among disadvantaged boys.

Findings from PISA 2000 suggested that the usually lower level of reading performance among socio-economically disadvantaged students is no longer evident if these students report high levels of engagement in reading (OECD, 2002). Other research too shows that disadvantaged students who are highly engaged in diverse reading activities, who enjoy reading and rely on appropriate learning strategies to solve reading tasks, appear to be able to compensate for fewer opportunities they have at home and in their schools by generating learning opportunities themselves (Guthrie, Schafer and Huang, 2001). Similarly, although girls generally outperform boys in reading (Cole, 1997; OECD, 2001; Smith and Wilhelm, 2009), when boys enjoy reading, when they read widely and adopt learning strategies extensively, they can attain higher levels of performance in reading than girls.

The aim of the chapter is to assess to what extent reading habits and approaches to learning contribute to the observed performance differences between boys and girls, and among socio-economic groups. If this relationship can be established and its causal nature inferred through other sources and methods (Annex A3.b), such analyses can provide insights for policy makers as to whether the gender gap in reading performance could be reduced if boys were keen readers and effective learners. These analyses could also determine whether socio-economic differences in reading performance could be reduced if disadvantaged students enjoyed reading, read widely for enjoyment, and adopted effective learning strategies.

As discussed in Volume I, *What Students Know and Can Do*, girls outperform boys in the PISA 2009 reading assessment in every participating country by an average, across OECD countries, of 39 PISA score points – the equivalent of an average school year. However, gender differences are much wider in some countries and economies than in others and also vary across different parts of the performance distribution. The gender gap is particularly wide in Finland, Slovenia, the Slovak Republic, Poland and the partner countries and economy Qatar, Dubai (UAE), Croatia, Montenegro, Kyrgyzstan, Jordan, Trinidad and Tobago, Lithuania, Bulgaria and Albania (see Table I.2.3). In contrast, in Chile and the Netherlands, and in the partner countries Colombia, Peru and Azerbaijan, the gender gap is comparatively small. Although girls have better reading skills than boys, on average, the gap is especially wide among low-achieving students (OECD, 2001; Grigg, Daane, Jin and Campbell, 2002; OECD, 2002; OECD, 2008a). In most countries and economies, boys greatly outnumber girls among those students who lack basic reading skills, or among students who do not attain Level 2 in reading proficiency (Figure I.2.2).

Volume II, *Overcoming Social Background*, confirms that in all countries and economies, students who come from socio-economically disadvantaged backgrounds show lower levels of reading performance in PISA 2009 than their better-off peers. Even countries and economies that have had successes in reducing socio-economic disparities have only been able to reduce, but not eliminate, the influence of socio-economic background on reading performance (Figures II.3.2 and II.3.3). Socio-economic differences are often compounded by racial and ethnic differences in achievement, as many poor children and adolescents are also from minority groups, and their native languages are often different than the languages in which reading is taught in school (Snow and Biancarosa, 2003; Strickland and Alvermann, 2004).

Despite the large body of evidence on the persistence of gender and social inequalities in reading performance, and on the different mechanisms involved in perpetuating the gender gap and social differentials (Volumes I and II), not enough is known about the extent to which engaging in reading and using learning strategies ameliorates gender and socio-economic differences in reading achievement.

INEQUALITIES IN READING PERFORMANCE AND THE ROLE OF ENGAGEMENT IN READING AND LEARNING STRATEGIES

Inequalities in reading performance are the result of a complex web of relationships and practices. Figure III.3.1 shows how this chapter attempts to disentangle the extent to which the associations between gender and reading performance, and socio-economic background and reading performance could be due to students' reading habits and the way in which they approach learning. The black arrows represent the hypothetical influence of gender and socio-economic background on reading habits and learning strategies, and the hypothetical influence of reading habits and learning strategies on reading performance. The grey arrows represent other factors that could be responsible for gender and socio-economic disparities in reading performance.

Figure III.3.1 depicts how findings presented in Volume I on the magnitude of gender differences in reading, and findings presented in Volume II on socio-economic inequities can be interpreted in the light of disparities in engagement in reading and learning strategies. The figure also shows the strength of the association between engagement, learning strategies and reading performance.

■ Figure III.3.1 ■
How engagement in reading activities and approaches to learning contribute to disparities in reading performance

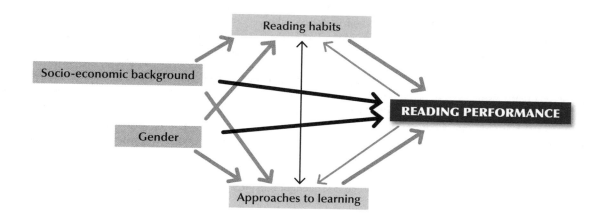

Why are boys less engaged in reading than girls? At least three explanations have been suggested. One focuses on differences between brain structure and function for boys and girls; but the links between these differences and different behaviour in areas such as reading have not been established empirically (Ruble, Martin and Berenbaum, 2006). A second focuses on socialisation issues around gender identity and how different activities are more or less appropriate for males and females. Reading is often defined as a feminine activity, which means that some males reject it as inappropriate (Osmont, 1987; Smith and Wilhelm, 2009; Ruble et al., 2006). Third, Smith and Wilhelm (2002, 2006) found that boys reject some types of reading, especially in school, but that they do enjoy certain kinds of reading related to other activities in which they participate. This research suggests that boys' interest in reading may be confined to certain types of reading.

PISA shows major gender differences in the extent to which boys and girls, but also students from socio-economically advantaged and disadvantaged backgrounds, report being engaged in reading and knowing about learning strategies (Chapter 2). These findings closely resemble findings in the literature on boys' general lack of interest in reading and the low levels of interest in reading among students from disadvantaged socio-economic backgrounds. Some observational and interview studies, for example, indicate that boys often feel that it is "inappropriate" and "contrary to their masculine identity" to show interest in school, in general, and in reading, in particular (Paechter, 1998; Francis, 2000; Warrington, Younger and Williams, 2000; Smith and Wilhelm, 2002; Smith and Wilhelm, 2006). PISA data cannot establish the extent to which the association between engagement in reading and knowledge of appropriate learning strategies can be considered causal. Observational studies, however, have illustrated that one of the major factors for boys' underachievement in language is their lack of interest in reading and writing, and engagement with literacy (Safford, O'Sullivan and Barrs, 2004). Boys also appear to experience greater peer pressure to conform to masculine identities than girls (Younger and Warrington, 1996; Warrington et al., 2000), and this identity is marked by a relative lack of interest in schooling and reading (Clark and Trafford, 1995).

Recent work has also highlighted how academic achievement can be determined by self-stereotyping and, implicitly, by people's attitudes and beliefs about their own identity. For example, Asian-American women performed better on a mathematics assessment when they were told the reason for doing the test was to identify ethnic differences in performance – because of the stereotype that Asians have higher quantitative skills than other ethnic groups (Steen, 1987) – but worse when they were told that the reason for them taking the assessment was to identify gender differences – because of the common stereotype that women have inferior quantitative skills than men (Benbow, 1988; Hedges and Nowell, 1995), compared with a control group that was not told anything about reasons for taking the assessment (Shih, Pittinsky and Ambady, 1999). Elderly people who had absorbed a negative stereotype of memory abilities also performed worse on a memory task than elderly people who had absorbed positive stereotypes of the elderly (Levy, 1996).

Other work on identity suggests that some minority students distance themselves from school as a way to protect their self-esteem. For instance, Osborne (1995, 1997) found that correlations of grades, test scores, and self-esteem are lower for African-American males than for other groups, and interpreted this finding as indicating that these students' identities and self-esteem are based on other qualities besides school achievement. Broader factors that are important to consider are some students' sense that they are treated differently by teachers because of their background, or that even if they do succeed in school, there will be no economic benefits for them later on because of their group membership and backgrounds (Murdock, 2009). Together, these findings provide for a better understanding of the nature of the relationships that are discussed below.

Enjoyment of reading and awareness of effective learning strategies to summarise information are two distinct, yet complementary, aspects of students' approaches to reading and learning. Chapter 2 shows how these factors are associated with reading performance. Enjoyment of reading is one of the motivating aspects of learning, while awareness of appropriate strategies to summarise information is a meta-cognitive and self-regulatory aspect of learning (Hacker, 2004; Schiefele, 2009; Zimmerman and Clearly, 2009). Since enjoyment of reading is closely associated with other indicators used to characterise engagement in reading activities, and an awareness of effective summarising strategies is closely associated with students' use of other effective learning strategies, this section develops models based on these two key indicators, even though the aim is to assess the potential role of engagement and learning strategies more broadly.

Reading habits and approaches to learning are potentially important mediators of gender inequalities in reading performance, but their role is more limited in the case of socio-economic inequities. On average across OECD countries, almost 70% of the difference in reading performance between boys and girls is the indirect result of disparities in how much boys and girls reported enjoying reading and knowing about effective strategies to summarise information. However, only about 30% of the difference in reading performance between socio-economically advantaged and disadvantaged students is the indirect result of disparities in how much socio-economically advantaged and disadvantaged students reported enjoying reading and knowing about effective strategies to summarise information.

■ Figure III.3.2 ■
How engagement in reading activities and learning strategies contribute to disparities in reading performance across OECD countries

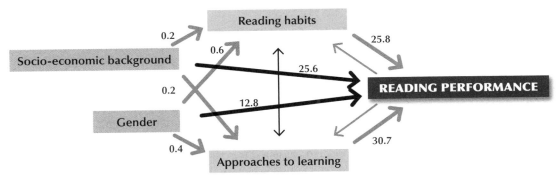

Source: OECD, *PISA 2009 Database*, Table III.3.10.
StatLink ⟨⟩ http://dx.doi.org/10.1787/888932360214

HOW READING HABITS AND APPROACHES TO LEARNING MEDIATE THE GENDER GAP IN READING PERFORMANCE

Tables III.3.1 and III.3.10 and Figure III.3.3 suggest that a large share of gender differences in reading performance may stem from disparities in the enjoyment of reading and knowledge about effective summarising strategies.

Figure III.3.3 shows countries and economies with a relatively large gender gap in reading performance, and illustrates the extent to which engagement in reading and approaches to learning could help narrow such a gap. The vertical axis plots countries on the basis of the score point difference in the reading assessment between boys and girls (Table I.2.3). The horizontal axis shows the extent to which the total gender gap in reading performance is mediated by enjoyment of reading and awareness of effective strategies to summarise information in different countries. Countries in the top-right corner of Figure III.3.3 are countries with a large gender gap in reading performance, where a large share of gender differences in reading are mediated by boys' and girls' engagement in reading and how positively they approach learning. In contrast, countries in the bottom-left corner of Figure III.3.3 are countries where differences in the reading performance of boys and girls are smaller, and where gender differences in reading performance are not strongly mediated by these actions and attitudes. Countries in the top-right corner of Figure III.3.3 are those where policies aimed at promoting engagement in reading and positive approaches to learning among boys could be particularly useful.

The fact that, on average, boys enjoy reading substantially less than girls and have less extensive knowledge about effective summarising strategies than girls explains a large part of the gender gap in reading performance in most countries and economies. In Finland, where boys score an average of 55 points lower than girls in the PISA reading assessment, differences in the extent to which boys and girls enjoy reading and are aware of effective learning strategies to summarise information represent almost 80% of the overall gender difference in reading performance.

■ Figure III.3.3 ■

The role of engagement in reading and approaches to learning as mediators of gender differences in reading performance

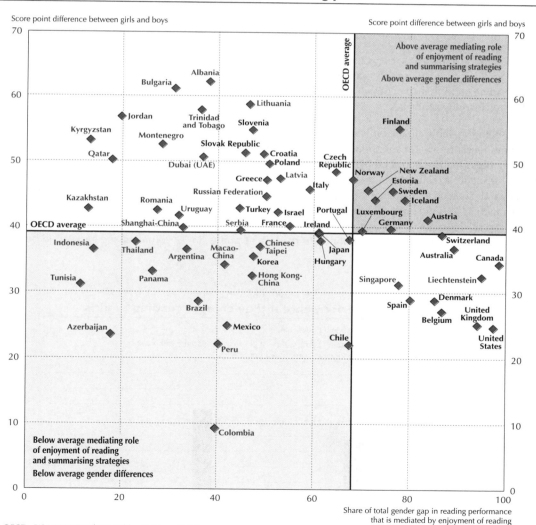

Source: OECD, *PISA 2009 Database*, Tables III.3.1 and I.2.3.
StatLink ⬛⬛⬛ http://dx.doi.org/10.1787/888932360214

In Poland and the partner country the Russian Federation, where gender disparities in the PISA reading assessment are above the OECD average, enjoyment of reading and awareness of effective learning strategies influence these differences far less, representing about half of the overall gender differences in reading performance. In the partner economy Shanghai-China, however, where boys and girls also show relatively large score point disparities in the PISA reading assessment (with a mean score difference of 40 points), the mediating role of engagement in reading and approaches to learning represents only about one-third of the overall gender differences in reading performance (Tables I.2.3, III.3.1 and III.3.10).

On average, boys enjoy reading less than girls. However, in all countries and economies that participated in PISA, differences in enjoyment of reading between genders are far smaller than differences in enjoyment levels within genders: on average across OECD countries, the difference in enjoyment of reading between boys and girls is 0.6 index points (Table III.1.1). This difference ranges from less than 0.3 in Korea and the partner countries Kazakhstan, Jordan, Colombia, Panama, Peru, Indonesia and Azerbaijan, to over 0.8 in Finland, Germany, Canada, Austria, Switzerland and the partner country Lithuania (Table III.1.1). The difference between the quarter of boys who reported enjoying reading the most in their country and the quarter who enjoy reading the least, however, is far greater: it is above 2.0 across OECD countries, ranging from 1.8 in Mexico to 2.8 in Switzerland and, among the partner countries, ranging from 1.2 in Indonesia to 2.7 in Liechtenstein (Table III.3.2). This means that while factors such as predisposition, temperament, peer pressure and socialisation may lead boys to enjoy reading less than girls in general, boys could be encouraged to enjoy reading more and to read more for enjoyment. Similarly, recent qualitative studies suggest that at least some adolescent girls lose interest in reading in secondary school, especially in the reading required for school. This is partly because of the kind of reading required and because girls and boys may be treated differently in classrooms (Guzetti, 2008, 2009; Guzetti and Gamboa, 2004). These findings show that it is not only boys who can lose interest in some forms of reading.

Results presented in Tables III.3.3 and III.3.4 show that the gap between boys and girls could be narrower if boys had higher levels of motivation to read and used effective learning strategies. Figures III.3.4 and III.3.5 illustrate the predicted reading performance of boys if boys enjoyed reading as much as girls and shared their levels of knowledge about effective learning strategies.[1]

Results presented in Table III.3.3 indicate that in all countries and economies that participated in PISA, if boys had the same levels of awareness about effective strategies to summarise information as girls in their countries, their reading performance would be higher. Table III.3.4 indicates that this would be the case in all countries and economies – except Kazakhstan – if the levels of boys' enjoyment of reading matched the levels that girls currently have. In Finland, Sweden and Germany the score point difference between what boys could achieve if they enjoyed reading as much as girls did and what they currently demonstrate in PISA is large: equivalent to 30 points or more, almost half a proficiency level. On average across OECD countries, the untapped potential of boys, represented by their unsatisfactory levels of internal motivation to read, is 23 points. In 32 countries, the gap would be predicted to be 20 score points narrower.

■ Figure III.3.4 ■
Boys' reading performance if they enjoyed reading as girls

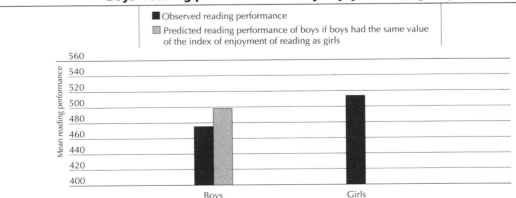

Source: OECD, *PISA 2009 Database,* Table III.3.4.
StatLink ᴬˢᴾ http://dx.doi.org/10.1787/888932360214

■ Figure III.3.5 ■

Boys' reading performance if they were as aware of effective summarising strategies as girls

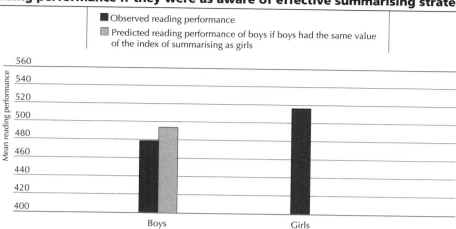

■ Observed reading performance
▨ Predicted reading performance of boys if boys had the same value
of the index of summarising as girls

Source: OECD, *PISA 2009 Database*, Table III.3.3.
StatLink ⬛⬛⬛ http://dx.doi.org/10.1787/888932360214

Table III.3.3 shows that in as many as 16 countries, if boys had the same levels of awareness about which summarising strategies were most effective as the girls in their countries do, their reading performance would be predicted to be at least 15 points higher. In Finland and the partner country Liechtenstein, the predicted change in reading performance that could occur if boys were equally aware as girls of the most effective strategies to summarise complex information would be more than 20 points.

HOW READING HABITS AND APPROACHES TO LEARNING MEDIATE SOCIO-ECONOMIC INEQUITIES IN READING PERFORMANCE

Some 15-year-olds who come from the most socio-economically disadvantaged homes, but who are highly engaged in reading and who approach learning positively, achieve higher reading scores than students who come from highly or moderately privileged families but who are poorly engaged in reading and do not approach their learning effectively. However, these students are relatively rare in the countries and economies that participate in PISA (Table III.2.13). The *PISA index of economic, social and cultural status* used to characterise students' socio-economic background is based on several components (Volume II, *Overcoming Social Background*, for a detailed description). Two of those components are parental education and the number of books that are available in the students' households. Educated parents and those who have many books in their homes are more likely to read to their children when they are young and to be positive role models for their children by being enthusiastic and engaged readers (Baker, Scher and Mackler, 1997; Klauda, 2009). One of the primary channels through which a socio-economically advantaged status[2] may determine reading achievement is by providing opportunities for students to develop high motivation to read and use effective learning strategies.

In most countries and economies, socio-economic inequities in reading performance can be partly explained by differences in students' reading habits and their approaches to learning (Tables III.3.1 and III.3.10). On average across OECD countries, approximately one-third of the association between reading performance and socio-economic background is mediated by the extent to which students enjoy reading and are aware of effective strategies to summarise information.[3] The role of enjoyment of reading and learning strategies is particularly pronounced in Switzerland, Iceland, Denmark, Australia, Norway, Belgium and in the partner country and economy Liechtenstein and Chinese Taipei. It is generally greater in OECD countries than in partner countries and economies.

Figure III.3.6 shows countries and economies with relatively large socio-economic disparities in reading performance and the extent to which engagement in reading and approaches to learning could help tackle such disparities. The vertical axis plots countries on the basis of the score point difference in reading that is associated with a one-unit change in the *PISA index of economic, social and cultural status* (Table II.3.12). This is the slope of the social gradient: the average difference in reading performance between students with a difference equal to one unit in the *PISA index of economic, social and cultural status*. The horizontal axis shows the extent to which the total association between socio-economic background and reading performance is mediated by enjoyment of reading and awareness of effective learning strategies to summarise information in different countries. Countries in the top-right corner of Figure III.3.6 are those with large socio-economic differences in reading performance and where the effect of socio-economic background on reading performance is mediated to a large extent by engagement in reading and approaches to learning. In contrast, countries in the bottom-left corner of Figure III.3.6 are those that show fewer socio-economic differences in reading performance and where the association between socio-economic background and reading performance is not particularly mediated by engagement in reading and approaches to learning. Countries in the top-right corner of Figure III.3.6 are those where policies aimed at promoting engagement in reading and positive approaches to learning among socio-economically disadvantaged students could be particularly useful.

Not all countries and economies show substantial socio-economic differences in reading performance. However, New Zealand, France, Hungary, Israel, Belgium, Australia, the Czech Republic, the United Kingdom and the partner country and economy Bulgaria and Dubai (UAE) all show relatively large socio-economic variations in reading performance,[4] and in all of them, a substantial share of the overall association between socio-economic background and reading performance is mediated by the extent to which students enjoy reading and know how to summarise complex information.[5]

■ Figure III.3.6 ■

The role of engagement in reading and approaches to learning as mediators of socio-economic disparities in reading performance

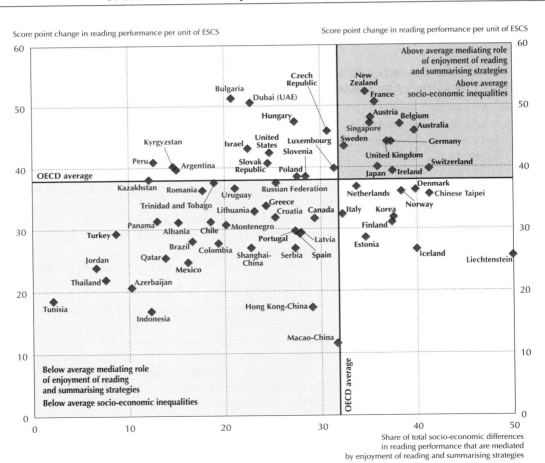

Source: OECD, *PISA 2009 Database*, Tables III.3.1 and II.3.2.
StatLink ⬛⬛ http://dx.doi.org/10.1787/888932360214

These countries could greatly reduce disparities in reading performance by promoting higher levels of engagement in reading activities and positive approaches to learning among socio-economically disadvantaged students. Iceland is a country where approximately 40% of the overall association between socio-economic status and reading performance is mediated by engagement in reading and approaches to learning. However, in Iceland, socio-economic disparities in reading performance are relatively small.[6] Among partner countries and economies, in Liechtenstein, almost 50% of the overall association between socio-economic status and reading performance is mediated by engagement in reading and approaches to learning. However, in Liechtenstein, socio-economic disparities in reading performance are relatively small.[7] The partner country and economy Bulgaria and Dubai (UAE) both show fairly large socio-economic disparities in reading performance, but engagement in reading and approaches to learning are not particularly important mediators of socio-economic inequities in reading performance in these countries and economies (Table III.3.1).[8]

Results presented in Tables III.3.5 and III.3.6 show that students from socio-economically disadvantaged backgrounds would be predicted to perform significantly closer to advantaged students if they had higher levels of engagement in reading and approached their learning more positively. Figures III.3.7 and III.3.8 illustrate the predicted reading performance of socio-economically disadvantaged students if these students enjoyed reading as much as students from more advantaged backgrounds and if they had similar levels of knowledge about effective learning strategies.[9]

Results presented in Table III.3.5 indicate that, in as many as 31 countries and economies, if the most socio-economically disadvantaged students had the same levels of awareness about summarising strategies as the most advantaged students in their countries and economies, their reading performance would be at least 15 points higher. In Belgium, Hungary, Germany, Switzerland, Austria, France, Luxembourg, New Zealand, Portugal and the partner countries and economy Liechtenstein, Uruguay and Dubai (UAE), the score point difference between what socio-economically disadvantaged students could achieve if they had the same levels of knowledge about effective summarising strategies as advantaged students is more than 20 points. On average across OECD countries, the untapped potential of socio-economically disadvantaged students, represented by their low levels of awareness about learning strategies, is 17 points. Across OECD countries, if disadvantaged students used effective learning strategies to the same extent as students from more advantaged backgrounds did, their performance gap would be almost 20% narrower. In Korea, Belgium, Finland and the partner country Liechtenstein, the gap would be 25% narrower.

Table III.3.6 also suggests that in as many as 27 countries and economies, if the most socio-economically disadvantaged students had the same levels of enjoyment of reading as the most advantaged students, their reading performance could be at least 15 points higher. In Ireland, Australia, New Zealand, France, Switzerland, Germany, the United Kingdom, Denmark, Hungary, Austria and the partner country and economy Chinese Taipei and Singapore, the predicted change in reading performance would be 20 points or more.

■ Figure III.3.7 ■
Reading performance of socio-economically disadvantaged students if they were as aware of effective summarising strategies as socio-economically advantaged students

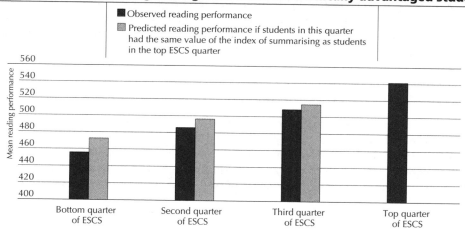

Note: Socio-economically disadvantaged (advantaged) students are students in the bottom (top) quarter of the PISA index of economic, social and cultural status (ESCS) within their country of assessment.
Source: OECD, *PISA 2009 Database*, Table III.3.5.
StatLink http://dx.doi.org/10.1787/888932360214

- Figure III.3.8 -

Reading performance of socio-economically disadvantaged students if they enjoyed reading as much as socio-economically advantaged students

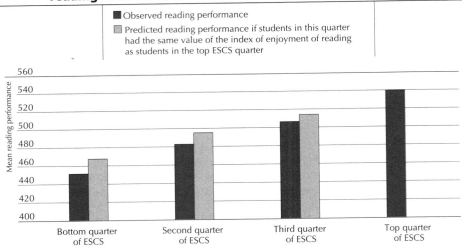

Note: Socio-economically disadvantaged (advantaged) students are students in the bottom (top) quarter of the PISA index of economic, social and cultural status (ESCS) within their country of assessment.
Source: OECD, *PISA 2009 Database*, Table III.3.6.
StatLink ᴍˢᴾ http://dx.doi.org/10.1787/888932360214

Reading proficiency is the key that allows students to build on the skill base they acquire at school and to go on to become lifelong learners. If young people leave formal education before they have learned how to learn, they will not be able to update their skills to meet the needs of a fast-changing and increasingly globalised labour market. Economic growth depends, to a large extent, on a workforce that is flexible and able to adapt to different needs. Countries that fail to ensure that disadvantaged students can escape from a cycle of low skills and low wages that are transmitted across generations not only pay a heavy human cost, but also significant costs in lost productivity and economic growth.

THE UNDERACHIEVEMENT OF DISADVANTAGED BOYS

Table III.3.7 identifies in socio-economically disadvantaged boys a group of students that is particularly likely to underperform in the PISA reading assessment in all countries and economies that participate in PISA. The low reading proficiency among socio-economically disadvantaged boys is of concern because, without the ability to read well enough to participate fully in society, these students and their future families will have fewer opportunities to escape poverty and deprivation. Societies characterised by low levels of social mobility and intergenerational transmission of deprivation are not only unfair societies, but may also be less productive because they do not make use of all their potential (Volume II of this report and OECD, 2008b). Socio-economically disadvantaged boys are also more likely to abandon school as soon as it is legally possible, even if they have no or few qualifications, and are unlikely to participate in other training or educational opportunities later in their lives.

Previous sections of this chapter have illustrated how enjoyment of reading and knowledge of effective summarising strategies may influence both gender and socio-economic differences in reading proficiency. Results presented in Tables III.3.8 and III.3.9 indicate that socio-economically disadvantaged boys could be predicted to catch up with advantaged girls if they had higher levels of motivation to read and used effective learning strategies. Figures III.3.9 and III.3.10 illustrate the predicted reading performance of boys if they enjoyed reading as much as girls did and had similar approaches to learning.[10]

Results presented in Table III.3.8 indicate that in all countries and economies that participated in PISA, if disadvantaged boys had the same levels of awareness about effective learning strategies as advantaged girls in their countries and economies do, their scores in reading would be predicted to be higher. Table III.3.9 similarly indicates that this would be the case in most countries and economies if the levels of these boys' enjoyment of reading matched the levels that socio-economically advantaged girls now have. In Australia, Finland, Switzerland, New Zealand and Germany, the score point difference between what socio-economically disadvantaged boys would be predicted to achieve if they enjoyed reading as much as advantaged girls do and what they currently demonstrate in PISA is large: equivalent to 45 points or more. On average across OECD countries, the untapped potential of socio-economically disadvantaged boys, represented by their low levels of internal motivation to read, is 35 points. Across OECD countries, if these boys had the same level of awareness of effective summarising strategies as socio-economically advantaged girls do, the gap between their performance and the average student's performance would be predicted to be a third narrower.

■ Figure III.3.9 ■

Reading performance of socio-economically disadvantaged boys if they were as aware of effective summarising strategies as socio-economically advantaged girls

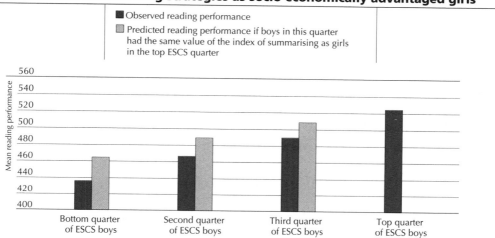

Note: Socio-economically disadvantaged (advantaged) students are students in the bottom (top) quarter of the PISA index of economic, social and cultural status (ESCS) within their country of assessment.
Source: OECD, *PISA 2009 Database,* Table III.3.8.
StatLink ⬛ᵐˢ▨ http://dx.doi.org/10.1787/888932360214

■ Figure III.3.10 ■

Reading performance of socio-economically disadvantaged boys if they enjoyed reading as much as socio-economically advantaged girls

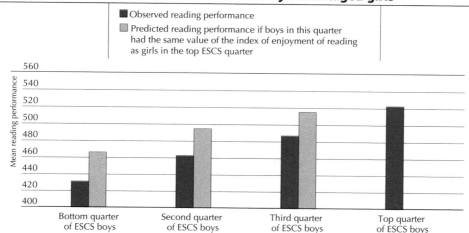

Note: Socio-economically disadvantaged (advantaged) students are students in the bottom (top) quarter of the PISA index of economic, social and cultural status (ESCS) within their country of assessment.
Source: OECD, *PISA 2009 Database,* Table III.3.9.
StatLink ⬛ᵐˢ▨ http://dx.doi.org/10.1787/888932360214

Notes

1. See the *PISA 2009 Technical Report* (OECD, forthcoming) for a detailed description of the modelling used to predict changes in reading performance.

2. In this context, "socio-economically advantaged students" refers to students in the top quarter of the *PISA index of economic, social and cultural status* in their country.

3. The share of the **total effect** of the *PISA index of economic, social and cultural status* (ESCS) on reading performance that is mediated by enjoyment of reading and awareness of effective learning strategies is calculated in the following way: two regressions were run. The first estimated reading performance as a function of ESCS, gender, immigration status and language spoken at home. The second regression estimated reading performance as a function of ESCS, gender, immigration status and language spoken at home, and enjoyment of reading and awareness of summarising strategies. The **indirect effect** of ESCS on reading performance is represented by the difference in the co-efficient for ESCS estimated in the first regression and the co-efficient for ESCS estimated in the second regression. The **share of ESCS mediated by enjoyment of reading and awareness of effective learning strategies** was calculated by dividing the **indirect effect** of ESCS over the ESCS co-efficient estimated in the first regression. These results are in line with those obtained using path models presented in Table III.3.10.

4. In all these countries, the score point difference that is associated with a difference of one standard deviation of the indicator of socio-economic background is 44 points or more.

5. In these countries, more than 20% of the association between the *PISA index of economic, social and cultural status* and reading performance is mediated by enjoyment of reading and knowledge of effective learning strategies.

6. In Iceland, a one-unit change in the *PISA index of economic, social and cultural status* is associated with a score point difference in reading of 27 points.

7. In Liechtenstein, a one-unit change in the *PISA index of economic, social and cultural status* is associated with a 26 score point difference in reading.

8. In Bulgaria and Dubai (UAE), the difference in reading performance between socio-economically advantaged and disadvantaged students is more than 50 points, and about 20% of socio-economic disparities can be explained by differences in levels of enjoyment of reading and knowledge of effective strategies to summarise information.

9. See the *PISA 2009 Technical Report* (OECD, forthcoming) for a detailed description of the modelling used to predict changes in reading performance.

10. See the *PISA 2009 Technical Report* (OECD, forthcoming) for a detailed description of the modelling used to predict changes in reading performance.

Policy Implications

To become effective learners, students need to be able to figure out what they need to learn and how to achieve their learning goals. They also need to master a wide repertoire of cognitive and meta-cognitive information-processing strategies to be able to develop efficient ways of learning. At the same time, fostering effective ways of learning, including goal setting, strategy selection and controlling and evaluating the learning process, should not come at the expense of students' enjoyment of reading and learning, since proficiency is the result of sustained practice and dedication, both of which go hand-in-hand with high levels of motivation to read and learn.

Research has consistently shown that by being engaged in reading and developing effective approaches to learning, students can build solid foundations to become proficient readers, thus paving their path towards becoming lifelong learners. PISA's findings on the relationships between reading performance, 15-year-olds' engagement in reading, and their knowledge and use of learning strategies are consistent with this research. In all countries that took part in PISA 2009, students who perform well in reading tend to be those students who have a deep understanding of which learning strategies are most effective in attaining different learning goals while also reading a wide variety of materials for their own enjoyment.

ENGAGEMENT IN READING MATTERS

Students who make reading an everyday part of their lives are able to build their reading proficiency through practice, which in turn can improve their confidence and encourage them to become more engaged in reading. In almost every country that took part in PISA 2009, the more students enjoy reading and the more engaged they become in reading for enjoyment – both off and on line – the higher their reading proficiency. Among different reading media, reading fiction shows the strongest association with reading performance: students who read fiction regularly score about half a proficiency level above the average. However, the positive association between reading online and performance in reading print media shows that reading books or magazines is not the only way in which being a keen reader is associated with being a good reader.

PISA shows that boys and, to some extent, socio-economically disadvantaged students, tend to be less engaged in reading than girls and socio-economically advantaged students: they are less likely to read for enjoyment on a daily basis, they tend to enjoy reading less, are less likely to read fiction and are less likely to read a variety of materials. As noted before, reading widely, and particularly reading fiction, are two of the factors that are most closely associated with high performance in reading. However, even if simpler reading materials may not lead students to become highly proficient readers, they can still be used by parents and teachers to help develop a habit of reading for enjoyment. Devising a structured approach that 'entices' disengaged readers to begin with easy and interesting texts, such as those found in magazines, and then gradually introducing more complex reading tasks and texts could be one way to improve the reading performance of those groups that currently underperform in reading.

Across OECD countries, over a third of students – and large numbers of students in almost all countries and economies participating in PISA – reported that they do not read any type of material for enjoyment regularly. Research suggests that creating conditions that promote reading practice, and letting students read what they want to read, could be beneficial.

Thus, it might be useful to provide a large supply of texts and activities that could stimulate students' interest in reading, such as organising book clubs, letting students use school facilities after school hours to access material online, under the supervision of responsible adults, or incorporating into school curricula those reading materials that are favourites among students who read for enjoyment, according to PISA results, namely magazines and newspapers. In contrast, the strong link between reading fiction and high reading performance indicates that some materials may be far too complex for weak readers to grasp. Obliging poor readers to engage in material that is beyond their skills may alienate them. Therefore, efforts to promote reading practice should not only take into account differences in reading preferences among students, but also differences in students' current reading abilities.

APPROACHES TO LEARNING MATTER

PISA measures approaches to learning strategies in two ways: by examining the extent to which students report employing certain strategies, and by looking at students' awareness of which strategies work best. The latter indicator, new to PISA 2009, is a more robust measure because it also provides for an external validation of students' knowledge of what works, rather than just their preferences. Across countries, students who are better-informed about what will help them learn tend to have substantially higher reading proficiency. This applies both to an awareness of strategies to understand and remember information as well as to strategies to summarise information. The reported use of strategies to control one's learning is also associated with higher student performance in every country, although, on average, this association is not as strong as an awareness of effective learning strategies.

Research has shown that students who take responsibility for their own learning – who employ "control strategies" in which they set their own learning goals and check their own progress – are able to learn more effectively. However, given the wide variety in students' levels of understanding about which techniques work, it is clear that giving all students more autonomy will not lead to better results across the board. Weaker students in particular need to be taught how to learn effectively.

PISA shows that an awareness of effective learning strategies is closely associated with proficiency in reading. Reading a lot is not enough: students who read a lot but who do not understand how to learn effectively perform worse in reading than students who read less but understand what effective learning entails. This confirms previous research that while enjoying reading is a necessary step towards becoming a better reader, it is not sufficient if it does not go hand-in-hand with a good understanding of how to use reading to learn effectively. This underlines the importance for parents, teachers and schools to provide students with the tools to become effective readers and learners. Developing an awareness of effective learning strategies can involve letting students experiment with different approaches, discussing with students what they find helpful and unhelpful, and encouraging them to reflect on the different approaches that they use to achieve learning goals.

LEVELLING THE PLAYING FIELD MATTERS

PISA identifies large gender and socio-economic gaps in reading performance, but also separate and complementary gaps in reading habits and approaches to learning. Boys are especially likely to be less engaged in reading than girls. Similarly, students from more disadvantaged backgrounds are less likely to have the levels of engagement in reading and knowledge of learning strategies that are associated with effective reading performance.

Differences in levels of engagement in reading and approaches to learning account for about one-third of socio-economic differences in reading performance, but over two-thirds of gender differences. For example, the difference in reading enjoyment between the bottom and top quarter of students by social background is smaller than the difference between boys and girls in all countries except Australia, Belgium, Denmark, France, Ireland, Japan, Korea, the United Kingdom and the partner country and economies Shanghai-China, Singapore and Chinese Taipei. While these are the countries where reading enjoyment is most closely linked to social background, the gender difference is much larger, because it affects half the population rather than just the difference between the top and bottom quarter.

Most boys and girls in the countries that took part in PISA 2009 sit side-by-side in the same classrooms and work with similar teachers. Yet, PISA reveals that in OECD countries, boys are on average 39 points behind girls in reading, the equivalent of an average year of schooling. PISA suggests that differences in how boys and girls approach learning and how engaged they are in reading account for most of the gap in reading performance between boys and girls, so much so that this gap would be predicted to shrink by 10 score points if boys approached learning as positively as girls, and by over 20 score points if they were as engaged in reading as girls. This does not mean that if boys' engagement and awareness of learning strategies rose by this amount, the increase would automatically translate into respective performance gains, since PISA does not measure causation. But the fact that most of the gender gap can be explained by boys being less engaged, and less engaged students having lower performance, is a good reason to look hard for more effective ways of increasing boys' interest in reading at school or at home.

PISA reveals that, although girls have higher mean reading performance, enjoy reading more and are more aware of effective strategies to summarise information than boys, differences within genders are far greater than those between the genders. Moreover, the size of the gender gap varies considerably across countries, suggesting that boys and girls do not have inherently different interests and academic strengths, but that these are mostly acquired and socially induced. The large gender gap in reading is not a mystery: it can be attributed to differences that have been identified in the attitudes and behaviours of boys and girls.

Volume V of this report, *Learning Trends*, reveals how the gender gap in reading engagement has widened in recent years, as has the gender gap in reading performance. But changing students' attitudes and behaviours may be inherently more difficult than providing equal access to high quality teachers and schools, two of the factors that explain the low performance of socio-economically disadvantaged students – an area where PISA shows that over the past decade, some countries have achieved significant progress. In the short term, this may require catering to boys' reading preferences, such as their relatively strong interest in reading newspapers and reading online, rather than designing a single model of engagement in reading. Over the longer term, shrinking the gender gap in reading performance will require the concerted effort of parents, teachers and society at large to change the stereotyped notions of what boys and girls excel in doing and what they enjoy doing.

Socio-economic disparities in engagement in reading and the use of effective learning strategies are smaller than gender differences. Nevertheless, if all students approached learning as positively as the quarter of students with the greatest socio-economic advantage, there could be large gains in their reading proficiency, especially among the least-advantaged students.

References

Aunola, K., E. Leskinen, T. Onatsu-Arvilommi and **J.E. Nurmi** (2002), "Three Methods for Studying Developmental Change: A Case of Reading Skills and Self-concept", *British Journal of Educational Psychology*, Vol. 72, No. 3, pp. 343-364.

Baker, L., D. Scher and **K. Mackler** (1997), "Home and Family Influences on Motivations for Reading", *Educational Psychologist*, Vol. 32, pp. 69-82.

Baker, L. and **A. Wigfield** (1999), "Dimensions of Children's Motivation for Reading and their Relations to Reading Activity and Reading Achievement", *Reading Research Quarterly*, Vol. 34, pp. 452-477.

Bempechat, J., N.V. Jimenez and **B.A. Boulay** (2002), "Cultural-Cognitive Issues in Academic Achievement: New Directions for Cross-National Research", in A.C. Porter and A. Gamoran (eds.), *Methodological Advances in Cross-National Surveys of Educational Achievement,* National Academic Press, Washington DC.

Benbow, C.P. (1988), "Sex Differences in Mathematical Reasoning Ability in Intellectually Talented Preadolescents: Their Nature, Effects, and Possible Causes", *Behavioral and Brain Science*, Vol. 11, pp. 169-232.

Boekaerts, M. (2009), "Goal-directed Behaviors in the Classroom", in K.R. Wentzel and A. Wigfield (eds.), *Handbook of Motivation at School*, Routledge, New York, pp. 105-122.

Ciepilewski, J. and **K.E. Stanovich** (1992), "Predicting Growth in Reading Ability from Children's Exposure to Print", *Journal of Experimental Child Psychology*, Vol. 54, pp. 74-89.

Clark and Trafford (1995), "Boys into Modern Languages: An Investigation of the Discrepancy in Attitudes and Performance between Boys and Girls in Modern Languages", *Gender and Education*, Vol. 7, pp. 315-325.

Cole, N. (1997), *The ETS Gender Study: How Females and Males Perform in Educational Settings*, Educational Testing Service, Princeton, NJ.

Cunningham, A.E. and **K.E. Stanovich** (1998), "Early Reading Acquisition and its Relation to Reading Experience and Ability 10 Years Later", *Developmental Psychology*, Vol. 33, No. 6, pp. 934-945.

Dempster, A.P., N.M. Laird and **D.B. Rubin** (1977), "Maximum likelihood from incomplete data via the EM algorithm", *Journal of the Royal Statistical Society, Series B,* Vol. 34, pp1-38.

Francis, B. (2000), *Boys, Girls, and Achievement: Addressing the Classroom Issue*, Routledge/Falmer Press, London.

Fredricks, J.A., P.C. Blumenfeld and **A.H. Paris** (2004), "School Engagement: Potential of the Concept, State of the Evidence", *Review of Educational Research*, Vol. 74, pp. 59-109.

Ganzeboom, H.B.G., P.M. De Graaf and **D.J. Treiman** (1992), "A Standard International Socio-economic Index of Occupational Status", *Social Science Research* Vol. 21, No. 1, Elsevier LTD., pp. 1-56.

Goldman, S.R. and **J.A. Rakestraw** (2000), "Structural Aspects of Constructing Meaning from Text", in M.L. Kamil, P.B. Mosenthal, P.D. Pearson and R. Barr (eds.), *Handbook of Reading Research*, Erlbaum, Mahwah, NJ, pp. 311-336.

Grigg, W.S., M.C. Daane, Y. Jin and **J.R. Campbell** (2001), *The Nation's Report Card: Reading 2002*, US Department of Education, Washington DC.

Guthrie, J.T. (2008), *Engaging Adolescents in Reading*, Corwin Press, Thousand Oaks, CA.

Guthrie, J.T. and **A. Wigfield** (2000), "Engagement and Motivation in Reading", in M.L. Kamil and P.B. Mosenthal (eds.), *Handbook of Reading Research*, Erlbaum, Mahwah, NJ, pp. 403-422.

Guthrie, J.T., A. Wigfield and **W. You** (in press), "Instructional Contexts for Engagement and Achievement in Reading", in S.L. Christenson (ed.), *Handbook of Research on Student Engagement*, Springer Science, New York.

Guzetti, B.J. (2008), "Adolescent Girls Performing Gender through Literacies: Marginalized or Resistant Youth?", in K. Sanford and R. Hammett (eds.), *Boys, Girls, and the Myths of Literacy*, Canadian Scholars Press, Toronto, pp. 219-233.

Guzetti, B.J. (2009), "Lessons on Literacy, Learning and Teaching: Listening to Adolescent Girls", in L. Christenbury, R. Bomer and P. Smagorinsky (eds.), *Handbook of Adolescent Literacy Research*, Guilford, New York, NY, pp. 372-385.

Guzetti, B.J. and **M. Gamboa** (2004), "Zines for Social Justice: Adolescent Girls Writing on their Own", *Reading Research Quarterly*, Vol. 39, pp. 408-436.

Hacker, D.J. (2004), "Self-regulated Comprehension during Normal Reading", in R. Ruddell and N. Unrau (eds.), *Theoretical Models and Processes of Reading*, 5th ed., International Reading Association, Newark, NJ, pp. 755-779.

Hedges. L.V., and **A. Nowell** (1995), "Sex Differences in Mental Test Scores, Variability, and Numbers of High-Scoring Individuals", *Science.* Vol. 269, pp. 41-45.

ILO (International Labour Organization) (1990), *International Standard Classification of Occupations* (ISCO-88), Geneva.

Levy, B. (1996), "Improving Memory in Old Age through Implicit Self-Stereotyping", *Journal of Personality and Social Psychology,* Vol. 71, pp. 1092-1107.

Lie, S. and **A. Turmo** (2005), "Cross-Country Comparability of Students' Self-Reports – Evidence from PISA 2003", Internal Working OECD/PISA document, TAG(0505)11.

Lüdtke, O., A. Robitzsch, U. Trautwein and **O. Köller** (2007), "Umgang mit fehlenden Werten in der psychologischen Forschung: Probleme und Lösungen" ("Handling of Missing Data in Psychological Research"), *Psychologische Rundschau,* Vol. 58, Deutsche Gesellschaft für Psychologie, pp. 103-117.

Kintsch, W. (2004), "The Construction-Integration Model of Text Comprehension and its Implications for Instruction", in R. Ruddell and N. Unrau (eds.), *Theoretical Models and Processes of Reading*, 5th ed., International Reading Association, Newark, DE, pp. 1270-1328.

Klauda, S.L. (2009), "The Role of Parents in Adolescents' Reading Motivation and Activity", *Educational Psychology Review*, Vol. 21, pp. 325-363.

McKenna, M.C., D.J. Kear and **Ellsworth** (1995), "Children's Attitudes toward Reading: A National Survey", *Reading Research Quarterly*, Vol. 30, No. 4, pp. 934-956.

Mills, K.A. (2010), "A Review of the 'Digital Turn' in New Literacy Studies", *Review of Educational Research*, Vol. 80, pp. 246-271.

Mullis, I.V.S, Martin, M.O., A.M. Kennedy and **Foy P.** (2007), *PIRLS 2006 International Report: IEA's Progress in International Reading Literacy Study in Primary School in 40 Countries*. Chestnut Hill, MA, Boston College.

Murdock, T.B (2009), "Achievement Motivation in Racial and Ethnic Context", in K.R. Wentzel and A. Wigfield (eds.), *Handbook of Motivation in School*, Taylor Francis, New York, pp. 433-461.

Nurmi, J.E., K. Aunola, K. Salmela-Aro and **M. Lindroos** (2003), "The Role of Success Expectation and Task-avoidance in Academic Performance and Satisfaction: Three Studies on Antecedents, Consequences and Correlates", *Contemporary Education Psychology*, Vol. 28, pp. 59-90.

OECD (1999), *Classifying Educational Programmes: Manual for ISCED-97 Implementation in OECD Countries*, OECD Publishing.

OECD (2001), *Knowledge and Skills for Life: First Results from PISA 2000*, OECD Publishing.

OECD (2002), *Reading for Change: Performance and Engagement across OECD Countries*, OECD Publishing.

OECD (2007a), *PISA 2006: Science Competencies for Tomorrow's World*, OECD Publishing.

OECD (2007b), *Understanding the Brain: The Birth of a Learning Science*, OECD Publishing.

OECD (2008a), *PISA Data Analysis Manual*, OECD Publishing.

OECD (2008b), *Growing Unequal? Income Distribution and Poverty in OECD Countries*, OECD Publishing.

OECD (2010), *PISA 2009 Framework: Key Competencies in Reading, Mathematics and Science,* OECD Publishing, Paris.

OECD (forthcoming), *PISA 2009 Technical Report*, OECD Publishing.

OECD and **Statistics Canada** (2000), *Literacy in the information age,* Final Report of the International Adult Literacy Survey.

Osborne, J.W. (1995), "Academic Self-Esteem and Race: A Look at the Underlying Assumptions of the Disidentification Hypothesis", *Personality and Social Psychology Bulletin*, Vol. 21, pp. 441-455.

Osborne, J.W. (1997), "Race and Academic Disidentification", *Journal of Educational Psychology*, Vol. 89, pp. 728-735.

Paechter, C. (1998), *Educating the Other: Gender, Power, and Schooling*, Falmer, London.

Pastor, D.A., K.E. Barron, B.J. Miller and **S.L. Davis** (2007), "A Latent Profile Analysis of College Students' Achievement Goal Orientation", Contemporary Educational Psychology, Vol. 32, No. 1, pp. 8-47.

Pinker, S. (1995), The Language Instinct: How the Mind Creates Language, Harper Collins, New York, NY.

Ruble, D.N., C.L. Martin and S.A. Berenbaum (2006), "Gender Development", in W. Damon (Series ed.) and N. Eisenberg (Vol. ed.), *Handbook of Child Psychology*, 6th ed., Vol. 3, Wiley, New York, NY, pp. 858-932.

Ryan, R.M. and E.L. Deci (2009), "Promoting Self-determined School Engagement: Motivation, Learning, and Well-being", in K.R. Wentzel and A. Wigfield (eds.), *Handbook of Motivation in School*, Taylor Francis, New York, pp. 171-196.

Safford, K., O. O'Sullivan and M. Barrs, M. (2004), *Boys on the Margin: Promoting Boys Literacy and Learning at Key Stage 2*, Centre for Literacy in Primary Education, London.

Schafer, J.L. and J.W. Graham (2002), "Missing Data: Our View of the State of the Art", *Psychological Methods,* Vol. 7, No. 2, American Psychological Association, pp. 147-177.

Schiefele, U. (2009), "Situational and Individual Interest", in K.R. Wentzel and A. Wigfield (eds.), *Handbook of Motivation in School*, Taylor Francis, New York, pp. 197-223.

Shih, M., T.L. Pittinsky, and N. Ambady (1999), "Stereotype Susceptibility: Identity Salience and Shifts in Quantitative Performance", *Psychological Science*, Vol. 10, No. 1, pp. 80-83.

Skinner, E.A., T.A. Kindermann and C. Furrer (2009), "A Motivational Perspective on Engagement and Disaffection: Conceptualization and Assessment of Children's Behavioral and Emotional Participation in Academic Activities in the Classroom", *Educational and Psychological Measurement*, Vol. 69, pp. 493-525.

Smith, C.M. (1996), "Differences in Adults' Reading Practices and Literacy Proficiencies", *Reading Research Quarterly,* Vol. 31, No. 2, pp. 196-219.

Smith, C.M., L. Mikulecky, M.W. Kibby and M.J. Dreher (2000), "What will be the Demands of Literacy in the Workplace in the Next Millennium?", *Reading Research Quarterly,* Vol. 35, No. 3, pp. 378-383.

Smith, M.W. and J. Wilhelm (2002), *"Reading don't Fix no Chevys": Literacy in the Lives of Young Men*, Heinemann, Portsmouth, NH.

Smith, M.W. and J. Wilhelm (2004), "'I just Like Being Good at It': The Importance of Competence in the Literate Lives of Young Men", *Journal of Adolescent and Adult Literacy*, Vol. 47, pp. 454-461.

Smith, M.W. and J. Wilhelm (2006), *Going with the Flow: How to Encourage Boys (and Girls) in their Literacy Learning*, Heinemann, Portsmouth, NH.

Smith, M.W. and J. Wilhelm (2009), "Boys and Literacy: Complexity and Multiplicity", in L. Christenbury, R. Bomer and P. Smagorinsky (eds.), *Handbook of Adolescent Literacy Research*, Guilford, New York, pp. 360-371.

Snow, C. and A. Biancarosa (2003), *Adolescent Literacy and the Achievement Gap: What Do we Know and Where Do we Go from Here?*, Carnegie Corporation, New York.

Stanovich, K.E. (1986), "Matthew Effects in Reading: Some Consequences of Individual Differences in the Acquisition of Literacy", *Reading Research Quarterly*, Vol. 21, pp. 360-406.

Stanovich, K.E. (2004), "Matthew Effects in Reading: Some Consequences of Individual Differences in the Acquisition of Literacy", in R. Ruddell and N. Unrau (eds.), *Theoretical Models and Processes of Reading*, International Reading Association, Newark, DE, pp. 454-516.

Steen, I.A. (1987), "Mathematics Education: A Predictor of Scientific Competitiveness", *Science*, Vol. 237, pp. 251-253.

Strickland, D.S. and D.E. Alvermann (2004), "Learning and Teaching Literacy in Grades 4-12: Issues and Challenges", in D.S. Strickland and D.E. Alvermann (eds.), *Bridging the Literacy Achievement Gap Grades 4-12*, Teachers College Press, New York, pp. 1-13.

Warm, T.A. (1985), "Weighted Maximum Likelihood Estimation of Ability Item Response Theory with Tests of Finite Length", *Technical Report CGI-TR-85-08*, U.S. Coast Guard Institute, Oklahoma City.

Warrington, M., M. Younger and J. Williams (2000), "Students' Attitudes, Image, and the Gender Gap", *British Educational Research Journal*, Vol. 26, No. 3, pp. 393-407.

Younger, M. and M. Warrington (1996), "Differential Achievement of Girls and Boys at GCSE: Some Observations from the Perspective of One School", *British Journal of Sociology of Education*, Vol. 17, No. 3, pp. 299-314.

Zimmerman, B.J. and T.J. Cleary (2009), "Motives to Self-regulate Learning: A Social Cognitive Account", in K.R. Wentzel and A. Wigfield (eds.), *Handbook of Motivation in School*, Taylor Francis, New York, pp. 1247-264.

Annex A

TECHNICAL BACKGROUND

All tables in Annex A are available on line

ANNEX A1

CONSTRUCTION OF READING SCALES AND INDICES FROM THE STUDENT, SCHOOL AND PARENT CONTEXT QUESTIONNAIRES

How the PISA 2009 reading assessments were designed, analysed and scaled

The development of the PISA 2009 reading tasks was co-ordinated by an international consortium of educational research institutions contracted by the OECD, under the guidance of a group of reading experts from participating countries. Participating countries contributed stimulus material and questions, which were reviewed, tried out and refined iteratively over the three years leading up to the administration of the assessment in 2009. The development process involved provisions for several rounds of commentary from participating countries, as well as small-scale piloting and a formal field trial in which samples of 15-year-olds from all participating countries took part. The reading expert group recommended the final selection of tasks, which included material submitted by 21 of the participating countries. The selection was made with regard to both their technical quality, assessed on the basis of their performance in the field trial and their cultural appropriateness and interest level for 15-year-olds, as judged by the participating countries. Another essential criterion for selecting the set of material as a whole was its fit to the framework described in *Volume 1, What Students Know and Can Do,* to maintain the balance across various categories of text, aspect and situation. Finally, it was carefully ensured that the set of questions covered a range of difficulty, allowing good measurement and description of the reading literacy of all 15-year-old students, from the least proficient to the highly able.

More than 130 print reading questions were used in PISA 2009, but each student in the sample only saw a fraction of the total pool because different sets of questions were given to different students. The reading questions selected for inclusion in PISA 2009 were organised into half-hour clusters. These, along with clusters of mathematics and science questions, were assembled into booklets containing four clusters each. Each participating student was then given a two-hour assessment. As reading was the focus of the PISA 2009 assessment, every booklet included at least one cluster of reading material. The clusters were rotated so that each cluster appeared in each of the four possible positions in the booklets, and each pair of clusters appeared in at least one of the 13 booklets that were used.

This design, similar to those used in previous PISA assessments, makes it possible to construct a single scale of reading proficiency, in which each question is associated with a particular point on the scale that indicates its difficulty, whereby each student's performance is associated with a particular point on the same scale that indicates his or her estimated proficiency. A description of the modelling technique used to construct this scale can be found in the *PISA 2009 Technical Report* (OECD, forthcoming).

The relative difficulty of tasks in a test is estimated by considering the proportion of test takers who answer each question correctly. The relative proficiency of students taking a particular test can be estimated by considering the proportion of test questions they answer correctly. A single continuous scale shows the relationship between the difficulty of questions and the proficiency of students. By constructing a scale that shows the difficulty of each question, it is possible to locate the level of reading literacy that the question represents. By showing the proficiency of each student on the same scale, it is possible to describe the level of reading literacy that the student possesses.

The location of student proficiency on this scale is set in relation to the particular group of questions used in the assessment. However, just as the sample of students taking PISA in 2009 is drawn to represent all the 15-year-olds in the participating countries, so the individual questions used in the assessment are designed to represent the definition of reading literacy adequately. Estimates of student proficiency reflect the kinds of tasks they would be expected to perform successfully. This means that students are likely to be able to complete questions successfully at or below the difficulty level associated with their own position on the scale (but they may not always do so). Conversely, they are unlikely to be able to successfully complete questions above the difficulty level associated with their position on the scale (but they may sometimes do so).

The further a student's proficiency is located above a given question, the more likely he or she is to successfully complete the question (and other questions of similar difficulty); the further the student's proficiency is located below a given question, the lower the probability that the student will be able to successfully complete the question, and other questions of similar difficulty.

How reading proficiency levels are defined in PISA 2009

PISA 2009 provides an overall reading literacy scale for the reading texts, drawing on all the questions in the reading assessment, as well as scales for three aspects and two text formats. The metric for the overall reading scale is based on a mean for OECD countries set at 500 in PISA 2000, with a standard deviation of 100. To help interpret what students' scores mean in substantive terms, the scale is divided into levels, based on a set of statistical principles, and then descriptions are generated, based on the tasks that are located within each level, to describe the kinds of skills and knowledge needed to successfully complete those tasks.

For PISA 2009, the range of difficulty of tasks allows for the description of seven levels of reading proficiency: Level 1b is the lowest described level, then Level 1a, Level 2, Level 3 and so on up to Level 6.

Students with a proficiency within the range of Level 1b are likely to be able to successfully complete Level 1b tasks (and others like them), but are unlikely to be able to complete tasks at higher levels. Level 6 reflects tasks that present the greatest challenge in terms of reading skills and knowledge. Students with scores in this range are likely to be able to complete reading tasks located at that level successfully, as well as all the other reading tasks in PISA.

PISA applies a standard methodology for constructing proficiency scales. Based on a student's performance on the tasks in the test, his or her score is generated and located in a specific part of the scale, thus allowing the score to be associated with a defined proficiency level. The level at which the student's score is located is the highest level for which he or she would be expected to answer correctly, most of a random selection of questions within the same level. Thus, for example, in an assessment composed of tasks spread uniformly across Level 3, students with a score located within Level 3 would be expected to complete at least 50% of the tasks successfully. Because a level covers a range of difficulty and proficiency, success rates across the band vary. Students near the bottom of the level would be likely to succeed on just over 50% of the tasks spread uniformly across the level, while students at the top of the level would be likely to succeed on well over 70% of the same tasks.

Figure I.2.12 in Volume I provides details of the nature of reading skills, knowledge and understanding required at each level of the reading scale.

Explanation of indices

This section explains the indices derived from the student, school and parent context questionnaires used in PISA 2009. Parent questionnaire indices are only available for the 14 countries that chose to administer the optional parent questionnaire.

Several PISA measures reflect indices that summarise responses from students, their parents or school representatives (typically principals) to a series of related questions. The questions were selected from a larger pool of questions on the basis of theoretical considerations and previous research. Structural equation modelling was used to confirm the theoretically expected behaviour of the indices and to validate their comparability across countries. For this purpose, a model was estimated separately for each country and collectively for all OECD countries.

For a detailed description of other PISA indices and details on the methods, see *PISA 2009 Technical Report* (OECD, forthcoming).

There are two types of indices: simple indices and scale indices.

Simple indices are the variables that are constructed through the arithmetic transformation or recoding of one or more items, in exactly the same way across assessments. Here, item responses are used to calculate meaningful variables, such as the recoding of the four-digit ISCO-88 codes into "Highest parents' socio-economic index (HISEI)" or, teacher-student ratio based on information from the school questionnaire.

Scale indices are the variables constructed through the scaling of multiple items. Unless otherwise indicated, the index was scaled using a weighted maximum likelihood estimate (WLE) (Warm, 1985), using a one-parameter item response model (a partial credit model was used in the case of items with more than two categories).

The scaling was done in three stages:

- The item parameters were estimated from equal-sized subsamples of students from each OECD country.

- The estimates were computed for all students and all schools by anchoring the item parameters obtained in the preceding step.

- The indices were then standardised so that the mean of the index value for the OECD student population was 0 and the standard deviation was 1 (countries being given equal weight in the standardisation process).

Sequential codes were assigned to the different response categories of the questions in the sequence in which the latter appeared in the student, school or parent questionnaires. Where indicated in this section, these codes were inverted for the purpose of constructing indices or scales. It is important to note that negative values for an index do not necessarily imply that students responded negatively to the underlying questions. A negative value merely indicates that the respondents answered less positively than all respondents did on average across OECD countries. Likewise, a positive value on an index indicates that the respondents answered more favourably, or more positively, than respondents did, on average, in OECD countries. Terms enclosed in brackets < > in the following descriptions were replaced in the national versions of the student, school and parent questionnaires by the appropriate national equivalent. For example, the term <qualification at ISCED level 5A> was translated in the United States into "Bachelor's degree, post-graduate certificate program, Master's degree program or first professional degree program". Similarly the term <classes in the language of assessment> in Luxembourg was translated into "German classes" or "French classes" depending on whether students received the German or French version of the assessment instruments.

In addition to simple and scaled indices described in this annex, there are a number of variables from the questionnaires that correspond to single items not used to construct indices. These non-recoded variables have prefix of "ST" for the questionnaire items in the student questionnaire, "SC" for the items in the school questionnaire, and "PA" for the items in the parent questionnaire. All the context questionnaires as well as the PISA international database, including all variables, are available through *www.pisa.oecd.org*.

Student-level simple indices

Age

The variable AGE is calculated as the difference between the middle month and the year in which students were assessed and their month and year of birth, expressed in years and months.

Study programme

In PISA 2009, study programmes available to 15-year-old students in each country were collected both through the student tracking form and the student questionnaire (ST02). All study programmes were classified using ISCED (OECD, 1999). In the PISA international database, all national programmes are indicated in a variable (PROGN) where the first three digits are the ISO code for a country, the fourth digit the sub-national category and the last two digits the nationally specific programme code.

The following internationally comparable indices were derived from the data on study programmes:

- Programme level (ISCEDL) indicates whether students are (1) primary education level (ISCED 1); (2) lower-secondary education level; or (3) upper secondary education level.
- Programme designation (ISCEDD) indicates the designation of the study programme: (1) = "A" (general programmes designed to give access to the next programme level); (2) = "B" (programmes designed to give access to vocational studies at the next programme level); (3) = "C" (programmes designed to give direct access to the labour market); or (4) = "M" (modular programmes that combine any or all of these characteristics).
- Programme orientation (ISCEDO) indicates whether the programme's curricular content is (1) general; (2) pre-vocational; (3) vocational; or (4) modular programmes that combine any or all of these characteristics.

Occupational status of parents

Occupational data for both a student's father and a student's mother were obtained by asking open-ended questions in the student questionnaire (ST9a, ST9b, ST12, ST13a, ST13b and ST16). The responses were coded to four-digit ISCO codes (ILO, 1990) and then mapped to Ganzeboom et al.'s SEI index (1992). Higher scores of SEI indicate higher levels of occupational status. The following three indices are obtained:

- Mother's occupational status (BMMJ).
- Father's occupational status (BFMJ).
- The highest occupational level of parents (HISEI) corresponds to the higher SEI score of either parent or to the only available parent's SEI score.

Educational level of parents

The educational level of parents is classified using ISCED (OECD, 1999) based on students' responses in the student questionnaire (ST10, ST11, ST14 and ST15). Please note that the question format for school education in PISA 2009 differs from the one used in PISA 2000, 2003 and 2006 but the method used to compute parental education is the same.

As in PISA 2000, 2003 and 2006, indices were constructed by selecting the highest level for each parent and then assigning them to the following categories: (0) None, (1) ISCED 1 (primary education), (2) ISCED 2 (lower secondary), (3) ISCED Level 3B or 3C (vocational/pre-vocational upper secondary), (4) ISCED 3A (upper secondary) and/or ISCED 4 (non-tertiary post-secondary), (5) ISCED 5B (vocational tertiary), (6) ISCED 5A, 6 (theoretically oriented tertiary and post-graduate). The following three indices with these categories are developed:

- Mother's educational level (MISCED).
- Father's educational level (FISCED).
- Highest educational level of parents (HISCED) corresponds to the higher ISCED level of either parent.

Highest educational level of parents was also converted into the number of years of schooling (PARED). For the conversion of level of education into years of schooling, see Table A1.1.

Immigration and language background

Information on the country of birth of students and their parents (ST17) is collected in a similar manner as in PISA 2000, PISA 2003 and PISA 2006 by using nationally specific ISO coded variables. The ISO codes of the country of birth for students and their parents are available in the PISA international database (COBN_S, COBN_M, and COBN_F).

The index on immigrant background (IMMIG) has the following categories: (1) native students (those students born in the country of assessment, or those with at least one parent born in that country; students who were born abroad with at least one parent born in the country of assessment are also classified as 'native' students), (2) second-generation students (those born in the country of assessment but whose parents were born in another country) and (3) first-generation students (those born outside the country of assessment and whose parents were also born in another country). Students with missing responses for either the student or for both parents, or for all three questions have been given missing values for this variable.

Students indicate the language they usually speak at home. The data are captured in nationally-specific language codes, which were recoded into variable ST19Q01 with the following two values: (1) language at home is the same as the language of assessment, and (2) language at home is a different language than the language of assessment.

[Part 1/1]

Table A1.1 **Levels of parental education converted into years of schooling**

	Did not go to school	Completed ISCED Level 1 (primary education)	Completed ISCED Level 2 (lower secondary education)	Completed ISCED Levels 3B or 3C (upper secondary education providing direct access to the labor market or to ISCED 5B programmes)	Completed ISCED Level 3A (upper secondary education providing access to ISCED 5A and 5B programmes) and/or ISCED Level 4 (non-tertiary post-secondary)	Completed ISCED Level 5A (university level tertiary education) or ISCED Level 6 (advanced research programmes)	Completed ISCED Level 5B (non-university tertiary education)
OECD							
Australia	0.0	6.0	10.0	11.0	12.0	15.0	14.0
Austria	0.0	4.0	9.0	12.0	12.5	17.0	15.0
Belgium	0.0	6.0	9.0	12.0	12.0	17.0	14.5
Canada	0.0	6.0	9.0	12.0	12.0	17.0	15.0
Chile	0.0	6.0	8.0	12.0	12.0	17.0	16.0
Czech Republic	0.0	5.0	9.0	11.0	13.0	16.0	16.0
Denmark	0.0	6.0	9.0	12.0	12.0	17.0	15.0
Estonia	0.0	4.0	9.0	12.0	12.0	16.0	15.0
Finland	0.0	6.0	9.0	12.0	12.0	16.5	14.5
France	0.0	5.0	9.0	12.0	12.0	15.0	14.0
Germany	0.0	4.0	10.0	13.0	13.0	18.0	15.0
Greece	0.0	6.0	9.0	11.5	12.0	17.0	15.0
Hungary	0.0	4.0	8.0	10.5	12.0	16.5	13.5
Iceland	0.0	7.0	10.0	13.0	14.0	18.0	16.0
Ireland	0.0	6.0	9.0	12.0	12.0	16.0	14.0
Israel	0.0	6.0	9.0	12.0	12.0	15.0	15.0
Italy	0.0	5.0	8.0	12.0	13.0	17.0	16.0
Japan	0.0	6.0	9.0	12.0	12.0	16.0	14.0
Korea	0.0	6.0	9.0	12.0	12.0	16.0	14.0
Luxembourg	0.0	6.0	9.0	12.0	13.0	17.0	16.0
Mexico	0.0	6.0	9.0	12.0	12.0	16.0	14.0
Netherlands	0.0	6.0	10.0	a	12.0	16.0	a
New Zealand	0.0	5.5	10.0	11.0	12.0	15.0	14.0
Norway	0.0	6.0	9.0	12.0	12.0	16.0	14.0
Poland	0.0	a	8.0	11.0	12.0	16.0	15.0
Portugal	0.0	6.0	9.0	12.0	12.0	17.0	15.0
Scotland	0.0	7.0	11.0	13.0	13.0	16.0	16.0
Slovak Republic	0.0	4.5	8.5	12.0	12.0	17.5	13.5
Slovenia	0.0	4.0	8.0	11.0	12.0	16.0	15.0
Spain	0.0	5.0	8.0	10.0	12.0	16.5	13.0
Sweden	0.0	6.0	9.0	11.5	12.0	15.5	14.0
Switzerland	0.0	6.0	9.0	12.5	12.5	17.5	14.5
Turkey	0.0	5.0	8.0	11.0	11.0	15.0	13.0
United Kingdom	0.0	6.0	9.0	12.0	13.0	16.0	15.0
United States	0.0	6.0	9.0	a	12.0	16.0	14.0
Partners							
Albania	0.0	6.0	9.0	12.0	12.0	16.0	16.0
Argentina	0.0	6.0	10.0	12.0	12.0	17.0	14.5
Azerbaijan	0.0	4.0	9.0	11.0	11.0	17.0	14.0
Brazil	0.0	4.0	8.0	11.0	11.0	16.0	14.5
Bulgaria	0.0	4.0	8.0	12.0	12.0	17.5	15.0
Colombia	0.0	5.0	9.0	11.0	11.0	15.5	14.0
Croatia	0.0	4.0	8.0	11.0	12.0	17.0	15.0
Dubai (UAE)	0.0	5.0	9.0	12.0	12.0	16.0	15.0
Hong Kong- China	0.0	6.0	9.0	11.0	13.0	16.0	14.0
Indonesia	0.0	6.0	9.0	12.0	12.0	15.0	14.0
Jordan	0.0	6.0	10.0	12.0	12.0	16.0	14.5
Kazakhstan	0.0	4.0	9.0	11.5	12.5	15.0	14.0
Kyrgyzstan	0.0	4.0	8.0	11.0	10.0	15.0	13.0
Latvia	0.0	3.0	8.0	11.0	11.0	16.0	16.0
Liechtenstein	0.0	5.0	9.0	11.0	13.0	17.0	14.0
Lithuania	0.0	3.0	8.0	11.0	11.0	16.0	15.0
Macao-China	0.0	6.0	9.0	11.0	12.0	16.0	15.0
Montenegro	0.0	4.0	8.0	11.0	12.0	16.0	15.0
Panama	0.0	6.0	9.0	12.0	12.0	16.0	a
Peru	0.0	6.0	9.0	11.0	11.0	17.0	14.0
Qatar	0.0	6.0	9.0	12.0	12.0	16.0	15.0
Romania	0.0	4.0	8.0	11.5	12.5	16.0	14.0
Russian Federation	0.0	4.0	9.0	11.5	12.0	15.0	a
Serbia	0.0	4.0	8.0	11.0	12.0	17.0	14.5
Shanghai-China	0.0	6.0	9.0	12.0	12.0	16.0	15.0
Singapore	0.0	6.0	8.0	10.5	10.5	12.5	12.5
Chinese Taipei	0.0	6.0	9.0	12.0	12.0	16.0	14.0
Thailand	0.0	6.0	9.0	12.0	12.0	16.0	14.0
Trinidad and Tobago	0.0	5.0	9.0	12.0	12.0	16.0	15.0
Tunisia	0.0	6.0	9.0	12.0	13.0	17.0	16.0
Uruguay	0.0	6.0	9.0	12.0	12.0	17.0	15.0

StatLink ᨑᨗᨔᨗ http://dx.doi.org/10.1787/888932343171

Relative grade

Data on the student's grade are obtained both from the student questionnaire (ST01) and from the student tracking form. As with all variables that are on both the tracking form and the questionnaire, inconsistencies between the two sources are reviewed and resolved during data-cleaning. In order to capture between-country variation, the relative grade index (GRADE) indicates whether students are at the modal grade in a country (value of 0), or whether they are below or above the modal grade level (+x grades, –x grades).

The relationship between the grade and student performance was estimated through a multilevel model accounting for the following background variables: *i*) the **PISA index of economic, social and cultural status**; *ii*) the **PISA index of economic, social and cultural status** squared; *iii*) the school mean of the **PISA index of economic, social and cultural status**; *iv*) an indicator as to whether students were foreign born first-generation students; *v*) the percentage of first-generation students in the school; and *vi*) students' gender.

Table A1.2 presents the results of the multilevel model. Column 1 in Table A1.2 estimates the score point difference that is associated with one grade level (or school year). This difference can be estimated for the 32 OECD countries in which a sizeable number of 15-year-olds in the PISA samples were enrolled in at least two different grades. The average score point difference between two grades is about 39 score points on the PISA reading scale. This implies that one school year corresponds to an average of 39 score points. Since 15-year-olds cannot be assumed to be distributed at random across the grade levels, adjustments had to be made for the above-mentioned contextual factors that may relate to the assignment of students to the different grade levels. These adjustments are documented in columns 2 to 7 of the table. While it is possible to estimate the typical performance difference among students in two adjacent grades net of the effects of selection and contextual factors, this difference cannot automatically be equated with the progress that students have made over the last school year but should be interpreted as a lower boundary of the progress achieved. This is not only because different students were assessed but also because the content of the PISA assessment was not expressly designed to match what students had learned in the preceding school year but more broadly to assess the cumulative outcome of learning in school up to age 15. For example, if the curriculum of the grades in which 15-year-olds are enrolled mainly includes material other than that assessed by PISA (which, in turn, may have been included in earlier school years) then the observed performance difference will underestimate student progress.

Learning time

Learning time in test language (LMINS) was computed by multiplying students' responses on the number of minutes on average in the test language class by number of test language class periods per week (ST28 and ST29). Comparable indices are computed for mathematics (MMINS) and science (SMINS).

Student-level scale indices

Family wealth

The *index of family wealth* (WEALTH) is based on the students' responses on whether they had the following at home: a room of their own, a link to the Internet, a dishwasher (treated as a country-specific item), a DVD player, and three other country-specific items (some items in ST20); and their responses on the number of cellular phones, televisions, computers, cars and the rooms with a bath or shower (ST21).

Home educational resources

The *index of home educational resources* (HEDRES) is based on the items measuring the existence of educational resources at home including a desk and a quiet place to study, a computer that students can use for schoolwork, educational software, books to help with students' school work, technical reference books and a dictionary (some items in ST20).

Cultural possessions

The *index of cultural possessions* (CULTPOSS) is based on the students' responses to whether they had the following at home: classic literature, books of poetry and works of art (some items in ST20).

Economic, social and cultural status

The *PISA index of economic, social and cultural status* (ESCS) was derived from the following three indices: highest occupational status of parents (HISEI), highest educational level of parents in years of education according to ISCED (PARED), and home possessions (HOMEPOS). The *index of home possessions* (HOMEPOS) comprises all items on the indices of WEALTH, CULTPOSS and HEDRES, as well as books in the home recoded into a four-level categorical variable (0-10 books, 11-25 or 26-100 books, 101-200 or 201-500 books, more than 500 books).

The *PISA index of economic, social and cultural status* (ESCS) was derived from a principal component analysis of standardised variables (each variable has an OECD mean of 0 and a standard deviation of 1), taking the factor scores for the first principal component as measures of the index of economic, social and cultural status.

[Part 1/1]

Table A1.2 A multilevel model to estimate grade effects in reading, accounting for some background variables

		Grade		Index of economic, social and cultural status		Index of economic, social and cultural status squared		School mean index of economic, social and cultural status		First Generation students		School percentage of first generation students		Gender – student is a girl		Intercept	
		Coef.	S.E.	Coef.	S.E.	Coef.	S.E.	Coef.	S.E.	Coef.	S.E.	Coef.	S.E.	Coef.	S.E.	Coef.	S.E.
OECD	Australia	33.2	(1.95)	30.0	(1.36)	-3.8	(1.05)	66.4	(1.87)	-7.4	(2.82)	0.1	(0.07)	32.9	(1.91)	466.0	(1.39)
	Austria	35.3	(2.18)	11.4	(1.66)	-0.5	(1.00)	89.7	(3.86)	-33.1	(6.11)	1.4	(0.13)	19.9	(2.67)	467.9	(2.45)
	Belgium	48.9	(1.98)	10.0	(1.12)	-0.1	(0.63)	79.9	(1.73)	-3.2	(5.18)	0.3	(0.11)	11.3	(1.81)	507.0	(1.70)
	Canada	45.0	(2.14)	19.4	(1.52)	1.5	(0.91)	33.9	(2.28)	-13.7	(3.18)	0.3	(0.04)	30.4	(1.60)	483.4	(1.76)
	Chile	35.5	(1.55)	8.6	(1.52)	0.3	(0.63)	37.4	(1.61)	c	c	c	c	13.8	(2.33)	478.6	(1.60)
	Czech Republic	44.6	(3.39)	13.4	(1.89)	-2.3	(1.47)	111.5	(3.12)	-8.9	(12.29)	0.4	(0.33)	32.3	(2.84)	460.7	(2.39)
	Denmark	36.1	(3.02)	27.9	(1.51)	-2.8	(1.10)	35.1	(2.91)	-37.5	(5.97)	0.0	(0.14)	25.5	(2.59)	474.0	(1.95)
	Estonia	44.4	(2.74)	14.1	(1.80)	1.6	(1.43)	52.1	(4.52)	-18.7	(14.08)	-3.3	(0.44)	36.7	(2.45)	485.8	(2.02)
	Finland	37.3	(3.60)	27.7	(1.66)	-2.5	(1.30)	10.4	(3.28)	-56.0	(13.09)	-0.1	(0.29)	51.5	(2.26)	500.6	(2.02)
	France	47.1	(5.14)	12.5	(1.70)	-1.9	(1.12)	81.6	(4.04)	-11.6	(9.24)	0.2	(0.15)	25.9	(2.67)	516.5	(2.35)
	Germany	34.4	(1.74)	9.2	(1.23)	-1.6	(0.74)	109.1	(2.16)	-13.2	(4.80)	0.2	(0.12)	27.2	(1.92)	458.0	(1.46)
	Greece	22.6	(10.86)	15.9	(1.46)	1.5	(1.07)	41.2	(2.84)	-15.0	(7.82)	0.0	(0.18)	36.2	(2.55)	469.0	(2.04)
	Hungary	25.6	(2.19)	8.3	(1.39)	0.9	(0.87)	74.8	(2.09)	2.8	(7.92)	0.0	(0.27)	21.4	(2.22)	494.1	(1.65)
	Iceland	c	c	29.8	(2.56)	-5.1	(1.56)	-3.8	(5.12)	-52.2	(11.45)	-1.3	(0.40)	44.9	(2.59)	469.1	(4.23)
	Ireland	18.2	(1.99)	29.7	(1.78)	-3.5	(1.44)	43.6	(2.68)	-32.8	(6.52)	-0.1	(0.20)	33.9	(3.62)	474.8	(2.77)
	Israel	36.6	(3.85)	19.9	(1.90)	3.4	(1.04)	104.7	(2.10)	-11.0	(6.13)	1.5	(0.08)	29.4	(2.81)	460.1	(2.13)
	Italy	36.1	(1.67)	4.5	(0.69)	-1.4	(0.42)	76.4	(1.07)	-29.7	(3.36)	0.2	(0.08)	24.0	(1.29)	491.4	(0.85)
	Japan	a	a	4.1	(1.51)	0.1	(1.47)	144.2	(2.40)	c	c	c	c	27.9	(2.43)	508.6	(1.58)
	Korea	31.2	(9.77)	12.9	(1.42)	1.9	(1.18)	64.9	(2.24)	a	a	a	a	30.6	(3.21)	537.7	(2.08)
	Luxembourg	45.3	(1.95)	16.6	(1.31)	-2.6	(1.08)	62.0	(2.89)	-10.4	(5.11)	-0.2	(0.10)	33.0	(2.22)	435.7	(2.40)
	Mexico	32.6	(1.59)	7.5	(0.92)	0.8	(0.34)	27.8	(0.80)	-41.9	(6.36)	-1.8	(0.15)	17.9	(1.03)	473.7	(1.02)
	Netherlands	26.6	(2.04)	6.0	(1.52)	-1.2	(1.02)	106.7	(2.32)	-11.6	(5.72)	1.7	(0.14)	15.3	(1.85)	484.5	(2.33)
	New Zealand	44.2	(4.15)	38.9	(1.82)	-1.7	(1.44)	56.3	(3.35)	-12.2	(3.84)	0.0	(0.10)	44.8	(2.62)	496.5	(2.44)
	Norway	37.6	(18.19)	34.2	(2.00)	-3.4	(1.62)	31.1	(4.32)	-33.4	(7.52)	0.4	(0.25)	48.3	(2.56)	453.2	(2.87)
	Poland	73.8	(4.44)	29.4	(1.59)	-1.8	(1.21)	19.4	(2.99)	c	c	c	c	44.2	(2.41)	498.9	(1.89)
	Portugal	48.9	(1.71)	12.0	(0.94)	1.0	(0.64)	21.3	(1.33)	-5.3	(5.75)	0.0	(0.23)	22.9	(1.84)	518.6	(1.92)
	Slovak Republic	34.2	(3.85)	14.7	(1.44)	-3.2	(0.98)	64.3	(6.30)	c	c	c	c	39.1	(2.58)	483.2	(2.33)
	Slovenia	22.8	(3.41)	4.8	(1.28)	0.0	(1.25)	100.2	(2.74)	-23.4	(7.48)	-0.2	(0.24)	27.7	(2.16)	452.4	(1.63)
	Spain	61.7	(1.22)	9.8	(0.83)	0.4	(0.64)	22.7	(1.25)	-29.7	(2.86)	0.4	(0.04)	18.0	(1.42)	511.3	(1.07)
	Sweden	63.8	(6.69)	31.4	(1.82)	-1.3	(1.04)	49.0	(6.55)	-38.8	(8.53)	0.3	(0.34)	43.2	(2.41)	454.4	(3.62)
	Switzerland	45.5	(2.75)	18.2	(1.27)	-1.0	(1.23)	59.5	(2.95)	-25.1	(3.99)	-0.7	(0.11)	27.0	(2.00)	488.8	(1.50)
	Turkey	33.7	(1.96)	7.7	(1.50)	0.3	(0.61)	46.3	(1.70)	c	c	c	c	27.9	(1.74)	524.0	(1.59)
	United Kingdom	35.9	(6.21)	27.7	(2.01)	-0.3	(1.51)	65.7	(2.49)	-13.6	(8.49)	-0.3	(0.13)	23.1	(2.48)	468.7	(1.73)
	United States	36.3	(2.17)	23.5	(1.70)	4.4	(1.15)	50.4	(2.56)	-5.6	(5.57)	0.8	(0.14)	25.4	(2.36)	463.5	(2.01)
Partners	Albania	11.9	(5.07)	20.8	(3.04)	3.2	(1.35)	43.0	(2.47)	c	c	c	c	56.5	(3.40)	421.5	(3.44)
	Argentina	33.6	(2.50)	11.2	(1.96)	0.9	(0.87)	52.6	(2.03)	-27.0	(10.55)	0.5	(0.20)	24.0	(2.38)	439.7	(2.32)
	Azerbaijan	13.2	(1.78)	10.5	(1.67)	1.3	(0.90)	36.4	(2.00)	-9.8	(12.34)	-0.3	(0.49)	22.6	(2.16)	390.9	(2.12)
	Brazil	36.1	(1.23)	7.7	(1.54)	1.3	(0.57)	38.3	(1.25)	-71.7	(17.16)	-0.9	(0.47)	20.2	(1.63)	445.5	(1.33)
	Bulgaria	27.8	(5.08)	15.7	(1.93)	0.2	(1.29)	75.7	(3.99)	c	c	c	c	42.1	(3.51)	423.7	(2.61)
	Colombia	33.2	(1.12)	6.9	(2.01)	0.9	(0.72)	39.4	(1.53)	c	c	c	c	3.2	(2.17)	477.7	(1.83)
	Croatia	31.8	(2.33)	10.3	(1.36)	-4.0	(0.99)	75.3	(2.01)	-13.0	(5.71)	-0.1	(0.22)	31.4	(2.56)	472.8	(1.69)
	Dubai (UAE)	34.6	(1.56)	15.2	(1.52)	3.2	(1.03)	25.9	(3.13)	21.5	(3.25)	1.1	(0.05)	28.2	(3.94)	362.4	(2.92)
	Hong Kong-China	33.6	(2.03)	-0.9	(1.70)	-1.0	(0.76)	41.9	(1.64)	23.4	(3.70)	-0.4	(0.06)	21.9	(2.42)	575.8	(1.83)
	Indonesia	14.4	(2.00)	4.7	(2.44)	0.9	(0.62)	29.1	(1.83)	c	c	c	c	28.0	(1.48)	430.8	(2.46)
	Jordan	47.6	(6.38)	17.7	(1.52)	0.7	(0.81)	26.9	(1.55)	-11.5	(7.50)	-0.2	(0.20)	48.1	(2.73)	415.5	(2.04)
	Kazakhstan	22.2	(2.42)	16.2	(2.12)	-1.7	(1.31)	55.7	(2.70)	-12.2	(6.78)	0.0	(0.10)	38.1	(2.23)	411.1	(1.57)
	Kyrgyzstan	20.8	(2.92)	18.3	(2.23)	1.7	(1.10)	75.2	(2.03)	-23.4	(21.78)	3.3	(0.50)	46.0	(2.45)	345.7	(1.83)
	Latvia	43.8	(3.07)	16.2	(1.89)	-0.8	(1.35)	37.0	(2.77)	c	c	c	c	38.9	(2.36)	479.6	(1.77)
	Liechtenstein	23.8	(7.40)	2.1	(4.18)	-5.3	(3.07)	112.5	(12.17)	-12.6	(10.22)	-0.7	(0.44)	20.3	(6.86)	499.8	(8.42)
	Lithuania	27.4	(2.87)	18.1	(1.56)	0.2	(1.04)	44.0	(2.45)	c	c	c	c	51.1	(2.34)	447.6	(1.87)
	Macao-China	36.7	(1.01)	1.8	(1.61)	-1.1	(0.78)	1.0	(4.75)	16.7	(2.17)	-0.1	(0.23)	14.1	(1.51)	511.0	(3.47)
	Montenegro	22.9	(3.44)	12.1	(1.38)	-0.3	(1.05)	64.2	(6.54)	-1.8	(6.69)	-1.2	(0.32)	39.3	(2.63)	409.5	(2.58)
	Panama	32.6	(3.41)	7.9	(2.42)	1.2	(0.79)	45.8	(2.60)	-3.4	(10.77)	-1.4	(0.16)	15.8	(4.48)	431.3	(3.22)
	Peru	27.5	(1.23)	10.5	(2.05)	0.9	(0.64)	47.2	(1.46)	c	c	c	c	8.3	(2.17)	445.6	(1.59)
	Qatar	30.7	(1.70)	5.3	(0.98)	0.4	(0.85)	12.7	(2.91)	31.5	(2.98)	1.7	(0.07)	31.4	(3.71)	302.5	(2.94)
	Romania	19.6	(4.19)	10.7	(1.63)	-0.3	(0.79)	63.9	(2.34)	c	c	c	c	13.7	(2.56)	446.4	(1.70)
	Russian Federation	31.0	(2.01)	18.2	(1.93)	-1.6	(1.40)	38.8	(3.32)	-9.1	(5.88)	-0.4	(0.22)	38.7	(2.28)	452.9	(1.89)
	Serbia	21.3	(4.48)	9.2	(1.25)	-0.8	(0.74)	55.1	(3.42)	1.2	(5.65)	0.3	(0.13)	27.1	(2.22)	425.1	(1.60)
	Shanghai-China	21.8	(3.34)	4.6	(1.41)	0.1	(0.85)	57.3	(1.48)	c	c	c	c	29.3	(1.98)	583.5	(2.04)
	Singapore	28.9	(2.09)	22.2	(2.19)	-2.8	(1.14)	104.7	(2.86)	0.4	(4.21)	-1.0	(0.13)	24.6	(2.57)	590.2	(2.76)
	Chinese Taipei	15.4	(4.12)	15.5	(1.50)	-1.2	(1.05)	82.8	(3.06)	c	c	c	c	36.8	(2.25)	515.6	(2.03)
	Thailand	22.1	(2.05)	10.4	(1.54)	2.4	(0.66)	28.8	(1.31)	a	a	a	a	31.3	(1.78)	454.6	(1.67)
	Trinidad and Tobago	35.3	(1.60)	-0.6	(2.00)	-0.2	(0.91)	123.2	(3.42)	-9.2	(13.59)	-0.7	(0.28)	40.4	(2.90)	484.9	(2.77)
	Tunisia	49.7	(1.57)	3.7	(1.76)	0.7	(0.56)	17.8	(1.25)	c	c	c	c	14.4	(1.84)	449.6	(1.63)
	Uruguay	41.4	(1.49)	12.4	(1.58)	0.5	(0.75)	29.7	(1.58)	c	c	c	c	30.1	(2.48)	464.2	(2.29)

StatLink http://dx.doi.org/10.1787/888932343171

Principal component analysis was also performed for each participating country to determine to what extent the components of the index operate in similar ways across countries. The analysis revealed that patterns of factor loading were very similar across countries, with all three components contributing to a similar extent to the index. For the occupational component, the average factor loading was 0.80, ranging from 0.66 to 0.87 across countries. For the educational component, the average factor loading was 0.79, ranging from 0.69 to 0.87 across countries. For the home possession component, the average factor loading was 0.73, ranging from 0.60 to 0.84 across countries. The reliability of the index ranged from 0.41 to 0.81. These results support the cross-national validity of the *PISA index of economic, social and cultural status*.

The imputation of components for students missing data on one component was done on the basis of a regression on the other two variables, with an additional random error component. The final values on the *PISA index of economic, social and cultural status* (ESCS) have an OECD mean of 0 and a standard deviation of 1.

Enjoyment of reading activities

The *index of enjoyment of reading activities* (ENJOY) was derived from students' level of agreement with the following statements (ST24): *i)* I read only if I have to; *ii)* reading is one of my favourite hobbies; *iii)* I like talking about books with other people; *iv)* I find it hard to finish books; *v)* I feel happy if I receive a book as a present; *vi)* for me, reading is a waste of time; *vii)* I enjoy going to a bookstore or a library; *viii)* I read only to get information that I need; *ix)* I cannot sit still and read for more than a few minutes; *x)* I like to express my opinions about books I have read; and *xi)* I like to exchange books with my friends.

As all items that are negatively phrased (items *i, iv, vi, viii* and *ix*) are inverted for scaling, higher values on this index indicate higher levels of enjoyment of reading.

Diversity of reading materials

The *index of diversity of reading materials* (DIVREAD) was derived from the frequency with which students read the following materials because they want to (ST25): magazines, comic books, fiction, non-fiction books and newspapers. Higher values on this index indicate higher diversity in reading.

Online reading activities

The *index of online reading activities* (ONLNREAD) was derived from the frequency with which students involved in the following reading activities (ST26): reading emails, <chat on line>, reading online news, using an online dictionary or encyclopaedia, searching online information to learn about a particular topic, taking part in online group discussions or forums and searching for practical information online. Higher values on this index indicate more frequent online reading activities.

Approaches to learning

How students approach learning is based on student responses in ST27 and measured through the following three indices: memorisation (MEMOR), elaboration (ELAB) and control strategies (CSTRAT).

The *index of memorisation* (MEMOR) was derived from the frequency with which students did the following when they were studying: *i)* try to memorise everything that is covered in the text; *ii)* try to memorise as many details as possible; *iii)* read the text so many times that they can recite it; and *iv)* read the text over and over again.

The *index of elaboration* (ELAB) was derived from the frequency with which students did the following when they were studying: *i)* try to relate new information to prior knowledge acquired in other subjects; *ii)* figure out how the information might be useful outside school; *iii)* try to understand the material better by relating it to my own experiences; and *iv)* figure out how the text information fits in with what happens in real life.

The *index of control strategies* (CSTRAT) was derived from students' reports on how often they did the following statements: *i)* when I study, I start by figuring out what exactly I need to learn; *ii)* when I study, I check if I understand what I have read; *iii)* when I study, I try to figure out which concepts I still haven't really understood; *iv)* when I study, I make sure that I remember the most important points in the text; and *v)* when I study and I don't understand something, I look for additional information to clarify this.

Higher values on the index indicate higher importance attached to the given strategy.

Teachers' stimulation of students' reading engagement

The *index of teachers' stimulation of students' reading engagement* (STIMREAD) was derived from students' reports on how often the following occurred in their lessons of the language of instruction (ST37): *i)* the teacher asks students to explain the meaning of a text; *ii)* the teacher asks questions that challenge students to get a better understanding of a text; *iii)* the teacher gives students enough time to think about their answers; *iv)* the teacher recommends a book or author to read; *v)* the teacher encourages students to express their opinion about a text; *vi)* the teacher helps students relate the stories they read to their lives; and *vii)* the teacher shows students how the information in texts builds on what they already know. Higher values on this index indicate higher teachers' stimulation of students' reading engagement.

Metacognition strategies: understanding and remembering

The *index of understanding and remembering* (UNDREM) was derived from students' reports on the usefulness of the following strategies for understanding and memorising the text (ST41): A) I concentrate on the parts of the text that are easy to understand; B) I quickly read through the text twice; C) After reading the text, I discuss its content with other people; D) I underline important parts of the text; E) I summarise the text in my own words; and F) I read the text aloud to another person.

This index was scored using a rater-scoring system. Through a variety of trial activities, both with reading experts and national centres, a preferred ordering of the strategies according to their effectiveness to achieve the intended goal was agreed. The experts' agreed order of the six items consisting this index is CDE > ABF. Scaling was conducted with two steps. First, a score was assigned to each student, which is a number that ranged from 0 to 1 and can be interpreted as the proportion of the total number of expert pair-wise relations that are consistent with the student ordering. For example, if the expert rule is (ABFD>CEG, 4′3=12 pair wise rules are created (*i.e.* A>C, A>E, A>G, B>C, B>E, B>G, F>C, F>E, F>G, D>C, D>E, D>G). If the responses of a student on this task follow 8 of the 12 rules, the student gets a score of 8/12 = 0.67. Second, these scores were standardised for the index to have a mean of 0 and a standard deviation of 1 across OECD countries. Higher values on this index indicate greater students' perception of usefulness of this strategy.

Metacognition strategies: summarising

The *index of summarising* (METASUM) was derived from students' reports on the usefulness of the following strategies for writing a summary of a long and rather difficult two-page text about fluctuations in the water levels of a lake in Africa (ST42): A) I write a summary. Then I check that each paragraph is covered in the summary, because the content of each paragraph should be included; B) I try to copy out accurately as many sentences as possible; C) before writing the summary, I read the text as many times as possible; D) I carefully check whether the most important facts in the text are represented in the summary; and E) I read through the text, underlining the most important sentences, then I write them in my own words as a summary.

This index was scored using a rater-scoring system. The experts' agreed order of the five items consisting this index is DE>AC>B. Higher values on this index indicate greater students' perception of usefulness of this strategy.

Reading for school

Students' engagement in reading for school is based on student responses to 17 items included in the last page of the test booklets and measured through the following four indices: *index of interpretation of literary texts* (RFSINTRP), *index of use of texts containing non-continuous materials* (RFSNCONT), *index of reading activities for traditional literature courses* (RFSTRLIT), *index of use of functional texts* (RFSFUMAT).

For each item students were asked to report whether they read different texts for school (either in the classroom or as homework) "many times", "two or three times", "once", or "not at all". All items are inverted for scaling, so that higher values on this index indicate higher levels of enjoyment of reading.

The *index of interpretation of literary texts* (RFSINTRP) was derived from the frequency with which students reported that in the past month they did the following: i) read fiction; ii) explain the cause of events in a text; iii) explain the way characters behave in a text; iv) explain the purpose of a text.

The *index of use of texts containing non-continuous materials* (RFSNCONT) was derived from the frequency with which students reported that in the past month they did the following: *i)* use texts that include diagrams or maps; *ii)* use texts that include tables or graphs; *iii)* find information from a graph, diagram or table; and *iv)* describe the way the information in a table or graph is organised.

The *index of reading activities for traditional literature courses* (RFSTRLIT) was derived from the frequency with which students reported that in the past month they did the following: *i)* read information texts about writers or books; *ii)* read poetry; *iii)* memorise a text by heart; *iv)* learn about the place of a text in the history of literature; *v)* learn about the life of the writer.

The *index of use of functional texts* (RFSFUMAT) was derived from the frequency with which students reported that in the past month they did the following: *i)* read newspaper reports and magazine articles; *ii)* read instructions or manuals telling how to make or do something (*e.g.* how a machine works); and *iii)* read advertising material (*e.g.* advertisements in magazines, posters).

ANNEX A2
THE PISA TARGET POPULATION, THE PISA SAMPLES AND THE DEFINITION OF SCHOOLS

Definition of the PISA target population

PISA 2009 provides an assessment of the cumulative yield of education and learning at a point at which most young adults are still enrolled in initial education.

A major challenge for an international survey is to ensure that international comparability of national target populations is guaranteed in such a venture.

Differences between countries in the nature and extent of pre-primary education and care, the age of entry into formal schooling and the institutional structure of educational systems do not allow the definition of internationally comparable grade levels of schooling. Consequently, international comparisons of educational performance typically define their populations with reference to a target age group. Some previous international assessments have defined their target population on the basis of the grade level that provides maximum coverage of a particular age cohort. A disadvantage of this approach is that slight variations in the age distribution of students across grade levels often lead to the selection of different target grades in different countries, or between education systems within countries, raising serious questions about the comparability of results across, and at times within, countries. In addition, because not all students of the desired age are usually represented in grade-based samples, there may be a more serious potential bias in the results if the unrepresented students are typically enrolled in the next higher grade in some countries and the next lower grade in others. This would exclude students with potentially higher levels of performance in the former countries and students with potentially lower levels of performance in the latter.

In order to address this problem, PISA uses an age-based definition for its target population, *i.e.* a definition that is not tied to the institutional structures of national education systems. PISA assesses students who were aged between 15 years and 3 (complete) months and 16 years and 2 (complete) months at the beginning of the assessment period, plus or minus a 1 month allowable variation, and who were enrolled in an educational institution with Grade 7 or higher, regardless of the grade levels or type of institution in which they were enrolled, and regardless of whether they were in full-time or part-time education. Educational institutions are generally referred to as schools in this publication, although some educational institutions (in particular, some types of vocational education establishments) may not be termed schools in certain countries. As expected from this definition, the average age of students across OECD countries was 15 years and 9 months. The range in country means was 2 months and 5 days (0.18 years), from the minimum country mean of 15 years and 8 months to the maximum country mean of 15 years and 10 months.

Given this definition of population, PISA makes statements about the knowledge and skills of a group of individuals who were born within a comparable reference period, but who may have undergone different educational experiences both in and outside of schools. In PISA, these knowledge and skills are referred to as the yield of education at an age that is common across countries. Depending on countries' policies on school entry, selection and promotion, these students may be distributed over a narrower or a wider range of grades across different education systems, tracks or streams. It is important to consider these differences when comparing PISA results across countries, as observed differences between students at age 15 may no longer appear as students' educational experiences converge later on.

If a country's scale scores in reading, scientific or mathematical literacy are significantly higher than those in another country, it cannot automatically be inferred that the schools or particular parts of the education system in the first country are more effective than those in the second. However, one can legitimately conclude that the cumulative impact of learning experiences in the first country, starting in early childhood and up to the age of 15, and embracing experiences both in school, home and beyond, have resulted in higher outcomes in the literacy domains that PISA measures.

The PISA target population did not include residents attending schools in a foreign country. It does, however, include foreign nationals attending schools in the country of assessment.

To accommodate countries that desired grade-based results for the purpose of national analyses, PISA 2009 provided a sampling option to supplement age-based sampling with grade-based sampling.

Population coverage

All countries attempted to maximise the coverage of 15-year-olds enrolled in education in their national samples, including students enrolled in special educational institutions. As a result, PISA 2009 reached standards of population coverage that are unprecedented in international surveys of this kind.

The sampling standards used in PISA permitted countries to exclude up to a total of 5% of the relevant population either by excluding schools or by excluding students within schools. All but 5 countries, Denmark (8.17%), Luxembourg (8.15%), Canada (6.00%), Norway (5.93%) and the United States (5.16%), achieved this standard, and in 36 countries and economies, the overall exclusion rate was less than 2%. When language exclusions were accounted for (*i.e.* removed from the overall exclusion rate), the United States no longer had an exclusion rate greater than 5%. For details, see *www.pisa.oecd.org*.

Exclusions within the above limits include:

- *At the school level: i)* schools that were geographically inaccessible or where the administration of the PISA assessment was not considered feasible; and *ii)* schools that provided teaching only for students in the categories defined under "within-school exclusions", such as schools for the blind. The percentage of 15-year-olds enrolled in such schools had to be less than 2.5% of the nationally desired target population [0.5% maximum for *i)* and 2% maximum for *ii)*]. The magnitude, nature and justification of school-level exclusions are documented in the *PISA 2009 Technical Report* (OECD, forthcoming).

- *At the student level: i)* students with an intellectual disability; *ii)* students with a functional disability; *iii)* students with limited assessment language proficiency; *iv)* other – a category defined by the national centres and approved by the international centre; and *v)* students taught in a language of instruction for the main domain for which no materials were available. Students could not be excluded solely because of low proficiency or common discipline problems. The percentage of 15-year-olds excluded within schools had to be less than 2.5% of the nationally desired target population.

Table A2.1 describes the target population of the countries participating in PISA 2009. Further information on the target population and the implementation of PISA sampling standards can be found in the *PISA 2009 Technical Report* (OECD, forthcoming).

- *Column 1* shows the **total number of 15-year-olds** according to the most recent available information, which in most countries meant the year 2008 as the year before the assessment.

- *Column 2* shows the number of 15-year-olds enrolled in schools in Grade 7 or above (as defined above), which is referred to as the **eligible population**.

- *Column 3* shows the **national desired target population**. Countries were allowed to exclude up to 0.5% of students *a priori* from the eligible population, essentially for practical reasons. The following *a priori* exclusions exceed this limit but were agreed with the PISA Consortium: Canada excluded 1.1% of its population from Territories and Aboriginal reserves; France excluded 1.7% of its students in its *territoires d'outre-mer* and other institutions; Indonesia excluded 4.7% of its students from four provinces because of security reasons; Kyrgyzstan excluded 2.3% of its population in remote, inaccessible schools; and Serbia excluded 2% of its students taught in Serbian in Kosovo.

- *Column 4* shows the **number of students enrolled in schools that were excluded from the national desired target population** either from the sampling frame or later in the field during data collection.

- *Column 5* shows the **size of the national desired target population after subtracting the students enrolled in excluded schools**. This is obtained by subtracting Column 4 from Column 3.

- *Column 6* shows the **percentage of students enrolled in excluded schools**. This is obtained by dividing Column 4 by Column 3 and multiplying by 100.

- *Column 7* shows the **number of students participating in PISA 2009**. Note that in some cases this number does not account for 15-year-olds assessed as part of additional national options.

- *Column 8* shows the **weighted number of participating students,** *i.e.* the number of students in the nationally defined target population that the PISA sample represents.

- Each country attempted to maximise the coverage of PISA's target population within the sampled schools. In the case of each sampled school, all eligible students, namely those 15 years of age, regardless of grade, were first listed. Sampled students who were to be excluded had still to be included in the sampling documentation, and a list drawn up stating the reason for their exclusion. *Column 9* indicates the **total number of excluded students,** which is further described and classified into specific categories in Table A2.2. *Column 10* indicates the **weighted number of excluded students,** *i.e.* the overall number of students in the nationally defined target population represented by the number of students excluded from the sample, which is also described and classified by exclusion categories in Table A2.2. Excluded students were excluded based on five categories: *i)* students with an intellectual disability – the student has a mental or emotional disability and is cognitively delayed such that he/she cannot perform in the PISA testing situation; *ii)* students with a functional disability – the student has a moderate to severe permanent physical disability such that he/she cannot perform in the PISA testing situation; *iii)* students with a limited assessment language proficiency – the student is unable to read or speak any of the languages of the assessment in the country and would be unable to overcome the language barrier in the testing situation (typically a student who has received less than one year of instruction in the languages of the assessment may be excluded); *iv)* other – a category defined by the national centres and approved by the international centre; and *v)* students taught in a language of instruction for the main domain for which no materials were available.

- *Column 11* shows the **percentage of students excluded within schools**. This is calculated as the weighted number of excluded students (Column 10), divided by the weighted number of excluded and participating students (Column 8 plus Column 10), then multiplied by 100.

[Part 1/2]
Table A2.1 **PISA target populations and samples**

		Population and sample information						
		Total population of 15-year-olds	Total enrolled population of 15-year-olds at Grade 7 or above	Total in national desired target population	Total school-level exclusions	Total in national desired target population after all school exclusions and before within-school exclusions	School-level exclusion rate (%)	Number of participating students	Weighted number of participating students
		(1)	(2)	(3)	(4)	(5)	(6)	(7)	(8)
OECD	Australia	286 334	269 669	269 669	7 057	262 612	2.62	14 251	240 851
	Austria	99 818	94 192	94 192	115	94 077	0.12	6 590	87 326
	Belgium	126 377	126 335	126 335	2 474	123 861	1.96	8 501	119 140
	Canada	430 791	426 590	422 052	2 370	419 682	0.56	23 207	360 286
	Chile	290 056	265 542	265 463	2 594	262 869	0.98	5 669	247 270
	Czech Republic	122 027	116 153	116 153	1 619	114 534	1.39	6 064	113 951
	Denmark	70 522	68 897	68 897	3 082	65 815	4.47	5 924	60 855
	Estonia	14 248	14 106	14 106	436	13 670	3.09	4 727	12 978
	Finland	66 198	66 198	66 198	1 507	64 691	2.28	5 810	61 463
	France	749 808	732 825	720 187	18 841	701 346	2.62	4 298	677 620
	Germany	852 044	852 044	852 044	7 138	844 906	0.84	4 979	766 993
	Greece	102 229	105 664	105 664	696	104 968	0.66	4 969	93 088
	Hungary	121 155	118 387	118 387	3 322	115 065	2.81	4 605	105 611
	Iceland	4 738	4 738	4 738	20	4 718	0.42	3 646	4 410
	Ireland	56 635	55 464	55 446	276	55 170	0.50	3 937	52 794
	Israel	122 701	112 254	112 254	1 570	110 684	1.40	5 761	103 184
	Italy	586 904	573 542	573 542	2 694	570 848	0.47	30 905	506 733
	Japan	1 211 642	1 189 263	1 189 263	22 955	1 166 308	1.93	6 088	1 113 403
	Korea	717 164	700 226	700 226	2 927	697 299	0.42	4 989	630 030
	Luxembourg	5 864	5 623	5 623	186	5 437	3.31	4 622	5 124
	Mexico	2 151 771	1 425 397	1 425 397	5 825	1 419 572	0.41	38 250	1 305 461
	Netherlands	199 000	198 334	198 334	6 179	192 155	3.12	4 760	183 546
	New Zealand	63 460	60 083	60 083	645	59 438	1.07	4 643	55 129
	Norway	63 352	62 948	62 948	1 400	61 548	2.22	4 660	57 367
	Poland	482 500	473 700	473 700	7 650	466 050	1.61	4 917	448 866
	Portugal	115 669	107 583	107 583	0	107 583	0.00	6 298	96 820
	Slovak Republic	72 826	72 454	72 454	1 803	70 651	2.49	4 555	69 274
	Slovenia	20 314	19 571	19 571	174	19 397	0.89	6 155	18 773
	Spain	433 224	425 336	425 336	3 133	422 203	0.74	25 887	387 054
	Sweden	121 486	121 216	121 216	2 323	118 893	1.92	4 567	113 054
	Switzerland	90 623	89 423	89 423	1 747	87 676	1.95	11 812	80 839
	Turkey	1 336 842	859 172	859 172	8 569	850 603	1.00	4 996	757 298
	United Kingdom	786 626	786 825	786 825	17 593	769 232	2.24	12 179	683 380
	United States	4 103 738	4 210 475	4 210 475	15 199	4 195 276	0.36	5 233	3 373 264
Partners	Albania	55 587	42 767	42 767	372	42 395	0.87	4 596	34 134
	Argentina	688 434	636 713	636 713	2 238	634 475	0.35	4 774	472 106
	Azerbaijan	185 481	184 980	184 980	1 886	183 094	1.02	4 727	105 886
	Brazil	3 292 022	2 654 489	2 654 489	15 571	2 638 918	0.59	20 127	2 080 159
	Bulgaria	80 226	70 688	70 688	1 369	69 319	1.94	4 507	57 833
	Colombia	893 057	582 640	582 640	412	582 228	0.07	7 921	522 388
	Croatia	48 491	46 256	46 256	535	45 721	1.16	4 994	43 065
	Dubai (UAE)	10 564	10 327	10 327	167	10 160	1.62	5 620	9 179
	Hong Kong-China	85 000	78 224	78 224	809	77 415	1.03	4 837	75 548
	Indonesia	4 267 801	3 158 173	3 010 214	10 458	2 999 756	0.35	5 136	2 259 118
	Jordan	117 732	107 254	107 254	0	107 254	0.00	6 486	104 056
	Kazakhstan	281 659	263 206	263 206	7 210	255 996	2.74	5 412	250 657
	Kyrgyzstan	116 795	93 989	91 793	1 149	90 644	1.25	4 986	78 493
	Latvia	28 749	28 149	28 149	943	27 206	3.35	4 502	23 362
	Liechtenstein	399	360	360	5	355	1.39	329	355
	Lithuania	51 822	43 967	43 967	522	43 445	1.19	4 528	40 530
	Macao-China	7 500	5 969	5 969	3	5 966	0.05	5 952	5 978
	Montenegro	8 500	8 493	8 493	10	8 483	0.12	4 825	7 728
	Panama	57 919	43 623	43 623	501	43 122	1.15	3 969	30 510
	Peru	585 567	491 514	490 840	984	489 856	0.20	5 985	427 607
	Qatar	10 974	10 665	10 665	114	10 551	1.07	9 078	9 806
	Romania	152 084	152 084	152 084	679	151 405	0.45	4 776	151 130
	Russian Federation	1 673 085	1 667 460	1 667 460	25 012	1 642 448	1.50	5 308	1 290 047
	Serbia	85 121	75 128	73 628	1 580	72 048	2.15	5 523	70 796
	Shanghai-China	112 000	100 592	100 592	1 287	99 305	1.28	5 115	97 045
	Singapore	54 982	54 212	54 212	633	53 579	1.17	5 283	51 874
	Chinese Taipei	329 249	329 189	329 189	1 778	327 411	0.54	5 831	297 203
	Thailand	949 891	763 679	763 679	8 438	755 241	1.10	6 225	691 916
	Trinidad and Tobago	19 260	17 768	17 768	0	17 768	0.00	4 778	14 938
	Tunisia	153 914	153 914	153 914	0	153 914	0.00	4 955	136 545
	Uruguay	53 801	43 281	43 281	30	43 251	0.07	5 957	33 971

Note: For a full explanation of the details in this table, please refer to the *PISA 2009 Technical Report* (OECD, forthcoming). The figure for total national population of 15-year-olds enrolled in Column 1 may occasionally be larger than the total number of 15-year-olds in Column 2 due to differing data sources. In Greece, Column 1 does not include immigrants but Column 2 does.
StatLink ⟳ http://dx.doi.org/10.1787/888932343190

[Part 2/2]

Table A2.1   **PISA target populations and samples**

	Population and sample information				Coverage indices		
	Number of excluded students	Weighted number of excluded students	Within-school exclusion rate (%)	Overall exclusion rate (%)	Coverage index 1: Coverage of national desired population	Coverage index 2: Coverage of national enrolled population	Coverage index 3: Coverage of 15-year-old population
	(9)	(10)	(11)	(12)	(13)	(14)	(15)
OECD Australia	313	4 389	1.79	4.36	0.956	0.956	0.841
Austria	45	607	0.69	0.81	0.992	0.992	0.875
Belgium	30	292	0.24	2.20	0.978	0.978	0.943
Canada	1 607	20 837	5.47	6.00	0.940	0.930	0.836
Chile	15	620	0.25	1.22	0.988	0.987	0.852
Czech Republic	24	423	0.37	1.76	0.982	0.982	0.934
Denmark	296	2 448	3.87	8.17	0.918	0.918	0.863
Estonia	32	97	0.74	3.81	0.962	0.962	0.911
Finland	77	717	1.15	3.40	0.966	0.966	0.928
France	1	304	0.04	2.66	0.973	0.957	0.904
Germany	28	3 591	0.47	1.30	0.987	0.987	0.900
Greece	142	2 977	3.10	3.74	0.963	0.963	0.911
Hungary	10	361	0.34	3.14	0.969	0.969	0.872
Iceland	187	189	4.10	4.50	0.955	0.955	0.931
Ireland	136	1 492	2.75	3.23	0.968	0.967	0.932
Israel	86	1 359	1.30	2.68	0.973	0.973	0.841
Italy	561	10 663	2.06	2.52	0.975	0.975	0.863
Japan	0	0	0.00	1.93	0.981	0.981	0.919
Korea	16	1 748	0.28	0.69	0.993	0.993	0.879
Luxembourg	196	270	5.01	8.15	0.919	0.919	0.874
Mexico	52	1 951	0.15	0.56	0.994	0.994	0.607
Netherlands	19	648	0.35	3.46	0.965	0.965	0.922
New Zealand	184	1 793	3.15	4.19	0.958	0.958	0.869
Norway	207	2 260	3.79	5.93	0.941	0.941	0.906
Poland	15	1 230	0.27	1.88	0.981	0.981	0.930
Portugal	115	1 544	1.57	1.57	0.984	0.984	0.837
Slovak Republic	106	1 516	2.14	4.58	0.954	0.954	0.951
Slovenia	43	138	0.73	1.61	0.984	0.984	0.924
Spain	775	12 673	3.17	3.88	0.961	0.961	0.893
Sweden	146	3 360	2.89	4.75	0.953	0.953	0.931
Switzerland	209	940	1.15	3.08	0.969	0.969	0.892
Turkey	11	1 497	0.20	1.19	0.988	0.988	0.566
United Kingdom	318	17 094	2.44	4.62	0.954	0.954	0.869
United States	315	170 542	4.81	5.16	0.948	0.948	0.822
Partners Albania	0	0	0.00	0.87	0.991	0.991	0.614
Argentina	14	1 225	0.26	0.61	0.994	0.994	0.686
Azerbaijan	0	0	0.00	1.02	0.990	0.990	0.571
Brazil	24	2 692	0.13	0.72	0.993	0.993	0.632
Bulgaria	0	0	0.00	1.94	0.981	0.981	0.721
Colombia	11	490	0.09	0.16	0.998	0.998	0.585
Croatia	34	273	0.63	1.78	0.982	0.982	0.888
Dubai (UAE)	5	7	0.07	1.69	0.983	0.983	0.869
Hong Kong-China	9	119	0.16	1.19	0.988	0.988	0.889
Indonesia	0	0	0.00	0.35	0.997	0.950	0.529
Jordan	24	443	0.42	0.42	0.996	0.996	0.884
Kazakhstan	82	3 844	1.51	4.21	0.958	0.958	0.890
Kyrgyzstan	86	1 384	1.73	2.96	0.970	0.948	0.672
Latvia	19	102	0.43	3.77	0.962	0.962	0.813
Liechtenstein	0	0	0.00	1.39	0.986	0.986	0.890
Lithuania	74	632	1.53	2.70	0.973	0.973	0.782
Macao-China	0	0	0.00	0.05	0.999	0.999	0.797
Montenegro	0	0	0.00	0.12	0.999	0.999	0.909
Panama	0	0	0.00	1.15	0.989	0.989	0.527
Peru	9	558	0.13	0.33	0.997	0.995	0.730
Qatar	28	28	0.28	1.35	0.986	0.986	0.894
Romania	0	0	0.00	0.45	0.996	0.996	0.994
Russian Federation	59	15 247	1.17	2.65	0.973	0.973	0.771
Serbia	10	133	0.19	2.33	0.977	0.957	0.832
Shanghai-China	7	130	0.13	1.41	0.986	0.986	0.866
Singapore	48	417	0.80	1.96	0.980	0.980	0.943
Chinese Taipei	32	1 662	0.56	1.09	0.989	0.989	0.903
Thailand	6	458	0.07	1.17	0.988	0.988	0.728
Trinidad and Tobago	11	36	0.24	0.24	0.998	0.998	0.776
Tunisia	7	184	0.13	0.13	0.999	0.999	0.887
Uruguay	14	67	0.20	0.26	0.997	0.997	0.631

Note: For a full explanation of the details in this table please refer to the *PISA 2009 Technical Report* (OECD, forthcoming). The figure for total national population of 15-year-olds enrolled in Column 1 may occasionally be larger than the total number of 15-year-olds in Column 2 due to differing data sources. In Greece, Column 1 does not include immigrants but Column 2 does.

StatLink ⫘⫘⫘ http://dx.doi.org/10.1787/888932343190

[Part 1/1]

Table A2.2 **Exclusions**

		Student exclusions (unweighted)					Student exclusion (weighted)					
	Number of excluded students with a disability (Code 1)	Number of excluded students with a disability (Code 2)	Number of excluded students because of language (Code 3)	Number of excluded students for other reasons (Code 4)	Number of excluded students because of no materials available in the language of instruction (Code 5)	Total number of excluded students	Weighted number of excluded students with a disability (Code 1)	Weighted number of excluded students with a disability (Code 2)	Weighted number of excluded students because of language (Code 3)	Weighted number of excluded students for other reasons (Code 4)	Number of excluded students because of no materials available in the language of instruction (Code 5)	Total weighted number of excluded students
	(1)	(2)	(3)	(4)	(5)	(6)	(7)	(8)	(9)	(10)	(11)	(12)
Australia	24	210	79	0	0	313	272	2 834	1 283	0	0	4 389
Austria	0	26	19	0	0	45	0	317	290	0	0	607
Belgium	3	17	10	0	0	30	26	171	95	0	0	292
Canada	49	1 458	100	0	0	1 607	428	19 082	1 326	0	0	20 837
Chile	5	10	0	0	0	15	177	443	0	0	0	620
Czech Republic	8	7	9	0	0	24	117	144	162	0	0	423
Denmark	13	182	35	66	0	296	165	1 432	196	656	0	2 448
Estonia	3	28	1	0	0	32	8	87	2	0	0	97
Finland	4	48	12	11	2	77	38	447	110	99	23	717
France	1	0	0	0	0	1	304	0	0	0	0	304
Germany	6	20	2	0	0	28	864	2 443	285	0	0	3 591
Greece	7	11	7	117	0	142	172	352	195	2 257	0	2 977
Hungary	0	1	0	9	0	10	0	48	0	313	0	361
Iceland	3	78	64	38	1	187	3	78	65	39	1	189
Ireland	4	72	25	35	0	136	51	783	262	396	0	1 492
Israel	10	69	7	0	0	86	194	1 049	116	0	0	1 359
Italy	45	348	168	0	0	561	748	6 241	3 674	0	0	10 663
Japan	0	0	0	0	0	0	0	0	0	0	0	0
Korea	7	9	0	0	0	16	994	753	0	0	0	1 748
Luxembourg	2	132	62	0	0	196	2	206	62	0	0	270
Mexico	25	25	2	0	0	52	1 010	905	36	0	0	1 951
Netherlands	6	13	0	0	0	19	178	470	0	0	0	648
New Zealand	19	84	78	0	3	184	191	824	749	0	29	1 793
Norway	8	160	39	0	0	207	90	1 756	414	0	0	2 260
Poland	2	13	0	0	0	15	169	1 061	0	0	0	1 230
Portugal	2	100	13	0	0	115	25	1 322	197	0	0	1 544
Slovak Republic	12	37	1	56	0	106	171	558	19	768	0	1 516
Slovenia	6	10	27	0	0	43	40	32	66	0	0	138
Spain	45	441	289	0	0	775	1 007	7 141	4 525	0	0	12 673
Sweden	115	0	31	0	0	146	2 628	0	732	0	0	3 360
Switzerland	11	106	92	0	0	209	64	344	532	0	0	940
Turkey	3	3	5	0	0	11	338	495	665	0	0	1 497
United Kingdom	40	247	31	0	0	318	2 438	13 482	1 174	0	0	17 094
United States	29	236	40	10	0	315	15 367	127 486	21 718	5 971	0	170 542
Albania	0	0	0	0	0	0	0	0	0	0	0	0
Argentina	4	10	0	0	0	14	288	937	0	0	0	1 225
Azerbaijan	0	0	0	0	0	0	0	0	0	0	0	0
Brazil	21	3	0	0	0	24	2 495	197	0	0	0	2 692
Bulgaria	0	0	0	0	0	0	0	0	0	0	0	0
Colombia	7	2	2	0	0	11	200	48	242	0	0	490
Croatia	4	30	0	0	0	34	34	239	0	0	0	273
Dubai (UAE)	1	1	3	0	0	5	2	2	3	0	0	7
Hong Kong-China	0	9	0	0	0	9	0	119	0	0	0	119
Indonesia	0	0	0	0	0	0	0	0	0	0	0	0
Jordan	11	7	6	0	0	24	166	149	127	0	0	443
Kazakhstan	10	17	0	0	55	82	429	828	0	0	2 587	3 844
Kyrgyzstan	68	13	5	0	0	86	1 093	211	80	0	0	1 384
Latvia	6	8	5	0	0	19	25	44	33	0	0	102
Liechtenstein	0	0	0	0	0	0	0	0	0	0	0	0
Lithuania	4	69	1	0	0	74	33	590	9	0	0	632
Macao-China	0	0	0	0	0	0	0	0	0	0	0	0
Montenegro	0	0	0	0	0	0	0	0	0	0	0	0
Panama	0	0	0	0	0	0	0	0	0	0	0	0
Peru	4	5	0	0	0	9	245	313	0	0	0	558
Qatar	9	18	1	0	0	28	9	18	1	0	0	28
Romania	0	0	0	0	0	0	0	0	0	0	0	0
Russian Federation	11	47	1	0	0	59	2 081	13 010	157	0	0	15 247
Serbia	4	5	0	0	1	10	66	53	0	0	13	133
Shanghai-China	1	6	0	0	0	7	19	111	0	0	0	130
Singapore	2	22	24	0	0	48	17	217	182	0	0	417
Chinese Taipei	13	19	0	0	0	32	684	977	0	0	0	1 662
Thailand	0	5	1	0	0	6	0	260	198	0	0	458
Trinidad and Tobago	1	10	0	0	0	11	3	33	0	0	0	36
Tunisia	4	1	2	0	0	7	104	21	58	0	0	184
Uruguay	2	9	3	0	0	14	14	34	18	0	0	67

Exclusion codes:
Code 1 Functional disability – student has a moderate to severe permanent physical disability.
Code 2 Intellectual disability – student has a mental or emotional disability and has either been tested as cognitively delayed or is considered in the professional opinion of qualified staff to be cognitively delayed.
Code 3 Limited assessment language proficiency – student is not a native speaker of any of the languages of the assessment in the country and has been resident in the country for less than one year.
Code 4 Other defined by the national centres and approved by the international centre.
Code 5 No materials available in the language of instruction.
Note: For a full explanation of other details in this table, please refer to the *PISA 2009 Technical Report* (OECD, forthcoming).
StatLink ⬛⬛ http://dx.doi.org/10.1787/888932343190

- **Column 12** shows the **overall exclusion rate**, which represents the weighted percentage of the national desired target population excluded from PISA either through school-level exclusions or through the exclusion of students within schools. It is calculated as the school-level exclusion rate (Column 6 divided by 100) plus within-school exclusion rate (Column 11 divided by 100) multiplied by 1 minus the school-level exclusion rate (Column 6 divided by 100). This result is then multiplied by 100. Five countries, Denmark, Luxembourg, Canada, Norway and the United States, had exclusion rates higher than 5%. When language exclusions were accounted for (*i.e.* removed from the overall exclusion rate), the United States no longer had an exclusion rate greater than 5%.

- **Column 13** presents an **index of the extent to which the national desired target population is covered by the PISA sample**. Denmark, Luxembourg, Canada, Norway and the United States were the only countries where the coverage is below 95%.

- **Column 14** presents an **index of the extent to which 15-year-olds enrolled in schools are covered by the PISA sample**. The index measures the overall proportion of the national enrolled population that is covered by the non-excluded portion of the student sample. The index takes into account both school-level and student-level exclusions. Values close to 100 indicate that the PISA sample represents the entire education system as defined for PISA 2009. The index is the weighted number of participating students (Column 8) divided by the weighted number of participating and excluded students (Column 8 plus Column 10), times the nationally defined target population (Column 5) divided by the eligible population (Column 2) (times 100).

- **Column 15** presents an **index of the coverage of the 15-year-old population**. This index is the weighted number of participating students (Column 8) divided by the total population of 15-year-old students (Column 1).

This high level of coverage contributes to the comparability of the assessment results. For example, even assuming that the excluded students would have systematically scored worse than those who participated, and that this relationship is moderately strong, an exclusion rate in the order of 5% would likely lead to an overestimation of national mean scores of less than 5 score points (on a scale with an international mean of 500 score points and a standard deviation of 100 score points). This assessment is based on the following calculations: if the correlation between the propensity of exclusions and student performance is 0.3, resulting mean scores would likely be overestimated by 1 score point if the exclusion rate is 1%, by 3 score points if the exclusion rate is 5%, and by 6 score points if the exclusion rate is 10%. If the correlation between the propensity of exclusions and student performance is 0.5, resulting mean scores would be overestimated by 1 score point if the exclusion rate is 1%, by 5 score points if the exclusion rate is 5%, and by 10 score points if the exclusion rate is 10%. For this calculation, a model was employed that assumes a bivariate normal distribution for performance and the propensity to participate. For details, see the *PISA 2009 Technical Report* (OECD, forthcoming).

Sampling procedures and response rates

The accuracy of any survey results depends on the quality of the information on which national samples are based as well as on the sampling procedures. Quality standards, procedures, instruments and verification mechanisms were developed for PISA that ensured that national samples yielded comparable data and that the results could be compared with confidence.

Most PISA samples were designed as two-stage stratified samples (where countries applied different sampling designs, these are documented in the *PISA 2009 Technical Report* [OECD, forthcoming]). The first stage consisted of sampling individual schools in which 15-year-old students could be enrolled. Schools were sampled systematically with probabilities proportional to size, the measure of size being a function of the estimated number of eligible (15-year-old) students enrolled. A minimum of 150 schools were selected in each country (where this number existed), although the requirements for national analyses often required a somewhat larger sample. As the schools were sampled, replacement schools were simultaneously identified, in case a sampled school chose not to participate in PISA 2009.

In the case of Iceland, Liechtenstein, Luxembourg, Macao-China and Qatar, all schools and all eligible students within schools were included in the sample.

Experts from the PISA Consortium performed the sample selection process for most participating countries and monitored it closely in those countries that selected their own samples. The second stage of the selection process sampled students within sampled schools. Once schools were selected, a list of each sampled school's 15-year-old students was prepared. From this list, 35 students were then selected with equal probability (all 15-year-old students were selected if fewer than 35 were enrolled). The number of students to be sampled per school could deviate from 35, but could not be less than 20.

Data-quality standards in PISA required minimum participation rates for schools as well as for students. These standards were established to minimise the potential for response biases. In the case of countries meeting these standards, it was likely that any bias resulting from non-response would be negligible, *i.e.* typically smaller than the sampling error.

A minimum response rate of 85% was required for the schools initially selected. Where the initial response rate of schools was between 65 and 85%, however, an acceptable school response rate could still be achieved through the use of replacement schools. This procedure brought with it a risk of increased response bias. Participating countries were, therefore, encouraged to persuade as many of the schools in the original sample as possible to participate. Schools with a student participation rate between 25% and 50% were not regarded as participating schools, but data from these schools were included in the database and contributed to the various estimations. Data from schools with a student participation rate of less than 25% were excluded from the database.

[Part 1/2]

Table A2.3 **Response rates**

		Initial sample – before school replacement					Final sample – after school replacement		
		Weighted school participation rate before replacement (%)	Weighted number of responding schools (weighted also by enrolment)	Weighted number of schools sampled (responding and non-responding) (weighted also by enrolment)	Number of responding schools (unweighted)	Number of responding and non-responding schools (unweighted)	Weighted school participation rate after replacement (%)	Weighted number of responding schools (weighted also by enrolment)	Weighted number of schools sampled (responding and non-responding) (weighted also by enrolment)
		(1)	(2)	(3)	(4)	(5)	(6)	(7)	(8)
OECD	Australia	97.78	265 659	271 696	342	357	98.85	268 780	271 918
	Austria	93.94	88 551	94 261	280	291	93.94	88 551	94 261
	Belgium	88.76	112 594	126 851	255	292	95.58	121 291	126 899
	Canada	88.04	362 152	411 343	893	1 001	89.64	368 708	411 343
	Chile	94.34	245 583	260 331	189	201	99.04	257 594	260 099
	Czech Republic	83.09	94 696	113 961	226	270	97.40	111 091	114 062
	Denmark	83.94	55 375	65 967	264	325	90.75	59 860	65 964
	Estonia	100.00	13 230	13 230	175	175	100.00	13 230	13 230
	Finland	98.65	62 892	63 751	201	204	100.00	63 748	63 751
	France	94.14	658 769	699 776	166	177	94.14	658 769	699 776
	Germany	98.61	826 579	838 259	223	226	100.00	838 259	838 259
	Greece	98.19	98 710	100 529	181	184	99.40	99 925	100 529
	Hungary	98.21	101 523	103 378	184	190	99.47	103 067	103 618
	Iceland	98.46	4 488	4 558	129	141	98.46	4 488	4 558
	Ireland	87.18	48 821	55 997	139	160	88.44	49 526	55 997
	Israel	92.03	103 141	112 069	170	186	95.40	106 918	112 069
	Italy	94.27	532 432	564 811	1 054	1 108	99.08	559 546	564 768
	Japan	87.77	999 408	1 138 694	171	196	94.99	1 081 662	1 138 694
	Korea	100.00	683 793	683 793	157	157	100.00	683 793	683 793
	Luxembourg	100.00	5 437	5 437	39	39	100.00	5 437	5 437
	Mexico	95.62	1 338 291	1 399 638	1 512	1 560	97.71	1 367 668	1 399 730
	Netherlands	80.40	154 471	192 140	155	194	95.54	183 555	192 118
	New Zealand	84.11	49 917	59 344	148	179	91.00	54 130	59 485
	Norway	89.61	55 484	61 920	183	207	96.53	59 759	61 909
	Poland	88.16	409 513	464 535	159	187	97.70	453 855	464 535
	Portugal	93.61	102 225	109 205	201	216	98.43	107 535	109 251
	Slovak Republic	93.33	67 284	72 092	180	191	99.01	71 388	72 105
	Slovenia	98.36	19 798	20 127	337	352	98.36	19 798	20 127
	Spain	99.53	422 692	424 705	888	892	99.53	422 692	424 705
	Sweden	99.91	120 693	120 802	189	191	99.91	120 693	120 802
	Switzerland	94.25	81 005	85 952	413	429	98.71	84 896	86 006
	Turkey	100.00	849 830	849 830	170	170	100.00	849 830	849 830
	United Kingdom	71.06	523 271	736 341	418	549	87.35	643 027	736 178
	United States	67.83	2 673 852	3 941 908	140	208	77.50	3 065 651	3 955 606
Partners	Albania	97.29	39 168	40 259	177	182	99.37	39 999	40 253
	Argentina	97.18	590 215	607 344	194	199	99.42	603 817	607 344
	Azerbaijan	99.86	168 646	168 890	161	162	100.00	168 890	168 890
	Brazil	93.13	2 435 250	2 614 824	899	976	94.75	2 477 518	2 614 806
	Bulgaria	98.16	56 922	57 991	173	178	99.10	57 823	58 346
	Colombia	90.21	507 649	562 728	260	285	94.90	533 899	562 587
	Croatia	99.19	44 561	44 926	157	159	99.86	44 862	44 926
	Dubai (UAE)	100.00	10 144	10 144	190	190	100.00	10 144	10 144
	Hong Kong-China	69.19	53 800	77 758	108	156	96.75	75 232	77 758
	Indonesia	94.54	2 337 438	2 472 502	172	183	100.00	2 473 528	2 473 528
	Jordan	100.00	105 906	105 906	210	210	100.00	105 906	105 906
	Kazakhstan	100.00	257 427	257 427	199	199	100.00	257 427	257 427
	Kyrgyzstan	98.53	88 412	89 733	171	174	99.47	89 260	89 733
	Latvia	97.46	26 986	27 689	180	185	99.39	27 544	27 713
	Liechtenstein	100.00	356	356	12	12	100.00	356	356
	Lithuania	98.13	41 759	42 555	192	197	99.91	42 526	42 564
	Macao-China	100.00	5 966	5 966	45	45	100.00	5 966	5 966
	Montenegro	100.00	8 527	8 527	52	52	100.00	8 527	8 527
	Panama	82.58	33 384	40 426	180	220	83.76	33 779	40 329
	Peru	100.00	480 640	480 640	240	240	100.00	480 640	480 640
	Qatar	97.30	10 223	10 507	149	154	97.30	10 223	10 507
	Romania	100.00	150 114	150 114	159	159	100.00	150 114	150 114
	Russian Federation	100.00	1 392 765	1 392 765	213	213	100.00	1 392 765	1 392 765
	Serbia	99.21	70 960	71 524	189	191	99.97	71 504	71 524
	Shanghai-China	99.32	98 841	99 514	151	152	100.00	99 514	99 514
	Singapore	96.19	51 552	53 592	168	175	97.88	52 454	53 592
	Chinese Taipei	99.34	322 005	324 141	157	158	100.00	324 141	324 141
	Thailand	98.01	737 225	752 193	225	230	100.00	752 392	752 392
	Trinidad and Tobago	97.21	17 180	17 673	155	160	97.21	17 180	17 673
	Tunisia	100.00	153 198	153 198	165	165	100.00	153 198	153 198
	Uruguay	98.66	42 820	43 400	229	233	98.66	42 820	43 400

StatLink http://dx.doi.org/10.1787/888932343190

[Part 2/2]

Table A2.3   **Response rates**

	Final sample – after school replacement		Final sample – students within schools after school replacement				
	Number of responding schools (unweighted)	Number of responding and non-responding schools (unweighted)	Weighted student participation rate after replacement (%)	Number of students assessed (weighted)	Number of students sampled (assessed and absent) (weighted)	Number of students assessed (unweighted)	Number of students sampled (assessed and absent) (unweighted)
	(9)	(10)	(11)	(12)	(13)	(14)	(15)
Australia	345	357	86.05	205 234	238 498	14 060	16 903
Austria	280	291	88.63	72 793	82 135	6 568	7 587
Belgium	275	292	91.38	104 263	114 097	8 477	9 245
Canada	908	1 001	79.52	257 905	324 342	22 383	27 603
Chile	199	201	92.88	227 551	244 995	5 663	6 097
Czech Republic	260	270	90.75	100 685	110 953	6 049	6 656
Denmark	285	325	89.29	49 236	55 139	5 924	6 827
Estonia	175	175	94.06	12 208	12 978	4 727	5 023
Finland	203	204	92.27	56 709	61 460	5 810	6 309
France	166	177	87.12	556 054	638 284	4 272	4 900
Germany	226	226	93.93	720 447	766 993	4 979	5 309
Greece	183	184	95.95	88 875	92 631	4 957	5 165
Hungary	187	190	93.25	97 923	105 015	4 605	4 956
Iceland	129	141	83.91	3 635	4 332	3 635	4 332
Ireland	141	160	83.81	39 248	46 830	3 896	4 654
Israel	176	186	89.45	88 480	98 918	5 761	6 440
Italy	1 095	1 108	92.13	462 655	502 190	30 876	33 390
Japan	185	196	95.32	1 010 801	1 060 382	6 077	6 377
Korea	157	157	98.76	622 187	630 030	4 989	5 057
Luxembourg	39	39	95.57	4 897	5 124	4 622	4 833
Mexico	1 531	1 560	95.13	1 214 827	1 276 982	38 213	40 125
Netherlands	185	194	89.78	157 912	175 897	4 747	5 286
New Zealand	161	179	84.65	42 452	50 149	4 606	5 476
Norway	197	207	89.92	49 785	55 366	4 660	5 194
Poland	179	187	85.87	376 767	438 739	4 855	5 674
Portugal	212	216	87.11	83 094	95 386	6 263	7 169
Slovak Republic	189	191	93.03	63 854	68 634	4 555	4 898
Slovenia	337	352	90.92	16 777	18 453	6 135	6 735
Spain	888	892	89.60	345 122	385 164	25 871	28 280
Sweden	189	191	92.97	105 026	112 972	4 567	4 912
Switzerland	425	429	93.58	74 712	79 836	11 810	12 551
Turkey	170	170	97.85	741 029	757 298	4 996	5 108
United Kingdom	481	549	86.96	520 121	598 110	12 168	14 046
United States	160	208	86.99	2 298 889	2 642 598	5 165	5 951
Albania	181	182	95.39	32 347	33 911	4 596	4 831
Argentina	198	199	88.25	414 166	469 285	4 762	5 423
Azerbaijan	162	162	99.14	105 095	106 007	4 691	4 727
Brazil	926	976	89.04	1 767 872	1 985 479	19 901	22 715
Bulgaria	176	178	97.34	56 096	57 630	4 499	4 617
Colombia	274	285	92.83	462 602	498 331	7 910	8 483
Croatia	158	159	93.76	40 321	43 006	4 994	5 326
Dubai (UAE)	190	190	90.39	8 297	9 179	5 620	6 218
Hong Kong-China	151	156	93.19	68 142	73 125	4 837	5 195
Indonesia	183	183	96.91	2 189 287	2 259 118	5 136	5 313
Jordan	210	210	95.85	99 734	104 056	6 486	6 777
Kazakhstan	199	199	98.49	246 872	250 657	5 412	5 489
Kyrgyzstan	173	174	98.04	76 523	78 054	4 986	5 086
Latvia	184	185	91.27	21 241	23 273	4 502	4 930
Liechtenstein	12	12	92.68	329	355	329	355
Lithuania	196	197	93.36	37 808	40 495	4 528	4 854
Macao-China	45	45	99.57	5 952	5 978	5 952	5 978
Montenegro	52	52	95.43	7 375	7 728	4 825	5 062
Panama	183	220	88.67	22 666	25 562	3 913	4 449
Peru	240	240	96.35	412 011	427 607	5 985	6 216
Qatar	149	154	93.63	8 990	9 602	8 990	9 602
Romania	159	159	99.47	150 331	151 130	4 776	4 803
Russian Federation	213	213	96.77	1 248 353	1 290 047	5 308	5 502
Serbia	190	191	95.37	67 496	70 775	5 522	5 804
Shanghai-China	152	152	98.89	95 966	97 045	5 115	5 175
Singapore	171	175	91.04	46 224	50 775	5 283	5 809
Chinese Taipei	158	158	95.30	283 239	297 203	5 831	6 108
Thailand	230	230	97.37	673 688	691 916	6 225	6 396
Trinidad and Tobago	155	160	85.92	12 275	14 287	4 731	5 518
Tunisia	165	165	96.93	132 354	136 545	4 955	5 113
Uruguay	229	233	87.03	29 193	33 541	5 924	6 815

StatLink http://dx.doi.org/10.1787/888932343190

PISA 2009 also required a minimum participation rate of 80% of students within participating schools. This minimum participation rate had to be met at the national level, not necessarily by each participating school. Follow-up sessions were required in schools in which too few students had participated in the original assessment sessions. Student participation rates were calculated over all original schools, and also over all schools, whether original sample or replacement schools, and from the participation of students in both the original assessment and any follow-up sessions. A student who participated in the original or follow-up cognitive sessions was regarded as a participant. Those who attended only the questionnaire session were included in the international database and contributed to the statistics presented in this publication if they provided at least a description of their father's or mother's occupation.

Table A2.3 shows the response rates for students and schools, before and after replacement.

- *Column 1* shows the **weighted participation rate of schools before replacement**. This is obtained by dividing Column 2 by Column 3.

- *Column 2* shows the **weighted number of responding schools before school replacement** (weighted by student enrolment).

- *Column 3* shows the **weighted number of sampled schools before school replacement** (including both responding and non-responding schools, weighted by student enrolment).

- *Column 4* shows the unweighted number **of responding schools before school replacement**.

- *Column 5* shows the unweighted **number of responding and non-responding schools before school replacement**.

- *Column 6* shows the **weighted participation rate of schools after replacement**. This is obtained by dividing Column 7 by Column 8.

- *Column 7* shows the **weighted number of responding schools after school replacement** (weighted by student enrolment).

- *Column 8* shows the **weighted number of schools sampled after school replacement** (including both responding and non-responding schools, weighted by student enrolment).

- *Column 9* shows the unweighted number of responding schools after school replacement.

- *Column 10* shows the unweighted number of responding and non-responding schools after school replacement.

- *Column 11* shows the **weighted student participation rate after replacement**. This is obtained by dividing Column 12 by Column 13.

- *Column 12* shows the **weighted number of students assessed**.

- *Column 13* shows the **weighted number of students sampled** (including both students who were assessed and students who were absent on the day of the assessment).

- *Column 14* shows the **unweighted number of students assessed.** Note that any students in schools with student-response rates less than 50% were not included in these rates (both weighted and unweighted).

- *Column 15* shows the **unweighted number of students sampled** (including both students that were assessed and students who were absent on the day of the assessment). Note that any students in schools where fewer than half of the eligible students were assessed were not included in these rates (neither weighted nor unweighted).

Definition of schools

In some countries, sub-units within schools were sampled instead of schools and this may affect the estimation of the between-school variance components. In Austria, the Czech Republic, Germany, Hungary, Japan, Romania and Slovenia, schools with more than one study programme were split into the units delivering these programmes. In the Netherlands, for schools with both lower and upper secondary programmes, schools were split into units delivering each programme level. In the Flemish Community of Belgium, in the case of multi-campus schools, implantations (campuses) were sampled, whereas in the French Community, in the case of multi-campus schools, the larger administrative units were sampled. In Australia, for schools with more than one campus, the individual campuses were listed for sampling. In Argentina, Croatia and Dubai (UAE), schools that had more than one campus had the locations listed for sampling. In Spain, the schools in the Basque region with multi-linguistic models were split into linguistic models for sampling.

Grade levels

Students assessed in PISA 2009 are at various grade levels. The percentage of students at each grade level is presented by country in Table A2.4a and by gender within each country in Table A2.4b.

[Part 1/1]

Table A2.4a **Percentage of students at each grade level**

		Grade level										
		7th grade		8th grade		9th grade		10th grade		11th grade		12th grade	
		%	S.E.	%	S.E.	%	S.E.	%	S.E.	%	S.E.	%	S.E.
OECD	Australia	0.0	(0.0)	0.1	(0.0)	10.4	(0.6)	70.8	(0.6)	18.6	(0.6)	0.1	(0.0)
	Austria	0.7	(0.2)	6.2	(1.0)	42.4	(0.9)	50.7	(1.0)	0.0	(0.0)	0.0	c
	Belgium	0.4	(0.2)	5.5	(0.5)	32.0	(0.6)	60.8	(0.7)	1.2	(0.1)	0.0	(0.0)
	Canada	0.0	(0.0)	1.2	(0.2)	13.6	(0.5)	84.1	(0.5)	1.1	(0.1)	0.0	(0.0)
	Chile	1.0	(0.2)	3.9	(0.5)	20.5	(0.8)	69.4	(1.0)	5.2	(0.3)	0.0	(0.0)
	Czech Republic	0.5	(0.2)	3.8	(0.3)	48.9	(1.0)	46.7	(1.1)	0.0	c	0.0	c
	Denmark	0.1	(0.0)	14.7	(0.6)	83.5	(0.8)	1.7	(0.5)	0.0	c	0.0	c
	Estonia	1.6	(0.3)	24.0	(0.7)	72.4	(0.9)	1.8	(0.3)	0.1	(0.1)	0.0	c
	Finland	0.5	(0.1)	11.8	(0.5)	87.3	(0.5)	0.0	c	0.4	(0.1)	0.0	c
	France	1.3	(0.9)	3.6	(0.7)	34.4	(1.2)	56.6	(1.5)	4.0	(0.7)	0.1	(0.0)
	Germany	1.2	(0.2)	11.0	(0.5)	54.8	(0.8)	32.5	(0.8)	0.4	(0.1)	0.0	(0.0)
	Greece	0.4	(0.2)	1.4	(0.5)	5.5	(0.8)	92.7	(1.0)	0.0	c	0.0	c
	Hungary	2.8	(0.6)	7.6	(1.1)	67.1	(1.4)	22.4	(0.9)	0.1	(0.1)	0.0	(0.0)
	Iceland	0.0	c	0.0	c	0.0	(0.0)	98.3	(0.1)	1.7	(0.1)	0.0	c
	Ireland	0.1	(0.0)	2.4	(0.3)	59.1	(1.0)	24.0	(1.4)	14.4	(1.1)	0.0	c
	Israel	0.0	c	0.3	(0.1)	17.9	(1.0)	81.3	(1.0)	0.5	(0.2)	0.0	(0.0)
	Italy	0.1	(0.1)	1.4	(0.3)	16.9	(0.4)	78.4	(0.6)	3.2	(0.3)	0.0	c
	Japan	0.0	c	0.0	c	0.0	c	100.0	(0.0)	0.0	c	0.0	c
	Korea	0.0	c	0.0	(0.0)	4.2	(0.9)	95.1	(0.9)	0.7	(0.1)	0.0	c
	Luxembourg	0.6	(0.1)	11.6	(0.2)	51.6	(0.3)	36.0	(0.2)	0.3	(0.0)	0.0	c
	Mexico	1.7	(0.1)	7.4	(0.3)	34.5	(0.8)	55.6	(0.9)	0.7	(0.2)	0.0	(0.0)
	Netherlands	0.2	(0.2)	2.7	(0.3)	46.2	(1.1)	50.5	(1.1)	0.5	(0.1)	0.0	c
	New Zealand	0.0	c	0.0	c	0.0	c	5.9	(0.4)	88.8	(0.5)	5.3	(0.3)
	Norway	0.0	c	0.0	c	0.5	(0.1)	99.3	(0.2)	0.2	(0.1)	0.0	c
	Poland	1.0	(0.2)	4.5	(0.4)	93.6	(0.6)	0.9	(0.3)	0.0	c	0.0	c
	Portugal	2.3	(0.3)	9.0	(0.8)	27.9	(1.6)	60.4	(2.2)	0.4	(0.1)	0.0	c
	Slovak Republic	1.0	(0.2)	2.6	(0.3)	35.7	(1.4)	56.9	(1.6)	3.8	(0.8)	0.0	(0.0)
	Slovenia	0.0	c	0.1	(0.1)	3.0	(0.7)	90.7	(0.7)	6.2	(0.2)	0.0	c
	Spain	0.1	(0.0)	9.9	(0.4)	26.5	(0.6)	63.4	(0.7)	0.0	(0.0)	0.0	c
	Sweden	0.1	(0.1)	3.2	(0.3)	95.1	(0.6)	1.6	(0.5)	0.0	c	0.0	c
	Switzerland	0.6	(0.1)	15.5	(0.9)	61.7	(1.3)	21.0	(1.1)	1.2	(0.5)	0.0	(0.0)
	Turkey	0.7	(0.1)	3.5	(0.8)	25.2	(1.3)	66.6	(1.5)	3.8	(0.3)	0.2	(0.1)
	United Kingdom	0.0	c	0.0	c	0.0	c	1.2	(0.1)	98.0	(0.1)	0.8	(0.0)
	United States	0.0	c	0.1	(0.1)	10.9	(0.8)	68.5	(1.0)	20.3	(0.7)	0.1	(0.1)
	OECD average	0.8	(0.1)	5.8	(0.1)	37.0	(0.2)	52.9	(0.2)	9.9	(0.1)	0.5	(0.0)
Partners	Albania	0.4	(0.1)	2.2	(0.3)	50.9	(2.0)	46.4	(2.0)	0.1	(0.0)	0.0	c
	Argentina	4.7	(0.9)	12.9	(1.3)	20.4	(1.2)	57.8	(2.1)	4.3	(0.5)	0.0	c
	Azerbaijan	0.6	(0.2)	5.3	(0.5)	49.4	(1.3)	44.3	(1.3)	0.4	(0.1)	0.0	c
	Brazil	6.8	(0.4)	18.0	(0.7)	37.5	(0.8)	35.7	(0.8)	2.1	(0.1)	0.0	c
	Bulgaria	1.5	(0.3)	6.1	(0.6)	88.7	(0.9)	3.8	(0.6)	0.0	c	0.0	c
	Colombia	4.4	(0.5)	10.3	(0.7)	22.1	(0.8)	42.3	(1.0)	21.0	(1.0)	0.0	c
	Croatia	0.0	c	0.2	(0.2)	77.5	(0.4)	22.3	(0.4)	0.0	c	0.0	c
	Dubai (UAE)	1.1	(0.1)	3.4	(0.1)	14.8	(0.4)	56.9	(0.5)	22.9	(0.4)	0.9	(0.1)
	Hong Kong-China	1.7	(0.2)	7.2	(0.5)	25.2	(0.5)	65.9	(0.9)	0.1	(0.0)	0.0	c
	Indonesia	1.5	(0.5)	6.5	(0.8)	46.0	(3.1)	40.5	(3.2)	5.0	(0.8)	0.5	(0.4)
	Jordan	0.1	(0.1)	1.3	(0.2)	7.0	(0.5)	91.6	(0.6)	0.0	c	0.0	c
	Kazakhstan	0.4	(0.1)	6.4	(0.4)	73.3	(1.9)	19.7	(2.0)	0.1	(0.1)	0.0	c
	Kyrgyzstan	0.2	(0.1)	7.9	(0.5)	71.4	(1.3)	19.8	(1.4)	0.7	(0.1)	0.0	c
	Latvia	2.7	(0.5)	15.5	(0.7)	79.4	(0.9)	2.4	(0.3)	0.1	(0.1)	0.0	(0.0)
	Liechtenstein	0.8	(0.5)	17.5	(1.1)	71.3	(0.8)	10.4	(1.0)	0.0	c	0.0	c
	Lithuania	0.5	(0.1)	10.2	(0.9)	80.9	(0.9)	8.4	(0.6)	0.0	(0.0)	0.0	c
	Macao-China	6.7	(0.1)	19.2	(0.2)	34.9	(0.1)	38.7	(0.1)	0.5	(0.1)	0.0	c
	Montenegro	0.0	c	2.5	(1.7)	82.7	(1.5)	14.8	(0.3)	0.0	c	0.0	c
	Panama	2.9	(0.8)	10.6	(1.6)	30.6	(3.3)	49.8	(4.5)	6.1	(1.4)	0.0	c
	Peru	4.0	(0.4)	8.9	(0.6)	17.1	(0.7)	44.6	(1.1)	25.4	(0.8)	0.0	c
	Qatar	1.7	(0.1)	3.6	(0.1)	13.5	(0.2)	62.6	(0.2)	18.2	(0.2)	0.4	(0.1)
	Romania	0.0	c	7.2	(1.0)	88.6	(1.1)	4.3	(0.6)	0.0	c	0.0	c
	Russian Federation	0.9	(0.2)	10.0	(0.7)	60.1	(1.8)	28.1	(1.6)	0.9	(0.2)	0.0	c
	Serbia	0.2	(0.1)	2.1	(0.5)	96.0	(0.6)	1.7	(0.2)	0.0	c	0.0	c
	Shanghai-China	1.0	(0.2)	4.1	(0.4)	37.4	(0.8)	57.1	(0.9)	0.4	(0.2)	0.0	(0.0)
	Singapore	1.0	(0.2)	2.6	(0.2)	34.7	(0.4)	61.6	(0.3)	0.0	c	0.0	(0.0)
	Chinese Taipei	0.0	c	0.1	(0.0)	34.4	(0.9)	65.5	(0.9)	0.0	(0.0)	0.0	c
	Thailand	0.1	(0.0)	0.5	(0.1)	23.2	(1.1)	73.5	(1.1)	2.7	(0.4)	0.0	c
	Trinidad and Tobago	2.1	(0.2)	8.8	(0.4)	25.3	(0.4)	56.1	(0.4)	7.7	(0.3)	0.0	c
	Tunisia	6.4	(0.4)	13.4	(0.6)	23.9	(0.9)	50.9	(1.4)	5.4	(0.4)	0.0	c
	Uruguay	7.1	(0.8)	10.6	(0.6)	21.5	(0.8)	56.2	(1.1)	4.6	(0.4)	0.0	c

StatLink ⫘ http://dx.doi.org/10.1787/888932343190

[Part 1/2]

Table A2.4b **Percentage of students at each grade level, by gender**

		Boys – grade level											
		7th grade		8th grade		9th grade		10th grade		11th grade		12th grade	
		%	S.E.	%	S.E.	%	S.E.	%	S.E.	%	S.E.	%	S.E.
OECD	Australia	0.0	c	0.1	(0.0)	13.1	(0.9)	69.6	(1.1)	17.1	(0.8)	0.1	(0.0)
	Austria	0.7	(0.2)	7.4	(1.2)	42.6	(1.3)	49.3	(1.3)	0.0	(0.0)	0.0	c
	Belgium	0.6	(0.2)	6.4	(0.7)	34.6	(0.9)	57.3	(1.0)	1.1	(0.2)	0.0	(0.0)
	Canada	0.0	(0.0)	1.4	(0.3)	14.6	(0.6)	82.9	(0.6)	1.1	(0.1)	0.0	(0.0)
	Chile	1.3	(0.3)	4.9	(0.6)	23.2	(1.0)	65.9	(1.3)	4.7	(0.3)	0.0	c
	Czech Republic	0.7	(0.2)	4.5	(0.5)	52.5	(2.2)	42.3	(2.4)	0.0	c	0.0	c
	Denmark	0.1	(0.0)	19.5	(0.9)	79.5	(1.0)	0.8	(0.3)	0.0	c	0.0	c
	Estonia	2.4	(0.5)	27.0	(1.0)	69.6	(1.1)	1.0	(0.3)	0.0	c	0.0	c
	Finland	0.6	(0.2)	14.0	(0.8)	85.2	(0.8)	0.0	c	0.2	(0.1)	0.0	c
	France	1.3	(0.9)	4.0	(0.6)	39.6	(1.5)	51.4	(1.9)	3.6	(0.8)	0.0	(0.0)
	Germany	1.4	(0.3)	13.1	(0.7)	56.1	(1.0)	28.8	(0.9)	0.6	(0.1)	0.0	c
	Greece	0.5	(0.2)	1.9	(0.5)	6.2	(1.2)	91.4	(1.5)	0.0	c	0.0	c
	Hungary	3.2	(0.8)	9.3	(1.3)	68.8	(1.6)	18.7	(0.9)	0.0	(0.0)	0.0	(0.0)
	Iceland	0.0	c	0.0	c	0.0	c	98.7	(0.2)	1.3	(0.2)	0.0	c
	Ireland	0.1	(0.0)	2.8	(0.5)	60.9	(1.3)	22.4	(1.5)	13.8	(1.4)	0.0	c
	Israel	0.0	c	0.5	(0.2)	19.9	(1.1)	78.7	(1.2)	1.0	(0.1)	0.0	c
	Italy	0.1	(0.1)	1.7	(0.4)	20.1	(0.6)	75.7	(0.7)	2.5	(0.3)	0.0	c
	Japan	0.0	c	0.0	c	0.0	c	100.0	(0.0)	0.0	c	0.0	c
	Korea	0.0	c	0.1	(0.1)	4.7	(1.3)	94.5	(1.4)	0.7	(0.2)	0.0	c
	Luxembourg	0.8	(0.2)	12.5	(0.4)	52.4	(0.5)	34.0	(0.4)	0.3	(0.1)	0.0	c
	Mexico	2.0	(0.2)	8.8	(0.5)	37.6	(0.9)	51.0	(0.9)	0.5	(0.2)	0.0	c
	Netherlands	0.4	(0.3)	3.0	(0.4)	48.9	(1.3)	47.3	(1.3)	0.3	(0.1)	0.0	c
	New Zealand	0.0	c	0.0	c	0.0	c	6.9	(0.5)	87.9	(0.6)	5.2	(0.5)
	Norway	0.0	c	0.0	c	0.5	(0.1)	99.2	(0.2)	0.3	(0.2)	0.0	c
	Poland	1.5	(0.3)	6.5	(0.6)	91.6	(0.7)	0.5	(0.2)	0.0	c	0.0	c
	Portugal	3.4	(0.5)	10.5	(0.9)	30.9	(2.0)	54.9	(2.6)	0.4	(0.1)	0.0	c
	Slovak Republic	1.4	(0.3)	3.7	(0.5)	40.1	(1.9)	51.6	(2.1)	3.3	(0.7)	0.0	c
	Slovenia	0.0	c	0.1	(0.1)	4.0	(1.2)	91.1	(1.2)	4.7	(0.4)	0.0	c
	Spain	0.1	(0.0)	12.2	(0.6)	28.7	(0.8)	58.9	(0.9)	0.0	(0.0)	0.0	c
	Sweden	0.0	(0.0)	4.1	(0.4)	94.7	(0.6)	1.1	(0.3)	0.0	c	0.0	c
	Switzerland	0.8	(0.2)	18.0	(1.2)	60.7	(1.8)	19.4	(1.8)	1.0	(0.4)	0.1	(0.1)
	Turkey	1.0	(0.2)	4.0	(0.9)	30.2	(1.4)	61.3	(1.7)	3.2	(0.3)	0.2	(0.1)
	United Kingdom	0.0	c	0.0	c	0.0	c	1.3	(0.2)	98.0	(0.2)	0.7	(0.1)
	United States	0.0	c	0.1	(0.0)	13.2	(1.0)	68.6	(1.4)	17.9	(0.9)	0.1	(0.1)
	OECD average	1.0	(0.1)	7.0	(0.1)	40.8	(0.2)	50.8	(0.2)	9.8	(0.1)	0.7	(0.0)
Partners	Albania	0.5	(0.2)	2.6	(0.4)	54.0	(2.0)	42.9	(2.1)	0.0	(0.0)	0.0	c
	Argentina	5.9	(1.1)	15.4	(1.4)	22.7	(1.5)	52.5	(2.4)	3.5	(0.5)	0.0	c
	Azerbaijan	0.6	(0.2)	4.7	(0.5)	47.8	(1.4)	46.5	(1.5)	0.3	(0.1)	0.0	c
	Brazil	8.4	(0.6)	21.0	(0.9)	37.8	(0.8)	31.1	(0.9)	1.7	(0.2)	0.0	c
	Bulgaria	2.0	(0.4)	7.4	(0.9)	86.9	(1.2)	3.7	(0.6)	0.0	c	0.0	c
	Colombia	5.5	(0.9)	11.5	(0.9)	21.9	(1.1)	42.4	(1.4)	18.7	(1.2)	0.0	c
	Croatia	0.0	c	0.1	(0.1)	79.1	(0.6)	20.7	(0.6)	0.0	c	0.0	c
	Dubai (UAE)	1.6	(0.2)	4.5	(0.3)	16.0	(0.6)	53.6	(0.7)	23.1	(0.6)	1.1	(0.2)
	Hong Kong-China	1.9	(0.3)	7.3	(0.6)	26.6	(0.7)	64.1	(1.0)	0.1	(0.1)	0.0	c
	Indonesia	1.8	(0.7)	8.2	(1.0)	49.3	(3.4)	36.2	(3.6)	4.0	(0.9)	0.5	(0.3)
	Jordan	0.1	(0.1)	1.2	(0.4)	7.5	(0.8)	91.2	(0.9)	0.0	c	0.0	c
	Kazakhstan	0.5	(0.1)	7.1	(0.6)	75.2	(2.2)	17.2	(2.3)	0.1	(0.0)	0.0	c
	Kyrgyzstan	0.2	(0.1)	8.9	(0.7)	72.9	(1.6)	17.4	(1.6)	0.5	(0.2)	0.0	c
	Latvia	3.6	(0.9)	19.9	(1.1)	74.7	(1.4)	1.6	(0.4)	0.1	(0.1)	0.0	(0.0)
	Liechtenstein	1.1	(0.7)	19.7	(1.6)	68.9	(1.2)	10.3	(1.2)	0.0	c	0.0	c
	Lithuania	0.6	(0.2)	12.3	(1.2)	80.0	(1.2)	7.2	(0.7)	0.0	c	0.0	c
	Macao-China	8.9	(0.2)	22.0	(0.2)	34.9	(0.2)	33.6	(0.2)	0.5	(0.1)	0.0	c
	Montenegro	0.0	c	3.0	(2.0)	85.0	(1.8)	12.0	(0.4)	0.0	c	0.0	c
	Panama	3.4	(1.1)	13.6	(2.5)	32.6	(4.4)	45.7	(5.5)	4.7	(1.8)	0.0	c
	Peru	4.9	(0.5)	11.2	(0.8)	18.8	(1.0)	42.3	(1.4)	22.9	(0.9)	0.0	c
	Qatar	1.9	(0.1)	4.3	(0.2)	14.8	(0.3)	60.4	(0.3)	18.2	(0.2)	0.4	(0.1)
	Romania	0.0	c	6.3	(1.1)	89.9	(1.3)	3.9	(0.7)	0.0	c	0.0	c
	Russian Federation	1.4	(0.3)	10.4	(0.9)	61.2	(1.9)	26.3	(1.9)	0.8	(0.2)	0.0	c
	Serbia	0.3	(0.1)	2.7	(0.7)	95.6	(0.8)	1.4	(0.2)	0.0	c	0.0	c
	Shanghai-China	1.2	(0.3)	5.1	(0.6)	38.8	(1.2)	54.7	(1.4)	0.2	(0.1)	0.0	c
	Singapore	0.8	(0.2)	2.9	(0.3)	35.7	(0.6)	60.6	(0.5)	0.0	c	0.0	c
	Chinese Taipei	0.0	c	0.2	(0.1)	35.2	(1.5)	64.7	(1.5)	0.0	c	0.0	c
	Thailand	0.2	(0.1)	0.8	(0.2)	26.3	(1.4)	70.5	(1.4)	2.2	(0.5)	0.0	c
	Trinidad and Tobago	2.7	(0.3)	10.7	(0.5)	28.4	(0.6)	51.0	(0.5)	7.1	(0.4)	0.0	c
	Tunisia	8.9	(0.6)	16.8	(0.9)	24.4	(1.1)	45.3	(1.5)	4.7	(0.5)	0.0	c
	Uruguay	9.1	(1.0)	12.0	(0.8)	24.9	(0.8)	50.4	(1.3)	3.6	(0.4)	0.0	c

StatLink http://dx.doi.org/10.1787/888932343190

[Part 2/2]

Table A2.4b **Percentage of students at each grade level, by gender**

		Girls – grade level										
		7th grade		8th grade		9th grade		10th grade		11th grade		12th grade	
		%	S.E.	%	S.E.	%	S.E.	%	S.E.	%	S.E.	%	S.E.
OECD	Australia	0.0	(0.0)	0.1	(0.0)	7.9	(0.5)	72.0	(0.8)	20.0	(0.8)	0.1	(0.0)
	Austria	0.6	(0.4)	5.0	(1.2)	42.2	(1.4)	52.1	(1.5)	0.0	(0.0)	0.0	c
	Belgium	0.3	(0.1)	4.5	(0.5)	29.3	(1.1)	64.5	(1.1)	1.3	(0.2)	0.0	(0.0)
	Canada	0.0	(0.0)	1.0	(0.2)	12.5	(0.5)	85.3	(0.5)	1.1	(0.1)	0.0	(0.0)
	Chile	0.7	(0.1)	2.9	(0.5)	17.7	(0.9)	73.0	(1.1)	5.6	(0.4)	0.0	(0.0)
	Czech Republic	0.3	(0.2)	3.1	(0.4)	44.8	(1.9)	51.8	(1.9)	0.0	c	0.0	c
	Denmark	0.1	(0.0)	10.0	(0.7)	87.3	(0.9)	2.5	(0.8)	0.0	c	0.0	c
	Estonia	0.9	(0.3)	20.8	(0.9)	75.4	(1.1)	2.7	(0.5)	0.2	(0.2)	0.0	c
	Finland	0.4	(0.1)	9.6	(0.6)	89.4	(0.6)	0.0	c	0.6	(0.2)	0.0	c
	France	1.3	(0.9)	3.2	(0.9)	29.4	(1.5)	61.6	(1.7)	4.4	(0.8)	0.1	(0.1)
	Germany	1.1	(0.2)	8.8	(0.6)	53.4	(1.1)	36.4	(1.1)	0.3	(0.1)	0.0	(0.0)
	Greece	0.2	(0.2)	0.9	(0.5)	4.9	(0.7)	94.0	(0.9)	0.0	c	0.0	c
	Hungary	2.3	(0.7)	5.9	(1.1)	65.4	(1.6)	26.2	(1.2)	0.2	(0.1)	0.0	c
	Iceland	0.0	c	0.0	c	0.0	(0.1)	97.9	(0.2)	2.1	(0.2)	0.0	c
	Ireland	0.1	(0.1)	2.0	(0.4)	57.3	(1.5)	25.7	(2.0)	15.1	(1.5)	0.0	c
	Israel	0.0	c	0.1	(0.1)	15.9	(1.0)	83.8	(1.1)	0.2	(0.1)	0.0	(0.0)
	Italy	0.2	(0.1)	1.0	(0.2)	13.5	(0.6)	81.4	(0.7)	3.9	(0.3)	0.0	c
	Japan	0.0	c	0.0	c	0.0	c	100.0	(0.0)	0.0	c	0.0	c
	Korea	0.0	c	0.0	c	3.6	(1.0)	95.6	(1.0)	0.8	(0.1)	0.0	c
	Luxembourg	0.4	(0.1)	10.6	(0.3)	50.8	(0.4)	38.0	(0.3)	0.2	(0.1)	0.0	c
	Mexico	1.5	(0.2)	6.1	(0.4)	31.5	(0.9)	60.1	(1.0)	0.8	(0.3)	0.0	(0.0)
	Netherlands	0.1	(0.1)	2.3	(0.4)	43.4	(1.4)	53.5	(1.3)	0.7	(0.2)	0.0	c
	New Zealand	0.0	c	0.0	c	0.1	(0.1)	4.8	(0.5)	89.8	(0.6)	5.4	(0.5)
	Norway	0.0	c	0.0	c	0.4	(0.1)	99.4	(0.2)	0.1	(0.1)	0.0	c
	Poland	0.6	(0.2)	2.5	(0.3)	95.6	(0.7)	1.3	(0.6)	0.0	c	0.0	c
	Portugal	1.4	(0.2)	7.7	(0.8)	25.1	(1.4)	65.4	(1.9)	0.4	(0.1)	0.0	c
	Slovak Republic	0.7	(0.2)	1.5	(0.3)	31.4	(1.8)	62.1	(2.1)	4.3	(0.9)	0.0	(0.0)
	Slovenia	0.0	c	0.0	c	1.9	(0.7)	90.3	(0.8)	7.8	(0.5)	0.0	c
	Spain	0.1	(0.1)	7.6	(0.4)	24.2	(0.7)	68.0	(0.8)	0.0	(0.0)	0.0	c
	Sweden	0.1	(0.1)	2.3	(0.3)	95.4	(0.7)	2.2	(0.7)	0.0	c	0.0	c
	Switzerland	0.4	(0.1)	12.9	(0.9)	62.6	(1.8)	22.7	(2.0)	1.4	(0.6)	0.0	c
	Turkey	0.4	(0.2)	2.9	(0.8)	19.8	(1.3)	72.3	(1.6)	4.4	(0.4)	0.2	(0.1)
	United Kingdom	0.0	c	0.0	c	0.0	c	1.0	(0.1)	98.1	(0.1)	0.9	(0.1)
	United States	0.0	c	0.2	(0.2)	8.5	(0.7)	68.4	(1.1)	22.8	(1.0)	0.1	(0.1)
	OECD average	0.6	(0.1)	5.0	(0.1)	35.6	(0.2)	55.0	(0.2)	10.2	(0.1)	0.5	(0.0)
Partners	Albania	0.2	(0.1)	1.8	(0.4)	47.6	(2.3)	50.2	(2.3)	0.2	(0.1)	0.0	c
	Argentina	3.6	(0.9)	10.7	(1.5)	18.4	(1.2)	62.3	(2.2)	4.9	(0.6)	0.0	c
	Azerbaijan	0.6	(0.3)	5.8	(0.6)	51.0	(1.5)	42.1	(1.4)	0.4	(0.1)	0.0	c
	Brazil	5.4	(0.4)	15.3	(0.6)	37.1	(0.9)	39.7	(0.9)	2.5	(0.2)	0.0	c
	Bulgaria	0.9	(0.3)	4.6	(0.7)	90.6	(1.0)	3.9	(0.7)	0.0	c	0.0	c
	Colombia	3.3	(0.4)	9.1	(0.8)	22.4	(1.0)	42.2	(1.1)	23.0	(1.1)	0.0	c
	Croatia	0.0	c	0.2	(0.2)	75.8	(0.6)	24.1	(0.5)	0.0	c	0.0	c
	Dubai (UAE)	0.6	(0.1)	2.2	(0.2)	13.5	(0.5)	60.4	(0.6)	22.7	(0.7)	0.6	(0.1)
	Hong Kong-China	1.5	(0.2)	7.1	(0.6)	23.5	(0.6)	67.9	(1.0)	0.0	c	0.0	c
	Indonesia	1.2	(0.3)	4.9	(0.8)	42.7	(3.7)	44.6	(3.8)	6.0	(1.1)	0.6	(0.5)
	Jordan	0.1	(0.0)	1.3	(0.3)	6.5	(0.7)	92.1	(0.9)	0.0	c	0.0	c
	Kazakhstan	0.4	(0.1)	5.7	(0.5)	71.5	(2.0)	22.3	(2.1)	0.2	(0.1)	0.0	c
	Kyrgyzstan	0.1	(0.1)	7.1	(0.6)	69.9	(1.5)	22.0	(1.6)	0.9	(0.2)	0.0	c
	Latvia	1.7	(0.4)	11.2	(0.6)	83.9	(0.8)	3.1	(0.4)	0.1	(0.1)	0.0	c
	Liechtenstein	0.6	(0.6)	15.0	(1.5)	74.0	(1.2)	10.4	(1.6)	0.0	c	0.0	c
	Lithuania	0.3	(0.1)	8.1	(0.8)	81.9	(0.9)	9.6	(0.7)	0.0	c	0.0	c
	Macao-China	4.4	(0.1)	16.3	(0.2)	34.9	(0.2)	43.9	(0.2)	0.5	(0.1)	0.0	c
	Montenegro	0.0	c	2.0	(1.4)	80.3	(1.3)	17.8	(0.4)	0.0	c	0.0	c
	Panama	2.4	(0.6)	7.7	(1.1)	28.7	(3.0)	53.8	(4.0)	7.5	(1.6)	0.0	c
	Peru	3.2	(0.4)	6.5	(0.6)	15.4	(0.8)	47.0	(1.2)	27.9	(1.2)	0.0	c
	Qatar	1.4	(0.1)	3.0	(0.1)	12.1	(0.2)	64.9	(0.2)	18.1	(0.2)	0.5	(0.1)
	Romania	0.0	c	8.1	(1.5)	87.3	(1.5)	4.7	(0.6)	0.0	c	0.0	c
	Russian Federation	0.5	(0.1)	9.7	(0.8)	59.0	(2.0)	29.8	(1.8)	1.0	(0.2)	0.0	c
	Serbia	0.1	(0.1)	1.4	(0.5)	96.4	(0.6)	2.0	(0.2)	0.0	c	0.0	c
	Shanghai-China	0.8	(0.2)	3.0	(0.4)	36.1	(1.0)	59.5	(1.0)	0.6	(0.2)	0.0	(0.0)
	Singapore	1.2	(0.2)	2.3	(0.3)	33.7	(0.5)	62.7	(0.4)	0.0	c	0.0	(0.0)
	Chinese Taipei	0.0	c	0.0	(0.0)	33.7	(1.5)	66.3	(1.5)	0.0	(0.0)	0.0	c
	Thailand	0.0	c	0.3	(0.1)	20.9	(1.4)	75.8	(1.4)	3.0	(0.4)	0.0	c
	Trinidad and Tobago	1.5	(0.3)	6.9	(0.5)	22.3	(0.6)	61.0	(0.6)	8.3	(0.4)	0.0	c
	Tunisia	4.2	(0.4)	10.3	(0.5)	23.4	(1.0)	56.1	(1.4)	6.0	(0.5)	0.0	c
	Uruguay	5.4	(0.6)	9.4	(0.5)	18.5	(0.9)	61.4	(1.2)	5.4	(0.6)	0.0	c

StatLink 🖳 http://dx.doi.org/10.1787/888932343190

Students in or out of the regular education system in Argentina

The low performance of 15-year-old students in Argentina is, to some extent, influenced by a fairly large proportion of 15-year-olds enrolled in programmes outside the regular education system. Table A2.5 shows the proportion of students inside and outside the regular education system, alongside their performance in PISA 2009.

Table A2.5 **Percentage of students and mean scores in reading, mathematics and science, according to whether students are in or out of the regular education system in Argentina**

| | Percentage of students | | Mean performance | | | | | |
| | | | Reading | | Mathematics | | Science | |
	%	S.E.	Mean	S.E.	Mean	S.E.	Mean	S.E.
Students in the regular educational system[1]	60.9	2.2	439	5.1	421	4.8	439	4.9
Students out of the regular educational system[2]	39.1	2.2	335	8.0	337	6.7	341	8.3

1. Students who are not in grade 10 or 11 and in programme 3, 4, 5, 6, 7 or 8.
2. Students who are in grade 10 or 11 and in programme 3, 4, 5, 6, 7 or 8.
StatLink 📈 http://dx.doi.org/10.1787/888932343190

ANNEX A3
STANDARD ERRORS, SIGNIFICANCE TESTS AND SUB-GROUP COMPARISONS

The statistics in this report represent estimates of national performance based on samples of students, rather than values that could be calculated if every student in every country had answered every question. Consequently, it is important to measure the degree of uncertainty of the estimates. In PISA, each estimate has an associated degree of uncertainty, which is expressed through a standard error. The use of confidence intervals provides a way to make inferences about the population means and proportions in a manner that reflects the uncertainty associated with the sample estimates. From an observed sample statistic and assuming a normal distribution, it can be inferred that the corresponding population result would lie within the confidence interval in 95 out of 100 replications of the measurement on different samples drawn from the same population.

In many cases, readers are primarily interested in whether a given value in a particular country is different from a second value in the same or another country, *e.g.* whether girls in a country perform better than boys in the same country. In the tables and charts used in this report, differences are labelled as statistically significant when a difference of that size, smaller or larger, would be observed less than 5% of the time, if there were actually no difference in corresponding population values. Similarly, the risk of reporting a correlation as significant if there is, in fact, no correlation between two measures, is contained at 5%.

Throughout the report, significance tests were undertaken to assess the statistical significance of the comparisons made. Except when noted statistical test evaluate whether the estimate is significantly different from zero. In specific cases statistical tests evaluate whether the estimates for individual countries are statistically different from the OECD average.

Gender differences

Gender differences in student performance or other indices were tested for statistical significance. Positive differences indicate higher scores for boys while negative differences indicate higher scores for girls. Generally, differences marked in bold in the tables in this volume are statistically significant at the 95% confidence level.

Performance differences between the top and bottom quartiles of PISA indices and scales

Differences in average performance between the top and bottom quarters of the PISA indices and scales were tested for statistical significance. Figures marked in bold indicate that performance between the top and bottom quarters of students on the respective index is statistically significantly different at the 95% confidence level.

Change in the performance per unit of the index

For many tables, the difference in student performance per unit of the index shown was calculated. Figures in bold indicate that the differences are statistically significantly different from zero at the 95% confidence level.

Relative risk or increased likelihood

The relative risk is a measure of association between an antecedent factor and an outcome factor. The relative risk is simply the ratio of two risks, *i.e.* the risk of observing the outcome when the antecedent is present and the risk of observing the outcome when the antecedent is not present. Figure A3.1 presents the notation that is used in the following.

■ Figure A3.1 ■
Labels used in a two-way table

P_{11}	P_{12}	$P_{1.}$
P_{21}	P_{22}	$P_{2.}$
$P_{.1}$	$P_{.2}$	$P_{..}$

$P_{..}$ is equal to $\frac{n_{..}}{n_{..}}$, with $n_{..}$ the total number of students and $P_{..}$ is therefore equal to 1, $P_{i.}$, $P_{.j}$ respectively represent the marginal probabilities for each row and for each column. The marginal probabilities are equal to the marginal frequencies divided by the total number of students. Finally, the P_{ij} represent the probabilities for each cell and are equal to the number of observations in a particular cell divided by the total number of observations.

In PISA, the rows represent the antecedent factor with the first row for "having the antecedent" and the second row for "not having the antecedent" and the columns represent the outcome with, the first column for "having the outcome" and the second column for "not having the outcome". The relative risk is then equal to:

$$RR = \frac{(P_{11}/P_{1.})}{(P_{21}/P_{2.})}$$

Figures in bold in the data tables presented in Annex B of this report indicate that the relative risk is statistically significantly different from 1 at the 95% confidence level.

Difference in reading performance between native students and students with an immigrant background

Differences in performance between native and non-native students were tested for statistical significance. For this purpose, first-generation and second-generation students were jointly considered as students with an immigrant background. Positive differences represent higher scores for native students, while negative differences represent higher scores for first-generation and second-generation students. Figures in bold in data tables presented in this volume indicate statistically significantly different scores at the 95% confidence level.

Effect sizes

Sometimes it is useful to compare differences in an index between groups, such as males and females, across countries. A problem that may occur in such instances is that the distribution of the index varies across groups or countries. One way to resolve this is to calculate an effect size that accounts for differences in the distributions. An effect size measures the difference between, say, the self-efficacy in reading of male and female students in a given country, relative to the average variation in self-efficacy in reading scores among male and female students in the country.

An effect size also allows a comparison of differences across measures that differ in their metric. For example, it is possible to compare effect sizes between the PISA indices and the PISA test scores, as when, for example, gender differences in performance in reading are compared with the gender differences in several of the indices.

In accordance with common practices, effect sizes less than 0.20 are considered small in this volume, effect sizes in the order of 0.50 are considered medium, and effect sizes greater than 0.80 are considered large. Many comparisons in this report consider differences only if the effect sizes are equal to or greater than 0.20, even if smaller differences are still statistically significant; figures in bold in data tables presented in Annex B of this report indicate values equal to or greater than 0.20. Values smaller than 0.20 but that due to rounding are shown as 0.20 in tables and figures have not been highlighted. Light shading represents the absolute value of effect size is equal or more than 0.2 and less than 0.5; medium shading represents the absolute value of effect size is equal or more than 0.5 and less than 0.8; and dark shading represents the absolute value of effect size is equal or more than 0.8.

The effect size between two sub-groups is calculated as:

$$\frac{m_1 - m_2}{\sqrt{\dfrac{\sigma_1^2 + \sigma_2^2}{2}}}, \ i.e.$$

m_1 and m_2 respectively represent the mean values for the sub-groups 1 and 2. σ_1^2 and σ_2^2 respectively represent the values of variance for the sub-groups 1 and 2. The effect size between the two sub-groups 1 and 2 is calculated as dividing the mean difference between the two sub-groups ($m_1 - m_2$), by the square root of the sum of the sub-group's variance ($\sigma_1^2 + \sigma_2^2$) divided by 2.

ANNEX A4
QUALITY ASSURANCE

Quality assurance procedures were implemented in all parts of PISA 2009, as was done for all previous PISA surveys.

The consistent quality and linguistic equivalence of the PISA 2009 assessment instruments were facilitated by providing countries with equivalent source versions of the assessment instruments in English and French, and requiring countries (other than those assessing students in English and French) to prepare and consolidate two independent translations using both source versions. Precise translation and adaptation guidelines were supplied, also including instructions for selecting and training the translators. For each country, the translation and format of the assessment instruments (including test materials, marking guides, questionnaires and manuals) were verified by expert translators appointed by the PISA Consortium before they were used in the PISA 2009 Field Trial and Main Study. These translators' mother tongue was the language of instruction in the country concerned and they were knowledgeable about education systems. For further information on the PISA translation procedures, see the *PISA 2009 Technical Report* (OECD, forthcoming).

The survey was implemented through standardised procedures. The PISA Consortium provided comprehensive manuals that explained the implementation of the survey, including precise instructions for the work of School Co-ordinators and scripts for Test Administrators to use during the assessment sessions. Proposed adaptations to survey procedures, or proposed modifications to the assessment session script, were submitted to the PISA Consortium for approval prior to verification. The PISA Consortium then verified the national translation and adaptation of these manuals.

To establish the credibility of PISA as valid and unbiased, and to encourage uniformity in administering the assessment sessions, Test Administrators in participating countries were selected using the following criteria: it was required that the Test Administrator not be the reading, mathematics or science instructor of any students in the sessions he or she would administer for PISA; it was recommended that the Test Administrator not be a member of the staff of any school where he or she would administer for PISA; and it was considered preferable that the Test Administrator not be a member of the staff of any school in the PISA sample. Participating countries organised an in-person training session for Test Administrators.

Participating countries were required to ensure that: Test Administrators worked with the School Co-ordinator to prepare the assessment session, including updating student tracking forms and identifying excluded students; no extra time was given for the cognitive items (while it was permissible to give extra time for the student questionnaire); no instrument was administered before the two one-hour parts of the cognitive session; Test Administrators recorded the student participation status on the student tracking forms and filled in a Session Report Form; no cognitive instrument was permitted to be photocopied; no cognitive instrument could be viewed by school staff before the assessment session; and Test Administrators returned the material to the National Centre immediately after the assessment sessions.

National Project Managers were encouraged to organise a follow-up session when more than 15% of the PISA sample was not able to attend the original assessment session.

National Quality Monitors from the PISA Consortium visited all National Centres to review data-collection procedures. Finally, School Quality Monitors from the PISA Consortium visited a sample of 15 schools during the assessment. For further information on the field operations, see the *PISA 2009 Technical Report* (OECD, forthcoming).

Marking procedures were designed to ensure consistent and accurate application of the marking guides outlined in the PISA Operations Manuals. National Project Managers were required to submit proposed modifications to these procedures to the Consortium for approval. Reliability studies to analyse the consistency of marking were implemented, these are discussed in more detail below.

Software specially designed for PISA facilitated data entry, detected common errors during data entry, and facilitated the process of data cleaning. Training sessions familiarised National Project Managers with these procedures.

For a description of the quality assurance procedures applied in PISA and in the results, see the *PISA 2009 Technical Report* (OECD, forthcoming).

The results of data adjudication show that the PISA Technical Standards were fully met in all countries and economies that participated in PISA 2009, though for one country, some serious doubts were raised. Analysis of the data for Azerbaijan suggest that the PISA Technical Standards may not have been fully met for the following four main reasons: *i)* the order of difficulty of the clusters is inconsistent with previous experience and the ordering varies across booklets; *ii)* the percentage correct on some items is higher than that of the highest scoring countries; *iii)* the difficulty of the clusters varies widely across booklets; and *iv)* the coding of items in Azerbaijan is at an extremely high level of agreement between independent coders, and was judged, on some items, to be too lenient. However, further investigation of the survey instruments, the procedures for test implementation and coding of student responses at the national level did not provide sufficient evidence of systematic errors or violations of the PISA Technical Standards. Azerbaijan's data are, therefore, included in the PISA 2009 international dataset.

For the PISA 2009 assessment in Austria, a dispute between teacher unions and the education minister has led to the announcement of a boycott of PISA which was withdrawn after the first week of testing. The boycott required the OECD to remove identifiable cases from the dataset. Although the Austrian dataset met the PISA 2009 technical standards after the removal of these cases, the negative atmosphere in regard to educational assessment has affected the conditions under which the assessment was administered and could have adversely affected student motivation to respond to the PISA tasks. The comparability of the 2009 data with data from earlier PISA assessments can therefore not be ensured and data for Austria have therefore been excluded from trend comparisons.

ANNEX A5
LATENT PROFILE ANALYSIS

This annex describes the methods used for the classification of students presented in Chapters 1 and 2. Latent profile analysis was performed to identify profiles of readers based on the extent to which students read comic books, magazines, newspapers, fiction and non-fiction books for enjoyment, as well as on their awareness of effective learning strategies to understand, remember and summarise information. The analysis shows how different reading patterns are associated with reading performance.

Method

A key aim of the report is to identify what it takes to be an effective learner – whereby effectiveness is measured in terms of performance on the PISA reading assessment – in different countries. Latent profile analysis was used to ascertain whether students could be reliably assigned to a small number of groups that share similar profiles. Unlike traditional cluster analysis, latent profile analysis is model-based, and so provides the opportunity to asses the validity of the latent profile classes rigorously.

Latent profile analysis is a method that allows researchers to ascertain whether individual observations – in the context of Chapter 2 of this Volume students – can be reliably assigned to a small number of groups that share similar profiles. In a sense, latent profile analysis "clusters" students into unique profile groups. Latent profile analysis assumes that the population distribution of the observed variables is a mixture of several normal distributions. Thus, each variable y_i, given the model parameters ($\theta = \pi_k, \mu_k, \Sigma_k$), can be represented as a weighted mixture of K classes, where K is specified by the analyst according to theory, although exploratory studies of the number of latent profiles can also be conducted. The distribution for each class was defined by a mean vector (μ_k) and a covariance vector (Σ_k) (Pastor et al, 2006). In functional form, $f(y_i \mid \theta) = \Sigma_{k=1}^{k} \pi_k f_k (y_i \mid \mu_k, \Sigma_k)$.

In the report, latent profile analysis was conducted with *multiple categorical latent variables*. This model assumes that there are several dimensions (*i.e.* latent variables) when classifying students into groups. Because latent profile analysis is model-based, several dimensions were hypothesised according to findings presented in the Volume on the strong association between reading performance and reading different types of materials and awareness of effective strategies to understand, remember and summarise information.

Figure A5.1 illustrates the two categorical latent variables model (a model with two dimensions) employed to estimate profiles of students in Chapter 2. Figure A5.1 shows how the first dimension, characterising the material students read several times a month or several times a week – *i.e.* categorical latent variable C1 – is identified by five variables: whether students read comic books, fiction, non-fiction, magazines and newspapers. The second dimension, characterising students' awareness of effective learning strategies – *i.e.* categorical latent variable C2 – is identified by two variables: awareness of effective strategies to understand and remember information and awareness of effective strategies summarise information. Means are specified to vary only across the classes within each dimension. After grouping students into classes within each dimension, groupings are assigned according to the combination of the two dimensions, C1 and C2. Three classes were extracted from the first dimension, and two classes were extracted from the second dimension, resulting in a total of 6 groups that students could be assigned (3 x 2). The models were estimated by maximum likelihood with robust standard errors.

Models were estimated for the 295,074 students in 34 OECD countries. Because all countries contributed equally to the analysis, students in larger countries were given a somewhat lower weight in estimates than students in smaller countries. Students from partner countries and economies were grouped into each class using estimates for the OECD countries: once the estimates for the 34 OECD countries were obtained, these coefficients were applied to partner countries and economies to find their fit within the classes obtained for OECD countries. The fit statistics for students in partner countries and economies using the OECD estimates were generally satisfactory and in line with those obtained for OECD countries.

Mplus software was used to estimate the latent profile analyses.

■ Figure A5.1 ■
Latent profile analysis with two categorical latent variables

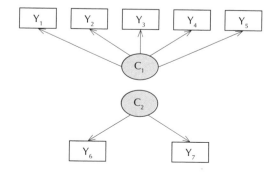

Missing data

Unfortunately, some information for the variables used in the latent profile analysis was not available for all students: 3 380 students had to be excluded from the analyses because of missing information, approximately 1.1% of entire sample. The model-based approach for categorical and continuous data implemented in Mplus was used to estimate parameters. Model-based approaches can estimate parameters even when data are missing (Lüdtke, Robitzsch, Trautwein & Köller, 2007). Specifically, Mplus uses the EM algorithm (for a detailed description, see Dempster, Laird & Rubin, 1977) and assumes that the missing data are missing at random (MAR). MAR means missing values on an observed variable are not dependent on that variable but may be a function of other variables. For example, if a student did not report whether he or she reads fiction several times a month or several times a week, the model assumes that this is not due to reading fiction, but may be due to other characteristics of the student (Schafer & Graham, 2002).

Models

The model has two dimensions (*i.e.* categorical latent variables): materials students read several times a month or several times a week and awareness of effective learning strategies in reading. The first dimension, material students read either several times a month or several times a week is characterised by five variables: whether students read comic books, magazines, newspapers, fiction and non-fiction books. The second dimension, awareness of learning strategies in reading, is characterised by two variables: awareness of effective strategies to understand and remember information and awareness of effective strategies to summarise information. Given the model fit, three classes were extracted from the first dimension, and two classes were extracted from the second dimension. Given the combination of these classes, students were assigned to 6 groups (3 x 2).

Entropy index

The entropy index value for the OECD countries and partner countries is 0.691 and 0.685 respectively. The entropy index is measured on a zero–to-one scale with a value of one indicating that students are perfectly classified. High values of the entropy index therefore indicate a good classification of students into different groups.

Annex B

TABLES OF RESULTS

All tables in Annex B are available on line

Annex B1: Results for countries and economies

Annex B2: Results for regions within countries

Adjudicated regions
Data for which adherence to the PISA sampling
standards and international comparability
was internationally adjudicated.

Non-adjudicated regions
Data for which adherence to the PISA sampling
standards at subnational levels was assessed
by the countries concerned.

In these countries, adherence to the PISA sampling
standards and international comparability was
internationally adjudicated only for the combined set
of all subnational entities.

Note: Unless otherwise specified, all the data contained in the following tables are drawn from the OECD PISA Database.

ANNEX B1
RESULTS FOR COUNTRIES AND ECONOMIES

[Part 1/2]

Index of enjoyment of reading and reading performance, by national quarters of this index

Table III.1.1 *Results based on students' self-reports*

	All students		Boys		Girls		Gender difference (B – G)		Bottom quarter		Second quarter		Third quarter		Top quarter	
	Mean index	S.E.	Mean index	S.E.	Mean index	S.E.	Dif.	S.E.	Mean index	S.E.	Mean index	S.E.	Mean index	S.E.	Mean index	S.E.
OECD																
Australia	0.00	(0.02)	-0.33	(0.02)	0.31	(0.02)	**-0.64**	(0.03)	**-1.36**	(0.01)	-0.37	(0.00)	0.31	(0.00)	**1.42**	(0.01)
Austria	-0.13	(0.03)	-0.55	(0.03)	0.26	(0.03)	**-0.81**	(0.04)	**-1.52**	(0.02)	-0.65	(0.01)	0.16	(0.01)	**1.47**	(0.02)
Belgium	-0.20	(0.02)	-0.45	(0.02)	0.07	(0.02)	**-0.52**	(0.03)	**-1.42**	(0.01)	-0.58	(0.00)	0.11	(0.01)	**1.11**	(0.01)
Canada	0.13	(0.01)	-0.28	(0.02)	0.55	(0.02)	**-0.83**	(0.02)	**-1.25**	(0.01)	-0.24	(0.00)	0.45	(0.00)	**1.57**	(0.01)
Chile	-0.06	(0.01)	-0.28	(0.02)	0.16	(0.02)	**-0.44**	(0.02)	**-1.01**	(0.01)	-0.37	(0.00)	0.10	(0.00)	**1.02**	(0.02)
Czech Republic	-0.13	(0.02)	-0.44	(0.02)	0.22	(0.02)	**-0.66**	(0.03)	**-1.21**	(0.01)	-0.46	(0.00)	0.10	(0.00)	**1.06**	(0.02)
Denmark	-0.09	(0.02)	-0.35	(0.02)	0.17	(0.02)	**-0.52**	(0.03)	**-1.17**	(0.01)	-0.40	(0.01)	0.15	(0.01)	**1.07**	(0.02)
Estonia	-0.03	(0.02)	-0.38	(0.02)	0.33	(0.02)	**-0.71**	(0.03)	**-1.07**	(0.01)	-0.37	(0.00)	0.20	(0.01)	**1.10**	(0.02)
Finland	0.05	(0.02)	-0.41	(0.02)	0.50	(0.02)	**-0.91**	(0.03)	**-1.25**	(0.02)	-0.28	(0.01)	0.36	(0.01)	**1.35**	(0.02)
France	0.01	(0.03)	-0.23	(0.03)	0.24	(0.03)	**-0.47**	(0.04)	**-1.26**	(0.01)	-0.33	(0.01)	0.34	(0.01)	**1.30**	(0.02)
Germany	0.07	(0.02)	-0.38	(0.02)	0.52	(0.03)	**-0.89**	(0.03)	**-1.33**	(0.01)	-0.45	(0.01)	0.42	(0.01)	**1.63**	(0.02)
Greece	0.07	(0.02)	-0.24	(0.02)	0.36	(0.02)	**-0.60**	(0.03)	**-0.95**	(0.01)	-0.22	(0.01)	0.29	(0.01)	**1.14**	(0.02)
Hungary	0.14	(0.02)	-0.15	(0.03)	0.43	(0.02)	**-0.58**	(0.04)	**-0.94**	(0.01)	-0.19	(0.01)	0.37	(0.01)	**1.30**	(0.02)
Iceland	-0.06	(0.02)	-0.38	(0.02)	0.25	(0.02)	**-0.63**	(0.03)	**-1.28**	(0.02)	-0.43	(0.01)	0.18	(0.01)	**1.27**	(0.02)
Ireland	-0.08	(0.02)	-0.30	(0.02)	0.15	(0.03)	**-0.45**	(0.04)	**-1.30**	(0.02)	-0.44	(0.01)	0.19	(0.01)	**1.23**	(0.02)
Israel	0.06	(0.02)	-0.26	(0.03)	0.35	(0.04)	**-0.60**	(0.04)	**-1.16**	(0.01)	-0.28	(0.00)	0.31	(0.01)	**1.35**	(0.02)
Italy	0.06	(0.01)	-0.27	(0.01)	0.41	(0.01)	**-0.68**	(0.02)	**-1.10**	(0.01)	-0.28	(0.00)	0.37	(0.00)	**1.27**	(0.01)
Japan	0.20	(0.02)	0.02	(0.03)	0.38	(0.02)	**-0.36**	(0.03)	**-1.07**	(0.01)	-0.19	(0.01)	0.48	(0.01)	**1.58**	(0.02)
Korea	0.13	(0.02)	0.00	(0.02)	0.27	(0.02)	**-0.27**	(0.03)	**-0.82**	(0.02)	-0.15	(0.01)	0.31	(0.00)	**1.17**	(0.02)
Luxembourg	-0.16	(0.02)	-0.51	(0.02)	0.20	(0.02)	**-0.71**	(0.03)	**-1.43**	(0.02)	-0.58	(0.01)	0.12	(0.01)	**1.25**	(0.02)
Mexico	0.14	(0.01)	-0.04	(0.01)	0.32	(0.01)	**-0.35**	(0.01)	**-0.77**	(0.01)	-0.13	(0.00)	0.32	(0.00)	**1.15**	(0.01)
Netherlands	-0.32	(0.03)	-0.66	(0.03)	0.02	(0.03)	**-0.69**	(0.03)	**-1.47**	(0.02)	-0.66	(0.01)	-0.03	(0.01)	**0.88**	(0.02)
New Zealand	0.13	(0.02)	-0.17	(0.02)	0.44	(0.02)	**-0.61**	(0.02)	**-1.07**	(0.02)	-0.21	(0.01)	0.40	(0.01)	**1.41**	(0.02)
Norway	-0.19	(0.02)	-0.50	(0.02)	0.13	(0.03)	**-0.63**	(0.03)	**-1.41**	(0.01)	-0.56	(0.01)	0.09	(0.01)	**1.12**	(0.02)
Poland	0.02	(0.02)	-0.36	(0.02)	0.39	(0.03)	**-0.75**	(0.03)	**-1.21**	(0.01)	-0.43	(0.00)	0.21	(0.01)	**1.49**	(0.02)
Portugal	0.21	(0.02)	-0.15	(0.02)	0.54	(0.02)	**-0.69**	(0.02)	**-0.87**	(0.01)	-0.09	(0.00)	0.44	(0.00)	**1.35**	(0.02)
Slovak Republic	-0.10	(0.02)	-0.36	(0.02)	0.15	(0.02)	**-0.51**	(0.02)	**-1.07**	(0.02)	-0.41	(0.00)	0.06	(0.01)	**1.02**	(0.02)
Slovenia	-0.20	(0.01)	-0.53	(0.02)	0.14	(0.02)	**-0.67**	(0.03)	**-1.35**	(0.01)	-0.55	(0.00)	0.06	(0.01)	**1.04**	(0.02)
Spain	-0.01	(0.01)	-0.28	(0.02)	0.26	(0.01)	**-0.55**	(0.02)	**-1.15**	(0.01)	-0.35	(0.00)	0.23	(0.00)	**1.22**	(0.01)
Sweden	-0.11	(0.02)	-0.47	(0.02)	0.26	(0.02)	**-0.72**	(0.03)	**-1.29**	(0.01)	-0.45	(0.01)	0.18	(0.01)	**1.14**	(0.02)
Switzerland	-0.04	(0.02)	-0.44	(0.02)	0.37	(0.03)	**-0.80**	(0.03)	**-1.46**	(0.02)	-0.50	(0.01)	0.32	(0.01)	**1.48**	(0.02)
Turkey	0.64	(0.02)	0.34	(0.02)	0.95	(0.02)	**-0.61**	(0.03)	**-0.34**	(0.01)	0.33	(0.00)	0.80	(0.00)	**1.77**	(0.02)
United Kingdom	-0.12	(0.02)	-0.37	(0.02)	0.13	(0.03)	**-0.50**	(0.03)	**-1.29**	(0.01)	-0.45	(0.00)	0.14	(0.01)	**1.13**	(0.02)
United States	-0.04	(0.03)	-0.35	(0.03)	0.28	(0.03)	**-0.63**	(0.03)	**-1.27**	(0.01)	-0.41	(0.00)	0.19	(0.01)	**1.33**	(0.02)
OECD average	0.00	(0.00)	-0.31	(0.00)	0.31	(0.00)	**-0.62**	(0.01)	**-1.17**	(0.00)	-0.36	(0.00)	0.26	(0.00)	**1.27**	(0.00)
Partners																
Albania	0.67	(0.02)	0.36	(0.02)	0.99	(0.02)	**-0.63**	(0.02)	**-0.21**	(0.01)	0.44	(0.00)	0.89	(0.00)	**1.56**	(0.01)
Argentina	-0.16	(0.02)	-0.34	(0.02)	-0.01	(0.02)	**-0.34**	(0.03)	**-1.02**	(0.01)	-0.43	(0.00)	0.00	(0.00)	**0.81**	(0.02)
Azerbaijan	0.39	(0.01)	0.29	(0.02)	0.50	(0.02)	**-0.22**	(0.03)	**-0.42**	(0.01)	0.16	(0.00)	0.57	(0.00)	**1.27**	(0.02)
Brazil	0.27	(0.01)	0.05	(0.01)	0.47	(0.02)	**-0.42**	(0.02)	**-0.64**	(0.01)	-0.01	(0.00)	0.45	(0.00)	**1.28**	(0.01)
Bulgaria	-0.02	(0.03)	-0.25	(0.03)	0.23	(0.03)	**-0.48**	(0.03)	**-1.01**	(0.02)	-0.31	(0.00)	0.17	(0.01)	**1.08**	(0.02)
Colombia	0.14	(0.02)	-0.02	(0.02)	0.28	(0.02)	**-0.29**	(0.03)	**-0.68**	(0.02)	-0.12	(0.00)	0.31	(0.00)	**1.05**	(0.01)
Croatia	-0.13	(0.02)	-0.44	(0.02)	0.22	(0.02)	**-0.66**	(0.03)	**-1.16**	(0.01)	-0.44	(0.00)	0.09	(0.00)	**1.00**	(0.02)
Dubai (UAE)	0.28	(0.01)	0.04	(0.02)	0.52	(0.02)	**-0.49**	(0.03)	**-0.80**	(0.01)	-0.05	(0.00)	0.52	(0.00)	**1.45**	(0.02)
Hong Kong-China	0.32	(0.01)	0.16	(0.02)	0.51	(0.02)	**-0.35**	(0.02)	**-0.54**	(0.01)	0.08	(0.00)	0.49	(0.00)	**1.27**	(0.01)
Indonesia	0.43	(0.01)	0.32	(0.01)	0.55	(0.01)	**-0.22**	(0.02)	**-0.16**	(0.01)	0.27	(0.00)	0.55	(0.00)	**1.07**	(0.01)
Jordan	0.37	(0.02)	0.22	(0.02)	0.52	(0.02)	**-0.30**	(0.03)	**-0.50**	(0.01)	0.12	(0.00)	0.56	(0.00)	**1.31**	(0.02)
Kazakhstan	0.54	(0.02)	0.39	(0.02)	0.70	(0.02)	**-0.30**	(0.02)	**-0.28**	(0.01)	0.31	(0.00)	0.72	(0.00)	**1.42**	(0.02)
Kyrgyzstan	0.39	(0.01)	0.19	(0.02)	0.57	(0.02)	**-0.38**	(0.02)	**-0.35**	(0.01)	0.14	(0.00)	0.52	(0.00)	**1.23**	(0.01)
Latvia	-0.04	(0.02)	-0.39	(0.02)	0.30	(0.02)	**-0.68**	(0.03)	**-0.98**	(0.01)	-0.34	(0.00)	0.18	(0.01)	**0.98**	(0.02)
Liechtenstein	-0.20	(0.05)	-0.57	(0.07)	0.21	(0.08)	**-0.78**	(0.11)	**-1.56**	(0.06)	-0.66	(0.02)	0.06	(0.03)	**1.34**	(0.07)
Lithuania	0.06	(0.02)	-0.44	(0.02)	0.57	(0.03)	**-1.00**	(0.03)	**-1.22**	(0.01)	-0.38	(0.01)	0.36	(0.01)	**1.48**	(0.02)
Macao-China	0.08	(0.01)	-0.13	(0.01)	0.28	(0.01)	**-0.41**	(0.02)	**-0.76**	(0.00)	-0.16	(0.00)	0.25	(0.00)	**0.97**	(0.01)
Montenegro	0.21	(0.01)	-0.04	(0.02)	0.47	(0.02)	**-0.52**	(0.02)	**-0.77**	(0.01)	-0.07	(0.00)	0.44	(0.01)	**1.25**	(0.01)
Panama	0.18	(0.02)	0.03	(0.03)	0.32	(0.03)	**-0.29**	(0.04)	**-0.71**	(0.02)	-0.12	(0.01)	0.34	(0.01)	**1.21**	(0.03)
Peru	0.35	(0.01)	0.21	(0.02)	0.48	(0.02)	**-0.27**	(0.02)	**-0.44**	(0.01)	0.11	(0.00)	0.50	(0.00)	**1.20**	(0.01)
Qatar	0.20	(0.01)	0.04	(0.01)	0.36	(0.01)	**-0.31**	(0.02)	**-0.74**	(0.01)	-0.08	(0.00)	0.37	(0.00)	**1.27**	(0.01)
Romania	0.10	(0.02)	-0.13	(0.02)	0.32	(0.02)	**-0.45**	(0.02)	**-0.73**	(0.01)	-0.16	(0.00)	0.27	(0.00)	**1.03**	(0.01)
Russian Federation	0.07	(0.01)	-0.15	(0.02)	0.29	(0.02)	**-0.44**	(0.02)	**-0.73**	(0.01)	-0.19	(0.00)	0.23	(0.00)	**0.99**	(0.01)
Serbia	0.04	(0.02)	-0.26	(0.02)	0.33	(0.03)	**-0.60**	(0.03)	**-0.97**	(0.01)	-0.26	(0.00)	0.24	(0.00)	**1.14**	(0.02)
Shanghai-China	0.57	(0.01)	0.39	(0.02)	0.75	(0.01)	**-0.35**	(0.02)	**-0.29**	(0.01)	0.36	(0.00)	0.78	(0.00)	**1.43**	(0.01)
Singapore	0.29	(0.01)	0.00	(0.02)	0.58	(0.02)	**-0.58**	(0.02)	**-0.81**	(0.01)	-0.03	(0.00)	0.51	(0.00)	**1.48**	(0.02)
Chinese Taipei	0.39	(0.02)	0.18	(0.02)	0.61	(0.03)	**-0.43**	(0.04)	**-0.59**	(0.01)	0.08	(0.00)	0.58	(0.00)	**1.51**	(0.02)
Thailand	0.54	(0.01)	0.36	(0.02)	0.67	(0.01)	**-0.31**	(0.02)	**-0.19**	(0.01)	0.32	(0.00)	0.67	(0.00)	**1.35**	(0.01)
Trinidad and Tobago	0.21	(0.01)	-0.08	(0.02)	0.49	(0.02)	**-0.57**	(0.02)	**-0.78**	(0.01)	-0.12	(0.00)	0.40	(0.01)	**1.34**	(0.02)
Tunisia	0.37	(0.02)	0.14	(0.03)	0.58	(0.02)	**-0.44**	(0.03)	**-0.67**	(0.01)	0.10	(0.00)	0.66	(0.00)	**1.39**	(0.01)
Uruguay	-0.14	(0.02)	-0.39	(0.02)	0.07	(0.02)	**-0.46**	(0.02)	**-1.17**	(0.01)	-0.44	(0.00)	0.08	(0.00)	**0.97**	(0.01)

Note: Values that are statistically significant are indicated in bold (see Annex A3).
StatLink 🔗 http://dx.doi.org/10.1787/888932343285

[Part 2/2]

Index of enjoyment of reading and reading performance, by national quarters of this index

Table III.1.1   *Results based on students' self-reports*

| | | Performance on the reading scale, by national quarters of this index | | | | | | | | Change in the reading score per unit of this index | | Increased likelihood of students in the bottom quarter of this index scoring in the bottom quarter of the national reading performance distribution | | Explained variance in student performance (r-squared x 100) | |
| | | Bottom quarter | | Second quarter | | Third quarter | | Top quarter | | | | | | | |
		Mean score	S.E.	Mean score	S.E.	Mean score	S.E.	Mean score	S.E.	Effect	S.E.	Ratio	S.E.	%	S.E.
OECD	Australia	454	(2.4)	489	(2.7)	536	(2.7)	588	(2.7)	44.9	(1.04)	2.7	(0.12)	26.0	(0.80)
	Austria	422	(3.5)	446	(3.8)	481	(4.2)	536	(4.2)	37.2	(1.63)	2.0	(0.15)	19.8	(1.40)
	Belgium	461	(2.4)	482	(3.2)	514	(3.7)	571	(2.9)	40.9	(1.21)	1.8	(0.10)	16.7	(0.93)
	Canada	473	(2.0)	506	(2.1)	542	(2.2)	582	(1.9)	35.7	(0.80)	2.5	(0.10)	20.1	(0.83)
	Chile	430	(3.3)	433	(4.1)	450	(3.7)	490	(3.6)	29.0	(1.57)	1.4	(0.09)	8.4	(0.84)
	Czech Republic	436	(3.3)	446	(3.7)	488	(2.8)	547	(3.5)	46.0	(1.53)	2.0	(0.11)	20.7	(1.10)
	Denmark	448	(3.1)	477	(3.4)	509	(2.9)	549	(3.1)	43.2	(1.46)	2.5	(0.16)	21.4	(1.27)
	Estonia	456	(3.2)	480	(3.2)	515	(3.3)	555	(3.4)	43.3	(1.71)	2.4	(0.17)	20.7	(1.28)
	Finland	475	(2.7)	518	(2.9)	557	(3.0)	596	(2.7)	43.3	(1.17)	3.2	(0.16)	27.0	(1.22)
	France	435	(4.9)	475	(3.7)	514	(4.0)	562	(4.1)	47.1	(2.28)	2.5	(0.16)	20.7	(1.55)
	Germany	451	(4.0)	468	(3.5)	520	(3.1)	562	(3.0)	36.6	(1.36)	2.3	(0.12)	21.0	(1.13)
	Greece	435	(6.2)	463	(6.0)	494	(4.6)	540	(3.3)	46.8	(2.35)	2.3	(0.15)	17.2	(1.36)
	Hungary	452	(3.8)	468	(3.5)	500	(4.9)	559	(3.4)	45.1	(1.92)	2.1	(0.16)	20.1	(1.61)
	Iceland	444	(2.8)	485	(2.7)	516	(3.3)	564	(2.5)	43.4	(1.37)	2.7	(0.18)	22.2	(1.12)
	Ireland	445	(3.9)	467	(3.6)	513	(4.0)	567	(3.0)	45.1	(1.56)	2.4	(0.15)	23.8	(1.36)
	Israel	455	(4.5)	447	(4.8)	479	(4.2)	534	(3.9)	30.1	(1.91)	1.2	(0.08)	7.9	(0.90)
	Italy	445	(2.3)	459	(2.0)	500	(2.2)	544	(2.1)	40.4	(1.02)	1.9	(0.07)	16.2	(0.71)
	Japan	471	(4.3)	505	(4.2)	540	(3.4)	573	(3.6)	35.8	(1.89)	2.3	(0.13)	15.0	(1.12)
	Korea	495	(4.5)	526	(3.6)	555	(3.5)	584	(3.4)	40.4	(2.29)	2.5	(0.15)	17.6	(1.35)
	Luxembourg	426	(2.7)	445	(2.9)	483	(3.4)	537	(2.7)	39.9	(1.34)	1.9	(0.12)	17.4	(1.09)
	Mexico	412	(2.3)	411	(2.4)	427	(2.3)	454	(2.4)	21.6	(1.12)	1.2	(0.04)	4.0	(0.40)
	Netherlands	464	(5.1)	487	(5.2)	522	(5.2)	560	(5.7)	38.5	(1.88)	2.0	(0.16)	16.7	(1.46)
	New Zealand	466	(3.3)	489	(3.2)	541	(3.8)	593	(3.2)	48.2	(1.56)	2.3	(0.15)	22.3	(1.37)
	Norway	450	(3.6)	484	(3.3)	518	(3.3)	564	(3.4)	42.1	(1.51)	2.5	(0.18)	22.2	(1.27)
	Poland	464	(3.4)	472	(3.5)	508	(3.3)	563	(3.1)	35.2	(1.31)	1.9	(0.13)	18.7	(1.19)
	Portugal	453	(3.4)	470	(3.7)	498	(3.3)	541	(3.3)	35.6	(1.59)	1.9	(0.11)	14.0	(1.00)
	Slovak Republic	451	(3.4)	447	(3.8)	479	(3.5)	538	(3.9)	39.8	(2.42)	1.5	(0.09)	14.3	(1.39)
	Slovenia	445	(2.3)	457	(2.4)	494	(2.4)	543	(2.6)	39.0	(1.39)	1.9	(0.10)	17.4	(1.09)
	Spain	439	(2.6)	461	(2.5)	493	(2.3)	537	(1.9)	38.4	(0.97)	2.2	(0.11)	17.8	(0.74)
	Sweden	442	(3.3)	474	(3.8)	515	(3.8)	563	(3.6)	46.8	(1.54)	2.4	(0.18)	21.7	(1.32)
	Switzerland	449	(3.1)	475	(2.9)	516	(3.0)	565	(3.2)	37.7	(1.20)	2.3	(0.14)	22.4	(1.13)
	Turkey	444	(4.3)	451	(3.8)	469	(3.6)	498	(4.7)	23.5	(2.03)	1.5	(0.11)	6.2	(0.94)
	United Kingdom	446	(3.2)	466	(2.6)	508	(3.2)	562	(2.7)	45.0	(1.52)	2.2	(0.13)	21.5	(1.34)
	United States	454	(2.8)	474	(4.3)	511	(4.2)	563	(5.0)	38.3	(1.81)	2.0	(0.12)	17.5	(1.30)
	OECD average	450	(0.6)	471	(0.6)	506	(0.6)	553	(0.6)	39.5	(0.28)	2.1	(0.02)	18.1	(0.20)
Partners	Albania	340	(5.5)	370	(5.4)	403	(4.7)	436	(4.3)	47.8	(2.83)	2.2	(0.22)	12.0	(1.28)
	Argentina	390	(4.9)	388	(5.6)	388	(5.3)	442	(6.6)	27.4	(3.65)	1.1	(0.07)	3.6	(0.91)
	Azerbaijan	342	(3.9)	357	(4.7)	373	(4.5)	386	(3.6)	22.8	(2.12)	1.7	(0.14)	4.5	(0.88)
	Brazil	397	(2.7)	399	(3.8)	411	(3.3)	444	(3.8)	25.8	(1.87)	1.2	(0.06)	4.6	(0.62)
	Bulgaria	407	(5.6)	407	(7.3)	432	(7.7)	493	(8.3)	38.3	(3.13)	1.3	(0.13)	8.7	(1.47)
	Colombia	407	(4.1)	402	(4.0)	418	(5.2)	429	(5.5)	14.4	(2.62)	1.0	(0.09)	1.4	(0.51)
	Croatia	441	(3.8)	454	(3.6)	484	(3.4)	526	(3.4)	37.1	(1.81)	1.9	(0.12)	13.8	(1.12)
	Dubai (UAE)	425	(2.4)	427	(2.6)	469	(2.6)	524	(2.6)	43.4	(1.27)	1.6	(0.08)	13.8	(0.86)
	Hong Kong-China	491	(2.9)	522	(3.6)	552	(2.7)	574	(3.1)	42.3	(2.03)	2.4	(0.14)	14.0	(1.12)
	Indonesia	393	(4.3)	395	(3.8)	404	(4.1)	417	(5.1)	21.2	(2.89)	1.3	(0.09)	2.5	(0.71)
	Jordan	394	(4.6)	386	(3.8)	412	(3.5)	446	(3.4)	27.5	(2.14)	1.4	(0.09)	5.2	(0.73)
	Kazakhstan	393	(4.8)	378	(4.2)	392	(3.4)	403	(4.3)	5.0	(2.97)	1.0	(0.07)	0.1	(0.18)
	Kyrgyzstan	304	(4.7)	300	(3.9)	322	(4.3)	343	(4.3)	23.8	(2.97)	1.4	(0.10)	2.5	(0.64)
	Latvia	450	(4.0)	459	(3.5)	492	(3.3)	536	(3.4)	42.0	(1.51)	1.9	(0.16)	17.1	(1.34)
	Liechtenstein	448	(8.3)	485	(8.4)	519	(7.8)	544	(8.4)	31.0	(3.45)	2.6	(0.52)	18.5	(3.78)
	Lithuania	429	(3.3)	445	(3.2)	478	(3.0)	526	(2.8)	34.3	(1.33)	2.0	(0.13)	18.3	(1.21)
	Macao-China	456	(2.0)	474	(1.9)	494	(1.8)	524	(1.7)	35.9	(1.32)	1.9	(0.09)	11.1	(0.74)
	Montenegro	378	(2.3)	389	(2.9)	413	(3.2)	457	(3.8)	36.7	(1.84)	1.5	(0.11)	10.4	(0.99)
	Panama	375	(7.1)	360	(8.4)	376	(7.2)	401	(7.3)	15.0	(3.31)	0.9	(0.14)	1.5	(0.66)
	Peru	373	(4.8)	351	(4.8)	366	(4.3)	398	(4.8)	18.3	(2.45)	0.9	(0.07)	1.5	(0.41)
	Qatar	355	(2.1)	348	(2.2)	377	(2.4)	429	(2.4)	35.7	(1.48)	1.3	(0.07)	6.7	(0.52)
	Romania	413	(5.0)	407	(4.7)	421	(4.5)	463	(5.1)	27.9	(2.92)	1.2	(0.10)	5.1	(1.00)
	Russian Federation	426	(4.0)	439	(4.5)	464	(3.2)	514	(4.6)	48.6	(2.70)	1.8	(0.12)	14.5	(1.35)
	Serbia	417	(3.3)	422	(3.1)	447	(3.1)	485	(3.4)	29.2	(1.71)	1.6	(0.11)	9.1	(1.08)
	Shanghai-China	515	(3.3)	550	(3.3)	570	(2.9)	590	(3.2)	39.8	(2.56)	2.4	(0.16)	12.2	(1.22)
	Singapore	473	(2.4)	505	(2.7)	546	(2.7)	583	(2.2)	43.3	(1.57)	2.4	(0.11)	17.3	(0.96)
	Chinese Taipei	444	(3.3)	477	(3.1)	515	(2.5)	551	(3.8)	45.9	(2.06)	2.7	(0.15)	21.7	(1.39)
	Thailand	397	(3.0)	412	(3.2)	429	(3.2)	451	(3.6)	31.8	(2.08)	1.8	(0.12)	7.7	(0.88)
	Trinidad and Tobago	398	(3.5)	389	(3.8)	417	(3.3)	471	(3.0)	33.6	(1.98)	1.2	(0.08)	6.8	(0.75)
	Tunisia	408	(4.3)	389	(3.8)	403	(3.5)	417	(4.0)	4.9	(2.13)	0.9	(0.07)	0.2	(0.21)
	Uruguay	401	(3.3)	409	(3.3)	430	(3.2)	472	(3.6)	30.0	(2.02)	1.4	(0.08)	6.9	(0.89)

Note: Values that are statistically significant are indicated in bold (see Annex A3).
StatLink http://dx.doi.org/10.1787/888932343285

[Part 1/1]
Proportion of students with low levels of enjoyment of reading, by reading proficiency level[1]
Table III.1.2   *Results based on students' self-reports*

| | | Percentage of students with low levels of enjoyment of reading | | | | | | | | |
| | | Level 1a or below | | Level 2 | | Level 3 | | Level 4 | | Level 5 or above | |
		%	S.E.	%	S.E.	%	S.E.	%	S.E.	%	S.E.
OECD	Australia	77.7	(1.1)	64.9	(1.5)	44.7	(1.3)	23.3	(1.0)	12.9	(1.4)
	Austria	71.4	(1.8)	60.0	(1.9)	43.3	(2.3)	23.0	(2.2)	13.9	(3.1)
	Belgium	65.6	(1.9)	65.4	(1.6)	51.2	(1.5)	30.9	(1.4)	15.5	(1.3)
	Canada	78.6	(1.3)	67.0	(1.1)	49.2	(1.0)	30.4	(1.0)	17.6	(1.5)
	Chile	59.7	(1.5)	50.1	(1.3)	37.9	(1.5)	23.9	(1.9)	c	c
	Czech Republic	75.5	(1.4)	60.4	(2.1)	42.9	(1.6)	21.8	(1.8)	10.2	(1.9)
	Denmark	73.6	(1.7)	63.0	(1.8)	41.9	(1.5)	22.5	(2.3)	c	c
	Estonia	79.8	(2.2)	67.7	(2.0)	48.4	(1.6)	27.5	(1.6)	14.2	(2.8)
	Finland	81.9	(2.5)	71.5	(1.8)	51.9	(1.7)	27.3	(1.6)	12.8	(1.8)
	France	71.8	(2.2)	61.0	(2.4)	43.6	(2.4)	25.1	(1.9)	14.3	(2.5)
	Germany	78.0	(1.5)	63.8	(1.6)	46.6	(1.6)	25.9	(2.0)	13.6	(2.3)
	Greece	73.1	(2.1)	58.3	(2.0)	42.9	(1.7)	27.7	(2.2)	15.6	(2.5)
	Hungary	71.3	(3.1)	62.6	(1.8)	46.2	(1.8)	22.5	(1.8)	11.0	(2.1)
	Iceland	75.5	(2.3)	61.2	(2.1)	45.1	(1.5)	27.7	(1.8)	12.5	(2.0)
	Ireland	77.6	(2.0)	67.8	(1.7)	44.2	(2.0)	21.3	(2.2)	c	c
	Israel	57.2	(2.1)	53.3	(2.1)	43.9	(1.9)	30.6	(1.7)	21.6	(2.2)
	Italy	68.5	(1.3)	56.8	(1.1)	40.1	(0.8)	23.4	(1.1)	12.6	(1.8)
	Japan	78.9	(2.1)	64.4	(1.6)	51.0	(1.7)	36.9	(1.5)	26.0	(2.1)
	Korea	84.9	(3.8)	70.2	(2.7)	52.0	(1.9)	33.4	(1.6)	23.4	(2.6)
	Luxembourg	70.2	(1.9)	58.2	(1.7)	40.8	(1.6)	24.8	(1.6)	11.8	(2.1)
	Mexico	53.7	(0.8)	46.7	(0.7)	37.2	(1.0)	23.0	(1.6)	c	c
	Netherlands	70.8	(2.8)	63.4	(2.4)	47.7	(2.0)	30.1	(2.4)	15.2	(2.6)
	New Zealand	77.1	(2.2)	67.6	(1.6)	51.9	(1.8)	29.3	(1.8)	14.7	(1.5)
	Norway	74.1	(1.9)	63.4	(1.8)	46.9	(1.7)	25.4	(1.5)	11.5	(1.9)
	Poland	76.7	(2.1)	69.6	(1.6)	50.7	(1.9)	30.8	(1.8)	15.0	(2.2)
	Portugal	69.8	(2.0)	58.2	(1.8)	43.5	(1.6)	26.1	(2.0)	15.8	(3.1)
	Slovak Republic	70.5	(1.7)	62.9	(1.7)	43.9	(1.9)	26.9	(2.4)	15.4	(3.4)
	Slovenia	70.9	(1.6)	62.0	(2.1)	41.4	(1.8)	24.1	(1.7)	c	c
	Spain	74.1	(1.4)	61.9	(1.6)	42.6	(1.2)	23.5	(1.4)	12.7	(2.2)
	Sweden	75.9	(2.0)	63.4	(1.8)	44.8	(1.8)	24.3	(2.1)	12.8	(2.1)
	Switzerland	74.7	(1.6)	64.8	(1.7)	45.3	(1.7)	25.1	(1.6)	11.7	(2.3)
	Turkey	67.5	(2.1)	56.7	(1.7)	47.2	(2.0)	36.2	(2.6)	c	c
	United Kingdom	76.0	(1.9)	62.8	(1.7)	44.8	(1.4)	24.8	(1.4)	12.5	(2.1)
	United States	71.8	(1.9)	60.7	(1.7)	44.9	(1.8)	27.6	(1.9)	17.7	(2.7)
	OECD average	73.1	(0.4)	62.2	(0.3)	45.4	(0.3)	26.6	(0.3)	14.8	(0.4)
Partners	Albania	59.2	(1.6)	36.3	(1.9)	27.2	(2.7)	19.4	(4.7)	c	c
	Argentina	56.7	(1.5)	53.5	(2.2)	43.5	(3.2)	26.4	(4.4)	c	c
	Azerbaijan	54.6	(1.2)	38.8	(2.0)	32.6	(3.8)	35.6	(19.6)	c	c
	Brazil	58.1	(0.9)	51.2	(1.7)	42.2	(1.8)	32.1	(3.0)	18.6	(3.6)
	Bulgaria	61.4	(1.9)	56.7	(2.2)	38.7	(2.4)	23.5	(3.3)	c	c
	Colombia	56.8	(1.8)	53.9	(1.8)	42.9	(2.3)	31.1	(3.9)	c	c
	Croatia	70.5	(1.7)	57.5	(1.9)	41.9	(1.9)	26.3	(2.3)	c	c
	Dubai (UAE)	68.6	(1.2)	56.5	(1.7)	43.2	(1.6)	26.7	(1.8)	13.7	(2.7)
	Hong Kong-China	79.4	(2.2)	68.1	(2.2)	50.0	(1.8)	35.1	(1.4)	29.8	(2.5)
	Indonesia	49.9	(1.5)	41.7	(1.9)	35.0	(2.6)	28.6	(6.6)	c	c
	Jordan	61.3	(1.3)	45.3	(1.5)	41.9	(2.2)	33.1	(3.8)	c	c
	Kazakhstan	48.8	(1.6)	47.4	(2.4)	48.9	(2.9)	38.0	(5.2)	c	c
	Kyrgyzstan	53.9	(1.2)	47.0	(3.1)	43.8	(4.6)	26.0	(6.9)	c	c
	Latvia	74.7	(2.0)	63.0	(2.1)	43.0	(2.1)	23.5	(2.1)	c	c
	Liechtenstein	76.1	(6.1)	73.0	(4.9)	41.0	(6.2)	31.3	(6.5)	c	c
	Lithuania	72.9	(2.0)	55.0	(1.7)	36.8	(1.5)	21.0	(2.0)	c	c
	Macao-China	69.6	(1.9)	58.6	(1.3)	43.5	(1.2)	28.8	(2.0)	22.4	(4.5)
	Montenegro	59.2	(1.4)	44.2	(2.2)	30.1	(1.9)	13.4	(2.8)	c	c
	Panama	54.6	(1.7)	46.5	(3.1)	44.5	(5.0)	36.3	(7.0)	c	c
	Peru	48.2	(1.2)	44.7	(2.4)	38.9	(2.9)	32.3	(4.5)	c	c
	Qatar	57.5	(0.7)	42.8	(1.5)	37.4	(1.9)	26.9	(2.3)	21.3	(4.2)
	Romania	55.4	(1.7)	47.7	(2.3)	39.6	(2.3)	27.3	(3.4)	c	c
	Russian Federation	68.1	(2.1)	56.3	(1.9)	40.5	(2.0)	24.7	(2.0)	c	c
	Serbia	62.0	(1.5)	48.3	(1.5)	33.7	(1.8)	21.2	(2.8)	c	c
	Shanghai-China	79.5	(3.8)	68.3	(2.4)	50.9	(1.5)	37.2	(1.4)	32.6	(1.7)
	Singapore	80.5	(1.5)	69.2	(1.5)	54.7	(1.4)	36.1	(2.0)	20.0	(2.3)
	Chinese Taipei	84.5	(1.4)	67.6	(1.5)	46.5	(1.4)	26.8	(2.0)	12.8	(2.5)
	Thailand	60.1	(1.3)	44.1	(1.6)	33.1	(2.0)	22.9	(4.2)	c	c
	Trinidad and Tobago	59.4	(1.3)	49.2	(1.8)	41.8	(1.8)	30.5	(2.7)	c	c
	Tunisia	45.1	(1.6)	41.5	(1.7)	42.0	(2.7)	38.7	(6.4)	c	c
	Uruguay	59.7	(1.4)	51.3	(2.2)	38.1	(1.7)	24.5	(3.2)	c	c

1. Students who reported levels of enjoyment of reading below their country average.
StatLink ⟐⟐ http://dx.doi.org/10.1787/888932343285

[Part 1/1]

Percentage of students and reading performance, by time spent reading for enjoyment

Table III.1.3 *Results based on students' self-reports*

	Percentage of students, by time spent on reading for enjoyment										Performance on the reading scale, by time spent on reading for enjoyment									
	I do not read for enjoyment		30 minutes or less a day		More than 30 minutes to less than 60 minutes a day		1 to 2 hours a day		More than 2 hours a day		I do not read for enjoyment		30 minutes or less a day		More than 30 minutes to less than 60 minutes a day		1 to 2 hours a day		More than 2 hours a day	
	%	S.E.	%	S.E.	%	S.E.	%	S.E.	%	S.E.	Mean score	S.E.	Mean score	S.E.	Mean score	S.E.	Mean score	S.E.	Mean score	S.E.
OECD																				
Australia	36.7	(0.6)	30.7	(0.5)	18.0	(0.5)	9.0	(0.3)	5.5	(0.3)	469	(2.2)	524	(2.6)	560	(3.0)	570	(3.5)	563	(4.0)
Austria	50.0	(0.9)	23.7	(0.6)	14.7	(0.7)	7.2	(0.4)	4.3	(0.3)	437	(3.1)	494	(3.5)	517	(5.7)	530	(5.8)	504	(9.8)
Belgium	44.4	(0.8)	26.2	(0.6)	17.2	(0.5)	9.1	(0.4)	3.1	(0.2)	469	(2.7)	532	(2.9)	547	(3.1)	548	(4.2)	523	(8.2)
Canada	31.1	(0.5)	30.5	(0.5)	19.0	(0.4)	13.3	(0.4)	6.0	(0.2)	481	(1.9)	530	(1.8)	555	(2.2)	565	(2.5)	559	(3.7)
Chile	39.7	(0.8)	35.9	(0.7)	15.5	(0.5)	6.4	(0.4)	2.5	(0.2)	437	(3.3)	449	(3.5)	472	(4.1)	478	(6.7)	499	(8.3)
Czech Republic	43.0	(0.8)	27.8	(0.7)	14.5	(0.5)	10.2	(0.5)	4.6	(0.3)	441	(3.2)	489	(3.5)	520	(4.5)	532	(4.0)	522	(6.7)
Denmark	33.6	(0.9)	41.1	(0.8)	15.5	(0.7)	7.4	(0.4)	2.3	(0.2)	464	(2.9)	503	(2.5)	518	(3.0)	537	(3.9)	536	(9.5)
Estonia	38.6	(1.1)	26.4	(0.8)	18.9	(0.7)	10.5	(0.4)	5.7	(0.4)	469	(2.8)	514	(3.4)	525	(3.9)	530	(4.5)	527	(6.1)
Finland	33.0	(0.8)	32.4	(0.7)	18.6	(0.6)	12.7	(0.5)	3.2	(0.3)	492	(2.5)	545	(2.7)	569	(3.3)	572	(4.8)	568	(9.1)
France	38.8	(1.0)	31.1	(0.8)	16.4	(0.7)	9.8	(0.5)	3.9	(0.3)	450	(4.4)	512	(3.8)	538	(4.9)	546	(5.9)	543	(8.8)
Germany	41.3	(0.9)	24.7	(0.8)	16.8	(0.6)	11.3	(0.5)	5.9	(0.4)	457	(3.5)	513	(3.3)	545	(3.5)	548	(4.5)	532	(6.8)
Greece	17.5	(0.8)	24.3	(0.8)	21.5	(0.7)	23.6	(0.7)	13.1	(0.6)	450	(7.5)	480	(6.5)	490	(4.6)	492	(4.1)	507	(4.9)
Hungary	25.5	(0.8)	34.7	(0.8)	22.1	(0.7)	13.6	(0.6)	4.2	(0.3)	453	(4.2)	490	(3.5)	517	(4.3)	533	(4.8)	536	(9.1)
Iceland	38.0	(0.8)	32.5	(0.8)	16.6	(0.5)	9.6	(0.5)	3.3	(0.3)	455	(2.5)	521	(2.6)	544	(3.8)	542	(4.5)	533	(9.4)
Ireland	41.9	(1.0)	26.0	(0.7)	16.3	(0.6)	11.7	(0.6)	4.1	(0.3)	458	(3.5)	505	(3.9)	540	(3.8)	550	(4.5)	549	(8.2)
Israel	34.5	(0.9)	26.5	(0.6)	16.3	(0.5)	15.8	(0.6)	6.9	(0.4)	460	(4.4)	483	(4.1)	498	(4.9)	492	(5.2)	484	(7.8)
Italy	33.9	(0.6)	28.5	(0.4)	18.9	(0.3)	13.7	(0.3)	5.0	(0.2)	449	(2.3)	489	(1.8)	516	(2.7)	521	(2.2)	528	(3.5)
Japan	44.2	(0.9)	25.4	(0.9)	16.4	(0.5)	9.6	(0.4)	4.4	(0.3)	492	(3.9)	536	(4.2)	550	(4.0)	552	(5.1)	537	(7.1)
Korea	38.5	(0.8)	29.8	(0.8)	19.1	(0.6)	8.4	(0.5)	4.2	(0.3)	518	(4.4)	550	(4.0)	558	(3.6)	560	(5.0)	535	(8.8)
Luxembourg	48.2	(0.8)	24.6	(0.7)	13.9	(0.6)	8.8	(0.4)	4.4	(0.3)	437	(1.9)	493	(3.3)	516	(3.7)	524	(4.8)	519	(7.2)
Mexico	23.8	(0.4)	44.4	(0.4)	18.6	(0.3)	10.3	(0.2)	2.9	(0.2)	421	(2.4)	420	(2.0)	444	(2.4)	430	(3.6)	437	(8.4)
Netherlands	48.6	(1.3)	30.8	(0.9)	12.6	(0.6)	6.3	(0.4)	1.8	(0.2)	478	(4.5)	534	(5.9)	552	(5.5)	541	(8.5)	514	(10.6)
New Zealand	31.3	(0.8)	33.1	(0.8)	19.7	(0.7)	10.2	(0.4)	5.6	(0.3)	472	(3.4)	525	(3.9)	558	(3.8)	574	(4.8)	573	(6.9)
Norway	40.0	(0.9)	32.9	(0.8)	16.8	(0.6)	6.9	(0.4)	3.4	(0.3)	465	(3.2)	523	(3.0)	540	(4.6)	542	(5.8)	528	(8.8)
Poland	32.2	(0.8)	30.4	(0.8)	17.6	(0.6)	12.5	(0.6)	7.4	(0.4)	463	(3.2)	498	(2.9)	526	(3.8)	544	(4.6)	549	(5.4)
Portugal	35.2	(0.7)	32.8	(0.6)	19.2	(0.5)	9.7	(0.4)	3.1	(0.2)	459	(3.0)	490	(3.8)	519	(3.6)	530	(4.9)	538	(5.7)
Slovak Republic	40.9	(1.1)	32.1	(0.8)	14.1	(0.6)	8.9	(0.5)	3.9	(0.3)	445	(3.6)	486	(3.1)	514	(4.7)	523	(5.2)	516	(9.3)
Slovenia	39.8	(0.7)	34.5	(0.7)	15.6	(0.5)	8.0	(0.5)	2.2	(0.2)	446	(1.7)	499	(2.4)	526	(3.1)	520	(5.3)	521	(10.8)
Spain	39.6	(0.7)	25.6	(0.5)	19.5	(0.5)	11.3	(0.4)	3.9	(0.2)	453	(2.4)	484	(2.5)	510	(2.5)	515	(3.1)	517	(4.2)
Sweden	37.3	(0.9)	34.0	(0.7)	17.4	(0.6)	8.2	(0.4)	3.1	(0.3)	455	(3.1)	515	(3.8)	539	(4.9)	539	(5.0)	532	(8.2)
Switzerland	44.6	(0.9)	30.1	(0.7)	14.4	(0.6)	8.0	(0.4)	2.9	(0.3)	461	(2.6)	521	(2.8)	548	(4.3)	558	(4.2)	533	(7.6)
Turkey	22.9	(0.7)	27.5	(0.6)	22.2	(0.7)	21.5	(0.7)	6.0	(0.4)	444	(4.1)	468	(3.6)	480	(3.9)	473	(4.5)	472	(7.6)
United Kingdom	39.6	(0.9)	31.5	(0.8)	15.5	(0.6)	9.8	(0.4)	3.6	(0.3)	458	(2.6)	505	(3.2)	531	(4.3)	549	(4.7)	539	(7.5)
United States	42.0	(1.0)	29.3	(0.8)	15.1	(0.5)	8.7	(0.4)	4.9	(0.3)	467	(3.0)	514	(4.8)	532	(6.0)	541	(5.9)	544	(6.6)
OECD average	37.4	(0.1)	30.3	(0.1)	17.2	(0.1)	10.6	(0.1)	4.5	(0.1)	460	(0.6)	504	(0.6)	527	(0.7)	532	(0.8)	527	(1.3)
Partners																				
Albania	7.4	(0.5)	23.4	(0.8)	26.1	(0.8)	30.5	(0.8)	12.6	(0.6)	361	(7.9)	365	(6.2)	393	(4.8)	407	(4.3)	397	(6.3)
Argentina	41.7	(1.0)	29.4	(0.8)	14.8	(0.6)	10.4	(0.4)	3.7	(0.3)	394	(5.5)	398	(5.2)	414	(6.0)	416	(9.0)	418	(10.4)
Azerbaijan	30.4	(1.1)	16.2	(0.7)	15.7	(0.4)	22.4	(0.8)	15.2	(0.8)	354	(3.8)	359	(5.2)	378	(5.4)	367	(4.4)	367	(4.8)
Brazil	21.8	(0.6)	39.5	(0.5)	20.3	(0.5)	12.9	(0.4)	5.5	(0.3)	396	(3.0)	403	(2.5)	428	(3.3)	431	(4.2)	429	(6.3)
Bulgaria	28.0	(1.3)	22.9	(0.9)	21.6	(0.8)	19.3	(0.9)	8.2	(0.5)	397	(7.1)	419	(7.5)	457	(7.0)	455	(7.9)	477	(11.2)
Colombia	29.5	(1.0)	39.1	(1.0)	16.9	(0.8)	10.7	(0.6)	3.7	(0.3)	415	(3.9)	410	(4.1)	431	(5.4)	406	(6.9)	392	(9.9)
Croatia	27.3	(0.9)	37.8	(0.7)	20.1	(0.6)	11.3	(0.6)	3.5	(0.3)	441	(4.0)	476	(3.1)	499	(4.2)	506	(4.6)	513	(8.2)
Dubai (UAE)	24.5	(0.6)	31.0	(0.7)	22.2	(0.6)	14.6	(0.6)	7.7	(0.4)	429	(2.8)	453	(2.6)	484	(3.2)	490	(4.2)	484	(5.6)
Hong Kong-China	19.5	(0.6)	35.9	(0.6)	23.5	(0.6)	13.8	(0.5)	7.3	(0.4)	498	(3.0)	532	(2.8)	554	(3.1)	552	(3.5)	532	(5.3)
Indonesia	12.1	(0.6)	39.0	(0.9)	26.7	(0.8)	15.2	(0.6)	8.0	(0.6)	380	(3.7)	390	(3.2)	414	(4.1)	412	(5.9)	429	(7.8)
Jordan	22.8	(0.7)	33.7	(0.7)	22.4	(0.7)	15.9	(0.7)	5.3	(0.4)	407	(3.8)	417	(3.5)	419	(4.1)	404	(4.3)	389	(6.7)
Kazakhstan	7.2	(0.5)	17.6	(0.8)	34.2	(0.9)	28.8	(0.9)	12.1	(0.8)	392	(7.5)	390	(5.0)	389	(3.6)	389	(3.6)	400	(5.1)
Kyrgyzstan	11.7	(0.6)	22.4	(0.7)	31.0	(0.7)	20.3	(0.6)	14.5	(0.7)	291	(5.9)	307	(3.8)	319	(3.8)	333	(4.5)	335	(5.4)
Latvia	29.7	(0.9)	26.4	(0.8)	21.1	(0.6)	15.8	(0.7)	7.1	(0.6)	454	(3.8)	477	(4.7)	501	(3.6)	515	(4.6)	516	(6.4)
Liechtenstein	52.0	(2.4)	24.8	(2.0)	13.5	(1.9)	c	c	c	c	467	(4.8)	532	(7.0)	541	(11.2)	c	c	c	c
Lithuania	28.1	(0.8)	28.1	(0.6)	19.9	(0.6)	17.1	(0.7)	6.7	(0.4)	433	(3.8)	468	(3.1)	490	(3.8)	495	(3.9)	492	(5.3)
Macao-China	19.8	(0.5)	35.8	(0.6)	23.3	(0.6)	13.1	(0.5)	8.0	(0.4)	457	(2.2)	484	(1.8)	501	(1.8)	506	(3.0)	502	(4.0)
Montenegro	20.8	(0.7)	24.8	(0.6)	22.6	(0.8)	24.0	(0.8)	7.8	(0.8)	383	(2.9)	405	(2.3)	417	(4.6)	428	(2.8)	410	(9.4)
Panama	28.3	(1.3)	38.6	(1.1)	15.4	(0.8)	12.4	(1.0)	5.3	(0.8)	376	(7.2)	371	(6.2)	398	(7.6)	367	(10.5)	405	(22.3)
Peru	13.7	(0.5)	41.1	(0.8)	22.9	(0.6)	16.8	(0.5)	5.5	(0.3)	382	(5.7)	370	(3.8)	381	(4.7)	359	(5.3)	363	(9.9)
Qatar	20.6	(0.5)	38.5	(0.5)	20.1	(0.4)	13.9	(0.4)	6.8	(0.3)	350	(2.9)	364	(1.8)	399	(2.4)	399	(3.2)	386	(5.5)
Romania	24.3	(0.9)	32.0	(0.8)	19.6	(0.7)	18.2	(0.7)	6.0	(0.5)	407	(5.1)	420	(4.7)	441	(4.5)	439	(4.7)	434	(9.1)
Russian Federation	21.4	(0.8)	31.1	(0.9)	27.5	(0.8)	13.2	(0.5)	6.9	(0.4)	427	(4.9)	452	(3.4)	472	(3.4)	489	(4.9)	498	(6.6)
Serbia	23.4	(0.8)	33.4	(0.7)	24.1	(0.6)	15.0	(0.6)	4.0	(0.3)	413	(3.4)	443	(2.9)	458	(3.2)	461	(3.4)	465	(7.5)
Shanghai-China	8.0	(0.4)	35.9	(0.8)	36.5	(0.7)	13.2	(0.5)	6.4	(0.3)	497	(5.5)	560	(2.6)	563	(2.9)	564	(3.7)	548	(4.8)
Singapore	22.5	(0.6)	29.0	(0.6)	23.6	(0.6)	16.1	(0.5)	8.8	(0.5)	483	(3.3)	524	(2.5)	544	(2.8)	548	(3.0)	558	(5.1)
Chinese Taipei	17.3	(0.6)	30.9	(0.7)	21.4	(0.7)	18.8	(0.6)	11.6	(0.4)	437	(4.1)	492	(3.2)	513	(3.4)	522	(3.1)	518	(3.6)
Thailand	9.2	(0.6)	42.5	(0.8)	27.6	(0.8)	15.3	(0.6)	5.5	(0.4)	385	(4.0)	411	(2.7)	430	(3.2)	447	(4.8)	465	(5.4)
Trinidad and Tobago	28.0	(0.7)	27.6	(0.7)	19.9	(0.7)	14.1	(0.5)	10.4	(0.5)	404	(2.8)	402	(3.3)	425	(4.2)	440	(4.9)	473	(5.4)
Tunisia	20.6	(0.8)	27.3	(0.9)	22.0	(0.7)	22.4	(0.7)	7.7	(0.5)	419	(4.4)	408	(3.9)	403	(3.6)	401	(4.3)	394	(5.3)
Uruguay	39.7	(0.8)	30.7	(0.7)	15.5	(0.5)	10.2	(0.4)	3.8	(0.3)	406	(3.0)	428	(3.4)	455	(4.6)	454	(5.0)	463	(7.3)

StatLink ▉▉▉ http://dx.doi.org/10.1787/888932343285

[Part 1/2]
Percentage of students and reading performance, by whether students spend any time reading for enjoyment and gender

Table III.1.4   *Results based on students' self-reports*

| | | Percentage of students, by time spent on reading for enjoyment | | | Percentage of students who read for enjoyment by gender | | | | | | Reading performance, by whether students read for enjoyment | | | |
| | | I do not read for enjoyment | | I read for enjoyment[1] | | Boys | | Girls | | Difference (B-G) | | I do not read for enjoyment | | I read for enjoyment | |
		%	S.E.	%	S.E.	%	S.E.	%	S.E.	%	S.E.	Mean score	S.E.	Mean score	S.E.
OECD	Australia	36.7	(0.6)	63.3	(0.6)	53.0	(0.8)	73.1	(0.8)	-20.1	(1.1)	469	(2.2)	545	(2.5)
	Austria	50.0	(0.9)	50.0	(0.9)	38.5	(1.0)	60.9	(1.2)	-22.4	(1.6)	437	(3.1)	507	(3.5)
	Belgium	44.4	(0.8)	55.6	(0.8)	46.2	(1.0)	65.4	(1.0)	-19.2	(1.4)	469	(2.7)	539	(2.4)
	Canada	31.1	(0.5)	68.9	(0.5)	56.2	(0.8)	81.6	(0.5)	-25.4	(0.8)	481	(1.9)	546	(1.5)
	Chile	39.7	(0.8)	60.3	(0.8)	50.7	(1.0)	70.3	(0.9)	-19.6	(1.3)	437	(3.3)	460	(3.3)
	Czech Republic	43.0	(0.8)	57.0	(0.8)	44.3	(1.0)	71.5	(1.2)	-27.2	(1.5)	441	(3.2)	507	(3.0)
	Denmark	33.6	(0.9)	66.4	(0.9)	57.3	(1.1)	75.3	(1.1)	-18.0	(1.4)	464	(2.9)	512	(2.0)
	Estonia	38.6	(1.1)	61.4	(1.1)	47.1	(1.4)	76.8	(1.2)	-29.8	(1.7)	469	(2.8)	521	(2.7)
	Finland	33.0	(0.8)	67.0	(0.8)	53.3	(1.1)	80.6	(1.0)	-27.3	(1.5)	450	(4.4)	526	(3.3)
	France	38.8	(1.0)	61.2	(1.0)	52.1	(1.3)	69.8	(1.3)	-17.7	(1.7)	457	(3.5)	530	(2.7)
	Germany	41.3	(0.9)	58.7	(0.9)	45.1	(1.1)	72.5	(1.1)	-27.4	(1.3)	450	(7.5)	490	(3.9)
	Greece	17.5	(0.8)	82.5	(0.8)	76.4	(1.1)	88.4	(0.9)	-12.0	(1.3)	453	(4.2)	509	(3.2)
	Hungary	25.5	(0.8)	74.5	(0.8)	65.7	(1.2)	83.5	(0.9)	-17.8	(1.5)	455	(2.5)	531	(1.6)
	Iceland	38.0	(0.8)	62.0	(0.8)	51.5	(1.3)	72.3	(1.0)	-20.8	(1.7)	458	(3.5)	527	(2.9)
	Ireland	41.9	(1.0)	58.1	(1.0)	52.5	(1.4)	63.8	(1.3)	-11.3	(1.8)	460	(4.4)	489	(3.3)
	Israel	34.5	(0.9)	65.5	(0.9)	55.2	(1.5)	75.1	(1.0)	-19.9	(1.7)	449	(2.3)	506	(1.6)
	Italy	33.9	(0.6)	66.1	(0.6)	53.9	(0.8)	79.0	(0.6)	-25.1	(1.1)	492	(3.9)	543	(3.5)
	Japan	44.2	(0.9)	55.8	(0.9)	53.6	(1.1)	58.2	(1.3)	-4.6	(1.5)	518	(4.4)	553	(3.4)
	Korea	38.5	(0.8)	61.5	(0.8)	60.5	(1.0)	62.6	(1.4)	-2.2	(1.8)	437	(1.9)	507	(2.1)
	Luxembourg	48.2	(0.8)	51.8	(0.8)	39.6	(1.1)	64.2	(1.0)	-24.6	(1.5)	421	(2.4)	428	(2.1)
	Mexico	23.8	(0.4)	76.2	(0.4)	69.5	(0.7)	82.8	(0.4)	-13.3	(0.7)	478	(4.5)	539	(5.4)
	Netherlands	48.6	(1.3)	51.4	(1.3)	35.8	(1.5)	66.8	(1.4)	-31.1	(1.5)	472	(3.4)	546	(2.7)
	New Zealand	31.3	(0.8)	68.7	(0.8)	59.4	(1.1)	78.3	(1.0)	-18.9	(1.4)	465	(3.2)	530	(2.7)
	Norway	40.0	(0.9)	60.0	(0.9)	50.4	(1.1)	70.0	(1.1)	-19.6	(1.5)	463	(3.2)	519	(2.6)
	Poland	32.2	(0.8)	67.8	(0.8)	53.1	(1.3)	82.5	(0.9)	-29.4	(1.4)	459	(3.0)	507	(3.2)
	Portugal	35.2	(0.7)	64.8	(0.7)	50.2	(1.0)	78.7	(0.8)	-28.4	(1.3)	445	(3.6)	500	(2.7)
	Slovak Republic	40.9	(1.1)	59.1	(1.1)	47.3	(1.5)	70.5	(1.1)	-23.2	(1.8)	446	(1.7)	509	(1.5)
	Slovenia	39.8	(0.7)	60.2	(0.7)	46.1	(1.2)	74.9	(0.8)	-28.8	(1.5)	453	(2.4)	500	(2.0)
	Spain	39.6	(0.7)	60.4	(0.7)	51.0	(0.9)	70.0	(0.8)	-19.0	(1.2)	455	(3.1)	525	(3.1)
	Sweden	37.3	(0.9)	62.7	(0.9)	50.7	(1.1)	75.0	(1.0)	-24.3	(1.3)	455	(3.1)	534	(2.7)
	Switzerland	44.6	(0.9)	55.4	(0.9)	43.6	(1.1)	67.6	(1.0)	-24.0	(1.3)	461	(2.6)	473	(3.4)
	Turkey	22.9	(0.7)	77.1	(0.7)	68.4	(1.0)	86.5	(1.0)	-18.1	(1.5)	444	(4.1)	521	(2.6)
	United Kingdom	39.6	(0.9)	60.4	(0.9)	50.7	(1.0)	69.7	(1.1)	-19.0	(1.4)	458	(2.6)	525	(4.4)
	United States	42.0	(1.0)	58.0	(1.0)	47.4	(1.2)	69.2	(1.3)	-21.8	(1.4)	467	(3.0)	525	(4.4)
	OECD average	37.4	(0.1)	62.6	(0.1)	52.2	(0.2)	73.1	(0.2)	-20.9	(0.2)	460	(0.6)	517	(0.5)
Partners	Albania	7.4	(0.5)	92.6	(0.5)	88.0	(0.8)	97.4	(0.4)	-9.3	(0.9)	361	(7.9)	391	(3.9)
	Argentina	41.7	(1.0)	58.3	(1.0)	49.4	(1.2)	65.8	(1.3)	-16.4	(1.7)	394	(5.5)	407	(4.8)
	Azerbaijan	30.4	(1.1)	69.6	(1.1)	67.1	(1.4)	72.1	(1.2)	-5.0	(1.5)	354	(3.8)	368	(3.6)
	Brazil	21.8	(0.6)	78.2	(0.6)	68.7	(1.0)	86.6	(0.5)	-17.9	(1.0)	396	(3.0)	416	(2.5)
	Bulgaria	28.0	(1.3)	72.0	(1.3)	61.9	(1.6)	82.7	(1.1)	-20.8	(1.6)	397	(7.1)	447	(6.8)
	Colombia	29.5	(1.0)	70.5	(1.0)	64.0	(1.4)	76.5	(1.0)	-12.5	(1.4)	415	(3.9)	414	(4.2)
	Croatia	27.3	(0.9)	72.7	(0.9)	62.1	(1.2)	84.7	(0.8)	-22.6	(1.5)	441	(4.0)	489	(2.8)
	Dubai (UAE)	24.5	(0.6)	75.5	(0.6)	69.5	(0.8)	81.7	(0.9)	-12.2	(1.2)	429	(2.8)	472	(1.5)
	Hong Kong-China	19.5	(0.6)	80.5	(0.6)	76.5	(0.8)	84.9	(0.9)	-8.4	(1.2)	498	(3.0)	542	(2.2)
	Indonesia	12.1	(0.6)	87.9	(0.6)	83.4	(0.9)	92.2	(0.6)	-8.8	(1.1)	380	(3.7)	405	(3.9)
	Jordan	22.8	(0.7)	77.2	(0.7)	73.1	(1.1)	81.3	(0.9)	-8.3	(1.4)	407	(3.8)	413	(3.1)
	Kazakhstan	7.2	(0.5)	92.8	(0.5)	90.6	(0.7)	95.0	(0.5)	-4.4	(0.8)	392	(7.5)	391	(3.0)
	Kyrgyzstan	11.7	(0.6)	88.3	(0.6)	84.0	(1.0)	92.3	(0.7)	-8.3	(1.1)	291	(5.9)	322	(3.1)
	Latvia	29.7	(0.9)	70.3	(0.9)	55.1	(1.5)	85.2	(0.9)	-30.1	(1.7)	454	(3.8)	497	(3.2)
	Liechtenstein	52.0	(2.4)	48.0	(2.4)	38.8	(3.4)	58.4	(3.7)	-19.6	(5.2)	467	(4.8)	534	(4.9)
	Lithuania	28.1	(0.8)	71.9	(0.8)	56.0	(1.1)	88.2	(0.7)	-32.2	(1.2)	433	(3.8)	483	(2.4)
	Macao-China	19.8	(0.5)	80.2	(0.5)	74.9	(0.7)	85.6	(0.6)	-10.7	(0.9)	457	(2.2)	495	(1.0)
	Montenegro	20.8	(0.7)	79.2	(0.7)	71.5	(1.2)	87.3	(0.7)	-15.8	(1.4)	383	(2.9)	416	(2.3)
	Panama	28.3	(1.3)	71.7	(1.3)	66.0	(1.9)	77.3	(1.6)	-11.3	(2.4)	376	(7.2)	379	(6.8)
	Peru	13.7	(0.5)	86.3	(0.5)	83.5	(0.8)	89.1	(0.6)	-5.5	(1.0)	382	(5.7)	370	(3.8)
	Qatar	20.6	(0.5)	79.4	(0.5)	73.8	(0.7)	84.9	(0.6)	-11.1	(0.9)	350	(2.9)	381	(1.1)
	Romania	24.3	(0.9)	75.7	(0.9)	66.4	(1.3)	84.6	(1.0)	-18.2	(1.4)	407	(5.1)	431	(4.2)
	Russian Federation	21.4	(0.8)	78.6	(0.8)	70.6	(1.2)	86.6	(0.9)	-16.0	(1.4)	427	(4.9)	469	(3.1)
	Serbia	23.4	(0.8)	76.6	(0.8)	66.0	(1.2)	87.3	(0.8)	-21.3	(1.3)	413	(3.4)	452	(2.3)
	Shanghai-China	8.0	(0.4)	92.0	(0.4)	89.0	(0.6)	95.0	(0.4)	-6.1	(0.6)	497	(5.5)	561	(2.3)
	Singapore	22.5	(0.6)	77.5	(0.6)	69.2	(0.9)	86.1	(0.7)	-16.9	(1.1)	483	(3.3)	539	(1.2)
	Chinese Taipei	17.3	(0.6)	82.7	(0.6)	77.5	(0.9)	88.0	(0.7)	-10.5	(1.1)	437	(4.1)	508	(2.5)
	Thailand	9.2	(0.5)	90.8	(0.5)	85.1	(0.9)	95.1	(0.4)	-9.9	(1.0)	385	(4.0)	426	(2.7)
	Trinidad and Tobago	28.0	(0.7)	72.0	(0.7)	62.9	(1.2)	80.8	(0.9)	-17.8	(1.5)	404	(2.8)	426	(1.9)
	Tunisia	20.6	(0.8)	79.4	(0.8)	72.9	(1.2)	85.1	(0.9)	-12.3	(1.4)	419	(4.4)	403	(2.8)
	Uruguay	39.7	(0.8)	60.3	(0.8)	46.9	(1.2)	72.1	(0.9)	-25.2	(1.5)	406	(3.0)	442	(2.8)

Note: Values that are statistically significant are indicated in bold (see Annex A3).
1. The "I read for enjoyment" category groups students who: read "30 minutes or less per day", students who read "between 30 minutes and 60 minutes", students who read "between 1 hour and 2 hours" and students who read "more than 2 hours daily".
StatLink ᴴᴵᴾ⌐ http://dx.doi.org/10.1787/888932343285

[Part 2/2]

Percentage of students and reading performance, by whether students spend any time reading for enjoyment and gender

Table III.1.4 *Results based on students' self-reports*

	Reading performance of boys, by whether they read for enjoyment				Reading performance of girls, by whether they read for enjoyment				Difference between boys and girls, by whether they read for enjoyment			
	I do not read for enjoyment		I read for enjoyment[1]		I do not read for enjoyment		I read for enjoyment		I do not read for enjoyment (B-G)		I read for enjoyment (B-G)	
	Mean score	S.E.	Mean score	S.E.	Mean score	S.E.	Mean score	S.E.	Score dif.	S.E.	Score dif.	S.E.
OECD												
Australia	460	(2.9)	**533**	(3.5)	484	(3.1)	**552**	(2.6)	**-25**	(3.9)	**-19**	(3.6)
Austria	429	(4.2)	**486**	(4.9)	449	(4.3)	**519**	(4.5)	**-20**	(6.1)	**-33**	(6.5)
Belgium	465	(3.6)	**531**	(3.8)	476	(3.7)	**545**	(2.7)	**-11**	(5.0)	**-14**	(4.3)
Canada	476	(2.2)	**535**	(2.1)	493	(3.0)	**554**	(1.7)	**-17**	(3.3)	**-19**	(2.2)
Chile	434	(3.8)	**446**	(4.6)	442	(4.2)	**470**	(3.7)	-8	(4.6)	**-24**	(5.0)
Czech Republic	433	(3.7)	**485**	(4.5)	459	(4.5)	**523**	(2.9)	**-26**	(5.5)	**-38**	(4.4)
Denmark	455	(3.6)	**501**	(2.8)	481	(4.1)	**520**	(2.6)	**-26**	(5.1)	**-19**	(3.6)
Estonia	462	(3.0)	**500**	(3.7)	486	(4.2)	**536**	(2.9)	**-24**	(4.3)	**-36**	(3.7)
Finland	479	(3.0)	**534**	(3.3)	522	(4.3)	**574**	(2.3)	**-43**	(5.2)	**-40**	(3.1)
France	439	(5.1)	**511**	(4.5)	467	(5.5)	**537**	(3.5)	**-28**	(6.1)	**-26**	(4.5)
Germany	452	(4.2)	**516**	(4.0)	467	(4.4)	**540**	(3.0)	**-15**	(5.1)	**-24**	(4.5)
Greece	437	(8.6)	**466**	(5.0)	475	(7.2)	**510**	(3.5)	**-38**	(7.5)	**-44**	(4.3)
Hungary	444	(4.9)	**492**	(4.1)	471	(5.3)	**522**	(3.8)	**-28**	(5.9)	**-29**	(4.5)
Iceland	440	(2.8)	**517**	(3.2)	481	(4.1)	**541**	(2.0)	**-41**	(4.7)	**-24**	(4.1)
Ireland	445	(5.1)	**509**	(4.3)	475	(3.5)	**543**	(3.2)	**-30**	(5.8)	**-34**	(5.0)
Israel	450	(5.2)	**467**	(5.2)	475	(5.2)	**504**	(3.7)	**-25**	(5.9)	**-37**	(5.7)
Italy	440	(2.7)	**487**	(2.3)	470	(3.6)	**520**	(1.9)	**-30**	(4.3)	**-34**	(2.7)
Japan	476	(5.9)	**524**	(5.3)	512	(3.9)	**562**	(4.8)	**-36**	(7.0)	**-38**	(7.4)
Korea	499	(6.1)	**538**	(4.8)	540	(5.3)	**569**	(3.8)	**-40**	(7.7)	**-31**	(5.8)
Luxembourg	429	(2.5)	**493**	(3.7)	451	(2.7)	**516**	(2.1)	**-22**	(3.6)	**-23**	(3.9)
Mexico	413	(2.9)	414	(2.3)	434	(2.8)	439	(2.2)	**-20**	(3.2)	**-25**	(1.8)
Netherlands	474	(4.7)	**538**	(5.8)	485	(5.2)	**539**	(5.7)	**-11**	(3.8)	-1	(3.7)
New Zealand	460	(4.1)	**529**	(4.1)	496	(4.3)	**558**	(3.0)	**-36**	(5.5)	**-29**	(4.6)
Norway	451	(3.6)	**510**	(3.4)	487	(3.7)	**545**	(3.1)	**-36**	(3.7)	**-35**	(3.5)
Poland	451	(3.4)	**499**	(3.4)	494	(4.7)	**532**	(2.8)	**-42**	(4.6)	**-33**	(3.3)
Portugal	451	(3.4)	**490**	(4.1)	476	(3.8)	**517**	(3.1)	**-25**	(4.1)	**-27**	(3.0)
Slovak Republic	432	(4.4)	**475**	(3.5)	470	(4.3)	**517**	(3.3)	**-38**	(5.1)	**-41**	(3.8)
Slovenia	433	(2.2)	**486**	(2.5)	474	(3.5)	**524**	(1.7)	**-41**	(4.3)	**-38**	(3.0)
Spain	446	(2.6)	**489**	(2.6)	466	(3.1)	**509**	(2.2)	**-20**	(3.1)	**-20**	(2.7)
Sweden	445	(3.8)	**508**	(3.7)	476	(4.0)	**537**	(3.4)	**-31**	(4.7)	**-29**	(3.5)
Switzerland	452	(3.3)	**522**	(3.4)	476	(3.5)	**542**	(2.7)	**-24**	(4.4)	**-20**	(2.7)
Turkey	438	(4.5)	**449**	(3.8)	460	(6.6)	**493**	(3.9)	**-22**	(6.9)	**-44**	(3.6)
United Kingdom	452	(3.4)	**514**	(4.2)	467	(3.0)	**526**	(3.5)	**-15**	(4.0)	**-12**	(5.7)
United States	462	(3.9)	**517**	(5.2)	474	(4.1)	**530**	(4.5)	**-12**	(5.4)	**-13**	(3.9)
OECD average	450	(0.7)	**500**	(0.7)	477	(0.7)	**528**	(0.6)	**-27**	(0.9)	**-28**	(0.7)
Partners												
Albania	356	(7.8)	361	(5.1)	388	(20.9)	419	(3.9)	-32	(21.0)	**-59**	(4.4)
Argentina	380	(6.0)	387	(5.8)	413	(6.2)	419	(5.1)	**-34**	(5.5)	**-32**	(5.0)
Azerbaijan	345	(4.4)	355	(4.3)	366	(4.3)	**379**	(3.6)	**-21**	(4.4)	**-24**	(3.3)
Brazil	393	(3.6)	399	(3.1)	402	(4.6)	428	(2.5)	-10	(5.3)	**-29**	(2.1)
Bulgaria	389	(7.5)	**415**	(8.1)	416	(9.5)	**472**	(5.9)	**-27**	(9.3)	**-58**	(5.7)
Colombia	415	(5.3)	406	(4.9)	415	(4.3)	420	(4.6)	-1	(6.1)	**-14**	(4.1)
Croatia	432	(4.6)	**465**	(3.4)	468	(5.2)	**509**	(3.8)	**-37**	(6.7)	**-44**	(4.6)
Dubai (UAE)	414	(3.8)	**448**	(2.2)	455	(4.2)	**493**	(1.8)	**-41**	(5.8)	**-45**	(2.8)
Hong Kong-China	489	(4.4)	**527**	(3.4)	514	(5.2)	**557**	(2.9)	**-25**	(7.7)	**-30**	(4.3)
Indonesia	372	(4.2)	386	(4.0)	397	(5.4)	422	(4.0)	**-25**	(6.3)	**-36**	(3.4)
Jordan	387	(5.4)	**386**	(4.2)	435	(6.4)	437	(4.0)	**-49**	(8.9)	**-51**	(5.6)
Kazakhstan	386	(7.8)	368	(3.2)	403	(11.5)	413	(3.4)	-17	(11.4)	**-44**	(2.9)
Kyrgyzstan	283	(7.1)	294	(3.8)	308	(8.1)	**344**	(3.2)	**-25**	(9.5)	**-50**	(3.1)
Latvia	446	(4.4)	**471**	(4.5)	476	(5.5)	**513**	(3.2)	**-30**	(6.5)	**-42**	(4.2)
Liechtenstein	457	(6.5)	**527**	(8.0)	484	(8.7)	**540**	(7.1)	**-26**	(11.8)	-12	(11.5)
Lithuania	425	(3.9)	**452**	(3.2)	462	(6.5)	**503**	(2.6)	**-37**	(6.0)	**-51**	(3.3)
Macao-China	448	(2.6)	**478**	(1.5)	473	(3.7)	**509**	(1.3)	**-26**	(4.4)	**-32**	(1.9)
Montenegro	370	(3.5)	**389**	(2.8)	412	(5.1)	**439**	(2.4)	**-42**	(6.3)	**-50**	(2.9)
Panama	359	(8.2)	363	(7.1)	399	(10.4)	392	(7.9)	**-40**	(12.3)	**-29**	(7.1)
Peru	382	(6.1)	357	(4.1)	383	(8.6)	383	(4.8)	-1	(8.9)	**-26**	(4.9)
Qatar	334	(3.4)	**357**	(1.9)	377	(4.2)	**401**	(1.2)	**-43**	(5.0)	**-44**	(2.3)
Romania	399	(5.4)	406	(4.8)	425	(7.2)	450	(4.3)	**-26**	(7.2)	**-43**	(4.6)
Russian Federation	415	(5.0)	**447**	(3.6)	452	(6.5)	**487**	(3.3)	**-37**	(5.7)	**-40**	(3.0)
Serbia	406	(3.8)	**433**	(3.4)	433	(4.7)	**467**	(2.5)	**-26**	(5.2)	**-34**	(3.5)
Shanghai-China	482	(5.9)	**543**	(2.9)	532	(8.4)	**578**	(2.3)	**-50**	(9.0)	**-35**	(2.9)
Singapore	475	(3.9)	**527**	(2.0)	500	(4.3)	**549**	(1.7)	**-24**	(5.1)	**-21**	(2.7)
Chinese Taipei	425	(4.9)	**493**	(3.6)	460	(5.8)	**522**	(3.8)	**-35**	(7.5)	**-28**	(5.5)
Thailand	376	(4.6)	**406**	(3.4)	405	(5.9)	**440**	(3.1)	**-29**	(6.8)	**-34**	(3.8)
Trinidad and Tobago	385	(3.7)	395	(3.4)	439	(4.9)	450	(1.8)	**-54**	(6.6)	**-55**	(3.8)
Tunisia	409	(5.1)	**385**	(3.2)	436	(5.2)	417	(3.0)	**-27**	(5.5)	**-32**	(2.8)
Uruguay	392	(3.4)	**421**	(4.2)	428	(4.1)	**453**	(2.9)	**-36**	(4.3)	**-32**	(4.2)

Note: Values that are statistically significant are indicated in bold (see Annex A3).
1. The "I read for enjoyment" category groups students who: read "30 minutes or less per day", students who read "between 30 minutes and 60 minutes", students who read "between 1 hour and 2 hours" and students who read "more than 2 hours daily".
StatLink ⟪ᵐˢ⟫ http://dx.doi.org/10.1787/888932343285

[Part 1/2]

Percentage of students and reading performance, by whether students spend any time reading for enjoyment and socio-economic background

Table III.1.5   *Results based on students' self-reports*

| | | Percentage of students who spend time reading for enjoyment. by quarter of ESCS[1] | | | | | | | | Performance on the reading scale of students who do not read for enjoyment. by quarter of ESCS | | | | | | | |
| | | Bottom quarter | | Second quarter | | Third quarter | | Top quarter | | Bottom quarter | | Second quarter | | Third quarter | | Top quarter | |
		%	S.E.	%	S.E.	%	S.E.	%	S.E.	Mean score	S.E.	Mean score	S.E.	Mean score	S.E.	Mean score	S.E.
OECD	Australia	52.5	(1.1)	59.7	(1.0)	66.6	(1.0)	75.1	(0.9)	441	(3.1)	468	(2.9)	487	(3.5)	509	(3.8)
	Austria	41.9	(1.9)	46.2	(1.4)	49.8	(1.9)	62.3	(1.8)	403	(4.2)	431	(4.6)	447	(5.0)	485	(4.7)
	Belgium	44.3	(1.3)	50.9	(1.5)	59.4	(1.3)	68.4	(1.0)	435	(3.3)	462	(3.9)	486	(3.5)	527	(3.4)
	Canada	61.0	(1.0)	66.0	(0.8)	70.4	(0.9)	78.3	(0.8)	463	(2.9)	476	(3.3)	493	(3.1)	508	(3.5)
	Chile	61.9	(1.4)	57.4	(1.5)	59.7	(1.3)	62.3	(1.4)	403	(5.0)	422	(4.6)	440	(4.2)	482	(4.7)
	Czech Republic	48.6	(1.7)	55.6	(1.5)	56.8	(1.4)	67.4	(1.4)	414	(3.8)	436	(4.3)	455	(4.7)	475	(4.9)
	Denmark	59.2	(1.5)	61.5	(1.7)	68.0	(1.8)	77.1	(1.3)	436	(4.1)	460	(5.0)	480	(4.1)	506	(5.1)
	Estonia	51.3	(2.2)	59.2	(1.8)	63.3	(1.8)	71.8	(1.5)	453	(4.9)	463	(4.5)	475	(4.5)	499	(4.4)
	Finland	59.0	(1.6)	67.0	(1.3)	67.1	(1.3)	75.1	(1.4)	472	(4.4)	485	(4.7)	506	(3.9)	516	(5.6)
	France	48.3	(1.9)	59.7	(1.8)	63.5	(1.7)	74.0	(1.6)	413	(5.4)	449	(7.6)	471	(6.8)	508	(7.8)
	Germany	44.4	(1.7)	57.0	(1.4)	61.3	(1.6)	73.2	(1.4)	422	(4.4)	462	(4.6)	477	(4.6)	501	(6.3)
	Greece	79.2	(1.8)	81.7	(1.3)	82.9	(1.0)	86.3	(1.2)	417	(10.6)	450	(8.5)	459	(7.8)	489	(8.3)
	Hungary	67.6	(1.9)	70.8	(1.5)	75.1	(1.5)	84.3	(1.2)	414	(6.5)	454	(5.5)	471	(5.6)	501	(8.0)
	Iceland	57.4	(1.7)	57.5	(1.7)	63.3	(1.7)	69.9	(1.5)	431	(4.9)	458	(4.8)	463	(4.1)	477	(4.6)
	Ireland	43.7	(2.1)	51.8	(1.7)	62.8	(1.6)	74.0	(1.4)	431	(4.7)	456	(5.1)	473	(5.2)	498	(4.7)
	Israel	64.8	(1.7)	62.5	(1.4)	66.8	(1.6)	68.2	(1.4)	415	(6.9)	451	(5.2)	481	(5.4)	506	(5.7)
	Italy	58.2	(1.0)	64.4	(0.9)	67.9	(0.8)	74.1	(0.8)	417	(3.8)	447	(2.9)	464	(3.2)	483	(3.2)
	Japan	48.6	(1.4)	52.2	(1.7)	58.1	(1.4)	64.9	(1.6)	466	(4.9)	484	(6.3)	514	(4.6)	525	(5.1)
	Korea	51.6	(1.6)	59.2	(1.4)	62.3	(1.7)	73.0	(1.2)	490	(6.9)	518	(4.2)	530	(6.2)	550	(5.4)
	Luxembourg	41.1	(1.5)	47.5	(1.7)	54.0	(1.3)	64.6	(1.6)	396	(3.6)	434	(4.0)	464	(3.8)	481	(4.9)
	Mexico	83.3	(0.6)	75.6	(0.7)	73.8	(0.8)	72.3	(0.9)	381	(3.9)	404	(2.6)	427	(2.8)	454	(3.6)
	Netherlands	44.3	(2.2)	46.9	(2.3)	51.6	(1.5)	63.1	(1.8)	456	(4.6)	465	(4.9)	494	(5.2)	513	(6.6)
	New Zealand	59.9	(1.7)	65.5	(1.5)	71.8	(1.5)	78.7	(1.3)	440	(5.7)	477	(4.6)	485	(6.4)	522	(6.0)
	Norway	54.0	(1.6)	56.4	(1.4)	60.8	(1.5)	68.9	(1.7)	439	(4.4)	460	(4.5)	480	(4.2)	490	(5.3)
	Poland	63.2	(1.3)	63.8	(1.5)	67.2	(1.5)	77.5	(1.4)	430	(4.8)	460	(4.3)	474	(4.7)	507	(6.2)
	Portugal	61.1	(1.5)	61.1	(1.5)	65.9	(1.3)	71.1	(1.5)	429	(5.0)	446	(4.3)	472	(4.4)	502	(4.5)
	Slovak Republic	51.2	(2.2)	56.9	(2.0)	61.1	(1.7)	67.5	(1.3)	415	(5.2)	441	(5.1)	460	(4.5)	481	(4.3)
	Slovenia	54.6	(1.4)	55.0	(1.6)	61.3	(1.5)	70.2	(1.4)	419	(4.0)	438	(3.2)	458	(3.9)	484	(5.0)
	Spain	51.9	(1.6)	58.0	(1.3)	62.9	(1.0)	68.8	(1.1)	424	(3.3)	446	(2.9)	466	(3.0)	495	(4.7)
	Sweden	55.5	(1.8)	59.3	(1.6)	65.2	(1.5)	71.2	(1.4)	424	(5.1)	451	(4.6)	476	(4.9)	489	(5.2)
	Switzerland	46.7	(2.0)	49.7	(1.3)	57.2	(1.2)	68.8	(1.5)	429	(3.4)	466	(3.9)	470	(4.2)	498	(4.8)
	Turkey	75.9	(1.4)	73.4	(1.5)	77.8	(1.3)	81.6	(1.1)	412	(6.5)	438	(5.7)	450	(6.3)	488	(6.0)
	United Kingdom	53.1	(1.8)	56.1	(1.6)	61.8	(1.5)	71.7	(1.3)	432	(3.6)	452	(3.8)	476	(4.2)	498	(5.0)
	United States	51.0	(1.7)	53.9	(1.4)	57.8	(2.0)	69.4	(1.5)	431	(4.0)	456	(3.9)	485	(4.5)	516	(5.6)
	OECD average	55.6	(0.3)	59.4	(0.3)	64.0	(0.2)	71.9	(0.2)	429	(0.9)	455	(0.8)	474	(0.8)	499	(0.9)
Partners	Albania	92.0	(1.3)	92.7	(0.9)	92.7	(1.0)	93.1	(0.8)	312	(14.8)	348	(10.7)	373	(13.4)	423	(13.3)
	Argentina	62.4	(1.6)	55.9	(2.0)	56.9	(1.7)	57.9	(1.7)	347	(5.9)	380	(7.5)	396	(5.7)	451	(8.4)
	Azerbaijan	64.3	(2.2)	68.3	(1.7)	71.1	(1.7)	74.3	(1.5)	342	(6.3)	350	(5.1)	354	(5.4)	378	(6.5)
	Brazil	80.3	(1.1)	79.6	(0.9)	75.3	(1.2)	77.9	(1.1)	358	(5.7)	387	(3.7)	401	(5.2)	433	(5.9)
	Bulgaria	65.1	(2.4)	72.4	(1.8)	72.3	(1.6)	78.7	(1.6)	349	(6.8)	396	(8.6)	415	(10.7)	460	(8.9)
	Colombia	73.9	(1.6)	69.0	(1.5)	68.9	(1.6)	70.3	(1.6)	377	(5.7)	398	(4.2)	428	(5.8)	452	(6.1)
	Croatia	68.5	(1.5)	69.1	(1.7)	74.9	(1.4)	78.6	(1.1)	417	(4.5)	435	(5.9)	450	(6.1)	477	(5.5)
	Dubai (UAE)	69.8	(1.2)	76.0	(1.2)	78.5	(1.0)	77.8	(1.3)	390	(5.0)	425	(5.0)	449	(6.7)	467	(5.9)
	Hong Kong-China	74.3	(1.3)	79.7	(1.2)	82.9	(1.0)	85.2	(1.2)	478	(5.4)	500	(5.9)	510	(5.9)	516	(6.8)
	Indonesia	85.1	(1.2)	86.3	(1.3)	88.4	(1.1)	91.5	(0.8)	376	(6.6)	371	(5.8)	382	(6.3)	402	(7.4)
	Jordan	75.7	(1.5)	79.3	(1.2)	79.2	(1.3)	74.7	(1.4)	364	(5.6)	406	(5.5)	413	(6.0)	443	(9.1)
	Kazakhstan	91.9	(0.9)	93.1	(0.8)	93.1	(0.7)	93.0	(0.9)	347	(9.7)	390	(11.3)	402	(12.4)	435	(12.0)
	Kyrgyzstan	84.3	(1.5)	89.1	(1.1)	89.9	(0.9)	90.2	(0.7)	258	(8.1)	282	(9.1)	295	(10.4)	353	(9.7)
	Latvia	64.2	(1.7)	65.3	(2.1)	72.9	(1.6)	78.8	(1.4)	432	(7.1)	446	(5.2)	472	(4.5)	482	(5.7)
	Liechtenstein	40.4	(5.2)	46.7	(4.9)	45.8	(5.7)	58.7	(5.3)	441	(10.8)	472	(8.9)	469	(11.6)	499	(14.4)
	Lithuania	67.5	(1.5)	71.1	(1.4)	71.4	(1.4)	78.3	(1.1)	408	(5.9)	427	(6.9)	438	(5.1)	473	(5.9)
	Macao-China	73.2	(1.1)	81.1	(1.1)	81.5	(0.9)	85.0	(1.0)	457	(3.7)	450	(4.7)	464	(4.5)	457	(5.2)
	Montenegro	80.4	(1.4)	77.6	(1.5)	78.0	(1.2)	80.9	(1.3)	354	(5.5)	379	(6.4)	384	(6.4)	417	(5.9)
	Panama	76.8	(1.8)	75.9	(2.2)	69.4	(2.1)	65.0	(2.4)	327	(10.5)	353	(6.3)	375	(10.2)	427	(11.9)
	Peru	90.0	(0.9)	88.3	(0.9)	83.9	(1.0)	83.1	(1.1)	298	(8.7)	362	(6.6)	393	(6.0)	436	(8.0)
	Qatar	79.2	(0.9)	79.6	(0.9)	78.7	(0.9)	80.3	(0.9)	312	(4.0)	344	(5.7)	373	(6.3)	372	(5.5)
	Romania	74.8	(1.4)	76.6	(1.3)	76.4	(1.6)	75.3	(1.4)	364	(8.7)	406	(6.6)	420	(7.3)	441	(6.7)
	Russian Federation	76.1	(1.4)	76.1	(1.2)	79.2	(1.3)	83.2	(1.0)	399	(6.9)	423	(5.6)	438	(7.1)	459	(5.5)
	Serbia	72.2	(1.5)	77.6	(1.2)	77.2	(1.3)	79.7	(1.1)	391	(5.6)	399	(4.8)	419	(5.2)	455	(5.2)
	Shanghai-China	87.8	(1.0)	91.2	(0.9)	93.2	(0.7)	95.9	(0.6)	476	(9.0)	499	(10.2)	508	(12.0)	539	(12.5)
	Singapore	68.2	(1.2)	75.9	(1.1)	79.9	(1.1)	86.2	(1.1)	453	(4.9)	480	(5.1)	507	(5.8)	521	(7.6)
	Chinese Taipei	74.3	(1.3)	80.0	(1.1)	86.3	(1.0)	90.7	(0.9)	414	(5.5)	437	(6.4)	461	(6.7)	470	(7.7)
	Thailand	90.3	(1.0)	89.7	(0.9)	90.7	(1.1)	92.7	(0.9)	372	(6.7)	373	(6.3)	389	(7.0)	417	(9.5)
	Trinidad and Tobago	72.2	(1.5)	72.1	(1.4)	73.4	(1.5)	70.9	(1.4)	357	(6.7)	394	(6.1)	410	(7.2)	461	(5.6)
	Tunisia	82.4	(1.4)	81.9	(1.2)	80.1	(1.3)	73.0	(1.3)	385	(6.2)	408	(6.6)	413	(7.1)	452	(6.2)
	Uruguay	58.4	(1.5)	58.7	(1.6)	59.8	(1.6)	64.9	(1.6)	361	(4.4)	392	(4.8)	414	(4.8)	469	(6.2)

Notes: Values that are statistically significant are indicated in bold (see Annex A3).
1. The "I read for enjoyment" category groups students who: read "30 minutes or less per day", students who read "between 30 minutes and 60 minutes", students who read "between 1 hour and 2 hours" and students who read "more than 2 hours daily".
StatLink ⫘⫘⫘ http://dx.doi.org/10.1787/888932343285

[Part 2/2]

Percentage of students and reading performance, by whether students spend any time reading for enjoyment and socio-economic background

Table III.1.5 *Results based on students' self-reports*

	Performance on the reading scale of students who spend time reading for enjoyment. by quarter of ESCS								Difference in reading performance that is associated with reading for enjoyment. by quarter of ESCS							
	Bottom quarter		Second quarter		Third quarter		Top quarter		Bottom quarter		Second quarter		Third quarter		Top quarter	
	Mean score	S.E.	Mean score	S.E.	Mean score	S.E.	Mean score	S.E.	Score dif.	S.E.	Score dif.	S.E.	Score dif.	S.E.	Score dif.	S.E.
OECD																
Australia	500	(3.1)	529	(2.8)	556	(3.0)	580	(3.3)	60	(4.0)	62	(3.4)	70	(3.4)	70	(4.6)
Austria	449	(7.3)	489	(5.4)	517	(4.6)	550	(4.5)	46	(7.7)	58	(5.9)	70	(6.7)	65	(5.6)
Belgium	477	(4.6)	516	(3.3)	553	(3.1)	587	(3.1)	42	(4.8)	54	(4.3)	66	(4.4)	60	(4.1)
Canada	515	(2.7)	535	(2.0)	550	(2.4)	576	(2.6)	52	(3.6)	59	(3.7)	58	(3.6)	68	(4.0)
Chile	413	(3.7)	444	(3.9)	469	(3.9)	513	(3.7)	10	(4.7)	22	(4.4)	29	(4.2)	30	(4.7)
Czech Republic	464	(4.0)	493	(4.0)	516	(3.8)	544	(4.5)	50	(4.8)	57	(4.5)	60	(5.3)	69	(5.8)
Denmark	469	(3.2)	502	(3.9)	522	(3.0)	545	(2.8)	33	(5.5)	42	(5.8)	43	(4.4)	39	(5.7)
Estonia	497	(4.2)	509	(3.9)	523	(3.4)	548	(4.5)	44	(6.0)	46	(5.4)	48	(5.5)	49	(6.1)
Finland	527	(3.9)	548	(3.1)	570	(3.0)	582	(2.8)	55	(5.3)	62	(5.9)	64	(4.4)	66	(6.5)
France	476	(6.4)	508	(4.8)	539	(3.9)	568	(4.7)	62	(7.0)	59	(8.9)	69	(7.3)	61	(7.0)
Germany	477	(5.2)	520	(3.1)	538	(3.9)	567	(3.3)	54	(6.3)	59	(5.3)	61	(5.3)	66	(6.8)
Greece	442	(6.7)	482	(4.9)	499	(4.0)	534	(3.5)	25	(8.2)	32	(7.3)	39	(8.3)	46	(8.6)
Hungary	445	(6.4)	497	(3.7)	517	(4.4)	563	(3.8)	31	(7.9)	43	(6.4)	46	(5.9)	62	(7.2)
Iceland	501	(3.9)	521	(4.1)	543	(3.5)	552	(3.6)	70	(6.3)	63	(6.1)	80	(5.4)	75	(6.3)
Ireland	487	(4.9)	515	(4.7)	533	(4.4)	555	(3.8)	56	(6.1)	60	(6.2)	61	(5.6)	57	(4.8)
Israel	431	(5.6)	475	(4.6)	513	(3.9)	538	(4.7)	16	(7.1)	25	(5.6)	33	(5.9)	32	(6.5)
Italy	461	(2.7)	495	(2.5)	518	(2.1)	542	(2.2)	44	(3.6)	48	(3.8)	54	(3.5)	58	(3.4)
Japan	502	(5.8)	534	(4.3)	554	(4.5)	575	(4.4)	35	(5.5)	50	(6.7)	40	(5.3)	50	(6.8)
Korea	516	(5.1)	546	(3.1)	559	(3.5)	580	(3.5)	25	(6.2)	27	(4.9)	29	(6.0)	30	(5.6)
Luxembourg	435	(5.3)	491	(4.1)	527	(3.6)	551	(3.2)	39	(6.8)	57	(6.1)	62	(5.5)	70	(6.0)
Mexico	387	(3.2)	417	(2.5)	438	(2.4)	476	(2.3)	6	(4.5)	13	(2.7)	12	(2.7)	22	(3.7)
Netherlands	497	(7.4)	525	(6.9)	543	(4.8)	576	(5.5)	41	(5.8)	61	(6.1)	50	(5.2)	63	(5.6)
New Zealand	499	(4.6)	526	(3.6)	553	(3.6)	593	(3.9)	59	(6.8)	50	(5.6)	68	(7.3)	71	(6.9)
Norway	492	(3.9)	522	(3.8)	542	(3.4)	557	(4.2)	53	(5.4)	62	(5.7)	63	(5.1)	67	(6.1)
Poland	479	(3.7)	505	(3.5)	521	(3.2)	562	(3.5)	48	(5.5)	46	(5.5)	47	(5.3)	55	(5.6)
Portugal	465	(4.4)	490	(3.9)	514	(3.5)	552	(3.8)	36	(4.9)	44	(4.9)	42	(4.3)	50	(5.0)
Slovak Republic	455	(5.5)	488	(3.5)	505	(3.9)	541	(4.6)	40	(5.3)	46	(5.8)	45	(5.8)	60	(5.9)
Slovenia	467	(3.7)	491	(3.4)	516	(3.4)	552	(3.1)	47	(5.6)	53	(4.6)	58	(5.5)	68	(6.1)
Spain	460	(4.1)	485	(2.6)	506	(2.5)	539	(3.0)	36	(3.9)	39	(3.4)	40	(3.5)	45	(4.1)
Sweden	474	(5.2)	514	(3.7)	537	(3.7)	565	(4.5)	51	(6.4)	63	(5.4)	61	(5.9)	76	(6.0)
Switzerland	490	(5.5)	519	(3.7)	535	(3.4)	574	(4.1)	62	(6.2)	53	(5.6)	65	(4.8)	76	(6.4)
Turkey	430	(3.6)	461	(3.4)	476	(3.9)	520	(4.8)	17	(6.3)	23	(5.3)	27	(6.4)	32	(5.7)
United Kingdom	470	(4.0)	508	(3.8)	531	(3.5)	561	(3.5)	39	(5.2)	56	(4.8)	55	(5.4)	63	(5.2)
United States	472	(4.3)	502	(4.3)	532	(4.4)	578	(4.8)	41	(4.9)	46	(4.7)	46	(6.0)	62	(5.4)
OECD average	471	(0.8)	503	(0.7)	525	(0.6)	556	(0.7)	42	(1.0)	48	(0.9)	52	(0.9)	57	(1.0)
Partners																
Albania	356	(6.2)	380	(4.6)	396	(4.5)	435	(5.0)	44	(13.9)	32	(11.5)	23	(13.7)	12	(11.6)
Argentina	347	(5.5)	381	(5.4)	421	(6.5)	484	(6.4)	0	(6.3)	1	(8.4)	25	(6.2)	32	(7.9)
Azerbaijan	340	(6.5)	357	(4.0)	373	(4.0)	397	(5.0)	-2	(5.8)	7	(5.7)	19	(5.5)	19	(6.5)
Brazil	379	(2.8)	403	(3.1)	415	(3.4)	468	(4.3)	21	(6.6)	16	(4.9)	14	(4.6)	35	(6.1)
Bulgaria	380	(6.7)	429	(6.5)	459	(7.5)	510	(6.3)	30	(7.6)	33	(7.5)	44	(10.5)	50	(10.1)
Colombia	370	(5.4)	399	(5.5)	421	(4.0)	466	(5.0)	-6	(6.5)	1	(5.6)	-7	(5.9)	13	(5.5)
Croatia	451	(4.4)	482	(4.1)	495	(4.1)	523	(3.7)	35	(4.8)	47	(6.2)	45	(6.5)	46	(5.0)
Dubai (UAE)	407	(3.4)	466	(3.2)	492	(3.1)	517	(3.2)	18	(6.5)	41	(6.1)	43	(7.4)	49	(7.0)
Hong Kong-China	520	(4.3)	534	(3.1)	548	(3.1)	564	(3.3)	41	(5.7)	33	(6.4)	38	(6.5)	48	(6.6)
Indonesia	388	(3.9)	392	(3.8)	406	(4.7)	433	(6.2)	11	(6.3)	20	(5.9)	24	(6.6)	31	(8.0)
Jordan	385	(4.1)	404	(3.6)	417	(4.0)	448	(5.2)	21	(5.8)	-2	(6.2)	4	(7.0)	5	(8.8)
Kazakhstan	349	(4.1)	383	(3.2)	399	(3.4)	432	(5.0)	2	(9.7)	-7	(11.4)	-3	(12.9)	-3	(10.9)
Kyrgyzstan	282	(3.9)	301	(4.0)	328	(4.4)	373	(5.9)	23	(7.7)	19	(9.3)	32	(10.8)	20	(8.9)
Latvia	469	(4.6)	483	(4.4)	500	(4.4)	529	(3.5)	38	(6.8)	37	(6.6)	28	(5.7)	47	(5.7)
Liechtenstein	494	(11.5)	538	(12.9)	542	(10.3)	552	(10.8)	53	(17.0)	66	(15.4)	73	(16.0)	53	(19.7)
Lithuania	441	(3.6)	467	(3.9)	493	(3.9)	526	(3.3)	33	(6.3)	40	(7.1)	55	(6.7)	53	(6.1)
Macao-China	479	(2.3)	494	(2.0)	499	(2.4)	505	(2.4)	22	(4.1)	44	(4.9)	35	(5.3)	47	(6.2)
Montenegro	374	(3.7)	411	(3.7)	425	(3.7)	455	(3.0)	20	(6.8)	32	(7.6)	40	(7.8)	38	(6.8)
Panama	340	(8.1)	353	(8.2)	378	(6.4)	460	(10.7)	12	(11.5)	0	(9.9)	2	(10.8)	32	(10.2)
Peru	304	(3.4)	354	(3.1)	392	(3.9)	435	(7.6)	6	(8.2)	-7	(6.6)	-1	(5.6)	-1	(6.5)
Qatar	345	(2.0)	372	(2.8)	405	(3.1)	401	(2.6)	34	(4.7)	28	(6.8)	32	(7.0)	29	(6.5)
Romania	387	(5.5)	424	(4.3)	437	(4.7)	475	(5.7)	23	(8.0)	18	(5.7)	17	(7.0)	34	(5.7)
Russian Federation	432	(3.2)	455	(3.8)	475	(3.1)	511	(5.2)	33	(6.7)	32	(5.3)	37	(6.5)	52	(6.5)
Serbia	423	(3.8)	444	(3.2)	453	(2.9)	486	(2.8)	32	(5.6)	45	(5.5)	35	(5.3)	30	(5.6)
Shanghai-China	527	(4.1)	550	(3.2)	568	(2.6)	596	(3.4)	51	(8.4)	52	(10.1)	60	(12.3)	57	(12.5)
Singapore	489	(2.9)	523	(3.6)	550	(2.6)	583	(3.1)	36	(5.7)	43	(5.9)	43	(6.0)	62	(7.7)
Chinese Taipei	476	(3.2)	497	(3.2)	512	(3.1)	542	(4.6)	62	(5.3)	59	(6.1)	51	(7.2)	72	(9.1)
Thailand	402	(3.8)	412	(2.8)	423	(2.7)	467	(4.9)	30	(6.6)	39	(6.0)	34	(7.5)	50	(10.8)
Trinidad and Tobago	387	(4.2)	417	(4.1)	432	(3.8)	477	(5.2)	30	(7.9)	23	(8.0)	22	(8.3)	16	(7.7)
Tunisia	378	(3.6)	392	(3.5)	406	(3.5)	440	(5.2)	-7	(6.7)	-16	(6.8)	-7	(7.0)	-12	(5.8)
Uruguay	385	(3.7)	419	(3.5)	455	(4.7)	501	(4.0)	24	(5.4)	27	(5.2)	41	(6.0)	33	(5.8)

Notes: Values that are statistically significant are indicated in bold (see Annex A3).
1. The "I read for enjoyment" category groups students who: read "30 minutes or less per day", students who read "between 30 minutes and 60 minutes", students who read "between 1 hour and 2 hours" and students who read "more than 2 hours daily".

StatLink ⟐ⓢ⟐ http://dx.doi.org/10.1787/888932343285

[Part 1/1]
Reading diverse materials and performance
Students who reported that they read the following materials because they want to "several times a month" or "several times a week"

Table III.1.6

Performance on the reading scale of students who read different materials:

	Does not read magazines		Reads magazines		Does not read comic books		Reads comic books		Does not read fiction (novels, narratives, stories)		Reads fiction (novels, narratives, stories)		Does not read non-fiction books		Reads non-fiction books		Does not read newspapers		Reads newspapers	
	Mean score	S.E.	Mean score	S.E.	Mean score	S.E.	Mean score	S.E.	Mean score	S.E.	Mean score	S.E.	Mean score	S.E.	Mean score	S.E.	Mean score	S.E.	Mean score	S.E.
OECD																				
Australia	524	(2.6)	510	(2.5)	517	(2.2)	517	(4.8)	488	(2.0)	564	(2.8)	510	(2.3)	544	(3.4)	510	(2.2)	523	(2.9)
Austria	470	(4.1)	478	(2.8)	478	(2.8)	458	(4.8)	456	(2.9)	530	(4.0)	474	(3.1)	483	(4.4)	458	(4.6)	479	(2.9)
Belgium	492	(3.8)	523	(2.2)	505	(2.6)	529	(2.7)	499	(2.4)	561	(3.1)	512	(2.1)	522	(5.6)	505	(2.9)	520	(2.4)
Canada	523	(1.6)	528	(1.9)	526	(1.5)	526	(2.6)	502	(1.6)	558	(1.7)	522	(1.5)	539	(2.5)	521	(1.7)	531	(1.9)
Chile	438	(3.7)	463	(2.9)	452	(3.2)	444	(3.7)	446	(3.1)	462	(3.8)	446	(3.0)	475	(4.1)	436	(3.5)	461	(3.2)
Czech Republic	476	(3.8)	485	(2.9)	482	(2.7)	484	(5.7)	470	(2.9)	541	(4.1)	479	(2.9)	505	(4.4)	477	(4.0)	485	(2.8)
Denmark	483	(3.4)	503	(2.0)	494	(2.4)	506	(2.9)	483	(2.3)	525	(2.7)	490	(2.2)	514	(2.7)	489	(2.5)	503	(2.5)
Estonia	488	(3.8)	506	(2.7)	506	(2.6)	476	(4.5)	493	(2.6)	531	(3.5)	493	(2.7)	521	(3.3)	485	(4.5)	506	(2.6)
Finland	510	(3.5)	551	(2.2)	530	(3.0)	540	(2.4)	517	(2.2)	590	(2.8)	532	(2.2)	558	(4.2)	523	(3.2)	540	(2.3)
France	483	(4.5)	505	(3.3)	493	(3.6)	507	(4.5)	477	(3.4)	549	(3.9)	497	(3.3)	494	(4.7)	491	(4.0)	504	(3.9)
Germany	503	(3.1)	506	(3.1)	506	(2.6)	499	(5.6)	483	(3.0)	551	(2.9)	504	(2.9)	509	(4.1)	495	(3.7)	511	(2.8)
Greece	473	(5.4)	490	(4.3)	483	(4.6)	483	(4.9)	472	(4.9)	523	(3.5)	482	(4.4)	504	(7.4)	482	(4.7)	484	(4.6)
Hungary	469	(4.6)	512	(2.8)	499	(3.1)	482	(4.6)	484	(3.1)	519	(4.6)	490	(3.3)	504	(3.9)	483	(5.0)	499	(3.0)
Iceland	488	(2.3)	511	(1.7)	495	(1.8)	516	(2.6)	484	(1.7)	549	(2.8)	496	(1.5)	528	(3.6)	457	(4.5)	511	(1.6)
Ireland	497	(4.0)	499	(3.1)	500	(3.0)	476	(6.7)	480	(3.1)	542	(3.5)	494	(3.0)	526	(5.1)	505	(4.2)	495	(3.0)
Israel	469	(4.1)	495	(3.4)	483	(3.6)	459	(4.7)	471	(3.6)	500	(4.2)	477	(3.5)	486	(4.5)	444	(5.1)	491	(3.3)
Italy	482	(1.9)	492	(1.7)	483	(1.7)	505	(2.5)	471	(1.8)	517	(1.9)	486	(1.6)	497	(3.9)	477	(1.9)	496	(1.7)
Japan	524	(4.5)	519	(3.4)	516	(4.7)	522	(3.4)	501	(4.0)	548	(3.3)	518	(3.5)	542	(4.8)	506	(4.0)	531	(3.5)
Korea	540	(3.5)	539	(4.5)	543	(3.9)	534	(4.1)	526	(4.0)	556	(3.1)	530	(3.7)	562	(3.6)	527	(3.7)	556	(3.6)
Luxembourg	463	(3.1)	479	(1.7)	475	(1.4)	470	(3.4)	452	(1.4)	527	(2.6)	471	(1.4)	487	(3.4)	472	(3.1)	474	(1.7)
Mexico	419	(2.4)	435	(1.8)	430	(2.1)	417	(1.9)	429	(2.0)	424	(2.2)	423	(1.9)	442	(2.6)	424	(2.1)	429	(2.0)
Netherlands	487	(5.3)	530	(5.0)	509	(5.2)	522	(6.2)	501	(5.5)	552	(5.1)	507	(5.3)	547	(5.8)	497	(5.8)	527	(5.2)
New Zealand	531	(3.2)	515	(2.6)	525	(2.6)	506	(5.8)	494	(2.6)	559	(3.0)	518	(2.5)	538	(3.4)	518	(2.9)	526	(2.8)
Norway	494	(3.2)	511	(2.7)	495	(2.9)	517	(2.8)	487	(2.6)	551	(3.4)	503	(2.6)	507	(3.7)	487	(4.0)	510	(2.4)
Poland	480	(3.5)	512	(2.6)	503	(2.6)	487	(5.0)	491	(2.5)	544	(4.0)	494	(2.7)	530	(3.8)	489	(3.6)	504	(2.7)
Portugal	492	(3.8)	489	(3.0)	491	(3.0)	486	(3.9)	479	(3.0)	518	(3.8)	485	(2.9)	519	(5.1)	494	(3.3)	486	(3.3)
Slovak Republic	448	(5.3)	487	(2.3)	478	(2.6)	481	(5.4)	469	(2.6)	524	(4.9)	473	(2.5)	504	(4.0)	470	(4.2)	482	(2.4)
Slovenia	471	(2.6)	491	(1.4)	488	(1.2)	474	(4.0)	476	(1.2)	538	(3.9)	478	(1.1)	527	(3.2)	480	(2.5)	488	(1.3)
Spain	479	(2.2)	484	(2.3)	482	(2.0)	485	(3.8)	466	(2.1)	519	(2.2)	473	(2.1)	523	(2.7)	478	(2.2)	487	(2.4)
Sweden	480	(3.6)	513	(2.9)	496	(2.9)	510	(4.0)	475	(2.7)	549	(3.3)	495	(2.7)	541	(5.5)	468	(3.9)	511	(2.8)
Switzerland	487	(3.2)	508	(2.4)	498	(2.5)	513	(3.2)	480	(2.4)	550	(3.3)	500	(2.3)	507	(4.5)	482	(3.4)	506	(2.5)
Turkey	467	(4.0)	465	(3.5)	470	(3.4)	451	(4.5)	462	(3.7)	468	(3.7)	472	(3.6)	450	(4.0)	444	(4.9)	468	(3.7)
United Kingdom	496	(3.1)	495	(2.2)	498	(2.2)	475	(4.9)	475	(2.3)	542	(3.0)	491	(2.3)	519	(3.7)	497	(2.6)	495	(2.5)
United States	500	(3.9)	502	(3.9)	502	(3.6)	488	(6.4)	483	(3.1)	532	(4.8)	502	(3.7)	498	(5.2)	499	(3.9)	504	(4.2)
OECD average	486	(0.6)	501	(0.5)	495	(0.5)	492	(0.8)	480	(0.5)	533	(0.6)	492	(0.5)	513	(0.7)	484	(0.6)	501	(0.5)
Partners																				
Albania	381	(4.8)	395	(4.2)	399	(4.8)	375	(3.9)	375	(4.7)	400	(4.2)	385	(3.8)	402	(6.5)	388	(5.0)	387	(3.9)
Argentina	387	(4.8)	415	(5.0)	404	(5.2)	400	(4.9)	402	(4.7)	406	(5.8)	402	(4.8)	404	(5.6)	397	(5.1)	407	(4.9)
Azerbaijan	360	(3.7)	375	(3.4)	366	(3.9)	368	(3.2)	360	(3.9)	373	(3.3)	367	(3.9)	367	(3.8)	359	(3.3)	372	(3.9)
Brazil	402	(2.7)	427	(3.3)	421	(3.1)	402	(2.5)	414	(2.8)	416	(3.5)	414	(2.7)	424	(4.1)	409	(2.9)	422	(3.3)
Bulgaria	404	(7.3)	451	(6.3)	441	(6.4)	409	(8.0)	420	(6.0)	461	(8.2)	424	(6.4)	460	(7.1)	416	(7.2)	448	(6.4)
Colombia	415	(3.8)	415	(4.2)	414	(4.2)	417	(3.6)	421	(3.3)	405	(5.0)	412	(3.4)	420	(5.5)	417	(3.5)	413	(4.5)
Croatia	463	(3.8)	482	(3.0)	479	(2.9)	465	(4.4)	466	(2.9)	515	(3.7)	468	(2.9)	522	(4.3)	455	(5.4)	479	(2.9)
Dubai (UAE)	448	(2.4)	467	(1.7)	469	(1.7)	448	(1.9)	442	(1.5)	489	(2.6)	459	(1.4)	467	(3.0)	448	(3.0)	466	(1.7)
Hong Kong-China	539	(2.4)	527	(2.7)	535	(2.1)	529	(3.1)	516	(2.4)	552	(2.5)	525	(2.3)	549	(2.9)	511	(4.0)	538	(2.2)
Indonesia	392	(3.5)	410	(4.4)	398	(3.8)	407	(4.0)	394	(4.0)	408	(3.9)	393	(3.6)	420	(4.3)	393	(3.5)	407	(4.2)
Jordan	398	(3.7)	422	(3.1)	399	(3.7)	420	(3.0)	410	(3.5)	406	(3.3)	409	(3.3)	405	(3.7)	390	(3.6)	422	(3.1)
Kazakhstan	383	(5.0)	393	(2.8)	403	(3.9)	371	(3.1)	391	(4.2)	391	(3.2)	404	(3.7)	379	(3.4)	395	(6.3)	390	(2.9)
Kyrgyzstan	307	(3.7)	332	(3.4)	326	(3.8)	307	(3.3)	310	(3.9)	323	(3.3)	318	(3.2)	323	(3.9)	290	(5.1)	326	(3.0)
Latvia	467	(4.3)	491	(2.9)	487	(3.0)	458	(5.8)	477	(3.0)	500	(4.0)	478	(3.0)	502	(3.9)	475	(4.0)	489	(3.0)
Liechtenstein	491	(7.8)	505	(4.9)	501	(4.0)	495	(10.3)	484	(4.0)	543	(7.5)	499	(3.9)	509	(12.1)	478	(6.7)	508	(4.4)
Lithuania	443	(3.7)	477	(2.4)	475	(2.5)	444	(3.1)	450	(2.7)	501	(2.5)	457	(2.6)	498	(3.0)	459	(3.5)	473	(2.5)
Macao-China	487	(1.5)	486	(1.4)	485	(1.1)	490	(1.5)	477	(1.2)	509	(1.8)	480	(1.0)	506	(1.8)	467	(1.7)	495	(1.1)
Montenegro	379	(2.8)	420	(2.4)	414	(1.8)	401	(3.1)	401	(3.4)	428	(4.2)	406	(1.7)	423	(4.5)	393	(3.2)	416	(2.0)
Panama	360	(7.3)	393	(5.8)	384	(7.1)	367	(6.8)	377	(6.6)	380	(6.4)	379	(5.6)	380	(9.4)	377	(9.8)	379	(5.6)
Peru	356	(3.8)	389	(4.3)	379	(4.8)	364	(3.5)	372	(5.0)	372	(3.6)	377	(4.5)	365	(3.7)	341	(4.1)	383	(4.0)
Qatar	363	(1.9)	383	(1.2)	373	(1.5)	378	(1.4)	363	(1.3)	394	(1.8)	374	(1.2)	379	(2.0)	366	(2.2)	380	(1.1)
Romania	404	(4.5)	439	(4.4)	428	(4.0)	412	(5.2)	421	(4.2)	437	(4.7)	424	(4.1)	432	(4.6)	422	(4.5)	430	(5.0)
Russian Federation	455	(4.6)	463	(3.0)	468	(3.0)	434	(4.3)	439	(3.4)	477	(3.3)	458	(3.5)	472	(3.9)	464	(5.0)	459	(3.0)
Serbia	424	(3.6)	449	(2.4)	448	(2.4)	423	(3.9)	437	(2.5)	460	(3.3)	441	(2.3)	468	(5.4)	431	(3.7)	447	(2.4)
Shanghai-China	547	(2.5)	563	(2.7)	561	(2.3)	543	(3.3)	548	(2.5)	563	(2.8)	554	(2.4)	561	(3.3)	531	(3.5)	566	(2.6)
Singapore	524	(1.9)	528	(1.5)	525	(1.5)	529	(2.2)	503	(1.6)	552	(1.7)	521	(1.5)	538	(1.9)	503	(3.3)	531	(1.3)
Chinese Taipei	498	(2.9)	494	(3.0)	496	(2.7)	496	(3.2)	478	(2.6)	516	(3.1)	485	(2.7)	515	(3.2)	478	(3.9)	503	(2.6)
Thailand	411	(3.1)	432	(2.6)	411	(3.4)	426	(2.5)	410	(2.9)	428	(2.8)	411	(2.7)	433	(3.6)	413	(3.6)	425	(2.6)
Trinidad and Tobago	414	(1.9)	429	(2.3)	423	(2.1)	417	(2.9)	409	(1.9)	439	(2.5)	414	(1.9)	439	(3.0)	393	(4.6)	426	(1.4)
Tunisia	398	(3.0)	412	(3.2)	411	(3.2)	392	(2.9)	407	(3.3)	402	(3.3)	405	(3.1)	404	(3.7)	391	(3.5)	413	(3.0)
Uruguay	411	(3.2)	444	(2.4)	431	(3.0)	419	(3.1)	426	(2.9)	438	(3.3)	425	(2.6)	450	(4.7)	421	(2.9)	446	(3.4)

Note: Values that are statistically significant are indicated in bold (see Annex A3).
StatLink 🔗 http://dx.doi.org/10.1787/888932343285

[Part 1/3
Reading diverse materials and performance, by gender

Table III.1.7 *Percentage of students who reported that they read the following materials because they want to "several times a month" or "several times a week"*

		Boys																			
		Does not read magazines		Reads magazines		Does not read comic books		Comic books		Does not read fiction (novels, narratives, stories)		Reads fiction (novels, narratives, stories)		Does not read non-fiction books		Reads non-fiction books		Does not read newspapers		Reads newspapers	
		Mean	S.E.	Mean	S.E.	Mean	S.E.	Mean	S.E.	Mean	S.E.	Mean	S.E.	Mean	S.E.	Mean	S.E.	Mean	S.E.	Mean	S.E.
OECD	Australia	505	(3.1)	**492**	(3.3)	499	(2.8)	498	(5.6)	477	(2.6)	**554**	(3.8)	490	(2.7)	**539**	(4.7)	491	(2.5)	**504**	(3.6)
	Austria	447	(4.6)	458	(4.3)	455	(3.9)	451	(6.3)	444	(3.9)	**513**	(7.1)	450	(4.1)	**469**	(5.2)	428	(6.8)	**459**	(4.1)
	Belgium	480	(4.0)	**516**	(3.4)	485	(3.9)	**524**	(3.1)	491	(3.2)	**559**	(4.9)	501	(3.0)	507	(8.0)	491	(4.4)	**508**	(3.4)
	Canada	507	(2.0)	511	(2.3)	508	(1.8)	515	(3.3)	494	(2.0)	**546**	(2.5)	503	(1.8)	**535**	(3.2)	502	(2.3)	**515**	(2.1)
	Chile	432	(4.2)	**451**	(4.1)	440	(4.0)	439	(4.5)	438	(3.7)	448	(5.4)	437	(3.7)	**459**	(6.4)	422	(4.3)	**453**	(4.3)
	Czech Republic	447	(4.5)	**467**	(3.9)	457	(3.5)	472	(7.1)	454	(3.7)	**534**	(8.0)	457	(3.9)	**486**	(6.1)	450	(4.5)	**464**	(4.0)
	Denmark	472	(3.7)	**489**	(2.6)	476	(2.9)	**498**	(3.7)	473	(3.0)	**513**	(3.4)	471	(2.8)	**509**	(3.2)	468	(3.2)	**492**	(3.0)
	Estonia	467	(4.0)	**487**	(3.1)	485	(2.9)	**463**	(5.3)	477	(2.9)	**502**	(5.1)	472	(3.0)	**501**	(3.9)	457	(4.9)	**486**	(3.0)
	Finland	494	(3.4)	**522**	(2.9)	489	(3.5)	**517**	(2.7)	500	(2.5)	**572**	(5.4)	501	(2.6)	**542**	(4.8)	489	(4.1)	**515**	(2.7)
	France	460	(5.9)	**489**	(4.2)	463	(4.9)	**497**	(5.3)	462	(4.5)	**536**	(5.6)	475	(4.6)	483	(6.3)	467	(5.1)	**486**	(4.9)
	Germany	474	(4.1)	**496**	(4.4)	485	(3.6)	494	(6.5)	472	(3.7)	**544**	(4.7)	482	(3.9)	**504**	(5.7)	468	(5.8)	**495**	(3.7)
	Greece	448	(5.9)	**468**	(6.2)	455	(6.0)	468	(6.0)	454	(5.9)	**500**	(6.5)	458	(5.6)	480	(9.8)	451	(6.4)	465	(5.5)
	Hungary	449	(5.1)	**497**	(4.0)	478	(4.2)	470	(5.6)	468	(3.8)	**502**	(6.8)	467	(4.3)	**493**	(4.9)	463	(5.5)	**482**	(4.1)
	Iceland	467	(3.1)	**492**	(2.9)	469	(2.7)	**498**	(4.0)	468	(2.1)	**530**	(5.5)	475	(2.1)	**510**	(6.2)	430	(5.4)	**491**	(2.5)
	Ireland	476	(5.1)	482	(4.4)	480	(4.2)	472	(8.3)	468	(4.3)	**517**	(6.4)	474	(4.2)	**515**	(7.5)	479	(6.5)	479	(4.1)
	Israel	454	(5.4)	**475**	(5.4)	463	(5.2)	**436**	(7.4)	456	(4.8)	**478**	(8.4)	456	(5.0)	470	(7.7)	418	(6.7)	**476**	(5.0)
	Italy	458	(2.5)	**474**	(2.5)	457	(2.5)	**493**	(3.1)	455	(2.5)	**494**	(2.8)	465	(2.3)	472	(7.6)	447	(2.8)	**478**	(2.4)
	Japan	502	(7.0)	501	(5.3)	486	(9.7)	505	(4.9)	483	(5.9)	**535**	(4.8)	500	(5.5)	**518**	(7.3)	482	(6.1)	**514**	(5.5)
	Korea	522	(4.8)	526	(6.4)	521	(6.1)	525	(5.3)	508	(5.4)	**545**	(4.3)	511	(4.9)	**556**	(5.9)	508	(5.6)	**541**	(4.5)
	Luxembourg	438	(3.9)	**465**	(2.5)	451	(2.4)	**463**	(4.4)	442	(2.1)	**520**	(5.6)	446	(2.1)	**481**	(4.3)	438	(4.6)	**461**	(2.3)
	Mexico	407	(2.6)	**423**	(2.1)	416	(2.4)	410	(2.1)	418	(2.4)	**407**	(2.7)	412	(2.2)	**424**	(2.9)	406	(2.6)	**421**	(2.2)
	Netherlands	477	(5.7)	**527**	(5.1)	491	(5.4)	**519**	(6.0)	493	(5.3)	**560**	(8.2)	498	(5.2)	**526**	(9.3)	479	(6.7)	**518**	(5.0)
	New Zealand	509	(4.5)	**492**	(4.0)	504	(3.5)	488	(7.2)	479	(3.5)	**543**	(5.0)	492	(3.5)	**531**	(5.2)	498	(3.7)	503	(4.6)
	Norway	476	(3.4)	**486**	(3.7)	464	(3.3)	**499**	(3.5)	470	(3.0)	**535**	(4.8)	478	(3.1)	**490**	(4.2)	455	(5.5)	**490**	(2.9)
	Poland	453	(4.1)	**495**	(2.9)	478	(2.9)	473	(6.3)	472	(2.7)	**517**	(7.3)	470	(2.9)	**512**	(5.6)	456	(4.6)	**483**	(3.0)
	Portugal	473	(4.3)	470	(3.7)	470	(3.3)	474	(5.2)	465	(3.5)	**502**	(6.6)	469	(3.5)	**488**	(7.4)	467	(4.6)	473	(3.7)
	Slovak Republic	425	(6.0)	**463**	(3.3)	451	(3.7)	**466**	(6.4)	448	(3.6)	**499**	(7.3)	444	(3.7)	**492**	(4.5)	436	(5.4)	**460**	(3.4)
	Slovenia	446	(3.1)	**467**	(2.1)	459	(1.9)	463	(4.4)	455	(1.6)	**506**	(6.8)	453	(1.7)	**507**	(5.6)	443	(3.8)	**465**	(1.9)
	Spain	465	(2.6)	471	(2.6)	466	(2.3)	**479**	(3.8)	457	(2.2)	**509**	(3.1)	462	(2.3)	**507**	(4.3)	459	(3.2)	**474**	(2.4)
	Sweden	463	(4.0)	**492**	(3.7)	468	(3.4)	**500**	(4.4)	463	(3.2)	**535**	(4.8)	473	(3.1)	**519**	(8.0)	443	(4.9)	**491**	(3.3)
	Switzerland	467	(3.8)	**492**	(3.1)	473	(3.2)	**502**	(3.5)	468	(2.9)	**545**	(4.2)	479	(2.8)	**498**	(5.2)	453	(4.9)	**489**	(3.0)
	Turkey	445	(4.0)	445	(4.3)	449	(3.7)	**433**	(5.2)	450	(4.1)	440	(4.1)	450	(3.9)	**434**	(4.7)	411	(5.7)	**449**	(3.9)
	United Kingdom	481	(4.2)	485	(3.4)	486	(3.5)	**467**	(6.7)	469	(3.4)	**532**	(4.7)	477	(3.4)	**516**	(5.4)	481	(4.2)	485	(3.9)
	United States	489	(4.5)	490	(5.0)	492	(4.3)	**470**	(7.3)	475	(3.8)	**524**	(5.9)	487	(4.5)	497	(6.3)	485	(4.1)	494	(5.6)
	OECD average	467	(0.7)	**484**	(0.7)	473	(0.7)	**481**	(0.9)	467	(0.6)	**518**	(1.0)	472	(0.6)	**499**	(1.0)	459	(0.8)	**484**	(0.6)
Partners	Albania	355	(5.9)	362	(5.5)	364	(6.1)	354	(5.7)	355	(5.4)	367	(6.4)	356	(4.7)	**376**	(8.5)	353	(6.3)	362	(4.9)
	Argentina	375	(5.1)	**393**	(6.5)	385	(5.7)	381	(6.0)	383	(5.2)	389	(8.8)	382	(5.4)	390	(8.2)	367	(5.3)	**396**	(6.2)
	Azerbaijan	350	(3.9)	**363**	(4.7)	354	(4.5)	358	(4.1)	350	(4.2)	**363**	(4.1)	356	(3.8)	356	(4.9)	344	(3.6)	**364**	(4.5)
	Brazil	392	(3.1)	**413**	(4.2)	405	(3.5)	**392**	(3.0)	401	(2.9)	396	(4.6)	400	(2.8)	401	(6.4)	391	(3.4)	**410**	(3.4)
	Bulgaria	386	(8.2)	**423**	(7.0)	412	(7.1)	**385**	(10.0)	399	(6.6)	**428**	(9.7)	393	(6.8)	**440**	(8.0)	380	(7.6)	**427**	(7.2)
	Colombia	409	(4.7)	410	(5.1)	405	(5.3)	415	(4.3)	415	(4.4)	**397**	(5.8)	408	(4.2)	414	(6.5)	410	(4.5)	409	(5.1)
	Croatia	438	(4.3)	**460**	(3.5)	452	(3.7)	455	(5.1)	447	(3.5)	**488**	(5.7)	446	(3.5)	**495**	(5.9)	429	(7.5)	**455**	(3.4)
	Dubai (UAE)	421	(3.5)	**444**	(2.8)	443	(2.7)	**425**	(3.2)	424	(2.3)	**462**	(4.1)	436	(2.2)	439	(5.0)	408	(4.7)	**444**	(2.4)
	Hong Kong-China	523	(3.4)	513	(4.3)	519	(3.8)	517	(3.6)	505	(3.6)	**536**	(3.8)	507	(3.6)	**537**	(4.0)	494	(5.5)	**523**	(3.5)
	Indonesia	375	(4.0)	**391**	(4.6)	377	(3.5)	**391**	(4.7)	380	(4.2)	387	(4.2)	377	(3.8)	**401**	(5.0)	370	(3.9)	**390**	(4.4)
	Jordan	373	(4.7)	**397**	(4.8)	374	(4.5)	**394**	(4.7)	384	(4.6)	377	(4.9)	380	(4.5)	384	(5.2)	359	(5.0)	**396**	(4.4)
	Kazakhstan	363	(5.1)	372	(3.1)	382	(3.9)	**348**	(3.6)	373	(5.0)	368	(3.3)	382	(4.3)	**360**	(3.5)	367	(6.9)	370	(3.1)
	Kyrgyzstan	284	(4.5)	**304**	(4.7)	300	(4.5)	**276**	(4.4)	290	(5.2)	294	(3.9)	290	(3.8)	298	(5.2)	262	(5.2)	**302**	(4.0)
	Latvia	446	(4.3)	**468**	(3.5)	463	(3.6)	**441**	(7.4)	457	(3.5)	470	(5.6)	456	(3.5)	**478**	(5.4)	446	(4.9)	**468**	(3.5)
	Liechtenstein	475	(9.0)	492	(7.8)	483	(6.8)	490	(12.2)	471	(5.5)	**544**	(12.7)	481	(6.1)	505	(13.3)	458	(10.2)	**494**	(6.6)
	Lithuania	417	(3.8)	**451**	(3.0)	444	(2.9)	**428**	(4.4)	432	(2.9)	**468**	(4.5)	432	(2.8)	**471**	(4.3)	428	(3.9)	**445**	(3.1)
	Macao-China	470	(1.8)	470	(2.2)	465	(1.7)	**477**	(2.1)	465	(1.6)	**487**	(3.0)	462	(1.6)	**491**	(2.5)	452	(2.3)	**478**	(1.6)
	Montenegro	363	(3.7)	**395**	(3.0)	386	(2.9)	383	(3.7)	380	(2.3)	**400**	(5.2)	380	(2.3)	**401**	(5.7)	365	(4.4)	**391**	(2.8)
	Panama	350	(6.8)	**376**	(7.5)	362	(7.9)	359	(8.2)	362	(7.1)	360	(7.9)	363	(6.4)	362	(10.9)	347	(10.3)	368	(6.8)
	Peru	350	(3.9)	**375**	(5.5)	366	(5.1)	354	(4.1)	365	(5.3)	356	(4.2)	366	(4.8)	**353**	(4.2)	331	(4.7)	**370**	(4.3)
	Qatar	338	(2.4)	**365**	(1.9)	346	(2.2)	**361**	(2.3)	344	(1.9)	**370**	(2.6)	352	(1.9)	355	(3.0)	333	(3.4)	**361**	(1.6)
	Romania	389	(4.8)	**418**	(5.3)	407	(4.3)	391	(7.9)	404	(4.6)	407	(5.6)	402	(4.5)	416	(6.1)	397	(5.8)	411	(4.6)
	Russian Federation	433	(5.1)	443	(3.6)	446	(3.6)	**412**	(5.3)	422	(4.2)	**457**	(3.9)	434	(3.8)	**455**	(5.0)	436	(5.2)	440	(3.5)
	Serbia	410	(3.8)	**432**	(3.6)	427	(3.3)	416	(5.2)	421	(3.3)	**434**	(4.6)	423	(3.1)	**447**	(7.4)	405	(5.4)	**429**	(3.2)
	Shanghai-China	527	(3.4)	**544**	(3.5)	542	(3.1)	**525**	(4.0)	533	(3.2)	539	(3.6)	532	(3.2)	**543**	(3.9)	508	(4.3)	**548**	(3.1)
	Singapore	510	(2.6)	513	(2.7)	508	(2.4)	**516**	(3.0)	493	(2.4)	**540**	(2.7)	503	(2.3)	**529**	(3.2)	476	(5.1)	**518**	(1.8)
	Chinese Taipei	474	(4.1)	482	(4.6)	473	(4.3)	**484**	(3.8)	464	(3.8)	**500**	(4.5)	465	(3.9)	**500**	(4.4)	451	(5.1)	**489**	(4.0)
	Thailand	392	(3.7)	**413**	(3.4)	388	(4.1)	**407**	(3.2)	396	(3.7)	405	(3.6)	390	(3.1)	**414**	(4.2)	388	(5.0)	**406**	(3.0)
	Trinidad and Tobago	384	(3.1)	**406**	(3.8)	389	(2.9)	398	(4.3)	387	(2.7)	**407**	(4.3)	390	(2.4)	**404**	(5.6)	354	(5.8)	**401**	(2.4)
	Tunisia	384	(3.3)	**396**	(4.5)	395	(3.4)	**373**	(3.8)	396	(3.7)	**378**	(4.1)	387	(3.3)	395	(4.6)	373	(5.1)	**399**	(3.3)
	Uruguay	398	(3.5)	**421**	(4.1)	408	(3.8)	402	(4.9)	408	(3.3)	407	(5.6)	407	(3.2)	412	(8.8)	396	(3.5)	**430**	(4.8)

Note: Values that are statistically significant are indicated in bold (see Annex A3).
StatLink http://dx.doi.org/10.1787/888932343285

[Part 2/3]
Reading diverse materials and performance, by gender
Table III.1.7 *Percentage of students who reported that they read the following materials because they want to "several times a month" or "several times a week"*

		Girls																			
		Does not read magazines		Reads magazines		Does not read comic books		Comic books		Does not read fiction (novels, narratives, stories)		Reads fiction (novels, narratives, stories)		Does not read non-fiction books		Reads non-fiction books		Does not read newspapers		Reads newspapers	
		Mean	S.E.	Mean	S.E.	Mean	S.E.	Mean	S.E.	Mean	S.E.	Mean	S.E.	Mean	S.E.	Mean	S.E.	Mean	S.E.	Mean	S.E.
OECD	Australia	544	(3.2)	**525**	(2.8)	533	(2.5)	**548**	(6.9)	502	(2.5)	**569**	(2.9)	530	(2.8)	**549**	(3.6)	525	(2.8)	**543**	(3.2)
	Austria	497	(5.2)	495	(3.9)	498	(3.8)	**471**	(8.6)	472	(3.9)	**536**	(4.7)	494	(3.8)	507	(7.4)	485	(6.0)	498	(3.9)
	Belgium	512	(5.5)	**528**	(2.7)	521	(2.9)	**536**	(4.9)	508	(2.9)	**562**	(3.5)	523	(2.9)	**537**	(5.1)	516	(3.5)	**535**	(3.5)
	Canada	545	(2.2)	540	(2.2)	542	(1.7)	546	(4.8)	516	(2.1)	**565**	(1.9)	542	(1.8)	543	(3.0)	537	(2.0)	**549**	(2.4)
	Chile	448	(4.9)	**471**	(3.4)	464	(3.7)	**452**	(4.6)	457	(3.8)	470	(4.2)	456	(3.5)	**486**	(5.0)	451	(4.1)	**470**	(3.9)
	Czech Republic	522	(3.9)	**502**	(3.3)	508	(3.1)	504	(6.0)	493	(3.2)	**543**	(4.4)	505	(3.1)	**524**	(5.2)	503	(4.4)	510	(3.2)
	Denmark	502	(5.0)	**513**	(2.4)	508	(2.7)	**522**	(5.2)	496	(2.8)	**532**	(3.8)	507	(2.7)	**519**	(4.1)	505	(3.0)	**516**	(3.5)
	Estonia	522	(5.4)	525	(2.7)	526	(2.9)	**504**	(6.4)	514	(3.0)	**546**	(4.2)	516	(3.0)	**542**	(4.2)	513	(5.7)	**527**	(2.8)
	Finland	541	(5.3)	**571**	(2.2)	555	(3.4)	**572**	(2.7)	542	(2.9)	**597**	(3.0)	561	(2.5)	**585**	(5.4)	555	(4.4)	**567**	(2.4)
	France	513	(4.9)	517	(3.6)	514	(3.4)	525	(5.9)	494	(3.8)	**556**	(4.3)	517	(3.8)	510	(7.6)	509	(4.2)	**526**	(4.7)
	Germany	532	(4.0)	**516**	(3.3)	524	(2.9)	510	(9.5)	498	(3.3)	**554**	(3.4)	524	(3.2)	520	(5.5)	516	(3.6)	**530**	(3.5)
	Greece	504	(5.6)	507	(3.7)	507	(3.6)	506	(6.1)	495	(4.2)	**532**	(3.7)	505	(3.5)	521	(9.0)	500	(4.1)	**523**	(4.0)
	Hungary	495	(5.9)	**524**	(3.3)	520	(3.2)	**495**	(6.3)	504	(3.5)	**529**	(5.2)	513	(3.6)	515	(4.8)	513	(7.0)	514	(3.4)
	Iceland	520	(4.2)	525	(2.0)	518	(2.2)	**538**	(3.8)	504	(2.4)	**559**	(2.9)	520	(2.3)	**539**	(4.1)	486	(5.7)	**531**	(2.0)
	Ireland	535	(4.1)	**510**	(3.5)	520	(3.1)	**484**	(10.0)	495	(3.3)	**559**	(3.7)	515	(3.1)	**536**	(6.4)	524	(3.9)	514	(3.7)
	Israel	489	(4.2)	**506**	(3.7)	503	(3.4)	**473**	(5.6)	489	(3.6)	**510**	(4.3)	496	(3.4)	500	(4.7)	475	(5.4)	**503**	(3.3)
	Italy	515	(2.2)	**506**	(2.1)	507	(1.9)	**532**	(3.6)	492	(2.0)	**531**	(2.4)	510	(1.9)	518	(5.7)	503	(2.2)	**518**	(2.2)
	Japan	553	(4.5)	**535**	(3.9)	531	(4.9)	**546**	(3.8)	524	(4.1)	**559**	(4.6)	537	(3.8)	**565**	(6.6)	527	(4.2)	**553**	(4.2)
	Korea	561	(3.6)	549	(5.7)	561	(4.1)	551	(4.3)	551	(4.3)	**565**	(4.0)	554	(4.2)	**567**	(4.1)	546	(3.9)	**574**	(4.5)
	Luxembourg	497	(4.4)	491	(1.9)	495	(1.7)	**482**	(6.1)	467	(2.2)	**530**	(3.1)	492	(1.7)	497	(5.7)	500	(4.2)	**489**	(2.3)
	Mexico	432	(2.8)	**445**	(1.8)	442	(2.2)	**427**	(2.5)	441	(2.2)	435	(2.6)	434	(2.1)	**459**	(2.9)	438	(2.4)	438	(2.3)
	Netherlands	504	(5.7)	**532**	(5.4)	522	(5.2)	529	(8.5)	510	(6.1)	**550**	(4.9)	516	(5.6)	**557**	(5.4)	512	(5.5)	**539**	(6.2)
	New Zealand	560	(3.5)	**535**	(2.9)	546	(2.8)	538	(7.9)	517	(3.3)	**569**	(3.6)	545	(2.9)	545	(4.3)	539	(3.3)	**551**	(3.1)
	Norway	527	(5.1)	528	(2.8)	519	(3.4)	**546**	(3.5)	511	(2.8)	**558**	(3.9)	529	(3.1)	525	(4.7)	516	(4.6)	**533**	(2.8)
	Poland	526	(4.1)	525	(3.2)	527	(2.9)	**509**	(7.1)	514	(2.9)	**555**	(4.1)	520	(3.1)	**544**	(4.1)	532	(4.5)	524	(3.1)
	Portugal	519	(4.6)	**504**	(2.9)	508	(3.0)	506	(4.9)	497	(3.1)	**525**	(3.5)	502	(2.8)	**536**	(5.0)	508	(3.3)	509	(3.4)
	Slovak Republic	490	(7.2)	**506**	(2.9)	506	(2.7)	492	(7.2)	494	(2.6)	**534**	(5.3)	501	(2.6)	**516**	(6.0)	505	(4.7)	503	(3.0)
	Slovenia	518	(4.1)	511	(1.7)	515	(1.5)	**495**	(6.3)	501	(1.8)	**552**	(4.0)	506	(1.9)	**540**	(3.7)	508	(3.2)	515	(1.9)
	Spain	498	(2.8)	495	(2.6)	496	(2.2)	500	(5.8)	478	(2.6)	**525**	(2.5)	485	(2.6)	**533**	(2.4)	490	(2.3)	**511**	(3.0)
	Sweden	507	(4.7)	**529**	(3.1)	521	(3.1)	528	(6.2)	493	(3.3)	**556**	(3.6)	517	(3.0)	**562**	(6.1)	495	(5.0)	**532**	(3.1)
	Switzerland	517	(4.7)	522	(2.6)	518	(2.6)	**531**	(4.9)	498	(2.8)	**553**	(3.6)	520	(2.8)	525	(6.0)	508	(4.0)	**524**	(2.8)
	Turkey	495	(5.3)	**482**	(3.9)	492	(4.3)	**474**	(5.5)	484	(5.1)	489	(4.4)	493	(4.4)	**472**	(4.9)	472	(7.0)	**490**	(4.2)
	United Kingdom	523	(4.3)	**501**	(2.8)	509	(2.8)	**490**	(7.1)	483	(3.0)	**547**	(3.8)	504	(2.8)	**522**	(5.1)	508	(3.4)	507	(3.3)
	United States	513	(4.0)	513	(4.4)	513	(3.8)	517	(8.6)	493	(3.3)	**537**	(5.2)	518	(3.7)	**499**	(6.4)	512	(4.4)	517	(4.8)
	OECD average	514	(0.8)	514	(0.6)	514	(0.5)	**511**	(1.1)	498	(0.6)	**541**	(0.7)	512	(0.5)	**527**	(0.9)	507	(0.7)	**520**	(0.6)
Partners	Albania	417	(4.8)	420	(4.5)	430	(5.0)	**399**	(4.3)	412	(6.0)	421	(4.1)	416	(4.1)	424	(7.5)	422	(5.3)	414	(4.3)
	Argentina	402	(6.1)	**427**	(5.2)	421	(5.4)	415	(5.7)	422	(5.1)	414	(6.2)	422	(5.0)	412	(6.4)	418	(5.7)	418	(5.2)
	Azerbaijan	372	(4.3)	**385**	(3.5)	378	(4.3)	379	(3.2)	374	(4.4)	381	(3.5)	380	(4.7)	376	(3.4)	374	(3.6)	381	(4.1)
	Brazil	417	(3.0)	**434**	(3.3)	435	(3.3)	**412**	(2.9)	432	(3.4)	423	(3.5)	426	(3.0)	**440**	(4.0)	423	(3.0)	**434**	(3.8)
	Bulgaria	445	(7.0)	**470**	(6.0)	470	(5.6)	**442**	(8.5)	450	(5.1)	**482**	(8.3)	458	(5.2)	**481**	(7.9)	459	(6.7)	468	(6.0)
	Colombia	422	(4.2)	418	(4.6)	421	(4.8)	420	(4.0)	428	(3.3)	**410**	(5.8)	417	(3.9)	424	(5.8)	423	(4.2)	417	(4.9)
	Croatia	508	(5.4)	502	(3.8)	505	(3.8)	**487**	(6.6)	492	(3.9)	**529**	(4.2)	494	(3.7)	**543**	(4.5)	481	(6.3)	**506**	(3.7)
	Dubai (UAE)	483	(3.4)	487	(2.1)	497	(2.2)	**470**	(2.7)	466	(2.2)	**509**	(2.7)	483	(1.8)	**494**	(3.5)	476	(3.8)	**491**	(2.0)
	Hong Kong-China	558	(3.2)	**543**	(3.3)	550	(2.8)	551	(5.1)	533	(3.2)	**565**	(3.3)	543	(3.1)	**565**	(4.1)	531	(5.3)	**554**	(2.9)
	Indonesia	411	(3.7)	**427**	(4.4)	419	(4.3)	422	(4.0)	413	(4.5)	424	(4.1)	412	(3.7)	**434**	(4.4)	412	(3.7)	**426**	(4.3)
	Jordan	431	(5.4)	439	(3.6)	429	(5.5)	441	(3.6)	438	(4.7)	430	(4.2)	438	(4.2)	427	(5.0)	417	(5.0)	**449**	(4.0)
	Kazakhstan	415	(6.6)	411	(3.3)	425	(4.3)	**392**	(3.8)	416	(4.8)	411	(3.6)	427	(4.1)	**399**	(3.9)	428	(7.5)	**410**	(3.3)
	Kyrgyzstan	335	(4.0)	**351**	(3.5)	349	(3.8)	**338**	(4.0)	338	(4.3)	345	(3.6)	345	(3.3)	343	(4.1)	335	(6.8)	345	(3.0)
	Latvia	504	(6.3)	508	(3.1)	510	(3.1)	**486**	(6.8)	502	(3.3)	**516**	(4.1)	503	(3.0)	**518**	(4.3)	506	(3.8)	509	(3.3)
	Liechtenstein	519	(13.1)	516	(6.3)	519	(4.8)	c	c	502	(6.3)	**542**	(9.8)	516	(5.4)	c	c	497	(10.0)	**525**	(6.8)
	Lithuania	497	(5.3)	499	(2.5)	505	(2.7)	**466**	(4.2)	479	(3.6)	**515**	(2.5)	489	(3.1)	**514**	(3.4)	493	(4.3)	501	(2.7)
	Macao-China	508	(2.0)	**500**	(1.6)	502	(1.4)	**509**	(2.4)	492	(1.7)	**521**	(2.2)	498	(1.3)	**521**	(2.5)	486	(2.8)	**510**	(1.4)
	Montenegro	410	(5.4)	**441**	(2.3)	439	(2.3)	**430**	(4.0)	428	(2.5)	**448**	(4.2)	433	(2.4)	**444**	(4.3)	418	(5.3)	**444**	(2.0)
	Panama	377	(10.2)	**405**	(6.3)	404	(8.0)	**377**	(7.9)	396	(8.7)	393	(7.4)	395	(6.4)	398	(10.7)	403	(11.7)	390	(5.7)
	Peru	364	(4.9)	**402**	(5.2)	393	(5.9)	**374**	(4.7)	382	(6.4)	384	(4.7)	388	(5.7)	376	(5.0)	350	(5.3)	**395**	(5.0)
	Qatar	400	(3.1)	397	(1.4)	405	(2.2)	**393**	(1.6)	386	(1.8)	**412**	(2.2)	396	(1.6)	402	(3.0)	394	(2.7)	400	(1.5)
	Romania	427	(6.1)	**453**	(4.2)	449	(4.4)	**431**	(6.1)	441	(4.5)	453	(5.2)	446	(4.5)	447	(5.0)	442	(4.8)	451	(5.7)
	Russian Federation	493	(6.0)	**479**	(3.1)	488	(3.8)	**459**	(5.3)	465	(4.8)	**491**	(3.4)	481	(3.7)	488	(4.3)	493	(5.3)	**477**	(3.2)
	Serbia	460	(5.0)	463	(2.7)	467	(2.6)	**436**	(5.6)	456	(2.8)	**475**	(3.4)	460	(2.5)	**487**	(5.9)	454	(4.0)	**465**	(2.6)
	Shanghai-China	569	(2.5)	**581**	(2.7)	577	(2.4)	570	(3.9)	566	(2.7)	**582**	(2.8)	572	(2.3)	**589**	(4.0)	556	(3.3)	**584**	(2.7)
	Singapore	544	(2.6)	541	(2.0)	539	(1.9)	**549**	(3.9)	518	(2.6)	**560**	(2.2)	540	(2.0)	546	(3.0)	525	(4.4)	**546**	(1.9)
	Chinese Taipei	521	(3.6)	**506**	(4.3)	514	(3.4)	514	(5.1)	498	(3.4)	**528**	(4.3)	506	(3.5)	**529**	(4.5)	507	(4.2)	517	(3.8)
	Thailand	433	(3.9)	441	(3.1)	435	(4.1)	439	(3.1)	429	(3.9)	**441**	(3.3)	430	(3.5)	**445**	(3.3)	433	(3.6)	439	(3.4)
	Trinidad and Tobago	449	(2.7)	447	(2.6)	455	(2.7)	**437**	(3.7)	438	(3.1)	**459**	(2.7)	441	(2.7)	**462**	(3.6)	445	(6.4)	448	(1.9)
	Tunisia	416	(4.0)	422	(3.3)	427	(3.7)	**406**	(3.1)	421	(3.4)	417	(3.5)	422	(3.3)	412	(4.8)	406	(3.4)	**427**	(3.2)
	Uruguay	430	(4.5)	**456**	(2.6)	452	(3.0)	**434**	(3.8)	445	(3.2)	453	(3.5)	442	(3.0)	**469**	(4.6)	441	(3.1)	**462**	(3.8)

Note: Values that are statistically significant are indicated in bold (see Annex A3).
StatLink http://dx.doi.org/10.1787/888932343285

[Part 3/3]
Reading diverse materials and performance, by gender
Percentage of students who reported that they read the following materials because they want to "several times a month" or "several times a week"

Table III.1.7

	Difference (Boys – Girls)																			
	Does not read magazines		Reads magazines		Does not read comic books		Comic books		Does not read fiction (novels, narratives, stories)		Reads fiction (novels, narratives, stories)		Does not read non-fiction books		Reads non-fiction books		Does not read newspapers		Reads newspapers	
	Score dif.	S.E.	Score dif.	S.E.	Score dif.	S.E.	Score dif.	S.E.	Score dif.	S.E.	Score dif.	S.E.	Score dif.	S.E.	Score dif.	S.E.	Score dif.	S.E.	Score dif.	S.E.
Australia	-39	(3.6)	-33	(3.5)	-34	(2.9)	-49	(8.2)	-25	(3.2)	-15	(3.7)	-41	(3.2)	-9	(4.8)	-34	(3.2)	-39	(3.9)
Austria	-50	(6.1)	-37	(6.3)	-44	(5.7)	-20	(11.3)	-28	(5.6)	-23	(8.6)	-44	(5.5)	-37	(9.0)	-57	(9.1)	-39	(6.0)
Belgium	-32	(5.7)	-12	(4.2)	-35	(4.5)	-12	(5.7)	-17	(3.9)	-3	(5.5)	-22	(4.2)	-31	(7.8)	-25	(5.2)	-27	(4.6)
Canada	-38	(2.9)	-29	(2.7)	-34	(2.0)	-32	(6.2)	-22	(2.5)	-18	(2.7)	-39	(2.2)	-8	(3.5)	-35	(2.7)	-34	(2.5)
Chile	-15	(5.1)	-19	(4.7)	-24	(4.4)	-13	(5.4)	-19	(4.4)	-22	(5.8)	-19	(4.0)	-27	(8.0)	-29	(4.7)	-17	(4.9)
Czech Republic	-75	(5.0)	-35	(4.7)	-51	(4.3)	-32	(7.9)	-39	(4.4)	-9	(8.4)	-49	(4.4)	-38	(7.6)	-53	(4.9)	-46	(5.0)
Denmark	-29	(5.6)	-24	(3.1)	-33	(3.2)	-24	(6.7)	-24	(3.5)	-19	(5.4)	-36	(3.4)	-10	(5.0)	-37	(4.0)	-24	(4.0)
Estonia	-54	(6.0)	-38	(2.8)	-42	(2.8)	-40	(7.2)	-38	(3.0)	-43	(6.2)	-45	(2.9)	-41	(4.8)	-56	(6.5)	-41	(3.1)
Finland	-47	(5.0)	-49	(2.8)	-66	(3.7)	-55	(2.7)	-43	(3.0)	-25	(5.8)	-60	(2.7)	-44	(6.0)	-65	(5.7)	-52	(2.5)
France	-53	(5.6)	-28	(4.1)	-51	(4.6)	-28	(6.8)	-32	(4.2)	-20	(5.9)	-41	(4.0)	-26	(10.4)	-42	(4.5)	-40	(5.7)
Germany	-58	(5.5)	-20	(4.6)	-40	(4.0)	-16	(10.5)	-26	(4.1)	-10	(5.5)	-43	(4.0)	-16	(7.9)	-48	(5.7)	-35	(4.4)
Greece	-56	(5.6)	-39	(5.5)	-52	(4.7)	-37	(7.7)	-42	(4.5)	-33	(7.1)	-47	(4.4)	-41	(11.8)	-49	(5.3)	-58	(5.6)
Hungary	-46	(5.7)	-27	(4.6)	-42	(4.0)	-25	(7.5)	-37	(4.1)	-27	(7.3)	-47	(4.5)	-22	(5.4)	-51	(7.3)	-32	(4.3)
Iceland	-53	(5.9)	-34	(3.5)	-49	(3.4)	-40	(5.8)	-37	(3.1)	-29	(6.1)	-45	(3.1)	-29	(7.0)	-56	(7.8)	-41	(3.4)
Ireland	-59	(5.9)	-28	(4.9)	-40	(4.7)	-12	(12.2)	-27	(4.7)	-42	(7.3)	-41	(4.5)	-21	(9.4)	-45	(6.7)	-36	(5.2)
Israel	-35	(5.7)	-31	(6.0)	-40	(5.3)	-38	(9.1)	-33	(5.0)	-33	(9.0)	-40	(5.3)	-30	(8.6)	-58	(7.5)	-26	(5.2)
Italy	-57	(3.2)	-32	(3.1)	-50	(2.8)	-39	(4.6)	-37	(3.0)	-37	(3.6)	-45	(2.8)	-46	(10.4)	-56	(3.4)	-40	(3.3)
Japan	-50	(8.6)	-34	(6.5)	-45	(11.3)	-41	(6.2)	-41	(7.1)	-24	(6.5)	-38	(6.8)	-46	(10.1)	-44	(7.1)	-39	(7.2)
Korea	-39	(5.8)	-24	(8.2)	-40	(7.1)	-26	(4.9)	-43	(6.6)	-20	(6.6)	-44	(6.1)	-11	(7.1)	-39	(6.7)	-33	(5.9)
Luxembourg	-58	(5.4)	-26	(2.8)	-43	(2.9)	-19	(7.7)	-25	(3.3)	-10	(6.6)	-46	(2.6)	-16	(7.4)	-62	(6.0)	-28	(2.2)
Mexico	-24	(2.6)	-22	(1.7)	-26	(1.9)	-16	(2.4)	-24	(2.1)	-29	(2.9)	-22	(1.8)	-35	(3.0)	-32	(2.5)	-17	(2.0)
Netherlands	-27	(4.7)	-5	(3.5)	-31	(3.0)	-10	(6.2)	-17	(2.8)	10	(6.5)	-19	(2.6)	-31	(8.6)	-33	(4.2)	-21	(4.1)
New Zealand	-51	(5.5)	-43	(4.7)	-42	(4.2)	-50	(10.8)	-38	(4.6)	-26	(4.6)	-52	(4.3)	-14	(6.6)	-40	(4.3)	-48	(5.6)
Norway	-51	(5.6)	-42	(3.4)	-55	(3.9)	-48	(4.3)	-40	(3.1)	-24	(5.5)	-51	(3.4)	-35	(5.2)	-61	(6.5)	-43	(2.9)
Poland	-73	(5.1)	-30	(3.2)	-49	(2.7)	-36	(9.1)	-41	(2.7)	-39	(7.5)	-50	(3.0)	-32	(6.1)	-76	(6.5)	-41	(2.9)
Portugal	-46	(5.0)	-30	(2.9)	-38	(2.5)	-32	(6.6)	-32	(2.9)	-23	(5.9)	-33	(2.6)	-48	(7.6)	-41	(4.4)	-36	(3.3)
Slovak Republic	-65	(8.4)	-43	(3.8)	-54	(3.8)	-26	(8.7)	-46	(3.5)	-35	(7.4)	-57	(3.6)	-24	(7.0)	-69	(6.1)	-43	(3.8)
Slovenia	-72	(5.5)	-44	(2.7)	-56	(2.6)	-32	(7.1)	-46	(2.6)	-46	(7.3)	-53	(2.8)	-33	(6.8)	-65	(5.1)	-50	(2.9)
Spain	-33	(3.4)	-24	(2.6)	-30	(2.2)	-21	(5.3)	-21	(2.5)	-16	(3.1)	-23	(2.5)	-27	(4.1)	-30	(3.1)	-37	(2.5)
Sweden	-44	(5.2)	-38	(3.6)	-53	(3.0)	-29	(6.3)	-31	(3.5)	-22	(5.1)	-44	(2.9)	-43	(8.9)	-52	(6.3)	-41	(3.3)
Switzerland	-50	(5.6)	-29	(2.8)	-45	(3.1)	-28	(4.9)	-30	(3.1)	-8	(4.3)	-41	(2.8)	-26	(4.1)	-54	(6.1)	-35	(2.5)
Turkey	-49	(5.0)	-37	(4.4)	-43	(3.9)	-41	(6.0)	-34	(5.1)	-49	(4.5)	-43	(4.1)	-38	(5.8)	-61	(8.1)	-42	(3.7)
United Kingdom	-42	(6.1)	-16	(4.4)	-23	(4.4)	-23	(10.2)	-14	(4.4)	-15	(5.9)	-27	(4.2)	-6	(7.5)	-28	(5.6)	-23	(5.3)
United States	-25	(4.7)	-24	(5.4)	-21	(3.4)	-47	(9.7)	-18	(3.7)	-13	(5.4)	-30	(3.5)	-2	(7.1)	-27	(3.7)	-23	(5.9)
OECD average	**-47**	**(0.9)**	**-30**	**(0.7)**	**-42**	**(0.7)**	**-30**	**(1.3)**	**-31**	**(0.7)**	**-23**	**(1.0)**	**-40**	**(0.7)**	**-28**	**(1.3)**	**-47**	**(1.0)**	**-36**	**(0.7)**
Albania	-61	(5.5)	-58	(5.2)	-66	(5.9)	-45	(6.2)	-56	(6.5)	-53	(6.5)	-60	(4.7)	-48	(9.0)	-68	(6.3)	-53	(4.9)
Argentina	-26	(5.3)	-34	(6.1)	-36	(4.4)	-33	(6.6)	-38	(4.7)	-25	(8.9)	-40	(4.4)	-23	(9.1)	-51	(5.3)	-21	(5.9)
Azerbaijan	-22	(3.3)	-22	(4.5)	-24	(4.4)	-21	(3.8)	-25	(3.6)	-18	(3.6)	-24	(3.5)	-20	(3.9)	-30	(3.1)	-17	(3.8)
Brazil	-26	(2.8)	-21	(3.3)	-31	(2.5)	-19	(3.3)	-31	(2.8)	-27	(3.4)	-25	(2.1)	-39	(6.3)	-32	(2.6)	-24	(2.9)
Bulgaria	-59	(7.8)	-47	(4.5)	-58	(5.2)	-57	(12.0)	-51	(5.3)	-54	(7.9)	-65	(5.1)	-40	(6.8)	-78	(7.3)	-42	(5.0)
Colombia	-13	(4.8)	-8	(4.7)	-16	(5.6)	-5	(3.9)	-13	(4.1)	-13	(6.2)	-10	(4.4)	-10	(5.3)	-13	(5.2)	-7	(4.4)
Croatia	-70	(6.6)	-41	(4.5)	-53	(5.0)	-32	(7.4)	-45	(4.7)	-40	(6.5)	-48	(4.8)	-48	(6.5)	-52	(9.7)	-51	(4.4)
Dubai (UAE)	-61	(5.2)	-43	(3.7)	-54	(3.7)	-45	(4.6)	-42	(3.4)	-46	(4.5)	-48	(3.0)	-55	(6.2)	-68	(5.9)	-46	(3.0)
Hong Kong-China	-36	(4.5)	-30	(5.5)	-31	(5.0)	-35	(5.9)	-27	(5.0)	-29	(5.0)	-36	(4.7)	-28	(5.7)	-37	(7.2)	-31	(4.6)
Indonesia	-36	(3.7)	-36	(3.9)	-42	(3.9)	-32	(3.9)	-33	(4.2)	-37	(4.0)	-35	(3.3)	-34	(5.0)	-41	(4.4)	-36	(3.6)
Jordan	-57	(7.2)	-42	(5.8)	-55	(7.1)	-48	(5.7)	-54	(6.5)	-53	(6.3)	-57	(6.1)	-43	(7.1)	-58	(7.2)	-53	(5.7)
Kazakhstan	-52	(6.2)	-39	(3.0)	-43	(3.1)	-44	(4.0)	-43	(5.4)	-43	(3.0)	-45	(4.2)	-40	(3.3)	-61	(7.6)	-39	(2.8)
Kyrgyzstan	-51	(4.4)	-47	(4.3)	-49	(3.4)	-61	(5.3)	-49	(5.4)	-51	(3.2)	-55	(3.1)	-45	(5.0)	-73	(6.6)	-43	(3.2)
Latvia	-58	(6.5)	-40	(3.3)	-47	(3.2)	-45	(8.9)	-45	(3.6)	-46	(5.7)	-48	(3.2)	-40	(5.7)	-59	(5.3)	-41	(3.3)
Liechtenstein	-44	(15.9)	-24	(10.4)	-36	(8.8)	-14	(24.6)	-31	(8.7)	1	(16.5)	-35	(8.5)	-12	(24.5)	-39	(15.2)	-31	(10.1)
Lithuania	-79	(5.6)	-47	(3.0)	-61	(3.0)	-39	(6.2)	-46	(3.8)	-47	(4.4)	-57	(3.2)	-43	(4.8)	-65	(5.0)	-55	(3.1)
Macao-China	-38	(2.3)	-30	(2.7)	-37	(2.1)	-32	(3.5)	-27	(2.3)	-34	(3.8)	-36	(2.1)	-30	(3.5)	-33	(3.8)	-32	(2.1)
Montenegro	-47	(6.9)	-46	(3.1)	-53	(3.9)	-47	(4.9)	-48	(3.6)	-48	(4.6)	-53	(3.4)	-44	(5.2)	-52	(7.2)	-53	(3.4)
Panama	-27	(8.7)	-28	(8.0)	-41	(8.8)	-18	(9.1)	-34	(9.6)	-33	(8.7)	-32	(6.8)	-36	(12.2)	-56	(13.4)	-22	(6.2)
Peru	-14	(4.5)	-27	(6.4)	-27	(5.7)	-20	(5.4)	-16	(6.0)	-28	(5.8)	-23	(5.6)	-24	(5.5)	-20	(5.9)	-25	(4.9)
Qatar	-63	(4.1)	-32	(2.3)	-59	(3.3)	-32	(2.9)	-41	(2.7)	-42	(3.3)	-44	(2.6)	-47	(4.5)	-61	(4.5)	-39	(2.3)
Romania	-38	(6.2)	-35	(4.6)	-42	(4.4)	-40	(10.0)	-37	(4.4)	-46	(6.3)	-44	(4.5)	-31	(6.8)	-44	(6.2)	-40	(4.3)
Russian Federation	-59	(5.9)	-36	(3.0)	-42	(3.0)	-48	(6.6)	-43	(5.0)	-35	(3.1)	-47	(3.5)	-33	(5.0)	-56	(4.9)	-37	(2.9)
Serbia	-50	(5.4)	-31	(3.7)	-40	(3.1)	-21	(7.4)	-34	(3.5)	-41	(4.7)	-37	(3.1)	-40	(8.1)	-49	(5.9)	-36	(3.4)
Shanghai-China	-42	(3.7)	-36	(3.5)	-35	(3.1)	-45	(4.8)	-33	(3.5)	-43	(3.6)	-39	(3.2)	-46	(4.8)	-48	(4.3)	-36	(3.1)
Singapore	-34	(3.6)	-28	(3.5)	-32	(3.0)	-32	(5.4)	-25	(3.9)	-21	(3.6)	-37	(3.2)	-17	(4.6)	-50	(6.8)	-28	(2.6)
Chinese Taipei	-47	(5.4)	-24	(6.6)	-42	(5.7)	-30	(6.3)	-34	(5.2)	-28	(6.5)	-40	(5.4)	-29	(6.3)	-56	(6.2)	-27	(5.8)
Thailand	-40	(4.6)	-28	(3.9)	-47	(5.0)	-32	(4.0)	-33	(4.9)	-36	(4.3)	-40	(4.1)	-31	(4.7)	-45	(5.3)	-33	(4.0)
Trinidad and Tobago	-65	(4.3)	-40	(4.5)	-66	(3.7)	-39	(5.5)	-50	(4.4)	-53	(4.9)	-50	(3.5)	-59	(7.1)	-91	(9.0)	-47	(3.2)
Tunisia	-32	(4.2)	-25	(4.3)	-31	(3.2)	-33	(3.7)	-25	(3.1)	-39	(4.1)	-35	(2.4)	-17	(5.8)	-33	(4.9)	-28	(2.9)
Uruguay	-32	(4.2)	-35	(4.1)	-43	(3.6)	-32	(6.0)	-36	(3.3)	-46	(6.4)	-35	(3.3)	-58	(9.4)	-46	(3.5)	-32	(5.6)

Note: Values that are statistically significant are indicated in bold (see Annex A3).
StatLink ⌨ http://dx.doi.org/10.1787/888932343285

[Part 1/2]

Table III.1.8 Percentage of students who read fiction, comic books and other materials

Percentage of students who reported that they read the following materials because they want to "several times a month" or "several times a week"

		Percentage of students who read different materials																			
		Fiction and others but no comics								Fiction and comics and others								Comics and others but no fiction			
		All students		Boys		Girls		Difference (B – G)		All students		Boys		Girls		Difference (B – G)		All students		Boys	
		%	S.E.	%	S.E.	%	S.E.	%	S.E.	%	S.E.	%	S.E.	%	S.E.	%	S.E.	%	S.E.	%	S.E.
OECD	Australia	33.5	(0.6)	23.2	(0.7)	43.3	(0.7)	**-20.1**	(0.9)	4.8	(0.3)	5.1	(0.3)	4.6	(0.4)	0.6	(0.5)	4.2	(0.2)	6.4	(0.3)
	Austria	22.7	(0.8)	11.4	(0.7)	33.2	(1.2)	**-21.8**	(1.4)	4.2	(0.3)	4.0	(0.4)	4.3	(0.6)	-0.3	(0.7)	9.5	(0.6)	14.1	(0.9)
	Belgium	12.6	(0.5)	5.9	(0.4)	19.5	(0.8)	**-13.6**	(0.9)	9.8	(0.4)	9.3	(0.5)	10.4	(0.6)	-1.1	(0.7)	21.9	(0.6)	30.4	(0.8)
	Canada	33.9	(0.5)	20.7	(0.6)	47.2	(0.8)	**-26.4**	(1.0)	8.2	(0.3)	8.9	(0.5)	7.5	(0.4)	**1.4**	(0.6)	6.2	(0.3)	9.3	(0.4)
	Chile	19.8	(0.6)	12.2	(0.7)	27.6	(1.0)	**-15.3**	(1.0)	10.8	(0.5)	9.8	(0.6)	12.0	(0.6)	**-2.2**	(0.8)	10.1	(0.5)	13.1	(0.6)
	Czech Republic	14.5	(0.7)	5.6	(0.5)	24.3	(1.1)	**-18.6**	(1.1)	3.1	(0.3)	2.1	(0.3)	4.3	(0.5)	**-2.2**	(0.5)	12.3	(0.6)	16.2	(0.9)
	Denmark	22.5	(0.6)	14.2	(0.9)	30.6	(1.0)	**-16.4**	(1.4)	8.0	(0.5)	8.7	(0.7)	7.3	(0.6)	1.4	(0.9)	12.7	(0.5)	19.2	(0.9)
	Estonia	20.9	(0.8)	13.4	(0.6)	29.0	(1.2)	**-15.6**	(1.1)	3.1	(0.3)	2.6	(0.4)	3.6	(0.5)	-1.0	(0.6)	10.3	(0.5)	15.1	(0.8)
	Finland	9.9	(0.5)	2.9	(0.4)	17.0	(0.9)	**-14.1**	(0.9)	16.2	(0.6)	10.2	(0.6)	22.2	(1.0)	**-12.1**	(1.1)	43.9	(0.8)	59.8	(1.2)
	France	17.4	(0.7)	8.3	(0.6)	26.0	(1.1)	**-17.7**	(1.1)	11.6	(0.5)	13.0	(0.8)	10.3	(0.7)	**2.7**	(1.0)	18.7	(0.7)	27.5	(1.0)
	Germany	28.5	(0.8)	15.3	(0.9)	41.7	(1.1)	**-26.4**	(1.2)	4.3	(0.3)	5.1	(0.5)	3.4	(0.3)	**1.7**	(0.6)	7.0	(0.4)	11.2	(0.7)
	Greece	15.2	(0.6)	7.4	(0.6)	22.7	(0.8)	**-15.3**	(0.9)	6.5	(0.4)	5.3	(0.5)	7.6	(0.6)	**-2.3**	(0.8)	18.2	(0.6)	25.2	(1.0)
	Hungary	21.2	(0.9)	14.5	(1.0)	28.0	(1.3)	**-13.5**	(1.4)	10.3	(0.6)	9.6	(0.7)	11.0	(0.8)	-1.3	(1.0)	16.2	(0.6)	18.7	(1.0)
	Iceland	16.2	(0.5)	8.2	(0.6)	24.0	(1.0)	**-15.7**	(1.2)	11.2	(0.5)	10.7	(0.6)	11.6	(0.7)	-0.9	(1.0)	19.8	(0.8)	24.5	(1.1)
	Ireland	26.9	(1.0)	20.1	(1.2)	33.8	(1.3)	**-13.6**	(1.8)	3.3	(0.3)	4.1	(0.5)	2.5	(0.3)	**1.6**	(0.6)	4.2	(0.3)	6.1	(0.6)
	Israel	21.0	(0.7)	13.7	(1.0)	27.9	(0.9)	**-14.2**	(1.4)	8.5	(0.5)	5.5	(0.5)	11.3	(0.7)	**-5.8**	(0.9)	8.9	(0.5)	8.5	(0.7)
	Italy	28.1	(0.4)	17.3	(0.5)	39.4	(0.6)	**-22.1**	(0.7)	6.9	(0.2)	7.5	(0.3)	6.3	(0.2)	**1.2**	(0.4)	10.4	(0.3)	15.6	(0.4)
	Japan	7.8	(0.5)	4.6	(0.4)	11.3	(0.8)	**-6.7**	(0.8)	34.2	(0.9)	32.1	(1.1)	36.5	(1.1)	**-4.4**	(1.4)	38.1	(1.0)	49.3	(1.2)
	Korea	22.8	(0.8)	15.0	(0.7)	31.3	(1.2)	**-16.3**	(1.4)	23.9	(0.7)	25.8	(0.9)	21.8	(0.9)	**4.0**	(1.1)	16.5	(0.7)	24.0	(1.1)
	Luxembourg	21.9	(0.6)	10.3	(0.7)	33.6	(1.0)	**-23.2**	(1.3)	7.0	(0.4)	6.5	(0.5)	7.6	(0.6)	-1.2	(0.8)	13.2	(0.5)	19.9	(0.9)
	Mexico	22.6	(0.4)	15.6	(0.5)	29.4	(0.5)	**-13.8**	(0.7)	15.3	(0.4)	15.5	(0.5)	15.0	(0.4)	0.4	(0.5)	11.6	(0.3)	16.1	(0.5)
	Netherlands	15.7	(0.7)	4.8	(0.5)	26.2	(1.2)	**-21.3**	(1.3)	5.9	(0.5)	5.3	(0.5)	6.5	(0.7)	-1.2	(0.8)	17.3	(0.7)	26.4	(1.2)
	New Zealand	37.4	(0.8)	27.1	(1.0)	48.0	(1.1)	**-21.0**	(1.4)	7.0	(0.4)	8.1	(0.6)	5.9	(0.5)	**2.1**	(0.7)	4.6	(0.3)	6.9	(0.5)
	Norway	13.5	(0.6)	5.9	(0.4)	21.4	(1.1)	**-15.4**	(1.1)	12.9	(0.5)	11.1	(0.8)	14.9	(0.8)	**-3.8**	(1.1)	29.3	(0.8)	39.6	(1.1)
	Poland	17.2	(0.7)	8.9	(0.6)	25.3	(1.0)	**-16.5**	(1.1)	3.0	(0.3)	2.6	(0.3)	3.3	(0.4)	-0.6	(0.5)	8.3	(0.4)	11.5	(0.7)
	Portugal	20.9	(0.6)	9.7	(0.5)	31.5	(1.1)	**-21.8**	(1.3)	7.2	(0.4)	6.7	(0.5)	7.6	(0.5)	-0.9	(0.7)	11.3	(0.5)	16.9	(0.7)
	Slovak Republic	14.0	(0.6)	7.9	(0.6)	20.0	(0.9)	**-12.2**	(1.1)	3.7	(0.3)	2.2	(0.4)	5.1	(0.5)	**-2.9**	(0.7)	9.5	(0.4)	9.2	(0.7)
	Slovenia	12.5	(0.6)	6.0	(0.5)	19.1	(1.1)	**-13.1**	(1.1)	2.9	(0.3)	2.8	(0.4)	2.9	(0.4)	-0.1	(0.6)	11.8	(0.4)	16.4	(0.8)
	Spain	24.4	(0.5)	14.9	(0.6)	34.3	(0.7)	**-19.5**	(1.0)	5.6	(0.3)	6.5	(0.4)	4.6	(0.3)	**2.0**	(0.5)	6.4	(0.2)	10.1	(0.4)
	Sweden	23.3	(0.8)	11.5	(0.8)	35.4	(1.2)	**-23.9**	(1.3)	9.0	(0.5)	8.4	(0.8)	9.6	(0.7)	-1.1	(1.1)	13.5	(0.5)	20.4	(0.9)
	Switzerland	20.9	(0.6)	9.9	(0.6)	32.1	(1.0)	**-22.2**	(1.1)	9.1	(0.3)	9.1	(0.4)	9.2	(0.5)	-0.2	(0.7)	14.9	(0.5)	21.8	(0.9)
	Turkey	40.0	(0.8)	29.0	(0.9)	51.9	(1.2)	**-22.9**	(1.5)	16.0	(0.6)	15.9	(0.8)	16.1	(0.9)	-0.2	(1.1)	6.6	(0.3)	8.6	(0.5)
	United Kingdom	28.3	(0.7)	19.9	(0.9)	36.2	(0.9)	**-16.3**	(1.3)	3.4	(0.3)	3.9	(0.4)	2.9	(0.3)	**1.0**	(0.5)	4.4	(0.3)	6.7	(0.5)
	United States	30.9	(1.0)	22.0	(1.2)	40.1	(1.2)	**-18.1**	(1.2)	5.9	(0.4)	6.0	(0.6)	5.8	(0.5)	0.2	(0.8)	4.5	(0.4)	6.7	(0.5)
	OECD average	21.7	(0.1)	12.9	(0.1)	30.7	(0.2)	**-17.8**	(0.2)	8.9	(0.1)	8.5	(0.1)	9.3	(0.1)	**-0.8**	(0.1)	13.4	(0.1)	18.6	(0.1)
Partners	Albania	26.9	(0.9)	15.8	(0.9)	38.3	(1.3)	**-22.6**	(1.5)	27.2	(1.1)	24.8	(1.5)	29.7	(1.3)	**-4.9**	(1.7)	16.2	(0.7)	21.8	(1.1)
	Argentina	16.2	(0.7)	11.1	(0.7)	20.5	(1.1)	**-9.4**	(1.3)	10.6	(0.5)	8.0	(0.7)	12.8	(0.7)	**-4.9**	(0.9)	18.6	(0.8)	20.0	(1.1)
	Azerbaijan	24.0	(0.9)	20.1	(1.0)	28.0	(1.3)	**-7.8**	(1.5)	28.3	(1.1)	26.1	(1.2)	30.5	(1.4)	**-4.3**	(1.6)	19.6	(0.9)	23.1	(1.3)
	Brazil	20.0	(0.5)	9.9	(0.6)	28.9	(0.8)	**-19.0**	(0.9)	15.5	(0.4)	11.2	(0.5)	19.3	(0.7)	**-8.1**	(0.8)	17.7	(0.6)	24.3	(0.8)
	Bulgaria	27.1	(1.4)	18.7	(1.2)	36.0	(1.8)	**-17.3**	(1.6)	7.1	(0.5)	6.4	(0.6)	7.8	(0.8)	-1.4	(1.0)	10.4	(0.6)	13.0	(0.9)
	Colombia	18.2	(0.8)	12.8	(1.0)	23.0	(1.2)	**-10.2**	(1.6)	19.4	(0.8)	17.7	(1.1)	21.0	(1.1)	**-3.4**	(1.5)	23.7	(0.8)	28.8	(1.3)
	Croatia	17.3	(0.7)	9.4	(0.7)	26.2	(1.2)	**-16.9**	(1.4)	4.8	(0.4)	5.0	(0.5)	4.6	(0.4)	0.4	(0.6)	13.8	(0.5)	19.2	(0.9)
	Dubai (UAE)	20.8	(0.6)	16.0	(0.8)	25.6	(1.0)	**-9.7**	(1.2)	19.5	(0.7)	17.0	(0.8)	22.0	(0.9)	**-5.0**	(1.2)	19.8	(0.5)	21.0	(0.7)
	Hong Kong-China	29.6	(0.8)	21.1	(1.1)	39.1	(1.2)	**-18.1**	(1.6)	18.9	(0.6)	21.0	(0.9)	16.6	(0.9)	**4.3**	(1.3)	11.4	(0.5)	16.5	(0.8)
	Indonesia	18.5	(0.6)	15.4	(0.9)	21.6	(0.9)	**-6.1**	(1.2)	40.9	(0.9)	36.4	(1.1)	45.4	(1.4)	**-8.9**	(1.8)	11.4	(0.6)	14.9	(0.9)
	Jordan	16.2	(0.5)	14.4	(0.8)	17.9	(0.8)	**-3.5**	(1.2)	19.7	(0.6)	18.1	(0.8)	21.3	(1.1)	**-3.2**	(1.3)	24.9	(0.7)	20.9	(1.1)
	Kazakhstan	40.5	(0.9)	37.7	(1.2)	43.4	(1.2)	**-5.7**	(1.6)	29.3	(1.1)	27.5	(1.3)	31.1	(1.2)	**-3.6**	(1.2)	8.4	(0.4)	9.0	(0.5)
	Kyrgyzstan	48.2	(1.1)	41.6	(1.5)	54.3	(1.5)	**-12.7**	(2.0)	18.5	(1.0)	18.0	(1.4)	19.0	(1.1)	-0.9	(1.4)	5.9	(0.4)	7.1	(0.7)
	Latvia	29.3	(1.1)	20.3	(1.2)	38.1	(1.7)	**-17.9**	(2.1)	3.5	(0.4)	3.2	(0.5)	3.7	(0.6)	-0.6	(0.8)	6.0	(0.5)	8.7	(0.8)
	Liechtenstein	19.2	(1.9)	9.9	(2.1)	29.4	(3.6)	**-19.5**	(4.4)	9.1	(1.3)	10.4	(2.1)	7.7	(1.9)	2.7	(3.1)	11.8	(1.8)	15.6	(2.8)
	Lithuania	31.7	(0.7)	18.3	(0.9)	45.2	(1.0)	**-26.9**	(1.3)	7.0	(0.4)	5.3	(0.5)	8.8	(0.7)	**-3.5**	(0.9)	12.3	(0.6)	17.0	(0.9)
	Macao-China	17.1	(0.5)	9.7	(0.5)	24.6	(0.8)	**-14.9**	(1.0)	14.9	(0.5)	12.8	(0.5)	17.1	(0.8)	**-4.4**	(0.9)	22.3	(0.6)	31.1	(0.9)
	Montenegro	23.5	(0.6)	15.9	(0.6)	31.2	(0.9)	**-15.3**	(1.1)	10.4	(0.5)	10.7	(0.7)	10.0	(0.7)	0.7	(1.0)	16.5	(0.6)	20.9	(1.0)
	Panama	19.7	(1.1)	12.8	(1.2)	26.4	(1.6)	**-13.6**	(1.9)	20.1	(1.0)	19.2	(1.4)	21.0	(1.4)	-1.8	(2.0)	14.7	(0.8)	17.4	(1.5)
	Peru	22.8	(0.6)	18.6	(0.9)	27.1	(0.9)	**-8.5**	(1.3)	32.8	(0.8)	30.0	(1.1)	35.7	(1.1)	**-5.6**	(1.7)	15.6	(0.5)	18.1	(0.7)
	Qatar	12.8	(0.4)	10.4	(0.5)	15.2	(0.5)	**-4.8**	(0.7)	27.2	(0.4)	22.9	(0.6)	31.3	(0.7)	**-8.4**	(1.0)	23.6	(0.4)	23.4	(0.6)
	Romania	26.6	(0.9)	18.4	(0.9)	34.3	(1.3)	**-15.9**	(1.6)	5.2	(0.4)	4.2	(0.5)	6.2	(0.5)	**-2.0**	(0.8)	6.7	(0.4)	7.5	(0.7)
	Russian Federation	48.4	(1.1)	39.6	(1.6)	56.9	(1.0)	**-17.3**	(1.6)	10.4	(0.6)	10.2	(0.7)	10.6	(0.8)	-0.4	(1.0)	6.4	(0.4)	7.8	(0.9)
	Serbia	22.7	(0.8)	14.8	(0.8)	30.6	(1.3)	**-15.8**	(1.3)	5.7	(0.3)	6.5	(0.6)	4.9	(0.4)	**1.6**	(0.7)	11.8	(0.5)	16.1	(0.8)
	Shanghai-China	34.3	(0.7)	26.5	(0.9)	42.0	(1.1)	**-15.5**	(1.4)	21.8	(0.6)	25.0	(1.0)	18.8	(0.9)	**6.2**	(1.3)	7.6	(0.4)	11.1	(0.7)
	Singapore	28.3	(0.8)	18.4	(1.0)	38.6	(1.1)	**-20.2**	(1.4)	19.9	(0.6)	21.0	(0.9)	18.7	(0.8)	2.2	(1.2)	13.1	(0.5)	18.7	(0.8)
	Chinese Taipei	20.9	(0.7)	13.6	(0.7)	28.2	(1.1)	**-14.6**	(1.3)	27.0	(0.7)	27.1	(0.8)	26.9	(1.0)	0.2	(1.3)	13.3	(0.5)	19.7	(0.8)
	Thailand	7.9	(0.4)	7.6	(0.6)	8.2	(0.5)	-0.6	(0.8)	57.2	(0.9)	45.9	(1.3)	65.8	(0.9)	**-19.8**	(1.5)	15.0	(0.5)	21.3	(0.8)
	Trinidad and Tobago	23.8	(0.7)	16.1	(0.9)	31.0	(1.1)	**-14.9**	(1.3)	19.3	(0.6)	17.9	(0.9)	20.6	(0.8)	**-2.7**	(1.3)	17.4	(0.6)	20.3	(0.9)
	Tunisia	24.7	(0.8)	20.3	(1.0)	28.7	(1.1)	**-8.4**	(1.4)	21.9	(0.7)	17.9	(0.9)	25.6	(1.0)	**-7.7**	(1.3)	12.1	(0.5)	12.7	(0.8)
	Uruguay	16.3	(0.6)	9.9	(0.7)	21.8	(0.9)	**-12.0**	(1.1)	11.0	(0.5)	9.1	(0.6)	12.7	(0.6)	**-3.6**	(0.7)	13.4	(0.5)	15.7	(0.7)

Note: Values that are statistically significant are indicated in bold (see Annex A3).

StatLink http://dx.doi.org/10.1787/888932343285

[Part 2/2]

Percentage of students who read fiction, comic books and other materials
Percentage of students who reported that they read the following materials because they want to "several times a month" or "several times a week"

Table III.1.8

| | Comics and others but no fiction | | | | Others than fiction or comics | | | | | | | | Nothing | | | | | | | |
| | Girls | | Difference (B – G) | | All students | | Boys | | Girls | | Difference (B – G) | | All students | | Boys | | Girls | | Difference (B – G) | |
	%	S.E.	%	S.E.	%	S.E.	%	S.E.	%	S.E.	%	S.E.	%	S.E.	%	S.E.	%	S.E.	%	S.E.
OECD																				
Australia	2.0	(0.3)	4.4	(0.4)	40.7	(0.6)	45.7	(0.8)	35.9	(0.8)	9.8	(1.0)	16.8	(0.4)	19.6	(0.6)	14.2	(0.5)	5.4	(0.8)
Austria	5.3	(0.6)	8.8	(1.1)	56.5	(0.8)	61.4	(1.2)	51.8	(1.2)	9.6	(1.7)	7.2	(0.4)	9.1	(0.6)	5.4	(0.5)	3.8	(0.8)
Belgium	13.3	(0.7)	17.1	(0.9)	41.3	(0.6)	37.8	(0.9)	44.9	(0.8)	-7.0	(1.1)	14.3	(0.6)	16.7	(0.8)	12.0	(0.7)	4.7	(1.0)
Canada	3.1	(0.2)	6.2	(0.5)	32.7	(0.5)	36.3	(0.7)	29.1	(0.7)	7.3	(1.0)	19.0	(0.5)	24.7	(0.7)	13.2	(0.5)	11.6	(0.8)
Chile	7.0	(0.6)	6.1	(0.7)	39.0	(0.9)	40.0	(1.2)	37.9	(1.0)	2.1	(1.3)	20.3	(0.6)	24.9	(1.0)	15.5	(0.7)	9.4	(1.1)
Czech Republic	8.0	(0.6)	8.2	(1.1)	56.5	(0.9)	59.3	(1.0)	53.4	(1.3)	5.9	(1.5)	13.6	(0.5)	16.8	(0.8)	10.0	(0.8)	6.7	(1.1)
Denmark	6.4	(0.5)	12.8	(1.2)	41.8	(0.9)	39.3	(1.1)	44.3	(1.1)	-5.0	(1.4)	15.0	(0.6)	18.7	(0.9)	11.4	(0.7)	7.3	(1.1)
Estonia	5.2	(0.5)	9.9	(1.0)	58.4	(0.9)	59.4	(1.2)	57.4	(1.2)	2.0	(1.6)	7.3	(0.5)	9.6	(0.8)	4.8	(0.4)	4.7	(0.8)
Finland	28.1	(1.1)	31.7	(1.6)	24.1	(0.7)	19.8	(0.9)	28.3	(1.1)	-8.5	(1.4)	5.8	(0.4)	7.3	(0.6)	4.4	(0.5)	2.9	(0.8)
France	10.5	(0.6)	17.0	(1.1)	37.2	(0.9)	33.8	(1.1)	40.3	(1.2)	-6.5	(1.5)	15.1	(0.6)	17.4	(0.9)	12.9	(0.7)	4.5	(1.1)
Germany	2.9	(0.3)	8.3	(0.8)	46.0	(0.9)	52.4	(1.2)	39.6	(1.1)	12.8	(1.3)	14.2	(0.6)	16.0	(0.8)	12.4	(0.7)	3.5	(1.0)
Greece	11.5	(0.8)	13.7	(1.3)	42.6	(0.9)	44.2	(1.1)	41.1	(1.1)	3.1	(1.1)	17.5	(0.7)	17.9	(1.0)	17.1	(0.8)	0.7	(1.2)
Hungary	13.7	(0.8)	5.0	(1.2)	41.0	(0.9)	41.9	(1.2)	40.1	(1.2)	1.8	(1.6)	11.3	(0.6)	15.2	(0.9)	7.2	(0.6)	8.0	(1.1)
Iceland	15.2	(0.9)	9.4	(1.3)	43.7	(0.9)	44.4	(1.4)	42.9	(1.1)	1.6	(1.8)	9.2	(0.5)	12.1	(0.8)	6.4	(0.6)	5.7	(1.1)
Ireland	2.3	(0.4)	3.8	(0.7)	54.0	(1.0)	56.4	(1.3)	51.5	(1.4)	4.9	(1.9)	11.6	(0.5)	13.3	(0.8)	9.9	(0.7)	3.4	(1.1)
Israel	9.3	(0.6)	-0.8	(0.7)	47.4	(0.9)	53.6	(1.3)	41.5	(1.1)	12.1	(1.7)	14.2	(0.5)	18.7	(0.8)	10.0	(0.7)	8.7	(1.1)
Italy	5.0	(0.2)	10.7	(0.5)	37.1	(0.5)	38.8	(0.7)	35.2	(0.6)	3.6	(0.8)	17.5	(0.4)	20.7	(0.5)	14.1	(0.4)	6.6	(0.6)
Japan	26.2	(0.9)	23.1	(1.1)	15.2	(0.5)	9.8	(0.6)	21.0	(0.8)	-11.2	(1.1)	4.6	(0.3)	4.3	(0.4)	5.0	(0.5)	-0.7	(0.6)
Korea	8.3	(0.6)	15.7	(1.3)	16.2	(0.6)	15.2	(0.8)	17.4	(0.8)	-2.2	(1.1)	20.5	(0.7)	20.0	(1.0)	21.2	(1.0)	-1.2	(1.6)
Luxembourg	6.5	(0.5)	13.3	(1.0)	48.3	(0.7)	51.5	(1.0)	45.0	(1.1)	6.4	(1.5)	9.6	(0.5)	11.9	(0.7)	7.2	(0.6)	4.6	(0.8)
Mexico	7.3	(0.3)	8.9	(0.6)	30.5	(0.5)	30.8	(0.7)	30.4	(0.5)	0.4	(0.8)	20.0	(0.4)	22.1	(0.5)	17.9	(0.5)	4.1	(0.7)
Netherlands	8.4	(0.7)	17.9	(1.4)	40.7	(1.2)	38.3	(1.5)	43.1	(1.6)	-4.8	(2.1)	20.4	(1.3)	25.2	(1.7)	15.8	(1.2)	9.4	(1.5)
New Zealand	2.3	(0.3)	4.6	(0.6)	35.7	(0.8)	38.4	(1.2)	33.0	(1.2)	5.4	(1.6)	15.2	(0.6)	19.6	(0.9)	10.7	(0.8)	8.9	(1.2)
Norway	18.5	(0.9)	21.0	(1.4)	36.0	(0.8)	33.3	(1.0)	38.8	(1.3)	-5.5	(1.7)	8.3	(0.5)	10.2	(0.7)	6.4	(0.5)	3.7	(0.8)
Poland	5.1	(0.5)	6.4	(0.9)	59.8	(0.8)	61.1	(1.0)	58.5	(1.1)	2.7	(1.4)	11.8	(0.5)	15.8	(0.8)	7.8	(0.5)	8.0	(1.0)
Portugal	6.1	(0.5)	10.8	(0.9)	45.6	(0.7)	50.0	(1.0)	41.5	(1.1)	8.5	(1.6)	15.0	(0.5)	16.7	(0.7)	13.3	(0.6)	3.4	(1.0)
Slovak Republic	9.9	(0.5)	-0.7	(0.8)	63.3	(0.8)	67.0	(1.1)	59.6	(1.2)	7.4	(1.6)	9.5	(0.6)	13.7	(1.0)	5.3	(0.5)	8.4	(1.1)
Slovenia	7.3	(0.5)	9.1	(1.0)	62.4	(0.7)	61.1	(1.0)	63.8	(1.1)	-2.7	(1.4)	10.3	(0.5)	13.8	(0.7)	6.9	(0.5)	6.9	(0.8)
Spain	2.6	(0.3)	7.5	(0.5)	43.5	(0.6)	47.6	(0.8)	39.3	(0.8)	8.3	(1.1)	20.1	(0.4)	20.9	(0.7)	19.2	(0.7)	1.7	(0.9)
Sweden	6.5	(0.6)	13.8	(1.1)	39.7	(0.9)	41.9	(1.1)	37.4	(1.2)	4.6	(1.4)	14.5	(0.6)	17.8	(0.9)	11.1	(0.7)	6.6	(1.1)
Switzerland	8.0	(0.5)	13.8	(0.8)	47.5	(0.7)	49.8	(0.9)	45.2	(1.0)	4.7	(1.3)	7.5	(0.4)	9.4	(0.7)	5.5	(0.5)	3.9	(0.9)
Turkey	4.5	(0.5)	4.0	(0.8)	32.2	(0.8)	40.4	(1.2)	23.4	(1.0)	17.1	(1.5)	5.1	(0.4)	6.1	(0.5)	4.1	(0.4)	2.0	(0.6)
United Kingdom	2.2	(0.3)	4.5	(0.6)	50.5	(0.9)	52.4	(1.0)	48.8	(0.9)	3.6	(1.3)	13.5	(0.5)	17.1	(0.7)	10.0	(0.7)	7.2	(1.0)
United States	2.1	(0.3)	4.6	(0.6)	33.6	(1.0)	36.3	(1.2)	30.7	(1.3)	5.5	(1.3)	25.2	(0.7)	29.0	(1.0)	21.3	(0.9)	7.8	(1.3)
OECD average	8.3	(0.1)	10.3	(0.2)	42.4	(0.1)	43.8	(0.2)	40.9	(0.2)	2.9	(0.2)	13.6	(0.1)	16.2	(0.2)	10.9	(0.2)	5.4	(0.2)
Partners																				
Albania	10.5	(0.9)	11.3	(1.3)	19.2	(0.9)	23.1	(1.3)	15.2	(1.0)	7.9	(1.5)	10.5	(0.7)	14.5	(1.0)	6.3	(0.7)	8.3	(1.1)
Argentina	17.5	(1.1)	2.5	(1.4)	35.7	(1.0)	36.9	(1.6)	34.7	(1.3)	2.2	(2.0)	18.9	(0.7)	24.1	(1.1)	14.5	(0.7)	9.6	(1.3)
Azerbaijan	15.9	(1.0)	7.2	(1.5)	14.4	(0.7)	13.7	(0.8)	15.1	(1.0)	-1.4	(1.3)	13.7	(0.8)	16.9	(1.2)	10.5	(0.9)	6.3	(1.5)
Brazil	11.9	(0.6)	12.4	(0.8)	25.7	(0.6)	27.2	(0.8)	24.4	(0.8)	2.8	(1.1)	21.6	(0.6)	27.4	(1.0)	15.5	(0.7)	11.9	(1.1)
Bulgaria	7.7	(0.8)	5.3	(1.2)	39.7	(1.1)	39.5	(1.4)	39.9	(1.6)	-0.3	(2.1)	15.6	(0.9)	22.3	(1.4)	8.6	(0.8)	13.7	(1.5)
Colombia	19.1	(0.9)	9.8	(1.7)	23.4	(0.7)	21.9	(1.1)	24.7	(1.0)	-2.8	(1.5)	15.3	(0.9)	18.8	(1.1)	12.2	(0.9)	6.6	(1.1)
Croatia	7.7	(0.6)	11.6	(1.1)	59.1	(0.8)	60.2	(1.0)	57.9	(1.2)	2.4	(1.7)	5.0	(0.4)	6.2	(0.6)	3.7	(0.4)	2.5	(0.8)
Dubai (UAE)	18.6	(0.9)	2.4	(1.2)	32.1	(0.5)	36.9	(0.9)	27.2	(1.1)	9.7	(1.3)	7.9	(0.4)	9.2	(0.6)	6.6	(0.5)	2.6	(0.8)
Hong Kong-China	5.7	(0.6)	10.8	(1.0)	33.9	(0.8)	34.0	(1.1)	33.8	(1.1)	0.1	(1.4)	6.2	(0.4)	7.5	(0.6)	4.7	(0.5)	2.8	(0.8)
Indonesia	8.0	(0.7)	7.0	(1.1)	17.1	(0.7)	19.4	(0.9)	14.8	(0.9)	4.6	(1.1)	12.1	(0.8)	13.8	(1.1)	10.3	(0.8)	3.5	(1.1)
Jordan	28.7	(0.8)	-7.9	(1.3)	23.3	(0.6)	27.0	(0.9)	19.8	(0.7)	7.3	(1.0)	15.9	(0.5)	19.6	(0.8)	12.3	(0.8)	7.2	(1.1)
Kazakhstan	7.8	(0.6)	1.3	(0.8)	17.8	(0.7)	20.1	(0.9)	15.4	(0.9)	4.8	(1.0)	4.0	(0.3)	5.6	(0.6)	2.4	(0.3)	3.2	(0.6)
Kyrgyzstan	4.8	(0.4)	2.3	(0.8)	19.3	(0.7)	20.4	(1.1)	18.2	(0.9)	2.3	(1.4)	8.1	(0.6)	12.8	(1.0)	3.8	(0.4)	9.0	(1.1)
Latvia	3.3	(0.5)	5.4	(0.9)	50.4	(1.1)	51.3	(1.2)	49.4	(1.7)	1.9	(1.9)	10.9	(0.6)	16.5	(1.0)	5.4	(0.7)	11.1	(1.2)
Liechtenstein	7.6	(2.1)	8.0	(3.5)	48.1	(2.7)	49.1	(3.6)	47.1	(4.2)	2.0	(5.7)	11.8	(1.8)	15.0	(2.9)	8.2	(1.7)	6.8	(3.3)
Lithuania	7.5	(0.6)	9.5	(0.9)	40.7	(0.7)	46.3	(1.2)	35.0	(1.0)	11.3	(1.3)	8.3	(0.4)	13.1	(0.7)	3.5	(0.5)	9.6	(0.8)
Macao-China	13.4	(0.7)	17.8	(1.1)	35.5	(0.6)	33.5	(0.8)	37.5	(0.9)	-4.1	(1.2)	10.2	(0.4)	13.0	(0.6)	7.4	(0.5)	5.5	(0.7)
Montenegro	11.9	(0.7)	9.0	(1.2)	42.4	(0.8)	43.0	(1.1)	41.8	(1.1)	1.2	(1.6)	7.2	(0.4)	9.4	(0.7)	5.0	(0.5)	4.4	(0.9)
Panama	12.1	(1.0)	5.3	(2.0)	32.8	(1.4)	35.3	(2.3)	30.3	(1.3)	5.1	(2.3)	12.7	(1.1)	15.3	(1.8)	10.3	(1.1)	5.0	(1.9)
Peru	13.1	(0.7)	5.0	(0.9)	21.5	(0.8)	24.7	(1.1)	18.3	(0.8)	6.5	(1.2)	7.2	(0.5)	8.5	(0.7)	5.8	(0.6)	2.7	(0.8)
Qatar	23.8	(0.6)	-0.4	(0.9)	24.9	(0.5)	28.6	(0.7)	21.3	(0.6)	7.2	(0.9)	11.5	(0.4)	14.7	(0.6)	8.4	(0.4)	6.3	(0.7)
Romania	5.9	(0.5)	1.6	(0.9)	44.0	(1.0)	46.8	(1.3)	41.3	(1.2)	5.5	(1.5)	17.6	(0.8)	23.2	(1.2)	12.3	(0.9)	10.9	(1.5)
Russian Federation	5.2	(0.4)	2.6	(1.2)	26.2	(0.8)	29.2	(1.0)	23.2	(1.0)	5.9	(1.2)	8.6	(0.6)	13.3	(1.0)	4.1	(0.5)	9.2	(1.1)
Serbia	7.4	(0.6)	8.7	(1.0)	52.0	(0.9)	51.5	(0.9)	52.6	(1.5)	-1.1	(1.7)	7.9	(0.4)	11.2	(0.7)	4.6	(0.4)	6.6	(0.8)
Shanghai-China	4.2	(0.4)	6.9	(0.8)	28.4	(0.8)	28.6	(1.1)	28.2	(0.9)	0.3	(1.1)	7.8	(0.5)	8.8	(0.7)	6.7	(0.5)	2.1	(0.8)
Singapore	7.3	(0.5)	11.4	(1.0)	32.4	(0.7)	34.6	(0.9)	30.2	(0.9)	4.5	(1.1)	6.3	(0.4)	7.3	(0.6)	5.2	(0.5)	2.1	(0.7)
Chinese Taipei	6.7	(0.5)	13.0	(0.9)	27.7	(0.7)	26.7	(0.8)	28.8	(1.1)	-2.1	(1.3)	11.1	(0.5)	12.8	(0.8)	9.4	(0.7)	3.4	(1.0)
Thailand	10.2	(0.6)	11.1	(1.0)	13.5	(0.6)	15.3	(1.0)	12.1	(0.7)	3.2	(1.2)	6.4	(0.4)	9.8	(0.8)	3.8	(0.4)	6.0	(0.9)
Trinidad and Tobago	14.7	(0.8)	5.6	(1.2)	32.1	(0.7)	35.7	(1.1)	28.8	(1.0)	6.9	(1.5)	7.4	(0.4)	10.0	(0.7)	4.9	(0.5)	5.1	(0.9)
Tunisia	11.5	(0.7)	1.2	(1.1)	29.3	(0.8)	34.4	(1.2)	24.8	(0.9)	9.6	(1.5)	12.0	(0.6)	14.8	(1.1)	9.4	(0.7)	5.3	(1.2)
Uruguay	11.5	(0.7)	4.2	(0.9)	30.2	(0.8)	27.5	(1.0)	32.6	(1.1)	-5.1	(1.4)	29.1	(0.7)	37.9	(1.1)	21.4	(0.9)	16.5	(1.4)

Note: Values that are statistically significant are indicated in bold (see Annex A3).
StatLink ⟹ http://dx.doi.org/10.1787/888932343285

[Part 1/2]
Reading performance of students who read fiction, comic books and others materials
Percentage of students who reported that they read the following materials because they want to "several times a month" or "several times a week"

Table III.1.9

	Performance on the reading scale of students reading different materials									
	All students					Boys				
	Fiction and others but no comics	Fiction and comics and others	Comics and others but no fiction	Others than fiction or comics	Nothing	Fiction and others but no comics	Fiction and comics and others	Comics and others but no fiction	Others than fiction or comics	Nothing
	Mean Score S.E.	Mean Score S.E.	Mean Score S.E.	Mean Score S.E.	Mean Score S.E.	Mean Score S.E.	Mean Score S.E.	Mean Score S.E.	Mean Score S.E.	Mean Score S.E.
Australia	566 (2.6)	546 (5.9)	485 (6.1)	491 (2.4)	483 (2.4)	559 (3.7)	531 (8.0)	475 (5.8)	480 (3.4)	473 (3.6)
Austria	536 (4.3)	498 (8.4)	441 (5.7)	464 (2.8)	420 (6.5)	517 (7.8)	502 (11.3)	437 (7.3)	451 (4.2)	410 (8.9)
Belgium	562 (4.0)	562 (4.0)	516 (3.1)	502 (2.7)	466 (4.8)	555 (8.9)	563 (4.8)	514 (3.4)	491 (4.2)	452 (5.2)
Canada	561 (1.8)	547 (3.3)	500 (3.3)	508 (1.8)	494 (2.4)	550 (2.9)	537 (4.3)	494 (4.2)	500 (2.4)	486 (3.0)
Chile	470 (4.3)	448 (4.4)	443 (4.6)	458 (3.1)	426 (4.3)	458 (7.5)	436 (5.4)	443 (5.6)	448 (3.8)	420 (4.7)
Czech Republic	545 (4.1)	525 (10.0)	474 (6.2)	474 (2.7)	451 (4.6)	537 (7.6)	527 (16.9)	466 (7.4)	459 (3.8)	428 (4.5)
Denmark	523 (3.2)	532 (4.5)	491 (3.6)	491 (2.7)	458 (3.7)	507 (5.2)	524 (5.6)	488 (4.5)	481 (3.6)	444 (4.3)
Estonia	535 (3.7)	499 (8.0)	469 (5.5)	501 (2.5)	461 (6.0)	510 (5.3)	462 (10.6)	464 (5.9)	486 (3.0)	444 (6.8)
Finland	588 (4.4)	593 (3.3)	522 (2.6)	521 (2.8)	475 (6.1)	566 (13.9)	574 (5.3)	508 (2.8)	490 (4.0)	458 (8.0)
France	557 (4.1)	538 (5.5)	489 (4.7)	481 (3.8)	451 (5.7)	551 (7.5)	528 (7.2)	484 (5.6)	463 (5.0)	426 (8.0)
Germany	553 (3.2)	546 (7.6)	472 (6.6)	490 (2.9)	467 (4.9)	545 (5.4)	542 (9.0)	474 (7.4)	481 (3.6)	444 (6.3)
Greece	523 (3.7)	524 (6.3)	469 (5.8)	481 (5.2)	457 (7.6)	495 (8.8)	507 (9.2)	461 (6.8)	460 (6.8)	429 (8.0)
Hungary	534 (4.5)	490 (8.3)	478 (4.4)	497 (3.1)	446 (5.9)	517 (7.1)	483 (10.4)	464 (5.8)	484 (4.2)	430 (6.7)
Iceland	553 (3.8)	544 (4.2)	501 (3.2)	488 (2.4)	430 (5.1)	533 (9.5)	528 (6.8)	486 (4.4)	473 (3.3)	411 (6.9)
Ireland	549 (3.3)	499 (11.7)	460 (6.7)	483 (3.0)	478 (6.1)	523 (5.9)	499 (15.9)	458 (8.0)	472 (4.1)	459 (8.5)
Israel	517 (4.9)	463 (6.8)	456 (6.0)	486 (4.0)	434 (5.5)	498 (10.4)	430 (11.0)	441 (8.1)	473 (5.4)	418 (6.9)
Italy	514 (1.9)	534 (3.5)	488 (2.8)	476 (2.0)	449 (2.8)	483 (3.1)	524 (5.0)	479 (3.3)	462 (2.7)	426 (3.7)
Japan	554 (6.0)	547 (3.3)	501 (4.0)	509 (4.9)	475 (9.5)	548 (8.8)	533 (4.9)	488 (5.1)	482 (10.6)	432 (14.9)
Korea	566 (3.7)	547 (3.9)	516 (5.0)	545 (4.6)	518 (5.0)	552 (5.2)	542 (5.1)	507 (5.8)	529 (5.8)	493 (8.4)
Luxembourg	535 (3.0)	503 (6.3)	454 (4.3)	457 (1.8)	432 (5.4)	530 (6.8)	505 (9.6)	451 (5.4)	447 (2.8)	412 (7.2)
Mexico	431 (2.6)	414 (2.2)	424 (2.2)	441 (1.9)	415 (2.8)	410 (4.0)	405 (2.5)	418 (2.7)	431 (2.4)	402 (3.5)
Netherlands	554 (5.6)	549 (7.3)	514 (7.1)	511 (5.3)	470 (6.0)	564 (11.6)	556 (8.2)	512 (6.4)	503 (5.2)	459 (6.8)
New Zealand	565 (3.1)	526 (7.9)	475 (8.1)	499 (3.1)	492 (4.5)	554 (4.6)	509 (10.8)	463 (9.6)	482 (4.2)	479 (5.7)
Norway	546 (4.2)	556 (4.4)	501 (3.0)	486 (2.8)	450 (5.6)	528 (7.4)	539 (6.4)	488 (3.6)	465 (3.5)	425 (6.9)
Poland	549 (4.1)	521 (9.7)	474 (5.7)	499 (2.6)	462 (4.6)	525 (7.8)	492 (13.7)	468 (6.8)	483 (3.0)	435 (5.0)
Portugal	526 (3.7)	498 (6.0)	480 (4.7)	481 (3.2)	473 (4.2)	516 (5.9)	483 (9.7)	472 (5.5)	468 (3.9)	451 (5.3)
Slovak Republic	533 (4.4)	506 (10.5)	475 (4.9)	475 (2.5)	427 (5.9)	512 (7.6)	478 (17.3)	465 (7.3)	455 (3.7)	408 (6.8)
Slovenia	546 (4.0)	510 (9.5)	465 (3.9)	483 (1.5)	450 (3.9)	514 (7.4)	486 (14.8)	459 (4.5)	461 (2.2)	430 (4.7)
Spain	522 (2.3)	508 (5.1)	466 (3.9)	471 (2.4)	454 (3.0)	513 (3.6)	500 (5.1)	466 (4.5)	463 (2.5)	440 (3.9)
Sweden	554 (3.4)	543 (5.9)	487 (4.3)	484 (2.8)	440 (4.1)	538 (6.0)	536 (7.4)	484 (4.9)	468 (3.5)	426 (5.3)
Switzerland	551 (3.4)	550 (4.5)	491 (3.8)	484 (2.5)	438 (4.3)	545 (5.2)	545 (5.6)	485 (3.9)	469 (3.3)	424 (5.3)
Turkey	477 (3.9)	450 (4.9)	458 (6.0)	467 (4.0)	438 (5.9)	448 (4.4)	429 (6.4)	446 (7.0)	456 (4.4)	413 (6.7)
United Kingdom	546 (3.1)	507 (8.2)	452 (5.0)	480 (2.7)	467 (4.1)	541 (4.9)	491 (11.9)	455 (5.8)	475 (4.2)	458 (5.0)
United States	538 (4.9)	502 (7.5)	469 (8.3)	489 (3.5)	479 (4.2)	537 (5.8)	479 (9.0)	463 (8.8)	481 (4.6)	474 (5.0)
OECD average	538 (0.7)	518 (1.1)	478 (0.9)	487 (0.5)	457 (0.9)	523 (1.2)	506 (1.6)	471 (1.0)	473 (0.7)	439 (1.1)
Albania	419 (5.0)	385 (4.7)	365 (5.7)	394 (6.2)	364 (9.0)	383 (7.6)	361 (7.7)	354 (6.1)	373 (7.7)	337 (9.4)
Argentina	420 (6.7)	389 (7.1)	407 (5.7)	418 (5.7)	374 (5.6)	406 (10.5)	369 (11.6)	386 (7.2)	402 (7.2)	357 (6.7)
Azerbaijan	379 (4.1)	372 (3.6)	367 (4.7)	371 (5.1)	347 (5.5)	370 (5.5)	362 (4.8)	357 (5.4)	361 (6.5)	337 (5.9)
Brazil	433 (4.3)	399 (3.2)	410 (3.2)	435 (3.4)	399 (3.7)	419 (7.2)	382 (4.3)	401 (3.7)	421 (4.4)	388 (4.1)
Bulgaria	476 (7.7)	420 (9.9)	406 (8.8)	447 (5.4)	370 (6.6)	445 (9.7)	387 (13.6)	388 (10.8)	430 (6.2)	360 (8.0)
Colombia	405 (6.8)	406 (4.9)	428 (3.6)	422 (4.8)	413 (4.3)	390 (9.0)	403 (5.9)	424 (4.7)	412 (6.7)	408 (5.5)
Croatia	522 (3.7)	493 (6.6)	457 (4.5)	471 (3.1)	429 (6.4)	492 (6.0)	484 (9.5)	450 (5.0)	449 (3.7)	417 (8.1)
Dubai (UAE)	518 (3.2)	461 (3.5)	437 (2.8)	453 (2.4)	416 (5.3)	493 (6.1)	435 (5.6)	419 (4.2)	437 (3.6)	389 (7.6)
Hong Kong-China	559 (2.4)	541 (3.8)	509 (4.0)	524 (2.7)	488 (6.8)	547 (4.6)	526 (4.5)	505 (4.5)	512 (4.4)	475 (9.2)
Indonesia	407 (4.5)	410 (4.1)	401 (5.2)	403 (4.8)	378 (3.8)	379 (4.4)	391 (5.0)	392 (5.6)	386 (4.7)	364 (5.1)
Jordan	401 (4.8)	412 (3.3)	429 (3.7)	419 (4.1)	372 (4.6)	370 (5.7)	384 (5.3)	405 (5.3)	398 (5.5)	347 (5.7)
Kazakhstan	407 (4.0)	369 (3.4)	377 (5.1)	402 (4.9)	378 (9.6)	385 (4.1)	348 (3.9)	352 (6.6)	386 (5.9)	364 (10.8)
Kyrgyzstan	334 (4.1)	311 (4.0)	306 (6.7)	337 (4.9)	267 (6.8)	306 (4.6)	280 (5.5)	277 (7.9)	324 (7.4)	257 (7.4)
Latvia	504 (4.3)	468 (8.4)	453 (6.5)	488 (3.0)	441 (5.2)	474 (6.4)	447 (13.3)	440 (8.3)	470 (3.7)	428 (5.4)
Liechtenstein	553 (8.4)	c c	480 (14.5)	490 (5.3)	462 (12.4)	c c	c c	c c	477 (8.9)	c c
Lithuania	509 (2.6)	465 (4.5)	435 (3.9)	462 (2.9)	413 (5.6)	475 (4.9)	448 (8.4)	425 (4.7)	469 (2.3)	403 (5.5)
Macao-China	512 (2.2)	505 (2.4)	480 (2.0)	483 (1.4)	448 (3.5)	486 (4.6)	487 (3.9)	473 (2.4)	469 (2.3)	437 (4.1)
Montenegro	442 (3.4)	408 (5.4)	400 (3.6)	412 (2.0)	347 (5.4)	416 (6.1)	383 (7.5)	386 (4.3)	388 (3.3)	338 (6.8)
Panama	400 (8.5)	368 (6.8)	377 (8.1)	391 (7.0)	353 (11.7)	372 (11.4)	357 (9.6)	368 (10.3)	374 (8.4)	338 (13.5)
Peru	383 (4.6)	367 (3.5)	365 (5.1)	394 (5.7)	335 (7.0)	365 (5.8)	352 (4.5)	363 (6.2)	384 (5.8)	327 (8.6)
Qatar	427 (3.6)	381 (2.1)	377 (1.9)	368 (2.4)	331 (3.7)	397 (5.9)	360 (3.3)	363 (3.3)	350 (3.0)	311 (4.7)
Romania	443 (4.6)	411 (6.7)	414 (7.1)	433 (4.2)	396 (6.0)	414 (6.0)	384 (10.5)	396 (9.7)	417 (4.5)	385 (6.6)
Russian Federation	485 (3.6)	447 (5.3)	419 (6.2)	451 (3.4)	423 (6.8)	467 (4.2)	425 (7.1)	402 (8.3)	434 (4.0)	412 (6.4)
Serbia	470 (3.4)	428 (5.6)	425 (4.3)	446 (2.6)	403 (5.6)	446 (4.9)	415 (8.2)	420 (5.1)	431 (3.5)	388 (6.6)
Shanghai-China	573 (3.0)	546 (3.5)	533 (4.9)	560 (2.5)	517 (5.3)	552 (4.2)	526 (4.3)	524 (5.2)	548 (3.3)	495 (6.5)
Singapore	555 (2.5)	547 (2.8)	503 (3.0)	509 (2.1)	473 (5.5)	548 (4.2)	545 (4.0)	499 (4.3)	498 (3.0)	453 (6.6)
Chinese Taipei	528 (3.5)	506 (3.5)	478 (4.0)	490 (2.7)	450 (5.2)	510 (6.0)	495 (4.7)	472 (4.6)	477 (4.7)	425 (6.3)
Thailand	422 (5.4)	429 (2.7)	415 (3.5)	425 (3.6)	370 (4.3)	389 (6.2)	408 (3.6)	407 (4.6)	406 (5.0)	359 (4.3)
Trinidad and Tobago	451 (3.7)	429 (4.3)	411 (4.3)	423 (2.9)	365 (6.5)	413 (6.5)	405 (6.5)	398 (5.7)	398 (4.0)	345 (8.6)
Tunisia	410 (4.3)	395 (3.4)	388 (4.7)	419 (3.5)	399 (5.3)	385 (5.4)	373 (4.9)	376 (7.0)	410 (4.1)	383 (7.7)
Uruguay	457 (4.6)	415 (4.4)	426 (4.5)	451 (4.0)	402 (3.9)	428 (7.7)	391 (8.6)	414 (5.7)	435 (5.1)	389 (4.5)

Note: Values that are statistically significant are indicated in bold (see Annex A3).
StatLink ᴬᴵˢᴸ http://dx.doi.org/10.1787/888932343285

[Part 1/2]

Reading performance of students who read fiction, comic books and others materials
Percentage of students who reported that they read the following materials because they want to "several times a month" or "several times a week"

Table III.1.9

| | Girls | | | | | | | | | | Difference (B − G) | | | | | | | | | |
| | Fiction and others but no comics | | Fiction and comics and others | | Comics and others but no fiction | | Others than fiction or comics | | Nothing | | Fiction and others but no comics | | Fiction and comics and others | | Comics and others but no fiction | | Others than fiction or comics | | Nothing | |
	Mean Score	S.E.	Mean Score	S.E.	Mean Score	S.E.	Mean Score	S.E.	Mean Score	S.E.	Score dif.	S.E.	Score dif.	S.E.	Score dif.	S.E.	Score dif.	S.E.	Score dif.	S.E.
OECD																				
Australia	570	(2.8)	563	(6.7)	515	(14.1)	504	(2.7)	496	(3.4)	-11	(3.7)	-32	(8.8)	-40	(15.1)	-25	(3.8)	-23	(5.1)
Austria	542	(4.7)	494	(13.6)	451	(9.4)	478	(3.9)	435	(8.0)	-25	(8.9)	9	(18.8)	-14	(12.3)	-27	(6.0)	-25	(11.6)
Belgium	565	(3.9)	560	(6.2)	520	(5.7)	512	(3.0)	486	(6.7)	-9	(8.9)	3	(7.9)	-6	(6.4)	-21	(4.7)	-33	(7.5)
Canada	566	(2.0)	559	(5.3)	519	(6.3)	518	(2.5)	510	(3.2)	-16	(3.2)	-21	(7.1)	-25	(8.4)	-19	(3.3)	-24	(4.2)
Chile	475	(4.8)	458	(5.2)	443	(7.0)	468	(3.9)	435	(6.3)	-17	(8.2)	-22	(6.3)	-1	(8.5)	-20	(4.9)	-15	(6.8)
Czech Republic	547	(4.5)	523	(11.5)	493	(7.2)	493	(3.4)	495	(7.7)	-10	(8.1)	4	(19.3)	-28	(8.8)	-35	(5.2)	-67	(8.4)
Denmark	531	(4.2)	541	(7.7)	501	(6.9)	501	(3.1)	480	(7.0)	-24	(7.0)	-17	(9.9)	-13	(8.7)	-20	(4.0)	-36	(8.6)
Estonia	548	(4.4)	528	(9.6)	487	(9.0)	519	(3.1)	496	(9.2)	-38	(6.5)	-66	(13.3)	-23	(9.2)	-33	(3.4)	-53	(11.3)
Finland	591	(4.6)	601	(3.7)	549	(3.8)	542	(3.3)	503	(3.9)	-25	(14.7)	-27	(6.0)	-41	(3.8)	-52	(4.6)	-45	(12.7)
France	558	(4.6)	550	(7.7)	500	(6.5)	496	(4.2)	484	(5.4)	-8	(8.5)	-22	(9.9)	-16	(7.5)	-34	(5.6)	-58	(8.9)
Germany	555	(3.6)	552	(11.8)	464	(12.8)	503	(3.8)	495	(5.6)	-10	(6.0)	-10	(13.7)	9	(14.2)	-22	(4.4)	-51	(7.6)
Greece	531	(3.6)	535	(8.9)	487	(7.8)	502	(4.3)	485	(8.1)	-37	(9.3)	-28	(13.0)	-26	(9.2)	-42	(5.7)	-56	(7.8)
Hungary	543	(4.6)	497	(10.5)	497	(5.7)	512	(3.9)	480	(9.7)	-25	(6.6)	-14	(12.6)	-33	(7.3)	-28	(5.1)	-50	(11.1)
Iceland	560	(3.7)	558	(5.6)	524	(4.8)	503	(2.9)	465	(7.9)	-27	(9.9)	-30	(9.2)	-38	(6.7)	-29	(4.1)	-54	(11.0)
Ireland	564	(3.7)	500	(14.4)	467	(14.3)	495	(3.7)	505	(6.4)	-41	(7.0)	-1	(20.5)	-10	(16.8)	-23	(4.9)	-46	(10.6)
Israel	526	(4.4)	479	(8.0)	469	(7.2)	501	(3.9)	462	(7.4)	-28	(10.6)	-48	(13.3)	-28	(10.0)	-28	(5.7)	-44	(9.7)
Italy	529	(2.5)	546	(4.7)	516	(4.5)	493	(2.4)	485	(2.8)	-46	(4.0)	-22	(6.2)	-37	(5.5)	-30	(3.3)	-59	(4.1)
Japan	556	(7.9)	560	(4.1)	528	(4.6)	522	(5.2)	515	(9.3)	-8	(12.0)	-27	(6.2)	-40	(6.8)	-40	(12.1)	-82	(18.0)
Korea	573	(4.5)	554	(4.9)	545	(5.9)	561	(5.6)	545	(5.3)	-21	(6.4)	-13	(6.5)	-38	(7.8)	-31	(7.2)	-52	(10.9)
Luxembourg	537	(3.3)	501	(8.0)	462	(7.5)	468	(2.6)	465	(7.8)	-7	(7.5)	4	(13.3)	-12	(9.8)	-22	(4.0)	-52	(10.4)
Mexico	442	(2.7)	424	(3.1)	437	(2.9)	451	(2.2)	430	(3.5)	-32	(4.4)	-19	(3.5)	-19	(3.6)	-20	(2.4)	-28	(4.3)
Netherlands	552	(5.4)	543	(8.7)	518	(11.5)	517	(5.9)	486	(6.4)	11	(10.6)	14	(9.0)	-6	(8.1)	-14	(4.6)	-28	(5.7)
New Zealand	572	(3.9)	549	(9.6)	511	(11.5)	518	(3.7)	517	(6.6)	-19	(5.6)	-39	(14.1)	-48	(14.8)	-35	(5.1)	-38	(9.1)
Norway	551	(4.6)	569	(5.7)	529	(3.9)	505	(3.2)	492	(8.0)	-23	(7.9)	-30	(8.5)	-41	(5.0)	-41	(3.7)	-67	(10.7)
Poland	558	(4.0)	544	(12.2)	487	(8.3)	516	(3.1)	515	(5.9)	-32	(7.6)	-52	(18.0)	-18	(9.8)	-32	(3.2)	-80	(7.3)
Portugal	528	(3.8)	511	(6.7)	501	(6.9)	497	(3.4)	499	(5.8)	-12	(5.6)	-28	(11.6)	-29	(8.3)	-28	(3.5)	-48	(7.6)
Slovak Republic	541	(4.8)	517	(13.1)	483	(5.8)	497	(2.8)	474	(9.2)	-30	(7.8)	-39	(22.5)	-18	(8.5)	-43	(3.8)	-65	(10.7)
Slovenia	556	(4.4)	533	(11.4)	480	(6.8)	505	(1.9)	492	(6.4)	-41	(8.3)	-47	(18.7)	-21	(8.0)	-44	(3.0)	-62	(8.2)
Spain	527	(2.5)	519	(7.2)	468	(8.2)	482	(2.9)	471	(4.0)	-14	(3.8)	-19	(6.8)	-2	(9.3)	-19	(2.7)	-31	(5.3)
Sweden	559	(3.6)	549	(8.0)	497	(7.0)	503	(3.6)	461	(6.2)	-22	(6.3)	-14	(9.9)	-12	(7.7)	-35	(4.4)	-35	(8.2)
Switzerland	552	(3.8)	554	(6.1)	507	(6.9)	501	(2.9)	463	(6.6)	-8	(5.6)	-9	(7.3)	-21	(6.9)	-32	(3.6)	-39	(8.4)
Turkey	495	(4.8)	473	(5.2)	482	(10.4)	488	(5.3)	478	(10.1)	-47	(5.1)	-44	(6.9)	-36	(12.3)	-31	(5.6)	-64	(11.7)
United Kingdom	549	(3.7)	528	(10.7)	443	(10.4)	486	(2.9)	480	(7.1)	-8	(5.9)	-37	(16.1)	12	(12.2)	-11	(4.9)	-21	(9.0)
United States	539	(5.5)	528	(10.0)	489	(15.4)	499	(4.1)	487	(5.1)	-1	(5.8)	-49	(12.2)	-26	(16.0)	-18	(5.3)	-13	(5.5)
OECD average	544	(0.7)	529	(1.5)	493	(1.4)	502	(0.6)	484	(1.2)	-21	(1.3)	-23	(2.1)	-22	(1.7)	-29	(0.8)	-45	(1.6)
Partners																				
Albania	434	(5.4)	406	(5.2)	389	(9.9)	427	(6.9)	428	(13.6)	-50	(7.7)	-45	(8.4)	-35	(10.4)	-54	(7.9)	-92	(14.7)
Argentina	426	(6.5)	400	(8.4)	427	(6.4)	432	(6.0)	399	(7.8)	-20	(9.6)	-31	(13.8)	-41	(8.1)	-30	(6.9)	-42	(9.7)
Azerbaijan	385	(4.9)	381	(3.9)	382	(5.5)	380	(6.1)	365	(7.0)	-15	(6.3)	-19	(4.8)	-25	(5.7)	-19	(7.6)	-28	(7.0)
Brazil	437	(4.2)	408	(3.7)	425	(4.7)	449	(3.5)	416	(5.8)	-18	(6.1)	-26	(5.0)	-24	(5.3)	-28	(4.3)	-29	(6.6)
Bulgaria	493	(7.9)	448	(12.6)	439	(9.2)	466	(5.6)	400	(8.6)	-48	(8.5)	-61	(17.0)	-51	(13.1)	-36	(5.4)	-40	(11.4)
Colombia	413	(7.8)	409	(5.8)	433	(3.7)	431	(5.1)	419	(5.8)	-23	(9.5)	-6	(6.3)	-10	(4.8)	-19	(6.8)	-11	(7.5)
Croatia	534	(4.2)	503	(8.7)	478	(7.5)	497	(4.0)	450	(11.1)	-42	(7.3)	-19	(12.5)	-28	(8.3)	-48	(5.0)	-32	(14.6)
Dubai (UAE)	534	(3.5)	481	(4.1)	458	(4.7)	474	(3.3)	453	(7.0)	-41	(7.3)	-46	(7.0)	-39	(5.8)	-37	(5.3)	-64	(10.7)
Hong Kong-China	566	(3.2)	562	(5.8)	522	(7.9)	537	(3.6)	511	(9.8)	-20	(6.0)	-36	(7.1)	-17	(9.0)	-25	(5.9)	-36	(13.7)
Indonesia	426	(5.4)	424	(4.0)	416	(7.1)	425	(6.0)	398	(3.8)	-47	(6.4)	-33	(4.4)	-24	(7.6)	-38	(5.8)	-34	(5.7)
Jordan	425	(7.0)	434	(3.7)	446	(4.6)	446	(5.2)	410	(7.7)	-54	(8.7)	-51	(6.5)	-41	(6.7)	-48	(7.4)	-63	(10.1)
Kazakhstan	427	(4.5)	389	(4.1)	407	(6.8)	423	(5.8)	411	(13.6)	-43	(3.6)	-41	(4.3)	-55	(9.1)	-38	(6.5)	-47	(15.8)
Kyrgyzstan	354	(4.4)	338	(4.7)	345	(9.0)	350	(5.4)	298	(11.7)	-48	(4.0)	-58	(6.4)	-68	(11.9)	-27	(8.1)	-40	(12.5)
Latvia	519	(4.2)	486	(10.9)	485	(9.5)	506	(3.4)	482	(10.2)	-46	(6.2)	-39	(17.4)	-45	(12.8)	-36	(4.1)	-54	(10.7)
Liechtenstein	549	(8.9)	c	c	c	c	505	(6.7)	c	c	c	c	c	c	c	c	-28	(12.1)	c	c
Lithuania	523	(2.6)	475	(5.7)	458	(6.2)	486	(3.7)	455	(10.4)	-49	(5.0)	-26	(10.6)	-33	(7.6)	-42	(4.2)	-52	(10.0)
Macao-China	523	(2.3)	518	(3.8)	498	(3.7)	496	(2.1)	466	(5.2)	-37	(5.1)	-31	(6.1)	-25	(4.6)	-26	(3.3)	-28	(6.0)
Montenegro	455	(4.0)	435	(6.4)	426	(5.7)	437	(2.7)	365	(9.0)	-39	(7.2)	-52	(9.6)	-40	(6.4)	-49	(4.7)	-27	(11.7)
Panama	413	(9.8)	377	(7.4)	388	(11.7)	410	(8.2)	374	(13.2)	-42	(13.8)	-20	(10.4)	-20	(15.0)	-36	(10.2)	-36	(15.0)
Peru	395	(6.0)	379	(4.7)	368	(7.5)	408	(7.5)	348	(11.0)	-29	(7.9)	-27	(6.4)	-5	(8.8)	-23	(7.1)	-22	(13.3)
Qatar	447	(4.5)	396	(2.8)	390	(2.9)	391	(3.7)	367	(5.4)	-50	(7.4)	-36	(4.4)	-27	(4.9)	-41	(4.7)	-56	(6.9)
Romania	459	(5.3)	428	(8.7)	436	(8.3)	451	(4.8)	415	(8.4)	-45	(7.1)	-44	(14.3)	-40	(12.1)	-34	(4.8)	-30	(8.6)
Russian Federation	497	(3.7)	468	(7.4)	444	(8.2)	472	(4.3)	456	(13.5)	-30	(3.4)	-42	(9.8)	-43	(12.2)	-38	(4.8)	-44	(12.5)
Serbia	482	(3.7)	445	(7.0)	434	(7.5)	461	(3.2)	440	(10.0)	-36	(5.0)	-30	(10.6)	-14	(8.9)	-30	(3.9)	-52	(12.4)
Shanghai-China	586	(3.1)	573	(4.1)	557	(10.1)	573	(2.8)	545	(6.7)	-34	(4.5)	-48	(5.2)	-33	(11.3)	-24	(3.8)	-50	(8.8)
Singapore	559	(3.0)	564	(4.5)	512	(5.8)	521	(3.0)	504	(9.0)	-11	(4.8)	-31	(6.6)	-13	(4.8)	-23	(4.6)	-51	(11.3)
Chinese Taipei	537	(4.9)	518	(5.0)	498	(9.0)	503	(3.5)	484	(5.9)	-27	(8.6)	-23	(6.9)	-26	(10.4)	-26	(6.5)	-59	(7.3)
Thailand	445	(6.7)	440	(3.2)	427	(5.1)	443	(4.8)	391	(8.0)	-56	(8.3)	-33	(4.4)	-21	(6.7)	-37	(6.6)	-32	(8.4)
Trinidad and Tobago	469	(4.3)	449	(5.1)	426	(5.8)	452	(4.6)	403	(11.5)	-56	(7.5)	-44	(7.5)	-30	(8.6)	-54	(6.5)	-58	(15.2)
Tunisia	426	(4.4)	409	(3.7)	401	(5.4)	430	(4.7)	421	(5.8)	-41	(4.4)	-36	(5.2)	-24	(8.1)	-20	(5.5)	-38	(8.2)
Uruguay	469	(4.8)	430	(5.2)	441	(5.5)	463	(3.5)	423	(5.0)	-41	(8.2)	-40	(10.2)	-28	(6.7)	-28	(5.1)	-34	(5.5)

Note: Values that are statistically significant are indicated in bold (see Annex A3).

StatLink 📊 http://dx.doi.org/10.1787/888932343285

[Part 1/2]
Index of diversity of reading materials and performance, by national quarters of this index

Table III.1.10 *Results based on students' self-reports*

| | Index of diversity of reading materials | | | | | | | | | | | | | | | |
| | All students | | Boys | | Girls | | Gender difference (B – G) | | Bottom quarter | | Second quarter | | Third quarter | | Top quarter | |
	Mean index	S.E.	Mean index	S.E.	Mean index	S.E.	Dif.	S.E.	Mean index	S.E.	Mean index	S.E.	Mean index	S.E.	Mean index	S.E.
OECD																
Australia	-0.12	(0.01)	-0.19	(0.02)	-0.06	(0.01)	**-0.13**	(0.02)	-1.25	(0.01)	-0.34	(0.00)	0.15	(0.00)	**0.95**	(0.01)
Austria	0.01	(0.02)	-0.04	(0.03)	0.06	(0.02)	**-0.09**	(0.03)	-1.08	(0.03)	-0.19	(0.00)	0.29	(0.00)	**1.08**	(0.02)
Belgium	-0.08	(0.02)	-0.12	(0.03)	-0.05	(0.02)	**-0.07**	(0.03)	-1.34	(0.03)	-0.30	(0.00)	0.23	(0.00)	**1.03**	(0.01)
Canada	-0.11	(0.01)	-0.24	(0.02)	0.01	(0.01)	**-0.25**	(0.02)	-1.35	(0.02)	-0.33	(0.00)	0.21	(0.00)	**1.15**	(0.01)
Chile	-0.02	(0.02)	-0.19	(0.02)	0.16	(0.02)	**-0.35**	(0.03)	-1.31	(0.03)	-0.24	(0.00)	0.33	(0.00)	**0.83**	(0.02)
Czech Republic	-0.16	(0.02)	-0.30	(0.02)	0.00	(0.02)	**-0.30**	(0.03)	-1.24	(0.02)	-0.36	(0.00)	0.12	(0.00)	**1.21**	(0.01)
Denmark	0.07	(0.02)	-0.01	(0.03)	0.15	(0.02)	**-0.16**	(0.03)	-1.20	(0.03)	-0.13	(0.01)	0.41	(0.00)	**1.19**	(0.02)
Estonia	0.30	(0.01)	0.23	(0.02)	0.38	(0.02)	**-0.14**	(0.03)	-0.64	(0.02)	0.13	(0.00)	0.54	(0.00)	**1.44**	(0.02)
Finland	0.45	(0.02)	0.36	(0.02)	0.55	(0.02)	**-0.19**	(0.02)	-0.55	(0.02)	0.24	(0.00)	0.70	(0.00)	**1.05**	(0.02)
France	-0.07	(0.02)	-0.07	(0.03)	-0.07	(0.02)	0.00	(0.03)	-1.28	(0.02)	-0.28	(0.00)	0.23	(0.00)	**0.90**	(0.02)
Germany	-0.18	(0.02)	-0.20	(0.03)	-0.15	(0.02)	-0.05	(0.03)	-1.36	(0.03)	-0.38	(0.00)	0.13	(0.00)	**0.70**	(0.02)
Greece	-0.32	(0.02)	-0.32	(0.03)	-0.33	(0.02)	0.02	(0.03)	-1.41	(0.03)	-0.54	(0.00)	-0.05	(0.00)	**1.53**	(0.02)
Hungary	0.28	(0.02)	0.14	(0.03)	0.42	(0.03)	**-0.29**	(0.04)	-1.12	(0.03)	0.07	(0.01)	0.63	(0.00)	**1.38**	(0.02)
Iceland	0.19	(0.02)	0.02	(0.03)	0.36	(0.03)	**-0.35**	(0.04)	-1.07	(0.03)	-0.03	(0.01)	0.48	(0.00)	**0.88**	(0.02)
Ireland	-0.13	(0.02)	-0.20	(0.03)	-0.06	(0.02)	**-0.14**	(0.03)	-1.18	(0.02)	-0.33	(0.00)	0.12	(0.00)	**1.31**	(0.03)
Israel	-0.08	(0.02)	-0.35	(0.04)	0.17	(0.03)	**-0.52**	(0.04)	-1.54	(0.03)	-0.36	(0.00)	0.26	(0.01)	**0.69**	(0.01)
Italy	-0.31	(0.01)	-0.40	(0.01)	-0.22	(0.01)	**-0.18**	(0.02)	-1.45	(0.03)	-0.47	(0.00)	-0.01	(0.00)	**1.56**	(0.02)
Japan	0.38	(0.02)	0.39	(0.02)	0.38	(0.02)	0.02	(0.03)	-0.77	(0.02)	0.12	(0.00)	0.63	(0.00)	**1.23**	(0.02)
Korea	0.01	(0.02)	-0.03	(0.03)	0.06	(0.03)	**-0.09**	(0.04)	-1.26	(0.02)	-0.25	(0.01)	0.32	(0.00)	**1.17**	(0.02)
Luxembourg	0.06	(0.02)	0.02	(0.02)	0.10	(0.02)	**-0.08**	(0.03)	-1.14	(0.02)	-0.15	(0.00)	0.37	(0.00)	**1.14**	(0.01)
Mexico	-0.08	(0.01)	-0.10	(0.01)	-0.06	(0.01)	**-0.04**	(0.01)	-1.35	(0.01)	-0.34	(0.00)	0.06	(0.01)	**1.00**	(0.01)
Netherlands	-0.32	(0.04)	-0.49	(0.05)	-0.16	(0.04)	**-0.33**	(0.04)	-1.81	(0.04)	-0.54	(0.01)	0.32	(0.00)	**1.11**	(0.02)
New Zealand	0.05	(0.01)	-0.03	(0.02)	0.13	(0.02)	**-0.16**	(0.03)	-1.06	(0.02)	-0.19	(0.00)	0.32	(0.00)	**1.11**	(0.02)
Norway	0.32	(0.02)	0.22	(0.03)	0.43	(0.03)	**-0.20**	(0.04)	-0.90	(0.03)	0.10	(0.00)	0.62	(0.00)	**1.47**	(0.03)
Poland	0.00	(0.02)	-0.19	(0.03)	0.18	(0.02)	**-0.37**	(0.03)	-1.12	(0.02)	-0.20	(0.00)	0.29	(0.00)	**1.02**	(0.01)
Portugal	-0.09	(0.01)	-0.14	(0.02)	-0.05	(0.01)	**-0.09**	(0.02)	-1.19	(0.02)	-0.32	(0.00)	0.17	(0.00)	**0.96**	(0.02)
Slovak Republic	-0.01	(0.02)	-0.20	(0.02)	0.17	(0.02)	**-0.37**	(0.03)	-1.11	(0.02)	-0.22	(0.00)	0.25	(0.00)	**1.02**	(0.02)
Slovenia	0.03	(0.01)	-0.07	(0.02)	0.14	(0.02)	**-0.20**	(0.03)	-0.98	(0.02)	-0.17	(0.00)	0.28	(0.00)	**1.00**	(0.02)
Spain	-0.30	(0.01)	-0.31	(0.02)	-0.28	(0.01)	-0.02	(0.02)	-1.49	(0.02)	-0.50	(0.00)	0.01	(0.00)	**0.80**	(0.01)
Sweden	-0.01	(0.02)	-0.17	(0.03)	0.15	(0.02)	**-0.32**	(0.03)	-1.33	(0.03)	-0.20	(0.00)	0.34	(0.00)	**1.14**	(0.02)
Switzerland	0.15	(0.02)	0.09	(0.03)	0.20	(0.02)	**-0.12**	(0.03)	-0.97	(0.02)	-0.07	(0.00)	0.40	(0.00)	**1.22**	(0.01)
Turkey	0.49	(0.01)	0.43	(0.02)	0.54	(0.02)	**-0.11**	(0.03)	-0.56	(0.02)	0.21	(0.00)	0.70	(0.00)	**1.59**	(0.02)
United Kingdom	-0.11	(0.02)	-0.21	(0.02)	-0.02	(0.02)	**-0.19**	(0.03)	-1.23	(0.02)	-0.32	(0.00)	0.15	(0.00)	**0.95**	(0.01)
United States	-0.32	(0.02)	-0.40	(0.03)	-0.24	(0.02)	**-0.16**	(0.03)	-1.61	(0.03)	-0.54	(0.00)	0.01	(0.00)	**0.86**	(0.03)
OECD average	0.00	(0.00)	-0.09	(0.00)	0.09	(0.00)	**-0.18**	(0.01)	-1.18	(0.00)	-0.22	(0.00)	0.29	(0.00)	**1.11**	(0.00)
Partners																
Albania	0.33	(0.03)	0.21	(0.03)	0.45	(0.03)	**-0.24**	(0.03)	-0.89	(0.03)	0.06	(0.01)	0.61	(0.01)	**1.52**	(0.02)
Argentina	0.07	(0.02)	-0.10	(0.03)	0.20	(0.03)	**-0.30**	(0.04)	-1.23	(0.03)	-0.21	(0.01)	0.37	(0.01)	**1.33**	(0.03)
Azerbaijan	0.41	(0.04)	0.31	(0.05)	0.51	(0.05)	**-0.20**	(0.05)	-1.31	(0.05)	0.10	(0.01)	0.80	(0.01)	**2.04**	(0.03)
Brazil	-0.05	(0.02)	-0.24	(0.02)	0.12	(0.02)	**-0.36**	(0.03)	-1.37	(0.02)	-0.32	(0.00)	0.28	(0.00)	**1.21**	(0.01)
Bulgaria	0.03	(0.04)	-0.17	(0.05)	0.23	(0.03)	**-0.40**	(0.05)	-1.37	(0.05)	-0.18	(0.01)	0.37	(0.01)	**1.28**	(0.03)
Colombia	0.30	(0.03)	0.14	(0.04)	0.45	(0.03)	**-0.31**	(0.04)	-1.07	(0.02)	0.00	(0.01)	0.62	(0.00)	**1.67**	(0.02)
Croatia	0.17	(0.02)	0.09	(0.02)	0.27	(0.02)	**-0.18**	(0.03)	-0.80	(0.02)	-0.05	(0.00)	0.40	(0.00)	**1.14**	(0.02)
Dubai (UAE)	0.47	(0.02)	0.42	(0.02)	0.53	(0.02)	**-0.12**	(0.03)	-0.74	(0.02)	0.20	(0.00)	0.75	(0.00)	**1.69**	(0.02)
Hong Kong-China	0.46	(0.02)	0.45	(0.03)	0.48	(0.02)	-0.03	(0.03)	-0.69	(0.02)	0.23	(0.00)	0.73	(0.00)	**1.58**	(0.02)
Indonesia	0.60	(0.03)	0.49	(0.04)	0.71	(0.04)	**-0.22**	(0.05)	-0.89	(0.03)	0.23	(0.01)	0.91	(0.01)	**2.15**	(0.03)
Jordan	0.14	(0.02)	0.00	(0.03)	0.28	(0.03)	**-0.28**	(0.04)	-1.44	(0.02)	-0.13	(0.00)	0.51	(0.00)	**1.61**	(0.02)
Kazakhstan	1.03	(0.03)	0.95	(0.04)	1.10	(0.03)	**-0.15**	(0.03)	-0.28	(0.02)	0.65	(0.01)	1.25	(0.01)	**2.48**	(0.03)
Kyrgyzstan	0.53	(0.02)	0.37	(0.03)	0.68	(0.02)	**-0.31**	(0.03)	-0.78	(0.02)	0.23	(0.00)	0.79	(0.00)	**1.88**	(0.03)
Latvia	0.13	(0.02)	-0.05	(0.03)	0.30	(0.03)	**-0.35**	(0.03)	-0.91	(0.03)	-0.05	(0.01)	0.39	(0.00)	**1.08**	(0.02)
Liechtenstein	0.04	(0.05)	0.01	(0.07)	0.06	(0.06)	-0.05	(0.10)	-1.23	(0.09)	-0.18	(0.02)	0.28	(0.01)	**1.27**	(0.09)
Lithuania	0.33	(0.02)	0.10	(0.03)	0.56	(0.02)	**-0.46**	(0.03)	-0.86	(0.02)	0.10	(0.00)	0.62	(0.00)	**1.44**	(0.02)
Macao-China	0.17	(0.01)	0.06	(0.02)	0.29	(0.02)	**-0.22**	(0.02)	-1.01	(0.02)	-0.05	(0.00)	0.47	(0.00)	**1.29**	(0.02)
Montenegro	0.32	(0.01)	0.25	(0.03)	0.39	(0.02)	**-0.14**	(0.04)	-0.81	(0.02)	0.07	(0.00)	0.56	(0.00)	**1.45**	(0.02)
Panama	0.24	(0.03)	0.13	(0.06)	0.36	(0.03)	**-0.22**	(0.06)	-1.11	(0.06)	-0.09	(0.01)	0.50	(0.01)	**1.66**	(0.06)
Peru	0.62	(0.02)	0.54	(0.03)	0.70	(0.02)	**-0.17**	(0.04)	-0.62	(0.02)	0.33	(0.00)	0.89	(0.00)	**1.89**	(0.02)
Qatar	0.54	(0.01)	0.39	(0.02)	0.70	(0.02)	**-0.31**	(0.03)	-1.02	(0.02)	0.21	(0.00)	0.84	(0.00)	**2.14**	(0.02)
Romania	-0.08	(0.02)	-0.21	(0.03)	0.04	(0.03)	**-0.26**	(0.03)	-1.28	(0.04)	-0.30	(0.00)	0.21	(0.00)	**1.05**	(0.02)
Russian Federation	0.27	(0.02)	0.13	(0.02)	0.40	(0.02)	**-0.27**	(0.03)	-0.91	(0.02)	0.00	(0.00)	0.53	(0.00)	**1.46**	(0.02)
Serbia	0.08	(0.01)	-0.01	(0.02)	0.17	(0.02)	**-0.18**	(0.02)	-0.97	(0.02)	-0.11	(0.00)	0.33	(0.00)	**1.08**	(0.02)
Shanghai-China	0.43	(0.02)	0.47	(0.03)	0.39	(0.02)	0.08	(0.03)	-0.71	(0.02)	0.15	(0.00)	0.66	(0.00)	**1.63**	(0.03)
Singapore	0.53	(0.02)	0.49	(0.02)	0.57	(0.02)	**-0.08**	(0.03)	-0.61	(0.02)	0.24	(0.00)	0.75	(0.00)	**1.74**	(0.02)
Chinese Taipei	0.49	(0.02)	0.47	(0.03)	0.51	(0.02)	-0.04	(0.03)	-0.89	(0.03)	0.17	(0.00)	0.75	(0.00)	**1.92**	(0.02)
Thailand	0.99	(0.02)	0.73	(0.03)	1.19	(0.02)	**-0.47**	(0.03)	-0.27	(0.02)	0.70	(0.00)	1.20	(0.00)	**2.34**	(0.02)
Trinidad and Tobago	0.41	(0.02)	0.24	(0.03)	0.57	(0.02)	**-0.33**	(0.04)	-0.89	(0.02)	0.08	(0.01)	0.67	(0.01)	**1.76**	(0.02)
Tunisia	0.31	(0.02)	0.17	(0.03)	0.43	(0.02)	**-0.26**	(0.03)	-0.90	(0.02)	0.03	(0.00)	0.59	(0.00)	**1.52**	(0.02)
Uruguay	-0.42	(0.02)	-0.66	(0.03)	-0.20	(0.03)	**-0.46**	(0.04)	-2.02	(0.03)	-0.66	(0.00)	0.01	(0.01)	**1.00**	(0.02)

Note: Values that are statistically significant are indicated in bold (see Annex A3).
StatLink http://dx.doi.org/10.1787/888932343285

[Part 2/2]

Index of diversity of reading materials and performance, by national quarters of this index

Table III.1.10 — *Results based on students' self-reports*

	Performance on the reading scale, by national quarters of this index								Change in the reading score per unit of this index		Increased likelihood of students in the bottom quarter of this index scoring in the bottom quarter of the national reading performance distribution		Explained variance in student performance (r-squared x 100)	
	Bottom quarter		Second quarter		Third quarter		Top quarter							
	Mean score	S.E.	Mean score	S.E.	Mean score	S.E.	Mean score	S.E.	Effect	S.E.	Ratio	S.E.	%	S.E.
Australia	482	(2.5)	510	(3.1)	530	(2.9)	544	(3.2)	24.7	(1.41)	1.7	(0.08)	5.5	(0.55)
Austria	442	(4.0)	472	(4.1)	489	(3.8)	498	(4.4)	23.0	(2.16)	1.7	(0.11)	4.6	(0.84)
Belgium	469	(3.3)	508	(3.0)	528	(3.0)	543	(3.1)	29.3	(1.39)	2.0	(0.10)	9.2	(0.88)
Canada	500	(2.2)	523	(2.1)	535	(2.2)	545	(2.3)	18.4	(0.98)	1.6	(0.07)	4.3	(0.45)
Chile	422	(4.0)	446	(3.7)	463	(3.6)	470	(3.5)	16.5	(1.34)	1.7	(0.10)	4.2	(0.65)
Czech Republic	449	(3.9)	476	(3.2)	494	(4.0)	509	(3.9)	25.9	(1.75)	1.8	(0.11)	6.2	(0.76)
Denmark	465	(3.5)	494	(3.2)	505	(3.1)	519	(2.6)	22.0	(1.23)	1.8	(0.11)	7.5	(0.82)
Estonia	471	(4.2)	503	(3.5)	514	(3.4)	517	(3.6)	23.0	(2.26)	1.8	(0.11)	4.6	(0.93)
Finland	494	(3.1)	527	(3.1)	549	(3.2)	575	(3.1)	37.9	(1.72)	2.2	(0.13)	13.7	(1.18)
France	451	(5.7)	496	(4.6)	514	(4.3)	526	(4.3)	30.9	(2.68)	2.0	(0.14)	8.2	(1.15)
Germany	469	(4.0)	505	(3.8)	518	(3.7)	526	(3.3)	23.9	(1.89)	1.8	(0.12)	6.4	(0.93)
Greece	456	(6.5)	483	(5.6)	496	(4.9)	498	(3.9)	21.8	(2.24)	1.5	(0.13)	4.1	(0.82)
Hungary	465	(4.5)	504	(3.9)	504	(4.2)	504	(4.1)	14.8	(1.58)	1.9	(0.14)	3.4	(0.73)
Iceland	453	(3.1)	497	(3.0)	516	(2.8)	540	(2.8)	30.1	(1.47)	2.2	(0.17)	11.4	(1.04)
Ireland	472	(4.8)	494	(3.9)	507	(4.2)	517	(4.0)	19.3	(2.39)	1.4	(0.10)	3.2	(0.74)
Israel	447	(5.4)	486	(4.1)	489	(5.1)	491	(4.4)	13.2	(1.81)	1.5	(0.10)	2.2	(0.55)
Italy	448	(2.6)	485	(2.2)	499	(2.2)	514	(2.1)	29.5	(1.26)	2.0	(0.06)	8.0	(0.61)
Japan	489	(4.6)	519	(4.7)	530	(3.8)	544	(3.7)	20.7	(1.76)	1.7	(0.09)	4.2	(0.61)
Korea	511	(4.8)	539	(4.3)	549	(3.8)	559	(3.6)	17.0	(1.87)	1.8	(0.11)	4.9	(0.94)
Luxembourg	440	(3.0)	468	(2.9)	487	(3.4)	498	(2.9)	21.7	(1.77)	1.7	(0.12)	4.5	(0.71)
Mexico	413	(2.8)	429	(2.2)	433	(2.4)	427	(2.3)	5.1	(0.86)	1.3	(0.05)	0.4	(0.13)
Netherlands	465	(5.1)	503	(5.4)	531	(6.1)	548	(5.2)	26.4	(1.67)	2.3	(0.21)	12.9	(1.57)
New Zealand	496	(3.8)	525	(3.4)	534	(3.6)	534	(4.5)	15.7	(1.85)	1.4	(0.09)	2.0	(0.47)
Norway	466	(3.9)	500	(3.5)	515	(2.7)	535	(3.8)	25.9	(1.89)	2.0	(0.11)	8.5	(1.07)
Poland	464	(3.4)	501	(3.2)	516	(3.4)	523	(3.7)	24.1	(1.71)	2.0	(0.11)	6.2	(0.89)
Portugal	471	(3.7)	492	(4.1)	498	(3.8)	499	(3.6)	12.3	(1.87)	1.5	(0.08)	1.7	(0.46)
Slovak Republic	447	(4.2)	469	(3.9)	490	(3.3)	506	(3.6)	25.8	(2.19)	1.8	(0.11)	6.8	(0.99)
Slovenia	452	(2.9)	478	(3.5)	497	(2.5)	514	(2.9)	26.3	(1.75)	1.9	(0.12)	6.4	(0.77)
Spain	445	(2.9)	477	(2.5)	493	(2.3)	512	(2.6)	25.7	(1.16)	2.0	(0.08)	8.1	(0.68)
Sweden	449	(3.7)	489	(3.6)	517	(3.5)	541	(4.0)	33.6	(1.65)	2.3	(0.14)	13.5	(1.21)
Switzerland	460	(3.7)	499	(2.8)	513	(3.2)	532	(3.4)	29.9	(1.50)	2.0	(0.11)	9.0	(0.84)
Turkey	457	(5.1)	475	(4.1)	471	(4.0)	455	(4.2)	-0.3	(1.74)	1.2	(0.10)	0.0	(0.03)
United Kingdom	466	(3.0)	493	(3.6)	512	(2.7)	511	(3.3)	19.2	(1.36)	1.6	(0.08)	3.5	(0.52)
United States	473	(4.0)	508	(4.2)	513	(4.6)	508	(5.4)	11.4	(1.67)	1.5	(0.09)	1.5	(0.43)
OECD average	462	(0.7)	493	(0.6)	507	(0.6)	517	(0.6)	21.9	(0.30)	1.8	(0.02)	5.9	(0.14)
Albania	368	(6.8)	396	(5.0)	395	(4.6)	387	(5.1)	8.1	(2.66)	1.4	(0.15)	0.7	(0.46)
Argentina	377	(5.4)	409	(6.2)	410	(5.8)	406	(5.4)	8.2	(1.98)	1.4	(0.11)	0.7	(0.33)
Azerbaijan	347	(4.2)	368	(3.8)	371	(4.6)	368	(4.2)	6.2	(1.04)	1.5	(0.11)	1.4	(0.48)
Brazil	393	(3.2)	417	(3.0)	424	(3.5)	416	(3.9)	8.0	(1.24)	1.3	(0.06)	0.8	(0.25)
Bulgaria	378	(6.2)	441	(7.6)	462	(6.9)	446	(7.6)	23.7	(2.54)	2.2	(0.17)	5.9	(1.23)
Colombia	404	(4.1)	417	(4.7)	424	(4.2)	409	(5.3)	1.9	(1.74)	1.2	(0.09)	0.1	(0.13)
Croatia	442	(3.8)	471	(3.5)	486	(3.6)	504	(3.4)	27.8	(1.46)	2.0	(0.12)	7.0	(0.74)
Dubai (UAE)	438	(2.9)	461	(3.5)	476	(3.5)	467	(3.0)	10.3	(1.78)	1.4	(0.09)	1.0	(0.34)
Hong Kong-China	513	(3.2)	537	(2.8)	543	(3.0)	541	(3.3)	11.5	(1.55)	1.5	(0.09)	1.8	(0.50)
Indonesia	383	(3.8)	401	(4.2)	410	(4.5)	414	(4.6)	8.1	(1.27)	1.5	(0.12)	2.4	(0.72)
Jordan	378	(4.3)	409	(4.2)	423	(3.6)	420	(3.3)	13.2	(1.15)	1.9	(0.12)	3.8	(0.65)
Kazakhstan	402	(5.3)	406	(4.5)	385	(3.8)	369	(3.5)	-10.2	(2.00)	0.9	(0.08)	1.7	(0.63)
Kyrgyzstan	292	(4.6)	326	(4.2)	328	(4.4)	317	(3.7)	7.0	(1.58)	1.5	(0.10)	0.6	(0.27)
Latvia	459	(4.6)	487	(3.8)	496	(3.7)	494	(3.9)	17.0	(2.41)	1.7	(0.13)	3.2	(0.85)
Liechtenstein	466	(8.6)	494	(9.3)	510	(8.4)	530	(9.8)	20.8	(5.31)	1.8	(0.39)	7.2	(3.61)
Lithuania	430	(3.5)	472	(3.6)	487	(3.3)	486	(3.1)	22.1	(1.66)	2.1	(0.13)	6.1	(0.82)
Macao-China	459	(2.2)	486	(1.7)	499	(2.0)	504	(1.9)	17.8	(1.12)	1.8	(0.08)	5.2	(0.65)
Montenegro	375	(3.0)	412	(2.8)	426	(3.2)	422	(4.2)	18.4	(2.36)	1.8	(0.12)	3.6	(0.88)
Panama	359	(11.3)	379	(7.7)	387	(7.6)	377	(6.9)	4.0	(2.58)	1.4	(0.21)	0.2	(0.30)
Peru	351	(5.1)	372	(5.3)	385	(4.3)	374	(3.9)	8.7	(1.68)	1.5	(0.07)	0.9	(0.34)
Qatar	346	(2.3)	377	(2.5)	392	(3.1)	381	(2.5)	10.0	(0.82)	1.7	(0.07)	1.4	(0.22)
Romania	403	(5.1)	430	(4.8)	433	(4.8)	434	(5.2)	13.2	(2.37)	1.6	(0.11)	2.1	(0.80)
Russian Federation	442	(5.2)	466	(4.7)	475	(3.0)	457	(3.8)	5.9	(1.92)	1.5	(0.12)	0.4	(0.29)
Serbia	423	(3.5)	442	(3.6)	453	(3.4)	452	(3.6)	13.6	(1.80)	1.5	(0.09)	2.0	(0.54)
Shanghai-China	539	(3.2)	559	(3.4)	564	(3.3)	561	(3.5)	9.2	(1.54)	1.4	(0.09)	1.3	(0.44)
Singapore	501	(2.6)	526	(2.8)	536	(3.1)	541	(2.7)	13.7	(1.32)	1.6	(0.09)	2.0	(0.38)
Chinese Taipei	467	(3.5)	500	(3.1)	510	(3.2)	506	(3.8)	11.8	(1.42)	1.8	(0.11)	2.8	(0.63)
Thailand	396	(3.2)	424	(3.2)	432	(3.3)	435	(3.4)	13.1	(1.12)	1.9	(0.13)	4.1	(0.63)
Trinidad and Tobago	389	(3.4)	428	(3.7)	428	(3.5)	431	(3.4)	14.8	(1.60)	1.7	(0.12)	2.3	(0.48)
Tunisia	397	(4.1)	406	(4.1)	407	(3.7)	407	(3.5)	4.6	(1.55)	1.1	(0.08)	0.3	(0.20)
Uruguay	392	(4.3)	429	(3.4)	444	(3.3)	442	(3.7)	16.6	(1.37)	1.8	(0.10)	4.5	(0.71)

Note: Values that are statistically significant are indicated in bold (see Annex A3).
StatLink ⬛🖳⬛ http://dx.doi.org/10.1787/888932343285

[Part 1/1]
Table III.1.11 Proportion of students with low levels of reading diversity, by reading proficiency level[1]
Results based on students' self-reports

		Percentage of students with low levels of diversity of reading activities									
		Level 1a or below		Level 2		Level 3		Level 4		Level 5 or above	
		%	S.E.	%	S.E.	%	S.E.	%	S.E.	%	S.E.
OECD	Australia	61.1	(1.6)	56.0	(1.3)	47.1	(1.1)	37.9	(1.0)	28.5	(1.5)
	Austria	60.9	(1.9)	53.5	(2.1)	46.1	(1.7)	35.2	(1.9)	33.2	(3.3)
	Belgium	61.8	(2.0)	55.3	(1.9)	44.1	(1.6)	33.6	(1.3)	22.6	(1.7)
	Canada	58.8	(1.8)	52.1	(1.2)	45.5	(1.1)	39.7	(1.0)	30.0	(1.6)
	Chile	61.4	(1.5)	49.6	(1.5)	42.7	(2.0)	34.2	(2.8)	c	c
	Czech Republic	63.5	(1.5)	52.6	(1.6)	44.4	(1.4)	34.9	(1.6)	27.1	(3.1)
	Denmark	59.4	(1.8)	52.6	(2.1)	43.0	(1.6)	31.4	(1.8)	c	c
	Estonia	58.3	(2.5)	50.8	(2.7)	42.4	(2.4)	34.3	(2.4)	24.6	(3.3)
	Finland	74.6	(2.7)	63.9	(2.2)	52.5	(1.5)	40.1	(1.7)	24.4	(2.0)
	France	61.5	(2.4)	49.3	(2.1)	40.5	(1.7)	33.5	(1.8)	25.6	(2.6)
	Germany	62.4	(1.8)	55.8	(2.1)	47.0	(1.8)	39.4	(1.7)	31.1	(4.3)
	Greece	55.0	(2.1)	50.5	(1.8)	43.9	(2.0)	38.6	(2.3)	29.8	(3.9)
	Hungary	57.6	(1.9)	45.0	(2.1)	42.4	(1.7)	39.3	(1.9)	33.6	(2.8)
	Iceland	72.6	(1.8)	60.0	(2.5)	48.8	(1.9)	37.1	(1.7)	27.2	(2.6)
	Ireland	57.0	(2.2)	52.8	(2.2)	47.3	(1.8)	40.3	(2.2)	c	c
	Israel	50.5	(1.8)	49.2	(1.7)	45.4	(2.0)	36.7	(1.6)	33.2	(2.5)
	Italy	57.8	(1.0)	46.2	(0.9)	40.1	(0.7)	30.8	(0.9)	22.6	(1.6)
	Japan	69.0	(2.0)	58.5	(2.0)	52.8	(1.7)	47.6	(1.7)	42.8	(2.8)
	Korea	73.0	(4.6)	58.4	(1.9)	53.2	(1.8)	44.8	(1.9)	36.4	(3.2)
	Luxembourg	59.2	(1.7)	48.2	(1.6)	42.8	(1.8)	36.0	(2.4)	24.5	(2.9)
	Mexico	47.8	(0.8)	44.8	(0.9)	42.0	(1.1)	37.0	(1.7)	c	c
	Netherlands	68.7	(3.3)	57.7	(2.9)	43.4	(2.3)	29.1	(2.0)	18.0	(2.6)
	New Zealand	55.5	(2.2)	52.2	(1.9)	51.4	(1.7)	46.1	(1.8)	37.5	(2.1)
	Norway	64.7	(2.0)	50.9	(2.0)	41.6	(1.7)	32.8	(1.9)	25.8	(2.9)
	Poland	66.0	(2.4)	56.8	(1.9)	47.8	(1.5)	39.0	(1.7)	31.5	(2.5)
	Portugal	53.1	(1.9)	49.2	(1.6)	44.5	(1.6)	38.8	(1.8)	31.3	(3.9)
	Slovak Republic	69.2	(2.0)	54.2	(2.1)	46.2	(1.8)	39.1	(2.2)	32.7	(4.7)
	Slovenia	65.6	(1.6)	54.5	(1.8)	44.9	(1.8)	36.5	(2.3)	c	c
	Spain	60.7	(1.4)	49.8	(1.5)	40.0	(1.1)	28.4	(1.7)	17.6	(2.3)
	Sweden	69.8	(2.2)	58.9	(2.2)	47.6	(1.7)	32.0	(1.8)	19.8	(2.2)
	Switzerland	70.5	(1.7)	62.7	(1.9)	51.8	(1.5)	44.0	(2.0)	31.5	(3.1)
	Turkey	48.5	(1.9)	47.0	(1.5)	50.8	(1.6)	53.0	(2.2)	c	c
	United Kingdom	58.4	(1.6)	51.2	(1.7)	43.5	(1.3)	36.5	(1.6)	30.0	(2.3)
	United States	52.9	(2.1)	47.6	(1.7)	46.5	(1.6)	39.8	(1.8)	31.8	(3.1)
	OECD average	61.4	(0.4)	52.9	(0.3)	45.7	(0.3)	37.6	(0.3)	28.7	(0.5)
Partners	Albania	47.5	(1.8)	43.6	(2.0)	44.9	(3.0)	45.3	(6.1)	c	c
	Argentina	51.1	(1.5)	46.9	(1.7)	47.1	(2.6)	40.5	(5.3)	c	c
	Azerbaijan	51.0	(1.3)	44.1	(2.4)	47.9	(4.5)	45.1	(12.5)	c	c
	Brazil	55.1	(0.8)	51.1	(1.4)	47.3	(1.9)	44.6	(3.3)	46.7	(4.8)
	Bulgaria	58.7	(2.0)	44.3	(2.2)	36.7	(1.6)	34.3	(2.5)	c	c
	Colombia	48.4	(1.7)	46.4	(2.0)	42.9	(2.5)	42.5	(3.6)	c	c
	Croatia	68.1	(1.5)	57.4	(1.7)	48.2	(1.6)	39.0	(2.6)	c	c
	Dubai (UAE)	54.0	(1.4)	48.9	(1.8)	44.5	(1.6)	41.4	(2.2)	38.2	(4.2)
	Hong Kong-China	58.9	(3.0)	49.2	(2.5)	50.2	(1.5)	45.5	(1.5)	38.6	(2.5)
	Indonesia	58.8	(1.2)	49.2	(1.7)	38.6	(2.8)	36.3	(9.4)	c	c
	Jordan	50.9	(1.1)	36.7	(1.6)	38.4	(2.4)	36.9	(4.7)	c	c
	Kazakhstan	48.8	(1.6)	59.5	(1.8)	70.9	(2.6)	74.7	(4.3)	c	c
	Kyrgyzstan	47.7	(1.2)	43.1	(3.3)	45.8	(4.0)	51.8	(8.2)	c	c
	Latvia	55.0	(3.1)	43.8	(2.1)	39.2	(1.6)	33.1	(2.1)	c	c
	Liechtenstein	60.4	(8.1)	62.6	(7.7)	42.8	(6.0)	32.3	(6.9)	c	c
	Lithuania	59.5	(2.1)	46.1	(1.4)	36.0	(1.8)	29.1	(2.5)	26.6	(4.6)
	Macao-China	65.8	(1.5)	56.8	(1.3)	47.8	(1.3)	39.6	(2.2)	30.2	(4.4)
	Montenegro	53.4	(1.4)	42.1	(2.0)	37.3	(2.2)	30.2	(3.6)	c	c
	Panama	53.6	(1.6)	47.0	(3.1)	50.5	(3.6)	50.9	(6.2)	c	c
	Peru	54.0	(1.1)	46.9	(1.5)	46.1	(2.5)	50.3	(5.4)	c	c
	Qatar	57.5	(0.6)	48.2	(1.4)	51.0	(1.7)	54.5	(2.6)	56.3	(5.2)
	Romania	48.9	(1.6)	42.5	(1.6)	41.0	(1.8)	36.5	(3.9)	c	c
	Russian Federation	54.3	(2.2)	48.9	(2.0)	44.7	(1.6)	46.4	(2.6)	c	c
	Serbia	52.9	(1.5)	46.5	(1.5)	39.9	(1.6)	35.8	(2.7)	c	c
	Shanghai-China	62.1	(4.2)	54.5	(2.3)	53.7	(1.5)	52.5	(1.4)	44.0	(1.6)
	Singapore	56.8	(2.2)	53.0	(1.7)	46.9	(1.4)	41.7	(1.7)	37.2	(1.7)
	Chinese Taipei	60.7	(1.9)	52.7	(1.7)	48.3	(1.1)	40.9	(1.7)	34.9	(3.7)
	Thailand	64.5	(1.3)	52.7	(1.3)	50.5	(2.3)	50.7	(4.0)	c	c
	Trinidad and Tobago	56.3	(1.3)	51.7	(1.6)	47.7	(1.9)	47.3	(2.7)	c	c
	Tunisia	47.8	(1.3)	46.0	(1.7)	44.5	(2.2)	42.9	(5.5)	c	c
	Uruguay	55.7	(1.3)	46.8	(1.5)	40.0	(2.3)	36.0	(3.2)	c	c

1. Students who reported levels of diversity of reading below their country average.
StatLink http://dx.doi.org/10.1787/888932343285

[Part 1/2]

Index of online reading activities and performance, by national quarters of this index

Table III.1.12 *Results based on students' self-reports*

| | Index of online reading activities | | | | | | | | | | | | | | | |
| | All students | | Boys | | Girls | | Gender difference (B – G) | | Bottom quarter | | Second quarter | | Third quarter | | Top quarter | |
	Mean index	S.E.	Mean index	S.E.	Mean index	S.E.	Dif.	S.E.	Mean index	S.E.	Mean index	S.E.	Mean index	S.E.	Mean index	S.E.
Australia	-0.08	(0.01)	-0.09	(0.02)	-0.07	(0.02)	-0.02	(0.02)	**-1.06**	(0.01)	-0.37	(0.00)	0.11	(0.00)	**1.02**	(0.02)
Austria	0.06	(0.02)	0.08	(0.03)	0.04	(0.02)	0.04	(0.03)	**-0.99**	(0.02)	-0.21	(0.00)	0.28	(0.01)	**1.17**	(0.02)
Belgium	-0.18	(0.01)	-0.14	(0.02)	-0.22	(0.01)	**0.08**	(0.02)	**-1.06**	(0.02)	-0.44	(0.00)	-0.01	(0.00)	**0.80**	(0.01)
Canada	-0.04	(0.01)	-0.03	(0.02)	-0.04	(0.02)	0.00	(0.02)	**-1.09**	(0.01)	-0.34	(0.00)	0.16	(0.00)	**1.12**	(0.02)
Chile	-0.22	(0.03)	-0.20	(0.04)	-0.25	(0.03)	0.06	(0.04)	**-1.51**	(0.02)	-0.58	(0.00)	0.05	(0.00)	**1.15**	(0.02)
Czech Republic	0.53	(0.02)	0.61	(0.03)	0.43	(0.02)	**0.17**	(0.03)	**-0.61**	(0.02)	0.21	(0.00)	0.73	(0.01)	**1.77**	(0.02)
Denmark	0.15	(0.01)	0.23	(0.02)	0.06	(0.02)	**0.17**	(0.02)	**-0.76**	(0.01)	-0.13	(0.00)	0.32	(0.01)	**1.14**	(0.02)
Estonia	0.50	(0.01)	0.58	(0.03)	0.42	(0.02)	**0.17**	(0.03)	**-0.50**	(0.02)	0.20	(0.00)	0.68	(0.00)	**1.63**	(0.02)
Finland	-0.04	(0.01)	0.01	(0.02)	-0.08	(0.02)	**0.10**	(0.03)	**-0.94**	(0.01)	-0.30	(0.00)	0.13	(0.00)	**0.96**	(0.02)
France	-0.13	(0.02)	-0.12	(0.02)	-0.14	(0.02)	0.03	(0.03)	**-1.20**	(0.02)	-0.34	(0.00)	0.11	(0.00)	**0.91**	(0.02)
Germany	0.12	(0.02)	0.16	(0.03)	0.08	(0.02)	**0.08**	(0.03)	**-0.94**	(0.02)	-0.12	(0.00)	0.37	(0.00)	**1.19**	(0.02)
Greece	-0.15	(0.02)	0.00	(0.04)	-0.30	(0.03)	**0.30**	(0.05)	**-1.56**	(0.03)	-0.57	(0.01)	0.15	(0.01)	**1.37**	(0.03)
Hungary	0.38	(0.03)	0.44	(0.03)	0.33	(0.03)	**0.11**	(0.04)	**-0.89**	(0.02)	0.09	(0.00)	0.66	(0.00)	**1.67**	(0.02)
Iceland	0.20	(0.01)	0.33	(0.02)	0.08	(0.02)	**0.25**	(0.03)	**-0.82**	(0.02)	-0.07	(0.00)	0.42	(0.00)	**1.29**	(0.02)
Ireland	-0.50	(0.02)	-0.52	(0.03)	-0.48	(0.03)	-0.04	(0.04)	**-1.54**	(0.02)	-0.78	(0.00)	-0.33	(0.00)	**0.64**	(0.03)
Israel	-0.02	(0.02)	-0.07	(0.04)	0.02	(0.02)	**-0.09**	(0.04)	**-1.33**	(0.03)	-0.32	(0.00)	0.28	(0.01)	**1.28**	(0.02)
Italy	-0.04	(0.01)	-0.02	(0.02)	-0.06	(0.01)	0.03	(0.02)	**-1.50**	(0.02)	-0.34	(0.00)	0.30	(0.00)	**1.38**	(0.01)
Japan	-0.49	(0.02)	-0.56	(0.03)	-0.43	(0.03)	**-0.13**	(0.03)	**-1.64**	(0.03)	-0.71	(0.00)	-0.24	(0.00)	**0.61**	(0.02)
Korea	-0.21	(0.02)	-0.27	(0.03)	-0.13	(0.02)	**-0.14**	(0.03)	**-1.19**	(0.02)	-0.43	(0.00)	0.02	(0.00)	**0.78**	(0.02)
Luxembourg	0.02	(0.01)	0.05	(0.02)	-0.02	(0.01)	**0.07**	(0.03)	**-1.07**	(0.02)	-0.25	(0.00)	0.25	(0.00)	**1.15**	(0.02)
Mexico	-0.54	(0.02)	-0.54	(0.02)	-0.54	(0.02)	0.00	(0.02)	**-1.96**	(0.03)	-0.83	(0.00)	-0.20	(0.00)	**0.83**	(0.01)
Netherlands	0.09	(0.02)	0.12	(0.03)	0.07	(0.02)	0.05	(0.03)	**-0.75**	(0.02)	-0.17	(0.00)	0.25	(0.00)	**1.04**	(0.02)
New Zealand	-0.29	(0.02)	-0.33	(0.02)	-0.24	(0.02)	**-0.09**	(0.03)	**-1.33**	(0.02)	-0.56	(0.00)	-0.07	(0.00)	**0.82**	(0.02)
Norway	0.17	(0.02)	0.23	(0.03)	0.12	(0.02)	**0.11**	(0.03)	**-0.78**	(0.02)	-0.10	(0.00)	0.36	(0.00)	**1.22**	(0.02)
Poland	0.44	(0.02)	0.51	(0.03)	0.37	(0.02)	**0.14**	(0.04)	**-0.93**	(0.03)	0.20	(0.00)	0.74	(0.00)	**1.75**	(0.02)
Portugal	0.13	(0.01)	0.24	(0.02)	0.02	(0.02)	**0.22**	(0.03)	**-0.89**	(0.02)	-0.20	(0.00)	0.31	(0.00)	**1.29**	(0.02)
Slovak Republic	0.06	(0.02)	0.11	(0.03)	0.00	(0.02)	**0.11**	(0.04)	**-1.21**	(0.02)	-0.26	(0.00)	0.33	(0.01)	**1.37**	(0.02)
Slovenia	0.27	(0.01)	0.33	(0.02)	0.20	(0.02)	**0.13**	(0.02)	**-0.83**	(0.02)	-0.04	(0.00)	0.47	(0.00)	**1.46**	(0.02)
Spain	-0.11	(0.01)	-0.07	(0.02)	-0.16	(0.01)	**0.08**	(0.02)	**-1.13**	(0.01)	-0.40	(0.00)	0.09	(0.00)	**0.98**	(0.01)
Sweden	0.03	(0.01)	0.12	(0.02)	-0.07	(0.01)	**0.19**	(0.02)	**-0.90**	(0.02)	-0.27	(0.00)	0.20	(0.00)	**1.08**	(0.02)
Switzerland	0.00	(0.02)	0.02	(0.02)	-0.03	(0.02)	**0.05**	(0.02)	**-1.00**	(0.02)	-0.26	(0.00)	0.20	(0.00)	**1.06**	(0.02)
Turkey	-0.05	(0.03)	0.06	(0.03)	-0.16	(0.04)	**0.22**	(0.04)	**-1.58**	(0.04)	-0.41	(0.01)	0.32	(0.01)	**1.49**	(0.02)
United Kingdom	0.11	(0.01)	0.13	(0.02)	0.08	(0.01)	**0.05**	(0.02)	**-0.88**	(0.02)	-0.18	(0.00)	0.29	(0.00)	**1.20**	(0.02)
United States	-0.16	(0.02)	-0.25	(0.03)	-0.06	(0.02)	**-0.18**	(0.03)	**-1.31**	(0.02)	-0.49	(0.00)	0.06	(0.01)	**1.10**	(0.02)
OECD average	0.00	(0.00)	0.03	(0.00)	-0.03	(0.00)	**0.07**	(0.01)	**-1.11**	(0.00)	-0.29	(0.00)	0.23	(0.00)	**1.17**	(0.00)
Albania	-0.62	(0.05)	-0.42	(0.06)	-0.83	(0.05)	**0.41**	(0.06)	**-2.22**	(0.09)	-0.97	(0.01)	-0.21	(0.01)	**0.93**	(0.03)
Argentina	-0.52	(0.04)	-0.41	(0.04)	-0.62	(0.05)	**0.21**	(0.04)	**-1.99**	(0.04)	-0.81	(0.01)	-0.16	(0.01)	**0.88**	(0.02)
Azerbaijan	-1.55	(0.05)	-1.36	(0.07)	-1.74	(0.06)	**0.37**	(0.07)	**-3.97**	(0.06)	-1.82	(0.00)	-1.01	(0.01)	**0.61**	(0.03)
Brazil	-0.61	(0.03)	-0.58	(0.04)	-0.64	(0.03)	0.07	(0.03)	**-2.40**	(0.03)	-0.91	(0.01)	-0.17	(0.01)	**1.03**	(0.02)
Bulgaria	0.26	(0.05)	0.23	(0.06)	0.30	(0.04)	-0.07	(0.06)	**-1.50**	(0.05)	-0.06	(0.01)	0.67	(0.01)	**1.94**	(0.03)
Colombia	-0.39	(0.04)	-0.37	(0.04)	-0.41	(0.05)	0.04	(0.05)	**-1.86**	(0.05)	-0.63	(0.01)	-0.01	(0.01)	**0.94**	(0.03)
Croatia	0.11	(0.02)	0.19	(0.03)	0.01	(0.03)	**0.18**	(0.04)	**-1.23**	(0.02)	-0.21	(0.00)	0.40	(0.00)	**1.48**	(0.02)
Dubai (UAE)	0.18	(0.01)	0.22	(0.02)	0.13	(0.02)	**0.09**	(0.03)	**-1.13**	(0.03)	-0.12	(0.00)	0.45	(0.00)	**1.50**	(0.02)
Hong Kong-China	0.38	(0.02)	0.42	(0.03)	0.33	(0.02)	**0.10**	(0.03)	**-0.65**	(0.02)	0.10	(0.00)	0.58	(0.00)	**1.48**	(0.02)
Indonesia	-1.41	(0.06)	-1.39	(0.06)	-1.42	(0.07)	0.03	(0.06)	**-3.16**	(0.05)	-1.63	(0.01)	-0.93	(0.01)	**0.09**	(0.02)
Jordan	-0.98	(0.04)	-0.96	(0.06)	-1.00	(0.06)	0.04	(0.08)	**-3.04**	(0.04)	-1.27	(0.01)	-0.49	(0.01)	**0.86**	(0.03)
Kazakhstan	-1.08	(0.05)	-1.07	(0.06)	-1.09	(0.06)	0.03	(0.05)	**-2.90**	(0.04)	-1.60	(0.01)	-0.61	(0.01)	**0.78**	(0.03)
Kyrgyzstan	-1.83	(0.05)	-1.86	(0.06)	-1.81	(0.05)	-0.05	(0.05)	**-4.22**	(0.05)	-1.98	(0.01)	-1.18	(0.01)	**0.05**	(0.02)
Latvia	0.28	(0.02)	0.29	(0.03)	0.27	(0.03)	0.02	(0.04)	**-0.86**	(0.02)	-0.04	(0.01)	0.52	(0.01)	**1.49**	(0.02)
Liechtenstein	-0.01	(0.05)	0.11	(0.08)	-0.15	(0.07)	**0.26**	(0.11)	**-0.99**	(0.09)	-0.22	(0.01)	0.16	(0.01)	**0.99**	(0.07)
Lithuania	0.54	(0.02)	0.55	(0.03)	0.53	(0.02)	0.02	(0.04)	**-0.77**	(0.03)	0.27	(0.01)	0.84	(0.01)	**1.82**	(0.02)
Macao-China	-0.02	(0.01)	-0.02	(0.02)	-0.01	(0.01)	-0.01	(0.02)	**-0.99**	(0.02)	-0.28	(0.00)	0.19	(0.00)	**1.01**	(0.02)
Montenegro	-0.17	(0.02)	-0.04	(0.03)	-0.30	(0.03)	**0.25**	(0.04)	**-1.75**	(0.03)	-0.50	(0.01)	0.21	(0.01)	**1.38**	(0.02)
Panama	-0.64	(0.08)	-0.63	(0.08)	-0.65	(0.09)	0.01	(0.07)	**-2.55**	(0.07)	-0.94	(0.01)	-0.14	(0.01)	**1.07**	(0.03)
Peru	-0.75	(0.04)	-0.72	(0.05)	-0.78	(0.05)	0.05	(0.05)	**-2.59**	(0.05)	-0.89	(0.01)	-0.27	(0.00)	**0.75**	(0.02)
Qatar	0.23	(0.02)	0.16	(0.03)	0.30	(0.02)	**-0.14**	(0.03)	**-1.53**	(0.03)	-0.08	(0.00)	0.62	(0.00)	**1.92**	(0.02)
Romania	-0.16	(0.04)	-0.10	(0.05)	-0.21	(0.04)	**0.11**	(0.05)	**-1.97**	(0.06)	-0.43	(0.01)	0.32	(0.01)	**1.45**	(0.02)
Russian Federation	-0.58	(0.05)	-0.48	(0.06)	-0.67	(0.04)	**0.19**	(0.04)	**-2.34**	(0.04)	-1.04	(0.01)	-0.13	(0.01)	**1.19**	(0.02)
Serbia	-0.39	(0.03)	-0.29	(0.03)	-0.50	(0.03)	**0.22**	(0.04)	**-1.93**	(0.02)	-0.88	(0.01)	-0.02	(0.01)	**1.25**	(0.03)
Shanghai-China	-0.35	(0.02)	-0.31	(0.04)	-0.38	(0.03)	0.07	(0.03)	**-1.44**	(0.02)	-0.63	(0.00)	-0.12	(0.00)	**0.80**	(0.02)
Singapore	0.13	(0.02)	0.20	(0.04)	0.07	(0.02)	**0.13**	(0.02)	**-0.96**	(0.02)	-0.19	(0.00)	0.34	(0.00)	**1.35**	(0.02)
Chinese Taipei	-0.19	(0.01)	-0.16	(0.02)	-0.23	(0.02)	**0.06**	(0.03)	**-1.20**	(0.02)	-0.47	(0.00)	-0.01	(0.00)	**0.90**	(0.02)
Thailand	-0.78	(0.03)	-0.76	(0.05)	-0.79	(0.04)	0.03	(0.06)	**-2.34**	(0.04)	-1.11	(0.01)	-0.43	(0.01)	**0.76**	(0.02)
Trinidad and Tobago	-0.65	(0.04)	-0.75	(0.03)	-0.55	(0.03)	**-0.19**	(0.04)	**-2.14**	(0.04)	-0.98	(0.01)	-0.30	(0.01)	**0.83**	(0.02)
Tunisia	-1.14	(0.06)	-1.04	(0.07)	-1.22	(0.05)	**0.18**	(0.05)	**-3.06**	(0.08)	-1.51	(0.01)	-0.69	(0.01)	**0.71**	(0.04)
Uruguay	-0.19	(0.02)	-0.19	(0.03)	-0.19	(0.02)	0.00	(0.03)	**-1.62**	(0.02)	-0.55	(0.00)	0.13	(0.01)	**1.27**	(0.02)

Note: Values that are statistically significant are indicated in bold (see Annex A3).
StatLink ⟐ﺴ⅃ http://dx.doi.org/10.1787/888932343285

[Part 2/2]
Index of online reading activities and performance, by national quarters of this index

Table III.1.12   *Results based on students' self-reports*

		Performance on the reading scale, by national quarters of this index								Change in the reading score per unit of this index		Increased likelihood of students in the bottom quarter of this index scoring in the bottom quarter of the national reading performance distribution		Explained variance in student performance (r-squared x 100)	
		Bottom quarter		Second quarter		Third quarter		Top quarter							
		Mean score	S.E.	Mean score	S.E.	Mean score	S.E.	Mean score	S.E.	Effect	S.E.	Ratio	S.E.	%	S.E.
OECD	Australia	478	(3.1)	516	(2.6)	534	(2.7)	538	(4.0)	26.0	(1.65)	1.9	(0.08)	5.5	(0.64)
	Austria	447	(4.5)	479	(3.6)	489	(4.3)	486	(4.0)	15.9	(2.11)	1.7	(0.11)	2.2	(0.57)
	Belgium	492	(2.8)	522	(2.8)	524	(3.5)	511	(3.2)	10.5	(1.75)	1.5	(0.08)	0.7	(0.24)
	Canada	501	(2.2)	528	(2.2)	537	(2.0)	536	(2.8)	14.1	(1.25)	1.6	(0.07)	2.2	(0.38)
	Chile	414	(3.8)	448	(3.9)	463	(3.5)	477	(4.1)	20.7	(1.49)	2.1	(0.14)	7.7	(1.11)
	Czech Republic	460	(4.2)	491	(3.4)	491	(3.7)	485	(3.4)	8.2	(1.54)	1.6	(0.10)	0.8	(0.31)
	Denmark	474	(3.1)	498	(3.4)	507	(3.1)	505	(2.9)	14.0	(1.86)	1.6	(0.10)	1.8	(0.47)
	Estonia	479	(4.2)	505	(4.2)	509	(4.1)	512	(3.8)	12.1	(2.05)	1.6	(0.11)	1.7	(0.53)
	Finland	517	(3.3)	539	(3.4)	544	(3.4)	544	(3.3)	14.5	(1.87)	1.5	(0.09)	1.8	(0.45)
	France	454	(5.6)	504	(4.4)	513	(4.1)	515	(4.0)	28.3	(2.71)	2.1	(0.13)	5.8	(0.94)
	Germany	485	(4.1)	507	(3.5)	516	(3.9)	509	(3.7)	10.5	(2.16)	1.5	(0.09)	1.1	(0.43)
	Greece	470	(5.5)	481	(5.7)	493	(5.3)	489	(4.7)	6.9	(1.72)	1.3	(0.10)	0.8	(0.38)
	Hungary	457	(5.6)	503	(4.1)	510	(4.0)	508	(3.8)	20.8	(2.08)	2.3	(0.20)	5.9	(1.12)
	Iceland	483	(3.6)	511	(3.2)	509	(2.5)	503	(3.2)	8.7	(2.03)	1.5	(0.10)	0.7	(0.32)
	Ireland	468	(4.5)	502	(4.1)	510	(3.8)	512	(3.9)	18.9	(2.39)	1.6	(0.11)	3.6	(0.81)
	Israel	439	(5.9)	487	(5.0)	497	(3.8)	489	(3.5)	18.1	(2.22)	1.8	(0.12)	3.4	(0.80)
	Italy	462	(2.3)	489	(2.2)	499	(2.0)	497	(2.0)	12.6	(0.81)	1.6	(0.05)	2.5	(0.34)
	Japan	484	(5.0)	521	(3.9)	538	(3.1)	539	(4.2)	21.3	(1.52)	1.8	(0.09)	4.4	(0.67)
	Korea	519	(4.8)	546	(3.9)	552	(3.6)	539	(4.5)	13.7	(2.15)	1.5	(0.09)	2.1	(0.64)
	Luxembourg	454	(3.6)	482	(3.4)	481	(3.1)	476	(3.1)	8.1	(2.04)	1.4	(0.10)	0.6	(0.29)
	Mexico	384	(3.0)	420	(2.3)	443	(2.3)	455	(2.1)	22.3	(1.42)	2.2	(0.08)	9.8	(0.99)
	Netherlands	481	(6.7)	517	(5.5)	521	(5.1)	528	(5.4)	19.2	(2.70)	1.9	(0.14)	2.8	(0.73)
	New Zealand	486	(3.9)	525	(3.8)	541	(3.7)	538	(4.2)	23.9	(1.99)	1.8	(0.10)	4.5	(0.72)
	Norway	488	(4.0)	511	(3.7)	510	(3.2)	506	(3.2)	7.4	(1.88)	1.5	(0.09)	0.5	(0.25)
	Poland	465	(3.6)	507	(3.4)	519	(3.5)	514	(3.2)	17.0	(1.52)	2.0	(0.12)	4.5	(0.76)
	Portugal	476	(4.8)	499	(3.9)	497	(3.8)	489	(3.2)	4.2	(1.82)	1.4	(0.09)	0.2	(0.16)
	Slovak Republic	439	(4.4)	486	(3.9)	492	(3.4)	495	(3.1)	20.4	(1.97)	2.2	(0.16)	5.8	(1.06)
	Slovenia	461	(3.1)	489	(3.2)	499	(3.1)	493	(2.6)	11.9	(1.39)	1.6	(0.11)	1.7	(0.40)
	Spain	456	(3.1)	485	(2.7)	494	(2.3)	492	(2.4)	15.5	(1.18)	1.7	(0.08)	2.5	(0.37)
	Sweden	475	(3.9)	502	(4.1)	513	(3.7)	505	(3.9)	12.6	(1.88)	1.5	(0.10)	1.2	(0.35)
	Switzerland	487	(3.3)	512	(3.4)	509	(3.1)	496	(3.6)	4.9	(1.88)	1.4	(0.07)	0.2	(0.17)
	Turkey	444	(4.5)	465	(4.2)	476	(4.2)	473	(4.5)	10.3	(1.48)	1.5	(0.12)	2.6	(0.78)
	United Kingdom	467	(2.9)	499	(2.7)	509	(3.5)	507	(3.7)	16.1	(2.07)	1.7	(0.09)	2.3	(0.60)
	United States	472	(4.3)	496	(5.2)	516	(4.8)	518	(4.7)	16.5	(1.87)	1.6	(0.09)	3.0	(0.65)
	OECD average	468	(0.7)	499	(0.6)	507	(0.6)	505	(0.6)	14.9	(0.32)	1.7	(0.02)	2.8	(0.11)
Partners	Albania	358	(5.9)	391	(5.1)	396	(5.7)	401	(5.8)	14.2	(2.18)	1.6	(0.16)	3.8	(1.24)
	Argentina	344	(4.8)	393	(4.7)	429	(5.3)	437	(6.0)	28.4	(2.15)	2.2	(0.17)	10.2	(1.31)
	Azerbaijan	342	(4.7)	363	(4.4)	370	(4.1)	382	(4.1)	6.8	(0.96)	1.6	(0.14)	2.8	(0.76)
	Brazil	372	(2.5)	406	(3.1)	434	(3.9)	439	(3.3)	18.1	(0.88)	1.9	(0.10)	7.7	(0.69)
	Bulgaria	355	(6.1)	440	(6.4)	464	(7.0)	468	(6.4)	29.4	(1.60)	3.0	(0.29)	14.7	(1.59)
	Colombia	374	(4.9)	409	(4.2)	432	(3.8)	438	(4.7)	21.4	(1.76)	2.1	(0.17)	8.6	(1.28)
	Croatia	443	(4.5)	482	(3.9)	491	(3.9)	488	(3.2)	14.3	(1.37)	1.9	(0.11)	3.4	(0.61)
	Dubai (UAE)	434	(3.1)	470	(2.8)	474	(3.2)	463	(3.0)	12.9	(1.30)	1.6	(0.09)	1.9	(0.40)
	Hong Kong-China	517	(3.6)	537	(3.0)	544	(3.0)	535	(2.9)	8.5	(2.07)	1.4	(0.08)	0.9	(0.41)
	Indonesia	377	(3.3)	392	(3.7)	414	(4.3)	426	(6.5)	12.4	(1.59)	1.8	(0.16)	6.7	(1.62)
	Jordan	373	(4.2)	413	(3.8)	413	(3.8)	429	(4.5)	14.2	(1.24)	1.9	(0.12)	6.8	(1.11)
	Kazakhstan	370	(3.7)	386	(3.9)	388	(4.3)	418	(5.9)	12.3	(1.49)	1.4	(0.09)	4.5	(1.07)
	Kyrgyzstan	283	(4.5)	317	(3.6)	331	(4.6)	336	(6.1)	10.7	(1.42)	1.5	(0.13)	3.5	(0.85)
	Latvia	462	(4.4)	488	(4.1)	494	(4.3)	492	(3.4)	9.5	(2.31)	1.6	(0.13)	1.3	(0.64)
	Liechtenstein	491	(8.8)	515	(7.7)	502	(10.2)	490	(8.5)	1.6	(4.69)	1.0	(0.24)	0.0	(0.30)
	Lithuania	435	(3.9)	476	(3.6)	485	(2.9)	479	(3.4)	15.9	(1.52)	2.0	(0.13)	3.8	(0.69)
	Macao-China	467	(2.0)	488	(2.0)	496	(2.1)	496	(2.2)	13.2	(1.39)	1.6	(0.07)	2.1	(0.44)
	Montenegro	379	(3.2)	415	(2.6)	427	(3.4)	416	(3.8)	10.2	(1.63)	1.7	(0.16)	2.1	(0.65)
	Panama	324	(6.7)	364	(5.2)	394	(9.2)	421	(7.8)	22.9	(2.43)	2.1	(0.24)	12.4	(2.44)
	Peru	310	(3.7)	370	(3.7)	394	(4.2)	410	(6.6)	26.1	(1.69)	2.8	(0.18)	14.7	(1.50)
	Qatar	335	(2.5)	387	(2.5)	396	(2.5)	378	(2.0)	11.5	(0.83)	1.8	(0.07)	2.2	(0.32)
	Romania	376	(5.6)	424	(4.9)	453	(4.3)	448	(4.5)	19.1	(1.58)	2.4	(0.20)	9.5	(1.45)
	Russian Federation	429	(5.9)	451	(3.7)	474	(4.1)	486	(4.6)	14.5	(1.69)	1.7	(0.13)	5.6	(1.21)
	Serbia	409	(3.1)	441	(3.1)	459	(3.3)	461	(3.3)	14.5	(1.10)	1.8	(0.11)	5.1	(0.75)
	Shanghai-China	541	(3.7)	562	(3.4)	562	(2.9)	558	(3.4)	5.2	(1.63)	1.3	(0.10)	0.4	(0.23)
	Singapore	500	(2.3)	529	(3.0)	537	(2.8)	539	(2.8)	16.0	(1.27)	1.6	(0.09)	2.5	(0.41)
	Chinese Taipei	480	(3.7)	503	(3.2)	507	(3.4)	494	(3.2)	7.0	(1.37)	1.4	(0.08)	0.5	(0.20)
	Thailand	395	(3.4)	415	(2.7)	428	(3.4)	448	(4.1)	14.1	(1.28)	1.7	(0.12)	6.6	(0.99)
	Trinidad and Tobago	373	(3.4)	416	(3.9)	442	(3.2)	445	(3.6)	22.6	(1.17)	1.9	(0.12)	6.6	(0.72)
	Tunisia	382	(3.5)	411	(3.1)	408	(4.2)	416	(5.2)	9.2	(1.44)	1.5	(0.11)	2.9	(0.97)
	Uruguay	378	(3.5)	426	(3.6)	452	(3.6)	453	(4.0)	21.8	(1.39)	2.2	(0.16)	7.1	(0.87)

Note: Values that are statistically significant are indicated in bold (see Annex A3).
StatLink ⟦⟧ http://dx.doi.org/10.1787/888932343285

[Part 1/1]

Proportion of students with low levels of online reading activities, by reading proficiency level[1]

Table III.1.13 *Results based on students' self-reports*

	Percentage of students with low levels of online reading activities									
	Level 1a or below		Level 2		Level 3		Level 4		Level 5 or above	
	%	S.E.	%	S.E.	%	S.E.	%	S.E.	%	S.E.
OECD Australia	70.6	(1.5)	65.0	(1.2)	56.0	(1.2)	48.8	(1.3)	41.5	(2.2)
Austria	57.2	(2.1)	48.9	(2.4)	44.5	(2.0)	40.5	(2.6)	39.7	(4.0)
Belgium	56.5	(1.7)	53.7	(1.8)	54.1	(1.7)	51.7	(1.3)	48.1	(2.2)
Canada	65.8	(1.6)	57.9	(1.5)	54.7	(1.4)	49.8	(1.4)	44.6	(2.0)
Chile	67.0	(1.7)	55.0	(1.5)	43.9	(2.1)	34.8	(3.4)	c	c
Czech Republic	59.3	(1.9)	50.5	(1.5)	47.6	(1.6)	50.0	(2.0)	51.0	(3.3)
Denmark	65.3	(2.0)	55.6	(1.8)	51.5	(1.6)	47.5	(2.2)	c	c
Estonia	63.7	(2.8)	58.0	(1.9)	50.3	(1.9)	49.5	(2.2)	47.4	(3.9)
Finland	63.5	(2.6)	58.8	(2.3)	55.1	(1.5)	53.1	(1.5)	47.3	(2.5)
France	62.0	(1.9)	48.3	(2.1)	42.3	(1.8)	39.1	(1.9)	36.5	(2.6)
Germany	59.0	(2.8)	54.9	(2.0)	49.2	(1.5)	47.8	(2.0)	44.4	(3.2)
Greece	55.6	(2.4)	53.4	(1.8)	49.7	(1.4)	47.4	(2.1)	40.0	(3.0)
Hungary	66.7	(2.4)	48.5	(2.0)	40.4	(1.8)	42.6	(2.2)	43.8	(3.4)
Iceland	55.7	(2.0)	49.5	(2.2)	47.6	(1.5)	46.3	(1.8)	49.2	(4.4)
Ireland	61.1	(2.6)	57.7	(2.5)	52.0	(1.8)	44.7	(2.6)	c	c
Israel	59.4	(1.9)	52.3	(1.7)	48.3	(1.7)	43.4	(2.0)	41.4	(3.3)
Italy	60.8	(0.9)	50.7	(1.0)	46.9	(1.1)	44.3	(1.1)	44.7	(1.7)
Japan	63.7	(2.1)	57.2	(2.3)	47.5	(1.5)	39.9	(1.5)	36.3	(2.1)
Korea	69.5	(4.2)	54.5	(2.0)	49.3	(1.7)	50.5	(1.4)	48.6	(2.6)
Luxembourg	54.0	(1.9)	49.0	(2.3)	45.9	(1.8)	48.5	(2.2)	49.8	(3.2)
Mexico	64.6	(0.8)	46.9	(0.8)	34.4	(1.1)	24.6	(2.3)	c	c
Netherlands	65.3	(2.7)	62.7	(2.2)	55.8	(2.3)	50.6	(2.0)	46.7	(3.3)
New Zealand	59.7	(2.4)	55.7	(2.0)	49.1	(1.8)	42.2	(1.8)	34.2	(2.4)
Norway	59.1	(2.9)	51.9	(2.3)	49.3	(1.6)	49.9	(1.9)	54.7	(3.0)
Poland	67.4	(2.4)	55.3	(1.9)	47.7	(1.8)	44.1	(2.3)	37.4	(3.1)
Portugal	57.1	(2.2)	55.2	(1.4)	55.0	(1.4)	53.4	(1.8)	54.2	(5.4)
Slovak Republic	63.2	(1.9)	48.3	(2.1)	42.1	(1.9)	37.3	(2.0)	41.2	(4.2)
Slovenia	62.8	(1.8)	58.1	(1.8)	53.7	(1.6)	50.3	(2.1)	c	c
Spain	59.5	(1.6)	49.6	(1.5)	44.9	(1.4)	43.4	(1.6)	35.7	(3.1)
Sweden	60.1	(2.2)	55.1	(2.0)	49.8	(1.9)	45.9	(2.1)	46.7	(3.1)
Switzerland	53.9	(1.9)	51.6	(1.6)	49.7	(1.5)	51.6	(1.9)	52.6	(3.7)
Turkey	58.6	(2.2)	53.0	(1.9)	45.9	(2.1)	42.5	(2.8)	c	c
United Kingdom	64.3	(2.1)	58.4	(1.7)	54.1	(1.6)	50.4	(2.3)	44.5	(2.8)
United States	64.3	(1.9)	56.2	(1.6)	50.6	(2.4)	42.2	(2.3)	36.2	(3.3)
OECD average	61.7	(0.4)	54.0	(0.3)	48.8	(0.3)	45.5	(0.4)	44.2	(0.6)
Partners Albania	52.0	(1.7)	44.3	(2.5)	36.5	(3.7)	28.9	(4.5)	c	c
Argentina	61.5	(1.6)	43.0	(2.1)	29.9	(2.2)	21.0	(3.3)	c	c
Azerbaijan	57.6	(1.6)	41.5	(2.5)	41.5	(5.6)	34.4	(16.2)	c	c
Brazil	56.3	(1.0)	41.6	(1.8)	28.4	(1.5)	18.1	(2.4)	14.7	(4.3)
Bulgaria	66.4	(1.7)	46.3	(2.0)	36.6	(2.0)	32.1	(3.1)	c	c
Colombia	60.0	(1.8)	44.5	(2.0)	33.4	(2.1)	21.5	(4.2)	c	c
Croatia	63.1	(1.6)	55.0	(1.5)	47.5	(1.4)	43.6	(2.7)	c	c
Dubai (UAE)	54.0	(1.1)	47.4	(1.7)	48.1	(1.9)	44.8	(2.4)	44.2	(4.5)
Hong Kong-China	62.7	(3.2)	51.1	(2.5)	48.3	(1.6)	46.6	(1.3)	46.4	(2.2)
Indonesia	53.6	(2.2)	35.9	(2.5)	17.5	(3.1)	8.0	(5.9)	c	c
Jordan	51.8	(1.4)	42.4	(1.7)	34.4	(2.6)	27.8	(5.2)	c	c
Kazakhstan	56.7	(2.2)	51.0	(2.1)	39.3	(2.5)	28.9	(4.2)	c	c
Kyrgyzstan	52.1	(1.5)	33.4	(2.7)	16.5	(3.8)	5.5	(3.8)	c	c
Latvia	64.6	(2.9)	54.1	(2.1)	50.0	(1.7)	50.4	(1.9)	c	c
Liechtenstein	46.7	(6.6)	53.0	(6.1)	50.9	(5.2)	53.9	(7.5)	c	c
Lithuania	61.0	(1.8)	46.7	(2.2)	42.4	(1.8)	38.5	(2.3)	c	c
Macao-China	60.6	(1.8)	55.2	(1.5)	49.8	(1.2)	42.6	(1.8)	41.4	(5.0)
Montenegro	54.0	(1.5)	45.6	(1.7)	40.0	(2.1)	31.2	(4.1)	c	c
Panama	54.6	(2.3)	37.4	(4.2)	13.8	(3.8)	5.2	(3.4)	c	c
Peru	55.5	(1.4)	31.4	(1.6)	23.4	(3.2)	15.1	(6.2)	c	c
Qatar	49.3	(0.7)	39.8	(1.6)	40.1	(2.0)	38.4	(3.0)	30.2	(4.5)
Romania	60.7	(1.8)	40.0	(1.9)	30.2	(2.1)	20.7	(3.4)	c	c
Russian Federation	64.5	(2.3)	56.3	(2.3)	45.4	(2.4)	33.3	(2.8)	c	c
Serbia	64.2	(1.5)	53.9	(1.6)	43.6	(2.0)	36.2	(2.7)	c	c
Shanghai-China	55.6	(4.5)	54.4	(2.5)	53.9	(2.0)	51.6	(1.7)	47.0	(2.2)
Singapore	66.3	(1.8)	56.1	(2.0)	54.9	(1.9)	50.5	(1.6)	46.1	(1.9)
Chinese Taipei	60.0	(1.7)	53.3	(1.8)	53.0	(1.5)	53.3	(1.7)	50.8	(3.1)
Thailand	56.8	(1.6)	45.3	(1.4)	30.4	(1.8)	14.9	(3.6)	c	c
Trinidad and Tobago	58.5	(1.2)	47.9	(1.7)	38.0	(1.9)	28.2	(3.4)	c	c
Tunisia	49.8	(1.8)	46.7	(2.0)	38.4	(2.8)	27.1	(5.8)	c	c
Uruguay	64.0	(1.2)	48.3	(1.5)	38.5	(1.6)	30.8	(3.3)	c	c

1. Students who reported levels of diversity of reading below their country average.
StatLink ᐸᔆᔆᔆᕒ http://dx.doi.org/10.1787/888932343285

[Part 1/2]
Index of understanding and remembering and reading performance, by national quarters of this index

Table III.1.14 *Results based on students' self-reports*

| | Index of understanding and remembering | | | | | | | | | | | | | | | |
| | All students | | Boys | | Girls | | Gender difference (B – G) | | Bottom quarter | | Second quarter | | Third quarter | | Top quarter | |
	Mean index	S.E.	Mean index	S.E.	Mean index	S.E.	Dif.	S.E.	Mean index	S.E.	Mean index	S.E.	Mean index	S.E.	Mean index	S.E.
OECD																
Australia	0.02	(0.01)	-0.13	(0.02)	0.15	(0.02)	**-0.28**	(0.02)	**-1.35**	(0.01)	**-0.31**	(0.00)	**0.46**	(0.00)	**1.26**	(0.00)
Austria	0.18	(0.02)	0.00	(0.03)	0.36	(0.03)	**-0.36**	(0.04)	**-1.24**	(0.02)	**-0.03**	(0.01)	**0.63**	(0.01)	**1.37**	(0.00)
Belgium	0.22	(0.02)	0.10	(0.02)	0.33	(0.02)	**-0.23**	(0.03)	**-1.16**	(0.01)	**-0.01**	(0.01)	**0.67**	(0.01)	**1.36**	(0.00)
Canada	-0.03	(0.01)	-0.17	(0.02)	0.12	(0.01)	**-0.29**	(0.02)	**-1.37**	(0.01)	**-0.49**	(0.01)	**0.32**	(0.00)	**1.23**	(0.01)
Chile	-0.09	(0.02)	-0.15	(0.03)	-0.03	(0.03)	**-0.11**	(0.03)	**-1.43**	(0.01)	**-0.33**	(0.01)	**0.39**	(0.00)	**1.16**	(0.01)
Czech Republic	-0.02	(0.02)	-0.18	(0.03)	0.15	(0.03)	**-0.33**	(0.04)	**-1.31**	(0.01)	**-0.33**	(0.01)	**0.39**	(0.00)	**1.31**	(0.00)
Denmark	0.16	(0.02)	0.02	(0.03)	0.30	(0.02)	**-0.28**	(0.03)	**-1.17**	(0.02)	**-0.06**	(0.01)	**0.56**	(0.00)	**1.35**	(0.00)
Estonia	0.23	(0.02)	0.06	(0.03)	0.42	(0.02)	**-0.36**	(0.03)	**-1.12**	(0.02)	**0.04**	(0.01)	**0.59**	(0.01)	**1.32**	(0.00)
Finland	0.03	(0.02)	-0.25	(0.03)	0.30	(0.02)	**-0.56**	(0.03)	**-1.37**	(0.01)	**-0.26**	(0.01)	**0.48**	(0.01)	**1.25**	(0.01)
France	0.17	(0.02)	0.05	(0.03)	0.28	(0.03)	**-0.22**	(0.03)	**-1.19**	(0.01)	**-0.04**	(0.01)	**0.59**	(0.01)	**1.32**	(0.00)
Germany	0.30	(0.02)	0.15	(0.03)	0.44	(0.03)	**-0.29**	(0.03)	**-1.15**	(0.01)	**0.10**	(0.01)	**0.83**	(0.01)	**1.42**	(0.00)
Greece	-0.07	(0.01)	-0.16	(0.02)	0.01	(0.02)	**-0.18**	(0.03)	**-1.23**	(0.02)	**-0.36**	(0.01)	**0.26**	(0.00)	**1.04**	(0.01)
Hungary	0.05	(0.02)	-0.07	(0.03)	0.16	(0.03)	**-0.23**	(0.04)	**-1.24**	(0.02)	**-0.24**	(0.01)	**0.43**	(0.00)	**1.24**	(0.01)
Iceland	-0.19	(0.02)	-0.40	(0.03)	0.02	(0.02)	**-0.41**	(0.02)	**-1.56**	(0.01)	**-0.53**	(0.01)	**0.23**	(0.00)	**1.10**	(0.01)
Ireland	0.16	(0.02)	0.08	(0.03)	0.23	(0.02)	**-0.14**	(0.04)	**-1.12**	(0.02)	**-0.03**	(0.01)	**0.50**	(0.01)	**1.27**	(0.01)
Israel	-0.16	(0.02)	-0.23	(0.02)	-0.10	(0.02)	**-0.13**	(0.03)	**-1.46**	(0.01)	**-0.50**	(0.01)	**0.23**	(0.00)	**1.08**	(0.01)
Italy	0.25	(0.01)	0.12	(0.01)	0.39	(0.01)	**-0.27**	(0.02)	**-0.98**	(0.01)	**0.11**	(0.00)	**0.58**	(0.00)	**1.30**	(0.00)
Japan	0.12	(0.02)	0.01	(0.03)	0.25	(0.02)	**-0.23**	(0.03)	**-1.16**	(0.02)	**-0.03**	(0.01)	**0.46**	(0.01)	**1.22**	(0.01)
Korea	0.03	(0.03)	-0.07	(0.04)	0.15	(0.03)	**-0.23**	(0.05)	**-1.33**	(0.02)	**-0.25**	(0.01)	**0.45**	(0.01)	**1.26**	(0.01)
Luxembourg	-0.17	(0.01)	-0.34	(0.02)	0.01	(0.02)	**-0.35**	(0.03)	**-1.53**	(0.01)	**-0.56**	(0.01)	**0.26**	(0.01)	**1.15**	(0.01)
Mexico	-0.25	(0.01)	-0.29	(0.01)	-0.21	(0.01)	**-0.08**	(0.02)	**-1.57**	(0.01)	**-0.66**	(0.00)	**0.16**	(0.00)	**1.07**	(0.00)
Netherlands	0.10	(0.04)	-0.01	(0.04)	0.21	(0.04)	**-0.22**	(0.03)	**-1.30**	(0.01)	**-0.18**	(0.01)	**0.56**	(0.01)	**1.33**	(0.00)
New Zealand	-0.04	(0.02)	-0.18	(0.03)	0.11	(0.02)	**-0.28**	(0.03)	**-1.37**	(0.01)	**-0.39**	(0.01)	**0.39**	(0.01)	**1.22**	(0.01)
Norway	-0.30	(0.02)	-0.45	(0.02)	-0.14	(0.03)	**-0.30**	(0.03)	**-1.62**	(0.01)	**-0.71**	(0.01)	**0.12**	(0.01)	**1.03**	(0.01)
Poland	-0.16	(0.02)	-0.30	(0.02)	-0.02	(0.02)	**-0.27**	(0.03)	**-1.45**	(0.01)	**-0.54**	(0.01)	**0.23**	(0.01)	**1.12**	(0.01)
Portugal	-0.07	(0.02)	-0.19	(0.03)	0.04	(0.03)	**-0.23**	(0.03)	**-1.43**	(0.01)	**-0.38**	(0.01)	**0.39**	(0.00)	**1.15**	(0.01)
Slovak Republic	-0.19	(0.02)	-0.32	(0.02)	-0.05	(0.03)	**-0.37**	(0.03)	**-1.51**	(0.01)	**-0.52**	(0.01)	**0.19**	(0.01)	**1.04**	(0.01)
Slovenia	-0.07	(0.01)	-0.25	(0.02)	0.12	(0.02)	**-0.37**	(0.02)	**-1.18**	(0.01)	**-0.07**	(0.00)	**0.48**	(0.00)	**1.26**	(0.00)
Spain	0.13	(0.01)	0.00	(0.02)	0.25	(0.02)	**-0.25**	(0.02)	**-1.18**	(0.01)	**-0.07**	(0.00)	**0.48**	(0.00)	**1.14**	(0.01)
Sweden	-0.17	(0.02)	-0.34	(0.03)	0.01	(0.03)	**-0.35**	(0.03)	**-1.54**	(0.01)	**-0.57**	(0.01)	**0.28**	(0.01)	**1.14**	(0.01)
Switzerland	0.20	(0.02)	0.01	(0.02)	0.40	(0.03)	**-0.39**	(0.03)	**-1.24**	(0.01)	**-0.04**	(0.01)	**0.71**	(0.01)	**1.39**	(0.00)
Turkey	-0.23	(0.02)	-0.32	(0.03)	-0.13	(0.02)	**-0.19**	(0.03)	**-1.50**	(0.01)	**-0.57**	(0.01)	**0.18**	(0.00)	**0.98**	(0.00)
United Kingdom	0.09	(0.02)	-0.01	(0.02)	0.19	(0.02)	**-0.20**	(0.03)	**-1.23**	(0.01)	**-0.17**	(0.01)	**0.49**	(0.00)	**1.27**	(0.00)
United States	-0.21	(0.02)	-0.31	(0.03)	-0.11	(0.02)	**-0.20**	(0.03)	**-1.55**	(0.01)	**-0.60**	(0.01)	**0.19**	(0.00)	**1.09**	(0.01)
OECD average	0.00	(0.00)	-0.13	(0.00)	0.13	(0.00)	**-0.27**	(0.01)	**-1.33**	(0.00)	**-0.29**	(0.00)	**0.42**	(0.00)	**1.21**	(0.00)
Partners																
Albania	0.21	(0.03)	0.05	(0.04)	0.37	(0.03)	**-0.31**	(0.04)	**-1.21**	(0.02)	**0.00**	(0.01)	**0.65**	(0.01)	**1.40**	(0.00)
Argentina	-0.27	(0.02)	-0.32	(0.03)	-0.23	(0.04)	-0.09	(0.04)	**-1.58**	(0.01)	**-0.66**	(0.01)	**0.15**	(0.01)	**0.99**	(0.01)
Azerbaijan	-0.69	(0.03)	-0.72	(0.04)	-0.66	(0.03)	-0.05	(0.04)	**-1.88**	(0.00)	**-1.17**	(0.01)	**-0.39**	(0.01)	**0.68**	(0.02)
Brazil	-0.35	(0.02)	-0.43	(0.02)	-0.27	(0.02)	**-0.17**	(0.02)	**-1.62**	(0.01)	**-0.77**	(0.00)	**0.04**	(0.00)	**0.96**	(0.01)
Bulgaria	-0.36	(0.03)	-0.52	(0.04)	-0.18	(0.03)	**-0.34**	(0.05)	**-1.65**	(0.01)	**-0.74**	(0.01)	**0.05**	(0.01)	**0.90**	(0.01)
Colombia	-0.38	(0.02)	-0.40	(0.03)	-0.36	(0.03)	-0.04	(0.04)	**-1.69**	(0.01)	**-0.84**	(0.01)	**0.00**	(0.01)	**1.01**	(0.01)
Croatia	-0.10	(0.02)	-0.22	(0.02)	0.03	(0.03)	**-0.26**	(0.03)	**-1.41**	(0.01)	**-0.40**	(0.01)	**0.31**	(0.00)	**1.09**	(0.01)
Dubai (UAE)	-0.03	(0.01)	-0.11	(0.02)	0.05	(0.02)	**-0.16**	(0.03)	**-1.38**	(0.01)	**-0.38**	(0.01)	**0.40**	(0.00)	**1.23**	(0.01)
Hong Kong-China	-0.20	(0.02)	-0.33	(0.03)	-0.06	(0.03)	**-0.27**	(0.03)	**-1.52**	(0.01)	**-0.56**	(0.01)	**0.21**	(0.01)	**1.05**	(0.01)
Indonesia	-0.32	(0.03)	-0.42	(0.03)	-0.23	(0.03)	**-0.18**	(0.04)	**-1.57**	(0.01)	**-0.69**	(0.01)	**0.05**	(0.01)	**0.90**	(0.02)
Jordan	-0.49	(0.02)	-0.59	(0.03)	-0.41	(0.03)	**-0.18**	(0.04)	**-1.81**	(0.01)	**-0.89**	(0.01)	**-0.08**	(0.01)	**0.80**	(0.01)
Kazakhstan	-0.33	(0.02)	-0.39	(0.03)	-0.27	(0.02)	**-0.12**	(0.03)	**-1.65**	(0.01)	**-0.71**	(0.00)	**0.08**	(0.01)	**0.97**	(0.01)
Kyrgyzstan	-0.69	(0.03)	-0.75	(0.03)	-0.62	(0.03)	**-0.13**	(0.03)	**-1.86**	(0.00)	**-1.09**	(0.01)	**-0.43**	(0.01)	**0.64**	(0.02)
Latvia	-0.21	(0.03)	-0.35	(0.02)	-0.07	(0.04)	**-0.28**	(0.04)	**-1.47**	(0.01)	**-0.60**	(0.01)	**0.16**	(0.01)	**1.06**	(0.01)
Liechtenstein	0.01	(0.05)	-0.23	(0.08)	0.27	(0.06)	**-0.51**	(0.10)	**-1.43**	(0.04)	**-0.41**	(0.03)	**0.52**	(0.02)	**1.33**	(0.02)
Lithuania	-0.15	(0.02)	-0.32	(0.02)	0.01	(0.02)	**-0.33**	(0.03)	**-1.40**	(0.01)	**-0.53**	(0.01)	**0.22**	(0.00)	**1.09**	(0.01)
Macao-China	-0.10	(0.01)	-0.25	(0.02)	0.05	(0.02)	**-0.30**	(0.02)	**-1.34**	(0.01)	**-0.46**	(0.01)	**0.29**	(0.00)	**1.12**	(0.01)
Montenegro	-0.28	(0.02)	-0.38	(0.03)	-0.17	(0.02)	**-0.21**	(0.04)	**-1.66**	(0.01)	**-0.67**	(0.01)	**0.19**	(0.01)	**1.03**	(0.01)
Panama	-0.43	(0.04)	-0.48	(0.05)	-0.39	(0.05)	-0.10	(0.06)	**-1.73**	(0.01)	**-0.85**	(0.01)	**-0.03**	(0.01)	**0.88**	(0.01)
Peru	-0.42	(0.02)	-0.45	(0.02)	-0.40	(0.03)	-0.05	(0.04)	**-1.66**	(0.01)	**-0.83**	(0.01)	**-0.07**	(0.01)	**0.87**	(0.01)
Qatar	-0.44	(0.01)	-0.47	(0.02)	-0.41	(0.02)	**-0.05**	(0.02)	**-1.79**	(0.00)	**-0.84**	(0.01)	**0.00**	(0.01)	**0.87**	(0.01)
Romania	-0.33	(0.02)	-0.42	(0.03)	-0.25	(0.03)	**-0.16**	(0.04)	**-1.64**	(0.01)	**-0.72**	(0.01)	**0.07**	(0.01)	**0.95**	(0.01)
Russian Federation	-0.11	(0.03)	-0.25	(0.03)	0.02	(0.03)	**-0.27**	(0.03)	**-1.42**	(0.01)	**-0.45**	(0.01)	**0.29**	(0.00)	**1.15**	(0.01)
Serbia	-0.05	(0.02)	-0.15	(0.03)	0.06	(0.02)	**-0.21**	(0.03)	**-1.34**	(0.01)	**-0.33**	(0.01)	**0.34**	(0.00)	**1.13**	(0.01)
Shanghai-China	0.14	(0.02)	0.01	(0.02)	0.26	(0.02)	**-0.26**	(0.03)	**-1.18**	(0.01)	**-0.13**	(0.01)	**0.53**	(0.01)	**1.33**	(0.00)
Singapore	0.05	(0.01)	0.02	(0.02)	0.09	(0.02)	**-0.07**	(0.02)	**-1.22**	(0.01)	**-0.25**	(0.01)	**0.45**	(0.00)	**1.23**	(0.01)
Chinese Taipei	-0.13	(0.02)	-0.23	(0.02)	-0.02	(0.02)	**-0.21**	(0.02)	**-1.35**	(0.01)	**-0.47**	(0.01)	**0.24**	(0.00)	**1.08**	(0.01)
Thailand	-0.30	(0.02)	-0.46	(0.03)	-0.17	(0.03)	**-0.29**	(0.04)	**-1.64**	(0.01)	**-0.71**	(0.01)	**0.12**	(0.01)	**1.04**	(0.01)
Trinidad and Tobago	-0.14	(0.02)	-0.28	(0.02)	-0.01	(0.02)	**-0.28**	(0.03)	**-1.53**	(0.01)	**-0.52**	(0.01)	**0.30**	(0.00)	**1.19**	(0.01)
Tunisia	-0.39	(0.02)	-0.43	(0.03)	-0.35	(0.03)	-0.09	(0.04)	**-1.63**	(0.01)	**-0.80**	(0.01)	**-0.01**	(0.01)	**0.89**	(0.01)
Uruguay	-0.26	(0.01)	-0.33	(0.02)	-0.19	(0.02)	**-0.14**	(0.03)	**-1.59**	(0.01)	**-0.64**	(0.01)	**0.19**	(0.01)	**1.01**	(0.01)

Note: Values that are statistically significant are indicated in bold (see Annex A3).
StatLink ⟦⟧ http://dx.doi.org/10.1787/888932343285

[Part 2/2]

Index of understanding and remembering and reading performance, by national quarters of this index

Table III.1.14 *Results based on students' self-reports*

| | Performance on the reading scale, by national quarters of this index | | | | | | | | Change in the reading score per unit of this index | | Increased likelihood of students in the bottom quarter of this index scoring in the bottom quarter of the national reading performance distribution | | Explained variance in student performance (r-squared x 100) | |
| | Bottom quarter | | Second quarter | | Third quarter | | Top quarter | | | | | | | |
	Mean score	S.E.	Mean score	S.E.	Mean score	S.E.	Mean score	S.E.	Effect	S.E.	Ratio	S.E.	%	S.E.
OECD														
Australia	466	(2.8)	508	(2.6)	535	(2.5)	566	(2.8)	38.5	(1.16)	2.5	(0.09)	16.4	(0.76)
Austria	420	(4.0)	464	(3.7)	493	(4.1)	530	(3.5)	41.7	(1.92)	2.5	(0.16)	18.8	(1.39)
Belgium	455	(3.1)	502	(2.9)	536	(2.6)	573	(2.5)	46.5	(1.38)	2.9	(0.14)	23.2	(1.07)
Canada	490	(2.4)	519	(2.4)	540	(2.3)	559	(2.1)	27.2	(0.92)	2.0	(0.07)	9.4	(0.61)
Chile	411	(3.3)	438	(3.5)	466	(3.3)	499	(3.3)	32.6	(1.54)	2.2	(0.16)	17.0	(1.21)
Czech Republic	436	(3.9)	472	(3.4)	498	(3.3)	530	(3.8)	37.9	(1.56)	2.2	(0.15)	16.7	(1.19)
Denmark	449	(3.0)	488	(3.2)	510	(3.2)	541	(2.5)	37.0	(1.42)	2.6	(0.16)	18.4	(1.23)
Estonia	459	(3.7)	494	(4.0)	518	(3.5)	541	(3.1)	33.2	(1.51)	2.4	(0.18)	15.1	(1.16)
Finland	490	(3.4)	523	(3.6)	555	(3.3)	581	(2.5)	35.4	(1.22)	2.5	(0.15)	17.6	(1.00)
France	448	(5.0)	495	(4.1)	522	(4.4)	550	(4.3)	41.1	(2.45)	2.6	(0.15)	15.9	(1.33)
Germany	449	(3.9)	495	(4.1)	531	(2.9)	556	(2.8)	40.8	(1.69)	2.9	(0.19)	20.8	(1.33)
Greece	460	(5.0)	483	(5.0)	492	(5.4)	508	(5.2)	22.5	(1.93)	1.6	(0.11)	4.5	(0.80)
Hungary	449	(4.9)	488	(4.0)	510	(3.6)	540	(3.8)	36.3	(2.40)	2.3	(0.16)	15.4	(1.57)
Iceland	459	(3.1)	497	(3.6)	515	(2.9)	544	(3.1)	32.2	(1.66)	2.1	(0.13)	12.2	(1.16)
Ireland	455	(5.0)	501	(3.8)	512	(3.1)	540	(3.5)	35.2	(2.02)	2.5	(0.20)	12.9	(1.29)
Israel	434	(5.3)	474	(4.4)	496	(3.8)	529	(3.6)	37.5	(2.03)	2.2	(0.15)	11.9	(1.10)
Italy	438	(2.6)	483	(2.1)	504	(2.0)	530	(1.8)	40.6	(1.26)	2.4	(0.08)	14.6	(0.69)
Japan	468	(5.7)	523	(4.5)	537	(3.6)	558	(3.0)	40.3	(2.49)	2.5	(0.13)	14.3	(1.39)
Korea	494	(5.5)	533	(3.8)	555	(3.0)	578	(3.0)	33.2	(2.17)	2.7	(0.18)	17.9	(1.74)
Luxembourg	424	(2.8)	463	(3.1)	495	(2.8)	532	(2.5)	40.0	(1.31)	2.4	(0.14)	17.0	(1.05)
Mexico	398	(2.1)	415	(2.1)	437	(2.4)	469	(2.1)	27.3	(0.78)	1.8	(0.06)	11.3	(0.55)
Netherlands	463	(5.5)	496	(5.7)	529	(5.7)	565	(4.4)	38.5	(1.82)	2.4	(0.20)	20.2	(1.58)
New Zealand	473	(3.4)	516	(3.6)	543	(3.4)	570	(3.1)	37.8	(1.52)	2.5	(0.15)	14.5	(1.07)
Norway	460	(3.5)	496	(2.9)	517	(3.1)	549	(3.2)	33.1	(1.40)	2.2	(0.11)	14.1	(1.08)
Poland	471	(3.2)	492	(3.3)	517	(4.0)	542	(3.2)	28.0	(1.47)	1.8	(0.10)	10.4	(0.99)
Portugal	439	(3.7)	481	(3.9)	508	(3.3)	536	(3.1)	35.5	(1.32)	2.7	(0.17)	19.3	(1.22)
Slovak Republic	439	(3.7)	472	(3.8)	493	(3.4)	520	(3.5)	32.2	(1.88)	2.1	(0.13)	12.2	(1.28)
Slovenia	441	(2.5)	476	(2.7)	501	(2.7)	533	(2.6)	36.0	(1.21)	2.4	(0.12)	16.9	(1.17)
Spain	444	(2.8)	480	(2.7)	495	(2.3)	514	(2.2)	29.7	(1.17)	2.2	(0.08)	10.5	(0.72)
Sweden	453	(3.3)	480	(3.3)	518	(3.9)	557	(3.2)	39.5	(1.39)	2.1	(0.14)	18.4	(1.13)
Switzerland	442	(3.4)	487	(2.9)	525	(2.8)	559	(2.9)	44.4	(1.57)	3.0	(0.14)	24.4	(1.31)
Turkey	431	(3.5)	462	(4.1)	477	(3.9)	496	(4.2)	26.2	(1.52)	2.1	(0.14)	9.8	(0.98)
United Kingdom	457	(2.8)	486	(3.1)	514	(3.5)	538	(3.5)	33.6	(1.61)	2.1	(0.15)	12.1	(1.10)
United States	463	(3.9)	485	(4.4)	518	(4.7)	544	(3.8)	31.8	(1.37)	1.9	(0.11)	11.3	(0.96)
OECD average	451	(0.7)	487	(0.6)	512	(0.6)	541	(0.6)	35.4	(0.28)	2.3	(0.02)	15.2	(0.20)
Partners														
Albania	348	(4.2)	382	(5.6)	413	(6.1)	434	(5.7)	34.1	(2.23)	2.0	(0.18)	13.1	(1.61)
Argentina	374	(5.5)	405	(5.3)	425	(5.8)	452	(6.1)	30.5	(2.45)	1.8	(0.13)	9.0	(1.27)
Azerbaijan	351	(4.0)	366	(4.5)	377	(4.3)	394	(4.8)	16.4	(2.00)	1.5	(0.14)	5.0	(1.22)
Brazil	383	(2.8)	405	(3.0)	427	(3.9)	463	(3.6)	31.0	(1.26)	1.7	(0.10)	11.6	(0.81)
Bulgaria	389	(7.1)	429	(7.6)	461	(6.8)	492	(7.5)	40.8	(2.47)	2.2	(0.19)	14.0	(1.51)
Colombia	387	(4.1)	403	(4.1)	428	(3.9)	470	(4.2)	31.2	(1.69)	1.9	(0.14)	15.5	(1.37)
Croatia	430	(3.6)	471	(4.1)	493	(3.2)	520	(3.5)	35.0	(1.55)	2.4	(0.15)	15.8	(1.11)
Dubai (UAE)	411	(2.9)	451	(3.1)	479	(2.7)	519	(2.7)	40.9	(1.32)	2.3	(0.13)	15.5	(0.95)
Hong Kong-China	491	(3.6)	532	(3.3)	549	(2.8)	564	(2.6)	28.8	(1.44)	2.3	(0.14)	11.8	(1.05)
Indonesia	377	(3.6)	398	(4.2)	412	(4.1)	432	(4.4)	22.0	(1.46)	1.9	(0.13)	10.5	(1.15)
Jordan	385	(4.0)	411	(3.5)	420	(4.1)	435	(4.0)	18.8	(1.55)	1.5	(0.11)	4.8	(0.75)
Kazakhstan	346	(2.9)	382	(4.2)	402	(3.7)	437	(4.5)	34.3	(1.62)	2.2	(0.13)	14.8	(1.19)
Kyrgyzstan	284	(4.4)	315	(3.8)	328	(3.8)	371	(5.3)	34.9	(2.29)	1.8	(0.12)	12.3	(1.40)
Latvia	451	(3.5)	472	(3.5)	498	(3.4)	523	(3.4)	28.7	(1.40)	2.0	(0.13)	12.7	(1.16)
Liechtenstein	450	(8.4)	485	(8.4)	506	(8.1)	558	(7.4)	36.5	(3.86)	2.9	(0.63)	22.2	(4.26)
Lithuania	436	(4.0)	457	(3.4)	480	(2.9)	515	(3.7)	32.2	(2.11)	1.9	(0.12)	13.3	(1.50)
Macao-China	464	(2.0)	482	(2.5)	493	(2.2)	510	(2.0)	19.0	(1.07)	1.7	(0.08)	5.8	(0.64)
Montenegro	370	(3.3)	405	(2.8)	430	(3.0)	460	(2.7)	33.4	(1.42)	2.3	(0.17)	15.2	(1.15)
Panama	338	(5.7)	366	(7.4)	401	(8.6)	426	(7.2)	34.9	(2.40)	2.0	(0.20)	13.5	(1.32)
Peru	345	(4.3)	367	(4.8)	383	(5.1)	422	(5.7)	31.1	(2.30)	1.7	(0.13)	10.2	(1.25)
Qatar	335	(2.4)	376	(2.8)	391	(2.7)	436	(2.8)	37.7	(1.20)	1.7	(0.08)	11.6	(0.70)
Romania	385	(5.0)	418	(5.4)	440	(4.9)	471	(4.4)	32.8	(1.95)	2.1	(0.16)	14.3	(1.38)
Russian Federation	421	(4.3)	451	(3.8)	479	(3.8)	508	(3.6)	34.1	(1.83)	2.2	(0.15)	15.0	(1.30)
Serbia	404	(3.5)	441	(2.6)	460	(3.0)	485	(3.2)	32.4	(1.51)	2.4	(0.13)	14.9	(1.12)
Shanghai-China	519	(3.4)	556	(2.7)	564	(3.4)	586	(2.7)	27.3	(1.25)	2.2	(0.10)	10.9	(0.83)
Singapore	487	(2.4)	513	(2.7)	543	(3.1)	563	(2.5)	31.9	(1.38)	2.0	(0.11)	9.8	(0.82)
Chinese Taipei	456	(3.9)	495	(3.1)	507	(3.2)	528	(3.8)	30.6	(1.90)	2.2	(0.13)	11.7	(1.17)
Thailand	396	(3.3)	410	(3.2)	429	(3.1)	453	(4.1)	21.9	(1.54)	1.7	(0.12)	10.0	(1.13)
Trinidad and Tobago	377	(3.3)	418	(3.5)	446	(5.3)	483	(3.3)	37.9	(1.54)	2.3	(0.15)	13.7	(1.12)
Tunisia	388	(3.5)	395	(3.5)	412	(3.3)	433	(4.5)	18.1	(1.52)	1.4	(0.08)	4.5	(0.69)
Uruguay	389	(3.4)	425	(3.9)	445	(3.5)	475	(3.8)	31.9	(1.36)	2.0	(0.14)	11.2	(0.86)

Note: Values that are statistically significant are indicated in bold (see Annex A3).
StatLink ⬛⬛⬛ http://dx.doi.org/10.1787/888932343285

[Part 1/1]
Proportion of students with low levels of understanding and remembering, by reading proficiency level[1]

Table III.1.15   *Results based on students' self-reports*

	Percentage of students with low levels of understanding and remembering									
	Level 1a or below		Level 2		Level 3		Level 4		Level 5 or above	
	%	S.E.	%	S.E.	%	S.E.	%	S.E.	%	S.E.
OECD										
Australia	77.8	(1.1)	64.0	(1.2)	48.2	(1.4)	35.8	(1.6)	25.3	(1.4)
Austria	65.8	(1.9)	48.3	(2.1)	33.5	(1.7)	19.2	(1.7)	13.8	(2.9)
Belgium	71.8	(1.6)	57.9	(1.7)	39.7	(1.6)	23.0	(1.3)	13.9	(1.3)
Canada	74.0	(1.6)	63.5	(1.7)	51.4	(1.2)	40.3	(1.0)	33.2	(1.3)
Chile	66.2	(1.6)	48.0	(1.7)	29.5	(1.7)	16.7	(2.4)	c	c
Czech Republic	72.5	(1.7)	61.7	(1.8)	45.9	(1.9)	29.0	(2.0)	19.4	(2.5)
Denmark	72.3	(1.9)	54.9	(1.8)	37.1	(1.5)	23.4	(1.6)	c	c
Estonia	65.4	(2.2)	53.5	(1.7)	35.6	(1.4)	22.2	(1.6)	12.3	(1.9)
Finland	81.5	(2.2)	69.1	(2.1)	52.1	(1.7)	33.9	(1.9)	22.4	(2.2)
France	69.7	(1.8)	51.5	(1.8)	36.9	(1.8)	28.4	(1.7)	18.2	(2.3)
Germany	70.5	(2.1)	49.5	(1.7)	32.1	(1.6)	17.6	(1.5)	10.9	(1.5)
Greece	54.2	(2.6)	46.3	(1.9)	39.5	(1.4)	34.4	(1.9)	27.6	(3.2)
Hungary	72.5	(2.6)	58.2	(1.9)	46.5	(1.6)	29.5	(1.8)	20.6	(2.7)
Iceland	69.6	(2.2)	55.6	(2.5)	44.9	(2.0)	33.1	(2.2)	23.8	(3.1)
Ireland	69.1	(2.5)	49.6	(2.3)	37.1	(2.1)	31.3	(2.6)	c	c
Israel	65.3	(1.8)	52.4	(2.2)	41.2	(2.2)	30.1	(2.1)	22.6	(2.4)
Italy	60.9	(1.0)	44.0	(1.0)	30.6	(1.0)	20.8	(0.8)	14.5	(1.2)
Japan	70.6	(1.9)	54.7	(1.9)	40.8	(1.7)	32.6	(1.3)	26.1	(1.7)
Korea	84.2	(3.6)	69.9	(2.7)	53.0	(1.6)	35.4	(1.4)	25.6	(2.7)
Luxembourg	72.1	(1.4)	55.9	(1.7)	39.8	(1.9)	26.5	(1.7)	17.3	(2.8)
Mexico	65.5	(0.8)	50.7	(1.1)	33.7	(1.2)	21.5	(1.6)	c	c
Netherlands	72.8	(2.4)	62.7	(2.0)	44.8	(1.8)	26.4	(1.9)	14.5	(2.0)
New Zealand	78.7	(2.0)	66.3	(1.9)	55.0	(2.2)	39.9	(1.5)	31.6	(2.3)
Norway	76.0	(1.9)	62.8	(1.6)	50.7	(1.5)	37.0	(2.0)	24.9	(2.7)
Poland	67.6	(2.1)	60.4	(1.9)	46.1	(1.7)	33.1	(1.7)	21.1	(2.9)
Portugal	72.4	(1.6)	52.4	(1.6)	35.0	(1.5)	21.5	(1.7)	13.8	(3.2)
Slovak Republic	68.4	(1.7)	53.2	(1.8)	41.6	(1.8)	30.7	(3.4)	17.4	(5.1)
Slovenia	65.0	(1.7)	53.2	(1.9)	34.3	(1.7)	19.4	(1.7)	c	c
Spain	64.3	(1.5)	49.7	(1.3)	37.0	(1.2)	27.9	(1.3)	22.0	(3.6)
Sweden	73.5	(1.7)	62.2	(1.8)	46.0	(2.0)	26.6	(2.2)	15.8	(2.4)
Switzerland	76.4	(1.6)	55.5	(1.4)	36.4	(1.4)	21.3	(1.7)	9.1	(1.7)
Turkey	66.7	(1.8)	51.8	(1.5)	40.4	(1.5)	33.1	(2.3)	c	c
United Kingdom	70.8	(2.1)	56.4	(1.8)	43.4	(1.7)	32.1	(2.0)	21.9	(2.9)
United States	68.6	(2.1)	61.5	(1.9)	46.9	(1.7)	33.4	(2.5)	23.4	(2.4)
OECD average	70.4	(0.3)	56.1	(0.3)	41.4	(0.3)	28.4	(0.3)	20.1	(0.5)
Partners										
Albania	52.6	(1.9)	31.3	(2.2)	18.1	(2.2)	8.4	(2.7)	c	c
Argentina	62.0	(1.3)	48.4	(2.1)	37.7	(3.1)	26.4	(4.1)	c	c
Azerbaijan	63.3	(1.5)	49.0	(2.0)	37.6	(4.6)	23.4	(10.2)	c	c
Brazil	67.4	(0.7)	54.3	(1.1)	40.2	(1.5)	22.0	(2.2)	10.9	(2.7)
Bulgaria	72.4	(1.6)	56.3	(2.2)	42.6	(2.2)	31.0	(2.3)	c	c
Colombia	72.2	(1.4)	56.0	(1.8)	35.1	(2.2)	16.8	(4.2)	c	c
Croatia	66.9	(1.8)	51.4	(1.7)	32.8	(1.7)	21.9	(1.9)	c	c
Dubai (UAE)	70.3	(1.3)	56.7	(1.6)	40.0	(1.5)	30.2	(2.0)	22.2	(3.7)
Hong Kong-China	77.5	(2.4)	63.1	(2.2)	49.1	(2.0)	37.5	(1.9)	29.9	(2.6)
Indonesia	64.5	(1.4)	46.6	(1.9)	33.7	(3.1)	24.6	(10.6)	c	c
Jordan	56.2	(1.4)	48.3	(1.7)	34.0	(2.5)	25.5	(4.0)	c	c
Kazakhstan	64.1	(1.1)	45.7	(1.7)	31.7	(2.0)	17.7	(3.9)	c	c
Kyrgyzstan	62.6	(1.2)	40.3	(2.7)	24.4	(3.1)	12.5	(4.9)	c	c
Latvia	71.4	(2.2)	59.4	(1.8)	44.4	(1.9)	27.4	(2.1)	c	c
Liechtenstein	80.7	(5.8)	66.5	(7.5)	39.2	(5.3)	32.5	(7.3)	c	c
Lithuania	65.7	(1.9)	54.2	(1.9)	40.9	(2.2)	24.7	(2.3)	c	c
Macao-China	60.6	(1.9)	49.0	(1.4)	40.7	(1.2)	32.4	(1.9)	26.5	(4.4)
Montenegro	64.3	(1.1)	45.2	(2.2)	30.2	(2.4)	21.1	(3.5)	c	c
Panama	59.6	(1.9)	35.9	(3.0)	26.1	(3.4)	15.0	(4.7)	c	c
Peru	54.5	(1.2)	40.3	(1.7)	26.5	(2.9)	13.2	(3.3)	c	c
Qatar	56.4	(0.7)	43.0	(1.6)	28.2	(2.0)	16.4	(2.6)	9.9	(2.9)
Romania	69.5	(1.8)	51.4	(1.7)	36.6	(2.0)	23.3	(3.8)	c	c
Russian Federation	66.0	(1.9)	49.0	(1.8)	33.6	(1.7)	20.4	(2.5)	c	c
Serbia	69.4	(1.3)	53.4	(1.7)	37.7	(1.7)	25.3	(2.4)	c	c
Shanghai-China	73.2	(3.4)	62.0	(2.0)	51.5	(1.5)	39.2	(1.3)	29.8	(2.2)
Singapore	74.0	(2.0)	61.7	(1.8)	49.1	(1.4)	39.5	(1.9)	30.8	(2.1)
Chinese Taipei	69.1	(1.9)	50.9	(1.6)	40.2	(1.6)	33.0	(1.5)	24.6	(3.4)
Thailand	64.3	(1.3)	49.0	(1.5)	34.4	(1.6)	18.3	(4.0)	c	c
Trinidad and Tobago	63.3	(1.5)	42.8	(2.0)	30.9	(2.3)	19.3	(2.9)	c	c
Tunisia	65.0	(1.3)	54.3	(1.9)	42.2	(2.7)	37.0	(4.3)	c	c
Uruguay	64.0	(1.2)	50.3	(1.5)	36.1	(2.1)	27.9	(3.0)	c	c

1. Students who reported levels of diversity of reading below their country average.
StatLink ᵐˢᵖ http://dx.doi.org/10.1787/888932343285

[Part 1/2]
Index of summarising and reading performance, by national quarters of this index
Table III.1.16 *Results based on students' self-reports*

	Index of summarising															
	All students		Boys		Girls		Gender difference (B – G)		Bottom quarter		Second quarter		Third quarter		Top quarter	
	Mean index	S.E.	Mean index	S.E.	Mean index	S.E.	Dif.	S.E.	Mean index	S.E.	Mean index	S.E.	Mean index	S.E.	Mean index	S.E.
Australia	-0.09	(0.02)	-0.30	(0.02)	0.11	(0.02)	**-0.42**	(0.03)	**-1.54**	(0.01)	**-0.33**	(0.01)	0.40	(0.00)	1.12	(0.00)
Austria	0.07	(0.02)	-0.16	(0.02)	0.28	(0.03)	**-0.43**	(0.04)	**-1.34**	(0.01)	**-0.15**	(0.01)	0.56	(0.00)	1.21	(0.00)
Belgium	0.17	(0.02)	0.04	(0.02)	0.30	(0.03)	**-0.26**	(0.03)	**-1.24**	(0.01)	0.04	(0.01)	0.63	(0.00)	1.25	(0.00)
Canada	0.02	(0.01)	-0.19	(0.01)	0.24	(0.01)	**-0.43**	(0.02)	**-1.40**	(0.01)	**-0.16**	(0.00)	0.49	(0.00)	1.17	(0.00)
Chile	-0.15	(0.02)	-0.26	(0.02)	-0.03	(0.02)	**-0.24**	(0.03)	**-1.44**	(0.01)	**-0.39**	(0.01)	0.30	(0.01)	0.94	(0.01)
Czech Republic	0.11	(0.02)	-0.09	(0.03)	0.32	(0.03)	**-0.40**	(0.04)	**-1.31**	(0.01)	**-0.08**	(0.01)	0.60	(0.00)	1.21	(0.00)
Denmark	0.18	(0.02)	-0.01	(0.03)	0.37	(0.03)	**-0.38**	(0.03)	**-1.17**	(0.02)	0.05	(0.01)	0.61	(0.00)	1.21	(0.01)
Estonia	0.15	(0.02)	-0.05	(0.03)	0.35	(0.02)	**-0.41**	(0.03)	**-1.08**	(0.02)	**-0.07**	(0.01)	0.55	(0.00)	1.18	(0.01)
Finland	0.08	(0.02)	-0.22	(0.03)	0.38	(0.02)	**-0.60**	(0.03)	**-1.30**	(0.02)	**-0.10**	(0.01)	0.55	(0.00)	1.19	(0.01)
France	0.24	(0.02)	0.14	(0.03)	0.33	(0.03)	**-0.19**	(0.03)	**-1.04**	(0.02)	0.12	(0.01)	0.62	(0.01)	1.25	(0.01)
Germany	0.12	(0.02)	-0.04	(0.03)	0.28	(0.03)	**-0.32**	(0.03)	**-1.34**	(0.01)	0.01	(0.01)	0.61	(0.00)	1.22	(0.01)
Greece	-0.11	(0.02)	-0.21	(0.03)	-0.01	(0.02)	**-0.21**	(0.03)	**-1.38**	(0.02)	**-0.29**	(0.00)	0.30	(0.01)	0.93	(0.01)
Hungary	-0.01	(0.03)	-0.19	(0.03)	0.17	(0.04)	**-0.36**	(0.04)	**-1.43**	(0.02)	**-0.22**	(0.01)	0.44	(0.00)	1.17	(0.01)
Iceland	-0.17	(0.02)	-0.42	(0.03)	0.08	(0.02)	**-0.51**	(0.03)	**-1.66**	(0.01)	**-0.34**	(0.01)	0.36	(0.01)	0.97	(0.01)
Ireland	0.14	(0.02)	-0.01	(0.03)	0.29	(0.03)	**-0.30**	(0.03)	**-1.20**	(0.01)	**-0.02**	(0.01)	0.57	(0.00)	1.21	(0.01)
Israel	-0.16	(0.02)	-0.32	(0.03)	-0.01	(0.02)	**-0.31**	(0.04)	**-1.62**	(0.01)	**-0.41**	(0.01)	0.35	(0.01)	1.04	(0.01)
Italy	0.28	(0.01)	0.16	(0.01)	0.42	(0.01)	**-0.26**	(0.02)	**-0.92**	(0.01)	0.17	(0.00)	0.64	(0.00)	1.24	(0.00)
Japan	-0.01	(0.02)	-0.19	(0.04)	0.18	(0.02)	**-0.37**	(0.04)	**-1.52**	(0.02)	**-0.14**	(0.01)	0.47	(0.00)	1.15	(0.00)
Korea	0.04	(0.03)	-0.10	(0.04)	0.20	(0.03)	**-0.30**	(0.05)	**-1.45**	(0.02)	**-0.10**	(0.01)	0.52	(0.00)	1.19	(0.01)
Luxembourg	-0.04	(0.01)	-0.23	(0.02)	0.15	(0.03)	**-0.38**	(0.03)	**-1.48**	(0.01)	**-0.27**	(0.01)	0.42	(0.01)	1.16	(0.01)
Mexico	-0.06	(0.01)	-0.17	(0.01)	0.05	(0.02)	**-0.22**	(0.02)	**-1.44**	(0.01)	**-0.28**	(0.00)	0.38	(0.00)	1.09	(0.00)
Netherlands	-0.14	(0.04)	-0.29	(0.04)	-0.01	(0.04)	**-0.28**	(0.03)	**-1.60**	(0.02)	**-0.41**	(0.01)	0.38	(0.00)	1.05	(0.01)
New Zealand	-0.14	(0.02)	-0.33	(0.04)	0.05	(0.02)	**-0.38**	(0.04)	**-1.60**	(0.01)	**-0.39**	(0.01)	0.38	(0.01)	1.06	(0.01)
Norway	0.13	(0.02)	-0.10	(0.03)	0.35	(0.03)	**-0.45**	(0.03)	**-1.23**	(0.02)	**-0.02**	(0.01)	0.56	(0.00)	1.19	(0.01)
Poland	-0.02	(0.02)	-0.20	(0.02)	0.15	(0.03)	**-0.35**	(0.03)	**-1.47**	(0.01)	**-0.23**	(0.01)	0.47	(0.00)	1.14	(0.01)
Portugal	0.02	(0.02)	-0.19	(0.03)	0.21	(0.03)	**-0.40**	(0.03)	**-1.49**	(0.01)	**-0.13**	(0.01)	0.51	(0.00)	1.19	(0.01)
Slovak Republic	-0.11	(0.02)	-0.32	(0.04)	0.09	(0.03)	**-0.41**	(0.04)	**-1.57**	(0.02)	**-0.33**	(0.01)	0.39	(0.01)	1.06	(0.01)
Slovenia	-0.19	(0.02)	-0.40	(0.02)	0.01	(0.03)	**-0.41**	(0.03)	**-1.64**	(0.01)	**-0.45**	(0.01)	0.32	(0.01)	1.00	(0.01)
Spain	0.08	(0.01)	-0.07	(0.02)	0.23	(0.02)	**-0.31**	(0.02)	**-1.13**	(0.01)	**-0.12**	(0.01)	0.47	(0.00)	1.10	(0.00)
Sweden	-0.14	(0.03)	-0.34	(0.03)	0.06	(0.03)	**-0.40**	(0.03)	**-1.62**	(0.01)	**-0.41**	(0.01)	0.39	(0.01)	1.10	(0.01)
Switzerland	0.13	(0.02)	-0.07	(0.02)	0.34	(0.03)	**-0.41**	(0.03)	**-1.28**	(0.01)	**-0.02**	(0.01)	0.61	(0.00)	1.23	(0.01)
Turkey	-0.36	(0.02)	-0.52	(0.03)	-0.19	(0.03)	**-0.32**	(0.03)	**-1.71**	(0.01)	**-0.61**	(0.01)	0.09	(0.00)	0.79	(0.01)
United Kingdom	-0.06	(0.02)	-0.18	(0.03)	0.05	(0.03)	**-0.23**	(0.03)	**-1.45**	(0.01)	**-0.29**	(0.01)	0.39	(0.01)	1.11	(0.01)
United States	-0.18	(0.02)	-0.34	(0.03)	-0.02	(0.03)	**-0.33**	(0.03)	**-1.61**	(0.01)	**-0.45**	(0.01)	0.33	(0.01)	1.00	(0.01)
OECD average	-0.01	(0.00)	-0.18	(0.00)	0.17	(0.00)	**-0.35**	(0.01)	**-1.40**	(0.00)	**-0.20**	(0.00)	0.46	(0.00)	1.12	(0.00)
Albania	-0.12	(0.03)	-0.23	(0.03)	-0.01	(0.04)	**-0.23**	(0.04)	**-1.40**	(0.02)	**-0.33**	(0.00)	0.31	(0.01)	0.94	(0.01)
Argentina	-0.24	(0.03)	-0.35	(0.03)	-0.14	(0.04)	**-0.20**	(0.04)	**-1.58**	(0.02)	**-0.47**	(0.01)	0.22	(0.01)	0.88	(0.01)
Azerbaijan	-0.93	(0.03)	-0.93	(0.03)	-0.92	(0.04)	-0.02	(0.04)	**-2.01**	(0.00)	**-1.55**	(0.01)	**-0.57**	(0.00)	0.42	(0.02)
Brazil	-0.32	(0.02)	-0.40	(0.02)	-0.25	(0.02)	**-0.15**	(0.02)	**-1.65**	(0.01)	**-0.52**	(0.01)	0.09	(0.00)	0.81	(0.01)
Bulgaria	-0.38	(0.04)	-0.52	(0.04)	-0.24	(0.03)	**-0.28**	(0.04)	**-1.78**	(0.01)	**-0.69**	(0.01)	0.10	(0.01)	0.83	(0.01)
Colombia	-0.24	(0.03)	-0.28	(0.03)	-0.21	(0.04)	-0.08	(0.04)	**-1.58**	(0.02)	**-0.51**	(0.01)	0.21	(0.01)	0.90	(0.01)
Croatia	-0.10	(0.02)	-0.30	(0.03)	0.12	(0.03)	**-0.42**	(0.04)	**-1.55**	(0.01)	**-0.35**	(0.01)	0.40	(0.00)	1.09	(0.01)
Dubai (UAE)	-0.11	(0.01)	-0.22	(0.03)	-0.01	(0.02)	**-0.22**	(0.03)	**-1.53**	(0.01)	**-0.32**	(0.01)	0.36	(0.01)	1.03	(0.01)
Hong Kong-China	-0.53	(0.03)	-0.63	(0.03)	-0.41	(0.03)	**-0.22**	(0.04)	**-1.94**	(0.00)	**-0.91**	(0.01)	-0.03	(0.01)	0.78	(0.01)
Indonesia	-0.54	(0.03)	-0.61	(0.04)	-0.48	(0.04)	**-0.13**	(0.04)	**-1.94**	(0.01)	**-0.84**	(0.01)	-0.12	(0.01)	0.73	(0.01)
Jordan	-0.58	(0.02)	-0.70	(0.03)	-0.46	(0.03)	**-0.24**	(0.04)	**-1.92**	(0.00)	**-0.91**	(0.01)	-0.16	(0.01)	0.67	(0.01)
Kazakhstan	-0.54	(0.02)	-0.65	(0.03)	-0.44	(0.03)	**-0.21**	(0.03)	**-1.89**	(0.01)	**-0.91**	(0.01)	-0.14	(0.01)	0.77	(0.01)
Kyrgyzstan	-0.88	(0.02)	-0.91	(0.03)	-0.85	(0.03)	-0.06	(0.03)	**-2.01**	(0.00)	**-1.41**	(0.01)	**-0.54**	(0.01)	0.45	(0.02)
Latvia	-0.20	(0.02)	-0.38	(0.03)	-0.02	(0.03)	**-0.36**	(0.04)	**-1.53**	(0.01)	**-0.53**	(0.01)	0.28	(0.01)	0.99	(0.01)
Liechtenstein	0.00	(0.04)	-0.24	(0.07)	0.27	(0.07)	**-0.51**	(0.10)	**-1.38**	(0.05)	**-0.26**	(0.03)	0.44	(0.02)	1.18	(0.02)
Lithuania	-0.17	(0.02)	-0.35	(0.02)	0.01	(0.02)	**-0.36**	(0.03)	**-1.46**	(0.01)	**-0.46**	(0.01)	0.28	(0.01)	0.95	(0.01)
Macao-China	-0.28	(0.01)	-0.39	(0.02)	-0.17	(0.02)	**-0.22**	(0.02)	**-1.65**	(0.01)	**-0.55**	(0.00)	0.21	(0.00)	0.87	(0.01)
Montenegro	-0.57	(0.02)	-0.62	(0.02)	-0.51	(0.02)	**-0.11**	(0.03)	**-1.93**	(0.00)	**-0.93**	(0.01)	-0.14	(0.01)	0.74	(0.01)
Panama	-0.50	(0.04)	-0.57	(0.05)	-0.42	(0.05)	**-0.15**	(0.06)	**-1.91**	(0.01)	**-0.78**	(0.01)	-0.07	(0.01)	0.78	(0.02)
Peru	-0.33	(0.02)	-0.42	(0.02)	-0.24	(0.03)	**-0.19**	(0.04)	**-1.66**	(0.01)	**-0.56**	(0.01)	0.06	(0.01)	0.82	(0.01)
Qatar	-0.46	(0.01)	-0.52	(0.02)	-0.41	(0.01)	**-0.10**	(0.02)	**-1.90**	(0.00)	**-0.78**	(0.01)	0.00	(0.01)	0.82	(0.01)
Romania	-0.11	(0.03)	-0.23	(0.03)	0.00	(0.03)	**-0.22**	(0.03)	**-1.40**	(0.02)	**-0.31**	(0.00)	0.32	(0.01)	0.95	(0.01)
Russian Federation	-0.33	(0.03)	-0.50	(0.03)	-0.18	(0.03)	**-0.32**	(0.03)	**-1.68**	(0.01)	**-0.63**	(0.01)	0.11	(0.01)	0.87	(0.01)
Serbia	-0.40	(0.02)	-0.54	(0.02)	-0.26	(0.03)	**-0.28**	(0.03)	**-1.74**	(0.01)	**-0.71**	(0.01)	0.05	(0.01)	0.80	(0.01)
Shanghai-China	0.06	(0.01)	-0.03	(0.02)	0.15	(0.02)	**-0.18**	(0.03)	**-1.18**	(0.02)	**-0.09**	(0.01)	0.46	(0.00)	1.07	(0.01)
Singapore	0.17	(0.01)	0.04	(0.02)	0.30	(0.02)	**-0.26**	(0.03)	**-1.31**	(0.02)	0.10	(0.01)	0.65	(0.00)	1.23	(0.00)
Chinese Taipei	-0.40	(0.02)	-0.48	(0.03)	-0.32	(0.04)	**-0.15**	(0.05)	**-1.87**	(0.01)	**-0.69**	(0.01)	0.13	(0.01)	0.82	(0.01)
Thailand	-0.67	(0.02)	-0.75	(0.02)	-0.60	(0.02)	**-0.15**	(0.03)	**-1.93**	(0.00)	**-1.04**	(0.01)	**-0.29**	(0.01)	0.59	(0.01)
Trinidad and Tobago	-0.24	(0.02)	-0.37	(0.03)	-0.13	(0.02)	**-0.24**	(0.03)	**-1.68**	(0.01)	**-0.47**	(0.01)	0.26	(0.01)	0.93	(0.01)
Tunisia	-0.32	(0.02)	-0.37	(0.03)	-0.27	(0.03)	**-0.10**	(0.03)	**-1.57**	(0.01)	**-0.51**	(0.01)	0.04	(0.01)	0.76	(0.01)
Uruguay	-0.18	(0.02)	-0.29	(0.02)	-0.10	(0.02)	**-0.19**	(0.03)	**-1.57**	(0.01)	**-0.41**	(0.00)	0.29	(0.01)	0.95	(0.01)

Note: Values that are statistically significant are indicated in bold (see Annex A3).
StatLink ᵐˢˡ http://dx.doi.org/10.1787/888932343285

[Part 2/2]
Index of summarising and reading performance, by national quarters of this index

Table III.1.16 *Results based on students' self-reports*

		Performance on the reading scale, by national quarters of this index								Change in the reading score per unit of this index		Increased likelihood of students in the bottom quarter of this index scoring in the bottom quarter of the national reading performance distribution		Explained variance in student performance (r-squared x 100)	
		Bottom quarter		Second quarter		Third quarter		Top quarter							
		Mean score	S.E.	Mean score	S.E.	Mean score	S.E.	Mean score	S.E.	Effect	S.E.	Ratio	S.E.	%	S.E.
OECD	Australia	454	(2.1)	509	(2.5)	544	(2.5)	571	(2.8)	43.8	(0.99)	3.0	(0.12)	22.4	(0.73)
	Austria	411	(3.6)	465	(4.2)	498	(3.7)	534	(3.6)	46.9	(1.79)	3.0	(0.21)	22.9	(1.23)
	Belgium	442	(2.8)	509	(2.9)	541	(3.5)	573	(2.7)	50.8	(1.31)	3.6	(0.18)	27.9	(0.97)
	Canada	476	(1.9)	520	(2.1)	544	(2.2)	568	(1.9)	35.3	(0.81)	2.5	(0.10)	15.7	(0.68)
	Chile	405	(3.9)	448	(3.4)	468	(3.0)	491	(3.9)	34.8	(1.66)	2.6	(0.14)	16.4	(1.26)
	Czech Republic	416	(3.2)	471	(3.4)	513	(2.8)	537	(2.7)	46.9	(1.43)	3.5	(0.24)	26.8	(1.01)
	Denmark	443	(2.8)	499	(2.8)	511	(2.9)	539	(2.6)	38.7	(1.22)	3.0	(0.20)	19.8	(1.16)
	Estonia	454	(4.0)	494	(3.6)	518	(3.4)	544	(2.8)	38.9	(1.78)	2.6	(0.21)	18.2	(1.54)
	Finland	473	(2.7)	537	(2.9)	559	(2.9)	581	(2.7)	42.4	(1.20)	3.5	(0.19)	23.6	(1.16)
	France	433	(4.5)	500	(4.8)	532	(4.3)	548	(3.9)	51.2	(2.17)	3.4	(0.25)	21.8	(1.61)
	Germany	440	(3.8)	502	(3.4)	531	(3.6)	557	(3.1)	44.8	(1.52)	3.5	(0.24)	25.0	(1.32)
	Greece	436	(5.2)	480	(4.6)	501	(5.2)	523	(4.6)	36.3	(1.77)	2.2	(0.14)	12.6	(1.06)
	Hungary	434	(4.8)	481	(4.1)	520	(3.6)	550	(3.5)	45.2	(2.14)	3.1	(0.23)	26.1	(1.78)
	Iceland	440	(3.1)	502	(3.6)	529	(3.3)	545	(3.6)	40.0	(1.63)	3.1	(0.18)	19.5	(1.41)
	Ireland	447	(4.2)	496	(3.3)	524	(3.4)	541	(3.4)	38.9	(1.74)	2.8	(0.22)	17.2	(1.24)
	Israel	423	(4.3)	465	(4.2)	506	(3.8)	542	(3.9)	44.4	(1.76)	2.5	(0.15)	18.8	(1.25)
	Italy	431	(2.8)	483	(2.1)	507	(2.1)	535	(1.8)	48.0	(1.36)	2.8	(0.11)	19.5	(0.82)
	Japan	444	(5.6)	521	(3.5)	551	(3.0)	571	(3.2)	48.6	(2.21)	3.6	(0.20)	25.9	(1.52)
	Korea	477	(4.6)	542	(3.3)	563	(3.2)	579	(2.9)	38.9	(1.71)	3.9	(0.26)	26.1	(1.59)
	Luxembourg	412	(3.2)	467	(4.0)	501	(3.0)	535	(2.6)	45.7	(1.39)	3.0	(0.19)	21.7	(1.25)
	Mexico	384	(2.1)	414	(2.5)	445	(1.9)	476	(1.8)	35.4	(0.90)	2.4	(0.08)	17.8	(0.67)
	Netherlands	455	(5.4)	496	(4.6)	533	(5.2)	569	(4.1)	42.3	(1.70)	2.8	(0.26)	25.3	(1.50)
	New Zealand	458	(2.9)	512	(3.8)	550	(4.5)	581	(3.0)	46.3	(1.32)	2.8	(0.15)	23.0	(1.10)
	Norway	447	(3.7)	508	(2.9)	525	(3.1)	545	(3.1)	41.4	(1.41)	3.1	(0.16)	19.8	(1.24)
	Poland	449	(3.1)	489	(3.2)	525	(3.2)	553	(3.6)	39.7	(1.41)	2.9	(0.20)	21.2	(1.35)
	Portugal	420	(3.2)	492	(3.0)	515	(2.8)	536	(3.2)	42.1	(1.31)	4.0	(0.21)	26.0	(1.19)
	Slovak Republic	422	(4.2)	469	(3.9)	504	(3.3)	529	(3.2)	40.7	(1.89)	2.8	(0.20)	22.1	(1.65)
	Slovenia	432	(2.5)	473	(3.4)	511	(3.3)	535	(3.4)	39.7	(1.27)	2.7	(0.17)	21.3	(1.35)
	Spain	430	(2.7)	480	(2.4)	501	(2.5)	524	(2.2)	41.1	(0.94)	2.8	(0.11)	18.5	(0.69)
	Sweden	440	(2.9)	488	(3.7)	525	(3.5)	554	(3.2)	41.5	(1.36)	2.8	(0.16)	21.2	(1.14)
	Switzerland	432	(3.0)	495	(3.1)	527	(3.1)	557	(3.0)	48.0	(1.48)	3.5	(0.19)	26.2	(1.22)
	Turkey	427	(3.3)	455	(4.0)	480	(3.6)	506	(4.3)	31.7	(1.42)	2.2	(0.14)	14.8	(1.04)
	United Kingdom	445	(3.2)	487	(3.6)	513	(3.1)	547	(3.0)	39.4	(1.23)	2.5	(0.14)	17.9	(1.10)
	United States	455	(3.2)	484	(4.3)	520	(4.4)	553	(4.5)	36.3	(1.67)	2.1	(0.13)	15.1	(1.13)
	OECD average	**438**	**(0.6)**	**489**	**(0.6)**	**519**	**(0.6)**	**545**	**(0.6)**	**41.9**	**(0.26)**	**3.0**	**(0.03)**	**21.1**	**(0.21)**
Partners	Albania	348	(4.4)	395	(4.5)	411	(4.9)	427	(5.8)	32.9	(2.18)	2.2	(0.20)	10.3	(1.30)
	Argentina	361	(5.4)	400	(4.9)	427	(5.9)	462	(6.2)	40.0	(2.79)	2.2	(0.19)	14.5	(1.73)
	Azerbaijan	359	(3.6)	366	(4.5)	381	(4.3)	382	(5.4)	10.2	(1.94)	1.2	(0.11)	1.8	(0.72)
	Brazil	374	(2.6)	408	(3.1)	429	(3.3)	465	(4.2)	35.5	(1.58)	2.1	(0.10)	13.6	(0.97)
	Bulgaria	379	(5.6)	426	(7.5)	465	(6.8)	494	(6.7)	45.4	(2.41)	2.4	(0.22)	18.2	(1.62)
	Colombia	376	(3.9)	408	(3.8)	435	(4.3)	466	(4.4)	35.8	(1.74)	2.3	(0.19)	17.6	(1.42)
	Croatia	419	(3.6)	469	(3.6)	503	(3.5)	524	(3.1)	39.5	(1.51)	3.0	(0.20)	22.5	(1.21)
	Dubai (UAE)	400	(3.4)	448	(3.8)	490	(2.9)	519	(2.9)	47.1	(1.55)	2.6	(0.16)	20.1	(1.15)
	Hong Kong-China	493	(3.4)	520	(3.0)	552	(3.3)	570	(3.4)	29.2	(1.27)	2.2	(0.15)	13.6	(1.05)
	Indonesia	378	(3.7)	396	(4.0)	412	(4.1)	434	(4.9)	21.0	(1.61)	1.9	(0.14)	10.6	(1.23)
	Jordan	381	(3.9)	398	(4.1)	431	(3.8)	438	(3.8)	23.0	(1.43)	1.6	(0.10)	6.9	(0.78)
	Kazakhstan	349	(3.2)	372	(3.0)	403	(3.5)	444	(4.6)	36.3	(1.68)	2.1	(0.13)	16.5	(1.33)
	Kyrgyzstan	293	(4.3)	307	(3.7)	328	(4.1)	371	(5.1)	32.4	(2.31)	1.5	(0.12)	10.7	(1.40)
	Latvia	442	(3.8)	470	(3.6)	503	(3.9)	529	(3.3)	34.1	(1.62)	2.4	(0.17)	18.4	(1.49)
	Liechtenstein	441	(8.0)	479	(9.7)	525	(7.7)	553	(6.9)	43.1	(3.98)	3.4	(0.72)	26.8	(4.42)
	Lithuania	427	(3.2)	457	(3.4)	485	(2.9)	516	(3.3)	36.4	(1.69)	2.3	(0.13)	16.4	(1.35)
	Macao-China	455	(2.1)	482	(1.7)	502	(2.6)	510	(2.3)	22.2	(0.95)	2.0	(0.12)	8.3	(0.66)
	Montenegro	378	(3.3)	398	(3.4)	432	(3.0)	457	(3.1)	31.6	(1.47)	1.9	(0.12)	13.1	(1.12)
	Panama	341	(7.5)	363	(7.3)	395	(6.4)	433	(8.9)	34.9	(2.82)	1.9	(0.16)	13.6	(1.78)
	Peru	331	(4.6)	365	(4.0)	390	(5.3)	431	(5.7)	39.3	(2.68)	2.2	(0.15)	15.2	(1.65)
	Qatar	338	(2.2)	363	(2.6)	396	(2.9)	428	(3.0)	34.7	(1.25)	1.5	(0.08)	10.0	(0.68)
	Romania	377	(5.1)	419	(4.5)	442	(4.4)	470	(4.7)	38.1	(2.34)	2.5	(0.17)	16.2	(1.46)
	Russian Federation	421	(4.2)	449	(4.1)	476	(3.9)	509	(3.5)	35.0	(1.66)	2.2	(0.15)	15.6	(1.31)
	Serbia	398	(3.0)	431	(3.0)	467	(2.8)	492	(3.3)	37.4	(1.34)	2.6	(0.16)	21.1	(1.30)
	Shanghai-China	511	(3.3)	557	(3.0)	574	(3.0)	584	(2.7)	32.9	(1.45)	2.6	(0.15)	13.7	(0.99)
	Singapore	460	(3.0)	517	(2.8)	553	(3.1)	577	(2.2)	45.1	(1.38)	3.1	(0.17)	22.2	(1.24)
	Chinese Taipei	447	(3.7)	488	(3.2)	518	(3.4)	533	(3.9)	32.6	(1.90)	2.6	(0.16)	16.0	(1.37)
	Thailand	402	(2.8)	407	(2.8)	429	(3.2)	449	(3.9)	19.5	(1.54)	1.4	(0.09)	7.0	(0.95)
	Trinidad and Tobago	375	(3.4)	418	(3.4)	453	(3.6)	481	(4.2)	41.0	(1.76)	2.2	(0.16)	15.1	(1.32)
	Tunisia	381	(3.1)	402	(3.4)	415	(4.5)	434	(4.3)	22.4	(1.75)	1.6	(0.10)	5.9	(0.85)
	Uruguay	373	(3.1)	424	(3.4)	453	(3.0)	483	(3.9)	43.0	(1.34)	2.7	(0.17)	19.8	(0.95)

Note: Values that are statistically significant are indicated in bold (see Annex A3).
StatLink ⋯ http://dx.doi.org/10.1787/888932343285

[Part 1/1]
Proportion of students with low levels of summarising, by reading proficiency level[1]
Table III.1.17 *Results based on students' self-reports*

| | Percentage of students with low levels of summarising | | | | | | | | | |
| | Level 1a or below | | Level 2 | | Level 3 | | Level 4 | | Level 5 or above | |
	%	S.E.	%	S.E.	%	S.E.	%	S.E.	%	S.E.
Australia	77.8	(1.1)	62.4	(1.4)	43.8	(1.2)	25.1	(1.0)	14.7	(1.0)
Austria	65.9	(1.8)	43.9	(2.6)	28.8	(2.3)	14.0	(1.5)	6.3	(2.3)
Belgium	83.8	(1.2)	64.2	(1.5)	43.2	(1.5)	25.1	(1.2)	14.7	(1.4)
Canada	68.5	(1.7)	54.8	(1.4)	40.0	(1.0)	25.5	(1.0)	15.3	(1.2)
Chile	68.3	(1.4)	48.9	(1.4)	33.3	(1.4)	22.9	(2.1)	c	c
Czech Republic	83.3	(1.6)	60.4	(1.9)	37.7	(1.9)	20.9	(1.6)	14.4	(2.0)
Denmark	75.9	(2.3)	55.6	(2.0)	38.4	(1.6)	25.8	(1.8)	c	c
Estonia	77.5	(2.1)	63.6	(1.9)	46.4	(1.8)	29.3	(1.7)	21.3	(3.2)
Finland	75.5	(2.6)	62.0	(2.0)	40.5	(1.6)	21.4	(1.6)	10.7	(1.7)
France	78.3	(2.0)	57.2	(2.4)	36.9	(1.8)	27.3	(1.8)	18.9	(2.3)
Germany	81.3	(2.1)	64.5	(2.1)	41.8	(1.8)	24.8	(1.4)	15.0	(2.1)
Greece	63.0	(2.3)	55.7	(2.0)	40.3	(1.6)	28.1	(1.9)	15.7	(2.1)
Hungary	75.7	(2.3)	58.3	(2.4)	33.0	(1.7)	15.7	(1.6)	6.2	(1.6)
Iceland	74.8	(2.2)	56.6	(2.2)	41.8	(1.8)	27.2	(2.2)	13.2	(2.4)
Ireland	81.0	(1.8)	58.4	(2.1)	42.1	(1.9)	31.7	(1.8)	c	c
Israel	71.6	(1.7)	57.5	(2.0)	39.7	(1.6)	24.0	(1.8)	15.5	(2.5)
Italy	70.0	(1.1)	51.5	(1.0)	33.9	(0.9)	22.5	(0.8)	15.4	(1.4)
Japan	79.5	(1.9)	55.4	(2.3)	34.6	(1.7)	19.4	(1.3)	10.4	(1.9)
Korea	82.7	(3.2)	66.6	(2.0)	41.4	(1.8)	20.7	(1.2)	13.6	(1.5)
Luxembourg	69.9	(1.8)	49.7	(2.0)	30.3	(1.5)	21.1	(2.0)	11.8	(2.8)
Mexico	62.4	(0.9)	40.3	(0.8)	22.6	(0.9)	10.8	(1.2)	c	c
Netherlands	75.8	(2.5)	67.6	(2.1)	44.7	(1.9)	22.9	(1.5)	9.2	(1.7)
New Zealand	76.4	(2.3)	65.5	(2.1)	48.4	(1.6)	28.0	(1.6)	15.7	(1.6)
Norway	77.0	(2.3)	56.9	(2.1)	45.0	(1.9)	33.7	(1.7)	20.1	(2.3)
Poland	72.0	(2.3)	57.9	(1.8)	33.7	(1.7)	19.4	(1.4)	9.1	(1.7)
Portugal	74.3	(1.8)	50.2	(1.7)	27.5	(1.4)	15.1	(1.4)	10.3	(3.3)
Slovak Republic	73.1	(1.8)	54.2	(1.9)	31.5	(1.8)	18.8	(2.6)	9.6	(2.6)
Slovenia	75.5	(1.6)	60.9	(1.7)	39.1	(1.6)	20.9	(1.7)	c	c
Spain	65.0	(1.4)	45.8	(1.7)	27.6	(1.0)	18.5	(1.0)	10.9	(1.9)
Sweden	76.2	(1.8)	61.6	(2.1)	42.5	(1.8)	24.6	(1.6)	12.6	(1.8)
Switzerland	81.3	(1.3)	63.9	(1.8)	41.2	(1.5)	24.1	(1.5)	15.1	(2.7)
Turkey	61.3	(1.3)	44.6	(1.4)	26.7	(1.6)	15.0	(1.9)	c	c
United Kingdom	70.1	(1.8)	55.2	(1.7)	37.1	(1.5)	23.1	(1.5)	14.4	(2.3)
United States	72.3	(1.8)	60.9	(1.9)	46.4	(1.6)	30.7	(2.2)	15.1	(2.0)
OECD average	74.0	(0.3)	56.8	(0.3)	37.7	(0.3)	22.9	(0.3)	13.4	(0.4)
Albania	57.3	(1.9)	41.2	(2.2)	29.2	(2.6)	18.1	(5.0)	c	c
Argentina	64.7	(1.5)	47.1	(1.9)	31.4	(2.7)	22.7	(4.2)	c	c
Azerbaijan	55.1	(1.7)	43.1	(2.5)	39.5	(3.9)	19.9	(10.9)	c	c
Brazil	68.1	(0.9)	52.9	(1.4)	38.8	(1.9)	25.3	(2.6)	13.3	(3.4)
Bulgaria	61.9	(1.6)	41.7	(2.2)	24.4	(1.8)	13.6	(1.8)	c	c
Colombia	68.0	(1.8)	49.4	(2.2)	29.2	(2.0)	16.4	(3.3)	c	c
Croatia	73.7	(1.7)	55.6	(1.7)	31.5	(2.0)	18.9	(2.4)	c	c
Dubai (UAE)	68.4	(1.3)	50.8	(1.6)	32.7	(1.5)	18.0	(1.6)	11.9	(2.8)
Hong Kong-China	75.6	(2.4)	64.4	(2.0)	53.3	(2.0)	34.7	(2.2)	19.5	(2.4)
Indonesia	56.2	(1.4)	36.9	(1.9)	21.8	(2.4)	7.9	(5.0)	c	c
Jordan	60.3	(1.2)	43.6	(1.4)	28.8	(2.4)	19.9	(5.2)	c	c
Kazakhstan	60.9	(1.1)	39.0	(1.5)	22.0	(2.0)	10.3	(2.8)	c	c
Kyrgyzstan	55.1	(1.1)	29.1	(2.9)	16.5	(3.0)	13.0	(5.8)	c	c
Latvia	75.5	(2.5)	64.1	(1.9)	42.4	(2.0)	22.3	(1.9)	c	c
Liechtenstein	82.1	(5.6)	57.4	(6.4)	32.6	(6.8)	16.0	(5.6)	c	c
Lithuania	69.6	(1.7)	57.9	(1.7)	37.3	(1.6)	22.8	(2.0)	c	c
Macao-China	69.3	(1.6)	60.0	(1.5)	47.0	(1.4)	36.2	(1.8)	27.0	(4.1)
Montenegro	62.4	(1.2)	45.6	(1.7)	29.4	(2.4)	13.9	(3.7)	c	c
Panama	56.6	(2.3)	34.6	(3.2)	21.1	(5.1)	13.7	(6.5)	c	c
Peru	66.4	(0.9)	47.3	(1.7)	30.5	(2.7)	15.3	(4.2)	c	
Qatar	54.4	(0.7)	39.5	(1.4)	22.6	(1.4)	9.6	(1.6)	3.2	(2.0)
Romania	64.0	(1.6)	43.4	(2.1)	30.5	(1.9)	16.3	(2.8)	c	c
Russian Federation	61.9	(1.7)	44.7	(1.5)	29.5	(1.6)	16.8	(2.6)	c	c
Serbia	67.1	(1.2)	44.2	(1.4)	21.5	(1.4)	9.6	(1.9)	c	c
Shanghai-China	72.0	(3.5)	58.1	(2.3)	41.9	(2.0)	28.2	(1.5)	17.4	(1.4)
Singapore	82.5	(1.8)	62.5	(2.1)	43.2	(2.1)	27.6	(1.5)	15.4	(1.6)
Chinese Taipei	71.2	(1.8)	52.9	(1.8)	34.5	(1.6)	21.3	(1.6)	11.6	(3.0)
Thailand	65.3	(1.1)	53.1	(1.3)	33.7	(1.9)	19.7	(3.1)	c	c
Trinidad and Tobago	68.5	(1.4)	49.6	(2.1)	34.1	(2.2)	23.7	(2.4)	c	c
Tunisia	64.5	(1.5)	53.8	(1.9)	41.7	(3.2)	32.5	(4.6)	c	c
Uruguay	68.1	(1.0)	48.7	(1.8)	31.1	(1.9)	19.3	(2.4)	c	c

1. Students who reported levels of diversity of reading below their country average.
StatLink http://dx.doi.org/10.1787/888932343285

[Part 1/2]
Index of control strategies and reading performance, by national quarters of this index

Table III.1.18 *Results based on students' self-reports*

	All students		Boys		Girls		Gender difference (B – G)		Bottom quarter		Second quarter		Third quarter		Top quarter	
	Mean index	S.E.	Mean index	S.E.	Mean index	S.E.	Dif.	S.E.	Mean index	S.E.	Mean index	S.E.	Mean index	S.E.	Mean index	S.E.
OECD																
Australia	0.06	(0.02)	-0.10	(0.02)	0.21	(0.02)	**-0.31**	(0.03)	**-1.29**	(0.01)	-0.23	(0.00)	0.36	(0.00)	**1.40**	(0.01)
Austria	0.25	(0.02)	0.15	(0.03)	0.35	(0.02)	**-0.19**	(0.04)	**-0.90**	(0.02)	-0.03	(0.00)	0.50	(0.01)	**1.44**	(0.02)
Belgium	0.05	(0.02)	-0.06	(0.02)	0.16	(0.02)	**-0.22**	(0.03)	**-1.11**	(0.02)	-0.20	(0.00)	0.31	(0.00)	**1.19**	(0.01)
Canada	0.10	(0.01)	-0.09	(0.02)	0.30	(0.01)	**-0.39**	(0.02)	**-1.25**	(0.01)	-0.12	(0.00)	0.40	(0.00)	**1.39**	(0.01)
Chile	0.23	(0.02)	0.16	(0.02)	0.30	(0.02)	**-0.15**	(0.03)	**-0.92**	(0.02)	-0.05	(0.00)	0.48	(0.00)	**1.40**	(0.02)
Czech Republic	-0.01	(0.02)	-0.14	(0.02)	0.14	(0.02)	**-0.27**	(0.03)	**-1.11**	(0.02)	-0.25	(0.00)	0.24	(0.00)	**1.09**	(0.02)
Denmark	-0.24	(0.02)	-0.34	(0.02)	-0.15	(0.02)	**-0.19**	(0.03)	**-1.33**	(0.02)	-0.47	(0.00)	0.02	(0.00)	**0.80**	(0.01)
Estonia	-0.14	(0.01)	-0.26	(0.02)	-0.02	(0.02)	**-0.24**	(0.03)	**-1.15**	(0.02)	-0.37	(0.00)	0.08	(0.00)	**0.88**	(0.02)
Finland	-0.34	(0.02)	-0.45	(0.02)	-0.22	(0.02)	**-0.23**	(0.03)	**-1.51**	(0.02)	-0.60	(0.00)	-0.07	(0.00)	**0.82**	(0.02)
France	0.03	(0.02)	-0.14	(0.03)	0.19	(0.02)	**-0.33**	(0.03)	**-1.20**	(0.02)	-0.21	(0.00)	0.32	(0.00)	**1.21**	(0.02)
Germany	0.21	(0.02)	0.06	(0.02)	0.35	(0.02)	**-0.30**	(0.03)	**-0.95**	(0.02)	-0.06	(0.00)	0.45	(0.01)	**1.39**	(0.02)
Greece	-0.03	(0.02)	-0.23	(0.03)	0.17	(0.02)	**-0.40**	(0.04)	**-1.26**	(0.03)	-0.27	(0.01)	0.27	(0.00)	**1.15**	(0.02)
Hungary	0.12	(0.02)	0.01	(0.03)	0.23	(0.02)	**-0.22**	(0.03)	**-0.97**	(0.02)	-0.13	(0.00)	0.34	(0.00)	**1.24**	(0.02)
Iceland	-0.23	(0.02)	-0.34	(0.02)	-0.13	(0.02)	**-0.22**	(0.03)	**-1.44**	(0.02)	-0.53	(0.01)	0.03	(0.00)	**1.00**	(0.02)
Ireland	0.00	(0.02)	-0.11	(0.03)	0.11	(0.02)	**-0.21**	(0.04)	**-1.28**	(0.03)	-0.26	(0.01)	0.30	(0.00)	**1.24**	(0.02)
Israel	0.36	(0.02)	0.15	(0.03)	0.55	(0.02)	**-0.40**	(0.04)	**-0.94**	(0.02)	0.00	(0.00)	0.63	(0.00)	**1.74**	(0.01)
Italy	0.14	(0.01)	-0.06	(0.01)	0.36	(0.01)	**-0.42**	(0.02)	**-1.01**	(0.01)	-0.07	(0.00)	0.40	(0.00)	**1.25**	(0.01)
Japan	-0.55	(0.02)	-0.57	(0.03)	-0.53	(0.03)	-0.04	(0.04)	**-1.85**	(0.02)	-0.79	(0.00)	-0.23	(0.00)	**0.66**	(0.01)
Korea	-0.27	(0.02)	-0.34	(0.04)	-0.20	(0.03)	**-0.14**	(0.05)	**-1.50**	(0.03)	-0.53	(0.00)	0.02	(0.00)	**0.91**	(0.02)
Luxembourg	0.08	(0.01)	-0.10	(0.02)	0.27	(0.02)	**-0.37**	(0.03)	**-1.18**	(0.02)	-0.17	(0.00)	0.36	(0.00)	**1.31**	(0.02)
Mexico	-0.01	(0.01)	-0.12	(0.01)	0.10	(0.01)	**-0.22**	(0.02)	**-1.25**	(0.01)	-0.32	(0.00)	0.26	(0.00)	**1.28**	(0.01)
Netherlands	-0.11	(0.03)	-0.19	(0.03)	-0.03	(0.03)	**-0.16**	(0.03)	**-1.20**	(0.03)	-0.31	(0.00)	0.13	(0.00)	**0.94**	(0.02)
New Zealand	0.17	(0.02)	-0.01	(0.03)	0.35	(0.02)	**-0.36**	(0.04)	**-1.12**	(0.02)	-0.10	(0.00)	0.45	(0.01)	**1.45**	(0.02)
Norway	-0.42	(0.02)	-0.50	(0.02)	-0.35	(0.02)	**-0.15**	(0.04)	**-1.63**	(0.02)	-0.64	(0.00)	-0.11	(0.00)	**0.69**	(0.02)
Poland	0.08	(0.02)	-0.11	(0.02)	0.26	(0.02)	**-0.37**	(0.02)	**-1.04**	(0.02)	-0.23	(0.00)	0.30	(0.00)	**1.28**	(0.02)
Portugal	0.11	(0.02)	-0.10	(0.03)	0.32	(0.03)	**-0.43**	(0.03)	**-1.05**	(0.02)	-0.19	(0.00)	0.35	(0.00)	**1.34**	(0.02)
Slovak Republic	-0.11	(0.02)	-0.28	(0.03)	0.05	(0.02)	**-0.34**	(0.03)	**-1.25**	(0.03)	-0.34	(0.00)	0.15	(0.00)	**0.99**	(0.02)
Slovenia	0.15	(0.01)	0.00	(0.02)	0.31	(0.02)	**-0.31**	(0.02)	**-0.97**	(0.02)	-0.12	(0.00)	0.38	(0.00)	**1.32**	(0.02)
Spain	0.12	(0.01)	-0.01	(0.01)	0.25	(0.01)	**-0.26**	(0.02)	**-1.16**	(0.01)	-0.13	(0.00)	0.41	(0.00)	**1.34**	(0.01)
Sweden	-0.08	(0.02)	-0.21	(0.02)	0.05	(0.02)	**-0.26**	(0.03)	**-1.24**	(0.02)	-0.32	(0.00)	0.19	(0.00)	**1.04**	(0.02)
Switzerland	0.08	(0.02)	-0.10	(0.02)	0.27	(0.02)	**-0.38**	(0.02)	**-1.14**	(0.02)	-0.19	(0.00)	0.36	(0.00)	**1.30**	(0.02)
Turkey	0.23	(0.01)	0.08	(0.02)	0.38	(0.02)	**-0.30**	(0.02)	**-0.80**	(0.02)	-0.06	(0.00)	0.39	(0.00)	**1.37**	(0.02)
United Kingdom	0.08	(0.02)	-0.01	(0.02)	0.16	(0.02)	**-0.17**	(0.02)	**-1.08**	(0.02)	-0.17	(0.00)	0.33	(0.00)	**1.22**	(0.02)
United States	-0.04	(0.02)	-0.17	(0.02)	0.09	(0.03)	**-0.27**	(0.03)	**-1.42**	(0.02)	-0.31	(0.01)	0.25	(0.00)	**1.31**	(0.02)
OECD average	0.00	(0.00)	-0.13	(0.00)	0.14	(0.00)	**-0.27**	(0.01)	**-1.19**	(0.00)	-0.26	(0.00)	0.27	(0.00)	**1.19**	(0.00)
Partners																
Albania	0.38	(0.02)	0.21	(0.02)	0.56	(0.02)	**-0.35**	(0.03)	**-0.57**	(0.03)	0.16	(0.00)	0.61	(0.00)	**1.34**	(0.02)
Argentina	0.26	(0.02)	0.14	(0.03)	0.37	(0.02)	**-0.22**	(0.03)	**-0.91**	(0.02)	0.00	(0.01)	0.52	(0.01)	**1.45**	(0.01)
Azerbaijan	0.24	(0.03)	0.09	(0.04)	0.39	(0.03)	**-0.31**	(0.04)	**-1.16**	(0.03)	-0.06	(0.01)	0.51	(0.01)	**1.66**	(0.02)
Brazil	-0.05	(0.02)	-0.16	(0.02)	0.05	(0.02)	**-0.21**	(0.02)	**-1.16**	(0.01)	-0.29	(0.00)	0.19	(0.00)	**1.07**	(0.01)
Bulgaria	0.06	(0.02)	-0.11	(0.03)	0.24	(0.02)	**-0.34**	(0.04)	**-1.30**	(0.02)	-0.23	(0.00)	0.38	(0.01)	**1.38**	(0.03)
Colombia	0.15	(0.02)	0.03	(0.03)	0.25	(0.02)	**-0.22**	(0.03)	**-0.98**	(0.01)	-0.20	(0.00)	0.38	(0.01)	**1.39**	(0.02)
Croatia	0.11	(0.02)	-0.02	(0.02)	0.26	(0.02)	**-0.27**	(0.03)	**-0.95**	(0.02)	-0.16	(0.00)	0.33	(0.00)	**1.23**	(0.02)
Dubai (UAE)	0.57	(0.01)	0.46	(0.02)	0.69	(0.02)	**-0.23**	(0.03)	**-0.56**	(0.02)	0.26	(0.00)	0.81	(0.00)	**1.78**	(0.02)
Hong Kong-China	-0.14	(0.02)	-0.17	(0.03)	-0.11	(0.03)	-0.06	(0.04)	**-1.24**	(0.02)	-0.44	(0.00)	0.09	(0.00)	**1.02**	(0.02)
Indonesia	-0.19	(0.02)	-0.29	(0.02)	-0.09	(0.02)	**-0.20**	(0.02)	**-1.02**	(0.02)	-0.41	(0.00)	0.00	(0.00)	**0.68**	(0.01)
Jordan	0.24	(0.02)	0.07	(0.03)	0.41	(0.03)	**-0.34**	(0.04)	**-1.17**	(0.03)	-0.05	(0.00)	0.54	(0.00)	**1.64**	(0.02)
Kazakhstan	0.22	(0.02)	0.11	(0.03)	0.33	(0.03)	**-0.21**	(0.03)	**-0.82**	(0.02)	-0.10	(0.00)	0.39	(0.00)	**1.40**	(0.02)
Kyrgyzstan	0.17	(0.02)	-0.03	(0.02)	0.36	(0.02)	**-0.39**	(0.03)	**-0.98**	(0.02)	-0.16	(0.00)	0.39	(0.00)	**1.44**	(0.02)
Latvia	-0.16	(0.02)	-0.27	(0.02)	-0.06	(0.02)	**-0.20**	(0.03)	**-1.07**	(0.01)	-0.41	(0.00)	0.03	(0.00)	**0.79**	(0.02)
Liechtenstein	0.07	(0.06)	-0.08	(0.08)	0.23	(0.07)	**-0.30**	(0.10)	**-1.11**	(0.08)	-0.19	(0.02)	0.36	(0.01)	**1.19**	(0.06)
Lithuania	-0.08	(0.02)	-0.25	(0.02)	0.10	(0.02)	**-0.35**	(0.02)	**-1.09**	(0.01)	-0.35	(0.00)	0.15	(0.00)	**0.99**	(0.02)
Macao-China	-0.53	(0.01)	-0.55	(0.01)	-0.51	(0.01)	-0.04	(0.02)	**-1.56**	(0.01)	-0.81	(0.00)	-0.31	(0.00)	**0.55**	(0.02)
Montenegro	0.50	(0.02)	0.33	(0.03)	0.67	(0.02)	**-0.34**	(0.03)	**-0.69**	(0.02)	0.18	(0.00)	0.72	(0.01)	**1.79**	(0.02)
Panama	0.40	(0.03)	0.38	(0.04)	0.42	(0.03)	-0.04	(0.05)	**-0.82**	(0.04)	0.06	(0.01)	0.63	(0.01)	**1.72**	(0.03)
Peru	0.22	(0.02)	0.13	(0.02)	0.32	(0.02)	**-0.19**	(0.03)	**-0.91**	(0.02)	-0.08	(0.00)	0.45	(0.00)	**1.45**	(0.02)
Qatar	0.33	(0.01)	0.16	(0.02)	0.51	(0.02)	**-0.36**	(0.02)	**-1.01**	(0.02)	0.01	(0.00)	0.60	(0.00)	**1.73**	(0.01)
Romania	0.07	(0.03)	-0.13	(0.03)	0.27	(0.03)	**-0.40**	(0.04)	**-1.16**	(0.03)	-0.24	(0.01)	0.34	(0.00)	**1.36**	(0.02)
Russian Federation	-0.14	(0.02)	-0.24	(0.02)	-0.05	(0.02)	**-0.18**	(0.02)	**-1.16**	(0.01)	-0.38	(0.00)	0.08	(0.00)	**0.89**	(0.01)
Serbia	0.37	(0.02)	0.24	(0.02)	0.51	(0.02)	**-0.27**	(0.03)	**-0.78**	(0.02)	0.08	(0.00)	0.60	(0.00)	**1.59**	(0.02)
Shanghai-China	-0.28	(0.01)	-0.32	(0.02)	-0.24	(0.02)	**-0.08**	(0.02)	**-1.24**	(0.02)	-0.52	(0.00)	-0.07	(0.00)	**0.72**	(0.02)
Singapore	0.30	(0.01)	0.26	(0.02)	0.33	(0.02)	**-0.07**	(0.02)	**-0.81**	(0.01)	0.00	(0.00)	0.50	(0.00)	**1.50**	(0.02)
Chinese Taipei	-0.39	(0.02)	-0.46	(0.02)	-0.31	(0.03)	**-0.15**	(0.04)	**-1.61**	(0.02)	-0.69	(0.00)	-0.10	(0.00)	**0.85**	(0.02)
Thailand	-0.44	(0.01)	-0.51	(0.02)	-0.38	(0.02)	**-0.12**	(0.02)	**-1.29**	(0.01)	-0.68	(0.00)	-0.24	(0.00)	**0.46**	(0.02)
Trinidad and Tobago	0.24	(0.01)	0.09	(0.02)	0.39	(0.02)	**-0.30**	(0.03)	**-0.91**	(0.02)	-0.07	(0.00)	0.47	(0.00)	**1.47**	(0.02)
Tunisia	0.15	(0.02)	-0.04	(0.03)	0.32	(0.02)	**-0.37**	(0.03)	**-1.01**	(0.02)	-0.14	(0.00)	0.40	(0.00)	**1.34**	(0.02)
Uruguay	0.04	(0.02)	-0.13	(0.02)	0.19	(0.02)	**-0.32**	(0.03)	**-1.34**	(0.02)	-0.25	(0.01)	0.39	(0.00)	**1.35**	(0.02)

Note: Values that are statistically significant are indicated in bold (see Annex A3).
StatLink 🖳 http://dx.doi.org/10.1787/888932343285

[Part 2/2]
Index of control strategies and reading performance, by national quarters of this index

Table III.1.18   *Results based on students' self-reports*

| | | Performance on the reading scale, by national quarters of this index | | | | | | | Change in the reading score per unit of this index | | Increased likelihood of students in the bottom quarter of this index scoring in the bottom quarter of the national reading performance distribution | | Explained variance in student performance (r-squared x 100) | |
| | | Bottom quarter | | Second quarter | | Third quarter | | Top quarter | | | | | | | |
		Mean score	S.E.	Mean score	S.E.	Mean score	S.E.	Mean score	S.E.	Effect	S.E.	Ratio	S.E.	%	S.E.
OECD	Australia	462	(2.6)	510	(2.3)	535	(2.9)	560	(3.0)	33.1	(1.09)	2.5	(0.10)	14.1	(0.74)
	Austria	449	(3.9)	475	(4.4)	484	(4.1)	495	(3.6)	17.0	(1.71)	1.6	(0.10)	2.8	(0.50)
	Belgium	468	(3.1)	510	(3.0)	527	(2.5)	545	(3.8)	30.2	(1.78)	2.1	(0.12)	8.7	(0.99)
	Canada	483	(2.2)	520	(1.7)	539	(2.1)	562	(2.4)	25.8	(1.01)	2.2	(0.08)	10.0	(0.69)
	Chile	413	(3.7)	449	(3.6)	463	(3.5)	478	(4.2)	25.3	(1.53)	2.0	(0.13)	8.2	(0.93)
	Czech Republic	443	(3.4)	478	(3.8)	496	(3.5)	511	(3.7)	28.7	(1.31)	2.0	(0.11)	8.5	(0.76)
	Denmark	469	(3.3)	495	(3.6)	507	(3.5)	512	(2.7)	18.9	(1.54)	1.7	(0.11)	4.0	(0.65)
	Estonia	482	(3.9)	497	(3.4)	507	(4.0)	520	(3.3)	17.6	(2.28)	1.5	(0.10)	3.1	(0.79)
	Finland	503	(3.4)	531	(3.1)	545	(3.0)	565	(3.6)	25.6	(1.57)	1.9	(0.11)	8.1	(0.98)
	France	438	(5.9)	489	(4.4)	520	(4.1)	544	(4.1)	41.4	(2.63)	2.5	(0.19)	15.7	(1.65)
	Germany	471	(4.5)	501	(3.3)	515	(3.5)	531	(3.5)	22.9	(1.80)	1.8	(0.10)	5.8	(0.84)
	Greece	444	(6.4)	482	(5.4)	494	(4.3)	512	(4.0)	27.4	(1.97)	2.0	(0.14)	8.2	(1.08)
	Hungary	467	(4.4)	493	(4.0)	508	(4.3)	509	(4.8)	16.9	(2.69)	1.6	(0.11)	2.8	(0.90)
	Iceland	462	(3.7)	503	(3.1)	509	(3.4)	533	(3.1)	25.0	(1.78)	2.0	(0.11)	7.1	(1.01)
	Ireland	457	(4.4)	492	(4.4)	514	(3.9)	528	(3.6)	27.6	(1.86)	2.0	(0.12)	9.3	(1.20)
	Israel	439	(5.7)	482	(4.4)	494	(3.7)	497	(4.0)	20.1	(2.02)	1.9	(0.11)	4.0	(0.75)
	Italy	448	(2.5)	483	(2.1)	502	(2.4)	514	(1.9)	28.0	(1.11)	1.9	(0.07)	7.7	(0.58)
	Japan	474	(5.4)	511	(5.0)	540	(3.5)	556	(3.6)	32.5	(2.10)	2.2	(0.13)	11.2	(1.11)
	Korea	488	(5.6)	540	(3.5)	555	(3.2)	575	(3.5)	34.2	(2.04)	2.8	(0.19)	18.7	(1.85)
	Luxembourg	435	(3.0)	469	(2.8)	487	(2.9)	503	(2.9)	25.1	(1.54)	2.0	(0.13)	6.3	(0.73)
	Mexico	394	(2.5)	421	(2.3)	436	(2.2)	452	(2.0)	20.4	(0.92)	1.8	(0.06)	6.0	(0.46)
	Netherlands	475	(5.6)	511	(6.7)	522	(4.8)	539	(6.0)	25.6	(1.97)	1.9	(0.14)	7.0	(1.06)
	New Zealand	473	(3.8)	514	(2.7)	539	(3.6)	565	(3.9)	32.2	(1.40)	2.1	(0.12)	11.1	(0.97)
	Norway	469	(3.3)	501	(3.4)	515	(3.3)	532	(3.8)	25.7	(1.57)	1.9	(0.11)	7.5	(0.83)
	Poland	464	(3.6)	495	(3.6)	514	(3.0)	531	(3.9)	27.1	(1.62)	2.0	(0.14)	8.5	(0.94)
	Portugal	440	(3.5)	481	(3.2)	504	(3.4)	536	(3.2)	35.7	(1.53)	2.5	(0.16)	16.4	(1.14)
	Slovak Republic	443	(4.9)	476	(3.4)	488	(3.9)	506	(3.4)	25.1	(2.08)	1.9	(0.11)	6.7	(1.03)
	Slovenia	449	(2.4)	484	(2.7)	494	(2.8)	515	(3.2)	24.0	(1.74)	2.0	(0.11)	6.4	(0.91)
	Spain	440	(3.0)	478	(2.3)	498	(2.6)	510	(2.3)	27.1	(1.20)	2.1	(0.08)	10.4	(0.84)
	Sweden	459	(4.0)	500	(3.8)	513	(3.8)	527	(4.3)	26.8	(1.98)	2.0	(0.12)	6.7	(1.00)
	Switzerland	468	(3.4)	491	(2.9)	511	(3.6)	535	(3.2)	24.8	(1.46)	1.7	(0.09)	7.1	(0.74)
	Turkey	435	(4.4)	463	(4.0)	477	(3.9)	485	(4.1)	20.7	(1.68)	1.9	(0.12)	5.1	(0.76)
	United Kingdom	455	(3.1)	494	(3.0)	513	(3.2)	522	(3.1)	27.2	(1.39)	2.0	(0.12)	7.5	(0.79)
	United States	461	(3.6)	499	(4.9)	510	(5.0)	533	(4.8)	22.0	(1.58)	1.9	(0.11)	6.6	(0.86)
	OECD average	456	(0.7)	492	(0.6)	508	(0.6)	525	(0.6)	26.1	(0.30)	2.0	(0.02)	8.2	(0.16)
Partners	Albania	340	(5.9)	390	(4.5)	408	(5.2)	414	(4.6)	37.0	(3.15)	2.2	(0.18)	9.2	(1.67)
	Argentina	363	(6.3)	401	(6.2)	418	(5.9)	426	(5.0)	25.6	(2.12)	1.8	(0.13)	5.5	(0.80)
	Azerbaijan	341	(4.7)	362	(4.1)	376	(4.5)	381	(3.5)	13.1	(1.57)	1.7	(0.15)	4.1	(1.03)
	Brazil	379	(2.9)	407	(2.6)	423	(3.3)	446	(4.0)	26.6	(1.42)	1.7	(0.08)	6.8	(0.67)
	Bulgaria	394	(7.0)	436	(7.6)	453	(7.4)	447	(7.5)	19.2	(1.94)	1.8	(0.15)	3.6	(0.71)
	Colombia	399	(4.2)	413	(4.5)	419	(4.3)	427	(5.1)	9.0	(2.02)	1.2	(0.11)	1.0	(0.47)
	Croatia	453	(4.2)	478	(3.4)	483	(3.5)	491	(3.7)	15.5	(1.88)	1.6	(0.09)	2.5	(0.58)
	Dubai (UAE)	419	(3.0)	464	(2.9)	475	(3.0)	483	(2.9)	25.4	(1.45)	1.9	(0.09)	5.1	(0.56)
	Hong Kong-China	490	(3.2)	532	(3.1)	546	(2.5)	565	(3.0)	28.1	(1.51)	2.3	(0.15)	9.6	(0.95)
	Indonesia	385	(3.8)	401	(4.3)	408	(4.6)	415	(4.8)	16.2	(2.10)	1.4	(0.11)	3.0	(0.74)
	Jordan	358	(4.5)	408	(3.6)	426	(3.6)	437	(3.4)	27.0	(1.44)	2.6	(0.14)	11.8	(1.18)
	Kazakhstan	380	(4.4)	395	(4.0)	397	(3.8)	392	(3.8)	4.2	(1.76)	1.3	(0.08)	0.2	(0.15)
	Kyrgyzstan	295	(4.2)	325	(4.5)	330	(3.8)	319	(4.0)	9.7	(1.65)	1.7	(0.10)	1.0	(0.34)
	Latvia	465	(4.3)	480	(3.7)	488	(3.9)	504	(4.0)	18.8	(2.24)	1.5	(0.14)	3.3	(0.73)
	Liechtenstein	467	(10.1)	501	(8.8)	512	(10.2)	518	(7.7)	20.4	(5.16)	1.9	(0.35)	5.5	(2.60)
	Lithuania	441	(3.7)	467	(3.0)	476	(3.1)	493	(3.7)	22.4	(1.90)	1.7	(0.11)	4.9	(0.75)
	Macao-China	466	(2.0)	481	(2.3)	495	(1.8)	506	(2.1)	18.4	(1.26)	1.6	(0.09)	4.5	(0.60)
	Montenegro	388	(3.2)	409	(3.5)	423	(3.4)	418	(3.4)	10.7	(2.54)	1.5	(0.12)	1.4	(0.64)
	Panama	351	(6.6)	376	(8.0)	397	(7.9)	388	(6.7)	15.1	(2.38)	1.6	(0.19)	2.5	(0.73)
	Peru	350	(4.7)	377	(4.3)	381	(4.9)	376	(5.4)	9.3	(2.06)	1.4	(0.08)	0.8	(0.35)
	Qatar	320	(2.1)	367	(2.4)	402	(2.2)	410	(2.1)	28.6	(1.08)	2.1	(0.11)	7.6	(0.57)
	Romania	390	(4.9)	426	(4.6)	440	(4.8)	446	(4.9)	21.1	(1.72)	2.0	(0.14)	6.0	(0.96)
	Russian Federation	439	(4.5)	454	(3.9)	467	(3.8)	482	(4.3)	18.7	(1.98)	1.5	(0.10)	3.1	(0.63)
	Serbia	423	(3.7)	439	(3.0)	456	(3.4)	454	(3.5)	11.7	(1.53)	1.5	(0.11)	1.8	(0.50)
	Shanghai-China	527	(3.1)	548	(3.2)	565	(3.5)	584	(3.1)	26.5	(1.76)	1.8	(0.10)	7.5	(0.86)
	Singapore	488	(3.1)	526	(2.6)	538	(2.6)	553	(2.7)	25.9	(1.63)	1.9	(0.11)	6.1	(0.74)
	Chinese Taipei	440	(3.5)	488	(2.8)	519	(2.9)	536	(3.9)	35.0	(1.59)	3.0	(0.18)	17.8	(1.25)
	Thailand	397	(2.9)	416	(2.8)	431	(3.1)	443	(4.0)	23.6	(1.95)	1.8	(0.12)	5.9	(0.90)
	Trinidad and Tobago	372	(3.9)	408	(4.2)	439	(3.6)	460	(3.6)	35.5	(2.07)	2.1	(0.12)	9.6	(1.07)
	Tunisia	373	(3.5)	400	(3.7)	415	(3.7)	429	(3.8)	22.5	(1.66)	1.7	(0.11)	6.4	(0.94)
	Uruguay	387	(3.4)	425	(3.2)	446	(3.1)	456	(3.9)	24.3	(1.30)	2.0	(0.11)	7.5	(0.75)

Note: Values that are statistically significant are indicated in bold (see Annex A3).
StatLink ᝍᝍ http://dx.doi.org/10.1787/888932343285

[Part 1/1]
Proportion of students with low levels of control strategies, by reading proficiency level[1]
Table III.1.19   *Results based on students' self-reports*

		Percentage of students with low levels of control strategies								
		Level 1a or below		Level 2		Level 3		Level 4		Level 5 or above	
		%	S.E.	%	S.E.	%	S.E.	%	S.E.	%	S.E.
OECD	Australia	75.1	(1.2)	64.8	(1.3)	51.6	(1.3)	37.2	(1.3)	25.8	(1.7)
	Austria	65.2	(1.5)	57.6	(1.7)	54.7	(1.7)	46.6	(1.9)	40.9	(3.9)
	Belgium	67.7	(1.9)	62.7	(2.1)	54.3	(1.8)	40.1	(1.3)	31.0	(1.9)
	Canada	70.2	(1.6)	60.2	(1.2)	49.1	(1.0)	37.4	(1.0)	c	c
	Chile	69.9	(1.6)	59.0	(1.2)	46.6	(1.8)	40.1	(2.4)	31.0	(3.8)
	Czech Republic	71.0	(1.7)	59.6	(1.8)	52.0	(1.8)	43.2	(2.2)	c	c
	Denmark	62.1	(1.9)	60.4	(1.9)	51.9	(1.8)	42.9	(1.9)	32.5	(4.0)
	Estonia	61.3	(2.6)	52.4	(1.9)	47.0	(1.4)	42.9	(1.9)	32.5	(4.0)
	Finland	64.2	(3.2)	58.4	(2.2)	50.3	(1.6)	39.6	(1.5)	27.6	(2.2)
	France	76.1	(1.9)	60.8	(2.1)	48.9	(2.3)	35.3	(2.0)	24.6	(2.4)
	Germany	59.6	(2.4)	51.7	(1.8)	44.4	(1.8)	35.4	(2.0)	25.2	(3.2)
	Greece	69.5	(2.0)	57.1	(2.0)	49.0	(1.8)	42.9	(2.3)	34.8	(3.9)
	Hungary	59.9	(3.0)	53.5	(2.0)	48.3	(1.5)	38.4	(2.0)	34.6	(3.5)
	Iceland	68.7	(2.0)	58.3	(2.0)	53.2	(1.6)	44.9	(1.8)	33.6	(3.4)
	Ireland	71.6	(2.0)	60.0	(2.0)	50.2	(1.6)	38.8	(2.2)	c	c
	Israel	64.7	(1.8)	52.3	(1.8)	47.7	(1.5)	45.5	(1.9)	45.1	(3.2)
	Italy	62.4	(1.1)	49.7	(1.1)	41.3	(0.9)	33.8	(1.0)	27.2	(1.8)
	Japan	68.2	(2.4)	55.1	(1.7)	41.1	(1.5)	30.9	(1.7)	23.3	(1.9)
	Korea	83.9	(4.4)	72.2	(2.1)	58.3	(1.5)	44.4	(1.4)	29.1	(2.1)
	Luxembourg	64.0	(1.7)	52.2	(1.9)	44.5	(1.6)	38.4	(2.1)	28.9	(3.0)
	Mexico	65.6	(0.7)	54.7	(0.8)	43.3	(0.8)	32.6	(2.0)	c	c
	Netherlands	59.7	(3.2)	56.5	(2.2)	45.0	(2.0)	34.9	(2.0)	23.7	(2.7)
	New Zealand	66.6	(2.4)	58.5	(2.1)	48.7	(1.7)	36.2	(2.2)	23.8	(1.9)
	Norway	64.2	(2.1)	56.6	(2.3)	45.6	(1.7)	38.6	(2.3)	26.6	(2.9)
	Poland	72.2	(2.4)	59.8	(1.7)	50.5	(1.6)	38.6	(2.0)	31.5	(2.8)
	Portugal	74.8	(1.6)	59.4	(1.5)	45.2	(1.5)	28.3	(1.6)	17.4	(3.8)
	Slovak Republic	59.7	(1.8)	51.1	(1.8)	42.7	(1.6)	33.5	(2.4)	22.7	(3.8)
	Slovenia	61.8	(1.8)	54.5	(1.8)	46.2	(1.7)	33.9	(2.4)	c	c
	Spain	66.3	(1.2)	54.2	(1.3)	42.4	(1.3)	31.0	(1.7)	21.4	(3.4)
	Sweden	60.8	(2.1)	51.3	(2.0)	43.0	(1.5)	35.3	(2.0)	25.2	(3.0)
	Switzerland	64.1	(1.9)	60.1	(1.9)	50.4	(1.7)	36.9	(2.0)	26.9	(2.5)
	Turkey	74.1	(1.9)	61.2	(1.7)	54.3	(1.7)	49.4	(2.3)	c	c
	United Kingdom	65.6	(1.9)	56.7	(1.7)	46.9	(1.5)	38.4	(2.2)	28.4	(2.8)
	United States	58.7	(1.7)	51.9	(2.0)	42.9	(1.7)	33.8	(1.9)	21.3	(2.7)
	OECD average	66.7	(0.4)	57.2	(0.3)	48.0	(0.3)	38.1	(0.3)	28.2	(0.6)
Partners	Albania	56.7	(1.7)	39.0	(2.2)	32.1	(2.5)	30.7	(4.7)	c	c
	Argentina	62.8	(1.3)	51.4	(2.2)	45.6	(2.6)	38.3	(3.9)	c	c
	Azerbaijan	59.5	(1.3)	46.3	(2.1)	41.1	(4.2)	48.1	(14.0)	c	c
	Brazil	52.9	(0.9)	40.7	(1.4)	31.0	(1.8)	20.8	(2.8)	13.0	(4.1)
	Bulgaria	57.9	(1.6)	48.7	(2.2)	44.0	(2.3)	40.2	(3.4)	c	c
	Colombia	53.8	(1.9)	50.5	(2.0)	42.4	(2.2)	33.2	(3.6)	c	c
	Croatia	57.8	(1.8)	54.1	(1.6)	47.0	(1.6)	42.5	(1.8)	c	c
	Dubai (UAE)	64.4	(1.2)	56.7	(1.7)	47.9	(1.9)	47.9	(3.0)	41.8	(4.0)
	Hong Kong-China	71.5	(2.8)	63.6	(2.2)	55.2	(1.7)	40.3	(1.8)	27.2	(2.4)
	Indonesia	58.2	(1.3)	48.8	(1.7)	39.2	(2.6)	35.1	(7.4)	c	c
	Jordan	66.0	(1.2)	47.1	(1.6)	41.4	(2.2)	33.9	(4.2)	c	c
	Kazakhstan	61.5	(1.3)	61.5	(1.7)	63.6	(2.3)	56.7	(6.2)	c	c
	Kyrgyzstan	49.8	(1.1)	48.6	(2.9)	55.6	(3.8)	44.4	(11.8)	c	c
	Latvia	61.7	(2.9)	56.0	(2.4)	49.4	(1.8)	41.4	(2.6)	c	c
	Liechtenstein	62.0	(7.4)	56.6	(5.8)	47.0	(5.5)	41.0	(5.6)	c	c
	Lithuania	58.9	(1.9)	49.6	(1.5)	42.1	(2.0)	34.6	(2.0)	c	c
	Macao-China	69.8	(1.7)	62.8	(1.2)	54.5	(1.5)	45.0	(1.7)	40.7	(4.3)
	Montenegro	62.5	(1.6)	56.9	(2.0)	52.8	(2.2)	49.8	(4.5)	c	c
	Panama	54.7	(1.6)	45.4	(3.1)	40.2	(3.3)	40.6	(5.8)	c	c
	Peru	59.5	(1.1)	57.2	(2.0)	55.1	(2.6)	47.1	(4.7)	c	c
	Qatar	61.5	(0.7)	42.7	(1.5)	35.9	(2.0)	31.5	(2.7)	22.4	(4.5)
	Romania	61.7	(1.6)	47.7	(2.0)	42.2	(2.4)	37.3	(3.7)	c	c
	Russian Federation	56.3	(1.9)	51.7	(1.7)	44.8	(1.5)	36.9	(2.3)	c	c
	Serbia	58.8	(1.4)	51.1	(1.3)	46.5	(1.8)	36.2	(3.1)	c	c
	Shanghai-China	76.7	(3.7)	71.2	(2.4)	64.5	(1.7)	54.5	(1.4)	38.7	(1.7)
	Singapore	73.9	(1.8)	63.1	(1.8)	58.4	(1.5)	49.7	(1.5)	42.6	(2.4)
	Chinese Taipei	77.4	(1.8)	62.2	(1.8)	42.7	(1.6)	28.1	(1.5)	16.1	(2.7)
	Thailand	63.4	(1.3)	48.8	(1.3)	40.2	(1.8)	25.7	(4.1)	c	c
	Trinidad and Tobago	69.1	(1.4)	55.1	(2.2)	45.9	(2.0)	37.0	(3.2)	c	c
	Tunisia	56.9	(1.4)	43.4	(1.7)	35.2	(2.1)	28.3	(4.8)	c	c
	Uruguay	62.5	(1.1)	49.5	(1.5)	39.3	(1.9)	32.6	(3.2)	c	c

1. Students who reported levels of diversity of reading below their country average.
StatLink ⌐⌐⌐ http://dx.doi.org/10.1787/888932343285

[Part 1/2]

Index of memorisation strategies and reading performance, by national quarters of this index

Table III.1.20 *Results based on students' self-reports*

	All students		Boys		Girls		Gender difference (B – G)		Bottom quarter		Second quarter		Third quarter		Top quarter	
	Mean index	S.E.	Mean index	S.E.	Mean index	S.E.	Dif.	S.E.	Mean index	S.E.	Mean index	S.E.	Mean index	S.E.	Mean index	S.E.
OECD																
Australia	-0.06	(0.01)	-0.17	(0.02)	0.05	(0.02)	**-0.22**	(0.02)	**-1.30**	(0.02)	-0.31	(0.00)	0.24	(0.00)	**1.14**	(0.01)
Austria	0.45	(0.02)	0.34	(0.02)	0.55	(0.03)	**-0.21**	(0.03)	**-0.69**	(0.02)	0.22	(0.00)	0.69	(0.00)	**1.57**	(0.02)
Belgium	-0.15	(0.02)	-0.24	(0.02)	-0.06	(0.02)	**-0.19**	(0.03)	**-1.37**	(0.02)	-0.38	(0.00)	0.15	(0.00)	**0.99**	(0.01)
Canada	-0.02	(0.01)	-0.16	(0.02)	0.12	(0.02)	**-0.28**	(0.02)	**-1.35**	(0.02)	-0.27	(0.00)	0.30	(0.00)	**1.22**	(0.01)
Chile	0.20	(0.02)	0.18	(0.02)	0.22	(0.02)	-0.04	(0.03)	**-0.91**	(0.01)	-0.06	(0.00)	0.43	(0.00)	**1.32**	(0.02)
Czech Republic	0.18	(0.02)	0.07	(0.03)	0.30	(0.02)	**-0.23**	(0.03)	**-1.04**	(0.02)	-0.08	(0.01)	0.46	(0.00)	**1.36**	(0.02)
Denmark	-0.18	(0.02)	-0.22	(0.02)	-0.15	(0.02)	**-0.08**	(0.03)	**-1.22**	(0.02)	-0.39	(0.00)	0.07	(0.00)	**0.81**	(0.01)
Estonia	0.08	(0.01)	-0.01	(0.02)	0.18	(0.02)	**-0.19**	(0.02)	**-0.97**	(0.02)	-0.11	(0.00)	0.32	(0.00)	**1.09**	(0.02)
Finland	-0.25	(0.01)	-0.33	(0.02)	-0.17	(0.02)	**-0.17**	(0.02)	**-1.36**	(0.02)	-0.44	(0.00)	0.02	(0.00)	**0.79**	(0.01)
France	-0.11	(0.02)	-0.22	(0.03)	0.00	(0.02)	**-0.22**	(0.03)	**-1.24**	(0.02)	-0.34	(0.00)	0.20	(0.00)	**0.94**	(0.02)
Germany	0.22	(0.02)	0.11	(0.02)	0.32	(0.02)	**-0.20**	(0.03)	**-0.85**	(0.02)	-0.02	(0.00)	0.47	(0.00)	**1.25**	(0.02)
Greece	-0.08	(0.02)	-0.26	(0.02)	0.09	(0.03)	**-0.35**	(0.04)	**-1.42**	(0.02)	-0.35	(0.01)	0.25	(0.00)	**1.19**	(0.02)
Hungary	0.74	(0.02)	0.62	(0.02)	0.87	(0.02)	**-0.25**	(0.02)	**-0.33**	(0.02)	0.46	(0.00)	0.94	(0.00)	**1.89**	(0.02)
Iceland	-0.34	(0.02)	-0.36	(0.02)	-0.31	(0.02)	-0.05	(0.03)	**-1.52**	(0.02)	-0.57	(0.00)	-0.05	(0.01)	**0.79**	(0.02)
Ireland	-0.01	(0.02)	-0.14	(0.03)	0.13	(0.02)	**-0.26**	(0.04)	**-1.21**	(0.02)	-0.25	(0.01)	0.28	(0.00)	**1.16**	(0.02)
Israel	0.22	(0.02)	0.13	(0.03)	0.31	(0.03)	**-0.18**	(0.04)	**-1.11**	(0.02)	-0.12	(0.00)	0.52	(0.00)	**1.60**	(0.02)
Italy	-0.17	(0.01)	-0.26	(0.01)	-0.07	(0.01)	**-0.20**	(0.01)	**-1.36**	(0.01)	-0.38	(0.00)	0.15	(0.00)	**0.92**	(0.01)
Japan	-0.70	(0.02)	-0.70	(0.02)	-0.71	(0.03)	0.01	(0.03)	**-2.05**	(0.02)	-0.91	(0.00)	-0.36	(0.00)	**0.51**	(0.02)
Korea	0.08	(0.02)	-0.02	(0.03)	0.19	(0.02)	**-0.21**	(0.03)	**-1.12**	(0.03)	-0.08	(0.00)	0.38	(0.00)	**1.13**	(0.01)
Luxembourg	0.23	(0.01)	0.09	(0.02)	0.36	(0.02)	**-0.27**	(0.03)	**-0.92**	(0.02)	-0.01	(0.01)	0.51	(0.00)	**1.33**	(0.02)
Mexico	0.01	(0.01)	-0.04	(0.01)	0.06	(0.01)	**-0.11**	(0.02)	**-1.15**	(0.01)	-0.30	(0.00)	0.27	(0.00)	**1.21**	(0.01)
Netherlands	-0.25	(0.03)	-0.26	(0.03)	-0.24	(0.03)	-0.02	(0.03)	**-1.46**	(0.02)	-0.46	(0.01)	0.03	(0.00)	**0.87**	(0.03)
New Zealand	0.05	(0.02)	-0.09	(0.03)	0.19	(0.02)	**-0.27**	(0.03)	**-1.12**	(0.02)	-0.20	(0.00)	0.31	(0.00)	**1.19**	(0.02)
Norway	-0.44	(0.02)	-0.44	(0.02)	-0.45	(0.02)	0.02	(0.03)	**-1.71**	(0.02)	-0.68	(0.00)	-0.10	(0.00)	**0.71**	(0.02)
Poland	0.42	(0.02)	0.25	(0.02)	0.60	(0.02)	**-0.35**	(0.03)	**-0.65**	(0.02)	0.18	(0.00)	0.64	(0.00)	**1.53**	(0.02)
Portugal	-0.27	(0.01)	-0.36	(0.02)	-0.18	(0.02)	**-0.18**	(0.03)	**-1.46**	(0.02)	-0.51	(0.00)	0.01	(0.00)	**0.87**	(0.01)
Slovak Republic	-0.33	(0.03)	-0.42	(0.03)	-0.25	(0.04)	**-0.18**	(0.04)	**-1.66**	(0.02)	-0.64	(0.01)	0.00	(0.01)	**0.97**	(0.02)
Slovenia	0.06	(0.01)	0.02	(0.02)	0.11	(0.02)	**-0.09**	(0.02)	**-1.06**	(0.02)	-0.18	(0.00)	0.33	(0.01)	**1.17**	(0.02)
Spain	0.34	(0.01)	0.24	(0.02)	0.43	(0.02)	**-0.19**	(0.02)	**-1.02**	(0.02)	0.04	(0.00)	0.63	(0.00)	**1.69**	(0.01)
Sweden	0.19	(0.02)	0.12	(0.03)	0.25	(0.02)	**-0.13**	(0.03)	**-0.98**	(0.02)	-0.05	(0.01)	0.46	(0.00)	**1.32**	(0.01)
Switzerland	0.00	(0.01)	-0.09	(0.02)	0.09	(0.02)	**-0.18**	(0.02)	**-1.11**	(0.01)	-0.24	(0.00)	0.25	(0.00)	**1.08**	(0.02)
Turkey	-0.04	(0.02)	-0.09	(0.03)	0.01	(0.02)	**-0.10**	(0.03)	**-1.12**	(0.02)	-0.29	(0.00)	0.22	(0.00)	**1.02**	(0.02)
United Kingdom	0.04	(0.01)	-0.02	(0.02)	0.10	(0.02)	**-0.12**	(0.02)	**-1.05**	(0.02)	-0.19	(0.00)	0.28	(0.00)	**1.13**	(0.02)
United States	-0.04	(0.02)	-0.15	(0.03)	0.06	(0.03)	**-0.21**	(0.03)	**-1.40**	(0.02)	-0.31	(0.00)	0.29	(0.00)	**1.25**	(0.02)
OECD average	0.00	(0.00)	-0.09	(0.00)	0.09	(0.00)	**-0.17**	(0.01)	**-1.18**	(0.00)	-0.24	(0.00)	0.28	(0.00)	**1.15**	(0.00)
Partners																
Albania	0.77	(0.02)	0.61	(0.03)	0.94	(0.03)	**-0.33**	(0.04)	**-0.28**	(0.03)	0.54	(0.01)	1.00	(0.00)	**1.83**	(0.02)
Argentina	0.32	(0.02)	0.28	(0.03)	0.35	(0.02)	-0.07	(0.03)	**-0.89**	(0.02)	0.05	(0.00)	0.58	(0.00)	**1.52**	(0.02)
Azerbaijan	0.62	(0.02)	0.49	(0.04)	0.75	(0.02)	**-0.26**	(0.04)	**-0.65**	(0.03)	0.37	(0.01)	0.87	(0.01)	**1.87**	(0.02)
Brazil	0.11	(0.01)	0.00	(0.02)	0.21	(0.01)	**-0.21**	(0.02)	**-0.98**	(0.01)	-0.11	(0.00)	0.37	(0.00)	**1.18**	(0.01)
Bulgaria	0.38	(0.02)	0.23	(0.03)	0.54	(0.03)	**-0.31**	(0.04)	**-1.02**	(0.03)	0.10	(0.01)	0.70	(0.00)	**1.74**	(0.02)
Colombia	0.32	(0.03)	0.23	(0.03)	0.41	(0.04)	**-0.18**	(0.04)	**-0.89**	(0.02)	-0.01	(0.00)	0.58	(0.00)	**1.61**	(0.02)
Croatia	0.51	(0.01)	0.41	(0.02)	0.63	(0.02)	**-0.22**	(0.03)	**-0.56**	(0.02)	0.25	(0.00)	0.75	(0.00)	**1.60**	(0.01)
Dubai (UAE)	0.43	(0.01)	0.38	(0.02)	0.48	(0.02)	**-0.10**	(0.03)	**-0.77**	(0.01)	0.15	(0.01)	0.68	(0.00)	**1.65**	(0.02)
Hong Kong-China	0.13	(0.01)	0.06	(0.02)	0.21	(0.02)	**-0.15**	(0.03)	**-0.88**	(0.02)	-0.13	(0.00)	0.33	(0.00)	**1.19**	(0.02)
Indonesia	0.34	(0.01)	0.25	(0.02)	0.42	(0.02)	**-0.17**	(0.03)	**-0.47**	(0.01)	0.15	(0.00)	0.52	(0.00)	**1.15**	(0.02)
Jordan	0.61	(0.02)	0.50	(0.03)	0.72	(0.02)	**-0.22**	(0.04)	**-0.75**	(0.02)	0.35	(0.00)	0.92	(0.00)	**1.92**	(0.02)
Kazakhstan	0.50	(0.02)	0.47	(0.02)	0.54	(0.02)	-0.07	(0.02)	**-0.48**	(0.01)	0.25	(0.00)	0.69	(0.00)	**1.55**	(0.02)
Kyrgyzstan	0.53	(0.02)	0.40	(0.02)	0.65	(0.02)	**-0.24**	(0.03)	**-0.54**	(0.02)	0.26	(0.00)	0.75	(0.00)	**1.64**	(0.02)
Latvia	0.13	(0.02)	0.07	(0.03)	0.19	(0.02)	**-0.12**	(0.03)	**-0.89**	(0.02)	-0.06	(0.01)	0.36	(0.01)	**1.12**	(0.02)
Liechtenstein	0.10	(0.05)	0.00	(0.08)	0.21	(0.06)	**-0.20**	(0.10)	**-1.05**	(0.09)	-0.07	(0.02)	0.42	(0.01)	**1.09**	(0.05)
Lithuania	0.19	(0.02)	0.09	(0.02)	0.29	(0.02)	**-0.19**	(0.03)	**-0.78**	(0.01)	-0.04	(0.00)	0.42	(0.00)	**1.14**	(0.01)
Macao-China	-0.16	(0.01)	-0.20	(0.02)	-0.12	(0.01)	**-0.08**	(0.02)	**-1.13**	(0.01)	-0.38	(0.00)	0.06	(0.00)	**0.80**	(0.01)
Montenegro	0.70	(0.02)	0.61	(0.03)	0.79	(0.02)	**-0.19**	(0.03)	**-0.44**	(0.02)	0.40	(0.00)	0.90	(0.00)	**1.93**	(0.02)
Panama	0.56	(0.03)	0.61	(0.03)	0.51	(0.04)	0.10	(0.05)	**-0.68**	(0.03)	0.23	(0.01)	0.79	(0.01)	**1.89**	(0.03)
Peru	0.18	(0.02)	0.22	(0.02)	0.15	(0.02)	0.07	(0.02)	**-0.95**	(0.02)	-0.10	(0.00)	0.42	(0.00)	**1.35**	(0.02)
Qatar	0.59	(0.01)	0.41	(0.02)	0.76	(0.02)	**-0.34**	(0.02)	**-0.80**	(0.02)	0.26	(0.00)	0.89	(0.00)	**1.99**	(0.02)
Romania	0.22	(0.02)	0.04	(0.02)	0.39	(0.03)	**-0.35**	(0.03)	**-1.01**	(0.03)	-0.07	(0.01)	0.49	(0.01)	**1.47**	(0.02)
Russian Federation	0.20	(0.02)	0.16	(0.02)	0.24	(0.02)	**-0.08**	(0.02)	**-0.84**	(0.01)	-0.03	(0.00)	0.46	(0.00)	**1.20**	(0.01)
Serbia	0.49	(0.02)	0.36	(0.02)	0.62	(0.02)	**-0.26**	(0.03)	**-0.69**	(0.02)	0.19	(0.00)	0.73	(0.00)	**1.73**	(0.02)
Shanghai-China	-0.07	(0.01)	-0.14	(0.01)	0.00	(0.02)	**-0.14**	(0.02)	**-1.02**	(0.02)	-0.31	(0.00)	0.19	(0.00)	**0.87**	(0.01)
Singapore	0.06	(0.01)	0.04	(0.02)	0.08	(0.02)	-0.04	(0.03)	**-1.00**	(0.02)	-0.22	(0.00)	0.28	(0.00)	**1.19**	(0.02)
Chinese Taipei	-0.13	(0.02)	-0.26	(0.02)	0.01	(0.02)	**-0.28**	(0.02)	**-1.27**	(0.02)	-0.37	(0.00)	0.13	(0.00)	**1.00**	(0.02)
Thailand	0.06	(0.01)	-0.06	(0.02)	0.16	(0.02)	**-0.23**	(0.03)	**-0.82**	(0.02)	-0.15	(0.00)	0.24	(0.00)	**0.98**	(0.02)
Trinidad and Tobago	0.38	(0.02)	0.27	(0.02)	0.49	(0.02)	**-0.22**	(0.02)	**-0.73**	(0.01)	0.08	(0.00)	0.59	(0.00)	**1.60**	(0.02)
Tunisia	0.24	(0.02)	0.11	(0.03)	0.36	(0.02)	**-0.25**	(0.04)	**-0.95**	(0.02)	0.00	(0.00)	0.54	(0.00)	**1.38**	(0.02)
Uruguay	0.06	(0.02)	-0.05	(0.02)	0.15	(0.02)	**-0.20**	(0.03)	**-1.25**	(0.02)	-0.24	(0.01)	0.34	(0.00)	**1.38**	(0.02)

Note: Values that are statistically significant are indicated in bold (see Annex A3).
StatLink http://dx.doi.org/10.1787/888932343285

[Part 2/2]
Index of memorisation strategies and reading performance, by national quarters of this index
Table III.1.20 *Results based on students' self-reports*

	Bottom quarter Mean score	S.E.	Second quarter Mean score	S.E.	Third quarter Mean score	S.E.	Top quarter Mean score	S.E.	Change in the reading score per unit of this index Effect	S.E.	Increased likelihood of students in the bottom quarter of this index scoring in the bottom quarter of the national reading performance distribution Ratio	S.E.	Explained variance in student performance (r-squared x 100) %	S.E.
OECD														
Australia	**503**	(3.3)	520	(2.9)	525	(2.8)	**520**	(2.7)	**9.7**	(1.17)	**1.3**	(0.06)	1.0	(0.24)
Austria	**488**	(4.4)	479	(4.0)	471	(4.1)	**464**	(4.2)	**-8.9**	(2.00)	0.8	(0.06)	0.7	(0.32)
Belgium	**527**	(3.2)	524	(2.8)	511	(2.8)	**489**	(3.6)	**-12.4**	(1.46)	0.9	(0.05)	1.5	(0.35)
Canada	523	(2.1)	527	(2.3)	527	(2.3)	526	(2.2)	3.3	(0.99)	1.1	(0.05)	0.2	(0.09)
Chile	**442**	(4.4)	453	(3.8)	453	(3.5)	**454**	(3.9)	**5.2**	(1.79)	**1.3**	(0.08)	0.3	(0.22)
Czech Republic	**489**	(3.9)	491	(3.9)	481	(3.6)	**468**	(3.5)	**-6.4**	(1.55)	1.0	(0.07)	0.5	(0.24)
Denmark	**504**	(3.9)	505	(3.4)	496	(3.0)	**479**	(3.1)	**-9.5**	(2.01)	0.9	(0.06)	0.9	(0.40)
Estonia	**507**	(4.6)	506	(3.9)	498	(3.8)	**493**	(3.4)	**-6.7**	(2.23)	0.9	(0.08)	0.5	(0.31)
Finland	534	(3.3)	538	(3.6)	537	(3.3)	536	(3.2)	2.9	(1.68)	**1.1**	(0.07)	0.1	(0.10)
France	478	(6.3)	506	(4.7)	508	(4.2)	498	(3.8)	**11.0**	(2.68)	**1.4**	(0.10)	0.9	(0.44)
Germany	**506**	(4.3)	513	(4.3)	507	(3.8)	**492**	(3.4)	**-5.1**	(1.78)	**1.1**	(0.09)	0.2	(0.17)
Greece	479	(6.8)	487	(4.4)	480	(4.9)	486	(4.7)	**5.3**	(1.87)	**1.2**	(0.10)	0.4	(0.25)
Hungary	**487**	(5.3)	499	(4.7)	500	(4.6)	**491**	(4.9)	3.3	(2.50)	**1.3**	(0.10)	0.1	(0.17)
Iceland	**507**	(3.5)	499	(3.5)	508	(3.1)	**492**	(3.4)	-1.0	(1.90)	0.9	(0.07)	0.0	(0.04)
Ireland	**490**	(5.4)	501	(4.5)	500	(3.4)	**500**	(3.2)	**7.0**	(2.35)	**1.2**	(0.10)	0.5	(0.36)
Israel	**489**	(5.6)	477	(5.6)	474	(4.0)	**472**	(3.6)	-5.6	(1.94)	1.0	(0.07)	0.3	(0.23)
Italy	**501**	(2.4)	495	(2.0)	484	(2.2)	**467**	(2.3)	**-10.1**	(1.27)	0.9	(0.03)	1.0	(0.25)
Japan	**508**	(5.6)	527	(4.7)	523	(4.8)	**523**	(3.7)	**6.5**	(1.82)	**1.3**	(0.07)	0.5	(0.25)
Korea	**503**	(5.7)	545	(3.8)	553	(3.4)	**557**	(3.2)	**24.6**	(2.47)	**2.3**	(0.14)	**8.7**	(1.58)
Luxembourg	**457**	(3.2)	477	(2.8)	481	(3.1)	**478**	(3.2)	**10.2**	(1.72)	**1.5**	(0.10)	0.9	(0.29)
Mexico	422	(2.6)	428	(2.8)	430	(2.3)	422	(2.2)	-0.1	(0.83)	**1.1**	(0.04)	0.0	(0.01)
Netherlands	**541**	(6.1)	523	(5.3)	503	(5.8)	**481**	(5.6)	**-21.9**	(1.76)	0.6	(0.07)	**5.7**	(0.87)
New Zealand	**516**	(3.9)	528	(3.7)	529	(3.8)	**518**	(4.1)	3.1	(2.00)	**1.2**	(0.07)	0.1	(0.12)
Norway	499	(4.0)	508	(3.8)	508	(3.7)	502	(3.5)	**3.8**	(1.53)	**1.2**	(0.07)	0.2	(0.14)
Poland	**490**	(4.1)	505	(3.7)	504	(3.5)	**505**	(3.5)	**7.2**	(1.89)	**1.4**	(0.08)	0.5	(0.27)
Portugal	500	(3.9)	483	(4.2)	491	(3.6)	487	(3.4)	-2.7	(1.50)	0.8	(0.06)	0.1	(0.10)
Slovak Republic	**504**	(4.6)	487	(3.0)	471	(3.5)	**449**	(5.3)	**-18.1**	(2.26)	0.6	(0.06)	**4.6**	(1.11)
Slovenia	**501**	(2.7)	494	(2.7)	485	(3.0)	**462**	(3.4)	**-15.9**	(1.75)	0.9	(0.06)	**2.8**	(0.61)
Spain	475	(3.8)	486	(2.7)	486	(2.4)	481	(2.5)	**4.2**	(1.35)	**1.3**	(0.06)	0.3	(0.19)
Sweden	482	(4.8)	501	(3.1)	508	(3.6)	506	(4.0)	**10.3**	(1.97)	**1.4**	(0.08)	1.0	(0.40)
Switzerland	**504**	(3.4)	511	(3.2)	502	(3.3)	**489**	(3.4)	**-5.8**	(1.56)	1.0	(0.07)	0.3	(0.17)
Turkey	486	(5.3)	465	(4.6)	457	(3.7)	449	(3.7)	**-15.1**	(2.03)	0.7	(0.06)	**2.7**	(0.66)
United Kingdom	489	(3.4)	504	(3.4)	504	(3.4)	486	(2.8)	1.2	(1.59)	**1.2**	(0.07)	0.0	(0.04)
United States	**507**	(4.4)	505	(4.8)	500	(5.1)	**490**	(4.1)	-4.4	(1.59)	1.0	(0.07)	0.2	(0.18)
OECD average	**495**	(0.8)	500	(0.7)	497	(0.6)	**489**	(0.6)	-0.9	(0.31)	**1.1**	(0.01)	1.1	(0.08)
Partners														
Albania	370	(7.3)	390	(5.5)	393	(5.4)	395	(4.8)	**13.1**	(3.34)	**1.6**	(0.13)	1.3	(0.70)
Argentina	409	(6.7)	410	(6.3)	397	(5.9)	391	(4.4)	-5.7	(2.09)	1.0	(0.08)	0.3	(0.20)
Azerbaijan	346	(4.5)	371	(4.7)	372	(3.7)	366	(4.3)	**7.6**	(1.68)	**1.5**	(0.12)	1.1	(0.53)
Brazil	396	(3.4)	414	(3.2)	420	(3.5)	424	(3.1)	**12.1**	(1.30)	**1.4**	(0.06)	1.3	(0.29)
Bulgaria	422	(8.9)	442	(8.3)	438	(6.4)	428	(6.5)	4.7	(2.04)	**1.4**	(0.10)	0.2	(0.22)
Colombia	426	(4.9)	420	(3.8)	411	(4.1)	399	(5.2)	**-11.5**	(2.00)	0.8	(0.08)	1.8	(0.60)
Croatia	471	(4.5)	487	(3.6)	478	(3.6)	468	(3.5)	-1.4	(1.81)	**1.2**	(0.09)	0.0	(0.06)
Dubai (UAE)	484	(3.7)	470	(3.3)	455	(2.9)	432	(2.8)	**-20.5**	(1.61)	0.8	(0.05)	**3.6**	(0.56)
Hong Kong-China	**518**	(3.3)	537	(3.0)	540	(3.5)	**539**	(3.3)	**8.2**	(1.77)	**1.5**	(0.09)	0.7	(0.31)
Indonesia	391	(4.0)	402	(4.2)	406	(4.4)	409	(4.5)	**11.2**	(2.16)	**1.3**	(0.11)	1.3	(0.51)
Jordan	367	(4.6)	413	(4.3)	425	(3.5)	423	(3.8)	**20.8**	(1.50)	**2.2**	(0.13)	**6.5**	(0.89)
Kazakhstan	398	(5.0)	391	(3.9)	392	(3.6)	381	(3.6)	**-9.0**	(2.29)	1.0	(0.08)	0.7	(0.36)
Kyrgyzstan	**289**	(3.9)	329	(4.4)	324	(4.5)	**325**	(4.1)	**12.9**	(1.90)	**1.7**	(0.11)	1.4	(0.41)
Latvia	487	(4.6)	487	(3.4)	484	(4.2)	480	(4.2)	-3.0	(2.38)	1.0	(0.10)	0.1	(0.14)
Liechtenstein	504	(10.0)	512	(6.8)	497	(9.8)	485	(9.7)	-5.5	(7.14)	**1.1**	(0.27)	0.4	(1.08)
Lithuania	475	(4.4)	472	(3.0)	469	(2.9)	459	(4.0)	**-8.4**	(2.38)	1.0	(0.08)	0.6	(0.33)
Macao-China	**477**	(2.2)	486	(2.6)	490	(2.3)	**494**	(2.4)	**9.2**	(1.38)	**1.3**	(0.06)	1.0	(0.29)
Montenegro	423	(3.3)	420	(3.2)	408	(4.5)	384	(3.2)	**-14.5**	(1.86)	0.9	(0.08)	**2.3**	(0.61)
Panama	384	(9.0)	383	(7.1)	381	(6.3)	362	(7.1)	-6.9	(2.69)	1.0	(0.10)	0.5	(0.42)
Peru	391	(6.1)	380	(4.4)	368	(4.6)	346	(4.4)	**-18.7**	(2.31)	0.8	(0.07)	**3.2**	(0.76)
Qatar	367	(2.8)	384	(2.1)	378	(2.3)	369	(1.9)	1.9	(1.15)	**1.5**	(0.06)	0.0	(0.04)
Romania	411	(6.6)	430	(4.6)	432	(4.0)	426	(4.9)	**6.8**	(2.01)	**1.5**	(0.12)	0.6	(0.35)
Russian Federation	**469**	(5.5)	463	(4.0)	457	(3.5)	**452**	(3.8)	**-7.5**	(2.30)	0.9	(0.07)	0.5	(0.30)
Serbia	461	(3.5)	451	(3.1)	436	(3.4)	424	(3.4)	**-14.7**	(1.70)	0.8	(0.06)	**3.0**	(0.65)
Shanghai-China	**550**	(3.6)	555	(3.6)	559	(3.0)	**560**	(3.3)	4.9	(1.80)	**1.1**	(0.07)	0.2	(0.18)
Singapore	**541**	(2.8)	532	(3.5)	524	(3.1)	**508**	(2.5)	**-14.1**	(1.42)	0.8	(0.06)	1.7	(0.35)
Chinese Taipei	**465**	(4.2)	490	(3.4)	511	(3.1)	**516**	(3.0)	**20.7**	(1.56)	**2.0**	(0.12)	**5.5**	(0.77)
Thailand	396	(3.0)	414	(3.4)	432	(2.8)	444	(3.9)	**24.8**	(1.62)	**1.8**	(0.12)	**6.7**	(0.77)
Trinidad and Tobago	**403**	(3.9)	419	(3.6)	422	(4.2)	**435**	(3.3)	**12.1**	(2.03)	**1.5**	(0.09)	1.1	(0.35)
Tunisia	404	(4.7)	408	(4.0)	405	(3.2)	400	(3.2)	-1.3	(2.02)	**1.1**	(0.08)	0.0	(0.09)
Uruguay	425	(4.5)	438	(3.7)	431	(3.4)	419	(3.8)	-1.4	(1.65)	**1.2**	(0.07)	0.0	(0.07)

Note: Values that are statistically significant are indicated in bold (see Annex A3).
StatLink ᵃᵐˢ᠊ http://dx.doi.org/10.1787/888932343285

[Part 1/1]

Table III.1.21 **Proportion of students with low levels of memorisation strategies, by reading proficiency level[1]**
Results based on students' self-reports

	Percentage of students with low levels of memorisation strategies									
	Level 1a or below		Level 2		Level 3		Level 4		Level 5 or above	
	%	S.E.	%	S.E.	%	S.E.	%	S.E.	%	S.E.
OECD Australia	56.2	(1.5)	50.0	(1.4)	47.1	(1.1)	46.0	(1.1)	47.0	(1.5)
Austria	50.6	(1.8)	51.0	(1.8)	55.1	(1.7)	60.6	(2.4)	68.6	(4.2)
Belgium	44.4	(1.8)	46.3	(1.7)	51.8	(1.6)	57.8	(1.5)	65.5	(2.0)
Canada	51.0	(1.8)	46.8	(1.4)	44.2	(0.9)	45.7	(1.1)	49.7	(1.7)
Chile	56.9	(1.6)	51.9	(1.6)	51.0	(1.6)	54.3	(2.9)	c	c
Czech Republic	51.9	(1.8)	46.2	(1.6)	51.0	(1.8)	61.2	(2.2)	68.9	(2.9)
Denmark	48.6	(2.2)	52.1	(1.7)	54.6	(1.6)	61.5	(2.4)	c	c
Estonia	40.3	(2.8)	36.7	(1.9)	40.4	(1.4)	45.0	(1.8)	51.3	(3.4)
Finland	49.3	(2.8)	43.3	(2.2)	39.9	(1.6)	41.4	(1.7)	45.8	(2.4)
France	56.5	(2.3)	50.1	(2.3)	48.2	(1.9)	49.4	(2.1)	50.4	(2.8)
Germany	52.0	(1.9)	46.7	(1.8)	47.8	(2.2)	56.4	(2.2)	60.9	(3.5)
Greece	51.9	(2.1)	46.9	(1.8)	46.9	(1.9)	51.0	(1.9)	56.0	(4.7)
Hungary	62.5	(2.9)	54.3	(1.8)	55.9	(1.7)	59.6	(1.7)	62.7	(4.5)
Iceland	49.5	(2.2)	45.7	(2.7)	46.1	(1.9)	48.6	(2.2)	50.9	(3.0)
Ireland	49.3	(2.7)	44.0	(2.1)	44.6	(1.7)	45.7	(1.9)	c	c
Israel	52.3	(1.6)	46.6	(1.6)	47.9	(1.9)	55.3	(2.2)	70.6	(3.3)
Italy	46.5	(1.1)	46.4	(1.1)	53.3	(1.0)	60.9	(0.9)	68.5	(1.5)
Japan	49.6	(2.3)	44.3	(2.4)	42.2	(1.8)	42.4	(2.0)	46.0	(2.7)
Korea	74.8	(4.7)	52.4	(2.2)	38.0	(1.3)	30.8	(1.3)	30.9	(2.2)
Luxembourg	57.5	(1.4)	46.8	(1.9)	46.9	(1.8)	48.4	(1.9)	50.8	(4.0)
Mexico	48.3	(0.7)	47.2	(0.8)	46.7	(1.0)	50.9	(2.1)	c	c
Netherlands	31.7	(2.5)	32.5	(1.9)	39.3	(2.0)	53.2	(2.1)	63.9	(2.4)
New Zealand	48.2	(2.7)	42.8	(2.1)	42.8	(1.9)	44.9	(2.1)	46.1	(2.1)
Norway	53.7	(2.4)	50.7	(1.8)	49.4	(1.7)	52.2	(1.8)	51.3	(2.7)
Poland	65.8	(2.5)	54.0	(1.9)	54.5	(1.2)	56.2	(2.0)	61.8	(2.7)
Portugal	48.1	(1.6)	41.3	(1.7)	42.1	(1.4)	48.4	(1.8)	51.9	(3.7)
Slovak Republic	38.5	(1.9)	40.1	(2.1)	50.0	(2.2)	63.3	(3.6)	74.1	(4.6)
Slovenia	38.7	(1.9)	35.6	(1.8)	44.5	(1.9)	55.3	(2.4)	c	c
Spain	52.7	(1.8)	42.5	(1.4)	42.4	(1.2)	49.1	(1.4)	57.7	(3.1)
Sweden	62.6	(2.5)	52.8	(2.0)	49.7	(1.6)	50.7	(1.8)	51.5	(2.9)
Switzerland	44.0	(2.0)	42.9	(1.9)	46.1	(1.6)	50.9	(1.8)	53.3	(2.9)
Turkey	42.0	(1.9)	42.3	(1.7)	52.7	(1.8)	64.3	(2.5)	c	c
United Kingdom	48.0	(1.6)	40.9	(1.5)	43.2	(1.4)	45.4	(1.4)	48.2	(2.7)
United States	47.6	(1.8)	43.6	(1.7)	45.1	(1.7)	51.9	(2.5)	57.1	(3.3)
OECD average	50.6	(0.4)	45.8	(0.3)	47.1	(0.3)	51.7	(0.3)	55.8	(0.6)
Partners Albania	56.5	(1.4)	47.5	(2.2)	54.0	(2.8)	61.8	(5.9)	c	c
Argentina	43.4	(1.2)	43.5	(1.8)	51.4	(2.3)	64.6	(3.5)	c	c
Azerbaijan	47.2	(1.1)	42.3	(2.0)	43.9	(4.8)	49.4	(13.2)	c	c
Brazil	59.9	(0.8)	54.0	(1.2)	52.8	(2.0)	51.0	(2.6)	52.5	(5.6)
Bulgaria	45.7	(2.1)	39.9	(2.3)	39.8	(2.4)	48.9	(4.0)	c	c
Colombia	45.7	(1.7)	49.5	(1.9)	56.4	(2.1)	61.8	(3.8)	c	c
Croatia	51.3	(1.7)	50.0	(1.5)	50.4	(1.4)	57.3	(1.8)	c	c
Dubai (UAE)	46.8	(1.3)	49.9	(1.7)	59.1	(1.8)	72.3	(2.2)	77.7	(3.5)
Hong Kong-China	70.3	(2.8)	61.1	(2.5)	57.2	(1.6)	56.0	(1.8)	59.1	(2.4)
Indonesia	49.7	(1.4)	41.6	(1.6)	39.9	(2.8)	47.4	(9.8)	c	c
Jordan	54.5	(1.2)	37.9	(1.3)	37.6	(2.3)	35.4	(5.9)	c	c
Kazakhstan	51.6	(1.4)	54.9	(2.0)	60.4	(3.1)	61.7	(4.4)	c	c
Kyrgyzstan	52.0	(1.1)	45.9	(2.2)	47.5	(3.3)	49.4	(7.5)	c	c
Latvia	55.7	(2.7)	55.0	(2.1)	57.0	(1.8)	59.7	(2.5)	c	c
Liechtenstein	41.3	(7.4)	33.0	(5.3)	34.2	(5.8)	46.9	(6.5)	c	c
Lithuania	52.1	(2.0)	49.8	(1.6)	53.2	(1.9)	59.2	(2.4)	c	c
Macao-China	62.1	(1.6)	57.4	(1.4)	54.5	(1.1)	52.3	(2.2)	51.1	(4.0)
Montenegro	53.0	(1.3)	60.0	(1.6)	68.8	(2.1)	81.5	(4.4)	c	c
Panama	48.3	(1.7)	51.5	(3.2)	60.0	(4.0)	69.0	(4.5)	c	c
Peru	50.1	(1.0)	59.8	(1.8)	66.7	(2.2)	73.8	(4.4)	c	c
Qatar	48.0	(0.8)	39.2	(1.2)	50.7	(1.8)	67.8	(2.6)	84.0	(3.8)
Romania	54.5	(1.7)	49.3	(1.8)	51.3	(2.3)	58.0	(3.9)	c	c
Russian Federation	49.3	(1.9)	48.5	(1.6)	52.8	(1.5)	58.2	(2.5)	c	c
Serbia	46.5	(1.4)	50.6	(1.6)	60.4	(1.6)	71.7	(2.7)	c	c
Shanghai-China	58.2	(3.7)	54.0	(2.5)	49.7	(1.5)	48.2	(1.2)	49.3	(1.9)
Singapore	41.7	(1.9)	38.3	(1.8)	42.4	(1.6)	50.1	(1.9)	55.6	(2.0)
Chinese Taipei	73.5	(1.6)	58.0	(1.4)	47.9	(1.5)	44.6	(1.6)	44.4	(3.1)
Thailand	54.8	(1.3)	38.9	(1.4)	28.0	(2.1)	19.0	(3.3)	c	c
Trinidad and Tobago	49.5	(1.5)	40.3	(1.6)	43.1	(2.2)	45.6	(3.0)	c	c
Tunisia	47.2	(1.4)	47.5	(1.8)	52.4	(2.1)	59.9	(5.5)	c	c
Uruguay	45.3	(1.1)	41.2	(1.7)	45.4	(1.9)	55.7	(3.0)	c	c

1. Students who reported levels of diversity of reading below their country average.
StatLink http://dx.doi.org/10.1787/888932343285

[Part 1/2]
Index of elaboration strategies and reading performance, by national quarters of this index

Table III.1.22 *Results based on students' self-reports*

	All students		Boys		Girls		Gender difference (B – G)		Bottom quarter		Second quarter		Third quarter		Top quarter	
	Mean index	S.E.	Mean index	S.E.	Mean index	S.E.	Dif.	S.E.	Mean index	S.E.	Mean index	S.E.	Mean index	S.E.	Mean index	S.E.
OECD																
Australia	-0.14	(0.01)	-0.10	(0.02)	-0.18	(0.01)	0.08	(0.02)	-1.45	(0.01)	-0.36	(0.00)	0.19	(0.00)	1.07	(0.01)
Austria	0.19	(0.02)	0.26	(0.02)	0.12	(0.03)	0.14	(0.03)	-1.11	(0.02)	-0.08	(0.00)	0.52	(0.00)	1.41	(0.02)
Belgium	-0.32	(0.01)	-0.23	(0.02)	-0.40	(0.02)	0.17	(0.03)	-1.62	(0.01)	-0.53	(0.00)	0.01	(0.00)	0.87	(0.01)
Canada	-0.21	(0.01)	-0.16	(0.02)	-0.25	(0.01)	0.09	(0.02)	-1.61	(0.01)	-0.45	(0.00)	0.16	(0.00)	1.08	(0.01)
Chile	0.13	(0.01)	0.16	(0.02)	0.09	(0.02)	0.07	(0.02)	-1.17	(0.02)	-0.14	(0.00)	0.44	(0.00)	1.36	(0.02)
Czech Republic	0.12	(0.02)	0.14	(0.02)	0.09	(0.02)	0.05	(0.03)	-1.06	(0.02)	-0.12	(0.00)	0.41	(0.00)	1.23	(0.01)
Denmark	0.10	(0.02)	0.13	(0.02)	0.07	(0.02)	0.06	(0.03)	-1.09	(0.02)	-0.12	(0.00)	0.41	(0.00)	1.20	(0.01)
Estonia	0.10	(0.01)	0.13	(0.02)	0.07	(0.02)	0.07	(0.03)	-0.98	(0.02)	-0.11	(0.00)	0.37	(0.00)	1.12	(0.02)
Finland	-0.15	(0.01)	-0.12	(0.02)	-0.17	(0.02)	0.04	(0.03)	-1.38	(0.02)	-0.36	(0.00)	0.17	(0.00)	0.94	(0.01)
France	-0.18	(0.02)	-0.13	(0.02)	-0.24	(0.02)	0.11	(0.02)	-1.44	(0.02)	-0.41	(0.01)	0.16	(0.00)	0.94	(0.02)
Germany	0.09	(0.02)	0.17	(0.02)	0.02	(0.02)	0.15	(0.02)	-1.12	(0.02)	-0.14	(0.00)	0.41	(0.01)	1.22	(0.02)
Greece	0.05	(0.02)	0.08	(0.02)	0.01	(0.02)	0.07	(0.03)	-1.28	(0.02)	-0.18	(0.01)	0.39	(0.00)	1.27	(0.02)
Hungary	0.20	(0.02)	0.27	(0.02)	0.12	(0.02)	0.15	(0.02)	-0.94	(0.02)	-0.04	(0.00)	0.47	(0.00)	1.31	(0.02)
Iceland	-0.03	(0.02)	-0.01	(0.02)	-0.06	(0.02)	0.06	(0.03)	-1.32	(0.02)	-0.25	(0.00)	0.28	(0.01)	1.16	(0.02)
Ireland	-0.20	(0.02)	-0.12	(0.03)	-0.28	(0.03)	0.17	(0.04)	-1.58	(0.02)	-0.44	(0.01)	0.15	(0.00)	1.07	(0.02)
Israel	0.10	(0.02)	0.14	(0.03)	0.06	(0.03)	0.08	(0.03)	-1.28	(0.02)	-0.20	(0.00)	0.43	(0.00)	1.45	(0.02)
Italy	-0.07	(0.01)	-0.05	(0.01)	-0.09	(0.01)	0.04	(0.01)	-1.37	(0.01)	-0.30	(0.00)	0.28	(0.00)	1.11	(0.01)
Japan	-0.74	(0.02)	-0.63	(0.03)	-0.85	(0.03)	0.22	(0.04)	-2.11	(0.01)	-1.07	(0.01)	-0.34	(0.00)	0.58	(0.01)
Korea	0.09	(0.02)	0.10	(0.03)	0.08	(0.03)	0.03	(0.04)	-1.18	(0.02)	-0.13	(0.00)	0.42	(0.00)	1.25	(0.01)
Luxembourg	0.01	(0.01)	0.10	(0.02)	-0.08	(0.02)	0.18	(0.02)	-1.23	(0.02)	-0.20	(0.00)	0.32	(0.00)	1.15	(0.02)
Mexico	0.21	(0.01)	0.20	(0.01)	0.21	(0.01)	-0.01	(0.02)	-0.98	(0.02)	-0.07	(0.00)	0.50	(0.00)	1.38	(0.01)
Netherlands	-0.20	(0.02)	-0.10	(0.02)	-0.31	(0.02)	0.21	(0.03)	-1.40	(0.02)	-0.42	(0.01)	0.10	(0.00)	0.89	(0.02)
New Zealand	-0.06	(0.01)	-0.04	(0.02)	-0.08	(0.02)	0.04	(0.03)	-1.28	(0.02)	-0.26	(0.00)	0.26	(0.00)	1.05	(0.02)
Norway	-0.08	(0.02)	-0.03	(0.02)	-0.13	(0.03)	0.10	(0.03)	-1.42	(0.02)	-0.30	(0.00)	0.29	(0.01)	1.11	(0.01)
Poland	0.24	(0.02)	0.25	(0.02)	0.23	(0.02)	0.02	(0.03)	-0.87	(0.02)	-0.01	(0.00)	0.49	(0.00)	1.36	(0.02)
Portugal	0.39	(0.01)	0.32	(0.02)	0.45	(0.02)	-0.13	(0.03)	-0.62	(0.01)	0.15	(0.00)	0.63	(0.00)	1.41	(0.02)
Slovak Republic	-0.04	(0.02)	-0.03	(0.02)	-0.06	(0.02)	0.03	(0.03)	-1.21	(0.02)	-0.24	(0.00)	0.24	(0.00)	1.04	(0.02)
Slovenia	0.20	(0.02)	0.27	(0.02)	0.14	(0.02)	0.13	(0.02)	-0.99	(0.02)	-0.07	(0.01)	0.50	(0.00)	1.38	(0.02)
Spain	-0.07	(0.01)	-0.02	(0.02)	-0.12	(0.01)	0.10	(0.02)	-1.42	(0.01)	-0.32	(0.00)	0.29	(0.00)	1.18	(0.01)
Sweden	-0.09	(0.02)	-0.06	(0.03)	-0.13	(0.02)	0.07	(0.03)	-1.38	(0.02)	-0.33	(0.00)	0.23	(0.00)	1.10	(0.02)
Switzerland	0.06	(0.01)	0.12	(0.02)	-0.01	(0.02)	0.13	(0.02)	-1.12	(0.01)	-0.15	(0.00)	0.37	(0.00)	1.13	(0.01)
Turkey	0.44	(0.01)	0.40	(0.02)	0.48	(0.02)	-0.07	(0.03)	-0.58	(0.02)	0.19	(0.00)	0.68	(0.00)	1.47	(0.01)
United Kingdom	-0.03	(0.02)	0.03	(0.02)	-0.09	(0.02)	0.12	(0.02)	-1.26	(0.01)	-0.26	(0.00)	0.29	(0.00)	1.10	(0.02)
United States	-0.11	(0.02)	-0.09	(0.03)	-0.12	(0.02)	0.03	(0.04)	-1.55	(0.02)	-0.35	(0.01)	0.26	(0.01)	1.23	(0.02)
OECD average	0.00	(0.00)	0.04	(0.00)	-0.04	(0.00)	0.08	(0.00)	-1.25	(0.00)	-0.24	(0.00)	0.32	(0.00)	1.17	(0.00)
Partners																
Albania	0.49	(0.02)	0.44	(0.02)	0.55	(0.02)	-0.11	(0.03)	-0.44	(0.02)	0.26	(0.00)	0.73	(0.00)	1.42	(0.02)
Argentina	0.14	(0.02)	0.14	(0.02)	0.13	(0.03)	0.01	(0.03)	-1.19	(0.02)	-0.12	(0.01)	0.48	(0.00)	1.38	(0.02)
Azerbaijan	0.76	(0.02)	0.68	(0.04)	0.85	(0.03)	-0.18	(0.04)	-0.56	(0.03)	0.48	(0.00)	1.04	(0.01)	2.09	(0.02)
Brazil	0.24	(0.01)	0.19	(0.02)	0.27	(0.02)	-0.08	(0.02)	-0.93	(0.01)	-0.04	(0.00)	0.53	(0.00)	1.40	(0.02)
Bulgaria	0.15	(0.02)	0.17	(0.02)	0.13	(0.03)	0.04	(0.04)	-1.24	(0.03)	-0.13	(0.00)	0.50	(0.00)	1.46	(0.02)
Colombia	0.52	(0.02)	0.49	(0.03)	0.56	(0.02)	-0.07	(0.04)	-0.66	(0.02)	0.22	(0.00)	0.80	(0.00)	1.73	(0.01)
Croatia	0.27	(0.01)	0.29	(0.02)	0.24	(0.02)	0.05	(0.03)	-0.84	(0.02)	0.00	(0.00)	0.52	(0.00)	1.39	(0.02)
Dubai (UAE)	0.48	(0.01)	0.50	(0.02)	0.46	(0.02)	0.05	(0.03)	-0.71	(0.02)	0.21	(0.00)	0.75	(0.00)	1.68	(0.02)
Hong Kong-China	0.00	(0.02)	0.08	(0.02)	-0.09	(0.02)	0.17	(0.03)	-1.13	(0.02)	-0.23	(0.00)	0.25	(0.01)	1.10	(0.02)
Indonesia	0.25	(0.01)	0.21	(0.02)	0.29	(0.02)	-0.08	(0.02)	-0.58	(0.01)	0.07	(0.00)	0.44	(0.00)	1.07	(0.01)
Jordan	0.62	(0.01)	0.54	(0.02)	0.70	(0.02)	-0.16	(0.03)	-0.65	(0.02)	0.37	(0.00)	0.92	(0.00)	1.84	(0.02)
Kazakhstan	0.52	(0.02)	0.48	(0.02)	0.56	(0.03)	-0.08	(0.03)	-0.56	(0.02)	0.25	(0.00)	0.75	(0.00)	1.65	(0.02)
Kyrgyzstan	0.57	(0.02)	0.45	(0.02)	0.68	(0.03)	-0.23	(0.03)	-0.50	(0.02)	0.27	(0.00)	0.78	(0.00)	1.73	(0.02)
Latvia	0.13	(0.01)	0.15	(0.02)	0.11	(0.02)	0.03	(0.02)	-0.88	(0.02)	-0.09	(0.00)	0.39	(0.00)	1.10	(0.01)
Liechtenstein	-0.02	(0.05)	0.10	(0.08)	-0.15	(0.07)	0.25	(0.11)	-1.28	(0.05)	-0.25	(0.02)	0.31	(0.02)	1.14	(0.05)
Lithuania	0.18	(0.01)	0.18	(0.02)	0.18	(0.02)	0.00	(0.02)	-0.85	(0.01)	-0.07	(0.00)	0.45	(0.00)	1.18	(0.01)
Macao-China	-0.09	(0.01)	-0.04	(0.02)	-0.13	(0.01)	0.09	(0.02)	-1.17	(0.01)	-0.27	(0.00)	0.16	(0.00)	0.94	(0.01)
Montenegro	0.53	(0.02)	0.56	(0.03)	0.50	(0.02)	0.06	(0.03)	-0.71	(0.02)	0.24	(0.00)	0.79	(0.00)	1.79	(0.03)
Panama	0.49	(0.02)	0.55	(0.04)	0.44	(0.03)	0.10	(0.06)	-0.77	(0.03)	0.22	(0.01)	0.80	(0.01)	1.72	(0.02)
Peru	0.44	(0.02)	0.44	(0.02)	0.45	(0.02)	-0.01	(0.02)	-0.68	(0.02)	0.18	(0.00)	0.70	(0.00)	1.57	(0.02)
Qatar	0.64	(0.01)	0.62	(0.02)	0.66	(0.01)	-0.05	(0.02)	-0.61	(0.01)	0.32	(0.00)	0.89	(0.00)	1.95	(0.01)
Romania	0.32	(0.02)	0.26	(0.02)	0.38	(0.03)	-0.12	(0.03)	-0.83	(0.03)	0.07	(0.01)	0.60	(0.00)	1.44	(0.02)
Russian Federation	0.06	(0.02)	0.10	(0.02)	0.02	(0.02)	0.08	(0.03)	-1.12	(0.02)	-0.15	(0.00)	0.34	(0.00)	1.17	(0.02)
Serbia	0.44	(0.02)	0.49	(0.02)	0.40	(0.02)	0.09	(0.03)	-0.79	(0.03)	0.16	(0.00)	0.72	(0.00)	1.67	(0.02)
Shanghai-China	0.16	(0.01)	0.22	(0.02)	0.09	(0.02)	0.13	(0.02)	-0.81	(0.02)	-0.11	(0.00)	0.38	(0.00)	1.16	(0.02)
Singapore	0.24	(0.02)	0.35	(0.02)	0.12	(0.02)	0.23	(0.03)	-0.86	(0.02)	-0.05	(0.00)	0.51	(0.00)	1.37	(0.02)
Chinese Taipei	0.12	(0.02)	0.12	(0.02)	0.12	(0.02)	0.00	(0.03)	-1.02	(0.02)	-0.13	(0.00)	0.40	(0.00)	1.24	(0.02)
Thailand	0.27	(0.01)	0.24	(0.02)	0.30	(0.02)	-0.06	(0.02)	-0.53	(0.01)	0.04	(0.00)	0.45	(0.01)	1.12	(0.02)
Trinidad and Tobago	0.29	(0.01)	0.27	(0.02)	0.32	(0.02)	-0.05	(0.03)	-0.83	(0.02)	0.00	(0.01)	0.55	(0.01)	1.45	(0.02)
Tunisia	0.53	(0.02)	0.42	(0.03)	0.63	(0.03)	-0.21	(0.03)	-0.58	(0.02)	0.27	(0.00)	0.78	(0.00)	1.67	(0.02)
Uruguay	-0.04	(0.02)	-0.02	(0.03)	-0.06	(0.02)	0.03	(0.04)	-1.46	(0.02)	-0.32	(0.01)	0.34	(0.01)	1.28	(0.01)

Note: Values that are statistically significant are indicated in bold (see Annex A3).
StatLink ᴍᴸᴾ http://dx.doi.org/10.1787/888932343285

[Part 2/2]

Index of elaboration strategies and reading performance, by national quarters of this index

Table III.1.22 *Results based on students' self-reports*

	Bottom quarter Mean score	S.E.	Second quarter Mean score	S.E.	Third quarter Mean score	S.E.	Top quarter Mean score	S.E.	Change in the reading score per unit of this index Effect	S.E.	Increased likelihood of students in the bottom quarter of this index scoring in the bottom quarter of the national reading performance distribution Ratio	S.E.	Explained variance in student performance (r-squared x 100) %	S.E.
OECD														
Australia	**508**	(2.6)	510	(3.0)	523	(2.7)	**527**	(3.1)	**10.0**	(1.07)	**1.2**	(0.05)	1.1	(0.22)
Austria	477	(4.1)	473	(3.9)	473	(4.0)	480	(3.9)	1.9	(1.58)	0.9	(0.06)	0.0	(0.08)
Belgium	513	(2.9)	515	(3.4)	515	(3.6)	508	(4.2)	-0.3	(1.53)	0.9	(0.05)	0.0	(0.02)
Canada	526	(2.0)	522	(2.2)	527	(2.5)	527	(2.2)	2.6	(0.85)	0.9	(0.04)	0.1	(0.06)
Chile	**448**	(3.5)	446	(4.2)	447	(3.6)	**462**	(3.9)	**5.2**	(1.45)	1.0	(0.06)	0.4	(0.23)
Czech Republic	471	(3.3)	474	(3.9)	486	(3.9)	**498**	(3.7)	**12.4**	(1.42)	**1.2**	(0.09)	1.7	(0.40)
Denmark	**490**	(3.3)	489	(3.3)	498	(2.9)	**507**	(3.1)	**8.7**	(1.55)	1.1	(0.08)	1.0	(0.35)
Estonia	496	(4.1)	494	(3.5)	504	(3.8)	**513**	(3.7)	**9.3**	(2.01)	1.0	(0.07)	0.9	(0.41)
Finland	**523**	(3.0)	529	(3.1)	541	(3.5)	**551**	(3.6)	**13.1**	(1.58)	**1.2**	(0.08)	2.1	(0.50)
France	491	(5.2)	496	(4.4)	503	(4.0)	502	(4.5)	7.0	(2.22)	1.1	(0.08)	0.4	(0.25)
Germany	511	(3.4)	497	(3.9)	506	(3.5)	505	(3.9)	0.5	(1.47)	**0.8**	(0.07)	0.0	(0.03)
Greece	**473**	(5.4)	477	(5.5)	487	(5.0)	**495**	(5.0)	**11.7**	(1.64)	1.1	(0.08)	1.6	(0.44)
Hungary	493	(4.1)	498	(4.3)	496	(3.9)	491	(4.9)	0.0	(1.91)	1.0	(0.09)	0.0	(0.03)
Iceland	**492**	(3.4)	491	(3.4)	512	(3.3)	**512**	(3.1)	**10.4**	(1.84)	1.1	(0.10)	1.2	(0.43)
Ireland	**493**	(4.3)	496	(3.9)	497	(3.8)	**506**	(3.7)	**5.9**	(1.67)	1.0	(0.07)	0.4	(0.24)
Israel	**494**	(4.3)	478	(4.7)	477	(4.7)	**464**	(4.9)	**-8.5**	(1.51)	**0.7**	(0.05)	0.7	(0.26)
Italy	**483**	(2.1)	487	(2.1)	488	(2.2)	**491**	(2.1)	**5.3**	(0.95)	1.0	(0.04)	0.3	(0.11)
Japan	**494**	(4.2)	525	(3.6)	520	(5.0)	**543**	(4.2)	**16.8**	(1.47)	**1.5**	(0.07)	3.2	(0.52)
Korea	**512**	(5.0)	528	(4.2)	552	(3.5)	**566**	(3.7)	**24.0**	(2.11)	**1.7**	(0.11)	9.1	(1.33)
Luxembourg	482	(2.4)	468	(4.0)	474	(3.2)	471	(2.8)	-2.3	(1.53)	**0.8**	(0.06)	0.0	(0.06)
Mexico	**420**	(2.3)	422	(2.6)	427	(2.2)	**435**	(2.4)	**6.0**	(0.77)	1.1	(0.05)	0.5	(0.12)
Netherlands	511	(6.5)	510	(6.3)	515	(6.0)	511	(5.6)	2.1	(1.73)	0.9	(0.08)	0.1	(0.08)
New Zealand	526	(3.6)	519	(3.9)	523	(3.8)	523	(4.4)	1.7	(2.04)	**0.8**	(0.07)	0.0	(0.06)
Norway	**485**	(3.4)	499	(3.3)	509	(3.7)	**524**	(4.0)	**16.1**	(1.43)	**1.4**	(0.09)	3.3	(0.56)
Poland	493	(3.7)	495	(4.5)	505	(3.5)	**512**	(3.6)	**7.8**	(1.67)	1.1	(0.10)	0.7	(0.27)
Portugal	**464**	(3.9)	485	(4.0)	497	(3.8)	**513**	(3.5)	**22.3**	(1.68)	**1.6**	(0.10)	4.8	(0.64)
Slovak Republic	**471**	(3.4)	472	(3.7)	481	(4.2)	**489**	(3.9)	**9.5**	(1.80)	1.1	(0.08)	0.9	(0.35)
Slovenia	**482**	(2.4)	477	(3.3)	489	(2.8)	**494**	(3.3)	**4.4**	(1.59)	0.9	(0.06)	0.2	(0.17)
Spain	**469**	(2.8)	483	(2.6)	484	(2.8)	**491**	(2.4)	**9.0**	(1.15)	**1.2**	(0.05)	1.2	(0.29)
Sweden	**488**	(4.2)	492	(4.3)	504	(4.0)	**515**	(4.8)	**12.4**	(1.86)	**1.2**	(0.08)	1.6	(0.50)
Switzerland	503	(2.8)	501	(3.9)	500	(3.7)	501	(3.6)	0.6	(1.51)	0.9	(0.05)	0.0	(0.03)
Turkey	**453**	(4.5)	463	(4.1)	466	(4.1)	**478**	(4.2)	**11.0**	(1.64)	**1.3**	(0.08)	1.3	(0.37)
United Kingdom	494	(3.4)	491	(3.6)	501	(3.5)	498	(3.5)	4.4	(1.43)	1.0	(0.08)	0.2	(0.13)
United States	504	(5.3)	498	(4.2)	502	(4.9)	499	(5.0)	0.2	(1.56)	0.9	(0.06)	0.0	(0.03)
OECD average	**489**	(0.7)	491	(0.7)	498	(0.6)	**503**	(0.7)	**7.1**	(0.27)	**1.1**	(0.01)	1.2	(0.06)
Partners														
Albania	**369**	(5.8)	389	(5.9)	396	(4.8)	**402**	(4.7)	**17.1**	(3.26)	**1.4**	(0.12)	1.9	(0.71)
Argentina	406	(5.4)	395	(5.7)	400	(5.6)	409	(5.7)	2.6	(2.03)	0.9	(0.06)	0.1	(0.10)
Azerbaijan	**350**	(4.3)	364	(4.3)	373	(4.2)	**375**	(4.0)	**9.5**	(1.74)	**1.4**	(0.12)	1.9	(0.71)
Brazil	412	(3.5)	411	(3.0)	412	(3.2)	**421**	(3.9)	3.9	(1.36)	1.0	(0.06)	0.2	(0.11)
Bulgaria	**425**	(7.1)	423	(6.8)	445	(8.0)	**441**	(7.2)	**7.0**	(2.00)	1.1	(0.09)	0.5	(0.29)
Colombia	410	(4.6)	416	(4.0)	417	(4.5)	417	(5.2)	1.5	(1.79)	1.0	(0.08)	0.0	(0.08)
Croatia	478	(4.0)	478	(3.7)	476	(3.6)	471	(3.7)	-2.2	(1.64)	0.9	(0.07)	0.1	(0.08)
Dubai (UAE)	465	(3.0)	463	(2.9)	457	(2.8)	457	(3.1)	-3.7	(1.72)	0.9	(0.06)	0.1	(0.10)
Hong Kong-China	**527**	(3.2)	523	(3.3)	544	(3.0)	**540**	(3.1)	**9.2**	(1.38)	**1.2**	(0.08)	1.0	(0.30)
Indonesia	391	(4.0)	400	(3.5)	408	(4.3)	**411**	(5.1)	**12.3**	(1.92)	**1.3**	(0.09)	1.6	(0.48)
Jordan	**373**	(4.5)	409	(4.0)	418	(3.4)	**429**	(3.6)	**21.7**	(1.39)	**2.0**	(0.10)	6.2	(0.76)
Kazakhstan	**404**	(4.8)	388	(3.8)	386	(3.8)	**386**	(4.0)	**-7.8**	(2.05)	**0.8**	(0.07)	0.6	(0.32)
Kyrgyzstan	309	(4.9)	323	(4.8)	319	(3.9)	321	(4.3)	2.6	(2.06)	**1.3**	(0.08)	0.1	(0.10)
Latvia	**482**	(4.2)	478	(3.9)	486	(3.9)	**491**	(4.1)	**5.3**	(2.16)	1.1	(0.13)	0.3	(0.24)
Liechtenstein	499	(8.7)	500	(8.9)	493	(9.5)	507	(9.0)	2.6	(4.69)	1.1	(0.29)	0.1	(0.48)
Lithuania	467	(3.5)	463	(3.2)	472	(3.5)	474	(3.7)	4.3	(1.73)	1.0	(0.06)	0.2	(0.14)
Macao-China	**470**	(2.0)	479	(2.0)	492	(2.0)	**505**	(1.8)	**16.2**	(1.18)	**1.4**	(0.08)	3.4	(0.48)
Montenegro	406	(2.7)	412	(2.6)	413	(3.4)	407	(4.6)	-0.6	(1.98)	1.0	(0.06)	0.0	(0.05)
Panama	377	(7.8)	382	(7.1)	377	(7.6)	378	(7.1)	-1.2	(2.32)	1.1	(0.13)	0.0	(0.07)
Peru	371	(5.1)	374	(4.1)	371	(4.2)	370	(5.2)	-2.8	(1.99)	1.0	(0.06)	0.1	(0.10)
Qatar	370	(2.7)	378	(2.6)	374	(2.1)	**378**	(2.1)	**2.0**	(1.29)	**1.2**	(0.05)	0.0	(0.04)
Romania	416	(5.1)	424	(5.1)	431	(5.2)	**431**	(4.7)	**7.4**	(1.82)	**1.3**	(0.10)	0.6	(0.32)
Russian Federation	459	(4.1)	457	(4.1)	460	(4.0)	468	(4.4)	4.0	(1.81)	1.0	(0.09)	0.2	(0.16)
Serbia	436	(3.0)	444	(3.4)	445	(3.0)	448	(3.4)	2.7	(1.36)	**1.2**	(0.08)	0.1	(0.11)
Shanghai-China	**544**	(2.9)	549	(3.6)	562	(3.1)	**570**	(3.5)	**14.8**	(1.68)	**1.3**	(0.11)	2.3	(0.53)
Singapore	526	(2.9)	526	(3.0)	525	(2.6)	528	(2.7)	0.7	(1.58)	0.9	(0.07)	0.0	(0.03)
Chinese Taipei	**460**	(4.0)	483	(3.6)	516	(2.9)	**524**	(3.5)	**28.3**	(1.75)	**2.1**	(0.13)	9.9	(1.02)
Thailand	**404**	(3.4)	419	(3.2)	424	(3.1)	**439**	(3.6)	**18.4**	(1.98)	**1.5**	(0.10)	3.1	(0.64)
Trinidad and Tobago	424	(4.0)	413	(3.0)	419	(3.7)	427	(3.9)	2.9	(2.12)	1.0	(0.08)	0.1	(0.09)
Tunisia	**392**	(3.6)	397	(3.4)	406	(3.6)	**422**	(4.1)	**13.4**	(1.54)	**1.3**	(0.08)	2.1	(0.47)
Uruguay	427	(3.5)	430	(3.6)	429	(3.9)	429	(3.8)	1.6	(1.42)	1.0	(0.08)	0.0	(0.06)

Note: Values that are statistically significant are indicated in bold (see Annex A3).
StatLink ᗏᔒᔎ http://dx.doi.org/10.1787/888932343285

[Part 1/1]
Proportion of students with low levels of elaboration strategies, by reading proficiency level[1]

Table III.1.23   *Results based on students' self-reports*

		Percentage of students with low levels of elaboration strategies								
		Level 1a or below		Level 2		Level 3		Level 4		Level 5 or above	
		%	S.E.	%	S.E.	%	S.E.	%	S.E.	%	S.E.
OECD	Australia	53.6	(1.5)	53.0	(1.3)	49.0	(1.0)	45.0	(1.1)	41.2	(1.4)
	Austria	47.4	(1.7)	46.6	(1.9)	50.7	(1.7)	46.5	(2.1)	45.5	(3.1)
	Belgium	34.7	(1.7)	42.2	(1.6)	43.0	(1.5)	42.8	(1.1)	36.7	(2.0)
	Canada	51.1	(1.6)	50.9	(1.3)	52.8	(1.0)	51.9	(1.1)	46.6	(1.5)
	Chile	52.4	(1.3)	53.2	(1.5)	50.0	(1.8)	44.7	(2.5)	c	c
	Czech Republic	59.6	(1.8)	53.7	(1.5)	51.1	(1.5)	45.9	(2.0)	38.8	(3.0)
	Denmark	57.3	(2.3)	54.7	(2.1)	51.5	(1.6)	45.6	(2.2)	c	c
	Estonia	57.7	(2.8)	54.5	(1.8)	52.8	(1.9)	50.0	(2.3)	38.1	(3.6)
	Finland	55.5	(3.4)	55.4	(2.3)	51.3	(1.4)	48.1	(1.7)	36.2	(2.0)
	France	52.5	(2.4)	50.7	(2.2)	50.7	(1.8)	46.5	(1.8)	46.9	(2.8)
	Germany	52.5	(2.1)	53.4	(1.7)	52.6	(1.7)	53.3	(1.8)	46.8	(3.1)
	Greece	58.4	(2.2)	56.9	(1.6)	52.4	(1.6)	48.7	(2.4)	43.1	(3.6)
	Hungary	47.6	(2.5)	46.6	(2.1)	50.5	(1.5)	47.4	(1.7)	45.2	(3.7)
	Iceland	53.8	(2.2)	49.6	(2.2)	45.4	(1.6)	39.3	(2.1)	35.1	(3.6)
	Ireland	50.9	(2.7)	53.5	(1.9)	51.3	(1.8)	50.7	(2.4)	c	c
	Israel	46.2	(1.8)	50.6	(2.1)	56.4	(1.8)	57.3	(2.1)	55.5	(2.7)
	Italy	44.3	(1.0)	46.5	(0.9)	47.0	(0.9)	42.9	(1.1)	34.7	(1.8)
	Japan	52.0	(1.8)	50.5	(1.8)	48.7	(1.5)	40.3	(1.4)	32.2	(1.8)
	Korea	79.1	(4.5)	66.3	(2.3)	54.6	(1.5)	43.6	(1.3)	33.4	(2.3)
	Luxembourg	40.5	(1.8)	43.0	(2.1)	43.5	(1.5)	43.7	(1.8)	40.3	(3.5)
	Mexico	51.0	(0.7)	48.6	(0.8)	44.4	(1.1)	38.0	(1.8)	c	c
	Netherlands	50.6	(2.8)	53.8	(2.2)	55.2	(1.6)	53.1	(1.9)	43.1	(3.0)
	New Zealand	42.0	(2.1)	43.4	(1.9)	49.4	(1.7)	47.2	(2.0)	39.9	(2.4)
	Norway	54.5	(2.2)	52.5	(2.0)	45.6	(1.8)	40.0	(2.4)	29.0	(3.8)
	Poland	53.2	(2.6)	47.5	(2.3)	46.1	(1.6)	43.3	(1.6)	38.8	(2.7)
	Portugal	68.1	(1.8)	59.5	(1.7)	52.5	(1.3)	44.2	(1.5)	40.0	(3.6)
	Slovak Republic	47.0	(1.9)	47.3	(1.7)	44.1	(1.7)	37.5	(1.9)	33.9	(4.2)
	Slovenia	50.4	(1.5)	51.0	(1.6)	49.3	(1.9)	43.4	(2.3)	c	c
	Spain	49.6	(1.5)	48.7	(1.3)	45.3	(1.2)	41.1	(1.5)	31.9	(2.7)
	Sweden	52.0	(2.3)	51.0	(2.0)	47.6	(1.5)	43.5	(2.6)	33.8	(3.2)
	Switzerland	50.3	(1.7)	53.8	(1.6)	56.0	(1.4)	54.7	(2.0)	48.1	(3.2)
	Turkey	58.1	(1.5)	52.3	(1.4)	48.2	(1.7)	47.3	(3.1)	c	c
	United Kingdom	46.0	(1.8)	44.8	(1.8)	44.8	(1.6)	42.0	(2.5)	38.8	(2.7)
	United States	47.3	(1.9)	48.6	(2.0)	48.1	(1.6)	48.3	(1.8)	47.4	(3.0)
	OECD average	52.0	(0.4)	51.0	(0.3)	49.5	(0.3)	45.8	(0.3)	40.0	(0.6)
Partners	Albania	52.0	(1.7)	44.8	(2.2)	42.9	(2.6)	43.9	(4.8)	c	c
	Argentina	50.4	(1.5)	50.6	(2.1)	50.6	(2.3)	45.1	(3.5)	c	c
	Azerbaijan	51.9	(1.3)	41.7	(2.1)	40.6	(4.1)	52.5	(15.2)	c	c
	Brazil	47.6	(1.0)	47.9	(1.3)	46.2	(2.0)	43.1	(2.4)	35.1	(5.1)
	Bulgaria	53.6	(1.4)	50.2	(1.8)	47.3	(2.0)	44.0	(2.8)	c	c
	Colombia	49.2	(1.6)	49.8	(1.9)	45.5	(2.3)	40.6	(3.3)	c	c
	Croatia	44.0	(1.7)	46.1	(1.4)	48.1	(1.5)	48.1	(2.3)	c	c
	Dubai (UAE)	46.9	(1.3)	47.9	(2.0)	49.2	(1.9)	52.5	(2.7)	53.8	(4.2)
	Hong Kong-China	58.5	(2.7)	51.6	(2.1)	46.6	(1.6)	43.1	(1.7)	38.3	(2.5)
	Indonesia	49.7	(1.3)	43.3	(1.8)	33.3	(2.8)	38.5	(8.2)	c	c
	Jordan	61.5	(1.0)	49.5	(1.3)	46.1	(2.2)	39.9	(4.5)	c	c
	Kazakhstan	45.0	(1.3)	49.6	(1.8)	55.5	(2.8)	51.3	(5.5)	c	c
	Kyrgyzstan	46.8	(1.4)	50.5	(2.8)	53.5	(4.2)	55.0	(10.2)	c	c
	Latvia	55.4	(2.9)	52.3	(2.0)	50.2	(1.8)	47.6	(3.2)	c	c
	Liechtenstein	38.6	(7.2)	45.8	(7.7)	40.1	(6.5)	47.8	(7.1)	c	c
	Lithuania	51.8	(2.0)	51.1	(1.8)	48.8	(1.7)	46.3	(2.1)	c	c
	Macao-China	61.1	(1.7)	52.0	(1.2)	45.4	(1.4)	37.2	(1.9)	33.5	(5.0)
	Montenegro	47.6	(1.6)	48.9	(1.7)	48.0	(2.1)	42.5	(4.2)	c	c
	Panama	46.8	(1.5)	47.7	(3.0)	50.0	(4.6)	53.7	(6.0)	c	c
	Peru	51.3	(1.1)	54.3	(1.7)	51.9	(2.2)	50.2	(6.1)	c	c
	Qatar	54.7	(0.7)	52.4	(1.3)	56.5	(1.8)	60.1	(2.7)	62.6	(4.4)
	Romania	45.0	(1.5)	41.2	(1.5)	41.1	(2.3)	37.6	(4.2)	c	c
	Russian Federation	57.1	(2.3)	55.4	(2.0)	53.8	(1.9)	51.5	(1.9)	c	c
	Serbia	52.7	(1.4)	51.7	(1.3)	49.0	(1.6)	45.3	(3.0)	c	c
	Shanghai-China	64.5	(3.2)	59.2	(2.5)	56.1	(1.8)	51.1	(1.8)	43.4	(1.9)
	Singapore	47.0	(2.0)	46.9	(1.8)	49.7	(1.5)	48.4	(1.5)	46.3	(1.8)
	Chinese Taipei	76.4	(1.5)	59.3	(1.6)	47.8	(1.7)	38.3	(2.1)	29.7	(4.0)
	Thailand	53.0	(1.4)	42.6	(1.3)	37.1	(1.9)	32.8	(5.8)	c	c
	Trinidad and Tobago	46.7	(1.4)	45.8	(1.8)	46.3	(2.3)	47.0	(3.4)	c	c
	Tunisia	51.9	(1.2)	44.7	(1.6)	41.7	(2.3)	33.6	(4.5)	c	c
	Uruguay	44.8	(1.2)	45.0	(1.6)	46.0	(1.7)	42.9	(2.8)	c	c

1. Students who reported levels of diversity of reading below their country average.
StatLink ⧉ http://dx.doi.org/10.1787/888932343285

[Part 1/1]

Table III.1.24 Unadjusted and adjusted score point differences associated with reading different types of materials

Results based on students' self-reports

		Students who read either several times a month or several times a week:																			
		Unadjusted score point differences										Adjusted score point differences[1]									
		Magazines		Comic books		Fiction		Non-fiction books		Newspapers		Magazines		Comic books		Fiction		Non-fiction books		Newspapers	
		Score dif.	S.E.	Score dif.	S.E.	Score dif.	S.E.	Score dif.	S.E.	Score dif.	S.E.	Score dif.	S.E.	Score dif.	S.E.	Score dif.	S.E.	Score dif.	S.E.	Score dif.	S.E.
OECD	Australia	**-13.8**	(2.0)	0.6	(4.1)	**75.6**	(2.3)	**34.0**	(3.0)	**12.3**	(2.1)	**-16.7**	(1.7)	**4.6**	(3.5)	**58.1**	(2.0)	**22.3**	2.7	**10.6**	(1.9)
	Austria	**7.4**	(3.6)	**-20.4**	(4.4)	**73.6**	(4.3)	8.7	(4.8)	**21.2**	(4.3)	-0.9	(3.3)	**-8.7**	(4.2)	**56.3**	(3.4)	**11.5**	4.4	**15.9**	(4.1)
	Belgium	**31.2**	(3.6)	**24.3**	(2.8)	**62.6**	(3.5)	**10.6**	(4.6)	**14.7**	(3.2)	**15.5**	(3.1)	**17.8**	(2.6)	**46.3**	(2.8)	**8.7**	3.6	**12.7**	(2.8)
	Canada	**5.0**	(1.9)	1.0	(2.6)	**55.9**	(1.8)	**16.6**	(2.6)	**10.0**	(2.2)	**-6.7**	(1.8)	**6.3**	(2.6)	**43.5**	(1.7)	**10.4**	2.3	**8.2**	(2.1)
	Chile	**24.6**	(2.9)	**-7.2**	(3.0)	**15.9**	(2.7)	**29.2**	(3.2)	**24.8**	(3.1)	**13.5**	(2.8)	**-2.8**	(2.6)	**9.8**	(2.9)	**21.1**	2.7	**16.1**	(2.8)
	Czech Republic	**9.2**	(3.1)	1.7	(5.0)	**70.7**	(4.1)	**25.8**	(3.8)	**7.8**	(3.2)	1.9	(2.9)	**5.9**	(4.1)	**49.8**	(3.4)	**18.1**	3.7	**8.8**	(3.0)
	Denmark	**19.7**	(3.1)	**12.8**	(3.3)	**41.3**	(2.8)	**23.9**	(2.6)	**13.6**	(2.8)	**8.7**	(2.8)	**17.5**	(3.0)	**30.2**	(2.7)	**17.3**	2.4	**14.5**	(2.6)
	Estonia	**17.8**	(3.5)	**-30.0**	(4.5)	**37.6**	(3.3)	**27.8**	(3.2)	**21.5**	(4.2)	5.8	(3.1)	**-20.2**	(4.1)	**27.9**	(2.9)	**23.4**	2.8	**15.4**	(3.6)
	Finland	**39.8**	(3.4)	**10.1**	(3.0)	**73.2**	(2.9)	**26.2**	(3.9)	**17.5**	(2.9)	**21.6**	(3.2)	**18.8**	(2.7)	**53.8**	(2.8)	**30.0**	3.6	**15.5**	(2.8)
	France	**20.2**	(3.6)	**14.1**	(4.3)	**72.3**	(4.8)	-2.4	(5.9)	**13.5**	(4.2)	**5.3**	(3.3)	**15.7**	(4.1)	**50.8**	(4.5)	2.2	5.3	**13.6**	(3.9)
	Germany	3.8	(2.9)	-6.8	(5.2)	**68.4**	(3.2)	5.8	(4.8)	**15.2**	(3.7)	0.2	(2.6)	**6.4**	(4.2)	**45.8**	(2.8)	**6.8**	4.4	**8.9**	(3.4)
	Greece	**17.2**	(4.2)	-0.1	(4.1)	**50.3**	(4.7)	**22.9**	(6.7)	2.6	(3.6)	5.7	(3.6)	**4.3**	(3.7)	**29.0**	(3.7)	5.1	5.6	**10.3**	(3.2)
	Hungary	**42.1**	(4.5)	**-17.3**	(3.8)	**35.6**	(4.1)	**14.3**	(3.6)	**15.8**	(4.6)	**27.3**	(3.1)	**-8.7**	(2.9)	**18.9**	(3.2)	**9.4**	3.0	**10.9**	(3.6)
	Iceland	**23.8**	(2.8)	**20.9**	(3.3)	**65.6**	(3.3)	**32.3**	(3.7)	**55.4**	(4.5)	**12.3**	(2.9)	**24.4**	(3.5)	**54.1**	(3.2)	**25.6**	3.8	**41.4**	(4.6)
	Ireland	0.3	(4.1)	**-24.1**	(6.3)	**62.8**	(3.5)	**32.3**	(5.1)	**-10.3**	(3.6)	-7.0	(3.5)	**-9.6**	(5.8)	**47.4**	(3.1)	**23.1**	4.7	-2.3	(3.0)
	Israel	**24.3**	(4.1)	**-25.2**	(5.1)	**30.3**	(4.4)	**9.0**	(4.0)	**46.1**	(4.6)	**11.0**	(3.6)	**-24.6**	(4.9)	**17.1**	(4.1)	4.4	3.6	**32.0**	(4.4)
	Italy	**9.2**	(1.7)	**22.6**	(2.6)	**47.2**	(2.4)	**12.4**	(4.2)	**18.4**	(1.8)	**0.3**	(1.4)	**22.7**	(2.4)	**29.5**	(1.7)	**3.7**	4.0	**13.5**	(1.5)
	Japan	-4.7	(3.5)	6.6	(3.6)	**46.9**	(3.7)	**23.8**	(4.0)	**24.2**	(3.2)	**-12.4**	(3.2)	**11.8**	(3.1)	**37.2**	(3.1)	**14.0**	4.2	**20.9**	(2.9)
	Korea	-1.0	(3.3)	**-9.4**	(3.9)	**30.6**	(2.8)	**31.0**	(3.5)	**28.8**	(3.2)	**-12.4**	(3.0)	**-0.9**	(3.4)	**20.8**	(2.4)	**21.1**	3.0	**17.4**	(2.7)
	Luxembourg	**14.4**	(3.9)	-4.7	(3.9)	**74.3**	(3.1)	**16.7**	(3.8)	2.7	(4.0)	4.0	(3.7)	**-0.5**	(3.8)	**47.6**	(3.0)	**9.1**	3.4	**9.2**	(3.8)
	Mexico	**15.7**	(1.8)	**-12.4**	(1.5)	**-5.1**	(1.6)	**19.1**	(2.1)	**5.9**	(1.5)	**3.3**	(1.4)	**-10.0**	(1.5)	**-5.0**	(1.4)	**14.3**	1.9	**3.0**	(1.4)
	Netherlands	**42.5**	(3.6)	**13.9**	(3.6)	**51.9**	(4.8)	**40.2**	(4.3)	**29.5**	(4.3)	**28.4**	(3.2)	**14.7**	(3.7)	**41.7**	(4.6)	**32.6**	4.1	**29.2**	(3.6)
	New Zealand	**-15.3**	(3.6)	**-20.0**	(5.9)	**64.4**	(3.6)	**20.5**	(3.5)	**7.5**	(3.2)	**-19.6**	(2.8)	**-5.8**	(4.8)	**46.3**	(3.1)	**13.0**	3.2	4.6	(3.0)
	Norway	**16.3**	(2.9)	**22.9**	(2.9)	**62.7**	(3.4)	3.5	(3.3)	**23.4**	(3.6)	**-0.6**	(2.7)	**27.2**	(2.7)	**47.7**	(2.8)	**0.9**	2.9	**18.4**	(3.2)
	Poland	**32.1**	(3.2)	**-17.6**	(4.7)	**54.0**	(3.7)	**36.3**	(3.7)	**15.5**	(3.3)	**17.5**	(2.8)	**-10.5**	(3.8)	**30.8**	(3.1)	**20.3**	3.4	**10.1**	(3.0)
	Portugal	-2.1	(2.8)	-4.1	(2.8)	**39.1**	(3.1)	**33.6**	(4.4)	**-7.8**	(2.7)	**-7.8**	(2.6)	**-0.8**	(2.4)	**20.3**	(2.9)	**17.0**	3.7	2.4	(2.5)
	Slovak Republic	**38.4**	(5.0)	3.9	(5.0)	**58.1**	(4.9)	**32.6**	(3.7)	**11.3**	(3.8)	**19.3**	(4.0)	**-0.4**	(4.5)	**38.8**	(4.0)	**25.2**	3.3	**6.7**	(3.2)
	Slovenia	**20.5**	(3.3)	**-14.4**	(4.4)	**62.3**	(4.4)	**48.7**	(3.5)	**8.2**	(3.2)	5.0	(2.9)	**-7.0**	(4.0)	**39.7**	(3.7)	**28.6**	3.4	**13.0**	(2.8)
	Spain	**5.0**	(1.9)	3.9	(3.4)	**53.7**	(2.0)	**51.2**	(2.6)	**9.0**	(2.2)	**-3.8**	(1.8)	**10.0**	(3.2)	**40.0**	(2.2)	**34.8**	2.1	**9.6**	(2.2)
	Sweden	**33.3**	(3.1)	**12.6**	(3.5)	**75.7**	(3.1)	**47.0**	(5.2)	**42.9**	(3.6)	**18.3**	(3.0)	**17.2**	(3.2)	**57.2**	(3.0)	**35.5**	5.1	**32.7**	(3.3)
	Switzerland	**20.5**	(2.5)	**15.3**	(2.9)	**69.7**	(2.9)	6.4	(3.9)	**24.5**	(3.3)	**9.9**	(2.5)	**14.3**	(2.9)	**52.2**	(2.7)	**10.3**	3.5	**22.4**	(3.1)
	Turkey	-2.4	(2.8)	**-18.2**	(3.5)	**6.9**	(2.7)	**-21.0**	(3.0)	**21.0**	(4.6)	**-16.0**	(2.5)	**-17.8**	(2.9)	-0.5	(2.5)	**-13.7**	2.6	**9.3**	(4.4)
	United Kingdom	-2.1	(3.0)	**-22.5**	(4.9)	**66.6**	(3.1)	**29.0**	(3.8)	-2.1	(2.9)	**-7.6**	(2.6)	**-8.9**	(4.9)	**54.6**	(2.7)	**23.2**	3.2	3.7	(2.8)
	United States	1.8	(2.7)	**-15.3**	(5.8)	**48.9**	(3.7)	-4.3	(4.4)	4.0	(3.6)	**-6.5**	(2.5)	**-7.4**	(5.3)	**35.4**	(2.9)	-5.3	4.1	1.5	(3.1)
	OECD average	**6.8**	(0.9)	2.1	(1.4)	**42.2**	(1.1)	**11.7**	(1.5)	**9.0**	(1.2)	**-4.2**	(0.8)	**8.7**	(1.2)	**32.3**	(0.9)	**8.3**	1.4	**8.8**	(0.9)
Partners	Albania	**14.0**	(4.4)	**-22.6**	(4.6)	**24.9**	(4.5)	**17.3**	(6.0)	-2.9	(4.1)	-5.8	(3.6)	**-20.1**	(4.1)	**4.0**	(4.1)	6.9	5.3	-1.5	(3.1)
	Argentina	**27.6**	(3.9)	-6.1	(5.1)	4.3	(4.9)	2.9	(4.9)	**10.1**	(4.1)	**10.3**	(3.2)	-3.0	(4.1)	2.6	(3.8)	**2.8**	3.6	**5.8**	(3.4)
	Azerbaijan	**14.7**	(3.2)	1.6	(2.9)	**12.5**	(3.4)	-1.3	(3.9)	**14.4**	(3.1)	4.3	(2.9)	**0.3**	(2.7)	4.3	(3.3)	**-6.0**	3.7	**10.0**	(3.1)
	Brazil	**24.5**	(2.7)	**-18.3**	(2.7)	1.7	(2.7)	**12.4**	(3.3)	**14.1**	(3.1)	**10.4**	(2.5)	**-13.5**	(2.3)	**-4.8**	(2.4)	**8.1**	3.0	**6.8**	(2.8)
	Bulgaria	**44.4**	(4.9)	**-30.7**	(6.0)	**41.8**	(6.1)	**36.3**	(4.8)	**30.2**	(4.6)	**12.7**	(3.9)	**-17.0**	(4.6)	**18.6**	(4.7)	**19.0**	4.2	**14.5**	(4.1)
	Colombia	0.4	(3.2)	3.9	(3.2)	**-16.3**	(3.8)	7.1	(4.4)	-2.2	(3.9)	-3.4	(3.0)	5.1	(2.9)	**-14.9**	(3.4)	5.6	3.5	-1.5	(3.1)
	Croatia	**19.0**	(3.6)	**-12.9**	(3.9)	**49.8**	(3.7)	**54.0**	(4.2)	**22.8**	(5.0)	**6.2**	(3.0)	**-6.9**	(3.8)	**29.5**	(3.5)	**33.6**	3.7	**17.8**	(3.9)
	Dubai (UAE)	**18.2**	(3.3)	**-21.3**	(2.7)	**47.6**	(3.4)	**7.9**	(3.5)	**18.2**	(4.0)	3.8	(3.0)	**-12.3**	(2.6)	**23.6**	(3.1)	**1.7**	3.1	**20.4**	(3.3)
	Hong Kong-China	**-11.8**	(2.9)	**-6.7**	(2.6)	**35.7**	(2.5)	**24.9**	(3.0)	**27.0**	(4.4)	**-18.7**	(2.7)	**-2.4**	(2.6)	**25.7**	(2.3)	**20.2**	2.9	**18.5**	(4.0)
	Indonesia	**18.4**	(3.3)	**9.4**	(2.5)	**13.7**	(2.5)	**26.7**	(2.4)	**14.9**	(2.9)	**8.2**	(2.9)	**3.9**	(2.0)	**4.3**	(2.4)	**17.8**	2.1	**10.1**	(2.3)
	Jordan	**23.7**	(2.9)	**21.4**	(2.9)	-4.4	(3.0)	-3.4	(3.0)	**30.9**	(2.9)	**8.0**	(2.8)	**8.8**	(2.8)	**-7.2**	(2.8)	**-4.0**	2.7	**22.9**	(2.7)
	Kazakhstan	**9.6**	(4.0)	**-32.6**	(4.0)	-0.3	(3.7)	**-24.9**	(3.6)	-6.1	(5.4)	-4.1	(3.2)	**-32.8**	(3.6)	**-9.6**	(3.2)	**-26.0**	3.2	**-9.3**	(4.4)
	Kyrgyzstan	**25.4**	(3.7)	**-17.5**	(4.3)	**13.5**	(3.9)	**6.6**	(3.2)	**32.6**	(4.2)	2.2	(3.7)	**-19.3**	(3.5)	**-0.4**	(3.3)	**-0.7**	2.8	**15.8**	(3.7)
	Latvia	**24.9**	(3.7)	**-28.8**	(5.3)	**22.9**	(3.5)	**24.2**	(3.2)	**14.1**	(3.3)	**9.1**	(2.9)	**-20.7**	(5.3)	**12.1**	(3.2)	**10.4**	2.8	**10.4**	(3.1)
	Liechtenstein	12.2	(11.3)	-4.0	(12.8)	**58.8**	(9.6)	8.9	(14.9)	**29.0**	(9.6)	3.5	(12.0)	**-2.8**	(12.6)	**49.5**	(9.6)	**11.5**	15.5	**29.4**	(10.6)
	Lithuania	**34.3**	(3.5)	**-29.9**	(3.2)	**51.3**	(2.7)	**40.0**	(3.2)	**13.5**	(3.6)	**15.1**	(3.3)	**-16.1**	(2.7)	**27.4**	(2.4)	**23.6**	2.8	**9.9**	(2.9)
	Macao-China	-1.4	(2.3)	**5.0**	(1.9)	**31.8**	(2.4)	**25.6**	(2.1)	**27.6**	(2.0)	**-6.4**	(2.4)	**8.1**	(1.9)	**23.7**	(2.2)	**21.3**	1.9	**22.1**	(2.0)
	Montenegro	**41.1**	(3.6)	**-11.9**	(3.9)	**29.6**	(3.5)	**19.5**	(3.5)	**21.2**	(3.8)	**22.5**	(3.7)	**-9.9**	(3.8)	**18.8**	(3.2)	**14.1**	3.4	**14.7**	(3.3)
	Panama	**31.9**	(5.2)	**-14.8**	(6.5)	4.3	(5.2)	3.4	(6.5)	0.3	(8.8)	**16.9**	(5.3)	-8.7	(4.7)	0.6	(4.6)	3.2	5.4	**12.4**	(6.4)
	Peru	**32.4**	(3.1)	**-14.8**	(3.1)	-1.2	(3.4)	**-11.7**	(3.3)	**41.1**	(3.9)	**11.7**	(2.7)	**-9.7**	(2.5)	-3.0	(2.8)	**-5.0**	2.6	**18.4**	(3.5)
	Qatar	**18.3**	(2.6)	4.5	(2.3)	**31.4**	(2.6)	4.8	(2.8)	**12.2**	(2.8)	**8.4**	(2.5)	**-0.7**	(2.2)	**17.4**	(2.4)	**1.1**	2.4	**15.0**	(2.3)
	Romania	**34.3**	(4.0)	**-15.9**	(4.0)	**16.6**	(3.8)	**8.4**	(3.3)	8.6	(5.1)	**15.1**	(3.1)	**-16.6**	(3.5)	**5.9**	(3.2)	0.7	3.3	**3.6**	(4.0)
	Russian Federation	**7.2**	(3.2)	**-31.8**	(4.3)	**38.1**	(3.6)	**16.0**	(3.4)	-3.6	(4.2)	-3.4	(2.9)	**-21.2**	(4.0)	**26.1**	(2.8)	**8.9**	2.7	-0.5	(3.2)
	Serbia	**26.3**	(3.3)	**-23.1**	(3.8)	**23.9**	(3.3)	**29.3**	(4.8)	**16.2**	(3.4)	**10.4**	(3.2)	**-19.1**	(3.8)	**12.9**	(3.2)	**20.3**	4.3	**11.6**	(3.2)
	Shanghai-China	**16.4**	(2.3)	**-19.0**	(2.8)	**14.8**	(2.6)	**7.2**	(2.7)	**34.3**	(3.9)	**7.0**	(1.9)	**-13.2**	(2.3)	**8.6**	(2.4)	**7.0**	2.6	**24.3**	(3.1)
	Singapore	3.9	(2.7)	4.3	(2.9)	**48.9**	(2.6)	**16.9**	(2.6)	**28.5**	(3.9)	**-6.1**	(2.5)	**6.9**	(2.7)	**31.6**	(2.5)	**6.1**	2.3	**21.2**	(3.8)
	Chinese Taipei	-3.6	(2.8)	0.9	(2.5)	**37.2**	(2.8)	**29.5**	(3.0)	**24.9**	(3.5)	**-8.8**	(2.8)	**1.3**	(2.5)	**24.1**	(2.2)	**18.5**	2.5	**13.1**	(3.1)
	Thailand	**20.8**	(2.5)	**14.9**	(2.1)	**17.8**	(2.4)	**21.7**	(2.3)	**12.7**	(2.9)	**10.1**	(2.1)	**11.4**	(2.1)	**10.5**	(2.2)	**17.3**	2.0	**7.8**	(2.6)
	Trinidad and Tobago	**14.2**	(3.4)	-6.3	(4.2)	**29.7**	(3.5)	**25.8**	(4.1)	**28.5**	(5.7)	1.9	(3.1)	**-2.7**	(4.1)	**22.3**	(3.8)	**17.4**	4.1	**19.8**	(4.5)
	Tunisia	**13.7**	(2.6)	**-19.1**	(2.9)	-4.1	(3.3)	-1.1	(3.8)	**21.9**	(2.9)	0.0	(2.6)	**-18.6**	(2.6)	**-7.3**	(3.1)	**-3.1**	3.4	**14.7**	(3.2)
	Uruguay	**32.4**	(3.0)	**-12.2**	(3.9)	**13.3**	(4.0)	**25.7**	(4.9)	**24.9**	(4.0)	**15.8**	(2.6)	**-2.2**	(3.4)	**5.3**	(3.3)	**13.3**	4.4	**13.9**	(3.3)

Notes: Values that are statistically significant are indicated in bold (see Annex A3).
Comparisons are derived using as the reference group students who do not read for enjoyment any material at least several times a month or several times a week introducing indicators for each material in the same regression.
1. Adjusted models account for gender, PISA index of economic, social and cultural status, immigration status and language spoken at home

StatLink http://dx.doi.org/10.1787/888932343285

[Part 1/2]

Unadjusted and adjusted score point differences associated with reading different types of materials, by gender

Table III.1.25 *Results based on students' self-reports*

		Boys who read either several times a month or several times a week:																			
		Unadjusted score point differences										Adjusted score point differences[1]									
		Magazines		Comic books		Fiction		Non-fiction books		Newspapers		Magazines		Comic books		Fiction		Non-fiction books		Newspapers	
		Score dif.	S.E.	Score dif.	S.E.	Score dif.	S.E.	Score dif.	S.E.	Score dif.	S.E.	Score dif.	S.E.	Score dif.	S.E.	Score dif.	S.E.	Score dif.	S.E.	Score dif.	S.E.
OECD	Australia	**-13.0**	(2.7)	0.5	(5.1)	**76.8**	(3.7)	**49.3**	(4.2)	**12.6**	(3.0)	**-15.5**	(2.5)	-4.1	(4.5)	**60.0**	(3.4)	**32.5**	4.1	**6.8**	(2.9)
	Austria	**11.5**	(4.5)	-3.5	(6.1)	**69.3**	(7.7)	**19.3**	(5.3)	**31.9**	(7.1)	3.6	(4.6)	-2.6	(5.7)	**54.9**	(6.4)	**11.2**	4.7	**18.5**	(6.5)
	Belgium	**36.8**	(3.9)	**39.3**	(3.9)	**68.6**	(5.4)	6.7	(7.3)	**17.6**	(4.6)	**21.9**	(3.6)	**22.9**	(3.6)	**53.1**	(4.7)	8.6	5.1	**10.3**	(3.9)
	Canada	3.8	(2.5)	**7.1**	(3.4)	**52.2**	(2.8)	**31.4**	(3.3)	**13.4**	(2.8)	**-3.5**	(2.4)	6.9	(3.6)	**44.7**	(2.7)	**24.8**	2.9	**7.2**	(2.7)
	Chile	**19.5**	(3.6)	-0.9	(3.9)	**10.1**	(4.2)	**21.1**	(5.3)	**30.8**	(4.3)	**13.2**	(3.5)	-0.7	(3.5)	7.6	(4.2)	**17.5**	4.7	**21.5**	(3.7)
	Czech Republic	**19.7**	(3.8)	**14.8**	(6.3)	**79.7**	(7.9)	**29.6**	(6.2)	**13.8**	(3.9)	**16.1**	(4.1)	**12.5**	(5.5)	**66.5**	(7.2)	**23.4**	5.8	**11.6**	(4.2)
	Denmark	**16.4**	(3.9)	**23.0**	(4.4)	**39.7**	(4.4)	**37.2**	(3.7)	**23.4**	(3.8)	**11.9**	(3.6)	**20.6**	(4.1)	**30.5**	(4.5)	**27.8**	3.7	**17.2**	(3.7)
	Estonia	**19.5**	(4.1)	**-21.5**	(5.3)	**25.4**	(5.0)	**29.0**	(4.0)	**29.2**	(5.1)	**13.7**	(3.5)	**-20.0**	(4.9)	**23.6**	(5.1)	**24.0**	3.7	**19.8**	(4.9)
	Finland	**27.4**	(3.8)	**28.3**	(3.7)	**72.7**	(5.2)	**41.0**	(4.8)	**25.0**	(4.2)	**21.8**	(3.6)	**25.5**	(3.6)	**66.0**	(4.8)	**36.4**	4.6	**20.9**	(4.0)
	France	**26.9**	(5.6)	**34.2**	(6.3)	**75.1**	(7.0)	10.3	(7.1)	**18.8**	(5.5)	**11.4**	(5.1)	**19.5**	(5.7)	**54.9**	(5.9)	6.5	6.8	**16.4**	(5.1)
	Germany	**21.4**	(4.3)	9.5	(5.6)	**71.8**	(4.9)	**22.7**	(6.4)	**26.2**	(5.6)	**14.1**	(3.8)	**10.2**	(4.4)	**53.1**	(4.2)	**14.1**	5.9	**12.4**	(5.2)
	Greece	**21.1**	(5.2)	**13.2**	(5.6)	**46.0**	(7.4)	**21.5**	(9.5)	**15.0**	(4.7)	**12.5**	(5.0)	6.9	(4.8)	**35.5**	(6.7)	5.3	9.2	6.3	(4.6)
	Hungary	**47.9**	(5.4)	-8.7	(5.7)	**35.7**	(6.6)	**26.9**	(5.1)	**19.9**	(5.6)	**34.5**	(4.2)	-2.5	(4.5)	**21.2**	(4.9)	**15.9**	4.3	**15.1**	(4.6)
	Iceland	**25.2**	(4.3)	**29.5**	(5.1)	**62.5**	(5.9)	**36.7**	(6.2)	**61.3**	(6.6)	**20.6**	(4.4)	**27.1**	(5.4)	**57.9**	(6.2)	**35.3**	6.3	**48.3**	(6.9)
	Ireland	6.0	(5.1)	-7.3	(7.9)	**50.5**	(5.9)	**41.6**	(7.3)	0.3	(5.9)	5.0	(4.8)	0.1	(7.2)	**41.0**	(4.8)	**31.7**	6.5	-1.2	(4.8)
	Israel	**20.2**	(5.8)	**-28.4**	(8.1)	**21.8**	(8.4)	11.7	(7.3)	**57.7**	(6.3)	7.6	(5.2)	**-27.4**	(8.2)	**14.4**	(7.0)	8.8	6.8	**46.1**	(6.5)
	Italy	**15.6**	(2.2)	**36.3**	(3.3)	**39.6**	(3.2)	9.9	(7.4)	**30.1**	(2.6)	**9.5**	(1.9)	**24.2**	(2.8)	**32.1**	(2.8)	9.3	5.6	**19.5**	(2.3)
	Japan	-0.2	(5.1)	**18.5**	(7.1)	**51.5**	(3.9)	**18.1**	(5.6)	**29.9**	(4.6)	-6.9	(5.1)	10.7	(5.9)	**42.5**	(3.3)	9.0	6.1	**21.8**	(4.1)
	Korea	2.8	(4.4)	3.4	(5.7)	**37.6**	(3.6)	**45.0**	(5.4)	**32.6**	(4.5)	-7.7	(4.3)	4.1	(5.0)	**31.0**	(3.8)	**35.0**	4.9	**18.3**	(4.4)
	Luxembourg	**24.3**	(4.8)	**11.2**	(5.2)	**77.5**	(6.2)	**34.9**	(4.9)	**23.2**	(5.7)	**14.4**	(4.9)	4.7	(5.2)	**51.5**	(5.9)	**16.5**	4.5	**19.7**	(5.4)
	Mexico	**15.0**	(2.5)	**-5.2**	(2.2)	**-11.3**	(3.0)	**13.1**	(2.9)	**14.5**	(2.5)	**7.5**	(2.2)	**-7.3**	(2.1)	-4.9	(2.5)	**11.1**	2.6	**7.1**	(2.2)
	Netherlands	**49.8**	(5.0)	**28.4**	(4.6)	**66.6**	(7.3)	**28.5**	(7.4)	**39.0**	(6.0)	**39.4**	(5.0)	**21.4**	(4.7)	**57.2**	(7.1)	**24.2**	7.3	**34.4**	(5.5)
	New Zealand	**-16.0**	(5.1)	**-16.0**	(7.2)	**64.1**	(5.1)	**39.0**	(5.2)	4.8	(4.7)	**-17.7**	(4.1)	-11.8	(6.0)	**49.3**	(4.5)	**24.9**	4.5	-1.1	(4.4)
	Norway	**9.9**	(4.0)	**35.3**	(3.9)	**63.9**	(5.5)	**11.9**	(4.1)	**34.3**	(5.6)	5.8	(3.9)	**31.3**	(3.7)	**54.4**	(4.9)	**7.8**	3.9	**26.5**	(5.2)
	Poland	**42.5**	(4.4)	-6.0	(6.6)	**45.1**	(7.5)	**41.8**	(5.9)	**26.9**	(4.9)	**31.6**	(3.9)	-7.5	(5.3)	**34.1**	(5.7)	**28.6**	5.6	**23.3**	(4.6)
	Portugal	-2.0	(4.0)	4.7	(4.0)	**36.8**	(6.1)	**18.3**	(7.1)	5.6	(4.5)	-4.6	(3.7)	1.3	(3.4)	**24.3**	(5.2)	5.9	6.6	3.6	(4.0)
	Slovak Republic	**37.6**	(5.8)	**15.2**	(6.2)	**55.9**	(7.3)	**50.1**	(4.7)	**23.6**	(4.9)	**25.3**	(5.1)	11.4	(6.2)	**40.2**	(6.4)	**38.6**	4.4	**16.3**	(4.6)
	Slovenia	**22.2**	(4.1)	3.5	(5.0)	**49.7**	(7.3)	**53.2**	(6.2)	**21.3**	(4.5)	**14.2**	(3.8)	0.1	(4.7)	**35.5**	(6.1)	**34.1**	5.8	**17.2**	(4.0)
	Spain	**6.7**	(2.6)	**13.3**	(3.6)	**52.0**	(3.1)	**45.4**	(4.3)	**14.8**	(3.3)	-2.3	(2.4)	**11.8**	(3.3)	**42.0**	(2.9)	**33.7**	3.6	4.2	(2.7)
	Sweden	**28.4**	(4.8)	**30.6**	(4.5)	**74.1**	(5.2)	**46.6**	(8.2)	**47.1**	(5.4)	**20.7**	(4.5)	**21.5**	(4.4)	**60.3**	(4.6)	**34.2**	7.9	**35.4**	(4.9)
	Switzerland	**24.8**	(4.0)	**29.2**	(4.0)	**76.9**	(4.2)	**18.8**	(4.8)	**36.3**	(5.2)	**16.5**	(3.9)	**21.2**	(3.7)	**62.6**	(4.3)	**13.4**	4.5	**28.5**	(5.1)
	Turkey	0.2	(3.7)	**-14.8**	(4.4)	**-9.1**	(3.7)	**-16.0**	(4.3)	**32.5**	(6.1)	**-12.6**	(3.5)	**-17.9**	(3.7)	-5.1	(3.4)	**-11.7**	3.6	**17.1**	(5.3)
	United Kingdom	4.6	(3.8)	**-18.0**	(6.4)	**63.8**	(4.7)	**40.4**	(5.3)	3.6	(4.5)	2.5	(3.4)	-8.6	(6.4)	**54.6**	(4.7)	**32.5**	4.6	5.6	(4.3)
	United States	1.3	(4.5)	**-22.3**	(7.4)	**48.8**	(4.8)	9.4	(5.9)	8.2	(4.7)	-5.9	(4.1)	**-17.7**	(6.5)	**36.2**	(4.4)	2.4	5.2	1.7	(4.1)
	OECD average	**9.0**	(1.3)	**7.3**	(2.0)	**39.3**	(1.6)	**18.1**	(2.0)	**13.3**	(1.4)	-0.1	(1.3)	**8.2**	(1.7)	**34.5**	(1.3)	**13.6**	1.7	**9.1**	(1.2)
Partners	Albania	7.8	(6.1)	-8.4	(6.7)	12.5	(6.8)	**20.2**	(8.2)	6.9	(5.3)	**-1.6**	(5.1)	**-14.3**	(6.0)	5.7	(5.6)	13.4	7.2	2.5	(5.0)
	Argentina	**19.6**	(5.9)	-6.5	(6.3)	6.4	(8.5)	9.9	(8.3)	**28.9**	(6.1)	8.8	(4.3)	-3.3	(5.5)	9.1	(6.4)	9.6	6.2	**14.3**	(5.0)
	Azerbaijan	**12.4**	(4.8)	3.0	(4.6)	**13.5**	(4.2)	-0.3	(4.7)	**22.1**	(4.2)	5.8	(4.5)	1.6	(4.0)	**8.4**	(4.0)	-4.9	4.6	**16.5**	(4.3)
	Brazil	**22.2**	(4.4)	**-11.5**	(4.0)	-4.1	(3.8)	2.8	(5.9)	**18.6**	(3.5)	**14.6**	(4.0)	**-8.3**	(3.8)	-0.2	(3.7)	4.3	5.4	**11.3**	(3.4)
	Bulgaria	**35.0**	(6.7)	**-26.4**	(9.0)	**28.4**	(6.8)	**47.8**	(6.5)	**45.3**	(5.8)	**16.6**	(6.1)	**-15.3**	(7.5)	**14.7**	(5.9)	**25.0**	5.4	**23.0**	(4.9)
	Colombia	-0.7	(4.1)	**10.6**	(4.3)	**-18.2**	(5.1)	6.0	(5.7)	-1.1	(4.7)	-1.9	(3.8)	**11.5**	(4.2)	**-14.6**	(4.8)	5.0	4.7	-1.4	(4.0)
	Croatia	**22.6**	(3.7)	5.1	(4.9)	**42.1**	(5.7)	**49.3**	(5.8)	**25.2**	(7.2)	**15.8**	(3.6)	1.2	(4.7)	**32.1**	(5.9)	**34.3**	5.4	**16.7**	(5.7)
	Dubai (UAE)	**22.8**	(5.3)	**-17.9**	(4.6)	**38.3**	(5.0)	**3.8**	(6.0)	**36.3**	(6.1)	5.5	(4.3)	**-12.7**	(4.1)	**18.6**	(4.7)	2.3	5.0	**24.1**	(5.1)
	Hong Kong-China	**-10.3**	(3.9)	-2.6	(3.7)	**31.2**	(3.5)	**29.9**	(3.9)	**29.5**	(6.1)	**-16.2**	(3.9)	-4.4	(3.4)	**24.4**	(3.3)	**23.3**	3.6	**21.1**	(5.3)
	Indonesia	**15.3**	(4.2)	**13.7**	(3.6)	5.8	(3.5)	**23.5**	(3.9)	**18.9**	(4.3)	**9.8**	(3.9)	**8.3**	(3.0)	3.0	(3.5)	**19.1**	3.3	**12.1**	(3.7)
	Jordan	**22.5**	(4.0)	**20.1**	(3.5)	-7.7	(4.3)	**5.0**	(4.2)	**36.2**	(4.4)	**14.0**	(4.3)	**12.9**	(3.7)	**-9.5**	(4.1)	1.6	4.2	**23.9**	(4.0)
	Kazakhstan	8.3	(4.5)	**-34.3**	(4.3)	-4.4	(4.7)	**-22.3**	(4.4)	3.2	(6.3)	-0.2	(4.1)	**-32.9**	(3.9)	**-10.1**	(4.4)	**-24.2**	4.1	-1.1	(5.4)
	Kyrgyzstan	**20.6**	(5.5)	**-23.2**	(5.4)	4.0	(5.3)	**10.0**	(4.8)	**37.0**	(5.4)	4.0	(5.4)	**-21.9**	(4.9)	-3.4	(5.1)	4.0	4.0	**23.7**	(5.1)
	Latvia	**22.6**	(3.9)	**-20.6**	(7.4)	**12.8**	(5.2)	**22.4**	(5.0)	**22.2**	(4.8)	**16.7**	(3.6)	**-17.3**	(7.6)	10.2	(5.5)	**11.5**	4.7	**18.4**	(4.9)
	Liechtenstein	15.1	(14.4)	11.1	(16.1)	**73.0**	(14.8)	21.0	(17.2)	**33.6**	(14.1)	10.0	(15.9)	2.8	(17.2)	**72.8**	(16.5)	16.8	19.8	**41.1**	(16.6)
	Lithuania	**34.5**	(4.2)	**-14.1**	(4.4)	**36.2**	(4.9)	**38.7**	(4.5)	**17.2**	(4.4)	**25.4**	(4.4)	**-8.6**	(4.0)	**29.0**	(4.8)	**31.0**	4.4	**12.4**	(4.2)
	Macao-China	-0.1	(3.1)	**12.3**	(2.9)	**21.2**	(3.8)	**28.6**	(3.2)	**25.9**	(2.8)	-1.5	(3.3)	**10.6**	(2.9)	**22.0**	(3.7)	**23.8**	2.9	**22.8**	(2.8)
	Montenegro	**31.6**	(4.6)	-2.8	(5.5)	**22.0**	(5.1)	**23.2**	(5.4)	**25.2**	(5.2)	**23.3**	(4.9)	-10.1	(5.5)	**18.2**	(4.5)	**19.4**	5.2	**15.3**	(5.0)
	Panama	**24.3**	(6.8)	-2.6	(9.4)	-1.5	(8.1)	0.9	(10.1)	19.1	(11.1)	**16.5**	(5.4)	1.1	(7.1)	0.9	(7.4)	3.6	8.6	**19.9**	(8.4)
	Peru	**25.0**	(4.9)	**-12.0**	(4.1)	**-10.2**	(5.0)	**-13.8**	(4.1)	**39.0**	(4.5)	**11.5**	(3.8)	**-8.2**	(3.7)	-6.4	(4.0)	-4.5	3.6	**15.8**	(4.2)
	Qatar	**25.1**	(3.4)	**13.0**	(3.6)	**25.4**	(3.5)	2.7	(4.0)	**25.8**	(4.1)	**16.3**	(3.5)	5.1	(3.2)	**13.4**	(3.3)	1.3	3.3	**20.0**	(3.8)
	Romania	**28.7**	(4.6)	**-15.9**	(6.9)	3.2	(5.0)	**14.1**	(5.4)	**13.7**	(5.5)	**16.7**	(3.8)	**-15.8**	(6.3)	0.5	(4.7)	6.3	5.5	3.9	(4.6)
	Russian Federation	**9.6**	(4.4)	**-31.6**	(5.4)	**35.2**	(4.5)	**23.6**	(4.8)	4.8	(4.6)	4.9	(4.0)	**-26.3**	(4.7)	**29.6**	(4.0)	**16.7**	4.1	5.4	(4.2)
	Serbia	**24.2**	(4.0)	-8.9	(4.7)	**14.0**	(4.4)	**26.4**	(6.4)	**24.7**	(5.4)	**17.2**	(4.0)	**-13.0**	(4.5)	**10.3**	(4.2)	**20.7**	5.9	**17.2**	(4.9)
	Shanghai-China	**18.0**	(3.4)	**-17.5**	(3.4)	**6.5**	(3.3)	**10.9**	(3.6)	**40.0**	(4.5)	**9.8**	(3.3)	**-17.3**	(3.1)	3.9	(3.0)	4.1	3.5	**29.1**	(3.6)
	Singapore	3.0	(3.9)	**8.9**	(4.1)	**46.8**	(4.0)	**26.3**	(4.2)	**41.7**	(5.6)	-5.1	(3.8)	**8.1**	(3.6)	**34.3**	(4.2)	**13.8**	4.0	**30.7**	(5.8)
	Chinese Taipei	8.3	(4.4)	**12.0**	(3.3)	**36.0**	(4.0)	**35.5**	(4.1)	**38.1**	(5.5)	0.1	(4.2)	3.2	(3.4)	**25.4**	(3.4)	**22.5**	3.5	**23.9**	(4.6)
	Thailand	**20.5**	(3.3)	**19.5**	(2.9)	**8.5**	(3.3)	**23.9**	(3.3)	**18.1**	(4.0)	**17.6**	(3.2)	**19.7**	(2.9)	**9.2**	(3.1)	**21.0**	2.8	**14.1**	(4.1)
	Trinidad and Tobago	**21.3**	(5.6)	7.8	(5.8)	**19.3**	(5.3)	**14.1**	(6.6)	**41.6**	(7.1)	**11.2**	(5.4)	7.5	(5.8)	**19.7**	(5.4)	**13.0**	6.4	**28.4**	(6.7)
	Tunisia	**13.0**	(4.6)	**-22.4**	(3.7)	**-16.9**	(5.0)	8.3	(4.5)	**24.6**	(5.3)	5.1	(4.3)	**-19.6**	(3.7)	**-14.5**	(4.7)	4.9	4.3	**18.0**	(5.4)
	Uruguay	**22.4**	(4.3)	-5.6	(6.3)	0.6	(6.2)	6.9	(9.2)	**35.1**	(5.8)	**17.1**	(3.8)	4.0	(5.2)	3.4	(5.5)	-0.8	7.8	**16.8**	(5.2)

Notes: Values that are statistically significant are indicated in bold (see Annex A3).
Comparisons are derived using as the reference group students who do not read for enjoyment any material at least several times a month or several times a week introducing indicators for each material in the same regression.
1. Adjusted models account for gender, PISA index of economic, social and cultural status, immigration status and language spoken at home.
StatLink http://dx.doi.org/10.1787/888932343285

[Part 2/2]
Unadjusted and adjusted score point differences associated with reading different types of materials, by gender
Table III.1.25 *Results based on students' self-reports*

		Girls who read either several times a month or several times a week:																			
		Unadjusted score point differences										Adjusted score point differences[1]									
		Magazines		Comic books		Fiction		Non-fiction books		Newspapers		Magazines		Comic books		Fiction		Non-fiction books		Newspapers	
		Score dif.	S.E.	Score dif.	S.E.	Score dif.	S.E.	Score dif.	S.E.	Score dif.	S.E.	Score dif.	S.E.	Score dif.	S.E.	Score dif.	S.E.	Score dif.	S.E.	Score dif.	S.E.
OECD	Australia	**-18.6**	(2.8)	**14.4**	(6.0)	**66.8**	(2.7)	**18.4**	(3.5)	**18.1**	(2.8)	**-17.9**	(2.4)	**18.3**	(5.5)	**56.7**	(2.5)	**13.4**	3.3	**13.9**	(2.2)
	Austria	-3.2	(5.0)	**-28.6**	(8.9)	**64.3**	(5.1)	12.5	(7.2)	**14.0**	(6.2)	-5.4	(4.5)	**-18.6**	(7.7)	**57.9**	(4.5)	**10.8**	8.3	**13.3**	(6.4)
	Belgium	**15.8**	(5.0)	**16.1**	(4.6)	**53.9**	(3.6)	**15.0**	(4.9)	**19.6**	(4.0)	**7.0**	(4.8)	**10.5**	(3.9)	**42.2**	(3.3)	**9.0**	4.6	**15.0**	(3.8)
	Canada	-5.0	(2.8)	4.8	(5.0)	**49.2**	(2.3)	0.6	(3.1)	**12.6**	(2.8)	**-9.8**	(2.5)	5.5	(4.8)	**42.7**	(2.2)	**-2.2**	3.0	**9.2**	(2.6)
	Chile	**22.5**	(4.1)	**-11.8**	(3.9)	**13.3**	(3.5)	**30.4**	(4.3)	**18.4**	(3.6)	**13.6**	(3.8)	**-5.7**	(3.5)	**11.6**	(3.4)	**23.7**	3.5	**10.6**	(3.5)
	Czech Republic	**-19.2**	(4.3)	-4.5	(6.0)	**49.7**	(4.6)	**18.9**	(4.9)	7.1	(4.5)	**-16.5**	(3.7)	**-3.9**	(5.4)	**43.4**	(3.7)	**12.6**	4.9	6.3	(4.0)
	Denmark	**10.6**	(5.0)	**13.3**	(5.6)	**35.7**	(4.3)	**11.4**	(4.4)	**11.1**	(4.1)	**4.6**	(4.4)	**12.7**	(5.2)	**30.2**	(4.2)	**7.4**	3.8	**12.5**	(3.8)
	Estonia	1.1	(5.0)	**-23.0**	(7.0)	**31.0**	(4.7)	**25.5**	(4.5)	**15.1**	(5.7)	-5.0	(4.9)	**-20.6**	(6.7)	**30.4**	(4.1)	**22.9**	4.3	11.0	(5.6)
	Finland	**29.0**	(5.3)	**17.0**	(3.8)	**54.2**	(3.9)	**24.2**	(5.6)	**12.2**	(4.3)	**21.2**	(5.0)	**13.5**	(3.4)	**48.3**	(3.7)	**20.5**	4.7	**10.4**	(4.1)
	France	3.7	(4.5)	10.5	(5.5)	**61.6**	(5.3)	-7.8	(8.9)	**15.7**	(5.6)	-2.1	(4.4)	**9.2**	(4.9)	**47.8**	(4.8)	**-4.4**	7.4	**11.0**	(5.1)
	Germany	**-16.1**	(4.3)	-13.2	(10.0)	**56.1**	(4.1)	-4.4	(6.0)	**13.9**	(4.2)	**-13.0**	(3.7)	**-2.5**	(8.9)	**40.9**	(3.7)	**-3.9**	6.1	5.7	(4.1)
	Greece	2.6	(5.7)	-0.7	(5.7)	**36.8**	(4.6)	**16.9**	(8.3)	**24.4**	(4.3)	-2.0	(4.7)	**0.8**	(5.6)	**26.2**	(4.2)	**5.1**	6.8	**15.2**	(4.0)
	Hungary	**28.5**	(6.0)	**-23.1**	(4.6)	**25.3**	(4.9)	2.7	(4.2)	0.3	(6.5)	**19.5**	(4.4)	**-15.5**	(3.7)	**17.1**	(4.0)	2.7	3.8	**5.2**	(5.2)
	Iceland	5.2	(4.7)	**20.7**	(4.5)	**55.7**	(3.9)	**19.3**	(4.8)	**45.8**	(6.3)	**3.0**	(4.3)	**21.3**	(4.5)	**51.7**	(3.6)	**19.5**	4.6	**34.1**	(6.3)
	Ireland	**-27.5**	(4.4)	**-36.3**	(9.9)	**64.6**	(4.2)	**20.9**	(6.2)	**-9.8**	(4.1)	**-20.6**	(4.3)	**-27.7**	(9.0)	**52.7**	(3.9)	**15.3**	6.2	-3.1	(4.0)
	Israel	**16.2**	(4.8)	**-30.6**	(5.9)	**22.9**	(4.4)	4.2	(4.3)	**27.1**	(5.3)	**13.5**	(4.5)	**-22.8**	(5.8)	**18.9**	(4.3)	**0.4**	4.2	**16.4**	(4.9)
	Italy	**-9.7**	(2.1)	**25.7**	(3.2)	**38.2**	(2.7)	8.1	(5.8)	**15.6**	(2.3)	**-9.4**	(2.1)	**18.9**	(3.4)	**27.9**	(2.2)	**0.0**	5.5	**7.6**	(2.2)
	Japan	**-17.3**	(3.6)	**14.8**	(4.0)	**34.6**	(4.4)	**27.1**	(6.0)	**26.0**	(4.2)	**-19.1**	(3.3)	**12.5**	(4.0)	**32.0**	(4.1)	**19.0**	6.1	**19.9**	(3.8)
	Korea	**-12.5**	(4.2)	**-9.9**	(3.5)	**14.8**	(3.3)	**12.5**	(3.7)	**27.2**	(4.3)	**-16.3**	(3.9)	**-7.7**	(3.4)	**9.8**	(2.9)	**7.1**	3.4	**16.3**	(3.3)
	Luxembourg	-5.5	(5.3)	-11.8	(6.6)	**62.8**	(4.2)	6.4	(6.3)	-11.0	(5.7)	-8.2	(5.2)	**-9.3**	(5.9)	**45.6**	(3.7)	-3.3	5.7	0.6	(5.2)
	Mexico	**12.7**	(2.3)	**-15.0**	(2.0)	**-6.5**	(2.1)	**24.1**	(2.5)	1.3	(2.0)	-0.6	(1.8)	**-13.1**	(2.0)	**-4.9**	(1.8)	**17.4**	2.3	-1.0	(1.8)
	Netherlands	**27.4**	(4.2)	6.6	(6.0)	**40.2**	(5.4)	**40.4**	(5.7)	**26.7**	(4.9)	**16.6**	(3.4)	**4.6**	(4.8)	**35.2**	(4.9)	**37.2**	5.0	**24.1**	(4.0)
	New Zealand	**-25.4**	(4.1)	-7.9	(8.6)	**52.4**	(4.6)	-0.2	(4.7)	**12.6**	(3.7)	**-21.8**	(3.3)	**4.8**	(7.7)	**43.8**	(4.2)	**1.7**	4.6	**10.2**	(3.7)
	Norway	0.6	(4.5)	**28.2**	(4.1)	**47.5**	(3.7)	-3.8	(4.9)	**18.5**	(4.0)	**-9.2**	(4.3)	**22.7**	(3.9)	**43.8**	(3.4)	**-6.4**	4.4	**10.6**	(3.9)
	Poland	-1.5	(4.2)	**-18.2**	(6.9)	**42.4**	(3.9)	**24.5**	(4.1)	-7.6	(4.6)	-1.1	(3.8)	**-16.1**	(5.9)	**29.8**	(3.3)	**13.7**	3.8	-6.5	(4.1)
	Portugal	**-15.8**	(4.4)	-2.0	(4.8)	**27.5**	(3.4)	**34.6**	(4.7)	0.7	(3.4)	**-11.9**	(3.8)	**-3.3**	(4.5)	**18.4**	(3.2)	**24.4**	4.0	0.9	(3.2)
	Slovak Republic	**15.6**	(7.7)	-11.7	(6.8)	**42.6**	(4.9)	**16.2**	(5.6)	-1.7	(4.8)	10.7	(6.7)	**-9.5**	(6.1)	**38.2**	(4.2)	**12.8**	4.9	-2.3	(4.0)
	Slovenia	-6.5	(4.8)	**-19.7**	(6.7)	**51.0**	(4.8)	**33.8**	(4.5)	6.5	(4.1)	**-8.6**	(4.2)	**-19.5**	(6.5)	**41.9**	(4.3)	**24.7**	4.2	**9.2**	(3.7)
	Spain	-2.8	(3.2)	4.3	(5.7)	**48.0**	(2.6)	**48.4**	(3.2)	**21.1**	(2.9)	-5.2	(2.9)	**5.9**	(5.3)	**38.5**	(2.7)	**35.6**	2.6	**15.8**	(2.6)
	Sweden	**23.2**	(4.3)	6.8	(5.8)	**63.5**	(4.2)	**44.1**	(5.9)	**38.0**	(4.9)	**15.4**	(4.0)	**10.4**	(4.7)	**55.5**	(3.6)	**36.7**	5.6	**29.8**	(4.4)
	Switzerland	4.4	(4.3)	**13.5**	(4.4)	**54.5**	(3.9)	4.4	(6.1)	**17.3**	(3.9)	**1.9**	(4.0)	**5.6**	(4.2)	**45.5**	(3.5)	**5.9**	6.3	**18.1**	(3.8)
	Turkey	**-13.3**	(3.9)	**-17.2**	(4.6)	4.1	(4.3)	**-20.5**	(3.8)	**17.5**	(6.1)	**-19.4**	(3.5)	**-17.7**	(3.7)	5.0	(3.4)	**-16.0**	3.7	2.9	(6.1)
	United Kingdom	**-22.7**	(4.1)	**-18.1**	(7.2)	**64.4**	(4.0)	**17.8**	(4.9)	-1.0	(4.0)	**-18.8**	(3.9)	**-9.0**	(8.4)	**54.7**	(3.4)	**15.2**	4.2	2.2	(3.8)
	United States	-0.3	(3.9)	3.8	(8.4)	**43.5**	(4.7)	**-19.7**	(5.8)	4.0	(5.2)	-7.1	(3.7)	**9.5**	(7.7)	**34.8**	(3.9)	**-12.9**	5.0	1.1	(4.3)
	OECD average	-2.2	(1.2)	**5.4**	(1.9)	**36.0**	(1.4)	**4.2**	(1.9)	**9.9**	(1.6)	**-8.5**	(1.2)	**9.3**	(1.6)	**30.4**	(1.1)	**3.2**	1.7	**8.5**	(1.2)
Partners	Albania	2.5	(5.0)	**-30.1**	(5.8)	6.7	(6.0)	7.9	(7.6)	**-10.6**	(5.3)	**-9.4**	(4.8)	**-26.2**	(5.2)	2.1	(5.2)	0.8	7.2	-5.5	(4.2)
	Argentina	**22.9**	(5.6)	-7.7	(5.7)	-7.2	(5.9)	-9.8	(5.6)	0.0	(5.4)	**11.7**	(4.7)	-3.0	(4.7)	-1.4	(4.9)	-1.9	5.0	**-1.7**	(4.8)
	Azerbaijan	**12.6**	(4.3)	1.4	(4.3)	6.1	(4.4)	-4.3	(4.8)	7.2	(3.8)	3.0	(4.0)	-0.8	(4.1)	0.0	(4.4)	-7.0	4.4	3.7	(3.9)
	Brazil	**16.9**	(3.3)	**-22.1**	(3.2)	**-8.5**	(3.8)	**16.4**	(4.0)	**11.9**	(3.7)	**7.0**	(3.2)	**-18.2**	(2.6)	**-7.4**	(3.0)	**10.7**	3.4	**2.8**	(3.2)
	Bulgaria	**24.7**	(5.8)	**-27.4**	(8.3)	**33.1**	(7.7)	**23.5**	(6.0)	7.5	(6.2)	7.2	(4.9)	**-18.4**	(7.4)	**22.0**	(5.5)	**12.6**	5.1	4.9	(5.3)
	Colombia	-3.0	(4.2)	-1.0	(4.5)	**-18.2**	(4.9)	6.5	(4.8)	-4.2	(5.1)	-4.9	(4.1)	-0.8	(3.8)	**-15.1**	(4.4)	6.4	4.0	-1.5	(4.0)
	Croatia	-6.6	(4.9)	**-18.4**	(6.1)	**37.4**	(4.2)	**48.5**	(4.7)	**25.3**	(5.4)	-7.9	(4.3)	**-21.6**	(5.6)	**27.6**	(4.1)	**32.8**	4.5	**18.8**	(5.3)
	Dubai (UAE)	4.7	(4.7)	**-27.4**	(3.8)	**43.5**	(4.0)	**10.4**	(4.1)	**14.3**	(4.8)	0.0	(4.5)	**-14.3**	(4.0)	**28.4**	(4.2)	**2.7**	4.3	**16.8**	(4.2)
	Hong Kong-China	**-15.8**	(3.4)	1.5	(4.6)	**32.6**	(3.8)	**21.4**	(4.5)	**23.6**	(5.4)	**-21.4**	(3.1)	**0.3**	(4.1)	**27.3**	(3.5)	**16.6**	4.3	**15.9**	(5.0)
	Indonesia	**16.0**	(3.4)	3.7	(3.1)	**10.7**	(3.4)	**22.7**	(2.9)	**14.9**	(3.2)	6.4	(3.4)	**-0.2**	(2.7)	**5.5**	(3.3)	**16.7**	2.7	**8.4**	(3.0)
	Jordan	**8.9**	(3.9)	**11.7**	(4.2)	**-8.6**	(4.1)	**-10.1**	(3.7)	**31.5**	(3.8)	**2.6**	(3.3)	4.9	(3.8)	-5.0	(3.9)	**-9.4**	3.4	**22.0**	(3.5)
	Kazakhstan	-5.1	(6.2)	**-33.1**	(4.8)	-5.7	(4.7)	**-27.6**	(4.2)	**-19.8**	(6.8)	**-9.9**	(5.0)	**-32.5**	(4.5)	**-9.0**	(3.9)	**-27.8**	4.0	**-18.2**	(5.9)
	Kyrgyzstan	**16.1**	(4.7)	**-10.4**	(5.2)	7.9	(4.8)	-0.9	(4.0)	7.6	(6.4)	0.8	(4.3)	**-16.7**	(4.3)	3.1	(4.0)	-4.6	4.3	6.0	(5.4)
	Latvia	3.5	(5.8)	**-24.6**	(6.2)	**13.8**	(4.2)	**14.4**	(3.9)	2.5	(3.5)	-1.4	(4.3)	**-25.6**	(5.9)	**13.6**	(3.9)	**9.3**	3.6	2.2	(3.3)
	Liechtenstein	-4.2	(16.5)	-14.9	(22.4)	**39.8**	(13.5)	-0.4	(24.3)	**29.9**	(14.2)	-3.7	(16.4)	**-13.4**	(16.5)	**38.8**	(11.9)	**4.4**	20.4	21.4	(15.1)
	Lithuania	1.6	(5.0)	**-37.9**	(4.6)	**36.7**	(3.3)	**24.8**	(4.0)	8.0	(4.4)	-0.7	(4.2)	**-25.6**	(4.6)	**26.2**	(2.5)	**18.4**	3.4	**7.7**	(3.5)
	Macao-China	**-8.4**	(2.8)	**7.4**	(2.9)	**28.4**	(3.1)	**22.5**	(2.9)	**24.8**	(3.3)	**-10.9**	(2.9)	**5.7**	(2.9)	**25.3**	(2.9)	**18.8**	2.8	**21.4**	(3.3)
	Montenegro	**29.6**	(6.2)	-9.4	(5.1)	**21.9**	(4.1)	**14.6**	(4.3)	**23.7**	(5.2)	**21.8**	(6.1)	**-9.2**	(5.0)	**19.3**	(4.1)	**9.3**	4.5	**14.0**	(4.7)
	Panama	**27.9**	(6.5)	**-24.7**	(6.6)	-0.7	(7.6)	5.4	(6.6)	-13.6	(9.9)	**16.8**	(8.5)	**-19.1**	(5.6)	-0.5	(5.6)	0.4	6.4	**8.9**	(7.4)
	Peru	**37.1**	(3.7)	**-17.9**	(4.7)	1.4	(4.5)	**-11.5**	(4.6)	**44.0**	(5.2)	**11.4**	(3.7)	**-11.2**	(3.2)	-0.4	(3.6)	**-5.8**	3.5	**20.3**	(4.7)
	Qatar	-4.5	(3.8)	**-11.7**	(3.2)	**26.2**	(3.5)	5.9	(4.0)	4.9	(3.7)	-0.8	(3.4)	**-6.8**	(2.9)	**20.4**	(3.1)	1.9	3.6	**10.7**	(3.0)
	Romania	**24.4**	(5.3)	**-16.8**	(5.9)	**12.1**	(4.8)	1.4	(4.5)	9.6	(6.2)	**13.3**	(4.8)	**-17.3**	(5.0)	**9.6**	(4.1)	-4.3	4.1	**3.3**	(5.1)
	Russian Federation	**-15.3**	(4.4)	**-28.6**	(6.2)	**26.8**	(4.5)	7.4	(4.3)	**-14.7**	(4.6)	**-13.1**	(3.8)	**-15.5**	(6.4)	**22.0**	(3.5)	1.3	3.7	-5.6	(3.8)
	Serbia	3.9	(5.4)	**-29.0**	(6.2)	**20.4**	(4.0)	**28.7**	(6.2)	**11.9**	(4.1)	-1.6	(4.8)	**-29.4**	(5.8)	**14.8**	(4.1)	**20.1**	5.6	6.6	(3.7)
	Shanghai-China	**11.3**	(2.8)	-7.2	(4.1)	**16.0**	(3.3)	**17.6**	(3.7)	**27.4**	(4.2)	4.2	(2.5)	**-8.0**	(3.6)	**13.8**	(3.3)	**10.8**	3.4	**19.8**	(4.0)
	Singapore	-3.1	(3.5)	**9.6**	(4.7)	**42.7**	(3.9)	6.0	(4.0)	**20.7**	(5.2)	**-6.8**	(3.3)	**5.7**	(4.4)	**29.0**	(3.9)	**-1.1**	3.6	**13.1**	(4.9)
	Chinese Taipei	**-15.2**	(3.1)	-0.9	(3.8)	**29.5**	(3.7)	**23.3**	(3.5)	**8.9**	(3.4)	**-17.6**	(2.9)	**-0.7**	(3.5)	**22.9**	(3.1)	**14.3**	3.1	1.9	(3.0)
	Thailand	**8.4**	(2.9)	3.4	(3.1)	**11.7**	(3.4)	**14.7**	(2.9)	6.0	(3.4)	4.3	(2.7)	**4.0**	(3.1)	**11.8**	(3.2)	**14.6**	2.8	2.8	(3.0)
	Trinidad and Tobago	-2.0	(4.2)	**-16.8**	(5.5)	**21.6**	(5.0)	**22.9**	(5.4)	2.5	(7.2)	-6.2	(4.0)	**-12.3**	(5.1)	**24.7**	(5.1)	**20.8**	5.1	10.8	(6.6)
	Tunisia	6.5	(4.1)	**-20.4**	(4.0)	-2.3	(3.7)	-8.4	(5.3)	**20.5**	(3.2)	-4.4	(3.8)	**-17.7**	(3.6)	-1.4	(3.1)	**-9.9**	4.9	**11.7**	(3.1)
	Uruguay	**25.4**	(4.3)	**-17.6**	(4.3)	**8.7**	(4.2)	**27.4**	(5.1)	**20.1**	(4.4)	**14.6**	(3.5)	**-7.5**	(4.1)	**6.4**	(3.6)	**20.7**	4.5	**11.2**	(3.5)

Notes: Values that are statistically significant are indicated in bold (see Annex A3).
Comparisons are derived using as the reference group students who do not read for enjoyment any material at least several times a month or several times a week introducing indicators for each material in the same regression.
1. Adjusted models account for gender, PISA index of economic, social and cultural status, immigration status and language spoken at home.
StatLink http://dx.doi.org/10.1787/888932343285

[Part 1/2]
Engagement in reading and learning strategies, and change in reading performance

Table III.1.26   *Results based on students' self-reports*

	Engagement in reading											
	Enjoyment of reading				Diversity of reading materials				Online reading activities			
	Change in the reading score per unit of this index		Adjusted change[1] in the reading score per unit of this index		Change in the reading score per unit of this index		Adjusted change[1] in the reading score per unit of this index		Change in the reading score per unit of this index		Adjusted change[1] in the reading score per unit of this index	
	Score dif.	S.E.	Score dif.	S.E.	Score dif.	S.E.	Score dif.	S.E.	Score dif.	S.E.	Score dif.	S.E.
Australia	**44.9**	(1.0)	**37.5**	(0.9)	**24.7**	(1.4)	**17.0**	(1.2)	**26.0**	(1.7)	**17.0**	(1.3)
Austria	**37.2**	(1.6)	**30.3**	(1.5)	**23.0**	(2.2)	**17.9**	(2.0)	**15.9**	(2.1)	**13.4**	(2.0)
Belgium	**40.9**	(1.2)	**33.1**	(1.3)	**29.3**	(1.4)	**21.6**	(1.3)	**10.5**	(1.7)	**6.6**	(1.7)
Canada	**35.7**	(0.8)	**31.3**	(0.8)	**18.4**	(1.0)	**12.7**	(1.0)	**14.1**	(1.2)	**9.7**	(1.2)
Chile	**29.0**	(1.6)	**23.3**	(1.6)	**16.5**	(1.3)	**10.8**	(1.3)	**20.7**	(1.5)	**8.6**	(1.3)
Czech Republic	**46.0**	(1.5)	**35.9**	(1.5)	**25.9**	(1.7)	**18.6**	(1.6)	**8.2**	(1.5)	**4.6**	(1.6)
Denmark	**43.2**	(1.5)	**37.0**	(1.5)	**22.0**	(1.2)	**16.8**	(1.3)	**14.0**	(1.9)	**11.5**	(1.6)
Estonia	**43.3**	(1.7)	**36.1**	(1.7)	**23.0**	(2.3)	**15.7**	(2.1)	**12.1**	(2.0)	**9.1**	(1.8)
Finland	**43.3**	(1.2)	**36.0**	(1.3)	**37.9**	(1.7)	**30.1**	(1.7)	**14.5**	(1.9)	**12.9**	(1.6)
France	**47.1**	(2.3)	**36.5**	(2.2)	**30.9**	(2.7)	**23.0**	(2.5)	**28.3**	(2.7)	**17.7**	(2.5)
Germany	**36.6**	(1.4)	**27.0**	(1.2)	**23.9**	(1.9)	**16.7**	(1.7)	**10.5**	(2.2)	**4.5**	(1.7)
Greece	**46.8**	(2.3)	**35.2**	(1.9)	**21.8**	(2.2)	**14.6**	(1.7)	**6.9**	(1.7)	1.1	(1.3)
Hungary	**45.1**	(1.9)	**30.4**	(1.8)	**14.8**	(1.6)	**9.0**	(1.4)	**20.8**	(2.1)	**8.6**	(1.5)
Iceland	**43.4**	(1.4)	**37.9**	(1.4)	**30.1**	(1.5)	**24.6**	(1.5)	**8.7**	(2.0)	**8.9**	(1.7)
Ireland	**45.1**	(1.6)	**37.3**	(1.5)	**19.3**	(2.4)	**14.2**	(1.9)	**18.9**	(2.4)	**13.8**	(2.0)
Israel	**30.1**	(1.9)	**22.6**	(1.8)	**13.2**	(1.8)	**6.5**	(1.6)	**18.1**	(2.2)	**6.1**	(2.0)
Italy	**40.4**	(1.0)	**30.3**	(0.9)	**29.5**	(1.3)	**19.8**	(1.0)	**12.6**	(0.8)	**5.2**	(0.8)
Japan	**35.8**	(1.9)	**30.2**	(1.5)	**20.7**	(1.8)	**15.6**	(1.5)	**21.3**	(1.5)	**15.8**	(1.5)
Korea	**40.4**	(2.3)	**32.7**	(2.0)	**17.0**	(1.9)	**10.7**	(1.7)	**13.7**	(2.2)	**7.6**	(1.6)
Luxembourg	**39.9**	(1.3)	**29.0**	(1.4)	**21.7**	(1.8)	**14.4**	(1.8)	**8.1**	(2.0)	3.1	(1.8)
Mexico	**21.6**	(1.1)	**18.8**	(1.0)	**5.1**	(0.9)	**1.5**	(0.8)	**22.3**	(1.4)	**10.0**	(1.3)
Netherlands	**38.5**	(1.9)	**34.6**	(2.0)	**26.4**	(1.7)	**21.7**	(1.6)	**19.2**	(2.7)	**16.3**	(2.2)
New Zealand	**48.2**	(1.6)	**37.3**	(1.6)	**15.7**	(1.8)	**8.1**	(1.6)	**23.9**	(2.0)	**12.8**	(1.8)
Norway	**42.1**	(1.5)	**35.9**	(1.5)	**25.9**	(1.9)	**19.2**	(1.7)	**7.4**	(1.9)	**5.2**	(1.6)
Poland	**35.2**	(1.3)	**24.7**	(1.4)	**24.1**	(1.7)	**14.5**	(1.5)	**17.0**	(1.5)	**8.9**	(1.4)
Portugal	**35.6**	(1.6)	**26.5**	(1.3)	**12.3**	(1.9)	**6.7**	(1.5)	**4.2**	(1.8)	1.2	(1.6)
Slovak Republic	**39.8**	(2.4)	**27.9**	(1.9)	**25.8**	(2.2)	**15.1**	(1.9)	**20.4**	(2.0)	**11.8**	(1.6)
Slovenia	**39.0**	(1.4)	**26.6**	(1.3)	**26.3**	(1.7)	**17.0**	(1.5)	**11.9**	(1.4)	**7.3**	(1.4)
Spain	**38.4**	(1.0)	**31.7**	(1.0)	**25.7**	(1.2)	**19.3**	(1.1)	**15.5**	(1.2)	**9.5**	(1.0)
Sweden	**46.8**	(1.5)	**39.6**	(1.7)	**33.6**	(1.6)	**26.0**	(1.5)	**12.6**	(1.9)	**10.9**	(1.8)
Switzerland	**37.7**	(1.2)	**30.7**	(1.3)	**29.9**	(1.5)	**23.7**	(1.4)	**4.9**	(1.9)	2.7	(1.9)
Turkey	**23.5**	(2.0)	**17.3**	(1.8)	-0.3	(1.7)	**-5.5**	(1.6)	**10.3**	(1.5)	-1.2	(1.4)
United Kingdom	**45.0**	(1.5)	**39.3**	(1.3)	**19.2**	(1.4)	**15.9**	(1.4)	**16.1**	(2.1)	**10.8**	(1.8)
United States	**38.3**	(1.8)	**31.1**	(1.5)	**11.4**	(1.7)	**5.6**	(1.5)	**16.5**	(1.9)	**6.9**	(1.6)
OECD average	**35.0**	(0.7)	**29.3**	(0.5)	**15.5**	(0.5)	**11.1**	(0.5)	**17.8**	(0.6)	**7.0**	(0.5)
Albania	**47.8**	(2.8)	**28.7**	(2.8)	**8.1**	(2.7)	-1.6	(2.0)	**14.2**	(2.2)	**7.3**	(1.8)
Argentina	**27.4**	(3.6)	**21.8**	(3.2)	**8.2**	(2.0)	**3.9**	(1.7)	**28.4**	(2.2)	**13.1**	(1.6)
Azerbaijan	**22.8**	(2.1)	**18.1**	(2.3)	**6.2**	(1.0)	**3.3**	(1.1)	**6.8**	(1.0)	**3.3**	(0.9)
Brazil	**25.8**	(1.9)	**19.5**	(1.6)	**8.0**	(1.2)	**2.9**	(1.1)	**18.1**	(0.9)	**9.2**	(1.0)
Bulgaria	**38.3**	(3.1)	**22.9**	(2.8)	**23.7**	(2.5)	**9.9**	(1.9)	**29.4**	(1.6)	**14.5**	(1.4)
Colombia	**14.4**	(2.6)	**13.8**	(2.0)	1.9	(1.7)	0.6	(1.5)	**21.4**	(1.8)	**10.2**	(1.4)
Croatia	**37.1**	(1.8)	**26.1**	(1.6)	**27.8**	(1.5)	**17.6**	(1.4)	**14.3**	(1.4)	**7.9**	(1.2)
Dubai (UAE)	**43.4**	(1.3)	**27.9**	(1.3)	**10.3**	(1.8)	**4.8**	(1.3)	**12.9**	(1.3)	**3.4**	(1.3)
Hong Kong-China	**42.3**	(2.0)	**35.0**	(1.9)	**11.5**	(1.5)	**7.1**	(1.5)	**8.5**	(2.1)	**4.7**	(1.8)
Indonesia	**21.2**	(2.9)	**12.6**	(2.8)	**8.1**	(1.3)	**3.5**	(1.1)	**12.4**	(1.6)	**8.5**	(1.2)
Jordan	**27.5**	(2.1)	**19.6**	(2.0)	**13.2**	(1.4)	**6.8**	(1.2)	**14.2**	(1.2)	**8.6**	(0.9)
Kazakhstan	5.0	(3.0)	-4.2	(2.8)	**-10.2**	(2.0)	**-13.4**	(1.7)	**12.3**	(1.5)	**4.7**	(1.1)
Kyrgyzstan	**23.8**	(3.0)	**13.5**	(2.9)	**7.0**	(1.6)	-1.4	(1.4)	**10.7**	(1.4)	**3.2**	(1.2)
Latvia	**42.0**	(2.0)	**30.0**	(1.7)	**17.0**	(2.4)	**8.3**	(2.1)	**9.5**	(2.3)	2.8	(2.0)
Liechtenstein	**31.0**	(3.4)	**28.3**	(3.6)	**20.8**	(5.3)	**24.2**	(5.6)	1.6	(4.7)	4.9	(6.0)
Lithuania	**34.3**	(1.3)	**21.6**	(1.4)	**22.1**	(1.7)	**12.0**	(1.5)	**15.9**	(1.5)	**8.5**	(1.3)
Macao-China	**35.9**	(1.3)	**28.6**	(1.3)	**17.8**	(1.1)	**14.5**	(1.0)	**13.2**	(1.4)	**12.3**	(1.4)
Montenegro	**36.7**	(1.8)	**25.4**	(2.1)	**18.4**	(2.4)	**11.4**	(1.9)	**10.2**	(1.6)	3.1	(1.8)
Panama	**15.0**	(3.3)	**14.6**	(2.9)	4.0	(2.6)	3.0	(2.3)	**22.9**	(2.4)	**9.7**	(2.0)
Peru	**18.3**	(2.5)	**16.4**	(1.9)	**8.7**	(1.7)	1.3	(1.5)	**26.1**	(1.7)	**9.2**	(1.3)
Qatar	**35.7**	(1.5)	**21.0**	(1.3)	**10.0**	(0.8)	**5.8**	(0.7)	**11.5**	(0.8)	**4.2**	(0.8)
Romania	**27.9**	(2.9)	**15.8**	(2.4)	**13.2**	(2.4)	3.2	(1.7)	**19.1**	(1.6)	**11.2**	(1.3)
Russian Federation	**48.6**	(2.7)	**36.8**	(2.4)	**5.9**	(1.9)	2.3	(1.5)	**14.5**	(1.7)	**7.2**	(1.1)
Serbia	**29.2**	(1.7)	**20.3**	(1.8)	**13.6**	(1.8)	**6.3**	(1.8)	**14.5**	(1.1)	**8.6**	(1.1)
Shanghai-China	**39.8**	(2.6)	**27.8**	(2.2)	**9.2**	(1.5)	**4.8**	(1.3)	**5.2**	(1.6)	**-4.1**	(1.5)
Singapore	**43.3**	(1.6)	**33.2**	(1.7)	**13.7**	(1.3)	**6.7**	(1.2)	**16.0**	(1.3)	**7.8**	(1.3)
Chinese Taipei	**45.9**	(2.1)	**35.5**	(1.7)	**11.8**	(1.4)	**6.5**	(1.3)	**7.0**	(1.4)	1.3	(1.4)
Thailand	**31.8**	(2.1)	**24.9**	(1.8)	**13.1**	(1.1)	**8.2**	(0.9)	**14.1**	(1.3)	**6.2**	(1.0)
Trinidad and Tobago	**33.6**	(2.0)	**23.8**	(2.1)	**14.8**	(1.6)	**9.5**	(1.7)	**22.6**	(1.2)	**11.9**	(1.5)
Tunisia	**4.9**	(2.1)	**4.4**	(1.9)	**4.6**	(1.5)	-0.7	(1.5)	**9.2**	(1.4)	2.2	(1.4)
Uruguay	**30.0**	(2.0)	**19.7**	(1.8)	**16.6**	(1.4)	**9.9**	(1.3)	**21.8**	(1.4)	**7.7**	(1.3)

Note: Values that are statistically significant are indicated in bold (see Annex A3).
1. Adjusted models account for gender, the PISA index of economic, social and cultural status, immigration status and language spoken at home.
StatLink ᴬᴵ°ᴸ° http://dx.doi.org/10.1787/888932343285

[Part 2/2]
Table III.1.26 Engagement in reading and learning strategies, and change in reading performance
Results based on students' self-reports

		Learning strategies																			
		Memorisation strategies				Elaboration strategies				Control strategies				Understanding and rememberin				Summarising			
		Change in the reading score per unit of this index		Adjusted change[1] in the reading score per unit of this index		Change in the reading score per unit of this index		Adjusted change[1] in the reading score per unit of this index		Change in the reading score per unit of this index		Adjusted change[1] in the reading score per unit of this index		Change in the reading score per unit of this index		Adjusted change[1] in the reading score per unit of this index		Change in the reading score per unit of this index		Adjusted change[1] in the reading score per unit of this index	
		Score dif.	S.E.	Score dif.	S.E.	Score dif.	S.E.	Score dif.	S.E.	Score dif.	S.E.	Score dif.	S.E.	Score dif.	S.E.	Score dif.	S.E.	Score dif.	S.E.	Score dif.	S.E.
OECD	Australia	**9.7**	(1.2)	**3.7**	(1.1)	**10.0**	(1.1)	**6.4**	(0.8)	**33.1**	(1.1)	**25.1**	(0.9)	**38.5**	(1.2)	**30.5**	(1.0)	**43.8**	(1.0)	**36.2**	(0.9)
	Austria	**-8.9**	(2.0)	**-10.7**	(1.8)	1.9	(1.6)	-0.8	(1.6)	**17.0**	(1.7)	**11.0**	(1.5)	**41.7**	(1.9)	**32.2**	(1.8)	**46.9**	(1.8)	**37.6**	(1.6)
	Belgium	**-12.4**	(1.5)	**-10.2**	(1.3)	-0.3	(1.5)	-0.8	(1.3)	**30.2**	(1.8)	**22.0**	(1.4)	**46.5**	(1.4)	**37.3**	(1.2)	**50.8**	(1.3)	**41.6**	(1.1)
	Canada	**3.3**	(1.0)	-0.6	(0.9)	**2.6**	(0.9)	0.4	(0.8)	**25.8**	(1.0)	**19.7**	(1.0)	**27.2**	(0.9)	**22.8**	(0.9)	**35.3**	(0.8)	**30.0**	(0.8)
	Chile	**5.2**	(1.8)	**3.2**	(1.5)	**5.2**	(1.4)	1.8	(1.3)	**25.3**	(1.5)	**18.1**	(1.3)	**32.6**	(1.5)	**25.9**	(1.4)	**34.8**	(1.7)	**27.0**	(1.4)
	Czech Republic	**-6.4**	(1.6)	**-9.0**	(1.5)	**12.4**	(1.4)	**8.7**	(1.5)	**28.7**	(1.3)	**19.8**	(1.3)	**37.9**	(1.6)	**30.1**	(1.4)	**46.9**	(1.4)	**39.8**	(1.4)
	Denmark	**-9.5**	(2.0)	**-8.7**	(1.7)	**8.7**	(1.5)	**4.8**	(1.6)	**18.9**	(1.5)	**14.4**	(1.5)	**37.0**	(1.4)	**29.1**	(1.4)	**38.7**	(1.2)	**30.9**	(1.3)
	Estonia	**-6.7**	(2.2)	**-9.7**	(2.1)	**9.3**	(2.0)	**6.8**	(1.9)	**17.6**	(2.3)	**10.0**	(2.2)	**33.2**	(1.5)	**26.8**	(1.3)	**38.9**	(1.8)	**31.4**	(1.7)
	Finland	2.9	(1.7)	-1.3	(1.4)	**13.1**	(1.6)	**11.2**	(1.3)	**25.6**	(1.6)	**19.6**	(1.3)	**35.4**	(1.2)	**27.4**	(1.2)	**42.4**	(1.2)	**34.1**	(1.2)
	France	**11.0**	(2.7)	**5.7**	(2.3)	**7.0**	(2.2)	3.7	(2.0)	**41.4**	(2.6)	**30.4**	(2.1)	**41.1**	(2.5)	**30.6**	(2.1)	**51.2**	(2.2)	**40.4**	(2.0)
	Germany	**-5.1**	(1.8)	**-6.5**	(1.5)	0.5	(1.5)	-0.3	(1.4)	**22.9**	(1.8)	**15.3**	(1.5)	**40.8**	(1.7)	**31.2**	(1.4)	**44.8**	(1.5)	**34.5**	(1.4)
	Greece	**5.3**	(1.9)	-0.7	(1.5)	**11.7**	(1.6)	**6.7**	(1.5)	**27.4**	(2.0)	**18.2**	(1.6)	**22.5**	(1.9)	**17.4**	(1.8)	**36.3**	(1.8)	**28.3**	(1.5)
	Hungary	3.3	(2.5)	0.9	(1.9)	0.0	(1.9)	-2.6	(1.7)	**16.9**	(2.7)	**9.2**	(2.0)	**36.3**	(2.4)	**26.8**	(1.6)	**45.2**	(2.1)	**33.7**	(1.6)
	Iceland	-1.0	(1.9)	**-3.8**	(1.8)	**10.4**	(1.8)	**7.4**	(1.7)	**25.0**	(1.8)	**18.6**	(1.8)	**32.2**	(1.7)	**26.5**	(1.7)	**40.0**	(1.6)	**34.3**	(1.7)
	Ireland	**7.0**	(2.3)	1.9	(1.8)	**5.9**	(1.7)	**4.3**	(1.4)	**27.6**	(1.9)	**19.3**	(1.6)	**35.2**	(2.0)	**27.1**	(1.7)	**38.9**	(1.7)	**31.5**	(1.5)
	Israel	**-5.6**	(1.9)	**-8.1**	(1.5)	**-8.5**	(1.5)	**-9.6**	(1.3)	**20.1**	(2.0)	**11.0**	(1.7)	**37.5**	(2.0)	**30.1**	(1.8)	**44.4**	(1.8)	**35.9**	(1.5)
	Italy	**-10.1**	(1.3)	**-12.4**	(1.1)	**5.3**	(0.9)	**2.8**	(0.9)	**28.0**	(1.1)	**17.0**	(0.9)	**40.6**	(1.3)	**30.2**	(0.9)	**48.0**	(1.4)	**37.5**	(1.0)
	Japan	**6.5**	(1.8)	3.1	(1.7)	**16.8**	(1.5)	**13.8**	(1.2)	**32.5**	(2.1)	**26.6**	(1.9)	**40.3**	(2.5)	**35.0**	(1.9)	**48.6**	(2.2)	**43.0**	(1.7)
	Korea	**24.6**	(2.5)	**18.9**	(2.1)	**24.0**	(2.1)	**18.8**	(1.9)	**34.2**	(2.0)	**28.1**	(1.9)	**33.2**	(2.2)	**28.0**	(1.9)	**38.9**	(1.7)	**33.4**	(1.6)
	Luxembourg	**10.2**	(1.7)	**4.8**	(1.7)	-2.3	(1.5)	**-3.3**	(1.6)	**25.1**	(1.5)	**15.5**	(1.5)	**40.0**	(1.3)	**29.9**	(1.4)	**45.7**	(1.4)	**34.4**	(1.7)
	Mexico	-0.1	(0.8)	**-3.2**	(0.8)	**6.0**	(0.8)	**3.7**	(0.7)	**20.4**	(0.9)	**14.1**	(0.8)	**27.3**	(0.8)	**21.6**	(0.7)	**35.4**	(0.9)	**28.5**	(0.8)
	Netherlands	**-21.9**	(1.8)	**-18.0**	(1.6)	2.1	(1.7)	1.2	(1.4)	**25.6**	(2.0)	**22.0**	(1.9)	**38.5**	(1.8)	**32.6**	(1.7)	**42.3**	(1.7)	**37.3**	(1.6)
	New Zealand	3.1	(2.0)	-2.9	(1.7)	1.7	(2.0)	-0.4	(1.7)	**32.2**	(1.4)	**21.9**	(1.4)	**37.8**	(1.5)	**27.6**	(1.3)	**46.3**	(1.3)	**36.5**	(1.2)
	Norway	**3.8**	(1.5)	2.2	(1.5)	**16.1**	(1.4)	**13.4**	(1.4)	**25.7**	(1.6)	**20.1**	(1.5)	**33.1**	(1.4)	**26.2**	(1.4)	**41.4**	(1.4)	**33.0**	(1.4)
	Poland	**7.2**	(1.9)	0.1	(1.7)	**7.8**	(1.7)	**3.6**	(1.5)	**27.1**	(1.6)	**16.3**	(1.5)	**28.0**	(1.5)	**20.3**	(1.3)	**39.7**	(1.4)	**31.2**	(1.4)
	Portugal	-2.7	(1.5)	**-5.5**	(1.3)	**22.3**	(1.7)	**12.6**	(1.4)	**35.7**	(1.5)	**24.2**	(1.3)	**35.5**	(1.3)	**28.2**	(1.2)	**42.1**	(1.3)	**33.9**	(1.2)
	Slovak Republic	**-18.1**	(2.3)	**-16.4**	(1.6)	**9.5**	(1.8)	**5.9**	(1.4)	**25.1**	(2.1)	**15.8**	(1.8)	**32.2**	(1.9)	**23.7**	(1.7)	**40.7**	(1.9)	**31.8**	(1.6)
	Slovenia	**-15.9**	(1.7)	**-14.4**	(1.4)	**4.4**	(1.6)	2.6	(1.4)	**24.0**	(1.7)	**14.8**	(1.5)	**36.0**	(1.2)	**27.0**	(1.3)	**39.7**	(1.3)	**30.1**	(1.2)
	Spain	**4.2**	(1.4)	**2.5**	(1.1)	**9.0**	(1.2)	**5.4**	(0.9)	**27.1**	(1.2)	**20.1**	(1.0)	**29.7**	(1.2)	**24.2**	(1.0)	**41.1**	(0.9)	**34.2**	(1.0)
	Sweden	**10.3**	(2.0)	**5.9**	(1.7)	**12.4**	(1.9)	**10.4**	(1.5)	**26.8**	(2.0)	**20.7**	(1.6)	**39.5**	(1.4)	**30.9**	(1.4)	**41.5**	(1.4)	**33.6**	(1.3)
	Switzerland	**-5.8**	(1.6)	**-5.8**	(1.3)	0.6	(1.5)	0.2	(1.5)	**24.8**	(1.5)	**18.0**	(1.5)	**44.4**	(1.6)	**35.0**	(1.4)	**48.0**	(1.5)	**38.9**	(1.4)
	Turkey	**-15.1**	(2.0)	**-12.8**	(1.6)	**11.0**	(1.6)	**8.1**	(1.5)	**20.7**	(1.7)	**14.7**	(1.4)	**26.2**	(1.5)	**21.1**	(1.4)	**31.7**	(1.4)	**24.8**	(1.3)
	United Kingdom	1.2	(1.6)	-1.4	(1.4)	**4.4**	(1.4)	1.6	(1.2)	**27.2**	(1.4)	**20.4**	(1.4)	**33.6**	(1.6)	**26.8**	(1.5)	**39.4**	(1.2)	**32.8**	(1.2)
	United States	**-4.4**	(1.6)	**-7.4**	(1.6)	0.2	(1.6)	**-3.3**	(1.4)	**22.0**	(1.6)	**13.8**	(1.3)	**31.8**	(1.4)	**25.5**	(1.3)	**36.3**	(1.7)	**29.6**	(1.4)
	OECD average	**-2.0**	(0.6)	**-4.0**	(0.6)	**1.7**	(0.6)	**1.1**	(0.5)	**22.5**	(0.6)	**15.6**	(0.5)	**34.7**	(0.5)	**27.1**	(0.5)	**40.0**	(0.6)	**32.3**	(0.5)
Partners	Albania	**13.1**	(3.3)	4.3	(2.8)	**17.1**	(3.3)	**10.1**	(2.9)	**37.0**	(3.1)	**23.7**	(3.3)	**34.1**	(2.2)	**26.6**	(2.0)	**32.9**	(2.2)	**24.9**	(2.0)
	Argentina	**-5.7**	(2.1)	**-6.3**	(1.7)	2.6	(2.0)	0.7	(1.7)	**25.6**	(2.1)	**16.5**	(1.7)	**30.5**	(2.4)	**22.8**	(1.7)	**40.0**	(2.8)	**28.3**	(2.2)
	Azerbaijan	**7.6**	(1.7)	**4.9**	(1.6)	**9.5**	(1.7)	**6.6**	(1.6)	**13.1**	(1.6)	**9.3**	(1.6)	**16.4**	(2.0)	**14.9**	(2.0)	**10.2**	(1.9)	**7.8**	(1.9)
	Brazil	**12.1**	(1.3)	**5.5**	(1.3)	**3.9**	(1.4)	1.6	(1.2)	**26.6**	(1.4)	**18.6**	(1.3)	**31.0**	(1.3)	**23.9**	(1.1)	**35.5**	(1.6)	**28.3**	(1.3)
	Bulgaria	**4.7**	(2.0)	-1.8	(1.7)	**7.0**	(2.0)	1.7	(1.7)	**19.2**	(1.9)	**8.8**	(1.6)	**40.8**	(2.5)	**27.4**	(2.2)	**45.4**	(2.4)	**32.4**	(1.9)
	Colombia	**-11.5**	(2.0)	**-10.2**	(1.8)	1.5	(1.8)	0.9	(1.6)	**9.0**	(2.0)	**5.6**	(1.7)	**31.2**	(1.7)	**25.3**	(1.4)	**35.8**	(1.7)	**29.3**	(1.5)
	Croatia	-1.4	(1.8)	**-5.1**	(1.5)	-2.2	(1.6)	**-3.9**	(1.5)	**15.5**	(1.9)	**8.0**	(1.5)	**35.0**	(1.6)	**28.2**	(1.4)	**39.5**	(1.5)	**32.5**	(1.2)
	Dubai (UAE)	**-20.5**	(1.6)	**-15.8**	(1.6)	**-3.7**	(1.7)	**-3.5**	(1.5)	**25.4**	(1.4)	**13.0**	(1.3)	**40.9**	(1.3)	**27.4**	(1.5)	**47.1**	(1.5)	**31.6**	(1.4)
	Hong Kong-China	**8.2**	(1.8)	**3.6**	(1.6)	**9.2**	(1.4)	**6.8**	(1.3)	**28.1**	(1.5)	**23.7**	(1.2)	**28.8**	(1.4)	**24.5**	(1.2)	**29.2**	(1.3)	**25.9**	(1.2)
	Indonesia	**11.2**	(2.2)	**5.6**	(2.0)	**12.3**	(1.9)	**6.4**	(1.7)	**16.2**	(2.1)	**9.4**	(1.9)	**22.0**	(1.5)	**18.1**	(1.3)	**21.0**	(1.6)	**17.8**	(1.4)
	Jordan	**20.8**	(1.5)	**13.3**	(1.5)	**21.7**	(1.4)	**14.0**	(1.4)	**27.0**	(1.4)	**17.9**	(1.5)	**18.8**	(1.6)	**14.5**	(1.4)	**23.0**	(1.4)	**16.6**	(1.3)
	Kazakhstan	**-9.0**	(2.3)	**-11.8**	(2.0)	**-7.8**	(2.1)	**-12.0**	(1.8)	**4.2**	(1.8)	**-3.0**	(1.6)	**34.3**	(1.6)	**29.8**	(1.4)	**36.3**	(1.7)	**30.8**	(1.4)
	Kyrgyzstan	**12.9**	(1.9)	**4.8**	(1.8)	2.6	(2.1)	-1.7	(1.7)	**9.7**	(1.6)	**3.4**	(1.6)	**34.9**	(2.3)	**24.4**	(1.7)	**32.4**	(2.3)	**23.0**	(1.7)
	Latvia	-3.0	(2.3)	**-6.5**	(2.0)	**5.3**	(2.2)	1.8	(1.8)	**18.8**	(2.2)	**9.9**	(2.1)	**28.7**	(1.4)	**22.0**	(1.3)	**34.1**	(1.6)	**27.1**	(1.5)
	Liechtenstein	-5.5	(7.1)	-3.2	(6.9)	2.6	(4.7)	5.7	(4.7)	**20.4**	(5.2)	**20.7**	(5.1)	**36.5**	(3.9)	**31.0**	(4.3)	**43.1**	(4.0)	**38.3**	(4.2)
	Lithuania	**-8.4**	(2.4)	**-12.2**	(1.9)	**4.3**	(1.7)	0.5	(1.6)	**22.4**	(1.9)	**9.9**	(1.8)	**32.2**	(2.1)	**22.4**	(1.7)	**36.4**	(1.7)	**26.0**	(1.6)
	Macao-China	**9.2**	(1.4)	**8.0**	(1.3)	**16.2**	(1.2)	**15.6**	(1.2)	**18.4**	(1.3)	**19.7**	(1.3)	**19.0**	(1.1)	**16.0**	(1.0)	**22.2**	(1.0)	**20.9**	(0.9)
	Montenegro	**-14.5**	(1.9)	**-14.4**	(1.7)	-0.6	(2.0)	-0.7	(1.6)	**10.7**	(2.5)	**4.7**	(2.4)	**33.4**	(1.4)	**27.5**	(1.4)	**31.6**	(1.5)	**26.4**	(1.4)
	Panama	**-6.9**	(2.7)	-2.5	(2.5)	-1.2	(2.3)	1.1	(2.0)	**15.1**	(2.4)	**11.6**	(2.1)	**34.9**	(2.4)	**25.1**	(2.5)	**34.9**	(2.8)	**27.0**	(2.1)
	Peru	**-18.7**	(2.3)	**-15.6**	(1.8)	-2.8	(2.0)	**-4.1**	(1.7)	**9.3**	(2.1)	2.9	(1.6)	**31.1**	(2.3)	**21.6**	(1.4)	**39.3**	(2.7)	**26.0**	(1.6)
	Qatar	1.9	(1.1)	**-3.1**	(1.0)	2.0	(1.3)	-0.3	(1.1)	**28.6**	(1.1)	**15.4**	(1.1)	**37.7**	(1.2)	**26.9**	(1.2)	**34.7**	(1.2)	**24.7**	(1.1)
	Romania	**6.8**	(2.0)	1.2	(1.6)	**7.4**	(1.8)	0.5	(1.4)	**21.1**	(1.7)	**12.5**	(1.5)	**32.8**	(2.0)	**25.9**	(1.8)	**38.1**	(2.3)	**30.0**	(2.0)
	Russian Federation	**-7.5**	(2.3)	**-8.1**	(2.0)	**4.0**	(1.8)	2.0	(1.6)	**18.7**	(2.0)	**11.5**	(1.8)	**34.1**	(1.8)	**26.6**	(1.5)	**35.0**	(1.7)	**27.5**	(1.5)
	Serbia	**-14.7**	(1.7)	**-14.4**	(1.4)	**2.7**	(1.4)	1.6	(1.3)	**11.7**	(1.5)	**6.3**	(1.3)	**32.4**	(1.5)	**27.0**	(1.4)	**37.4**	(1.3)	**31.6**	(1.4)
	Shanghai-China	**4.9**	(1.8)	0.1	(1.6)	**14.8**	(1.7)	**9.6**	(1.6)	**26.5**	(1.8)	**18.8**	(1.6)	**27.3**	(1.3)	**22.1**	(1.1)	**32.9**	(1.4)	**26.8**	(1.3)
	Singapore	**-14.1**	(1.4)	**-13.4**	(1.3)	0.7	(1.6)	-0.9	(1.5)	**25.9**	(1.6)	**17.4**	(1.6)	**31.9**	(1.4)	**25.5**	(1.2)	**45.1**	(1.4)	**37.1**	(1.3)
	Chinese Taipei	**20.7**	(1.6)	**11.7**	(1.4)	**28.3**	(1.7)	**20.5**	(1.4)	**35.0**	(1.6)	**26.8**	(1.3)	**30.6**	(1.9)	**23.2**	(1.4)	**32.6**	(1.9)	**26.0**	(1.5)
	Thailand	**24.8**	(1.6)	**18.8**	(1.4)	**18.4**	(2.0)	**13.8**	(1.7)	**23.6**	(2.0)	**18.1**	(1.5)	**21.9**	(1.5)	**17.0**	(1.0)	**19.5**	(1.5)	**14.8**	(1.1)
	Trinidad and Tobago	**12.1**	(2.0)	**5.7**	(1.7)	2.9	(2.1)	-0.6	(2.1)	**35.5**	(2.1)	**24.3**	(2.0)	**37.9**	(1.5)	**29.0**	(1.6)	**41.0**	(1.8)	**33.0**	(1.8)
	Tunisia	-1.3	(2.0)	-2.5	(1.8)	**13.4**	(1.5)	**9.4**	(1.5)	**22.5**	(1.7)	**17.7**	(1.6)	**18.1**	(1.5)	**15.8**	(1.4)	**22.4**	(1.8)	**20.2**	(1.6)
	Uruguay	-1.4	(1.7)	**-2.9**	(1.4)	1.6	(1.4)	-0.2	(1.2)	**24.3**	(1.3)	**15.2**	(1.3)	**31.9**	(1.4)	**22.6**	(1.3)	**43.0**	(1.3)	**32.7**	(1.2)

Note: Values that are statistically significant are indicated in bold (see Annex A3).
1. Adjusted models account for gender, the PISA index of economic, social and cultural status, immigration status and language spoken at home.
StatLink http://dx.doi.org/10.1787/888932343285

[Part 1/1]
Percentage of students, by reader profile
Table III.1.27 *Results based on students' self-reports*

	Group 1 %	Group 1 S.E.	Group 2 %	Group 2 S.E.	Group 3 %	Group 3 S.E.	Group 4 %	Group 4 S.E.	Group 5 %	Group 5 S.E.	Group 6 %	Group 6 S.E.
OECD												
Australia	21.0	(0.5)	13.9	(0.4)	34.2	(0.6)	5.3	(0.2)	8.2	(0.3)	17.5	(0.5)
Austria	16.6	(0.7)	33.1	(0.8)	24.1	(0.7)	3.4	(0.3)	13.3	(0.5)	9.4	(0.4)
Belgium	16.6	(0.6)	29.6	(0.6)	32.0	(0.8)	2.0	(0.2)	8.1	(0.4)	11.6	(0.5)
Canada	23.3	(0.5)	13.4	(0.3)	37.0	(0.5)	6.0	(0.2)	5.8	(0.3)	14.5	(0.4)
Chile	17.7	(0.6)	19.7	(0.7)	32.5	(0.7)	6.4	(0.4)	7.2	(0.4)	16.5	(0.6)
Czech Republic	12.5	(0.6)	35.0	(0.8)	28.0	(0.8)	1.5	(0.2)	12.2	(0.7)	10.8	(0.6)
Denmark	22.0	(0.7)	26.2	(0.7)	30.6	(0.8)	3.8	(0.3)	6.7	(0.4)	10.6	(0.6)
Estonia	17.8	(0.7)	43.1	(0.9)	19.3	(0.8)	3.1	(0.3)	10.7	(0.5)	6.0	(0.4)
Finland	20.4	(0.7)	39.3	(0.9)	17.0	(0.6)	2.1	(0.2)	13.4	(0.5)	7.9	(0.5)
France	18.5	(0.7)	27.5	(0.8)	36.8	(0.8)	1.9	(0.2)	6.2	(0.4)	9.1	(0.6)
Germany	18.3	(0.7)	22.5	(0.7)	35.9	(0.9)	3.0	(0.3)	9.0	(0.5)	11.6	(0.5)
Greece	11.6	(0.6)	22.9	(0.7)	38.6	(0.8)	3.2	(0.3)	9.0	(0.5)	14.8	(0.7)
Hungary	21.3	(0.8)	30.8	(0.9)	20.5	(0.7)	5.7	(0.5)	11.0	(0.5)	10.7	(0.6)
Iceland	18.4	(0.6)	30.3	(0.8)	20.5	(0.7)	4.5	(0.3)	12.7	(0.5)	13.5	(0.6)
Ireland	20.2	(0.8)	24.7	(0.8)	34.4	(0.9)	3.0	(0.3)	7.4	(0.5)	10.3	(0.6)
Israel	16.7	(0.5)	19.7	(0.6)	31.8	(0.9)	5.8	(0.4)	8.5	(0.4)	17.5	(0.7)
Italy	18.4	(0.4)	20.8	(0.3)	45.2	(0.5)	2.2	(0.1)	3.7	(0.2)	9.7	(0.3)
Japan	27.9	(0.9)	26.2	(0.6)	19.2	(0.6)	7.2	(0.3)	11.6	(0.7)	7.9	(0.5)
Korea	25.8	(0.9)	9.3	(0.4)	41.2	(0.9)	5.9	(0.4)	3.2	(0.3)	14.5	(0.7)
Luxembourg	19.5	(0.6)	30.1	(0.7)	21.7	(0.7)	4.1	(0.3)	13.0	(0.6)	11.7	(0.5)
Mexico	19.9	(0.3)	16.6	(0.3)	36.0	(0.4)	7.4	(0.2)	5.5	(0.2)	14.7	(0.3)
Netherlands	14.3	(0.8)	19.8	(1.0)	31.5	(0.9)	4.3	(0.3)	9.7	(0.7)	20.4	(1.3)
New Zealand	23.9	(0.7)	12.7	(0.6)	30.3	(0.7)	8.5	(0.5)	7.9	(0.4)	16.7	(0.5)
Norway	19.4	(0.7)	37.0	(0.7)	22.5	(0.7)	2.8	(0.2)	9.8	(0.5)	8.6	(0.5)
Poland	13.1	(0.6)	37.1	(0.6)	21.7	(0.6)	3.4	(0.3)	14.2	(0.6)	10.6	(0.5)
Portugal	19.2	(0.6)	24.0	(0.7)	32.1	(0.7)	4.0	(0.3)	9.0	(0.5)	11.7	(0.6)
Slovak Republic	12.8	(0.6)	39.4	(0.9)	16.8	(0.5)	3.3	(0.3)	17.7	(0.6)	10.0	(0.5)
Slovenia	10.4	(0.6)	34.5	(0.8)	20.9	(0.7)	2.7	(0.3)	18.7	(0.6)	12.9	(0.5)
Spain	19.8	(0.5)	18.7	(0.5)	41.5	(0.5)	2.9	(0.2)	5.6	(0.4)	11.6	(0.5)
Sweden	19.9	(0.7)	22.7	(0.7)	24.3	(0.6)	5.1	(0.3)	12.2	(0.5)	15.6	(0.6)
Switzerland	20.6	(0.6)	33.2	(0.8)	22.5	(0.6)	3.2	(0.2)	11.3	(0.5)	9.1	(0.5)
Turkey	24.7	(0.6)	12.8	(0.5)	24.6	(0.8)	15.5	(0.6)	8.2	(0.4)	14.2	(0.6)
United Kingdom	18.9	(0.6)	20.7	(0.5)	31.1	(0.7)	5.2	(0.3)	10.2	(0.5)	13.9	(0.6)
United States	19.0	(0.8)	10.9	(0.6)	36.7	(0.8)	6.5	(0.4)	6.4	(0.4)	20.4	(0.8)
OECD average	18.8	(0.1)	25.2	(0.1)	29.2	(0.1)	4.6	(0.1)	9.6	(0.1)	12.5	(0.1)
Partners												
Albania	35.6	(0.9)	14.7	(0.6)	23.4	(1.0)	11.5	(0.9)	6.1	(0.4)	8.7	(0.6)
Argentina	17.0	(0.8)	22.9	(0.8)	29.5	(0.9)	7.6	(0.5)	9.8	(0.6)	13.1	(0.7)
Azerbaijan	21.8	(0.9)	10.2	(0.6)	15.1	(0.7)	26.7	(1.0)	10.9	(0.6)	15.3	(0.7)
Brazil	20.9	(0.5)	15.6	(0.4)	28.9	(0.6)	10.2	(0.4)	7.9	(0.3)	16.4	(0.5)
Bulgaria	21.6	(1.5)	20.4	(0.8)	20.2	(0.7)	10.4	(0.6)	11.3	(0.6)	16.1	(1.0)
Colombia	23.9	(1.0)	22.4	(0.8)	20.9	(1.0)	11.2	(0.7)	9.5	(0.5)	12.2	(0.6)
Croatia	16.6	(0.8)	36.4	(0.7)	15.4	(0.5)	4.7	(0.3)	17.7	(0.6)	9.3	(0.5)
Dubai (UAE)	29.0	(0.7)	26.5	(0.6)	15.7	(0.6)	9.7	(0.4)	11.5	(0.5)	7.6	(0.3)
Hong Kong-China	27.7	(0.8)	13.6	(0.6)	12.3	(0.5)	19.2	(0.6)	14.2	(0.6)	13.1	(0.6)
Indonesia	32.2	(1.0)	10.6	(0.6)	14.3	(0.6)	24.6	(0.9)	6.4	(0.4)	11.9	(0.7)
Jordan	16.9	(0.6)	17.1	(0.6)	19.7	(0.6)	16.2	(0.7)	11.8	(0.5)	18.3	(0.7)
Kazakhstan	34.9	(0.8)	10.9	(0.5)	6.3	(0.4)	33.1	(1.0)	9.2	(0.4)	5.6	(0.4)
Kyrgyzstan	26.6	(1.0)	7.3	(0.4)	9.3	(0.5)	36.0	(0.9)	7.9	(0.5)	12.9	(0.5)
Latvia	20.3	(0.8)	25.1	(1.0)	17.5	(0.7)	10.1	(0.7)	14.0	(0.6)	13.0	(0.8)
Liechtenstein	22.9	(2.1)	26.5	(2.5)	20.7	(2.0)	4.6	(1.0)	11.5	(1.8)	13.8	(1.7)
Lithuania	27.6	(0.7)	25.0	(0.7)	13.4	(0.5)	9.4	(0.4)	15.2	(0.6)	9.4	(0.5)
Macao-China	20.5	(0.5)	23.0	(0.6)	18.4	(0.5)	9.8	(0.4)	14.4	(0.4)	13.8	(0.5)
Montenegro	18.6	(0.6)	23.4	(0.6)	12.2	(0.6)	14.1	(0.6)	19.3	(0.5)	12.3	(0.5)
Panama	20.7	(1.0)	16.7	(1.0)	19.3	(1.3)	16.5	(1.1)	12.6	(0.8)	14.2	(0.9)
Peru	34.2	(0.8)	16.1	(0.6)	14.6	(0.5)	18.1	(0.7)	8.0	(0.4)	9.1	(0.5)
Qatar	22.8	(0.4)	19.7	(0.4)	16.4	(0.4)	15.4	(0.4)	14.0	(0.4)	11.7	(0.3)
Romania	21.4	(0.9)	22.3	(0.8)	29.3	(1.0)	6.3	(0.4)	8.1	(0.6)	12.6	(0.7)
Russian Federation	33.9	(1.0)	12.0	(0.5)	14.8	(0.5)	18.7	(0.5)	8.9	(0.4)	11.7	(0.6)
Serbia	16.7	(0.7)	26.4	(0.6)	15.9	(0.6)	9.9	(0.4)	18.8	(0.6)	12.3	(0.4)
Shanghai-China	41.4	(0.8)	17.4	(0.6)	19.9	(0.7)	10.5	(0.5)	4.3	(0.3)	6.5	(0.4)
Singapore	39.3	(0.8)	20.0	(0.6)	19.1	(0.5)	7.6	(0.3)	6.7	(0.3)	7.4	(0.4)
Chinese Taipei	29.1	(0.9)	14.6	(0.6)	15.7	(0.5)	16.6	(0.6)	10.2	(0.4)	13.7	(0.6)
Thailand	30.7	(0.7)	9.3	(0.5)	6.5	(0.4)	33.6	(0.7)	9.4	(0.5)	10.5	(0.5)
Trinidad and Tobago	29.1	(0.8)	19.8	(0.7)	19.8	(0.5)	12.2	(0.5)	9.1	(0.4)	10.0	(0.5)
Tunisia	28.8	(0.8)	15.7	(0.7)	20.3	(0.7)	14.5	(0.8)	8.7	(0.5)	11.9	(0.5)
Uruguay	18.2	(0.5)	16.8	(0.7)	36.3	(0.6)	5.9	(0.3)	5.2	(0.3)	17.7	(0.6)

Note: Group 1: "Wide and deep"; Group 2: "Narrow and deep"; Group 3: "Highly restricted and deep"; Group 4: "Wide and surface"; Group 5: "Narrow and surface"; Group 6: "Highly restricted and surface".
StatLink ⟨⟩ http://dx.doi.org/10.1787/888932343285

PISA 2009 RESULTS: LEARNING TO LEARN – VOLUME III

[Part 1/2]
Reading performance, by reader profile
Table III.1.28 *Results based on students' self-reports*

	Before accounting for student background variables											
	Group 1		Group 2		Group 3		Group 4		Group 5		Group 6	
	Mean score	S.E.	Mean score	S.E.	Mean score	S.E.	Mean score	S.E.	Mean score	S.E.	Mean score	S.E.
OECD												
Australia	570	(2.9)	510	(3.1)	537	(2.7)	496	(3.9)	449	(3.2)	455	(2.4)
Austria	540	(4.3)	480	(3.0)	492	(4.3)	437	(7.8)	413	(4.0)	401	(5.1)
Belgium	571	(3.4)	531	(2.8)	515	(2.7)	459	(8.2)	443	(4.1)	427	(3.8)
Canada	566	(2.0)	521	(2.9)	536	(1.6)	500	(4.0)	473	(3.4)	468	(2.4)
Chile	485	(3.7)	477	(3.5)	454	(3.7)	422	(4.3)	418	(5.1)	399	(3.9)
Czech Republic	548	(4.6)	494	(2.9)	495	(3.8)	443	(11.5)	419	(4.6)	408	(3.3)
Denmark	535	(2.9)	508	(2.6)	497	(3.2)	458	(5.8)	441	(4.4)	426	(4.4)
Estonia	541	(3.4)	510	(2.8)	501	(3.5)	464	(8.5)	446	(4.1)	435	(6.3)
Finland	601	(2.5)	543	(2.5)	533	(3.8)	522	(8.2)	474	(2.8)	448	(6.4)
France	558	(4.1)	504	(3.5)	499	(4.5)	462	(16.6)	425	(6.1)	393	(6.4)
Germany	560	(3.3)	507	(3.3)	518	(3.0)	459	(7.3)	439	(5.3)	430	(4.5)
Greece	540	(4.4)	494	(4.5)	492	(4.9)	472	(8.0)	434	(7.9)	431	(5.7)
Hungary	539	(3.9)	513	(3.4)	497	(4.7)	434	(9.0)	453	(3.8)	420	(6.4)
Iceland	564	(3.1)	516	(2.5)	507	(3.6)	479	(7.1)	452	(4.1)	430	(3.8)
Ireland	547	(4.2)	491	(3.5)	507	(3.5)	473	(9.3)	435	(6.0)	435	(6.2)
Israel	518	(4.7)	503	(4.2)	490	(4.2)	433	(7.2)	442	(5.2)	419	(4.8)
Italy	524	(2.2)	496	(1.9)	493	(1.7)	438	(5.4)	417	(4.0)	400	(4.6)
Japan	565	(3.3)	533	(3.6)	543	(3.4)	473	(5.8)	438	(7.0)	431	(7.2)
Korea	574	(3.0)	556	(4.8)	551	(2.9)	493	(5.9)	466	(6.5)	468	(5.6)
Luxembourg	537	(3.0)	476	(2.8)	490	(3.1)	450	(7.7)	417	(4.0)	398	(4.9)
Mexico	446	(2.4)	449	(2.2)	435	(2.3)	381	(3.1)	399	(2.8)	381	(2.7)
Netherlands	575	(4.7)	550	(4.7)	516	(4.9)	492	(7.0)	472	(6.7)	446	(4.9)
New Zealand	569	(3.4)	520	(4.2)	548	(3.5)	489	(5.5)	447	(5.1)	462	(4.1)
Norway	559	(3.7)	512	(2.4)	505	(3.0)	480	(8.3)	441	(4.7)	419	(5.4)
Poland	560	(4.2)	519	(2.8)	500	(3.5)	479	(7.3)	457	(3.7)	432	(4.9)
Portugal	532	(3.9)	501	(3.0)	510	(3.0)	429	(6.5)	420	(4.0)	415	(4.2)
Slovak Republic	543	(4.8)	495	(2.7)	482	(4.4)	452	(10.0)	434	(3.9)	407	(5.8)
Slovenia	555	(3.8)	504	(2.4)	500	(2.9)	468	(7.5)	440	(2.9)	426	(3.1)
Spain	532	(2.0)	489	(2.4)	484	(2.3)	448	(6.1)	422	(4.4)	411	(3.5)
Sweden	567	(3.3)	510	(3.1)	501	(4.1)	483	(6.6)	458	(3.6)	428	(3.8)
Switzerland	562	(3.1)	508	(2.5)	508	(3.1)	456	(7.0)	432	(3.1)	418	(3.9)
Turkey	482	(4.1)	480	(4.5)	488	(4.7)	428	(3.5)	439	(4.9)	433	(4.3)
United Kingdom	548	(3.5)	492	(2.9)	509	(3.4)	473	(5.5)	441	(4.5)	446	(3.5)
United States	539	(6.1)	503	(4.7)	516	(4.1)	473	(5.7)	454	(5.5)	458	(3.5)
OECD average	546	(0.6)	506	(0.6)	504	(0.6)	462	(1.3)	440	(0.8)	427	(0.8)
Partners												
Albania	410	(4.5)	392	(5.2)	392	(7.3)	353	(5.5)	348	(8.4)	335	(5.8)
Argentina	426	(6.9)	426	(5.9)	404	(5.3)	351	(7.6)	380	(6.9)	359	(5.9)
Azerbaijan	372	(4.6)	366	(5.6)	347	(4.8)	368	(3.5)	364	(5.3)	354	(4.5)
Brazil	434	(4.5)	440	(3.3)	425	(3.3)	374	(2.8)	389	(4.0)	372	(2.8)
Bulgaria	487	(8.6)	457	(6.6)	426	(7.3)	401	(7.8)	407	(6.0)	367	(6.6)
Colombia	419	(5.5)	438	(4.5)	429	(4.7)	368	(5.4)	395	(4.9)	386	(3.9)
Croatia	532	(3.8)	493	(3.1)	479	(4.4)	449	(5.8)	428	(3.6)	405	(4.8)
Dubai (UAE)	509	(2.6)	469	(2.3)	461	(3.3)	417	(4.5)	404	(3.5)	382	(5.0)
Hong Kong-China	574	(2.7)	543	(3.7)	543	(4.2)	518	(3.1)	496	(3.6)	490	(4.0)
Indonesia	423	(4.3)	420	(5.8)	394	(4.7)	389	(3.9)	385	(5.6)	372	(3.6)
Jordan	426	(3.9)	441	(3.9)	409	(4.9)	384	(4.0)	409	(4.6)	374	(4.2)
Kazakhstan	420	(4.0)	422	(4.9)	415	(8.7)	358	(2.7)	364	(4.9)	355	(6.6)
Kyrgyzstan	341	(4.7)	344	(8.1)	300	(6.5)	307	(3.4)	311	(5.1)	285	(5.0)
Latvia	521	(3.9)	505	(3.2)	491	(4.9)	456	(4.9)	453	(4.1)	431	(4.7)
Liechtenstein	563	(7.2)	510	(8.6)	495	(8.7)	443	(18.7)	446	(13.4)	444	(10.6)
Lithuania	515	(3.0)	476	(3.3)	455	(4.7)	455	(4.3)	429	(3.4)	411	(4.9)
Macao-China	522	(2.3)	495	(1.9)	488	(2.2)	480	(3.1)	466	(2.2)	444	(2.8)
Montenegro	451	(3.9)	427	(3.2)	398	(4.6)	394	(5.6)	395	(2.8)	358	(3.9)
Panama	405	(7.1)	399	(9.9)	385	(10.2)	348	(8.5)	360	(7.6)	338	(10.1)
Peru	389	(4.4)	405	(6.4)	367	(5.7)	340	(3.4)	349	(6.8)	323	(6.1)
Qatar	420	(2.9)	386	(2.7)	370	(3.4)	351	(2.9)	350	(2.6)	327	(3.0)
Romania	453	(4.9)	447	(4.6)	430	(4.1)	382	(6.5)	390	(7.6)	368	(5.6)
Russian Federation	493	(3.7)	459	(4.4)	470	(4.8)	441	(3.8)	420	(4.1)	411	(5.6)
Serbia	484	(3.8)	465	(3.1)	453	(4.1)	413	(4.4)	414	(3.3)	389	(4.0)
Shanghai-China	577	(2.9)	571	(3.6)	554	(2.9)	511	(4.5)	508	(5.7)	491	(5.3)
Singapore	566	(1.8)	525	(2.9)	527	(3.0)	472	(4.7)	452	(4.7)	439	(4.7)
Chinese Taipei	536	(3.5)	510	(3.3)	504	(3.3)	476	(3.7)	451	(3.9)	442	(4.5)
Thailand	446	(3.8)	441	(3.8)	415	(5.7)	411	(2.4)	407	(4.2)	381	(3.8)
Trinidad and Tobago	457	(3.7)	437	(4.0)	415	(4.3)	382	(4.0)	382	(5.6)	356	(5.0)
Tunisia	414	(3.5)	421	(4.2)	416	(4.2)	381	(3.9)	393	(6.1)	372	(3.8)
Uruguay	455	(3.6)	461	(4.1)	437	(3.5)	381	(5.3)	392	(5.8)	370	(3.7)

Notes: Values that are statistically significant are indicated in bold (see Annex A3). Performance difference between each group and group 1.
Student background variables: Gender, immigrant background, language spoken at home and the PISA index of economic, social and cultural status
Group 1: "Wide and deep"; Group 2: "Narrow and deep"; Group 3: "Highly restricted and deep"; Group 4: "Wide and surface"; Group 5: "Narrow and surface";
Group 6: "Highly restricted and surface".
StatLink ᵐˢᵖ http://dx.doi.org/10.1787/888932343285

[Part 2/2]
Reading performance, by reader profile
Table III.1.28 *Results based on students' self-reports*

						After accounting for student background variables						
	Group 1		Group 2		Group 3		Group 4		Group 5		Group 6	
	Mean score	S.E.	Mean score	S.E.	Mean score	S.E.	Mean score	S.E.	Mean score	S.E.	Mean score	S.E.
OECD												
Australia	544	(8.3)	498	(7.5)	522	(8.2)	482	(8.1)	447	(8.4)	453	(7.4)
Austria	489	(6.2)	445	(6.5)	457	(6.6)	414	(9.4)	388	(6.8)	404	(7.0)
Belgium	516	(6.5)	485	(6.5)	475	(6.1)	429	(9.0)	413	(6.8)	460	(4.1)
Canada	537	(4.2)	503	(4.3)	518	(3.7)	480	(5.3)	459	(4.7)	460	(4.1)
Chile	391	(25.0)	386	(25.6)	371	(24.7)	343	(25.1)	340	(25.0)	417	(12.3)
Czech Republic	529	(12.9)	491	(12.4)	491	(12.5)	431	(15.8)	427	(12.2)	417	(12.3)
Denmark	475	(4.9)	458	(5.2)	446	(5.0)	416	(7.8)	400	(6.8)	388	(6.2)
Estonia	461	(8.9)	436	(8.5)	430	(8.7)	392	(11.6)	383	(8.9)	380	(9.5)
Finland	506	(10.7)	462	(10.9)	453	(10.8)	439	(13.3)	406	(10.2)	381	(10.7)
France	488	(10.5)	451	(10.6)	445	(10.4)	412	(18.6)	388	(11.7)	363	(10.5)
Germany	505	(5.6)	472	(5.9)	478	(5.7)	396	(16.7)	376	(18.0)	410	(6.9)
Greece	448	(16.4)	426	(16.0)	421	(17.1)	396	(16.7)	411	(21.1)	375	(16.3)
Hungary	471	(20.5)	458	(20.4)	445	(21.1)	397	(22.1)	411	(21.1)	392	(22.2)
Iceland	484	(12.4)	442	(12.8)	438	(12.5)	412	(14.2)	387	(12.4)	369	(12.6)
Ireland	488	(10.4)	446	(9.9)	459	(9.9)	424	(14.2)	404	(10.6)	401	(11.0)
Israel	506	(9.1)	497	(8.3)	491	(8.1)	442	(9.3)	447	(9.2)	433	(9.1)
Italy	450	(4.2)	435	(4.0)	432	(4.2)	382	(7.3)	370	(5.2)	362	(4.2)
Japan	524	(35.4)	497	(35.4)	509	(35.2)	442	(35.1)	413	(35.3)	409	(36.1)
Korea	429	(49.9)	415	(49.5)	416	(50.1)	359	(49.4)	339	(49.5)	344	(49.3)
Luxembourg	500	(4.5)	458	(3.8)	467	(4.9)	425	(7.5)	413	(5.5)	400	(5.7)
Mexico	314	(8.7)	318	(8.4)	310	(8.5)	262	(8.7)	276	(8.9)	267	(9.0)
Netherlands	553	(8.5)	533	(8.7)	506	(9.4)	482	(10.4)	465	(9.8)	442	(9.2)
New Zealand	508	(5.5)	473	(6.0)	495	(5.7)	442	(6.6)	416	(5.9)	429	(5.5)
Norway	493	(6.7)	455	(5.8)	452	(6.1)	427	(9.4)	398	(7.6)	385	(7.3)
Poland	555	(33.5)	533	(32.8)	522	(33.1)	495	(32.2)	483	(33.2)	467	(32.9)
Portugal	474	(9.0)	458	(8.3)	464	(8.1)	393	(9.3)	391	(8.9)	386	(8.3)
Slovak Republic	512	(18.0)	478	(18.2)	471	(17.6)	440	(19.1)	428	(17.7)	412	(18.0)
Slovenia	490	(6.5)	456	(5.6)	453	(5.3)	405	(7.0)	386	(5.8)	380	(5.2)
Spain	477	(4.5)	443	(4.4)	441	(4.6)	428	(8.4)	414	(5.7)	390	(6.6)
Sweden	500	(5.9)	456	(5.6)	450	(6.4)	437	(8.0)	410	(4.1)	400	(4.3)
Switzerland	514	(4.3)	475	(3.9)	476	(4.2)	409	(26.2)	418	(26.7)	423	(26.0)
Turkey	449	(25.7)	448	(26.0)	463	(26.2)	409	(26.2)	412	(6.9)	417	(6.7)
United Kingdom	501	(5.8)	459	(5.2)	471	(6.1)	445	(7.6)	459	(6.8)	463	(5.3)
United States	525	(5.7)	495	(5.7)	512	(4.8)	468	(6.2)	459	(6.8)	463	(5.3)
OECD average	488	(2.7)	460	(2.7)	460	(2.7)	421	(2.9)	406	(2.8)	397	(2.8)
Partners												
Albania	326	(28.7)	321	(29.1)	328	(28.2)	285	(29.7)	285	(29.2)	283	(28.6)
Argentina	344	(20.1)	338	(20.0)	330	(20.2)	295	(21.4)	311	(20.6)	300	(20.3)
Azerbaijan	370	(10.5)	367	(10.8)	357	(10.8)	369	(10.6)	367	(10.7)	363	(10.2)
Brazil	275	(17.5)	282	(17.4)	272	(16.9)	224	(17.4)	241	(16.7)	232	(16.9)
Bulgaria	366	(21.7)	354	(22.1)	342	(21.8)	311	(21.4)	315	(21.3)	296	(22.1)
Colombia	266	(28.9)	282	(29.1)	278	(29.1)	226	(29.7)	247	(29.5)	243	(28.4)
Croatia	487	(12.4)	464	(11.9)	455	(11.8)	423	(12.2)	409	(11.9)	394	(12.2)
Dubai (UAE)	489	(3.4)	468	(2.9)	460	(3.5)	430	(4.8)	422	(4.4)	410	(5.2)
Hong Kong-China	505	(8.6)	482	(9.5)	485	(8.7)	456	(9.1)	437	(9.0)	437	(8.3)
Indonesia	305	(17.8)	308	(18.2)	288	(19.2)	278	(18.3)	279	(18.7)	270	(18.4)
Jordan	370	(12.6)	380	(12.5)	361	(12.1)	336	(11.9)	356	(12.1)	338	(11.7)
Kazakhstan	410	(9.8)	417	(9.8)	418	(12.2)	357	(9.2)	369	(10.5)	368	(11.1)
Kyrgyzstan	368	(14.5)	367	(14.1)	346	(15.3)	343	(14.0)	353	(14.0)	341	(14.8)
Latvia	474	(11.8)	464	(11.2)	457	(11.3)	422	(10.9)	422	(11.1)	412	(10.6)
Liechtenstein	534	(15.7)	488	(16.7)	478	(13.4)	430	(25.2)	433	(17.5)	425	(15.5)
Lithuania	448	(10.0)	425	(10.4)	411	(10.9)	401	(10.8)	393	(10.0)	380	(10.3)
Macao-China	456	(3.5)	435	(3.3)	430	(3.6)	417	(4.0)	407	(3.3)	389	(3.9)
Montenegro	393	(15.3)	377	(14.0)	358	(15.0)	346	(15.4)	350	(14.2)	328	(14.3)
Panama	329	(25.0)	333	(28.2)	325	(25.4)	293	(24.1)	303	(24.8)	279	(24.6)
Peru	234	(16.9)	240	(16.9)	225	(17.1)	198	(16.8)	209	(17.2)	198	(17.0)
Qatar	428	(3.3)	408	(3.9)	399	(3.6)	379	(3.5)	379	(3.4)	369	(3.7)
Romania	353	(33.3)	351	(33.4)	343	(33.4)	294	(33.9)	304	(33.8)	296	(33.1)
Russian Federation	430	(7.8)	402	(9.0)	414	(8.4)	388	(8.1)	374	(8.2)	371	(9.2)
Serbia	464	(11.3)	451	(11.1)	446	(12.1)	404	(11.6)	409	(10.8)	393	(11.5)
Shanghai-China	487	(18.2)	484	(18.2)	472	(18.0)	432	(18.4)	434	(19.1)	423	(18.6)
Singapore	537	(3.9)	509	(4.3)	512	(4.9)	458	(6.3)	444	(6.6)	443	(6.5)
Chinese Taipei	472	(19.5)	454	(19.2)	453	(19.2)	424	(18.1)	405	(19.0)	402	(19.0)
Thailand	421	(4.1)	419	(4.2)	402	(5.8)	395	(3.4)	394	(4.8)	374	(4.5)
Trinidad and Tobago	386	(17.2)	372	(16.0)	358	(17.2)	328	(17.3)	318	(16.8)	312	(16.9)
Tunisia	324	(29.8)	328	(30.9)	334	(29.9)	295	(30.1)	305	(31.2)	293	(30.0)
Uruguay	377	(32.5)	384	(32.1)	368	(32.9)	323	(33.4)	331	(33.9)	320	(33.5)

Notes: Values that are statistically significant are indicated in bold (see Annex A3). Performance difference between each group and group 1.
Student background variables: Gender, immigrant background, language spoken at home and the PISA index of economic, social and cultural status
Group 1: "Wide and deep"; Group 2: "Narrow and deep"; Group 3: "Highly restricted and deep"; Group 4: "Wide and surface"; Group 5: "Narrow and surface"; Group 6: "Highly restricted and surface".
StatLink ⃗⃝🇪 http://dx.doi.org/10.1787/888932343285

[Part 1/2]
Percentage of students, by reader profile and gender
Table III.1.29 *Results based on students' self-reports*

		Boys										
		Group 1		Group 2		Group 3		Group 4		Group 5		Group 6	
		%	S.E.	%	S.E.	%	S.E.	%	S.E.	%	S.E.	%	S.E.
OECD	Australia	14.6	(0.6)	15.6	(0.6)	30.6	(0.7)	5.1	(0.4)	5.2	(0.3)	22.8	(0.7)
	Austria	9.2	(0.6)	35.2	(1.0)	21.4	(0.9)	2.9	(0.4)	8.6	(0.7)	13.1	(0.6)
	Belgium	10.6	(0.5)	34.4	(0.9)	29.0	(0.9)	1.6	(0.2)	5.3	(0.5)	13.6	(0.7)
	Canada	14.4	(0.5)	15.3	(0.5)	36.3	(0.7)	5.9	(0.3)	3.3	(0.2)	19.8	(0.5)
	Chile	10.4	(0.6)	18.6	(0.9)	35.3	(0.9)	5.5	(0.5)	5.5	(0.5)	21.3	(0.8)
	Czech Republic	5.3	(0.4)	35.8	(1.1)	27.0	(1.1)	0.8	(0.2)	8.0	(0.8)	15.1	(0.9)
	Denmark	15.4	(0.8)	29.0	(0.9)	28.5	(1.0)	3.7	(0.4)	4.2	(0.4)	14.2	(0.9)
	Estonia	10.4	(0.7)	43.5	(1.2)	19.2	(1.0)	3.4	(0.4)	6.3	(0.5)	8.6	(0.7)
	Finland	9.3	(0.6)	40.2	(1.2)	16.1	(0.8)	1.9	(0.3)	5.7	(0.5)	11.5	(0.8)
	France	14.1	(0.8)	31.5	(1.0)	33.5	(1.1)	1.3	(0.2)	4.3	(0.5)	11.4	(0.9)
	Germany	12.7	(1.0)	28.0	(1.0)	30.5	(1.2)	2.2	(0.3)	5.6	(0.5)	14.6	(0.8)
	Greece	5.7	(0.5)	29.1	(1.2)	32.3	(1.2)	2.8	(0.4)	4.6	(0.4)	16.5	(0.9)
	Hungary	15.4	(1.0)	29.2	(1.3)	21.6	(0.9)	5.5	(0.6)	8.5	(0.7)	14.7	(1.0)
	Iceland	11.3	(0.7)	27.2	(1.1)	20.6	(0.9)	4.2	(0.5)	8.6	(0.7)	19.9	(1.0)
	Ireland	14.8	(1.0)	23.1	(1.0)	36.0	(1.2)	2.9	(0.4)	5.8	(0.5)	14.1	(1.0)
	Israel	9.7	(0.8)	17.8	(0.8)	34.6	(1.2)	4.7	(0.5)	7.8	(0.6)	24.0	(1.3)
	Italy	12.2	(0.4)	23.7	(0.5)	43.6	(0.6)	2.0	(0.2)	2.1	(0.2)	13.3	(0.5)
	Japan	22.9	(1.1)	28.1	(0.9)	15.2	(0.7)	7.9	(0.5)	6.4	(0.5)	9.5	(0.7)
	Korea	22.1	(1.1)	10.6	(0.6)	38.3	(1.1)	5.8	(0.5)	1.8	(0.3)	18.7	(1.1)
	Luxembourg	11.1	(0.6)	34.4	(0.9)	19.3	(0.9)	3.3	(0.4)	8.7	(0.6)	14.8	(0.8)
	Mexico	14.6	(0.4)	18.7	(0.4)	34.5	(0.6)	7.6	(0.3)	3.8	(0.2)	17.2	(0.5)
	Netherlands	6.3	(0.6)	23.2	(1.2)	30.9	(1.3)	2.2	(0.3)	6.8	(0.6)	24.7	(1.6)
	New Zealand	17.4	(0.9)	13.6	(0.7)	28.9	(0.9)	8.0	(0.6)	5.0	(0.4)	21.4	(0.9)
	Norway	11.6	(0.8)	37.7	(1.1)	22.0	(0.9)	2.4	(0.3)	5.5	(0.5)	12.4	(0.8)
	Poland	6.5	(0.5)	33.7	(0.9)	24.8	(1.0)	2.9	(0.4)	12.3	(0.8)	16.0	(0.8)
	Portugal	9.4	(0.6)	29.4	(1.0)	28.1	(1.0)	3.2	(0.5)	4.1	(0.4)	15.7	(0.8)
	Slovak Republic	6.6	(0.6)	37.5	(1.4)	17.4	(0.9)	2.4	(0.3)	13.5	(0.8)	14.0	(0.9)
	Slovenia	5.1	(0.4)	32.1	(1.0)	20.3	(0.9)	2.5	(0.4)	14.3	(0.7)	17.1	(0.8)
	Spain	13.0	(0.6)	22.3	(0.7)	38.0	(0.6)	2.7	(0.3)	2.4	(0.3)	15.3	(0.6)
	Sweden	10.8	(0.6)	24.1	(1.0)	24.3	(0.8)	3.8	(0.4)	8.1	(0.6)	20.7	(0.9)
	Switzerland	12.7	(0.6)	35.5	(1.1)	21.3	(0.9)	3.1	(0.3)	7.3	(0.4)	12.3	(0.8)
	Turkey	17.7	(0.7)	13.9	(0.6)	22.5	(1.0)	16.3	(0.7)	5.3	(0.5)	18.6	(0.9)
	United Kingdom	13.0	(0.6)	21.3	(0.7)	32.0	(0.8)	4.9	(0.4)	8.8	(0.6)	17.0	(0.7)
	United States	14.0	(0.8)	12.6	(0.8)	34.5	(0.9)	5.8	(0.5)	4.2	(0.4)	24.6	(1.2)
	OECD average	12.1	(0.1)	26.6	(0.2)	27.9	(0.2)	4.2	(0.1)	6.4	(0.1)	16.4	(0.2)
Partners	Albania	24.6	(1.1)	17.6	(0.9)	25.6	(1.3)	11.5	(0.8)	4.0	(0.5)	12.6	(0.9)
	Argentina	10.8	(0.8)	21.3	(1.1)	32.3	(1.2)	6.9	(0.7)	7.7	(0.8)	16.4	(1.0)
	Azerbaijan	18.5	(1.1)	10.6	(0.7)	16.6	(1.1)	25.1	(1.0)	9.9	(0.7)	17.4	(0.8)
	Brazil	11.9	(0.5)	17.1	(0.6)	31.3	(0.8)	7.0	(0.5)	5.8	(0.4)	22.4	(0.8)
	Bulgaria	13.5	(1.3)	19.0	(1.0)	23.4	(1.2)	9.8	(0.6)	10.1	(0.7)	22.0	(1.3)
	Colombia	19.1	(1.3)	22.1	(1.0)	23.3	(1.2)	9.8	(0.9)	8.7	(0.7)	15.4	(0.9)
	Croatia	9.3	(0.7)	34.7	(1.0)	16.4	(0.8)	4.5	(0.4)	13.1	(0.8)	13.3	(0.8)
	Dubai (UAE)	21.8	(0.8)	28.7	(0.8)	15.4	(0.8)	10.3	(0.6)	8.9	(0.6)	9.8	(0.6)
	Hong Kong-China	22.1	(1.0)	15.8	(0.8)	11.6	(0.7)	19.0	(0.8)	11.8	(0.8)	15.3	(0.8)
	Indonesia	25.3	(1.0)	11.9	(0.9)	15.3	(0.7)	24.3	(1.1)	4.5	(0.5)	14.8	(0.9)
	Jordan	12.6	(0.7)	14.2	(0.7)	21.0	(0.9)	18.0	(1.0)	11.4	(0.7)	21.9	(1.0)
	Kazakhstan	28.6	(1.0)	10.8	(0.5)	7.6	(0.6)	35.1	(1.2)	7.9	(0.6)	7.6	(0.6)
	Kyrgyzstan	22.9	(1.1)	7.2	(0.7)	11.7	(0.8)	33.0	(1.2)	7.6	(0.6)	17.1	(1.0)
	Latvia	12.7	(1.0)	22.3	(1.1)	19.8	(1.1)	8.7	(0.8)	10.7	(0.8)	19.2	(1.3)
	Liechtenstein	15.5	(2.3)	27.1	(3.4)	18.2	(2.8)	4.5	(1.6)	5.3	(1.7)	17.5	(2.6)
	Lithuania	14.7	(0.8)	27.6	(1.0)	16.2	(0.8)	7.7	(0.6)	10.2	(0.6)	13.8	(0.7)
	Macao-China	12.9	(0.5)	25.2	(0.9)	19.1	(0.7)	8.4	(0.4)	11.6	(0.6)	17.1	(0.6)
	Montenegro	14.2	(0.8)	24.2	(1.0)	13.0	(0.7)	12.1	(0.9)	17.5	(0.8)	15.5	(0.8)
	Panama	14.9	(1.2)	16.2	(1.3)	22.1	(1.9)	15.1	(1.4)	11.1	(1.3)	17.4	(1.5)
	Peru	28.2	(1.1)	17.7	(0.8)	15.3	(0.7)	17.9	(0.8)	6.2	(0.4)	11.2	(0.7)
	Qatar	18.3	(0.5)	20.0	(0.5)	19.4	(0.5)	13.6	(0.5)	13.5	(0.5)	14.1	(0.5)
	Romania	13.5	(0.8)	23.8	(1.0)	30.3	(1.2)	5.8	(0.6)	5.7	(0.6)	16.2	(0.9)
	Russian Federation	26.1	(1.3)	11.7	(0.7)	16.0	(0.8)	18.2	(0.7)	6.7	(0.6)	16.9	(0.9)
	Serbia	11.1	(0.7)	24.0	(1.1)	16.9	(0.9)	8.8	(0.5)	15.3	(0.9)	17.0	(0.7)
	Shanghai-China	36.0	(0.9)	20.1	(0.9)	18.3	(0.9)	12.1	(0.7)	2.9	(0.3)	7.7	(0.5)
	Singapore	30.8	(1.0)	23.1	(0.8)	20.4	(0.9)	8.0	(0.5)	4.9	(0.4)	9.4	(0.6)
	Chinese Taipei	24.3	(0.9)	16.4	(0.9)	15.5	(0.6)	15.3	(0.7)	7.5	(0.7)	15.5	(0.8)
	Thailand	22.7	(1.0)	10.3	(0.6)	8.9	(0.6)	30.3	(1.1)	6.9	(0.5)	15.1	(0.8)
	Trinidad and Tobago	19.8	(1.1)	19.5	(1.0)	23.9	(0.9)	13.0	(0.8)	8.6	(0.6)	14.3	(0.8)
	Tunisia	21.7	(0.9)	16.9	(0.9)	22.1	(1.1)	14.1	(1.0)	7.4	(0.6)	15.0	(0.8)
	Uruguay	11.5	(0.9)	15.5	(0.7)	38.9	(0.8)	5.4	(0.5)	4.3	(0.4)	22.6	(0.9)

Notes: Values that are statistically significant are indicated in bold (see Annex A3).
Group 1: "Wide and deep"; Group 2: "Narrow and deep"; Group 3: "Highly restricted and deep"; Group 4: "Wide and surface"; Group 5: "Narrow and surface"; Group 6: "Highly restricted and surface"
StatLink ⌐¶⌐ http://dx.doi.org/10.1787/888932343285

[Part 2/2]
Percentage of students, by reader profile and gender
Table III.1.29 *Results based on students' self-reports*

		Girls											Gender difference in the share of Group 1 (B-G)		Gender difference in the share of Group 1 and 2 (B-G)	
		Group 1		Group 2		Group 3		Group 4		Group 5		Group 6					
		%	S.E.	%	S.E.	%	S.E.	%	S.E.	%	S.E.	%	S.E.	% dif.	S.E.	% dif.	S.E.
OECD	Australia	27.1	(0.7)	12.2	(0.5)	37.6	(0.7)	5.4	(0.3)	11.3	(0.5)	12.5	(0.5)	-13	(0.8)	-9	(1.1)
	Austria	23.7	(1.1)	31.2	(1.0)	26.8	(0.9)	3.8	(0.4)	18.3	(0.7)	6.0	(0.6)	-14	(1.3)	-10	(1.6)
	Belgium	22.8	(0.9)	24.8	(0.8)	35.2	(1.0)	2.5	(0.3)	10.8	(0.6)	9.5	(0.5)	-12	(1.0)	-3	(1.5)
	Canada	32.2	(0.7)	11.5	(0.5)	37.7	(0.7)	6.1	(0.4)	8.2	(0.5)	9.1	(0.4)	-18	(0.8)	-14	(0.9)
	Chile	25.4	(0.9)	20.7	(0.9)	29.5	(0.9)	7.3	(0.5)	8.9	(0.7)	11.5	(0.7)	-15	(0.9)	-17	(1.3)
	Czech Republic	20.7	(1.0)	34.0	(1.1)	29.1	(1.1)	2.4	(0.3)	16.0	(0.9)	5.9	(0.7)	-15	(1.3)	-14	(1.7)
	Denmark	28.6	(1.0)	23.5	(1.0)	32.7	(1.0)	3.9	(0.4)	9.3	(0.6)	7.1	(0.6)	-13	(1.2)	-8	(1.5)
	Estonia	25.7	(1.0)	42.7	(1.2)	19.4	(1.1)	2.8	(0.5)	14.9	(0.9)	3.2	(0.4)	-15	(1.0)	-14	(1.5)
	Finland	31.5	(1.1)	38.4	(1.2)	17.9	(0.8)	2.3	(0.2)	21.0	(0.9)	4.3	(0.4)	-22	(1.2)	-20	(1.4)
	France	22.8	(1.0)	23.7	(0.9)	39.9	(1.1)	2.5	(0.4)	8.2	(0.7)	6.9	(0.6)	-9	(1.3)	-1	(1.5)
	Germany	23.7	(1.0)	17.0	(0.8)	41.2	(1.2)	3.9	(0.5)	11.9	(0.7)	8.7	(0.8)	-11	(1.3)	0	(1.6)
	Greece	17.2	(0.8)	16.9	(0.9)	44.6	(1.3)	3.5	(0.4)	13.6	(0.9)	13.2	(0.8)	-11	(0.9)	1	(1.5)
	Hungary	27.2	(1.2)	32.3	(1.3)	19.5	(1.0)	5.9	(0.7)	13.5	(0.8)	6.6	(0.7)	-12	(1.5)	-15	(2.0)
	Iceland	25.5	(1.0)	33.4	(1.1)	20.4	(1.0)	4.9	(0.5)	16.8	(0.8)	7.2	(0.6)	-14	(1.1)	-20	(1.7)
	Ireland	25.7	(1.1)	26.3	(1.1)	32.8	(1.1)	3.1	(0.3)	9.0	(0.7)	6.4	(0.6)	-11	(1.5)	-14	(1.7)
	Israel	23.2	(0.8)	21.5	(0.9)	29.2	(1.1)	6.8	(0.6)	9.2	(0.6)	11.5	(0.7)	-13	(1.3)	-17	(1.8)
	Italy	25.0	(0.5)	17.8	(0.4)	47.0	(0.5)	2.3	(0.2)	5.2	(0.3)	5.8	(0.3)	-13	(0.7)	-7	(0.9)
	Japan	33.1	(1.1)	24.3	(0.8)	23.5	(0.9)	6.5	(0.5)	16.4	(1.0)	6.1	(0.6)	-10	(1.3)	-6	(1.7)
	Korea	29.9	(1.3)	7.9	(0.5)	44.4	(1.4)	6.1	(0.5)	4.5	(0.4)	9.9	(0.5)	-8	(1.6)	-5	(1.8)
	Luxembourg	27.9	(1.0)	25.7	(1.0)	24.2	(1.0)	4.9	(0.5)	17.1	(0.8)	8.5	(0.6)	-17	(1.1)	-8	(1.5)
	Mexico	25.0	(0.5)	14.5	(0.5)	37.4	(0.5)	7.1	(0.3)	7.4	(0.3)	12.3	(0.4)	-10	(0.6)	-6	(0.8)
	Netherlands	22.2	(1.3)	16.4	(1.1)	32.1	(1.2)	6.3	(0.6)	12.6	(0.9)	16.1	(1.2)	-16	(1.2)	-9	(1.4)
	New Zealand	30.5	(1.0)	11.7	(0.6)	31.8	(1.2)	9.0	(0.7)	10.7	(0.7)	11.9	(0.9)	-13	(1.4)	-11	(1.7)
	Norway	27.5	(1.2)	36.3	(1.1)	22.9	(0.9)	3.2	(0.4)	13.9	(0.8)	4.7	(0.5)	-16	(1.4)	-14	(1.7)
	Poland	19.6	(1.0)	40.4	(0.9)	18.6	(0.7)	4.0	(0.4)	16.1	(0.8)	5.2	(0.5)	-13	(1.0)	-20	(1.4)
	Portugal	28.5	(1.0)	18.8	(0.9)	36.0	(0.9)	4.8	(0.5)	14.2	(0.8)	7.8	(0.6)	-19	(1.2)	-9	(1.3)
	Slovak Republic	18.9	(0.9)	41.2	(1.1)	16.3	(0.9)	4.2	(0.4)	22.0	(0.9)	6.0	(0.5)	-12	(1.0)	-16	(2.1)
	Slovenia	15.8	(1.0)	37.0	(1.2)	21.5	(1.0)	2.9	(0.4)	22.9	(0.9)	8.5	(0.5)	-11	(1.0)	-16	(1.3)
	Spain	26.9	(0.6)	14.9	(0.6)	45.0	(0.7)	3.0	(0.3)	8.7	(0.6)	7.8	(0.5)	-14	(0.9)	-6	(0.9)
	Sweden	29.3	(1.2)	21.3	(0.9)	24.3	(1.1)	6.5	(0.5)	16.3	(0.8)	10.4	(0.8)	-19	(1.4)	-16	(1.4)
	Switzerland	28.8	(0.9)	30.8	(1.2)	23.8	(0.9)	3.4	(0.3)	15.2	(0.8)	5.9	(0.6)	-16	(1.1)	-11	(1.6)
	Turkey	32.2	(1.0)	11.6	(0.7)	26.9	(1.2)	14.6	(0.9)	10.9	(0.5)	9.4	(0.8)	-15	(1.3)	-12	(1.5)
	United Kingdom	24.5	(0.9)	20.0	(0.8)	30.3	(1.0)	5.6	(0.4)	11.7	(0.7)	10.8	(0.7)	-11	(1.2)	-10	(1.2)
	United States	24.3	(1.1)	9.0	(0.7)	39.2	(1.0)	7.3	(0.6)	8.6	(0.6)	16.0	(0.8)	-10	(1.0)	-7	(1.2)
	OECD average	25.7	(0.2)	23.8	(0.2)	30.5	(0.2)	5.0	(0.1)	12.8	(0.1)	8.6	(0.1)	-14	(0.2)	-11	(0.3)
Partners	Albania	47.1	(1.5)	11.8	(0.7)	21.2	(1.2)	11.4	(1.3)	8.1	(0.7)	4.5	(0.5)	-22	(1.8)	-17	(1.5)
	Argentina	22.2	(1.0)	24.3	(1.1)	27.1	(1.1)	8.3	(0.8)	12.3	(0.9)	10.3	(0.8)	-11	(1.1)	-14	(1.7)
	Azerbaijan	25.1	(1.3)	9.9	(0.9)	13.5	(0.9)	28.3	(1.3)	11.8	(0.8)	13.2	(1.0)	-7	(1.5)	-6	(1.6)
	Brazil	28.8	(0.8)	14.3	(0.6)	26.9	(0.7)	13.0	(0.5)	10.2	(0.5)	11.2	(0.6)	-17	(0.9)	-14	(1.0)
	Bulgaria	30.3	(1.8)	22.0	(1.2)	16.7	(0.8)	11.0	(1.1)	12.3	(0.8)	9.9	(0.7)	-17	(1.5)	-20	(1.6)
	Colombia	28.2	(1.2)	22.7	(1.3)	18.7	(1.2)	12.4	(1.0)	10.3	(0.7)	9.3	(0.8)	-9	(1.7)	-10	(1.9)
	Croatia	24.7	(1.2)	38.3	(1.0)	14.3	(0.7)	4.8	(0.5)	21.7	(0.9)	4.7	(0.5)	-15	(1.3)	-19	(1.6)
	Dubai (UAE)	36.5	(1.1)	24.3	(0.9)	16.1	(0.8)	9.1	(0.5)	14.0	(0.7)	5.2	(0.4)	-15	(1.3)	-10	(1.3)
	Hong Kong-China	34.0	(1.3)	11.1	(0.8)	13.0	(0.7)	19.4	(0.8)	16.3	(0.8)	10.7	(0.7)	-12	(1.5)	-7	(1.7)
	Indonesia	38.9	(1.4)	9.2	(0.8)	13.4	(0.8)	24.8	(1.3)	8.3	(0.7)	9.1	(0.7)	-14	(1.6)	-11	(1.7)
	Jordan	21.3	(1.0)	19.9	(0.9)	18.4	(0.8)	14.3	(0.8)	12.2	(0.8)	14.7	(0.8)	-9	(1.2)	-14	(1.4)
	Kazakhstan	41.5	(1.1)	11.0	(0.8)	4.9	(0.4)	31.1	(1.2)	10.4	(0.6)	3.6	(0.4)	-13	(1.3)	-13	(1.4)
	Kyrgyzstan	30.1	(1.2)	7.4	(0.5)	7.2	(0.4)	38.9	(1.1)	8.3	(0.7)	8.9	(0.7)	-7	(1.3)	-7	(1.3)
	Latvia	27.7	(1.3)	27.8	(1.5)	15.3	(0.9)	11.5	(1.1)	17.3	(1.0)	7.0	(0.7)	-15	(1.5)	-20	(1.8)
	Liechtenstein	31.1	(3.8)	25.8	(3.6)	23.5	(2.9)	4.6	(1.8)	17.0	(2.8)	9.7	(2.5)	-16	(4.6)	-14	(5.2)
	Lithuania	40.9	(1.2)	22.4	(0.9)	10.5	(0.6)	11.1	(0.6)	20.0	(0.8)	4.9	(0.5)	-26	(1.5)	-21	(1.7)
	Macao-China	28.3	(0.8)	20.8	(0.8)	17.7	(0.8)	11.2	(0.7)	17.2	(0.6)	10.5	(0.5)	-15	(1.0)	-11	(1.2)
	Montenegro	23.3	(0.9)	22.6	(0.9)	11.4	(0.7)	16.2	(0.7)	21.0	(0.8)	9.0	(0.6)	-9	(1.2)	-8	(1.6)
	Panama	26.5	(1.4)	17.2	(1.3)	16.5	(1.5)	17.8	(1.3)	14.2	(1.3)	11.0	(1.0)	-12	(1.8)	-13	(2.3)
	Peru	40.3	(1.1)	14.4	(0.8)	13.8	(0.7)	18.4	(0.8)	9.7	(0.6)	6.9	(0.6)	-12	(1.6)	-9	(1.6)
	Qatar	27.3	(0.6)	19.4	(0.6)	13.3	(0.5)	17.3	(0.5)	14.6	(0.6)	9.2	(0.5)	-9	(0.8)	-8	(0.9)
	Romania	29.1	(1.2)	20.8	(1.0)	28.3	(1.2)	6.8	(0.7)	10.5	(0.9)	9.2	(0.8)	-16	(1.3)	-13	(1.8)
	Russian Federation	41.5	(1.2)	12.4	(0.9)	13.6	(0.5)	19.3	(1.0)	11.0	(0.6)	6.6	(0.5)	-15	(1.5)	-16	(1.7)
	Serbia	22.4	(1.2)	28.8	(1.0)	14.9	(0.8)	11.0	(0.6)	22.1	(0.8)	7.5	(0.4)	-11	(1.3)	-16	(1.5)
	Shanghai-China	46.7	(1.0)	14.7	(0.7)	21.4	(1.0)	8.9	(0.6)	5.8	(0.5)	5.3	(0.5)	-11	(1.2)	-5	(1.4)
	Singapore	48.0	(1.2)	16.7	(0.8)	17.8	(0.7)	7.2	(0.5)	8.3	(0.5)	5.3	(0.4)	-17	(1.5)	-11	(1.4)
	Chinese Taipei	34.0	(1.4)	12.7	(0.8)	15.9	(0.7)	18.0	(0.7)	12.9	(0.7)	11.8	(0.7)	-10	(1.6)	-6	(1.9)
	Thailand	36.7	(1.1)	8.5	(0.6)	4.7	(0.4)	36.1	(1.0)	12.7	(0.8)	7.0	(0.5)	-14	(1.6)	-12	(1.7)
	Trinidad and Tobago	38.0	(1.1)	20.1	(0.9)	15.9	(0.8)	11.4	(0.7)	9.5	(0.7)	6.0	(0.6)	-18	(1.5)	-19	(1.6)
	Tunisia	35.2	(1.0)	14.6	(0.8)	18.7	(0.9)	14.9	(1.0)	10.2	(0.8)	9.2	(0.6)	-13	(1.2)	-11	(1.4)
	Uruguay	24.1	(0.7)	17.9	(0.9)	34.0	(1.0)	6.4	(0.5)	6.2	(0.4)	13.4	(0.8)	-13	(0.9)	-15	(1.3)

Notes: Values that are statistically significant are indicated in bold (see Annex A3).
Group 1: "Wide and deep"; Group 2: "Narrow and deep"; Group 3: "Highly restricted and deep"; Group 4: "Wide and surface"; Group 5: "Narrow and surface"; Group 6: "Highly restricted and surface"
StatLink ᐧᐧᒲᔕᐧ http://dx.doi.org/10.1787/888932343285

[Part 1/4]

Percentage of students, by reader profile and socio-economic background

Table III.1.30 *Results based on students' self-reports*

		Bottom quarter										
		Group 1		Group 2		Group 3		Group 4		Group 5		Group 6	
		%	S.E.	%	S.E.	%	S.E.	%	S.E.	%	S.E.	%	S.E.
OECD	Australia	14.9	(0.8)	12.9	(0.7)	31.7	(1.0)	5.1	(0.4)	11.7	(0.7)	23.8	(0.9)
	Austria	10.1	(1.0)	30.1	(1.4)	24.5	(1.5)	3.8	(0.6)	17.8	(1.1)	13.8	(0.9)
	Belgium	10.6	(0.6)	24.4	(1.0)	32.6	(1.3)	2.9	(0.5)	10.3	(0.9)	19.2	(0.9)
	Canada	17.2	(0.8)	13.4	(0.8)	39.9	(1.1)	5.5	(0.5)	5.6	(0.5)	18.3	(0.7)
	Chile	13.8	(1.1)	15.6	(1.0)	31.4	(1.4)	8.3	(0.6)	7.5	(0.7)	23.5	(1.3)
	Czech Republic	8.5	(1.0)	32.8	(1.5)	27.1	(1.4)	1.9	(0.5)	16.1	(1.2)	13.4	(1.0)
	Denmark	14.8	(1.0)	25.4	(1.5)	30.0	(1.4)	4.4	(0.5)	9.0	(0.8)	16.1	(1.1)
	Estonia	14.8	(1.1)	41.7	(2.1)	20.6	(1.3)	2.2	(0.6)	12.2	(1.2)	8.3	(0.9)
	Finland	12.3	(1.0)	38.7	(1.7)	17.9	(1.3)	1.8	(0.4)	17.7	(1.1)	11.7	(1.0)
	France	11.3	(1.2)	25.0	(1.7)	38.1	(1.7)	2.5	(0.6)	8.2	(0.9)	14.6	(1.2)
	Germany	10.0	(1.0)	21.4	(1.2)	35.1	(1.5)	3.9	(0.7)	12.6	(0.9)	17.0	(1.2)
	Greece	5.9	(0.9)	19.4	(1.4)	40.2	(1.5)	2.9	(0.6)	10.9	(1.0)	20.9	(1.5)
	Hungary	15.7	(1.3)	25.2	(1.7)	20.4	(1.2)	8.3	(1.3)	13.0	(1.2)	17.4	(1.2)
	Iceland	15.1	(1.3)	28.9	(1.7)	19.0	(1.3)	5.7	(0.8)	13.9	(1.1)	17.3	(1.1)
	Ireland	13.7	(1.4)	30.0	(1.8)	29.4	(1.8)	2.3	(0.5)	11.0	(1.0)	13.5	(1.1)
	Israel	13.5	(0.9)	15.9	(1.0)	30.2	(1.5)	7.9	(0.8)	9.5	(0.9)	23.1	(1.4)
	Italy	12.9	(0.6)	18.3	(0.7)	47.2	(0.9)	2.3	(0.3)	4.4	(0.3)	14.9	(0.8)
	Japan	21.4	(1.2)	24.2	(1.2)	19.3	(1.0)	8.5	(0.7)	14.9	(1.0)	11.6	(1.0)
	Korea	14.5	(1.2)	5.1	(0.6)	46.0	(1.7)	6.7	(0.7)	3.8	(0.7)	24.0	(1.6)
	Luxembourg	12.7	(1.1)	29.2	(1.4)	19.3	(1.3)	3.7	(0.5)	16.3	(1.2)	18.8	(1.2)
	Mexico	17.3	(0.7)	10.2	(0.5)	38.9	(0.9)	8.3	(0.6)	5.1	(0.4)	20.1	(0.9)
	Netherlands	8.9	(1.1)	14.5	(1.6)	34.8	(2.0)	6.1	(0.8)	10.7	(1.2)	25.1	(2.5)
	New Zealand	18.8	(1.3)	11.6	(1.1)	27.2	(1.3)	8.4	(1.0)	11.0	(1.1)	22.9	(1.2)
	Norway	14.3	(1.2)	32.9	(1.5)	23.2	(1.4)	3.1	(0.5)	13.4	(1.0)	13.2	(1.0)
	Poland	8.8	(0.9)	32.4	(1.4)	21.9	(1.3)	3.6	(0.7)	18.3	(1.2)	14.8	(1.1)
	Portugal	13.5	(1.1)	21.5	(1.2)	31.4	(1.4)	5.7	(0.7)	11.2	(0.9)	16.8	(1.1)
	Slovak Republic	8.5	(0.9)	35.1	(1.5)	17.5	(1.3)	3.4	(0.6)	21.2	(1.3)	14.4	(1.3)
	Slovenia	7.2	(1.0)	30.7	(1.5)	20.0	(1.2)	2.2	(0.5)	23.2	(1.3)	16.6	(1.1)
	Spain	12.3	(0.7)	15.7	(0.8)	46.1	(1.0)	2.6	(0.4)	6.7	(0.8)	16.7	(1.0)
	Sweden	12.2	(0.9)	21.0	(1.3)	26.1	(1.5)	3.9	(0.6)	14.1	(1.0)	22.6	(1.3)
	Switzerland	13.3	(1.1)	30.6	(1.2)	24.0	(1.1)	3.9	(0.5)	14.2	(1.0)	14.2	(1.1)
	Turkey	23.2	(1.3)	7.7	(0.7)	24.2	(1.2)	18.7	(1.2)	7.5	(0.7)	18.8	(1.2)
	United Kingdom	11.9	(1.1)	23.2	(1.1)	27.6	(1.1)	6.4	(0.7)	13.4	(1.1)	17.6	(1.1)
	United States	16.6	(1.1)	9.3	(0.9)	34.3	(1.5)	6.5	(0.7)	7.6	(0.9)	25.7	(1.4)
	OECD average	13.2	(0.2)	22.8	(0.2)	29.3	(0.2)	5.1	(0.1)	11.9	(0.2)	17.7	(0.2)
Partners	Albania	32.4	(2.4)	9.8	(1.2)	27.8	(3.1)	13.2	(2.2)	5.7	(1.1)	11.0	(1.5)
	Argentina	16.4	(1.3)	15.9	(1.3)	29.4	(1.5)	10.9	(1.1)	10.2	(1.3)	17.3	(1.1)
	Azerbaijan	16.8	(1.5)	9.0	(1.2)	21.0	(1.3)	23.0	(1.7)	10.3	(1.4)	19.9	(1.7)
	Brazil	19.6	(0.8)	10.0	(0.7)	28.6	(1.0)	13.1	(0.7)	8.0	(0.6)	20.8	(1.0)
	Bulgaria	12.3	(1.3)	18.6	(1.5)	23.3	(1.8)	11.3	(1.4)	11.6	(1.4)	22.8	(1.6)
	Colombia	22.1	(2.0)	18.3	(1.2)	20.4	(1.7)	15.3	(1.5)	9.7	(1.0)	14.4	(1.3)
	Croatia	10.5	(1.1)	34.9	(1.4)	16.4	(1.0)	4.6	(0.7)	19.9	(1.3)	13.9	(1.0)
	Dubai (UAE)	20.2	(1.3)	25.4	(1.1)	15.5	(1.2)	11.5	(1.0)	15.2	(1.0)	12.1	(0.8)
	Hong Kong-China	20.9	(1.2)	13.1	(1.2)	14.5	(1.0)	17.1	(1.0)	14.4	(1.0)	20.1	(1.2)
	Indonesia	25.8	(1.2)	8.0	(1.1)	20.0	(1.3)	24.4	(1.8)	5.3	(0.6)	16.4	(1.4)
	Jordan	16.6	(1.1)	10.2	(0.9)	20.5	(1.1)	16.6	(1.3)	10.3	(1.0)	26.0	(1.4)
	Kazakhstan	30.3	(1.7)	10.3	(1.2)	6.7	(0.8)	34.0	(1.9)	11.0	(0.9)	7.5	(1.0)
	Kyrgyzstan	19.8	(1.3)	4.5	(0.7)	12.5	(1.1)	36.1	(1.7)	8.9	(0.8)	18.2	(1.2)
	Latvia	17.0	(1.7)	21.9	(1.7)	16.0	(1.8)	12.1	(1.5)	13.1	(1.2)	19.7	(2.3)
	Liechtenstein	11.3	(3.1)	21.7	(4.3)	24.5	(4.5)	7.3	(2.8)	17.2	(4.2)	17.7	(4.1)
	Lithuania	21.5	(1.4)	22.6	(1.3)	14.1	(1.0)	9.1	(1.0)	19.7	(1.2)	13.1	(1.0)
	Macao-China	14.2	(0.8)	19.4	(1.1)	22.4	(0.9)	8.4	(0.8)	15.2	(1.0)	20.6	(1.2)
	Montenegro	13.6	(1.3)	19.9	(1.2)	14.0	(1.2)	16.0	(1.8)	19.0	(1.1)	17.5	(1.3)
	Panama	14.6	(1.4)	17.4	(1.7)	17.5	(2.2)	20.8	(2.0)	13.8	(1.8)	15.9	(2.2)
	Peru	29.3	(1.4)	9.4	(1.0)	16.8	(1.1)	21.6	(1.3)	8.9	(1.0)	14.0	(1.1)
	Qatar	19.4	(1.0)	17.5	(0.8)	15.5	(0.8)	16.6	(0.8)	16.0	(0.8)	15.0	(0.7)
	Romania	19.2	(1.6)	17.0	(1.3)	30.3	(1.8)	7.6	(0.8)	7.3	(0.9)	18.7	(1.7)
	Russian Federation	29.8	(1.5)	11.5	(1.2)	13.1	(1.0)	20.2	(1.5)	9.9	(1.1)	15.5	(1.3)
	Serbia	14.2	(1.1)	20.3	(1.3)	18.0	(1.4)	10.8	(0.9)	19.1	(1.2)	17.5	(1.0)
	Shanghai-China	35.4	(1.1)	14.1	(1.0)	23.7	(1.3)	11.1	(1.0)	4.8	(0.6)	10.9	(0.9)
	Singapore	27.7	(1.3)	21.7	(1.2)	21.9	(1.1)	7.5	(0.7)	8.3	(0.7)	13.0	(0.8)
	Chinese Taipei	21.7	(1.1)	10.9	(1.0)	17.8	(1.1)	18.4	(1.0)	11.0	(0.8)	20.2	(1.2)
	Thailand	28.6	(1.1)	6.3	(0.7)	6.8	(0.7)	38.3	(1.6)	8.8	(0.8)	11.3	(1.0)
	Trinidad and Tobago	27.1	(1.4)	17.0	(1.2)	19.0	(1.2)	16.2	(1.1)	7.6	(0.9)	13.2	(1.2)
	Tunisia	26.4	(1.0)	10.5	(0.8)	25.4	(1.5)	15.8	(1.3)	6.7	(0.8)	15.1	(1.1)
	Uruguay	14.3	(0.8)	12.7	(1.0)	33.7	(1.3)	8.0	(0.7)	5.5	(0.6)	25.8	(1.2)

Notes: Values that are statistically significant are indicated in bold (see Annex A3).
Group 1: "Wide and deep"; Group 2: "Narrow and deep"; Group 3: "Highly restricted and deep"; Group 4: "Wide and surface"; Group 5: "Narrow and surface"; Group 6: "Highly restricted and surface".
StatLink ⌁ http://dx.doi.org/10.1787/888932343285

[Part 2/4]
Percentage of students, by reader profile and socio-economic background
Table III.1.30   *Results based on students' self-reports*

		Second quarter										
		Group 1		Group 2		Group 3		Group 4		Group 5		Group 6	
		%	S.E.	%	S.E.	%	S.E.	%	S.E.	%	S.E.	%	S.E.
OECD	Australia	17.2	(0.7)	15.1	(0.8)	33.4	(1.1)	5.8	(0.5)	8.1	(0.5)	20.4	(0.9)
	Austria	14.3	(1.1)	34.2	(1.5)	24.0	(1.3)	3.6	(0.6)	14.5	(1.4)	9.6	(1.0)
	Belgium	13.8	(1.0)	27.9	(1.1)	33.1	(1.5)	2.1	(0.4)	9.4	(0.7)	13.5	(1.0)
	Canada	20.7	(0.7)	12.8	(0.7)	36.6	(1.0)	6.4	(0.4)	6.8	(0.6)	16.5	(0.7)
	Chile	16.7	(1.1)	16.9	(1.0)	33.6	(1.4)	6.9	(0.8)	7.7	(0.8)	18.3	(1.3)
	Czech Republic	10.9	(0.9)	36.6	(1.4)	27.1	(1.2)	0.8	(0.2)	13.0	(1.0)	11.7	(1.1)
	Denmark	18.8	(1.4)	24.1	(1.4)	34.3	(1.5)	4.2	(0.5)	7.7	(0.8)	11.1	(1.1)
	Estonia	16.2	(1.3)	41.7	(1.7)	20.0	(1.6)	2.7	(0.5)	12.0	(1.1)	7.7	(0.8)
	Finland	18.3	(1.4)	40.9	(1.7)	15.8	(1.2)	2.2	(0.4)	14.3	(1.2)	8.4	(0.8)
	France	15.7	(1.2)	28.4	(1.5)	36.5	(1.6)	1.9	(0.5)	7.2	(0.8)	10.6	(1.1)
	Germany	17.0	(1.0)	22.9	(1.3)	36.0	(1.6)	3.5	(0.6)	8.9	(0.8)	11.7	(1.1)
	Greece	10.6	(1.0)	21.9	(1.3)	41.9	(1.6)	2.5	(0.6)	8.1	(1.1)	14.8	(1.0)
	Hungary	18.2	(1.3)	34.0	(1.6)	20.3	(1.2)	6.3	(0.8)	11.8	(1.0)	9.6	(1.0)
	Iceland	16.4	(1.3)	29.6	(1.8)	22.0	(1.4)	3.9	(0.7)	13.8	(1.1)	14.4	(1.2)
	Ireland	16.3	(1.2)	25.8	(1.4)	34.7	(1.7)	3.3	(0.6)	8.5	(1.0)	11.3	(1.0)
	Israel	14.9	(1.0)	19.2	(1.0)	31.5	(1.5)	6.1	(0.7)	9.1	(0.7)	19.3	(1.4)
	Italy	17.0	(0.8)	21.6	(0.7)	44.9	(0.9)	2.0	(0.2)	4.2	(0.3)	10.4	(0.5)
	Japan	24.8	(1.4)	24.7	(1.2)	20.1	(1.0)	7.5	(0.7)	14.3	(1.2)	8.7	(0.8)
	Korea	22.4	(1.2)	9.2	(0.9)	44.0	(1.6)	5.9	(0.6)	3.7	(0.7)	14.6	(1.0)
	Luxembourg	16.1	(1.2)	31.0	(1.4)	22.4	(1.2)	3.8	(0.5)	14.7	(1.2)	12.0	(1.1)
	Mexico	19.1	(0.6)	16.1	(0.5)	35.2	(0.7)	8.1	(0.4)	5.9	(0.3)	15.7	(0.5)
	Netherlands	14.0	(1.3)	18.0	(1.3)	31.4	(1.6)	2.7	(0.5)	10.2	(1.1)	23.6	(1.6)
	New Zealand	20.8	(1.3)	14.2	(1.2)	30.6	(1.4)	7.8	(0.8)	8.7	(0.9)	17.8	(1.2)
	Norway	17.2	(1.2)	37.3	(1.4)	22.5	(1.4)	3.3	(0.6)	10.9	(0.9)	8.7	(0.9)
	Poland	10.1	(1.2)	40.0	(1.6)	22.2	(1.1)	3.1	(0.6)	13.6	(1.0)	11.1	(0.8)
	Portugal	17.4	(1.3)	22.9	(1.4)	30.9	(1.4)	4.6	(0.7)	11.0	(1.0)	13.1	(1.0)
	Slovak Republic	12.4	(1.2)	40.1	(1.7)	17.0	(1.1)	3.1	(0.5)	17.7	(1.1)	9.9	(1.0)
	Slovenia	7.4	(0.9)	34.5	(1.7)	19.3	(1.2)	3.2	(0.6)	20.7	(1.4)	15.0	(1.2)
	Spain	17.2	(0.7)	18.1	(1.0)	42.6	(1.0)	3.5	(0.4)	5.7	(0.5)	12.7	(0.7)
	Sweden	17.2	(1.2)	23.9	(1.3)	24.5	(1.5)	5.4	(0.8)	13.1	(1.1)	15.9	(1.2)
	Switzerland	16.8	(1.0)	34.6	(1.7)	23.6	(1.4)	3.1	(0.4)	11.9	(0.9)	10.0	(0.8)
	Turkey	21.4	(1.1)	13.3	(1.0)	25.6	(1.3)	15.0	(1.1)	8.8	(0.9)	15.6	(1.1)
	United Kingdom	17.4	(1.2)	21.3	(1.1)	29.2	(1.3)	5.2	(0.6)	11.5	(0.8)	15.4	(1.1)
	United States	16.6	(1.2)	10.5	(0.8)	37.7	(1.2)	6.3	(0.7)	6.7	(0.7)	22.3	(1.3)
	OECD average	16.5	(0.2)	25.4	(0.2)	29.5	(0.2)	4.6	(0.1)	10.4	(0.2)	13.6	(0.2)
Partners	Albania	34.3	(1.8)	15.4	(1.2)	22.4	(1.5)	11.9	(1.4)	7.1	(0.9)	8.9	(1.1)
	Argentina	15.2	(1.3)	23.3	(1.5)	29.0	(1.7)	7.8	(0.9)	11.1	(1.0)	13.5	(1.3)
	Azerbaijan	21.1	(1.6)	9.6	(1.0)	14.8	(1.3)	28.5	(1.7)	10.3	(1.0)	15.6	(1.3)
	Brazil	20.1	(1.0)	16.8	(0.9)	27.8	(1.2)	10.4	(0.7)	7.7	(0.5)	17.0	(0.7)
	Bulgaria	18.9	(1.8)	19.9	(1.3)	21.0	(1.4)	11.0	(1.2)	11.3	(1.2)	17.8	(1.9)
	Colombia	23.2	(1.5)	21.2	(1.3)	18.4	(1.5)	11.9	(0.9)	11.1	(1.1)	14.0	(1.2)
	Croatia	12.4	(1.0)	34.7	(1.4)	17.5	(1.2)	5.3	(0.6)	19.8	(1.2)	10.3	(1.0)
	Dubai (UAE)	28.6	(1.4)	27.1	(1.4)	17.0	(1.4)	10.1	(0.9)	10.5	(0.9)	6.6	(0.7)
	Hong Kong-China	25.8	(1.3)	14.2	(1.1)	14.0	(1.1)	19.3	(1.3)	13.9	(1.0)	12.9	(1.0)
	Indonesia	29.6	(1.7)	10.1	(0.9)	14.1	(1.2)	25.5	(1.6)	7.4	(1.0)	13.3	(1.0)
	Jordan	18.1	(1.2)	16.9	(1.1)	19.9	(1.2)	16.3	(1.2)	11.2	(0.9)	17.3	(1.1)
	Kazakhstan	33.5	(1.5)	10.1	(0.9)	5.3	(0.7)	35.3	(1.6)	9.6	(0.9)	6.2	(0.8)
	Kyrgyzstan	25.8	(1.6)	6.9	(0.7)	7.5	(0.8)	37.8	(1.7)	8.2	(0.9)	14.0	(1.0)
	Latvia	16.9	(1.5)	23.8	(1.5)	18.4	(1.4)	10.8	(1.2)	16.4	(1.5)	13.7	(1.3)
	Liechtenstein	24.9	(4.4)	30.9	(5.3)	20.7	(4.6)	1.1	(1.1)	10.3	(3.8)	12.1	(3.2)
	Lithuania	24.1	(1.3)	24.8	(1.3)	14.0	(1.1)	9.6	(0.8)	17.1	(1.2)	10.3	(0.9)
	Macao-China	18.1	(0.9)	23.5	(1.1)	19.1	(1.1)	10.2	(0.8)	14.2	(1.0)	14.7	(0.8)
	Montenegro	18.4	(1.2)	20.3	(1.1)	13.1	(1.1)	14.5	(1.2)	20.3	(1.3)	13.5	(1.1)
	Panama	20.4	(1.8)	15.4	(1.8)	17.2	(1.7)	17.6	(2.0)	14.2	(1.5)	15.3	(1.4)
	Peru	35.2	(1.2)	14.5	(0.9)	14.1	(0.9)	20.2	(1.1)	7.5	(0.7)	8.5	(0.8)
	Qatar	20.3	(0.9)	19.7	(0.9)	18.8	(0.9)	15.3	(0.7)	13.0	(0.8)	12.9	(0.7)
	Romania	21.1	(1.5)	18.4	(1.3)	32.2	(1.8)	7.0	(0.9)	8.0	(0.9)	13.1	(1.0)
	Russian Federation	29.9	(1.6)	14.4	(1.1)	13.3	(0.9)	20.7	(1.3)	10.9	(0.8)	11.1	(1.3)
	Serbia	13.3	(1.1)	27.3	(1.3)	14.4	(0.9)	10.1	(0.7)	22.7	(1.2)	12.2	(0.9)
	Shanghai-China	39.5	(1.5)	14.8	(1.2)	22.6	(1.4)	11.1	(0.8)	5.1	(0.6)	7.1	(0.8)
	Singapore	34.7	(1.4)	20.3	(1.3)	21.2	(1.1)	7.4	(0.7)	8.1	(0.7)	8.2	(0.8)
	Chinese Taipei	24.1	(1.3)	15.5	(1.2)	16.1	(0.9)	17.2	(1.1)	11.1	(0.8)	15.9	(1.0)
	Thailand	27.3	(1.2)	8.8	(0.8)	5.8	(0.7)	37.9	(1.3)	8.8	(0.7)	11.2	(1.0)
	Trinidad and Tobago	28.0	(1.5)	17.4	(1.4)	20.1	(1.4)	12.0	(1.0)	11.5	(1.0)	10.9	(0.9)
	Tunisia	30.3	(1.5)	14.2	(1.3)	21.3	(1.3)	14.9	(1.2)	7.5	(0.7)	11.8	(1.1)
	Uruguay	18.4	(1.2)	15.2	(1.0)	35.0	(1.4)	6.7	(0.7)	5.8	(0.7)	19.1	(1.3)

Notes: Values that are statistically significant are indicated in bold (see Annex A3).
Group 1: "Wide and deep"; Group 2: "Narrow and deep"; Group 3: "Highly restricted and deep"; Group 4: "Wide and surface"; Group 5: "Narrow and surface"; Group 6: "Highly restricted and surface".
StatLink ᵃˢᵖ http://dx.doi.org/10.1787/888932343285

[Part 3/4]
Percentage of students, by reader profile and socio-economic background
Table III.1.30 | *Results based on students' self-reports*

		Third quarter										
		Group 1		Group 2		Group 3		Group 4		Group 5		Group 6	
		%	S.E.	%	S.E.	%	S.E.	%	S.E.	%	S.E.	%	S.E.

		%	S.E.	%	S.E.	%	S.E.	%	S.E.	%	S.E.	%	S.E.
OECD	Australia	22.6	(0.8)	13.6	(0.6)	36.7	(1.1)	5.0	(0.5)	7.5	(0.6)	14.7	(0.7)
	Austria	16.7	(1.3)	34.8	(1.4)	24.2	(1.2)	3.1	(0.7)	12.2	(0.9)	8.9	(0.9)
	Belgium	18.4	(0.8)	32.6	(1.1)	30.5	(1.2)	1.5	(0.3)	8.0	(0.7)	9.0	(0.7)
	Canada	23.1	(0.8)	13.6	(0.6)	39.0	(0.9)	5.7	(0.4)	5.5	(0.5)	13.2	(0.7)
	Chile	18.5	(1.1)	19.7	(1.2)	33.5	(1.2)	5.8	(0.7)	7.9	(0.7)	14.5	(0.9)
	Czech Republic	12.6	(1.1)	34.8	(1.6)	29.0	(1.7)	1.6	(0.4)	10.8	(1.1)	11.2	(0.9)
	Denmark	23.3	(1.4)	26.1	(1.5)	31.2	(1.7)	3.6	(0.6)	6.5	(0.7)	9.2	(1.1)
	Estonia	17.9	(1.2)	43.1	(1.5)	19.0	(1.2)	3.4	(0.5)	11.9	(1.1)	4.6	(0.7)
	Finland	22.1	(1.2)	38.9	(1.6)	17.9	(1.1)	1.8	(0.4)	12.6	(1.0)	6.6	(0.8)
	France	18.5	(1.1)	29.4	(1.5)	38.9	(1.5)	1.1	(0.3)	5.3	(0.5)	6.7	(0.9)
	Germany	18.8	(1.2)	21.5	(1.4)	38.2	(1.5)	2.6	(0.5)	7.9	(0.9)	10.8	(0.8)
	Greece	12.4	(0.8)	24.3	(1.4)	37.1	(1.5)	3.0	(0.5)	9.0	(0.8)	14.1	(1.0)
	Hungary	20.0	(1.5)	34.4	(1.8)	19.4	(1.3)	4.1	(0.6)	11.8	(1.0)	10.1	(1.2)
	Iceland	18.5	(1.2)	30.8	(1.6)	22.0	(1.3)	3.7	(0.7)	12.1	(1.1)	13.0	(1.2)
	Ireland	22.7	(1.5)	22.4	(1.3)	37.7	(1.4)	2.7	(0.5)	5.8	(0.9)	8.9	(1.0)
	Israel	18.8	(1.1)	20.3	(1.2)	33.5	(1.4)	4.7	(0.6)	8.0	(0.8)	14.5	(1.0)
	Italy	20.3	(0.6)	20.9	(0.6)	45.2	(0.8)	2.3	(0.3)	3.5	(0.3)	7.8	(0.4)
	Japan	29.0	(1.6)	29.3	(1.0)	20.0	(0.9)	6.5	(0.6)	9.2	(1.0)	5.8	(0.7)
	Korea	28.2	(1.4)	9.9	(0.9)	41.6	(1.4)	5.4	(0.5)	3.3	(0.5)	11.8	(1.3)
	Luxembourg	21.2	(1.2)	31.3	(1.3)	22.7	(1.3)	5.0	(0.6)	9.7	(1.0)	10.2	(0.9)
	Mexico	19.7	(0.7)	19.3	(0.7)	34.8	(0.7)	7.7	(0.5)	5.8	(0.4)	12.6	(0.5)
	Netherlands	14.3	(1.2)	21.1	(1.5)	32.1	(1.5)	3.7	(0.5)	10.3	(1.0)	18.5	(1.4)
	New Zealand	24.1	(1.2)	12.0	(1.0)	31.6	(1.4)	10.7	(1.0)	6.6	(0.8)	15.1	(1.1)
	Norway	18.6	(1.2)	41.3	(1.6)	22.9	(1.3)	2.2	(0.5)	7.4	(0.8)	7.8	(0.9)
	Poland	12.5	(1.0)	39.3	(1.5)	20.7	(1.1)	3.0	(0.5)	14.3	(1.0)	10.3	(1.0)
	Portugal	18.9	(1.1)	26.1	(1.4)	31.6	(1.4)	3.6	(0.5)	8.6	(0.8)	11.2	(1.0)
	Slovak Republic	12.3	(1.0)	43.9	(1.7)	14.1	(1.0)	3.2	(0.6)	18.0	(1.3)	8.6	(1.1)
	Slovenia	10.5	(1.1)	36.1	(1.6)	20.7	(1.5)	2.9	(0.5)	18.4	(1.2)	11.4	(1.0)
	Spain	21.7	(0.8)	19.2	(1.0)	41.1	(0.9)	2.8	(0.3)	5.3	(0.6)	10.0	(0.7)
	Sweden	22.6	(1.3)	22.5	(1.1)	25.3	(1.2)	5.5	(0.6)	12.5	(1.0)	11.7	(1.0)
	Switzerland	20.6	(1.2)	34.1	(1.6)	22.0	(1.2)	3.2	(0.5)	12.1	(0.8)	7.8	(0.8)
	Turkey	23.8	(1.2)	13.2	(1.0)	25.5	(1.6)	15.4	(1.1)	8.6	(0.7)	13.8	(1.0)
	United Kingdom	19.7	(1.2)	19.9	(1.1)	33.9	(1.2)	5.3	(0.7)	9.7	(0.9)	11.6	(0.9)
	United States	17.7	(1.2)	11.2	(1.1)	36.8	(1.4)	7.0	(0.9)	7.5	(0.8)	20.0	(1.4)
	OECD average	19.4	(0.2)	26.2	(0.2)	29.7	(0.2)	4.4	(0.1)	9.2	(0.1)	11.1	(0.2)
Partners	Albania	35.1	(1.7)	17.3	(1.2)	21.3	(1.5)	11.5	(1.0)	6.5	(0.7)	8.6	(1.0)
	Argentina	18.0	(1.2)	24.2	(1.5)	28.5	(1.4)	6.3	(0.8)	10.8	(1.2)	12.3	(1.4)
	Azerbaijan	23.1	(1.4)	10.9	(1.0)	12.2	(1.2)	28.4	(1.4)	12.1	(1.1)	13.3	(1.3)
	Brazil	21.0	(1.2)	16.7	(0.9)	28.9	(1.0)	10.3	(0.7)	7.8	(0.5)	15.4	(1.0)
	Bulgaria	24.7	(2.1)	21.0	(1.4)	18.4	(1.3)	9.3	(1.2)	13.3	(1.4)	13.5	(1.1)
	Colombia	24.3	(1.5)	24.0	(1.1)	20.6	(1.1)	10.2	(1.0)	9.7	(1.3)	11.4	(0.9)
	Croatia	19.4	(1.2)	37.8	(1.5)	14.0	(1.0)	4.5	(0.6)	17.1	(1.1)	7.1	(0.8)
	Dubai (UAE)	32.8	(1.4)	27.3	(1.3)	15.2	(1.1)	8.2	(0.8)	11.0	(1.0)	5.9	(0.6)
	Hong Kong-China	29.0	(1.4)	13.1	(1.0)	10.9	(0.8)	19.1	(1.1)	17.1	(1.1)	10.7	(0.9)
	Indonesia	35.1	(1.4)	10.7	(1.2)	13.0	(0.9)	24.2	(1.3)	5.7	(0.6)	11.5	(1.0)
	Jordan	15.9	(0.9)	20.1	(1.1)	19.3	(1.3)	16.6	(1.0)	12.4	(1.1)	15.7	(1.2)
	Kazakhstan	34.1	(1.3)	12.7	(0.9)	6.6	(0.7)	32.0	(1.4)	9.3	(0.9)	5.4	(0.7)
	Kyrgyzstan	29.2	(1.5)	7.2	(0.7)	8.7	(0.8)	36.3	(1.4)	7.9	(0.9)	10.8	(0.9)
	Latvia	21.0	(1.6)	26.2	(1.4)	18.6	(1.3)	9.4	(1.0)	13.8	(1.2)	11.0	(0.9)
	Liechtenstein	23.6	(4.6)	28.3	(5.0)	15.8	(4.1)	8.8	(2.5)	10.1	(3.7)	13.9	(3.9)
	Lithuania	28.7	(1.6)	25.1	(1.2)	13.0	(0.9)	11.1	(0.8)	13.6	(1.0)	8.4	(0.8)
	Macao-China	22.4	(1.2)	25.1	(1.3)	16.5	(1.0)	9.7	(0.8)	15.2	(1.0)	10.9	(0.8)
	Montenegro	18.7	(1.1)	26.4	(1.3)	11.8	(0.9)	13.2	(1.0)	20.1	(1.2)	9.9	(1.0)
	Panama	23.3	(1.8)	16.6	(1.6)	17.6	(1.7)	14.7	(1.5)	12.8	(1.6)	14.9	(2.0)
	Peru	37.4	(1.4)	17.1	(1.0)	12.6	(0.8)	17.4	(1.2)	7.6	(0.7)	8.0	(0.8)
	Qatar	25.3	(1.0)	21.8	(0.9)	16.6	(0.8)	12.8	(0.7)	13.6	(0.8)	10.0	(0.6)
	Romania	22.0	(1.5)	24.9	(1.2)	27.2	(1.5)	5.8	(0.7)	9.5	(1.1)	10.7	(1.0)
	Russian Federation	36.0	(1.6)	11.3	(1.0)	14.9	(1.0)	18.1	(1.2)	8.7	(0.9)	10.9	(0.7)
	Serbia	15.7	(1.1)	29.0	(1.3)	14.4	(1.1)	10.6	(1.1)	18.1	(1.1)	12.4	(1.2)
	Shanghai-China	42.4	(1.5)	18.6	(1.1)	18.7	(1.2)	11.3	(0.8)	4.0	(0.6)	4.9	(0.6)
	Singapore	42.6	(1.3)	21.8	(1.2)	18.3	(1.0)	7.9	(0.6)	4.7	(0.6)	4.5	(0.6)
	Chinese Taipei	29.8	(1.3)	16.5	(1.1)	15.9	(0.9)	17.5	(1.1)	9.7	(0.8)	10.8	(0.9)
	Thailand	29.7	(1.3)	9.3	(0.9)	6.8	(0.7)	32.8	(1.2)	10.5	(0.9)	11.0	(0.9)
	Trinidad and Tobago	32.4	(1.8)	20.5	(1.4)	18.7	(1.2)	11.6	(1.0)	8.2	(1.0)	8.6	(1.0)
	Tunisia	30.4	(1.5)	17.2	(1.4)	16.8	(1.2)	14.5	(1.4)	10.2	(0.9)	11.0	(1.1)
	Uruguay	18.1	(1.2)	19.0	(1.3)	36.2	(1.4)	5.3	(0.8)	5.3	(0.6)	15.9	(1.2)

Notes: Values that are statistically significant are indicated in bold (see Annex A3).
Group 1: "Wide and deep"; Group 2: "Narrow and deep"; Group 3: "Highly restricted and deep"; Group 4: "Wide and surface"; Group 5: "Narrow and surface"; Group 6: "Highly restricted and surface".
StatLink 🖳 http://dx.doi.org/10.1787/888932343285

[Part 4/4]
Percentage of students, by reader profile and socio-economic background
Table III.1.30 *Results based on students' self-reports*

| | | Top quarter | | | | | | | | | | | Difference in the share of Group 1 between the bottom and the top quarter of ESCS | | Difference in the share of Group 1 and 2 between the bottom and the top quarter of ESCS | |
| | | Group 1 | | Group 2 | | Group 3 | | Group 4 | | Group 5 | | Group 6 | | | | | |
		%	S.E.	%	S.E.	%	S.E.	%	S.E.	%	S.E.	%	S.E.	% dif.	S.E.	% dif.	S.E.
OECD	Australia	29.7	(1.1)	14.1	(0.9)	35.3	(1.2)	5.1	(0.4)	5.3	(0.5)	10.3	(0.7)	**-15**	(1.3)	**-16**	(1.5)
	Austria	26.0	(1.3)	33.8	(1.3)	23.1	(1.3)	3.1	(0.5)	8.9	(0.8)	5.1	(0.8)	**-16**	(1.6)	**-20**	(1.9)
	Belgium	24.2	(1.1)	34.2	(1.3)	31.8	(1.3)	1.6	(0.3)	4.5	(0.5)	3.7	(0.5)	**-13**	(1.2)	**-23**	(1.9)
	Canada	32.3	(1.1)	13.7	(0.7)	32.9	(1.1)	6.5	(0.5)	5.2	(0.5)	9.4	(0.6)	**-15**	(1.3)	**-15**	(1.3)
	Chile	22.1	(1.2)	26.4	(1.1)	31.4	(1.0)	4.6	(0.5)	5.9	(0.7)	9.6	(0.8)	**-8**	(1.5)	**-19**	(1.6)
	Czech Republic	18.1	(1.3)	35.6	(1.3)	28.6	(1.4)	1.8	(0.4)	9.2	(1.0)	6.6	(0.7)	**-10**	(1.6)	**-12**	(2.8)
	Denmark	31.4	(1.7)	29.4	(1.6)	26.7	(1.8)	3.0	(0.6)	3.7	(0.6)	5.8	(0.8)	**-17**	(2.1)	**-21**	(2.3)
	Estonia	22.4	(1.1)	46.4	(1.5)	17.4	(1.3)	3.7	(0.7)	7.0	(1.0)	3.1	(0.6)	**-8**	(1.4)	**-12**	(2.4)
	Finland	28.8	(1.3)	39.0	(1.5)	16.4	(1.1)	2.6	(0.5)	8.7	(0.9)	4.5	(0.6)	**-16**	(1.6)	**-17**	(2.1)
	France	29.2	(1.5)	27.6	(1.5)	33.9	(1.6)	1.9	(0.4)	3.6	(0.6)	3.8	(0.6)	**-18**	(1.7)	**-20**	(2.2)
	Germany	27.9	(1.5)	24.3	(1.2)	34.9	(1.4)	1.9	(0.4)	5.7	(0.7)	5.6	(0.6)	**-18**	(1.8)	**-21**	(2.0)
	Greece	17.4	(1.1)	26.1	(1.3)	35.1	(1.6)	4.4	(0.7)	7.9	(0.9)	9.2	(1.0)	**-11**	(1.4)	**-18**	(2.1)
	Hungary	31.3	(1.5)	29.6	(1.4)	22.1	(1.3)	4.1	(0.7)	7.2	(0.9)	5.6	(0.8)	**-15**	(2.0)	**-20**	(2.7)
	Iceland	23.8	(1.3)	32.2	(1.5)	18.6	(1.4)	4.9	(0.7)	11.1	(1.0)	9.3	(1.0)	**-9**	(1.7)	**-12**	(2.2)
	Ireland	28.2	(1.6)	20.6	(1.2)	36.1	(1.5)	3.4	(0.6)	4.3	(0.9)	7.6	(1.0)	**-14**	(2.2)	-5	(2.7)
	Israel	19.8	(1.3)	24.0	(1.2)	32.2	(1.1)	4.3	(0.6)	7.2	(0.7)	12.6	(0.9)	**-6**	(1.5)	**-14**	(1.9)
	Italy	23.5	(0.7)	22.6	(0.5)	43.5	(0.7)	2.0	(0.3)	2.9	(0.3)	5.5	(0.4)	**-11**	(0.9)	**-15**	(1.1)
	Japan	36.5	(1.5)	27.4	(1.2)	17.6	(1.1)	6.1	(0.6)	7.9	(0.7)	4.6	(0.5)	**-15**	(1.8)	**-18**	(2.1)
	Korea	38.2	(1.5)	13.2	(1.0)	33.1	(1.3)	5.6	(0.8)	2.1	(0.5)	7.7	(0.9)	**-24**	(1.9)	**-32**	(2.1)
	Luxembourg	28.1	(1.3)	29.5	(1.4)	22.7	(1.2)	3.9	(0.6)	10.5	(0.7)	5.3	(0.6)	**-6**	(1.0)	**-16**	(1.2)
	Mexico	23.2	(0.6)	20.8	(0.7)	34.9	(0.7)	5.3	(0.3)	5.4	(0.4)	10.4	(0.7)	**-12**	(1.7)	**-23**	(2.3)
	Netherlands	20.4	(1.5)	25.5	(1.6)	27.9	(1.6)	4.8	(0.7)	7.6	(0.9)	13.7	(1.7)	**-14**	(1.8)	**-14**	(2.1)
	New Zealand	32.6	(1.5)	12.5	(1.1)	32.4	(1.5)	7.0	(0.7)	4.9	(0.6)	10.6	(0.9)	**-13**	(1.6)	**-17**	(2.2)
	Norway	27.6	(1.5)	36.6	(1.4)	21.4	(1.3)	2.6	(0.5)	7.4	(0.9)	6.3	(0.7)	**-12**	(1.6)	**-17**	(2.2)
	Poland	21.2	(1.4)	36.9	(1.5)	21.3	(1.2)	4.0	(0.6)	10.3	(0.9)	5.3	(0.6)	**-13**	(1.8)	**-17**	(2.2)
	Portugal	26.8	(1.3)	25.5	(1.1)	34.8	(1.6)	2.3	(0.5)	5.4	(0.6)	6.7	(0.8)	**-10**	(1.5)	**-13**	(2.2)
	Slovak Republic	18.2	(1.2)	38.7	(1.5)	18.4	(0.9)	3.5	(0.6)	14.3	(1.1)	6.7	(0.8)	**-9**	(1.6)	**-15**	(2.4)
	Slovenia	16.4	(1.3)	37.1	(1.8)	23.7	(1.4)	2.5	(0.6)	12.0	(1.1)	6.7	(0.6)	**-16**	(1.3)	**-22**	(1.4)
	Spain	28.3	(1.0)	21.7	(0.9)	36.2	(0.9)	2.4	(0.2)	4.7	(0.5)	6.7	(0.6)	**-16**	(1.7)	**-19**	(2.0)
	Sweden	28.0	(1.5)	24.2	(1.2)	21.6	(1.3)	5.5	(0.7)	9.4	(1.0)	11.4	(1.1)	**-19**	(1.8)	**-22**	(1.8)
	Switzerland	32.0	(1.3)	33.5	(1.4)	20.6	(0.9)	2.7	(0.5)	7.0	(0.7)	4.2	(0.6)	**-7**	(1.9)	**-16**	(2.1)
	Turkey	30.2	(1.4)	17.0	(1.1)	23.4	(1.4)	12.9	(1.2)	8.0	(0.7)	8.3	(0.8)	**-15**	(1.8)	**-11**	(2.1)
	United Kingdom	27.3	(1.2)	18.3	(0.8)	33.8	(1.3)	4.2	(0.5)	6.4	(0.7)	10.0	(0.9)	**-8**	(1.6)	**-12**	(1.9)
	United States	25.1	(1.4)	12.5	(1.4)	38.1	(1.5)	6.4	(0.7)	4.0	(0.5)	13.8	(1.0)	**-13**	(0.3)	**-17**	(0.4)
	OECD average	26.4	(0.2)	26.8	(0.2)	28.3	(0.2)	4.1	(0.1)	6.9	(0.1)	7.5	(0.1)	**-13**	(0.3)	**-17**	(0.4)
Partners	Albania	41.1	(1.6)	16.3	(1.2)	21.8	(1.4)	9.3	(1.1)	5.1	(0.7)	6.3	(1.0)	**-9**	(2.9)	**-15**	(3.2)
	Argentina	18.2	(1.4)	28.6	(1.3)	31.4	(1.2)	5.1	(0.7)	7.4	(0.8)	9.3	(0.7)	-2	(1.9)	**-15**	(2.2)
	Azerbaijan	26.2	(1.6)	11.4	(1.2)	12.1	(0.9)	27.0	(1.6)	10.7	(0.9)	12.7	(1.0)	**-9**	(2.3)	**-12**	(2.6)
	Brazil	23.0	(1.1)	19.1	(0.8)	30.5	(1.2)	6.9	(0.6)	8.2	(0.7)	12.3	(0.8)	-3	(1.4)	**-13**	(1.8)
	Bulgaria	30.7	(2.3)	22.4	(1.1)	17.7	(1.1)	9.8	(1.0)	8.8	(0.9)	10.5	(1.2)	**-18**	(2.5)	**-22**	(3.0)
	Colombia	26.0	(1.8)	26.2	(1.6)	24.0	(1.7)	7.3	(0.9)	7.4	(0.9)	9.1	(1.0)	-4	(2.7)	**-12**	(3.1)
	Croatia	24.1	(1.4)	38.1	(1.3)	13.8	(1.1)	4.1	(0.7)	13.9	(0.9)	5.9	(0.7)	**-14**	(1.7)	**-17**	(2.2)
	Dubai (UAE)	34.6	(1.5)	26.3	(1.5)	15.3	(1.1)	9.1	(0.9)	9.3	(0.8)	5.4	(0.5)	**-14**	(2.0)	**-15**	(2.1)
	Hong Kong-China	35.2	(1.5)	14.1	(1.0)	9.5	(1.0)	21.0	(1.3)	11.5	(1.0)	8.6	(0.9)	**-14**	(1.8)	**-15**	(2.0)
	Indonesia	38.3	(1.8)	13.4	(1.2)	10.0	(0.9)	24.3	(1.7)	7.2	(0.8)	6.7	(0.7)	**-13**	(2.1)	**-18**	(2.7)
	Jordan	17.0	(1.0)	21.3	(1.0)	19.3	(1.3)	15.1	(1.1)	13.5	(1.0)	13.8	(1.1)	0	(1.4)	**-12**	(1.7)
	Kazakhstan	41.9	(1.6)	10.6	(0.9)	6.3	(0.7)	31.1	(1.8)	6.5	(0.8)	3.5	(0.5)	**-11**	(2.3)	**-12**	(2.6)
	Kyrgyzstan	31.6	(1.7)	10.4	(1.0)	8.7	(0.8)	34.1	(1.8)	6.7	(0.9)	8.4	(0.8)	**-12**	(2.0)	**-18**	(2.7)
	Latvia	26.6	(1.8)	28.8	(1.7)	17.0	(1.2)	7.6	(1.0)	12.6	(1.1)	7.5	(0.9)	**-10**	(2.6)	**-16**	(2.9)
	Liechtenstein	32.3	(5.3)	25.7	(4.9)	21.2	(4.9)	0.0	(0.0)	8.6	(3.5)	11.9	(3.0)	**-22**	(6.0)	**-25**	(7.8)
	Lithuania	36.6	(1.5)	27.3	(1.2)	12.3	(1.0)	7.8	(0.9)	10.4	(0.9)	5.6	(0.8)	**-13**	(1.5)	**-18**	(1.8)
	Macao-China	27.4	(1.2)	24.2	(1.1)	15.7	(1.1)	10.8	(0.8)	13.2	(0.9)	8.9	(0.7)	**-11**	(1.8)	**-18**	(1.9)
	Montenegro	24.0	(1.3)	27.2	(1.5)	10.0	(1.1)	12.8	(1.2)	17.8	(1.0)	8.0	(0.7)	**-10**	(2.4)	**-10**	(3.2)
	Panama	25.0	(2.0)	17.6	(1.5)	24.4	(1.9)	12.8	(1.8)	9.2	(1.3)	11.0	(1.4)	**-6**	(2.2)	**-20**	(2.5)
	Peru	35.0	(1.7)	23.4	(1.4)	14.8	(1.0)	13.3	(1.3)	7.8	(0.9)	5.6	(0.7)	**-7**	(1.3)	**-9**	(1.5)
	Qatar	26.2	(0.9)	20.0	(0.9)	14.3	(0.8)	17.0	(0.7)	13.6	(0.8)	8.8	(0.6)	-4	(2.1)	**-16**	(2.5)
	Romania	23.4	(1.4)	28.7	(1.6)	27.4	(1.7)	4.9	(0.7)	7.5	(0.9)	8.1	(0.9)	**-10**	(1.9)	**-9**	(2.2)
	Russian Federation	39.7	(1.5)	10.8	(0.6)	17.9	(0.8)	16.1	(1.0)	6.1	(0.8)	9.5	(1.0)	**-9**	(1.7)	**-18**	(2.4)
	Serbia	23.5	(1.4)	29.1	(1.3)	16.9	(0.9)	8.1	(0.8)	15.2	(1.2)	7.1	(0.7)	**-13**	(1.8)	**-21**	(1.9)
	Shanghai-China	48.4	(1.4)	22.0	(1.0)	14.6	(1.0)	8.5	(0.8)	3.4	(0.4)	3.2	(0.4)	**-13**	(1.8)	**-19**	(1.9)
	Singapore	52.2	(1.7)	16.2	(1.2)	14.9	(1.1)	7.5	(0.8)	5.5	(0.6)	3.8	(0.7)	**-25**	(2.0)	**-19**	(1.9)
	Chinese Taipei	41.3	(1.7)	15.6	(1.0)	12.9	(1.0)	13.4	(1.1)	9.2	(1.0)	7.3	(0.8)	**-20**	(1.9)	**-24**	(2.1)
	Thailand	37.3	(1.8)	12.9	(1.2)	6.7	(0.7)	25.5	(1.4)	9.4	(0.8)	8.2	(0.9)	-2	(2.1)	**-15**	(2.3)
	Trinidad and Tobago	29.3	(1.5)	24.4	(1.6)	20.9	(1.3)	9.0	(0.9)	8.9	(1.0)	7.5	(0.8)	-2	(2.1)	**-10**	(2.2)
	Tunisia	28.1	(1.4)	21.1	(1.3)	17.5	(1.3)	12.9	(1.1)	10.3	(1.2)	10.0	(0.8)	-2	(1.8)	**-12**	(2.2)
	Uruguay	21.6	(1.1)	20.7	(1.4)	40.2	(1.6)	3.6	(0.5)	4.1	(0.7)	9.7	(1.0)	**-7**	(1.3)	**-15**	(2.0)

Notes: Values that are statistically significant are indicated in bold (see Annex A3).
Group 1: "Wide and deep"; Group 2: "Narrow and deep"; Group 3: "Highly restricted and deep"; Group 4: "Wide and surface"; Group 5: "Narrow and surface"; Group 6: "Highly restricted and surface".
StatLink ⟨⟩ http://dx.doi.org/10.1787/888932343285

[Part 1/1]

Percentage of students reading the following types of texts

Percentage of students who reported that they had to read the following types of texts for school (in the classroom or for homework) more than two times during the last month

Table III.2.1

| | Percentage of students who read the following types of texts for school | | | | | | | | | | | | | | | |
| | Information texts about writers or books | | Poetry | | Texts that include diagrams or maps | | Fiction (*e.g.* novels, short stories) | | Newspaper reports and magazine articles | | Instructions or manuals telling you how to make or do something (*e.g.* how a machine works) | | Texts that include tables or graphs | | Advertising material (*e.g.* advertisements in magazines, posters) | |
	%	S.E.	%	S.E.	%	S.E.	%	S.E.	%	S.E.	%	S.E.	%	S.E.	%	S.E.
Australia	55.0	(0.7)	37.2	(1.0)	64.2	(0.6)	61.6	(0.8)	53.9	(0.8)	31.1	(0.5)	70.1	(0.6)	46.6	(0.7)
Austria	37.2	(0.9)	23.5	(1.1)	44.8	(1.0)	54.0	(0.9)	51.8	(1.0)	28.3	(0.9)	52.4	(1.0)	36.7	(1.1)
Belgium	52.7	(0.9)	36.0	(0.9)	59.9	(0.8)	56.0	(1.0)	52.1	(0.8)	27.9	(0.8)	63.4	(0.8)	38.7	(0.7)
Canada	52.5	(0.5)	35.9	(0.7)	65.6	(0.6)	65.2	(0.5)	51.9	(0.6)	37.6	(0.5)	71.2	(0.5)	45.0	(0.6)
Chile	69.9	(0.6)	40.7	(1.1)	61.4	(0.9)	70.5	(0.7)	54.9	(1.1)	43.9	(0.9)	64.3	(0.9)	57.2	(0.9)
Czech Republic	39.6	(1.3)	21.4	(0.9)	39.9	(0.9)	29.4	(0.8)	39.7	(0.8)	27.5	(0.9)	39.7	(0.9)	29.2	(0.8)
Denmark	63.1	(1.1)	53.7	(1.4)	52.5	(1.0)	70.4	(0.9)	61.0	(0.8)	29.2	(0.8)	57.1	(0.9)	55.0	(1.0)
Estonia	59.0	(1.0)	56.5	(1.0)	62.5	(0.9)	64.0	(1.0)	45.4	(1.0)	38.6	(0.9)	69.5	(0.8)	33.9	(1.1)
Finland	50.1	(1.0)	26.7	(1.0)	63.3	(0.9)	50.2	(1.2)	38.2	(1.0)	25.2	(0.7)	64.0	(1.0)	31.9	(0.9)
France	60.5	(0.9)	46.6	(1.5)	69.3	(0.9)	55.5	(0.9)	44.2	(0.8)	35.3	(0.8)	74.7	(0.8)	45.5	(0.9)
Germany	49.7	(0.9)	41.9	(1.1)	60.4	(0.9)	70.8	(0.8)	51.4	(1.1)	23.1	(0.6)	65.2	(0.8)	35.2	(0.9)
Greece	40.9	(0.9)	41.2	(1.0)	37.1	(0.9)	59.9	(1.1)	51.7	(0.9)	30.8	(0.9)	36.1	(0.8)	51.0	(1.0)
Hungary	55.9	(0.9)	66.9	(1.2)	51.0	(1.0)	57.5	(1.2)	35.0	(0.9)	26.1	(0.8)	58.9	(1.1)	38.2	(1.0)
Iceland	38.6	(0.8)	35.0	(0.7)	38.7	(0.7)	57.5	(0.8)	28.1	(0.8)	22.0	(0.8)	52.2	(0.8)	28.3	(0.7)
Ireland	54.1	(0.9)	65.2	(1.1)	64.6	(1.0)	65.0	(1.1)	44.6	(1.0)	26.4	(0.8)	65.1	(0.8)	50.6	(1.1)
Israel	45.9	(0.9)	38.2	(1.3)	43.3	(1.1)	52.4	(1.2)	44.1	(0.9)	28.0	(0.7)	55.6	(1.0)	35.1	(0.9)
Italy	57.5	(0.5)	66.2	(0.6)	43.6	(0.5)	71.4	(0.4)	46.0	(0.6)	18.3	(0.5)	45.4	(0.5)	26.5	(0.4)
Japan	43.2	(0.7)	31.9	(1.3)	41.3	(0.9)	53.0	(0.9)	37.5	(1.1)	29.1	(0.8)	41.0	(0.8)	24.4	(0.6)
Korea	46.0	(1.0)	53.6	(1.2)	51.8	(1.0)	60.0	(1.1)	36.9	(1.3)	26.4	(0.9)	43.5	(1.0)	27.7	(0.8)
Luxembourg	46.6	(0.8)	32.4	(0.6)	48.1	(0.6)	63.0	(0.8)	43.6	(0.8)	19.4	(0.7)	51.2	(0.7)	31.5	(0.9)
Mexico	70.7	(0.5)	42.1	(0.6)	65.5	(0.5)	59.2	(0.6)	65.2	(0.5)	49.9	(0.6)	65.2	(0.5)	67.1	(0.5)
Netherlands	53.7	(0.9)	15.7	(1.3)	45.2	(0.7)	55.6	(1.1)	50.6	(1.0)	30.2	(0.9)	75.3	(0.8)	39.9	(1.0)
New Zealand	46.9	(1.0)	30.9	(1.1)	55.2	(0.8)	64.9	(0.8)	44.7	(0.9)	30.9	(0.7)	67.0	(0.8)	44.5	(0.8)
Norway	58.8	(1.1)	31.0	(1.2)	52.1	(1.0)	64.7	(1.0)	38.9	(1.2)	18.5	(0.6)	56.7	(1.0)	26.8	(1.1)
Poland	63.7	(1.0)	54.5	(1.1)	67.7	(0.9)	70.1	(0.8)	52.1	(1.0)	39.5	(1.0)	66.2	(0.8)	44.2	(1.0)
Portugal	62.6	(0.9)	66.8	(0.9)	36.6	(0.7)	48.8	(0.8)	50.2	(0.8)	27.1	(0.8)	54.9	(0.7)	48.7	(0.8)
Slovak Republic	47.7	(1.3)	44.8	(1.2)	40.2	(1.2)	42.2	(1.2)	44.2	(1.0)	33.9	(1.0)	48.8	(1.3)	36.1	(0.9)
Slovenia	36.9	(0.7)	36.9	(0.7)	47.8	(0.8)	54.5	(0.7)	36.8	(0.8)	31.2	(0.8)	46.2	(0.9)	34.3	(0.8)
Spain	66.2	(0.6)	61.8	(0.8)	48.7	(0.8)	57.2	(0.6)	46.6	(0.7)	31.9	(0.6)	53.8	(0.6)	42.0	(0.8)
Sweden	42.3	(1.2)	14.2	(0.9)	41.4	(0.9)	60.0	(0.8)	39.2	(1.0)	31.0	(0.9)	57.9	(0.8)	26.5	(0.8)
Switzerland	41.3	(0.9)	26.6	(1.1)	52.0	(1.1)	56.3	(1.0)	45.8	(1.0)	29.6	(0.8)	59.2	(1.1)	32.2	(1.0)
Turkey	69.3	(0.9)	76.9	(0.8)	55.4	(0.9)	84.9	(0.7)	62.6	(0.8)	44.1	(0.9)	55.8	(1.0)	53.9	(0.9)
United Kingdom	60.2	(0.8)	66.4	(1.6)	57.0	(0.7)	61.6	(1.1)	45.1	(1.1)	24.6	(0.7)	67.2	(0.8)	47.2	(1.0)
United States	64.9	(0.8)	42.7	(1.3)	70.7	(0.8)	73.1	(0.8)	47.7	(1.0)	41.7	(1.0)	73.7	(0.7)	36.6	(1.0)
OECD average	53.0	(0.2)	43.0	(0.2)	52.9	(0.1)	60.0	(0.2)	46.5	(0.2)	30.5	(0.1)	58.5	(0.1)	39.6	(0.1)
Albania	75.8	(0.9)	78.9	(0.9)	50.0	(1.4)	77.7	(0.9)	56.8	(1.2)	35.5	(1.0)	48.6	(1.3)	45.5	(1.2)
Argentina	62.0	(0.9)	41.2	(1.5)	58.1	(1.2)	67.4	(0.9)	59.7	(1.2)	38.5	(1.1)	53.0	(1.3)	54.6	(1.1)
Azerbaijan	75.2	(1.2)	62.9	(1.2)	59.4	(1.3)	71.1	(1.1)	62.5	(1.2)	62.4	(1.4)	59.0	(1.2)	49.2	(1.2)
Brazil	62.6	(0.7)	61.2	(0.7)	54.5	(0.9)	58.9	(0.8)	55.3	(0.8)	35.6	(0.7)	60.5	(0.7)	53.4	(0.8)
Bulgaria	54.4	(1.2)	48.2	(1.0)	49.8	(0.9)	68.7	(1.1)	60.7	(0.9)	49.8	(1.2)	58.6	(1.2)	58.5	(0.9)
Colombia	73.0	(1.1)	41.5	(1.1)	61.2	(0.8)	57.4	(1.0)	57.9	(1.2)	40.7	(1.0)	66.1	(0.9)	58.0	(0.8)
Croatia	28.2	(0.9)	25.9	(0.7)	31.7	(0.8)	38.1	(0.9)	42.1	(0.8)	26.8	(0.6)	34.9	(1.0)	35.3	(0.7)
Dubai (UAE)	59.3	(0.8)	59.5	(0.6)	62.7	(0.7)	65.1	(0.7)	55.8	(0.8)	41.2	(0.9)	64.2	(0.8)	47.2	(0.8)
Hong Kong-China	63.1	(0.8)	53.2	(1.1)	42.8	(0.9)	60.0	(1.0)	71.2	(0.8)	20.1	(0.8)	45.0	(1.0)	39.0	(0.7)
Indonesia	71.7	(1.0)	70.1	(1.3)	58.0	(1.2)	79.8	(1.0)	64.9	(1.1)	47.1	(1.3)	62.0	(1.1)	69.4	(0.9)
Jordan	61.6	(0.9)	58.7	(0.9)	52.1	(0.9)	62.6	(0.7)	48.2	(1.0)	50.8	(0.8)	58.0	(1.0)	46.8	(0.8)
Kazakhstan	77.4	(0.8)	55.6	(1.0)	58.0	(0.9)	80.2	(0.7)	75.4	(0.8)	50.5	(1.0)	62.3	(1.0)	64.8	(0.8)
Kyrgyzstan	71.6	(1.2)	64.4	(1.6)	44.1	(1.2)	79.0	(1.1)	63.5	(1.2)	39.0	(1.1)	54.3	(1.1)	55.8	(1.1)
Latvia	60.7	(1.0)	53.9	(1.2)	58.6	(0.9)	75.4	(1.0)	44.4	(1.1)	32.6	(1.0)	61.1	(1.0)	45.9	(1.0)
Liechtenstein	40.4	(2.9)	25.6	(2.4)	51.1	(2.6)	57.7	(2.5)	37.0	(2.7)	22.3	(2.2)	57.9	(2.6)	28.3	(2.5)
Lithuania	59.7	(1.0)	43.0	(1.0)	55.8	(1.0)	67.7	(0.9)	42.6	(1.1)	32.3	(0.9)	53.2	(1.0)	39.2	(1.0)
Macao-China	57.9	(0.6)	56.6	(0.6)	50.1	(0.6)	50.1	(0.7)	64.7	(0.6)	29.0	(0.6)	46.8	(0.7)	46.8	(0.6)
Montenegro	61.9	(0.8)	65.3	(0.8)	25.9	(0.7)	76.9	(0.6)	44.6	(0.8)	34.9	(0.8)	37.1	(0.8)	37.6	(0.8)
Panama	63.7	(1.5)	41.4	(2.4)	62.5	(1.2)	55.6	(1.2)	53.1	(1.6)	51.8	(1.5)	50.3	(1.9)	39.5	(1.5)
Peru	79.8	(0.8)	54.6	(0.9)	64.3	(0.8)	68.4	(0.8)	58.6	(1.0)	46.0	(0.9)	59.9	(0.8)	58.9	(0.8)
Qatar	62.5	(0.5)	60.3	(0.5)	56.7	(0.5)	58.7	(0.6)	51.8	(0.6)	49.0	(0.6)	56.1	(0.5)	49.9	(0.5)
Romania	69.7	(1.4)	68.0	(1.3)	55.5	(1.4)	69.4	(1.1)	47.3	(1.5)	41.8	(1.3)	57.9	(1.2)	48.5	(1.3)
Russian Federation	70.3	(0.9)	60.4	(1.0)	56.5	(1.1)	80.0	(1.0)	70.3	(0.6)	49.9	(1.0)	66.2	(1.3)	67.0	(0.9)
Serbia	59.7	(0.9)	57.9	(1.0)	25.4	(0.8)	72.2	(0.8)	37.4	(0.8)	27.1	(0.8)	39.2	(0.7)	34.5	(0.8)
Shanghai-China	56.9	(0.8)	50.8	(0.9)	37.6	(0.8)	61.4	(0.9)	66.3	(0.8)	24.9	(0.7)	33.1	(0.7)	43.3	(0.8)
Singapore	51.2	(0.8)	24.8	(0.6)	69.7	(0.6)	66.7	(0.6)	82.0	(0.6)	36.8	(0.7)	73.9	(0.7)	51.7	(0.7)
Chinese Taipei	52.6	(0.8)	43.6	(0.8)	49.5	(1.1)	60.7	(0.8)	72.4	(0.7)	32.0	(0.7)	51.9	(1.0)	61.0	(0.8)
Thailand	70.2	(0.8)	66.4	(0.9)	61.9	(0.8)	79.8	(0.6)	77.5	(0.8)	55.8	(0.9)	59.0	(0.7)	74.6	(0.9)
Trinidad and Tobago	53.4	(0.8)	67.2	(0.7)	66.5	(0.8)	69.0	(0.8)	61.0	(1.0)	49.1	(0.9)	70.5	(0.9)	56.7	(0.9)
Tunisia	61.3	(1.0)	66.6	(1.0)	64.5	(0.9)	63.7	(1.0)	52.6	(1.0)	48.8	(1.1)	63.5	(0.9)	63.8	(1.0)
Uruguay	66.7	(0.8)	52.1	(1.0)	48.1	(1.0)	57.4	(0.7)	40.1	(0.7)	34.3	(0.9)	58.4	(0.8)	52.3	(0.9)

StatLink ᴍˢᴾ http://dx.doi.org/10.1787/888932343285

[Part 1/1]
Percentage of students doing the following tasks for school
Percentage of students who reported that they had to do the following types of tasks for school (in the classroom or for homework) more than two times during the last month

Table III.2.2

| | Percentage of students who do the following tasks for school: | | | | | | | | | | | | | | | | | |
| | Find information from a graph, diagram or table | | Explain the cause of events in a text | | Explain the way characters behave in a text | | Learn about the life of the writer | | Explain the purpose of a text | | Memorise a text by heart (e.g. a poem or part of a play) | | Learn about the place of a text in the history of literature | | Describe the way the information in a table or graph is organised | | Explain the connection between different parts of a text | |
	%	S.E.	%	S.E.	%	S.E.	%	S.E.	%	S.E.	%	S.E.	%	S.E.	%	S.E.	%	S.E.
OECD																		
Australia	73.6	(0.5)	66.5	(0.5)	68.3	(0.7)	23.7	(0.7)	66.7	(0.7)	18.5	(0.5)	33.0	(0.7)	43.3	(0.8)	43.2	(0.6)
Austria	40.7	(0.9)	44.5	(0.9)	44.0	(1.1)	22.0	(0.9)	47.4	(1.0)	13.4	(0.8)	22.1	(1.0)	24.3	(0.9)	25.2	(0.8)
Belgium	59.7	(0.8)	54.4	(0.7)	50.3	(0.8)	22.7	(0.6)	58.3	(0.8)	21.2	(0.8)	30.4	(0.7)	33.0	(0.7)	34.8	(0.8)
Canada	74.2	(0.6)	71.1	(0.4)	61.3	(0.6)	23.1	(0.4)	61.4	(1.0)	34.2	(0.9)	44.6	(0.8)	44.5	(0.9)	46.1	(0.8)
Chile	64.9	(0.9)	68.1	(0.8)	62.6	(0.8)	39.0	(1.0)	61.4	(1.0)	34.2	(0.9)	44.6	(0.8)	44.5	(0.9)	46.1	(0.8)
Czech Republic	38.7	(0.8)	40.2	(1.1)	40.5	(1.1)	35.6	(1.3)	49.2	(1.2)	17.5	(0.7)	19.6	(0.7)	24.7	(0.8)	22.2	(0.9)
Denmark	66.2	(0.9)	67.6	(0.8)	69.4	(0.9)	40.8	(1.3)	74.5	(0.8)	15.5	(0.6)	34.1	(1.0)	33.2	(0.9)	42.1	(0.7)
Estonia	70.8	(0.8)	66.7	(0.8)	65.2	(1.0)	45.6	(1.3)	64.5	(0.9)	31.6	(1.1)	28.6	(0.8)	30.1	(0.9)	33.1	(0.8)
Finland	55.9	(0.9)	49.7	(0.8)	37.2	(1.0)	30.0	(0.9)	42.6	(0.9)	11.8	(0.5)	24.4	(0.9)	23.7	(0.7)	23.4	(0.7)
France	80.3	(0.7)	71.4	(0.8)	70.4	(0.8)	49.0	(1.2)	70.5	(0.9)	20.7	(0.8)	41.9	(1.2)	43.9	(0.7)	49.5	(0.8)
Germany	63.5	(0.9)	64.6	(0.7)	58.6	(0.9)	22.7	(0.7)	66.9	(0.7)	13.9	(0.8)	19.5	(0.7)	39.5	(0.8)	40.6	(0.9)
Greece	33.4	(1.0)	66.4	(1.0)	68.1	(1.0)	44.2	(1.0)	64.4	(0.9)	30.1	(1.0)	33.3	(0.9)	26.2	(0.8)	38.4	(0.8)
Hungary	60.2	(1.0)	67.3	(1.0)	62.4	(1.0)	56.2	(1.4)	64.1	(1.0)	46.5	(1.5)	34.1	(1.0)	34.2	(0.9)	42.2	(0.8)
Iceland	37.6	(0.8)	41.0	(0.8)	38.6	(0.8)	16.7	(0.7)	33.3	(0.8)	13.9	(0.6)	19.6	(0.7)	22.6	(0.8)	19.2	(0.7)
Ireland	71.2	(0.9)	63.9	(1.0)	69.6	(0.9)	28.8	(0.9)	51.4	(0.8)	43.2	(1.0)	30.3	(0.8)	35.9	(0.9)	39.5	(0.9)
Israel	52.0	(0.9)	62.5	(0.9)	56.3	(0.9)	32.5	(1.0)	69.9	(0.5)	21.9	(0.5)	46.3	(0.5)	29.2	(0.4)	36.0	(0.4)
Italy	37.7	(0.5)	66.7	(0.5)	63.8	(0.5)	67.7	(0.6)	69.9	(0.5)	21.9	(0.5)	46.3	(0.5)	29.2	(0.4)	36.0	(0.4)
Japan	48.2	(0.8)	54.8	(0.8)	59.1	(0.8)	33.6	(0.9)	52.3	(0.6)	41.2	(0.9)	32.6	(0.8)	31.5	(0.5)	35.6	(0.7)
Korea	39.2	(1.1)	36.1	(1.0)	43.0	(1.0)	35.9	(1.0)	37.9	(1.1)	20.6	(0.7)	35.1	(1.0)	30.7	(1.0)	39.8	(1.0)
Luxembourg	47.4	(0.8)	60.3	(0.7)	62.1	(0.7)	22.2	(0.6)	56.7	(0.8)	15.8	(0.5)	20.4	(0.6)	30.0	(0.7)	37.7	(0.7)
Mexico	66.3	(0.5)	70.0	(0.5)	59.8	(0.5)	43.9	(0.6)	72.0	(0.4)	46.3	(0.6)	49.0	(0.4)	54.8	(0.5)	57.7	(0.5)
Netherlands	76.2	(0.8)	51.0	(1.0)	42.6	(0.9)	21.5	(1.2)	69.3	(0.9)	17.0	(0.8)	15.8	(0.8)	30.9	(0.8)	37.9	(0.8)
New Zealand	72.6	(0.9)	62.1	(0.7)	65.3	(0.8)	16.8	(0.7)	62.1	(0.7)	18.6	(0.7)	23.6	(0.7)	42.3	(0.8)	38.2	(0.7)
Norway	65.9	(0.9)	58.7	(0.9)	49.8	(1.1)	48.2	(1.5)	47.6	(1.0)	25.3	(0.9)	35.9	(1.1)	37.9	(0.9)	32.8	(0.8)
Poland	72.1	(0.9)	73.8	(0.7)	76.7	(0.8)	60.8	(1.2)	67.7	(0.8)	30.6	(1.1)	38.9	(0.9)	39.4	(0.9)	43.5	(0.8)
Portugal	60.6	(0.8)	72.8	(0.7)	74.0	(0.8)	59.5	(0.9)	74.3	(0.7)	22.9	(0.7)	44.4	(0.8)	46.7	(0.7)	43.7	(0.8)
Slovak Republic	45.0	(1.2)	60.2	(1.2)	60.9	(1.2)	45.4	(1.2)	56.4	(1.2)	28.7	(1.2)	28.6	(0.9)	28.2	(1.2)	32.1	(1.1)
Slovenia	49.7	(0.8)	59.2	(0.8)	53.8	(0.7)	33.4	(0.7)	62.8	(0.8)	15.7	(0.6)	36.7	(0.7)	26.6	(0.7)	32.6	(0.8)
Spain	51.8	(0.8)	71.7	(0.6)	65.4	(0.7)	58.6	(0.9)	67.5	(0.7)	28.9	(0.7)	52.0	(0.7)	39.8	(0.7)	42.1	(0.7)
Sweden	53.8	(0.9)	54.8	(1.0)	45.6	(0.9)	28.8	(1.4)	54.3	(0.9)	17.5	(0.7)	20.2	(0.9)	26.2	(0.8)	33.6	(0.8)
Switzerland	53.0	(0.9)	53.2	(1.0)	47.8	(1.0)	22.1	(0.9)	51.7	(0.8)	18.9	(0.9)	16.6	(0.6)	29.4	(0.8)	32.1	(0.7)
Turkey	62.5	(1.0)	79.8	(0.7)	77.6	(0.8)	76.4	(0.8)	84.5	(0.6)	52.8	(1.2)	67.3	(0.7)	47.6	(0.9)	62.8	(0.8)
United Kingdom	75.7	(0.7)	65.5	(0.7)	73.9	(0.9)	33.8	(0.9)	73.8	(0.8)	26.3	(0.8)	29.9	(0.7)	46.5	(0.8)	48.7	(0.9)
United States	79.9	(0.8)	74.2	(0.7)	75.6	(0.8)	45.4	(1.2)	73.9	(1.0)	21.0	(0.9)	57.4	(1.1)	56.1	(1.0)	60.4	(0.9)
OECD average	58.8	(0.1)	61.5	(0.1)	59.6	(0.1)	37.8	(0.2)	61.3	(0.1)	24.9	(0.1)	33.4	(0.1)	35.9	(0.1)	39.2	(0.1)
Partners																		
Albania	52.6	(1.2)	74.3	(0.9)	80.0	(1.0)	86.5	(0.7)	80.0	(1.0)	67.1	(1.5)	66.6	(1.0)	47.7	(1.3)	54.3	(1.1)
Argentina	45.1	(1.2)	74.2	(0.9)	66.4	(1.0)	41.4	(1.2)	68.2	(1.0)	35.4	(0.9)	44.4	(1.0)	38.8	(1.0)	47.3	(1.1)
Azerbaijan	63.8	(1.3)	68.6	(1.2)	65.2	(1.1)	76.1	(1.1)	70.0	(1.0)	65.4	(1.2)	62.2	(1.2)	48.0	(1.4)	54.2	(1.5)
Brazil	61.8	(0.8)	67.7	(0.7)	68.5	(0.7)	50.5	(0.8)	72.2	(0.6)	40.6	(0.6)	50.9	(0.7)	50.1	(0.8)	51.7	(0.6)
Bulgaria	52.0	(1.1)	66.3	(1.2)	71.9	(1.1)	59.9	(1.2)	67.3	(1.1)	39.1	(1.7)	52.0	(1.1)	38.9	(1.1)	47.5	(0.9)
Colombia	64.4	(1.1)	71.9	(0.9)	69.2	(0.9)	61.3	(1.1)	76.7	(0.9)	46.7	(1.2)	60.0	(1.0)	54.0	(0.9)	56.1	(1.1)
Croatia	23.9	(0.9)	44.4	(1.0)	47.1	(0.9)	30.6	(0.9)	44.8	(0.9)	10.6	(0.5)	19.8	(0.6)	14.7	(0.5)	21.0	(0.6)
Dubai (UAE)	66.8	(0.8)	70.8	(0.7)	69.4	(0.7)	48.3	(0.7)	69.5	(0.7)	42.7	(0.8)	42.9	(0.7)	51.7	(0.7)	52.1	(0.7)
Hong Kong-China	63.7	(0.9)	76.2	(0.6)	68.3	(0.8)	51.8	(1.1)	75.7	(0.7)	55.1	(1.3)	32.9	(1.0)	38.1	(0.8)	47.6	(0.8)
Indonesia	68.3	(1.0)	72.4	(0.9)	62.8	(1.0)	45.4	(1.2)	72.7	(1.1)	61.9	(0.9)	39.3	(0.9)	46.0	(1.1)	46.8	(1.0)
Jordan	66.8	(1.1)	76.5	(0.8)	63.8	(0.8)	62.0	(1.0)	75.0	(0.8)	71.6	(0.8)	47.8	(1.0)	54.5	(1.0)	56.3	(1.0)
Kazakhstan	63.3	(0.9)	73.4	(0.9)	75.1	(0.8)	79.4	(0.7)	75.5	(0.7)	79.4	(0.7)	73.6	(0.8)	56.1	(0.9)	61.7	(0.9)
Kyrgyzstan	50.6	(1.3)	67.3	(1.3)	70.4	(1.3)	74.4	(1.1)	70.7	(1.2)	73.3	(1.0)	55.2	(1.1)	39.1	(1.1)	50.6	(1.1)
Latvia	63.8	(0.9)	64.9	(1.0)	61.0	(1.2)	46.0	(1.2)	68.5	(0.9)	38.9	(1.3)	36.6	(1.1)	41.8	(0.9)	40.3	(1.0)
Liechtenstein	62.0	(2.7)	53.5	(3.1)	42.6	(2.3)	20.2	(2.2)	48.3	(2.4)	15.4	(1.6)	15.8	(1.6)	35.3	(2.4)	31.8	(2.5)
Lithuania	60.4	(1.0)	72.3	(0.9)	70.5	(0.9)	67.8	(0.9)	72.5	(0.8)	31.6	(1.1)	47.3	(0.9)	29.9	(0.9)	33.4	(0.9)
Macao-China	54.4	(0.7)	63.5	(0.7)	58.5	(0.8)	67.1	(0.6)	69.3	(0.6)	72.6	(0.5)	54.8	(0.7)	34.9	(0.7)	47.7	(0.7)
Montenegro	37.2	(1.0)	71.2	(0.8)	79.4	(0.6)	67.9	(0.7)	74.2	(0.7)	45.9	(1.1)	54.0	(0.8)	27.0	(0.7)	37.4	(0.8)
Panama	48.6	(1.6)	57.3	(1.3)	52.3	(1.5)	48.1	(1.5)	57.4	(1.6)	52.5	(1.5)	55.0	(1.2)	39.4	(1.6)	44.8	(1.4)
Peru	61.0	(0.9)	75.0	(0.7)	74.0	(0.8)	71.6	(0.8)	72.4	(0.8)	62.6	(1.2)	67.5	(0.9)	52.3	(0.9)	62.1	(0.9)
Qatar	62.1	(0.5)	65.5	(0.5)	59.8	(0.5)	52.7	(0.5)	62.5	(0.5)	57.3	(0.6)	50.5	(0.6)	48.2	(0.6)	47.5	(0.5)
Romania	57.4	(1.2)	75.2	(1.1)	79.7	(1.0)	69.4	(1.4)	72.4	(1.2)	49.0	(1.5)	44.7	(1.3)	43.0	(1.3)	44.6	(1.3)
Russian Federation	60.6	(1.1)	76.2	(1.0)	80.5	(0.8)	75.9	(0.8)	69.5	(1.0)	62.9	(1.1)	52.1	(1.0)	45.6	(0.8)	49.7	(1.1)
Serbia	31.9	(1.0)	68.6	(0.9)	76.1	(0.9)	47.1	(1.1)	69.2	(0.8)	36.3	(1.2)	47.9	(0.9)	23.9	(0.9)	28.3	(0.8)
Shanghai-China	58.4	(0.8)	75.5	(0.8)	70.6	(0.9)	55.6	(0.9)	73.7	(0.7)	82.4	(0.5)	47.0	(0.8)	34.5	(0.7)	48.9	(0.7)
Singapore	77.3	(0.6)	75.1	(0.6)	62.0	(0.6)	26.1	(0.6)	71.0	(0.8)	30.0	(0.7)	29.9	(0.7)	58.2	(0.8)	54.5	(0.7)
Chinese Taipei	65.5	(0.9)	60.8	(0.8)	57.6	(0.7)	53.7	(1.1)	60.2	(0.9)	61.7	(1.1)	51.5	(0.9)	44.8	(0.9)	51.4	(0.8)
Thailand	60.4	(0.9)	70.0	(0.8)	68.3	(0.8)	54.0	(1.0)	67.2	(0.8)	72.6	(0.7)	70.7	(0.9)	51.0	(0.9)	58.0	(0.8)
Trinidad and Tobago	71.8	(0.7)	71.1	(0.8)	69.4	(0.8)	41.0	(0.8)	58.3	(1.0)	42.5	(0.9)	44.9	(0.9)	54.1	(0.8)	51.2	(0.8)
Tunisia	70.0	(0.8)	76.1	(1.0)	69.0	(0.7)	57.3	(1.0)	72.7	(0.7)	54.4	(1.0)	45.6	(1.0)	50.5	(1.0)	52.8	(0.9)
Uruguay	53.9	(0.8)	74.4	(0.7)	70.3	(0.8)	56.2	(1.0)	66.2	(0.9)	35.2	(1.0)	51.0	(1.0)	41.8	(0.8)	44.3	(0.9)

StatLink ⟨⟩ http://dx.doi.org/10.1787/888932343285

[Part 1/2]

Index of interpretation of literary texts and reading performance, by national quarters of this index

Table III.2.3 *Results based on students' self-reports*

	Index of interpretation of literary texts															
	All students		Boys		Girls		Gender difference (B – G)		Bottom quarter		Second quarter		Third quarter		Top quarter	
	Mean index	S.E.	Mean index	S.E.	Mean index	S.E.	Dif.	S.E.	Mean index	S.E.	Mean index	S.E.	Mean index	S.E.	Mean index	S.E.
Australia	0.15	(0.02)	0.06	(0.02)	0.23	(0.02)	**-0.17**	(0.02)	**-0.96**	(0.01)	-0.17	(0.00)	0.34	(0.00)	**1.37**	(0.01)
Austria	-0.38	(0.02)	-0.51	(0.02)	-0.25	(0.03)	**-0.26**	(0.04)	**-1.55**	(0.02)	-0.63	(0.00)	-0.13	(0.00)	**0.79**	(0.02)
Belgium	-0.17	(0.02)	-0.22	(0.02)	-0.13	(0.02)	**-0.09**	(0.03)	**-1.31**	(0.02)	-0.46	(0.00)	0.05	(0.00)	**1.03**	(0.02)
Canada	0.15	(0.01)	0.07	(0.02)	0.22	(0.02)	**-0.15**	(0.02)	**-1.11**	(0.01)	-0.20	(0.00)	0.39	(0.00)	**1.52**	(0.01)
Chile	0.14	(0.02)	0.03	(0.02)	0.26	(0.03)	**-0.22**	(0.03)	**-0.95**	(0.02)	-0.19	(0.00)	0.34	(0.00)	**1.37**	(0.01)
Czech Republic	-0.58	(0.03)	-0.74	(0.03)	-0.40	(0.03)	**-0.34**	(0.04)	**-1.85**	(0.02)	-0.82	(0.00)	-0.29	(0.00)	**0.65**	(0.02)
Denmark	0.29	(0.02)	0.16	(0.03)	0.42	(0.02)	**-0.26**	(0.03)	**-0.83**	(0.01)	-0.06	(0.00)	0.47	(0.01)	**1.58**	(0.02)
Estonia	0.15	(0.02)	0.03	(0.02)	0.28	(0.02)	**-0.24**	(0.03)	**-0.87**	(0.02)	-0.16	(0.00)	0.32	(0.01)	**1.31**	(0.02)
Finland	-0.44	(0.02)	-0.52	(0.02)	-0.37	(0.02)	**-0.15**	(0.03)	**-1.56**	(0.02)	-0.70	(0.00)	-0.21	(0.00)	**0.70**	(0.02)
France	0.19	(0.02)	0.09	(0.02)	0.28	(0.02)	**-0.19**	(0.02)	**-0.93**	(0.02)	-0.09	(0.00)	0.41	(0.00)	**1.36**	(0.02)
Germany	0.12	(0.02)	0.02	(0.02)	0.23	(0.02)	**-0.21**	(0.03)	**-0.94**	(0.02)	-0.20	(0.00)	0.32	(0.00)	**1.30**	(0.02)
Greece	0.16	(0.02)	-0.12	(0.03)	0.42	(0.02)	**-0.54**	(0.04)	**-1.08**	(0.03)	-0.15	(0.01)	0.37	(0.01)	**1.48**	(0.02)
Hungary	0.06	(0.02)	-0.08	(0.03)	0.19	(0.03)	**-0.27**	(0.03)	**-0.97**	(0.02)	-0.26	(0.00)	0.23	(0.00)	**1.23**	(0.02)
Iceland	-0.49	(0.02)	-0.55	(0.03)	-0.43	(0.03)	**-0.12**	(0.04)	**-1.64**	(0.02)	-0.74	(0.00)	-0.27	(0.01)	**0.69**	(0.03)
Ireland	0.03	(0.02)	0.02	(0.03)	0.05	(0.03)	**-0.03**	(0.04)	**-1.15**	(0.03)	-0.26	(0.00)	0.27	(0.01)	**1.26**	(0.02)
Israel	-0.02	(0.02)	-0.17	(0.03)	0.12	(0.03)	**-0.28**	(0.04)	**-1.20**	(0.02)	-0.32	(0.00)	0.19	(0.00)	**1.24**	(0.02)
Italy	0.29	(0.01)	0.18	(0.02)	0.41	(0.02)	**-0.23**	(0.02)	**-0.89**	(0.01)	-0.07	(0.00)	0.50	(0.00)	**1.63**	(0.01)
Japan	-0.21	(0.02)	-0.30	(0.03)	-0.13	(0.03)	**-0.17**	(0.03)	**-1.78**	(0.02)	-0.49	(0.01)	0.13	(0.00)	**1.28**	(0.02)
Korea	-0.51	(0.03)	-0.62	(0.03)	-0.39	(0.04)	**-0.23**	(0.05)	**-1.84**	(0.02)	-0.78	(0.00)	-0.21	(0.00)	**0.79**	(0.02)
Luxembourg	-0.01	(0.01)	-0.14	(0.02)	0.14	(0.02)	**-0.28**	(0.03)	**-1.11**	(0.02)	-0.29	(0.00)	0.19	(0.00)	**1.20**	(0.02)
Mexico	0.09	(0.01)	0.02	(0.01)	0.16	(0.01)	**-0.14**	(0.01)	**-0.84**	(0.01)	-0.18	(0.00)	0.26	(0.00)	**1.12**	(0.01)
Netherlands	-0.15	(0.02)	-0.24	(0.02)	-0.07	(0.03)	**-0.18**	(0.03)	**-1.17**	(0.02)	-0.43	(0.00)	0.01	(0.00)	**0.97**	(0.02)
New Zealand	0.04	(0.02)	-0.07	(0.02)	0.15	(0.02)	**-0.22**	(0.03)	**-1.05**	(0.02)	-0.24	(0.00)	0.24	(0.00)	**1.22**	(0.02)
Norway	-0.18	(0.02)	-0.21	(0.02)	-0.14	(0.03)	**-0.07**	(0.03)	**-1.30**	(0.02)	-0.47	(0.00)	0.03	(0.00)	**1.03**	(0.02)
Poland	0.38	(0.02)	0.18	(0.02)	0.58	(0.03)	**-0.40**	(0.03)	**-0.78**	(0.02)	0.01	(0.00)	0.58	(0.01)	**1.72**	(0.02)
Portugal	0.17	(0.01)	0.02	(0.02)	0.31	(0.02)	**-0.29**	(0.02)	**-0.89**	(0.01)	-0.12	(0.00)	0.39	(0.00)	**1.29**	(0.01)
Slovak Republic	-0.18	(0.03)	-0.33	(0.03)	-0.04	(0.03)	**-0.30**	(0.04)	**-1.44**	(0.02)	-0.46	(0.01)	0.09	(0.00)	**1.08**	(0.02)
Slovenia	-0.08	(0.02)	-0.24	(0.02)	0.10	(0.02)	**-0.34**	(0.03)	**-1.19**	(0.02)	-0.36	(0.00)	0.13	(0.01)	**1.12**	(0.02)
Spain	0.10	(0.01)	-0.03	(0.01)	0.23	(0.02)	**-0.25**	(0.02)	**-0.96**	(0.01)	-0.18	(0.00)	0.29	(0.00)	**1.23**	(0.01)
Sweden	-0.20	(0.02)	-0.28	(0.02)	-0.11	(0.03)	**-0.17**	(0.03)	**-1.28**	(0.02)	-0.48	(0.00)	0.00	(0.00)	**0.98**	(0.02)
Switzerland	-0.24	(0.02)	-0.34	(0.02)	-0.14	(0.03)	**-0.20**	(0.03)	**-1.35**	(0.01)	-0.51	(0.00)	-0.03	(0.00)	**0.91**	(0.01)
Turkey	0.79	(0.02)	0.56	(0.03)	1.04	(0.02)	**-0.48**	(0.03)	**-0.48**	(0.02)	0.39	(0.01)	1.06	(0.01)	**2.19**	(0.00)
United Kingdom	0.20	(0.02)	0.13	(0.02)	0.27	(0.03)	**-0.15**	(0.03)	**-0.86**	(0.02)	-0.10	(0.00)	0.39	(0.00)	**1.37**	(0.02)
United States	0.42	(0.02)	0.35	(0.02)	0.49	(0.02)	**-0.14**	(0.02)	**-0.75**	(0.02)	0.08	(0.00)	0.63	(0.00)	**1.72**	(0.02)
OECD average	0.00	(0.00)	-0.11	(0.00)	0.12	(0.00)	**-0.23**	(0.01)	**-1.14**	(0.00)	-0.30	(0.00)	0.22	(0.00)	**1.23**	(0.00)
Albania	0.64	(0.02)	0.38	(0.03)	0.89	(0.03)	**-0.51**	(0.04)	**-0.55**	(0.02)	0.24	(0.01)	0.92	(0.01)	**1.95**	(0.01)
Argentina	0.25	(0.02)	0.10	(0.03)	0.38	(0.03)	**-0.27**	(0.03)	**-0.83**	(0.02)	-0.08	(0.01)	0.47	(0.01)	**1.46**	(0.02)
Azerbaijan	0.28	(0.03)	0.20	(0.03)	0.36	(0.03)	**-0.15**	(0.04)	**-0.77**	(0.02)	-0.05	(0.01)	0.45	(0.01)	**1.48**	(0.03)
Brazil	0.23	(0.02)	0.10	(0.02)	0.34	(0.02)	**-0.24**	(0.02)	**-0.92**	(0.01)	-0.11	(0.00)	0.43	(0.00)	**1.52**	(0.01)
Bulgaria	0.29	(0.03)	0.07	(0.04)	0.51	(0.03)	**-0.44**	(0.04)	**-0.94**	(0.02)	-0.08	(0.00)	0.50	(0.00)	**1.68**	(0.01)
Colombia	0.24	(0.02)	0.14	(0.02)	0.33	(0.03)	**-0.19**	(0.03)	**-0.83**	(0.02)	-0.05	(0.00)	0.44	(0.00)	**1.39**	(0.02)
Croatia	-0.43	(0.02)	-0.57	(0.02)	-0.27	(0.02)	**-0.30**	(0.03)	**-1.53**	(0.02)	-0.67	(0.00)	-0.20	(0.00)	**0.69**	(0.02)
Dubai (UAE)	0.24	(0.01)	0.11	(0.02)	0.37	(0.02)	**-0.27**	(0.03)	**-0.89**	(0.02)	-0.07	(0.00)	0.45	(0.01)	**1.47**	(0.02)
Hong Kong-China	0.23	(0.02)	0.11	(0.02)	0.37	(0.03)	**-0.26**	(0.03)	**-0.95**	(0.02)	-0.06	(0.00)	0.44	(0.00)	**1.50**	(0.02)
Indonesia	0.39	(0.02)	0.25	(0.03)	0.53	(0.03)	**-0.27**	(0.03)	**-0.62**	(0.01)	0.03	(0.00)	0.57	(0.01)	**1.60**	(0.02)
Jordan	0.32	(0.02)	0.14	(0.03)	0.49	(0.03)	**-0.35**	(0.04)	**-0.80**	(0.02)	-0.02	(0.00)	0.51	(0.01)	**1.59**	(0.02)
Kazakhstan	0.51	(0.02)	0.36	(0.02)	0.66	(0.03)	**-0.30**	(0.03)	**-0.54**	(0.01)	0.13	(0.00)	0.71	(0.01)	**1.74**	(0.01)
Kyrgyzstan	0.43	(0.03)	0.24	(0.04)	0.61	(0.03)	**-0.36**	(0.04)	**-0.72**	(0.03)	0.06	(0.00)	0.64	(0.01)	**1.74**	(0.01)
Latvia	0.21	(0.02)	0.09	(0.02)	0.33	(0.03)	**-0.24**	(0.03)	**-0.78**	(0.02)	-0.09	(0.00)	0.36	(0.01)	**1.35**	(0.02)
Liechtenstein	-0.33	(0.04)	-0.46	(0.05)	-0.18	(0.07)	**-0.28**	(0.09)	**-1.38**	(0.06)	-0.57	(0.01)	-0.11	(0.01)	**0.75**	(0.07)
Lithuania	0.36	(0.02)	0.12	(0.02)	0.60	(0.03)	**-0.48**	(0.03)	**-0.75**	(0.02)	-0.03	(0.00)	0.54	(0.00)	**1.70**	(0.02)
Macao-China	-0.04	(0.01)	-0.23	(0.02)	0.15	(0.02)	**-0.37**	(0.02)	**-1.14**	(0.01)	-0.30	(0.00)	0.17	(0.00)	**1.09**	(0.01)
Montenegro	0.62	(0.02)	0.42	(0.02)	0.83	(0.02)	**-0.41**	(0.03)	**-0.68**	(0.02)	0.19	(0.01)	0.92	(0.01)	**2.05**	(0.01)
Panama	-0.10	(0.03)	-0.15	(0.04)	-0.05	(0.03)	**-0.10**	(0.04)	**-1.10**	(0.03)	-0.41	(0.01)	0.10	(0.01)	**1.03**	(0.03)
Peru	0.35	(0.02)	0.23	(0.04)	0.47	(0.02)	**-0.24**	(0.03)	**-0.63**	(0.02)	0.03	(0.00)	0.54	(0.00)	**1.47**	(0.02)
Qatar	0.03	(0.01)	-0.01	(0.02)	0.06	(0.02)	**-0.08**	(0.02)	**-1.07**	(0.01)	-0.26	(0.00)	0.21	(0.00)	**1.22**	(0.01)
Romania	0.50	(0.03)	0.27	(0.03)	0.72	(0.04)	**-0.45**	(0.03)	**-0.71**	(0.03)	0.10	(0.00)	0.73	(0.01)	**1.86**	(0.01)
Russian Federation	0.49	(0.02)	0.30	(0.03)	0.67	(0.03)	**-0.36**	(0.02)	**-0.61**	(0.02)	0.17	(0.00)	0.72	(0.01)	**1.68**	(0.02)
Serbia	0.47	(0.02)	0.29	(0.03)	0.63	(0.03)	**-0.34**	(0.03)	**-0.83**	(0.02)	0.06	(0.00)	0.74	(0.01)	**1.90**	(0.01)
Shanghai-China	0.35	(0.02)	0.21	(0.02)	0.49	(0.03)	**-0.28**	(0.03)	**-0.86**	(0.02)	-0.01	(0.00)	0.56	(0.00)	**1.70**	(0.01)
Singapore	0.20	(0.01)	0.09	(0.02)	0.31	(0.02)	**-0.23**	(0.02)	**-0.98**	(0.01)	-0.11	(0.00)	0.40	(0.00)	**1.49**	(0.02)
Chinese Taipei	-0.04	(0.02)	-0.16	(0.03)	0.07	(0.03)	**-0.24**	(0.03)	**-1.36**	(0.02)	-0.34	(0.00)	0.22	(0.00)	**1.29**	(0.02)
Thailand	0.26	(0.01)	0.09	(0.02)	0.38	(0.02)	**-0.29**	(0.02)	**-0.65**	(0.01)	-0.02	(0.00)	0.40	(0.00)	**1.31**	(0.02)
Trinidad and Tobago	0.18	(0.02)	-0.01	(0.03)	0.35	(0.02)	**-0.36**	(0.03)	**-1.02**	(0.02)	-0.13	(0.01)	0.40	(0.01)	**1.47**	(0.02)
Tunisia	0.40	(0.02)	0.19	(0.03)	0.59	(0.02)	**-0.40**	(0.03)	**-0.73**	(0.02)	0.04	(0.00)	0.58	(0.01)	**1.69**	(0.01)
Uruguay	0.21	(0.02)	0.05	(0.02)	0.35	(0.02)	**-0.30**	(0.03)	**-0.93**	(0.02)	-0.09	(0.00)	0.41	(0.00)	**1.44**	(0.02)

Note: Values that are statistically significant are indicated in bold (see Annex A3).
StatLink ᐧᎷᏕᐅ http://dx.doi.org/10.1787/888932343285

[Part 2/2]
Index of interpretation of literary texts and reading performance, by national quarters of this index

Table III.2.3 *Results based on students' self-reports*

	Bottom quarter		Second quarter		Third quarter		Top quarter		Change in the reading score per unit of this index		Increased likelihood of students in the bottom quarter of this index scoring in the bottom quarter of the national reading performance distribution		Explained variance in student performance (r-squared x 100)	
	Mean score	S.E.	Mean score	S.E.	Mean score	S.E.	Mean score	S.E.	Effect	S.E.	Ratio	S.E.	%	S.E.
OECD														
Australia	490	(2.8)	513	(2.7)	529	(2.7)	546	(3.1)	23.0	(1.21)	1.7	(0.06)	5.1	(0.48)
Austria	449	(4.5)	469	(4.3)	478	(3.9)	496	(4.5)	19.5	(2.11)	1.5	(0.10)	3.5	(0.74)
Belgium	489	(3.5)	515	(2.9)	516	(3.6)	518	(3.2)	13.3	(1.71)	1.5	(0.08)	1.6	(0.42)
Canada	514	(2.3)	519	(2.1)	529	(2.1)	545	(2.2)	11.8	(1.02)	1.3	(0.07)	1.9	(0.32)
Chile	449	(3.7)	446	(3.9)	450	(4.3)	460	(3.2)	5.5	(1.34)	1.1	(0.07)	0.4	(0.20)
Czech Republic	461	(3.7)	475	(3.4)	486	(3.4)	501	(4.7)	16.0	(1.68)	1.3	(0.11)	3.1	(0.63)
Denmark	471	(3.3)	496	(3.3)	506	(3.0)	514	(3.1)	17.4	(1.51)	1.7	(0.10)	4.1	(0.70)
Estonia	496	(3.6)	498	(4.0)	507	(3.3)	514	(3.4)	8.7	(1.63)	1.3	(0.10)	0.9	(0.31)
Finland	529	(3.4)	538	(3.6)	536	(3.4)	544	(3.2)	6.3	(1.53)	1.2	(0.07)	0.5	(0.22)
France	474	(4.6)	502	(4.3)	511	(4.5)	523	(4.7)	20.1	(2.07)	1.7	(0.11)	3.4	(0.66)
Germany	477	(4.4)	493	(3.5)	505	(3.6)	520	(3.6)	18.6	(2.01)	1.5	(0.10)	3.2	(0.65)
Greece	452	(6.8)	479	(5.2)	500	(4.5)	507	(4.6)	20.7	(2.16)	1.8	(0.13)	5.1	(1.01)
Hungary	479	(5.1)	492	(4.3)	500	(4.1)	512	(4.0)	14.2	(1.91)	1.4	(0.11)	2.0	(0.50)
Iceland	484	(3.2)	508	(3.2)	515	(3.5)	513	(3.2)	11.2	(1.71)	1.5	(0.10)	1.3	(0.40)
Ireland	496	(4.0)	504	(4.1)	504	(3.8)	505	(3.8)	3.6	(1.94)	1.2	(0.08)	0.2	(0.17)
Israel	479	(5.8)	479	(5.1)	478	(5.2)	476	(4.2)	-2.0	(2.23)	1.0	(0.08)	0.0	(0.07)
Italy	481	(2.1)	488	(2.2)	497	(2.4)	498	(2.2)	7.3	(1.00)	1.3	(0.05)	0.6	(0.16)
Japan	497	(4.9)	511	(4.1)	531	(3.2)	548	(3.9)	16.3	(1.58)	1.4	(0.09)	4.1	(0.74)
Korea	509	(3.9)	530	(4.7)	547	(3.7)	578	(3.4)	25.5	(1.25)	2.0	(0.13)	12.0	(1.04)
Luxembourg	439	(3.5)	462	(2.7)	485	(3.8)	513	(2.7)	31.0	(1.51)	1.8	(0.12)	8.1	(0.76)
Mexico	421	(2.5)	423	(2.5)	430	(2.5)	441	(2.6)	10.1	(1.08)	1.2	(0.04)	0.9	(0.18)
Netherlands	490	(5.7)	512	(5.8)	518	(6.2)	521	(6.0)	14.1	(1.96)	1.5	(0.13)	2.0	(0.55)
New Zealand	507	(4.3)	519	(3.7)	527	(3.9)	545	(4.2)	15.3	(2.35)	1.4	(0.10)	2.0	(0.61)
Norway	493	(3.7)	505	(4.5)	510	(3.5)	514	(4.0)	9.3	(1.65)	1.2	(0.07)	1.0	(0.33)
Poland	476	(4.4)	500	(3.9)	506	(3.5)	524	(3.5)	18.7	(1.82)	1.7	(0.11)	4.3	(0.80)
Portugal	470	(4.2)	491	(3.6)	497	(3.7)	503	(3.4)	13.1	(1.52)	1.6	(0.10)	1.8	(0.42)
Slovak Republic	467	(4.1)	480	(3.7)	485	(3.8)	488	(3.8)	9.2	(2.03)	1.3	(0.10)	1.1	(0.47)
Slovenia	454	(2.7)	476	(2.9)	501	(3.3)	511	(3.2)	24.6	(1.64)	1.8	(0.11)	6.7	(0.89)
Spain	465	(3.3)	479	(2.2)	491	(2.7)	502	(1.8)	17.5	(1.41)	1.5	(0.06)	3.2	(0.50)
Sweden	486	(4.1)	495	(3.8)	509	(4.2)	515	(4.0)	11.7	(1.86)	1.2	(0.09)	1.3	(0.41)
Switzerland	476	(3.5)	496	(3.2)	506	(3.7)	528	(3.5)	21.2	(1.67)	1.6	(0.09)	4.4	(0.66)
Turkey	445	(4.7)	459	(5.0)	481	(3.9)	489	(4.0)	17.5	(1.37)	1.7	(0.09)	4.8	(0.70)
United Kingdom	483	(3.0)	493	(3.7)	504	(3.4)	510	(3.3)	11.4	(1.78)	1.3	(0.08)	1.2	(0.36)
United States	474	(4.1)	500	(4.3)	508	(4.3)	521	(5.0)	17.5	(1.64)	1.5	(0.09)	3.2	(0.58)
OECD average	477	(0.7)	492	(0.7)	502	(0.6)	513	(0.6)	14.7	(0.29)	1.5	(0.02)	2.9	(0.10)
Partners														
Albania	367	(5.9)	387	(4.6)	416	(5.4)	439	(5.1)	28.0	(2.15)	1.8	(0.16)	9.0	(1.26)
Argentina	398	(6.6)	411	(5.3)	417	(5.8)	421	(5.8)	10.1	(2.33)	1.3	(0.11)	0.8	(0.39)
Azerbaijan	366	(3.9)	371	(4.5)	384	(4.8)	391	(4.9)	12.1	(1.99)	1.3	(0.11)	2.3	(0.75)
Brazil	398	(2.8)	407	(2.9)	432	(3.3)	450	(3.8)	20.7	(1.30)	1.4	(0.07)	4.8	(0.52)
Bulgaria	413	(7.1)	439	(8.2)	455	(8.3)	462	(8.0)	17.6	(2.78)	1.5	(0.11)	2.9	(0.89)
Colombia	401	(4.6)	412	(5.4)	426	(4.6)	427	(5.0)	11.4	(1.95)	1.3	(0.11)	1.4	(0.50)
Croatia	458	(3.8)	483	(3.4)	489	(3.4)	484	(3.7)	11.4	(1.74)	1.5	(0.09)	1.5	(0.43)
Dubai (UAE)	452	(3.0)	456	(3.0)	476	(3.3)	494	(3.2)	16.9	(1.57)	1.4	(0.09)	2.4	(0.46)
Hong Kong-China	504	(3.4)	529	(3.0)	544	(3.1)	563	(3.1)	22.5	(1.72)	1.8	(0.13)	7.3	(1.03)
Indonesia	392	(4.8)	403	(4.5)	409	(5.0)	417	(5.5)	9.3	(1.94)	1.3	(0.09)	1.5	(0.61)
Jordan	386	(4.3)	400	(4.4)	419	(3.9)	432	(3.6)	18.2	(1.59)	1.7	(0.12)	4.0	(0.65)
Kazakhstan	369	(4.7)	384	(4.1)	400	(4.0)	420	(4.6)	21.1	(1.90)	1.5	(0.11)	4.4	(0.78)
Kyrgyzstan	292	(4.4)	309	(4.6)	330	(5.1)	359	(6.9)	25.5	(2.91)	1.6	(0.12)	6.2	(1.29)
Latvia	477	(4.0)	482	(3.5)	484	(3.5)	501	(4.3)	12.0	(1.82)	1.2	(0.10)	1.7	(0.51)
Liechtenstein	474	(7.2)	491	(8.0)	508	(10.4)	527	(9.6)	23.0	(5.38)	1.4	(0.28)	6.2	(2.91)
Lithuania	445	(3.6)	463	(3.1)	480	(3.2)	492	(3.1)	19.3	(1.41)	1.7	(0.14)	4.7	(0.66)
Macao-China	465	(1.9)	478	(2.9)	495	(2.1)	509	(2.0)	17.7	(1.05)	1.6	(0.08)	4.5	(0.49)
Montenegro	384	(2.7)	406	(3.0)	420	(3.7)	440	(2.8)	21.4	(1.19)	1.7	(0.12)	6.3	(0.73)
Panama	371	(8.8)	375	(6.3)	391	(8.6)	399	(7.4)	13.5	(4.09)	1.1	(0.15)	1.5	(0.91)
Peru	357	(5.2)	366	(5.3)	382	(5.1)	392	(4.8)	15.8	(2.14)	1.4	(0.10)	1.9	(0.50)
Qatar	361	(2.5)	357	(2.4)	380	(2.8)	415	(2.7)	21.7	(1.53)	1.1	(0.08)	3.2	(0.45)
Romania	398	(5.3)	421	(5.1)	435	(4.7)	453	(4.7)	20.7	(1.93)	1.9	(0.13)	5.7	(1.03)
Russian Federation	440	(3.7)	461	(4.1)	472	(4.2)	489	(3.8)	19.2	(1.53)	1.6	(0.11)	4.1	(0.62)
Serbia	428	(3.4)	442	(3.5)	456	(3.2)	460	(3.4)	11.8	(1.59)	1.5	(0.10)	2.4	(0.63)
Shanghai-China	522	(3.3)	550	(3.8)	571	(2.8)	584	(2.9)	22.9	(1.32)	2.1	(0.13)	8.5	(0.90)
Singapore	490	(2.7)	517	(3.1)	541	(3.0)	561	(3.1)	27.4	(1.43)	1.9	(0.10)	7.8	(0.77)
Chinese Taipei	468	(3.5)	490	(3.1)	508	(3.2)	522	(3.3)	19.4	(1.47)	1.7	(0.10)	6.0	(0.77)
Thailand	405	(3.1)	416	(3.6)	428	(3.4)	440	(4.1)	17.3	(1.83)	1.5	(0.10)	3.7	(0.67)
Trinidad and Tobago	407	(3.5)	417	(3.9)	446	(3.6)	466	(4.0)	24.1	(1.78)	1.5	(0.11)	5.0	(0.71)
Tunisia	393	(4.0)	396	(4.2)	413	(3.9)	423	(4.3)	11.9	(1.75)	1.3	(0.09)	1.8	(0.53)
Uruguay	410	(4.2)	429	(4.1)	448	(3.7)	446	(3.7)	14.8	(2.07)	1.5	(0.10)	2.2	(0.56)

The heading "Performance on the reading scale, by national quarters of this index" spans the Bottom, Second, Third and Top quarter columns.

Note: Values that are statistically significant are indicated in bold (see Annex A3).
StatLink ⟨⟩ http://dx.doi.org/10.1787/888932343285

[Part 1/2]
Index of use of texts containing non-continuous materials and reading performance, by national quarters of this index

Table III.2.4 *Results based on students' self-reports*

	All students		Boys		Girls		Gender difference (B – G)		Bottom quarter		Second quarter		Third quarter		Top quarter	
	Mean index	S.E.	Mean index	S.E.	Mean index	S.E.	Dif.	S.E.	Mean index	S.E.	Mean index	S.E.	Mean index	S.E.	Mean index	S.E.
OECD																
Australia	0.33	(0.02)	0.34	(0.02)	0.32	(0.02)	0.02	(0.03)	**-0.80**	(0.01)	0.01	(0.00)	0.53	(0.00)	**1.59**	(0.01)
Austria	-0.31	(0.02)	-0.23	(0.03)	-0.39	(0.02)	**0.16**	(0.04)	**-1.52**	(0.01)	-0.56	(0.00)	-0.05	(0.00)	**0.87**	(0.02)
Belgium	0.08	(0.02)	0.08	(0.02)	0.07	(0.02)	0.01	(0.02)	**-1.07**	(0.01)	-0.20	(0.00)	0.30	(0.00)	**1.28**	(0.02)
Canada	0.41	(0.01)	0.41	(0.02)	0.42	(0.02)	-0.02	(0.02)	**-0.81**	(0.01)	0.08	(0.00)	0.64	(0.00)	**1.75**	(0.01)
Chile	0.18	(0.02)	0.17	(0.02)	0.18	(0.03)	-0.01	(0.03)	**-0.92**	(0.02)	-0.10	(0.00)	0.40	(0.00)	**1.32**	(0.02)
Czech Republic	-0.44	(0.02)	-0.44	(0.02)	-0.44	(0.03)	0.00	(0.04)	**-1.68**	(0.01)	-0.68	(0.00)	-0.15	(0.00)	**0.74**	(0.02)
Denmark	0.00	(0.02)	0.03	(0.02)	-0.04	(0.02)	**0.06**	(0.02)	**-1.12**	(0.02)	-0.26	(0.00)	0.21	(0.00)	**1.15**	(0.02)
Estonia	0.20	(0.02)	0.18	(0.02)	0.21	(0.02)	-0.03	(0.03)	**-0.77**	(0.02)	-0.04	(0.00)	0.40	(0.00)	**1.20**	(0.02)
Finland	0.00	(0.02)	-0.01	(0.03)	0.01	(0.02)	-0.02	(0.03)	**-1.16**	(0.02)	-0.26	(0.00)	0.22	(0.00)	**1.20**	(0.02)
France	0.50	(0.02)	0.50	(0.03)	0.49	(0.02)	0.01	(0.03)	**-0.64**	(0.02)	0.18	(0.01)	0.70	(0.00)	**1.73**	(0.02)
Germany	0.15	(0.02)	0.18	(0.03)	0.13	(0.02)	0.05	(0.03)	**-0.97**	(0.02)	-0.15	(0.00)	0.36	(0.00)	**1.37**	(0.02)
Greece	-0.54	(0.02)	-0.43	(0.02)	-0.64	(0.02)	**0.21**	(0.03)	**-1.73**	(0.01)	-0.73	(0.00)	-0.24	(0.00)	**0.55**	(0.02)
Hungary	-0.01	(0.02)	0.01	(0.02)	-0.03	(0.03)	0.04	(0.03)	**-1.03**	(0.02)	-0.24	(0.00)	0.20	(0.01)	**1.02**	(0.02)
Iceland	-0.38	(0.01)	-0.37	(0.02)	-0.40	(0.02)	0.04	(0.03)	**-1.56**	(0.01)	-0.64	(0.01)	-0.13	(0.01)	**0.78**	(0.02)
Ireland	0.17	(0.02)	0.21	(0.03)	0.14	(0.02)	**0.07**	(0.03)	**-1.03**	(0.03)	-0.06	(0.00)	0.42	(0.01)	**1.37**	(0.02)
Israel	-0.10	(0.02)	-0.09	(0.03)	-0.10	(0.03)	0.01	(0.04)	**-1.31**	(0.01)	-0.37	(0.00)	0.16	(0.00)	**1.14**	(0.02)
Italy	-0.37	(0.01)	-0.29	(0.01)	-0.46	(0.01)	**0.17**	(0.02)	**-1.57**	(0.01)	-0.61	(0.00)	-0.08	(0.00)	**0.79**	(0.01)
Japan	-0.40	(0.02)	-0.35	(0.03)	-0.44	(0.03)	**0.09**	(0.03)	**-1.93**	(0.01)	-0.66	(0.01)	-0.02	(0.00)	**1.03**	(0.02)
Korea	-0.30	(0.03)	-0.36	(0.03)	-0.23	(0.04)	**-0.13**	(0.05)	**-1.70**	(0.02)	-0.57	(0.00)	0.00	(0.01)	**1.07**	(0.02)
Luxembourg	-0.17	(0.01)	-0.14	(0.02)	-0.20	(0.02)	**0.06**	(0.02)	**-1.34**	(0.01)	-0.43	(0.00)	0.07	(0.00)	**1.03**	(0.02)
Mexico	0.32	(0.01)	0.31	(0.01)	0.32	(0.01)	-0.01	(0.01)	**-0.74**	(0.01)	0.02	(0.00)	0.50	(0.00)	**1.49**	(0.01)
Netherlands	0.18	(0.01)	0.24	(0.02)	0.12	(0.02)	**0.12**	(0.03)	**-0.87**	(0.02)	-0.05	(0.00)	0.40	(0.00)	**1.23**	(0.02)
New Zealand	0.21	(0.02)	0.17	(0.02)	0.24	(0.03)	**-0.07**	(0.03)	**-0.96**	(0.01)	-0.06	(0.00)	0.43	(0.00)	**1.42**	(0.02)
Norway	0.04	(0.02)	0.03	(0.03)	0.06	(0.03)	-0.03	(0.03)	**-1.20**	(0.02)	-0.25	(0.00)	0.28	(0.00)	**1.33**	(0.02)
Poland	0.31	(0.02)	0.29	(0.02)	0.32	(0.03)	-0.03	(0.03)	**-0.82**	(0.02)	0.00	(0.00)	0.50	(0.00)	**1.55**	(0.02)
Portugal	-0.07	(0.01)	-0.09	(0.02)	-0.06	(0.02)	-0.03	(0.03)	**-1.31**	(0.01)	-0.34	(0.00)	0.19	(0.00)	**1.18**	(0.02)
Slovak Republic	-0.33	(0.03)	-0.27	(0.03)	-0.40	(0.04)	**0.13**	(0.04)	**-1.60**	(0.01)	-0.60	(0.00)	-0.02	(0.00)	**0.88**	(0.02)
Slovenia	-0.22	(0.01)	-0.22	(0.02)	-0.22	(0.02)	-0.01	(0.02)	**-1.37**	(0.01)	-0.45	(0.00)	0.02	(0.00)	**0.93**	(0.02)
Spain	-0.10	(0.02)	-0.08	(0.02)	-0.13	(0.02)	**0.05**	(0.02)	**-1.29**	(0.01)	-0.37	(0.00)	0.16	(0.00)	**1.09**	(0.02)
Sweden	-0.17	(0.02)	-0.16	(0.02)	-0.18	(0.02)	0.02	(0.03)	**-1.26**	(0.01)	-0.42	(0.00)	0.07	(0.00)	**0.93**	(0.02)
Switzerland	-0.08	(0.02)	-0.04	(0.02)	-0.12	(0.03)	**0.08**	(0.03)	**-1.18**	(0.02)	-0.32	(0.00)	0.15	(0.00)	**1.04**	(0.02)
Turkey	0.09	(0.02)	0.08	(0.02)	0.09	(0.03)	-0.01	(0.04)	**-1.08**	(0.02)	-0.19	(0.00)	0.33	(0.00)	**1.30**	(0.02)
United Kingdom	0.27	(0.02)	0.27	(0.02)	0.26	(0.02)	0.01	(0.02)	**-0.88**	(0.02)	-0.03	(0.00)	0.47	(0.00)	**1.50**	(0.02)
United States	0.57	(0.02)	0.57	(0.02)	0.57	(0.03)	0.01	(0.03)	**-0.61**	(0.02)	0.22	(0.00)	0.77	(0.01)	**1.90**	(0.01)
OECD average	0.00	(0.00)	0.02	(0.00)	-0.01	(0.00)	**0.03**	(0.01)	**-1.17**	(0.00)	-0.27	(0.00)	0.24	(0.00)	**1.20**	(0.00)
Partners																
Albania	-0.06	(0.02)	-0.05	(0.03)	-0.06	(0.03)	0.01	(0.03)	**-1.16**	(0.03)	-0.27	(0.01)	0.18	(0.00)	**1.01**	(0.02)
Argentina	-0.11	(0.03)	-0.11	(0.03)	-0.10	(0.03)	-0.01	(0.03)	**-1.24**	(0.02)	-0.36	(0.00)	0.16	(0.01)	**1.01**	(0.02)
Azerbaijan	0.16	(0.02)	0.23	(0.02)	0.09	(0.03)	**0.13**	(0.04)	**-0.95**	(0.02)	-0.06	(0.01)	0.42	(0.01)	**1.23**	(0.03)
Brazil	0.19	(0.02)	0.20	(0.02)	0.18	(0.02)	0.01	(0.02)	**-1.01**	(0.01)	-0.12	(0.00)	0.42	(0.00)	**1.46**	(0.02)
Bulgaria	-0.05	(0.02)	-0.05	(0.03)	-0.05	(0.03)	0.00	(0.04)	**-1.16**	(0.02)	-0.27	(0.00)	0.19	(0.00)	**1.03**	(0.02)
Colombia	0.29	(0.02)	0.28	(0.03)	0.30	(0.03)	-0.02	(0.04)	**-0.93**	(0.02)	-0.01	(0.01)	0.52	(0.00)	**1.59**	(0.02)
Croatia	-0.70	(0.02)	-0.62	(0.02)	-0.77	(0.03)	**0.15**	(0.03)	**-1.82**	(0.01)	-0.90	(0.00)	-0.40	(0.00)	**0.34**	(0.01)
Dubai (UAE)	0.33	(0.01)	0.31	(0.02)	0.34	(0.02)	-0.04	(0.03)	**-0.90**	(0.02)	0.01	(0.01)	0.55	(0.00)	**1.64**	(0.02)
Hong Kong-China	-0.15	(0.02)	-0.20	(0.02)	-0.10	(0.03)	**-0.09**	(0.03)	**-1.38**	(0.02)	-0.40	(0.00)	0.14	(0.00)	**1.03**	(0.02)
Indonesia	0.23	(0.02)	0.22	(0.03)	0.24	(0.02)	-0.02	(0.04)	**-0.78**	(0.02)	-0.04	(0.00)	0.41	(0.00)	**1.33**	(0.03)
Jordan	0.24	(0.02)	0.18	(0.03)	0.31	(0.03)	**-0.13**	(0.04)	**-0.91**	(0.02)	-0.04	(0.00)	0.46	(0.00)	**1.45**	(0.02)
Kazakhstan	0.24	(0.02)	0.25	(0.02)	0.24	(0.02)	0.01	(0.02)	**-0.74**	(0.02)	-0.02	(0.00)	0.42	(0.00)	**1.30**	(0.02)
Kyrgyzstan	-0.08	(0.03)	-0.08	(0.04)	-0.08	(0.03)	0.00	(0.03)	**-1.24**	(0.03)	-0.34	(0.01)	0.17	(0.01)	**1.08**	(0.04)
Latvia	0.18	(0.02)	0.24	(0.02)	0.12	(0.03)	**0.12**	(0.03)	**-0.86**	(0.02)	-0.10	(0.00)	0.37	(0.00)	**1.31**	(0.03)
Liechtenstein	0.02	(0.05)	0.04	(0.05)	-0.01	(0.08)	0.05	(0.10)	**-1.11**	(0.06)	-0.26	(0.00)	0.23	(0.02)	**1.20**	(0.07)
Lithuania	-0.01	(0.02)	-0.01	(0.02)	-0.01	(0.02)	0.00	(0.02)	**-0.99**	(0.02)	-0.24	(0.00)	0.20	(0.00)	**1.00**	(0.01)
Macao-China	-0.17	(0.01)	-0.23	(0.02)	-0.11	(0.02)	**-0.12**	(0.02)	**-1.32**	(0.01)	-0.40	(0.00)	0.10	(0.00)	**0.95**	(0.02)
Montenegro	-0.58	(0.02)	-0.50	(0.02)	-0.66	(0.02)	**0.16**	(0.03)	**-1.87**	(0.02)	-0.84	(0.01)	-0.24	(0.01)	**0.65**	(0.02)
Panama	-0.02	(0.03)	0.01	(0.04)	-0.06	(0.04)	0.07	(0.04)	**-1.18**	(0.03)	-0.32	(0.01)	0.22	(0.01)	**1.18**	(0.03)
Peru	0.22	(0.02)	0.19	(0.02)	0.26	(0.02)	**-0.07**	(0.03)	**-0.80**	(0.02)	-0.03	(0.00)	0.42	(0.00)	**1.30**	(0.02)
Qatar	0.13	(0.01)	0.23	(0.01)	0.04	(0.02)	**0.19**	(0.02)	**-1.15**	(0.01)	-0.12	(0.00)	0.40	(0.00)	**1.39**	(0.02)
Romania	0.07	(0.03)	0.05	(0.03)	0.09	(0.04)	-0.04	(0.04)	**-1.13**	(0.02)	-0.22	(0.00)	0.31	(0.01)	**1.33**	(0.04)
Russian Federation	0.16	(0.02)	0.20	(0.02)	0.12	(0.03)	**0.08**	(0.03)	**-0.92**	(0.02)	-0.11	(0.00)	0.37	(0.00)	**1.30**	(0.02)
Serbia	-0.65	(0.02)	-0.55	(0.03)	-0.74	(0.03)	**0.18**	(0.04)	**-1.94**	(0.01)	-0.92	(0.01)	-0.33	(0.01)	**0.60**	(0.02)
Shanghai-China	-0.34	(0.02)	-0.31	(0.02)	-0.38	(0.03)	**0.07**	(0.03)	**-1.65**	(0.02)	-0.61	(0.00)	-0.03	(0.01)	**0.93**	(0.02)
Singapore	0.57	(0.02)	0.52	(0.02)	0.62	(0.02)	**-0.10**	(0.03)	**-0.74**	(0.02)	0.20	(0.00)	0.78	(0.00)	**2.05**	(0.01)
Chinese Taipei	0.05	(0.03)	0.00	(0.03)	0.10	(0.03)	**-0.10**	(0.04)	**-1.32**	(0.02)	-0.26	(0.00)	0.31	(0.00)	**1.46**	(0.02)
Thailand	0.15	(0.02)	0.16	(0.02)	0.14	(0.02)	0.02	(0.03)	**-0.82**	(0.02)	-0.09	(0.00)	0.35	(0.00)	**1.15**	(0.02)
Trinidad and Tobago	0.39	(0.02)	0.34	(0.02)	0.44	(0.02)	**-0.10**	(0.03)	**-0.87**	(0.02)	0.08	(0.00)	0.62	(0.01)	**1.75**	(0.02)
Tunisia	0.39	(0.02)	0.35	(0.03)	0.44	(0.03)	**-0.09**	(0.04)	**-0.73**	(0.02)	0.07	(0.00)	0.59	(0.00)	**1.65**	(0.02)
Uruguay	-0.03	(0.02)	-0.03	(0.02)	-0.02	(0.02)	-0.01	(0.03)	**-1.23**	(0.02)	-0.27	(0.00)	0.24	(0.00)	**1.15**	(0.02)

Note: Values that are statistically significant are indicated in bold (see Annex A3).
StatLink ⬛▰▱ http://dx.doi.org/10.1787/888932343285

[Part 2/2]
Index of use of texts containing non-continuous materials and reading performance, by national quarters of this index

Table III.2.4   *Results based on students' self-reports*

	Bottom quarter Mean score	S.E.	Second quarter Mean score	S.E.	Third quarter Mean score	S.E.	Top quarter Mean score	S.E.	Change in the reading score per unit of this index Effect	S.E.	Increased likelihood of students in the bottom quarter of this index scoring in the bottom quarter of the national reading performance distribution Ratio	S.E.	Explained variance in student performance (r-squared x 100) %	S.E.
Australia	**499**	(2.9)	512	(2.5)	526	(2.6)	**541**	(3.6)	**16.8**	(1.37)	**1.4**	(0.06)	2.9	(0.45)
Austria	**463**	(3.7)	473	(4.5)	474	(4.2)	**481**	(3.6)	**8.6**	(2.00)	**1.2**	(0.09)	0.7	(0.31)
Belgium	**504**	(3.3)	506	(3.3)	513	(3.2)	**516**	(3.2)	**4.5**	(1.54)	**1.2**	(0.06)	0.2	(0.12)
Canada	**510**	(2.3)	524	(2.0)	530	(2.2)	**543**	(2.4)	**12.8**	(0.98)	**1.4**	(0.07)	2.1	(0.32)
Chile	450	(4.0)	449	(3.4)	451	(3.8)	455	(3.9)	**3.1**	(1.48)	1.0	(0.07)	0.1	(0.12)
Czech Republic	477	(3.8)	483	(3.8)	482	(4.2)	482	(4.0)	2.9	(1.77)	1.0	(0.08)	0.1	(0.11)
Denmark	**478**	(3.4)	496	(3.0)	503	(3.4)	**511**	(3.1)	**12.9**	(1.59)	**1.5**	(0.10)	2.1	(0.50)
Estonia	**492**	(3.6)	506	(3.6)	505	(4.3)	**559**	(3.7)	**8.3**	(2.04)	**1.2**	(0.10)	0.7	(0.33)
Finland	**514**	(3.1)	530	(3.1)	544	(3.1)	**559**	(3.3)	**17.0**	(1.42)	**1.5**	(0.11)	3.6	(0.60)
France	**476**	(4.4)	495	(4.7)	513	(4.3)	**526**	(4.4)	**20.5**	(1.94)	**1.6**	(0.10)	3.7	(0.65)
Germany	**490**	(3.6)	497	(4.0)	499	(4.2)	**471**	(3.7)	**6.8**	(1.59)	**1.2**	(0.07)	0.5	(0.22)
Greece	**489**	(6.0)	493	(4.3)	485	(4.3)	471	(6.1)	**-6.0**	(2.11)	0.9	(0.08)	0.3	(0.22)
Hungary	**494**	(4.8)	497	(4.8)	494	(4.2)	499	(4.3)	3.0	(2.23)	1.0	(0.08)	0.1	(0.12)
Iceland	**491**	(3.2)	508	(4.1)	507	(3.3)	**515**	(2.9)	**7.3**	(1.85)	**1.3**	(0.12)	0.5	(0.26)
Ireland	499	(4.6)	502	(3.4)	503	(4.1)	506	(4.2)	**3.8**	(1.79)	1.1	(0.09)	0.2	(0.16)
Israel	480	(4.5)	484	(4.1)	477	(5.6)	471	(5.6)	-2.0	(2.09)	0.9	(0.09)	0.0	(0.07)
Italy	**509**	(2.1)	498	(2.2)	482	(2.0)	**474**	(2.6)	**-13.1**	(1.14)	**0.7**	(0.03)	1.8	(0.29)
Japan	**516**	(4.2)	522	(4.2)	521	(3.5)	530	(4.4)	4.1	(1.69)	1.1	(0.06)	0.2	(0.19)
Korea	**509**	(4.0)	531	(4.0)	546	(4.1)	**577**	(3.5)	**23.2**	(1.12)	**2.0**	(0.16)	10.8	(1.00)
Luxembourg	**461**	(3.2)	470	(3.2)	474	(3.3)	**494**	(2.9)	**13.1**	(1.54)	**1.2**	(0.08)	1.5	(0.35)
Mexico	**423**	(2.5)	425	(2.6)	427	(2.3)	**439**	(2.7)	**6.8**	(1.08)	1.0	(0.05)	0.5	(0.17)
Netherlands	**493**	(5.6)	509	(5.5)	513	(6.1)	526	(6.5)	**15.0**	(1.66)	**1.4**	(0.11)	2.2	(0.48)
New Zealand	**502**	(3.7)	520	(3.7)	527	(3.7)	**550**	(3.4)	**16.8**	(1.55)	**1.4**	(0.09)	2.6	(0.48)
Norway	**485**	(3.3)	500	(3.5)	510	(3.7)	**528**	(3.2)	**15.0**	(1.42)	**1.5**	(0.10)	2.9	(0.57)
Poland	**491**	(3.6)	502	(3.5)	503	(3.7)	**511**	(3.6)	**7.8**	(1.47)	**1.2**	(0.08)	0.7	(0.26)
Portugal	**483**	(3.7)	480	(3.9)	488	(4.1)	**509**	(4.1)	**9.1**	(1.30)	1.1	(0.08)	1.1	(0.32)
Slovak Republic	476	(3.9)	480	(3.7)	485	(3.8)	479	(4.7)	2.6	(2.36)	1.0	(0.09)	0.1	(0.15)
Slovenia	**464**	(2.4)	480	(2.9)	490	(2.9)	**509**	(3.1)	**18.3**	(1.47)	**1.5**	(0.08)	3.6	(0.61)
Spain	**482**	(3.1)	485	(2.7)	483	(2.5)	487	(2.7)	2.1	(1.42)	1.0	(0.06)	0.1	(0.08)
Sweden	**496**	(3.9)	499	(3.9)	502	(3.7)	**509**	(4.2)	**6.4**	(1.78)	1.1	(0.07)	0.4	(0.20)
Switzerland	**496**	(3.7)	496	(4.1)	502	(3.5)	**513**	(3.7)	**6.8**	(2.32)	**1.1**	(0.06)	0.4	(0.30)
Turkey	467	(4.7)	468	(4.2)	462	(4.3)	476	(4.4)	**3.7**	(1.57)	1.0	(0.08)	0.2	(0.15)
United Kingdom	**476**	(2.6)	493	(3.7)	504	(3.8)	**516**	(3.6)	**16.1**	(1.38)	**1.4**	(0.09)	2.8	(0.48)
United States	**488**	(4.5)	498	(5.0)	503	(4.3)	**514**	(4.1)	**9.8**	(1.67)	**1.3**	(0.08)	1.0	(0.36)
OECD average	**486**	(0.7)	494	(0.6)	498	(0.7)	**507**	(0.7)	**8.3**	(0.29)	**1.2**	(0.01)	1.5	(0.07)
Albania	402	(5.0)	398	(5.2)	407	(5.4)	401	(5.5)	-2.6	(2.17)	1.0	(0.10)	0.1	(0.11)
Argentina	**401**	(5.4)	416	(5.8)	413	(5.8)	**417**	(6.9)	5.7	(2.72)	1.1	(0.10)	0.3	(0.23)
Azerbaijan	**380**	(4.5)	382	(4.6)	376	(4.4)	374	(4.8)	-2.4	(1.89)	1.0	(0.11)	0.1	(0.15)
Brazil	**412**	(2.6)	410	(3.2)	423	(4.2)	**442**	(4.1)	**13.5**	(1.51)	1.0	(0.06)	2.2	(0.47)
Bulgaria	440	(6.7)	446	(8.3)	444	(8.6)	441	(8.0)	0.4	(2.71)	**1.2**	(0.10)	0.0	(0.04)
Colombia	**405**	(4.8)	412	(4.2)	420	(4.8)	**429**	(4.5)	**9.0**	(1.73)	**1.2**	(0.10)	1.1	(0.44)
Croatia	**468**	(3.7)	481	(3.4)	488	(3.4)	**477**	(3.9)	**4.3**	(1.83)	**1.2**	(0.08)	0.2	(0.16)
Dubai (UAE)	**462**	(3.3)	459	(3.4)	464	(3.5)	**493**	(3.1)	**10.7**	(1.54)	1.1	(0.08)	1.1	(0.32)
Hong Kong-China	**523**	(3.1)	530	(3.3)	538	(3.1)	**548**	(3.8)	**10.5**	(1.56)	**1.3**	(0.09)	1.6	(0.46)
Indonesia	404	(5.6)	405	(5.0)	409	(4.2)	403	(5.1)	-1.5	(1.83)	1.1	(0.09)	0.0	(0.09)
Jordan	**399**	(4.2)	406	(3.8)	407	(4.3)	**423**	(4.3)	**9.5**	(1.95)	1.1	(0.08)	1.1	(0.44)
Kazakhstan	396	(5.3)	387	(4.1)	391	(4.0)	399	(4.6)	2.3	(2.36)	1.0	(0.08)	0.0	(0.11)
Kyrgyzstan	**326**	(5.1)	328	(4.9)	324	(5.6)	312	(6.5)	**-8.3**	(3.17)	0.8	(0.09)	0.6	(0.47)
Latvia	492	(3.2)	483	(3.2)	480	(4.2)	490	(4.7)	0.3	(1.82)	**0.8**	(0.06)	0.0	(0.04)
Liechtenstein	495	(8.6)	492	(10.5)	501	(9.4)	513	(10.1)	9.0	(5.89)	1.0	(0.23)	1.1	(1.27)
Lithuania	**460**	(3.2)	466	(3.5)	475	(3.6)	**480**	(3.9)	**9.5**	(1.71)	1.1	(0.07)	0.8	(0.29)
Macao-China	**478**	(2.0)	481	(2.0)	490	(1.9)	**498**	(2.2)	**7.9**	(1.10)	**1.2**	(0.06)	0.9	(0.25)
Montenegro	**422**	(3.3)	419	(3.1)	412	(3.3)	398	(3.2)	**-9.9**	(1.41)	0.8	(0.08)	1.2	(0.33)
Panama	**377**	(6.8)	373	(7.2)	386	(8.5)	398	(7.9)	8.8	(3.07)	0.9	(0.10)	0.8	(0.51)
Peru	**369**	(5.3)	370	(4.7)	374	(4.8)	384	(6.0)	7.2	(2.25)	1.1	(0.09)	0.4	(0.26)
Qatar	**388**	(2.2)	362	(2.7)	367	(2.7)	396	(2.5)	**4.2**	(1.21)	**0.6**	(0.04)	0.1	(0.09)
Romania	427	(5.4)	426	(4.8)	423	(4.9)	431	(5.5)	2.8	(2.65)	1.0	(0.10)	0.1	(0.19)
Russian Federation	**464**	(3.9)	463	(4.1)	470	(3.7)	466	(4.9)	1.7	(1.82)	1.0	(0.08)	0.0	(0.07)
Serbia	447	(3.1)	450	(3.6)	448	(2.8)	442	(3.8)	-2.4	(1.71)	0.9	(0.06)	0.1	(0.12)
Shanghai-China	**545**	(3.3)	554	(2.8)	560	(3.1)	**569**	(3.4)	**9.0**	(1.38)	**1.3**	(0.08)	1.4	(0.44)
Singapore	**489**	(2.7)	514	(3.0)	536	(2.9)	**569**	(2.3)	**26.7**	(1.28)	**1.9**	(0.09)	9.2	(0.81)
Chinese Taipei	**463**	(3.5)	489	(3.4)	505	(3.2)	**531**	(3.5)	**22.8**	(1.38)	**1.9**	(0.12)	8.9	(0.87)
Thailand	**426**	(3.3)	422	(3.2)	424	(3.2)	417	(3.6)	**-4.2**	(1.40)	1.0	(0.08)	0.2	(0.15)
Trinidad and Tobago	**398**	(4.0)	420	(4.3)	440	(4.7)	**476**	(4.0)	**28.1**	(1.73)	**1.7**	(0.12)	7.4	(0.92)
Tunisia	**402**	(3.5)	399	(4.4)	403	(3.8)	**422**	(4.5)	**8.6**	(1.86)	1.1	(0.10)	0.9	(0.38)
Uruguay	429	(3.8)	439	(3.9)	437	(4.0)	428	(4.4)	-0.7	(1.86)	1.0	(0.07)	0.0	(0.03)

Note: Values that are statistically significant are indicated in bold (see Annex A3).
StatLink ⟨⟩ http://dx.doi.org/10.1787/888932343285

[Part 1/2]

Index of reading activities for traditional literature courses and reading performance, by national quarters of this index

Table III.2.5   *Results based on students' self-reports*

| | Index of reading activities for traditional literature courses | | | | | | | | | | | | | | | |
| | All students | | Boys | | Girls | | Gender difference (B – G) | | Bottom quarter | | Second quarter | | Third quarter | | Top quarter | |
	Mean index	S.E.	Mean index	S.E.	Mean index	S.E.	Dif.	S.E.	Mean index	S.E.	Mean index	S.E.	Mean index	S.E.	Mean index	S.E.
OECD																
Australia	-0.14	(0.02)	-0.17	(0.02)	-0.11	(0.02)	**-0.05**	(0.02)	-1.32	(0.01)	-0.34	(0.00)	0.17	(0.00)	0.94	(0.01)
Austria	-0.57	(0.02)	-0.67	(0.03)	-0.48	(0.03)	**-0.19**	(0.04)	-1.97	(0.01)	-0.79	(0.01)	-0.18	(0.00)	0.64	(0.02)
Belgium	-0.16	(0.02)	-0.18	(0.02)	-0.13	(0.02)	**-0.05**	(0.03)	-1.34	(0.01)	-0.34	(0.00)	0.15	(0.00)	0.89	(0.01)
Canada	-0.16	(0.01)	-0.16	(0.02)	-0.17	(0.02)	0.00	(0.02)	-1.45	(0.01)	-0.35	(0.00)	0.17	(0.00)	0.98	(0.01)
Chile	0.26	(0.01)	0.23	(0.02)	0.29	(0.02)	**-0.06**	(0.02)	-0.77	(0.01)	0.01	(0.00)	0.51	(0.00)	1.28	(0.01)
Czech Republic	-0.32	(0.03)	-0.39	(0.03)	-0.24	(0.03)	**-0.15**	(0.03)	-1.57	(0.02)	-0.51	(0.01)	0.01	(0.00)	0.77	(0.01)
Denmark	0.12	(0.02)	0.08	(0.02)	0.15	(0.02)	**-0.07**	(0.02)	-0.94	(0.02)	-0.07	(0.00)	0.39	(0.00)	1.11	(0.02)
Estonia	0.28	(0.02)	0.22	(0.02)	0.34	(0.03)	**-0.13**	(0.03)	-0.79	(0.02)	0.07	(0.00)	0.55	(0.00)	1.28	(0.02)
Finland	-0.32	(0.03)	-0.35	(0.03)	-0.28	(0.03)	**-0.07**	(0.03)	-1.60	(0.02)	-0.51	(0.00)	0.05	(0.00)	0.79	(0.02)
France	0.21	(0.02)	0.17	(0.03)	0.25	(0.03)	**-0.08**	(0.03)	-0.89	(0.02)	0.01	(0.00)	0.50	(0.00)	1.23	(0.02)
Germany	-0.32	(0.02)	-0.36	(0.03)	-0.28	(0.02)	**-0.08**	(0.03)	-1.54	(0.02)	-0.49	(0.01)	0.02	(0.00)	0.75	(0.01)
Greece	0.01	(0.02)	-0.07	(0.03)	0.09	(0.03)	**-0.16**	(0.03)	-1.17	(0.03)	-0.17	(0.00)	0.32	(0.00)	1.07	(0.02)
Hungary	0.45	(0.03)	0.37	(0.03)	0.53	(0.03)	**-0.16**	(0.03)	-0.55	(0.02)	0.23	(0.00)	0.70	(0.00)	1.42	(0.02)
Iceland	-0.50	(0.02)	-0.46	(0.02)	-0.54	(0.03)	0.07	(0.03)	-1.88	(0.02)	-0.71	(0.01)	-0.14	(0.00)	0.72	(0.02)
Ireland	0.18	(0.02)	0.17	(0.03)	0.19	(0.03)	-0.02	(0.04)	-1.03	(0.03)	-0.04	(0.00)	0.49	(0.00)	1.29	(0.02)
Israel	-0.15	(0.03)	-0.21	(0.04)	-0.10	(0.03)	**-0.11**	(0.05)	-1.54	(0.02)	-0.42	(0.00)	0.19	(0.00)	1.17	(0.02)
Italy	0.44	(0.01)	0.35	(0.02)	0.54	(0.01)	**-0.19**	(0.02)	-0.62	(0.01)	0.26	(0.00)	0.71	(0.00)	1.43	(0.01)
Japan	-0.15	(0.02)	-0.12	(0.03)	-0.18	(0.03)	0.06	(0.04)	-1.73	(0.02)	-0.37	(0.01)	0.27	(0.00)	1.25	(0.01)
Korea	-0.02	(0.03)	-0.13	(0.03)	0.10	(0.04)	**-0.23**	(0.05)	-1.46	(0.02)	-0.19	(0.00)	0.35	(0.00)	1.20	(0.02)
Luxembourg	-0.35	(0.01)	-0.38	(0.02)	-0.33	(0.02)	-0.05	(0.03)	-1.55	(0.02)	-0.54	(0.01)	-0.03	(0.00)	0.70	(0.01)
Mexico	0.40	(0.01)	0.38	(0.01)	0.41	(0.01)	**-0.03**	(0.01)	-0.65	(0.00)	0.17	(0.00)	0.65	(0.00)	1.42	(0.02)
Netherlands	-0.43	(0.02)	-0.46	(0.03)	-0.41	(0.02)	-0.04	(0.03)	-1.52	(0.02)	-0.63	(0.00)	-0.12	(0.00)	0.54	(0.01)
New Zealand	-0.39	(0.02)	-0.42	(0.02)	-0.35	(0.03)	**-0.06**	(0.03)	-1.62	(0.02)	-0.58	(0.00)	-0.06	(0.00)	0.72	(0.01)
Norway	0.08	(0.03)	0.07	(0.03)	0.08	(0.03)	-0.01	(0.03)	-1.11	(0.02)	-0.13	(0.00)	0.37	(0.00)	1.18	(0.02)
Poland	0.41	(0.02)	0.34	(0.02)	0.48	(0.03)	**-0.14**	(0.03)	-0.65	(0.02)	0.19	(0.00)	0.65	(0.00)	1.45	(0.02)
Portugal	0.41	(0.02)	0.31	(0.02)	0.50	(0.02)	**-0.19**	(0.02)	-0.60	(0.02)	0.22	(0.00)	0.66	(0.00)	1.36	(0.01)
Slovak Republic	0.01	(0.03)	-0.04	(0.03)	0.07	(0.04)	**-0.11**	(0.04)	-1.27	(0.03)	-0.19	(0.00)	0.36	(0.00)	1.15	(0.02)
Slovenia	-0.15	(0.01)	-0.21	(0.02)	-0.09	(0.02)	**-0.11**	(0.03)	-1.33	(0.02)	-0.34	(0.01)	0.16	(0.00)	0.91	(0.02)
Spain	0.48	(0.02)	0.39	(0.02)	0.57	(0.02)	**-0.17**	(0.02)	-0.61	(0.01)	0.28	(0.00)	0.75	(0.00)	1.49	(0.02)
Sweden	-0.47	(0.03)	-0.46	(0.03)	-0.48	(0.03)	0.03	(0.03)	-1.80	(0.02)	-0.67	(0.01)	-0.09	(0.00)	0.68	(0.01)
Switzerland	-0.46	(0.02)	-0.50	(0.03)	-0.41	(0.02)	**-0.09**	(0.04)	-1.73	(0.02)	-0.65	(0.01)	-0.10	(0.00)	0.65	(0.01)
Turkey	1.00	(0.02)	0.89	(0.02)	1.13	(0.03)	**-0.24**	(0.03)	-0.11	(0.02)	0.73	(0.00)	1.23	(0.00)	2.16	(0.02)
United Kingdom	0.18	(0.02)	0.15	(0.02)	0.20	(0.03)	**-0.06**	(0.03)	-0.88	(0.02)	-0.02	(0.00)	0.42	(0.00)	1.18	(0.02)
United States	0.27	(0.02)	0.24	(0.03)	0.30	(0.02)	**-0.06**	(0.03)	-0.82	(0.02)	0.06	(0.00)	0.53	(0.00)	1.31	(0.02)
OECD average	0.00	(0.00)	-0.04	(0.00)	0.05	(0.00)	**-0.09**	(0.01)	-1.19	(0.00)	-0.20	(0.00)	0.31	(0.00)	1.09	(0.00)
Partners																
Albania	1.21	(0.02)	1.11	(0.03)	1.31	(0.03)	**-0.20**	(0.03)	0.24	(0.02)	0.95	(0.01)	1.38	(0.01)	2.29	(0.02)
Argentina	0.22	(0.02)	0.22	(0.03)	0.23	(0.03)	-0.01	(0.03)	-0.88	(0.02)	0.00	(0.00)	0.50	(0.00)	1.27	(0.02)
Azerbaijan	1.02	(0.03)	0.98	(0.03)	1.06	(0.03)	-0.09	(0.04)	-0.02	(0.03)	0.72	(0.00)	1.21	(0.01)	2.15	(0.03)
Brazil	0.53	(0.01)	0.48	(0.02)	0.57	(0.02)	**-0.09**	(0.02)	-0.65	(0.02)	0.27	(0.00)	0.78	(0.00)	1.72	(0.02)
Bulgaria	0.42	(0.02)	0.31	(0.04)	0.53	(0.02)	**-0.22**	(0.05)	-0.76	(0.03)	0.19	(0.00)	0.71	(0.01)	1.54	(0.02)
Colombia	0.61	(0.02)	0.57	(0.02)	0.65	(0.03)	**-0.08**	(0.03)	-0.45	(0.02)	0.36	(0.00)	0.85	(0.00)	1.68	(0.02)
Croatia	-0.47	(0.02)	-0.54	(0.02)	-0.39	(0.02)	**-0.14**	(0.02)	-1.67	(0.02)	-0.67	(0.00)	-0.14	(0.00)	0.59	(0.01)
Dubai (UAE)	0.41	(0.01)	0.35	(0.02)	0.46	(0.02)	**-0.11**	(0.03)	-0.84	(0.02)	0.17	(0.00)	0.72	(0.00)	1.58	(0.02)
Hong Kong-China	0.39	(0.03)	0.29	(0.03)	0.51	(0.04)	**-0.22**	(0.04)	-0.82	(0.02)	0.15	(0.00)	0.64	(0.00)	1.60	(0.03)
Indonesia	0.68	(0.03)	0.68	(0.04)	0.68	(0.02)	0.00	(0.04)	-0.27	(0.02)	0.41	(0.00)	0.85	(0.00)	1.73	(0.04)
Jordan	0.77	(0.02)	0.76	(0.04)	0.79	(0.03)	-0.03	(0.04)	-0.35	(0.02)	0.54	(0.00)	0.99	(0.00)	1.91	(0.02)
Kazakhstan	1.18	(0.02)	1.04	(0.02)	1.31	(0.03)	**-0.26**	(0.03)	0.13	(0.02)	0.85	(0.00)	1.36	(0.00)	2.37	(0.02)
Kyrgyzstan	1.03	(0.03)	0.90	(0.04)	1.15	(0.03)	**-0.25**	(0.04)	-0.15	(0.04)	0.75	(0.01)	1.26	(0.00)	2.26	(0.03)
Latvia	0.37	(0.02)	0.37	(0.03)	0.36	(0.03)	0.01	(0.04)	-0.64	(0.02)	0.15	(0.00)	0.59	(0.00)	1.37	(0.02)
Liechtenstein	-0.52	(0.05)	-0.56	(0.06)	-0.47	(0.07)	-0.09	(0.09)	-1.87	(0.05)	-0.71	(0.02)	-0.15	(0.02)	0.64	(0.06)
Lithuania	0.46	(0.02)	0.36	(0.02)	0.57	(0.02)	**-0.21**	(0.02)	-0.47	(0.02)	0.26	(0.00)	0.68	(0.00)	1.37	(0.02)
Macao-China	0.80	(0.01)	0.62	(0.02)	0.98	(0.02)	**-0.36**	(0.02)	-0.53	(0.02)	0.46	(0.00)	1.05	(0.00)	2.20	(0.02)
Montenegro	0.74	(0.02)	0.63	(0.02)	0.85	(0.02)	**-0.22**	(0.03)	-0.34	(0.02)	0.49	(0.00)	0.95	(0.00)	1.87	(0.02)
Panama	0.56	(0.03)	0.60	(0.04)	0.52	(0.04)	0.07	(0.04)	-0.54	(0.02)	0.30	(0.01)	0.79	(0.01)	1.69	(0.03)
Peru	0.96	(0.02)	0.88	(0.02)	1.03	(0.02)	**-0.14**	(0.03)	-0.03	(0.02)	0.68	(0.00)	1.15	(0.00)	2.02	(0.02)
Qatar	0.61	(0.01)	0.62	(0.02)	0.60	(0.01)	0.02	(0.02)	-0.53	(0.01)	0.38	(0.00)	0.83	(0.00)	1.75	(0.02)
Romania	0.76	(0.04)	0.61	(0.04)	0.89	(0.05)	**-0.28**	(0.04)	-0.44	(0.03)	0.46	(0.00)	0.98	(0.00)	2.02	(0.05)
Russian Federation	0.91	(0.02)	0.77	(0.03)	1.05	(0.02)	**-0.28**	(0.03)	-0.19	(0.02)	0.61	(0.00)	1.15	(0.00)	2.08	(0.02)
Serbia	0.45	(0.02)	0.38	(0.03)	0.51	(0.02)	**-0.13**	(0.03)	-0.71	(0.02)	0.19	(0.00)	0.71	(0.00)	1.60	(0.02)
Shanghai-China	0.70	(0.02)	0.62	(0.02)	0.79	(0.02)	**-0.17**	(0.03)	-0.45	(0.02)	0.43	(0.00)	0.93	(0.00)	1.89	(0.02)
Singapore	-0.29	(0.01)	-0.35	(0.02)	-0.22	(0.02)	**-0.13**	(0.03)	-1.65	(0.02)	-0.52	(0.01)	0.08	(0.00)	0.93	(0.02)
Chinese Taipei	0.45	(0.03)	0.32	(0.03)	0.59	(0.04)	**-0.27**	(0.05)	-1.00	(0.02)	0.21	(0.00)	0.77	(0.00)	1.83	(0.03)
Thailand	0.86	(0.02)	0.76	(0.02)	0.94	(0.02)	**-0.18**	(0.02)	-0.06	(0.02)	0.61	(0.00)	1.04	(0.00)	1.85	(0.02)
Trinidad and Tobago	0.34	(0.02)	0.23	(0.02)	0.43	(0.03)	**-0.19**	(0.04)	-0.95	(0.02)	0.09	(0.01)	0.65	(0.01)	1.55	(0.02)
Tunisia	0.68	(0.02)	0.55	(0.03)	0.81	(0.02)	**-0.26**	(0.03)	-0.39	(0.02)	0.44	(0.00)	0.92	(0.00)	1.74	(0.02)
Uruguay	0.45	(0.02)	0.34	(0.02)	0.54	(0.02)	**-0.21**	(0.03)	-0.73	(0.02)	0.24	(0.00)	0.73	(0.00)	1.54	(0.02)

Note: Values that are statistically significant are indicated in bold (see Annex A3).
StatLink http://dx.doi.org/10.1787/888932343285

[Part 2/2]

Index of reading activities for traditional literature courses and reading performance, by national quarters of this index

Table III.2.5 *Results based on students' self-reports*

| | Performance on the reading scale, by national quarters of this index | | | | | | | | Change in the reading score per unit of this index | | Increased likelihood of students in the bottom quarter of this index scoring in the bottom quarter of the national reading performance distribution | | Explained variance in student performance (r-squared x 100) | |
| | Bottom quarter | | Second quarter | | Third quarter | | Top quarter | | | | | | | |
	Mean score	S.E.	Mean score	S.E.	Mean score	S.E.	Mean score	S.E.	Effect	S.E.	Ratio	S.E.	%	S.E.
Australia	520	(2.8)	524	(3.0)	521	(2.8)	513	(3.4)	-2.7	(1.41)	0.9	(0.04)	0.1	(0.07)
Austria	456	(4.3)	477	(3.7)	486	(3.8)	473	(4.7)	6.2	(2.07)	1.2	(0.09)	0.4	(0.29)
Belgium	492	(3.7)	512	(2.9)	521	(3.5)	514	(3.7)	11.3	(1.87)	1.4	(0.09)	1.1	(0.37)
Canada	536	(2.1)	530	(2.4)	528	(2.3)	513	(2.2)	-8.4	(1.11)	0.8	(0.04)	0.9	(0.23)
Chile	467	(3.6)	462	(3.7)	444	(4.1)	430	(4.0)	-17.9	(1.66)	0.6	(0.06)	3.4	(0.57)
Czech Republic	469	(3.8)	487	(4.1)	489	(4.3)	478	(5.0)	4.4	(2.20)	1.2	(0.11)	0.2	(0.21)
Denmark	496	(2.9)	503	(3.3)	500	(3.6)	488	(3.6)	-3.2	(1.84)	1.0	(0.06)	0.1	(0.12)
Estonia	507	(3.8)	503	(3.8)	506	(3.7)	498	(4.3)	-1.8	(1.79)	1.1	(0.07)	0.0	(0.09)
Finland	536	(3.8)	539	(3.4)	538	(3.3)	534	(3.8)	-3.7	(1.72)	1.0	(0.07)	0.1	(0.14)
France	488	(4.4)	512	(3.7)	508	(5.3)	502	(5.5)	7.7	(2.98)	1.2	(0.09)	0.4	(0.34)
Germany	510	(3.5)	512	(4.2)	498	(3.5)	475	(4.3)	-15.2	(2.09)	0.8	(0.07)	2.2	(0.58)
Greece	481	(6.0)	489	(4.6)	491	(4.6)	475	(5.1)	0.1	(2.37)	1.1	(0.09)	0.0	(0.05)
Hungary	490	(4.5)	497	(4.5)	497	(3.7)	498	(5.5)	2.8	(2.55)	1.1	(0.09)	0.1	(0.12)
Iceland	500	(3.7)	519	(3.1)	517	(3.1)	484	(3.9)	-7.2	(1.79)	1.1	(0.08)	0.6	(0.32)
Ireland	518	(4.2)	511	(3.5)	499	(4.8)	481	(4.4)	-13.6	(1.92)	0.7	(0.07)	2.1	(0.57)
Israel	514	(4.0)	498	(4.4)	470	(4.8)	429	(5.9)	-27.8	(1.84)	0.5	(0.05)	7.7	(0.94)
Italy	480	(2.1)	492	(2.0)	494	(2.3)	498	(2.4)	9.2	(1.35)	1.2	(0.05)	0.7	(0.21)
Japan	514	(5.1)	531	(3.6)	529	(3.9)	514	(4.9)	1.1	(2.04)	1.1	(0.08)	0.0	(0.09)
Korea	511	(4.1)	541	(4.6)	551	(3.7)	561	(4.0)	18.4	(1.35)	1.9	(0.15)	6.6	(0.94)
Luxembourg	472	(2.9)	482	(2.9)	479	(3.0)	465	(3.1)	-2.6	(1.52)	1.0	(0.07)	0.1	(0.07)
Mexico	448	(2.3)	434	(2.5)	421	(2.4)	411	(2.9)	-16.3	(1.17)	0.6	(0.03)	2.7	(0.36)
Netherlands	508	(5.9)	518	(5.8)	519	(5.1)	497	(7.3)	-3.7	(2.53)	1.0	(0.09)	0.1	(0.18)
New Zealand	536	(3.6)	536	(3.8)	523	(4.4)	503	(4.2)	-12.4	(2.20)	0.8	(0.06)	1.3	(0.46)
Norway	499	(3.6)	510	(3.3)	509	(3.5)	503	(4.1)	1.9	(1.89)	1.1	(0.08)	0.0	(0.08)
Poland	502	(3.8)	510	(3.5)	502	(3.3)	492	(4.1)	-2.8	(1.99)	1.0	(0.08)	0.1	(0.11)
Portugal	479	(3.8)	495	(3.8)	496	(4.0)	491	(4.4)	5.8	(1.77)	1.3	(0.10)	0.3	(0.19)
Slovak Republic	485	(4.5)	491	(3.4)	482	(3.9)	461	(3.7)	-7.7	(2.13)	0.9	(0.09)	0.7	(0.40)
Slovenia	470	(2.5)	488	(2.8)	492	(3.7)	491	(3.0)	9.2	(1.57)	1.3	(0.07)	0.9	(0.30)
Spain	467	(2.9)	486	(2.6)	491	(2.5)	493	(2.8)	12.0	(1.39)	1.5	(0.08)	1.5	(0.35)
Sweden	510	(4.2)	508	(3.7)	501	(3.7)	486	(4.9)	-9.2	(1.89)	0.9	(0.06)	0.9	(0.38)
Switzerland	506	(3.0)	504	(3.6)	505	(3.7)	490	(4.5)	-5.4	(1.71)	0.8	(0.06)	0.3	(0.19)
Turkey	466	(5.2)	471	(4.4)	473	(4.2)	464	(4.2)	-0.4	(1.70)	1.1	(0.08)	0.0	(0.03)
United Kingdom	500	(3.7)	510	(3.1)	498	(3.8)	481	(3.2)	-8.5	(1.89)	0.9	(0.06)	0.6	(0.27)
United States	503	(4.2)	505	(4.3)	503	(4.2)	493	(6.9)	-3.8	(2.66)	0.8	(0.08)	0.1	(0.19)
OECD average	**495**	(0.7)	503	(0.6)	500	(0.7)	**488**	(0.7)	-2.5	(0.33)	1.0	(0.01)	1.1	(0.06)
Albania	394	(5.7)	404	(5.8)	406	(4.4)	403	(4.7)	3.8	(2.27)	1.2	(0.11)	0.1	(0.16)
Argentina	429	(5.8)	426	(6.9)	407	(5.5)	383	(5.4)	-21.7	(2.27)	0.7	(0.07)	3.5	(0.75)
Azerbaijan	375	(4.0)	376	(4.5)	379	(4.8)	380	(4.6)	3.0	(2.22)	1.0	(0.11)	0.1	(0.26)
Brazil	430	(3.4)	423	(3.1)	423	(3.6)	408	(3.8)	-7.0	(1.25)	0.8	(0.05)	0.5	(0.19)
Bulgaria	458	(7.2)	455	(6.8)	444	(8.6)	412	(8.6)	-14.0	(3.37)	0.7	(0.07)	1.5	(0.69)
Colombia	425	(4.0)	426	(4.9)	415	(4.8)	398	(5.1)	-12.7	(1.95)	0.8	(0.08)	1.7	(0.50)
Croatia	470	(3.6)	485	(3.5)	493	(3.4)	466	(3.9)	0.8	(1.54)	1.1	(0.08)	0.0	(0.03)
Dubai (UAE)	499	(3.2)	479	(3.4)	456	(3.4)	443	(3.5)	-20.6	(1.77)	0.6	(0.05)	3.9	(0.65)
Hong Kong-China	513	(3.5)	534	(3.0)	542	(3.0)	551	(3.4)	16.7	(1.67)	1.6	(0.11)	4.2	(0.83)
Indonesia	415	(5.3)	407	(4.6)	404	(4.5)	395	(5.5)	-11.7	(2.43)	0.8	(0.07)	2.1	(0.83)
Jordan	405	(4.3)	411	(4.0)	410	(3.8)	411	(4.2)	2.8	(1.82)	1.2	(0.08)	0.1	(0.12)
Kazakhstan	389	(4.6)	383	(4.1)	395	(4.0)	404	(3.9)	7.6	(1.88)	1.1	(0.08)	0.6	(0.28)
Kyrgyzstan	304	(4.5)	322	(5.4)	332	(5.0)	330	(6.4)	8.4	(3.00)	1.3	(0.11)	0.7	(0.47)
Latvia	504	(4.1)	491	(3.1)	482	(3.8)	467	(4.8)	-15.3	(2.23)	0.6	(0.08)	2.5	(0.76)
Liechtenstein	501	(8.3)	501	(9.0)	509	(9.0)	491	(9.9)	-4.3	(4.96)	0.9	(0.25)	0.3	(0.67)
Lithuania	470	(3.9)	471	(3.5)	476	(3.9)	464	(3.9)	-2.3	(2.44)	1.1	(0.08)	0.0	(0.09)
Macao-China	457	(2.0)	474	(1.9)	496	(2.2)	520	(2.2)	20.6	(0.92)	1.8	(0.10)	9.2	(0.76)
Montenegro	414	(3.2)	416	(2.6)	417	(2.7)	401	(3.0)	-3.6	(1.59)	1.0	(0.06)	0.1	(0.12)
Panama	396	(7.4)	391	(10.4)	377	(8.1)	367	(5.5)	-12.3	(2.87)	0.7	(0.10)	1.4	(0.65)
Peru	385	(6.2)	373	(5.0)	370	(4.9)	368	(4.8)	-8.4	(2.52)	1.0	(0.08)	0.5	(0.30)
Qatar	407	(2.4)	374	(2.3)	365	(2.4)	366	(2.3)	-14.1	(1.38)	0.6	(0.04)	1.4	(0.27)
Romania	430	(6.0)	430	(4.8)	426	(4.7)	422	(5.1)	-2.0	(2.53)	1.0	(0.10)	0.1	(0.16)
Russian Federation	461	(5.0)	461	(3.8)	470	(4.6)	469	(4.0)	3.8	(1.78)	1.1	(0.08)	0.2	(0.16)
Serbia	442	(3.6)	455	(2.7)	451	(3.5)	437	(3.5)	-1.7	(1.70)	1.0	(0.08)	0.0	(0.08)
Shanghai-China	528	(3.4)	553	(3.2)	566	(3.2)	580	(2.9)	21.1	(1.38)	1.8	(0.11)	6.8	(0.86)
Singapore	540	(2.5)	534	(2.7)	526	(3.0)	509	(2.8)	-10.1	(1.33)	0.7	(0.05)	1.2	(0.31)
Chinese Taipei	454	(3.4)	488	(3.2)	505	(2.9)	541	(3.9)	28.1	(1.64)	2.2	(0.13)	14.5	(1.39)
Thailand	410	(3.3)	421	(3.7)	429	(3.6)	428	(3.5)	7.6	(1.54)	1.4	(0.11)	0.7	(0.28)
Trinidad and Tobago	450	(4.0)	435	(5.1)	427	(4.5)	421	(4.3)	-10.0	(1.95)	0.7	(0.07)	0.9	(0.35)
Tunisia	403	(4.4)	403	(3.9)	405	(4.2)	416	(4.3)	4.5	(2.05)	1.1	(0.09)	0.2	(0.21)
Uruguay	426	(4.7)	443	(4.2)	440	(3.5)	424	(4.2)	1.6	(2.35)	1.1	(0.08)	0.0	(0.07)

Note: Values that are statistically significant are indicated in bold (see Annex A3).
StatLink ⟐⟐⟐ http://dx.doi.org/10.1787/888932343285

[Part 1/2]

Index of use of functional texts and reading performance, by national quarters of this index

Table III.2.6 *Results based on students' self-reports*

	All students Mean index	S.E.	Boys Mean index	S.E.	Girls Mean index	S.E.	Gender difference (B – G) Dif.	S.E.	Bottom quarter Mean index	S.E.	Second quarter Mean index	S.E.	Third quarter Mean index	S.E.	Top quarter Mean index	S.E.
Australia	0.14	(0.01)	0.18	(0.02)	0.11	(0.02)	**0.07**	(0.02)	**-1.02**	(0.01)	-0.06	(0.00)	0.42	(0.00)	**1.23**	(0.01)
Austria	0.01	(0.02)	0.01	(0.03)	0.02	(0.02)	-0.02	(0.04)	**-1.20**	(0.01)	-0.21	(0.00)	0.31	(0.00)	**1.15**	(0.02)
Belgium	0.03	(0.02)	0.03	(0.02)	0.03	(0.02)	0.00	(0.02)	**-1.19**	(0.01)	-0.21	(0.00)	0.32	(0.00)	**1.21**	(0.02)
Canada	0.19	(0.01)	0.21	(0.02)	0.16	(0.01)	**0.05**	(0.02)	**-0.98**	(0.01)	-0.05	(0.00)	0.46	(0.00)	**1.31**	(0.01)
Chile	0.36	(0.02)	0.32	(0.02)	0.40	(0.03)	**-0.08**	(0.03)	**-0.81**	(0.02)	0.12	(0.00)	0.65	(0.00)	**1.50**	(0.02)
Czech Republic	-0.17	(0.02)	-0.09	(0.03)	-0.25	(0.03)	**0.16**	(0.04)	**-1.53**	(0.01)	-0.53	(0.01)	0.16	(0.01)	**1.22**	(0.02)
Denmark	0.27	(0.01)	0.23	(0.02)	0.30	(0.02)	**-0.06**	(0.03)	**-0.84**	(0.02)	0.06	(0.01)	0.53	(0.00)	**1.32**	(0.02)
Estonia	0.06	(0.02)	0.07	(0.03)	0.04	(0.03)	0.03	(0.04)	**-1.29**	(0.02)	-0.20	(0.01)	0.39	(0.01)	**1.32**	(0.02)
Finland	-0.21	(0.02)	-0.16	(0.03)	-0.26	(0.02)	**0.09**	(0.03)	**-1.49**	(0.01)	-0.48	(0.01)	0.12	(0.00)	**1.01**	(0.02)
France	0.09	(0.02)	0.12	(0.02)	0.07	(0.02)	0.06	(0.02)	**-1.26**	(0.01)	-0.22	(0.01)	0.42	(0.01)	**1.42**	(0.02)
Germany	-0.07	(0.02)	-0.08	(0.02)	-0.06	(0.02)	-0.01	(0.03)	**-1.23**	(0.01)	-0.24	(0.00)	0.22	(0.00)	**0.96**	(0.02)
Greece	0.21	(0.02)	0.29	(0.03)	0.13	(0.03)	**0.15**	(0.03)	**-1.11**	(0.02)	-0.06	(0.01)	0.52	(0.00)	**1.48**	(0.02)
Hungary	-0.17	(0.02)	-0.08	(0.03)	-0.26	(0.03)	**0.18**	(0.04)	**-1.51**	(0.01)	-0.47	(0.01)	0.19	(0.01)	**1.09**	(0.02)
Iceland	-0.40	(0.01)	-0.39	(0.02)	-0.40	(0.02)	0.01	(0.03)	**-1.69**	(0.00)	-0.75	(0.01)	-0.06	(0.01)	**0.90**	(0.02)
Ireland	0.03	(0.02)	0.06	(0.03)	0.01	(0.03)	0.05	(0.04)	**-1.17**	(0.01)	-0.19	(0.01)	0.35	(0.00)	**1.14**	(0.02)
Israel	-0.08	(0.02)	-0.06	(0.03)	-0.10	(0.03)	0.04	(0.04)	**-1.38**	(0.01)	-0.35	(0.01)	0.25	(0.00)	**1.14**	(0.02)
Italy	-0.28	(0.01)	-0.21	(0.02)	-0.35	(0.01)	**0.15**	(0.02)	**-1.47**	(0.00)	-0.51	(0.00)	0.05	(0.00)	**0.83**	(0.01)
Japan	-0.35	(0.02)	-0.27	(0.03)	-0.43	(0.03)	**0.16**	(0.03)	**-1.69**	(0.00)	-0.84	(0.01)	0.05	(0.00)	**1.08**	(0.01)
Korea	-0.22	(0.02)	-0.24	(0.03)	-0.20	(0.03)	-0.04	(0.04)	**-1.47**	(0.01)	-0.43	(0.01)	0.11	(0.00)	**0.92**	(0.02)
Luxembourg	-0.19	(0.01)	-0.16	(0.02)	-0.21	(0.02)	0.04	(0.03)	**-1.35**	(0.01)	-0.44	(0.00)	0.11	(0.00)	**0.94**	(0.02)
Mexico	0.62	(0.01)	0.60	(0.01)	0.65	(0.01)	**-0.05**	(0.01)	**-0.36**	(0.01)	0.38	(0.00)	0.82	(0.00)	**1.65**	(0.02)
Netherlands	0.05	(0.02)	0.02	(0.02)	0.07	(0.03)	-0.05	(0.03)	**-1.11**	(0.02)	-0.18	(0.00)	0.34	(0.00)	**1.15**	(0.02)
New Zealand	0.02	(0.02)	0.03	(0.02)	0.02	(0.02)	0.00	(0.03)	**-1.21**	(0.01)	-0.20	(0.00)	0.33	(0.00)	**1.17**	(0.02)
Norway	-0.36	(0.03)	-0.31	(0.03)	-0.41	(0.03)	**0.10**	(0.03)	**-1.67**	(0.00)	-0.62	(0.01)	-0.02	(0.01)	**0.87**	(0.02)
Poland	0.22	(0.02)	0.30	(0.02)	0.13	(0.03)	**0.17**	(0.03)	**-1.22**	(0.01)	-0.08	(0.01)	0.56	(0.01)	**1.60**	(0.02)
Portugal	0.07	(0.02)	0.11	(0.02)	0.04	(0.02)	**0.07**	(0.03)	**-1.19**	(0.01)	-0.15	(0.00)	0.39	(0.00)	**1.24**	(0.01)
Slovak Republic	0.00	(0.02)	0.06	(0.03)	-0.07	(0.03)	**0.14**	(0.04)	**-1.45**	(0.01)	-0.38	(0.01)	0.34	(0.01)	**1.47**	(0.02)
Slovenia	-0.09	(0.02)	-0.02	(0.02)	-0.16	(0.02)	**0.13**	(0.02)	**-1.38**	(0.01)	-0.37	(0.01)	0.21	(0.01)	**1.18**	(0.02)
Spain	0.06	(0.01)	0.08	(0.02)	0.03	(0.02)	**0.06**	(0.02)	**-1.16**	(0.01)	-0.18	(0.00)	0.36	(0.00)	**1.21**	(0.02)
Sweden	-0.19	(0.02)	-0.20	(0.02)	-0.19	(0.02)	0.00	(0.03)	**-1.44**	(0.01)	-0.43	(0.01)	0.13	(0.01)	**0.97**	(0.01)
Switzerland	-0.07	(0.02)	-0.06	(0.02)	-0.08	(0.03)	0.02	(0.03)	**-1.28**	(0.01)	-0.27	(0.00)	0.23	(0.00)	**1.04**	(0.01)
Turkey	0.40	(0.02)	0.42	(0.03)	0.38	(0.03)	0.05	(0.04)	**-0.97**	(0.02)	0.17	(0.00)	0.72	(0.00)	**1.69**	(0.02)
United Kingdom	-0.02	(0.02)	-0.04	(0.03)	-0.01	(0.02)	-0.03	(0.03)	**-1.29**	(0.01)	-0.23	(0.00)	0.30	(0.00)	**1.12**	(0.02)
United States	0.11	(0.02)	0.09	(0.03)	0.13	(0.03)	-0.03	(0.04)	**-1.11**	(0.02)	-0.13	(0.00)	0.41	(0.00)	**1.27**	(0.02)
OECD average	0.00	(0.00)	0.03	(0.00)	-0.02	(0.00)	**0.05**	(0.01)	**-1.25**	(0.00)	-0.26	(0.00)	0.32	(0.00)	**1.20**	(0.00)
Albania	0.25	(0.02)	0.33	(0.03)	0.17	(0.03)	**0.16**	(0.03)	**-0.89**	(0.02)	0.03	(0.01)	0.52	(0.01)	**1.33**	(0.02)
Argentina	0.35	(0.02)	0.34	(0.03)	0.37	(0.03)	-0.03	(0.03)	**-0.78**	(0.02)	0.11	(0.00)	0.61	(0.00)	**1.47**	(0.02)
Azerbaijan	0.59	(0.02)	0.59	(0.03)	0.60	(0.03)	0.00	(0.04)	**-0.55**	(0.03)	0.32	(0.01)	0.78	(0.01)	**1.82**	(0.02)
Brazil	0.29	(0.02)	0.31	(0.02)	0.27	(0.02)	0.04	(0.02)	**-0.99**	(0.02)	0.05	(0.00)	0.59	(0.00)	**1.52**	(0.01)
Bulgaria	0.61	(0.02)	0.60	(0.03)	0.63	(0.03)	-0.03	(0.04)	**-0.69**	(0.02)	0.29	(0.00)	0.85	(0.00)	**1.99**	(0.03)
Colombia	0.40	(0.02)	0.38	(0.02)	0.42	(0.03)	-0.04	(0.03)	**-0.70**	(0.02)	0.15	(0.00)	0.65	(0.01)	**1.50**	(0.02)
Croatia	-0.11	(0.02)	-0.05	(0.02)	-0.16	(0.03)	**0.11**	(0.04)	**-1.49**	(0.01)	-0.44	(0.01)	0.26	(0.00)	**1.25**	(0.02)
Dubai (UAE)	0.30	(0.02)	0.32	(0.02)	0.28	(0.02)	0.04	(0.03)	**-0.97**	(0.02)	0.05	(0.00)	0.60	(0.00)	**1.51**	(0.02)
Hong Kong-China	0.12	(0.02)	0.12	(0.02)	0.12	(0.02)	0.01	(0.04)	**-0.97**	(0.02)	-0.11	(0.00)	0.38	(0.00)	**1.19**	(0.02)
Indonesia	0.66	(0.02)	0.63	(0.03)	0.69	(0.03)	-0.06	(0.04)	**-0.36**	(0.02)	0.38	(0.01)	0.85	(0.01)	**1.76**	(0.02)
Jordan	0.34	(0.02)	0.33	(0.03)	0.36	(0.02)	-0.03	(0.04)	**-0.88**	(0.02)	0.09	(0.01)	0.61	(0.00)	**1.55**	(0.02)
Kazakhstan	0.79	(0.02)	0.78	(0.02)	0.79	(0.02)	-0.01	(0.03)	**-0.21**	(0.02)	0.51	(0.00)	0.97	(0.00)	**1.86**	(0.02)
Kyrgyzstan	0.46	(0.03)	0.43	(0.04)	0.50	(0.03)	**-0.07**	(0.03)	**-0.67**	(0.02)	0.22	(0.00)	0.71	(0.00)	**1.61**	(0.03)
Latvia	0.14	(0.02)	0.22	(0.03)	0.07	(0.03)	**0.15**	(0.03)	**-1.07**	(0.02)	-0.11	(0.00)	0.45	(0.01)	**1.30**	(0.02)
Liechtenstein	-0.30	(0.05)	-0.27	(0.07)	-0.34	(0.07)	0.07	(0.10)	**-1.53**	(0.03)	-0.58	(0.02)	0.07	(0.02)	**0.82**	(0.06)
Lithuania	0.08	(0.02)	0.16	(0.03)	0.01	(0.03)	**0.15**	(0.03)	**-1.21**	(0.01)	-0.21	(0.01)	0.38	(0.01)	**1.37**	(0.02)
Macao-China	0.21	(0.01)	0.14	(0.01)	0.28	(0.02)	**-0.14**	(0.02)	**-0.96**	(0.01)	0.01	(0.00)	0.51	(0.00)	**1.28**	(0.01)
Montenegro	0.04	(0.02)	0.11	(0.03)	-0.03	(0.02)	**0.14**	(0.04)	**-1.46**	(0.01)	-0.31	(0.01)	0.44	(0.01)	**1.50**	(0.02)
Panama	0.32	(0.03)	0.36	(0.04)	0.27	(0.03)	**0.09**	(0.04)	**-0.82**	(0.03)	0.06	(0.01)	0.59	(0.00)	**1.44**	(0.03)
Peru	0.49	(0.02)	0.47	(0.02)	0.51	(0.02)	-0.04	(0.03)	**-0.57**	(0.02)	0.24	(0.00)	0.70	(0.00)	**1.60**	(0.02)
Qatar	0.35	(0.01)	0.42	(0.02)	0.28	(0.01)	**0.14**	(0.02)	**-0.92**	(0.01)	0.12	(0.00)	0.64	(0.00)	**1.55**	(0.01)
Romania	0.23	(0.04)	0.23	(0.04)	0.24	(0.05)	-0.01	(0.04)	**-1.13**	(0.02)	-0.07	(0.01)	0.56	(0.01)	**1.57**	(0.02)
Russian Federation	0.73	(0.02)	0.70	(0.02)	0.76	(0.03)	-0.05	(0.03)	**-0.41**	(0.02)	0.46	(0.00)	0.97	(0.00)	**1.89**	(0.02)
Serbia	-0.20	(0.02)	-0.12	(0.03)	-0.27	(0.03)	**0.15**	(0.05)	**-1.69**	(0.00)	-0.76	(0.01)	0.21	(0.01)	**1.44**	(0.02)
Shanghai-China	0.16	(0.01)	0.18	(0.02)	0.14	(0.02)	0.04	(0.03)	**-1.07**	(0.01)	-0.05	(0.00)	0.48	(0.00)	**1.29**	(0.02)
Singapore	0.47	(0.01)	0.48	(0.02)	0.45	(0.02)	0.03	(0.02)	**-0.57**	(0.02)	0.22	(0.00)	0.69	(0.00)	**1.52**	(0.01)
Chinese Taipei	0.46	(0.02)	0.46	(0.02)	0.45	(0.02)	0.01	(0.03)	**-0.77**	(0.02)	0.26	(0.00)	0.72	(0.00)	**1.61**	(0.02)
Thailand	0.85	(0.01)	0.81	(0.02)	0.88	(0.02)	**-0.07**	(0.02)	**-0.11**	(0.02)	0.63	(0.00)	1.00	(0.00)	**1.86**	(0.02)
Trinidad and Tobago	0.47	(0.02)	0.46	(0.03)	0.47	(0.03)	-0.02	(0.04)	**-0.83**	(0.02)	0.22	(0.01)	0.73	(0.00)	**1.75**	(0.02)
Tunisia	0.56	(0.02)	0.47	(0.03)	0.64	(0.03)	**-0.18**	(0.03)	**-0.57**	(0.02)	0.30	(0.00)	0.77	(0.00)	**1.73**	(0.02)
Uruguay	0.13	(0.02)	0.17	(0.02)	0.11	(0.03)	0.06	(0.03)	**-1.15**	(0.01)	-0.09	(0.00)	0.45	(0.00)	**1.33**	(0.02)

Note: Values that are statistically significant are indicated in bold (see Annex A3).
StatLink ᵃₛₗ http://dx.doi.org/10.1787/888932343285

[Part 2/2]

Index of use of functional texts and reading performance, by national quarters of this index

Table III.2.6   *Results based on students' self-reports*

| | Performance on the reading scale, by national quarters of this index | | | | | | | | Change in the reading score per unit of this index | | Increased likelihood of students in the bottom quarter of this index scoring in the bottom quarter of the national reading performance distribution | | Explained variance in student performance (r-squared x 100) | |
| | Bottom quarter | | Second quarter | | Third quarter | | Top quarter | | | | | | | |
	Mean score	S.E.	Mean score	S.E.	Mean score	S.E.	Mean score	S.E.	Effect	S.E.	Ratio	S.E.	%	S.E.
OECD														
Australia	532	(3.9)	527	(2.6)	514	(2.9)	505	(2.7)	-12.6	(1.57)	0.8	(0.05)	1.4	(0.35)
Austria	496	(4.0)	488	(3.9)	469	(4.3)	441	(4.1)	-21.9	(1.85)	0.7	(0.06)	4.3	(0.74)
Belgium	531	(3.1)	531	(3.3)	505	(3.3)	473	(3.7)	-22.9	(1.49)	0.7	(0.06)	4.9	(0.65)
Canada	539	(1.9)	534	(2.3)	526	(2.2)	507	(2.5)	-12.3	(1.04)	0.8	(0.04)	1.6	(0.28)
Chile	464	(4.4)	452	(3.8)	447	(3.7)	445	(4.0)	-8.8	(1.99)	0.6	(0.05)	5.8	(0.84)
Czech Republic	501	(3.5)	500	(3.8)	478	(3.8)	486	(3.7)	-6.9	(1.59)	0.9	(0.06)	0.5	(0.25)
Denmark	504	(3.7)	502	(3.2)	496	(3.1)	486	(3.7)	-14.3	(1.42)	0.6	(0.06)	3.2	(0.63)
Estonia	524	(3.4)	510	(3.8)	497	(3.5)	484	(3.4)	-16.9	(1.50)	0.7	(0.05)	3.7	(0.65)
Finland	552	(3.2)	551	(3.7)	533	(3.5)	511	(3.5)	-17.3	(1.51)	0.7	(0.05)	3.2	(0.52)
France	523	(4.3)	520	(4.4)	492	(4.5)	476	(4.1)	-18.7	(1.80)	0.7	(0.06)	3.0	(0.57)
Germany	513	(3.8)	512	(3.7)	497	(3.5)	473	(4.2)	-16.2	(1.81)	0.7	(0.07)	3.1	(0.69)
Greece	506	(5.1)	492	(5.4)	479	(4.9)	460	(5.3)	-28.2	(1.66)	0.4	(0.05)	10.2	(1.08)
Hungary	534	(3.6)	510	(4.4)	478	(4.5)	462	(4.0)	-19.9	(1.62)	0.8	(0.07)	4.7	(0.75)
Iceland	518	(3.3)	525	(3.4)	505	(3.2)	474	(2.9)	-15.0	(1.94)	0.7	(0.08)	2.5	(0.62)
Ireland	516	(4.0)	515	(4.1)	500	(4.1)	479	(3.8)	-24.9	(1.79)	0.7	(0.06)	5.2	(0.70)
Israel	502	(4.7)	500	(4.3)	471	(5.0)	440	(4.8)	-26.2	(1.15)	0.6	(0.04)	6.5	(0.53)
Italy	514	(1.9)	509	(2.2)	490	(2.6)	451	(2.5)	-13.2	(1.59)	0.8	(0.07)	2.3	(0.56)
Japan	533	(4.5)	537	(4.0)	523	(4.1)	496	(4.2)	0.6	(1.62)	1.1	(0.09)	0.0	(0.03)
Korea	537	(3.9)	549	(4.2)	538	(4.5)	540	(4.0)	-26.2	(1.75)	0.6	(0.06)	5.4	(0.70)
Luxembourg	498	(3.4)	496	(4.3)	471	(3.5)	434	(2.8)	-2.2	(1.09)	1.0	(0.04)	0.0	(0.05)
Mexico	431	(2.8)	428	(2.7)	428	(2.5)	428	(2.6)	-18.3	(1.77)	0.7	(0.06)	3.5	(0.65)
Netherlands	531	(5.6)	518	(6.8)	504	(5.7)	489	(5.2)	-23.9	(1.77)	0.6	(0.05)	5.1	(0.66)
New Zealand	551	(3.4)	542	(3.6)	515	(3.8)	490	(3.9)	-20.1	(1.58)	0.6	(0.05)	4.8	(0.72)
Norway	523	(3.0)	524	(3.8)	502	(3.8)	474	(3.9)	-19.8	(1.31)	0.5	(0.05)	6.1	(0.78)
Poland	535	(3.5)	504	(3.3)	490	(3.9)	477	(3.4)	-16.8	(1.40)	0.6	(0.05)	3.6	(0.58)
Portugal	510	(3.8)	500	(3.9)	483	(3.6)	467	(3.5)	-19.6	(1.55)	0.6	(0.07)	6.4	(0.91)
Slovak Republic	507	(4.1)	497	(3.5)	465	(3.7)	451	(3.8)	-21.2	(1.28)	0.6	(0.04)	5.8	(0.68)
Slovenia	512	(2.8)	498	(3.6)	477	(3.5)	456	(3.0)	-17.7	(1.08)	0.7	(0.05)	3.8	(0.48)
Spain	504	(2.8)	494	(2.3)	480	(2.3)	459	(2.9)	-13.4	(1.68)	0.8	(0.07)	1.8	(0.44)
Sweden	513	(3.6)	511	(3.8)	502	(4.3)	480	(4.2)	-13.7	(2.23)	0.8	(0.06)	1.8	(0.59)
Switzerland	513	(3.5)	515	(3.8)	498	(3.5)	481	(3.9)	-8.7	(1.52)	0.7	(0.07)	1.3	(0.44)
Turkey	483	(4.9)	468	(4.6)	466	(4.9)	458	(3.9)	-14.9	(1.51)	0.7	(0.04)	2.3	(0.46)
United Kingdom	510	(3.2)	511	(2.9)	494	(3.3)	475	(3.6)	-20.1	(1.59)	0.7	(0.06)	4.0	(0.57)
United States	521	(4.7)	516	(4.6)	495	(4.6)	471	(3.7)						
OECD average	514	(0.6)	508	(0.7)	491	(0.7)	472	(0.6)	-16.8	(0.27)	0.7	(0.01)	3.6	(0.11)
Partners														
Albania	415	(5.3)	403	(4.7)	398	(5.9)	394	(5.7)	-9.2	(2.39)	0.8	(0.10)	0.8	(0.43)
Argentina	420	(6.3)	419	(5.8)	411	(5.5)	398	(5.8)	-7.8	(2.66)	0.9	(0.08)	0.5	(0.32)
Azerbaijan	382	(4.3)	375	(4.5)	376	(4.5)	383	(4.8)	0.7	(1.80)	1.0	(0.09)	0.0	(0.07)
Brazil	428	(2.9)	423	(3.3)	425	(4.2)	416	(3.5)	-3.1	(1.37)	0.8	(0.05)	0.1	(0.10)
Bulgaria	463	(8.2)	441	(8.1)	438	(7.6)	432	(6.8)	-12.3	(1.89)	0.9	(0.08)	1.5	(0.43)
Colombia	415	(5.0)	419	(4.6)	420	(4.5)	415	(4.5)	-0.5	(1.64)	1.1	(0.09)	0.0	(0.04)
Croatia	499	(4.2)	488	(3.6)	473	(3.5)	455	(3.5)	-16.5	(1.33)	0.7	(0.06)	4.3	(0.67)
Dubai (UAE)	498	(3.3)	475	(3.4)	461	(3.2)	446	(3.4)	-19.0	(1.72)	0.6	(0.05)	3.3	(0.58)
Hong Kong-China	541	(3.1)	547	(2.9)	535	(2.9)	516	(4.0)	-9.5	(1.74)	0.8	(0.07)	1.0	(0.36)
Indonesia	390	(4.7)	401	(4.8)	411	(4.3)	420	(6.4)	11.7	(2.50)	1.5	(0.12)	2.2	(0.92)
Jordan	414	(4.5)	407	(3.9)	407	(3.8)	411	(4.6)	0.2	(1.92)	1.0	(0.07)	0.0	(0.04)
Kazakhstan	392	(4.6)	387	(4.3)	394	(4.1)	400	(4.6)	1.3	(1.97)	1.1	(0.08)	0.0	(0.06)
Kyrgyzstan	322	(5.4)	318	(5.4)	332	(5.5)	320	(5.5)	-1.0	(2.84)	1.1	(0.08)	0.0	(0.07)
Latvia	508	(3.8)	490	(4.5)	477	(4.0)	470	(4.2)	-16.0	(1.44)	0.6	(0.06)	3.8	(0.66)
Liechtenstein	507	(8.6)	512	(8.9)	492	(8.9)	492	(11.6)	-7.4	(5.53)	0.8	(0.23)	0.7	(1.04)
Lithuania	496	(3.0)	484	(3.4)	458	(3.0)	442	(3.5)	-21.1	(1.37)	0.5	(0.05)	6.3	(0.79)
Macao-China	494	(2.0)	488	(2.4)	482	(2.5)	482	(1.9)	-4.9	(1.02)	0.9	(0.05)	0.3	(0.14)
Montenegro	439	(3.6)	425	(3.2)	398	(2.9)	390	(3.3)	-17.3	(1.33)	0.6	(0.07)	4.9	(0.73)
Panama	409	(9.1)	380	(7.3)	378	(6.7)	370	(7.5)	-14.4	(2.54)	0.7	(0.09)	1.9	(0.65)
Peru	378	(5.2)	375	(5.1)	372	(5.4)	374	(4.6)	-2.5	(2.25)	1.0	(0.08)	0.1	(0.09)
Qatar	407	(2.0)	375	(2.3)	365	(2.6)	367	(2.7)	-16.5	(1.29)	0.6	(0.03)	2.1	(0.31)
Romania	439	(5.9)	427	(4.6)	423	(5.0)	419	(5.6)	-6.7	(2.37)	0.8	(0.09)	0.7	(0.46)
Russian Federation	473	(5.0)	465	(3.9)	468	(3.9)	458	(3.3)	-6.7	(1.55)	1.0	(0.07)	0.5	(0.23)
Serbia	463	(3.1)	459	(3.8)	439	(3.0)	427	(3.0)	-11.8	(1.10)	0.7	(0.06)	3.2	(0.58)
Shanghai-China	575	(3.1)	557	(3.4)	546	(3.5)	549	(3.3)	-11.0	(1.42)	0.7	(0.07)	1.7	(0.44)
Singapore	543	(2.8)	533	(3.0)	521	(3.1)	512	(2.5)	-12.1	(1.48)	0.7	(0.05)	1.2	(0.28)
Chinese Taipei	505	(4.2)	497	(4.2)	492	(3.3)	494	(2.6)	-4.1	(1.59)	1.0	(0.06)	0.2	(0.17)
Thailand	399	(3.1)	421	(3.8)	428	(3.5)	441	(3.0)	17.5	(1.26)	1.8	(0.10)	3.8	(0.54)
Trinidad and Tobago	447	(4.5)	428	(4.4)	433	(3.8)	430	(3.8)	-6.4	(1.90)	0.9	(0.08)	0.4	(0.22)
Tunisia	403	(4.0)	400	(3.7)	409	(4.6)	415	(4.0)	3.7	(1.72)	1.1	(0.11)	0.0	(0.16)
Uruguay	449	(3.7)	440	(4.2)	431	(4.3)	415	(3.8)	-13.3	(1.62)	0.8	(0.08)	1.8	(0.47)

Note: Values that are statistically significant are indicated in bold (see Annex A3).
StatLink ᵇᵐˢ⅃ http://dx.doi.org/10.1787/888932343285

[Part 1/1]

Percentage of students who read diverse materials

Percentage of students who reported that they read the following materials because they want to "several times a month" or "several times a week"

Table III.2.7

		Percentage of students who read diverse materials								
		Magazines		Comic books		Fiction (novels, narratives, stories)		Non-fiction books		Newspapers
		%	S.E.	%	S.E.	%	S.E.	%	S.E.	%	S.E.
OECD	Australia	50.0	(0.6)	9.0	(0.4)	38.3	(0.6)	20.0	(0.4)	53.7	(0.7)
	Austria	66.3	(0.8)	13.7	(0.7)	26.8	(0.8)	17.2	(0.7)	81.9	(0.8)
	Belgium	65.8	(0.7)	31.8	(0.7)	22.5	(0.7)	13.7	(0.6)	50.4	(0.9)
	Canada	48.1	(0.5)	14.4	(0.4)	42.0	(0.6)	20.0	(0.4)	47.9	(0.8)
	Chile	49.6	(0.8)	20.9	(0.6)	30.6	(0.8)	16.4	(0.6)	58.5	(0.9)
	Czech Republic	68.3	(0.8)	15.4	(0.6)	17.5	(0.8)	12.0	(0.6)	66.0	(0.8)
	Denmark	65.5	(0.8)	20.6	(0.7)	30.5	(0.8)	27.1	(0.7)	51.7	(0.9)
	Estonia	72.4	(0.8)	13.4	(0.6)	24.0	(0.8)	31.9	(1.0)	80.1	(0.7)
	Finland	64.9	(0.8)	60.1	(0.9)	26.1	(0.8)	15.5	(0.5)	75.4	(0.8)
	France	62.5	(0.8)	30.4	(0.8)	28.9	(1.0)	12.0	(0.5)	46.7	(1.1)
	Germany	54.9	(0.8)	11.3	(0.5)	32.8	(0.8)	17.2	(0.8)	61.8	(1.0)
	Greece	60.5	(0.9)	24.7	(0.7)	21.5	(0.7)	7.2	(0.4)	42.8	(0.9)
	Hungary	60.7	(1.0)	26.6	(0.8)	31.5	(1.0)	34.9	(0.8)	71.8	(0.9)
	Iceland	58.2	(0.9)	30.9	(0.8)	27.3	(0.7)	17.1	(0.7)	82.0	(0.7)
	Ireland	57.1	(0.9)	7.5	(0.5)	30.3	(1.0)	16.0	(0.7)	67.5	(0.9)
	Israel	38.8	(0.9)	17.5	(0.6)	29.7	(0.7)	26.5	(1.0)	74.7	(0.8)
	Italy	48.8	(0.5)	17.4	(0.3)	35.0	(0.5)	4.9	(0.2)	53.4	(0.5)
	Japan	64.5	(0.8)	72.4	(0.8)	42.0	(1.1)	11.1	(0.4)	57.6	(0.9)
	Korea	21.2	(0.6)	40.5	(1.0)	46.6	(0.8)	30.0	(0.9)	45.1	(1.2)
	Luxembourg	68.7	(0.8)	20.3	(0.7)	28.8	(0.7)	19.3	(0.5)	70.7	(0.6)
	Mexico	46.9	(0.5)	27.1	(0.4)	37.9	(0.4)	18.7	(0.3)	47.8	(0.5)
	Netherlands	57.2	(1.4)	23.1	(0.9)	21.5	(1.0)	12.6	(0.6)	48.5	(1.5)
	New Zealand	53.1	(1.0)	11.6	(0.5)	44.3	(0.8)	25.4	(0.7)	53.1	(0.9)
	Norway	60.6	(0.9)	42.2	(0.9)	26.3	(0.8)	27.2	(0.8)	73.4	(0.8)
	Poland	65.8	(0.7)	11.3	(0.5)	20.1	(0.7)	20.8	(0.8)	79.1	(0.6)
	Portugal	63.8	(0.7)	18.6	(0.5)	28.0	(0.6)	14.2	(0.5)	51.5	(0.7)
	Slovak Republic	79.9	(0.7)	13.3	(0.6)	17.8	(0.7)	19.9	(0.9)	72.4	(0.7)
	Slovenia	72.6	(0.7)	14.8	(0.5)	15.4	(0.7)	16.3	(0.6)	71.7	(0.9)
	Spain	51.3	(0.7)	12.0	(0.4)	30.1	(0.5)	18.3	(0.4)	45.1	(0.7)
	Sweden	58.2	(0.9)	22.5	(0.7)	32.4	(0.9)	9.9	(0.6)	71.6	(0.9)
	Switzerland	66.8	(0.7)	24.1	(0.6)	30.1	(0.7)	15.0	(0.5)	79.5	(0.8)
	Turkey	48.4	(1.0)	22.8	(0.6)	56.0	(0.8)	26.9	(0.7)	86.5	(0.6)
	United Kingdom	59.6	(0.8)	7.8	(0.4)	31.5	(0.7)	19.5	(0.5)	61.2	(0.8)
	United States	46.8	(0.7)	10.4	(0.6)	36.6	(1.1)	20.5	(0.8)	37.0	(1.0)
	OECD average	58.2	(0.1)	22.4	(0.1)	30.6	(0.1)	18.7	(0.1)	62.3	(0.1)
Partners	Albania	44.6	(1.1)	43.7	(1.2)	53.7	(1.1)	22.1	(0.8)	60.2	(1.2)
	Argentina	52.6	(0.9)	29.3	(0.9)	26.9	(0.9)	28.5	(0.9)	49.0	(1.1)
	Azerbaijan	44.2	(1.1)	48.2	(1.1)	52.1	(1.1)	48.6	(1.4)	51.0	(1.1)
	Brazil	48.9	(0.6)	33.5	(0.7)	35.7	(0.6)	15.1	(0.4)	44.3	(0.8)
	Bulgaria	61.8	(1.1)	17.7	(0.8)	34.3	(1.5)	29.6	(1.0)	57.2	(1.1)
	Colombia	54.0	(0.9)	43.2	(0.9)	37.7	(1.1)	33.1	(1.2)	57.8	(1.6)
	Croatia	71.1	(0.8)	18.6	(0.5)	22.1	(0.8)	15.9	(0.7)	88.4	(0.5)
	Dubai (UAE)	67.0	(0.7)	39.3	(0.7)	40.2	(0.8)	26.8	(0.6)	72.8	(0.7)
	Hong Kong-China	48.5	(0.9)	30.4	(0.8)	48.5	(0.8)	35.0	(0.9)	84.1	(0.7)
	Indonesia	55.2	(1.2)	52.3	(0.9)	59.3	(1.0)	36.1	(1.2)	65.4	(1.1)
	Jordan	43.7	(0.6)	44.5	(0.8)	36.0	(0.8)	26.2	(0.7)	58.2	(0.9)
	Kazakhstan	76.8	(0.9)	37.6	(1.1)	69.8	(0.9)	52.6	(1.2)	85.1	(0.7)
	Kyrgyzstan	50.2	(0.8)	24.9	(1.2)	67.1	(0.8)	38.3	(0.9)	78.8	(0.8)
	Latvia	71.1	(1.1)	9.5	(0.6)	32.8	(1.1)	25.9	(0.8)	65.2	(1.0)
	Liechtenstein	64.8	(2.6)	20.9	(2.1)	28.3	(2.3)	14.9	(2.0)	72.1	(2.4)
	Lithuania	75.5	(0.7)	19.4	(0.7)	38.7	(0.7)	30.2	(0.8)	72.4	(0.8)
	Macao-China	48.2	(0.6)	37.3	(0.6)	32.0	(0.6)	26.8	(0.7)	71.7	(0.5)
	Montenegro	73.7	(0.6)	26.9	(0.7)	34.1	(0.6)	25.9	(0.8)	71.5	(0.7)
	Panama	55.3	(1.2)	34.8	(1.3)	39.7	(1.3)	20.3	(1.0)	66.8	(1.7)
	Peru	47.9	(0.9)	48.6	(0.7)	55.4	(0.9)	39.9	(0.8)	73.9	(1.0)
	Qatar	60.1	(0.4)	50.6	(0.5)	39.9	(0.5)	33.2	(0.4)	68.0	(0.5)
	Romania	62.7	(1.0)	11.9	(0.5)	31.8	(1.0)	22.8	(0.6)	50.3	(1.4)
	Russian Federation	67.3	(0.9)	17.3	(0.9)	58.7	(1.0)	26.3	(0.7)	64.1	(1.1)
	Serbia	73.1	(0.8)	17.8	(0.6)	28.4	(0.8)	11.1	(0.7)	75.4	(0.6)
	Shanghai-China	54.6	(0.8)	29.5	(0.8)	56.2	(0.8)	27.3	(0.8)	71.1	(0.8)
	Singapore	53.9	(0.7)	33.0	(0.7)	48.2	(0.8)	33.1	(0.7)	83.5	(0.7)
	Chinese Taipei	46.6	(0.6)	40.3	(0.7)	47.8	(0.8)	37.2	(0.8)	72.0	(0.7)
	Thailand	53.1	(1.0)	72.2	(0.8)	65.1	(0.8)	50.5	(0.7)	72.0	(0.9)
	Trinidad and Tobago	44.3	(0.7)	36.7	(0.8)	42.9	(0.9)	31.6	(0.7)	83.1	(0.5)
	Tunisia	48.5	(1.0)	34.0	(0.8)	46.8	(1.0)	29.0	(1.0)	62.0	(0.9)
	Uruguay	50.5	(0.8)	24.7	(0.6)	27.5	(0.7)	15.8	(0.6)	32.7	(0.9)

StatLink ᴴᵀᴸ᠍᠊᠍ http://dx.doi.org/10.1787/888932343285

[Part 1/2]
Percentage of boys and girls who read diverse materials
Percentage of boys and girls who reported that they read the following materials because they want to "several times a month" or "several times a week"

Table III.2.8

| | Magazines | | | | | | Comic books | | | | | | Fiction | | | | | |
| | Boys | | Girls | | Difference (B – G) | | Boys | | Girls | | Difference (B – G) | | Boys | | Girls | | Difference (B – G) | |
	%	S.E.	%	S.E.	% dif.	S.E.	%	S.E.	%	S.E.	% dif.	S.E.	%	S.E.	%	S.E.	% dif.	S.E.
OECD																		
Australia	47.1	(0.8)	52.7	(0.7)	**-5.6**	(1.0)	11.6	(0.4)	6.6	(0.5)	**5.0**	(0.7)	28.3	(0.8)	47.8	(0.8)	**-19.5**	(1.0)
Austria	63.0	(1.1)	69.5	(1.1)	**-6.5**	(1.5)	18.1	(1.0)	9.6	(0.8)	**8.4**	(1.3)	15.6	(0.8)	37.4	(1.2)	**-21.9**	(1.5)
Belgium	57.4	(1.0)	74.4	(0.8)	**-17.1**	(1.2)	39.7	(0.9)	23.7	(0.9)	**16.0**	(1.2)	15.2	(0.6)	29.9	(1.0)	**-14.6**	(1.2)
Canada	39.7	(0.7)	56.5	(0.8)	**-16.8**	(1.2)	18.2	(0.6)	10.6	(0.5)	**7.6**	(0.7)	29.5	(0.8)	54.5	(0.8)	**-25.1**	(1.1)
Chile	39.2	(1.1)	60.4	(0.9)	**-21.3**	(1.3)	22.9	(0.8)	18.9	(0.7)	**3.9**	(1.0)	22.0	(0.8)	39.6	(1.1)	**-17.6**	(1.0)
Czech Republic	63.1	(1.0)	74.2	(1.0)	**-11.1**	(1.4)	18.3	(1.0)	12.2	(0.7)	**6.1**	(1.1)	7.7	(0.6)	28.5	(1.2)	**-20.8**	(1.1)
Denmark	55.0	(1.1)	75.9	(1.0)	**-21.0**	(1.3)	27.9	(1.2)	13.5	(0.8)	**14.3**	(1.5)	22.8	(1.0)	38.1	(1.1)	**-15.2**	(1.3)
Estonia	67.0	(1.3)	78.1	(0.9)	**-11.1**	(1.5)	17.7	(0.9)	8.8	(0.8)	**8.9**	(1.3)	16.0	(0.8)	32.5	(1.1)	**-16.5**	(1.2)
Finland	53.8	(1.3)	76.0	(0.9)	**-22.2**	(1.5)	70.0	(1.1)	50.3	(1.2)	**19.6**	(1.5)	13.0	(0.7)	39.2	(1.2)	**-26.1**	(1.3)
France	56.5	(1.2)	68.2	(1.1)	**-11.7**	(1.6)	40.6	(1.3)	20.7	(0.9)	**19.9**	(1.5)	21.1	(1.1)	36.2	(1.3)	**-15.1**	(1.5)
Germany	53.4	(1.2)	56.3	(1.1)	**-2.9**	(1.6)	16.2	(0.7)	6.5	(0.5)	**9.7**	(0.9)	20.4	(1.0)	45.1	(1.1)	**-24.7**	(1.3)
Greece	55.2	(1.1)	65.6	(1.1)	**-10.4**	(1.4)	30.5	(1.0)	19.1	(0.9)	**11.5**	(1.3)	12.6	(0.8)	30.1	(0.9)	**-17.5**	(1.2)
Hungary	56.0	(1.2)	65.4	(1.3)	**-9.5**	(1.6)	28.3	(1.0)	24.9	(1.1)	**3.3**	(1.4)	24.1	(1.3)	38.9	(1.3)	**-14.8**	(1.7)
Iceland	48.8	(1.3)	67.5	(1.1)	**-18.7**	(1.7)	35.1	(1.2)	26.8	(1.1)	**8.3**	(1.5)	18.9	(0.8)	35.7	(1.2)	**-16.8**	(1.5)
Ireland	45.6	(1.2)	68.8	(1.3)	**-23.2**	(1.7)	10.2	(0.8)	4.8	(0.5)	**5.5**	(0.9)	24.4	(1.4)	36.3	(1.3)	**-12.0**	(1.8)
Israel	29.6	(1.3)	47.4	(1.2)	**-17.8**	(1.8)	14.0	(0.8)	20.8	(0.9)	**-6.8**	(1.2)	19.2	(1.1)	39.5	(1.0)	**-20.3**	(1.6)
Italy	42.2	(0.6)	55.8	(0.6)	**-13.6**	(0.7)	23.1	(0.5)	11.3	(0.3)	**11.8**	(0.5)	24.9	(0.6)	45.7	(0.6)	**-20.8**	(0.8)
Japan	60.8	(1.1)	68.5	(0.8)	**-7.7**	(1.3)	81.4	(0.7)	62.7	(1.1)	**18.7**	(1.4)	36.7	(1.2)	47.8	(1.2)	**-11.1**	(1.3)
Korea	17.2	(0.8)	25.6	(1.0)	**-8.5**	(1.3)	49.8	(1.4)	30.2	(1.0)	**19.6**	(1.7)	40.8	(1.1)	53.2	(1.2)	**-12.4**	(1.7)
Luxembourg	64.2	(1.2)	73.2	(1.0)	**-9.0**	(1.4)	26.3	(1.1)	14.2	(0.8)	**12.1**	(1.3)	16.8	(0.8)	41.0	(1.1)	**-24.2**	(1.4)
Mexico	42.8	(0.7)	50.9	(0.5)	**-8.1**	(0.7)	31.8	(0.6)	22.5	(0.5)	**9.3**	(0.7)	31.1	(0.7)	44.4	(0.5)	**-13.3**	(0.8)
Netherlands	46.2	(1.3)	67.9	(1.4)	**-21.7**	(1.8)	30.1	(1.4)	14.9	(1.1)	**16.7**	(1.5)	10.1	(0.7)	32.7	(1.5)	**-22.6**	(1.4)
New Zealand	47.6	(1.2)	58.8	(1.4)	**-11.2**	(1.8)	14.9	(0.9)	8.2	(0.6)	**6.7**	(1.0)	34.8	(1.1)	53.9	(1.0)	**-19.1**	(1.5)
Norway	49.6	(1.2)	72.0	(1.2)	**-22.4**	(1.6)	50.5	(1.3)	33.4	(1.1)	**17.1**	(1.6)	16.9	(0.8)	36.2	(1.4)	**-19.3**	(1.5)
Poland	56.9	(1.1)	74.7	(0.9)	**-17.8**	(1.4)	14.1	(0.8)	8.4	(0.6)	**5.7**	(0.9)	11.5	(0.7)	28.6	(1.1)	**-17.1**	(1.2)
Portugal	56.1	(0.9)	71.3	(1.0)	**-15.2**	(1.3)	23.7	(0.8)	13.7	(0.8)	**10.0**	(1.1)	16.4	(0.8)	39.2	(1.1)	**-22.8**	(1.5)
Slovak Republic	73.3	(1.0)	86.2	(0.8)	**-12.9**	(1.5)	11.4	(0.7)	15.1	(0.8)	**-3.7**	(1.0)	10.3	(0.7)	25.2	(1.1)	**-14.9**	(1.2)
Slovenia	64.9	(1.0)	80.5	(0.9)	**-15.6**	(1.3)	19.2	(0.9)	10.4	(0.7)	**8.8**	(1.2)	8.9	(0.6)	22.1	(1.1)	**-13.2**	(1.2)
Spain	46.0	(0.8)	56.8	(0.9)	**-10.8**	(0.9)	16.7	(0.6)	7.2	(0.5)	**9.6**	(0.7)	21.4	(0.7)	39.0	(0.7)	**-17.6**	(1.0)
Sweden	49.7	(1.2)	66.9	(1.1)	**-17.3**	(1.4)	28.7	(1.1)	16.1	(0.9)	**12.6**	(1.5)	20.1	(0.9)	45.1	(1.3)	**-24.9**	(1.5)
Switzerland	61.0	(1.0)	72.8	(0.9)	**-11.8**	(1.5)	30.8	(0.9)	17.3	(0.8)	**13.5**	(1.2)	19.1	(0.8)	41.5	(1.1)	**-22.4**	(1.4)
Turkey	43.8	(1.1)	53.2	(1.4)	**-9.4**	(1.6)	24.6	(0.8)	20.8	(1.0)	**3.8**	(1.3)	45.0	(1.1)	67.7	(1.0)	**-22.7**	(1.6)
United Kingdom	48.1	(0.9)	70.7	(1.0)	**-22.6**	(1.5)	10.5	(0.6)	5.2	(0.4)	**5.3**	(0.7)	23.8	(1.0)	38.9	(1.0)	**-15.1**	(1.4)
United States	44.3	(1.2)	49.3	(1.0)	**-5.0**	(1.5)	12.7	(0.9)	7.9	(0.6)	**4.8**	(1.0)	27.8	(1.2)	45.8	(1.3)	**-18.0**	(1.2)
OECD average	51.3	(0.2)	65.1	(0.2)	**-13.7**	(0.2)	27.1	(0.2)	17.6	(0.1)	**9.5**	(0.2)	21.4	(0.2)	39.9	(0.2)	**-18.5**	(0.2)
Partners																		
Albania	37.3	(1.3)	52.3	(1.4)	**-15.0**	(1.7)	47.0	(1.6)	40.2	(1.3)	**6.8**	(1.6)	40.5	(1.5)	67.1	(1.5)	**-26.6**	(1.9)
Argentina	41.6	(1.2)	61.8	(1.1)	**-20.3**	(1.5)	28.0	(1.3)	30.4	(1.2)	-2.5	(1.7)	19.4	(1.0)	33.4	(1.3)	**-14.0**	(1.6)
Azerbaijan	39.3	(1.4)	49.3	(1.6)	**-10.1**	(1.9)	49.7	(1.6)	46.7	(1.4)	3.0	(1.9)	46.2	(1.2)	58.1	(1.6)	**-11.9**	(1.7)
Brazil	36.7	(0.8)	59.7	(0.9)	**-23.0**	(1.1)	35.5	(0.9)	31.7	(0.8)	**3.7**	(0.9)	21.2	(0.6)	48.4	(0.9)	**-27.3**	(1.1)
Bulgaria	49.1	(1.3)	75.3	(1.2)	**-26.2**	(1.7)	19.7	(1.2)	15.6	(1.0)	**4.1**	(1.5)	25.1	(1.5)	43.9	(1.7)	**-18.8**	(1.7)
Colombia	43.2	(1.2)	63.8	(1.1)	**-20.6**	(1.6)	46.6	(1.5)	40.2	(1.3)	**6.4**	(2.1)	30.6	(1.6)	44.1	(1.3)	**-13.6**	(1.9)
Croatia	64.7	(0.9)	78.3	(0.9)	**-13.5**	(1.2)	24.4	(0.9)	12.1	(0.7)	**12.3**	(1.2)	14.4	(0.8)	30.7	(1.3)	**-16.3**	(1.4)
Dubai (UAE)	63.5	(1.0)	70.7	(1.0)	**-7.2**	(1.4)	38.0	(0.9)	40.6	(1.0)	-2.6	(1.4)	33.0	(1.0)	47.7	(1.2)	**-14.7**	(1.5)
Hong Kong-China	46.9	(1.2)	50.3	(1.2)	**-3.4**	(1.6)	37.6	(1.2)	22.4	(1.0)	**15.2**	(1.5)	41.9	(1.0)	55.8	(1.2)	**-14.0**	(1.5)
Indonesia	51.4	(1.3)	59.0	(1.6)	**-7.7**	(1.8)	51.3	(1.1)	53.3	(1.2)	-2.1	(1.6)	51.6	(1.3)	66.8	(1.3)	**-15.3**	(1.8)
Jordan	35.2	(0.9)	52.1	(1.0)	**-16.9**	(1.4)	39.1	(1.0)	49.8	(1.1)	**-10.7**	(1.4)	32.8	(1.1)	39.2	(1.2)	**-6.4**	(1.6)
Kazakhstan	71.2	(1.0)	82.6	(1.0)	**-11.4**	(1.1)	36.4	(1.3)	38.8	(1.3)	-2.4	(1.8)	65.3	(1.1)	74.4	(1.1)	**-9.1**	(1.4)
Kyrgyzstan	42.8	(1.2)	57.0	(0.9)	**-14.2**	(1.4)	25.8	(1.6)	24.1	(1.2)	1.7	(1.6)	60.4	(1.0)	73.3	(1.0)	**-12.9**	(1.4)
Latvia	61.9	(1.3)	80.0	(1.2)	**-18.2**	(1.4)	12.0	(0.9)	7.1	(0.8)	**4.9**	(1.1)	23.3	(1.3)	42.0	(1.7)	**-18.6**	(2.0)
Liechtenstein	57.7	(3.7)	72.7	(3.4)	**-15.1**	(5.0)	26.2	(3.2)	15.0	(2.8)	**11.1**	(4.4)	20.1	(2.8)	37.2	(3.9)	**-17.1**	(4.9)
Lithuania	67.2	(1.1)	84.0	(0.7)	**-16.8**	(1.3)	22.5	(1.1)	16.4	(0.9)	**6.1**	(1.5)	23.6	(0.9)	53.9	(1.1)	**-30.3**	(1.4)
Macao-China	44.2	(0.8)	52.3	(0.9)	**-8.1**	(1.1)	43.9	(0.9)	30.5	(0.9)	**13.4**	(1.4)	22.4	(0.6)	41.7	(1.1)	**-19.3**	(1.2)
Montenegro	65.3	(1.2)	82.3	(0.8)	**-16.9**	(1.6)	31.8	(1.1)	21.8	(0.9)	**10.1**	(1.5)	27.0	(0.9)	41.4	(0.9)	**-14.5**	(1.2)
Panama	44.7	(2.0)	65.5	(1.5)	**-20.8**	(2.7)	36.5	(2.2)	33.1	(1.3)	3.4	(2.6)	31.9	(1.5)	47.3	(1.8)	**-15.3**	(2.0)
Peru	44.6	(1.2)	51.2	(1.2)	**-6.5**	(1.5)	48.1	(1.1)	49.0	(1.2)	-0.9	(1.7)	48.3	(1.3)	62.5	(1.0)	**-14.2**	(1.5)
Qatar	51.9	(0.7)	68.2	(0.7)	**-16.3**	(1.0)	45.9	(0.7)	55.2	(0.7)	**-9.3**	(1.1)	33.2	(0.7)	46.4	(0.7)	**-13.2**	(1.0)
Romania	52.5	(1.4)	72.4	(1.2)	**-19.9**	(1.8)	11.7	(0.7)	12.1	(0.7)	-0.3	(1.0)	22.7	(1.0)	40.5	(1.4)	**-17.8**	(1.5)
Russian Federation	58.6	(1.3)	75.8	(0.9)	**-17.1**	(1.3)	18.7	(1.2)	16.0	(1.0)	2.7	(1.2)	49.7	(1.6)	67.5	(1.0)	**-17.8**	(1.7)
Serbia	62.1	(1.1)	84.1	(0.9)	**-22.0**	(1.4)	22.9	(1.0)	12.7	(0.7)	**10.2**	(1.2)	21.3	(0.8)	35.5	(1.3)	**-14.2**	(1.5)
Shanghai-China	52.2	(1.1)	56.8	(1.0)	**-4.6**	(1.3)	36.1	(1.2)	23.0	(1.0)	**13.1**	(1.6)	51.5	(1.0)	60.8	(1.0)	**-9.3**	(1.2)
Singapore	47.7	(1.1)	60.3	(1.1)	**-12.6**	(1.3)	39.7	(1.1)	26.0	(1.0)	**13.7**	(1.5)	39.4	(1.1)	57.3	(1.1)	**-17.8**	(1.4)
Chinese Taipei	46.9	(0.9)	46.4	(1.0)	0.5	(1.4)	46.9	(0.9)	33.6	(1.2)	**13.3**	(1.4)	40.7	(1.0)	55.0	(1.1)	**-14.3**	(1.4)
Thailand	41.0	(1.2)	62.2	(1.0)	**-21.3**	(1.2)	67.2	(1.2)	75.9	(0.7)	**-8.7**	(1.3)	53.5	(1.2)	73.9	(0.8)	**-20.4**	(1.4)
Trinidad and Tobago	39.3	(1.0)	49.2	(1.1)	**-9.9**	(1.5)	38.0	(1.2)	35.5	(1.0)	2.5	(1.6)	33.8	(1.2)	51.4	(1.2)	**-17.6**	(1.7)
Tunisia	40.8	(1.3)	55.6	(1.3)	**-14.8**	(1.8)	30.5	(0.9)	37.1	(1.3)	**-6.6**	(1.5)	38.3	(1.3)	54.5	(1.1)	**-16.2**	(1.5)
Uruguay	36.9	(1.0)	62.3	(1.0)	**-25.4**	(1.3)	24.9	(0.9)	24.5	(0.9)	0.4	(1.2)	19.2	(1.0)	34.7	(1.0)	**-15.5**	(1.3)

Note: Values that are statistically significant are indicated in bold (see Annex A3).
StatLink ᵃˢᵖ http://dx.doi.org/10.1787/888932343285

[Part 2/2]
Percentage of boys and girls who read diverse materials
Percentage of boys and girls who reported that they read the following materials because they want to "several times a month" or "several times a week"

Table III.2.8

	Non-fiction books						Newspapers					
	Boys		Girls		Difference (B – G)		Boys		Girls		Difference (B – G)	
	%	S.E.	%	S.E.	% dif.	S.E.	%	S.E.	%	S.E.	% dif.	S.E.
OECD												
Australia	18.9	(0.6)	21.1	(0.5)	**-2.2**	(0.8)	58.1	(0.9)	49.5	(0.9)	**8.6**	(1.2)
Austria	22.6	(0.9)	12.1	(0.9)	**10.5**	(1.2)	82.7	(0.8)	81.1	(1.2)	1.6	(1.3)
Belgium	13.9	(0.7)	13.5	(0.7)	0.4	(0.8)	57.8	(1.2)	42.8	(1.0)	**15.1**	(1.4)
Canada	18.6	(0.6)	21.3	(0.6)	**-2.6**	(0.8)	52.2	(1.0)	43.7	(0.9)	**8.6**	(1.0)
Chile	12.7	(0.7)	20.1	(0.9)	**-7.4**	(1.0)	58.3	(1.4)	58.7	(1.0)	-0.4	(1.4)
Czech Republic	11.4	(0.8)	12.7	(0.7)	-1.3	(0.9)	68.4	(1.2)	63.4	(1.0)	**5.0**	(1.7)
Denmark	27.7	(0.9)	26.6	(1.0)	1.1	(1.3)	57.6	(1.1)	45.9	(1.2)	**11.7**	(1.5)
Estonia	31.5	(1.0)	32.3	(1.3)	-0.8	(1.4)	80.7	(1.0)	79.6	(1.0)	1.1	(1.4)
Finland	19.3	(0.7)	11.7	(0.6)	**7.6**	(0.8)	76.0	(1.1)	74.8	(0.9)	1.2	(1.2)
France	15.0	(0.8)	9.1	(0.7)	**5.9**	(1.1)	51.4	(1.4)	42.3	(1.3)	**9.1**	(1.6)
Germany	21.9	(1.1)	12.4	(0.8)	**9.5**	(1.2)	67.3	(1.2)	56.3	(1.3)	**11.0**	(1.4)
Greece	6.0	(0.5)	8.3	(0.7)	**-2.3**	(0.9)	58.7	(1.2)	27.6	(1.3)	**31.1**	(1.8)
Hungary	35.7	(1.2)	34.1	(1.1)	1.6	(1.5)	66.7	(1.2)	76.9	(1.2)	**-10.2**	(1.7)
Iceland	13.0	(0.8)	21.2	(1.1)	**-8.3**	(1.3)	80.9	(1.0)	83.0	(0.8)	-2.1	(1.1)
Ireland	15.0	(1.0)	17.1	(0.8)	-2.1	(1.2)	73.4	(1.2)	61.4	(1.3)	**12.0**	(1.8)
Israel	25.1	(1.4)	27.8	(1.2)	-2.7	(1.8)	71.4	(1.0)	77.8	(1.0)	**-6.4**	(1.3)
Italy	4.3	(0.2)	5.7	(0.3)	**-1.4**	(0.4)	58.1	(0.7)	48.5	(0.7)	**9.6**	(0.8)
Japan	10.6	(0.6)	11.7	(0.6)	-1.2	(0.8)	61.9	(1.1)	53.0	(1.2)	**8.9**	(1.5)
Korea	27.4	(1.3)	33.0	(1.2)	**-5.6**	(1.8)	46.6	(1.5)	43.4	(1.8)	3.2	(2.3)
Luxembourg	24.9	(0.8)	13.6	(0.7)	**11.3**	(1.2)	73.5	(0.8)	67.8	(1.0)	**5.7**	(1.4)
Mexico	18.4	(0.5)	18.9	(0.5)	-0.5	(0.7)	51.6	(0.7)	44.1	(0.6)	**7.5**	(0.8)
Netherlands	8.2	(0.7)	16.8	(1.1)	**-8.6**	(1.3)	54.7	(1.9)	42.4	(1.6)	**12.3**	(1.7)
New Zealand	24.1	(1.0)	26.7	(1.0)	-2.6	(1.4)	54.3	(1.2)	51.9	(1.4)	2.3	(1.9)
Norway	28.0	(1.1)	26.5	(1.1)	1.5	(1.4)	75.6	(1.0)	71.1	(1.2)	**4.5**	(1.5)
Poland	17.9	(1.0)	23.6	(0.9)	**-5.7**	(1.2)	76.1	(0.8)	82.1	(0.7)	**-6.0**	(1.1)
Portugal	10.4	(0.5)	17.8	(0.7)	**-7.3**	(1.0)	66.2	(1.0)	37.5	(1.0)	**28.7**	(1.4)
Slovak Republic	20.2	(1.1)	19.6	(1.2)	0.6	(1.4)	72.1	(1.1)	72.8	(1.0)	-0.8	(1.6)
Slovenia	12.5	(0.7)	20.1	(1.0)	**-7.6**	(1.2)	75.6	(1.0)	67.8	(1.2)	**7.8**	(1.4)
Spain	13.4	(0.6)	23.3	(0.7)	**-9.9**	(1.0)	58.1	(0.9)	31.8	(0.9)	**26.3**	(1.1)
Sweden	9.3	(0.7)	10.6	(0.8)	-1.3	(0.9)	71.4	(1.1)	71.8	(1.0)	-0.5	(1.3)
Switzerland	19.6	(0.8)	10.3	(0.5)	**9.3**	(0.9)	81.1	(1.0)	77.9	(0.9)	**3.1**	(1.2)
Turkey	29.7	(1.0)	23.8	(1.0)	**5.9**	(1.3)	88.1	(0.8)	84.9	(0.8)	**3.3**	(1.0)
United Kingdom	18.8	(0.9)	20.1	(0.6)	-1.3	(1.1)	67.7	(1.1)	54.9	(0.9)	**12.8**	(1.2)
United States	18.5	(1.0)	22.7	(1.1)	**-4.2**	(1.4)	41.2	(1.1)	32.6	(1.5)	**8.7**	(1.7)
OECD average	18.4	(0.1)	19.0	(0.2)	**-0.6**	(0.2)	65.7	(0.2)	58.9	(0.2)	**6.9**	(0.2)
Partners												
Albania	20.1	(1.1)	24.3	(1.1)	**-4.2**	(1.5)	61.4	(1.3)	58.9	(1.6)	2.5	(1.6)
Argentina	22.4	(1.3)	33.6	(1.2)	**-11.1**	(1.9)	53.4	(1.5)	45.3	(1.3)	**8.1**	(1.7)
Azerbaijan	46.6	(1.7)	50.7	(1.7)	**-4.1**	(1.9)	51.8	(1.3)	50.2	(1.5)	1.5	(1.8)
Brazil	13.3	(0.6)	16.6	(0.6)	**-3.3**	(1.0)	46.2	(1.2)	42.6	(1.0)	3.6	(1.3)
Bulgaria	29.3	(1.5)	29.9	(1.2)	-0.6	(1.8)	54.7	(1.7)	59.7	(1.1)	**-5.0**	(1.8)
Colombia	29.5	(1.4)	36.3	(1.3)	**-6.8**	(1.4)	54.9	(1.7)	60.5	(1.8)	**-5.6**	(1.7)
Croatia	13.2	(0.8)	19.0	(1.2)	**-5.8**	(1.4)	89.3	(0.8)	87.4	(0.8)	1.8	(1.1)
Dubai (UAE)	26.2	(0.9)	27.3	(1.0)	-1.1	(1.5)	77.3	(0.8)	68.0	(1.0)	**9.3**	(1.3)
Hong Kong-China	36.3	(1.2)	33.6	(1.0)	2.7	(1.4)	84.0	(1.0)	84.3	(0.9)	-0.3	(1.1)
Indonesia	31.1	(1.3)	41.0	(1.4)	**-9.8**	(1.7)	67.7	(1.4)	63.2	(1.3)	**4.6**	(1.5)
Jordan	27.0	(1.0)	25.5	(1.0)	1.5	(1.3)	60.8	(1.3)	55.7	(1.2)	**5.1**	(1.8)
Kazakhstan	52.6	(1.3)	52.5	(1.5)	0.1	(1.4)	84.2	(0.8)	86.0	(0.8)	-1.9	(0.9)
Kyrgyzstan	36.4	(1.2)	40.0	(1.1)	**-3.5**	(1.6)	72.8	(1.1)	84.4	(0.8)	**-11.6**	(1.1)
Latvia	20.5	(0.9)	31.2	(1.3)	**-10.6**	(1.6)	63.5	(1.3)	66.8	(1.3)	-3.3	(1.8)
Liechtenstein	17.7	(2.8)	11.7	(2.4)	5.9	(3.6)	75.0	(3.3)	68.8	(3.4)	6.3	(4.7)
Lithuania	22.9	(0.9)	37.6	(1.1)	**-14.7**	(1.3)	71.8	(1.0)	73.0	(1.1)	-1.2	(1.3)
Macao-China	26.9	(0.8)	26.8	(0.9)	0.1	(1.1)	68.8	(0.7)	74.6	(0.8)	**-5.7**	(1.0)
Montenegro	25.5	(1.1)	26.4	(1.0)	-0.9	(1.3)	74.2	(1.1)	68.8	(1.3)	5.4	(2.0)
Panama	20.4	(1.6)	20.2	(1.1)	0.2	(1.8)	68.9	(2.3)	64.6	(2.1)	4.3	(2.8)
Peru	37.9	(1.0)	42.1	(1.2)	**-4.2**	(1.6)	74.7	(1.1)	73.2	(1.3)	1.5	(1.5)
Qatar	32.7	(0.7)	33.7	(0.7)	-1.0	(1.1)	70.4	(0.7)	65.5	(0.7)	**5.0**	(1.0)
Romania	22.1	(0.9)	23.5	(1.0)	-1.5	(1.4)	54.1	(1.5)	46.7	(1.7)	**7.4**	(1.7)
Russian Federation	25.8	(0.8)	26.8	(1.0)	-1.1	(1.2)	62.6	(1.1)	65.6	(1.5)	-3.0	(1.5)
Serbia	10.3	(0.7)	11.9	(0.8)	-1.6	(0.9)	77.2	(0.9)	73.6	(1.0)	**3.5**	(1.4)
Shanghai-China	33.6	(1.0)	21.0	(1.0)	**12.6**	(1.2)	70.5	(1.2)	71.7	(0.9)	-1.2	(1.4)
Singapore	32.0	(0.9)	34.1	(0.9)	-2.1	(1.2)	85.2	(0.8)	81.7	(0.9)	**3.4**	(0.9)
Chinese Taipei	37.1	(0.9)	37.2	(1.1)	-0.1	(1.3)	70.8	(0.9)	73.1	(0.9)	-2.3	(1.3)
Thailand	45.5	(1.1)	54.4	(1.0)	**-8.9**	(1.5)	70.4	(1.1)	73.1	(1.1)	-2.7	(1.4)
Trinidad and Tobago	25.9	(1.0)	37.1	(1.2)	**-11.2**	(1.6)	80.2	(0.9)	85.9	(0.8)	**-5.7**	(1.3)
Tunisia	30.1	(1.1)	28.0	(1.2)	2.1	(1.4)	63.0	(1.2)	61.2	(1.3)	1.8	(1.7)
Uruguay	11.7	(0.7)	19.4	(0.9)	**-7.7**	(1.0)	35.5	(1.1)	30.3	(1.2)	**5.2**	(1.4)

Note: Values that are statistically significant are indicated in bold (see Annex A3).
StatLink ⟐⟐ http://dx.doi.org/10.1787/888932343285

[Part 1/1]
Percentage of students doing diverse online reading activities
Percentage of students who reported that they were involved in the following online reading activities
Table III.2.9 *"several times a week" or "several times a day"*

		Reading emails		Chat on line (e.g. <MSN®>)		Reading online news		Using an online dictionary or encyclopedia (e.g. <Wikipedia®>)		Searching online information to learn about a practical topic		Taking part in online group discussions or forums		Searching for practical information online (e.g. schedules, events, tips, recipes)	
		%	S.E.	%	S.E.	%	S.E.	%	S.E.	%	S.E.	%	S.E.	%	S.E.
OECD	Australia	66.7	(0.6)	74.7	(0.5)	31.7	(0.5)	33.7	(0.7)	55.8	(0.6)	17.0	(0.5)	32.1	(0.6)
	Austria	67.6	(0.9)	76.6	(0.8)	60.4	(0.9)	37.6	(1.2)	53.7	(1.1)	13.5	(0.6)	37.9	(1.0)
	Belgium	73.7	(0.6)	80.9	(0.5)	31.0	(0.7)	23.6	(0.6)	33.8	(0.6)	16.0	(0.5)	27.4	(0.6)
	Canada	70.7	(0.5)	77.0	(0.4)	33.8	(0.6)	35.7	(0.8)	48.0	(0.6)	15.9	(0.4)	34.5	(0.6)
	Chile	48.3	(1.0)	64.5	(1.1)	25.6	(0.8)	42.1	(1.1)	57.3	(1.1)	15.4	(0.6)	30.8	(0.8)
	Czech Republic	75.8	(0.7)	84.5	(0.6)	63.3	(0.9)	55.3	(0.9)	61.7	(0.9)	30.7	(0.7)	55.1	(0.7)
	Denmark	76.1	(0.7)	86.0	(0.6)	47.8	(0.8)	44.6	(1.0)	60.7	(0.9)	14.4	(0.6)	33.6	(0.7)
	Estonia	71.1	(0.8)	90.8	(0.8)	67.9	(0.8)	51.6	(0.9)	55.1	(0.7)	33.3	(0.7)	51.0	(0.9)
	Finland	64.0	(0.7)	80.8	(0.5)	35.0	(0.8)	39.4	(0.9)	30.0	(0.9)	26.1	(0.6)	28.4	(0.8)
	France	63.0	(0.8)	77.1	(0.8)	45.0	(0.9)	32.4	(0.8)	38.4	(0.7)	9.5	(0.5)	41.9	(1.0)
	Germany	65.3	(0.9)	82.6	(0.6)	62.0	(0.8)	40.9	(0.9)	52.0	(0.9)	15.7	(0.6)	36.1	(0.9)
	Greece	52.2	(1.0)	58.1	(1.1)	34.4	(0.9)	29.1	(0.9)	54.5	(1.0)	21.4	(0.6)	38.1	(0.8)
	Hungary	79.0	(0.9)	79.0	(0.9)	48.9	(0.9)	47.9	(1.0)	55.5	(1.0)	40.6	(0.9)	53.4	(1.0)
	Iceland	63.9	(0.8)	88.8	(0.5)	59.2	(0.7)	38.3	(0.7)	49.5	(0.8)	33.1	(0.8)	36.7	(0.8)
	Ireland	46.0	(1.0)	60.3	(1.2)	19.7	(0.8)	20.4	(0.7)	32.2	(0.9)	14.9	(0.7)	24.1	(0.7)
	Israel	58.9	(0.9)	57.0	(0.9)	51.7	(1.0)	42.7	(0.9)	50.1	(0.9)	24.3	(0.8)	38.4	(0.8)
	Italy	54.1	(0.5)	70.8	(0.5)	55.4	(0.5)	39.8	(0.5)	51.8	(0.5)	19.8	(0.3)	31.3	(0.4)
	Japan	88.3	(0.5)	15.6	(0.5)	44.4	(0.8)	32.6	(0.7)	46.1	(0.8)	2.8	(0.3)	21.5	(0.6)
	Korea	28.1	(0.9)	57.4	(1.2)	68.6	(0.9)	34.8	(0.9)	59.4	(1.0)	6.1	(0.4)	48.3	(0.9)
	Luxembourg	68.9	(0.7)	79.6	(0.6)	58.1	(0.7)	35.3	(0.6)	46.2	(0.8)	17.7	(0.6)	31.3	(0.7)
	Mexico	39.9	(0.6)	48.1	(0.8)	24.9	(0.6)	42.0	(0.5)	56.2	(0.5)	9.6	(0.3)	23.8	(0.4)
	Netherlands	91.1	(0.5)	90.5	(0.7)	45.1	(0.9)	32.5	(1.3)	47.9	(1.2)	15.9	(0.8)	23.2	(1.0)
	New Zealand	60.6	(0.7)	56.9	(0.9)	27.3	(0.7)	30.1	(0.8)	50.2	(0.8)	16.5	(0.6)	28.5	(0.7)
	Norway	65.8	(0.8)	86.4	(0.5)	45.0	(1.0)	53.8	(1.0)	53.4	(0.8)	22.1	(0.7)	34.1	(0.9)
	Poland	54.6	(0.8)	78.9	(0.9)	74.3	(0.8)	58.2	(1.0)	72.6	(0.8)	27.8	(0.8)	47.8	(0.9)
	Portugal	67.2	(0.7)	80.0	(0.7)	43.9	(0.8)	44.1	(0.8)	60.9	(0.6)	18.8	(0.6)	35.5	(0.8)
	Slovak Republic	66.6	(0.8)	75.5	(0.8)	35.9	(0.8)	33.1	(0.9)	50.0	(1.0)	35.5	(0.9)	34.5	(0.8)
	Slovenia	70.4	(0.7)	83.2	(0.7)	58.8	(0.7)	34.7	(0.7)	49.2	(0.8)	29.3	(0.6)	37.7	(0.8)
	Spain	55.0	(0.6)	77.5	(0.5)	35.1	(0.5)	46.4	(0.8)	50.9	(0.5)	11.8	(0.4)	29.6	(0.6)
	Sweden	59.5	(0.9)	84.7	(0.7)	36.4	(0.9)	39.3	(0.9)	50.6	(0.9)	13.9	(0.5)	40.7	(0.9)
	Switzerland	70.0	(0.7)	78.6	(0.6)	52.1	(0.7)	34.2	(0.8)	64.9	(0.9)	23.4	(0.8)	31.8	(0.7)
	Turkey	50.7	(1.1)	60.4	(1.0)	51.5	(0.9)	43.9	(1.0)	54.3	(0.8)	20.6	(0.6)	33.0	(0.6)
	United Kingdom	74.8	(0.7)	83.5	(0.5)	43.7	(0.7)	39.9	(0.8)	54.3	(0.8)	14.6	(0.5)	36.9	(0.8)
	United States	57.4	(0.8)	64.5	(1.0)	35.7	(1.0)	35.0	(1.0)	46.7	(0.9)	14.6	(0.5)	36.9	(0.8)
	OECD average	63.7	(0.1)	73.3	(0.1)	45.7	(0.1)	39.0	(0.1)	51.3	(0.1)	19.6	(0.1)	35.5	(0.1)
Partners	Albania	35.4	(1.5)	40.7	(1.6)	20.8	(0.8)	22.1	(0.9)	42.2	(1.3)	22.1	(0.8)	32.7	(1.0)
	Argentina	44.6	(1.5)	58.7	(1.8)	27.7	(1.0)	32.9	(1.2)	38.2	(1.2)	12.6	(0.7)	25.4	(0.9)
	Azerbaijan	16.3	(1.0)	18.1	(1.0)	21.0	(1.0)	19.5	(1.0)	24.7	(1.0)	14.1	(0.6)	20.5	(1.0)
	Brazil	40.8	(0.8)	56.2	(0.9)	38.1	(0.8)	30.2	(0.6)	36.1	(0.8)	10.9	(0.5)	28.6	(0.6)
	Bulgaria	52.4	(1.0)	84.9	(1.0)	53.2	(1.1)	49.0	(1.5)	57.6	(1.4)	37.1	(1.2)	41.9	(1.3)
	Colombia	55.2	(1.4)	57.4	(1.6)	28.5	(1.0)	50.0	(1.5)	53.1	(1.4)	10.2	(0.6)	28.5	(0.8)
	Croatia	59.6	(0.8)	70.6	(0.8)	52.7	(0.7)	38.8	(1.1)	59.2	(0.8)	20.6	(0.6)	32.8	(0.8)
	Dubai (UAE)	68.3	(0.6)	72.9	(0.6)	43.1	(0.7)	47.3	(0.7)	61.9	(0.6)	28.6	(0.6)	42.1	(0.7)
	Hong Kong-China	54.7	(0.9)	82.6	(0.6)	59.9	(0.8)	53.2	(0.9)	41.9	(1.0)	52.1	(0.8)	44.3	(0.8)
	Indonesia	19.0	(1.0)	13.7	(1.1)	22.2	(1.3)	11.9	(1.0)	22.0	(1.3)	9.9	(0.8)	18.4	(1.1)
	Jordan	27.8	(1.0)	28.4	(0.9)	27.8	(0.8)	26.3	(0.9)	39.9	(1.0)	13.5	(0.6)	28.4	(0.9)
	Kazakhstan	29.6	(1.3)	26.2	(1.4)	26.1	(1.3)	20.5	(1.1)	26.5	(1.2)	13.2	(0.8)	15.4	(0.8)
	Kyrgyzstan	15.1	(0.8)	8.4	(0.5)	17.3	(0.8)	12.5	(0.7)	17.5	(0.8)	7.7	(0.5)	15.4	(0.6)
	Latvia	65.4	(0.9)	71.7	(1.1)	56.5	(1.0)	48.5	(1.1)	47.8	(1.0)	39.5	(1.0)	41.7	(1.1)
	Liechtenstein	70.6	(2.5)	79.8	(2.0)	56.9	(2.8)	34.8	(2.3)	45.9	(2.2)	12.6	(1.8)	30.8	(1.9)
	Lithuania	68.9	(0.9)	84.7	(0.8)	58.9	(0.9)	61.8	(1.0)	71.0	(0.9)	49.0	(0.8)	44.7	(0.9)
	Macao-China	41.0	(0.6)	85.2	(0.5)	49.5	(0.6)	35.7	(0.6)	27.2	(0.6)	31.0	(0.6)	33.3	(0.6)
	Montenegro	48.1	(0.7)	53.9	(0.7)	50.4	(0.8)	38.3	(0.7)	51.7	(0.7)	26.8	(0.9)	26.5	(0.9)
	Panama	39.0	(2.0)	53.4	(2.4)	24.8	(1.4)	37.7	(2.3)	48.4	(2.6)	15.0	(1.2)	25.2	(1.3)
	Peru	36.2	(1.1)	42.9	(1.3)	23.1	(0.9)	36.4	(1.3)	50.7	(1.2)	14.1	(0.5)	22.0	(0.7)
	Qatar	64.1	(0.5)	67.6	(0.5)	51.2	(0.6)	48.3	(0.5)	62.9	(0.5)	42.0	(0.5)	42.9	(0.5)
	Romania	49.0	(1.3)	63.4	(1.3)	28.5	(0.9)	36.7	(1.1)	52.3	(1.2)	37.4	(0.9)	37.6	(0.9)
	Russian Federation	40.3	(1.2)	58.1	(1.6)	36.1	(1.2)	28.1	(1.1)	37.6	(1.4)	18.0	(0.9)	20.5	(0.9)
	Serbia	38.7	(1.0)	46.2	(1.0)	31.6	(0.9)	28.3	(0.8)	41.7	(1.0)	23.0	(0.6)	37.4	(0.8)
	Shanghai-China	23.6	(0.7)	62.8	(0.8)	37.7	(1.0)	39.1	(1.0)	32.7	(0.8)	20.9	(0.7)	20.8	(0.7)
	Singapore	61.8	(0.8)	77.2	(0.6)	45.6	(0.8)	47.7	(0.8)	50.7	(0.8)	21.1	(0.6)	37.8	(0.6)
	Chinese Taipei	35.6	(0.7)	66.8	(0.8)	46.8	(0.7)	20.7	(0.6)	32.1	(0.8)	19.0	(0.6)	39.9	(0.6)
	Thailand	28.0	(0.9)	32.3	(1.1)	22.9	(0.9)	16.9	(0.8)	34.5	(0.9)	22.4	(0.7)	23.2	(0.9)
	Trinidad and Tobago	38.8	(0.9)	38.2	(0.7)	22.0	(0.6)	28.3	(0.7)	41.7	(0.7)	15.9	(0.6)	26.6	(0.7)
	Tunisia	19.1	(1.0)	27.3	(1.2)	22.0	(1.1)	20.0	(0.9)	32.9	(1.1)	15.3	(0.8)	23.2	(0.8)
	Uruguay	50.4	(0.8)	64.2	(0.9)	37.0	(0.7)	48.2	(1.0)	58.0	(0.9)	17.9	(0.6)	24.0	(0.6)

StatLink http://dx.doi.org/10.1787/888932343285

[Part 1/3]
Percentage of boys and girls doing diverse online reading activities
Percentage of boys and girls who reported that they were involved in the following online reading activities "several times a week" or "several times a day"

Table III.2.10

	Reading emails						<Chat on line> (e.g. <MSN®>)						Reading online news					
	Boys		Girls		Difference (B – G)		Boys		Girls		Difference (B – G)		Boys		Girls		Difference (B – G)	
	%	S.E.	%	S.E.	% dif.	S.E.	%	S.E.	%	S.E.	% dif.	S.E.	%	S.E.	%	S.E.	% dif.	S.E.
OECD																		
Australia	63.2	(0.9)	70.1	(0.8)	**-6.9**	(1.1)	72.6	(0.7)	76.8	(0.7)	**-4.2**	(1.0)	31.9	(0.8)	31.4	(0.7)	0.5	(1.0)
Austria	64.0	(1.4)	71.1	(1.2)	**-7.1**	(1.7)	74.4	(1.1)	78.7	(1.3)	**-4.2**	(1.7)	58.5	(1.2)	62.2	(1.5)	-3.8	(1.9)
Belgium	73.0	(0.9)	74.4	(0.8)	-1.4	(1.1)	79.7	(0.8)	82.1	(0.7)	**-2.4**	(1.0)	35.4	(1.0)	26.5	(0.9)	**9.0**	(1.3)
Canada	65.3	(0.7)	76.2	(0.6)	**-10.9**	(0.8)	74.7	(0.6)	79.4	(0.6)	**-4.7**	(0.7)	35.9	(0.8)	31.7	(0.7)	**4.2**	(1.0)
Chile	47.3	(1.4)	49.4	(0.9)	-2.1	(1.3)	63.2	(1.4)	65.8	(1.3)	-2.7	(1.5)	27.3	(1.1)	23.8	(1.1)	**3.6**	(1.5)
Czech Republic	72.8	(1.0)	79.1	(0.9)	**-6.2**	(1.3)	84.1	(0.8)	84.9	(0.8)	-0.7	(1.0)	68.6	(1.1)	57.3	(1.2)	**11.3**	(1.6)
Denmark	74.5	(1.0)	77.6	(1.1)	**-3.1**	(1.5)	83.9	(0.8)	88.1	(0.7)	**-4.3**	(1.1)	54.2	(1.1)	41.6	(0.9)	**12.6**	(1.3)
Estonia	67.9	(1.2)	74.5	(1.1)	**-6.6**	(1.6)	88.9	(1.1)	92.9	(0.7)	**-4.0**	(1.0)	69.1	(1.2)	66.6	(1.0)	2.5	(1.5)
Finland	60.6	(1.0)	67.5	(1.0)	**-6.9**	(1.3)	77.9	(0.8)	83.6	(0.8)	**-5.7**	(1.1)	40.9	(1.1)	29.1	(1.0)	**11.8**	(1.5)
France	59.8	(1.2)	65.9	(1.0)	**-6.0**	(1.6)	74.2	(1.1)	79.9	(1.0)	**-5.7**	(1.3)	48.2	(1.2)	41.9	(1.0)	**6.3**	(1.7)
Germany	63.9	(1.2)	66.6	(1.2)	-2.8	(1.6)	82.2	(0.9)	83.1	(1.0)	-0.8	(1.4)	62.2	(1.0)	61.8	(1.2)	0.4	(1.5)
Greece	55.2	(1.2)	49.4	(1.3)	5.8	(1.7)	61.9	(1.3)	54.3	(1.4)	7.6	(1.6)	41.0	(1.3)	28.1	(1.1)	**12.8**	(1.6)
Hungary	75.7	(1.3)	82.3	(1.0)	**-6.6**	(1.5)	77.9	(1.2)	80.1	(1.1)	-2.2	(1.5)	52.5	(1.4)	45.4	(1.3)	**7.1**	(1.9)
Iceland	60.6	(1.2)	67.1	(0.9)	**-6.6**	(1.4)	87.1	(0.7)	90.5	(0.7)	-3.4	(1.1)	65.2	(1.1)	53.3	(1.5)	**11.8**	(1.7)
Ireland	42.4	(1.1)	49.7	(1.5)	**-7.4**	(1.8)	53.1	(1.7)	67.6	(1.4)	**-14.5**	(2.0)	22.6	(1.1)	16.7	(1.0)	**5.9**	(1.4)
Israel	52.8	(1.4)	65.2	(1.0)	**-12.4**	(1.7)	54.4	(1.4)	59.8	(1.0)	**-5.4**	(1.6)	52.1	(1.5)	51.3	(1.3)	0.8	(1.9)
Italy	52.1	(0.6)	56.2	(0.6)	**-4.2**	(0.7)	70.4	(0.6)	71.2	(0.6)	-0.8	(0.8)	57.7	(0.7)	52.9	(0.5)	**4.9**	(0.9)
Japan	85.1	(0.7)	91.6	(0.5)	**-6.5**	(0.7)	16.2	(0.7)	14.9	(0.6)	1.2	(0.9)	47.3	(1.1)	41.4	(1.1)	**5.9**	(1.5)
Korea	24.6	(1.2)	32.0	(1.2)	**-7.4**	(1.6)	56.5	(1.8)	58.5	(1.6)	-2.1	(2.4)	65.7	(1.2)	71.9	(1.1)	**-6.3**	(1.5)
Luxembourg	65.7	(1.1)	72.1	(0.9)	**-6.4**	(1.4)	77.5	(1.0)	81.6	(0.8)	**-4.1**	(1.3)	58.7	(1.0)	57.5	(0.9)	1.2	(1.3)
Mexico	38.4	(0.8)	41.4	(0.7)	**-3.0**	(0.8)	46.8	(1.0)	49.4	(0.8)	**-2.6**	(0.9)	26.9	(0.8)	23.0	(0.5)	**3.9**	(0.7)
Netherlands	87.3	(0.8)	94.8	(0.6)	**-7.5**	(0.8)	88.4	(1.1)	92.6	(0.6)	**-4.2**	(1.1)	50.6	(1.3)	39.7	(1.3)	**10.8**	(1.8)
New Zealand	54.5	(1.1)	66.9	(0.9)	**-12.4**	(1.5)	53.4	(1.3)	60.6	(1.0)	**-7.2**	(1.4)	26.7	(1.0)	27.9	(1.0)	-1.2	(1.4)
Norway	65.3	(1.2)	66.3	(1.3)	-1.1	(1.8)	84.6	(0.8)	88.2	(0.8)	**-3.6**	(1.2)	53.7	(1.3)	35.9	(1.1)	**17.9**	(1.4)
Poland	56.0	(1.2)	53.3	(1.2)	2.7	(1.7)	79.1	(1.1)	78.7	(1.1)	0.4	(1.3)	74.5	(1.0)	74.1	(1.0)	0.4	(1.3)
Portugal	66.3	(1.0)	68.0	(0.9)	-1.7	(1.4)	79.5	(1.0)	80.5	(0.8)	-1.0	(1.1)	52.9	(1.1)	35.2	(1.1)	**17.7**	(1.5)
Slovak Republic	64.8	(1.2)	68.3	(1.1)	**-3.5**	(1.7)	73.6	(1.1)	77.4	(0.9)	**-3.8**	(1.4)	36.4	(1.2)	35.3	(1.3)	1.1	(1.9)
Slovenia	68.0	(1.2)	72.9	(1.0)	**-4.8**	(1.7)	80.9	(1.0)	85.5	(0.9)	**-4.6**	(1.3)	62.6	(1.0)	55.0	(1.2)	**7.6**	(1.4)
Spain	54.3	(0.9)	55.8	(0.9)	-1.6	(1.3)	75.1	(0.7)	80.0	(0.7)	**-4.9**	(1.0)	44.3	(0.8)	25.7	(0.7)	**18.6**	(1.1)
Sweden	57.0	(1.1)	62.1	(1.2)	**-5.1**	(1.5)	85.3	(0.9)	84.1	(1.0)	1.2	(1.1)	43.7	(1.0)	29.0	(1.2)	**14.7**	(1.5)
Switzerland	67.2	(1.0)	72.9	(1.0)	**-5.7**	(1.4)	76.8	(0.9)	80.5	(0.7)	**-3.7**	(1.1)	53.8	(1.0)	50.3	(0.9)	**3.5**	(1.4)
Turkey	53.1	(1.3)	48.2	(1.3)	4.8	(1.5)	65.8	(1.2)	54.8	(1.4)	**11.0**	(1.5)	56.7	(1.1)	45.8	(1.3)	**10.9**	(1.5)
United Kingdom	71.2	(0.9)	78.2	(0.9)	**-7.0**	(1.2)	81.8	(0.8)	85.1	(0.8)	**-3.3**	(1.1)	46.9	(1.1)	40.6	(1.0)	**6.4**	(1.5)
United States	51.4	(1.1)	63.8	(1.1)	**-12.4**	(1.4)	60.5	(1.3)	68.7	(1.1)	**-8.2**	(1.4)	35.7	(1.3)	35.7	(1.0)	0.0	(1.3)
OECD average	61.2	(0.2)	66.2	(0.2)	**-5.0**	(0.2)	71.8	(0.2)	74.7	(0.2)	**-2.9**	(0.2)	48.8	(0.2)	42.5	(0.2)	**6.3**	(0.3)
Partners																		
Albania	44.1	(1.5)	26.4	(2.0)	**17.7**	(2.0)	53.6	(1.7)	27.5	(1.9)	**26.1**	(1.9)	25.3	(1.0)	16.2	(1.1)	**9.1**	(1.4)
Argentina	45.2	(1.5)	44.0	(2.1)	1.2	(2.1)	59.9	(1.7)	57.6	(2.3)	2.3	(2.0)	32.7	(1.4)	23.4	(1.0)	**9.3**	(1.2)
Azerbaijan	21.4	(1.4)	11.0	(1.1)	**10.5**	(1.4)	24.8	(1.4)	11.0	(1.0)	**13.8**	(1.3)	25.1	(1.3)	16.7	(1.3)	**8.3**	(1.7)
Brazil	38.6	(1.1)	42.6	(0.9)	**-4.0**	(1.2)	55.0	(1.1)	57.2	(1.0)	-2.3	(1.1)	40.5	(1.0)	36.0	(1.0)	**4.5**	(1.0)
Bulgaria	51.3	(1.3)	53.5	(1.4)	-2.2	(1.8)	82.9	(1.5)	87.0	(1.0)	**-4.1**	(1.6)	52.7	(1.8)	53.8	(1.4)	-1.1	(2.3)
Colombia	53.4	(1.5)	56.8	(1.8)	-3.4	(2.0)	56.0	(1.7)	58.6	(1.9)	-2.5	(1.8)	29.5	(1.4)	27.5	(1.1)	1.9	(1.4)
Croatia	58.2	(1.1)	61.1	(1.2)	-3.0	(1.5)	69.6	(1.1)	71.8	(1.2)	-2.3	(1.6)	57.8	(1.0)	46.9	(1.1)	**10.9**	(1.4)
Dubai (UAE)	67.9	(1.0)	68.8	(0.9)	-0.9	(1.4)	74.1	(0.9)	71.6	(0.9)	2.5	(1.4)	47.6	(0.8)	38.4	(1.3)	**9.2**	(1.6)
Hong Kong-China	50.5	(1.3)	59.5	(1.4)	**-9.0**	(1.8)	82.3	(0.8)	82.9	(0.8)	-0.6	(1.1)	61.9	(1.1)	57.6	(1.0)	**4.3**	(1.4)
Indonesia	20.2	(1.2)	17.8	(1.3)	2.3	(1.5)	15.0	(1.4)	12.3	(1.4)	2.7	(1.5)	24.9	(1.6)	19.6	(1.5)	**5.4**	(1.5)
Jordan	30.3	(1.4)	25.4	(1.6)	4.9	(2.3)	33.6	(1.4)	23.3	(1.4)	**10.3**	(2.1)	30.8	(1.2)	24.9	(1.2)	**5.9**	(1.8)
Kazakhstan	28.9	(1.5)	30.4	(1.5)	-1.6	(1.5)	26.5	(1.5)	26.0	(1.5)	0.6	(1.3)	27.1	(1.5)	25.1	(1.3)	2.0	(1.2)
Kyrgyzstan	15.8	(0.9)	14.4	(0.9)	1.4	(1.0)	10.6	(0.8)	6.4	(0.6)	**4.2**	(1.0)	19.0	(1.0)	15.6	(1.0)	**3.4**	(1.1)
Latvia	63.0	(1.2)	67.7	(1.2)	**-4.6**	(1.5)	70.7	(1.4)	72.6	(1.4)	-1.9	(1.8)	58.2	(1.3)	54.8	(1.5)	3.4	(2.0)
Liechtenstein	72.1	(2.8)	68.9	(4.1)	3.2	(5.0)	79.5	(2.5)	80.1	(3.0)	-0.6	(3.7)	56.2	(4.1)	57.7	(3.7)	-1.5	(5.4)
Lithuania	68.7	(1.1)	69.0	(1.1)	-0.3	(1.4)	84.6	(0.9)	84.8	(1.0)	-0.2	(1.4)	57.5	(1.1)	60.3	(1.2)	-2.8	(1.4)
Macao-China	36.3	(0.8)	45.7	(0.8)	**-9.5**	(1.1)	85.0	(0.7)	85.4	(0.6)	-0.4	(1.0)	50.6	(0.9)	48.3	(0.7)	2.3	(1.3)
Montenegro	51.0	(1.1)	45.1	(1.1)	5.9	(1.7)	57.5	(1.1)	50.1	(1.2)	**7.4**	(1.7)	53.5	(1.1)	47.1	(1.0)	**6.5**	(1.3)
Panama	39.5	(2.3)	38.5	(2.2)	1.0	(2.2)	51.8	(2.2)	54.9	(3.2)	-3.1	(2.6)	26.7	(1.7)	22.9	(1.6)	3.9	(1.7)
Peru	36.0	(1.3)	36.3	(1.5)	-0.3	(1.8)	43.2	(1.5)	42.6	(1.7)	0.7	(1.9)	25.2	(1.1)	20.9	(1.0)	**4.3**	(1.2)
Qatar	62.2	(0.7)	66.0	(0.7)	**-3.8**	(1.0)	65.2	(0.7)	69.9	(0.7)	**-4.6**	(0.9)	51.4	(0.8)	50.9	(0.7)	0.5	(1.0)
Romania	48.3	(1.6)	49.6	(1.7)	-1.4	(2.1)	62.7	(1.7)	64.1	(1.5)	-1.5	(1.8)	33.5	(1.2)	23.8	(1.0)	**9.7**	(1.3)
Russian Federation	41.1	(1.3)	39.4	(1.3)	1.7	(1.3)	61.4	(1.6)	54.9	(1.8)	**6.5**	(1.3)	39.6	(1.4)	32.7	(1.3)	**7.0**	(1.4)
Serbia	41.3	(1.4)	36.1	(1.0)	**5.2**	(1.5)	48.0	(1.0)	44.5	(1.4)	**3.6**	(1.4)	35.6	(1.2)	27.5	(1.0)	**8.1**	(1.4)
Shanghai-China	24.8	(1.0)	22.4	(1.1)	2.4	(1.4)	67.3	(1.1)	58.4	(1.2)	**8.9**	(1.6)	40.7	(1.1)	34.8	(1.3)	**5.9**	(1.4)
Singapore	59.8	(1.1)	63.9	(1.1)	**-4.2**	(1.2)	78.9	(0.8)	75.5	(0.8)	**3.4**	(1.1)	48.2	(1.1)	43.0	(1.0)	**5.2**	(1.3)
Chinese Taipei	35.4	(0.9)	35.9	(1.1)	-0.5	(1.5)	69.8	(0.9)	63.9	(1.2)	**5.9**	(1.4)	49.5	(0.9)	44.0	(1.2)	**5.5**	(1.4)
Thailand	29.8	(1.4)	26.6	(1.0)	3.2	(1.5)	34.8	(1.7)	30.4	(1.5)	4.4	(2.2)	24.6	(1.2)	21.6	(1.0)	3.0	(1.4)
Trinidad and Tobago	35.8	(1.2)	41.6	(1.3)	**-5.7**	(1.8)	36.5	(1.1)	39.9	(1.0)	**-3.4**	(1.5)	20.2	(1.0)	23.8	(0.9)	-3.6	(1.4)
Tunisia	22.9	(1.3)	15.7	(1.0)	7.2	(1.4)	33.9	(1.6)	21.5	(1.2)	**12.4**	(1.4)	26.1	(1.4)	18.4	(1.1)	**7.7**	(1.3)
Uruguay	47.1	(1.0)	53.4	(1.1)	**-6.3**	(1.5)	62.7	(1.1)	65.6	(1.1)	-2.9	(1.5)	38.8	(1.1)	35.5	(0.9)	3.2	(1.5)

Note: Values that are statistically significant are indicated in bold (see Annex A3).
StatLink ⫘ http://dx.doi.org/10.1787/888932343285

[Part 2/3]
Percentage of boys and girls doing diverse online reading activities
Percentage of boys and girls who reported that they were involved in the following online reading activities "several times a week" or "several times a day"

Table III.2.10

	Using an online dictionary or encyclopaedia (e.g. <Wikipedia®>)						Searching online information to learn about a particular topic					
	Boys		Girls		Difference (B – G)		Boys		Girls		Difference (B – G)	
	%	S.E.	%	S.E.	% dif.	S.E.	%	S.E.	%	S.E.	% dif.	S.E.
OECD												
Australia	33.6	(0.9)	33.8	(0.9)	-0.2	(1.2)	54.4	(0.8)	57.2	(0.9)	-2.7	(1.2)
Austria	36.2	(1.5)	39.0	(1.5)	-2.8	(1.8)	56.6	(1.3)	51.0	(1.4)	5.6	(1.5)
Belgium	24.5	(0.9)	22.8	(0.8)	1.7	(1.2)	37.4	(0.8)	30.2	(1.0)	7.2	(1.3)
Canada	36.5	(0.9)	35.0	(1.0)	1.5	(1.1)	50.0	(0.8)	45.9	(0.9)	4.1	(1.1)
Chile	41.2	(1.4)	42.9	(1.3)	-1.7	(1.5)	58.4	(1.2)	56.1	(1.3)	2.3	(1.4)
Czech Republic	56.0	(1.2)	54.4	(1.4)	1.6	(2.0)	64.3	(1.2)	58.7	(1.3)	5.6	(1.8)
Denmark	45.7	(1.3)	43.5	(1.1)	2.2	(1.5)	66.3	(1.3)	55.2	(1.1)	11.1	(1.6)
Estonia	51.4	(1.2)	51.9	(1.2)	-0.5	(1.5)	59.2	(1.1)	50.8	(1.1)	8.4	(1.5)
Finland	43.2	(1.1)	35.5	(1.2)	7.7	(1.4)	37.4	(1.1)	22.7	(1.1)	14.6	(1.4)
France	32.8	(1.2)	32.0	(1.1)	0.8	(1.6)	40.3	(1.1)	36.6	(1.1)	3.7	(1.7)
Germany	40.7	(1.2)	41.0	(1.3)	-0.3	(1.7)	54.2	(1.2)	49.7	(1.2)	4.5	(1.7)
Greece	29.9	(1.2)	28.3	(1.2)	1.6	(1.5)	59.9	(1.4)	49.2	(1.3)	10.7	(1.8)
Hungary	47.4	(1.4)	48.5	(1.3)	-1.1	(1.7)	57.6	(1.2)	53.4	(1.2)	4.2	(1.5)
Iceland	45.4	(1.0)	31.3	(1.0)	14.1	(1.4)	59.0	(1.1)	40.1	(1.1)	18.9	(1.7)
Ireland	22.6	(1.2)	18.2	(0.9)	4.5	(1.5)	35.0	(1.4)	29.5	(1.4)	5.5	(2.1)
Israel	40.0	(1.1)	45.6	(1.2)	-5.6	(1.6)	50.1	(1.2)	50.0	(1.2)	0.1	(1.5)
Italy	38.4	(0.7)	41.3	(0.6)	-2.9	(0.8)	52.7	(0.7)	50.9	(0.6)	1.8	(0.9)
Japan	33.0	(1.0)	32.1	(0.8)	0.9	(1.3)	48.6	(1.1)	43.5	(1.0)	5.0	(1.4)
Korea	32.4	(1.1)	37.5	(1.4)	-5.1	(1.8)	58.9	(1.4)	59.9	(1.5)	-1.0	(2.0)
Luxembourg	35.1	(0.8)	35.4	(0.9)	-0.3	(1.2)	50.9	(1.1)	41.5	(1.0)	9.4	(1.5)
Mexico	41.5	(0.7)	42.5	(0.6)	-1.0	(0.8)	54.9	(0.7)	57.6	(0.7)	-2.7	(0.8)
Netherlands	32.0	(1.6)	33.0	(1.6)	-1.0	(1.8)	50.2	(1.7)	45.6	(1.5)	4.6	(2.0)
New Zealand	29.8	(0.9)	30.4	(1.1)	-0.6	(1.2)	49.0	(1.1)	51.4	(1.0)	-2.4	(1.4)
Norway	53.7	(1.2)	53.9	(1.2)	-0.2	(1.5)	55.4	(1.1)	51.2	(1.1)	4.3	(1.6)
Poland	55.5	(1.3)	60.9	(1.2)	-5.3	(1.5)	72.7	(1.0)	72.6	(1.2)	0.2	(1.5)
Portugal	43.2	(1.2)	45.0	(1.0)	-1.7	(1.5)	61.9	(0.9)	60.0	(0.9)	1.9	(1.3)
Slovak Republic	33.6	(1.2)	32.5	(1.1)	1.1	(1.7)	54.6	(1.5)	45.5	(1.0)	9.0	(1.8)
Slovenia	36.3	(1.0)	33.0	(1.1)	3.3	(1.5)	52.7	(1.2)	45.6	(1.0)	7.2	(1.5)
Spain	44.2	(1.1)	48.7	(0.9)	-4.6	(1.3)	51.0	(0.7)	50.8	(0.8)	0.2	(1.1)
Sweden	41.6	(1.0)	37.1	(1.3)	4.5	(1.4)	54.0	(1.1)	47.1	(1.2)	6.9	(1.5)
Switzerland	35.1	(1.0)	33.3	(1.3)	1.8	(1.7)	47.8	(0.9)	42.9	(1.3)	4.9	(1.5)
Turkey	44.7	(1.1)	43.0	(1.3)	1.7	(1.5)	66.8	(1.0)	62.9	(1.2)	3.9	(1.4)
United Kingdom	40.3	(1.0)	39.4	(1.2)	0.9	(1.5)	54.3	(1.0)	54.2	(1.0)	0.1	(1.3)
United States	31.4	(1.3)	38.7	(1.2)	-7.3	(1.6)	44.8	(1.4)	48.8	(1.3)	-4.0	(2.0)
OECD average	39.1	(0.2)	38.9	(0.2)	0.2	(0.3)	53.6	(0.2)	49.1	(0.2)	4.5	(0.3)
Partners												
Albania	24.4	(1.4)	19.8	(1.2)	4.6	(1.9)	45.0	(1.5)	39.2	(1.7)	5.8	(2.0)
Argentina	33.5	(1.4)	32.3	(1.5)	1.2	(1.7)	41.9	(1.7)	35.1	(1.3)	6.7	(1.7)
Azerbaijan	22.6	(1.4)	16.2	(1.2)	6.4	(1.6)	29.7	(1.4)	19.3	(1.2)	10.4	(1.6)
Brazil	30.1	(0.9)	30.4	(0.8)	-0.3	(1.0)	37.7	(1.0)	34.6	(0.9)	3.1	(1.0)
Bulgaria	46.4	(1.9)	51.7	(1.7)	-5.4	(2.1)	55.9	(1.9)	59.4	(1.5)	-3.5	(2.0)
Colombia	50.5	(1.9)	49.6	(1.6)	0.9	(2.0)	54.9	(1.8)	51.5	(1.5)	3.4	(1.8)
Croatia	40.5	(1.3)	37.0	(1.4)	3.5	(1.6)	62.4	(1.1)	55.6	(1.2)	6.8	(1.6)
Dubai (UAE)	46.4	(1.0)	48.2	(1.1)	-1.8	(1.5)	61.2	(0.9)	62.6	(1.0)	-1.3	(1.4)
Hong Kong-China	53.5	(1.4)	52.8	(1.2)	0.7	(1.7)	44.1	(1.2)	39.5	(1.4)	4.6	(1.7)
Indonesia	13.4	(1.1)	10.5	(1.2)	2.8	(1.3)	23.6	(1.5)	20.4	(1.5)	3.2	(1.6)
Jordan	27.2	(1.2)	25.5	(1.4)	1.7	(1.9)	41.5	(1.3)	38.4	(1.5)	3.1	(2.1)
Kazakhstan	20.5	(1.2)	20.5	(1.3)	0.1	(1.2)	27.6	(1.4)	25.3	(1.3)	2.3	(1.2)
Kyrgyzstan	12.4	(0.8)	12.6	(0.8)	-0.2	(0.8)	19.0	(1.1)	16.1	(0.9)	2.9	(1.3)
Latvia	46.1	(1.4)	50.8	(1.5)	-4.7	(1.8)	47.1	(1.3)	48.5	(1.3)	-1.4	(1.7)
Liechtenstein	38.4	(3.5)	30.7	(3.7)	7.7	(5.4)	53.9	(3.6)	36.9	(3.2)	17.0	(5.2)
Lithuania	59.8	(1.3)	63.7	(1.1)	-3.9	(1.4)	73.0	(1.1)	68.9	(1.1)	4.1	(1.3)
Macao-China	36.5	(1.0)	34.8	(0.8)	1.7	(1.2)	27.8	(0.8)	26.6	(0.8)	1.3	(1.3)
Montenegro	39.0	(1.2)	37.6	(1.0)	1.4	(1.6)	55.0	(1.1)	48.3	(1.0)	6.8	(1.6)
Panama	36.5	(2.2)	38.9	(3.3)	-2.3	(3.2)	47.7	(2.7)	49.1	(2.9)	-1.4	(2.5)
Peru	35.9	(1.4)	37.0	(1.6)	-1.1	(1.6)	48.8	(1.4)	52.7	(1.4)	-4.0	(1.6)
Qatar	46.6	(0.7)	50.1	(0.7)	-3.5	(1.1)	59.5	(0.8)	66.2	(0.7)	-6.8	(1.1)
Romania	35.9	(1.3)	37.5	(1.4)	-1.5	(1.7)	53.0	(1.5)	51.6	(1.3)	1.4	(1.7)
Russian Federation	28.3	(1.2)	27.9	(1.3)	0.5	(1.1)	40.6	(1.7)	34.8	(1.5)	5.8	(1.6)
Serbia	30.0	(1.1)	26.5	(1.1)	3.5	(1.4)	45.2	(1.2)	38.1	(1.2)	7.1	(1.4)
Shanghai-China	37.7	(1.3)	40.5	(1.2)	-2.8	(1.5)	32.6	(0.9)	32.7	(1.0)	-0.1	(1.2)
Singapore	48.1	(1.0)	47.2	(1.1)	0.9	(1.4)	54.2	(1.0)	47.0	(1.0)	7.2	(1.3)
Chinese Taipei	21.6	(0.8)	19.8	(0.9)	1.8	(1.2)	33.4	(1.0)	30.8	(1.2)	2.6	(1.6)
Thailand	18.0	(1.0)	16.1	(0.9)	2.0	(1.0)	33.8	(1.4)	35.0	(1.2)	-1.2	(1.8)
Trinidad and Tobago	25.7	(0.9)	30.9	(1.1)	-5.2	(1.4)	38.5	(1.1)	44.8	(1.0)	-6.3	(1.5)
Tunisia	20.9	(1.3)	19.1	(0.8)	1.7	(1.2)	34.1	(1.5)	31.9	(1.2)	2.2	(1.5)
Uruguay	46.3	(1.3)	49.9	(1.2)	-3.6	(1.5)	56.4	(1.2)	59.5	(1.1)	-3.1	(1.4)

Note: Values that are statistically significant are indicated in bold (see Annex A3).
StatLink ᴍᴸᴾ http://dx.doi.org/10.1787/888932343285

[Part 3/3]
Percentage of boys and girls doing diverse online reading activities
Percentage of boys and girls who reported that they were involved in the following online reading activities "several times a week" or "several times a day"

Table III.2.10

		Taking part in online group discussions or forums					Searching for practical information online (e.g. schedules, events, tips, recipes)					
		Boys		Girls		Difference (B – G)		Boys		Girls		Difference (B – G)
		%	S.E.	%	S.E.	% dif.	S.E.	%	S.E.	%	S.E.	% dif.	S.E.
OECD	Australia	20.4	(0.6)	13.7	(0.6)	6.7	(0.8)	33.7	(0.7)	30.6	(0.8)	3.1	(1.1)
	Austria	19.9	(1.0)	7.3	(0.5)	12.5	(1.1)	40.3	(1.2)	35.7	(1.4)	4.7	(1.9)
	Belgium	20.2	(0.7)	11.7	(0.6)	8.5	(0.8)	28.6	(0.9)	26.2	(0.9)	2.4	(1.3)
	Canada	20.1	(0.7)	11.7	(0.5)	8.4	(0.8)	36.2	(0.8)	32.8	(0.8)	3.5	(1.0)
	Chile	18.0	(1.0)	12.6	(0.7)	5.4	(1.1)	32.0	(0.9)	29.5	(1.2)	2.6	(1.4)
	Czech Republic	36.5	(0.9)	24.1	(1.0)	12.4	(1.4)	54.9	(1.2)	55.4	(1.1)	-0.6	(1.7)
	Denmark	19.3	(1.0)	9.6	(0.6)	9.7	(1.2)	36.1	(1.1)	31.2	(0.9)	4.9	(1.5)
	Estonia	44.7	(1.1)	21.2	(1.0)	23.5	(1.5)	49.6	(1.1)	52.5	(1.3)	-2.9	(1.7)
	Finland	30.7	(0.9)	21.6	(0.8)	9.1	(1.2)	28.8	(1.0)	28.0	(1.0)	0.8	(1.4)
	France	14.0	(0.7)	5.2	(0.5)	8.8	(0.9)	42.6	(1.3)	41.2	(1.4)	1.3	(1.9)
	Germany	21.5	(0.8)	10.0	(0.7)	11.5	(1.0)	36.9	(1.1)	35.4	(1.2)	1.5	(1.4)
	Greece	27.4	(1.0)	15.5	(0.8)	11.9	(1.3)	44.4	(1.4)	32.0	(1.0)	12.4	(1.7)
	Hungary	46.8	(1.2)	34.4	(1.2)	12.3	(1.8)	53.4	(1.3)	53.5	(1.5)	-0.1	(2.0)
	Iceland	40.8	(1.2)	25.4	(1.1)	15.4	(1.7)	40.7	(1.0)	32.7	(1.2)	8.0	(1.6)
	Ireland	17.2	(1.1)	12.5	(0.9)	4.7	(1.4)	27.1	(1.1)	21.0	(0.9)	6.1	(1.4)
	Israel	31.3	(1.3)	17.0	(0.7)	14.2	(1.4)	36.1	(1.1)	40.9	(1.1)	-4.8	(1.6)
	Italy	23.6	(0.5)	15.8	(0.4)	7.8	(0.6)	32.4	(0.5)	30.1	(0.5)	2.3	(0.7)
	Japan	3.9	(0.4)	1.6	(0.3)	2.2	(0.5)	18.2	(0.9)	25.0	(0.8)	-6.8	(1.1)
	Korea	7.2	(0.6)	5.0	(0.5)	2.2	(0.8)	46.6	(1.2)	50.1	(1.2)	-3.5	(1.6)
	Luxembourg	23.6	(0.9)	11.7	(0.7)	11.9	(1.3)	34.6	(1.0)	27.9	(1.0)	6.8	(1.4)
	Mexico	11.1	(0.4)	8.3	(0.3)	2.8	(0.5)	26.0	(0.6)	21.7	(0.6)	4.2	(0.8)
	Netherlands	20.9	(1.1)	11.1	(0.8)	9.8	(1.2)	25.3	(1.2)	21.1	(1.2)	4.1	(1.5)
	New Zealand	19.5	(0.9)	13.4	(0.7)	6.1	(1.1)	29.7	(1.0)	27.3	(0.9)	2.4	(1.2)
	Norway	23.6	(0.9)	20.5	(1.1)	3.1	(1.4)	31.8	(1.2)	36.5	(1.2)	-4.7	(1.5)
	Poland	35.1	(1.1)	20.5	(0.9)	14.6	(1.3)	50.2	(1.1)	45.4	(1.3)	4.8	(1.6)
	Portugal	27.0	(0.9)	11.0	(0.6)	16.0	(1.1)	37.1	(1.1)	34.0	(0.9)	3.2	(1.2)
	Slovak Republic	43.6	(1.3)	27.6	(1.1)	16.0	(1.6)	37.7	(1.1)	31.5	(1.0)	6.2	(1.3)
	Slovenia	35.9	(0.9)	22.6	(0.9)	13.4	(1.4)	39.3	(1.1)	36.0	(1.0)	3.2	(1.4)
	Spain	15.7	(0.6)	7.8	(0.4)	7.9	(0.7)	30.8	(0.8)	28.3	(0.8)	2.5	(1.1)
	Sweden	27.4	(1.0)	10.8	(0.6)	16.5	(1.2)	37.3	(1.1)	37.3	(1.1)	0.0	(1.6)
	Switzerland	18.6	(0.7)	9.0	(0.5)	9.6	(0.9)	40.5	(1.0)	40.9	(1.3)	-0.5	(1.7)
	Turkey	28.7	(1.0)	17.7	(1.0)	11.0	(1.4)	31.7	(1.0)	31.9	(1.1)	-0.2	(1.4)
	United Kingdom	23.6	(0.8)	17.7	(0.7)	5.9	(1.0)	34.8	(0.9)	31.2	(0.8)	3.6	(1.1)
	United States	16.1	(0.8)	13.1	(0.7)	2.9	(1.1)	35.3	(1.0)	38.5	(1.3)	-3.2	(1.6)
	OECD average	24.5	(0.2)	14.7	(0.1)	9.8	(0.2)	36.5	(0.2)	34.5	(0.2)	2.0	(0.2)
Partners	Albania	29.4	(1.5)	14.6	(0.9)	14.8	(1.8)	38.4	(1.5)	26.8	(1.4)	11.6	(2.1)
	Argentina	17.4	(1.1)	8.6	(0.6)	8.8	(1.1)	27.8	(1.2)	23.3	(1.0)	4.5	(1.3)
	Azerbaijan	17.9	(1.0)	10.0	(0.8)	7.9	(1.3)	25.5	(1.3)	15.2	(1.1)	10.3	(1.5)
	Brazil	14.0	(0.7)	8.2	(0.5)	5.9	(0.8)	29.2	(0.8)	28.1	(0.8)	1.1	(1.0)
	Bulgaria	41.9	(1.9)	32.1	(1.4)	9.8	(2.2)	41.2	(1.8)	42.7	(1.3)	-1.6	(2.0)
	Colombia	11.2	(0.9)	9.2	(0.7)	2.1	(1.1)	30.5	(1.1)	26.6	(1.0)	3.9	(1.3)
	Croatia	26.5	(0.9)	14.1	(0.8)	12.5	(1.2)	35.9	(1.0)	29.4	(1.0)	6.4	(1.3)
	Dubai (UAE)	33.3	(0.9)	23.8	(0.9)	9.4	(1.4)	43.0	(1.0)	41.2	(1.1)	1.7	(1.5)
	Hong Kong-China	59.5	(1.0)	43.7	(1.0)	15.8	(1.3)	45.8	(1.1)	42.5	(1.2)	3.2	(1.7)
	Indonesia	11.0	(0.9)	8.9	(1.0)	2.1	(1.1)	20.6	(1.3)	16.4	(1.5)	4.2	(1.6)
	Jordan	17.5	(0.9)	9.5	(0.7)	8.0	(1.2)	30.5	(1.2)	26.4	(1.3)	4.1	(1.8)
	Kazakhstan	14.6	(1.0)	11.8	(0.8)	2.8	(1.0)	17.0	(1.0)	13.7	(1.0)	3.4	(1.0)
	Kyrgyzstan	9.3	(0.7)	6.3	(0.5)	3.0	(0.8)	15.2	(0.8)	15.6	(0.8)	-0.5	(1.0)
	Latvia	43.8	(1.3)	35.2	(1.3)	8.6	(1.7)	41.8	(1.4)	41.7	(1.6)	0.2	(2.0)
	Liechtenstein	20.5	(3.2)	3.9	(1.6)	16.7	(3.8)	39.8	(3.4)	20.7	(3.0)	19.1	(5.1)
	Lithuania	52.1	(1.1)	45.8	(1.0)	6.3	(1.5)	42.8	(1.1)	46.6	(1.1)	-3.8	(1.3)
	Macao-China	33.9	(0.8)	28.1	(0.8)	5.7	(1.1)	35.4	(0.8)	31.1	(0.8)	4.2	(1.1)
	Montenegro	32.5	(1.1)	20.9	(1.1)	11.6	(1.4)	31.4	(1.6)	21.5	(0.9)	10.0	(1.8)
	Panama	15.7	(1.7)	14.3	(1.2)	1.5	(1.7)	24.7	(1.4)	25.8	(1.5)	-1.0	(1.4)
	Peru	16.3	(0.8)	11.8	(0.6)	4.5	(1.0)	21.7	(0.9)	22.2	(1.0)	-0.4	(1.3)
	Qatar	45.1	(0.7)	38.9	(0.7)	6.3	(1.1)	40.8	(0.8)	44.9	(0.8)	-4.1	(1.2)
	Romania	42.9	(1.4)	32.2	(1.1)	10.7	(1.8)	38.9	(1.3)	36.3	(1.1)	2.6	(1.7)
	Russian Federation	21.5	(1.1)	14.5	(0.8)	7.0	(1.1)	24.1	(1.2)	17.0	(1.0)	7.1	(1.3)
	Serbia	27.5	(1.0)	18.4	(0.8)	9.1	(1.3)	44.0	(1.1)	30.8	(1.0)	13.3	(1.5)
	Shanghai-China	23.7	(1.1)	18.1	(0.9)	5.6	(1.3)	23.5	(1.1)	18.1	(0.9)	5.4	(1.3)
	Singapore	25.6	(1.0)	16.3	(0.8)	9.3	(1.3)	40.2	(0.9)	35.4	(0.9)	4.8	(1.4)
	Chinese Taipei	23.0	(0.8)	15.0	(0.8)	7.9	(1.1)	42.0	(0.8)	37.8	(0.9)	4.3	(1.3)
	Thailand	25.3	(1.2)	20.1	(0.9)	5.2	(1.5)	24.5	(1.3)	22.2	(1.0)	2.2	(1.3)
	Trinidad and Tobago	17.7	(0.9)	14.1	(0.8)	3.6	(1.2)	25.8	(1.0)	27.4	(0.9)	-1.6	(1.4)
	Tunisia	19.0	(1.3)	12.0	(0.8)	7.0	(1.3)	24.4	(1.3)	22.1	(1.0)	2.2	(1.6)
	Uruguay	20.8	(0.8)	15.4	(0.8)	5.4	(1.1)	26.6	(0.9)	21.7	(0.8)	4.9	(1.1)

Note: Values that are statistically significant are indicated in bold (see Annex A3).
StatLink ᵃˢᵖ http://dx.doi.org/10.1787/888932343285

[Part 1/1]

Table III.2.11 Percentage of students according to what they enjoy about reading

Percentage of students who report "agree" or "strongly agree" on the following reading activities

		Percentage of students according to what they enjoy about reading																					
		I read only if I have to		Reading is one of my favourite hobbies		I like talking about books with other people		I find it hard to finish books		I feel happy if I receive a book as a present		For me, reading is a waste of time		I enjoy going to a bookstore or a library		I read only to get information that I need		I cannot sit still and read for more than a few minutes		I like to express my opinions about books I have read		I like to exchange books with my friends	
		%	S.E.	%	S.E.	%	S.E.	%	S.E.	%	S.E.	%	S.E.	%	S.E.	%	S.E.	%	S.E.	%	S.E.	%	S.E.
OECD	Australia	40.9	(0.6)	35.5	(0.8)	38.8	(0.7)	32.7	(0.5)	50.6	(0.6)	25.9	(0.5)	46.6	(0.7)	42.3	(0.8)	23.6	(0.5)	46.1	(0.7)	32.1	(0.7)
	Austria	49.1	(0.9)	27.2	(0.8)	26.8	(0.9)	32.7	(0.9)	42.2	(1.0)	35.1	(0.7)	29.4	(0.9)	52.7	(1.1)	21.7	(0.8)	58.5	(0.9)	28.0	(1.0)
	Belgium	44.5	(0.7)	24.1	(0.6)	28.9	(0.7)	34.5	(0.8)	36.9	(0.7)	34.6	(0.8)	36.7	(0.7)	47.3	(0.7)	28.3	(0.7)	56.1	(0.8)	32.8	(0.7)
	Canada	37.3	(0.5)	38.6	(0.5)	43.2	(0.5)	27.4	(0.5)	49.6	(0.7)	22.1	(0.5)	54.0	(0.6)	38.7	(0.6)	22.2	(0.5)	53.9	(0.5)	40.4	(0.5)
	Chile	34.8	(0.8)	32.1	(0.6)	47.4	(0.8)	46.5	(0.8)	38.3	(0.9)	17.8	(0.6)	33.7	(0.8)	64.8	(0.8)	33.0	(0.8)	66.1	(0.8)	32.9	(0.7)
	Czech Republic	40.8	(0.8)	33.4	(0.7)	34.9	(0.9)	34.3	(0.7)	43.8	(0.9)	32.5	(0.8)	34.5	(0.8)	51.8	(0.9)	32.5	(0.8)	48.5	(0.9)	29.3	(0.8)
	Denmark	45.4	(1.0)	24.2	(0.7)	36.7	(1.0)	25.2	(0.8)	42.8	(1.0)	25.9	(0.9)	34.7	(0.9)	47.5	(0.9)	19.6	(0.7)	73.6	(0.8)	18.6	(0.8)
	Estonia	44.3	(0.9)	28.7	(0.8)	35.2	(0.9)	30.6	(0.8)	40.7	(1.0)	22.7	(0.8)	41.4	(0.8)	52.0	(1.0)	18.1	(0.6)	59.8	(1.1)	27.5	(0.9)
	Finland	34.7	(0.8)	34.0	(0.8)	34.1	(0.9)	27.7	(0.7)	52.1	(0.8)	27.3	(0.8)	47.6	(0.9)	36.3	(0.8)	14.5	(0.6)	58.3	(0.8)	26.4	(0.7)
	France	33.9	(1.0)	31.2	(1.0)	42.6	(1.2)	39.2	(1.0)	41.5	(1.0)	25.8	(1.0)	47.2	(1.1)	43.5	(1.2)	26.5	(0.9)	64.4	(1.0)	45.7	(0.9)
	Germany	39.1	(0.8)	32.6	(0.8)	32.2	(0.8)	27.5	(0.7)	48.5	(0.8)	29.5	(0.7)	34.5	(0.8)	44.6	(0.8)	17.0	(0.5)	60.5	(0.7)	33.4	(0.7)
	Greece	42.8	(1.1)	29.1	(0.8)	37.7	(1.0)	38.6	(0.9)	42.7	(1.0)	13.0	(0.6)	45.5	(1.1)	39.2	(1.2)	30.9	(0.8)	75.0	(0.8)	49.8	(1.1)
	Hungary	32.5	(1.1)	34.8	(1.0)	38.8	(1.0)	20.9	(0.7)	55.4	(1.1)	22.2	(0.8)	46.5	(1.0)	47.4	(0.9)	19.5	(0.9)	64.7	(1.0)	37.0	(1.0)
	Iceland	47.8	(0.9)	24.0	(0.8)	33.0	(0.8)	29.8	(0.8)	60.8	(0.8)	25.0	(0.7)	40.5	(0.8)	41.6	(0.8)	25.7	(0.7)	47.6	(0.9)	27.0	(0.7)
	Ireland	39.2	(1.0)	31.7	(0.9)	34.7	(1.1)	40.4	(1.0)	45.8	(0.9)	24.1	(0.9)	40.0	(0.9)	44.9	(1.1)	31.6	(0.9)	44.2	(1.2)	32.5	(1.2)
	Israel	38.8	(0.9)	40.7	(1.0)	41.0	(0.9)	31.4	(0.7)	47.0	(1.0)	23.6	(0.8)	42.2	(1.0)	47.0	(1.0)	25.9	(0.8)	58.8	(0.8)	41.7	(0.9)
	Italy	28.8	(0.5)	39.8	(0.5)	44.2	(0.5)	38.4	(0.4)	48.8	(0.5)	21.5	(0.5)	39.4	(0.6)	47.8	(0.5)	30.4	(0.5)	68.9	(0.5)	47.4	(0.5)
	Japan	47.5	(0.8)	42.0	(0.9)	43.6	(0.8)	28.4	(0.7)	45.6	(0.8)	15.2	(0.6)	66.5	(0.7)	24.2	(0.7)	20.6	(0.6)	27.5	(0.7)	39.3	(0.8)
	Korea	54.8	(0.9)	39.1	(0.8)	38.5	(0.8)	32.4	(0.8)	55.2	(1.0)	9.5	(0.5)	42.2	(1.0)	31.0	(0.8)	15.9	(0.6)	41.6	(0.9)	48.5	(0.9)
	Luxembourg	47.7	(0.8)	26.2	(0.8)	25.6	(0.7)	29.9	(0.8)	36.9	(0.7)	33.4	(0.8)	29.4	(0.7)	49.0	(0.7)	25.9	(0.6)	57.7	(0.8)	28.7	(0.7)
	Mexico	41.1	(0.6)	49.3	(0.5)	48.2	(0.4)	39.2	(0.4)	57.3	(0.5)	12.2	(0.3)	46.9	(0.5)	55.4	(0.5)	23.9	(0.4)	64.0	(0.4)	49.0	(0.4)
	Netherlands	52.7	(1.4)	19.1	(1.0)	18.9	(0.9)	25.6	(0.8)	40.4	(1.2)	33.9	(1.3)	28.6	(0.9)	49.3	(1.4)	26.7	(1.1)	40.4	(1.1)	25.0	(1.1)
	New Zealand	38.0	(0.8)	37.5	(0.8)	42.7	(0.9)	30.6	(0.7)	56.5	(0.8)	18.1	(0.7)	54.4	(0.9)	39.7	(0.9)	18.3	(0.7)	48.8	(0.9)	38.3	(0.9)
	Norway	44.4	(0.9)	22.0	(0.7)	28.1	(0.8)	28.8	(0.7)	40.4	(0.9)	29.9	(0.8)	31.2	(0.7)	50.3	(0.9)	24.9	(0.7)	62.0	(0.9)	24.0	(0.7)
	Poland	44.2	(0.8)	37.1	(0.9)	38.9	(0.7)	34.5	(0.7)	41.1	(0.9)	26.8	(0.8)	42.7	(1.0)	53.6	(0.7)	29.9	(0.8)	53.9	(0.8)	36.8	(0.9)
	Portugal	22.0	(0.6)	35.6	(0.8)	48.6	(0.8)	29.4	(0.7)	52.9	(0.6)	18.8	(0.5)	54.0	(0.8)	42.9	(0.9)	31.3	(0.7)	70.6	(0.7)	50.0	(0.7)
	Slovak Republic	41.6	(0.9)	33.1	(0.8)	30.7	(0.9)	35.0	(0.8)	46.4	(0.9)	29.6	(0.8)	33.7	(0.8)	56.4	(0.9)	32.9	(0.8)	47.9	(0.8)	32.7	(0.8)
	Slovenia	52.8	(0.7)	23.2	(0.6)	34.5	(0.8)	34.1	(0.7)	37.5	(0.7)	33.4	(0.7)	35.0	(0.6)	53.1	(0.8)	27.9	(0.7)	54.9	(0.7)	33.0	(0.8)
	Spain	43.7	(0.7)	33.7	(0.5)	42.4	(0.7)	44.2	(0.6)	35.3	(0.5)	17.7	(0.6)	30.4	(0.6)	46.2	(0.7)	22.8	(0.5)	68.5	(0.7)	43.9	(0.5)
	Sweden	39.4	(0.7)	27.2	(0.7)	33.6	(0.9)	23.9	(0.7)	35.6	(0.9)	27.7	(0.7)	35.2	(0.9)	41.6	(0.9)	20.6	(0.7)	48.5	(1.0)	25.7	(0.7)
	Switzerland	43.4	(1.0)	29.5	(0.6)	31.2	(0.8)	31.7	(0.7)	45.0	(0.8)	31.3	(0.8)	39.6	(0.9)	45.8	(0.8)	21.6	(0.6)	57.6	(0.9)	32.3	(1.0)
	Turkey	21.1	(0.7)	65.4	(0.8)	67.4	(0.9)	32.7	(0.8)	77.2	(0.8)	7.8	(0.5)	74.6	(0.8)	31.5	(0.9)	30.2	(0.7)	84.8	(0.7)	76.8	(0.8)
	United Kingdom	41.8	(0.8)	27.1	(0.6)	35.0	(0.9)	37.1	(0.8)	49.1	(0.7)	23.4	(0.7)	34.2	(0.8)	48.2	(0.8)	28.0	(0.7)	44.0	(0.9)	29.0	(0.9)
	United States	49.7	(1.0)	30.5	(1.1)	40.9	(1.0)	31.0	(1.0)	37.9	(1.0)	25.8	(0.9)	53.8	(1.0)	47.1	(1.1)	28.3	(0.9)	51.1	(1.0)	34.4	(0.9)
	OECD average	41.2	(0.1)	32.9	(0.1)	37.6	(0.1)	32.5	(0.1)	46.4	(0.1)	24.2	(0.1)	42.0	(0.1)	45.7	(0.2)	25.0	(0.1)	56.7	(0.1)	36.2	(0.1)
Partners	Albania	36.5	(1.0)	67.7	(0.9)	72.6	(0.8)	22.4	(0.8)	84.8	(0.7)	6.3	(0.5)	81.3	(0.7)	37.4	(1.1)	21.5	(0.7)	88.9	(0.7)	84.1	(0.9)
	Argentina	57.7	(1.0)	32.2	(0.9)	38.8	(1.0)	55.1	(1.0)	46.3	(1.1)	19.6	(0.8)	36.2	(1.0)	66.4	(1.0)	35.1	(1.0)	61.2	(1.0)	35.2	(1.3)
	Azerbaijan	40.4	(1.2)	76.6	(1.1)	68.0	(1.0)	49.9	(1.1)	74.1	(1.0)	14.6	(0.6)	74.3	(1.0)	52.0	(1.1)	26.7	(0.9)	80.5	(0.7)	61.4	(1.1)
	Brazil	15.6	(0.5)	48.1	(0.8)	51.3	(0.7)	35.3	(0.6)	51.4	(0.6)	7.6	(0.3)	53.4	(0.6)	40.7	(0.8)	30.4	(0.6)	68.9	(0.7)	45.2	(0.7)
	Bulgaria	47.6	(1.3)	36.3	(1.3)	36.3	(1.4)	31.0	(0.8)	43.0	(1.4)	21.6	(1.2)	47.6	(1.3)	56.8	(1.4)	30.9	(1.0)	59.8	(1.2)	43.2	(1.4)
	Colombia	36.1	(0.9)	45.2	(1.2)	44.1	(1.1)	50.6	(0.8)	61.3	(1.2)	8.7	(0.5)	56.6	(1.2)	48.8	(1.0)	43.8	(1.0)	75.1	(0.7)	49.4	(1.1)
	Croatia	46.3	(1.0)	21.6	(0.7)	33.7	(1.0)	35.8	(0.9)	40.5	(0.9)	26.5	(0.9)	39.2	(1.2)	58.0	(1.0)	24.8	(0.8)	54.9	(1.0)	34.3	(0.9)
	Dubai (UAE)	43.6	(0.6)	52.2	(0.8)	53.1	(0.7)	35.7	(0.7)	59.0	(0.8)	15.1	(0.5)	63.1	(0.6)	48.1	(0.7)	28.8	(0.7)	68.5	(0.6)	61.7	(0.6)
	Hong Kong-China	42.9	(0.9)	64.9	(0.8)	60.6	(0.8)	23.2	(0.6)	58.5	(1.0)	9.2	(0.4)	64.8	(0.8)	37.7	(0.8)	16.4	(0.5)	60.0	(0.7)	55.2	(0.9)
	Indonesia	32.4	(1.0)	77.3	(0.9)	73.6	(0.9)	38.2	(0.9)	85.4	(0.7)	4.3	(0.4)	80.1	(0.9)	52.8	(1.0)	28.4	(0.7)	73.6	(0.9)	81.7	(0.7)
	Jordan	25.2	(0.8)	67.2	(0.8)	58.0	(0.8)	38.1	(0.7)	70.0	(0.9)	18.8	(0.6)	63.7	(0.9)	57.8	(1.0)	31.3	(0.8)	76.7	(0.6)	69.4	(0.8)
	Kazakhstan	19.2	(0.7)	78.4	(0.9)	68.6	(1.0)	22.5	(0.7)	71.7	(1.0)	9.6	(0.4)	76.5	(0.8)	51.8	(0.9)	12.0	(0.6)	80.9	(0.8)	70.1	(1.0)
	Kyrgyzstan	48.3	(1.0)	80.1	(0.8)	66.0	(1.0)	36.6	(0.7)	74.9	(1.0)	17.0	(0.8)	74.8	(0.8)	60.0	(0.9)	25.1	(0.8)	79.3	(0.8)	72.7	(0.8)
	Latvia	42.7	(1.0)	29.4	(0.9)	38.9	(1.1)	31.3	(0.8)	41.1	(1.1)	26.6	(1.0)	43.6	(1.2)	54.6	(1.1)	23.3	(0.8)	64.8	(1.0)	33.2	(0.9)
	Liechtenstein	51.0	(2.4)	21.2	(2.2)	21.1	(2.1)	29.3	(2.1)	40.4	(2.6)	38.9	(2.6)	28.8	(2.2)	51.6	(2.6)	21.2	(2.3)	53.5	(2.9)	23.3	(2.1)
	Lithuania	49.8	(0.9)	39.1	(0.8)	41.5	(0.8)	35.9	(0.8)	53.1	(0.9)	23.4	(0.7)	47.6	(0.8)	55.5	(0.8)	24.1	(0.9)	54.4	(0.8)	41.2	(0.9)
	Macao-China	49.9	(0.6)	49.6	(0.6)	50.9	(0.7)	34.2	(0.6)	46.0	(0.6)	13.6	(0.4)	52.2	(0.5)	57.0	(0.6)	15.9	(0.4)	53.4	(0.6)	39.2	(0.6)
	Montenegro	37.6	(0.7)	40.2	(0.9)	55.9	(0.9)	30.8	(0.9)	59.6	(0.9)	14.2	(0.4)	43.5	(0.8)	49.6	(0.9)	23.1	(0.6)	74.4	(0.6)	61.2	(0.7)
	Panama	43.3	(1.3)	53.3	(1.1)	50.6	(1.5)	41.8	(1.2)	61.7	(1.5)	13.8	(1.0)	44.8	(1.4)	51.3	(1.4)	30.3	(1.1)	67.7	(1.3)	50.2	(1.4)
	Peru	40.5	(0.8)	62.2	(0.9)	64.0	(0.9)	38.1	(0.8)	70.6	(0.9)	9.7	(0.5)	58.9	(0.9)	50.1	(0.9)	23.8	(0.7)	79.5	(0.7)	62.5	(0.8)
	Qatar	42.8	(0.5)	57.6	(0.5)	48.8	(0.6)	35.9	(0.5)	57.4	(0.5)	22.7	(0.4)	59.6	(0.6)	51.4	(0.5)	32.3	(0.5)	66.2	(0.5)	57.8	(0.5)
	Romania	31.8	(1.1)	40.2	(1.1)	47.7	(1.0)	39.6	(1.1)	65.0	(1.1)	23.3	(0.8)	55.3	(1.2)	60.6	(1.2)	28.1	(0.8)	65.9	(1.1)	53.0	(1.2)
	Russian Federation	38.0	(0.9)	37.9	(1.0)	41.3	(1.0)	28.8	(0.7)	43.0	(1.0)	18.1	(0.7)	44.9	(1.0)	59.5	(0.9)	13.6	(0.6)	66.7	(1.0)	43.3	(1.0)
	Serbia	45.2	(0.9)	29.4	(0.9)	41.6	(0.9)	31.9	(0.8)	52.5	(0.9)	20.7	(0.7)	35.4	(1.0)	53.5	(0.9)	21.1	(0.7)	64.5	(0.9)	48.6	(0.9)
	Shanghai-China	11.0	(0.5)	69.9	(0.8)	64.6	(0.9)	23.2	(0.7)	69.1	(0.7)	6.3	(0.4)	68.8	(0.8)	34.8	(0.9)	8.1	(0.4)	69.5	(0.8)	70.7	(0.8)
	Singapore	35.3	(0.6)	53.6	(0.8)	48.1	(0.6)	34.9	(0.6)	57.1	(0.6)	13.2	(0.4)	71.7	(0.6)	40.9	(0.7)	18.6	(0.6)	54.0	(0.7)	45.4	(0.7)
	Chinese Taipei	50.7	(1.0)	64.0	(0.9)	65.1	(0.9)	23.7	(0.8)	67.9	(0.7)	10.3	(0.5)	65.0	(1.0)	44.7	(1.0)	17.7	(0.7)	60.2	(0.9)	57.7	(1.0)
	Thailand	24.3	(0.7)	82.0	(0.6)	66.9	(0.6)	31.5	(0.8)	73.4	(0.7)	9.3	(0.5)	83.8	(0.6)	33.3	(0.8)	20.2	(0.6)	77.8	(0.7)	75.0	(0.7)
	Trinidad and Tobago	36.6	(0.8)	45.4	(0.8)	52.0	(0.9)	40.9	(0.9)	52.4	(0.9)	9.7	(0.5)	64.6	(0.7)	45.5	(0.9)	30.9	(0.8)	62.5	(0.8)	50.2	(0.8)
	Tunisia	32.4	(1.0)	57.3	(1.1)	56.1	(1.0)	30.8	(0.7)	65.6	(1.0)	12.9	(0.6)	61.9	(1.0)	50.5	(0.8)	26.8	(0.7)	74.5	(0.9)	67.1	(1.0)
	Uruguay	49.6	(0.9)	31.8	(0.7)	32.8	(0.9)	44.3	(0.8)	48.9	(0.9)	18.5	(0.7)	32.9	(0.8)	56.5	(0.8)	30.3	(0.8)	53.4	(0.8)	37.5	(0.8)

StatLink http://dx.doi.org/10.1787/888932343285

[Part 1/2]
Effect sizes for gender differences in engagement in reading and approaches to learning
Table III.2.12 *Results based on students' self-reports*

Effect size in favour of boys
- from 0.2 to 0.5
- from 0.5 to 0.8
- equal or greater than 0.8

Effect size in favour of girls
- from -0.2 to -0.5
- from -0.5 to -0.8
- equal or less than -0.8

	Enjoyment of reading		Diversity of reading materials		Online reading activities		Index of interpretation of literary texts		Index of use of texts containing non-continuous materials		Index of reading activities for traditional literature courses	
	Effect size	S.E.	Effect size	S.E.	Effect size	S.E.	Effect size	S.E.	Effect size	S.E.	Effect size	S.E.
OECD												
Australia	-0.60	(0.02)	-0.14	(0.02)	-0.03	(0.02)	-0.18	(0.03)	0.02	(0.03)	-0.06	(0.03)
Austria	-0.72	(0.04)	-0.10	(0.03)	0.04	(0.04)	-0.27	(0.04)	0.17	(0.04)	-0.18	(0.04)
Belgium	-0.54	(0.03)	-0.07	(0.03)	0.10	(0.03)	-0.09	(0.03)	0.01	(0.03)	-0.05	(0.03)
Canada	-0.79	(0.02)	-0.25	(0.02)	0.00	(0.02)	-0.15	(0.02)	-0.02	(0.02)	0.00	(0.02)
Chile	-0.56	(0.03)	-0.34	(0.03)	0.05	(0.03)	-0.24	(0.03)	-0.01	(0.04)	-0.07	(0.03)
Czech Republic	-0.78	(0.04)	-0.35	(0.03)	0.18	(0.04)	-0.34	(0.04)	0.00	(0.04)	-0.16	(0.04)
Denmark	-0.61	(0.03)	-0.15	(0.03)	0.21	(0.03)	-0.27	(0.03)	0.07	(0.03)	-0.08	(0.02)
Estonia	-0.90	(0.04)	-0.19	(0.04)	0.19	(0.04)	-0.28	(0.03)	-0.04	(0.04)	-0.15	(0.03)
Finland	-0.97	(0.03)	-0.23	(0.03)	0.12	(0.03)	-0.16	(0.03)	-0.02	(0.03)	-0.07	(0.03)
France	-0.48	(0.04)	0.00	(0.03)	0.03	(0.03)	-0.21	(0.03)	0.01	(0.03)	-0.09	(0.03)
Germany	-0.82	(0.03)	-0.05	(0.03)	0.09	(0.04)	-0.23	(0.03)	0.05	(0.03)	-0.09	(0.03)
Greece	-0.77	(0.04)	0.02	(0.04)	0.26	(0.04)	-0.55	(0.04)	0.24	(0.03)	-0.17	(0.04)
Hungary	-0.68	(0.05)	-0.26	(0.03)	0.10	(0.03)	-0.30	(0.03)	0.05	(0.04)	-0.19	(0.04)
Iceland	-0.64	(0.03)	-0.33	(0.03)	0.28	(0.03)	-0.12	(0.03)	0.04	(0.03)	0.07	(0.03)
Ireland	-0.45	(0.04)	-0.17	(0.04)	-0.04	(0.05)	-0.03	(0.04)	0.07	(0.04)	-0.03	(0.04)
Israel	-0.63	(0.05)	-0.44	(0.04)	-0.08	(0.04)	-0.29	(0.04)	0.01	(0.04)	-0.10	(0.04)
Italy	-0.77	(0.02)	-0.20	(0.02)	0.03	(0.02)	-0.24	(0.02)	0.18	(0.02)	-0.23	(0.02)
Japan	-0.34	(0.03)	0.02	(0.03)	-0.13	(0.03)	-0.14	(0.03)	0.07	(0.03)	0.05	(0.03)
Korea	-0.34	(0.04)	-0.09	(0.04)	-0.16	(0.04)	-0.22	(0.05)	-0.12	(0.05)	-0.21	(0.05)
Luxembourg	-0.70	(0.03)	-0.08	(0.03)	0.08	(0.03)	-0.30	(0.03)	0.07	(0.02)	-0.05	(0.03)
Mexico	-0.47	(0.02)	-0.04	(0.01)	0.00	(0.02)	-0.18	(0.02)	-0.01	(0.02)	-0.04	(0.01)
Netherlands	-0.78	(0.04)	-0.28	(0.03)	0.06	(0.04)	-0.20	(0.04)	0.14	(0.03)	-0.05	(0.03)
New Zealand	-0.65	(0.03)	-0.17	(0.03)	-0.11	(0.03)	-0.24	(0.03)	-0.07	(0.04)	-0.07	(0.03)
Norway	-0.65	(0.03)	-0.20	(0.04)	0.13	(0.04)	-0.07	(0.04)	-0.03	(0.03)	-0.01	(0.03)
Poland	-0.74	(0.03)	-0.41	(0.03)	0.13	(0.03)	-0.41	(0.03)	-0.03	(0.03)	-0.16	(0.03)
Portugal	-0.84	(0.03)	-0.10	(0.03)	0.25	(0.03)	-0.33	(0.03)	-0.03	(0.03)	-0.24	(0.03)
Slovak Republic	-0.63	(0.04)	-0.42	(0.04)	0.10	(0.03)	-0.29	(0.04)	0.14	(0.04)	-0.11	(0.04)
Slovenia	-0.75	(0.04)	-0.24	(0.03)	0.13	(0.03)	-0.37	(0.03)	-0.01	(0.03)	-0.12	(0.03)
Spain	-0.60	(0.02)	-0.02	(0.02)	0.09	(0.03)	-0.29	(0.02)	0.05	(0.03)	-0.20	(0.02)
Sweden	-0.80	(0.03)	-0.31	(0.03)	0.23	(0.03)	-0.18	(0.03)	0.02	(0.03)	0.03	(0.03)
Switzerland	-0.73	(0.03)	-0.12	(0.03)	0.06	(0.03)	-0.22	(0.03)	0.09	(0.04)	-0.10	(0.04)
Turkey	-0.75	(0.03)	-0.12	(0.03)	0.18	(0.03)	-0.49	(0.03)	-0.01	(0.04)	-0.25	(0.03)
United Kingdom	-0.53	(0.03)	-0.20	(0.03)	0.05	(0.02)	-0.16	(0.03)	0.01	(0.03)	-0.07	(0.03)
United States	-0.63	(0.03)	-0.15	(0.03)	-0.18	(0.03)	-0.15	(0.03)	0.01	(0.03)	-0.07	(0.03)
OECD average	-0.67	(0.01)	-0.18	(0.01)	0.07	(0.01)	-0.24	(0.01)	0.03	(0.01)	-0.10	(0.01)
Partners												
Albania	-0.98	(0.03)	-0.24	(0.03)	0.31	(0.05)	-0.54	(0.04)	0.01	(0.04)	-0.24	(0.04)
Argentina	-0.47	(0.04)	-0.28	(0.03)	0.18	(0.04)	-0.30	(0.04)	-0.01	(0.03)	-0.01	(0.04)
Azerbaijan	-0.32	(0.04)	-0.14	(0.04)	0.20	(0.04)	-0.17	(0.04)	0.15	(0.04)	-0.10	(0.05)
Brazil	-0.56	(0.02)	-0.34	(0.02)	0.05	(0.02)	-0.25	(0.02)	0.01	(0.02)	-0.09	(0.02)
Bulgaria	-0.60	(0.04)	-0.36	(0.04)	-0.05	(0.04)	-0.43	(0.04)	0.00	(0.04)	-0.23	(0.05)
Colombia	-0.43	(0.04)	-0.28	(0.04)	0.04	(0.04)	-0.21	(0.04)	-0.02	(0.04)	-0.09	(0.04)
Croatia	-0.81	(0.03)	-0.22	(0.03)	0.17	(0.03)	-0.33	(0.03)	0.18	(0.03)	-0.16	(0.03)
Dubai (UAE)	-0.56	(0.03)	-0.12	(0.03)	0.08	(0.03)	-0.28	(0.03)	-0.04	(0.03)	-0.11	(0.03)
Hong Kong-China	-0.49	(0.03)	-0.03	(0.03)	0.11	(0.03)	-0.27	(0.03)	-0.10	(0.03)	-0.21	(0.04)
Indonesia	-0.46	(0.04)	-0.18	(0.04)	0.02	(0.04)	-0.31	(0.04)	-0.02	(0.04)	0.00	(0.05)
Jordan	-0.42	(0.04)	-0.22	(0.03)	0.03	(0.05)	-0.37	(0.04)	-0.14	(0.05)	-0.03	(0.04)
Kazakhstan	-0.45	(0.03)	-0.13	(0.03)	0.02	(0.03)	-0.33	(0.04)	0.01	(0.03)	-0.29	(0.04)
Kyrgyzstan	-0.62	(0.03)	-0.28	(0.03)	-0.03	(0.03)	-0.38	(0.04)	0.00	(0.04)	-0.25	(0.04)
Latvia	-0.97	(0.04)	-0.42	(0.04)	0.02	(0.04)	-0.28	(0.03)	0.14	(0.03)	0.01	(0.04)
Liechtenstein	-0.72	(0.11)	-0.05	(0.09)	0.30	(0.11)	-0.31	(0.10)	0.05	(0.11)	-0.09	(0.09)
Lithuania	-1.05	(0.03)	-0.49	(0.03)	0.02	(0.03)	-0.51	(0.03)	0.00	(0.03)	-0.28	(0.03)
Macao-China	-0.60	(0.03)	-0.23	(0.02)	-0.02	(0.02)	-0.42	(0.03)	-0.13	(0.02)	-0.33	(0.02)
Montenegro	-0.67	(0.03)	-0.15	(0.04)	0.20	(0.03)	-0.40	(0.03)	0.16	(0.03)	-0.24	(0.03)
Panama	-0.38	(0.05)	-0.19	(0.05)	0.01	(0.04)	-0.12	(0.05)	0.07	(0.04)	0.08	(0.05)
Peru	-0.42	(0.03)	-0.16	(0.03)	0.04	(0.04)	-0.28	(0.03)	-0.08	(0.03)	-0.17	(0.03)
Qatar	-0.39	(0.02)	-0.23	(0.02)	-0.10	(0.02)	-0.08	(0.02)	0.18	(0.02)	0.02	(0.02)
Romania	-0.66	(0.03)	-0.26	(0.04)	0.08	(0.04)	-0.46	(0.04)	-0.04	(0.04)	-0.28	(0.03)
Russian Federation	-0.67	(0.03)	-0.27	(0.03)	0.13	(0.03)	-0.40	(0.03)	0.09	(0.03)	-0.30	(0.04)
Serbia	-0.74	(0.04)	-0.20	(0.03)	0.17	(0.03)	-0.32	(0.03)	0.18	(0.04)	-0.14	(0.04)
Shanghai-China	-0.52	(0.03)	0.08	(0.03)	0.07	(0.03)	-0.28	(0.03)	0.07	(0.03)	-0.17	(0.03)
Singapore	-0.66	(0.03)	-0.08	(0.03)	0.14	(0.02)	-0.23	(0.02)	-0.09	(0.02)	-0.13	(0.03)
Chinese Taipei	-0.51	(0.04)	-0.03	(0.03)	0.07	(0.03)	-0.22	(0.03)	-0.09	(0.04)	-0.24	(0.05)
Thailand	-0.51	(0.03)	-0.43	(0.03)	0.03	(0.04)	-0.37	(0.03)	0.02	(0.04)	-0.22	(0.03)
Trinidad and Tobago	-0.69	(0.03)	-0.29	(0.04)	-0.15	(0.03)	-0.36	(0.04)	-0.10	(0.03)	-0.19	(0.03)
Tunisia	-0.55	(0.03)	-0.26	(0.03)	0.12	(0.03)	-0.43	(0.03)	-0.09	(0.03)	-0.29	(0.04)
Uruguay	-0.56	(0.03)	-0.37	(0.03)	0.00	(0.03)	-0.32	(0.03)	-0.01	(0.03)	-0.22	(0.03)

Note: Values that are statistically significant are indicated in bold (see Annex A3).
StatLink ⎙ http://dx.doi.org/10.1787/888932343285

[Part 2/2]
Effect sizes for gender differences in engagement in reading and approaches to learning

Table III.2.12 *Results based on students' self-reports*

Effect size in favour of boys
- from 0.2 to 0.5
- from 0.5 to 0.8
- equal or greater than 0.8

Effect size in favour of girls
- from -0.2 to -0.5
- from -0.5 to -0.8
- equal or less than -0.8

	Index of use of functional texts		Memorisation strategies		Elaboration strategies		Control strategies		Understanding and remembering		Summarising	
	Effect size	S.E.	Effect size	S.E.	Effect size	S.E.	Effect size	S.E.	Effect size	S.E.	Effect size	S.E.
OECD												
Australia	**0.08**	(0.02)	**-0.22**	(0.02)	**0.08**	(0.02)	**-0.29**	(0.02)	**-0.28**	(0.02)	**-0.41**	(0.03)
Austria	-0.02	(0.04)	**-0.22**	(0.04)	**0.14**	(0.03)	**-0.20**	(0.04)	**-0.36**	(0.04)	**-0.45**	(0.04)
Belgium	0.00	(0.03)	**-0.20**	(0.03)	**0.17**	(0.03)	**-0.23**	(0.03)	**-0.24**	(0.03)	**-0.27**	(0.03)
Canada	**0.05**	(0.02)	**-0.26**	(0.02)	**0.09**	(0.02)	**-0.36**	(0.02)	**-0.29**	(0.02)	**-0.44**	(0.02)
Chile	**-0.09**	(0.03)	-0.04	(0.03)	**0.07**	(0.03)	**-0.16**	(0.03)	**-0.11**	(0.03)	**-0.25**	(0.03)
Czech Republic	**0.15**	(0.03)	**-0.24**	(0.03)	**0.06**	(0.03)	**-0.30**	(0.03)	**-0.35**	(0.04)	**-0.41**	(0.03)
Denmark	**-0.07**	(0.03)	**-0.09**	(0.03)	0.07	(0.03)	**-0.22**	(0.03)	**-0.39**	(0.03)	**-0.46**	(0.03)
Estonia	0.03	(0.04)	**-0.23**	(0.03)	0.08	(0.04)	**-0.24**	(0.03)	**-0.57**	(0.03)	**-0.65**	(0.03)
Finland	**0.09**	(0.03)	**-0.19**	(0.03)	0.05	(0.03)	**-0.24**	(0.03)	**-0.23**	(0.03)	**-0.21**	(0.03)
France	0.05	(0.03)	**-0.25**	(0.04)	**0.12**	(0.03)	**-0.33**	(0.03)	**-0.29**	(0.04)	**-0.32**	(0.04)
Germany	-0.02	(0.03)	**-0.23**	(0.03)	**0.16**	(0.03)	**-0.41**	(0.03)	**-0.20**	(0.03)	**-0.22**	(0.04)
Greece	**0.15**	(0.03)	**-0.34**	(0.04)	**0.07**	(0.03)	**-0.25**	(0.04)	**-0.24**	(0.04)	**-0.37**	(0.05)
Hungary	**0.18**	(0.04)	**-0.28**	(0.03)	**0.16**	(0.03)	**-0.22**	(0.03)	**-0.42**	(0.03)	**-0.51**	(0.03)
Iceland	0.01	(0.03)	**-0.05**	(0.03)	0.06	(0.03)	**-0.21**	(0.04)	**-0.16**	(0.04)	**-0.32**	(0.04)
Ireland	0.05	(0.04)	**-0.27**	(0.04)	**0.16**	(0.03)	**-0.38**	(0.03)	**-0.14**	(0.03)	**-0.30**	(0.04)
Israel	0.04	(0.04)	**-0.16**	(0.04)	0.07	(0.03)	**-0.45**	(0.02)	**-0.31**	(0.02)	**-0.31**	(0.02)
Italy	**0.16**	(0.02)	**-0.21**	(0.02)	**0.04**	(0.02)	-0.04	(0.04)	**-0.26**	(0.04)	**-0.36**	(0.04)
Japan	**0.14**	(0.03)	0.01	(0.03)	**0.21**	(0.04)	**-0.15**	(0.05)	**-0.23**	(0.05)	**-0.29**	(0.05)
Korea	-0.04	(0.04)	**-0.23**	(0.04)	0.03	(0.04)	**-0.37**	(0.03)	**-0.35**	(0.03)	**-0.37**	(0.03)
Luxembourg	0.05	(0.03)	**-0.29**	(0.03)	**0.19**	(0.03)	**-0.22**	(0.02)	**-0.08**	(0.02)	**-0.22**	(0.02)
Mexico	**-0.06**	(0.02)	**-0.11**	(0.02)	-0.01	(0.02)	**-0.18**	(0.03)	**-0.22**	(0.03)	**-0.27**	(0.03)
Netherlands	-0.05	(0.03)	-0.02	(0.03)	**0.23**	(0.03)	**-0.35**	(0.03)	**-0.28**	(0.04)	**-0.38**	(0.03)
New Zealand	0.00	(0.04)	**-0.29**	(0.03)	0.05	(0.03)	**-0.15**	(0.04)	**-0.30**	(0.03)	**-0.48**	(0.03)
Norway	**0.11**	(0.03)	0.02	(0.03)	0.09	(0.03)	**-0.39**	(0.03)	**-0.28**	(0.03)	**-0.35**	(0.03)
Poland	**0.16**	(0.03)	**-0.39**	(0.03)	0.02	(0.03)	**-0.45**	(0.03)	**-0.22**	(0.03)	**-0.40**	(0.03)
Portugal	**0.07**	(0.03)	**-0.19**	(0.03)	**-0.15**	(0.03)	**-0.37**	(0.04)	**-0.29**	(0.03)	**-0.41**	(0.04)
Slovak Republic	**0.12**	(0.04)	**-0.17**	(0.04)	0.03	(0.04)	**-0.34**	(0.03)	**-0.38**	(0.03)	**-0.40**	(0.03)
Slovenia	**0.13**	(0.03)	**-0.09**	(0.03)	**0.14**	(0.03)	**-0.26**	(0.02)	**-0.27**	(0.02)	**-0.35**	(0.02)
Spain	**0.06**	(0.02)	**-0.17**	(0.02)	**0.10**	(0.02)	**-0.28**	(0.03)	**-0.35**	(0.03)	**-0.39**	(0.03)
Sweden	0.00	(0.03)	**-0.14**	(0.03)	0.07	(0.03)	**-0.38**	(0.02)	**-0.39**	(0.03)	**-0.43**	(0.03)
Switzerland	0.02	(0.03)	**-0.20**	(0.03)	**0.14**	(0.02)	**-0.34**	(0.03)	**-0.19**	(0.03)	**-0.33**	(0.03)
Turkey	0.05	(0.04)	**-0.12**	(0.03)	**-0.09**	(0.03)	**-0.18**	(0.02)	**-0.21**	(0.03)	**-0.23**	(0.04)
United Kingdom	-0.03	(0.03)	**-0.14**	(0.03)	**0.13**	(0.03)	**-0.24**	(0.03)	**-0.20**	(0.03)	**-0.32**	(0.03)
United States	-0.04	(0.04)	**-0.19**	(0.03)	0.03	(0.03)	**-0.28**	(0.01)	**-0.27**	(0.01)	**-0.36**	(0.01)
OECD average	**0.05**	(0.01)	**-0.18**	(0.01)	**0.08**	(0.01)	**-0.28**	(0.01)	**-0.27**	(0.01)	**-0.36**	(0.01)
Partners												
Albania	**0.18**	(0.04)	**-0.39**	(0.04)	**-0.14**	(0.03)	**-0.45**	(0.03)	**-0.31**	(0.04)	**-0.25**	(0.04)
Argentina	-0.03	(0.04)	**-0.07**	(0.03)	0.01	(0.03)	**-0.23**	(0.03)	**-0.09**	(0.04)	**-0.21**	(0.04)
Azerbaijan	0.00	(0.05)	**-0.25**	(0.04)	**-0.17**	(0.04)	**-0.27**	(0.03)	-0.05	(0.04)	-0.02	(0.04)
Brazil	0.04	(0.02)	**-0.24**	(0.02)	**-0.08**	(0.02)	**-0.23**	(0.02)	**-0.17**	(0.02)	**-0.15**	(0.02)
Bulgaria	-0.03	(0.04)	**-0.28**	(0.04)	0.03	(0.04)	**-0.32**	(0.03)	**-0.35**	(0.05)	**-0.28**	(0.04)
Colombia	-0.05	(0.04)	**-0.18**	(0.04)	-0.07	(0.04)	**-0.23**	(0.03)	-0.04	(0.04)	-0.08	(0.04)
Croatia	**0.11**	(0.03)	**-0.25**	(0.03)	0.05	(0.03)	**-0.31**	(0.03)	**-0.27**	(0.03)	**-0.42**	(0.04)
Dubai (UAE)	0.04	(0.03)	**-0.10**	(0.03)	0.05	(0.03)	**-0.25**	(0.03)	**-0.16**	(0.03)	**-0.22**	(0.03)
Hong Kong-China	0.01	(0.03)	**-0.17**	(0.03)	**0.19**	(0.03)	-0.06	(0.04)	**-0.28**	(0.03)	**-0.21**	(0.04)
Indonesia	-0.07	(0.04)	**-0.26**	(0.04)	**-0.12**	(0.03)	**-0.29**	(0.03)	**-0.19**	(0.04)	**-0.13**	(0.04)
Jordan	-0.03	(0.04)	**-0.20**	(0.04)	**-0.16**	(0.03)	**-0.30**	(0.04)	**-0.18**	(0.04)	**-0.25**	(0.04)
Kazakhstan	-0.01	(0.03)	**-0.09**	(0.03)	**-0.09**	(0.03)	**-0.24**	(0.03)	**-0.12**	(0.03)	**-0.21**	(0.03)
Kyrgyzstan	**-0.07**	(0.04)	**-0.28**	(0.03)	**-0.25**	(0.03)	**-0.40**	(0.03)	**-0.14**	(0.03)	-0.06	(0.04)
Latvia	**0.16**	(0.04)	**-0.15**	(0.04)	0.04	(0.04)	**-0.27**	(0.04)	**-0.29**	(0.04)	**-0.37**	(0.04)
Liechtenstein	0.07	(0.11)	**-0.23**	(0.10)	**0.26**	(0.11)	**-0.32**	(0.10)	**-0.49**	(0.09)	**-0.53**	(0.11)
Lithuania	**0.15**	(0.03)	**-0.25**	(0.03)	0.00	(0.03)	**-0.43**	(0.03)	**-0.35**	(0.03)	**-0.39**	(0.03)
Macao-China	**-0.15**	(0.02)	**-0.09**	(0.03)	**0.10**	(0.02)	-0.05	(0.02)	**-0.32**	(0.02)	**-0.23**	(0.03)
Montenegro	**0.12**	(0.03)	**-0.19**	(0.03)	0.06	(0.03)	**-0.35**	(0.03)	**-0.20**	(0.03)	**-0.11**	(0.03)
Panama	**0.10**	(0.05)	0.10	(0.05)	0.10	(0.06)	-0.04	(0.05)	-0.09	(0.06)	-0.15	(0.06)
Peru	-0.04	(0.03)	**0.08**	(0.03)	-0.01	(0.03)	**-0.20**	(0.03)	-0.05	(0.04)	**-0.10**	(0.04)
Qatar	**0.14**	(0.02)	**-0.31**	(0.02)	**-0.05**	(0.02)	**-0.33**	(0.02)	**-0.05**	(0.02)	**-0.10**	(0.02)
Romania	-0.01	(0.04)	**-0.35**	(0.03)	**-0.13**	(0.03)	**-0.39**	(0.04)	**-0.16**	(0.04)	**-0.24**	(0.04)
Russian Federation	-0.06	(0.04)	**-0.09**	(0.02)	**0.09**	(0.03)	**-0.22**	(0.03)	**-0.27**	(0.03)	**-0.33**	(0.03)
Serbia	**0.12**	(0.04)	**-0.27**	(0.03)	**0.09**	(0.03)	**-0.29**	(0.03)	**-0.22**	(0.03)	**-0.28**	(0.03)
Shanghai-China	0.04	(0.03)	**-0.18**	(0.02)	**0.16**	(0.02)	**-0.09**	(0.03)	**-0.27**	(0.03)	**-0.20**	(0.03)
Singapore	0.03	(0.03)	-0.05	(0.03)	**0.25**	(0.03)	**-0.07**	(0.03)	**-0.07**	(0.03)	**-0.26**	(0.03)
Chinese Taipei	0.01	(0.03)	**-0.29**	(0.02)	-0.01	(0.03)	**-0.14**	(0.04)	**-0.22**	(0.03)	**-0.15**	(0.04)
Thailand	**-0.09**	(0.03)	**-0.30**	(0.04)	**-0.09**	(0.03)	**-0.17**	(0.03)	**-0.28**	(0.04)	**-0.15**	(0.03)
Trinidad and Tobago	-0.02	(0.04)	**-0.24**	(0.03)	-0.06	(0.03)	**-0.31**	(0.03)	**-0.27**	(0.03)	**-0.24**	(0.04)
Tunisia	**-0.19**	(0.03)	**-0.27**	(0.04)	**-0.24**	(0.04)	**-0.39**	(0.03)	**-0.09**	(0.04)	**-0.11**	(0.03)
Uruguay	0.06	(0.03)	**-0.19**	(0.03)	0.03	(0.03)	**-0.29**	(0.03)	**-0.14**	(0.03)	**-0.19**	(0.03)

Note: Values that are statistically significant are indicated in bold (see Annex A3).
StatLink ᴹᵠᵖ http://dx.doi.org/10.1787/888932343285

[Part 1/2]
Effect sizes for socio-economic differences in engagement in reading and approaches to learning[1]

Table III.2.13 *Results based on students' self-reports*

Effect size in favour of students with a high socio-economic background:
- from 0.2 to 0.5
- from 0.5 to 0.8
- equal or greater than 0.8

Effect size in favour of students with a low socio-economic background:
- from -0.2 to -0.5
- from -0.5 to -0.8
- equal or less than -0.8

	Enjoyment of reading		Diversity of reading materials		Online reading activities		Index of interpretation of literary texts		Index of use of texts containing non-continuous materials		Index of reading activities for traditional literature courses	
	Effect size	S.E.	Effect size	S.E.	Effect size	S.E.	Effect size	S.E.	Effect size	S.E.	Effect size	S.E.
OECD												
Australia	0.59	(0.03)	0.44	(0.03)	0.58	(0.03)	0.45	(0.03)	0.30	(0.03)	0.23	(0.03)
Austria	0.54	(0.05)	0.48	(0.05)	0.49	(0.05)	0.39	(0.05)	0.23	(0.04)	0.29	(0.05)
Belgium	0.59	(0.03)	0.55	(0.04)	0.32	(0.04)	0.30	(0.04)	0.13	(0.04)	0.42	(0.04)
Canada	0.42	(0.03)	0.46	(0.04)	0.49	(0.03)	0.29	(0.03)	0.23	(0.03)	0.20	(0.03)
Chile	0.22	(0.05)	0.26	(0.05)	1.25	(0.05)	0.05	(0.04)	0.10	(0.05)	-0.19	(0.05)
Czech Republic	0.43	(0.05)	0.34	(0.05)	0.52	(0.04)	0.19	(0.05)	0.21	(0.05)	0.18	(0.04)
Denmark	0.66	(0.04)	0.49	(0.04)	0.42	(0.05)	0.27	(0.05)	0.34	(0.05)	0.11	(0.05)
Estonia	0.45	(0.05)	0.37	(0.04)	0.66	(0.05)	0.23	(0.05)	0.18	(0.05)	0.14	(0.05)
Finland	0.45	(0.04)	0.47	(0.04)	0.32	(0.05)	0.25	(0.05)	0.34	(0.04)	0.11	(0.04)
France	0.61	(0.05)	0.54	(0.04)	0.57	(0.05)	0.37	(0.05)	0.38	(0.05)	0.32	(0.06)
Germany	0.66	(0.05)	0.51	(0.05)	0.40	(0.04)	0.29	(0.05)	0.22	(0.05)	-0.02	(0.05)
Greece	0.44	(0.05)	0.54	(0.05)	0.80	(0.05)	0.23	(0.06)	0.12	(0.05)	0.11	(0.05)
Hungary	0.65	(0.05)	0.21	(0.05)	0.72	(0.05)	0.18	(0.05)	0.08	(0.05)	0.07	(0.06)
Iceland	0.37	(0.04)	0.37	(0.05)	0.28	(0.04)	0.30	(0.05)	0.29	(0.05)	0.26	(0.05)
Ireland	0.72	(0.06)	0.28	(0.05)	0.50	(0.05)	-0.02	(0.05)	0.11	(0.06)	-0.16	(0.05)
Israel	0.24	(0.05)	0.16	(0.03)	0.56	(0.04)	-0.09	(0.05)	0.09	(0.04)	-0.29	(0.06)
Italy	0.48	(0.03)	0.55	(0.03)	0.65	(0.02)	0.15	(0.03)	-0.08	(0.03)	0.27	(0.03)
Japan	0.40	(0.04)	0.46	(0.04)	0.34	(0.04)	0.33	(0.04)	0.16	(0.04)	0.22	(0.04)
Korea	0.53	(0.05)	0.69	(0.05)	0.35	(0.05)	0.68	(0.05)	0.63	(0.06)	0.61	(0.05)
Luxembourg	0.54	(0.04)	0.43	(0.04)	0.30	(0.05)	0.48	(0.05)	0.42	(0.05)	0.27	(0.05)
Mexico	-0.03	(0.03)	0.24	(0.03)	1.39	(0.02)	0.15	(0.02)	0.11	(0.03)	-0.11	(0.03)
Netherlands	0.45	(0.06)	0.49	(0.05)	0.24	(0.05)	0.12	(0.05)	0.18	(0.05)	0.12	(0.05)
New Zealand	0.59	(0.05)	0.36	(0.04)	0.66	(0.05)	0.22	(0.04)	0.31	(0.05)	0.02	(0.05)
Norway	0.42	(0.05)	0.49	(0.04)	0.35	(0.05)	0.24	(0.05)	0.34	(0.04)	0.26	(0.05)
Poland	0.52	(0.05)	0.29	(0.04)	0.93	(0.05)	0.25	(0.05)	0.16	(0.05)	-0.03	(0.05)
Portugal	0.34	(0.04)	0.28	(0.04)	0.39	(0.04)	0.26	(0.04)	0.25	(0.04)	0.16	(0.05)
Slovak Republic	0.40	(0.05)	0.37	(0.04)	0.80	(0.05)	0.14	(0.04)	0.21	(0.05)	-0.03	(0.06)
Slovenia	0.45	(0.05)	0.36	(0.05)	0.53	(0.04)	0.26	(0.05)	0.35	(0.04)	0.34	(0.05)
Spain	0.50	(0.04)	0.56	(0.03)	0.43	(0.04)	0.27	(0.03)	0.07	(0.03)	0.34	(0.03)
Sweden	0.45	(0.05)	0.56	(0.05)	0.43	(0.04)	0.22	(0.05)	0.27	(0.05)	0.03	(0.05)
Switzerland	0.59	(0.05)	0.51	(0.04)	0.31	(0.03)	0.34	(0.05)	0.14	(0.05)	0.10	(0.05)
Turkey	0.01	(0.05)	0.17	(0.04)	1.26	(0.05)	0.27	(0.05)	0.20	(0.05)	0.01	(0.04)
United Kingdom	0.59	(0.05)	0.24	(0.05)	0.39	(0.04)	0.32	(0.04)	0.40	(0.04)	0.06	(0.04)
United States	0.52	(0.04)	0.31	(0.04)	0.54	(0.06)	0.32	(0.05)	0.24	(0.05)	0.17	(0.06)
OECD average	0.46	(0.01)	0.41	(0.01)	0.56	(0.01)	0.26	(0.01)	0.23	(0.01)	0.14	(0.01)
Partners												
Albania	0.20	(0.05)	0.33	(0.07)	1.32	(0.05)	0.34	(0.06)	0.07	(0.06)	0.06	(0.06)
Argentina	0.03	(0.05)	0.10	(0.05)	1.32	(0.06)	0.06	(0.05)	0.28	(0.08)	-0.14	(0.06)
Azerbaijan	0.23	(0.05)	0.44	(0.06)	1.14	(0.06)	0.16	(0.06)	0.03	(0.06)	0.06	(0.06)
Brazil	0.10	(0.04)	0.20	(0.03)	1.25	(0.04)	0.35	(0.04)	0.32	(0.04)	0.09	(0.03)
Bulgaria	0.47	(0.06)	0.50	(0.07)	1.03	(0.06)	0.28	(0.06)	0.19	(0.05)	-0.03	(0.05)
Colombia	0.00	(0.07)	0.02	(0.07)	1.22	(0.05)	0.27	(0.05)	0.24	(0.06)	-0.05	(0.05)
Croatia	0.33	(0.04)	0.52	(0.05)	0.98	(0.05)	0.20	(0.05)	0.28	(0.05)	0.21	(0.05)
Dubai (UAE)	0.30	(0.04)	0.16	(0.04)	0.64	(0.04)	0.39	(0.04)	0.23	(0.05)	-0.02	(0.04)
Hong Kong-China	0.43	(0.05)	0.44	(0.05)	0.48	(0.04)	0.52	(0.05)	0.49	(0.04)	0.46	(0.05)
Indonesia	0.03	(0.06)	0.60	(0.05)	1.08	(0.06)	0.20	(0.06)	-0.07	(0.07)	0.01	(0.08)
Jordan	-0.02	(0.05)	0.39	(0.05)	1.26	(0.05)	0.15	(0.04)	0.17	(0.05)	0.09	(0.05)
Kazakhstan	0.18	(0.05)	0.15	(0.06)	1.26	(0.05)	0.39	(0.05)	0.27	(0.06)	0.24	(0.05)
Kyrgyzstan	0.07	(0.05)	0.39	(0.05)	0.96	(0.05)	0.47	(0.07)	0.17	(0.07)	0.27	(0.08)
Latvia	0.41	(0.05)	0.29	(0.07)	0.77	(0.06)	0.18	(0.05)	0.07	(0.05)	-0.05	(0.06)
Liechtenstein	0.33	(0.15)	0.26	(0.12)	0.26	(0.16)	0.33	(0.16)	-0.09	(0.17)	0.22	(0.14)
Lithuania	0.43	(0.05)	0.29	(0.05)	0.78	(0.05)	0.20	(0.05)	0.30	(0.05)	-0.04	(0.05)
Macao-China	0.46	(0.03)	0.52	(0.03)	0.67	(0.04)	0.43	(0.03)	0.51	(0.04)	0.31	(0.03)
Montenegro	0.27	(0.04)	0.43	(0.05)	1.17	(0.05)	0.24	(0.05)	0.10	(0.06)	-0.05	(0.05)
Panama	-0.08	(0.05)	-0.08	(0.06)	1.64	(0.07)	0.44	(0.07)	0.47	(0.07)	0.02	(0.09)
Peru	-0.06	(0.05)	0.23	(0.04)	1.38	(0.06)	0.31	(0.06)	0.28	(0.05)	-0.07	(0.05)
Qatar	0.12	(0.03)	0.21	(0.03)	0.66	(0.03)	0.32	(0.03)	0.32	(0.03)	-0.07	(0.03)
Romania	0.13	(0.06)	0.35	(0.05)	1.26	(0.05)	0.29	(0.05)	0.26	(0.07)	0.03	(0.07)
Russian Federation	0.38	(0.05)	0.00	(0.05)	1.23	(0.05)	0.31	(0.05)	0.11	(0.04)	0.07	(0.04)
Serbia	0.27	(0.05)	0.41	(0.04)	1.15	(0.05)	0.17	(0.04)	0.16	(0.05)	0.15	(0.04)
Shanghai-China	0.50	(0.04)	0.52	(0.04)	0.85	(0.04)	0.63	(0.04)	0.42	(0.05)	0.58	(0.05)
Singapore	0.68	(0.04)	0.46	(0.03)	0.61	(0.04)	0.56	(0.03)	0.45	(0.04)	0.20	(0.04)
Chinese Taipei	0.74	(0.05)	0.48	(0.04)	0.37	(0.04)	0.46	(0.04)	0.59	(0.04)	0.68	(0.05)
Thailand	-0.01	(0.05)	0.16	(0.04)	1.32	(0.06)	0.14	(0.05)	-0.12	(0.04)	-0.02	(0.04)
Trinidad and Tobago	0.02	(0.04)	0.02	(0.05)	1.07	(0.05)	0.25	(0.05)	0.41	(0.05)	-0.03	(0.05)
Tunisia	-0.32	(0.05)	0.31	(0.05)	1.44	(0.05)	0.09	(0.05)	0.08	(0.05)	0.05	(0.06)
Uruguay	0.24	(0.05)	0.33	(0.05)	1.17	(0.05)	0.26	(0.04)	0.12	(0.05)	0.12	(0.05)

Note: Values that are statistically significant are indicated in bold (see Annex A3).
1. Top minus bottom quarter of the PISA index of economic, social and cultural status (ESCS).
StatLink ᵃˢᵖᵇ http://dx.doi.org/10.1787/888932343285

[Part 2/2]
Effect sizes for socio-economic differences in engagement in reading and approaches to learning[1]

Table III.2.13 *Results based on students' self-reports*

Effect size in favour of students with a high socio-economic background:
- from 0.2 to 0.5
- from 0.5 to 0.8
- equal or greater than 0.8

Effect size in favour of students with a low socio-economic background:
- from -0.2 to -0.5
- from -0.5 to -0.8
- equal or less than -0.8

	Index of use of functional texts		Memorisation strategies		Elaboration strategies		Control strategies		Understanding and remembering		Summarising	
	Effect size	S.E.	Effect size	S.E.	Effect size	S.E.	Effect size	S.E.	Effect size	S.E.	Effect size	S.E.
OECD												
Australia	0.01	(0.03)	0.27	(0.03)	0.34	(0.03)	0.63	(0.03)	0.51	(0.03)	0.51	(0.03)
Austria	-0.16	(0.04)	-0.03	(0.04)	0.29	(0.04)	0.38	(0.05)	0.55	(0.05)	0.56	(0.04)
Belgium	-0.29	(0.04)	-0.15	(0.04)	0.16	(0.04)	0.56	(0.04)	0.23	(0.03)	0.26	(0.02)
Canada	0.03	(0.03)	0.22	(0.03)	0.37	(0.03)	0.55	(0.03)	0.54	(0.05)	0.50	(0.05)
Chile	-0.18	(0.05)	0.10	(0.05)	0.25	(0.04)	0.50	(0.05)	0.36	(0.04)	0.43	(0.04)
Czech Republic	-0.17	(0.05)	-0.10	(0.04)	0.37	(0.04)	0.43	(0.04)	0.52	(0.05)	0.50	(0.05)
Denmark	0.06	(0.05)	-0.02	(0.05)	0.43	(0.05)	0.39	(0.04)	0.31	(0.05)	0.32	(0.06)
Estonia	0.11	(0.04)	0.02	(0.05)	0.37	(0.05)	0.33	(0.05)	0.32	(0.05)	0.42	(0.04)
Finland	0.02	(0.05)	0.23	(0.04)	0.37	(0.04)	0.49	(0.04)	0.48	(0.06)	0.52	(0.06)
France	-0.03	(0.05)	0.13	(0.05)	0.31	(0.04)	0.66	(0.05)	0.56	(0.06)	0.59	(0.05)
Germany	-0.18	(0.05)	-0.11	(0.05)	0.23	(0.04)	0.35	(0.04)	0.19	(0.04)	0.40	(0.05)
Greece	-0.09	(0.05)	0.11	(0.05)	0.48	(0.05)	0.38	(0.05)	0.43	(0.06)	0.63	(0.07)
Hungary	-0.33	(0.05)	-0.09	(0.06)	0.21	(0.05)	0.27	(0.06)	0.30	(0.05)	0.28	(0.05)
Iceland	0.01	(0.05)	0.19	(0.05)	0.43	(0.05)	0.50	(0.05)	0.43	(0.06)	0.34	(0.06)
Ireland	-0.07	(0.05)	0.16	(0.05)	0.36	(0.05)	0.59	(0.05)	0.39	(0.05)	0.49	(0.05)
Israel	-0.20	(0.05)	-0.05	(0.05)	0.11	(0.05)	0.27	(0.04)	0.41	(0.02)	0.45	(0.03)
Italy	-0.21	(0.03)	-0.08	(0.02)	0.29	(0.02)	0.39	(0.03)	0.25	(0.05)	0.39	(0.05)
Japan	-0.04	(0.05)	0.22	(0.04)	0.45	(0.04)	0.53	(0.04)	0.43	(0.05)	0.51	(0.05)
Korea	0.28	(0.06)	0.43	(0.05)	0.67	(0.04)	0.78	(0.05)	0.48	(0.04)	0.52	(0.04)
Luxembourg	-0.20	(0.05)	0.05	(0.04)	0.24	(0.04)	0.34	(0.04)	0.39	(0.02)	0.44	(0.03)
Mexico	0.01	(0.03)	0.13	(0.03)	0.20	(0.03)	0.36	(0.03)	0.49	(0.07)	0.42	(0.05)
Netherlands	-0.15	(0.05)	-0.32	(0.05)	0.25	(0.04)	0.41	(0.05)	0.50	(0.05)	0.50	(0.04)
New Zealand	-0.15	(0.04)	0.21	(0.05)	0.28	(0.04)	0.66	(0.05)	0.41	(0.04)	0.40	(0.05)
Norway	0.02	(0.04)	0.24	(0.05)	0.46	(0.04)	0.51	(0.05)	0.41	(0.05)	0.48	(0.04)
Poland	-0.18	(0.04)	0.05	(0.04)	0.26	(0.04)	0.44	(0.04)	0.50	(0.05)	0.55	(0.05)
Portugal	-0.17	(0.05)	0.05	(0.05)	0.53	(0.04)	0.73	(0.04)	0.36	(0.05)	0.40	(0.05)
Slovak Republic	-0.21	(0.06)	-0.30	(0.06)	0.35	(0.05)	0.38	(0.05)	0.38	(0.04)	0.48	(0.05)
Slovenia	-0.16	(0.04)	-0.17	(0.04)	0.33	(0.05)	0.39	(0.05)	0.26	(0.04)	0.38	(0.03)
Spain	-0.15	(0.04)	0.04	(0.05)	0.41	(0.03)	0.51	(0.03)	0.50	(0.05)	0.41	(0.05)
Sweden	0.14	(0.05)	0.22	(0.04)	0.41	(0.04)	0.42	(0.04)	0.64	(0.04)	0.54	(0.04)
Switzerland	-0.14	(0.04)	-0.09	(0.05)	0.22	(0.04)	0.39	(0.04)	0.21	(0.04)	0.35	(0.04)
Turkey	0.00	(0.05)	-0.26	(0.05)	0.07	(0.04)	0.17	(0.05)	0.21	(0.04)	0.35	(0.04)
United Kingdom	-0.10	(0.04)	0.16	(0.04)	0.30	(0.04)	0.53	(0.05)	0.41	(0.04)	0.52	(0.05)
United States	-0.17	(0.05)	0.11	(0.04)	0.25	(0.05)	0.58	(0.04)	0.44	(0.04)	0.47	(0.05)
OECD average	-0.09	(0.01)	0.05	(0.01)	0.33	(0.01)	0.46	(0.01)	0.42	(0.01)	0.46	(0.01)
Partners												
Albania	0.16	(0.06)	0.03	(0.06)	0.30	(0.05)	0.40	(0.06)	0.26	(0.07)	0.29	(0.07)
Argentina	-0.03	(0.06)	-0.09	(0.04)	0.12	(0.05)	0.33	(0.05)	0.41	(0.07)	0.60	(0.07)
Azerbaijan	0.15	(0.06)	0.16	(0.06)	0.27	(0.06)	0.39	(0.03)	0.47	(0.04)	0.44	(0.04)
Brazil	0.17	(0.04)	0.22	(0.03)	0.08	(0.03)	0.39	(0.03)	0.52	(0.07)	0.53	(0.07)
Bulgaria	-0.09	(0.05)	0.05	(0.05)	0.36	(0.05)	0.31	(0.06)	0.58	(0.06)	0.56	(0.07)
Colombia	-0.01	(0.05)	-0.17	(0.06)	0.07	(0.04)	0.23	(0.06)	0.35	(0.05)	0.37	(0.05)
Croatia	-0.10	(0.05)	-0.02	(0.04)	0.21	(0.04)	0.29	(0.05)	0.39	(0.04)	0.51	(0.05)
Dubai (UAE)	-0.18	(0.05)	-0.21	(0.04)	0.05	(0.04)	0.29	(0.04)	0.16	(0.05)	0.22	(0.05)
Hong Kong-China	0.17	(0.04)	0.31	(0.04)	0.57	(0.04)	0.63	(0.05)	0.31	(0.05)	0.28	(0.07)
Indonesia	0.38	(0.06)	0.17	(0.05)	0.36	(0.05)	0.30	(0.05)	0.22	(0.05)	0.28	(0.04)
Jordan	0.07	(0.04)	0.41	(0.05)	0.40	(0.05)	0.55	(0.05)	0.34	(0.05)	0.30	(0.06)
Kazakhstan	0.25	(0.05)	0.10	(0.05)	0.23	(0.04)	0.32	(0.05)	0.53	(0.06)	0.50	(0.07)
Kyrgyzstan	0.17	(0.07)	0.22	(0.05)	0.14	(0.05)	0.12	(0.05)	0.35	(0.07)	0.38	(0.06)
Latvia	-0.08	(0.06)	0.09	(0.05)	0.38	(0.04)	0.35	(0.05)	0.50	(0.16)	0.58	(0.17)
Liechtenstein	0.02	(0.15)	-0.03	(0.16)	0.33	(0.15)	0.24	(0.14)	0.41	(0.05)	0.48	(0.05)
Lithuania	-0.17	(0.05)	-0.05	(0.05)	0.31	(0.06)	0.44	(0.05)	0.20	(0.04)	0.27	(0.04)
Macao-China	0.21	(0.04)	0.39	(0.04)	0.51	(0.04)	0.66	(0.04)	0.35	(0.05)	0.41	(0.05)
Montenegro	-0.13	(0.04)	-0.29	(0.05)	0.08	(0.06)	0.17	(0.05)	0.52	(0.08)	0.54	(0.08)
Panama	-0.17	(0.08)	-0.34	(0.07)	-0.11	(0.07)	-0.04	(0.07)	0.48	(0.07)	0.65	(0.07)
Peru	0.11	(0.05)	-0.16	(0.05)	0.01	(0.05)	0.19	(0.04)	0.23	(0.04)	0.25	(0.03)
Qatar	0.02	(0.03)	0.07	(0.03)	0.09	(0.03)	0.30	(0.03)	0.38	(0.06)	0.45	(0.05)
Romania	0.09	(0.06)	0.02	(0.06)	0.25	(0.05)	0.31	(0.06)	0.47	(0.04)	0.39	(0.05)
Russian Federation	0.03	(0.05)	-0.13	(0.05)	0.20	(0.05)	0.25	(0.04)	0.32	(0.05)	0.43	(0.05)
Serbia	-0.08	(0.04)	-0.33	(0.05)	0.20	(0.05)	0.20	(0.05)	0.20	(0.05)	0.30	(0.05)
Shanghai-China	0.03	(0.05)	0.16	(0.04)	0.61	(0.05)	0.61	(0.04)	0.30	(0.04)	0.41	(0.04)
Singapore	0.00	(0.04)	-0.04	(0.04)	0.26	(0.04)	0.53	(0.04)	0.38	(0.05)	0.43	(0.05)
Chinese Taipei	0.09	(0.05)	0.44	(0.04)	0.68	(0.04)	0.75	(0.05)	0.28	(0.05)	0.33	(0.05)
Thailand	0.29	(0.05)	0.19	(0.05)	0.22	(0.05)	0.25	(0.05)	0.44	(0.05)	0.43	(0.04)
Trinidad and Tobago	-0.11	(0.06)	0.07	(0.04)	0.08	(0.05)	0.40	(0.05)	0.15	(0.04)	0.15	(0.05)
Tunisia	0.17	(0.06)	-0.05	(0.06)	0.18	(0.05)	0.27	(0.05)	0.53	(0.05)	0.67	(0.05)
Uruguay	-0.08	(0.04)	0.01	(0.04)	0.13	(0.04)	0.46	(0.04)	0.53	(0.05)	0.67	(0.05)

Note: Values that are statistically significant are indicated in bold (see Annex A3).
1. Top minus bottom quarter of the PISA index of economic, social and cultural status (ESCS).
StatLink http://dx.doi.org/10.1787/888932343285

[Part 1/2]

Effect sizes for the difference between students with and without an immigrant background in engagement in reading and approaches to learning

Table III.2.14 *Results based on students' self-reports*

Effect size in favour of students without an immigrant background:
- from 0.2 to 0.5
- from 0.5 to 0.8
- equal or greater than 0.8

Effect size in favour of students with an immigrant background:
- from -0.2 to -0.5
- from -0.5 to -0.8
- equal or less than -0.8

	Enjoyment of reading		Diversity of reading materials		Online reading activities		Index of interpretation of literary texts		Index of use of texts containing non-continuous materials		Index of reading activities for traditional literature courses	
	Effect size	S.E.	Effect size	S.E.	Effect size	S.E.	Effect size	S.E.	Effect size	S.E.	Effect size	S.E.
OECD												
Australia	-0.19	(0.03)	-0.18	(0.03)	-0.36	(0.03)	-0.25	(0.03)	-0.08	(0.03)	-0.19	(0.03)
Austria	0.02	(0.05)	-0.15	(0.05)	-0.18	(0.06)	-0.24	(0.05)	-0.08	(0.05)	-0.19	(0.03)
Belgium	-0.04	(0.05)	0.08	(0.05)	-0.22	(0.04)	-0.09	(0.04)	-0.18	(0.04)	-0.28	(0.06)
Canada	-0.08	(0.02)	-0.21	(0.03)	-0.49	(0.03)	-0.22	(0.03)	-0.12	(0.03)	-0.10	(0.05)
Chile	c	c	c	c	c	c	c	c	c	c	-0.30	(0.03)
Czech Republic	-0.06	(0.09)	-0.09	(0.11)	0.08	(0.11)	-0.15	(0.09)	-0.21	(0.09)	-0.19	(0.10)
Denmark	-0.16	(0.04)	-0.17	(0.04)	-0.11	(0.04)	-0.04	(0.04)	-0.04	(0.04)	-0.21	(0.04)
Estonia	-0.08	(0.06)	0.11	(0.06)	-0.19	(0.05)	-0.28	(0.06)	-0.05	(0.07)	-0.21	(0.04)
Finland	-0.17	(0.09)	0.23	(0.10)	-0.13	(0.12)	-0.14	(0.11)	0.12	(0.09)	-0.41	(0.08)
France	0.00	(0.05)	-0.01	(0.06)	-0.09	(0.05)	-0.12	(0.07)	0.07	(0.05)	-0.27	(0.12)
Germany	0.11	(0.04)	0.05	(0.04)	-0.02	(0.05)	-0.04	(0.05)	-0.06	(0.04)	-0.23	(0.07)
Greece	0.11	(0.07)	0.17	(0.06)	0.07	(0.07)	0.00	(0.07)	-0.12	(0.07)	-0.16	(0.06)
Hungary	-0.12	(0.10)	0.13	(0.10)	0.07	(0.09)	-0.04	(0.11)	-0.18	(0.12)	-0.13	(0.07)
Iceland	0.00	(0.11)	-0.03	(0.12)	-0.01	(0.14)	0.15	(0.12)	-0.06	(0.14)	-0.12	(0.12)
Ireland	-0.22	(0.06)	-0.13	(0.06)	-0.44	(0.07)	0.01	(0.06)	0.05	(0.06)	-0.06	(0.11)
Israel	-0.03	(0.04)	0.11	(0.04)	0.02	(0.06)	0.06	(0.04)	0.03	(0.04)	-0.07	(0.07)
Italy	0.08	(0.04)	0.17	(0.04)	0.26	(0.05)	0.01	(0.05)	-0.25	(0.04)	0.11	(0.04)
Japan	c	c	c	c	c	c	c	c	c	c	0.23	(0.05)
Korea	c	c	c	c	c	c	c	c	c	c	c	c
Luxembourg	0.07	(0.03)	0.01	(0.03)	-0.01	(0.03)	0.00	(0.03)	-0.12	(0.03)	-0.16	(0.04)
Mexico	0.09	(0.07)	0.10	(0.07)	0.44	(0.06)	0.07	(0.08)	0.13	(0.07)	-0.20	(0.07)
Netherlands	-0.19	(0.06)	-0.09	(0.05)	-0.19	(0.08)	-0.17	(0.08)	-0.06	(0.05)	-0.30	(0.06)
New Zealand	-0.21	(0.03)	-0.29	(0.04)	-0.29	(0.04)	-0.20	(0.03)	-0.06	(0.04)	-0.35	(0.03)
Norway	-0.16	(0.06)	0.10	(0.08)	-0.13	(0.07)	-0.24	(0.07)	-0.01	(0.06)	-0.27	(0.09)
Poland	c	c	c	c	c	c	c	c	c	c	c	c
Portugal	-0.10	(0.07)	-0.01	(0.07)	0.02	(0.07)	-0.17	(0.07)	-0.12	(0.06)	0.01	(0.06)
Slovak Republic	c	c	c	c	c	c	c	c	c	c	c	c
Slovenia	0.17	(0.06)	0.08	(0.04)	0.08	(0.06)	-0.08	(0.07)	0.00	(0.06)	-0.16	(0.06)
Spain	0.05	(0.04)	0.04	(0.04)	-0.02	(0.04)	0.08	(0.04)	-0.05	(0.04)	0.16	(0.04)
Sweden	-0.08	(0.05)	0.11	(0.05)	-0.15	(0.06)	-0.25	(0.07)	-0.14	(0.05)	-0.23	(0.07)
Switzerland	0.04	(0.03)	0.06	(0.03)	-0.13	(0.03)	-0.18	(0.05)	-0.14	(0.05)	-0.31	(0.04)
Turkey	c	c	c	c	c	c	c	c	c	c	c	c
United Kingdom	-0.29	(0.05)	-0.33	(0.05)	-0.30	(0.05)	-0.20	(0.05)	-0.16	(0.06)	-0.24	(0.07)
United States	-0.04	(0.04)	-0.11	(0.04)	-0.22	(0.05)	-0.15	(0.05)	0.02	(0.04)	-0.16	(0.04)
OECD average	-0.05	(0.01)	-0.01	(0.01)	-0.09	(0.01)	-0.10	(0.01)	-0.07	(0.01)	-0.16	(0.01)
Partners												
Albania	c	c	c	c	c	c	c	c	c	c	c	c
Argentina	0.01	(0.10)	0.17	(0.10)	0.14	(0.11)	0.21	(0.09)	0.28	(0.10)	0.05	(0.09)
Azerbaijan	0.11	(0.11)	0.00	(0.07)	0.11	(0.10)	-0.15	(0.15)	-0.05	(0.09)	-0.10	(0.17)
Brazil	-0.03	(0.10)	0.15	(0.17)	0.27	(0.15)	0.15	(0.18)	0.15	(0.14)	0.07	(0.15)
Bulgaria	c	c	c	c	c	c	c	c	c	c	c	c
Colombia	-0.14	(0.23)	0.29	(0.19)	-0.02	(0.19)	0.36	(0.21)	0.13	(0.18)	-0.16	(0.27)
Croatia	0.08	(0.05)	0.09	(0.06)	0.03	(0.06)	-0.03	(0.05)	-0.02	(0.05)	-0.01	(0.05)
Dubai (UAE)	-0.34	(0.03)	-0.14	(0.03)	-0.09	(0.03)	-0.03	(0.03)	-0.22	(0.04)	0.40	(0.04)
Hong Kong-China	0.03	(0.03)	0.11	(0.03)	0.19	(0.03)	0.04	(0.03)	0.07	(0.03)	0.04	(0.04)
Indonesia	c	c	c	c	c	c	c	c	c	c	c	c
Jordan	0.06	(0.06)	-0.02	(0.04)	-0.28	(0.05)	0.01	(0.04)	0.03	(0.05)	0.05	(0.04)
Kazakhstan	0.02	(0.09)	-0.01	(0.07)	-0.02	(0.06)	0.08	(0.06)	-0.02	(0.05)	0.11	(0.06)
Kyrgyzstan	0.26	(0.11)	0.08	(0.10)	-0.26	(0.12)	-0.17	(0.11)	-0.09	(0.17)	-0.10	(0.13)
Latvia	-0.01	(0.09)	-0.14	(0.11)	-0.25	(0.12)	-0.36	(0.07)	-0.22	(0.09)	-0.47	(0.08)
Liechtenstein	-0.07	(0.12)	0.04	(0.11)	0.05	(0.14)	-0.13	(0.11)	-0.03	(0.11)	-0.22	(0.11)
Lithuania	0.19	(0.12)	0.29	(0.14)	-0.09	(0.09)	-0.02	(0.13)	0.01	(0.13)	0.15	(0.12)
Macao-China	-0.06	(0.03)	0.06	(0.03)	0.10	(0.03)	0.00	(0.03)	0.10	(0.03)	-0.05	(0.03)
Montenegro	0.27	(0.07)	0.05	(0.09)	-0.09	(0.06)	0.07	(0.07)	0.08	(0.07)	0.18	(0.07)
Panama	0.07	(0.15)	0.10	(0.09)	0.26	(0.22)	0.23	(0.21)	-0.17	(0.10)	-0.34	(0.14)
Peru	c	c	c	c	c	c	c	c	c	c	c	c
Qatar	-0.27	(0.02)	0.02	(0.02)	-0.07	(0.02)	-0.18	(0.02)	-0.09	(0.02)	0.07	(0.02)
Romania	c	c	c	c	c	c	c	c	c	c	c	c
Russian Federation	0.05	(0.06)	0.03	(0.08)	0.03	(0.07)	0.05	(0.05)	-0.05	(0.05)	-0.05	(0.06)
Serbia	-0.07	(0.06)	0.07	(0.04)	0.01	(0.06)	0.14	(0.06)	0.02	(0.04)	0.17	(0.05)
Shanghai-China	c	c	c	c	c	c	c	c	c	c	c	c
Singapore	-0.21	(0.04)	-0.10	(0.04)	-0.08	(0.05)	-0.05	(0.04)	-0.05	(0.04)	-0.10	(0.04)
Chinese Taipei	c	c	c	c	c	c	c	c	c	c	c	c
Thailand	c	c	c	c	c	c	c	c	c	c	c	c
Trinidad and Tobago	-0.11	(0.10)	0.21	(0.11)	-0.43	(0.08)	-0.01	(0.10)	0.13	(0.12)	0.00	(0.10)
Tunisia	c	c	c	c	c	c	c	c	c	c	c	c
Uruguay	c	c	c	c	c	c	c	c	c	c	c	c

Note: Values that are statistically significant are indicated in bold (see Annex A3).
StatLink http://dx.doi.org/10.1787/888932343285

[Part 2/2]
Effect sizes for the difference between students with and without an immigrant background in engagement in reading and approaches to learning

Table III.2.14   *Results based on students' self-reports*

Effect size in favour of students without an immigrant background:
- from 0.2 to 0.5
- from 0.5 to 0.8
- equal or greater than 0.8

Effect size in favour of students with an immigrant background:
- from -0.2 to -0.5
- from -0.5 to -0.8
- equal or less than -0.8

	Index of use of functional texts		Memorisation strategies		Elaboration strategies		Control strategies		Understanding and remembering		Summarising	
	Effect size	S.E.	Effect size	S.E.	Effect size	S.E.	Effect size	S.E.	Effect size	S.E.	Effect size	S.E.
OECD												
Australia	-0.03	(0.04)	**-0.26**	(0.03)	**-0.19**	(0.02)	**-0.28**	(0.03)	**-0.12**	(0.03)	**-0.14**	(0.03)
Austria	**-0.22**	(0.05)	**-0.08**	(0.04)	**0.15**	(0.04)	0.05	(0.05)	**0.27**	(0.05)	**0.33**	(0.06)
Belgium	**-0.24**	(0.04)	**-0.30**	(0.04)	-0.07	(0.04)	-0.06	(0.05)	**0.27**	(0.04)	**0.34**	(0.05)
Canada	**-0.19**	(0.03)	**-0.27**	(0.02)	**-0.20**	(0.03)	**-0.28**	(0.03)	0.02	(0.03)	0.03	(0.02)
Chile	c	c	c	c	c	c	c	c	c	c	c	c
Czech Republic	**-0.24**	(0.10)	-0.02	(0.09)	-0.07	(0.10)	-0.09	(0.11)	0.11	(0.10)	0.07	(0.11)
Denmark	**-0.16**	(0.05)	**-0.41**	(0.04)	**-0.11**	(0.04)	**-0.30**	(0.04)	**0.28**	(0.06)	**0.32**	(0.07)
Estonia	-0.01	(0.06)	**-0.29**	(0.07)	-0.07	(0.08)	0.05	(0.07)	0.07	(0.08)	**0.20**	(0.08)
Finland	**-0.31**	(0.09)	**-0.49**	(0.10)	**-0.31**	(0.09)	**-0.51**	(0.10)	**0.16**	(0.06)	**0.23**	(0.06)
France	**-0.15**	(0.04)	**-0.30**	(0.06)	-0.11	(0.06)	-0.05	(0.07)	**0.33**	(0.04)	**0.35**	(0.04)
Germany	**-0.23**	(0.04)	**-0.15**	(0.04)	0.01	(0.04)	**0.17**	(0.06)	0.04	(0.07)	**0.26**	(0.07)
Greece	**-0.19**	(0.05)	0.12	(0.06)	**0.16**	(0.07)	-0.15	(0.10)	0.07	(0.12)	-0.07	(0.11)
Hungary	0.19	(0.10)	0.00	(0.12)	0.01	(0.09)	0.06	(0.12)	**0.26**	(0.11)	**0.36**	(0.11)
Iceland	**-0.40**	(0.11)	-0.19	(0.13)	-0.11	(0.10)	-0.12	(0.07)	**0.12**	(0.06)	**0.17**	(0.07)
Ireland	-0.09	(0.06)	**-0.15**	(0.06)	**-0.24**	(0.06)	0.01	(0.04)	0.00	(0.04)	0.06	(0.04)
Israel	0.05	(0.04)	-0.02	(0.04)	**0.17**	(0.04)	**0.14**	(0.05)	**0.36**	(0.05)	**0.35**	(0.04)
Italy	**-0.21**	(0.04)	**-0.20**	(0.04)	0.02	(0.04)	0.01	(0.04)	**0.17**	(0.04)	**0.19**	(0.04)
Japan	c	c	c	c	c	c	c	c	c	c	c	c
Korea	c	c	c	c	0.03	(0.03)	-0.02	(0.03)	**0.12**	(0.03)	**0.16**	(0.03)
Luxembourg	**-0.27**	(0.04)	-0.01	(0.03)	0.03	(0.03)	**0.33**	(0.07)	**0.42**	(0.07)	**0.61**	(0.07)
Mexico	0.01	(0.07)	0.02	(0.08)	0.09	(0.06)	**-0.17**	(0.07)	**0.20**	(0.09)	**0.29**	(0.07)
Netherlands	**-0.31**	(0.05)	**-0.60**	(0.04)	**-0.11**	(0.04)	**-0.34**	(0.03)	-0.01	(0.04)	-0.03	(0.04)
New Zealand	**-0.16**	(0.04)	**-0.39**	(0.03)	**-0.32**	(0.03)	**-0.34**	(0.03)	0.03	(0.07)	**0.16**	(0.06)
Norway	**-0.29**	(0.06)	**-0.30**	(0.07)	**-0.15**	(0.05)	**-0.24**	(0.06)	c	c	c	c
Poland	c	c	c	c	c	c	c	c	c	c	c	c
Portugal	0.01	(0.06)	0.03	(0.06)	0.01	(0.05)	0.07	(0.07)	0.11	(0.07)	**0.14**	(0.07)
Slovak Republic	c	c	c	c	c	c	0.00	(0.05)	**0.19**	(0.06)	**0.22**	(0.06)
Slovenia	**-0.24**	(0.06)	**-0.32**	(0.05)	0.00	(0.06)	**0.11**	(0.04)	**0.17**	(0.04)	**0.16**	(0.04)
Spain	**-0.16**	(0.04)	-0.06	(0.04)	-0.03	(0.03)	**-0.34**	(0.05)	**0.17**	(0.06)	**0.21**	(0.06)
Sweden	**-0.32**	(0.07)	**-0.22**	(0.05)	**-0.25**	(0.06)	**-0.34**	(0.05)	**0.21**	(0.04)	**0.24**	(0.04)
Switzerland	**-0.17**	(0.04)	**-0.22**	(0.04)	-0.02	(0.04)	-0.07	(0.04)	**0.21**	(0.04)	**0.24**	(0.04)
Turkey	c	c	c	c	c	c	c	c	c	c	c	c
United Kingdom	**-0.25**	(0.06)	**-0.35**	(0.05)	**-0.24**	(0.05)	**-0.32**	(0.05)	0.06	(0.04)	0.02	(0.05)
United States	**-0.12**	(0.05)	**-0.13**	(0.04)	-0.08	(0.04)	-0.04	(0.04)	0.00	(0.04)	0.03	(0.05)
OECD average	**-0.17**	(0.01)	**-0.20**	(0.01)	**-0.07**	(0.01)	**-0.09**	(0.01)	**0.15**	(0.01)	**0.19**	(0.01)
Partners												
Albania	c	c	c	c	c	c	c	c	0.10	(0.10)	0.14	(0.10)
Argentina	**0.23**	(0.08)	0.12	(0.10)	0.09	(0.08)	**0.20**	(0.09)	-0.17	(0.12)	-0.02	(0.12)
Azerbaijan	0.09	(0.12)	-0.11	(0.09)	0.05	(0.09)	-0.05	(0.12)	0.27	(0.16)	**0.50**	(0.19)
Brazil	-0.12	(0.20)	**0.40**	(0.15)	0.17	(0.16)	**0.42**	(0.17)	c	c	c	c
Bulgaria	c	c	c	c	c	c	c	c	c	c	c	c
Colombia	-0.14	(0.21)	-0.23	(0.24)	-0.17	(0.29)	0.11	(0.23)	0.49	(0.33)	0.27	(0.20)
Croatia	-0.06	(0.06)	-0.04	(0.05)	0.01	(0.05)	0.00	(0.05)	0.09	(0.05)	0.03	(0.05)
Dubai (UAE)	**0.17**	(0.03)	**0.24**	(0.02)	0.04	(0.03)	**-0.24**	(0.03)	**-0.43**	(0.03)	**-0.49**	(0.04)
Hong Kong-China	0.01	(0.03)	0.05	(0.03)	**0.15**	(0.03)	**0.08**	(0.04)	-0.02	(0.03)	-0.03	(0.04)
Indonesia	c	c	c	c	c	c	c	c	c	c	c	c
Jordan	**0.08**	(0.04)	-0.06	(0.05)	-0.05	(0.05)	-0.07	(0.05)	0.00	(0.04)	-0.02	(0.04)
Kazakhstan	-0.04	(0.05)	-0.01	(0.07)	-0.06	(0.07)	0.00	(0.06)	0.00	(0.06)	-0.10	(0.06)
Kyrgyzstan	0.03	(0.11)	0.09	(0.11)	**0.31**	(0.15)	0.08	(0.15)	**-0.43**	(0.10)	-0.21	(0.11)
Latvia	**-0.30**	(0.08)	**-0.27**	(0.08)	**-0.17**	(0.08)	-0.14	(0.08)	0.04	(0.09)	0.09	(0.08)
Liechtenstein	-0.20	(0.11)	**-0.35**	(0.14)	0.07	(0.14)	0.02	(0.13)	0.16	(0.11)	0.17	(0.11)
Lithuania	-0.07	(0.14)	0.17	(0.12)	0.09	(0.12)	0.18	(0.13)	0.20	(0.12)	0.00	(0.13)
Macao-China	0.04	(0.03)	0.05	(0.03)	0.04	(0.03)	0.04	(0.03)	-0.02	(0.03)	0.00	(0.03)
Montenegro	0.11	(0.07)	**0.13**	(0.06)	0.11	(0.07)	0.08	(0.07)	-0.10	(0.07)	0.02	(0.08)
Panama	0.13	(0.15)	**0.47**	(0.10)	**0.35**	(0.11)	**0.31**	(0.14)	0.11	(0.13)	0.10	(0.20)
Peru	c	c	c	c	c	c	c	c	c	c	c	c
Qatar	**0.07**	(0.02)	0.01	(0.02)	-0.03	(0.02)	**-0.34**	(0.02)	**-0.37**	(0.02)	**-0.32**	(0.02)
Romania	c	c	c	c	c	c	c	c	c	c	c	c
Russian Federation	0.00	(0.05)	0.01	(0.07)	-0.04	(0.05)	-0.04	(0.05)	0.06	(0.06)	0.09	(0.07)
Serbia	0.03	(0.06)	0.03	(0.04)	-0.04	(0.05)	-0.07	(0.04)	**-0.15**	(0.06)	-0.11	(0.07)
Shanghai-China	c	c	c	c	c	c	c	c	c	c	c	c
Singapore	-0.05	(0.04)	0.05	(0.04)	-0.04	(0.04)	-0.07	(0.04)	-0.07	(0.04)	-0.04	(0.05)
Chinese Taipei	c	c	c	c	c	c	c	c	c	c	c	c
Thailand	c	c	c	c	c	c	c	c	c	c	c	c
Trinidad and Tobago	**0.19**	(0.09)	0.10	(0.10)	**0.22**	(0.07)	0.10	(0.09)	-0.09	(0.09)	-0.13	(0.11)
Tunisia	c	c	c	c	c	c	c	c	c	c	c	c
Uruguay	c	c	c	c	c	c	c	c	c	c	c	c

Note: Values that are statistically significant are indicated in bold (see Annex A3).
StatLink ⟐⟐ http://dx.doi.org/10.1787/888932343285

[Part 1/2]
Effect sizes for the difference between students who speak and those who do not speak the language of assessment at home in engagement in reading and approaches to learning

Table III.2.15 *Results based on students' self-reports*

Effect size in favour of students who speak the language of assessment at home:
- from 0.2 to 0.5
- from 0.5 to 0.8
- equal or greater than 0.8

Effect size in favour of students who do not speak the language of assessment at home:
- from -0.2 to -0.5
- from -0.5 to -0.8
- equal or less than -0.8

	Enjoyment of reading		Diversity of reading materials		Online reading activities		Index of interpretation of literary texts		Index of use of texts containing non-continuous materials		Index of reading activities for traditional literature courses	
	Effect size	S.E.	Effect size	S.E.	Effect size	S.E.	Effect size	S.E.	Effect size	S.E.	Effect size	S.E.
OECD												
Australia	-0.19	(0.04)	-0.32	(0.04)	-0.38	(0.05)	-0.26	(0.05)	-0.14	(0.03)	-0.25	(0.03)
Austria	0.10	(0.06)	-0.08	(0.06)	-0.20	(0.06)	-0.12	(0.05)	-0.09	(0.06)	-0.18	(0.06)
Belgium	0.21	(0.03)	0.05	(0.03)	-0.01	(0.04)	0.02	(0.04)	0.02	(0.03)	-0.02	(0.03)
Canada	-0.02	(0.03)	-0.14	(0.04)	-0.31	(0.03)	-0.19	(0.04)	-0.04	(0.03)	-0.22	(0.03)
Chile	c	c	c	c	c	c	c	c	c	c	c	c
Czech Republic	-0.05	(0.11)	0.10	(0.16)	0.14	(0.15)	-0.07	(0.14)	-0.25	(0.15)	-0.35	(0.12)
Denmark	-0.09	(0.06)	-0.07	(0.08)	-0.10	(0.05)	0.04	(0.06)	0.00	(0.05)	-0.14	(0.06)
Estonia	0.03	(0.10)	0.28	(0.09)	0.01	(0.09)	-0.26	(0.10)	-0.06	(0.08)	-0.22	(0.08)
Finland	0.04	(0.08)	0.26	(0.06)	-0.08	(0.06)	-0.08	(0.08)	0.08	(0.07)	-0.11	(0.08)
France	0.12	(0.07)	0.05	(0.06)	0.09	(0.08)	0.01	(0.07)	0.03	(0.08)	-0.13	(0.09)
Germany	0.14	(0.05)	0.07	(0.05)	-0.07	(0.06)	-0.01	(0.06)	-0.07	(0.05)	-0.18	(0.06)
Greece	0.14	(0.08)	0.22	(0.10)	0.10	(0.09)	0.10	(0.08)	-0.22	(0.09)	-0.09	(0.12)
Hungary	-0.21	(0.15)	0.15	(0.19)	0.01	(0.27)	0.06	(0.18)	-0.12	(0.15)	-0.65	(0.30)
Iceland	-0.05	(0.11)	0.02	(0.11)	0.07	(0.12)	0.17	(0.12)	-0.17	(0.12)	0.02	(0.12)
Ireland	-0.09	(0.06)	-0.08	(0.07)	-0.34	(0.12)	-0.09	(0.07)	-0.01	(0.08)	-0.32	(0.09)
Israel	-0.09	(0.05)	0.14	(0.05)	-0.01	(0.06)	-0.02	(0.06)	-0.01	(0.04)	0.02	(0.05)
Italy	0.38	(0.03)	0.30	(0.03)	0.39	(0.03)	0.12	(0.03)	-0.12	(0.03)	0.20	(0.03)
Japan	c	c	c	c	c	c	c	c	c	c	c	c
Korea	c	c	c	c	c	c	c	c	c	c	c	c
Luxembourg	0.34	(0.05)	0.21	(0.05)	0.04	(0.05)	0.28	(0.05)	0.32	(0.06)	0.18	(0.06)
Mexico	-0.13	(0.05)	0.16	(0.06)	0.64	(0.07)	0.08	(0.06)	0.15	(0.05)	-0.20	(0.08)
Netherlands	-0.10	(0.07)	-0.02	(0.08)	-0.21	(0.08)	-0.09	(0.08)	-0.11	(0.06)	-0.18	(0.08)
New Zealand	-0.06	(0.04)	-0.28	(0.05)	-0.24	(0.05)	-0.17	(0.05)	-0.03	(0.05)	-0.45	(0.04)
Norway	-0.10	(0.06)	0.14	(0.06)	-0.08	(0.06)	-0.23	(0.06)	0.03	(0.06)	-0.27	(0.07)
Poland	c	c	c	c	c	c	c	c	c	c	c	c
Portugal	-0.03	(0.10)	0.12	(0.11)	-0.07	(0.13)	-0.04	(0.11)	-0.23	(0.12)	0.16	(0.11)
Slovak Republic	0.04	(0.07)	0.09	(0.09)	0.46	(0.12)	-0.23	(0.08)	0.05	(0.10)	-0.31	(0.07)
Slovenia	0.06	(0.08)	-0.02	(0.07)	0.03	(0.09)	-0.02	(0.08)	0.01	(0.08)	-0.16	(0.07)
Spain	-0.01	(0.03)	-0.02	(0.04)	0.12	(0.03)	0.13	(0.03)	0.01	(0.03)	0.06	(0.04)
Sweden	-0.07	(0.06)	0.11	(0.07)	-0.10	(0.07)	-0.24	(0.07)	-0.13	(0.06)	-0.26	(0.08)
Switzerland	0.11	(0.04)	0.09	(0.03)	-0.10	(0.04)	-0.11	(0.04)	-0.07	(0.05)	-0.21	(0.04)
Turkey	-0.03	(0.11)	0.25	(0.08)	0.67	(0.12)	0.31	(0.10)	-0.05	(0.09)	-0.01	(0.09)
United Kingdom	-0.20	(0.06)	-0.26	(0.06)	-0.27	(0.06)	-0.12	(0.06)	-0.17	(0.06)	-0.32	(0.07)
United States	0.06	(0.04)	-0.07	(0.04)	-0.10	(0.05)	-0.06	(0.04)	0.03	(0.05)	-0.17	(0.04)
OECD average	0.01	(0.01)	0.05	(0.01)	0.00	(0.02)	-0.04	(0.01)	-0.04	(0.01)	-0.16	(0.02)
Partners												
Albania	0.15	(0.14)	-0.07	(0.23)	-0.38	(0.19)	0.07	(0.18)	0.31	(0.15)	-0.05	(0.24)
Argentina	-0.21	(0.20)	0.00	(0.15)	0.14	(0.19)	0.16	(0.22)	0.08	(0.18)	0.16	(0.19)
Azerbaijan	0.11	(0.08)	0.06	(0.07)	-0.38	(0.12)	-0.09	(0.09)	0.19	(0.07)	0.02	(0.07)
Brazil	0.04	(0.13)	-0.23	(0.12)	-0.21	(0.14)	0.15	(0.17)	0.06	(0.15)	-0.06	(0.12)
Bulgaria	-0.01	(0.08)	0.19	(0.09)	0.64	(0.07)	0.13	(0.08)	-0.11	(0.06)	-0.24	(0.07)
Colombia	-0.38	(0.25)	-0.19	(0.20)	-0.64	(0.19)	-0.12	(0.21)	-0.02	(0.19)	-0.60	(0.19)
Croatia	0.09	(0.20)	0.42	(0.16)	0.16	(0.13)	0.12	(0.12)	0.17	(0.11)	-0.07	(0.16)
Dubai (UAE)	0.06	(0.03)	-0.04	(0.03)	0.00	(0.03)	0.07	(0.03)	0.00	(0.03)	0.20	(0.03)
Hong Kong-China	0.11	(0.07)	0.20	(0.05)	0.13	(0.13)	-0.05	(0.10)	-0.10	(0.08)	0.17	(0.06)
Indonesia	0.03	(0.04)	0.20	(0.04)	0.42	(0.07)	0.03	(0.04)	-0.07	(0.05)	-0.02	(0.05)
Jordan	-0.10	(0.08)	-0.06	(0.09)	-0.48	(0.10)	-0.05	(0.07)	-0.02	(0.09)	-0.02	(0.09)
Kazakhstan	0.26	(0.05)	0.19	(0.05)	-0.04	(0.06)	-0.10	(0.05)	-0.11	(0.05)	-0.08	(0.05)
Kyrgyzstan	0.15	(0.05)	-0.04	(0.08)	-0.24	(0.06)	-0.05	(0.06)	-0.01	(0.06)	-0.19	(0.06)
Latvia	0.07	(0.08)	0.09	(0.12)	0.12	(0.07)	0.00	(0.08)	-0.07	(0.10)	0.03	(0.06)
Liechtenstein	0.17	(0.15)	0.27	(0.14)	-0.25	(0.22)	-0.31	(0.15)	-0.13	(0.16)	-0.38	(0.15)
Lithuania	0.12	(0.08)	0.15	(0.07)	0.09	(0.07)	-0.06	(0.09)	-0.03	(0.08)	-0.10	(0.09)
Macao-China	-0.05	(0.05)	-0.23	(0.04)	-0.50	(0.04)	-0.13	(0.04)	-0.48	(0.05)	0.46	(0.04)
Montenegro	0.35	(0.12)	-0.20	(0.20)	-0.08	(0.17)	-0.01	(0.11)	-0.36	(0.14)	-0.14	(0.14)
Panama	-0.13	(0.09)	-0.04	(0.12)	0.41	(0.19)	0.12	(0.12)	0.00	(0.11)	-0.15	(0.13)
Peru	0.10	(0.05)	0.34	(0.07)	0.89	(0.07)	0.21	(0.07)	0.08	(0.10)	0.03	(0.08)
Qatar	-0.07	(0.02)	-0.02	(0.02)	-0.15	(0.02)	-0.28	(0.02)	-0.41	(0.03)	0.12	(0.02)
Romania	0.40	(0.17)	0.48	(0.21)	0.31	(0.23)	0.31	(0.11)	0.10	(0.12)	0.10	(0.14)
Russian Federation	0.02	(0.07)	-0.16	(0.09)	0.52	(0.11)	0.06	(0.05)	0.00	(0.07)	-0.23	(0.07)
Serbia	0.25	(0.13)	0.10	(0.11)	0.06	(0.08)	0.19	(0.12)	-0.19	(0.10)	0.00	(0.10)
Shanghai-China	0.35	(0.17)	0.19	(0.09)	0.37	(0.13)	0.38	(0.12)	-0.06	(0.11)	0.28	(0.13)
Singapore	0.37	(0.03)	0.18	(0.03)	0.20	(0.03)	0.29	(0.03)	0.18	(0.03)	0.03	(0.03)
Chinese Taipei	0.29	(0.05)	0.13	(0.03)	0.08	(0.03)	0.20	(0.04)	0.21	(0.04)	0.24	(0.04)
Thailand	-0.11	(0.04)	0.06	(0.04)	0.50	(0.04)	-0.05	(0.04)	-0.12	(0.04)	-0.12	(0.04)
Trinidad and Tobago	0.10	(0.10)	0.13	(0.11)	-0.14	(0.09)	0.13	(0.09)	-0.01	(0.12)	-0.04	(0.10)
Tunisia	c	c	c	c	c	c	c	c	c	c	c	c
Uruguay	-0.04	(0.08)	-0.08	(0.09)	0.34	(0.10)	0.12	(0.10)	0.09	(0.10)	0.02	(0.09)

Note: Values that are statistically significant are indicated in bold (see Annex A3).
StatLink ᴍᴸ᯽ http://dx.doi.org/10.1787/888932343285

[Part 2/2]
Effect sizes for the difference between students who speak and those who do not speak the language of assessment at home in engagement in reading and approaches to learning

Table III.2.15 *Results based on students' self-reports*

Effect size in favour of students who speak the language of assessment at home:
- from 0.2 to 0.5
- from 0.5 to 0.8
- equal or greater than 0.8

Effect size in favour of students who do not speak the language of assessment at home:
- from -0.2 to -0.5
- from -0.5 to -0.8
- equal or less than -0.8

	Index of use of functional texts		Memorisation strategies		Elaboration strategies		Control strategies		Understanding and remembering		Summarising	
	Effect size	S.E.	Effect size	S.E.	Effect size	S.E.	Effect size	S.E.	Effect size	S.E.	Effect size	S.E.
OECD												
Australia	-0.10	(0.05)	-0.34	(0.05)	-0.32	(0.04)	-0.32	(0.05)	-0.05	(0.03)	-0.06	(0.04)
Austria	-0.23	(0.06)	-0.03	(0.05)	0.21	(0.04)	0.17	(0.05)	0.28	(0.05)	0.35	(0.06)
Belgium	-0.08	(0.03)	-0.03	(0.04)	-0.08	(0.03)	0.07	(0.03)	0.23	(0.04)	0.17	(0.03)
Canada	-0.10	(0.04)	-0.20	(0.03)	-0.24	(0.03)	-0.21	(0.03)	0.02	(0.03)	0.05	(0.03)
Chile	c	c	c	c	c	c	c	c	c	c	c	c
Czech Republic	-0.06	(0.12)	0.00	(0.17)	-0.28	(0.12)	-0.19	(0.14)	0.17	(0.11)	0.16	(0.12)
Denmark	-0.12	(0.07)	-0.35	(0.07)	-0.13	(0.06)	-0.24	(0.07)	0.26	(0.06)	0.17	(0.05)
Estonia	-0.30	(0.10)	0.05	(0.10)	-0.02	(0.09)	-0.10	(0.11)	0.03	(0.09)	0.10	(0.08)
Finland	-0.25	(0.07)	-0.44	(0.08)	-0.21	(0.07)	-0.30	(0.07)	0.19	(0.07)	0.21	(0.06)
France	-0.17	(0.07)	-0.18	(0.06)	-0.22	(0.06)	0.08	(0.06)	0.22	(0.07)	0.34	(0.06)
Germany	-0.16	(0.05)	-0.20	(0.05)	-0.10	(0.05)	0.00	(0.05)	0.33	(0.05)	0.36	(0.05)
Greece	-0.05	(0.08)	0.05	(0.09)	0.10	(0.07)	0.16	(0.07)	0.06	(0.08)	0.29	(0.09)
Hungary	0.06	(0.16)	-0.18	(0.21)	-0.37	(0.10)	-0.38	(0.27)	0.55	(0.18)	0.56	(0.26)
Iceland	-0.28	(0.11)	-0.25	(0.11)	-0.29	(0.10)	-0.08	(0.11)	0.09	(0.11)	0.39	(0.09)
Ireland	-0.21	(0.07)	-0.09	(0.08)	-0.27	(0.07)	-0.03	(0.07)	0.32	(0.07)	0.27	(0.07)
Israel	-0.04	(0.06)	0.06	(0.05)	0.02	(0.05)	0.07	(0.05)	0.02	(0.06)	0.06	(0.05)
Italy	-0.21	(0.03)	-0.01	(0.03)	0.07	(0.02)	0.29	(0.03)	0.32	(0.02)	0.34	(0.03)
Japan	c	c	c	c	c	c	c	c	c	c	c	c
Korea	c	c	c	c	c	c	c	c	c	c	c	c
Luxembourg	0.12	(0.05)	-0.14	(0.05)	-0.10	(0.05)	0.13	(0.06)	0.32	(0.05)	0.36	(0.05)
Mexico	0.14	(0.06)	-0.02	(0.05)	-0.10	(0.04)	0.11	(0.05)	0.28	(0.06)	0.40	(0.05)
Netherlands	-0.40	(0.06)	-0.47	(0.07)	-0.10	(0.07)	-0.09	(0.10)	0.22	(0.10)	0.19	(0.08)
New Zealand	-0.23	(0.04)	-0.38	(0.04)	-0.37	(0.05)	-0.21	(0.04)	0.16	(0.05)	0.21	(0.04)
Norway	-0.29	(0.05)	-0.28	(0.05)	-0.14	(0.05)	-0.22	(0.05)	0.10	(0.06)	0.22	(0.06)
Poland	c	c	c	c	c	c	c	c	c	c	c	c
Portugal	-0.07	(0.12)	0.20	(0.14)	-0.08	(0.11)	-0.05	(0.10)	0.14	(0.09)	0.12	(0.12)
Slovak Republic	-0.22	(0.10)	-0.22	(0.09)	-0.05	(0.09)	0.05	(0.09)	0.13	(0.09)	0.24	(0.10)
Slovenia	-0.22	(0.06)	-0.25	(0.07)	0.02	(0.08)	0.03	(0.08)	0.17	(0.07)	0.20	(0.07)
Spain	0.01	(0.03)	0.16	(0.03)	0.02	(0.02)	0.13	(0.03)	0.05	(0.03)	0.08	(0.03)
Sweden	-0.26	(0.08)	-0.12	(0.07)	-0.21	(0.08)	-0.29	(0.07)	0.20	(0.07)	0.24	(0.08)
Switzerland	-0.13	(0.05)	-0.20	(0.04)	-0.08	(0.04)	-0.07	(0.04)	0.26	(0.04)	0.31	(0.04)
Turkey	0.03	(0.12)	-0.10	(0.07)	-0.02	(0.12)	-0.03	(0.08)	0.11	(0.07)	0.14	(0.08)
United Kingdom	-0.23	(0.07)	-0.43	(0.05)	-0.30	(0.05)	-0.27	(0.06)	0.12	(0.05)	0.07	(0.06)
United States	-0.13	(0.05)	0.00	(0.05)	-0.05	(0.03)	0.07	(0.04)	0.06	(0.04)	0.08	(0.06)
OECD average	-0.14	(0.01)	-0.15	(0.01)	-0.12	(0.01)	-0.06	(0.02)	0.18	(0.01)	0.22	(0.02)
Partners												
Albania	0.00	(0.18)	0.10	(0.14)	-0.09	(0.19)	0.00	(0.19)	0.52	(0.16)	0.10	(0.15)
Argentina	0.36	(0.16)	0.28	(0.17)	-0.16	(0.19)	0.24	(0.18)	0.16	(0.21)	0.13	(0.14)
Azerbaijan	0.34	(0.08)	0.11	(0.07)	0.18	(0.09)	0.09	(0.08)	-0.08	(0.09)	-0.31	(0.12)
Brazil	-0.02	(0.11)	0.10	(0.14)	-0.29	(0.15)	-0.01	(0.16)	0.21	(0.15)	0.28	(0.14)
Bulgaria	0.07	(0.05)	0.03	(0.06)	0.05	(0.05)	0.10	(0.07)	0.26	(0.05)	0.35	(0.07)
Colombia	-0.08	(0.23)	-0.11	(0.21)	-0.32	(0.19)	0.02	(0.25)	-0.23	(0.31)	-0.05	(0.22)
Croatia	0.19	(0.09)	0.28	(0.12)	0.19	(0.14)	0.24	(0.18)	0.19	(0.20)	0.07	(0.22)
Dubai (UAE)	-0.01	(0.03)	0.00	(0.03)	-0.04	(0.03)	-0.14	(0.03)	-0.03	(0.04)	-0.09	(0.03)
Hong Kong-China	-0.15	(0.06)	0.02	(0.05)	-0.03	(0.06)	-0.09	(0.08)	0.10	(0.07)	0.01	(0.06)
Indonesia	0.03	(0.04)	0.09	(0.04)	0.09	(0.03)	0.10	(0.04)	-0.05	(0.05)	-0.01	(0.05)
Jordan	-0.16	(0.08)	0.07	(0.09)	0.00	(0.07)	-0.01	(0.09)	0.02	(0.08)	0.15	(0.09)
Kazakhstan	-0.13	(0.04)	0.10	(0.06)	0.13	(0.05)	0.14	(0.06)	-0.04	(0.07)	-0.15	(0.06)
Kyrgyzstan	0.12	(0.05)	-0.19	(0.04)	0.12	(0.04)	0.18	(0.04)	-0.33	(0.05)	-0.40	(0.05)
Latvia	-0.13	(0.07)	0.05	(0.06)	-0.21	(0.06)	0.07	(0.08)	0.13	(0.09)	0.07	(0.08)
Liechtenstein	-0.36	(0.15)	-0.39	(0.15)	0.02	(0.16)	0.00	(0.16)	0.40	(0.14)	0.60	(0.20)
Lithuania	-0.17	(0.08)	-0.08	(0.08)	-0.04	(0.09)	0.01	(0.08)	0.15	(0.06)	0.09	(0.06)
Macao-China	-0.01	(0.05)	-0.40	(0.04)	-0.24	(0.04)	-0.75	(0.04)	-0.08	(0.04)	-0.35	(0.04)
Montenegro	-0.12	(0.15)	-0.05	(0.13)	0.02	(0.13)	0.26	(0.11)	0.23	(0.14)	0.40	(0.16)
Panama	-0.09	(0.18)	0.21	(0.12)	0.12	(0.08)	0.28	(0.12)	0.27	(0.14)	0.22	(0.13)
Peru	-0.01	(0.09)	-0.02	(0.09)	0.13	(0.07)	0.25	(0.07)	0.24	(0.07)	0.15	(0.08)
Qatar	-0.10	(0.02)	0.05	(0.02)	0.07	(0.02)	-0.20	(0.02)	-0.22	(0.02)	-0.16	(0.02)
Romania	0.13	(0.11)	0.20	(0.21)	0.30	(0.21)	0.36	(0.21)	0.43	(0.11)	0.25	(0.15)
Russian Federation	-0.08	(0.07)	-0.17	(0.07)	-0.09	(0.05)	-0.01	(0.07)	0.29	(0.10)	0.33	(0.07)
Serbia	-0.23	(0.11)	-0.26	(0.09)	-0.01	(0.13)	0.03	(0.13)	0.02	(0.10)	0.38	(0.11)
Shanghai-China	-0.17	(0.13)	0.10	(0.13)	0.24	(0.12)	0.25	(0.11)	0.28	(0.13)	0.51	(0.11)
Singapore	-0.08	(0.03)	-0.09	(0.03)	0.06	(0.03)	0.20	(0.03)	0.12	(0.03)	0.23	(0.03)
Chinese Taipei	-0.05	(0.04)	0.16	(0.04)	0.15	(0.04)	0.22	(0.04)	0.12	(0.04)	0.17	(0.04)
Thailand	0.03	(0.03)	0.00	(0.04)	-0.02	(0.04)	-0.01	(0.04)	0.05	(0.04)	0.09	(0.04)
Trinidad and Tobago	0.06	(0.10)	0.06	(0.10)	-0.09	(0.10)	0.32	(0.10)	0.44	(0.11)	0.35	(0.10)
Tunisia	c	c	c	c	c	c	c	c	c	c	c	c
Uruguay	-0.14	(0.10)	-0.01	(0.09)	-0.01	(0.09)	0.18	(0.11)	0.06	(0.09)	0.13	(0.11)

Note: Values that are statistically significant are indicated in bold (see Annex A3).
StatLink 🔗 http://dx.doi.org/10.1787/888932343285

[Part 1/1]

Table III.2.16

Index of enjoyment of reading and index of summarising, by quarter of the PISA index of economic, social and cultural status (ESCS)

	Index of enjoyment of reading								Index of summarising							
	Bottom quarter of ESCS		Second quarter of ESCS		Third quarter of ESCS		Top quarter of ESCS		Bottom quarter of ESCS		Second quarter of ESCS		Third quarter of ESCS		Top quarter of ESCS	
	Mean index	S.E.	Mean index	S.E.	Mean index	S.E.	Mean index	S.E.	Mean index	S.E.	Mean index	S.E.	Mean index	S.E.	Mean index	S.E.
Australia	-0.29	(0.02)	-0.13	(0.02)	0.09	(0.02)	**0.35**	(0.03)	**-0.34**	(0.02)	**-0.18**	(0.02)	0.01	(0.02)	**0.17**	(0.03)
Austria	-0.38	(0.04)	-0.30	(0.04)	-0.09	(0.04)	**0.25**	(0.04)	**-0.20**	(0.03)	0.05	(0.04)	0.07	(0.03)	**0.34**	(0.03)
Belgium	-0.44	(0.03)	-0.34	(0.03)	-0.12	(0.03)	**0.14**	(0.02)	**-0.14**	(0.03)	0.07	(0.03)	0.25	(0.03)	**0.49**	(0.02)
Canada	-0.07	(0.02)	0.05	(0.02)	0.18	(0.02)	**0.38**	(0.03)	**-0.08**	(0.02)	-0.06	(0.02)	0.07	(0.02)	**0.17**	(0.02)
Chile	-0.11	(0.02)	-0.17	(0.02)	-0.05	(0.03)	**0.07**	(0.03)	**-0.36**	(0.03)	**-0.24**	(0.03)	-0.09	(0.03)	**0.10**	(0.03)
Czech Republic	-0.29	(0.03)	-0.21	(0.03)	-0.10	(0.03)	**0.08**	(0.03)	**-0.10**	(0.04)	0.07	(0.04)	0.12	(0.04)	**0.32**	(0.03)
Denmark	-0.35	(0.02)	-0.20	(0.03)	-0.02	(0.03)	**0.22**	(0.02)	**-0.06**	(0.04)	0.12	(0.04)	0.26	(0.03)	**0.41**	(0.03)
Estonia	-0.21	(0.03)	-0.12	(0.03)	0.02	(0.03)	**0.18**	(0.03)	0.04	(0.04)	0.06	(0.04)	0.17	(0.03)	**0.32**	(0.03)
Finland	-0.19	(0.03)	0.02	(0.03)	0.11	(0.03)	**0.27**	(0.03)	**-0.11**	(0.03)	0.03	(0.03)	0.14	(0.03)	**0.29**	(0.03)
France	-0.24	(0.04)	-0.09	(0.04)	0.05	(0.04)	**0.36**	(0.03)	**-0.03**	(0.04)	0.17	(0.03)	0.37	(0.03)	**0.44**	(0.03)
Germany	-0.28	(0.03)	0.03	(0.03)	0.13	(0.04)	**0.44**	(0.04)	**-0.18**	(0.04)	0.11	(0.03)	0.18	(0.03)	**0.39**	(0.02)
Greece	-0.10	(0.03)	0.02	(0.03)	0.07	(0.02)	**0.27**	(0.03)	**-0.30**	(0.04)	-0.11	(0.03)	-0.10	(0.04)	**0.08**	(0.04)
Hungary	-0.09	(0.03)	0.02	(0.03)	0.14	(0.03)	**0.48**	(0.03)	**-0.32**	(0.05)	-0.03	(0.04)	0.03	(0.04)	**0.29**	(0.04)
Iceland	-0.25	(0.03)	-0.11	(0.03)	-0.02	(0.04)	**0.13**	(0.04)	**-0.32**	(0.03)	-0.19	(0.04)	-0.12	(0.03)	-0.04	(0.03)
Ireland	-0.42	(0.04)	-0.19	(0.03)	0.03	(0.03)	**0.26**	(0.04)	**-0.03**	(0.04)	0.08	(0.04)	0.22	(0.03)	**0.30**	(0.04)
Israel	-0.04	(0.03)	-0.04	(0.02)	0.11	(0.04)	**0.21**	(0.04)	**-0.43**	(0.04)	**-0.22**	(0.03)	-0.03	(0.03)	**0.07**	(0.03)
Italy	-0.15	(0.02)	-0.01	(0.02)	0.11	(0.02)	**0.29**	(0.02)	0.07	(0.02)	0.25	(0.02)	0.35	(0.02)	**0.46**	(0.01)
Japan	0.01	(0.03)	0.10	(0.04)	0.26	(0.03)	**0.44**	(0.03)	**-0.21**	(0.04)	-0.10	(0.04)	0.11	(0.03)	**0.18**	(0.03)
Korea	-0.07	(0.03)	0.08	(0.03)	0.15	(0.03)	**0.35**	(0.03)	**-0.24**	(0.05)	0.04	(0.03)	0.10	(0.04)	**0.28**	(0.03)
Luxembourg	-0.40	(0.03)	-0.26	(0.03)	-0.11	(0.03)	**0.16**	(0.03)	**-0.31**	(0.03)	-0.12	(0.03)	0.06	(0.03)	**0.21**	(0.03)
Mexico	0.20	(0.02)	0.10	(0.01)	0.09	(0.01)	0.17	(0.02)	**-0.27**	(0.02)	-0.14	(0.02)	-0.02	(0.02)	**0.16**	(0.02)
Netherlands	-0.49	(0.04)	-0.40	(0.04)	-0.32	(0.03)	-0.06	(0.04)	**-0.34**	(0.06)	**-0.24**	(0.05)	-0.09	(0.04)	**0.09**	(0.04)
New Zealand	-0.11	(0.03)	-0.01	(0.03)	0.21	(0.03)	**0.47**	(0.04)	**-0.36**	(0.04)	**-0.20**	(0.04)	-0.12	(0.04)	**0.14**	(0.03)
Norway	-0.37	(0.03)	-0.29	(0.03)	-0.14	(0.03)	0.05	(0.03)	**-0.09**	(0.03)	0.11	(0.03)	0.19	(0.03)	**0.29**	(0.03)
Poland	-0.16	(0.03)	-0.12	(0.03)	-0.04	(0.03)	**0.39**	(0.04)	**-0.28**	(0.03)	-0.04	(0.03)	0.02	(0.03)	**0.20**	(0.03)
Portugal	0.08	(0.02)	0.14	(0.03)	0.24	(0.03)	**0.38**	(0.03)	**-0.22**	(0.04)	-0.08	(0.04)	0.06	(0.03)	**0.32**	(0.03)
Slovak Republic	-0.25	(0.02)	-0.17	(0.03)	-0.07	(0.03)	**0.09**	(0.03)	**-0.34**	(0.04)	-0.11	(0.04)	-0.07	(0.04)	**0.07**	(0.04)
Slovenia	-0.37	(0.02)	-0.33	(0.03)	-0.14	(0.03)	0.05	(0.04)	**-0.39**	(0.03)	-0.33	(0.03)	-0.15	(0.04)	**0.09**	(0.03)
Spain	-0.25	(0.03)	-0.06	(0.02)	0.05	(0.02)	**0.21**	(0.02)	**-0.08**	(0.03)	0.03	(0.03)	0.11	(0.04)	**0.26**	(0.02)
Sweden	-0.30	(0.03)	-0.21	(0.03)	-0.03	(0.03)	**0.14**	(0.03)	**-0.36**	(0.04)	-0.18	(0.04)	-0.05	(0.03)	**0.07**	(0.03)
Switzerland	-0.31	(0.05)	-0.17	(0.03)	-0.03	(0.03)	**0.36**	(0.03)	**-0.12**	(0.03)	0.11	(0.03)	0.16	(0.03)	**0.40**	(0.03)
Turkey	0.67	(0.03)	0.61	(0.03)	0.59	(0.03)	0.68	(0.03)	**-0.52**	(0.03)	**-0.39**	(0.03)	-0.35	(0.04)	-0.19	(0.03)
United Kingdom	-0.35	(0.03)	-0.24	(0.03)	-0.06	(0.03)	**0.20**	(0.03)	**-0.30**	(0.03)	-0.13	(0.03)	0.01	(0.03)	**0.20**	(0.04)
United States	-0.25	(0.03)	-0.16	(0.04)	-0.02	(0.04)	**0.28**	(0.04)	**-0.39**	(0.03)	**-0.26**	(0.03)	-0.16	(0.04)	**0.07**	(0.03)
OECD average	-0.19	(0.01)	-0.09	(0.01)	0.04	(0.01)	**0.26**	(0.01)	**-0.23**	(0.01)	-0.06	(0.01)	0.05	(0.01)	**0.22**	(0.01)
Albania	0.62	(0.03)	0.63	(0.03)	0.67	(0.02)	0.76	(0.02)	**-0.23**	(0.05)	-0.18	(0.05)	-0.11	(0.04)	0.03	(0.03)
Argentina	-0.14	(0.03)	-0.21	(0.02)	-0.18	(0.03)	-0.12	(0.03)	**-0.50**	(0.05)	**-0.33**	(0.04)	-0.20	(0.04)	0.06	(0.04)
Azerbaijan	0.31	(0.03)	0.37	(0.02)	0.44	(0.02)	0.46	(0.02)	**-1.00**	(0.05)	-1.00	(0.04)	-0.94	(0.04)	-0.79	(0.06)
Brazil	0.27	(0.02)	0.25	(0.02)	0.22	(0.02)	0.35	(0.02)	**-0.53**	(0.02)	-0.36	(0.02)	-0.29	(0.02)	-0.11	(0.03)
Bulgaria	-0.16	(0.03)	-0.10	(0.03)	-0.04	(0.04)	0.24	(0.04)	**-0.64**	(0.04)	**-0.46**	(0.05)	-0.34	(0.05)	-0.12	(0.04)
Colombia	0.17	(0.04)	0.10	(0.03)	0.12	(0.03)	0.17	(0.03)	**-0.48**	(0.06)	**-0.41**	(0.04)	-0.18	(0.03)	0.06	(0.04)
Croatia	-0.23	(0.02)	-0.24	(0.03)	-0.10	(0.03)	0.06	(0.04)	**-0.28**	(0.03)	-0.19	(0.03)	-0.05	(0.03)	0.09	(0.04)
Dubai (UAE)	0.12	(0.03)	0.24	(0.03)	0.38	(0.03)	0.38	(0.03)	**-0.43**	(0.03)	-0.09	(0.03)	0.00	(0.03)	0.07	(0.03)
Hong Kong-China	0.17	(0.02)	0.29	(0.03)	0.37	(0.02)	0.48	(0.03)	**-0.62**	(0.04)	**-0.55**	(0.04)	-0.54	(0.04)	-0.39	(0.04)
Indonesia	0.41	(0.02)	0.44	(0.02)	0.45	(0.02)	0.43	(0.02)	**-0.66**	(0.04)	-0.63	(0.04)	-0.53	(0.04)	-0.37	(0.05)
Jordan	0.37	(0.02)	0.40	(0.02)	0.38	(0.03)	0.35	(0.03)	**-0.74**	(0.03)	**-0.56**	(0.03)	-0.55	(0.04)	-0.47	(0.03)
Kazakhstan	0.49	(0.03)	0.53	(0.03)	0.53	(0.03)	0.62	(0.03)	**-0.68**	(0.04)	-0.63	(0.03)	-0.49	(0.03)	-0.37	(0.05)
Kyrgyzstan	0.36	(0.03)	0.39	(0.02)	0.38	(0.02)	0.41	(0.02)	**-1.10**	(0.03)	-0.98	(0.03)	-0.84	(0.04)	-0.61	(0.05)
Latvia	-0.17	(0.03)	-0.12	(0.03)	-0.02	(0.03)	0.15	(0.03)	**-0.37**	(0.05)	**-0.26**	(0.03)	-0.15	(0.03)	0.00	(0.04)
Liechtenstein	-0.43	(0.11)	-0.14	(0.10)	-0.19	(0.13)	-0.04	(0.13)	**-0.32**	(0.10)	0.12	(0.10)	-0.06	(0.10)	0.26	(0.11)
Lithuania	-0.13	(0.04)	0.00	(0.03)	0.07	(0.03)	0.32	(0.03)	**-0.37**	(0.03)	**-0.24**	(0.03)	-0.15	(0.03)	0.07	(0.03)
Macao-China	-0.09	(0.02)	0.05	(0.02)	0.10	(0.02)	0.24	(0.02)	**-0.41**	(0.02)	-0.33	(0.02)	-0.24	(0.03)	-0.14	(0.03)
Montenegro	0.11	(0.02)	0.21	(0.02)	0.21	(0.02)	0.32	(0.02)	**-0.78**	(0.04)	-0.63	(0.03)	-0.49	(0.03)	-0.37	(0.03)
Panama	0.24	(0.04)	0.19	(0.03)	0.12	(0.04)	0.17	(0.04)	**-0.71**	(0.06)	-0.65	(0.05)	-0.48	(0.05)	-0.18	(0.06)
Peru	0.36	(0.02)	0.38	(0.02)	0.32	(0.02)	0.32	(0.02)	**-0.65**	(0.04)	-0.40	(0.04)	-0.26	(0.04)	-0.06	(0.05)
Qatar	0.16	(0.01)	0.19	(0.02)	0.21	(0.02)	0.26	(0.02)	**-0.66**	(0.02)	**-0.48**	(0.02)	-0.32	(0.02)	-0.40	(0.02)
Romania	0.06	(0.03)	0.09	(0.03)	0.10	(0.03)	0.16	(0.03)	**-0.33**	(0.04)	-0.14	(0.03)	-0.08	(0.03)	0.09	(0.04)
Russian Federation	-0.03	(0.02)	0.01	(0.03)	0.09	(0.02)	0.24	(0.03)	**-0.52**	(0.05)	**-0.39**	(0.03)	-0.30	(0.03)	-0.13	(0.03)
Serbia	-0.05	(0.03)	0.00	(0.03)	0.01	(0.03)	0.18	(0.03)	**-0.56**	(0.03)	**-0.51**	(0.03)	-0.40	(0.03)	-0.14	(0.03)
Shanghai-China	0.38	(0.02)	0.55	(0.02)	0.63	(0.02)	0.73	(0.02)	**-0.06**	(0.03)	0.02	(0.03)	0.09	(0.03)	**0.21**	(0.02)
Singapore	0.01	(0.02)	0.18	(0.03)	0.34	(0.03)	0.62	(0.03)	**-0.05**	(0.03)	0.10	(0.03)	0.27	(0.03)	**0.36**	(0.03)
Chinese Taipei	0.13	(0.02)	0.28	(0.02)	0.44	(0.02)	0.74	(0.03)	**-0.60**	(0.03)	**-0.47**	(0.03)	-0.36	(0.03)	-0.16	(0.04)
Thailand	0.55	(0.02)	0.53	(0.02)	0.52	(0.02)	0.55	(0.03)	**-0.79**	(0.03)	**-0.73**	(0.03)	-0.67	(0.03)	-0.47	(0.03)
Trinidad and Tobago	0.20	(0.03)	0.20	(0.03)	0.25	(0.03)	0.21	(0.03)	**-0.45**	(0.04)	**-0.30**	(0.04)	-0.20	(0.04)	-0.02	(0.03)
Tunisia	0.50	(0.03)	0.43	(0.02)	0.32	(0.03)	0.24	(0.03)	**-0.38**	(0.04)	-0.30	(0.03)	-0.36	(0.04)	-0.25	(0.04)
Uruguay	-0.21	(0.03)	-0.21	(0.02)	-0.14	(0.03)	0.00	(0.03)	**-0.48**	(0.03)	**-0.29**	(0.03)	-0.13	(0.03)	**0.16**	(0.03)

Note: Values that are statistically significant are indicated in bold (see Annex A3).
StatLink ⌐ᖵᒲ http://dx.doi.org/10.1787/888932343285

[Part 1/1]
Effect of socio-economic background and gender on reading performance
Table III.3.1 **and the mediating role of enjoyment of reading and summarising strategies**

		Score point difference in reading performance							Indirect effects			
		Total effect of the PISA index of economic, social and cultural status (ESCS)[1]		Total gender effect[2]		ESCS effect when controlling for the indirect effect of enjoyment of reading and summarising strategies		Gender effect when controlling for the indirect effect of enjoyment of reading and summarising strategies		Indirect effect ESCS		Indirect effect gender	
		Coef.	S.E.	Coef.	S.E.	Coef.	S.E.	Coef.	S.E.	Coef.	S.E.	Coef.	S.E.
OECD	Australia	47.2	(1.2)	37.3	(1.8)	28.4	(1.1)	4.0	(1.7)	18.7	(0.7)	33.2	(1.1)
	Austria	43.8	(1.7)	41.4	(2.8)	28.4	(1.6)	6.8	(2.7)	15.4	(0.9)	34.7	(1.7)
	Belgium	45.3	(1.2)	28.9	(2.1)	28.0	(1.1)	3.8	(1.9)	17.3	(0.7)	25.0	(1.3)
	Canada	32.2	(1.1)	34.8	(1.7)	22.7	(1.0)	0.5	(1.6)	9.4	(0.5)	34.4	(1.0)
	Chile	31.5	(1.0)	22.1	(2.4)	25.6	(0.9)	7.2	(2.3)	5.8	(0.4)	14.9	(1.0)
	Czech Republic	47.0	(1.7)	50.3	(2.4)	32.6	(1.6)	17.8	(2.3)	14.4	(0.9)	32.5	(1.6)
	Denmark	33.2	(1.4)	30.3	(2.4)	20.0	(1.3)	4.5	(2.4)	13.2	(0.7)	25.8	(1.4)
	Estonia	29.3	(1.6)	46.0	(2.8)	19.1	(1.5)	12.6	(2.9)	10.1	(0.8)	33.4	(1.8)
	Finland	29.9	(1.5)	54.5	(2.3)	18.7	(1.3)	12.2	(2.2)	11.2	(0.8)	42.4	(1.7)
	France	48.4	(1.8)	41.5	(3.2)	31.1	(1.8)	18.7	(2.9)	17.2	(1.0)	22.8	(1.7)
	Germany	41.7	(1.5)	41.1	(2.5)	26.1	(1.4)	9.9	(2.3)	15.6	(0.8)	31.2	(1.6)
	Greece	32.2	(1.5)	48.6	(2.8)	24.4	(1.5)	24.2	(2.7)	7.8	(0.7)	24.4	(1.5)
	Hungary	48.0	(1.4)	41.5	(2.6)	34.9	(1.4)	16.0	(2.5)	13.1	(0.8)	25.5	(1.5)
	Iceland	26.9	(1.9)	45.7	(3.1)	16.1	(1.7)	9.6	(3.1)	10.7	(0.9)	36.0	(1.9)
	Ireland	41.0	(1.7)	39.6	(3.0)	25.6	(1.6)	15.4	(2.8)	15.4	(1.0)	24.2	(1.6)
	Israel	47.8	(1.8)	47.3	(2.9)	37.1	(1.7)	22.5	(3.0)	10.7	(0.8)	24.8	(1.7)
	Italy	30.0	(0.8)	45.2	(1.5)	20.4	(0.8)	18.5	(1.6)	9.7	(0.4)	26.7	(0.8)
	Japan	40.1	(1.8)	36.7	(2.7)	25.7	(1.5)	14.3	(2.4)	14.4	(1.0)	22.4	(1.4)
	Korea	31.1	(1.4)	33.5	(2.5)	19.4	(1.2)	17.6	(2.2)	11.7	(0.8)	15.9	(1.3)
	Luxembourg	35.4	(1.5)	43.1	(2.9)	24.3	(1.5)	12.9	(2.8)	11.1	(0.7)	30.2	(1.8)
	Mexico	23.7	(0.5)	27.7	(1.3)	19.9	(0.5)	16.1	(1.2)	3.8	(0.2)	11.7	(0.6)
	Netherlands	35.2	(1.7)	26.8	(2.7)	23.3	(1.6)	-1.6	(2.6)	11.9	(0.9)	28.4	(1.8)
	New Zealand	52.3	(1.8)	45.6	(2.7)	34.2	(1.6)	13.1	(2.5)	18.1	(1.0)	32.5	(1.6)
	Norway	34.8	(1.8)	49.0	(2.6)	21.4	(1.6)	15.7	(2.4)	13.3	(0.9)	33.4	(1.6)
	Poland	39.6	(1.4)	50.9	(2.5)	28.7	(1.3)	25.1	(2.5)	10.9	(0.7)	25.8	(1.4)
	Portugal	30.5	(0.9)	40.8	(2.2)	22.2	(0.9)	13.3	(2.1)	8.3	(0.5)	27.5	(1.4)
	Slovak Republic	40.1	(1.6)	52.8	(2.5)	30.3	(1.5)	28.7	(2.4)	9.8	(0.7)	24.1	(1.4)
	Slovenia	38.5	(1.4)	56.8	(2.5)	27.6	(1.4)	30.0	(2.5)	11.0	(0.7)	26.7	(1.5)
	Spain	28.4	(0.9)	29.8	(1.7)	20.5	(0.8)	5.9	(1.6)	7.9	(0.4)	23.9	(0.9)
	Sweden	40.5	(1.7)	46.2	(2.7)	27.4	(1.6)	10.9	(2.5)	13.1	(0.9)	35.3	(1.7)
	Switzerland	35.8	(1.4)	39.3	(2.2)	21.0	(1.2)	5.2	(2.0)	14.8	(0.7)	34.1	(1.4)
	Turkey	27.6	(0.9)	37.3	(2.2)	25.2	(0.9)	20.7	(2.2)	2.4	(0.4)	16.6	(1.2)
	United Kingdom	44.1	(1.5)	25.9	(2.5)	27.8	(1.4)	1.5	(2.2)	16.3	(0.8)	24.3	(1.3)
	United States	42.9	(1.7)	26.6	(2.6)	32.3	(1.6)	0.7	(2.6)	10.6	(0.7)	25.9	(1.4)
	OECD average	37.5	(0.3)	40.1	(0.4)	25.6	(0.2)	12.8	(0.4)	11.9	(0.1)	27.4	(0.3)
Partners	Albania	32.4	(1.6)	63.7	(3.5)	27.5	(1.6)	39.4	(3.8)	4.9	(0.6)	24.3	(2.1)
	Argentina	40.8	(1.3)	40.3	(3.3)	34.7	(1.3)	26.8	(3.3)	6.1	(0.6)	13.5	(1.5)
	Azerbaijan	20.7	(1.3)	24.7	(2.7)	18.6	(1.3)	20.4	(2.8)	2.1	(0.3)	4.4	(0.7)
	Brazil	29.2	(0.8)	34.5	(2.1)	24.4	(0.8)	22.1	(2.1)	4.9	(0.3)	12.4	(0.9)
	Bulgaria	47.7	(1.7)	60.8	(3.4)	37.8	(1.7)	42.1	(3.3)	9.9	(0.8)	18.8	(1.8)
	Colombia	28.0	(1.1)	12.9	(2.6)	22.6	(1.1)	7.8	(2.4)	5.4	(0.5)	5.1	(1.1)
	Croatia	32.0	(1.3)	51.7	(2.5)	23.9	(1.2)	26.1	(2.5)	8.1	(0.6)	25.5	(1.4)
	Dubai (UAE)	45.5	(1.6)	50.9	(2.7)	35.2	(1.6)	32.2	(2.5)	10.3	(0.8)	18.8	(1.3)
	Hong Kong-China	19.5	(1.3)	33.1	(2.6)	13.9	(1.2)	17.5	(2.4)	5.7	(0.6)	15.6	(1.2)
	Indonesia	18.3	(1.1)	37.7	(1.9)	16.0	(1.0)	32.4	(1.9)	2.2	(0.3)	5.3	(0.8)
	Jordan	25.6	(1.3)	58.9	(2.5)	23.9	(1.3)	47.3	(2.4)	1.7	(0.4)	11.6	(1.0)
	Kazakhstan	37.7	(1.5)	41.8	(2.7)	33.2	(1.5)	36.4	(2.6)	4.6	(0.6)	5.4	(1.1)
	Kyrgyzstan	37.9	(1.6)	52.3	(2.6)	32.4	(1.5)	45.3	(2.6)	5.6	(0.6)	6.9	(1.2)
	Latvia	30.0	(1.5)	48.9	(2.7)	21.7	(1.4)	23.0	(2.8)	8.4	(0.7)	25.9	(1.8)
	Liechtenstein	22.8	(5.6)	36.2	(8.6)	11.4	(5.0)	1.8	(8.0)	11.4	(2.5)	34.4	(5.4)
	Lithuania	33.4	(1.2)	59.9	(2.4)	25.7	(1.2)	32.1	(2.8)	7.7	(0.6)	27.8	(1.6)
	Macao-China	17.2	(1.2)	33.4	(2.1)	11.7	(1.2)	19.6	(2.0)	5.4	(0.4)	13.8	(0.9)
	Montenegro	32.0	(1.4)	55.3	(3.2)	25.6	(1.4)	39.6	(3.4)	6.4	(0.7)	15.7	(1.5)
	Panama	31.0	(1.7)	28.6	(4.8)	27.0	(1.7)	21.1	(4.6)	4.0	(0.7)	7.5	(1.7)
	Peru	38.6	(1.0)	21.5	(2.6)	33.7	(1.0)	12.9	(2.6)	4.9	(0.4)	8.6	(1.0)
	Qatar	27.3	(1.2)	55.1	(2.1)	23.5	(1.2)	45.3	(2.1)	3.8	(0.4)	9.8	(0.8)
	Romania	35.8	(1.4)	43.9	(2.6)	29.5	(1.5)	31.9	(2.6)	6.3	(0.6)	12.0	(1.3)
	Russian Federation	36.2	(1.5)	44.8	(2.3)	27.0	(1.5)	22.4	(2.3)	9.2	(0.7)	22.4	(1.4)
	Serbia	28.1	(1.3)	41.9	(2.3)	20.4	(1.3)	23.2	(2.3)	7.7	(0.6)	18.7	(1.3)
	Shanghai-China	26.2	(1.0)	38.8	(2.2)	20.2	(1.0)	26.1	(2.2)	5.9	(0.5)	12.7	(1.1)
	Singapore	42.0	(2.0)	30.0	(2.6)	27.3	(1.9)	6.7	(2.4)	14.8	(0.9)	23.3	(1.4)
	Chinese Taipei	33.6	(1.5)	35.4	(2.3)	19.7	(1.4)	18.2	(2.1)	13.9	(0.7)	17.3	(1.1)
	Thailand	22.7	(1.0)	40.1	(2.0)	20.9	(0.9)	30.9	(2.0)	1.7	(0.3)	9.1	(0.7)
	Trinidad and Tobago	39.1	(1.9)	59.4	(3.4)	31.7	(1.7)	37.8	(3.4)	7.4	(0.8)	21.6	(1.9)
	Tunisia	18.9	(1.0)	32.3	(2.5)	18.5	(1.0)	28.6	(2.5)	0.4	(0.3)	3.7	(0.9)
	Uruguay	37.7	(1.1)	45.6	(2.7)	29.8	(1.0)	31.1	(2.6)	7.9	(0.5)	14.5	(1.3)

Note: Values that are statistically significant are indicated in bold (see Annex A3).
1. Total ESCS effect represent the score point change in reading performance that is associated with a one unit change in ESCS when controlling for gender, immigration background and home language.
2. Total gender effect represent the score point change in reading performance that is associated with being a girl when controlling for ESCS, immigration status and home language.
ESCS effect when controlling for the indirect effect of enjoyment of reading and summarising strategies represents the score point change in reading performance that is associated with a one unit increase in ESCS when controlling for gender, immigration status, home language, enjoyment of reading and summarising strategies.
Gender effect when controlling for the indirect effect of enjoyment of reading and summarising strategies represents the score point change in reading performance that is associated with being a girl when controlling for ESCS, immigration status, home language, enjoyment of reading and summarising strategies.
StatLink ⟐⟐ http://dx.doi.org/10.1787/888932343285

[Part 1/2]

Index of enjoyment of reading and reading performance, by national quarters of this index and gender

Table III.3.2 *Results based on students' self-reports*

	Index of enjoyment															
	Boys								Girls							
	Bottom quarter		Second quarter		Third quarter		Top quarter		Bottom quarter		Second quarter		Third quarter		Top quarter	
	Mean index	S.E.	Mean index	S.E.	Mean index	S.E.	Mean index	S.E.	Mean index	S.E.	Mean index	S.E.	Mean index	S.E.	Mean index	S.E.
OECD																
Australia	-1.37	(0.01)	-0.39	(0.01)	0.29	(0.00)	1.30	(0.02)	-1.36	(0.02)	-0.36	(0.01)	0.33	(0.01)	1.47	(0.01)
Austria	-1.54	(0.02)	-0.65	(0.01)	0.14	(0.01)	1.27	(0.03)	-1.47	(0.03)	-0.64	(0.01)	0.18	(0.01)	1.53	(0.02)
Belgium	-1.45	(0.02)	-0.58	(0.00)	0.09	(0.01)	1.03	(0.02)	-1.37	(0.02)	-0.57	(0.01)	0.13	(0.01)	1.14	(0.01)
Canada	-1.28	(0.01)	-0.26	(0.01)	0.43	(0.01)	1.46	(0.01)	-1.19	(0.02)	-0.20	(0.01)	0.46	(0.01)	1.61	(0.02)
Chile	-1.02	(0.01)	-0.37	(0.00)	0.09	(0.01)	0.87	(0.02)	-0.99	(0.02)	-0.36	(0.00)	0.11	(0.00)	1.09	(0.02)
Czech Republic	-1.24	(0.02)	-0.47	(0.00)	0.07	(0.01)	0.94	(0.02)	-1.12	(0.02)	-0.45	(0.01)	0.12	(0.01)	1.10	(0.02)
Denmark	-1.20	(0.02)	-0.41	(0.01)	0.13	(0.01)	0.96	(0.03)	-1.11	(0.02)	-0.38	(0.01)	0.17	(0.01)	1.12	(0.02)
Estonia	-1.09	(0.01)	-0.37	(0.01)	0.16	(0.01)	0.94	(0.02)	-1.00	(0.02)	-0.36	(0.01)	0.24	(0.01)	1.15	(0.02)
Finland	-1.29	(0.02)	-0.30	(0.01)	0.33	(0.01)	1.17	(0.03)	-1.11	(0.03)	-0.26	(0.01)	0.39	(0.01)	1.40	(0.02)
France	-1.28	(0.02)	-0.35	(0.01)	0.34	(0.01)	1.25	(0.03)	-1.21	(0.02)	-0.31	(0.01)	0.34	(0.01)	1.32	(0.02)
Germany	-1.34	(0.02)	-0.46	(0.01)	0.39	(0.01)	1.39	(0.03)	-1.31	(0.03)	-0.42	(0.01)	0.45	(0.01)	1.70	(0.02)
Greece	-0.97	(0.02)	-0.24	(0.01)	0.27	(0.01)	1.04	(0.03)	-0.88	(0.02)	-0.21	(0.01)	0.30	(0.01)	1.17	(0.02)
Hungary	-0.96	(0.01)	-0.20	(0.01)	0.35	(0.01)	1.18	(0.03)	-0.88	(0.02)	-0.18	(0.01)	0.39	(0.01)	1.34	(0.02)
Iceland	-1.29	(0.02)	-0.43	(0.01)	0.15	(0.01)	1.12	(0.04)	-1.25	(0.03)	-0.42	(0.01)	0.20	(0.01)	1.32	(0.03)
Ireland	-1.31	(0.02)	-0.43	(0.01)	0.18	(0.01)	1.12	(0.03)	-1.27	(0.02)	-0.44	(0.01)	0.20	(0.01)	1.29	(0.03)
Israel	-1.18	(0.02)	-0.29	(0.01)	0.29	(0.01)	1.20	(0.04)	-1.12	(0.02)	-0.26	(0.01)	0.33	(0.01)	1.40	(0.02)
Italy	-1.14	(0.01)	-0.29	(0.00)	0.34	(0.00)	1.17	(0.01)	-1.02	(0.01)	-0.26	(0.00)	0.38	(0.00)	1.30	(0.01)
Japan	-1.11	(0.02)	-0.19	(0.01)	0.48	(0.01)	1.53	(0.02)	-1.02	(0.02)	-0.18	(0.01)	0.48	(0.01)	1.62	(0.02)
Korea	-0.82	(0.02)	-0.15	(0.01)	0.30	(0.01)	1.17	(0.03)	-0.81	(0.01)	-0.14	(0.01)	0.32	(0.00)	1.17	(0.02)
Luxembourg	-1.44	(0.02)	-0.59	(0.01)	0.09	(0.01)	1.08	(0.02)	-1.42	(0.03)	-0.56	(0.01)	0.14	(0.01)	1.31	(0.02)
Mexico	-0.79	(0.01)	-0.14	(0.00)	0.31	(0.00)	1.06	(0.01)	-0.74	(0.01)	-0.13	(0.00)	0.33	(0.00)	1.20	(0.02)
Netherlands	-1.48	(0.02)	-0.67	(0.01)	-0.06	(0.01)	0.76	(0.04)	-1.43	(0.03)	-0.64	(0.01)	-0.02	(0.01)	0.92	(0.02)
New Zealand	-1.09	(0.02)	-0.23	(0.01)	0.39	(0.01)	1.27	(0.02)	-1.04	(0.02)	-0.18	(0.01)	0.41	(0.01)	1.47	(0.02)
Norway	-1.42	(0.02)	-0.58	(0.01)	0.07	(0.01)	0.99	(0.03)	-1.39	(0.02)	-0.54	(0.01)	0.11	(0.01)	1.17	(0.02)
Poland	-1.22	(0.02)	-0.45	(0.01)	0.18	(0.01)	1.33	(0.04)	-1.16	(0.02)	-0.41	(0.01)	0.24	(0.01)	1.54	(0.02)
Portugal	-0.90	(0.02)	-0.11	(0.01)	0.42	(0.01)	1.19	(0.03)	-0.81	(0.02)	-0.07	(0.01)	0.46	(0.01)	1.40	(0.03)
Slovak Republic	-1.10	(0.02)	-0.42	(0.00)	0.05	(0.01)	0.95	(0.03)	-1.01	(0.02)	-0.41	(0.01)	0.07	(0.01)	1.04	(0.02)
Slovenia	-1.36	(0.02)	-0.55	(0.01)	0.03	(0.01)	0.89	(0.04)	-1.32	(0.03)	-0.53	(0.01)	0.08	(0.01)	1.09	(0.02)
Spain	-1.19	(0.01)	-0.36	(0.00)	0.21	(0.01)	1.11	(0.02)	-1.05	(0.01)	-0.34	(0.01)	0.24	(0.01)	1.27	(0.01)
Sweden	-1.31	(0.02)	-0.47	(0.01)	0.16	(0.01)	0.99	(0.03)	-1.24	(0.03)	-0.42	(0.01)	0.20	(0.01)	1.18	(0.02)
Switzerland	-1.48	(0.02)	-0.51	(0.01)	0.28	(0.01)	1.34	(0.03)	-1.39	(0.03)	-0.49	(0.01)	0.35	(0.01)	1.53	(0.02)
Turkey	-0.37	(0.02)	0.31	(0.01)	0.78	(0.01)	1.61	(0.03)	-0.26	(0.02)	0.35	(0.01)	0.82	(0.01)	1.83	(0.02)
United Kingdom	-1.31	(0.02)	-0.46	(0.01)	0.12	(0.01)	1.03	(0.03)	-1.24	(0.02)	-0.45	(0.01)	0.16	(0.01)	1.18	(0.02)
United States	-1.32	(0.02)	-0.41	(0.00)	0.17	(0.01)	1.16	(0.03)	-1.18	(0.02)	-0.40	(0.01)	0.22	(0.01)	1.41	(0.02)
OECD average	-1.20	(0.00)	-0.37	(0.00)	0.24	(0.00)	1.14	(0.01)	-1.12	(0.00)	-0.34	(0.00)	0.27	(0.00)	1.32	(0.00)
Partners																
Albania	-0.23	(0.01)	0.43	(0.01)	0.87	(0.01)	1.47	(0.02)	-0.13	(0.03)	0.46	(0.01)	0.90	(0.00)	1.59	(0.02)
Argentina	-1.03	(0.01)	-0.43	(0.01)	-0.01	(0.01)	0.72	(0.02)	-1.00	(0.02)	-0.42	(0.00)	0.01	(0.01)	0.84	(0.02)
Azerbaijan	-0.44	(0.01)	0.15	(0.01)	0.57	(0.01)	1.28	(0.03)	-0.39	(0.02)	0.17	(0.01)	0.57	(0.01)	1.26	(0.02)
Brazil	-0.65	(0.01)	-0.02	(0.00)	0.44	(0.00)	1.17	(0.01)	-0.61	(0.01)	0.00	(0.00)	0.46	(0.00)	1.33	(0.01)
Bulgaria	-1.03	(0.02)	-0.32	(0.01)	0.15	(0.01)	1.02	(0.03)	-0.97	(0.03)	-0.30	(0.00)	0.19	(0.01)	1.11	(0.03)
Colombia	-0.71	(0.02)	-0.13	(0.01)	0.29	(0.01)	0.97	(0.01)	-0.65	(0.01)	-0.11	(0.00)	0.33	(0.01)	1.09	(0.02)
Croatia	-1.19	(0.01)	-0.45	(0.01)	0.06	(0.01)	0.85	(0.03)	-1.06	(0.02)	-0.43	(0.01)	0.12	(0.01)	1.05	(0.02)
Dubai (UAE)	-0.81	(0.01)	-0.05	(0.01)	0.49	(0.01)	1.32	(0.03)	-0.79	(0.01)	-0.04	(0.01)	0.53	(0.01)	1.51	(0.02)
Hong Kong-China	-0.58	(0.02)	0.07	(0.00)	0.49	(0.01)	1.24	(0.02)	-0.46	(0.02)	0.10	(0.00)	0.49	(0.01)	1.28	(0.02)
Indonesia	-0.17	(0.01)	0.26	(0.00)	0.55	(0.00)	1.03	(0.02)	-0.13	(0.01)	0.27	(0.00)	0.56	(0.00)	1.09	(0.01)
Jordan	-0.47	(0.02)	0.11	(0.00)	0.56	(0.01)	1.19	(0.02)	-0.54	(0.01)	0.13	(0.01)	0.57	(0.01)	1.37	(0.02)
Kazakhstan	-0.29	(0.01)	0.31	(0.01)	0.71	(0.01)	1.38	(0.02)	-0.25	(0.01)	0.32	(0.00)	0.72	(0.00)	1.45	(0.02)
Kyrgyzstan	-0.36	(0.01)	0.14	(0.00)	0.51	(0.01)	1.16	(0.02)	-0.34	(0.02)	0.15	(0.01)	0.54	(0.01)	1.25	(0.02)
Latvia	-1.01	(0.02)	-0.35	(0.01)	0.14	(0.01)	0.91	(0.03)	-0.91	(0.02)	-0.32	(0.01)	0.20	(0.01)	0.99	(0.02)
Liechtenstein	-1.61	(0.06)	-0.68	(0.03)	0.06	(0.04)	1.08	(0.11)	-1.45	(0.12)	-0.62	(0.04)	0.06	(0.04)	1.43	(0.08)
Lithuania	-1.24	(0.02)	-0.40	(0.01)	0.33	(0.01)	1.25	(0.01)	-1.14	(0.03)	-0.34	(0.01)	0.38	(0.01)	1.53	(0.02)
Macao-China	-0.79	(0.01)	-0.16	(0.00)	0.24	(0.00)	0.89	(0.02)	-0.68	(0.01)	-0.15	(0.00)	0.26	(0.00)	1.01	(0.02)
Montenegro	-0.78	(0.01)	-0.08	(0.01)	0.42	(0.01)	1.20	(0.03)	-0.72	(0.02)	-0.06	(0.01)	0.45	(0.01)	1.27	(0.02)
Panama	-0.73	(0.03)	-0.12	(0.01)	0.34	(0.01)	1.12	(0.04)	-0.69	(0.02)	-0.11	(0.01)	0.33	(0.01)	1.26	(0.03)
Peru	-0.45	(0.01)	0.11	(0.00)	0.49	(0.01)	1.13	(0.02)	-0.41	(0.01)	0.12	(0.00)	0.51	(0.01)	1.24	(0.01)
Qatar	-0.76	(0.01)	-0.09	(0.00)	0.36	(0.00)	1.16	(0.02)	-0.72	(0.01)	-0.08	(0.01)	0.37	(0.00)	1.33	(0.01)
Romania	-0.74	(0.02)	-0.17	(0.00)	0.26	(0.01)	0.92	(0.02)	-0.71	(0.02)	-0.15	(0.01)	0.29	(0.01)	1.07	(0.02)
Russian Federation	-0.75	(0.01)	-0.20	(0.00)	0.22	(0.00)	0.93	(0.02)	-0.70	(0.02)	-0.18	(0.00)	0.24	(0.01)	1.02	(0.02)
Serbia	-1.01	(0.01)	-0.27	(0.00)	0.21	(0.01)	1.04	(0.04)	-0.88	(0.02)	-0.25	(0.01)	0.26	(0.00)	1.17	(0.02)
Shanghai-China	-0.32	(0.01)	0.35	(0.01)	0.77	(0.01)	1.44	(0.03)	-0.23	(0.01)	0.37	(0.00)	0.79	(0.00)	1.42	(0.01)
Singapore	-0.82	(0.02)	-0.05	(0.01)	0.49	(0.01)	1.40	(0.03)	-0.76	(0.02)	-0.02	(0.01)	0.53	(0.01)	1.52	(0.02)
Chinese Taipei	-0.63	(0.02)	0.07	(0.00)	0.57	(0.01)	1.43	(0.03)	-0.52	(0.02)	0.09	(0.01)	0.58	(0.01)	1.55	(0.02)
Thailand	-0.20	(0.01)	0.32	(0.00)	0.67	(0.01)	1.27	(0.02)	-0.17	(0.01)	0.32	(0.00)	0.68	(0.00)	1.38	(0.02)
Trinidad and Tobago	-0.79	(0.02)	-0.13	(0.01)	0.38	(0.01)	1.16	(0.03)	-0.75	(0.02)	-0.11	(0.01)	0.41	(0.01)	1.40	(0.02)
Tunisia	-0.70	(0.02)	0.09	(0.01)	0.64	(0.01)	1.33	(0.02)	-0.61	(0.02)	0.12	(0.01)	0.67	(0.01)	1.42	(0.02)
Uruguay	-1.20	(0.02)	-0.45	(0.01)	0.06	(0.01)	0.91	(0.02)	-1.12	(0.02)	-0.43	(0.00)	0.10	(0.01)	0.99	(0.02)

Note: Values that are statistically significant are indicated in bold (see Annex A3).
StatLink ᴍˢᴸ http://dx.doi.org/10.1787/888932343285

[Part 2/2]
Index of enjoyment of reading and reading performance, by national quarters of this index and gender

Table III.3.2 *Results based on students' self-reports*

	Performance on the reading scale, by national quarters of this index															
	Boys								Girls							
	Bottom quarter		Second quarter		Third quarter		Top quarter		Bottom quarter		Second quarter		Third quarter		Top quarter	
	Mean score	S.E.	Mean score	S.E.	Mean score	S.E.	Mean score	S.E.	Mean score	S.E.	Mean score	S.E.	Mean score	S.E.	Mean score	S.E.
Australia	447	(3.0)	484	(3.5)	536	(4.1)	587	(4.2)	468	(3.6)	495	(3.2)	535	(2.9)	588	(2.7)
Austria	420	(4.6)	438	(5.3)	474	(5.9)	523	(7.7)	427	(5.9)	455	(4.9)	488	(5.9)	540	(4.8)
Belgium	459	(3.4)	480	(4.8)	509	(6.0)	568	(4.4)	465	(3.5)	483	(4.5)	518	(4.0)	572	(3.1)
Canada	470	(2.4)	504	(2.8)	544	(2.9)	579	(3.0)	481	(3.2)	508	(2.7)	541	(2.5)	583	(2.0)
Chile	428	(4.2)	427	(5.1)	447	(5.4)	478	(6.8)	435	(4.8)	437	(4.9)	454	(4.0)	496	(4.2)
Czech Republic	430	(3.9)	439	(4.8)	479	(4.7)	535	(7.0)	449	(5.3)	459	(5.1)	497	(3.5)	552	(3.3)
Denmark	443	(3.7)	475	(4.2)	505	(4.4)	543	(4.2)	459	(4.2)	480	(4.5)	511	(3.0)	552	(3.5)
Estonia	451	(3.5)	475	(3.8)	507	(4.7)	538	(7.8)	471	(5.3)	489	(4.0)	520	(3.9)	559	(3.3)
Finland	466	(3.0)	511	(3.4)	547	(4.7)	584	(5.8)	505	(5.2)	529	(3.6)	563	(3.1)	598	(2.8)
France	428	(6.0)	469	(5.1)	505	(6.2)	546	(6.6)	450	(6.2)	482	(5.3)	521	(4.0)	570	(4.1)
Germany	447	(4.7)	463	(4.7)	521	(4.5)	551	(6.2)	461	(4.8)	475	(5.0)	520	(3.7)	565	(3.6)
Greece	429	(6.5)	456	(7.3)	480	(6.9)	521	(6.5)	452	(6.6)	473	(6.3)	504	(4.5)	545	(3.6)
Hungary	445	(4.5)	461	(4.8)	497	(5.7)	547	(7.5)	468	(5.2)	476	(5.3)	502	(7.9)	563	(3.1)
Iceland	435	(3.1)	474	(4.2)	510	(5.7)	556	(6.4)	463	(5.5)	500	(3.3)	520	(3.5)	568	(2.9)
Ireland	437	(5.2)	455	(5.4)	507	(6.2)	552	(5.6)	458	(4.7)	482	(4.4)	518	(4.9)	575	(3.1)
Israel	449	(5.5)	435	(6.0)	466	(6.7)	529	(8.8)	465	(5.3)	463	(5.2)	490	(4.7)	535	(4.2)
Italy	439	(2.8)	451	(2.8)	488	(3.2)	536	(3.3)	462	(3.1)	472	(2.8)	510	(2.7)	584	(4.8)
Japan	462	(5.6)	492	(6.8)	529	(4.9)	557	(5.7)	488	(5.2)	519	(4.5)	550	(4.7)	591	(4.1)
Korea	487	(6.1)	513	(5.0)	543	(5.2)	575	(5.1)	511	(5.6)	541	(4.6)	568	(4.4)	541	(3.3)
Luxembourg	423	(3.5)	438	(3.5)	480	(5.1)	526	(6.8)	433	(4.5)	456	(5.4)	485	(4.3)	541	(3.3)
Mexico	407	(2.7)	403	(2.9)	417	(2.9)	438	(3.8)	420	(2.8)	421	(2.9)	435	(2.7)	463	(2.5)
Netherlands	463	(5.5)	487	(5.6)	529	(5.7)	557	(9.4)	467	(6.3)	487	(6.2)	517	(6.2)	561	(5.3)
New Zealand	457	(4.2)	479	(4.3)	539	(6.2)	587	(5.9)	486	(4.5)	504	(4.4)	542	(4.3)	595	(3.9)
Norway	441	(3.9)	476	(4.0)	505	(4.3)	552	(5.5)	468	(5.3)	497	(4.4)	530	(3.8)	569	(3.7)
Poland	455	(3.7)	461	(4.0)	496	(5.3)	549	(6.7)	487	(5.5)	488	(4.2)	518	(3.6)	567	(3.2)
Portugal	448	(3.8)	462	(4.4)	490	(4.5)	541	(5.3)	467	(5.1)	480	(4.3)	504	(3.5)	541	(3.5)
Slovak Republic	441	(4.1)	434	(5.2)	463	(5.1)	512	(6.4)	471	(4.8)	466	(4.3)	492	(4.9)	546	(4.0)
Slovenia	436	(2.8)	444	(3.3)	476	(3.9)	527	(6.1)	466	(4.0)	478	(4.9)	510	(3.5)	548	(2.7)
Spain	435	(2.6)	459	(2.8)	487	(3.1)	532	(3.6)	447	(4.3)	464	(3.7)	498	(3.2)	539	(2.5)
Sweden	434	(3.8)	466	(4.6)	510	(5.3)	561	(6.2)	460	(4.8)	486	(4.6)	519	(4.2)	564	(3.7)
Switzerland	446	(3.3)	470	(3.9)	511	(4.6)	560	(4.7)	461	(6.1)	466	(5.7)	487	(4.4)	567	(3.5)
Turkey	438	(4.9)	440	(4.4)	448	(4.4)	470	(6.3)	461	(6.1)	466	(5.7)	487	(4.4)	509	(4.8)
United Kingdom	440	(3.3)	467	(4.1)	510	(4.2)	561	(5.5)	457	(5.5)	466	(3.2)	506	(4.4)	563	(3.1)
United States	451	(3.3)	472	(5.1)	511	(5.7)	569	(6.6)	460	(4.4)	477	(5.7)	511	(4.4)	561	(5.3)
OECD average	444	(0.7)	464	(0.8)	499	(0.9)	543	(1.0)	463	(0.9)	480	(0.8)	512	(0.7)	556	(0.6)
Albania	334	(5.5)	354	(7.0)	384	(7.4)	407	(8.7)	366	(9.3)	394	(6.4)	418	(5.0)	443	(4.7)
Argentina	380	(6.1)	376	(6.7)	370	(7.3)	424	(10.1)	406	(5.6)	399	(7.1)	401	(6.5)	450	(6.5)
Azerbaijan	337	(4.0)	348	(5.7)	369	(5.6)	369	(5.8)	352	(5.4)	365	(5.6)	378	(5.0)	396	(4.1)
Brazil	395	(3.1)	389	(4.2)	396	(4.7)	424	(5.7)	401	(4.1)	408	(3.9)	423	(3.2)	453	(3.7)
Bulgaria	399	(6.2)	390	(8.1)	409	(10.5)	457	(12.7)	423	(7.9)	433	(7.3)	452	(5.6)	508	(7.8)
Colombia	407	(4.8)	398	(5.1)	412	(6.7)	425	(7.9)	407	(5.2)	406	(4.5)	422	(6.1)	432	(5.9)
Croatia	434	(4.1)	443	(4.7)	462	(3.9)	509	(7.2)	459	(6.0)	474	(4.5)	501	(4.7)	533	(3.6)
Dubai (UAE)	416	(3.6)	411	(4.0)	454	(4.4)	504	(5.7)	444	(4.4)	449	(3.9)	483	(3.6)	533	(3.1)
Hong Kong-China	486	(4.0)	515	(4.5)	546	(4.6)	558	(4.9)	501	(4.9)	533	(4.0)	556	(3.6)	583	(3.8)
Indonesia	381	(4.4)	382	(4.4)	386	(5.0)	389	(5.9)	414	(6.6)	411	(3.8)	418	(4.7)	432	(5.1)
Jordan	372	(6.2)	367	(5.1)	392	(4.1)	416	(5.6)	427	(5.9)	410	(5.0)	430	(5.1)	462	(4.0)
Kazakhstan	382	(5.2)	359	(4.7)	367	(5.5)	371	(5.2)	413	(5.6)	402	(4.9)	410	(4.2)	422	(5.2)
Kyrgyzstan	294	(5.4)	276	(5.5)	297	(5.2)	305	(6.6)	329	(6.3)	327	(5.4)	341	(5.0)	358	(4.1)
Latvia	442	(4.2)	450	(4.6)	480	(5.3)	529	(7.2)	473	(5.8)	475	(4.9)	500	(4.2)	537	(3.6)
Liechtenstein	443	(9.8)	474	(11.3)	526	(11.2)	534	(13.2)	461	(15.6)	502	(12.7)	512	(11.9)	547	(10.3)
Lithuania	423	(3.4)	434	(4.1)	459	(4.4)	497	(7.0)	450	(6.3)	463	(4.8)	492	(3.3)	532	(2.9)
Macao-China	448	(2.4)	466	(2.6)	484	(3.0)	507	(3.2)	473	(3.6)	484	(3.1)	503	(2.8)	532	(2.1)
Montenegro	370	(2.8)	371	(4.3)	393	(5.4)	431	(5.4)	398	(5.3)	416	(4.3)	428	(4.0)	467	(4.8)
Panama	364	(7.8)	351	(8.2)	362	(9.7)	374	(10.7)	392	(10.0)	371	(11.7)	389	(9.4)	416	(7.8)
Peru	373	(5.2)	345	(5.1)	351	(4.8)	376	(6.1)	373	(6.5)	358	(6.5)	380	(6.2)	410	(5.8)
Qatar	345	(2.9)	331	(2.9)	361	(3.8)	404	(4.7)	367	(2.8)	371	(3.1)	393	(2.7)	442	(2.8)
Romania	405	(5.2)	396	(5.6)	400	(5.5)	432	(7.8)	428	(6.7)	424	(5.3)	437	(5.3)	474	(5.1)
Russian Federation	417	(4.0)	426	(4.7)	450	(5.5)	500	(7.3)	446	(6.3)	458	(5.2)	473	(3.3)	519	(4.7)
Serbia	411	(4.2)	416	(4.0)	429	(4.8)	468	(7.0)	431	(4.2)	433	(4.8)	461	(3.5)	491	(3.2)
Shanghai-China	506	(3.7)	539	(4.2)	555	(3.9)	571	(4.8)	534	(4.4)	562	(3.6)	580	(3.3)	601	(3.2)
Singapore	471	(3.0)	501	(3.7)	545	(4.4)	584	(3.9)	478	(4.2)	509	(3.8)	546	(3.4)	584	(2.8)
Chinese Taipei	436	(4.2)	472	(3.9)	507	(4.1)	538	(5.6)	460	(5.1)	483	(3.8)	521	(3.3)	558	(5.0)
Thailand	386	(3.8)	395	(4.2)	411	(4.7)	432	(5.7)	416	(4.2)	425	(3.4)	439	(3.4)	459	(4.2)
Trinidad and Tobago	382	(3.8)	373	(4.9)	394	(5.2)	447	(7.3)	428	(5.6)	414	(5.7)	437	(4.6)	478	(3.0)
Tunisia	400	(5.0)	375	(4.7)	382	(4.4)	399	(5.6)	424	(5.3)	404	(4.3)	418	(3.9)	426	(4.0)
Uruguay	393	(3.7)	396	(4.5)	412	(5.2)	451	(7.0)	417	(5.0)	422	(4.3)	443	(4.2)	480	(4.1)

Note: Values that are statistically significant are indicated in bold (see Annex A3).
StatLink ⧉ http://dx.doi.org/10.1787/888932343285

[Part 1/1]

Table III.3.3 **Predicted reading performance of boys if boys had the same value on the index of summarising as girls**

	Observed reading performance of boys	S.E.	Observed reading performance of girls	S.E.	Predicted reading performance of boys if boys had the same value on the index of summarising as girls	S.E.
OECD						
Australia	502	(2.8)	536	(2.6)	519	(2.4)
Austria	456	(3.8)	496	(3.7)	475	(3.5)
Belgium	506	(2.8)	527	(2.8)	519	(2.4)
Canada	510	(1.7)	543	(1.7)	525	(1.6)
Chile	443	(3.6)	464	(3.5)	451	(3.2)
Czech Republic	462	(3.6)	509	(2.9)	480	(2.9)
Denmark	483	(2.6)	512	(2.4)	497	(2.3)
Estonia	482	(2.9)	525	(2.8)	496	(2.5)
Finland	511	(2.5)	564	(2.4)	533	(2.4)
France	485	(3.9)	520	(3.5)	494	(3.2)
Germany	489	(3.7)	526	(3.0)	503	(3.0)
Greece	461	(5.6)	508	(3.5)	468	(5.1)
Hungary	478	(3.9)	514	(3.5)	494	(3.3)
Iceland	483	(2.1)	525	(1.9)	501	(2.3)
Ireland	484	(3.8)	520	(3.1)	495	(3.4)
Israel	465	(4.6)	501	(3.3)	478	(3.9)
Italy	467	(2.3)	512	(1.8)	479	(1.9)
Japan	503	(5.5)	542	(3.7)	520	(4.0)
Korea	524	(4.9)	558	(3.8)	535	(3.7)
Luxembourg	460	(2.1)	497	(1.6)	477	(2.1)
Mexico	417	(2.0)	442	(1.9)	424	(1.8)
Netherlands	502	(5.2)	524	(5.4)	513	(3.9)
New Zealand	504	(3.4)	546	(2.6)	521	(3.1)
Norway	484	(2.8)	529	(2.9)	501	(2.2)
Poland	480	(2.7)	527	(2.9)	493	(2.7)
Portugal	472	(3.4)	509	(2.8)	488	(2.8)
Slovak Republic	455	(3.5)	506	(2.6)	470	(2.9)
Slovenia	462	(1.6)	514	(1.5)	477	(1.7)
Spain	469	(2.2)	498	(2.1)	482	(2.0)
Sweden	481	(3.1)	524	(2.9)	496	(2.7)
Switzerland	484	(2.8)	522	(2.6)	503	(2.3)
Turkey	446	(3.7)	489	(4.3)	456	(3.5)
United Kingdom	486	(3.4)	509	(2.9)	495	(3.2)
United States	491	(4.2)	515	(3.8)	503	(3.9)
OECD average	479	(0.6)	516	(0.5)	493	(0.5)
Partners						
Albania	367	(4.8)	422	(4.1)	374	(4.8)
Argentina	394	(5.1)	429	(4.8)	402	(4.8)
Azerbaijan	360	(4.0)	385	(3.5)	360	(3.9)
Brazil	405	(2.9)	431	(2.7)	410	(2.7)
Bulgaria	413	(7.3)	470	(5.8)	425	(6.4)
Colombia	415	(4.1)	427	(3.6)	418	(3.6)
Croatia	456	(3.4)	504	(3.6)	471	(2.9)
Dubai (UAE)	441	(1.9)	488	(1.6)	450	(1.9)
Hong Kong-China	518	(3.3)	551	(2.9)	525	(3.0)
Indonesia	386	(3.9)	423	(3.9)	389	(3.6)
Jordan	385	(4.2)	438	(4.1)	390	(4.0)
Kazakhstan	371	(3.3)	413	(3.4)	378	(3.0)
Kyrgyzstan	298	(4.0)	348	(3.2)	300	(3.7)
Latvia	463	(3.3)	509	(3.0)	474	(3.0)
Liechtenstein	484	(4.5)	516	(4.5)	506	(5.2)
Lithuania	443	(2.7)	500	(2.5)	454	(2.6)
Macao-China	471	(1.3)	504	(1.2)	475	(1.3)
Montenegro	391	(2.4)	442	(2.0)	395	(2.3)
Panama	366	(6.5)	399	(7.3)	371	(5.6)
Peru	368	(4.4)	391	(5.1)	375	(4.0)
Qatar	360	(1.6)	401	(1.1)	363	(1.6)
Romania	406	(4.5)	447	(4.2)	414	(3.9)
Russian Federation	442	(3.8)	486	(3.4)	452	(3.1)
Serbia	428	(3.2)	466	(2.4)	438	(2.9)
Shanghai-China	536	(3.0)	576	(2.3)	542	(2.8)
Singapore	512	(1.7)	542	(1.5)	523	(1.4)
Chinese Taipei	479	(3.7)	514	(3.6)	484	(3.1)
Thailand	401	(3.2)	438	(3.1)	403	(3.1)
Trinidad and Tobago	404	(2.3)	456	(1.7)	414	(2.4)
Tunisia	392	(3.2)	423	(3.0)	394	(3.2)
Uruguay	414	(3.2)	451	(2.9)	422	(2.8)

Note: Observed reading performance refers to mean reading performance of students with non-missing information on the index of summarising.
StatLink ⟲ᴹ⟲ᴸ http://dx.doi.org/10.1787/888932343285

[Part 1/1]

Predicted reading performance of boys if boys had the same value on the index of enjoyment of reading as girls

Table III.3.4

		Observed reading performance of boys	S.E.	Observed reading performance of girls	S.E.	Predicted reading performance of boys if boys had the same value on the index of enjoyment of reading as girls	S.E.
OECD	Australia	498	(2.9)	534	(2.7)	526	(2.7)
	Austria	450	(3.7)	491	(3.9)	479	(3.7)
	Belgium	494	(3.4)	520	(2.9)	515	(3.3)
	Canada	509	(1.8)	542	(1.7)	538	(1.8)
	Chile	440	(3.8)	462	(3.6)	452	(3.9)
	Czech Republic	457	(3.6)	504	(3.0)	485	(3.7)
	Denmark	481	(2.5)	510	(2.5)	503	(2.3)
	Estonia	480	(2.9)	524	(2.8)	508	(3.1)
	Finland	508	(2.6)	564	(2.4)	544	(2.6)
	France	476	(4.2)	516	(3.5)	498	(3.6)
	Germany	481	(3.7)	520	(2.9)	512	(3.5)
	Greece	459	(5.6)	506	(3.6)	485	(4.6)
	Hungary	476	(3.9)	514	(3.6)	500	(3.5)
	Iceland	480	(2.1)	524	(1.9)	506	(2.2)
	Ireland	478	(4.2)	518	(3.2)	497	(4.0)
	Israel	460	(5.0)	496	(3.4)	476	(4.9)
	Italy	465	(2.2)	510	(1.9)	490	(2.2)
	Japan	504	(5.3)	541	(3.7)	516	(4.6)
	Korea	524	(4.7)	558	(3.8)	534	(4.0)
	Luxembourg	454	(2.0)	492	(1.6)	481	(2.3)
	Mexico	414	(2.1)	438	(2.1)	420	(2.1)
	Netherlands	495	(5.2)	521	(5.4)	522	(5.0)
	New Zealand	500	(3.5)	545	(2.6)	528	(3.5)
	Norway	481	(3.0)	528	(2.9)	505	(2.7)
	Poland	477	(2.8)	526	(2.9)	501	(2.6)
	Portugal	472	(3.4)	508	(2.9)	494	(3.4)
	Slovak Republic	453	(3.5)	503	(2.7)	471	(3.5)
	Slovenia	458	(1.5)	512	(1.4)	480	(1.8)
	Spain	468	(2.2)	496	(2.2)	489	(2.1)
	Sweden	475	(3.1)	522	(3.1)	507	(3.4)
	Switzerland	482	(2.8)	521	(2.7)	512	(3.0)
	Turkey	445	(3.7)	487	(4.2)	455	(4.1)
	United Kingdom	483	(3.4)	508	(2.9)	505	(3.1)
	United States	488	(4.2)	514	(3.7)	512	(4.4)
	OECD average	**475**	**(0.6)**	**514**	**(0.5)**	**498**	**(0.6)**
Partners	Albania	358	(5.0)	418	(4.0)	380	(5.2)
	Argentina	384	(5.0)	417	(4.8)	392	(5.3)
	Azerbaijan	353	(3.8)	376	(3.3)	358	(3.7)
	Brazil	398	(2.9)	426	(2.8)	407	(3.2)
	Bulgaria	407	(7.0)	464	(5.8)	422	(7.7)
	Colombia	409	(4.5)	419	(4.0)	413	(4.9)
	Croatia	452	(3.4)	503	(3.7)	472	(3.4)
	Dubai (UAE)	437	(1.8)	487	(1.5)	456	(1.9)
	Hong Kong-China	520	(3.3)	551	(2.8)	534	(3.1)
	Indonesia	384	(3.8)	420	(3.9)	387	(4.0)
	Jordan	383	(4.3)	436	(4.0)	389	(4.2)
	Kazakhstan	370	(3.2)	413	(3.4)	370	(3.2)
	Kyrgyzstan	291	(3.8)	342	(3.1)	296	(3.9)
	Latvia	460	(3.4)	507	(3.1)	484	(3.4)
	Liechtenstein	485	(4.6)	515	(4.6)	508	(5.6)
	Lithuania	440	(2.6)	499	(2.6)	468	(2.9)
	Macao-China	470	(1.3)	504	(1.2)	483	(1.3)
	Montenegro	384	(2.0)	435	(2.1)	399	(2.5)
	Panama	362	(6.6)	394	(7.1)	365	(6.9)
	Peru	361	(4.1)	383	(4.9)	365	(4.0)
	Qatar	355	(1.3)	398	(1.0)	365	(1.2)
	Romania	405	(4.4)	446	(4.2)	414	(4.6)
	Russian Federation	438	(3.6)	482	(3.4)	457	(3.4)
	Serbia	424	(3.2)	462	(2.5)	438	(3.4)
	Shanghai-China	536	(3.0)	576	(2.3)	549	(3.0)
	Singapore	512	(1.8)	542	(1.5)	536	(1.8)
	Chinese Taipei	479	(3.7)	514	(3.6)	498	(3.2)
	Thailand	401	(3.3)	438	(3.1)	409	(3.5)
	Trinidad and Tobago	390	(2.1)	446	(1.6)	404	(2.6)
	Tunisia	389	(3.1)	419	(3.0)	389	(3.0)
	Uruguay	407	(3.1)	446	(2.8)	419	(3.2)

Note: Observed reading performance refers to mean reading performance of students with non-missing information on the index of enjoyment of reading.
StatLink ⌨️ http://dx.doi.org/10.1787/888932343285

[Part 1/1]

Table III.3.5

Predicted reading performance of students from different socio-economic backgrounds if they had the same value on the index of summarising as socio-economically advantaged students[1]

	Bottom quarter ESCS				Second quarter ESCS				Third quarter ESCS				Top quarter ESCS	
	Observed reading performance	S.E.	Predicted reading performance if students in this quarter had the same value on the index of summarising as students in the top ESCS quarter	S.E.	Observed reading performance	S.E.	Predicted reading performance if students in this quarter had the same value on the index of summarising as students in the top ESCS quarter	S.E.	Observed reading performance	S.E.	Predicted reading performance if students in this quarter had the same value on the index of summarising as students in the top ESCS quarter	S.E.	Observed reading performance	S.E.
OECD														
Australia	475	(2.5)	495	(2.2)	507	(2.3)	521	(2.1)	535	(2.9)	541	(2.5)	564	(3.0)
Austria	432	(4.0)	454	(3.4)	463	(4.0)	476	(3.3)	486	(3.8)	496	(3.4)	527	(4.0)
Belgium	468	(3.0)	495	(2.6)	499	(3.3)	517	(2.6)	533	(2.5)	544	(2.2)	570	(2.8)
Canada	496	(2.1)	505	(2.1)	516	(1.8)	523	(1.6)	535	(2.1)	538	(2.0)	562	(2.4)
Chile	413	(3.4)	427	(3.0)	438	(3.7)	448	(3.5)	459	(3.5)	465	(3.1)	503	(3.4)
Czech Republic	447	(3.2)	466	(2.7)	473	(3.6)	484	(2.9)	494	(3.3)	502	(2.8)	526	(4.1)
Denmark	457	(2.7)	473	(2.7)	489	(3.4)	499	(3.1)	512	(2.8)	516	(2.5)	538	(2.4)
Estonia	478	(3.6)	488	(2.9)	491	(3.4)	500	(2.7)	507	(3.2)	512	(2.7)	535	(3.9)
Finland	507	(3.2)	523	(2.8)	528	(2.6)	539	(2.4)	550	(2.8)	556	(2.5)	567	(2.7)
France	454	(4.7)	475	(3.9)	490	(4.3)	502	(3.6)	518	(4.1)	521	(3.7)	556	(4.8)
Germany	457	(3.9)	479	(3.0)	505	(2.7)	515	(2.4)	520	(3.6)	528	(3.2)	553	(3.2)
Greece	439	(7.2)	451	(6.6)	479	(5.0)	485	(4.7)	495	(3.7)	500	(3.5)	529	(3.4)
Hungary	438	(5.4)	461	(4.0)	487	(3.4)	499	(2.9)	507	(4.1)	517	(3.4)	554	(4.1)
Iceland	474	(3.1)	485	(2.9)	496	(3.5)	502	(3.2)	515	(3.1)	518	(2.8)	532	(3.0)
Ireland	462	(3.3)	473	(2.9)	491	(3.6)	498	(3.0)	516	(3.7)	518	(3.4)	541	(3.5)
Israel	432	(4.7)	451	(4.1)	471	(3.9)	481	(3.6)	506	(3.5)	509	(3.3)	532	(4.1)
Italy	445	(2.9)	462	(2.2)	481	(2.0)	490	(1.7)	503	(1.9)	508	(1.7)	528	(2.2)
Japan	485	(4.7)	503	(3.5)	511	(4.7)	524	(3.3)	538	(3.8)	542	(3.2)	558	(3.6)
Korea	505	(5.0)	523	(3.5)	536	(2.8)	545	(2.4)	548	(3.8)	554	(3.0)	573	(4.5)
Luxembourg	419	(2.9)	440	(2.7)	468	(2.9)	480	(2.6)	501	(2.7)	507	(2.6)	530	(2.8)
Mexico	391	(2.7)	404	(2.4)	418	(2.3)	427	(1.9)	439	(2.1)	444	(1.8)	471	(2.1)
Netherlands	479	(5.9)	497	(3.9)	497	(5.7)	510	(4.8)	522	(4.8)	531	(3.8)	556	(5.5)
New Zealand	478	(3.9)	499	(3.8)	512	(3.4)	526	(2.7)	535	(3.2)	545	(2.8)	581	(3.5)
Norway	470	(3.4)	485	(3.0)	499	(2.9)	506	(2.6)	519	(3.0)	523	(2.7)	538	(3.9)
Poland	465	(3.3)	482	(3.0)	490	(3.0)	499	(2.9)	510	(2.9)	517	(2.8)	552	(3.7)
Portugal	452	(4.0)	473	(3.3)	474	(3.2)	490	(2.7)	500	(3.4)	510	(2.7)	538	(3.7)
Slovak Republic	440	(4.9)	455	(3.9)	472	(3.2)	479	(2.8)	489	(3.2)	494	(2.9)	524	(3.7)
Slovenia	449	(2.6)	466	(2.5)	472	(2.5)	487	(2.4)	496	(2.6)	505	(2.4)	535	(2.8)
Spain	446	(3.3)	458	(3.0)	471	(2.4)	479	(2.0)	493	(2.1)	498	(1.9)	526	(3.1)
Sweden	458	(3.8)	474	(3.4)	491	(3.1)	500	(2.7)	519	(3.2)	523	(2.7)	544	(4.3)
Switzerland	459	(3.8)	481	(3.0)	494	(2.6)	506	(2.2)	508	(3.0)	518	(2.5)	552	(3.7)
Turkey	426	(3.8)	436	(3.5)	456	(3.6)	462	(3.3)	471	(3.8)	476	(3.4)	515	(4.5)
United Kingdom	455	(3.0)	472	(2.9)	486	(3.0)	498	(2.8)	511	(2.7)	517	(2.7)	545	(3.2)
United States	455	(3.4)	470	(3.0)	485	(3.4)	496	(3.3)	512	(3.6)	520	(3.4)	561	(4.6)
OECD average	456	(0.7)	473	(0.6)	486	(0.6)	497	(0.5)	509	(0.6)	515	(0.5)	542	(0.6)
Partners														
Albania	359	(6.5)	367	(6.7)	383	(4.2)	389	(3.9)	401	(4.5)	406	(4.4)	440	(5.1)
Argentina	361	(4.9)	378	(4.9)	392	(4.8)	405	(4.5)	423	(5.9)	430	(5.3)	477	(6.0)
Azerbaijan	351	(6.6)	353	(6.8)	363	(3.6)	365	(3.6)	375	(3.7)	376	(3.6)	400	(4.9)
Brazil	382	(2.5)	396	(2.6)	408	(3.0)	416	(2.8)	419	(3.8)	425	(3.7)	466	(4.3)
Bulgaria	380	(7.0)	400	(6.3)	427	(6.8)	441	(5.7)	455	(7.7)	463	(6.9)	505	(5.5)
Colombia	382	(4.6)	399	(4.2)	408	(4.2)	422	(4.1)	429	(3.5)	437	(3.3)	467	(4.8)
Croatia	444	(3.9)	457	(3.2)	470	(3.8)	480	(3.3)	486	(3.9)	491	(3.4)	516	(3.8)
Dubai (UAE)	405	(2.7)	425	(2.7)	458	(2.8)	464	(2.6)	486	(2.8)	489	(2.4)	511	(2.8)
Hong Kong-China	509	(4.0)	516	(3.5)	527	(2.8)	532	(2.8)	542	(2.8)	546	(2.7)	557	(3.5)
Indonesia	389	(3.7)	395	(3.4)	392	(3.8)	397	(3.6)	406	(4.5)	409	(4.0)	433	(6.0)
Jordan	381	(3.6)	386	(3.5)	406	(3.4)	408	(3.2)	418	(3.7)	419	(3.5)	446	(5.2)
Kazakhstan	350	(4.1)	360	(3.8)	385	(3.2)	394	(3.0)	400	(3.6)	404	(3.4)	433	(5.2)
Kyrgyzstan	282	(4.5)	295	(4.4)	305	(4.2)	315	(4.1)	333	(4.4)	339	(4.1)	379	(6.2)
Latvia	459	(4.7)	471	(4.0)	472	(3.3)	480	(3.0)	495	(3.5)	501	(3.1)	520	(3.6)
Liechtenstein	462	(7.8)	486	(7.3)	503	(7.9)	509	(7.2)	503	(9.3)	515	(8.7)	530	(8.1)
Lithuania	432	(3.5)	447	(3.2)	460	(3.3)	470	(3.3)	479	(3.4)	487	(3.0)	515	(3.3)
Macao-China	473	(2.1)	479	(2.0)	487	(2.0)	490	(2.0)	492	(2.1)	494	(1.9)	498	(2.1)
Montenegro	377	(3.4)	388	(3.3)	412	(3.0)	419	(2.9)	423	(3.0)	426	(3.0)	455	(2.8)
Panama	343	(6.5)	357	(5.6)	361	(6.4)	373	(5.7)	379	(6.7)	386	(5.7)	453	(11.1)
Peru	313	(3.9)	331	(3.9)	363	(3.1)	374	(3.0)	399	(3.8)	405	(3.7)	442	(7.5)
Qatar	344	(1.8)	352	(1.9)	375	(2.4)	377	(2.5)	405	(2.7)	402	(2.5)	401	(2.5)
Romania	385	(5.5)	399	(4.6)	421	(4.4)	429	(3.8)	435	(4.6)	440	(4.1)	468	(5.0)
Russian Federation	429	(3.7)	441	(2.9)	451	(3.9)	459	(3.2)	471	(3.3)	476	(3.1)	505	(4.9)
Serbia	419	(3.7)	434	(3.6)	437	(2.9)	450	(2.7)	450	(2.9)	459	(2.6)	482	(2.7)
Shanghai-China	522	(4.2)	530	(3.6)	546	(3.2)	552	(3.1)	564	(2.5)	568	(2.5)	594	(3.5)
Singapore	478	(2.4)	495	(2.3)	513	(3.1)	524	(2.7)	542	(2.4)	546	(2.4)	575	(3.1)
Chinese Taipei	461	(3.4)	474	(3.0)	485	(3.4)	494	(3.0)	505	(2.9)	511	(2.4)	536	(4.5)
Thailand	400	(3.7)	405	(3.7)	408	(2.8)	413	(2.7)	418	(2.7)	422	(2.7)	463	(4.5)
Trinidad and Tobago	394	(3.6)	410	(3.7)	421	(3.4)	431	(3.4)	437	(3.3)	443	(3.3)	480	(4.0)
Tunisia	381	(3.6)	384	(3.6)	396	(3.9)	397	(3.7)	409	(3.4)	412	(3.3)	447	(5.1)
Uruguay	382	(3.2)	404	(3.1)	414	(3.4)	430	(3.4)	445	(3.8)	455	(3.3)	495	(4.1)

Note: Observed reading performance refers to mean reading performance of students with non-missing information on the index of summarising.
1. Socio-economically advantaged students are students in the top quarter of the PISA index of economic, social and cultural status (ESCS).
StatLink ⟐ http://dx.doi.org/10.1787/888932343285

[Part 1/1]

Predicted reading performance of students from different socio-economic backgrounds if they had the same value on the index of enjoyment of reading as socio-economically advantaged students[1]

Table III.3.6

| | Bottom quarter ESCS | | | | Second quarter ESCS | | | | Third quarter ESCS | | | | Top quarter ESCS | |
	Observed reading performance	S.E.	Predicted reading performance if students in this quarter had the same value on the index of summarising as students in the top ESCS quarter	S.E.	Observed reading performance	S.E.	Predicted reading performance if students in this quarter had the same value on the index of summarising as students in the top ESCS quarter	S.E.	Observed reading performance	S.E.	Predicted reading performance if students in this quarter had the same value on the index of summarising as students in the top ESCS quarter	S.E.	Observed reading performance	S.E.
OECD														
Australia	471	(2.6)	497	(2.3)	504	(2.4)	523	(2.1)	533	(2.9)	543	(2.7)	562	(3.1)
Austria	421	(4.2)	441	(4.1)	457	(4.2)	474	(4.0)	482	(3.7)	493	(3.2)	525	(4.0)
Belgium	452	(3.2)	471	(3.4)	488	(3.2)	504	(3.0)	525	(2.5)	533	(2.3)	567	(2.7)
Canada	495	(2.3)	510	(2.2)	515	(1.7)	525	(1.7)	534	(2.1)	541	(1.9)	562	(2.4)
Chile	410	(3.6)	414	(3.5)	435	(3.6)	441	(3.6)	457	(3.5)	460	(3.3)	502	(3.5)
Czech Republic	438	(3.1)	454	(2.8)	468	(3.8)	480	(3.4)	491	(3.5)	498	(3.2)	523	(4.0)
Denmark	455	(2.7)	476	(2.8)	485	(3.4)	501	(3.1)	510	(2.8)	519	(2.5)	536	(2.4)
Estonia	475	(3.6)	491	(3.7)	491	(3.4)	503	(3.0)	506	(3.1)	512	(2.8)	534	(3.9)
Finland	505	(3.3)	524	(3.1)	527	(2.7)	538	(2.3)	549	(2.9)	556	(2.6)	566	(2.8)
France	443	(5.1)	467	(4.9)	485	(4.5)	503	(3.6)	513	(4.3)	526	(3.5)	553	(4.7)
Germany	446	(3.8)	469	(3.3)	495	(2.8)	508	(2.6)	514	(3.5)	524	(2.9)	550	(3.4)
Greece	437	(7.1)	452	(6.3)	476	(5.1)	486	(4.2)	493	(3.7)	501	(3.5)	528	(3.4)
Hungary	435	(5.4)	456	(5.7)	485	(3.5)	502	(3.0)	506	(4.1)	518	(3.4)	553	(4.1)
Iceland	471	(3.2)	487	(3.3)	495	(3.3)	505	(2.9)	515	(3.0)	521	(2.7)	530	(2.9)
Ireland	455	(3.9)	482	(3.7)	487	(3.9)	505	(3.4)	511	(4.2)	520	(3.9)	540	(3.5)
Israel	426	(5.1)	432	(4.7)	466	(4.1)	472	(4.0)	503	(3.5)	506	(3.4)	528	(4.3)
Italy	444	(2.7)	460	(2.6)	478	(2.0)	489	(1.8)	501	(2.0)	508	(1.7)	526	(2.2)
Japan	486	(4.5)	500	(3.9)	512	(4.5)	523	(3.7)	538	(4.1)	544	(3.7)	559	(3.5)
Korea	505	(4.7)	520	(4.2)	535	(2.7)	545	(2.4)	548	(3.8)	555	(3.2)	573	(4.5)
Luxembourg	411	(2.7)	430	(2.9)	460	(3.0)	474	(2.6)	497	(2.8)	507	(2.9)	525	(2.9)
Mexico	387	(2.8)	386	(2.7)	414	(2.4)	415	(2.3)	435	(2.1)	436	(2.0)	470	(2.2)
Netherlands	473	(5.6)	488	(5.4)	492	(5.6)	504	(5.0)	519	(4.8)	527	(4.3)	553	(5.9)
New Zealand	474	(4.0)	499	(3.9)	509	(3.0)	529	(3.0)	533	(3.2)	544	(2.6)	579	(3.5)
Norway	467	(3.4)	484	(3.0)	496	(3.2)	509	(2.8)	518	(2.9)	526	(2.6)	536	(3.9)
Poland	463	(3.4)	480	(3.3)	489	(3.0)	505	(2.7)	507	(3.0)	520	(2.9)	551	(3.7)
Portugal	452	(4.2)	461	(4.0)	473	(3.3)	481	(3.1)	500	(3.3)	505	(3.1)	538	(3.8)
Slovak Republic	437	(4.9)	449	(4.7)	469	(3.4)	478	(3.2)	489	(3.2)	495	(3.0)	522	(3.6)
Slovenia	445	(2.6)	459	(2.6)	467	(2.4)	480	(2.4)	494	(2.6)	500	(2.5)	534	(2.6)
Spain	445	(3.3)	460	(2.7)	469	(2.3)	478	(1.9)	492	(2.1)	497	(2.0)	526	(3.3)
Sweden	451	(4.1)	470	(4.1)	488	(3.3)	503	(3.2)	515	(3.4)	522	(2.9)	544	(4.1)
Switzerland	457	(3.9)	479	(3.3)	493	(2.6)	510	(2.4)	507	(3.1)	520	(2.9)	550	(3.7)
Turkey	424	(3.8)	424	(3.8)	455	(3.6)	457	(3.4)	470	(3.8)	472	(3.7)	514	(4.5)
United Kingdom	451	(2.9)	473	(2.7)	483	(3.0)	500	(2.8)	509	(2.9)	520	(2.7)	544	(3.2)
United States	452	(3.6)	469	(3.4)	482	(3.4)	496	(3.5)	512	(3.6)	522	(3.3)	540	(4.7)
OECD average	452	(0.7)	468	(0.6)	483	(0.6)	496	(0.5)	507	(0.6)	514	(0.4)	540	(0.6)
Partners														
Albania	359	(6.5)	367	(6.7)	383	(4.2)	389	(3.9)	401	(4.5)	406	(4.4)	440	(5.1)
Argentina	361	(4.9)	378	(4.9)	392	(4.8)	405	(4.5)	423	(5.9)	430	(5.3)	477	(6.0)
Azerbaijan	351	(6.6)	353	(6.8)	363	(3.6)	365	(3.6)	375	(3.7)	376	(3.6)	400	(4.9)
Brazil	382	(2.5)	396	(2.6)	408	(3.0)	416	(2.8)	419	(3.8)	425	(3.7)	466	(4.3)
Bulgaria	380	(7.0)	400	(6.3)	427	(6.8)	441	(5.7)	455	(7.7)	463	(6.9)	505	(5.5)
Colombia	382	(4.6)	399	(4.2)	408	(4.2)	422	(4.1)	429	(3.5)	437	(3.3)	467	(4.8)
Croatia	444	(3.9)	457	(3.2)	470	(3.8)	480	(3.3)	486	(3.9)	491	(3.4)	516	(3.8)
Dubai (UAE)	405	(2.7)	425	(2.7)	458	(2.8)	464	(2.6)	486	(2.8)	489	(2.4)	511	(2.8)
Hong Kong-China	509	(4.0)	516	(3.5)	527	(2.8)	532	(2.8)	542	(2.8)	546	(2.7)	557	(3.5)
Indonesia	389	(3.7)	395	(3.4)	392	(3.8)	397	(3.6)	406	(4.5)	409	(4.0)	433	(6.0)
Jordan	381	(3.6)	386	(3.5)	406	(3.4)	408	(3.2)	418	(3.7)	419	(3.5)	446	(5.2)
Kazakhstan	350	(4.1)	360	(3.8)	385	(3.2)	394	(3.0)	400	(3.6)	404	(3.4)	433	(5.2)
Kyrgyzstan	282	(4.5)	295	(4.4)	305	(4.2)	315	(4.1)	333	(4.4)	339	(4.1)	379	(6.2)
Latvia	459	(4.7)	471	(4.0)	472	(3.3)	480	(3.0)	495	(3.5)	501	(3.1)	520	(3.6)
Liechtenstein	462	(7.8)	486	(7.3)	503	(7.9)	509	(7.2)	503	(9.3)	515	(8.7)	530	(8.1)
Lithuania	432	(3.5)	447	(3.2)	460	(3.3)	470	(3.3)	479	(3.4)	487	(3.0)	515	(3.3)
Macao-China	473	(2.1)	479	(2.0)	487	(2.0)	490	(2.0)	492	(2.1)	494	(1.9)	498	(2.1)
Montenegro	377	(3.4)	388	(3.3)	412	(3.0)	419	(2.9)	423	(3.0)	426	(3.0)	455	(2.8)
Panama	343	(6.5)	357	(5.6)	361	(6.4)	373	(5.7)	379	(6.7)	386	(5.7)	453	(11.1)
Peru	313	(3.9)	331	(3.9)	363	(3.1)	374	(3.0)	399	(3.8)	405	(3.7)	442	(7.5)
Qatar	344	(1.8)	352	(1.9)	375	(2.4)	377	(2.5)	405	(2.7)	402	(2.5)	401	(2.5)
Romania	385	(5.5)	399	(4.6)	421	(4.4)	429	(3.8)	435	(4.6)	440	(4.1)	468	(5.0)
Russian Federation	429	(3.7)	441	(2.9)	451	(3.9)	459	(3.2)	471	(3.3)	476	(3.1)	505	(4.9)
Serbia	419	(3.7)	434	(3.6)	437	(2.9)	450	(2.7)	450	(2.9)	459	(2.6)	482	(2.7)
Shanghai-China	522	(4.2)	530	(3.6)	546	(3.2)	552	(3.1)	564	(2.5)	568	(2.5)	594	(3.5)
Singapore	478	(2.4)	495	(2.3)	513	(3.1)	524	(2.7)	542	(2.4)	546	(2.4)	575	(3.1)
Chinese Taipei	461	(3.4)	474	(3.0)	485	(3.4)	494	(3.0)	505	(2.7)	511	(2.4)	536	(4.5)
Thailand	400	(3.7)	405	(3.7)	408	(2.8)	413	(2.7)	418	(2.7)	422	(2.7)	463	(4.5)
Trinidad and Tobago	394	(3.6)	410	(3.7)	421	(3.4)	431	(3.4)	437	(3.3)	443	(3.3)	480	(4.0)
Tunisia	381	(3.6)	384	(3.6)	396	(3.9)	397	(3.7)	409	(3.4)	412	(3.3)	447	(5.1)
Uruguay	382	(3.2)	404	(3.1)	414	(3.4)	430	(2.9)	445	(3.8)	455	(3.3)	495	(4.1)

Note: Observed reading performance refers to mean reading performance of students with non-missing information on the index of enjoyment of reading.
1. Socio-economically advantaged students are students in the top quarter of the PISA index of economic, social and cultural status (ESCS).
StatLink ⊟⊡⊟ http://dx.doi.org/10.1787/888932343285

[Part 1/1]

Table III.3.7 **Reading performance by gender and socio-economic background**

| | Performance of boys on the reading scale, by socio-economic background | | | | Performance of girls on the reading scale, by socio-economic background | | | | Differences in performance | | | | | | | |
| | Bottom quarter of ESCS | | Top quarter of ESCS | | Bottom quarter of ESCS | | Top quarter of ESCS | | Among girls between bottom quarter and top quarter of ESCS | | Among boys between bottom quarter and top quarter of ESCS | | Among girls and boys in the bottom quarter of ESCS | | Among girls and boys in the top quarter of ESCS | |
	Mean score	S.E.	Mean score	S.E.	Mean score	S.E.	Mean score	S.E.	Score dif.	S.E.	Score dif.	S.E.	Score dif.	S.E.	Score dif.	S.E.
Australia	439	(9.9)	544	(5.1)	484	(6.9)	574	(7.3)	**89**	(4.1)	**105**	(7.2)	**46**	(4.9)	**29**	(4.9)
Austria	400	(6.2)	511	(4.8)	445	(4.6)	542	(7.1)	**98**	(8.0)	**111**	(7.8)	**44**	(9.8)	**31**	(7.3)
Belgium	431	(6.3)	563	(8.2)	464	(4.6)	580	(5.8)	**116**	(7.2)	**132**	(7.1)	**33**	(7.9)	**17**	(5.1)
Canada	474	(3.3)	543	(2.7)	509	(2.7)	583	(4.5)	**75**	(4.9)	**69**	(4.3)	**35**	(3.6)	**41**	(5.1)
Chile	399	(5.8)	493	(5.2)	424	(7.8)	511	(4.8)	**87**	(8.1)	**94**	(8.4)	**25**	(6.3)	**19**	(7.0)
Czech Republic	415	(5.3)	494	(8.0)	459	(5.8)	552	(7.5)	**93**	(5.2)	**78**	(7.1)	**44**	(9.1)	**58**	(13.5)
Denmark	437	(4.4)	521	(3.6)	465	(5.8)	552	(5.1)	**86**	(5.2)	**84**	(6.3)	**28**	(8.3)	**31**	(5.6)
Estonia	450	(6.9)	515	(4.5)	495	(5.2)	556	(5.5)	**61**	(6.9)	**65**	(8.6)	**45**	(6.1)	**41**	(6.4)
Finland	480	(7.8)	539	(4.0)	531	(5.0)	590	(4.0)	**59**	(4.5)	**59**	(8.6)	**51**	(10.9)	**51**	(4.9)
France	419	(13.2)	536	(5.9)	464	(6.0)	568	(5.7)	**104**	(8.8)	**117**	(14.1)	**45**	(11.2)	**32**	(6.7)
Germany	438	(9.6)	532	(5.5)	463	(5.2)	575	(8.1)	**112**	(11.0)	**94**	(8.1)	**25**	(12.1)	**43**	(6.3)
Greece	407	(8.2)	506	(5.1)	467	(8.5)	551	(3.9)	**85**	(9.7)	**99**	(8.3)	**60**	(8.6)	**45**	(5.7)
Hungary	412	(7.5)	537	(5.2)	454	(6.8)	572	(5.2)	**118**	(7.8)	**125**	(9.5)	**42**	(7.0)	**35**	(5.7)
Iceland	444	(6.9)	513	(6.4)	485	(5.5)	549	(4.5)	**64**	(7.3)	**69**	(6.0)	**41**	(11.0)	**36**	(8.4)
Ireland	429	(7.5)	520	(4.9)	467	(5.5)	559	(5.1)	**93**	(5.8)	**91**	(8.8)	**38**	(7.4)	**40**	(6.0)
Israel	386	(13.4)	515	(15.9)	439	(7.0)	549	(4.9)	**110**	(8.1)	**129**	(10.6)	**54**	(16.1)	**34**	(16.7)
Italy	418	(6.0)	507	(3.4)	467	(4.2)	546	(2.8)	**79**	(4.4)	**89**	(8.0)	**50**	(4.2)	**39**	(4.0)
Japan	465	(10.8)	543	(5.9)	505	(6.5)	577	(7.3)	**73**	(7.4)	**78**	(9.0)	**40**	(9.4)	**35**	(8.4)
Korea	483	(7.9)	563	(8.5)	528	(6.4)	588	(7.6)	**60**	(8.2)	**80**	(14.3)	**44**	(11.3)	**25**	(6.8)
Luxembourg	385	(4.9)	508	(6.5)	434	(4.9)	546	(3.8)	**112**	(7.0)	**123**	(9.6)	**48**	(8.1)	**38**	(8.5)
Mexico	370	(4.4)	458	(3.2)	399	(3.7)	484	(2.6)	**85**	(3.8)	**88**	(6.0)	**28**	(5.6)	**26**	(3.2)
Netherlands	461	(6.8)	529	(9.8)	479	(6.2)	571	(5.4)	**92**	(6.2)	**68**	(7.6)	**18**	(6.7)	**42**	(8.7)
New Zealand	441	(6.1)	563	(8.7)	496	(5.6)	598	(4.9)	**102**	(5.9)	**122**	(9.4)	**54**	(6.8)	**34**	(7.7)
Norway	442	(5.4)	516	(4.6)	490	(4.1)	560	(6.2)	**70**	(7.3)	**74**	(5.3)	**48**	(5.2)	**44**	(7.5)
Poland	428	(7.4)	530	(4.4)	485	(4.0)	571	(6.2)	**85**	(6.7)	**102**	(9.0)	**58**	(8.2)	**41**	(5.9)
Portugal	427	(7.5)	526	(6.2)	470	(4.4)	555	(4.5)	**84**	(6.5)	**99**	(7.3)	**43**	(7.5)	**28**	(5.6)
Slovak Republic	408	(7.2)	490	(11.4)	453	(6.7)	545	(8.2)	**92**	(7.8)	**82**	(9.5)	**45**	(6.6)	**55**	(6.5)
Slovenia	407	(4.1)	510	(6.2)	473	(4.9)	555	(5.2)	**82**	(8.9)	**103**	(8.3)	**65**	(7.4)	**45**	(10.2)
Spain	427	(4.2)	509	(4.4)	453	(4.4)	537	(5.2)	**84**	(5.4)	**81**	(5.9)	**26**	(5.2)	**28**	(6.8)
Sweden	420	(6.5)	524	(7.8)	473	(5.9)	562	(8.4)	**89**	(11.5)	**104**	(12.1)	**54**	(8.9)	**38**	(14.1)
Switzerland	433	(4.0)	529	(4.4)	473	(7.4)	572	(8.8)	**98**	(15.0)	**97**	(5.2)	**41**	(7.6)	**42**	(9.8)
Turkey	404	(4.0)	488	(11.7)	443	(5.2)	529	(9.0)	**86**	(9.4)	**84**	(10.7)	**39**	(4.6)	**41**	(5.1)
United Kingdom	430	(6.4)	529	(5.0)	456	(6.0)	556	(5.3)	**100**	(7.0)	**99**	(5.4)	**26**	(5.4)	**27**	(6.5)
United States	433	(5.2)	550	(5.1)	467	(5.5)	571	(7.0)	**105**	(8.2)	**117**	(7.8)	**34**	(8.0)	**22**	(5.8)
OECD average	428	(1.2)	522	(1.2)	469	(1.0)	558	(1.0)	**89**	(1.3)	**94**	(1.5)	**42**	(1.4)	**36**	(1.3)
Albania	314	(8.3)	392	(10.5)	376	(7.5)	462	(7.7)	**86**	(8.0)	**79**	(10.6)	**62**	(8.2)	**70**	(8.2)
Argentina	321	(7.8)	453	(13.1)	362	(6.3)	490	(10.8)	**128**	(12.0)	**132**	(11.8)	**40**	(7.5)	**37**	(7.4)
Azerbaijan	329	(8.2)	379	(5.5)	350	(6.9)	406	(5.4)	**56**	(8.9)	**50**	(9.8)	**21**	(5.7)	**27**	(5.1)
Brazil	356	(3.3)	445	(6.1)	385	(4.7)	481	(6.7)	**96**	(10.1)	**89**	(7.5)	**29**	(4.1)	**36**	(4.6)
Bulgaria	333	(7.2)	475	(7.4)	399	(10.6)	527	(7.9)	**128**	(10.2)	**142**	(10.3)	**65**	(13.1)	**52**	(6.1)
Colombia	374	(11.1)	458	(10.9)	376	(7.4)	474	(8.3)	**98**	(7.3)	**84**	(8.9)	2	(6.7)	15	(8.3)
Croatia	420	(5.3)	488	(4.8)	463	(5.1)	544	(5.1)	**81**	(6.9)	**68**	(7.3)	**44**	(6.6)	**56**	(6.2)
Dubai (UAE)	369	(8.5)	483	(5.7)	430	(3.7)	523	(5.6)	**93**	(7.2)	**113**	(7.0)	**61**	(10.0)	**40**	(6.2)
Hong Kong-China	492	(4.5)	542	(6.7)	522	(8.5)	577	(4.5)	**56**	(9.2)	**50**	(8.6)	**30**	(8.3)	**35**	(8.2)
Indonesia	368	(5.1)	404	(12.7)	403	(6.2)	449	(7.1)	**46**	(11.1)	**36**	(13.1)	**36**	(7.6)	**45**	(8.1)
Jordan	338	(6.2)	415	(7.0)	401	(4.6)	464	(11.2)	**63**	(11.5)	**77**	(8.8)	**63**	(7.7)	**49**	(12.2)
Kazakhstan	328	(4.5)	416	(7.7)	370	(4.9)	455	(6.6)	**86**	(8.1)	**88**	(9.1)	**41**	(5.6)	**39**	(5.6)
Kyrgyzstan	248	(8.6)	343	(10.1)	300	(6.8)	396	(5.7)	**96**	(7.5)	**95**	(9.4)	**52**	(5.6)	**52**	(6.9)
Latvia	430	(8.1)	497	(4.6)	479	(5.5)	544	(4.6)	**65**	(6.7)	**67**	(9.3)	**49**	(7.4)	**47**	(5.7)
Liechtenstein	459	(26.6)	517	(10.2)	474	(13.1)	537	(19.8)	63	(29.8)	58	(32.0)	15	(24.5)	20	(20.9)
Lithuania	402	(4.8)	485	(4.7)	454	(4.4)	545	(4.2)	**92**	(5.9)	**83**	(7.2)	**52**	(5.9)	**60**	(5.6)
Macao-China	458	(4.6)	482	(3.6)	488	(3.0)	511	(4.6)	**24**	(4.2)	**24**	(5.9)	**30**	(4.5)	**29**	(5.9)
Montenegro	340	(6.0)	424	(3.3)	392	(3.7)	475	(3.9)	**84**	(5.7)	**83**	(6.5)	**51**	(7.7)	**51**	(5.5)
Panama	315	(15.6)	429	(24.2)	329	(11.1)	478	(12.9)	**149**	(20.0)	**113**	(35.9)	14	(9.6)	**49**	(18.0)
Peru	300	(7.7)	425	(11.0)	309	(6.0)	441	(10.5)	**132**	(13.5)	**126**	(8.1)	9	(6.3)	16	(16.0)
Qatar	306	(3.0)	370	(3.8)	360	(2.6)	419	(4.4)	**59**	(5.1)	**63**	(5.4)	**54**	(3.7)	**49**	(6.1)
Romania	355	(9.6)	444	(6.7)	398	(11.4)	488	(5.6)	**90**	(10.8)	**89**	(10.5)	**44**	(8.1)	**44**	(5.7)
Russian Federation	405	(6.1)	474	(5.7)	444	(5.1)	535	(11.3)	**91**	(9.7)	**69**	(8.0)	**39**	(5.0)	**61**	(11.6)
Serbia	391	(5.6)	458	(6.1)	435	(6.7)	501	(5.4)	**66**	(4.7)	**66**	(9.6)	**44**	(4.7)	**44**	(10.3)
Shanghai-China	505	(9.0)	575	(4.6)	541	(4.0)	614	(4.1)	**73**	(6.2)	**70**	(8.3)	**36**	(8.6)	**39**	(5.6)
Singapore	459	(8.2)	555	(4.8)	489	(3.8)	593	(4.0)	**104**	(4.7)	**97**	(8.4)	**30**	(6.9)	**37**	(4.3)
Chinese Taipei	443	(11.3)	523	(8.7)	483	(8.5)	548	(8.2)	**65**	(14.2)	**79**	(7.8)	**40**	(6.3)	25	(14.3)
Thailand	375	(5.8)	435	(10.1)	414	(4.2)	483	(6.8)	**69**	(8.5)	**59**	(13.4)	**38**	(6.8)	**48**	(14.0)
Trinidad and Tobago	337	(8.3)	436	(5.3)	401	(6.8)	503	(5.4)	**103**	(8.4)	**99**	(8.3)	**63**	(13.5)	**67**	(7.7)
Tunisia	367	(4.6)	414	(9.0)	386	(4.6)	461	(5.6)	**75**	(7.1)	**47**	(11.6)	19	(5.8)	**47**	(9.6)
Uruguay	345	(7.6)	467	(5.8)	388	(5.7)	509	(6.0)	**121**	(5.4)	**122**	(9.5)	**43**	(6.4)	**42**	(7.3)

Note: Values that are statistically significant are indicated in bold (see Annex A3).
StatLink http://dx.doi.org/10.1787/888932343285

[Part 1/1]

Predicted reading performance of boys from different socio-economic backgrounds if they had the same value on the index of summarising as socio-economically advantaged girls[1]

Table III.3.8

| | | Bottom quarter ESCS boys | | | | Second quarter ESCS boys | | | | Third quarter ESCS boys | | | | Top quarter ESCS boys | |
		Observed reading performance	S.E.	Predicted reading performance if boys in this quarter had the same value on the index of summarising as girls in the top ESCS quarter	S.E.	Observed reading performance	S.E.	Predicted reading performance if boys in this quarter had the same value on the index of summarising as girls in the top ESCS quarter	S.E.	Observed reading performance	S.E.	Predicted reading performance if boys in this quarter had the same value on the index of summarising as girls in the top ESCS quarter	S.E.	Observed reading performance	S.E.
OECD	Australia	454	(3.1)	489	(3.0)	488	(3.2)	517	(3.1)	518	(3.6)	539	(3.3)	549	(3.7)
	Austria	408	(5.3)	444	(5.2)	443	(5.2)	469	(4.7)	462	(5.1)	489	(5.2)	512	(4.9)
	Belgium	454	(3.8)	492	(3.7)	484	(4.2)	514	(3.6)	523	(3.4)	542	(3.2)	563	(3.9)
	Canada	481	(3.0)	503	(3.0)	500	(2.4)	521	(2.3)	519	(2.7)	535	(2.7)	543	(2.7)
	Chile	403	(4.3)	422	(4.3)	426	(4.7)	443	(4.2)	450	(4.5)	462	(4.1)	495	(5.1)
	Czech Republic	429	(4.1)	459	(3.7)	448	(4.9)	477	(4.4)	471	(4.8)	495	(4.0)	501	(5.1)
	Denmark	445	(3.5)	471	(3.5)	472	(4.3)	493	(4.0)	496	(4.0)	511	(3.7)	522	(3.4)
	Estonia	457	(4.5)	478	(4.1)	469	(4.4)	490	(3.8)	483	(3.8)	501	(3.4)	517	(4.4)
	Finland	481	(4.6)	516	(4.3)	501	(3.5)	530	(3.5)	522	(3.7)	546	(3.3)	541	(3.9)
	France	432	(6.4)	463	(5.5)	468	(6.3)	487	(5.5)	501	(5.4)	511	(4.9)	540	(5.7)
	Germany	440	(5.5)	471	(4.3)	485	(4.1)	507	(3.7)	498	(4.8)	521	(4.3)	535	(4.4)
	Greece	409	(8.5)	426	(8.3)	450	(7.1)	463	(7.0)	474	(4.9)	486	(4.6)	507	(4.9)
	Hungary	414	(5.8)	451	(5.3)	465	(4.4)	491	(4.1)	488	(5.3)	510	(4.7)	539	(5.1)
	Iceland	452	(4.9)	481	(4.8)	471	(4.7)	495	(4.6)	492	(4.4)	511	(4.2)	514	(4.7)
	Ireland	441	(5.4)	465	(4.7)	475	(5.2)	492	(4.6)	497	(5.0)	509	(4.6)	523	(4.6)
	Israel	404	(5.3)	438	(5.3)	448	(5.3)	473	(5.0)	487	(5.2)	503	(5.0)	514	(5.6)
	Italy	420	(4.0)	446	(3.3)	458	(2.8)	476	(2.6)	480	(2.8)	493	(2.6)	510	(2.8)
	Japan	465	(6.0)	496	(4.8)	489	(6.9)	518	(5.2)	525	(5.7)	543	(4.7)	541	(5.1)
	Korea	486	(6.2)	512	(4.7)	519	(3.7)	536	(3.2)	533	(5.6)	548	(4.3)	560	(6.0)
	Luxembourg	396	(4.4)	430	(4.1)	447	(4.3)	474	(3.9)	482	(3.8)	501	(3.9)	512	(4.4)
	Mexico	376	(3.5)	396	(3.2)	404	(2.3)	420	(2.1)	425	(2.8)	438	(2.4)	459	(2.9)
	Netherlands	472	(6.2)	500	(4.9)	485	(6.0)	512	(5.3)	513	(5.8)	535	(4.4)	537	(7.3)
	New Zealand	455	(5.5)	489	(6.0)	492	(4.4)	519	(4.1)	510	(4.4)	535	(3.9)	563	(5.4)
	Norway	445	(4.4)	474	(3.8)	475	(4.4)	496	(3.7)	496	(3.8)	513	(3.3)	516	(4.2)
	Poland	437	(4.9)	464	(4.5)	462	(3.6)	480	(3.7)	487	(3.7)	506	(3.9)	534	(4.1)
	Portugal	428	(4.8)	462	(4.5)	451	(4.3)	480	(3.9)	480	(4.7)	502	(3.9)	523	(4.5)
	Slovak Republic	416	(6.5)	444	(5.7)	444	(5.6)	464	(5.0)	457	(5.1)	475	(4.7)	499	(3.9)
	Slovenia	418	(3.5)	448	(3.4)	446	(3.7)	472	(3.7)	469	(3.6)	490	(3.4)	511	(4.0)
	Spain	433	(3.9)	456	(3.6)	455	(2.8)	475	(2.5)	478	(2.8)	494	(2.7)	511	(4.3)
	Sweden	435	(4.7)	464	(4.5)	471	(4.6)	494	(4.4)	497	(3.8)	516	(3.4)	523	(5.1)
	Switzerland	437	(3.7)	477	(3.5)	479	(3.8)	507	(3.1)	488	(3.8)	516	(3.3)	531	(4.2)
	Turkey	408	(3.8)	424	(3.8)	437	(4.2)	452	(3.9)	450	(4.6)	464	(4.5)	495	(5.0)
	United Kingdom	444	(4.2)	468	(4.4)	473	(4.6)	492	(4.3)	500	(4.8)	516	(4.4)	533	(4.2)
	United States	441	(4.1)	465	(3.8)	470	(4.9)	491	(4.9)	501	(5.4)	518	(4.9)	551	(4.4)
	OECD average	**436**	**(0.8)**	**464**	**(0.8)**	**466**	**(0.8)**	**489**	**(0.7)**	**490**	**(0.8)**	**508**	**(0.7)**	**524**	**(0.8)**
Partners	Albania	332	(8.7)	345	(9.2)	357	(5.8)	369	(5.6)	372	(5.6)	383	(5.9)	409	(6.6)
	Argentina	339	(7.2)	362	(6.8)	371	(5.7)	389	(5.6)	401	(6.5)	417	(6.1)	461	(7.4)
	Azerbaijan	339	(7.7)	342	(7.9)	351	(4.3)	353	(4.3)	363	(5.0)	365	(4.9)	388	(6.2)
	Brazil	367	(3.2)	385	(3.3)	394	(4.0)	408	(3.9)	400	(4.1)	413	(4.2)	450	(5.1)
	Bulgaria	351	(7.1)	380	(7.0)	398	(8.4)	419	(7.3)	424	(9.9)	442	(9.8)	482	(6.1)
	Colombia	378	(5.8)	396	(5.4)	400	(4.9)	418	(5.0)	421	(5.6)	432	(5.3)	459	(6.7)
	Croatia	423	(4.9)	449	(4.6)	446	(5.1)	468	(4.5)	462	(4.9)	479	(4.3)	491	(4.3)
	Dubai (UAE)	377	(4.1)	404	(3.8)	430	(4.9)	446	(4.5)	465	(3.8)	476	(3.5)	492	(4.0)
	Hong Kong-China	496	(4.1)	507	(3.7)	514	(4.4)	525	(4.3)	526	(4.3)	536	(4.0)	540	(5.1)
	Indonesia	374	(4.7)	382	(4.3)	372	(4.2)	380	(3.7)	383	(4.6)	390	(4.2)	413	(6.3)
	Jordan	351	(4.8)	361	(4.6)	381	(5.1)	387	(5.0)	389	(5.2)	395	(5.1)	420	(7.0)
	Kazakhstan	331	(4.4)	345	(4.4)	363	(4.1)	379	(3.9)	380	(4.4)	391	(4.1)	413	(6.1)
	Kyrgyzstan	256	(6.0)	272	(5.7)	279	(5.4)	290	(5.3)	307	(5.5)	317	(5.3)	352	(8.5)
	Latvia	432	(5.6)	453	(6.1)	445	(4.6)	464	(4.3)	474	(3.9)	490	(3.7)	498	(4.3)
	Liechtenstein	453	(13.0)	491	(12.8)	477	(14.2)	512	(13.4)	484	(11.9)	515	(11.8)	519	(9.4)
	Lithuania	405	(4.8)	427	(4.7)	428	(3.8)	448	(3.9)	451	(4.1)	468	(4.0)	485	(4.3)
	Macao-China	460	(2.9)	469	(2.9)	470	(3.0)	477	(3.0)	473	(2.9)	480	(2.8)	482	(3.3)
	Montenegro	352	(5.2)	366	(5.2)	381	(4.4)	393	(4.2)	394	(4.6)	402	(4.5)	433	(3.6)
	Panama	340	(9.2)	359	(8.1)	349	(8.9)	366	(7.8)	361	(9.9)	374	(8.9)	424	(13.7)
	Peru	306	(4.5)	330	(4.5)	351	(4.0)	366	(4.1)	387	(4.7)	400	(4.6)	431	(8.2)
	Qatar	319	(3.0)	331	(3.1)	350	(3.6)	355	(3.7)	386	(3.8)	387	(3.6)	380	(4.1)
	Romania	361	(7.0)	380	(6.4)	397	(5.5)	414	(4.9)	414	(5.3)	428	(4.9)	447	(5.8)
	Russian Federation	409	(4.7)	430	(4.2)	430	(4.9)	447	(4.1)	449	(4.2)	467	(3.6)	477	(5.5)
	Serbia	398	(4.4)	422	(4.8)	415	(4.6)	438	(4.5)	431	(4.2)	450	(3.6)	465	(3.6)
	Shanghai-China	502	(5.0)	514	(4.4)	527	(4.2)	537	(4.2)	544	(3.3)	552	(3.3)	574	(3.8)
	Singapore	465	(3.7)	492	(3.4)	499	(3.9)	520	(3.6)	530	(3.4)	543	(3.3)	556	(3.8)
	Chinese Taipei	443	(4.8)	458	(4.4)	467	(5.3)	480	(4.4)	488	(4.1)	496	(3.5)	521	(5.5)
	Thailand	376	(4.8)	383	(4.7)	388	(3.3)	395	(3.4)	395	(3.3)	401	(3.3)	440	(5.4)
	Trinidad and Tobago	368	(5.6)	391	(5.4)	394	(4.6)	414	(4.5)	409	(5.8)	423	(5.4)	450	(5.4)
	Tunisia	371	(4.0)	375	(4.1)	381	(5.3)	385	(5.3)	388	(4.6)	392	(4.5)	428	(6.5)
	Uruguay	362	(4.5)	392	(4.6)	390	(4.9)	412	(4.5)	423	(4.5)	440	(3.9)	475	(5.8)

Note: Observed reading performance refers to mean reading performance of students with non-missing information on the index of summarising.
1. Socio-economically advantaged students are students in the top quarter of the PISA index of economic, social and cultural status (ESCS).
StatLink ᒪᔿᔕᒪ http://dx.doi.org/10.1787/888932343285

[Part 1/1]

Table III.3.9

Predicted reading performance of boys from different socio-economic backgrounds if they had the same value on the index of enjoyment of reading as socio-economically advantaged girls[1]

	Bottom quarter ESCS boys				Second quarter ESCS boys				Third quarter ESCS boys				Top quarter ESCS boys	
	Observed reading performance	S.E.	Predicted reading performance if boys in this quarter had the same value on the index of enjoyment of reading as girls in the top ESCS quarter	S.E.	Observed reading performance	S.E.	Predicted reading performance if boys in this quarter had the same value on the index of enjoyment of reading as girls in the top ESCS quarter	S.E.	Observed reading performance	S.E.	Predicted reading performance if boys in this quarter had the same value on the index of enjoyment of reading as girls in the top ESCS quarter	S.E.	Observed reading performance	S.E.
OECD														
Australia	449	(3.3)	498	(3.3)	484	(3.2)	527	(3.3)	514	(3.8)	548	(3.6)	547	(3.7)
Austria	400	(5.1)	441	(5.6)	436	(5.7)	475	(5.8)	459	(5.3)	495	(5.4)	510	(4.9)
Belgium	437	(4.7)	472	(5.4)	472	(4.1)	504	(4.2)	512	(3.5)	538	(3.3)	558	(3.8)
Canada	479	(3.2)	520	(3.4)	498	(2.3)	535	(2.2)	517	(2.9)	550	(2.7)	543	(2.7)
Chile	398	(4.7)	413	(4.9)	422	(4.5)	439	(4.7)	448	(4.5)	462	(4.5)	493	(5.1)
Czech Republic	420	(4.2)	457	(4.2)	443	(4.9)	480	(5.3)	468	(4.8)	500	(4.8)	498	(5.0)
Denmark	442	(3.7)	481	(3.8)	468	(4.1)	501	(3.9)	494	(4.0)	521	(3.8)	521	(3.4)
Estonia	453	(4.5)	493	(5.3)	469	(4.3)	505	(4.5)	482	(3.9)	514	(4.1)	515	(4.3)
Finland	478	(4.6)	527	(4.5)	499	(3.8)	538	(3.5)	520	(3.7)	559	(3.9)	539	(3.8)
France	419	(6.6)	459	(7.0)	462	(6.1)	498	(5.0)	494	(5.7)	524	(5.2)	537	(5.6)
Germany	427	(5.7)	473	(5.6)	474	(3.9)	514	(3.9)	490	(4.6)	525	(4.5)	531	(4.5)
Greece	407	(8.3)	442	(8.1)	448	(7.2)	483	(6.1)	472	(5.1)	504	(4.6)	506	(4.7)
Hungary	411	(5.7)	449	(6.2)	463	(4.4)	499	(4.3)	485	(5.2)	518	(4.7)	537	(5.2)
Iceland	447	(5.0)	485	(5.3)	470	(4.3)	504	(4.2)	490	(4.2)	519	(3.9)	511	(4.6)
Ireland	433	(6.1)	476	(6.0)	469	(5.5)	506	(5.1)	490	(5.2)	517	(5.1)	521	(4.8)
Israel	400	(6.5)	420	(6.5)	443	(5.5)	462	(5.8)	484	(5.0)	501	(5.1)	509	(5.9)
Italy	419	(3.7)	454	(3.8)	455	(2.8)	486	(3.0)	477	(2.9)	506	(2.8)	508	(2.7)
Japan	467	(5.9)	492	(5.4)	491	(6.3)	512	(5.4)	524	(6.3)	539	(5.7)	543	(4.8)
Korea	486	(5.7)	508	(5.6)	518	(3.6)	535	(3.2)	532	(5.7)	549	(4.6)	561	(5.9)
Luxembourg	388	(4.1)	430	(4.9)	439	(4.5)	475	(4.4)	479	(3.9)	510	(4.1)	505	(4.7)
Mexico	373	(3.3)	380	(3.2)	400	(2.4)	409	(2.5)	419	(2.7)	428	(2.7)	458	(2.9)
Netherlands	464	(5.7)	502	(6.1)	479	(5.7)	515	(5.7)	507	(5.7)	540	(5.8)	533	(7.4)
New Zealand	448	(5.7)	495	(5.9)	488	(4.6)	530	(5.1)	507	(4.2)	541	(4.0)	561	(5.6)
Norway	441	(4.5)	480	(4.2)	471	(4.2)	506	(4.5)	495	(3.8)	523	(3.6)	515	(4.1)
Poland	435	(5.2)	469	(5.5)	461	(3.4)	495	(3.6)	483	(4.0)	514	(4.3)	532	(4.1)
Portugal	429	(5.1)	455	(5.2)	451	(4.4)	478	(4.5)	479	(4.6)	503	(4.6)	523	(4.6)
Slovak Republic	415	(6.3)	439	(6.3)	441	(5.6)	464	(5.5)	458	(5.0)	481	(5.0)	497	(3.9)
Slovenia	412	(3.1)	443	(3.3)	441	(3.6)	471	(3.9)	466	(3.4)	491	(3.4)	511	(3.7)
Spain	433	(3.8)	465	(3.4)	454	(2.6)	483	(2.5)	477	(2.8)	501	(2.9)	510	(4.6)
Sweden	427	(5.2)	471	(5.7)	466	(4.8)	509	(4.8)	491	(3.8)	528	(4.1)	521	(4.9)
Switzerland	436	(3.7)	482	(4.3)	477	(3.8)	516	(3.7)	487	(3.8)	525	(3.9)	531	(4.3)
Turkey	407	(3.8)	417	(4.1)	436	(4.4)	449	(4.4)	449	(4.9)	462	(5.0)	494	(5.1)
United Kingdom	439	(3.9)	479	(3.9)	468	(4.6)	507	(4.5)	497	(5.0)	528	(4.5)	530	(4.2)
United States	437	(4.2)	475	(4.8)	466	(5.0)	501	(5.3)	500	(5.4)	531	(5.6)	549	(4.5)
OECD average	431	(0.9)	466	(0.9)	462	(0.8)	494	(0.8)	487	(0.8)	515	(0.7)	522	(0.8)
Partners														
Albania	321	(7.8)	348	(7.8)	348	(5.7)	373	(5.7)	364	(6.0)	388	(6.1)	399	(7.0)
Argentina	326	(6.7)	334	(7.2)	359	(5.9)	369	(6.1)	391	(5.9)	400	(6.4)	453	(7.0)
Azerbaijan	332	(6.9)	339	(7.0)	344	(4.1)	351	(4.0)	356	(4.6)	362	(4.6)	380	(5.4)
Brazil	359	(3.2)	370	(3.4)	386	(4.0)	398	(4.2)	394	(4.0)	407	(4.0)	445	(5.0)
Bulgaria	345	(6.3)	365	(7.4)	390	(8.0)	409	(9.3)	419	(9.0)	437	(10.2)	479	(6.6)
Colombia	369	(6.2)	373	(6.7)	394	(5.0)	398	(5.3)	415	(5.8)	420	(6.0)	453	(6.5)
Croatia	419	(4.9)	445	(5.3)	444	(5.2)	470	(5.1)	458	(5.1)	481	(4.8)	487	(4.6)
Dubai (UAE)	376	(4.0)	401	(4.3)	428	(4.4)	449	(4.6)	459	(4.0)	479	(3.9)	486	(4.0)
Hong Kong-China	497	(4.2)	522	(4.5)	515	(4.3)	536	(4.4)	526	(4.4)	543	(4.3)	543	(4.6)
Indonesia	370	(4.7)	374	(4.9)	370	(4.1)	374	(4.2)	380	(4.4)	383	(4.5)	412	(6.1)
Jordan	352	(4.9)	358	(4.8)	378	(4.8)	382	(4.7)	383	(5.7)	388	(5.4)	420	(6.9)
Kazakhstan	331	(4.1)	329	(4.3)	362	(4.1)	360	(4.3)	380	(4.5)	378	(4.6)	411	(5.9)
Kyrgyzstan	250	(5.7)	256	(6.1)	271	(5.1)	275	(5.2)	300	(5.2)	305	(5.2)	345	(8.0)
Latvia	430	(6.5)	463	(6.4)	443	(4.6)	473	(4.3)	469	(4.2)	495	(4.6)	497	(4.4)
Liechtenstein	448	(12.9)	481	(13.1)	477	(14.4)	501	(13.7)	485	(11.4)	513	(11.8)	519	(9.3)
Lithuania	405	(4.2)	438	(4.8)	424	(4.4)	455	(4.5)	448	(3.7)	478	(4.2)	484	(4.1)
Macao-China	459	(2.9)	480	(2.9)	469	(3.0)	487	(3.0)	472	(2.8)	487	(2.8)	481	(3.3)
Montenegro	346	(4.2)	365	(4.6)	374	(4.1)	392	(4.2)	387	(4.4)	405	(4.8)	425	(3.2)
Panama	334	(9.0)	336	(9.1)	342	(8.6)	345	(8.7)	363	(8.1)	368	(8.0)	420	(13.3)
Peru	298	(3.5)	302	(3.4)	346	(3.6)	352	(3.5)	378	(4.8)	384	(4.8)	424	(7.9)
Qatar	315	(2.6)	326	(2.6)	347	(3.4)	360	(3.3)	378	(3.8)	391	(3.7)	379	(3.5)
Romania	359	(7.0)	369	(7.2)	397	(5.4)	408	(5.5)	414	(5.3)	424	(5.3)	446	(6.0)
Russian Federation	405	(4.2)	434	(4.0)	426	(4.5)	451	(4.5)	445	(4.2)	469	(4.1)	474	(5.5)
Serbia	391	(4.6)	409	(5.4)	412	(4.7)	430	(4.7)	425	(3.9)	443	(4.2)	461	(3.7)
Shanghai-China	502	(5.1)	521	(5.0)	527	(4.2)	542	(4.3)	545	(3.4)	557	(3.6)	574	(3.8)
Singapore	466	(3.8)	506	(4.3)	500	(3.9)	536	(3.7)	528	(3.6)	559	(3.6)	556	(3.9)
Chinese Taipei	442	(4.7)	481	(4.6)	467	(5.1)	500	(4.4)	489	(4.2)	515	(4.1)	522	(5.5)
Thailand	376	(4.8)	384	(4.8)	388	(3.4)	396	(3.5)	397	(3.4)	406	(3.5)	442	(5.3)
Trinidad and Tobago	350	(5.9)	365	(6.1)	383	(4.3)	398	(4.6)	394	(5.2)	408	(5.3)	438	(4.6)
Tunisia	368	(3.8)	369	(3.9)	379	(4.8)	380	(4.6)	387	(4.5)	389	(4.6)	421	(6.1)
Uruguay	353	(4.3)	367	(4.5)	383	(4.6)	398	(4.7)	416	(4.6)	428	(4.6)	470	(6.1)

Note: Observed reading performance refers to mean reading performance of students with non-missing information on the index of enjoyment of reading.
1. Socio-economically advantaged students are students in the top quarter of the PISA index of economic, social and cultural status (ESCS).
StatLink ᠍᠌᠍ http://dx.doi.org/10.1787/888932343285

[Part 1/2]

The role of enjoyment of reading and summarising strategies as mediators of socio-economic background and gender[1]

Table III.3.10

	Total effect (ESCS on reading performance)		Indirect effect of ESCS through enjoyment of reading		Indirect effect of ESCS through summarising strategies		Direct effect of ESCS		ESCS on enjoyment of reading		ESCS on summarising strategies		Total effect (Gender on reading performance)		Indirect effect of gender through enjoyment of reading		Indirect effect of gender through summarising strategies	
	Change in score	S.E.	Change in score	S.E.	Change in score	S.E.	Change in score	S.E.	Change in score	S.E.	Change in score	S.E.	Change in score	S.E.	Change in score	S.E.	Change in score	S.E.
OECD																		
Australia	47.2	(1.2)	10.6	(0.5)	8.2	(0.4)	28.4	(1.1)	0.3	(0.0)	0.3	(0.0)	37.3	(1.8)	20.1	(0.8)	13.2	(0.7)
Austria	43.8	(1.7)	7.0	(0.6)	8.4	(0.7)	28.4	(1.6)	0.3	(0.0)	0.3	(0.0)	41.4	(2.8)	20.1	(1.3)	14.6	(1.1)
Belgium	45.3	(1.2)	5.7	(0.4)	11.6	(0.6)	28.0	(1.1)	0.2	(0.0)	0.3	(0.0)	34.8	(1.7)	23.0	(0.8)	11.3	(0.6)
Canada	32.2	(1.1)	5.9	(0.4)	3.6	(0.3)	22.7	(1.0)	0.2	(0.0)	0.1	(0.0)	22.1	(2.4)	8.6	(0.7)	6.3	(0.7)
Chile	31.5	(1.0)	1.4	(0.2)	4.4	(0.3)	25.6	(0.9)	0.1	(0.0)	0.2	(0.0)	28.9	(2.1)	13.0	(0.8)	12.1	(1.0)
Czech Republic	47.0	(1.7)	5.7	(0.5)	8.7	(0.8)	32.6	(1.6)	0.2	(0.0)	0.2	(0.0)	50.3	(2.4)	17.6	(1.1)	14.8	(1.1)
Denmark	33.2	(1.4)	7.6	(0.6)	5.6	(0.5)	20.0	(1.3)	0.3	(0.0)	0.2	(0.0)	30.3	(2.4)	15.8	(1.1)	10.0	(0.9)
Estonia	29.3	(1.6)	6.1	(0.6)	4.1	(0.6)	19.1	(1.5)	0.2	(0.0)	0.1	(0.0)	46.0	(2.8)	21.9	(1.5)	11.6	(1.0)
Finland	29.9	(1.5)	6.2	(0.6)	5.0	(0.5)	18.7	(1.3)	0.2	(0.0)	0.2	(0.0)	54.5	(2.3)	25.9	(1.3)	16.4	(1.1)
France	48.4	(1.8)	7.9	(0.6)	9.3	(0.8)	31.1	(1.8)	0.3	(0.0)	0.3	(0.0)	41.5	(3.2)	14.8	(1.2)	8.0	(1.2)
Germany	41.7	(1.5)	6.8	(0.5)	8.8	(0.7)	26.1	(1.4)	0.1	(0.0)	0.1	(0.0)	48.6	(2.8)	19.1	(1.3)	5.3	(0.8)
Greece	32.2	(1.5)	4.5	(0.4)	3.3	(0.4)	24.4	(1.5)	0.1	(0.0)	0.3	(0.0)	41.5	(2.6)	13.7	(1.0)	11.8	(1.1)
Hungary	48.0	(1.4)	5.4	(0.4)	7.7	(0.6)	34.9	(1.4)	0.2	(0.0)	0.2	(0.0)	45.7	(3.1)	20.8	(1.4)	15.3	(1.3)
Iceland	26.9	(1.9)	6.1	(0.7)	4.6	(0.6)	16.1	(1.7)	0.2	(0.0)	0.2	(0.0)	39.6	(3.0)	14.8	(1.2)	9.4	(1.0)
Ireland	41.0	(1.7)	10.4	(0.8)	5.0	(0.6)	25.6	(1.6)	0.3	(0.0)	0.2	(0.0)	47.3	(2.9)	11.7	(1.2)	13.1	(1.2)
Israel	47.8	(1.8)	2.0	(0.3)	8.7	(0.7)	37.1	(1.7)	0.1	(0.0)	0.1	(0.0)	45.2	(1.5)	17.1	(0.6)	9.6	(0.5)
Italy	30.0	(0.8)	4.5	(0.2)	5.2	(0.3)	20.4	(0.8)	0.2	(0.0)	0.1	(0.0)	36.7	(2.7)	8.4	(0.8)	14.1	(1.2)
Japan	40.1	(1.8)	5.4	(0.5)	9.0	(0.8)	25.7	(1.5)	0.2	(0.0)	0.2	(0.0)	33.5	(2.5)	7.1	(0.8)	8.8	(1.0)
Korea	31.1	(1.4)	4.8	(0.5)	6.9	(0.6)	19.4	(1.2)	0.2	(0.0)	0.2	(0.0)	43.1	(2.9)	17.0	(1.3)	13.2	(1.2)
Luxembourg	35.4	(1.5)	4.8	(0.4)	6.3	(0.6)	24.3	(1.5)	0.2	(0.0)	0.2	(0.0)	27.7	(1.3)	5.0	(0.6)	6.6	(0.5)
Mexico	23.7	(0.7)	0.1	(0.1)	3.8	(0.2)	19.9	(0.5)	0.0	(0.0)	0.1	(0.0)	26.8	(2.7)	18.2	(1.3)	10.2	(1.2)
Netherlands	35.2	(1.7)	4.6	(0.5)	7.2	(0.7)	23.3	(1.6)	0.2	(0.0)	0.2	(0.0)	45.6	(2.7)	19.4	(1.2)	13.0	(1.1)
New Zealand	52.3	(1.8)	9.6	(0.7)	8.6	(0.7)	34.2	(1.6)	0.3	(0.0)	0.3	(0.0)	49.0	(2.6)	19.8	(1.2)	13.6	(1.0)
Norway	34.8	(1.8)	7.0	(0.7)	6.3	(0.6)	21.4	(1.6)	0.2	(0.0)	0.2	(0.0)	50.9	(2.5)	15.1	(1.0)	10.7	(1.0)
Poland	39.6	(1.4)	5.1	(0.4)	5.9	(0.5)	28.7	(1.3)	0.3	(0.0)	0.2	(0.0)	40.8	(2.2)	14.0	(0.9)	13.5	(1.0)
Portugal	30.5	(0.9)	2.4	(0.2)	6.0	(0.4)	22.2	(0.9)	0.1	(0.0)	0.2	(0.0)	52.8	(2.5)	11.5	(0.9)	12.6	(1.1)
Slovak Republic	40.1	(1.6)	3.7	(0.4)	6.1	(0.6)	30.3	(1.5)	0.2	(0.0)	0.2	(0.0)	56.8	(2.5)	14.6	(1.1)	12.2	(1.1)
Slovenia	38.5	(1.4)	4.4	(0.4)	6.6	(0.6)	27.6	(1.4)	0.2	(0.0)	0.2	(0.0)	29.8	(1.7)	14.5	(0.7)	9.4	(0.6)
Spain	28.4	(0.9)	4.2	(0.3)	3.7	(0.3)	20.5	(0.8)	0.2	(0.0)	0.1	(0.0)	46.2	(2.7)	23.1	(1.3)	12.2	(1.1)
Sweden	40.5	(1.7)	6.8	(0.6)	6.4	(0.6)	27.4	(1.6)	0.2	(0.0)	0.2	(0.0)	39.3	(2.2)	19.9	(1.0)	14.2	(1.0)
Switzerland	35.8	(1.4)	7.1	(0.5)	7.7	(0.5)	21.0	(1.2)	0.3	(0.0)	0.2	(0.0)	37.3	(2.2)	9.2	(0.9)	7.4	(0.8)
Turkey	27.6	(0.9)	-0.1	(0.2)	2.5	(0.3)	25.2	(0.9)	0.0	(0.0)	0.1	(0.0)	25.9	(2.5)	17.4	(1.0)	7.0	(0.8)
United Kingdom	44.1	(1.5)	9.2	(0.6)	7.1	(0.6)	27.8	(1.4)	0.3	(0.0)	0.3	(0.0)	26.6	(2.6)	17.3	(1.2)	8.6	(0.9)
United States	42.9	(1.7)	5.9	(0.5)	4.7	(0.5)	32.3	(1.6)	0.2	(0.0)	0.2	(0.0)						
OECD average	37.5	(0.3)	5.5	(0.1)	6.4	(0.1)	25.6	(0.2)	0.2	(0.0)	0.2	(0.0)	40.1	(0.4)	16.2	(0.2)	11.2	(0.2)
Partners																		
Albania	32.4	(1.6)	1.9	(0.4)	3.0	(0.5)	27.5	(1.6)	0.1	(0.0)	0.1	(0.0)	63.7	(3.5)	17.7	(1.8)	6.5	(1.0)
Argentina	40.8	(1.3)	0.4	(0.2)	5.7	(0.6)	34.7	(1.3)	0.0	(0.0)	0.2	(0.0)	40.3	(3.3)	6.4	(0.9)	7.1	(1.1)
Azerbaijan	20.7	(1.3)	1.3	(0.2)	0.8	(0.2)	18.6	(1.3)	0.1	(0.0)	0.1	(0.0)	24.7	(2.7)	4.2	(0.6)	0.2	(0.3)
Brazil	29.2	(0.8)	0.7	(0.1)	4.2	(0.3)	24.4	(0.8)	0.0	(0.0)	0.1	(0.0)	34.5	(2.1)	7.2	(0.6)	5.2	(0.7)
Bulgaria	47.7	(1.7)	2.7	(0.4)	7.2	(0.7)	37.8	(1.7)	0.2	(0.0)	0.2	(0.0)	60.8	(3.4)	8.7	(1.2)	10.1	(1.3)
Colombia	28.0	(1.1)	0.0	(0.1)	5.4	(0.5)	22.6	(1.1)	0.0	(0.0)	0.2	(0.0)	12.9	(2.6)	2.5	(0.5)	2.6	(1.0)
Croatia	32.0	(1.3)	2.5	(0.3)	5.6	(0.5)	23.9	(1.2)	0.1	(0.0)	0.2	(0.0)	51.7	(2.5)	12.3	(1.0)	13.3	(1.0)
Dubai (UAE)	45.5	(1.6)	2.9	(0.4)	7.4	(0.6)	35.2	(1.6)	0.1	(0.0)	0.2	(0.0)	50.9	(2.5)	12.0	(0.9)	6.8	(1.0)
Hong Kong-China	19.5	(1.3)	3.6	(0.4)	2.1	(0.4)	13.9	(1.2)	0.1	(0.0)	0.1	(0.0)	33.1	(2.6)	10.5	(0.9)	5.1	(0.8)
Indonesia	18.3	(1.1)	0.1	(0.1)	2.1	(0.3)	16.0	(1.0)	0.0	(0.0)	0.1	(0.0)	37.7	(1.9)	2.8	(0.5)	2.6	(0.6)
Jordan	25.6	(1.3)	0.0	(0.2)	1.7	(0.3)	23.9	(1.3)	0.0	(0.0)	0.1	(0.0)	58.9	(2.2)	6.8	(0.7)	4.8	(0.7)
Kazakhstan	37.7	(1.5)	-0.2	(0.1)	4.8	(0.6)	33.2	(1.5)	0.1	(0.0)	0.2	(0.0)	41.8	(2.7)	-1.0	(0.5)	6.4	(0.9)
Kyrgyzstan	37.9	(1.6)	0.2	(0.1)	5.4	(0.6)	32.4	(1.5)	0.0	(0.0)	0.2	(0.0)	52.3	(2.6)	5.3	(1.0)	1.7	(0.8)
Latvia	30.0	(1.5)	3.7	(0.4)	4.6	(0.6)	21.7	(1.4)	0.2	(0.0)	0.2	(0.0)	48.9	(2.7)	16.4	(1.4)	9.5	(1.0)
Liechtenstein	22.8	(5.6)	4.1	(1.5)	7.3	(2.0)	11.4	(5.0)	0.2	(0.1)	0.2	(0.1)	36.2	(8.6)	17.2	(3.6)	17.2	(4.1)
Lithuania	33.4	(1.2)	3.3	(0.4)	4.3	(0.4)	25.7	(1.2)	0.2	(0.0)	0.2	(0.0)	59.9	(2.4)	18.8	(1.3)	9.0	(0.9)
Macao-China	17.2	(1.2)	3.2	(0.3)	2.3	(0.3)	11.7	(1.2)	0.1	(0.0)	0.1	(0.0)	33.4	(2.1)	9.8	(0.7)	4.0	(0.5)
Montenegro	32.0	(1.4)	2.0	(0.3)	4.5	(0.6)	25.6	(1.4)	0.1	(0.0)	0.2	(0.0)	55.3	(3.2)	12.0	(1.1)	3.7	(1.0)
Panama	31.0	(1.7)	-0.3	(0.2)	4.3	(0.6)	27.0	(1.7)	0.0	(0.0)	0.2	(0.0)	28.6	(4.8)	3.9	(1.0)	3.7	(1.4)
Peru	38.6	(1.0)	-0.2	(0.1)	5.0	(0.4)	33.7	(1.0)	0.0	(0.0)	0.2	(0.0)	21.5	(2.6)	3.8	(0.6)	4.8	(0.8)
Qatar	27.3	(1.2)	1.1	(0.2)	2.7	(0.3)	23.5	(1.2)	0.1	(0.0)	0.1	(0.0)	55.1	(2.1)	6.7	(0.6)	3.2	(0.6)
Romania	35.8	(1.4)	0.7	(0.2)	5.6	(0.6)	29.5	(1.5)	0.1	(0.0)	0.2	(0.0)	44.8	(2.3)	14.0	(1.1)	8.4	(0.9)
Russian Federation	36.2	(1.5)	4.4	(0.5)	4.7	(0.5)	27.0	(1.5)	0.1	(0.0)	0.2	(0.0)	41.9	(2.3)	9.1	(0.9)	9.6	(1.0)
Serbia	28.1	(1.3)	1.6	(0.2)	6.1	(0.5)	20.4	(1.3)	0.1	(0.0)	0.2	(0.0)	38.8	(2.2)	8.3	(0.8)	4.4	(0.7)
Shanghai-China	26.2	(1.0)	3.1	(0.3)	2.8	(0.3)	20.2	(1.0)	0.1	(0.0)	0.1	(0.0)	30.0	(2.6)	14.5	(1.0)	8.8	(1.0)
Singapore	42.0	(2.0)	7.4	(0.5)	7.4	(0.7)	27.3	(1.9)	0.3	(0.0)	0.2	(0.0)	35.4	(2.3)	13.6	(0.9)	3.7	(0.7)
Chinese Taipei	33.6	(1.5)	8.9	(0.5)	5.0	(0.5)	19.7	(1.4)	0.3	(0.0)	0.2	(0.0)	40.1	(2.0)	7.1	(0.6)	2.0	(0.4)
Thailand	22.7	(1.0)	0.3	(0.2)	1.5	(0.2)	20.9	(0.9)	0.0	(0.0)	0.1	(0.0)						
Trinidad and Tobago	39.1	(1.9)	0.6	(0.3)	6.8	(0.7)	31.7	(1.7)	0.0	(0.0)	0.2	(0.0)	59.4	(3.4)	12.2	(1.4)	9.4	(1.3)
Tunisia	18.9	(1.0)	-0.3	(0.1)	0.7	(0.2)	18.5	(1.0)	-0.1	(0.0)	0.0	(0.0)	32.3	(2.5)	1.5	(0.7)	2.2	(0.6)
Uruguay	37.7	(1.1)	1.2	(0.2)	6.8	(0.5)	29.8	(1.0)	0.1	(0.0)	0.2	(0.0)	45.6	(2.7)	7.0	(0.8)	7.5	(1.0)

Note: Values that are statistically significant are indicated in bold (see Annex A3).
1. Socio-economic background is measured by the PISA index of economic, social and cultural status (ESCS).
StatLink ⟐⟐⟐ http://dx.doi.org/10.1787/888932343285

[Part 2/2]

Table III.3.10 **The role of enjoyment of reading and summarising strategies as mediators of socio-economic background and gender[1]**

	Direct effect of gender		Gender on enjoyment of reading		Gender on summarising strategies		Enjoyment of reading on reading performance		Summarising strategies on reading performance		Enjoyment of reading with summarising strategies		Language		Immigrant	
	Change in score	S.E.	Change in score	S.E.	Change in score	S.E.	Change in score	S.E.	Change in score	S.E.	Corr.	S.E.	Change in score	S.E.	Change in score	S.E.
OECD																
Australia	**4.0**	(1.7)	**0.6**	(0.0)	**0.4**	(0.0)	**31.2**	(0.8)	**30.4**	(0.8)	**0.3**	(0.0)	**-15.9**	(3.7)	**5.0**	(2.2)
Austria	**6.8**	(2.7)	**0.8**	(0.0)	**0.4**	(0.0)	**24.8**	(1.2)	**33.1**	(1.3)	**0.2**	(0.0)	-5.0	(7.6)	**-32.2**	(7.0)
Belgium	**3.8**	(1.9)	**0.5**	(0.0)	**0.3**	(0.0)	**24.1**	(1.1)	**39.8**	(1.1)	**0.2**	(0.0)	-4.5	(2.9)	**-38.7**	(3.8)
Canada	0.5	(1.6)	**0.8**	(0.0)	**0.4**	(0.0)	**27.5**	(0.8)	**25.9**	(0.8)	**0.2**	(0.0)	**-16.6**	(2.7)	0.8	(2.2)
Chile	**7.2**	(2.3)	**0.4**	(0.0)	**0.2**	(0.0)	**19.4**	(1.4)	**26.1**	(1.1)	**0.1**	(0.0)	c	c	c	c
Czech Republic	**17.8**	(2.3)	**0.7**	(0.0)	**0.4**	(0.0)	**26.2**	(1.4)	**35.4**	(1.2)	**0.2**	(0.0)	4.8	(14.2)	-16.7	(12.2)
Denmark	**4.5**	(2.4)	**0.5**	(0.0)	**0.4**	(0.0)	**30.1**	(1.5)	**26.0**	(1.2)	**0.2**	(0.0)	**-22.7**	(6.1)	**-35.8**	(4.9)
Estonia	**12.6**	(2.9)	**0.7**	(0.0)	**0.4**	(0.0)	**30.2**	(1.7)	**27.7**	(1.5)	**0.1**	(0.0)	**-28.7**	(6.4)	**-26.1**	(4.7)
Finland	**12.2**	(2.2)	**0.9**	(0.0)	**0.6**	(0.0)	**28.9**	(1.3)	**27.2**	(1.3)	**0.2**	(0.0)	**-32.9**	(6.4)	**-40.1**	(10.9)
France	**18.7**	(2.9)	**0.5**	(0.0)	**0.2**	(0.0)	**30.7**	(1.5)	**37.0**	(1.8)	**0.2**	(0.0)	**-22.0**	(7.3)	**-24.4**	(5.0)
Germany	**9.9**	(2.3)	**0.9**	(0.0)	**0.3**	(0.0)	**21.9**	(1.0)	**33.0**	(1.2)	**0.2**	(0.0)	**-16.8**	(5.6)	**-13.8**	(4.4)
Greece	**24.2**	(2.7)	**0.6**	(0.0)	**0.2**	(0.0)	**31.2**	(1.7)	**25.1**	(1.4)	**0.1**	(0.0)	**-37.5**	(9.5)	**-19.0**	(6.1)
Hungary	**16.0**	(2.5)	**0.6**	(0.0)	**0.4**	(0.0)	**23.0**	(1.4)	**30.2**	(1.4)	**0.2**	(0.0)	**-54.9**	(16.0)	9.9	(7.7)
Iceland	**9.6**	(3.1)	**0.6**	(0.0)	**0.5**	(0.0)	**32.4**	(1.6)	**29.2**	(1.6)	**0.2**	(0.0)	**-30.5**	(12.2)	**-34.4**	(13.8)
Ireland	**15.4**	(2.8)	**0.5**	(0.0)	**0.3**	(0.0)	**32.5**	(1.5)	**29.1**	(1.6)	**0.2**	(0.0)	-10.0	(6.7)	**-29.1**	(5.5)
Israel	**22.5**	(3.0)	**0.6**	(0.0)	**0.4**	(0.0)	**18.6**	(1.6)	**36.9**	(1.5)	**0.1**	(0.0)	**-15.9**	(5.5)	**16.7**	(4.0)
Italy	**18.5**	(1.6)	**0.7**	(0.0)	**0.3**	(0.0)	**24.9**	(0.8)	**35.6**	(0.9)	**0.1**	(0.0)	**-18.6**	(2.4)	**-36.2**	(3.8)
Japan	**14.3**	(2.4)	**0.4**	(0.0)	**0.4**	(0.0)	**23.7**	(1.1)	**39.6**	(1.3)	**0.2**	(0.0)	c	c	c	c
Korea	**17.6**	(2.2)	**0.3**	(0.0)	**0.3**	(0.0)	**26.7**	(1.4)	**30.7**	(1.1)	**0.1**	(0.0)	c	c	c	c
Luxembourg	**12.9**	(2.8)	**0.7**	(0.0)	**0.4**	(0.0)	**23.2**	(1.4)	**32.7**	(1.7)	**0.2**	(0.0)	**-20.0**	(5.5)	**-26.6**	(3.3)
Mexico	**16.1**	(1.2)	**0.4**	(0.0)	**0.2**	(0.0)	**14.1**	(0.8)	**28.2**	(0.7)	**0.1**	(0.0)	**-57.8**	(4.3)	**-67.3**	(6.8)
Netherlands	-1.6	(2.6)	**0.7**	(0.0)	**0.3**	(0.0)	**26.5**	(1.5)	**33.5**	(1.2)	**0.2**	(0.0)	-3.1	(6.7)	**-20.2**	(4.8)
New Zealand	**13.1**	(2.5)	**0.6**	(0.0)	**0.4**	(0.0)	**31.2**	(1.4)	**32.1**	(1.3)	**0.2**	(0.0)	**-41.6**	(4.5)	-3.0	(3.3)
Norway	**15.7**	(2.4)	**0.6**	(0.0)	**0.5**	(0.0)	**30.9**	(1.3)	**29.0**	(1.3)	**0.2**	(0.0)	**-32.4**	(6.6)	-16.7	(7.2)
Poland	**25.1**	(2.5)	**0.8**	(0.0)	**0.4**	(0.0)	**19.6**	(1.1)	**28.7**	(1.3)	**0.2**	(0.0)	c	c	c	c
Portugal	**13.3**	(2.1)	**0.7**	(0.0)	**0.4**	(0.0)	**19.8**	(1.2)	**31.8**	(1.1)	**0.1**	(0.0)	**-16.8**	(8.0)	**-20.0**	(4.5)
Slovak Republic	**28.7**	(2.4)	**0.5**	(0.0)	**0.4**	(0.0)	**22.2**	(1.5)	**30.1**	(1.2)	**0.1**	(0.0)	**-44.9**	(5.2)	c	c
Slovenia	**30.0**	(2.5)	**0.7**	(0.0)	**0.4**	(0.0)	**21.3**	(1.4)	**28.1**	(1.3)	**0.2**	(0.0)	**-21.1**	(7.5)	-9.3	(6.5)
Spain	**5.9**	(1.6)	**0.6**	(0.0)	**0.3**	(0.0)	**26.3**	(0.9)	**30.0**	(0.9)	**0.2**	(0.0)	-2.6	(2.1)	**-42.2**	(3.0)
Sweden	**10.9**	(2.5)	**0.7**	(0.0)	**0.4**	(0.0)	**32.0**	(1.5)	**29.4**	(1.4)	**0.2**	(0.0)	**-29.4**	(6.8)	**-28.1**	(6.1)
Switzerland	**5.2**	(2.0)	**0.8**	(0.0)	**0.4**	(0.0)	**24.6**	(1.0)	**34.0**	(1.2)	**0.2**	(0.0)	**-19.0**	(3.7)	**-17.1**	(3.3)
Turkey	**20.7**	(2.2)	**0.6**	(0.0)	**0.3**	(0.0)	**15.0**	(1.4)	**24.3**	(1.1)	**0.1**	(0.0)	**-26.8**	(6.8)	c	c
United Kingdom	1.5	(2.2)	**0.5**	(0.0)	**0.2**	(0.0)	**34.1**	(1.2)	**28.3**	(1.2)	**0.2**	(0.0)	**-34.6**	(6.5)	**-11.1**	(5.4)
United States	0.7	(2.6)	**0.6**	(0.0)	**0.3**	(0.0)	**27.1**	(1.4)	**25.6**	(1.2)	**0.2**	(0.0)	-4.6	(5.4)	2.9	(4.6)
OECD average	**12.8**	(0.4)	**0.6**	(0.0)	**0.4**	(0.0)	**25.8**	(0.2)	**30.7**	(0.2)	**0.2**	(0.0)	**-22.8**	(1.3)	**-20.5**	(1.2)
Partners																
Albania	**39.4**	(3.8)	**0.6**	(0.0)	**0.3**	(0.0)	**28.0**	(2.8)	**25.8**	(1.8)	**0.1**	(0.0)	-21.5	(13.0)	c	c
Argentina	**26.8**	(3.3)	**0.3**	(0.0)	**0.2**	(0.0)	**18.6**	(2.3)	**31.3**	(1.8)	**0.1**	(0.0)	**-72.6**	(18.6)	-5.5	(9.3)
Azerbaijan	**20.4**	(2.8)	**0.2**	(0.0)	0.0	(0.0)	**18.6**	(1.9)	**8.5**	(1.5)	0.0	(0.0)	**14.0**	(4.8)	1.0	(7.5)
Brazil	**22.1**	(2.1)	**0.4**	(0.0)	**0.2**	(0.0)	**16.6**	(1.3)	**28.4**	(1.2)	**0.1**	(0.0)	**-57.7**	(11.1)	**-84.0**	(15.3)
Bulgaria	**42.1**	(3.3)	**0.5**	(0.0)	**0.3**	(0.0)	**17.6**	(2.1)	**33.4**	(1.7)	**0.1**	(0.0)	**-56.3**	(5.5)	c	c
Colombia	**7.8**	(2.4)	**0.3**	(0.0)	**0.1**	(0.0)	**8.5**	(1.7)	**30.6**	(1.4)	**0.1**	(0.0)	**-66.2**	(20.7)	**-81.1**	(21.9)
Croatia	**26.1**	(2.5)	**0.7**	(0.0)	**0.4**	(0.0)	**18.5**	(1.4)	**30.6**	(1.1)	**0.2**	(0.0)	-7.9	(8.2)	-8.4	(3.9)
Dubai (UAE)	**32.2**	(2.5)	**0.5**	(0.0)	**0.2**	(0.0)	**24.6**	(1.4)	**30.5**	(1.4)	**0.1**	(0.0)	**-14.5**	(2.7)	**70.9**	(2.8)
Hong Kong-China	**17.5**	(2.4)	**0.4**	(0.0)	**0.2**	(0.0)	**29.7**	(1.9)	**22.9**	(1.1)	**0.1**	(0.0)	**-60.4**	(6.4)	**8.8**	(2.5)
Indonesia	**32.4**	(1.9)	**0.2**	(0.0)	**0.1**	(0.0)	**12.2**	(2.0)	**18.0**	(0.9)	0.0	(0.0)	**5.2**	(2.1)	c	c
Jordan	**47.3**	(2.4)	**0.3**	(0.0)	**0.3**	(0.0)	**22.3**	(1.7)	**18.6**	(1.3)	0.0	(0.0)	**-42.1**	(8.6)	7.8	(3.7)
Kazakhstan	**36.4**	(2.6)	**0.3**	(0.0)	**0.2**	(0.0)	-3.5	(1.8)	**31.4**	(1.2)	0.0	(0.0)	2.9	(3.5)	9.4	(3.5)
Kyrgyzstan	**45.3**	(2.6)	**0.4**	(0.0)	**0.1**	(0.0)	**13.8**	(2.4)	**25.0**	(1.6)	0.0	(0.0)	**23.5**	(3.4)	**30.5**	(11.3)
Latvia	**23.0**	(2.8)	**0.7**	(0.0)	**0.4**	(0.0)	**23.7**	(1.9)	**25.1**	(1.4)	**0.1**	(0.0)	-9.3	(5.5)	-9.2	(6.0)
Liechtenstein	1.8	(8.0)	**0.8**	(0.1)	**0.6**	(0.1)	**20.8**	(3.4)	**31.1**	(4.2)	**0.2**	(0.1)	-21.0	(15.0)	-11.6	(11.6)
Lithuania	**32.1**	(2.8)	**1.0**	(0.0)	**0.4**	(0.0)	**18.6**	(1.2)	**24.1**	(1.4)	**0.1**	(0.0)	**-21.2**	(5.7)	-9.7	(9.4)
Macao-China	**19.6**	(2.0)	**0.4**	(0.0)	**0.2**	(0.0)	**24.6**	(1.4)	**18.4**	(1.0)	**0.1**	(0.0)	**-59.3**	(3.0)	**4.3**	(2.1)
Montenegro	**39.6**	(3.4)	**0.5**	(0.0)	**0.1**	(0.0)	**22.7**	(1.8)	**26.8**	(1.4)	**0.1**	(0.0)	**-26.0**	(11.5)	**11.6**	(5.0)
Panama	**21.1**	(4.6)	**0.3**	(0.0)	**0.1**	(0.0)	**13.1**	(2.9)	**27.2**	(2.2)	0.0	(0.0)	**-54.0**	(10.5)	-10.5	(14.0)
Peru	**12.9**	(2.6)	**0.3**	(0.0)	**0.2**	(0.0)	**14.0**	(1.9)	**27.3**	(1.3)	0.0	(0.0)	**-66.5**	(6.6)	c	c
Qatar	**45.3**	(2.1)	**0.3**	(0.0)	**0.1**	(0.0)	**20.5**	(1.4)	**24.7**	(1.1)	**0.1**	(0.0)	**-14.6**	(2.3)	**89.2**	(2.2)
Romania	**31.9**	(2.6)	**0.5**	(0.0)	**0.2**	(0.0)	**11.0**	(1.8)	**30.2**	(1.6)	**0.1**	(0.0)	**-44.4**	(8.3)	c	c
Russian Federation	**22.4**	(2.3)	**0.5**	(0.0)	**0.3**	(0.0)	**31.1**	(2.0)	**25.2**	(1.4)	**0.1**	(0.0)	**-33.1**	(5.0)	**-12.9**	(4.2)
Serbia	**23.2**	(2.3)	**0.6**	(0.0)	**0.3**	(0.0)	**15.0**	(1.3)	**31.6**	(1.3)	**0.1**	(0.0)	-4.3	(8.5)	**13.2**	(3.7)
Shanghai-China	**26.1**	(2.2)	**0.4**	(0.0)	**0.2**	(0.0)	**23.5**	(1.8)	**25.0**	(1.3)	**0.1**	(0.0)	**-34.4**	(7.8)	c	c
Singapore	**6.7**	(2.4)	**0.6**	(0.0)	**0.3**	(0.0)	**25.3**	(1.4)	**34.5**	(1.3)	**0.2**	(0.0)	**-21.3**	(2.9)	-4.9	(4.0)
Chinese Taipei	**18.2**	(2.1)	**0.4**	(0.0)	**0.2**	(0.0)	**31.3**	(1.3)	**23.2**	(1.0)	**0.2**	(0.0)	**-16.6**	(2.7)	c	c
Thailand	**30.9**	(2.0)	**0.3**	(0.0)	**0.2**	(0.0)	**22.8**	(1.5)	**12.8**	(0.9)	**0.1**	(0.0)	-0.5	(1.9)	c	c
Trinidad and Tobago	**37.8**	(3.4)	**0.6**	(0.0)	**0.3**	(0.0)	**21.5**	(2.2)	**35.3**	(1.8)	**0.1**	(0.0)	**-50.0**	(11.5)	-4.6	(13.2)
Tunisia	**28.6**	(2.5)	**0.4**	(0.0)	**0.1**	(0.0)	**3.5**	(1.6)	**21.0**	(1.6)	0.0	(0.0)	c	c	c	c
Uruguay	**31.1**	(2.6)	**0.5**	(0.0)	**0.2**	(0.0)	**14.7**	(1.6)	**32.2**	(1.3)	**0.1**	(0.0)	**-22.1**	(8.7)	c	c

Note: Values that are statistically significant are indicated in bold (see Annex A3).
1. Socio-economic background is measured by the PISA index of economic, social and cultural status (ESCS).
StatLink ⟨ http://dx.doi.org/10.1787/888932343285

[Part 1/3]

Table III.3.11 **The role of teachers' stimulation of their students' enjoyment of reading**

	Total effect (ESCS on reading performance)		Indirect effect of ESCS through enjoyment of reading		Indirect effect of ESCS through teacher stimulation		Indirect effect of ESCS through summarising strategies		Direct effect of ESCS		ESCS on enjoyment of reading		ESCS on summarising strategies		Total effect (gender on reading performance)	
	Change in score	S.E.	Change in score	S.E.	Change in score	S.E.	Change in score	S.E.	Change in score	S.E.	Change in score	S.E.	Change in score	S.E.	Change in score	S.E.
OECD																
Australia	47.2	(1.2)	9.4	(0.5)	1.1	(0.1)	8.2	(0.4)	28.4	(1.1)	0.3	(0.0)	0.3	(0.0)	37.2	(1.8)
Austria	43.8	(1.7)	6.6	(0.6)	0.4	(0.1)	8.5	(0.7)	28.4	(1.6)	0.3	(0.0)	0.3	(0.0)	41.4	(2.8)
Belgium	45.3	(1.2)	5.4	(0.4)	0.3	(0.1)	11.6	(0.6)	27.9	(1.1)	0.2	(0.0)	0.3	(0.0)	28.9	(2.1)
Canada	32.2	(1.1)	5.2	(0.4)	0.7	(0.1)	3.6	(0.3)	22.7	(1.0)	0.2	(0.0)	0.1	(0.0)	34.8	(1.7)
Chile	31.5	(1.0)	1.3	(0.2)	0.1	(0.0)	4.4	(0.3)	25.6	(0.9)	0.1	(0.0)	0.2	(0.0)	22.1	(2.4)
Czech Republic	47.0	(1.7)	5.6	(0.5)	0.1	(0.0)	8.8	(0.8)	32.6	(1.6)	0.2	(0.0)	0.2	(0.0)	50.3	(2.4)
Denmark	33.2	(1.4)	7.3	(0.6)	0.3	(0.1)	5.6	(0.5)	20.0	(1.3)	0.2	(0.0)	0.2	(0.0)	30.3	(2.4)
Estonia	29.3	(1.6)	5.9	(0.6)	0.2	(0.1)	4.1	(0.6)	19.1	(1.5)	0.2	(0.0)	0.1	(0.0)	46.0	(2.8)
Finland	29.9	(1.5)	5.8	(0.6)	0.4	(0.1)	5.0	(0.5)	18.7	(1.3)	0.2	(0.0)	0.2	(0.0)	54.5	(2.3)
France	48.4	(1.8)	7.4	(0.6)	0.5	(0.1)	9.3	(0.8)	31.1	(1.8)	0.2	(0.0)	0.3	(0.0)	41.5	(3.2)
Germany	41.7	(1.5)	6.6	(0.5)	0.1	(0.1)	8.8	(0.7)	26.1	(1.4)	0.3	(0.0)	0.3	(0.0)	41.1	(2.5)
Greece	32.2	(1.5)	4.6	(0.5)	0.0	(0.1)	3.3	(0.4)	24.4	(1.5)	0.1	(0.0)	0.1	(0.0)	48.6	(2.8)
Hungary	48.0	(1.4)	5.3	(0.4)	0.1	(0.1)	7.7	(0.6)	34.9	(1.4)	0.3	(0.0)	0.3	(0.0)	41.5	(2.6)
Iceland	26.9	(1.9)	5.8	(0.7)	0.4	(0.1)	4.6	(0.6)	16.1	(1.7)	0.2	(0.0)	0.2	(0.0)	45.7	(3.1)
Ireland	41.0	(1.7)	10.1	(0.8)	0.2	(0.1)	5.0	(0.6)	25.6	(1.6)	0.3	(0.0)	0.2	(0.0)	39.6	(3.0)
Israel	47.7	(1.8)	2.3	(0.3)	-0.3	(0.1)	8.7	(0.7)	37.0	(1.7)	0.1	(0.0)	0.2	(0.0)	47.3	(2.9)
Italy	30.0	(0.8)	4.4	(0.2)	0.1	(0.0)	5.2	(0.3)	20.4	(0.8)	0.2	(0.0)	0.1	(0.0)	45.2	(1.5)
Japan	40.1	(1.8)	5.1	(0.5)	0.3	(0.1)	9.0	(0.8)	25.7	(1.5)	0.2	(0.0)	0.2	(0.0)	36.7	(2.7)
Korea	31.1	(1.4)	4.7	(0.5)	0.1	(0.0)	6.9	(0.6)	19.4	(1.2)	0.2	(0.0)	0.2	(0.0)	33.5	(2.5)
Luxembourg	35.4	(1.5)	4.7	(0.4)	0.2	(0.0)	6.3	(0.6)	24.3	(1.5)	0.2	(0.0)	0.2	(0.0)	43.1	(2.9)
Mexico	23.7	(0.5)	0.1	(0.1)	0.0	(0.0)	3.8	(0.2)	19.9	(0.5)	0.0	(0.0)	0.1	(0.0)	27.7	(1.3)
Netherlands	35.2	(1.7)	4.5	(0.5)	0.1	(0.1)	7.2	(0.7)	23.3	(1.6)	0.2	(0.0)	0.2	(0.0)	26.8	(2.7)
New Zealand	52.3	(1.8)	8.8	(0.7)	0.7	(0.1)	8.6	(0.7)	34.2	(1.6)	0.3	(0.0)	0.3	(0.0)	45.6	(2.7)
Norway	34.8	(1.8)	6.4	(0.7)	0.7	(0.1)	6.3	(0.6)	21.4	(1.6)	0.2	(0.0)	0.2	(0.0)	49.0	(2.6)
Poland	39.7	(1.4)	4.9	(0.4)	0.1	(0.0)	5.9	(0.5)	28.7	(1.3)	0.3	(0.0)	0.2	(0.0)	50.9	(2.5)
Portugal	30.5	(0.9)	2.1	(0.2)	0.2	(0.0)	6.0	(0.4)	22.2	(0.9)	0.1	(0.0)	0.2	(0.0)	40.8	(2.2)
Slovak Republic	40.1	(1.6)	3.7	(0.4)	0.0	(0.0)	6.1	(0.6)	30.3	(1.5)	0.2	(0.0)	0.2	(0.0)	52.8	(2.5)
Slovenia	38.5	(1.4)	4.3	(0.4)	0.1	(0.0)	6.6	(0.6)	27.6	(1.4)	0.2	(0.0)	0.2	(0.0)	56.8	(2.5)
Spain	28.4	(0.9)	4.2	(0.3)	0.1	(0.0)	3.7	(0.3)	20.5	(0.8)	0.1	(0.0)	0.1	(0.0)	29.8	(1.7)
Sweden	40.6	(1.7)	6.3	(0.6)	0.4	(0.1)	6.4	(0.6)	27.4	(1.6)	0.2	(0.0)	0.2	(0.0)	46.2	(2.7)
Switzerland	35.8	(1.4)	6.9	(0.5)	0.2	(0.1)	7.7	(0.5)	21.0	(1.2)	0.3	(0.0)	0.2	(0.0)	39.3	(2.2)
Turkey	27.6	(0.9)	-0.1	(0.2)	0.0	(0.0)	2.5	(0.3)	25.2	(0.9)	0.0	(0.0)	0.1	(0.0)	37.3	(2.2)
United Kingdom	44.1	(1.5)	8.3	(0.6)	0.9	(0.1)	7.1	(0.6)	27.9	(1.4)	0.2	(0.0)	0.3	(0.0)	25.9	(2.5)
United States	42.9	(1.6)	5.3	(0.5)	0.6	(0.1)	4.7	(0.5)	32.4	(1.6)	0.2	(0.0)	0.2	(0.0)	26.6	(2.6)
OECD average	37.5	(0.3)	5.3	(0.1)	0.3	(0.0)	6.4	(0.1)	25.6	(0.2)	0.2	(0.0)	0.2	(0.0)	40.1	(0.4)
Partners																
Albania	32.4	(1.6)	1.8	(0.4)	0.1	(0.1)	3.0	(0.5)	27.4	(1.6)	0.1	(0.0)	0.1	(0.0)	63.7	(3.5)
Argentina	40.8	(1.3)	0.4	(0.2)	-0.1	(0.0)	5.7	(0.6)	34.7	(1.3)	0.0	(0.0)	0.2	(0.0)	40.3	(3.3)
Azerbaijan	20.7	(1.3)	1.3	(0.2)	0.1	(0.0)	0.8	(0.2)	18.6	(1.3)	0.1	(0.0)	0.1	(0.0)	24.7	(2.7)
Brazil	29.2	(0.8)	0.6	(0.1)	0.1	(0.0)	4.2	(0.3)	24.4	(0.8)	0.0	(0.0)	0.1	(0.0)	34.5	(2.1)
Bulgaria	47.7	(1.7)	2.7	(0.4)	0.0	(0.0)	7.2	(0.7)	37.8	(1.7)	0.2	(0.0)	0.2	(0.0)	60.8	(3.4)
Colombia	28.0	(1.1)	0.0	(0.1)	0.0	(0.0)	5.4	(0.5)	22.6	(1.1)	0.0	(0.0)	0.2	(0.0)	12.9	(2.6)
Croatia	32.0	(1.3)	2.3	(0.3)	0.1	(0.0)	5.6	(0.5)	23.9	(1.2)	0.1	(0.0)	0.2	(0.0)	51.7	(2.5)
Dubai (UAE)	45.5	(1.6)	2.7	(0.4)	0.3	(0.1)	7.4	(0.6)	35.2	(1.6)	0.1	(0.0)	0.2	(0.0)	50.9	(2.7)
Hong Kong-China	19.5	(1.3)	3.2	(0.4)	0.4	(0.1)	2.1	(0.4)	13.9	(1.2)	0.1	(0.0)	0.1	(0.0)	33.1	(2.6)
Indonesia	18.3	(1.1)	0.1	(0.1)	0.0	(0.0)	2.1	(0.3)	16.0	(1.0)	0.0	(0.0)	0.1	(0.0)	37.7	(1.9)
Jordan	25.6	(1.3)	-0.2	(0.2)	0.1	(0.0)	1.7	(0.3)	23.9	(1.3)	0.0	(0.0)	0.1	(0.0)	58.9	(2.2)
Kazakhstan	37.7	(1.5)	-0.2	(0.1)	0.0	(0.0)	4.8	(0.6)	33.2	(1.5)	0.0	(0.0)	0.2	(0.0)	41.8	(2.7)
Kyrgyzstan	37.9	(1.6)	0.2	(0.1)	-0.1	(0.0)	5.4	(0.6)	32.4	(1.5)	0.0	(0.0)	0.2	(0.0)	52.2	(2.6)
Latvia	30.0	(1.5)	3.6	(0.4)	0.2	(0.1)	4.6	(0.6)	21.7	(1.4)	0.2	(0.0)	0.2	(0.0)	48.9	(2.7)
Liechtenstein	22.7	(5.6)	3.3	(1.4)	0.8	(0.3)	7.2	(2.0)	11.4	(5.0)	0.2	(0.1)	0.2	(0.1)	36.2	(8.6)
Lithuania	33.4	(1.2)	3.4	(0.3)	0.0	(0.0)	4.3	(0.4)	25.7	(1.2)	0.2	(0.0)	0.2	(0.0)	59.9	(2.4)
Macao-China	17.2	(1.2)	3.0	(0.3)	0.2	(0.0)	2.3	(0.3)	11.7	(1.2)	0.1	(0.0)	0.1	(0.0)	33.4	(2.1)
Montenegro	32.0	(1.4)	2.0	(0.3)	0.0	(0.1)	4.4	(0.6)	25.6	(1.4)	0.1	(0.0)	0.2	(0.0)	55.3	(3.2)
Panama	31.0	(1.7)	-0.3	(0.2)	0.0	(0.0)	4.3	(0.6)	27.0	(1.7)	0.0	(0.0)	0.2	(0.0)	28.6	(4.8)
Peru	38.6	(1.9)	-0.2	(0.1)	0.0	(0.0)	5.0	(0.4)	33.7	(1.2)	0.0	(0.0)	0.2	(0.0)	21.5	(2.6)
Qatar	27.3	(1.2)	1.0	(0.2)	0.1	(0.0)	2.7	(0.3)	23.5	(1.1)	0.0	(0.0)	0.1	(0.0)	55.1	(2.1)
Romania	35.8	(1.4)	0.6	(0.2)	0.1	(0.0)	5.6	(0.6)	29.5	(1.5)	0.1	(0.0)	0.2	(0.0)	43.9	(2.6)
Russian Federation	36.2	(1.5)	4.3	(0.5)	0.1	(0.0)	4.7	(0.5)	27.0	(1.5)	0.1	(0.0)	0.2	(0.0)	44.7	(2.3)
Serbia	28.1	(1.3)	1.5	(0.2)	0.1	(0.0)	6.0	(0.5)	20.4	(1.3)	0.1	(0.0)	0.2	(0.0)	41.9	(2.3)
Shanghai-China	26.2	(1.0)	2.8	(0.3)	0.3	(0.1)	2.8	(0.3)	20.2	(1.0)	0.1	(0.0)	0.1	(0.0)	38.8	(2.2)
Singapore	42.0	(2.0)	6.9	(0.5)	0.4	(0.1)	7.4	(0.7)	27.3	(1.9)	0.3	(0.0)	0.2	(0.0)	30.0	(2.6)
Chinese Taipei	33.6	(1.5)	8.5	(0.5)	0.4	(0.1)	5.0	(0.5)	19.7	(1.4)	0.3	(0.0)	0.2	(0.0)	35.4	(2.3)
Thailand	22.7	(1.0)	0.3	(0.2)	0.0	(0.0)	1.5	(0.2)	20.9	(0.9)	0.0	(0.0)	0.1	(0.0)	40.1	(2.0)
Trinidad and Tobago	39.1	(1.9)	0.4	(0.3)	0.1	(0.0)	6.8	(0.7)	31.7	(1.7)	0.0	(0.0)	0.2	(0.0)	59.4	(3.4)
Tunisia	18.9	(1.0)	-0.3	(0.1)	0.0	(0.0)	0.7	(0.2)	18.5	(1.0)	-0.1	(0.0)	0.0	(0.0)	32.3	(2.5)
Uruguay	37.7	(1.1)	1.1	(0.2)	0.1	(0.0)	6.8	(0.5)	29.8	(1.0)	0.1	(0.0)	0.2	(0.0)	45.6	(2.7)

Note: Values that are statistically significant are indicated in bold (see Annex A3).
StatLink 🔗 http://dx.doi.org/10.1787/888932343285

[Part 2/3]

Table III.3.11 **The role of teachers' stimulation of their students' enjoyment of reading**

	Indirect effect of gender through enjoyment of reading		Indirect effect of gender through teacher stimulation		Indirect effect of gender through summarising strategies		Direct effect of gender		Gender on enjoyment of reading		Gender on summarising strategies		Enjoyment of reading on reading performance		Summarising strategies on reading performance	
	Change in score	S.E.	Change in score	S.E.	Change in score	S.E.	Change in score	S.E.	Change in score	S.E.	Change in score	S.E.	Change in score	S.E.	Change in score	S.E.
OECD																
Australia	**19.7**	(0.8)	**0.4**	(0.1)	**13.1**	(0.7)	**4.0**	(1.7)	**0.6**	(0.0)	**0.4**	(0.0)	**31.2**	(0.8)	**30.4**	(0.8)
Austria	**20.3**	(1.3)	**-0.3**	(0.1)	**14.6**	(1.1)	**6.8**	(2.7)	**0.8**	(0.0)	**0.4**	(0.0)	**24.7**	(1.2)	**33.1**	(1.3)
Belgium	**12.9**	(0.8)	**0.1**	(0.1)	**12.1**	(1.0)	**3.8**	(1.9)	**0.5**	(0.0)	**0.3**	(0.0)	**24.0**	(1.1)	**39.8**	(1.1)
Canada	**22.8**	(0.8)	**0.3**	(0.1)	**11.3**	(0.6)	0.5	(1.6)	**0.8**	(0.0)	**0.4**	(0.0)	**27.5**	(0.8)	**25.9**	(0.8)
Chile	**8.6**	(0.7)	0.0	(0.1)	**6.3**	(0.7)	**7.2**	(2.3)	**0.4**	(0.0)	**0.2**	(0.0)	**19.4**	(1.4)	**26.1**	(1.1)
Czech Republic	**17.6**	(1.1)	0.1	(0.1)	**14.8**	(1.1)	**17.8**	(2.3)	**0.7**	(0.0)	**0.4**	(0.0)	**26.3**	(1.4)	**35.4**	(1.2)
Denmark	**15.9**	(1.1)	-0.1	(0.1)	**10.0**	(0.9)	4.5	(2.4)	**0.5**	(0.0)	**0.4**	(0.0)	**30.1**	(1.5)	**26.0**	(1.2)
Estonia	**21.6**	(1.5)	**0.2**	(0.1)	**11.6**	(1.0)	**12.6**	(2.9)	**0.7**	(0.0)	**0.4**	(0.0)	**30.2**	(1.7)	**27.7**	(1.5)
Finland	**26.5**	(1.3)	**-0.6**	(0.1)	**16.4**	(1.1)	**12.2**	(2.2)	**0.9**	(0.0)	**0.6**	(0.0)	**28.8**	(1.3)	**27.2**	(1.3)
France	**14.9**	(1.2)	-0.1	(0.2)	**8.0**	(1.2)	**18.7**	(2.9)	**0.5**	(0.0)	**0.2**	(0.0)	**30.7**	(1.5)	**37.0**	(1.8)
Germany	**19.8**	(1.2)	0.0	(0.1)	**11.4**	(1.1)	**9.9**	(2.3)	**0.9**	(0.0)	**0.3**	(0.0)	**21.9**	(1.0)	**33.1**	(1.2)
Greece	**18.9**	(1.3)	0.1	(0.1)	**5.3**	(0.8)	**24.3**	(2.7)	**0.6**	(0.0)	**0.2**	(0.0)	**31.1**	(1.7)	**25.1**	(1.4)
Hungary	**13.4**	(1.0)	**0.3**	(0.1)	**11.8**	(1.1)	**16.0**	(2.5)	**0.6**	(0.0)	**0.4**	(0.0)	**22.9**	(1.4)	**30.3**	(1.4)
Iceland	**20.7**	(1.4)	0.1	(0.1)	**15.3**	(1.3)	**9.6**	(3.1)	**0.6**	(0.0)	**0.5**	(0.0)	**32.4**	(1.6)	**29.1**	(1.6)
Ireland	**14.8**	(1.2)	0.0	(0.1)	**9.4**	(1.1)	**15.4**	(3.0)	**0.5**	(0.0)	**0.3**	(0.0)	**32.5**	(1.5)	**29.1**	(1.6)
Israel	**11.5**	(1.2)	**0.2**	(0.1)	**13.1**	(1.2)	**22.5**	(3.0)	**0.6**	(0.0)	**0.4**	(0.0)	**18.6**	(1.6)	**36.9**	(1.5)
Italy	**16.8**	(0.6)	**0.3**	(0.1)	**9.6**	(0.5)	**18.5**	(1.6)	**0.7**	(0.0)	**0.3**	(0.0)	**24.9**	(0.8)	**35.6**	(0.9)
Japan	**8.5**	(0.7)	0.0	(0.1)	**14.0**	(1.2)	**14.3**	(2.4)	**0.4**	(0.0)	**0.4**	(0.0)	**23.7**	(1.1)	**39.6**	(1.3)
Korea	**7.1**	(0.8)	0.0	(0.1)	**8.8**	(1.0)	**17.6**	(2.2)	**0.3**	(0.0)	**0.3**	(0.0)	**26.7**	(1.4)	**30.7**	(1.1)
Luxembourg	**17.0**	(1.3)	0.1	(0.1)	**13.2**	(1.2)	**12.9**	(2.8)	**0.7**	(0.0)	**0.4**	(0.0)	**23.2**	(1.4)	**32.7**	(1.7)
Mexico	**5.1**	(0.3)	0.0	(0.0)	**6.6**	(0.5)	**16.1**	(1.2)	**0.4**	(0.0)	**0.2**	(0.0)	**14.2**	(0.7)	**28.2**	(0.7)
Netherlands	**18.5**	(1.3)	-0.2	(0.1)	**10.2**	(1.2)	-1.6	(2.6)	**0.7**	(0.0)	**0.3**	(0.0)	**26.5**	(1.5)	**33.5**	(1.2)
New Zealand	**19.3**	(1.2)	0.1	(0.2)	**13.0**	(1.1)	**13.2**	(2.5)	**0.6**	(0.0)	**0.4**	(0.0)	**31.1**	(1.4)	**32.2**	(1.3)
Norway	**20.0**	(1.2)	-0.2	(0.2)	**13.6**	(1.2)	**15.6**	(2.4)	**0.6**	(0.0)	**0.5**	(0.0)	**30.9**	(1.3)	**29.0**	(1.3)
Poland	**14.7**	(1.0)	**0.4**	(0.1)	**10.7**	(1.0)	**25.1**	(2.5)	**0.7**	(0.0)	**0.4**	(0.0)	**19.6**	(1.1)	**28.7**	(1.3)
Portugal	**14.0**	(0.9)	0.1	(0.1)	**13.5**	(1.0)	**13.3**	(2.1)	**0.7**	(0.0)	**0.4**	(0.0)	**19.9**	(1.2)	**31.8**	(1.1)
Slovak Republic	**11.4**	(0.9)	**0.1**	(0.1)	**12.6**	(1.1)	**28.7**	(2.4)	**0.5**	(0.0)	**0.4**	(0.0)	**22.2**	(1.5)	**30.1**	(1.2)
Slovenia	**14.4**	(1.1)	**0.2**	(0.1)	**12.2**	(1.1)	**30.0**	(2.5)	**0.7**	(0.0)	**0.4**	(0.0)	**21.3**	(1.4)	**28.1**	(1.3)
Spain	**14.5**	(0.7)	0.0	(0.1)	**9.3**	(0.6)	**5.9**	(1.6)	**0.6**	(0.0)	**0.3**	(0.0)	**26.3**	(0.9)	**30.0**	(0.9)
Sweden	**23.1**	(1.3)	-0.1	(0.1)	**12.2**	(1.1)	**10.9**	(2.5)	**0.7**	(0.0)	**0.4**	(0.0)	**31.9**	(1.5)	**29.4**	(1.4)
Switzerland	**20.0**	(1.0)	-0.1	(0.1)	**14.2**	(1.0)	**5.2**	(2.0)	**0.8**	(0.0)	**0.4**	(0.0)	**24.5**	(1.0)	**34.0**	(1.2)
Turkey	**8.8**	(0.9)	**0.4**	(0.1)	**7.4**	(0.8)	**20.7**	(2.2)	**0.6**	(0.0)	**0.3**	(0.0)	**15.1**	(1.4)	**24.3**	(1.1)
United Kingdom	**17.6**	(1.0)	-0.2	(0.2)	**7.0**	(0.8)	1.5	(2.2)	**0.5**	(0.0)	**0.2**	(0.0)	**34.1**	(1.2)	**28.3**	(1.2)
United States	**17.0**	(1.1)	**0.3**	(0.1)	**8.6**	(0.9)	0.7	(2.6)	**0.6**	(0.0)	**0.3**	(0.0)	**27.1**	(1.4)	**25.6**	(1.2)
OECD average	**16.1**	(0.2)	**0.1**	(0.0)	**11.2**	(0.2)	**12.8**	(0.4)	**0.6**	(0.0)	**0.4**	(0.0)	**25.8**	(0.2)	**30.7**	(0.2)
Partners																
Albania	**17.5**	(1.8)	**0.3**	(0.1)	**6.5**	(1.0)	**39.4**	(3.8)	**0.6**	(0.0)	**0.3**	(0.0)	**28.0**	(2.8)	**25.8**	(1.8)
Argentina	**6.3**	(0.9)	0.1	(0.1)	**7.1**	(1.1)	**26.9**	(3.3)	**0.3**	(0.0)	**0.2**	(0.0)	**18.5**	(2.3)	**31.3**	(1.8)
Azerbaijan	**4.1**	(0.6)	0.1	(0.1)	0.2	(0.3)	**20.4**	(2.8)	**0.2**	(0.0)	0.0	(0.0)	**18.5**	(2.0)	**8.5**	(1.5)
Brazil	**7.1**	(0.6)	0.1	(0.1)	**5.2**	(0.7)	**22.1**	(2.1)	**0.4**	(0.0)	**0.2**	(0.0)	**16.6**	(1.3)	**28.4**	(1.2)
Bulgaria	**8.7**	(1.2)	0.1	(0.1)	**10.0**	(1.3)	**42.0**	(3.3)	**0.5**	(0.0)	**0.3**	(0.0)	**17.8**	(2.1)	**33.4**	(1.7)
Colombia	**2.4**	(0.5)	0.1	(0.1)	**2.6**	(0.7)	**7.8**	(2.4)	**0.3**	(0.0)	**0.1**	(0.0)	**8.5**	(1.7)	**30.6**	(1.4)
Croatia	**12.0**	(1.0)	**0.3**	(0.1)	**13.3**	(1.0)	**26.1**	(2.5)	**0.6**	(0.0)	**0.4**	(0.0)	**18.5**	(1.5)	**30.6**	(1.1)
Dubai (UAE)	**11.4**	(0.9)	**0.6**	(0.1)	**6.8**	(1.0)	**32.2**	(2.6)	**0.5**	(0.0)	**0.2**	(0.0)	**24.6**	(1.4)	**30.5**	(1.4)
Hong Kong-China	**10.4**	(0.9)	0.1	(0.1)	**5.1**	(0.8)	**17.4**	(2.4)	**0.3**	(0.0)	**0.2**	(0.0)	**29.8**	(1.9)	**22.9**	(1.1)
Indonesia	**2.8**	(0.5)	-0.1	(0.0)	**2.5**	(0.6)	**32.5**	(1.9)	**0.2**	(0.0)	**0.1**	(0.0)	**12.2**	(2.0)	**18.0**	(0.9)
Jordan	**6.4**	(0.7)	**0.6**	(0.1)	**4.8**	(0.7)	**47.1**	(2.4)	**0.3**	(0.0)	**0.3**	(0.0)	**22.8**	(1.7)	**18.6**	(1.3)
Kazakhstan	-1.0	(0.5)	-0.1	(0.0)	**6.4**	(0.9)	**36.4**	(2.6)	**0.3**	(0.0)	**0.2**	(0.0)	-3.4	(1.8)	**31.4**	(1.2)
Kyrgyzstan	**5.0**	(0.9)	**0.1**	(0.1)	**1.7**	(0.8)	**45.4**	(2.6)	**0.4**	(0.0)	**0.1**	(0.0)	**13.5**	(2.4)	**25.0**	(1.6)
Latvia	**16.3**	(1.4)	0.2	(0.1)	**9.5**	(1.0)	**23.0**	(2.8)	**0.7**	(0.0)	**0.4**	(0.0)	**23.7**	(1.9)	**25.1**	(1.4)
Liechtenstein	**16.9**	(3.5)	0.2	(0.4)	**17.2**	(4.1)	1.9	(8.0)	**0.8**	(0.1)	**0.6**	(0.1)	**20.8**	(3.3)	**31.1**	(4.2)
Lithuania	**18.7**	(1.3)	0.1	(0.1)	**9.0**	(1.0)	**32.0**	(2.8)	**1.0**	(0.0)	**0.4**	(0.0)	**18.6**	(1.2)	**24.1**	(1.4)
Macao-China	**9.8**	(0.7)	0.0	(0.0)	**4.0**	(0.5)	**19.6**	(2.0)	**0.4**	(0.0)	**0.2**	(0.0)	**24.6**	(1.4)	**18.4**	(1.8)
Montenegro	**11.5**	(1.0)	**0.4**	(0.1)	**3.7**	(1.0)	**39.6**	(3.4)	**0.5**	(0.0)	**0.1**	(0.0)	**22.8**	(1.8)	**26.7**	(1.4)
Panama	**4.0**	(1.0)	-0.1	(0.1)	**3.7**	(1.4)	**21.0**	(4.6)	**0.3**	(0.0)	**0.1**	(0.0)	**13.1**	(2.9)	**27.2**	(2.2)
Peru	**3.7**	(0.6)	0.1	(0.1)	**4.8**	(0.8)	**12.8**	(2.4)	**0.3**	(0.0)	**0.2**	(0.0)	**14.1**	(1.9)	**27.3**	(1.3)
Qatar	**6.5**	(0.6)	**0.2**	(0.1)	**3.2**	(0.6)	**45.2**	(2.1)	**0.3**	(0.0)	**0.1**	(0.0)	**20.7**	(1.4)	**24.7**	(1.1)
Romania	**4.8**	(0.8)	**0.2**	(0.1)	**7.0**	(1.0)	**31.9**	(2.6)	**0.4**	(0.0)	**0.2**	(0.0)	**11.1**	(1.8)	**30.2**	(1.6)
Russian Federation	**13.6**	(1.0)	**0.4**	(0.1)	**8.4**	(0.9)	**22.4**	(2.3)	**0.4**	(0.0)	**0.3**	(0.0)	**31.1**	(2.0)	**25.2**	(1.4)
Serbia	**8.9**	(0.9)	**0.2**	(0.1)	**9.6**	(1.0)	**23.1**	(2.3)	**0.6**	(0.0)	**0.3**	(0.0)	**15.0**	(1.3)	**31.6**	(1.3)
Shanghai-China	**8.2**	(0.8)	0.1	(0.1)	**4.4**	(0.7)	**26.1**	(2.4)	**0.3**	(0.0)	**0.2**	(0.0)	**23.6**	(1.8)	**24.9**	(1.3)
Singapore	**14.9**	(1.0)	**-0.4**	(0.1)	**8.8**	(1.0)	**6.7**	(2.4)	**0.6**	(0.0)	**0.3**	(0.0)	**25.3**	(1.4)	**34.5**	(1.3)
Chinese Taipei	**13.5**	(0.9)	0.0	(0.1)	**3.7**	(0.7)	**18.2**	(2.1)	**0.4**	(0.0)	**0.2**	(0.0)	**31.2**	(1.3)	**23.3**	(1.0)
Thailand	**6.7**	(0.6)	**0.4**	(0.1)	**2.0**	(0.4)	**30.9**	(2.0)	**0.3**	(0.0)	**0.2**	(0.0)	**22.9**	(1.5)	**12.8**	(0.9)
Trinidad and Tobago	**11.8**	(1.3)	**0.4**	(0.1)	**9.4**	(1.3)	**37.8**	(3.4)	**0.6**	(0.0)	**0.3**	(0.0)	**21.4**	(2.2)	**35.3**	(1.8)
Tunisia	**1.5**	(0.6)	0.1	(0.0)	**2.2**	(0.6)	**28.6**	(2.5)	**0.4**	(0.0)	**0.1**	(0.0)	**3.6**	(1.6)	**21.0**	(1.6)
Uruguay	**6.9**	(0.8)	0.1	(0.1)	**7.5**	(1.0)	**31.1**	(2.6)	**0.5**	(0.0)	**0.2**	(0.0)	**14.8**	(1.6)	**32.2**	(1.3)

Note: Values that are statistically significant are indicated in bold (see Annex A3).
StatLink ⟱ http://dx.doi.org/10.1787/888932343285

Table III.3.11 **The role of teachers' stimulation of their students' enjoyment of reading**

		Enjoyment of reading with summarising strategies		Teacher stimulation on enjoyment of reading activities		ESCS on teacher stimulation		Gender on teacher stimulation		Language		Immigrant	
		Corr.	S.E.	Change in score	S.E.	Change in score	S.E.	Change in score	S.E.	Change in score	S.E.	Change in score	S.E.
OECD	Australia	0.3	(0.0)	0.2	(0.0)	0.2	(0.0)	0.1	(0.0)	-15.9	(3.7)	5.0	(2.2)
	Austria	0.2	(0.0)	0.1	(0.0)	0.1	(0.0)	-0.1	(0.0)	-4.9	(7.6)	-32.2	(7.0)
	Belgium	0.2	(0.0)	0.2	(0.0)	0.1	(0.0)	0.0	(0.0)	-4.5	(2.9)	-38.6	(3.8)
	Canada	0.2	(0.0)	0.2	(0.0)	0.1	(0.0)	0.1	(0.0)	-16.6	(2.7)	0.8	(2.2)
	Chile	0.1	(0.0)	0.1	(0.0)	0.0	(0.0)	0.0	(0.0)	c	c	c	c
	Czech Republic	0.2	(0.0)	0.1	(0.0)	0.1	(0.0)	0.0	(0.0)	4.8	(14.2)	-16.6	(12.2)
	Denmark	0.2	(0.0)	0.1	(0.0)	0.1	(0.0)	0.0	(0.0)	-22.6	(6.1)	-35.8	(4.9)
	Estonia	0.1	(0.0)	0.1	(0.0)	0.0	(0.0)	0.1	(0.0)	-28.7	(6.4)	-26.0	(4.7)
	Finland	0.2	(0.0)	0.2	(0.0)	0.1	(0.0)	-0.1	(0.0)	-32.9	(6.4)	-40.2	(10.9)
	France	0.2	(0.0)	0.2	(0.0)	0.1	(0.0)	0.0	(0.0)	-22.1	(7.3)	-24.5	(5.0)
	Germany	0.2	(0.0)	0.1	(0.0)	0.0	(0.0)	0.0	(0.0)	-16.8	(5.6)	-13.8	(4.4)
	Greece	0.1	(0.0)	0.1	(0.0)	0.0	(0.0)	0.0	(0.0)	-37.5	(9.5)	-19.0	(6.1)
	Hungary	0.2	(0.0)	0.2	(0.0)	0.0	(0.0)	0.1	(0.0)	-54.9	(16.0)	9.9	(7.7)
	Iceland	0.2	(0.0)	0.1	(0.0)	0.1	(0.0)	0.0	(0.0)	-30.5	(12.2)	-34.3	(13.8)
	Ireland	0.2	(0.0)	0.1	(0.0)	0.1	(0.0)	0.0	(0.0)	-9.9	(6.7)	-29.1	(5.5)
	Israel	0.2	(0.0)	0.1	(0.0)	-0.1	(0.0)	0.1	(0.0)	-15.8	(5.5)	16.7	(4.0)
	Italy	0.1	(0.0)	0.1	(0.0)	0.0	(0.0)	0.1	(0.0)	-18.6	(2.4)	-36.2	(3.9)
	Japan	0.2	(0.0)	0.1	(0.0)	0.1	(0.0)	0.0	(0.0)	c	c	c	c
	Korea	0.1	(0.0)	0.1	(0.0)	0.1	(0.0)	0.0	(0.0)	c	c	c	c
	Luxembourg	0.2	(0.0)	0.1	(0.0)	0.1	(0.0)	0.0	(0.0)	-20.0	(5.5)	-26.6	(3.3)
	Mexico	0.1	(0.0)	0.2	(0.0)	0.0	(0.0)	0.0	(0.0)	-57.8	(4.3)	-67.4	(6.8)
	Netherlands	0.2	(0.0)	0.1	(0.0)	0.0	(0.0)	-0.1	(0.0)	-3.2	(6.7)	-20.2	(4.8)
	New Zealand	0.2	(0.0)	0.2	(0.0)	0.1	(0.0)	0.0	(0.0)	-41.7	(4.5)	-3.0	(3.3)
	Norway	0.1	(0.0)	0.2	(0.0)	0.1	(0.0)	0.0	(0.0)	-32.4	(6.6)	-16.7	(7.2)
	Poland	0.2	(0.0)	0.1	(0.0)	0.0	(0.0)	0.2	(0.0)	c	c	c	c
	Portugal	0.1	(0.0)	0.1	(0.0)	0.1	(0.0)	0.0	(0.0)	-16.8	(8.0)	-20.0	(4.5)
	Slovak Republic	0.1	(0.0)	0.1	(0.0)	0.0	(0.0)	0.1	(0.0)	-44.9	(5.2)	c	c
	Slovenia	0.2	(0.0)	0.1	(0.0)	0.1	(0.0)	0.2	(0.0)	-21.1	(7.5)	-9.3	(6.5)
	Spain	0.2	(0.0)	0.1	(0.0)	0.0	(0.0)	0.0	(0.0)	-2.5	(2.1)	-42.2	(3.0)
	Sweden	0.2	(0.0)	0.1	(0.0)	0.1	(0.0)	0.0	(0.0)	-29.4	(6.8)	-28.2	(6.1)
	Switzerland	0.2	(0.0)	0.1	(0.0)	0.1	(0.0)	0.0	(0.0)	-19.0	(3.7)	-17.1	(3.3)
	Turkey	0.1	(0.0)	0.2	(0.0)	0.0	(0.0)	0.2	(0.0)	-26.7	(6.8)	c	c
	United Kingdom	0.2	(0.0)	0.2	(0.0)	0.1	(0.0)	0.0	(0.0)	-34.7	(6.5)	-11.1	(5.4)
	United States	0.2	(0.0)	0.1	(0.0)	0.2	(0.0)	0.1	(0.0)	-4.6	(5.4)	2.9	(4.6)
	OECD average	0.2	(0.0)	0.1	(0.0)	0.1	(0.0)	0.0	(0.0)	-22.8	(1.3)	-20.5	(1.2)
Partners	Albania	0.1	(0.0)	0.1	(0.0)	0.0	(0.0)	0.1	(0.0)	-21.6	(13.0)	c	c
	Argentina	0.1	(0.0)	0.1	(0.0)	0.0	(0.0)	0.0	(0.0)	-72.8	(18.7)	-5.5	(9.3)
	Azerbaijan	0.0	(0.0)	0.1	(0.0)	0.0	(0.0)	0.1	(0.0)	14.0	(4.8)	1.1	(7.5)
	Brazil	0.1	(0.0)	0.1	(0.0)	0.0	(0.0)	0.0	(0.0)	-57.9	(11.1)	-83.7	(15.4)
	Bulgaria	0.1	(0.0)	0.1	(0.0)	0.0	(0.0)	0.1	(0.0)	-56.2	(5.5)	c	c
	Colombia	0.1	(0.0)	0.2	(0.0)	0.0	(0.0)	0.1	(0.0)	-66.2	(20.7)	-81.2	(21.9)
	Croatia	0.1	(0.0)	0.1	(0.0)	0.1	(0.0)	0.1	(0.0)	-7.9	(8.2)	-8.4	(3.9)
	Dubai (UAE)	0.1	(0.0)	0.1	(0.0)	0.1	(0.0)	0.2	(0.0)	-14.5	(2.7)	70.9	(2.8)
	Hong Kong-China	0.1	(0.0)	0.1	(0.0)	0.1	(0.0)	0.0	(0.0)	-60.4	(6.4)	8.8	(2.5)
	Indonesia	0.0	(0.0)	0.1	(0.0)	0.0	(0.0)	-0.1	(0.0)	5.2	(2.1)	c	c
	Jordan	0.0	(0.0)	0.1	(0.0)	0.1	(0.0)	0.2	(0.0)	-42.0	(8.5)	7.7	(3.7)
	Kazakhstan	0.0	(0.0)	0.1	(0.0)	0.1	(0.0)	0.1	(0.0)	2.9	(3.5)	9.4	(3.8)
	Kyrgyzstan	0.0	(0.0)	0.1	(0.0)	0.0	(0.0)	0.1	(0.0)	23.5	(3.4)	30.4	(11.3)
	Latvia	0.1	(0.0)	0.1	(0.0)	0.1	(0.0)	0.1	(0.0)	-9.4	(5.5)	-9.2	(6.0)
	Liechtenstein	0.2	(0.1)	0.2	(0.1)	0.2	(0.1)	0.1	(0.1)	-20.9	(15.0)	-11.6	(11.6)
	Lithuania	0.1	(0.0)	0.1	(0.0)	0.0	(0.0)	0.1	(0.0)	-21.2	(5.7)	-9.7	(9.4)
	Macao-China	0.1	(0.0)	0.1	(0.0)	0.1	(0.0)	0.0	(0.0)	-59.3	(3.0)	4.3	(2.1)
	Montenegro	0.1	(0.0)	0.1	(0.0)	0.0	(0.0)	0.1	(0.0)	-26.4	(11.6)	11.6	(5.0)
	Panama	0.0	(0.0)	0.1	(0.0)	0.0	(0.0)	-0.1	(0.1)	-53.9	(10.5)	-10.5	(14.0)
	Peru	0.1	(0.0)	0.1	(0.0)	0.0	(0.0)	0.1	(0.0)	-66.4	(6.6)	c	c
	Qatar	0.1	(0.0)	0.1	(0.0)	0.0	(0.0)	0.1	(0.0)	-14.6	(2.3)	89.2	(2.2)
	Romania	0.1	(0.0)	0.1	(0.0)	0.1	(0.0)	0.2	(0.0)	-44.3	(8.3)	c	c
	Russian Federation	0.1	(0.0)	0.1	(0.0)	0.0	(0.0)	0.2	(0.0)	-33.1	(5.0)	-12.9	(4.2)
	Serbia	0.1	(0.0)	0.1	(0.0)	0.1	(0.0)	0.1	(0.0)	-4.3	(8.5)	13.2	(3.7)
	Shanghai-China	0.1	(0.0)	0.1	(0.0)	0.1	(0.0)	0.0	(0.0)	-34.3	(7.8)	c	c
	Singapore	0.2	(0.0)	0.2	(0.0)	0.1	(0.0)	-0.1	(0.0)	-21.3	(2.9)	-4.9	(4.0)
	Chinese Taipei	0.2	(0.0)	0.1	(0.0)	0.1	(0.0)	0.0	(0.0)	-16.6	(2.7)	c	c
	Thailand	0.1	(0.0)	0.1	(0.0)	0.0	(0.0)	0.1	(0.0)	-0.5	(1.9)	c	c
	Trinidad and Tobago	0.1	(0.0)	0.1	(0.0)	0.1	(0.0)	0.2	(0.0)	-50.1	(11.5)	-4.8	(13.3)
	Tunisia	0.0	(0.0)	0.2	(0.0)	0.0	(0.0)	0.1	(0.0)	c	c	c	c
	Uruguay	0.1	(0.0)	0.1	(0.0)	0.1	(0.0)	0.1	(0.0)	-22.2	(8.7)	c	c

Note: Values that are statistically significant are indicated in bold (see Annex A3).
StatLink ᵐˢᵖ http://dx.doi.org/10.1787/888932343285

ANNEX B2
RESULTS FOR REGIONS WITHIN COUNTRIES

[Part 1/2]

Table S.III.a

Index of enjoyment of reading and reading performance, by national quarters of this index
Results based on students' self-reports

	Index of enjoyment of reading															
	All students		Males		Females		Gender difference (B – G)		Bottom quarter		Second quarter		Third quarter		Top quarter	
	Mean index	S.E.	Mean index	S.E.	Mean index	S.E.	Dif.	S.E.	Mean index	S.E.	Mean index	S.E.	Mean index	S.E.	Mean index	S.E.
Adjudicated																
Belgium (Flemish Community)	-0.34	(0.02)	-0.62	(0.03)	-0.05	(0.02)	**-0.57**	(0.04)	**-1.54**	(0.02)	-0.70	(0.01)	-0.04	(0.01)	**0.94**	(0.01)
Spain (Andalusia)	-0.11	(0.04)	-0.33	(0.04)	0.13	(0.05)	**-0.46**	(0.05)	**-1.18**	(0.02)	-0.44	(0.01)	0.10	(0.01)	**1.08**	(0.03)
Spain (Aragon)	-0.09	(0.03)	-0.33	(0.05)	0.16	(0.04)	**-0.49**	(0.06)	**-1.24**	(0.03)	-0.42	(0.01)	0.13	(0.01)	**1.17**	(0.04)
Spain (Asturias)	-0.02	(0.03)	-0.29	(0.05)	0.27	(0.04)	**-0.56**	(0.06)	**-1.25**	(0.03)	-0.38	(0.01)	0.26	(0.01)	**1.30**	(0.03)
Spain (Balearic Islands)	-0.02	(0.03)	-0.31	(0.05)	0.27	(0.04)	**-0.58**	(0.06)	**-1.17**	(0.03)	-0.38	(0.01)	0.23	(0.01)	**1.25**	(0.03)
Spain (Basque Country)	-0.04	(0.02)	-0.29	(0.02)	0.22	(0.02)	**-0.52**	(0.03)	**-1.15**	(0.02)	-0.36	(0.00)	0.21	(0.01)	**1.15**	(0.02)
Spain (Canary Islands)	-0.03	(0.03)	-0.26	(0.04)	0.21	(0.04)	**-0.47**	(0.05)	**-1.14**	(0.02)	-0.40	(0.01)	0.17	(0.01)	**1.24**	(0.03)
Spain (Cantabria)	-0.07	(0.03)	-0.29	(0.04)	0.15	(0.04)	**-0.44**	(0.05)	**-1.23**	(0.03)	-0.43	(0.01)	0.17	(0.01)	**1.19**	(0.03)
Spain (Castile and Leon)	0.10	(0.03)	-0.20	(0.04)	0.39	(0.04)	**-0.59**	(0.06)	**-1.09**	(0.03)	-0.26	(0.01)	0.36	(0.01)	**1.40**	(0.03)
Spain (Catalonia)	0.07	(0.02)	-0.21	(0.04)	0.37	(0.04)	**-0.58**	(0.06)	**-1.16**	(0.03)	-0.27	(0.01)	0.39	(0.01)	**1.35**	(0.03)
Spain (Ceuta and Melilla)	0.03	(0.03)	-0.22	(0.03)	0.27	(0.04)	**-0.49**	(0.04)	**-1.07**	(0.02)	-0.31	(0.01)	0.27	(0.01)	**1.24**	(0.04)
Spain (Galicia)	-0.04	(0.03)	-0.31	(0.03)	0.24	(0.05)	**-0.55**	(0.05)	**-1.12**	(0.02)	-0.38	(0.01)	0.22	(0.01)	**1.14**	(0.02)
Spain (La Rioja)	-0.04	(0.03)	-0.27	(0.05)	0.20	(0.04)	**-0.47**	(0.06)	**-1.17**	(0.03)	-0.39	(0.01)	0.20	(0.01)	**1.21**	(0.04)
Spain (Madrid)	0.05	(0.03)	-0.26	(0.04)	0.37	(0.04)	**-0.63**	(0.06)	**-1.08**	(0.03)	-0.30	(0.01)	0.31	(0.01)	**1.29**	(0.03)
Spain (Murcia)	0.02	(0.05)	-0.23	(0.05)	0.28	(0.05)	**-0.51**	(0.05)	**-1.12**	(0.03)	-0.33	(0.01)	0.26	(0.01)	**1.29**	(0.04)
Spain (Navarre)	-0.09	(0.04)	-0.31	(0.04)	0.15	(0.05)	**-0.46**	(0.05)	**-1.19**	(0.03)	-0.39	(0.01)	0.15	(0.01)	**1.09**	(0.03)
United Kingdom (Scotland)	-0.15	(0.03)	-0.37	(0.04)	0.08	(0.03)	**-0.45**	(0.04)	**-1.39**	(0.02)	-0.51	(0.01)	0.14	(0.01)	**1.17**	(0.03)
Non-adjudicated																
Belgium (French Community)	-0.02	(0.03)	-0.24	(0.03)	0.21	(0.04)	**-0.46**	(0.05)	**-1.25**	(0.02)	-0.39	(0.01)	0.29	(0.01)	**1.27**	(0.02)
Belgium (German-Speaking Community)	-0.09	(0.04)	-0.51	(0.05)	0.35	(0.06)	**-0.86**	(0.07)	**-1.49**	(0.03)	-0.62	(0.02)	0.30	(0.02)	**1.47**	(0.05)
Finland (Finnish Speaking)	0.06	(0.02)	-0.40	(0.02)	0.51	(0.03)	**-0.91**	(0.03)	**-1.24**	(0.02)	-0.27	(0.01)	0.38	(0.01)	**1.37**	(0.03)
Finland (Swedish Speaking)	-0.10	(0.03)	-0.55	(0.03)	0.33	(0.03)	**-0.88**	(0.05)	**-1.32**	(0.03)	-0.41	(0.01)	0.20	(0.01)	**1.12**	(0.03)
Italy (Provincia Abruzzo)	0.00	(0.04)	-0.32	(0.03)	0.36	(0.05)	**-0.68**	(0.06)	**-1.15**	(0.03)	-0.35	(0.01)	0.29	(0.01)	**1.22**	(0.02)
Italy (Provincia Autonoma di Bolzano)	-0.09	(0.03)	-0.53	(0.04)	0.35	(0.04)	**-0.88**	(0.05)	**-1.49**	(0.03)	-0.57	(0.01)	0.27	(0.01)	**1.43**	(0.03)
Italy (Provincia Basilicata)	0.13	(0.03)	-0.25	(0.04)	0.54	(0.05)	**-0.80**	(0.06)	**-0.99**	(0.03)	-0.20	(0.01)	0.45	(0.01)	**1.27**	(0.02)
Italy (Provincia Calabria)	0.13	(0.03)	-0.23	(0.03)	0.50	(0.05)	**-0.73**	(0.05)	**-0.94**	(0.02)	-0.20	(0.01)	0.41	(0.01)	**1.26**	(0.03)
Italy (Provincia Campania)	0.09	(0.04)	-0.17	(0.04)	0.42	(0.05)	**-0.59**	(0.05)	**-0.96**	(0.02)	-0.25	(0.01)	0.34	(0.01)	**1.22**	(0.02)
Italy (Provincia Emilia Romagna)	0.05	(0.03)	-0.25	(0.03)	0.33	(0.05)	**-0.59**	(0.07)	**-1.14**	(0.03)	-0.28	(0.01)	0.38	(0.01)	**1.24**	(0.03)
Italy (Provincia Friuli Venezia Giulia)	0.07	(0.04)	-0.33	(0.04)	0.49	(0.04)	**-0.82**	(0.03)	**-1.18**	(0.03)	-0.25	(0.01)	0.44	(0.01)	**1.27**	(0.03)
Italy (Provincia Lazio)	0.10	(0.04)	-0.23	(0.05)	0.48	(0.05)	**-0.72**	(0.06)	**-1.12**	(0.03)	-0.23	(0.01)	0.43	(0.01)	**1.33**	(0.03)
Italy (Provincia Liguria)	-0.02	(0.04)	-0.30	(0.04)	0.29	(0.05)	**-0.59**	(0.06)	**-1.23**	(0.03)	-0.38	(0.01)	0.32	(0.01)	**1.21**	(0.02)
Italy (Provincia Lombardia)	0.02	(0.04)	-0.34	(0.04)	0.42	(0.04)	**-0.76**	(0.06)	**-1.19**	(0.03)	-0.33	(0.01)	0.34	(0.01)	**1.27**	(0.03)
Italy (Provincia Marche)	-0.05	(0.05)	-0.41	(0.04)	0.39	(0.05)	**-0.81**	(0.07)	**-1.20**	(0.02)	-0.40	(0.01)	0.26	(0.01)	**1.16**	(0.03)
Italy (Provincia Molise)	0.04	(0.03)	-0.30	(0.04)	0.41	(0.03)	**-0.71**	(0.05)	**-1.04**	(0.02)	-0.28	(0.01)	0.35	(0.01)	**1.16**	(0.03)
Italy (Provincia Piemonte)	0.00	(0.04)	-0.32	(0.06)	0.31	(0.05)	**-0.63**	(0.07)	**-1.23**	(0.04)	-0.34	(0.01)	0.33	(0.01)	**1.26**	(0.03)
Italy (Provincia Puglia)	0.05	(0.04)	-0.26	(0.04)	0.35	(0.03)	**-0.61**	(0.05)	**-1.03**	(0.03)	-0.29	(0.01)	0.32	(0.01)	**1.21**	(0.03)
Italy (Provincia Sardegna)	0.08	(0.03)	-0.28	(0.04)	0.42	(0.05)	**-0.69**	(0.06)	**-1.10**	(0.02)	-0.35	(0.01)	0.35	(0.01)	**1.44**	(0.02)
Italy (Provincia Sicilia)	0.16	(0.04)	-0.12	(0.04)	0.43	(0.06)	**-0.55**	(0.07)	**-0.89**	(0.02)	-0.18	(0.01)	0.42	(0.01)	**1.30**	(0.02)
Italy (Provincia Toscana)	0.08	(0.03)	-0.26	(0.04)	0.45	(0.05)	**-0.72**	(0.07)	**-1.12**	(0.02)	-0.23	(0.01)	0.43	(0.01)	**1.23**	(0.03)
Italy (Provincia Trento)	0.02	(0.03)	-0.32	(0.04)	0.39	(0.04)	**-0.71**	(0.06)	**-1.28**	(0.03)	-0.32	(0.01)	0.38	(0.01)	**1.31**	(0.03)
Italy (Provincia Umbria)	0.10	(0.03)	-0.26	(0.03)	0.44	(0.04)	**-0.70**	(0.05)	**-1.09**	(0.02)	-0.25	(0.01)	0.42	(0.01)	**1.33**	(0.02)
Italy (Provincia Valle d'Aosta)	0.02	(0.03)	-0.31	(0.04)	0.34	(0.04)	**-0.66**	(0.05)	**-1.25**	(0.03)	-0.31	(0.01)	0.37	(0.01)	**1.27**	(0.03)
Italy (Provincia Veneto)	0.03	(0.05)	-0.38	(0.05)	0.43	(0.05)	**-0.82**	(0.07)	**-1.23**	(0.03)	-0.34	(0.01)	0.37	(0.01)	**1.34**	(0.02)
United Kingdom (England)	-0.11	(0.02)	-0.37	(0.03)	0.14	(0.02)	**-0.51**	(0.03)	**-1.27**	(0.04)	-0.44	(0.01)	0.15	(0.01)	**1.14**	(0.02)
United Kingdom (Northern Ireland)	-0.19	(0.03)	-0.42	(0.03)	0.02	(0.04)	**-0.45**	(0.05)	**-1.41**	(0.02)	-0.56	(0.01)	0.07	(0.01)	**1.12**	(0.03)
United Kingdom (Wales)	-0.18	(0.02)	-0.44	(0.03)	0.08	(0.03)	**-0.52**	(0.04)	**-1.31**	(0.02)	-0.51	(0.01)	0.06	(0.01)	**1.05**	(0.02)

Notes: Values that are statistically significant are indicated in bold (see Annex A3). See Table III.1.1 for national data.
StatLink ⌨️ http://dx.doi.org/10.1787/888932343304

[Part 2/2]
Index of enjoyment of reading and reading performance, by national quarters of this index

Table S.III.a   *Results based on students' self-reports*

| | Performance on the reading scale by quarters of this index | | | | | | | | Change in the reading score per unit of this index | | Increased likelihood of students in the bottom quarter of this index scoring in the bottom quarter of the reading performance distribution | | Explained variance in student performance (r-squared x 100) | |
| | Bottom quarter | | Second quarter | | Third quarter | | Top quarter | | | | | | | |
	Mean index	S.E.	Mean index	S.E.	Mean index	S.E.	Mean index	S.E.	Effect	S.E.	Ratio	S.E.	%	S.E.
Adjudicated														
Belgium (Flemish Community)	**471**	(3.0)	496	(3.0)	526	(4.1)	**580**	(3.8)	**41.5**	(1.72)	**2.0**	(0.13)	19.0	(1.49)
Spain (Andalusia)	**424**	(7.4)	437	(6.3)	469	(5.5)	**518**	(4.3)	**39.9**	(2.72)	**2.0**	(0.23)	16.7	(2.01)
Spain (Aragon)	**451**	(5.5)	479	(5.2)	505	(6.3)	**548**	(4.9)	**38.5**	(2.24)	**2.4**	(0.27)	19.1	(1.84)
Spain (Asturias)	**440**	(5.6)	472	(6.8)	505	(5.8)	**552**	(5.4)	**39.4**	(2.34)	**2.5**	(0.25)	19.4	(1.77)
Spain (Balearic Islands)	**416**	(7.9)	436	(6.4)	467	(5.8)	**518**	(6.4)	**39.4**	(2.88)	**2.0**	(0.27)	17.7	(1.95)
Spain (Basque Country)	**449**	(4.6)	476	(3.1)	508	(3.7)	**549**	(3.4)	**40.3**	(1.56)	**2.3**	(0.15)	20.0	(1.18)
Spain (Canary Islands)	**406**	(6.5)	431	(5.2)	457	(5.7)	**509**	(6.0)	**41.4**	(2.56)	**2.3**	(0.27)	19.1	(1.89)
Spain (Cantabria)	**441**	(4.9)	466	(5.7)	498	(5.5)	**551**	(5.9)	**41.6**	(2.44)	**2.3**	(0.22)	21.6	(2.24)
Spain (Castile and Leon)	**460**	(5.2)	483	(7.1)	516	(5.5)	**557**	(4.6)	**37.0**	(2.03)	**2.5**	(0.31)	19.4	(2.10)
Spain (Catalonia)	**459**	(6.4)	479	(6.0)	511	(6.0)	**548**	(5.4)	**33.2**	(2.32)	**2.1**	(0.21)	17.0	(2.02)
Spain (Ceuta and Melilla)	**400**	(4.8)	394	(5.8)	412	(5.9)	**456**	(5.9)	**23.2**	(3.22)	**1.1**	(0.13)	4.5	(1.23)
Spain (Galicia)	**437**	(5.5)	465	(5.1)	502	(4.0)	**544**	(6.1)	**46.2**	(2.45)	**2.5**	(0.26)	22.9	(2.26)
Spain (La Rioja)	**455**	(4.9)	473	(5.6)	510	(5.2)	**559**	(4.4)	**43.1**	(2.33)	**2.2**	(0.26)	21.1	(1.88)
Spain (Madrid)	**452**	(6.8)	485	(5.8)	524	(4.9)	**554**	(5.2)	**39.4**	(2.64)	**2.6**	(0.23)	20.2	(1.92)
Spain (Murcia)	**444**	(5.8)	464	(5.9)	483	(5.4)	**534**	(5.4)	**33.4**	(2.44)	**1.8**	(0.21)	16.5	(2.23)
Spain (Navarre)	**460**	(4.8)	475	(4.5)	502	(5.3)	**554**	(4.5)	**39.1**	(2.58)	**2.1**	(0.24)	18.3	(2.24)
United Kingdom (Scotland)	**446**	(4.2)	467	(3.4)	519	(4.2)	**575**	(4.3)	**47.0**	(2.03)	**2.6**	(0.19)	26.7	(1.49)
Non-adjudicated														
Belgium (French Community)	**441**	(4.7)	459	(6.1)	504	(6.0)	**565**	(4.1)	**47.3**	(1.91)	**1.9**	(0.17)	19.4	(1.16)
Belgium (German-Speaking Community)	**445**	(5.1)	472	(6.8)	511	(6.0)	**568**	(5.5)	**39.2**	(2.88)	**2.6**	(0.33)	26.7	(2.93)
Finland (Finnish Speaking)	**477**	(2.9)	521	(2.9)	558	(3.1)	**597**	(2.8)	**42.9**	(1.22)	**3.2**	(0.18)	26.8	(1.29)
Finland (Swedish Speaking)	**452**	(4.8)	485	(4.6)	534	(4.1)	**574**	(4.7)	**47.6**	(2.36)	**3.0**	(0.34)	29.1	(2.24)
Italy (Provincia Abruzzo)	**440**	(4.9)	462	(7.3)	491	(6.9)	**535**	(5.6)	**37.8**	(2.46)	**2.1**	(0.18)	16.1	(1.94)
Italy (Provincia Autonoma di Bolzano)	**446**	(4.5)	471	(4.5)	493	(10.2)	**550**	(5.2)	**33.9**	(1.66)	**2.2**	(0.26)	18.1	(2.15)
Italy (Provincia Basilicata)	**442**	(6.0)	446	(7.3)	485	(5.5)	**523**	(4.2)	**36.6**	(2.86)	**1.7**	(0.20)	14.7	(1.71)
Italy (Provincia Calabria)	**411**	(6.8)	419	(8.0)	456	(7.4)	**511**	(6.4)	**41.7**	(3.90)	**1.9**	(0.20)	16.9	(2.26)
Italy (Provincia Campania)	**413**	(8.2)	422	(8.7)	461	(7.3)	**512**	(5.7)	**42.9**	(3.59)	**1.7**	(0.17)	15.9	(1.97)
Italy (Provincia Emilia Romagna)	**455**	(4.2)	481	(5.3)	521	(5.7)	**562**	(4.9)	**45.1**	(2.47)	**2.3**	(0.23)	19.2	(2.25)
Italy (Provincia Friuli Venezia Giulia)	**467**	(6.6)	489	(5.1)	526	(5.9)	**574**	(5.3)	**41.9**	(2.69)	**2.2**	(0.24)	19.9	(2.02)
Italy (Provincia Lazio)	**434**	(5.9)	451	(6.2)	505	(5.6)	**537**	(7.5)	**42.7**	(3.26)	**2.2**	(0.31)	21.1	(2.95)
Italy (Provincia Liguria)	**441**	(16.6)	472	(7.9)	505	(9.8)	**551**	(5.2)	**41.9**	(5.73)	**2.5**	(0.24)	18.9	(2.37)
Italy (Provincia Lombardia)	**474**	(6.4)	500	(8.2)	538	(5.9)	**575**	(9.9)	**40.2**	(4.17)	**2.2**	(0.29)	19.4	(3.50)
Italy (Provincia Marche)	**454**	(9.9)	477	(9.4)	510	(6.2)	**558**	(5.0)	**42.8**	(4.06)	**2.2**	(0.24)	19.4	(2.66)
Italy (Provincia Molise)	**427**	(5.6)	448	(6.3)	487	(5.4)	**523**	(5.2)	**43.8**	(2.71)	**2.3**	(0.27)	20.4	(2.15)
Italy (Provincia Piemonte)	**451**	(6.3)	471	(8.0)	516	(6.6)	**552**	(7.0)	**38.7**	(3.07)	**2.1**	(0.34)	17.0	(2.88)
Italy (Provincia Puglia)	**457**	(6.6)	469	(6.8)	500	(6.2)	**537**	(6.8)	**35.4**	(2.98)	**1.9**	(0.20)	13.5	(2.36)
Italy (Provincia Sardegna)	**428**	(6.3)	436	(6.0)	487	(6.1)	**531**	(5.7)	**39.9**	(3.18)	**2.0**	(0.24)	19.4	(2.86)
Italy (Provincia Sicilia)	**415**	(8.9)	425	(9.1)	461	(11.5)	**523**	(8.7)	**47.5**	(4.22)	**1.9**	(0.23)	18.1	(2.70)
Italy (Provincia Toscana)	**442**	(6.9)	468	(5.7)	509	(6.2)	**557**	(5.2)	**45.1**	(3.07)	**2.5**	(0.27)	19.7	(2.07)
Italy (Provincia Trento)	**462**	(5.7)	482	(6.6)	528	(5.7)	**567**	(4.4)	**38.5**	(2.97)	**2.1**	(0.25)	18.8	(2.54)
Italy (Provincia Umbria)	**444**	(7.5)	465	(8.1)	506	(5.9)	**555**	(5.3)	**45.0**	(3.16)	**2.1**	(0.23)	19.6	(2.14)
Italy (Provincia Valle d'Aosta)	**467**	(4.4)	499	(7.0)	526	(5.4)	**566**	(4.6)	**36.2**	(2.42)	**2.2**	(0.29)	17.3	(1.85)
Italy (Provincia Veneto)	**457**	(8.4)	474	(6.4)	528	(6.4)	**565**	(5.7)	**41.0**	(3.31)	**2.4**	(0.23)	21.5	(2.61)
United Kingdom (England)	**446**	(3.9)	468	(3.3)	508	(3.8)	**562**	(3.1)	**44.7**	(1.80)	**2.2**	(0.15)	21.0	(1.57)
United Kingdom (Northern Ireland)	**451**	(5.7)	471	(5.2)	510	(6.0)	**567**	(4.6)	**42.4**	(2.31)	**2.1**	(0.22)	19.8	(1.95)
United Kingdom (Wales)	**425**	(4.0)	450	(4.5)	486	(4.2)	**546**	(4.4)	**47.6**	(1.93)	**2.4**	(0.16)	23.6	(1.47)

Notes: Values that are statistically significant are indicated in bold (see Annex A3). See Table III.1.1 for national data.
StatLink 🔗 http://dx.doi.org/10.1787/888932343304

[Part 1/1]

Table S.III.b **Percentage of students and reading performance, by time spent reading for enjoyment**
Results based on students' self-reports

	Percentage of students, by time spent on reading for enjoyment										Performance on the reading scale, by time spent on reading for enjoyment									
	I do not read for enjoyment		30 minutes or less a day		More than 30 minutes to less than 60 minutes a day		1 to 2 hours a day		More than 2 hours a day		I do not read for enjoyment		30 minutes or less a day		More than 30 minutes to less than 60 minutes a day		1 to 2 hours a day		More than 2 hours a day	
	%	S.E.	%	S.E.	%	S.E.	%	S.E.	%	S.E.	Mean score	S.E.	Mean score	S.E.	Mean score	S.E.	Mean score	S.E.	Mean score	S.E.
Adjudicated																				
Belgium (Flemish Community)	49.3	(1.03)	28.9	(0.68)	12.9	(0.65)	6.7	(0.37)	2.2	(0.21)	483	(2.9)	551	(3.0)	566	(4.6)	560	(5.8)	525	(12.7)
Spain (Andalusia)	43.0	(1.81)	25.0	(1.22)	17.8	(1.21)	10.8	(0.87)	3.4	(0.71)	435	(5.7)	464	(5.7)	490	(5.6)	499	(7.7)	516	(13.0)
Spain (Aragon)	36.5	(1.87)	24.5	(1.70)	19.6	(1.34)	11.5	(1.08)	7.9	(1.34)	465	(5.1)	498	(5.0)	519	(7.2)	534	(7.7)	518	(10.0)
Spain (Asturias)	37.0	(1.84)	27.0	(1.27)	19.4	(1.31)	12.6	(1.17)	4.1	(0.54)	450	(4.6)	492	(5.4)	528	(6.0)	540	(7.0)	529	(14.7)
Spain (Balearic Islands)	43.7	(1.23)	25.2	(1.48)	15.7	(1.25)	10.8	(0.70)	4.7	(0.58)	432	(6.2)	461	(8.5)	482	(7.2)	509	(10.1)	509	(13.0)
Spain (Basque Country)	43.4	(0.93)	25.9	(0.80)	18.4	(0.64)	9.4	(0.51)	2.8	(0.25)	465	(3.6)	508	(3.1)	527	(3.5)	527	(4.2)	517	(10.8)
Spain (Canary Islands)	38.7	(1.75)	27.1	(1.52)	16.5	(0.77)	12.3	(0.98)	5.4	(0.71)	424	(4.7)	441	(5.4)	480	(5.6)	485	(9.4)	505	(12.2)
Spain (Cantabria)	40.8	(1.47)	25.7	(1.28)	19.1	(1.09)	10.1	(0.83)	4.2	(0.47)	454	(4.3)	493	(5.7)	529	(4.7)	518	(9.6)	534	(14.0)
Spain (Castile and Leon)	32.6	(1.28)	27.3	(1.05)	22.6	(1.27)	13.1	(1.03)	4.4	(0.54)	469	(5.9)	503	(6.0)	527	(6.2)	539	(6.7)	542	(11.5)
Spain (Catalonia)	40.3	(1.20)	21.8	(1.10)	22.5	(1.09)	11.7	(1.06)	3.7	(0.45)	471	(5.6)	506	(7.4)	518	(5.6)	538	(8.3)	518	(13.0)
Spain (Ceuta and Melilla)	34.5	(1.20)	29.4	(1.44)	18.5	(1.13)	12.3	(0.99)	5.4	(0.63)	401	(4.8)	407	(5.3)	429	(7.6)	432	(9.0)	434	(16.2)
Spain (Galicia)	38.1	(1.83)	26.8	(1.48)	18.5	(1.17)	12.4	(0.99)	4.2	(0.53)	447	(4.2)	495	(5.2)	521	(5.6)	524	(9.3)	522	(11.6)
Spain (La Rioja)	39.2	(1.41)	26.4	(1.27)	21.0	(1.01)	10.5	(0.90)	2.9	(0.56)	469	(3.9)	500	(5.5)	526	(5.2)	541	(8.0)	518	(20.6)
Spain (Madrid)	35.9	(1.57)	25.4	(1.03)	23.1	(1.33)	11.6	(0.95)	4.0	(0.37)	470	(6.0)	507	(6.6)	534	(5.8)	530	(6.7)	540	(11.6)
Spain (Murcia)	37.9	(1.81)	29.4	(1.78)	16.8	(1.09)	11.7	(1.16)	4.2	(0.68)	458	(5.3)	477	(6.3)	502	(5.9)	521	(8.3)	518	(19.0)
Spain (Navarre)	40.9	(1.81)	28.5	(1.31)	17.7	(1.30)	9.7	(0.93)	3.2	(0.53)	472	(4.1)	497	(5.0)	539	(4.9)	530	(8.2)	504	(16.4)
United Kingdom (Scotland)	42.7	(1.33)	26.8	(0.90)	17.5	(0.83)	9.6	(0.68)	3.5	(0.38)	459	(3.0)	512	(4.6)	549	(4.1)	553	(7.4)	559	(11.1)
Non-adjudicated																				
Belgium (French Community)	38.1	(1.00)	22.8	(0.78)	22.8	(0.78)	12.0	(0.61)	4.3	(0.37)	448	(5.3)	501	(5.2)	533	(4.4)	539	(5.4)	521	(10.2)
Belgium (German-Speaking Community)	49.9	(1.79)	21.3	(1.42)	13.8	(1.35)	10.4	(1.16)	4.7	(0.84)	460	(3.9)	529	(6.5)	550	(8.1)	540	(9.8)	547	(15.1)
Finland (Finnish Speaking)	33.0	(0.79)	32.0	(0.70)	18.6	(0.64)	13.1	(0.57)	3.3	(0.37)	494	(2.7)	547	(2.9)	570	(3.5)	571	(4.2)	568	(9.4)
Finland (Swedish Speaking)	33.5	(1.44)	39.2	(1.32)	18.7	(1.18)	7.0	(0.66)	c	c	462	(4.1)	522	(3.9)	549	(5.5)	581	(7.6)	c	c
Italy (Provincia Abruzzo)	33.8	(1.56)	30.0	(1.08)	16.8	(1.14)	14.2	(0.97)	5.3	(0.67)	449	(6.0)	484	(7.3)	508	(7.9)	515	(7.9)	497	(20.4)
Italy (Provincia Autonoma di Bolzano)	48.0	(1.60)	24.1	(1.16)	14.7	(0.92)	10.0	(0.77)	3.3	(0.55)	459	(3.3)	508	(6.2)	538	(5.4)	529	(17.1)	519	(19.0)
Italy (Provincia Basilicata)	29.2	(1.31)	30.8	(1.29)	20.2	(0.99)	14.5	(1.03)	5.2	(0.67)	441	(6.1)	473	(5.2)	492	(5.8)	501	(7.5)	504	(15.2)
Italy (Provincia Calabria)	29.3	(1.62)	31.4	(1.06)	17.3	(0.94)	16.9	(1.01)	5.1	(0.52)	419	(7.6)	441	(6.5)	467	(6.9)	474	(8.9)	515	(10.7)
Italy (Provincia Campania)	32.9	(1.92)	31.2	(1.33)	16.0	(1.20)	13.6	(0.93)	6.3	(0.91)	422	(9.5)	442	(7.6)	483	(7.8)	488	(7.9)	501	(12.4)
Italy (Provincia Emilia Romagna)	33.4	(1.54)	30.5	(1.57)	21.0	(1.02)	11.5	(0.88)	3.6	(0.36)	457	(6.0)	516	(6.4)	534	(5.3)	535	(7.6)	542	(12.9)
Italy (Provincia Friuli Venezia Giulia)	32.3	(2.02)	29.1	(1.52)	21.7	(1.32)	12.5	(0.90)	4.4	(0.57)	470	(6.8)	522	(5.8)	542	(6.9)	548	(7.9)	537	(12.1)
Italy (Provincia Lazio)	32.5	(1.69)	26.6	(1.10)	18.8	(1.41)	15.9	(0.92)	6.3	(0.79)	440	(5.1)	483	(5.5)	508	(9.0)	522	(8.2)	516	(12.3)
Italy (Provincia Liguria)	36.8	(1.51)	28.4	(1.13)	18.5	(1.21)	11.6	(1.00)	4.7	(0.61)	449	(14.1)	495	(11.2)	529	(5.5)	538	(5.7)	542	(9.2)
Italy (Provincia Lombardia)	35.9	(2.17)	25.8	(1.16)	21.6	(1.43)	12.6	(1.09)	4.1	(0.60)	479	(7.5)	534	(5.5)	544	(12.2)	563	(7.9)	571	(10.6)
Italy (Provincia Marche)	37.4	(2.29)	30.0	(1.30)	19.4	(1.46)	9.8	(0.81)	3.3	(0.40)	462	(12.1)	506	(5.7)	532	(5.9)	538	(6.5)	537	(17.3)
Italy (Provincia Molise)	29.8	(1.35)	32.7	(1.46)	20.1	(1.31)	13.2	(0.99)	4.2	(0.64)	434	(4.8)	470	(5.7)	491	(4.9)	506	(7.2)	532	(14.2)
Italy (Provincia Piemonte)	35.5	(1.85)	27.8	(1.28)	19.2	(1.50)	13.3	(0.76)	4.2	(0.55)	456	(5.7)	507	(8.3)	529	(8.2)	526	(8.4)	524	(15.7)
Italy (Provincia Puglia)	34.7	(1.84)	29.2	(0.89)	19.1	(1.27)	13.0	(0.89)	4.0	(0.45)	462	(6.9)	490	(5.1)	515	(7.0)	514	(8.2)	528	(11.1)
Italy (Provincia Sardegna)	35.5	(1.46)	24.2	(1.02)	17.2	(1.43)	16.0	(1.11)	7.2	(0.74)	428	(4.8)	464	(5.6)	510	(5.8)	509	(8.1)	516	(9.0)
Italy (Provincia Sicilia)	32.6	(1.89)	29.1	(1.58)	16.9	(0.80)	15.4	(1.33)	6.0	(0.74)	419	(8.8)	451	(8.3)	480	(9.8)	498	(11.0)	511	(12.9)
Italy (Provincia Toscana)	31.7	(1.84)	26.7	(1.35)	22.7	(1.40)	13.0	(0.99)	5.8	(0.61)	444	(6.6)	510	(5.2)	519	(6.5)	527	(7.7)	532	(6.6)
Italy (Provincia Trento)	34.3	(1.61)	27.2	(1.24)	20.7	(1.33)	13.0	(1.05)	4.8	(0.57)	468	(5.3)	516	(4.9)	539	(7.3)	534	(8.1)	551	(8.7)
Italy (Provincia Umbria)	31.9	(1.34)	27.5	(1.45)	20.3	(1.18)	15.3	(1.05)	5.0	(0.63)	449	(7.3)	498	(6.9)	511	(6.1)	530	(8.8)	540	(8.6)
Italy (Provincia Valle d'Aosta)	32.6	(1.46)	30.5	(1.56)	20.1	(1.22)	10.8	(1.00)	5.9	(0.74)	477	(4.8)	516	(5.3)	546	(5.4)	547	(8.5)	550	(13.0)
Italy (Provincia Veneto)	34.0	(1.92)	29.3	(1.13)	18.0	(1.25)	14.0	(1.09)	4.8	(0.59)	462	(8.2)	512	(5.9)	537	(6.1)	541	(7.8)	564	(11.4)
United Kingdom (England)	39.0	(1.05)	32.2	(0.89)	15.4	(0.68)	9.8	(0.46)	3.6	(0.31)	459	(3.1)	505	(3.7)	530	(5.2)	549	(5.4)	537	(8.7)
United Kingdom (Northern Ireland)	43.3	(1.08)	28.4	(1.02)	14.4	(0.84)	10.0	(0.75)	3.9	(0.56)	466	(4.2)	507	(6.5)	544	(6.1)	552	(7.0)	543	(14.6)
United Kingdom (Wales)	41.5	(0.82)	30.0	(0.76)	14.8	(0.60)	10.1	(0.54)	3.7	(0.31)	438	(4.2)	485	(4.0)	522	(5.4)	529	(6.4)	532	(9.4)

Note: See Table III.1.3 for national data.
StatLink ⟨⟨🔢⟩⟩ http://dx.doi.org/10.1787/888932343304

[Part 1/1]
Percentage of students who read diverse materials
Percentage of students who reported that they read the following materials because they want
Table S.III.c   *to "several times a month" or "several times a week"*

	Percentage of students who read because they want to...									
	Magazines		Comic books		Fiction (novels, narratives, stories)		Non-fiction books		Newspapers	
	%	S.E.	%	S.E.	%	S.E.	%	S.E.	%	S.E.
Adjudicated										
Belgium (Flemish Community)	67.3	(1.08)	31.1	(0.77)	19.2	(0.81)	12.1	(0.68)	54.7	(1.03)
Spain (Andalusia)	49.6	(1.61)	10.6	(0.80)	27.1	(1.26)	17.2	(1.23)	41.5	(2.03)
Spain (Aragon)	55.6	(1.45)	11.8	(0.94)	28.8	(1.64)	16.1	(1.37)	47.4	(1.70)
Spain (Asturias)	60.0	(1.30)	13.6	(0.78)	33.1	(1.29)	20.9	(0.74)	57.4	(1.65)
Spain (Balearic Islands)	52.0	(1.39)	13.1	(1.08)	25.8	(1.23)	15.0	(0.90)	46.2	(1.19)
Spain (Basque Country)	58.5	(0.88)	12.1	(0.56)	30.7	(0.76)	22.0	(0.66)	56.3	(0.94)
Spain (Canary Islands)	49.5	(1.74)	11.5	(1.19)	31.1	(1.24)	16.9	(1.15)	42.5	(1.04)
Spain (Cantabria)	59.0	(1.23)	10.2	(0.91)	30.3	(1.05)	18.3	(0.87)	49.3	(1.63)
Spain (Castile and Leon)	57.7	(1.56)	12.8	(1.05)	37.2	(1.73)	23.3	(1.15)	52.5	(1.64)
Spain (Catalonia)	41.8	(1.95)	13.6	(1.18)	29.1	(1.21)	19.1	(1.01)	41.7	(1.73)
Spain (Ceuta and Melilla)	47.7	(1.19)	15.0	(0.73)	32.3	(1.29)	17.5	(1.04)	40.5	(1.29)
Spain (Galicia)	63.1	(1.30)	14.2	(0.92)	33.9	(1.53)	19.6	(1.21)	59.6	(1.68)
Spain (La Rioja)	56.1	(1.47)	13.3	(1.10)	31.9	(1.61)	18.8	(1.26)	49.7	(1.31)
Spain (Madrid)	48.8	(1.79)	13.2	(1.02)	33.5	(1.29)	18.1	(1.31)	48.3	(1.99)
Spain (Murcia)	51.3	(1.46)	11.9	(0.96)	30.9	(1.57)	16.1	(1.15)	42.8	(1.19)
Spain (Navarre)	57.8	(1.36)	10.5	(0.83)	30.2	(1.28)	19.3	(1.15)	61.9	(1.44)
United Kingdom (Scotland)	58.9	(1.09)	7.2	(0.48)	32.6	(1.28)	17.8	(0.83)	69.4	(0.98)
Non-adjudicated										
Belgium (French Community)	64.3	(0.91)	33.0	(1.18)	26.5	(1.04)	15.8	(0.92)	44.9	(1.35)
Belgium (German-Speaking Community)	50.1	(1.68)	10.8	(1.11)	31.8	(1.63)	9.1	(0.98)	59.8	(1.53)
Finland (Finnish Speaking)	64.4	(0.87)	60.9	(0.92)	26.0	(0.81)	15.9	(0.57)	75.0	(0.83)
Finland (Swedish Speaking)	72.5	(1.41)	48.3	(1.28)	27.4	(1.39)	8.8	(0.85)	81.3	(1.17)
Italy (Provincia Abruzzo)	47.5	(1.40)	17.3	(1.16)	34.0	(1.46)	4.9	(0.69)	49.2	(1.75)
Italy (Provincia Autonoma di Bolzano)	63.6	(1.74)	14.0	(1.19)	26.9	(1.09)	15.5	(1.00)	71.2	(1.35)
Italy (Provincia Basilicata)	48.1	(1.48)	17.8	(1.34)	40.3	(1.49)	5.3	(0.63)	54.9	(2.36)
Italy (Provincia Calabria)	48.8	(1.64)	16.3	(1.06)	38.0	(1.85)	7.2	(0.82)	52.6	(1.75)
Italy (Provincia Campania)	47.9	(1.70)	14.9	(0.96)	42.2	(1.56)	7.2	(1.04)	54.9	(1.82)
Italy (Provincia Emilia Romagna)	48.2	(1.24)	18.5	(1.17)	31.5	(1.27)	2.7	(0.38)	50.8	(2.32)
Italy (Provincia Friuli Venezia Giulia)	51.2	(1.20)	17.6	(0.97)	33.3	(1.51)	4.0	(0.63)	51.8	(1.81)
Italy (Provincia Lazio)	44.8	(2.13)	20.3	(1.22)	37.1	(1.48)	5.6	(0.76)	57.3	(2.21)
Italy (Provincia Liguria)	46.7	(1.48)	20.0	(1.68)	33.9	(1.42)	4.6	(0.67)	54.1	(1.41)
Italy (Provincia Lombardia)	51.7	(1.68)	20.3	(1.39)	32.2	(1.55)	3.7	(0.57)	55.3	(1.65)
Italy (Provincia Marche)	47.8	(1.45)	16.5	(1.18)	30.2	(1.86)	4.7	(0.63)	55.1	(2.41)
Italy (Provincia Molise)	49.4	(1.89)	14.3	(1.05)	35.6	(1.54)	4.3	(0.68)	46.5	(1.81)
Italy (Provincia Piemonte)	52.8	(2.35)	17.1	(1.29)	31.2	(2.02)	2.4	(0.41)	53.5	(1.87)
Italy (Provincia Puglia)	50.2	(1.90)	14.8	(0.92)	35.2	(1.67)	5.2	(0.72)	51.0	(2.11)
Italy (Provincia Sardegna)	49.6	(2.30)	17.7	(1.32)	32.7	(1.70)	4.2	(0.66)	60.8	(1.94)
Italy (Provincia Sicilia)	42.7	(1.49)	12.6	(1.23)	36.2	(1.75)	7.0	(0.76)	45.9	(1.38)
Italy (Provincia Toscana)	49.0	(1.65)	20.1	(1.09)	37.5	(1.51)	3.8	(0.55)	57.3	(1.51)
Italy (Provincia Trento)	49.8	(1.66)	17.9	(1.34)	34.2	(1.57)	4.6	(0.64)	56.1	(1.42)
Italy (Provincia Umbria)	50.0	(1.19)	17.7	(0.85)	36.3	(1.43)	5.1	(0.63)	49.2	(1.86)
Italy (Provincia Valle d'Aosta)	52.8	(1.63)	18.0	(1.22)	30.6	(1.60)	2.6	(0.54)	55.7	(1.58)
Italy (Provincia Veneto)	51.1	(1.62)	18.5	(1.03)	32.2	(1.97)	3.2	(0.47)	51.8	(1.86)
United Kingdom (England)	59.5	(0.92)	7.9	(0.43)	31.6	(0.86)	19.7	(0.62)	60.2	(0.93)
United Kingdom (Northern Ireland)	62.1	(1.14)	7.1	(0.51)	32.2	(1.04)	20.6	(0.68)	67.6	(1.23)
United Kingdom (Wales)	60.8	(0.88)	7.4	(0.52)	28.4	(0.92)	18.0	(0.79)	59.7	(0.81)

Note: See Table III.2.7 for national data.
StatLink ⪢ http://dx.doi.org/10.1787/888932343304

[Part 1/2]

Index of diversity of reading materials and performance, by national quarters of this index

Table S.III.d *Results based on students' self-reports*

	Index of diversity of reading activities															
	All students		Males		Females		Gender difference (B – G)		Bottom quarter		Second quarter		Third quarter		Top quarter	
	Mean index	S.E.	Mean index	S.E.	Mean index	S.E.	Dif.	S.E.	Mean index	S.E.	Mean index	S.E.	Mean index	S.E.	Mean index	S.E.
Adjudicated																
Belgium (Flemish Community)	-0.11	(0.02)	-0.21	(0.04)	-0.01	(0.03)	**-0.20**	(0.04)	**-1.41**	(0.04)	-0.33	(0.01)	0.21	(0.01)	**1.08**	(0.02)
Spain (Andalusia)	-0.43	(0.03)	-0.37	(0.04)	-0.49	(0.04)	**0.12**	(0.05)	**-1.65**	(0.04)	-0.67	(0.01)	-0.08	(0.01)	**0.70**	(0.03)
Spain (Aragon)	-0.28	(0.04)	-0.32	(0.06)	-0.24	(0.04)	-0.08	(0.05)	**-1.49**	(0.04)	-0.49	(0.01)	0.02	(0.01)	**0.84**	(0.03)
Spain (Asturias)	-0.07	(0.03)	-0.10	(0.04)	-0.04	(0.04)	-0.06	(0.05)	**-1.22**	(0.04)	-0.31	(0.01)	0.22	(0.01)	**1.03**	(0.03)
Spain (Balearic Islands)	-0.29	(0.03)	-0.39	(0.05)	-0.20	(0.03)	**-0.19**	(0.06)	**-1.50**	(0.04)	-0.48	(0.01)	0.01	(0.01)	**0.80**	(0.03)
Spain (Basque Country)	-0.11	(0.02)	-0.12	(0.03)	-0.09	(0.02)	-0.03	(0.03)	**-1.35**	(0.03)	-0.31	(0.00)	0.21	(0.01)	**1.03**	(0.02)
Spain (Canary Islands)	-0.38	(0.03)	-0.42	(0.05)	-0.34	(0.03)	-0.08	(0.05)	**-1.53**	(0.05)	-0.60	(0.01)	-0.10	(0.01)	**0.71**	(0.03)
Spain (Cantabria)	-0.25	(0.03)	-0.32	(0.04)	-0.18	(0.03)	**-0.14**	(0.04)	**-1.44**	(0.04)	-0.46	(0.01)	0.06	(0.01)	**0.85**	(0.03)
Spain (Castile and Leon)	-0.07	(0.02)	-0.11	(0.04)	-0.02	(0.02)	-0.08	(0.06)	**-1.16**	(0.04)	-0.28	(0.01)	0.19	(0.01)	**1.00**	(0.03)
Spain (Catalonia)	-0.28	(0.03)	-0.32	(0.04)	-0.24	(0.03)	-0.09	(0.06)	**-1.41**	(0.04)	-0.47	(0.01)	0.02	(0.01)	**0.74**	(0.03)
Spain (Ceuta and Melilla)	-0.34	(0.03)	-0.36	(0.05)	-0.32	(0.03)	-0.04	(0.06)	**-1.58**	(0.04)	-0.61	(0.01)	-0.05	(0.01)	**0.90**	(0.05)
Spain (Galicia)	-0.02	(0.03)	-0.05	(0.04)	0.01	(0.04)	-0.06	(0.05)	**-1.12**	(0.04)	-0.27	(0.01)	0.26	(0.01)	**1.04**	(0.03)
Spain (La Rioja)	-0.14	(0.03)	-0.12	(0.05)	-0.16	(0.03)	0.04	(0.06)	**-1.30**	(0.04)	-0.38	(0.01)	0.15	(0.01)	**0.98**	(0.04)
Spain (Madrid)	-0.26	(0.04)	-0.28	(0.05)	-0.25	(0.05)	-0.03	(0.04)	**-1.40**	(0.05)	-0.48	(0.01)	0.02	(0.01)	**0.82**	(0.03)
Spain (Murcia)	-0.33	(0.03)	-0.31	(0.04)	-0.36	(0.04)	0.05	(0.06)	**-1.47**	(0.04)	-0.57	(0.01)	-0.05	(0.01)	**0.76**	(0.03)
Spain (Navarre)	-0.09	(0.03)	-0.18	(0.05)	0.01	(0.03)	**-0.19**	(0.05)	**-1.25**	(0.04)	-0.29	(0.01)	0.21	(0.01)	**0.99**	(0.03)
United Kingdom (Scotland)	-0.06	(0.02)	-0.15	(0.04)	0.03	(0.03)	**-0.17**	(0.04)	**-1.15**	(0.02)	-0.27	(0.01)	0.22	(0.01)	**0.95**	(0.03)
Non-adjudicated																
Belgium (French Community)	-0.04	(0.03)	0.01	(0.04)	-0.10	(0.03)	**0.10**	(0.04)	**-1.25**	(0.04)	-0.27	(0.01)	0.26	(0.01)	**1.08**	(0.02)
Belgium (German-Speaking Community)	-0.35	(0.03)	-0.47	(0.05)	-0.22	(0.04)	**-0.26**	(0.06)	**-1.62**	(0.07)	-0.49	(0.01)	0.01	(0.01)	**0.72**	(0.03)
Finland (Finnish Speaking)	0.46	(0.02)	0.37	(0.02)	0.56	(0.02)	**-0.19**	(0.02)	**-0.54**	(0.02)	0.24	(0.00)	0.70	(0.00)	**1.44**	(0.02)
Finland (Swedish Speaking)	0.35	(0.03)	0.23	(0.05)	0.48	(0.03)	**-0.25**	(0.05)	**-0.74**	(0.04)	0.16	(0.01)	0.60	(0.01)	**1.41**	(0.04)
Italy (Provincia Abruzzo)	-0.41	(0.03)	-0.50	(0.04)	-0.30	(0.04)	**-0.21**	(0.05)	**-1.61**	(0.05)	-0.55	(0.01)	-0.06	(0.01)	**0.60**	(0.02)
Italy (Provincia Autonoma di Bolzano)	-0.10	(0.03)	-0.18	(0.04)	-0.03	(0.03)	**-0.15**	(0.05)	**-1.23**	(0.05)	-0.27	(0.01)	0.19	(0.01)	**0.90**	(0.02)
Italy (Provincia Basilicata)	-0.24	(0.04)	-0.34	(0.05)	-0.14	(0.04)	**-0.20**	(0.04)	**-1.33**	(0.04)	-0.41	(0.01)	0.06	(0.01)	**0.73**	(0.03)
Italy (Provincia Calabria)	-0.25	(0.04)	-0.37	(0.06)	-0.13	(0.05)	**-0.24**	(0.07)	**-1.36**	(0.04)	-0.47	(0.01)	0.02	(0.01)	**0.79**	(0.03)
Italy (Provincia Campania)	-0.25	(0.03)	-0.33	(0.05)	-0.16	(0.04)	**-0.17**	(0.06)	**-1.40**	(0.04)	-0.45	(0.01)	0.08	(0.01)	**0.76**	(0.03)
Italy (Provincia Emilia Romagna)	-0.34	(0.02)	-0.36	(0.03)	-0.32	(0.03)	-0.04	(0.04)	**-1.39**	(0.05)	-0.49	(0.01)	-0.05	(0.01)	**0.57**	(0.02)
Italy (Provincia Friuli Venezia Giulia)	-0.31	(0.04)	-0.43	(0.04)	-0.17	(0.03)	**-0.26**	(0.05)	**-1.38**	(0.05)	-0.48	(0.01)	-0.04	(0.01)	**0.68**	(0.03)
Italy (Provincia Lazio)	-0.26	(0.04)	-0.31	(0.04)	-0.19	(0.04)	-0.12	(0.04)	**-1.42**	(0.04)	-0.42	(0.01)	0.08	(0.01)	**0.73**	(0.02)
Italy (Provincia Liguria)	-0.30	(0.03)	-0.35	(0.06)	-0.25	(0.05)	-0.10	(0.08)	**-1.46**	(0.05)	-0.46	(0.01)	-0.01	(0.01)	**0.73**	(0.02)
Italy (Provincia Lombardia)	-0.27	(0.02)	-0.33	(0.03)	-0.19	(0.03)	**-0.14**	(0.05)	**-1.32**	(0.04)	-0.45	(0.01)	0.02	(0.01)	**0.68**	(0.02)
Italy (Provincia Marche)	-0.37	(0.05)	-0.46	(0.08)	-0.26	(0.03)	**-0.20**	(0.09)	**-1.45**	(0.06)	-0.52	(0.01)	-0.07	(0.01)	**0.58**	(0.02)
Italy (Provincia Molise)	-0.38	(0.04)	-0.49	(0.06)	-0.26	(0.04)	**-0.23**	(0.07)	**-1.45**	(0.06)	-0.55	(0.01)	-0.08	(0.01)	**0.57**	(0.02)
Italy (Provincia Piemonte)	-0.36	(0.04)	-0.45	(0.06)	-0.26	(0.05)	**-0.19**	(0.07)	**-1.52**	(0.07)	-0.50	(0.01)	-0.03	(0.01)	**0.63**	(0.02)
Italy (Provincia Puglia)	-0.33	(0.04)	-0.44	(0.04)	-0.22	(0.04)	**-0.22**	(0.04)	**-1.46**	(0.04)	-0.50	(0.01)	-0.03	(0.01)	**0.69**	(0.02)
Italy (Provincia Sardegna)	-0.31	(0.04)	-0.44	(0.07)	-0.19	(0.03)	**-0.25**	(0.07)	**-1.53**	(0.06)	-0.46	(0.01)	0.02	(0.01)	**0.73**	(0.02)
Italy (Provincia Sicilia)	-0.42	(0.04)	-0.54	(0.05)	-0.31	(0.04)	**-0.23**	(0.04)	**-1.70**	(0.06)	-0.58	(0.01)	-0.07	(0.01)	**0.67**	(0.03)
Italy (Provincia Toscana)	-0.25	(0.04)	-0.37	(0.06)	-0.12	(0.03)	**-0.26**	(0.05)	**-1.35**	(0.05)	-0.41	(0.01)	0.05	(0.01)	**0.71**	(0.02)
Italy (Provincia Trento)	-0.29	(0.03)	-0.40	(0.05)	-0.16	(0.04)	**-0.23**	(0.07)	**-1.43**	(0.05)	-0.46	(0.01)	0.03	(0.01)	**0.71**	(0.04)
Italy (Provincia Umbria)	-0.32	(0.03)	-0.39	(0.04)	-0.26	(0.03)	**-0.13**	(0.04)	**-1.40**	(0.04)	-0.47	(0.01)	-0.04	(0.01)	**0.62**	(0.02)
Italy (Provincia Valle d'Aosta)	-0.31	(0.02)	-0.29	(0.04)	-0.32	(0.03)	0.03	(0.05)	**-1.36**	(0.05)	-0.47	(0.01)	-0.02	(0.01)	**0.62**	(0.02)
Italy (Provincia Veneto)	-0.36	(0.04)	-0.51	(0.07)	-0.22	(0.04)	**-0.29**	(0.09)	**-1.56**	(0.05)	-0.48	(0.01)	-0.03	(0.01)	**0.65**	(0.03)
United Kingdom (England)	-0.12	(0.02)	-0.21	(0.03)	-0.03	(0.02)	**-0.19**	(0.03)	**-1.24**	(0.03)	-0.33	(0.01)	0.15	(0.01)	**0.95**	(0.02)
United Kingdom (Northern Ireland)	-0.05	(0.02)	-0.13	(0.03)	0.03	(0.03)	**-0.16**	(0.04)	**-1.08**	(0.02)	-0.28	(0.01)	0.21	(0.01)	**0.96**	(0.02)
United Kingdom (Wales)	-0.16	(0.02)	-0.25	(0.03)	-0.07	(0.02)	**-0.18**	(0.04)	**-1.29**	(0.02)	-0.37	(0.01)	0.12	(0.00)	**0.90**	(0.02)

Notes: Values that are statistically significant are indicated in bold (see Annex A3). See Table III.1.10 for national data.
StatLink ⛬ http://dx.doi.org/10.1787/888932343304

[Part 2/2]
Index of diversity of reading materials and performance, by national quarters of this index

Table S.III.d *Results based on students' self-reports*

| | Performance on the reading scale, by quarters of this index | | | | | | | | Change in the reading score per unit of this index | | Increased likelihood of students in the bottom quarter of this index scoring in the bottom quarter of the reading performance distribution | | Explained variance in student performance (r-squared x 100) | |
| | Bottom quarter | | Second quarter | | Third quarter | | Top quarter | | | | | | | |
	Mean index	S.E.	Mean index	S.E.	Mean index	S.E.	Mean index	S.E.	Effect	S.E.	Ratio	S.E.	%	S.E.
Adjudicated														
Belgium (Flemish Community)	**476**	(3.7)	518	(3.1)	544	(3.1)	**560**	(3.8)	**31.7**	(1.53)	**2.4**	(0.15)	13.7	(1.34)
Spain (Andalusia)	**423**	(7.4)	454	(6.5)	475	(6.2)	**493**	(6.7)	**26.0**	(3.27)	**2.1**	(0.24)	8.3	(2.09)
Spain (Aragon)	**457**	(6.3)	490	(4.8)	508	(6.0)	**528**	(5.8)	**25.2**	(2.52)	**2.2**	(0.23)	8.7	(1.52)
Spain (Asturias)	**446**	(6.2)	479	(6.7)	516	(5.7)	**523**	(6.3)	**33.2**	(2.69)	**2.2**	(0.22)	11.5	(1.85)
Spain (Balearic Islands)	**419**	(7.2)	455	(6.2)	470	(6.1)	**492**	(6.5)	**25.7**	(2.67)	**2.0**	(0.22)	7.5	(1.38)
Spain (Basque Country)	**465**	(4.5)	492	(3.3)	502	(3.8)	**520**	(3.8)	**20.2**	(1.50)	**1.8**	(0.12)	6.1	(0.87)
Spain (Canary Islands)	**418**	(6.3)	441	(6.9)	463	(6.2)	**475**	(6.1)	**23.3**	(3.10)	**1.7**	(0.23)	5.9	(1.42)
Spain (Cantabria)	**446**	(5.0)	479	(6.0)	500	(5.9)	**528**	(5.5)	**33.7**	(2.18)	**1.9**	(0.18)	13.8	(1.87)
Spain (Castile and Leon)	**471**	(5.6)	496	(7.7)	516	(6.5)	**531**	(6.1)	**25.6**	(2.83)	**1.9**	(0.24)	7.7	(1.59)
Spain (Catalonia)	**471**	(6.6)	489	(5.6)	508	(6.9)	**526**	(5.5)	**21.0**	(2.49)	**1.8**	(0.18)	5.5	(1.24)
Spain (Ceuta and Melilla)	**398**	(5.7)	417	(5.5)	419	(5.7)	**422**	(5.9)	**9.0**	(3.47)	**1.2**	(0.14)	0.8	(0.65)
Spain (Galicia)	**449**	(4.8)	480	(5.1)	497	(6.5)	**519**	(7.1)	**27.8**	(2.97)	**1.9**	(0.19)	8.9	(1.66)
Spain (La Rioja)	**461**	(5.8)	495	(5.8)	514	(6.1)	**523**	(6.7)	**24.9**	(3.49)	**1.9**	(0.23)	7.0	(1.86)
Spain (Madrid)	**461**	(7.2)	502	(6.2)	522	(5.4)	**531**	(6.1)	**27.3**	(3.10)	**2.2**	(0.21)	9.2	(1.60)
Spain (Murcia)	**454**	(7.2)	483	(6.5)	482	(5.7)	**506**	(7.4)	**19.4**	(2.87)	**1.6**	(0.20)	5.2	(1.58)
Spain (Navarre)	**460**	(5.1)	498	(4.4)	508	(5.0)	**524**	(5.5)	**25.6**	(2.66)	**1.9**	(0.19)	8.2	(1.52)
United Kingdom (Scotland)	**465**	(5.1)	493	(4.7)	517	(4.8)	**531**	(5.3)	**27.4**	(2.94)	**2.0**	(0.18)	6.8	(1.31)
Non-adjudicated														
Belgium (French Community)	**460**	(6.4)	497	(4.9)	507	(5.0)	**523**	(5.5)	**27.0**	(2.74)	**1.8**	(0.14)	6.2	(1.22)
Belgium (German-Speaking Community)	**458**	(6.3)	498	(6.2)	515	(5.9)	**532**	(6.2)	**25.7**	(3.37)	**2.1**	(0.26)	9.0	(2.18)
Finland (Finnish Speaking)	**497**	(3.4)	528	(3.3)	551	(3.2)	**575**	(3.4)	**37.8**	(1.78)	**2.1**	(0.13)	13.5	(1.23)
Finland (Swedish Speaking)	**467**	(5.0)	504	(5.1)	520	(4.7)	**558**	(4.4)	**36.5**	(3.00)	**2.2**	(0.25)	15.2	(2.10)
Italy (Provincia Abruzzo)	**449**	(8.1)	485	(7.0)	487	(6.5)	**508**	(5.9)	**26.2**	(3.54)	**1.9**	(0.19)	8.2	(2.31)
Italy (Provincia Autonoma di Bolzano)	**453**	(6.3)	485	(5.3)	497	(7.3)	**526**	(4.4)	**31.9**	(3.34)	**2.0**	(0.24)	10.1	(1.89)
Italy (Provincia Basilicata)	**446**	(5.4)	474	(6.9)	482	(7.6)	**491**	(6.5)	**20.3**	(2.96)	**1.6**	(0.22)	4.4	(1.54)
Italy (Provincia Calabria)	**424**	(8.4)	442	(7.8)	461	(6.0)	**469**	(7.4)	**20.1**	(4.23)	**1.6**	(0.23)	4.3	(1.84)
Italy (Provincia Campania)	**419**	(9.2)	453	(8.3)	463	(8.6)	**471**	(7.2)	**23.3**	(3.30)	**1.8**	(0.18)	5.3	(1.37)
Italy (Provincia Emilia Romagna)	**460**	(7.5)	499	(4.4)	516	(6.9)	**538**	(5.4)	**37.6**	(3.62)	**2.0**	(0.18)	9.8	(1.41)
Italy (Provincia Friuli Venezia Giulia)	**475**	(7.6)	511	(6.4)	526	(6.4)	**543**	(6.4)	**30.9**	(3.86)	**1.9**	(0.23)	8.6	(2.23)
Italy (Provincia Lazio)	**444**	(5.6)	481	(6.0)	493	(6.0)	**508**	(7.5)	**29.5**	(3.14)	**1.8**	(0.26)	8.9	(1.97)
Italy (Provincia Liguria)	**448**	(20.8)	492	(8.5)	506	(6.3)	**520**	(5.9)	**31.6**	(6.19)	**2.0**	(0.25)	10.0	(2.90)
Italy (Provincia Lombardia)	**482**	(8.2)	517	(6.3)	535	(7.3)	**552**	(7.1)	**34.7**	(3.51)	**2.0**	(0.23)	10.7	(1.81)
Italy (Provincia Marche)	**455**	(15.7)	500	(7.9)	507	(4.8)	**532**	(5.8)	**35.1**	(6.90)	**2.4**	(0.35)	10.9	(4.07)
Italy (Provincia Molise)	**435**	(6.7)	469	(5.3)	483	(6.8)	**496**	(5.5)	**29.4**	(3.24)	**1.9**	(0.27)	8.7	(1.96)
Italy (Provincia Piemonte)	**452**	(5.5)	491	(6.5)	508	(8.3)	**536**	(8.1)	**35.9**	(2.93)	**2.2**	(0.23)	12.3	(1.89)
Italy (Provincia Puglia)	**462**	(6.8)	491	(6.3)	503	(6.4)	**502**	(7.0)	**19.9**	(2.75)	**1.7**	(0.22)	4.4	(1.07)
Italy (Provincia Sardegna)	**430**	(7.3)	472	(6.6)	485	(4.3)	**491**	(9.0)	**27.7**	(4.01)	**2.0**	(0.24)	8.6	(2.75)
Italy (Provincia Sicilia)	**417**	(13.3)	457	(8.0)	461	(9.0)	**484**	(10.4)	**26.1**	(5.44)	**1.9**	(0.29)	7.1	(2.61)
Italy (Provincia Toscana)	**452**	(7.8)	491	(5.3)	510	(4.9)	**524**	(5.1)	**33.6**	(3.12)	**2.3**	(0.23)	10.2	(1.60)
Italy (Provincia Trento)	**469**	(6.0)	502	(5.9)	513	(5.0)	**550**	(5.0)	**33.4**	(3.82)	**1.9**	(0.22)	11.4	(2.30)
Italy (Provincia Umbria)	**453**	(9.4)	485	(7.0)	507	(5.3)	**521**	(6.2)	**33.8**	(4.15)	**1.9**	(0.20)	9.0	(1.87)
Italy (Provincia Valle d'Aosta)	**484**	(5.4)	505	(6.3)	523	(5.5)	**545**	(4.8)	**30.4**	(3.04)	**1.8**	(0.25)	8.5	(1.62)
Italy (Provincia Veneto)	**459**	(9.8)	503	(6.3)	524	(5.7)	**538**	(6.1)	**35.5**	(3.73)	**2.3**	(0.26)	14.3	(2.69)
United Kingdom (England)	**467**	(3.5)	494	(4.0)	513	(3.3)	**509**	(4.0)	**18.2**	(1.62)	**1.6**	(0.10)	3.2	(0.59)
United Kingdom (Northern Ireland)	**477**	(5.4)	498	(4.8)	511	(6.5)	**515**	(5.5)	**18.0**	(2.80)	**1.5**	(0.16)	2.5	(0.77)
United Kingdom (Wales)	**444**	(4.7)	470	(4.8)	490	(4.6)	**501**	(4.5)	**23.1**	(2.17)	**1.8**	(0.13)	5.3	(0.91)

Notes: Values that are statistically significant are indicated in bold (see Annex A3). See Table III.1.10 for national data.
StatLink ⌐╦┐ http://dx.doi.org/10.1787/888932343304

[Part 1/1]
Percentage of students doing diverse online reading
Percentage of students who reported that they were involved in the following online reading activities "several times a week" or "several times a day"

Table S.III.e

	Percentage of students doing diverse online reading activities													
	Reading emails		<Chat on line> (e.g. <MSN®>)		Reading online news		Using an online dictionary or encyclopedia (e.g. <Wikipedia®>)		Searching online information to learn about a practical topic		Taking part in online group discussions or forums		Searching for practical information online (e.g. schedules, events, tips, recipes)	
	%	S.E.	%	S.E.	%	S.E.	%	S.E.	%	S.E.	%	S.E.	%	S.E.
Adjudicated														
Belgium (Flemish Community)	78.7	(0.65)	81.9	(0.74)	21.9	(0.82)	19.5	(0.68)	27.3	(0.77)	12.2	(0.54)	17.8	(0.65)
Spain (Andalusia)	55.3	(1.29)	78.7	(1.19)	39.2	(1.39)	49.6	(1.93)	55.5	(1.56)	12.9	(0.94)	32.7	(1.46)
Spain (Aragon)	59.2	(1.32)	79.1	(1.46)	35.0	(1.39)	47.5	(1.40)	53.4	(1.33)	12.9	(0.80)	29.8	(1.59)
Spain (Asturias)	56.1	(1.28)	82.4	(1.21)	40.0	(1.27)	48.6	(1.10)	54.5	(1.39)	12.0	(0.71)	31.8	(1.17)
Spain (Balearic Islands)	54.9	(1.21)	77.6	(0.99)	34.4	(1.44)	42.1	(1.87)	44.3	(1.94)	10.8	(0.85)	28.4	(1.23)
Spain (Basque Country)	53.4	(0.81)	78.9	(0.57)	30.4	(0.80)	38.3	(0.96)	43.0	(0.77)	14.3	(0.59)	25.7	(0.68)
Spain (Canary Islands)	50.9	(1.49)	78.7	(1.11)	37.3	(1.71)	47.4	(1.57)	55.1	(1.86)	10.6	(0.90)	30.1	(1.31)
Spain (Cantabria)	56.4	(1.54)	79.9	(1.15)	39.0	(1.85)	46.5	(1.44)	54.8	(1.70)	9.7	(0.74)	29.7	(1.37)
Spain (Castile and Leon)	53.6	(1.48)	75.5	(1.46)	35.2	(1.57)	47.1	(1.92)	53.3	(1.59)	10.8	(0.89)	30.7	(1.46)
Spain (Catalonia)	57.2	(1.23)	80.0	(1.20)	34.6	(1.43)	46.6	(1.46)	40.6	(0.90)	12.2	(0.88)	26.4	(1.03)
Spain (Ceuta and Melilla)	54.0	(1.30)	75.4	(1.11)	46.5	(1.06)	56.2	(1.62)	61.5	(1.50)	16.1	(0.99)	37.3	(1.39)
Spain (Galicia)	52.9	(1.60)	69.1	(1.94)	28.0	(1.47)	37.8	(1.93)	38.6	(1.71)	10.3	(0.83)	25.3	(1.33)
Spain (La Rioja)	57.1	(1.48)	74.4	(1.54)	34.4	(1.40)	48.4	(1.52)	57.0	(1.61)	9.9	(0.88)	31.1	(1.52)
Spain (Madrid)	55.9	(1.54)	80.1	(1.03)	34.7	(1.66)	47.8	(2.16)	57.2	(1.51)	12.2	(0.91)	33.2	(1.20)
Spain (Murcia)	52.8	(1.86)	72.6	(1.40)	37.0	(1.55)	43.7	(1.83)	54.2	(1.60)	13.5	(0.97)	31.9	(1.32)
Spain (Navarre)	55.5	(1.43)	75.1	(1.05)	28.5	(1.39)	42.6	(1.90)	48.8	(1.55)	11.1	(0.82)	24.0	(1.28)
United Kingdom (Scotland)	67.9	(1.11)	78.1	(0.91)	38.5	(1.04)	30.9	(1.22)	43.5	(1.15)	17.5	(0.63)	28.5	(1.11)
Non-adjudicated														
Belgium (French Community)	67.6	(0.97)	79.7	(0.75)	42.1	(1.05)	28.8	(1.07)	42.1	(1.06)	20.7	(0.81)	39.6	(1.07)
Belgium (German-Speaking Community)	64.3	(1.61)	78.0	(1.40)	51.7	(1.92)	23.2	(1.46)	30.8	(1.40)	15.0	(1.41)	18.8	(1.35)
Finland (Finnish Speaking)	64.4	(0.78)	80.9	(0.66)	35.6	(0.80)	40.1	(0.99)	29.6	(0.92)	26.5	(0.66)	28.5	(0.80)
Finland (Swedish Speaking)	58.9	(1.39)	79.4	(1.27)	25.5	(1.35)	28.5	(1.15)	37.4	(1.17)	20.5	(1.20)	27.1	(1.10)
Italy (Provincia Abruzzo)	55.6	(1.19)	74.7	(1.08)	61.8	(1.45)	40.8	(1.62)	54.5	(1.50)	19.8	(1.19)	33.1	(1.51)
Italy (Provincia Autonoma di Bolzano)	53.9	(1.24)	62.5	(1.28)	45.0	(1.30)	32.2	(1.13)	47.6	(1.58)	11.2	(0.89)	27.0	(1.41)
Italy (Provincia Basilicata)	51.4	(1.31)	65.3	(1.68)	57.1	(1.71)	38.6	(1.63)	50.9	(1.38)	21.7	(1.26)	28.1	(1.39)
Italy (Provincia Calabria)	52.2	(1.36)	69.0	(1.84)	60.1	(1.43)	43.8	(1.51)	56.2	(1.37)	21.9	(1.36)	32.4	(1.39)
Italy (Provincia Campania)	54.1	(1.38)	77.8	(1.51)	68.2	(1.67)	46.8	(1.87)	58.7	(1.61)	24.8	(1.13)	35.2	(1.48)
Italy (Provincia Emilia Romagna)	53.2	(1.17)	72.4	(1.13)	51.9	(1.48)	36.7	(1.55)	46.7	(1.30)	17.5	(1.12)	30.3	(0.90)
Italy (Provincia Friuli Venezia Giulia)	52.6	(1.46)	64.8	(1.59)	46.6	(1.65)	35.4	(1.86)	46.4	(1.43)	17.7	(1.22)	30.1	(1.43)
Italy (Provincia Lazio)	56.6	(1.05)	79.6	(1.25)	61.8	(1.44)	46.3	(1.66)	56.9	(1.62)	23.6	(1.09)	36.1	(1.53)
Italy (Provincia Liguria)	57.2	(1.82)	74.4	(1.84)	52.8	(2.60)	37.4	(1.81)	52.2	(1.89)	19.5	(1.19)	35.9	(1.67)
Italy (Provincia Lombardia)	58.8	(1.65)	72.8	(1.35)	51.7	(1.71)	38.2	(1.51)	49.0	(1.65)	17.5	(1.33)	29.8	(1.37)
Italy (Provincia Marche)	53.3	(1.34)	77.6	(0.99)	55.3	(2.00)	35.6	(1.55)	47.0	(1.86)	17.2	(1.22)	27.5	(1.53)
Italy (Provincia Molise)	54.9	(1.79)	67.8	(1.50)	57.3	(1.60)	40.2	(1.69)	53.2	(1.79)	19.8	(1.33)	26.6	(1.49)
Italy (Provincia Piemonte)	55.5	(1.59)	69.3	(2.11)	49.4	(1.72)	32.2	(1.43)	45.9	(1.77)	18.3	(1.06)	29.7	(1.24)
Italy (Provincia Puglia)	52.3	(1.88)	66.8	(2.28)	56.7	(1.81)	40.8	(2.25)	52.6	(2.01)	19.6	(1.26)	29.4	(1.62)
Italy (Provincia Sardegna)	52.8	(2.41)	63.6	(2.75)	50.3	(2.04)	37.6	(1.85)	47.6	(1.90)	19.9	(1.20)	28.7	(1.55)
Italy (Provincia Sicilia)	52.7	(2.10)	68.8	(2.10)	56.5	(1.66)	42.5	(2.01)	55.3	(1.36)	21.7	(1.43)	30.1	(1.18)
Italy (Provincia Toscana)	59.6	(1.90)	77.7	(1.60)	56.8	(1.21)	40.7	(1.64)	53.3	(1.90)	18.8	(1.18)	32.3	(1.35)
Italy (Provincia Trento)	48.8	(1.38)	57.6	(1.27)	42.3	(1.36)	31.5	(1.12)	44.9	(1.28)	14.8	(1.19)	27.9	(1.08)
Italy (Provincia Umbria)	51.4	(1.40)	73.1	(0.89)	56.7	(1.27)	38.9	(1.42)	52.5	(1.38)	18.7	(1.18)	30.0	(1.67)
Italy (Provincia Valle d'Aosta)	52.6	(1.53)	64.2	(1.57)	45.4	(1.52)	30.1	(1.44)	43.9	(1.75)	17.7	(1.45)	27.1	(1.31)
Italy (Provincia Veneto)	44.6	(2.07)	52.8	(1.74)	42.9	(1.56)	33.3	(1.17)	46.3	(1.12)	15.7	(1.21)	29.8	(1.09)
United Kingdom (England)	76.0	(0.84)	84.1	(0.62)	44.1	(0.89)	41.0	(0.96)	55.6	(0.90)	20.9	(0.71)	33.4	(0.73)
United Kingdom (Northern Ireland)	66.8	(1.32)	79.1	(1.19)	43.8	(0.87)	37.2	(0.94)	53.1	(1.10)	17.5	(0.99)	31.0	(0.94)
United Kingdom (Wales)	70.8	(0.78)	84.8	(0.65)	45.7	(0.88)	37.8	(1.02)	50.1	(1.03)	21.5	(0.87)	33.3	(0.99)

Note: See Table III.2.9 for national data.
StatLink ⟨⟩ http://dx.doi.org/10.1787/888932343304

[Part 1/2]

Index of online reading activities and performance, by national quarters of this index

Table S.III.f *Results based on students' self-reports*

| | Index of online reading activities | | | | | | | | | | | | | | |
| | All students | | Males | | Females | | Gender difference (B – G) | | Bottom quarter | | Second quarter | | Third quarter | | Top quarter | |
	Mean index	S.E.	Mean index	S.E.	Mean index	S.E.	Dif.	S.E.	Mean index	S.E.	Mean index	S.E.	Mean index	S.E.	Mean index	S.E.
Adjudicated																
Belgium (Flemish Community)	-0.31	(0.01)	-0.28	(0.02)	-0.34	(0.02)	**0.06**	(0.03)	**-1.07**	(0.02)	-0.53	(0.00)	-0.17	(0.00)	**0.54**	(0.02)
Spain (Andalusia)	-0.04	(0.02)	0.02	(0.03)	-0.12	(0.03)	**0.14**	(0.05)	**-1.16**	(0.03)	-0.32	(0.01)	0.18	(0.01)	**1.13**	(0.04)
Spain (Aragon)	-0.04	(0.02)	-0.04	(0.03)	-0.04	(0.03)	0.00	(0.04)	**-1.01**	(0.03)	-0.32	(0.01)	0.15	(0.01)	**1.02**	(0.03)
Spain (Asturias)	-0.01	(0.02)	-0.01	(0.04)	-0.02	(0.02)	0.01	(0.04)	**-1.01**	(0.03)	-0.29	(0.01)	0.19	(0.01)	**1.05**	(0.04)
Spain (Balearic Islands)	-0.16	(0.03)	-0.16	(0.04)	-0.16	(0.03)	0.00	(0.04)	**-1.14**	(0.03)	-0.42	(0.01)	0.02	(0.01)	**0.89**	(0.03)
Spain (Basque Country)	-0.22	(0.01)	-0.21	(0.02)	-0.23	(0.02)	0.02	(0.03)	**-1.20**	(0.02)	-0.47	(0.00)	-0.02	(0.00)	**0.81**	(0.02)
Spain (Canary Islands)	-0.06	(0.03)	0.03	(0.04)	-0.16	(0.02)	**0.19**	(0.04)	**-1.05**	(0.03)	-0.38	(0.01)	0.14	(0.01)	**1.04**	(0.03)
Spain (Cantabria)	-0.08	(0.03)	-0.10	(0.03)	-0.05	(0.03)	-0.04	(0.03)	**-1.07**	(0.04)	-0.33	(0.01)	0.14	(0.01)	**0.92**	(0.03)
Spain (Castile and Leon)	-0.14	(0.04)	-0.13	(0.04)	-0.16	(0.04)	0.03	(0.05)	**-1.21**	(0.04)	-0.38	(0.01)	0.11	(0.01)	**0.86**	(0.03)
Spain (Catalonia)	-0.13	(0.02)	-0.08	(0.03)	-0.19	(0.02)	**0.11**	(0.04)	**-1.02**	(0.02)	-0.41	(0.01)	0.04	(0.01)	**1.47**	(0.04)
Spain (Ceuta and Melilla)	0.09	(0.03)	0.17	(0.05)	0.01	(0.04)	**0.16**	(0.06)	**-1.27**	(0.05)	-0.22	(0.01)	0.38	(0.01)	**0.83**	(0.03)
Spain (Galicia)	-0.35	(0.04)	-0.32	(0.05)	-0.38	(0.04)	0.06	(0.04)	**-1.53**	(0.04)	-0.62	(0.01)	-0.09	(0.01)	**0.96**	(0.04)
Spain (La Rioja)	-0.13	(0.03)	-0.12	(0.05)	-0.14	(0.04)	0.01	(0.07)	**-1.23**	(0.05)	-0.38	(0.01)	0.13	(0.01)	**1.01**	(0.03)
Spain (Madrid)	-0.03	(0.03)	0.03	(0.05)	-0.09	(0.04)	0.12	(0.06)	**-0.95**	(0.03)	-0.32	(0.01)	0.14	(0.01)	**1.10**	(0.03)
Spain (Murcia)	-0.10	(0.04)	-0.01	(0.07)	-0.19	(0.03)	**0.18**	(0.07)	**-1.23**	(0.04)	-0.43	(0.01)	0.15	(0.01)	**0.81**	(0.03)
Spain (Navarre)	-0.23	(0.03)	-0.24	(0.04)	-0.22	(0.03)	-0.02	(0.05)	**-1.24**	(0.04)	-0.49	(0.01)	-0.02	(0.01)	**1.02**	(0.03)
United Kingdom (Scotland)	-0.08	(0.02)	-0.08	(0.03)	-0.08	(0.03)	0.01	(0.03)	**-1.06**	(0.02)	-0.39	(0.01)	0.11	(0.01)	**1.02**	(0.03)
Non-adjudicated																
Belgium (French Community)	-0.02	(0.02)	0.04	(0.03)	-0.07	(0.02)	**0.11**	(0.04)	**-1.04**	(0.03)	-0.27	(0.00)	0.19	(0.00)	**1.05**	(0.02)
Belgium (German-Speaking Community)	-0.18	(0.03)	-0.14	(0.05)	-0.21	(0.03)	0.07	(0.06)	**-1.14**	(0.03)	-0.41	(0.01)	-0.01	(0.01)	**0.86**	(0.05)
Finland (Finnish Speaking)	-0.03	(0.01)	0.02	(0.02)	-0.08	(0.02)	**0.10**	(0.03)	**-0.93**	(0.01)	-0.29	(0.00)	0.14	(0.01)	**0.97**	(0.02)
Finland (Swedish Speaking)	-0.17	(0.02)	-0.18	(0.03)	-0.17	(0.03)	0.00	(0.04)	**-1.06**	(0.02)	-0.42	(0.01)	0.01	(0.01)	**0.78**	(0.03)
Italy (Provincia Abruzzo)	0.05	(0.03)	0.06	(0.04)	0.04	(0.05)	0.02	(0.07)	**-1.35**	(0.05)	-0.25	(0.01)	0.36	(0.01)	**1.45**	(0.03)
Italy (Provincia Autonoma di Bolzano)	-0.27	(0.03)	-0.29	(0.06)	-0.24	(0.03)	-0.06	(0.07)	**-1.49**	(0.04)	-0.55	(0.01)	0.01	(0.01)	**1.36**	(0.04)
Italy (Provincia Basilicata)	-0.10	(0.05)	-0.07	(0.06)	-0.13	(0.06)	0.06	(0.07)	**-1.59**	(0.04)	-0.43	(0.01)	0.27	(0.01)	**1.57**	(0.05)
Italy (Provincia Calabria)	0.03	(0.04)	0.06	(0.06)	0.01	(0.05)	0.05	(0.08)	**-1.54**	(0.04)	-0.31	(0.01)	0.41	(0.01)	**1.65**	(0.04)
Italy (Provincia Campania)	0.17	(0.04)	0.22	(0.05)	0.12	(0.06)	0.10	(0.08)	**-1.36**	(0.06)	-0.11	(0.01)	0.52	(0.01)	**1.24**	(0.04)
Italy (Provincia Emilia Romagna)	-0.11	(0.03)	-0.13	(0.05)	-0.09	(0.03)	-0.04	(0.05)	**-1.47**	(0.04)	-0.40	(0.01)	0.14	(0.01)	**1.16**	(0.04)
Italy (Provincia Friuli Venezia Giulia)	-0.18	(0.04)	-0.22	(0.05)	-0.13	(0.04)	-0.09	(0.06)	**-1.52**	(0.03)	-0.51	(0.01)	0.14	(0.01)	**1.55**	(0.04)
Italy (Provincia Lazio)	0.16	(0.03)	0.20	(0.05)	0.12	(0.04)	0.08	(0.08)	**-1.21**	(0.04)	-0.15	(0.01)	0.47	(0.01)	**1.39**	(0.05)
Italy (Provincia Liguria)	0.02	(0.05)	-0.02	(0.09)	0.07	(0.04)	-0.10	(0.10)	**-1.32**	(0.03)	-0.30	(0.01)	0.32	(0.01)	**1.24**	(0.03)
Italy (Provincia Lombardia)	-0.08	(0.04)	-0.10	(0.05)	-0.05	(0.04)	-0.05	(0.05)	**-1.47**	(0.04)	-0.34	(0.01)	0.26	(0.01)	**1.19**	(0.03)
Italy (Provincia Marche)	-0.06	(0.05)	-0.07	(0.09)	-0.05	(0.03)	-0.02	(0.10)	**-1.29**	(0.05)	-0.35	(0.01)	0.21	(0.01)	**1.41**	(0.05)
Italy (Provincia Molise)	-0.07	(0.04)	-0.11	(0.06)	-0.03	(0.05)	-0.07	(0.08)	**-1.64**	(0.06)	-0.37	(0.02)	0.31	(0.01)	**1.28**	(0.05)
Italy (Provincia Piemonte)	-0.14	(0.05)	-0.09	(0.07)	-0.18	(0.05)	0.09	(0.07)	**-1.55**	(0.09)	-0.43	(0.01)	0.16	(0.01)	**1.46**	(0.04)
Italy (Provincia Puglia)	-0.08	(0.06)	-0.04	(0.07)	-0.13	(0.06)	0.09	(0.07)	**-1.70**	(0.05)	-0.41	(0.01)	0.32	(0.01)	**1.44**	(0.04)
Italy (Provincia Sardegna)	-0.17	(0.06)	-0.17	(0.07)	-0.17	(0.07)	0.00	(0.08)	**-1.84**	(0.07)	-0.52	(0.01)	0.26	(0.01)	**1.48**	(0.05)
Italy (Provincia Sicilia)	-0.01	(0.05)	0.02	(0.07)	-0.05	(0.06)	0.07	(0.08)	**-1.57**	(0.05)	-0.34	(0.01)	0.38	(0.01)	**1.30**	(0.03)
Italy (Provincia Toscana)	0.03	(0.04)	0.07	(0.05)	-0.01	(0.05)	0.08	(0.07)	**-1.25**	(0.04)	-0.23	(0.01)	0.31	(0.01)	**1.00**	(0.04)
Italy (Provincia Trento)	-0.30	(0.03)	-0.32	(0.06)	-0.28	(0.04)	-0.03	(0.07)	**-1.57**	(0.06)	-0.60	(0.01)	-0.04	(0.01)	**1.28**	(0.04)
Italy (Provincia Umbria)	-0.04	(0.03)	-0.04	(0.05)	-0.05	(0.04)	0.00	(0.05)	**-1.37**	(0.05)	-0.34	(0.01)	0.26	(0.01)	**1.11**	(0.06)
Italy (Provincia Valle d'Aosta)	-0.25	(0.04)	-0.20	(0.07)	-0.30	(0.04)	0.10	(0.08)	**-1.64**	(0.05)	-0.55	(0.01)	0.09	(0.01)	**1.02**	(0.04)
Italy (Provincia Veneto)	-0.35	(0.04)	-0.40	(0.08)	-0.29	(0.04)	-0.11	(0.09)	**-1.73**	(0.05)	-0.66	(0.01)	-0.02	(0.01)	**1.22**	(0.02)
United Kingdom (England)	0.13	(0.02)	0.16	(0.03)	0.10	(0.02)	**0.05**	(0.03)	**-0.85**	(0.02)	-0.15	(0.00)	0.31	(0.01)	**1.13**	(0.03)
United Kingdom (Northern Ireland)	0.01	(0.02)	0.05	(0.03)	-0.02	(0.02)	0.07	(0.04)	**-0.99**	(0.03)	-0.29	(0.01)	0.19	(0.01)	**1.25**	(0.03)
United Kingdom (Wales)	0.10	(0.02)	0.11	(0.03)	0.08	(0.02)	0.03	(0.04)	**-0.94**	(0.02)	-0.21	(0.01)	0.29	(0.01)	**1.25**	(0.03)

Notes: Values that are statistically significant are indicated in bold (see Annex A3). See Table III.2.12 for national data.
StatLink ⟪⟫ http://dx.doi.org/10.1787/888932343304

[Part 2/2]

Index of online reading activities and performance, by national quarters of this index

Table S.III.f *Results based on students' self-reports*

| | Performance on the reading scale, by quarters of this index | | | | | | | | Change in the reading score per unit of this index | | Increased likelihood of students in the bottom quarter of this index scoring in the bottom quarter of the reading performance distribution | | Explained variance in student performance (r-squared x 100) | |
| | Bottom quarter | | Second quarter | | Third quarter | | Top quarter | | | | | | | |
	Mean index	S.E.	Mean index	S.E.	Mean index	S.E.	Mean index	S.E.	Effect	S.E.	Ratio	S.E.	%	S.E.
Adjudicated														
Belgium (Flemish Community)	**502**	(3.2)	530	(3.3)	538	(4.1)	527	(3.8)	**15.4**	(2.23)	**1.5**	(0.12)	1.4	(0.41)
Spain (Andalusia)	**428**	(8.2)	465	(6.6)	475	(6.1)	478	(6.8)	**20.1**	(3.27)	**1.9**	(0.29)	4.6	(1.51)
Spain (Aragon)	**471**	(5.2)	499	(5.3)	510	(7.1)	503	(5.3)	**13.0**	(2.26)	**1.6**	(0.17)	1.7	(0.62)
Spain (Asturias)	**469**	(6.5)	490	(6.2)	501	(7.9)	504	(6.0)	**15.1**	(2.94)	**1.5**	(0.13)	2.1	(0.79)
Spain (Balearic Islands)	**431**	(8.3)	459	(4.7)	474	(7.8)	472	(7.3)	**19.8**	(4.08)	**1.7**	(0.18)	3.3	(1.39)
Spain (Basque Country)	**478**	(4.1)	497	(3.6)	500	(3.8)	505	(4.0)	**12.5**	(1.79)	**1.4**	(0.09)	1.7	(0.49)
Spain (Canary Islands)	**433**	(7.4)	442	(5.7)	464	(6.4)	459	(4.7)	**11.4**	(2.88)	**1.5**	(0.19)	1.2	(0.57)
Spain (Cantabria)	**462**	(6.9)	489	(6.3)	498	(5.0)	505	(4.5)	**19.7**	(2.95)	**1.6**	(0.15)	3.8	(1.18)
Spain (Castile and Leon)	**472**	(5.4)	511	(6.5)	513	(7.2)	519	(5.1)	**18.5**	(2.46)	**1.8**	(0.19)	3.9	(0.87)
Spain (Catalonia)	**473**	(8.0)	500	(7.1)	508	(6.5)	512	(6.8)	**16.1**	(3.18)	**1.7**	(0.22)	2.4	(0.92)
Spain (Ceuta and Melilla)	**368**	(5.3)	418	(5.5)	442	(5.9)	430	(5.9)	**19.9**	(2.73)	**1.9**	(0.22)	5.0	(1.37)
Spain (Galicia)	**450**	(5.0)	489	(5.7)	502	(5.2)	505	(7.0)	**21.9**	(3.23)	**2.0**	(0.23)	6.5	(2.00)
Spain (La Rioja)	**472**	(5.4)	500	(6.6)	511	(5.5)	511	(5.7)	**17.5**	(3.24)	**1.4**	(0.16)	3.3	(1.32)
Spain (Madrid)	**487**	(6.0)	510	(6.8)	511	(5.5)	507	(6.2)	**10.8**	(3.24)	**1.4**	(0.14)	1.1	(0.60)
Spain (Murcia)	**454**	(6.5)	482	(8.0)	495	(5.4)	495	(5.4)	**15.9**	(2.97)	**1.8**	(0.26)	3.7	(1.33)
Spain (Navarre)	**475**	(6.6)	494	(5.3)	513	(5.2)	507	(5.6)	**15.9**	(3.52)	**1.7**	(0.18)	2.8	(1.23)
United Kingdom (Scotland)	**476**	(5.3)	499	(4.7)	516	(4.7)	516	(5.2)	**21.3**	(2.94)	**1.7**	(0.15)	4.0	(1.12)
Non-adjudicated														
Belgium (French Community)	**472**	(5.8)	505	(5.3)	511	(5.6)	499	(5.1)	**13.2**	(2.56)	**1.6**	(0.09)	1.2	(0.46)
Belgium (German-Speaking Community)	491	(7.4)	500	(6.4)	514	(6.5)	500	(6.3)	2.3	(4.52)	1.3	(0.19)	0.1	(0.26)
Finland (Finnish Speaking)	**519**	(3.6)	541	(3.7)	546	(4.0)	545	(3.7)	**13.9**	(1.96)	**1.4**	(0.09)	1.7	(0.46)
Finland (Swedish Speaking)	**493**	(5.3)	508	(5.7)	520	(5.2)	528	(5.7)	**19.0**	(3.68)	**1.4**	(0.16)	2.8	(1.04)
Italy (Provincia Abruzzo)	**456**	(8.9)	487	(7.7)	492	(6.3)	494	(6.1)	**12.1**	(2.56)	**1.8**	(0.22)	2.7	(1.15)
Italy (Provincia Autonoma di Bolzano)	**463**	(5.4)	497	(5.4)	502	(6.4)	499	(6.3)	**16.3**	(2.90)	**1.7**	(0.22)	3.3	(1.30)
Italy (Provincia Basilicata)	**451**	(7.8)	461	(7.0)	489	(4.8)	493	(4.7)	**13.5**	(2.86)	**1.5**	(0.17)	3.6	(1.32)
Italy (Provincia Calabria)	**419**	(7.4)	446	(6.5)	460	(5.8)	470	(7.3)	**14.0**	(2.10)	**1.7**	(0.17)	3.9	(1.04)
Italy (Provincia Campania)	**427**	(7.4)	451	(9.9)	466	(8.0)	462	(7.8)	**11.5**	(1.74)	**1.6**	(0.22)	2.4	(0.78)
Italy (Provincia Emilia Romagna)	**471**	(7.6)	506	(6.9)	520	(6.7)	515	(4.0)	**16.5**	(2.56)	**1.8**	(0.19)	3.8	(1.08)
Italy (Provincia Friuli Venezia Giulia)	**488**	(7.2)	520	(7.1)	523	(5.6)	524	(7.2)	**15.9**	(2.74)	**1.7**	(0.21)	3.8	(1.26)
Italy (Provincia Lazio)	**454**	(5.4)	483	(6.2)	497	(4.7)	493	(6.1)	**14.1**	(1.86)	**1.7**	(0.15)	3.2	(0.89)
Italy (Provincia Liguria)	**463**	(14.1)	496	(9.1)	498	(10.2)	510	(6.5)	**14.6**	(3.07)	**1.9**	(0.22)	3.0	(1.13)
Italy (Provincia Lombardia)	**500**	(9.2)	526	(6.2)	530	(6.1)	532	(7.6)	**13.0**	(2.90)	**1.6**	(0.19)	2.7	(1.28)
Italy (Provincia Marche)	**474**	(13.7)	496	(8.0)	509	(7.1)	516	(6.4)	**17.0**	(5.33)	**1.7**	(0.26)	3.9	(2.36)
Italy (Provincia Molise)	**436**	(6.7)	477	(5.8)	492	(5.4)	479	(5.1)	**14.4**	(2.17)	**2.0**	(0.21)	4.6	(1.34)
Italy (Provincia Piemonte)	**469**	(8.8)	499	(6.5)	507	(8.4)	510	(8.9)	**13.3**	(3.54)	**1.6**	(0.22)	2.8	(1.54)
Italy (Provincia Puglia)	**470**	(5.3)	487	(7.3)	499	(5.8)	503	(7.1)	**10.2**	(1.93)	**1.4**	(0.17)	2.4	(0.82)
Italy (Provincia Sardegna)	**440**	(10.0)	472	(4.8)	482	(6.0)	486	(7.7)	**15.2**	(2.86)	**1.9**	(0.27)	5.0	(1.84)
Italy (Provincia Sicilia)	**416**	(9.4)	451	(10.5)	474	(8.9)	480	(7.5)	**19.6**	(3.28)	**2.1**	(0.30)	6.2	(1.89)
Italy (Provincia Toscana)	**468**	(7.7)	497	(7.2)	508	(7.7)	505	(4.7)	**13.2**	(2.69)	**1.7**	(0.19)	2.2	(0.91)
Italy (Provincia Trento)	**488**	(5.9)	513	(7.4)	514	(5.2)	518	(5.7)	**11.4**	(2.71)	**1.6**	(0.14)	1.8	(0.90)
Italy (Provincia Umbria)	**461**	(6.6)	496	(6.5)	495	(8.5)	515	(5.6)	**18.7**	(2.92)	**1.6**	(0.16)	4.5	(1.24)
Italy (Provincia Valle d'Aosta)	506	(7.5)	518	(6.7)	515	(5.5)	517	(5.8)	3.6	(2.65)	1.2	(0.16)	0.2	(0.32)
Italy (Provincia Veneto)	**477**	(10.9)	507	(5.1)	520	(6.8)	520	(5.7)	**16.9**	(3.81)	**1.6**	(0.25)	4.7	(1.88)
United Kingdom (England)	**466**	(3.6)	501	(3.8)	510	(4.4)	507	(4.3)	**15.7**	(2.46)	**1.7**	(0.11)	2.2	(0.68)
United Kingdom (Northern Ireland)	**470**	(7.3)	507	(5.4)	514	(4.2)	512	(5.3)	**17.2**	(2.80)	**1.6**	(0.15)	2.5	(0.75)
United Kingdom (Wales)	**448**	(4.9)	477	(3.8)	489	(5.0)	494	(4.5)	**17.9**	(2.28)	**1.7**	(0.12)	3.2	(0.82)

Notes: Values that are statistically significant are indicated in bold (see Annex A3). See Table III.2.12 for national data.
StatLink ⫘⫘⫘ http://dx.doi.org/10.1787/888932343304

[Part 1/2]

Table S.III.g **Effect sizes for gender differences in engagement in reading and approaches to learning**

Effect size in favour of boys:
- from 0.2 to 0.5
- from 0.5 to 0.8
- equal or greater than 0.8

Effect size in favour of girls:
- from -0.2 to -0.5
- from -0.5 to -0.8
- equal or less than -0.8

	Enjoyment of reading		Diversity of reading activities		Online reading activities		Interpretation of literary texts		Use of texts containing non-continuous materials		Reading activities for traditional literature courses	
	Effect size	S.E.	Effect size	S.E.	Effect size	S.E.	Effect size	S.E.	Effect size	S.E.	Effect size	S.E.
Adjudicated												
Belgium (Flemish Community)	**-0.60**	(0.04)	**-0.20**	(0.04)	**0.09**	(0.04)	**-0.08**	(0.04)	0.04	(0.04)	-0.02	(0.04)
Spain (Andalusia)	**-0.52**	(0.05)	**0.12**	(0.05)	**0.15**	(0.05)	**-0.27**	(0.05)	0.02	(0.06)	**-0.20**	(0.05)
Spain (Aragon)	**-0.53**	(0.06)	-0.08	(0.06)	0.00	(0.05)	**-0.30**	(0.06)	-0.04	(0.05)	**-0.27**	(0.06)
Spain (Asturias)	**-0.56**	(0.06)	-0.07	(0.06)	0.01	(0.05)	**-0.33**	(0.06)	0.06	(0.05)	**-0.20**	(0.07)
Spain (Balearic Islands)	**-0.62**	(0.06)	**-0.19**	(0.07)	0.00	(0.05)	**-0.34**	(0.04)	0.04	(0.05)	**-0.26**	(0.05)
Spain (Basque Country)	**-0.58**	(0.03)	-0.03	(0.03)	0.02	(0.03)	**-0.29**	(0.03)	0.00	(0.04)	**-0.23**	(0.03)
Spain (Canary Islands)	**-0.51**	(0.06)	-0.08	(0.05)	**0.22**	(0.05)	**-0.28**	(0.04)	0.08	(0.06)	**-0.14**	(0.06)
Spain (Cantabria)	**-0.47**	(0.06)	**-0.15**	(0.04)	-0.05	(0.03)	**-0.35**	(0.04)	-0.05	(0.05)	**-0.19**	(0.04)
Spain (Castile and Leon)	**-0.62**	(0.06)	-0.09	(0.07)	0.03	(0.05)	**-0.38**	(0.04)	**0.16**	(0.06)	**-0.23**	(0.06)
Spain (Catalonia)	**-0.61**	(0.07)	-0.10	(0.06)	**0.13**	(0.06)	**-0.25**	(0.07)	0.09	(0.06)	**-0.20**	(0.06)
Spain (Ceuta and Melilla)	**-0.54**	(0.05)	-0.04	(0.06)	**0.13**	(0.06)	**-0.23**	(0.06)	0.06	(0.07)	**-0.11**	(0.05)
Spain (Galicia)	**-0.65**	(0.06)	-0.07	(0.06)	0.06	(0.04)	**-0.23**	(0.05)	0.01	(0.05)	**-0.23**	(0.06)
Spain (La Rioja)	**-0.50**	(0.07)	0.04	(0.06)	0.01	(0.07)	**-0.30**	(0.07)	0.04	(0.05)	**-0.13**	(0.06)
Spain (Madrid)	**-0.70**	(0.07)	-0.04	(0.06)	0.14	(0.08)	**-0.24**	(0.06)	0.09	(0.07)	**-0.12**	(0.06)
Spain (Murcia)	**-0.55**	(0.05)	0.06	(0.06)	**0.19**	(0.07)	**-0.25**	(0.05)	0.00	(0.05)	**-0.30**	(0.06)
Spain (Navarre)	**-0.52**	(0.07)	**-0.21**	(0.06)	-0.02	(0.06)	**-0.26**	(0.05)	0.02	(0.07)	**-0.26**	(0.05)
United Kingdom (Scotland)	**-0.45**	(0.04)	**-0.20**	(0.05)	0.01	(0.03)	**-0.15**	(0.04)	0.04	(0.04)	**-0.08**	(0.03)
Non-adjudicated												
Belgium (French Community)	**-0.47**	(0.05)	**0.11**	(0.04)	**0.12**	(0.04)	**-0.11**	(0.04)	-0.02	(0.05)	-0.08	(0.05)
Belgium (German-Speaking Community)	**-0.78**	(0.06)	**-0.26**	(0.06)	0.09	(0.07)	**-0.20**	(0.06)	**0.16**	(0.07)	**-0.27**	(0.07)
Finland (Finnish Speaking)	**-0.97**	(0.03)	**-0.23**	(0.03)	**0.13**	(0.03)	**-0.15**	(0.03)	-0.02	(0.03)	**-0.08**	(0.03)
Finland (Swedish Speaking)	**-1.01**	(0.06)	**-0.27**	(0.05)	0.00	(0.06)	**-0.29**	(0.06)	-0.09	(0.06)	0.03	(0.06)
Italy (Provincia Abruzzo)	**-0.78**	(0.07)	**-0.22**	(0.05)	0.02	(0.06)	**-0.18**	(0.07)	0.00	(0.08)	**-0.26**	(0.07)
Italy (Provincia Autonoma di Bolzano)	**-0.82**	(0.05)	**-0.17**	(0.05)	-0.05	(0.07)	**-0.32**	(0.05)	**0.18**	(0.06)	-0.06	(0.05)
Italy (Provincia Basilicata)	**-1.00**	(0.08)	**-0.23**	(0.06)	0.05	(0.06)	**-0.35**	(0.08)	**0.22**	(0.06)	**-0.17**	(0.07)
Italy (Provincia Calabria)	**-0.92**	(0.07)	**-0.26**	(0.07)	0.04	(0.07)	**-0.34**	(0.07)	**0.18**	(0.08)	**-0.31**	(0.07)
Italy (Provincia Campania)	**-0.73**	(0.06)	**-0.19**	(0.06)	0.08	(0.06)	**-0.38**	(0.05)	**0.19**	(0.05)	**-0.28**	(0.06)
Italy (Provincia Emilia Romagna)	**-0.66**	(0.07)	-0.05	(0.05)	-0.04	(0.05)	**-0.14**	(0.06)	**0.15**	(0.06)	**-0.14**	(0.07)
Italy (Provincia Friuli Venezia Giulia)	**-0.93**	(0.06)	**-0.30**	(0.05)	-0.08	(0.05)	**-0.27**	(0.06)	**0.21**	(0.05)	**-0.26**	(0.05)
Italy (Provincia Lazio)	**-0.79**	(0.07)	**-0.13**	(0.05)	0.07	(0.07)	**-0.24**	(0.07)	**0.19**	(0.06)	**-0.32**	(0.06)
Italy (Provincia Liguria)	**-0.64**	(0.07)	-0.11	(0.09)	-0.09	(0.09)	**-0.14**	(0.05)	**0.20**	(0.06)	**-0.23**	(0.05)
Italy (Provincia Lombardia)	**-0.84**	(0.06)	**-0.17**	(0.06)	-0.05	(0.04)	**-0.17**	(0.07)	**0.14**	(0.05)	**-0.25**	(0.08)
Italy (Provincia Marche)	**-0.95**	(0.08)	**-0.23**	(0.10)	-0.02	(0.09)	**-0.16**	(0.05)	**0.25**	(0.07)	**-0.12**	(0.06)
Italy (Provincia Molise)	**-0.89**	(0.07)	**-0.27**	(0.07)	-0.06	(0.06)	**-0.17**	(0.07)	**0.18**	(0.06)	**-0.20**	(0.07)
Italy (Provincia Piemonte)	**-0.67**	(0.06)	**-0.21**	(0.07)	0.07	(0.06)	**-0.25**	(0.06)	0.08	(0.06)	**-0.19**	(0.07)
Italy (Provincia Puglia)	**-0.74**	(0.06)	**-0.25**	(0.04)	0.07	(0.05)	**-0.25**	(0.08)	**0.18**	(0.07)	**-0.22**	(0.07)
Italy (Provincia Sardegna)	**-0.73**	(0.07)	**-0.26**	(0.07)	0.00	(0.06)	**-0.24**	(0.06)	**0.24**	(0.07)	**-0.21**	(0.06)
Italy (Provincia Sicilia)	**-0.66**	(0.08)	**-0.23**	(0.04)	0.06	(0.07)	**-0.33**	(0.08)	**0.30**	(0.07)	**-0.30**	(0.08)
Italy (Provincia Toscana)	**-0.83**	(0.08)	**-0.29**	(0.06)	0.08	(0.06)	**-0.30**	(0.05)	**0.12**	(0.06)	**-0.24**	(0.06)
Italy (Provincia Trento)	**-0.73**	(0.06)	**-0.26**	(0.08)	-0.03	(0.06)	**-0.16**	(0.06)	**0.29**	(0.06)	-0.13	(0.08)
Italy (Provincia Umbria)	**-0.79**	(0.06)	**-0.15**	(0.05)	0.00	(0.05)	**-0.20**	(0.08)	**0.18**	(0.06)	-0.09	(0.05)
Italy (Provincia Valle d'Aosta)	**-0.70**	(0.06)	0.04	(0.06)	0.08	(0.07)	**-0.19**	(0.06)	0.12	(0.07)	-0.12	(0.07)
Italy (Provincia Veneto)	**-0.88**	(0.08)	**-0.31**	(0.09)	-0.10	(0.08)	**-0.19**	(0.08)	**0.22**	(0.06)	**-0.32**	(0.11)
United Kingdom (England)	**-0.54**	(0.04)	**-0.20**	(0.03)	**0.06**	(0.03)	**-0.17**	(0.04)	0.00	(0.03)	-0.06	(0.04)
United Kingdom (Northern Ireland)	**-0.45**	(0.05)	**-0.19**	(0.05)	0.08	(0.04)	**-0.20**	(0.05)	0.00	(0.04)	**-0.15**	(0.05)
United Kingdom (Wales)	**-0.57**	(0.04)	**-0.20**	(0.04)	0.03	(0.04)	-0.05	(0.03)	**0.10**	(0.04)	**-0.08**	(0.04)

Notes: Values that are statistically significant are indicated in bold (see Annex A3). See Table III.2.13 for national data.
StatLink ⟨⟩ http://dx.doi.org/10.1787/888932343304

[Part 2/2]

Table S.III.g **Effect sizes for gender differences in engagement in reading and approaches to learning**

Effect size in favour of boys:
- from 0.2 to 0.5
- from 0.5 to 0.8
- equal or greater than 0.8

Effect size in favour of girls:
- from -0.2 to -0.5
- from -0.5 to -0.8
- equal or less than -0.8

	Use of functional texts		Memorisation strategies		Elaboration strategies		Control strategies		Understanding and remembering		Summarising	
	Effect size	S.E.	Effect size	S.E.	Effect size	S.E.	Effect size	S.E.	Effect size	S.E.	Effect size	S.E.
Adjudicated												
Belgium (Flemish Community)	**0.08**	(0.03)	**-0.13**	(0.03)	**0.16**	(0.03)	**-0.20**	(0.04)	**-0.22**	(0.05)	**-0.28**	(0.05)
Spain (Andalusia)	0.06	(0.05)	**-0.10**	(0.05)	**0.14**	(0.07)	**-0.22**	(0.06)	**-0.24**	(0.06)	**-0.31**	(0.05)
Spain (Aragon)	0.03	(0.06)	**-0.19**	(0.05)	0.11	(0.06)	**-0.25**	(0.06)	**-0.20**	(0.06)	**-0.33**	(0.05)
Spain (Asturias)	0.02	(0.07)	**-0.27**	(0.06)	0.12	(0.06)	**-0.34**	(0.06)	**-0.37**	(0.05)	**-0.28**	(0.06)
Spain (Balearic Islands)	-0.01	(0.07)	**-0.28**	(0.04)	0.10	(0.05)	**-0.35**	(0.04)	**-0.12**	(0.05)	**-0.22**	(0.07)
Spain (Basque Country)	0.04	(0.03)	**-0.25**	(0.04)	**0.09**	(0.03)	**-0.24**	(0.04)	**-0.18**	(0.04)	**-0.34**	(0.03)
Spain (Canary Islands)	0.08	(0.05)	**-0.13**	(0.05)	0.04	(0.05)	**-0.29**	(0.05)	**-0.19**	(0.05)	**-0.16**	(0.05)
Spain (Cantabria)	0.01	(0.06)	**-0.12**	(0.05)	**0.09**	(0.04)	**-0.21**	(0.05)	**-0.16**	(0.06)	**-0.28**	(0.06)
Spain (Castile and Leon)	-0.01	(0.04)	**-0.21**	(0.07)	0.07	(0.06)	**-0.26**	(0.06)	**-0.29**	(0.05)	**-0.31**	(0.06)
Spain (Catalonia)	-0.02	(0.05)	**-0.23**	(0.06)	0.09	(0.06)	**-0.30**	(0.05)	**-0.27**	(0.06)	**-0.37**	(0.05)
Spain (Ceuta and Melilla)	0.08	(0.07)	**-0.11**	(0.05)	0.08	(0.06)	**-0.21**	(0.05)	**-0.16**	(0.06)	**-0.24**	(0.05)
Spain (Galicia)	0.09	(0.05)	**-0.26**	(0.06)	0.05	(0.05)	**-0.25**	(0.05)	**-0.19**	(0.06)	**-0.32**	(0.05)
Spain (La Rioja)	**0.20**	(0.06)	**-0.15**	(0.06)	0.06	(0.06)	**-0.24**	(0.06)	**-0.33**	(0.06)	**-0.40**	(0.05)
Spain (Madrid)	**0.12**	(0.05)	**-0.13**	(0.06)	0.07	(0.07)	**-0.30**	(0.06)	**-0.32**	(0.05)	**-0.46**	(0.05)
Spain (Murcia)	**0.14**	(0.05)	**-0.18**	(0.06)	**0.20**	(0.05)	**-0.19**	(0.05)	**-0.19**	(0.05)	**-0.34**	(0.06)
Spain (Navarre)	0.03	(0.06)	**-0.28**	(0.05)	0.09	(0.06)	**-0.37**	(0.06)	**-0.23**	(0.06)	**-0.19**	(0.05)
United Kingdom (Scotland)	**0.10**	(0.04)	**-0.17**	(0.04)	**0.11**	(0.04)	**-0.17**	(0.04)	**-0.20**	(0.05)	**-0.18**	(0.04)
Non-adjudicated												
Belgium (French Community)	-0.09	(0.05)	**-0.27**	(0.04)	**0.19**	(0.04)	**-0.26**	(0.05)	**-0.25**	(0.04)	**-0.24**	(0.04)
Belgium (German-Speaking Community)	-0.05	(0.07)	**-0.27**	(0.07)	**0.34**	(0.06)	**-0.42**	(0.06)	**-0.52**	(0.06)	**-0.50**	(0.07)
Finland (Finnish Speaking)	**0.09**	(0.03)	**-0.19**	(0.03)	0.04	(0.03)	**-0.24**	(0.03)	**-0.57**	(0.03)	**-0.65**	(0.03)
Finland (Swedish Speaking)	0.08	(0.06)	**-0.16**	(0.05)	**0.16**	(0.05)	**-0.28**	(0.05)	**-0.61**	(0.06)	**-0.59**	(0.06)
Italy (Provincia Abruzzo)	0.04	(0.05)	**-0.21**	(0.06)	0.03	(0.06)	**-0.43**	(0.05)	**-0.31**	(0.07)	**-0.35**	(0.06)
Italy (Provincia Autonoma di Bolzano)	0.04	(0.05)	**-0.14**	(0.05)	**0.19**	(0.06)	**-0.34**	(0.06)	**-0.45**	(0.05)	**-0.42**	(0.05)
Italy (Provincia Basilicata)	**0.18**	(0.06)	**-0.13**	(0.06)	0.07	(0.05)	**-0.47**	(0.06)	**-0.26**	(0.05)	**-0.43**	(0.06)
Italy (Provincia Calabria)	**0.21**	(0.06)	**-0.26**	(0.05)	-0.08	(0.06)	**-0.55**	(0.05)	**-0.33**	(0.07)	**-0.36**	(0.07)
Italy (Provincia Campania)	**0.16**	(0.07)	**-0.10**	(0.05)	0.13	(0.07)	**-0.43**	(0.06)	**-0.26**	(0.07)	**-0.29**	(0.07)
Italy (Provincia Emilia Romagna)	**0.12**	(0.06)	**-0.21**	(0.06)	0.09	(0.06)	**-0.31**	(0.06)	**-0.23**	(0.09)	**-0.27**	(0.07)
Italy (Provincia Friuli Venezia Giulia)	**0.29**	(0.08)	**-0.22**	(0.09)	0.04	(0.05)	**-0.45**	(0.06)	**-0.42**	(0.06)	**-0.45**	(0.06)
Italy (Provincia Lazio)	0.12	(0.07)	**-0.36**	(0.05)	-0.03	(0.05)	**-0.61**	(0.07)	**-0.37**	(0.06)	**-0.36**	(0.07)
Italy (Provincia Liguria)	0.11	(0.10)	**-0.18**	(0.06)	0.05	(0.07)	**-0.42**	(0.09)	**-0.33**	(0.08)	**-0.42**	(0.07)
Italy (Provincia Lombardia)	0.17	(0.11)	**-0.24**	(0.05)	-0.05	(0.06)	**-0.41**	(0.07)	**-0.33**	(0.05)	**-0.24**	(0.06)
Italy (Provincia Marche)	**0.16**	(0.07)	**-0.24**	(0.07)	0.07	(0.07)	**-0.41**	(0.10)	**-0.35**	(0.05)	**-0.34**	(0.07)
Italy (Provincia Molise)	**0.31**	(0.06)	**-0.18**	(0.07)	**0.18**	(0.07)	**-0.49**	(0.06)	**-0.46**	(0.06)	**-0.43**	(0.07)
Italy (Provincia Piemonte)	**0.17**	(0.08)	**-0.34**	(0.05)	-0.01	(0.05)	**-0.39**	(0.08)	**-0.22**	(0.07)	**-0.28**	(0.07)
Italy (Provincia Puglia)	0.10	(0.06)	**-0.14**	(0.06)	0.07	(0.05)	**-0.55**	(0.05)	**-0.29**	(0.05)	**-0.28**	(0.06)
Italy (Provincia Sardegna)	**0.27**	(0.06)	**-0.11**	(0.07)	0.11	(0.06)	**-0.37**	(0.06)	**-0.39**	(0.07)	**-0.36**	(0.09)
Italy (Provincia Sicilia)	**0.27**	(0.06)	**-0.19**	(0.07)	**0.19**	(0.06)	**-0.45**	(0.06)	**-0.25**	(0.06)	**-0.18**	(0.07)
Italy (Provincia Toscana)	**0.15**	(0.07)	**-0.17**	(0.05)	**0.09**	(0.04)	**-0.49**	(0.06)	**-0.35**	(0.09)	**-0.45**	(0.06)
Italy (Provincia Trento)	**0.19**	(0.05)	**-0.24**	(0.05)	**0.13**	(0.06)	**-0.43**	(0.07)	**-0.41**	(0.07)	**-0.43**	(0.07)
Italy (Provincia Umbria)	0.09	(0.07)	**-0.17**	(0.06)	0.06	(0.05)	**-0.39**	(0.05)	**-0.27**	(0.07)	**-0.35**	(0.05)
Italy (Provincia Valle d'Aosta)	**0.19**	(0.07)	**-0.23**	(0.08)	0.10	(0.07)	**-0.22**	(0.07)	**-0.34**	(0.06)	**-0.26**	(0.07)
Italy (Provincia Veneto)	**0.16**	(0.06)	**-0.23**	(0.05)	-0.04	(0.05)	**-0.54**	(0.09)	**-0.34**	(0.09)	**-0.35**	(0.10)
United Kingdom (England)	-0.05	(0.04)	**-0.12**	(0.03)	**0.13**	(0.04)	**-0.17**	(0.03)	**-0.22**	(0.04)	**-0.24**	(0.04)
United Kingdom (Northern Ireland)	0.01	(0.06)	**-0.24**	(0.05)	**0.10**	(0.04)	**-0.28**	(0.05)	**-0.15**	(0.05)	**-0.26**	(0.07)
United Kingdom (Wales)	0.04	(0.03)	**-0.23**	(0.03)	**0.15**	(0.03)	**-0.22**	(0.04)	**-0.16**	(0.04)	**-0.23**	(0.04)

Notes: Values that are statistically significant are indicated in bold (see Annex A3). See Table III.2.13 for national data.

StatLink ᴍᴵᔕᴸ http://dx.doi.org/10.1787/888932343304

[Part 1/2]

Table S.III.h **Effect sizes for socio-economic differences in engagement in reading and approaches to learning[1]**

Effect size in favour of students with a high socio-economic background:
- from 0.2 to 0.5
- from 0.5 to 0.8
- equal or greater than 0.8

Effect size in favour of students with a low socio-economic background:
- from -0.2 to -0.5
- from -0.5 to -0.8
- equal or less than -0.8

	Enjoyment of reading		Diversity of reading activities		Online reading activities		Interpretation of literary texts		Use of texts containing non-continuous materials		Reading activities for traditional literature courses	
	Effect size	S.E.	Effect size	S.E.	Effect size	S.E.	Effect size	S.E.	Effect size	S.E.	Effect size	S.E.
Adjudicated												
Belgium (Flemish Community)	0.53	(0.04)	0.56	(0.05)	0.33	(0.04)	0.30	(0.05)	0.01	(0.05)	0.40	(0.05)
Spain (Andalusia)	0.64	(0.07)	0.68	(0.07)	0.64	(0.07)	0.33	(0.08)	0.26	(0.13)	0.27	(0.10)
Spain (Aragon)	0.49	(0.07)	0.47	(0.09)	0.48	(0.06)	0.20	(0.11)	0.05	(0.13)	0.54	(0.09)
Spain (Asturias)	0.51	(0.07)	0.49	(0.08)	0.37	(0.08)	0.06	(0.07)	0.10	(0.10)	0.30	(0.09)
Spain (Balearic Islands)	0.31	(0.06)	0.43	(0.06)	0.28	(0.08)	0.23	(0.08)	0.03	(0.09)	0.23	(0.11)
Spain (Basque Country)	0.40	(0.05)	0.51	(0.04)	0.28	(0.04)	0.22	(0.05)	0.04	(0.05)	0.30	(0.05)
Spain (Canary Islands)	0.50	(0.10)	0.62	(0.08)	0.54	(0.07)	0.30	(0.11)	0.12	(0.09)	0.44	(0.10)
Spain (Cantabria)	0.69	(0.06)	0.60	(0.07)	0.46	(0.10)	0.26	(0.11)	0.14	(0.08)	0.41	(0.09)
Spain (Castile and Leon)	0.52	(0.09)	0.50	(0.09)	0.49	(0.08)	0.13	(0.08)	0.10	(0.09)	0.24	(0.07)
Spain (Catalonia)	0.28	(0.09)	0.47	(0.06)	0.38	(0.08)	0.10	(0.08)	0.12	(0.07)	0.12	(0.08)
Spain (Ceuta and Melilla)	0.17	(0.09)	0.21	(0.07)	0.83	(0.08)	0.31	(0.08)	0.20	(0.08)	0.15	(0.08)
Spain (Galicia)	0.57	(0.08)	0.61	(0.07)	0.70	(0.09)	0.22	(0.08)	0.18	(0.08)	0.30	(0.08)
Spain (La Rioja)	0.56	(0.06)	0.53	(0.07)	0.43	(0.09)	0.18	(0.07)	-0.02	(0.08)	0.21	(0.09)
Spain (Madrid)	0.39	(0.07)	0.45	(0.06)	0.12	(0.08)	0.24	(0.09)	-0.25	(0.09)	0.35	(0.10)
Spain (Murcia)	0.55	(0.11)	0.61	(0.08)	0.79	(0.08)	0.24	(0.09)	0.02	(0.08)	0.29	(0.07)
Spain (Navarre)	0.45	(0.11)	0.49	(0.08)	0.32	(0.09)	0.06	(0.07)	0.04	(0.10)	0.33	(0.10)
United Kingdom (Scotland)	0.68	(0.07)	0.35	(0.06)	0.43	(0.07)	0.36	(0.06)	0.40	(0.06)	0.07	(0.06)
Non-adjudicated												
Belgium (French Community)	0.67	(0.06)	0.53	(0.06)	0.33	(0.05)	0.29	(0.06)	0.26	(0.06)	0.45	(0.06)
Belgium (German-Speaking Community)	0.54	(0.11)	0.49	(0.12)	0.44	(0.11)	0.29	(0.10)	0.34	(0.09)	0.31	(0.10)
Finland (Finnish Speaking)	0.46	(0.05)	0.48	(0.04)	0.31	(0.05)	0.26	(0.05)	0.36	(0.05)	0.15	(0.05)
Finland (Swedish Speaking)	0.46	(0.08)	0.52	(0.08)	0.49	(0.08)	0.20	(0.09)	0.21	(0.08)	-0.01	(0.08)
Italy (Provincia Abruzzo)	0.57	(0.09)	0.56	(0.08)	0.58	(0.06)	0.19	(0.10)	-0.15	(0.11)	0.34	(0.12)
Italy (Provincia Autonoma di Bolzano)	0.44	(0.09)	0.43	(0.09)	0.80	(0.06)	0.17	(0.08)	0.18	(0.08)	0.16	(0.08)
Italy (Provincia Basilicata)	0.48	(0.07)	0.37	(0.07)	0.82	(0.07)	0.01	(0.08)	0.06	(0.08)	0.09	(0.10)
Italy (Provincia Calabria)	0.50	(0.09)	0.48	(0.10)	0.88	(0.07)	0.30	(0.09)	-0.21	(0.07)	0.29	(0.10)
Italy (Provincia Campania)	0.61	(0.12)	0.55	(0.09)	0.68	(0.08)	0.16	(0.08)	0.02	(0.09)	0.25	(0.11)
Italy (Provincia Emilia Romagna)	0.67	(0.09)	0.80	(0.10)	0.60	(0.07)	0.31	(0.09)	-0.01	(0.06)	0.59	(0.08)
Italy (Provincia Friuli Venezia Giulia)	0.44	(0.08)	0.44	(0.09)	0.58	(0.06)	0.26	(0.07)	-0.02	(0.07)	0.39	(0.09)
Italy (Provincia Lazio)	0.50	(0.10)	0.57	(0.10)	0.63	(0.07)	0.19	(0.09)	-0.11	(0.09)	0.28	(0.10)
Italy (Provincia Liguria)	0.38	(0.13)	0.57	(0.07)	0.59	(0.09)	0.19	(0.07)	-0.32	(0.09)	0.49	(0.08)
Italy (Provincia Lombardia)	0.35	(0.11)	0.57	(0.09)	0.64	(0.08)	0.32	(0.10)	0.03	(0.10)	0.42	(0.08)
Italy (Provincia Marche)	0.28	(0.06)	0.46	(0.09)	0.51	(0.09)	0.09	(0.09)	-0.15	(0.10)	0.34	(0.08)
Italy (Provincia Molise)	0.40	(0.09)	0.55	(0.09)	0.81	(0.10)	0.27	(0.09)	-0.13	(0.09)	0.34	(0.09)
Italy (Provincia Piemonte)	0.69	(0.10)	0.80	(0.08)	0.64	(0.07)	0.19	(0.08)	-0.15	(0.08)	0.40	(0.12)
Italy (Provincia Puglia)	0.48	(0.09)	0.53	(0.08)	0.78	(0.08)	0.20	(0.10)	-0.09	(0.07)	0.27	(0.08)
Italy (Provincia Sardegna)	0.42	(0.08)	0.49	(0.08)	0.83	(0.08)	0.01	(0.08)	-0.01	(0.12)	0.39	(0.08)
Italy (Provincia Sicilia)	0.60	(0.07)	0.53	(0.10)	0.78	(0.10)	0.10	(0.10)	0.06	(0.08)	0.30	(0.12)
Italy (Provincia Toscana)	0.45	(0.07)	0.48	(0.08)	0.38	(0.08)	0.09	(0.08)	0.01	(0.09)	0.10	(0.08)
Italy (Provincia Trento)	0.45	(0.11)	0.46	(0.10)	0.53	(0.09)	0.23	(0.09)	-0.05	(0.10)	0.44	(0.09)
Italy (Provincia Umbria)	0.62	(0.08)	0.54	(0.06)	0.66	(0.07)	0.27	(0.11)	0.06	(0.08)	0.24	(0.09)
Italy (Provincia Valle d'Aosta)	0.58	(0.11)	0.66	(0.09)	0.62	(0.08)	0.22	(0.07)	0.03	(0.09)	0.34	(0.09)
Italy (Provincia Veneto)	0.56	(0.12)	0.60	(0.08)	0.68	(0.09)	0.31	(0.07)	-0.09	(0.09)	0.39	(0.08)
United Kingdom (England)	0.58	(0.05)	0.22	(0.05)	0.36	(0.05)	0.32	(0.05)	0.41	(0.05)	0.05	(0.05)
United Kingdom (Northern Ireland)	0.51	(0.06)	0.20	(0.06)	0.45	(0.08)	0.35	(0.08)	0.45	(0.07)	0.18	(0.07)
United Kingdom (Wales)	0.57	(0.06)	0.29	(0.06)	0.55	(0.05)	0.24	(0.05)	0.41	(0.05)	0.19	(0.06)

Notes: Values that are statistically significant are indicated in bold (see Annex A3). See Table III.2.13 for national data.
1. Top minus bottom quarter of the PISA index of economic, social and cultural status (ESCS).
StatLink ᵐˢ⁴ http://dx.doi.org/10.1787/888932343304

[Part 2/2]

Effect sizes for socio-economic differences in engagement in reading and approaches to learning[1]

Table S.III.h

Effect size in favour of students with a high socio-economic background:
- from 0.2 to 0.5
- from 0.5 to 0.8
- equal or greater than 0.8

Effect size in favour of students with a low socio-economic background:
- from -0.2 to -0.5
- from -0.5 to -0.8
- equal or less than -0.8

	Use of functional texts		Memorisation strategies		Elaboration strategies		Control strategies		Understanding and remembering		Summarising	
	Effect size	S.E.	Effect size	S.E.	Effect size	S.E.	Effect size	S.E.	Effect size	S.E.	Effect size	S.E.
Adjudicated												
Belgium (Flemish Community)	-0.36	(0.05)	-0.20	(0.05)	0.24	(0.05)	0.51	(0.05)	0.58	(0.06)	0.63	(0.05)
Spain (Andalusia)	-0.10	(0.10)	0.22	(0.10)	0.56	(0.09)	0.63	(0.09)	0.24	(0.09)	0.34	(0.05)
Spain (Aragon)	-0.09	(0.07)	0.03	(0.07)	0.44	(0.07)	0.53	(0.07)	0.00	(0.07)	0.32	(0.07)
Spain (Asturias)	-0.26	(0.09)	0.09	(0.07)	0.52	(0.06)	0.59	(0.06)	0.19	(0.08)	0.28	(0.09)
Spain (Balearic Islands)	-0.22	(0.07)	0.19	(0.09)	0.37	(0.07)	0.47	(0.12)	0.29	(0.10)	0.39	(0.11)
Spain (Basque Country)	-0.04	(0.04)	0.04	(0.05)	0.36	(0.04)	0.50	(0.04)	0.29	(0.05)	0.40	(0.05)
Spain (Canary Islands)	0.00	(0.07)	0.13	(0.09)	0.35	(0.08)	0.44	(0.08)	0.20	(0.09)	0.38	(0.11)
Spain (Cantabria)	-0.16	(0.10)	-0.04	(0.10)	0.45	(0.08)	0.57	(0.06)	0.32	(0.08)	0.55	(0.08)
Spain (Castile and Leon)	-0.21	(0.07)	0.14	(0.08)	0.43	(0.07)	0.49	(0.07)	0.24	(0.07)	0.31	(0.07)
Spain (Catalonia)	-0.26	(0.09)	-0.04	(0.07)	0.49	(0.07)	0.62	(0.07)	0.32	(0.10)	0.39	(0.10)
Spain (Ceuta and Melilla)	-0.16	(0.09)	0.03	(0.08)	0.08	(0.08)	0.17	(0.07)	0.27	(0.08)	0.50	(0.07)
Spain (Galicia)	0.11	(0.07)	0.16	(0.08)	0.39	(0.07)	0.43	(0.07)	0.19	(0.09)	0.17	(0.07)
Spain (La Rioja)	-0.25	(0.08)	0.03	(0.09)	0.16	(0.09)	0.41	(0.08)	0.35	(0.08)	0.30	(0.08)
Spain (Madrid)	-0.17	(0.06)	-0.16	(0.10)	0.25	(0.08)	0.53	(0.08)	0.26	(0.07)	0.51	(0.09)
Spain (Murcia)	-0.04	(0.09)	0.08	(0.08)	0.40	(0.10)	0.44	(0.11)	0.16	(0.07)	0.24	(0.08)
Spain (Navarre)	-0.07	(0.08)	-0.04	(0.07)	0.36	(0.09)	0.56	(0.09)	0.39	(0.08)	0.35	(0.08)
United Kingdom (Scotland)	0.03	(0.05)	0.14	(0.06)	0.31	(0.05)	0.57	(0.05)	0.49	(0.06)	0.54	(0.06)
Non-adjudicated												
Belgium (French Community)	-0.22	(0.05)	-0.10	(0.07)	0.05	(0.06)	0.60	(0.06)	0.71	(0.06)	0.75	(0.07)
Belgium (German-Speaking Community)	-0.18	(0.11)	0.08	(0.09)	0.23	(0.10)	0.50	(0.10)	0.45	(0.11)	0.36	(0.10)
Finland (Finnish Speaking)	0.03	(0.05)	0.20	(0.04)	0.38	(0.04)	0.50	(0.04)	0.33	(0.05)	0.44	(0.04)
Finland (Swedish Speaking)	0.01	(0.09)	0.41	(0.07)	0.41	(0.09)	0.54	(0.09)	0.49	(0.09)	0.38	(0.09)
Italy (Provincia Abruzzo)	-0.01	(0.08)	0.05	(0.09)	0.33	(0.09)	0.43	(0.09)	0.43	(0.09)	0.45	(0.10)
Italy (Provincia Autonoma di Bolzano)	-0.12	(0.07)	0.03	(0.07)	0.30	(0.07)	0.39	(0.08)	0.34	(0.09)	0.25	(0.09)
Italy (Provincia Basilicata)	-0.23	(0.10)	-0.15	(0.08)	0.39	(0.05)	0.39	(0.07)	0.35	(0.08)	0.26	(0.08)
Italy (Provincia Calabria)	-0.35	(0.09)	-0.09	(0.08)	0.28	(0.09)	0.40	(0.09)	0.41	(0.08)	0.48	(0.07)
Italy (Provincia Campania)	-0.03	(0.10)	-0.03	(0.10)	0.35	(0.08)	0.39	(0.10)	0.31	(0.09)	0.35	(0.09)
Italy (Provincia Emilia Romagna)	-0.16	(0.08)	0.01	(0.07)	0.51	(0.06)	0.67	(0.08)	0.47	(0.09)	0.53	(0.10)
Italy (Provincia Friuli Venezia Giulia)	-0.12	(0.06)	0.17	(0.08)	0.41	(0.07)	0.67	(0.10)	0.48	(0.11)	0.48	(0.14)
Italy (Provincia Lazio)	-0.30	(0.12)	0.00	(0.10)	0.39	(0.08)	0.34	(0.14)	0.28	(0.07)	0.40	(0.11)
Italy (Provincia Liguria)	-0.15	(0.07)	0.05	(0.10)	0.28	(0.07)	0.54	(0.09)	0.39	(0.10)	0.34	(0.15)
Italy (Provincia Lombardia)	-0.12	(0.11)	-0.19	(0.09)	0.39	(0.09)	0.46	(0.11)	0.39	(0.11)	0.51	(0.08)
Italy (Provincia Marche)	-0.14	(0.09)	0.05	(0.08)	0.24	(0.07)	0.34	(0.09)	0.40	(0.09)	0.46	(0.08)
Italy (Provincia Molise)	-0.21	(0.09)	0.14	(0.11)	0.31	(0.10)	0.42	(0.10)	0.51	(0.08)	0.50	(0.09)
Italy (Provincia Piemonte)	-0.20	(0.09)	0.05	(0.09)	0.34	(0.11)	0.46	(0.11)	0.51	(0.10)	0.43	(0.11)
Italy (Provincia Puglia)	-0.15	(0.06)	-0.03	(0.07)	0.41	(0.08)	0.37	(0.05)	0.27	(0.09)	0.32	(0.08)
Italy (Provincia Sardegna)	-0.15	(0.12)	0.04	(0.09)	0.36	(0.09)	0.35	(0.09)	0.37	(0.08)	0.35	(0.10)
Italy (Provincia Sicilia)	-0.20	(0.10)	-0.18	(0.09)	0.29	(0.09)	0.43	(0.10)	0.59	(0.12)	0.46	(0.13)
Italy (Provincia Toscana)	-0.12	(0.10)	-0.01	(0.08)	0.22	(0.09)	0.39	(0.05)	0.31	(0.10)	0.29	(0.09)
Italy (Provincia Trento)	-0.20	(0.08)	-0.09	(0.09)	0.30	(0.09)	0.55	(0.09)	0.43	(0.09)	0.48	(0.08)
Italy (Provincia Umbria)	-0.08	(0.08)	-0.06	(0.07)	0.45	(0.08)	0.49	(0.07)	0.35	(0.09)	0.39	(0.06)
Italy (Provincia Valle d'Aosta)	-0.25	(0.09)	0.16	(0.11)	0.42	(0.10)	0.48	(0.10)	0.40	(0.11)	0.42	(0.10)
Italy (Provincia Veneto)	-0.01	(0.10)	0.09	(0.08)	0.39	(0.08)	0.49	(0.11)	0.29	(0.09)	0.31	(0.11)
United Kingdom (England)	-0.12	(0.05)	0.16	(0.04)	0.30	(0.05)	0.54	(0.06)	0.39	(0.04)	0.52	(0.06)
United Kingdom (Northern Ireland)	-0.05	(0.07)	0.14	(0.07)	0.27	(0.07)	0.44	(0.06)	0.45	(0.08)	0.42	(0.07)
United Kingdom (Wales)	-0.09	(0.06)	0.33	(0.05)	0.32	(0.06)	0.55	(0.06)	0.41	(0.07)	0.38	(0.05)

Notes: Values that are statistically significant are indicated in bold (see Annex A3). See Table III.2.13 for national data.
1. Top minus bottom quarter of the PISA index of economic, social and cultural status (ESCS).
StatLink 🔗 http://dx.doi.org/10.1787/888932343304

[Part 1/1]

Percentage of students reading the following types of texts

Percentage of students who reported that they had to read the following types of texts for school (in the classroom or for homework) more than two times during the last month

Table S.III.i

	Read the following types of texts for school															
	Information texts about writers or books		Poetry		Texts that include diagrams or maps		Fiction (e.g., novels, short stories)		Newspaper reports and magazine articles		Instructions or manuals telling you how to make or do something (e.g., how a machine works)		Texts that include tables or graphs		Advertising material (e.g., advertisements in magazines, posters)	
	%	S.E.	%	S.E.	%	S.E.	%	S.E.	%	S.E.	%	S.E.	%	S.E.	%	S.E.
Adjudicated																
Belgium (Flemish Community)	46.7	(1.1)	36.6	(1.2)	53.9	(1.0)	54.0	(1.1)	54.5	(1.2)	25.0	(0.9)	58.2	(1.1)	35.4	(1.0)
Spain (Andalusia)	66.5	(1.8)	60.2	(2.2)	50.3	(2.3)	59.2	(2.0)	48.3	(1.7)	37.9	(1.6)	54.0	(2.2)	46.5	(1.9)
Spain (Aragon)	65.3	(1.2)	63.8	(1.7)	50.0	(1.5)	54.4	(1.6)	49.4	(2.1)	32.2	(1.4)	55.8	(1.5)	39.9	(1.5)
Spain (Asturias)	70.1	(1.3)	68.0	(1.8)	50.7	(1.9)	58.7	(1.6)	50.8	(1.9)	31.2	(1.3)	57.9	(1.9)	45.5	(1.9)
Spain (Balearic Islands)	59.6	(1.5)	57.9	(2.0)	45.2	(1.7)	54.3	(1.2)	49.5	(1.6)	29.8	(1.2)	48.4	(1.4)	39.4	(1.9)
Spain (Basque Country)	66.6	(0.9)	58.6	(1.6)	47.5	(0.9)	57.9	(0.9)	46.0	(1.2)	30.1	(0.8)	53.6	(1.0)	36.7	(0.9)
Spain (Canary Islands)	68.2	(1.6)	59.5	(1.9)	50.8	(1.5)	59.7	(1.6)	46.4	(1.8)	37.6	(1.8)	56.7	(2.0)	42.9	(1.1)
Spain (Cantabria)	67.6	(1.5)	60.3	(2.4)	51.0	(2.0)	58.4	(1.6)	50.3	(1.5)	31.4	(1.3)	53.3	(1.9)	42.4	(1.8)
Spain (Castile and Leon)	68.6	(1.4)	62.6	(2.1)	47.6	(1.5)	57.9	(2.1)	49.7	(2.0)	28.7	(1.5)	52.6	(1.6)	43.3	(1.9)
Spain (Catalonia)	66.3	(1.1)	64.0	(2.1)	52.0	(1.9)	53.3	(1.6)	44.5	(1.5)	25.6	(1.6)	57.0	(1.7)	37.3	(1.6)
Spain (Ceuta and Melilla)	69.4	(1.3)	68.3	(1.3)	54.0	(1.5)	54.9	(1.4)	51.4	(1.4)	42.6	(1.6)	60.0	(1.6)	47.3	(1.5)
Spain (Galicia)	61.8	(1.3)	57.3	(2.0)	45.9	(2.0)	56.6	(1.3)	46.6	(1.6)	28.4	(1.5)	53.3	(1.9)	37.9	(1.9)
Spain (La Rioja)	67.6	(1.4)	64.2	(1.5)	53.1	(1.7)	56.9	(1.7)	45.9	(1.5)	35.2	(1.6)	56.7	(1.6)	43.8	(1.6)
Spain (Madrid)	69.3	(1.6)	64.2	(2.4)	48.5	(1.5)	57.4	(1.5)	44.0	(2.1)	30.4	(1.7)	50.2	(1.6)	38.6	(1.8)
Spain (Murcia)	65.4	(1.6)	61.1	(1.8)	48.1	(1.7)	54.2	(1.2)	43.4	(1.4)	33.4	(1.4)	56.2	(1.5)	42.6	(1.3)
Spain (Navarre)	69.8	(1.3)	67.0	(1.7)	51.2	(1.7)	58.5	(1.2)	51.9	(1.5)	29.2	(1.5)	60.1	(1.6)	44.9	(1.4)
United Kingdom (Scotland)	53.6	(1.1)	50.1	(1.3)	53.3	(1.1)	64.0	(1.1)	35.9	(1.2)	27.6	(1.0)	67.0	(1.3)	30.0	(0.9)
Non-adjudicated																
Belgium (French Community)	60.3	(1.4)	35.4	(1.8)	67.7	(1.1)	58.3	(1.6)	49.2	(1.1)	31.8	(1.2)	70.1	(0.9)	43.1	(1.3)
Belgium (German-Speaking Community)	52.9	(1.9)	27.1	(1.4)	56.7	(1.7)	68.9	(1.7)	46.0	(1.8)	21.6	(1.5)	57.0	(1.8)	27.1	(1.8)
Finland (Finnish Speaking)	51.4	(1.1)	27.7	(1.1)	64.1	(1.0)	50.6	(1.3)	38.4	(1.1)	25.8	(0.7)	64.7	(0.8)	32.3	(0.9)
Finland (Swedish Speaking)	30.9	(1.4)	11.4	(0.9)	51.0	(1.5)	43.0	(1.6)	36.0	(1.4)	16.2	(1.0)	53.9	(1.6)	26.4	(1.3)
Italy (Provincia Abruzzo)	59.2	(1.6)	69.6	(1.8)	40.4	(1.7)	69.0	(1.8)	44.1	(2.7)	15.6	(1.2)	49.5	(1.1)	30.1	(1.3)
Italy (Provincia Autonoma di Bolzano)	42.4	(1.3)	35.2	(1.1)	42.0	(1.4)	65.7	(1.0)	51.9	(1.3)	29.0	(1.2)	46.1	(1.7)	30.5	(1.3)
Italy (Provincia Basilicata)	64.5	(1.3)	68.1	(2.1)	49.3	(2.2)	76.8	(1.3)	53.6	(2.1)	20.2	(1.5)	48.3	(1.9)	31.3	(1.6)
Italy (Provincia Calabria)	70.5	(1.7)	73.7	(1.9)	43.2	(1.6)	72.4	(1.9)	49.1	(1.9)	24.9	(1.7)	52.2	(1.9)	30.5	(2.2)
Italy (Provincia Campania)	71.1	(1.7)	75.6	(1.9)	48.5	(2.1)	79.3	(1.0)	51.3	(2.0)	23.1	(1.5)	41.9	(1.9)	21.5	(1.1)
Italy (Provincia Emilia Romagna)	50.0	(1.2)	62.9	(2.4)	37.5	(1.1)	69.7	(1.6)	41.3	(1.9)	13.1	(1.3)	47.0	(1.8)	23.2	(1.3)
Italy (Provincia Friuli Venezia Giulia)	51.8	(1.7)	55.2	(2.6)	42.8	(1.5)	71.5	(1.5)	47.5	(2.0)	18.3	(1.6)	42.1	(1.8)	22.9	(1.7)
Italy (Provincia Lazio)	57.8	(1.5)	67.3	(2.1)	43.7	(2.0)	70.1	(1.5)	38.1	(2.5)	19.2	(1.4)	42.5	(1.5)	21.2	(1.7)
Italy (Provincia Liguria)	56.4	(2.0)	68.3	(1.7)	35.9	(1.5)	72.0	(1.3)	36.9	(3.1)	15.6	(1.1)	40.8	(1.4)	23.6	(1.2)
Italy (Provincia Lombardia)	49.1	(1.7)	66.5	(2.2)	40.8	(1.5)	67.4	(1.5)	45.4	(2.1)	13.0	(1.3)	43.5	(1.5)	24.4	(1.6)
Italy (Provincia Marche)	55.1	(1.9)	64.9	(2.6)	43.4	(1.9)	74.1	(1.5)	54.6	(2.7)	15.6	(1.6)	47.5	(1.7)	30.0	(1.5)
Italy (Provincia Molise)	54.3	(1.8)	67.3	(1.4)	49.7	(1.7)	72.0	(1.4)	51.6	(1.6)	19.6	(1.1)	43.1	(1.5)	27.7	(2.0)
Italy (Provincia Piemonte)	50.5	(1.9)	58.1	(2.2)	39.2	(1.6)	71.3	(1.6)	42.9	(2.4)	17.5	(1.7)	51.0	(1.9)	34.5	(1.9)
Italy (Provincia Puglia)	67.2	(1.4)	72.8	(2.4)	50.0	(1.9)	72.9	(1.6)	54.7	(1.8)	19.4	(1.6)	45.3	(1.5)	28.0	(1.8)
Italy (Provincia Sardegna)	59.0	(1.8)	58.6	(2.2)	44.3	(1.7)	74.3	(1.7)	52.4	(2.8)	20.3	(1.5)	45.9	(2.2)	29.0	(1.8)
Italy (Provincia Sicilia)	64.1	(1.9)	68.5	(2.2)	46.0	(1.5)	72.4	(2.1)	43.7	(1.9)	24.9	(1.4)	45.9	(2.2)	21.7	(1.6)
Italy (Provincia Toscana)	56.4	(1.3)	66.1	(2.6)	42.7	(1.4)	73.2	(1.5)	40.6	(2.6)	14.3	(1.5)	48.0	(1.9)	23.0	(1.9)
Italy (Provincia Trento)	48.2	(1.2)	51.1	(1.8)	45.9	(1.4)	67.0	(1.8)	49.3	(1.4)	16.4	(1.2)	47.3	(1.3)	24.9	(1.2)
Italy (Provincia Umbria)	58.2	(2.0)	66.5	(2.3)	48.6	(1.7)	72.7	(1.6)	53.2	(2.3)	15.0	(1.2)	48.0	(1.6)	22.9	(1.1)
Italy (Provincia Valle d'Aosta)	39.4	(1.7)	44.4	(1.5)	45.2	(1.7)	68.6	(1.5)	53.0	(1.6)	16.3	(2.1)	44.0	(1.3)	25.5	(1.3)
Italy (Provincia Veneto)	47.0	(2.1)	58.0	(2.7)	43.1	(1.7)	65.6	(2.0)	44.5	(2.5)	16.3	(1.2)	44.0	(1.0)	49.0	(1.2)
United Kingdom (England)	60.5	(0.9)	68.8	(1.9)	56.8	(0.9)	61.2	(1.3)	46.4	(1.3)	23.6	(0.8)	66.4	(1.0)	49.0	(1.2)
United Kingdom (Northern Ireland)	66.5	(1.1)	61.9	(1.9)	66.3	(1.2)	60.8	(1.2)	41.5	(1.4)	31.4	(1.0)	78.2	(0.9)	47.2	(1.7)
United Kingdom (Wales)	60.9	(0.8)	56.2	(1.5)	58.6	(1.1)	65.2	(1.0)	40.2	(1.2)	30.1	(0.9)	72.9	(1.0)	44.5	(1.0)

Note: See Table III.2.1 for national data.
StatLink ⟨≡⟩ http://dx.doi.org/10.1787/888932343304

[Part 1/1]

Percentage of students doing the following tasks for school

Percentage of students who reported that they had to do the following kinds of tasks for school (in the classroom or for homework) two or more times during the last month

Table S.III.j

	Do the following tasks for school																	
	Find information from a graph, diagram or table		Explain the cause of events in a text		Explain the way characters behave in a text		Learn about the life of the writer		Explain the purpose of a text		Memorise a text by heart (e.g., a poem or part of a play)		Learn about the place of a text in the history of literature		Describe the way the information in a table or graph is organised		Explain the connection between different parts of a text	
	%	S.E.	%	S.E.	%	S.E.	%	S.E.	%	S.E.	%	S.E.	%	S.E.	%	S.E.	%	S.E.
Adjudicated																		
Belgium (Flemish Community)	52.6	(1.0)	48.8	(0.9)	44.0	(0.9)	18.0	(0.8)	57.4	(1.0)	23.3	(1.2)	29.1	(0.9)	29.1	(0.8)	28.1	(0.8)
Spain (Andalusia)	55.6	(2.2)	74.5	(1.5)	65.2	(1.3)	53.8	(2.2)	63.8	(2.0)	32.2	(2.0)	48.5	(1.9)	40.2	(1.8)	43.4	(1.6)
Spain (Aragon)	55.2	(1.9)	71.3	(1.6)	62.4	(1.5)	53.4	(2.4)	63.3	(1.6)	26.2	(2.1)	46.3	(2.1)	41.1	(1.5)	42.4	(1.3)
Spain (Asturias)	57.1	(1.7)	75.5	(1.2)	68.9	(1.7)	60.7	(1.8)	68.8	(1.4)	29.1	(1.4)	53.3	(2.0)	45.1	(1.6)	47.0	(1.5)
Spain (Balearic Islands)	45.1	(1.5)	61.7	(1.4)	57.6	(1.9)	58.2	(1.9)	63.8	(1.3)	28.3	(1.5)	50.8	(1.7)	37.4	(1.4)	37.9	(1.7)
Spain (Basque Country)	49.4	(1.3)	67.0	(0.8)	60.0	(1.2)	54.7	(1.4)	65.7	(0.9)	27.7	(0.9)	47.0	(1.2)	40.0	(1.1)	38.5	(0.9)
Spain (Canary Islands)	55.4	(1.9)	72.5	(1.4)	68.6	(1.8)	51.6	(2.2)	67.0	(1.5)	32.6	(1.4)	47.0	(2.1)	41.0	(1.2)	41.6	(1.5)
Spain (Cantabria)	50.3	(1.8)	76.8	(1.6)	69.4	(1.8)	57.3	(2.4)	71.1	(1.7)	25.5	(1.6)	50.7	(1.9)	38.5	(2.0)	42.2	(1.6)
Spain (Castile and Leon)	49.6	(1.4)	73.3	(1.6)	68.7	(1.7)	63.3	(1.5)	65.4	(2.1)	26.5	(1.6)	51.0	(1.8)	37.0	(1.3)	41.8	(1.8)
Spain (Catalonia)	51.0	(2.4)	66.3	(1.8)	60.6	(1.6)	59.3	(2.2)	67.6	(1.2)	27.0	(2.1)	54.9	(1.5)	43.4	(2.0)	39.7	(1.7)
Spain (Ceuta and Melilla)	59.2	(1.3)	76.9	(1.2)	72.1	(1.5)	61.4	(1.4)	68.0	(1.4)	42.7	(1.6)	58.7	(1.5)	48.0	(1.6)	49.6	(1.4)
Spain (Galicia)	51.3	(2.0)	73.2	(1.1)	65.2	(1.4)	60.3	(1.3)	65.2	(1.4)	25.3	(1.5)	47.9	(1.5)	39.0	(1.5)	41.7	(1.4)
Spain (La Rioja)	54.0	(1.5)	73.9	(1.3)	67.4	(1.3)	64.8	(1.5)	64.5	(1.5)	27.0	(1.4)	53.3	(1.4)	40.4	(1.5)	46.6	(1.4)
Spain (Madrid)	48.0	(1.8)	73.6	(1.4)	71.2	(1.7)	65.4	(1.7)	72.5	(1.8)	26.1	(2.2)	56.1	(1.6)	34.7	(1.6)	41.8	(1.2)
Spain (Murcia)	53.5	(2.0)	75.3	(1.2)	66.2	(1.9)	58.2	(2.5)	67.8	(2.0)	31.2	(1.9)	52.9	(1.9)	42.1	(2.1)	42.9	(1.9)
Spain (Navarre)	53.0	(1.4)	72.6	(1.5)	63.6	(1.5)	58.7	(2.0)	73.1	(1.3)	27.5	(1.4)	54.8	(1.9)	44.5	(1.4)	45.7	(1.3)
United Kingdom (Scotland)	76.8	(1.1)	64.6	(1.1)	67.0	(1.0)	18.7	(1.0)	63.0	(1.2)	29.1	(1.2)	19.3	(0.7)	44.1	(1.1)	41.6	(1.2)
Non-adjudicated																		
Belgium (French Community)	69.1	(1.1)	61.6	(1.0)	58.3	(1.5)	28.7	(1.1)	59.5	(1.1)	20.6	(1.1)	32.1	(1.1)	38.2	(1.1)	43.3	(1.1)
Belgium (German-Speaking Community)	42.9	(1.8)	49.2	(1.9)	51.5	(1.9)	29.6	(1.5)	55.8	(1.7)	13.6	(1.1)	29.9	(1.6)	26.3	(1.6)	34.4	(1.8)
Finland (Finnish Speaking)	56.2	(1.0)	50.5	(0.9)	38.0	(1.0)	30.8	(1.0)	43.2	(0.9)	11.9	(0.6)	25.2	(0.9)	23.9	(0.8)	23.3	(0.8)
Finland (Swedish Speaking)	50.9	(1.5)	37.0	(1.2)	26.1	(1.3)	18.0	(1.0)	33.8	(1.6)	11.0	(0.9)	12.1	(1.1)	19.4	(1.3)	23.7	(1.4)
Italy (Provincia Abruzzo)	32.7	(1.8)	65.8	(1.6)	70.1	(1.5)	70.9	(1.7)	69.1	(1.8)	20.3	(1.5)	45.6	(2.0)	24.6	(1.6)	33.8	(1.9)
Italy (Provincia Autonoma di Bolzano)	40.5	(1.2)	55.1	(1.4)	51.0	(1.2)	29.3	(1.1)	54.9	(1.2)	14.7	(1.0)	23.2	(0.9)	25.9	(1.1)	32.5	(1.2)
Italy (Provincia Basilicata)	38.9	(1.6)	73.6	(1.3)	75.9	(1.4)	75.3	(1.6)	77.3	(1.2)	28.0	(2.3)	50.5	(1.5)	30.7	(1.4)	42.2	(1.5)
Italy (Provincia Calabria)	41.1	(1.6)	73.0	(1.2)	73.9	(2.0)	81.0	(1.6)	75.3	(1.6)	35.2	(1.9)	52.0	(1.8)	31.3	(1.6)	39.7	(1.6)
Italy (Provincia Campania)	44.4	(1.9)	79.8	(1.1)	78.4	(1.2)	80.0	(2.1)	79.8	(1.1)	30.8	(2.3)	54.3	(2.2)	35.2	(2.0)	44.2	(1.9)
Italy (Provincia Emilia Romagna)	32.9	(1.3)	60.9	(1.5)	65.4	(1.7)	60.3	(1.9)	64.1	(1.5)	17.6	(1.4)	44.6	(1.4)	24.8	(1.4)	30.4	(1.3)
Italy (Provincia Friuli Venezia Giulia)	35.5	(1.6)	63.0	(1.2)	67.4	(2.0)	56.7	(1.8)	67.1	(1.7)	15.1	(1.3)	41.4	(1.6)	26.8	(1.7)	30.5	(1.5)
Italy (Provincia Lazio)	35.4	(1.6)	65.1	(1.6)	70.0	(1.7)	68.9	(1.5)	67.9	(1.8)	23.0	(1.7)	47.8	(1.6)	26.7	(1.6)	33.6	(1.5)
Italy (Provincia Liguria)	34.8	(1.7)	62.1	(1.5)	67.9	(1.8)	68.5	(2.7)	67.1	(1.7)	20.6	(1.4)	44.7	(1.4)	29.4	(2.1)	30.2	(1.6)
Italy (Provincia Lombardia)	34.1	(1.8)	59.3	(1.8)	62.8	(1.9)	60.5	(1.8)	69.9	(1.6)	16.9	(1.4)	40.2	(1.9)	25.4	(1.2)	31.4	(1.6)
Italy (Provincia Marche)	33.7	(1.5)	66.2	(1.7)	68.3	(1.5)	58.4	(2.1)	68.8	(1.3)	17.4	(1.2)	42.2	(1.3)	28.7	(1.7)	34.8	(1.4)
Italy (Provincia Molise)	40.2	(1.4)	65.7	(1.4)	67.9	(1.5)	66.9	(1.7)	71.8	(1.5)	25.7	(1.4)	43.2	(1.7)	32.2	(1.6)	39.4	(1.9)
Italy (Provincia Piemonte)	33.9	(1.4)	62.0	(1.9)	64.5	(1.7)	62.4	(2.8)	62.7	(1.4)	20.2	(1.4)	41.5	(1.8)	25.6	(1.2)	31.7	(1.6)
Italy (Provincia Puglia)	48.3	(2.0)	72.6	(1.6)	72.5	(1.6)	77.6	(2.0)	74.7	(1.6)	25.1	(1.5)	47.8	(1.9)	35.3	(1.9)	41.5	(1.6)
Italy (Provincia Sardegna)	39.2	(1.5)	71.7	(1.6)	73.0	(1.6)	66.9	(2.2)	69.1	(1.5)	24.7	(3.7)	48.7	(1.3)	32.2	(1.4)	38.3	(1.2)
Italy (Provincia Sicilia)	39.6	(2.3)	72.0	(1.6)	75.4	(1.8)	78.8	(1.4)	74.2	(1.4)	26.1	(2.0)	54.1	(1.8)	32.9	(2.0)	45.3	(1.7)
Italy (Provincia Toscana)	37.7	(1.6)	68.1	(1.4)	70.4	(1.5)	63.0	(2.1)	67.9	(1.7)	18.9	(1.5)	43.8	(1.6)	29.5	(1.4)	33.2	(1.9)
Italy (Provincia Trento)	38.0	(1.7)	56.4	(1.5)	58.4	(1.5)	52.3	(1.6)	59.7	(1.4)	13.1	(1.2)	35.0	(1.1)	29.4	(1.4)	28.7	(1.4)
Italy (Provincia Umbria)	37.1	(1.3)	68.7	(1.4)	71.3	(1.6)	64.4	(1.9)	72.9	(1.4)	16.4	(1.6)	47.0	(1.5)	29.9	(1.3)	39.6	(1.5)
Italy (Provincia Valle d'Aosta)	40.1	(1.6)	61.4	(1.6)	57.4	(1.5)	47.2	(1.8)	64.1	(1.5)	14.7	(0.9)	42.9	(1.4)	30.8	(1.4)	31.9	(1.7)
Italy (Provincia Veneto)	33.4	(1.7)	58.7	(1.5)	60.5	(1.9)	58.0	(2.0)	62.0	(1.6)	14.2	(1.3)	41.3	(1.5)	26.3	(1.6)	30.3	(1.3)
United Kingdom (England)	75.1	(0.8)	65.5	(0.9)	74.3	(1.0)	34.9	(1.1)	75.7	(0.9)	25.8	(1.0)	30.9	(0.9)	46.4	(1.0)	49.7	(1.0)
United Kingdom (Northern Ireland)	83.5	(1.0)	70.2	(1.1)	78.7	(1.1)	45.5	(1.7)	68.0	(1.3)	25.0	(1.4)	31.5	(1.1)	52.8	(1.5)	47.9	(1.1)
United Kingdom (Wales)	78.9	(0.8)	63.9	(0.9)	75.0	(1.0)	31.5	(1.1)	64.7	(1.0)	31.3	(1.3)	30.4	(1.0)	46.8	(0.9)	43.2	(1.0)

Note: See Table III.2.2 for national data.
StatLink ᴍᴷᴾ http://dx.doi.org/10.1787/888932343304

[Part 1/2]
Index of interpretation of literary texts and reading performance, by national quarters of this index

Table S.III.k   *Results based on students' self-reports*

	Index of interpretation of literary texts															
	All students		Males		Females		Gender difference (B – G)		Bottom quarter		Second quarter		Third quarter		Top quarter	
	Mean index	S.E.	Mean index	S.E.	Mean index	S.E.	Dif.	S.E.	Mean index	S.E.	Mean index	S.E.	Mean index	S.E.	Mean index	S.E.
Adjudicated																
Belgium (Flemish Community)	-0.29	(0.02)	-0.32	(0.03)	-0.25	(0.02)	**-0.07**	(0.03)	**-1.37**	(0.02)	**-0.54**	(0.00)	-0.06	(0.00)	**0.82**	(0.02)
Spain (Andalusia)	0.11	(0.03)	0.00	(0.03)	0.24	(0.04)	**-0.24**	(0.05)	**-0.96**	(0.03)	-0.17	(0.01)	0.31	(0.01)	**1.25**	(0.04)
Spain (Aragon)	0.02	(0.03)	-0.11	(0.05)	0.16	(0.04)	**-0.27**	(0.05)	**-1.05**	(0.03)	-0.25	(0.00)	0.23	(0.01)	**1.16**	(0.04)
Spain (Asturias)	0.19	(0.03)	0.06	(0.03)	0.35	(0.05)	**-0.29**	(0.06)	**-0.85**	(0.02)	-0.11	(0.01)	0.39	(0.01)	**1.34**	(0.03)
Spain (Balearic Islands)	-0.07	(0.02)	-0.22	(0.03)	0.08	(0.03)	**-0.31**	(0.04)	**-1.16**	(0.03)	-0.35	(0.01)	0.15	(0.01)	**1.08**	(0.03)
Spain (Basque Country)	0.02	(0.02)	-0.10	(0.02)	0.14	(0.02)	**-0.25**	(0.03)	**-1.00**	(0.02)	-0.26	(0.00)	0.20	(0.00)	**1.13**	(0.02)
Spain (Canary Islands)	0.15	(0.04)	0.02	(0.04)	0.28	(0.04)	**-0.26**	(0.04)	**-0.96**	(0.03)	-0.16	(0.01)	0.38	(0.01)	**1.34**	(0.02)
Spain (Cantabria)	0.22	(0.04)	0.07	(0.04)	0.38	(0.04)	**-0.31**	(0.04)	**-0.82**	(0.03)	-0.09	(0.01)	0.40	(0.01)	**1.38**	(0.03)
Spain (Castile and Leon)	0.12	(0.03)	-0.05	(0.04)	0.28	(0.04)	**-0.33**	(0.03)	**-0.94**	(0.03)	-0.15	(0.01)	0.31	(0.01)	**1.25**	(0.02)
Spain (Catalonia)	0.00	(0.02)	-0.10	(0.03)	0.10	(0.04)	**-0.20**	(0.06)	**-0.98**	(0.03)	-0.24	(0.01)	0.19	(0.01)	**1.01**	(0.03)
Spain (Ceuta and Melilla)	0.18	(0.03)	0.07	(0.04)	0.29	(0.04)	**-0.22**	(0.06)	**-0.93**	(0.03)	-0.10	(0.01)	0.41	(0.01)	**1.35**	(0.03)
Spain (Galicia)	0.10	(0.03)	0.00	(0.03)	0.21	(0.04)	**-0.21**	(0.05)	**-0.99**	(0.03)	-0.17	(0.01)	0.32	(0.01)	**1.26**	(0.03)
Spain (La Rioja)	0.11	(0.02)	-0.01	(0.03)	0.24	(0.04)	**-0.26**	(0.03)	**-0.90**	(0.03)	-0.18	(0.01)	0.29	(0.01)	**1.24**	(0.04)
Spain (Madrid)	0.21	(0.03)	0.10	(0.04)	0.32	(0.04)	**-0.22**	(0.06)	**-0.85**	(0.03)	-0.08	(0.01)	0.40	(0.01)	**1.37**	(0.03)
Spain (Murcia)	0.09	(0.03)	-0.02	(0.03)	0.20	(0.04)	**-0.22**	(0.04)	**-0.93**	(0.02)	-0.18	(0.01)	0.28	(0.01)	**1.20**	(0.03)
Spain (Navarre)	0.13	(0.02)	0.03	(0.03)	0.24	(0.04)	**-0.21**	(0.05)	**-0.84**	(0.03)	-0.16	(0.00)	0.28	(0.01)	**1.24**	(0.04)
United Kingdom (Scotland)	0.06	(0.02)	-0.01	(0.03)	0.12	(0.03)	**-0.14**	(0.04)	**-1.07**	(0.02)	-0.24	(0.00)	0.27	(0.01)	**1.26**	(0.02)
Non-adjudicated																
Belgium (French Community)	-0.03	(0.03)	-0.09	(0.03)	0.03	(0.04)	**-0.11**	(0.04)	**-1.24**	(0.03)	-0.32	(0.01)	0.19	(0.01)	**1.25**	(0.02)
Belgium (German-Speaking Community)	-0.15	(0.03)	-0.23	(0.05)	-0.07	(0.04)	**-0.17**	(0.05)	**-1.16**	(0.03)	-0.43	(0.01)	0.02	(0.01)	**0.95**	(0.05)
Finland (Finnish Speaking)	-0.43	(0.02)	-0.50	(0.03)	-0.36	(0.03)	**-0.14**	(0.03)	**-1.54**	(0.02)	-0.69	(0.00)	-0.19	(0.00)	**0.37**	(0.04)
Finland (Swedish Speaking)	-0.68	(0.03)	-0.81	(0.04)	-0.56	(0.03)	**-0.25**	(0.05)	**-1.75**	(0.03)	-0.90	(0.01)	-0.45	(0.01)	**0.37**	(0.04)
Italy (Provincia Abruzzo)	0.22	(0.04)	0.14	(0.05)	0.31	(0.05)	**-0.18**	(0.07)	**-0.93**	(0.05)	-0.09	(0.01)	0.45	(0.01)	**1.45**	(0.03)
Italy (Provincia Autonoma di Bolzano)	-0.14	(0.02)	-0.28	(0.03)	0.01	(0.03)	**-0.29**	(0.04)	**-1.22**	(0.03)	-0.43	(0.01)	0.08	(0.01)	**1.02**	(0.03)
Italy (Provincia Basilicata)	0.47	(0.04)	0.31	(0.04)	0.64	(0.06)	**-0.33**	(0.07)	**-0.66**	(0.02)	0.13	(0.01)	0.67	(0.01)	**1.73**	(0.02)
Italy (Provincia Calabria)	0.44	(0.04)	0.27	(0.06)	0.60	(0.04)	**-0.33**	(0.06)	**-0.72**	(0.04)	0.09	(0.01)	0.65	(0.01)	**1.73**	(0.03)
Italy (Provincia Campania)	0.65	(0.03)	0.49	(0.04)	0.86	(0.03)	**-0.37**	(0.05)	**-0.52**	(0.03)	0.22	(0.01)	0.92	(0.01)	**1.98**	(0.02)
Italy (Provincia Emilia Romagna)	0.13	(0.03)	0.06	(0.04)	0.19	(0.05)	**-0.13**	(0.06)	**-1.01**	(0.03)	-0.19	(0.01)	0.35	(0.01)	**1.36**	(0.03)
Italy (Provincia Friuli Venezia Giulia)	0.20	(0.03)	0.08	(0.05)	0.33	(0.04)	**-0.26**	(0.06)	**-0.92**	(0.03)	-0.11	(0.01)	0.39	(0.01)	**1.44**	(0.03)
Italy (Provincia Lazio)	0.27	(0.04)	0.16	(0.06)	0.40	(0.05)	**-0.24**	(0.07)	**-0.93**	(0.03)	-0.05	(0.01)	0.48	(0.01)	**1.58**	(0.03)
Italy (Provincia Liguria)	0.21	(0.03)	0.15	(0.04)	0.29	(0.04)	**-0.14**	(0.05)	**-0.97**	(0.03)	-0.13	(0.01)	0.41	(0.01)	**1.54**	(0.03)
Italy (Provincia Lombardia)	0.12	(0.04)	0.04	(0.04)	0.20	(0.06)	**-0.16**	(0.07)	**-1.00**	(0.03)	-0.21	(0.01)	0.33	(0.01)	**1.35**	(0.03)
Italy (Provincia Marche)	0.27	(0.03)	0.20	(0.04)	0.36	(0.03)	**-0.15**	(0.05)	**-0.82**	(0.03)	-0.07	(0.01)	0.43	(0.01)	**1.56**	(0.03)
Italy (Provincia Molise)	0.29	(0.03)	0.21	(0.04)	0.37	(0.05)	**-0.16**	(0.07)	**-0.83**	(0.03)	-0.09	(0.01)	0.49	(0.01)	**1.57**	(0.03)
Italy (Provincia Piemonte)	0.16	(0.04)	0.03	(0.04)	0.28	(0.05)	**-0.25**	(0.06)	**-1.02**	(0.03)	-0.17	(0.01)	0.36	(0.01)	**1.45**	(0.03)
Italy (Provincia Puglia)	0.42	(0.04)	0.30	(0.06)	0.55	(0.05)	**-0.25**	(0.07)	**-0.76**	(0.03)	0.07	(0.01)	0.62	(0.01)	**1.76**	(0.03)
Italy (Provincia Sardegna)	0.39	(0.04)	0.27	(0.05)	0.51	(0.05)	**-0.24**	(0.06)	**-0.85**	(0.03)	-0.01	(0.01)	0.65	(0.01)	**1.77**	(0.02)
Italy (Provincia Sicilia)	0.46	(0.05)	0.30	(0.07)	0.62	(0.06)	**-0.32**	(0.08)	**-0.71**	(0.03)	0.06	(0.01)	0.71	(0.01)	**1.78**	(0.02)
Italy (Provincia Toscana)	0.34	(0.04)	0.20	(0.04)	0.50	(0.04)	**-0.30**	(0.05)	**-0.82**	(0.02)	-0.06	(0.01)	0.52	(0.01)	**1.72**	(0.02)
Italy (Provincia Trento)	-0.01	(0.03)	-0.08	(0.05)	0.07	(0.04)	-0.15	(0.07)	**-1.12**	(0.03)	-0.29	(0.01)	0.18	(0.01)	**1.20**	(0.04)
Italy (Provincia Umbria)	0.33	(0.04)	0.22	(0.04)	0.43	(0.06)	**-0.20**	(0.08)	**-0.85**	(0.06)	-0.02	(0.01)	0.53	(0.01)	**1.65**	(0.03)
Italy (Provincia Valle d'Aosta)	0.06	(0.03)	-0.03	(0.04)	0.15	(0.03)	**-0.18**	(0.06)	**-1.05**	(0.04)	-0.25	(0.01)	0.27	(0.01)	**1.27**	(0.04)
Italy (Provincia Veneto)	0.05	(0.04)	-0.05	(0.06)	0.14	(0.04)	**-0.19**	(0.08)	**-1.16**	(0.04)	-0.29	(0.01)	0.28	(0.01)	**1.38**	(0.03)
United Kingdom (England)	0.22	(0.02)	0.14	(0.03)	0.29	(0.03)	**-0.15**	(0.03)	**-0.83**	(0.02)	-0.08	(0.00)	0.40	(0.00)	**1.38**	(0.02)
United Kingdom (Northern Ireland)	0.24	(0.03)	0.15	(0.04)	0.33	(0.04)	**-0.19**	(0.04)	**-0.84**	(0.02)	-0.10	(0.01)	0.43	(0.01)	**1.48**	(0.03)
United Kingdom (Wales)	0.14	(0.02)	0.12	(0.02)	0.16	(0.03)	-0.04	(0.03)	**-0.91**	(0.02)	-0.15	(0.00)	0.34	(0.01)	**1.29**	(0.02)

Notes: Values that are statistically significant are indicated in bold (see Annex A3). See Table III.2.3 for national data.
StatLink ⟐ http://dx.doi.org/10.1787/888932343304

[Part 2/2]

Index of interpretation of literary texts and reading performance, by national quarters of this index

Table S.III.k · *Results based on students' self-reports*

| | Performance on the reading scale, by quarters of this index | | | | | | | Change in the reading score per unit of this index | | Increased likelihood of students in the bottom quarter of this index scoring in the bottom quarter of the reading performance distribution | | Explained variance in student performance (r-squared x 100) | |
| | Bottom quarter | | Second quarter | | Third quarter | | Top quarter | | | | | | | |
	Mean index	S.E.	Mean index	S.E.	Mean index	S.E.	Mean index	S.E.	Effect	S.E.	Ratio	S.E.	%	S.E.
Adjudicated														
Belgium (Flemish Community)	**499**	(3.9)	525	(3.6)	529	(3.8)	**534**	(3.8)	**16.3**	(2.17)	**1.6**	(0.10)	2.5	(0.65)
Spain (Andalusia)	**438**	(8.8)	460	(6.8)	474	(7.1)	**489**	(4.9)	**22.7**	(2.99)	**1.9**	(0.25)	5.5	(1.51)
Spain (Aragon)	**465**	(6.2)	497	(5.7)	508	(5.9)	**522**	(4.2)	**24.6**	(2.64)	**2.0**	(0.24)	7.1	(1.41)
Spain (Asturias)	**476**	(7.7)	483	(7.1)	504	(6.3)	**503**	(6.4)	**13.9**	(3.28)	**1.4**	(0.14)	1.8	(0.86)
Spain (Balearic Islands)	**437**	(8.2)	451	(8.6)	473	(7.4)	**482**	(6.1)	**21.7**	(2.96)	**1.7**	(0.19)	5.1	(1.32)
Spain (Basque Country)	**481**	(4.6)	493	(4.0)	501	(3.8)	**507**	(3.0)	**13.0**	(2.30)	**1.4**	(0.10)	1.9	(0.66)
Spain (Canary Islands)	**435**	(7.4)	447	(6.6)	464	(6.6)	**474**	(6.6)	**18.9**	(3.50)	**1.6**	(0.16)	3.8	(1.39)
Spain (Cantabria)	**465**	(6.6)	488	(6.5)	498	(6.3)	**507**	(5.7)	**17.9**	(2.66)	**1.6**	(0.16)	3.3	(0.96)
Spain (Castile and Leon)	**487**	(6.6)	498	(6.4)	511	(6.9)	**525**	(4.5)	**18.3**	(3.11)	**1.5**	(0.16)	3.8	(1.17)
Spain (Catalonia)	**491**	(8.5)	496	(5.9)	501	(8.1)	**512**	(5.3)	**10.3**	(2.86)	**1.2**	(0.13)	1.1	(0.62)
Spain (Ceuta and Melilla)	**397**	(5.8)	422	(6.5)	436	(6.7)	**449**	(5.8)	**20.1**	(3.42)	**1.9**	(0.23)	3.4	(1.12)
Spain (Galicia)	**466**	(6.8)	486	(5.9)	496	(7.4)	**499**	(5.4)	**15.6**	(2.44)	**1.7**	(0.20)	2.7	(0.81)
Spain (La Rioja)	**479**	(5.7)	496	(5.8)	506	(5.4)	**516**	(5.4)	**16.1**	(2.98)	**1.5**	(0.21)	2.4	(0.83)
Spain (Madrid)	**496**	(7.2)	499	(5.1)	511	(5.8)	**522**	(6.0)	**10.8**	(3.35)	**1.4**	(0.16)	1.4	(0.84)
Spain (Murcia)	**471**	(7.4)	473	(7.2)	487	(6.3)	**494**	(5.3)	**10.5**	(3.23)	**1.3**	(0.13)	1.3	(0.79)
Spain (Navarre)	**486**	(5.3)	486	(6.4)	506	(4.4)	**512**	(5.1)	**14.7**	(3.37)	**1.3**	(0.13)	2.2	(1.00)
United Kingdom (Scotland)	**480**	(4.7)	496	(5.8)	514	(4.6)	**522**	(4.5)	**18.2**	(2.30)	**1.6**	(0.14)	3.5	(0.84)
Non-adjudicated														
Belgium (French Community)	**472**	(6.2)	500	(4.8)	501	(5.8)	**507**	(5.2)	**14.5**	(2.29)	**1.6**	(0.14)	1.9	(0.59)
Belgium (German-Speaking Community)	**485**	(6.0)	501	(7.3)	506	(6.6)	**507**	(7.5)	**12.5**	(4.03)	1.4	(0.23)	1.4	(0.92)
Finland (Finnish Speaking)	**531**	(3.8)	540	(3.4)	538	(3.5)	**545**	(3.3)	**5.8**	(1.64)	1.2	(0.08)	0.4	(0.22)
Finland (Swedish Speaking)	**502**	(5.1)	520	(5.1)	512	(5.0)	**519**	(5.5)	**7.8**	(3.32)	1.1	(0.16)	0.6	(0.52)
Italy (Provincia Abruzzo)	**475**	(6.9)	483	(7.5)	482	(6.6)	**492**	(5.6)	**7.3**	(4.70)	1.2	(0.16)	0.7	(0.89)
Italy (Provincia Autonoma di Bolzano)	**471**	(6.5)	493	(4.7)	498	(6.5)	**507**	(4.7)	**16.0**	(3.07)	**1.6**	(0.18)	2.6	(0.99)
Italy (Provincia Basilicata)	**452**	(8.7)	470	(6.3)	489	(6.9)	**492**	(6.5)	**14.7**	(3.77)	**1.7**	(0.22)	2.6	(1.29)
Italy (Provincia Calabria)	**427**	(7.9)	449	(6.5)	460	(8.0)	**480**	(6.8)	**19.8**	(4.35)	**1.7**	(0.26)	4.9	(1.96)
Italy (Provincia Campania)	**433**	(8.2)	463	(7.0)	458	(7.8)	**475**	(6.8)	**14.4**	(2.44)	**1.8**	(0.18)	2.6	(0.85)
Italy (Provincia Emilia Romagna)	**486**	(6.8)	505	(5.3)	519	(5.0)	**518**	(6.5)	**11.7**	(3.59)	**1.5**	(0.19)	1.4	(0.80)
Italy (Provincia Friuli Venezia Giulia)	**501**	(8.4)	512	(6.2)	522	(7.2)	**526**	(5.7)	**11.1**	(3.99)	1.4	(0.20)	1.4	(0.95)
Italy (Provincia Lazio)	**472**	(6.6)	483	(6.7)	488	(7.6)	**492**	(6.5)	**8.9**	(2.95)	1.2	(0.16)	1.0	(0.63)
Italy (Provincia Liguria)	485	(16.3)	490	(11.5)	500	(6.3)	504	(6.5)	10.6	(5.43)	1.2	(0.20)	1.3	(1.21)
Italy (Provincia Lombardia)	513	(6.0)	518	(9.1)	534	(7.0)	534	(7.8)	9.9	(3.90)	1.3	(0.17)	1.1	(0.85)
Italy (Provincia Marche)	496	(10.3)	502	(9.3)	505	(7.4)	506	(7.9)	4.6	(3.06)	1.1	(0.15)	0.2	(0.32)
Italy (Provincia Molise)	**456**	(6.1)	460	(7.8)	481	(6.1)	**491**	(6.5)	**14.1**	(3.05)	1.3	(0.17)	2.6	(1.10)
Italy (Provincia Piemonte)	**491**	(8.0)	488	(11.7)	505	(10.2)	**512**	(6.4)	**9.2**	(3.39)	1.2	(0.20)	1.0	(0.70)
Italy (Provincia Puglia)	**473**	(6.8)	486	(8.1)	498	(6.5)	**514**	(6.9)	**14.3**	(3.16)	**1.6**	(0.24)	2.8	(1.21)
Italy (Provincia Sardegna)	**466**	(7.4)	468	(7.7)	476	(6.0)	**476**	(6.4)	**4.6**	(3.12)	1.1	(0.14)	0.3	(0.37)
Italy (Provincia Sicilia)	**443**	(9.0)	451	(9.1)	479	(8.6)	**485**	(9.1)	**16.1**	(3.65)	**1.5**	(0.20)	2.9	(1.36)
Italy (Provincia Toscana)	**479**	(8.3)	493	(7.2)	507	(7.8)	**504**	(4.9)	**10.7**	(2.74)	1.4	(0.14)	1.3	(0.64)
Italy (Provincia Trento)	**500**	(6.0)	508	(6.5)	513	(6.0)	**524**	(5.5)	**11.4**	(3.48)	1.3	(0.17)	1.4	(0.87)
Italy (Provincia Umbria)	**480**	(8.5)	489	(8.5)	503	(7.7)	**506**	(5.6)	**12.6**	(3.19)	1.4	(0.20)	1.7	(0.86)
Italy (Provincia Valle d'Aosta)	**505**	(5.5)	512	(5.9)	521	(6.0)	**522**	(5.5)	**7.6**	(2.60)	1.3	(0.18)	0.7	(0.46)
Italy (Provincia Veneto)	498	(8.8)	507	(6.7)	510	(6.7)	513	(6.9)	5.4	(4.01)	1.2	(0.18)	0.4	(0.52)
United Kingdom (England)	**484**	(3.9)	494	(4.6)	503	(3.9)	**509**	(4.0)	**10.3**	(2.13)	1.3	(0.09)	1.0	(0.39)
United Kingdom (Northern Ireland)	**481**	(7.2)	499	(6.7)	510	(5.6)	**517**	(5.0)	**15.1**	(2.66)	**1.5**	(0.16)	2.2	(0.80)
United Kingdom (Wales)	**463**	(4.7)	477	(4.4)	485	(4.4)	**492**	(4.8)	**13.9**	(2.16)	1.4	(0.12)	1.8	(0.56)

Notes: Values that are statistically significant are indicated in bold (see Annex A3). See Table III.2.3 for national data.
StatLink ﹏᠊ᠷᠡᠯ http://dx.doi.org/10.1787/888932343304

[Part 1/2]
Index of use of texts containing non-continuous materials and reading performance, by national quarters of this index

Table S.III.I — *Results based on students' self-reports*

| | Index of use of texts containing non-continuous materials | | | | | | | | | | | | | | | |
| | All students | | Males | | Females | | Gender difference (B − G) | | Bottom quarter | | Second quarter | | Third quarter | | Top quarter | |
	Mean index	S.E.	Mean index	S.E.	Mean index	S.E.	Dif.	S.E.	Mean index	S.E.	Mean index	S.E.	Mean index	S.E.	Mean index	S.E.
Adjudicated																
Belgium (Flemish Community)	-0.08	(0.02)	-0.06	(0.03)	-0.10	(0.03)	0.04	(0.03)	**-1.18**	(0.02)	-0.31	(0.00)	0.17	(0.00)	**1.01**	(0.02)
Spain (Andalusia)	-0.05	(0.05)	-0.04	(0.05)	-0.06	(0.06)	0.02	(0.06)	**-1.20**	(0.04)	-0.34	(0.01)	0.21	(0.01)	**1.13**	(0.04)
Spain (Aragon)	-0.05	(0.03)	-0.07	(0.04)	-0.03	(0.04)	-0.04	(0.05)	**-1.24**	(0.03)	-0.28	(0.01)	0.20	(0.01)	**1.31**	(0.04)
Spain (Asturias)	0.01	(0.04)	0.04	(0.06)	-0.02	(0.05)	0.06	(0.06)	**-1.27**	(0.02)	-0.26	(0.01)	0.26	(0.01)	**0.96**	(0.03)
Spain (Balearic Islands)	-0.25	(0.04)	-0.23	(0.04)	-0.27	(0.06)	0.04	(0.05)	**-1.52**	(0.04)	-0.48	(0.01)	0.04	(0.01)	**1.15**	(0.02)
Spain (Basque Country)	-0.11	(0.03)	-0.11	(0.02)	-0.12	(0.04)	0.00	(0.04)	**-1.35**	(0.02)	-0.41	(0.00)	0.16	(0.00)	**1.13**	(0.03)
Spain (Canary Islands)	-0.06	(0.04)	-0.02	(0.04)	-0.10	(0.05)	0.08	(0.06)	**-1.24**	(0.02)	-0.31	(0.01)	0.19	(0.01)	**1.14**	(0.04)
Spain (Cantabria)	-0.09	(0.05)	-0.12	(0.05)	-0.07	(0.06)	-0.05	(0.05)	**-1.31**	(0.02)	-0.38	(0.01)	0.17	(0.01)	**1.00**	(0.04)
Spain (Castile and Leon)	-0.15	(0.04)	-0.08	(0.05)	-0.23	(0.06)	**0.15**	(0.06)	**-1.37**	(0.02)	-0.40	(0.01)	0.15	(0.01)	**1.08**	(0.04)
Spain (Catalonia)	-0.05	(0.05)	-0.01	(0.06)	-0.09	(0.06)	0.08	(0.06)	**-1.20**	(0.04)	-0.27	(0.01)	0.20	(0.01)	**1.29**	(0.03)
Spain (Ceuta and Melilla)	0.10	(0.03)	0.13	(0.04)	0.08	(0.04)	0.05	(0.06)	**-1.06**	(0.04)	-0.17	(0.01)	0.34	(0.01)	**1.15**	(0.03)
Spain (Galicia)	-0.11	(0.04)	-0.10	(0.04)	-0.11	(0.06)	0.01	(0.06)	**-1.36**	(0.02)	-0.40	(0.01)	0.18	(0.01)	**1.30**	(0.05)
Spain (La Rioja)	0.02	(0.03)	0.04	(0.03)	0.00	(0.04)	0.04	(0.05)	**-1.17**	(0.03)	-0.28	(0.01)	0.24	(0.01)	**1.00**	(0.05)
Spain (Madrid)	-0.21	(0.04)	-0.16	(0.04)	-0.25	(0.06)	0.09	(0.07)	**-1.46**	(0.03)	-0.44	(0.01)	0.06	(0.01)	**1.07**	(0.03)
Spain (Murcia)	-0.08	(0.04)	-0.08	(0.04)	-0.08	(0.05)	0.00	(0.05)	**-1.27**	(0.03)	-0.31	(0.01)	0.18	(0.01)	**1.26**	(0.04)
Spain (Navarre)	0.03	(0.04)	0.04	(0.06)	0.02	(0.04)	0.02	(0.07)	**-1.14**	(0.03)	-0.26	(0.01)	0.27	(0.01)	**1.46**	(0.02)
United Kingdom (Scotland)	0.23	(0.03)	0.25	(0.04)	0.20	(0.03)	0.04	(0.04)	**-0.97**	(0.03)	-0.05	(0.01)	0.46	(0.01)	**1.55**	(0.02)
Non-adjudicated																
Belgium (French Community)	0.28	(0.03)	0.27	(0.03)	0.29	(0.04)	-0.02	(0.05)	**-0.90**	(0.02)	-0.02	(0.01)	0.49	(0.01)	**1.02**	(0.04)
Belgium (German-Speaking Community)	-0.16	(0.03)	-0.08	(0.05)	-0.24	(0.04)	**0.15**	(0.06)	**-1.29**	(0.04)	-0.43	(0.01)	0.06	(0.01)	**1.23**	(0.02)
Finland (Finnish Speaking)	0.02	(0.02)	0.01	(0.03)	0.03	(0.02)	-0.02	(0.03)	**-1.14**	(0.02)	-0.25	(0.00)	0.24	(0.00)	**0.79**	(0.03)
Finland (Swedish Speaking)	-0.24	(0.03)	-0.28	(0.04)	-0.20	(0.04)	-0.08	(0.05)	**-1.33**	(0.03)	-0.44	(0.01)	0.00	(0.01)	**0.69**	(0.06)
Italy (Provincia Abruzzo)	-0.45	(0.05)	-0.45	(0.05)	-0.45	(0.07)	0.00	(0.08)	**-1.62**	(0.03)	-0.68	(0.01)	-0.06	(0.01)	**0.82**	(0.03)
Italy (Provincia Autonoma di Bolzano)	-0.34	(0.02)	-0.25	(0.04)	-0.42	(0.04)	**0.17**	(0.06)	**-1.52**	(0.03)	-0.59	(0.01)	-0.06	(0.01)	**0.81**	(0.02)
Italy (Provincia Basilicata)	-0.31	(0.03)	-0.21	(0.04)	-0.41	(0.04)	**0.20**	(0.05)	**-1.50**	(0.03)	-0.51	(0.01)	-0.03	(0.01)	**0.78**	(0.03)
Italy (Provincia Calabria)	-0.33	(0.04)	-0.24	(0.04)	-0.41	(0.06)	**0.17**	(0.07)	**-1.52**	(0.03)	-0.55	(0.01)	-0.03	(0.01)	**0.95**	(0.04)
Italy (Provincia Campania)	-0.19	(0.04)	-0.12	(0.05)	-0.29	(0.05)	**0.17**	(0.04)	**-1.33**	(0.02)	-0.70	(0.01)	-0.22	(0.01)	**0.63**	(0.04)
Italy (Provincia Emilia Romagna)	-0.49	(0.03)	-0.42	(0.04)	-0.56	(0.04)	**0.14**	(0.06)	**-1.69**	(0.02)	-0.62	(0.01)	-0.12	(0.01)	**0.74**	(0.03)
Italy (Provincia Friuli Venezia Giulia)	-0.40	(0.04)	-0.30	(0.04)	-0.50	(0.05)	**0.20**	(0.05)	**-1.60**	(0.03)	-0.66	(0.01)	-0.15	(0.00)	**0.74**	(0.02)
Italy (Provincia Lazio)	-0.44	(0.04)	-0.35	(0.05)	-0.54	(0.06)	**0.18**	(0.06)	**-1.69**	(0.03)	-0.74	(0.01)	-0.20	(0.01)	**0.73**	(0.03)
Italy (Provincia Liguria)	-0.49	(0.04)	-0.40	(0.05)	-0.60	(0.05)	**0.20**	(0.06)	**-1.75**	(0.03)	-0.70	(0.01)	-0.22	(0.01)	**0.69**	(0.03)
Italy (Provincia Lombardia)	-0.47	(0.03)	-0.40	(0.03)	-0.53	(0.04)	**0.13**	(0.04)	**-1.63**	(0.03)	-0.65	(0.01)	-0.11	(0.01)	**0.70**	(0.03)
Italy (Provincia Marche)	-0.41	(0.04)	-0.31	(0.05)	-0.53	(0.05)	**0.23**	(0.06)	**-1.59**	(0.03)	-0.65	(0.01)	-0.02	(0.01)	**0.78**	(0.03)
Italy (Provincia Molise)	-0.30	(0.03)	-0.22	(0.04)	-0.38	(0.04)	**0.16**	(0.06)	**-1.46**	(0.04)	-0.50	(0.01)	-0.20	(0.01)	**0.70**	(0.03)
Italy (Provincia Piemonte)	-0.48	(0.03)	-0.44	(0.04)	-0.52	(0.05)	0.08	(0.06)	**-1.73**	(0.03)	-0.70	(0.01)	-0.20	(0.01)	**1.04**	(0.04)
Italy (Provincia Puglia)	-0.17	(0.04)	-0.07	(0.05)	-0.26	(0.06)	**0.18**	(0.07)	**-1.41**	(0.03)	-0.42	(0.01)	0.12	(0.01)	**0.88**	(0.04)
Italy (Provincia Sardegna)	-0.37	(0.03)	-0.24	(0.05)	-0.48	(0.05)	**0.24**	(0.07)	**-1.66**	(0.03)	-0.64	(0.01)	-0.05	(0.01)	**0.84**	(0.04)
Italy (Provincia Sicilia)	-0.29	(0.04)	-0.15	(0.05)	-0.42	(0.05)	**0.27**	(0.06)	**-1.44**	(0.03)	-0.53	(0.01)	-0.02	(0.01)	**0.75**	(0.03)
Italy (Provincia Toscana)	-0.37	(0.04)	-0.32	(0.04)	-0.43	(0.04)	**0.11**	(0.05)	**-1.57**	(0.03)	-0.60	(0.01)	-0.07	(0.01)	**0.80**	(0.03)
Italy (Provincia Trento)	-0.33	(0.03)	-0.21	(0.04)	-0.47	(0.04)	**0.26**	(0.05)	**-1.49**	(0.03)	-0.57	(0.01)	-0.08	(0.01)	**0.79**	(0.04)
Italy (Provincia Umbria)	-0.35	(0.03)	-0.26	(0.05)	-0.43	(0.04)	**0.17**	(0.06)	**-1.56**	(0.03)	-0.58	(0.01)	-0.06	(0.01)	**0.80**	(0.03)
Italy (Provincia Valle d'Aosta)	-0.32	(0.03)	-0.26	(0.05)	-0.37	(0.04)	0.11	(0.06)	**-1.50**	(0.03)	-0.55	(0.01)	-0.03	(0.01)	**0.69**	(0.03)
Italy (Provincia Veneto)	-0.45	(0.04)	-0.35	(0.05)	-0.55	(0.04)	**0.20**	(0.06)	**-1.64**	(0.02)	-0.69	(0.01)	-0.16	(0.01)	**0.69**	(0.03)
United Kingdom (England)	0.25	(0.02)	0.25	(0.03)	0.25	(0.03)	0.00	(0.03)	**-0.89**	(0.02)	-0.03	(0.00)	0.46	(0.00)	**1.48**	(0.02)
United Kingdom (Northern Ireland)	0.55	(0.03)	0.55	(0.03)	0.55	(0.03)	0.00	(0.04)	**-0.60**	(0.03)	0.21	(0.01)	0.77	(0.01)	**1.82**	(0.03)
United Kingdom (Wales)	0.35	(0.02)	0.40	(0.03)	0.31	(0.03)	**0.10**	(0.03)	**-0.73**	(0.02)	0.04	(0.00)	0.53	(0.00)	**1.58**	(0.02)

Notes: Values that are statistically significant are indicated in bold (see Annex A3). See Table II.2.4 for national data.
StatLink ⟨ms⟩ http://dx.doi.org/10.1787/888932343304

[Part 2/2]
Index of use of texts containing non-continuous materials and reading performance, by national quarters of this index
Table S.III.I · *Results based on students' self-reports*

| | Performance on the reading scale, by quarters of this index | | | | | | | | Change in the reading score per unit of this index | | Increased likelihood of students in the bottom quarter of this index scoring in the bottom quarter of the reading performance distribution | | Explained variance in student performance (r-squared x 100) | |
| | Bottom quarter | | Second quarter | | Third quarter | | Top quarter | | | | | | | |
	Mean index	S.E.	Mean index	S.E.	Mean index	S.E.	Mean index	S.E.	Effect	S.E.	Ratio	S.E.	%	S.E.
Adjudicated														
Belgium (Flemish Community)	524	(3.8)	520	(4.1)	521	(3.5)	521	(3.8)	-0.5	(2.27)	1.0	(0.07)	0.0	(0.05)
Spain (Andalusia)	**455**	(7.7)	468	(7.4)	459	(9.1)	**479**	(5.9)	**9.5**	(3.47)	1.3	(0.19)	1.1	(0.81)
Spain (Aragon)	**485**	(5.3)	492	(5.2)	501	(6.2)	**514**	(8.3)	**11.2**	(3.62)	1.2	(0.16)	1.6	(1.10)
Spain (Asturias)	492	(6.5)	496	(6.3)	492	(5.7)	487	(8.0)	-1.2	(2.92)	1.0	(0.12)	0.0	(0.13)
Spain (Balearic Islands)	459	(8.4)	456	(7.1)	461	(5.5)	467	(7.5)	4.9	(3.46)	1.1	(0.15)	0.3	(0.50)
Spain (Basque Country)	496	(3.9)	495	(3.9)	494	(4.0)	497	(4.2)	1.2	(1.72)	0.9	(0.08)	0.0	(0.07)
Spain (Canary Islands)	450	(6.2)	456	(6.7)	457	(7.5)	457	(7.0)	3.1	(4.03)	1.1	(0.15)	0.1	(0.33)
Spain (Cantabria)	482	(6.6)	489	(5.2)	496	(7.4)	490	(6.2)	4.2	(2.77)	1.0	(0.12)	0.2	(0.30)
Spain (Castile and Leon)	497	(6.2)	503	(5.4)	506	(6.3)	**514**	(7.7)	**6.6**	(3.12)	1.2	(0.14)	0.6	(0.46)
Spain (Catalonia)	506	(6.9)	499	(6.4)	494	(8.2)	500	(7.9)	-1.6	(3.45)	0.8	(0.14)	0.0	(0.18)
Spain (Ceuta and Melilla)	426	(6.6)	420	(5.8)	422	(7.6)	436	(6.2)	4.7	(3.21)	1.0	(0.15)	0.2	(0.29)
Spain (Galicia)	484	(5.8)	482	(6.6)	488	(6.6)	492	(6.4)	3.9	(2.90)	1.0	(0.15)	0.2	(0.32)
Spain (La Rioja)	**508**	(6.2)	507	(5.9)	490	(5.9)	**490**	(6.2)	**-6.6**	(3.16)	0.8	(0.13)	0.5	(0.49)
Spain (Madrid)	514	(8.1)	508	(5.7)	506	(5.4)	501	(6.0)	-4.6	(3.16)	0.9	(0.15)	0.3	(0.41)
Spain (Murcia)	483	(7.5)	475	(6.6)	479	(6.4)	488	(6.7)	3.7	(2.94)	1.0	(0.15)	0.2	(0.31)
Spain (Navarre)	**506**	(6.3)	499	(5.1)	496	(5.5)	**491**	(5.6)	-4.2	(3.03)	0.9	(0.15)	0.2	(0.36)
United Kingdom (Scotland)	**487**	(4.3)	495	(4.7)	508	(4.2)	**521**	(4.6)	**14.0**	(1.89)	**1.3**	(0.12)	2.2	(0.57)
Non-adjudicated														
Belgium (French Community)	**469**	(5.8)	493	(6.7)	509	(5.5)	**509**	(5.1)	**15.2**	(2.09)	**1.6**	(0.13)	2.0	(0.53)
Belgium (German-Speaking Community)	**477**	(7.4)	498	(7.4)	508	(7.3)	**516**	(5.4)	**16.3**	(3.60)	**1.5**	(0.22)	2.9	(1.22)
Finland (Finnish Speaking)	**515**	(3.4)	532	(3.7)	546	(3.3)	**560**	(3.3)	**16.9**	(1.53)	**1.5**	(0.10)	3.6	(0.65)
Finland (Swedish Speaking)	**500**	(6.4)	516	(6.6)	510	(5.8)	**527**	(6.0)	**11.9**	(3.07)	**1.3**	(0.17)	1.5	(0.75)
Italy (Provincia Abruzzo)	**498**	(7.9)	494	(7.6)	477	(6.7)	**464**	(7.7)	**-14.4**	(4.58)	0.7	(0.15)	2.3	(1.45)
Italy (Provincia Autonoma di Bolzano)	493	(5.4)	493	(4.7)	502	(4.6)	482	(6.1)	-0.5	(2.66)	1.0	(0.12)	0.0	(0.07)
Italy (Provincia Basilicata)	**495**	(6.0)	475	(6.6)	470	(8.4)	**465**	(7.4)	**-11.8**	(2.63)	0.6	(0.11)	1.6	(0.78)
Italy (Provincia Calabria)	**469**	(6.3)	459	(5.4)	454	(6.9)	**435**	(7.3)	**-13.9**	(3.25)	0.7	(0.11)	2.1	(0.93)
Italy (Provincia Campania)	**474**	(6.7)	465	(7.7)	446	(9.0)	**445**	(8.0)	**-13.0**	(3.69)	0.7	(0.13)	1.8	(1.02)
Italy (Provincia Emilia Romagna)	**519**	(6.9)	512	(6.2)	499	(6.7)	**499**	(5.1)	**-8.1**	(3.25)	0.8	(0.11)	0.6	(0.50)
Italy (Provincia Friuli Venezia Giulia)	**530**	(7.0)	518	(7.8)	509	(7.8)	**505**	(6.6)	**-9.2**	(3.52)	0.7	(0.13)	0.9	(0.70)
Italy (Provincia Lazio)	**503**	(7.5)	499	(4.8)	479	(7.1)	**455**	(8.7)	**-16.9**	(3.94)	0.7	(0.13)	3.2	(1.41)
Italy (Provincia Liguria)	**509**	(9.1)	502	(6.7)	495	(8.3)	**472**	(17.1)	**-13.8**	(4.19)	0.7	(0.09)	2.2	(1.11)
Italy (Provincia Lombardia)	**540**	(6.4)	524	(8.0)	520	(6.6)	**514**	(7.0)	**-9.3**	(2.75)	0.7	(0.10)	1.0	(0.56)
Italy (Provincia Marche)	**515**	(6.1)	510	(9.3)	496	(10.1)	**488**	(8.9)	**-9.8**	(3.88)	0.7	(0.14)	1.0	(0.74)
Italy (Provincia Molise)	**488**	(6.0)	476	(5.0)	466	(6.6)	**459**	(4.6)	**-12.0**	(2.85)	0.7	(0.12)	1.6	(0.79)
Italy (Provincia Piemonte)	**519**	(9.2)	510	(7.7)	496	(7.2)	**470**	(10.0)	**-17.7**	(3.28)	0.6	(0.15)	3.2	(1.21)
Italy (Provincia Puglia)	503	(6.2)	493	(6.3)	489	(7.3)	487	(7.5)	-5.4	(3.35)	0.8	(0.14)	0.4	(0.49)
Italy (Provincia Sardegna)	**491**	(7.0)	478	(8.7)	464	(6.5)	**454**	(6.9)	**-14.0**	(3.04)	0.6	(0.11)	2.4	(1.05)
Italy (Provincia Sicilia)	478	(7.3)	470	(8.4)	452	(9.1)	457	(11.5)	-6.6	(4.14)	0.7	(0.13)	0.4	(0.54)
Italy (Provincia Toscana)	507	(6.2)	508	(4.8)	486	(8.1)	482	(7.9)	-9.5	(3.97)	0.8	(0.13)	0.9	(0.72)
Italy (Provincia Trento)	521	(5.5)	514	(6.2)	505	(6.6)	504	(5.4)	-5.5	(2.88)	0.8	(0.11)	0.3	(0.34)
Italy (Provincia Umbria)	**511**	(6.2)	495	(7.0)	490	(7.6)	**484**	(8.0)	**-10.2**	(3.18)	0.7	(0.11)	1.0	(0.63)
Italy (Provincia Valle d'Aosta)	**531**	(5.3)	512	(6.7)	510	(7.8)	**507**	(5.4)	**-9.3**	(3.19)	0.7	(0.12)	1.0	(0.72)
Italy (Provincia Veneto)	**528**	(6.2)	509	(6.4)	504	(7.0)	**487**	(7.3)	**-15.6**	(3.51)	0.6	(0.09)	2.7	(1.11)
United Kingdom (England)	**477**	(3.5)	493	(4.6)	505	(4.4)	**516**	(4.2)	**16.4**	(1.65)	**1.4**	(0.09)	2.8	(0.59)
United Kingdom (Northern Ireland)	**475**	(5.0)	497	(5.4)	510	(6.1)	**525**	(6.1)	**20.0**	(2.20)	**1.6**	(0.15)	4.1	(0.99)
United Kingdom (Wales)	**457**	(4.1)	478	(4.3)	487	(4.6)	**494**	(5.1)	**15.1**	(2.05)	**1.5**	(0.14)	2.3	(0.64)

Notes: Values that are statistically significant are indicated in bold (see Annex A3). See Table III.2.4 for national data.
StatLink ⟥⟤ http://dx.doi.org/10.1787/888932343304

[Part 1/2]

Index of reading activities for traditional literature courses and reading performance, by national quarters of this index

Table S.III.m *Results based on students' self-reports*

| | Index of reading activities for traditional literature courses | | | | | | | | | | | | | | | |
| | All students | | Males | | Females | | Gender difference (B – G) | | Bottom quarter | | Second quarter | | Third quarter | | Top quarter | |
	Mean index	S.E.	Mean index	S.E.	Mean index	S.E.	Dif.	S.E.	Mean index	S.E.	Mean index	S.E.	Mean index	S.E.	Mean index	S.E.
Adjudicated																
Belgium (Flemish Community)	-0.20	(0.02)	-0.21	(0.03)	-0.19	(0.03)	-0.02	(0.03)	-1.33	(0.02)	-0.37	(0.00)	0.11	(0.00)	0.78	(0.01)
Spain (Andalusia)	0.45	(0.03)	0.37	(0.04)	0.54	(0.05)	-0.18	(0.05)	-0.64	(0.03)	0.22	(0.01)	0.72	(0.01)	1.49	(0.03)
Spain (Aragon)	0.39	(0.04)	0.27	(0.05)	0.51	(0.04)	-0.24	(0.06)	-0.75	(0.04)	0.20	(0.01)	0.68	(0.01)	1.56	(0.03)
Spain (Asturias)	0.55	(0.04)	0.47	(0.05)	0.64	(0.04)	-0.17	(0.06)	-0.55	(0.03)	0.36	(0.01)	0.82	(0.01)	1.40	(0.03)
Spain (Balearic Islands)	0.41	(0.03)	0.30	(0.03)	0.52	(0.04)	-0.22	(0.04)	-0.64	(0.04)	0.21	(0.01)	0.66	(0.01)	1.47	(0.02)
Spain (Basque Country)	0.40	(0.03)	0.30	(0.03)	0.51	(0.03)	-0.21	(0.03)	-0.74	(0.02)	0.18	(0.00)	0.67	(0.00)	1.44	(0.03)
Spain (Canary Islands)	0.40	(0.04)	0.34	(0.05)	0.46	(0.05)	-0.12	(0.05)	-0.72	(0.06)	0.21	(0.01)	0.66	(0.01)	1.46	(0.03)
Spain (Cantabria)	0.45	(0.04)	0.37	(0.05)	0.53	(0.04)	-0.16	(0.03)	-0.65	(0.04)	0.25	(0.01)	0.72	(0.01)	1.51	(0.03)
Spain (Castile and Leon)	0.50	(0.03)	0.40	(0.04)	0.60	(0.04)	-0.20	(0.05)	-0.59	(0.04)	0.30	(0.01)	0.77	(0.01)	1.44	(0.03)
Spain (Catalonia)	0.49	(0.03)	0.41	(0.04)	0.58	(0.04)	-0.17	(0.05)	-0.53	(0.04)	0.32	(0.01)	0.75	(0.01)	1.75	(0.03)
Spain (Ceuta and Melilla)	0.69	(0.03)	0.64	(0.04)	0.74	(0.03)	-0.10	(0.05)	-0.42	(0.03)	0.46	(0.01)	0.95	(0.01)	1.51	(0.02)
Spain (Galicia)	0.41	(0.03)	0.31	(0.04)	0.52	(0.04)	-0.21	(0.05)	-0.76	(0.04)	0.18	(0.01)	0.71	(0.01)	1.53	(0.04)
Spain (La Rioja)	0.53	(0.02)	0.48	(0.04)	0.59	(0.03)	-0.11	(0.05)	-0.50	(0.04)	0.33	(0.01)	0.76	(0.01)	1.61	(0.03)
Spain (Madrid)	0.59	(0.04)	0.54	(0.05)	0.64	(0.04)	-0.10	(0.05)	-0.45	(0.03)	0.37	(0.01)	0.82	(0.01)	1.50	(0.04)
Spain (Murcia)	0.50	(0.04)	0.37	(0.05)	0.63	(0.05)	-0.25	(0.05)	-0.56	(0.03)	0.31	(0.01)	0.76	(0.01)	1.65	(0.04)
Spain (Navarre)	0.56	(0.04)	0.45	(0.04)	0.68	(0.04)	-0.24	(0.04)	-0.57	(0.03)	0.34	(0.01)	0.82	(0.01)	1.50	(0.04)
United Kingdom (Scotland)	-0.14	(0.02)	-0.18	(0.03)	-0.10	(0.03)	-0.07	(0.03)	-1.23	(0.02)	-0.35	(0.00)	0.13	(0.01)	0.89	(0.02)
Non-adjudicated																
Belgium (French Community)	-0.10	(0.03)	-0.14	(0.03)	-0.06	(0.04)	-0.08	(0.04)	-1.36	(0.02)	-0.30	(0.01)	0.22	(0.01)	1.01	(0.02)
Belgium (German-Speaking Community)	-0.25	(0.03)	-0.36	(0.04)	-0.13	(0.04)	-0.24	(0.06)	-1.42	(0.04)	-0.42	(0.01)	0.08	(0.01)	0.75	(0.04)
Finland (Finnish Speaking)	-0.29	(0.03)	-0.33	(0.03)	-0.25	(0.03)	-0.08	(0.03)	-1.56	(0.02)	-0.47	(0.00)	0.08	(0.00)	0.33	(0.02)
Finland (Swedish Speaking)	-0.77	(0.03)	-0.75	(0.04)	-0.79	(0.03)	0.03	(0.06)	-1.99	(0.02)	-1.02	(0.01)	-0.40	(0.01)	0.33	(0.02)
Italy (Provincia Abruzzo)	0.48	(0.04)	0.38	(0.06)	0.60	(0.04)	-0.22	(0.06)	-0.58	(0.04)	0.33	(0.01)	0.74	(0.01)	1.45	(0.04)
Italy (Provincia Autonoma di Bolzano)	-0.31	(0.02)	-0.33	(0.04)	-0.28	(0.03)	-0.06	(0.05)	-1.53	(0.03)	-0.50	(0.01)	0.03	(0.01)	0.77	(0.03)
Italy (Provincia Basilicata)	0.63	(0.03)	0.56	(0.04)	0.70	(0.05)	-0.14	(0.05)	-0.36	(0.06)	0.44	(0.01)	0.87	(0.01)	1.58	(0.03)
Italy (Provincia Calabria)	0.79	(0.03)	0.66	(0.05)	0.92	(0.04)	-0.26	(0.06)	-0.19	(0.04)	0.56	(0.01)	1.00	(0.01)	1.78	(0.04)
Italy (Provincia Campania)	0.78	(0.04)	0.68	(0.05)	0.90	(0.05)	-0.22	(0.05)	-0.18	(0.04)	0.57	(0.01)	1.00	(0.01)	1.71	(0.03)
Italy (Provincia Emilia Romagna)	0.28	(0.02)	0.22	(0.05)	0.34	(0.03)	-0.12	(0.05)	-0.80	(0.03)	0.13	(0.01)	0.55	(0.01)	1.23	(0.02)
Italy (Provincia Friuli Venezia Giulia)	0.19	(0.04)	0.08	(0.05)	0.31	(0.05)	-0.23	(0.04)	-0.93	(0.05)	0.01	(0.01)	0.49	(0.01)	1.19	(0.03)
Italy (Provincia Lazio)	0.47	(0.04)	0.34	(0.05)	0.62	(0.04)	-0.28	(0.06)	-0.64	(0.04)	0.31	(0.01)	0.74	(0.01)	1.48	(0.03)
Italy (Provincia Liguria)	0.44	(0.04)	0.35	(0.05)	0.53	(0.03)	-0.18	(0.04)	-0.56	(0.03)	0.28	(0.01)	0.69	(0.01)	1.20	(0.03)
Italy (Provincia Lombardia)	0.28	(0.03)	0.18	(0.05)	0.38	(0.04)	-0.20	(0.06)	-0.75	(0.03)	0.11	(0.01)	0.54	(0.01)	1.19	(0.03)
Italy (Provincia Marche)	0.29	(0.03)	0.25	(0.04)	0.34	(0.03)	-0.09	(0.05)	-0.71	(0.04)	0.12	(0.01)	0.55	(0.01)	1.45	(0.03)
Italy (Provincia Molise)	0.45	(0.03)	0.37	(0.05)	0.54	(0.04)	-0.17	(0.06)	-0.60	(0.06)	0.27	(0.01)	0.69	(0.01)	1.28	(0.03)
Italy (Provincia Piemonte)	0.29	(0.05)	0.20	(0.04)	0.37	(0.07)	-0.17	(0.06)	-0.85	(0.04)	0.13	(0.01)	0.58	(0.01)	1.55	(0.03)
Italy (Provincia Puglia)	0.63	(0.04)	0.54	(0.05)	0.71	(0.05)	-0.17	(0.06)	-0.30	(0.03)	0.43	(0.01)	0.83	(0.01)	1.52	(0.06)
Italy (Provincia Sardegna)	0.43	(0.06)	0.33	(0.06)	0.53	(0.07)	-0.19	(0.06)	-0.72	(0.04)	0.21	(0.01)	0.72	(0.01)	1.58	(0.03)
Italy (Provincia Sicilia)	0.67	(0.04)	0.56	(0.05)	0.78	(0.04)	-0.22	(0.05)	-0.24	(0.04)	0.47	(0.01)	0.88	(0.01)	1.31	(0.02)
Italy (Provincia Toscana)	0.38	(0.03)	0.29	(0.04)	0.48	(0.04)	-0.19	(0.05)	-0.63	(0.04)	0.21	(0.01)	0.62	(0.01)	1.05	(0.03)
Italy (Provincia Trento)	0.06	(0.03)	0.01	(0.04)	0.12	(0.05)	-0.11	(0.07)	-1.07	(0.04)	-0.12	(0.01)	0.37	(0.01)	1.31	(0.02)
Italy (Provincia Umbria)	0.41	(0.03)	0.38	(0.03)	0.45	(0.04)	-0.07	(0.04)	-0.51	(0.03)	0.22	(0.01)	0.64	(0.01)	1.00	(0.03)
Italy (Provincia Valle d'Aosta)	0.01	(0.03)	-0.04	(0.04)	0.06	(0.04)	-0.10	(0.06)	-1.11	(0.05)	-0.16	(0.01)	0.31	(0.01)	1.11	(0.02)
Italy (Provincia Veneto)	0.17	(0.04)	0.04	(0.06)	0.30	(0.05)	-0.26	(0.09)	-0.91	(0.05)	-0.01	(0.01)	0.49	(0.01)	1.20	(0.02)
United Kingdom (England)	0.21	(0.03)	0.18	(0.03)	0.23	(0.03)	-0.05	(0.03)	-0.83	(0.03)	0.01	(0.00)	0.45	(0.00)	1.20	(0.02)
United Kingdom (Northern Ireland)	0.24	(0.03)	0.17	(0.05)	0.30	(0.04)	-0.13	(0.05)	-0.88	(0.04)	0.03	(0.01)	0.52	(0.00)	1.27	(0.02)
United Kingdom (Wales)	0.13	(0.02)	0.09	(0.03)	0.16	(0.02)	-0.07	(0.03)	-0.94	(0.02)	-0.08	(0.00)	0.38	(0.00)	1.15	(0.02)

Notes: Values that are statistically significant are indicated in bold (see Annex A3). See Table III.2.5 for national data.
StatLink ⟨⟩ http://dx.doi.org/10.1787/888932343304

[Part 2/2]
Index of reading activities for traditional literature courses and reading performance, by national quarters of this index
Table S.III.m *Results based on students' self-reports*

	Performance on the reading scale, by quarters of this index								Change in the reading score per unit of this index		Increased likelihood of students in the bottom quarter of this index scoring in the bottom quarter of the reading performance distribution		Explained variance in student performance (r-squared x 100)	
	Bottom quarter		Second quarter		Third quarter		Top quarter							
	Mean index	S.E.	Mean index	S.E.	Mean index	S.E.	Mean index	S.E.	Effect	S.E.	Ratio	S.E.	%	S.E.
Adjudicated														
Belgium (Flemish Community)	502	(3.9)	525	(3.1)	534	(4.1)	526	(4.6)	12.4	(2.53)	1.5	(0.12)	1.3	(0.55)
Spain (Andalusia)	451	(9.0)	465	(6.9)	472	(5.9)	474	(6.2)	9.7	(3.97)	1.3	(0.18)	1.0	(0.82)
Spain (Aragon)	470	(6.5)	498	(4.7)	503	(5.4)	520	(5.8)	21.2	(3.04)	1.9	(0.25)	5.3	(1.66)
Spain (Asturias)	472	(6.7)	497	(6.1)	499	(6.4)	498	(7.2)	13.0	(3.22)	1.4	(0.13)	1.5	(0.77)
Spain (Balearic Islands)	434	(8.5)	473	(7.6)	467	(5.8)	469	(6.7)	15.7	(3.90)	1.7	(0.18)	2.3	(1.26)
Spain (Basque Country)	488	(5.3)	498	(3.3)	494	(3.7)	502	(4.0)	5.6	(2.27)	1.3	(0.11)	0.4	(0.31)
Spain (Canary Islands)	440	(6.4)	447	(6.2)	464	(7.4)	466	(6.1)	11.7	(3.25)	1.3	(0.16)	1.4	(0.72)
Spain (Cantabria)	474	(6.5)	484	(5.8)	499	(6.7)	501	(6.1)	12.4	(3.96)	1.3	(0.17)	1.5	(0.96)
Spain (Castile and Leon)	490	(5.3)	503	(7.2)	510	(5.8)	517	(7.4)	14.7	(3.07)	1.3	(0.15)	2.3	(1.02)
Spain (Catalonia)	499	(6.9)	501	(5.5)	505	(6.3)	496	(7.8)	2.3	(2.88)	1.0	(0.10)	0.1	(0.17)
Spain (Ceuta and Melilla)	423	(6.8)	421	(6.6)	423	(5.9)	434	(6.3)	5.2	(3.56)	1.2	(0.15)	0.2	(0.30)
Spain (Galicia)	464	(6.3)	495	(6.3)	491	(6.6)	497	(5.9)	14.1	(3.47)	1.7	(0.19)	2.3	(1.15)
Spain (La Rioja)	485	(5.4)	499	(5.8)	503	(5.5)	508	(6.5)	7.6	(3.69)	1.4	(0.16)	0.5	(0.49)
Spain (Madrid)	485	(7.2)	508	(5.7)	519	(5.8)	516	(6.8)	13.4	(3.86)	1.6	(0.17)	2.0	(1.12)
Spain (Murcia)	470	(6.6)	483	(7.4)	486	(7.1)	486	(6.7)	6.4	(2.62)	1.3	(0.19)	0.5	(0.38)
Spain (Navarre)	475	(5.9)	499	(5.7)	508	(5.0)	509	(5.0)	12.5	(3.47)	1.6	(0.22)	1.9	(1.02)
United Kingdom (Scotland)	508	(5.0)	515	(5.9)	504	(5.7)	484	(4.7)	-7.1	(2.48)	0.9	(0.09)	0.5	(0.32)
Non-adjudicated														
Belgium (French Community)	477	(6.2)	494	(5.5)	505	(6.5)	503	(6.1)	12.0	(2.97)	1.3	(0.14)	1.2	(0.62)
Belgium (German-Speaking Community)	485	(6.1)	505	(6.9)	509	(7.5)	501	(6.9)	6.6	(3.70)	1.4	(0.20)	0.4	(0.45)
Finland (Finnish Speaking)	538	(4.0)	540	(3.5)	541	(3.5)	535	(3.8)	-1.9	(1.91)	1.0	(0.08)	0.0	(0.10)
Finland (Swedish Speaking)	526	(5.6)	514	(6.1)	522	(5.1)	491	(5.3)	-13.6	(2.78)	0.7	(0.10)	2.2	(0.91)
Italy (Provincia Abruzzo)	458	(6.0)	488	(8.2)	490	(6.1)	495	(7.9)	14.8	(5.72)	1.6	(0.22)	2.0	(1.53)
Italy (Provincia Autonoma di Bolzano)	494	(5.0)	492	(5.6)	499	(5.4)	484	(6.3)	-2.0	(3.04)	1.0	(0.12)	0.0	(0.15)
Italy (Provincia Basilicata)	463	(7.5)	474	(7.0)	479	(6.1)	487	(6.6)	10.6	(3.66)	1.3	(0.19)	1.0	(0.75)
Italy (Provincia Calabria)	440	(5.6)	449	(7.8)	458	(8.4)	471	(7.1)	13.9	(3.67)	1.4	(0.20)	1.8	(0.91)
Italy (Provincia Campania)	436	(6.1)	459	(8.5)	466	(8.6)	467	(10.1)	15.5	(4.91)	1.5	(0.24)	2.0	(1.33)
Italy (Provincia Emilia Romagna)	480	(6.0)	509	(5.0)	510	(6.6)	529	(3.9)	24.0	(2.58)	1.6	(0.15)	4.5	(1.00)
Italy (Provincia Friuli Venezia Giulia)	489	(7.3)	512	(6.3)	526	(6.6)	534	(6.5)	21.9	(4.33)	1.6	(0.19)	4.7	(1.76)
Italy (Provincia Lazio)	467	(8.3)	482	(5.6)	487	(8.1)	500	(8.8)	18.3	(4.42)	1.4	(0.22)	3.2	(1.63)
Italy (Provincia Liguria)	466	(10.6)	501	(8.4)	495	(8.5)	517	(10.2)	23.6	(3.87)	1.6	(0.22)	4.2	(1.14)
Italy (Provincia Lombardia)	510	(7.5)	518	(5.9)	524	(6.1)	546	(7.7)	17.9	(3.61)	1.2	(0.20)	2.6	(1.08)
Italy (Provincia Marche)	484	(11.0)	506	(8.0)	508	(6.5)	511	(7.3)	13.9	(3.99)	1.5	(0.17)	1.5	(0.74)
Italy (Provincia Molise)	458	(5.0)	473	(5.7)	480	(4.4)	476	(6.4)	9.1	(3.31)	1.3	(0.16)	0.9	(0.62)
Italy (Provincia Piemonte)	482	(7.1)	495	(8.9)	513	(10.3)	504	(8.2)	12.6	(3.65)	1.3	(0.20)	1.4	(0.86)
Italy (Provincia Puglia)	487	(7.9)	487	(7.1)	493	(8.0)	504	(5.9)	7.1	(4.45)	1.1	(0.16)	0.4	(0.54)
Italy (Provincia Sardegna)	454	(5.3)	464	(5.8)	481	(7.2)	488	(8.0)	15.7	(3.34)	1.3	(0.21)	2.6	(1.19)
Italy (Provincia Sicilia)	453	(7.0)	462	(9.9)	465	(10.3)	476	(10.0)	13.9	(4.63)	1.2	(0.19)	1.3	(0.88)
Italy (Provincia Toscana)	480	(7.0)	501	(5.6)	497	(5.5)	505	(6.8)	11.7	(3.15)	1.3	(0.18)	1.0	(0.55)
Italy (Provincia Trento)	489	(6.8)	512	(6.3)	517	(6.2)	525	(5.7)	14.3	(3.90)	1.4	(0.19)	1.9	(1.00)
Italy (Provincia Umbria)	478	(8.6)	493	(6.6)	506	(6.3)	502	(8.1)	14.9	(4.35)	1.4	(0.19)	1.4	(0.81)
Italy (Provincia Valle d'Aosta)	503	(4.6)	507	(5.7)	525	(6.8)	524	(6.2)	7.8	(2.58)	1.2	(0.16)	0.6	(0.40)
Italy (Provincia Veneto)	479	(7.8)	510	(7.4)	516	(5.1)	522	(8.9)	22.0	(4.45)	1.6	(0.22)	4.3	(1.70)
United Kingdom (England)	500	(4.5)	511	(3.8)	499	(4.3)	480	(3.8)	-9.1	(2.33)	0.9	(0.07)	0.7	(0.34)
United Kingdom (Northern Ireland)	498	(6.9)	505	(5.3)	506	(5.4)	497	(6.9)	-0.5	(3.55)	1.1	(0.11)	0.0	(0.09)
United Kingdom (Wales)	487	(4.9)	486	(5.2)	478	(4.5)	466	(4.9)	-7.2	(2.55)	0.9	(0.08)	0.5	(0.30)

Notes: Values that are statistically significant are indicated in bold (see Annex A3). See Table III.2.5 for national data.
StatLink ⟐ http://dx.doi.org/10.1787/888932343304

[Part 1/2]

Index of use of functional texts and reading performance, by national quarters of this index

Table S.III.n *Results based on students' self-reports*

	Index of use of functional texts															
	All students		Males		Females		Gender difference (B – G)		Bottom quarter		Second quarter		Third quarter		Top quarter	
	Mean index	S.E.	Mean index	S.E.	Mean index	S.E.	Dif.	S.E.	Mean index	S.E.	Mean index	S.E.	Mean index	S.E.	Mean index	S.E.
Adjudicated																
Belgium (Flemish Community)	0.01	(0.02)	0.05	(0.03)	-0.02	(0.02)	**0.07**	(0.03)	**-1.14**	(0.01)	-0.21	(0.00)	0.31	(0.00)	**1.09**	(0.02)
Spain (Andalusia)	0.15	(0.04)	0.17	(0.04)	0.12	(0.05)	0.06	(0.05)	**-1.10**	(0.03)	-0.05	(0.01)	0.45	(0.01)	**1.27**	(0.04)
Spain (Aragon)	0.06	(0.03)	0.07	(0.03)	0.05	(0.04)	0.03	(0.05)	**-1.13**	(0.03)	-0.16	(0.01)	0.35	(0.01)	**1.18**	(0.03)
Spain (Asturias)	0.12	(0.04)	0.13	(0.05)	0.11	(0.04)	0.02	(0.06)	**-1.11**	(0.03)	-0.15	(0.01)	0.42	(0.01)	**1.32**	(0.03)
Spain (Balearic Islands)	0.07	(0.02)	0.06	(0.04)	0.07	(0.03)	-0.01	(0.06)	**-1.18**	(0.02)	-0.18	(0.01)	0.37	(0.01)	**1.25**	(0.03)
Spain (Basque Country)	-0.03	(0.02)	-0.01	(0.03)	-0.05	(0.03)	0.04	(0.03)	**-1.25**	(0.01)	-0.23	(0.00)	0.28	(0.00)	**1.08**	(0.02)
Spain (Canary Islands)	0.11	(0.03)	0.15	(0.04)	0.07	(0.05)	0.07	(0.05)	**-1.10**	(0.02)	-0.11	(0.01)	0.41	(0.01)	**1.25**	(0.04)
Spain (Cantabria)	0.09	(0.03)	0.09	(0.04)	0.08	(0.04)	0.01	(0.05)	**-1.11**	(0.02)	-0.15	(0.01)	0.39	(0.01)	**1.21**	(0.02)
Spain (Castile and Leon)	0.08	(0.04)	0.08	(0.04)	0.09	(0.04)	-0.01	(0.04)	**-1.14**	(0.02)	-0.17	(0.01)	0.36	(0.01)	**1.27**	(0.03)
Spain (Catalonia)	-0.05	(0.03)	-0.06	(0.05)	-0.04	(0.03)	-0.01	(0.04)	**-1.26**	(0.02)	-0.26	(0.01)	0.26	(0.01)	**1.06**	(0.03)
Spain (Ceuta and Melilla)	0.24	(0.03)	0.28	(0.05)	0.20	(0.04)	0.08	(0.07)	**-1.08**	(0.03)	0.02	(0.01)	0.58	(0.01)	**1.45**	(0.03)
Spain (Galicia)	-0.01	(0.04)	0.04	(0.04)	-0.05	(0.04)	0.08	(0.05)	**-1.21**	(0.02)	-0.22	(0.01)	0.29	(0.01)	**1.12**	(0.03)
Spain (La Rioja)	0.07	(0.03)	0.16	(0.04)	-0.04	(0.05)	**0.20**	(0.06)	**-1.26**	(0.03)	-0.19	(0.01)	0.42	(0.01)	**1.29**	(0.03)
Spain (Madrid)	0.00	(0.04)	0.06	(0.04)	-0.06	(0.05)	0.11	(0.05)	**-1.23**	(0.03)	-0.21	(0.01)	0.26	(0.01)	**1.17**	(0.03)
Spain (Murcia)	0.04	(0.02)	0.10	(0.03)	-0.03	(0.03)	**0.13**	(0.05)	**-1.17**	(0.03)	-0.19	(0.01)	0.34	(0.01)	**1.17**	(0.03)
Spain (Navarre)	0.10	(0.03)	0.11	(0.04)	0.09	(0.04)	0.03	(0.06)	**-1.06**	(0.02)	-0.13	(0.01)	0.37	(0.01)	**1.22**	(0.03)
United Kingdom (Scotland)	-0.25	(0.02)	-0.20	(0.03)	-0.30	(0.02)	**0.09**	(0.04)	**-1.47**	(0.01)	-0.52	(0.01)	0.08	(0.00)	**0.92**	(0.02)
Non-adjudicated																
Belgium (French Community)	0.06	(0.03)	0.02	(0.04)	0.11	(0.03)	-0.09	(0.05)	**-1.26**	(0.02)	-0.21	(0.01)	0.36	(0.01)	**1.35**	(0.03)
Belgium (German-Speaking Community)	-0.22	(0.03)	-0.24	(0.05)	-0.20	(0.03)	-0.05	(0.06)	**-1.37**	(0.03)	-0.44	(0.01)	0.07	(0.01)	**0.85**	(0.03)
Finland (Finnish Speaking)	-0.20	(0.02)	-0.16	(0.03)	-0.25	(0.02)	**0.09**	(0.03)	**-1.49**	(0.01)	-0.47	(0.01)	0.13	(0.00)	**1.02**	(0.02)
Finland (Swedish Speaking)	-0.35	(0.03)	-0.31	(0.05)	-0.38	(0.03)	0.07	(0.06)	**-1.52**	(0.01)	-0.60	(0.01)	-0.03	(0.01)	**0.76**	(0.03)
Italy (Provincia Abruzzo)	-0.36	(0.05)	-0.34	(0.06)	-0.38	(0.05)	0.04	(0.04)	**-1.57**	(0.01)	-0.59	(0.01)	-0.03	(0.01)	**0.75**	(0.03)
Italy (Provincia Autonoma di Bolzano)	-0.05	(0.02)	-0.03	(0.03)	-0.07	(0.03)	0.04	(0.05)	**-1.21**	(0.02)	-0.23	(0.01)	0.24	(0.01)	**1.00**	(0.03)
Italy (Provincia Basilicata)	-0.12	(0.04)	-0.04	(0.05)	-0.21	(0.04)	**0.16**	(0.05)	**-1.28**	(0.02)	-0.29	(0.01)	0.11	(0.01)	**0.97**	(0.04)
Italy (Provincia Calabria)	-0.14	(0.03)	-0.04	(0.05)	-0.24	(0.04)	**0.20**	(0.04)	**-1.41**	(0.02)	-0.39	(0.01)	0.19	(0.01)	**1.04**	(0.03)
Italy (Provincia Campania)	-0.13	(0.04)	-0.07	(0.06)	-0.21	(0.04)	**0.14**	(0.06)	**-1.33**	(0.02)	-0.29	(0.01)	0.17	(0.01)	**0.91**	(0.02)
Italy (Provincia Emilia Romagna)	-0.41	(0.03)	-0.36	(0.04)	-0.46	(0.04)	**0.10**	(0.05)	**-1.54**	(0.01)	-0.60	(0.01)	-0.15	(0.01)	**0.64**	(0.03)
Italy (Provincia Friuli Venezia Giulia)	-0.28	(0.03)	-0.15	(0.05)	-0.41	(0.04)	**0.26**	(0.07)	**-1.45**	(0.02)	-0.50	(0.01)	0.03	(0.01)	**0.80**	(0.02)
Italy (Provincia Lazio)	-0.41	(0.05)	-0.35	(0.06)	-0.47	(0.06)	0.12	(0.06)	**-1.67**	(0.00)	-0.66	(0.01)	-0.08	(0.01)	**0.79**	(0.04)
Italy (Provincia Liguria)	-0.48	(0.05)	-0.44	(0.08)	-0.54	(0.05)	0.10	(0.09)	**-1.69**	(0.01)	-0.72	(0.02)	-0.16	(0.01)	**0.63**	(0.03)
Italy (Provincia Lombardia)	-0.36	(0.03)	-0.29	(0.04)	-0.44	(0.06)	0.15	(0.09)	**-1.52**	(0.01)	-0.55	(0.01)	-0.06	(0.00)	**0.67**	(0.03)
Italy (Provincia Marche)	-0.23	(0.05)	-0.16	(0.06)	-0.30	(0.05)	**0.14**	(0.06)	**-1.37**	(0.02)	-0.40	(0.01)	0.08	(0.01)	**0.80**	(0.03)
Italy (Provincia Molise)	-0.16	(0.02)	-0.03	(0.04)	-0.30	(0.04)	**0.28**	(0.06)	**-1.36**	(0.03)	-0.35	(0.01)	0.10	(0.01)	**0.95**	(0.04)
Italy (Provincia Piemonte)	-0.30	(0.04)	-0.22	(0.05)	-0.38	(0.05)	**0.15**	(0.07)	**-1.53**	(0.01)	-0.55	(0.01)	0.03	(0.01)	**0.83**	(0.03)
Italy (Provincia Puglia)	-0.07	(0.03)	-0.03	(0.04)	-0.12	(0.05)	0.09	(0.06)	**-1.24**	(0.02)	-0.25	(0.01)	0.17	(0.01)	**1.02**	(0.03)
Italy (Provincia Sardegna)	-0.21	(0.04)	-0.08	(0.05)	-0.33	(0.05)	**0.26**	(0.06)	**-1.49**	(0.02)	-0.41	(0.01)	0.11	(0.01)	**0.96**	(0.03)
Italy (Provincia Sicilia)	-0.19	(0.03)	-0.07	(0.05)	-0.31	(0.04)	**0.24**	(0.05)	**-1.38**	(0.02)	-0.41	(0.01)	0.10	(0.01)	**0.92**	(0.03)
Italy (Provincia Toscana)	-0.43	(0.04)	-0.37	(0.06)	-0.50	(0.04)	**0.13**	(0.06)	**-1.63**	(0.01)	-0.65	(0.01)	-0.12	(0.01)	**0.68**	(0.03)
Italy (Provincia Trento)	-0.28	(0.02)	-0.20	(0.04)	-0.37	(0.03)	**0.16**	(0.04)	**-1.42**	(0.02)	-0.47	(0.01)	0.00	(0.00)	**0.76**	(0.04)
Italy (Provincia Umbria)	-0.24	(0.03)	-0.20	(0.04)	-0.28	(0.04)	0.08	(0.06)	**-1.36**	(0.02)	-0.41	(0.01)	0.05	(0.01)	**0.75**	(0.03)
Italy (Provincia Valle d'Aosta)	-0.27	(0.03)	-0.19	(0.05)	-0.35	(0.03)	**0.16**	(0.06)	**-1.40**	(0.02)	-0.48	(0.01)	0.03	(0.01)	**0.76**	(0.04)
Italy (Provincia Veneto)	-0.34	(0.04)	-0.27	(0.04)	-0.41	(0.05)	**0.14**	(0.06)	**-1.53**	(0.01)	-0.55	(0.01)	0.00	(0.01)	**0.72**	(0.03)
United Kingdom (England)	0.00	(0.02)	-0.03	(0.03)	0.02	(0.03)	-0.04	(0.04)	**-1.26**	(0.02)	-0.22	(0.01)	0.33	(0.00)	**1.14**	(0.02)
United Kingdom (Northern Ireland)	0.00	(0.03)	0.00	(0.04)	-0.01	(0.04)	0.01	(0.06)	**-1.25**	(0.02)	-0.23	(0.01)	0.32	(0.01)	**1.15**	(0.02)
United Kingdom (Wales)	-0.03	(0.02)	-0.01	(0.02)	-0.05	(0.02)	0.04	(0.03)	**-1.27**	(0.02)	-0.22	(0.01)	0.29	(0.00)	**1.08**	(0.02)

Notes: Values that are statistically significant are indicated in bold (see Annex A3). See Table III.2.6 for national data.
StatLink ᴍ⛛ᴘ http://dx.doi.org/10.1787/888932343304

[Part 2/2]
Index of use of functional texts and reading performance, by national quarters of this index
Table S.III.n   *Results based on students' self-reports*

| | Performance on the reading scale, by quarters of this index | | | | | | | | Change in the reading score per unit of this index | | Increased likelihood of students in the bottom quarter of this index scoring in the bottom quarter of the reading performance distribution | | Explained variance in student performance (r-squared x 100) | |
| | Bottom quarter | | Second quarter | | Third quarter | | Top quarter | | | | | | | |
	Mean index	S.E.	Mean index	S.E.	Mean index	S.E.	Mean index	S.E.	Effect	S.E.	Ratio	S.E.	%	S.E.
Adjudicated														
Belgium (Flemish Community)	**549**	(4.3)	540	(3.6)	516	(4.5)	**482**	(4.1)	**-27.7**	(2.23)	**0.5**	(0.06)	7.2	(1.19)
Spain (Andalusia)	**481**	(7.6)	475	(6.4)	462	(7.0)	**443**	(7.2)	**-15.7**	(2.95)	0.8	(0.12)	3.0	(1.14)
Spain (Aragon)	**507**	(5.6)	508	(5.3)	498	(6.9)	**480**	(5.9)	**-11.5**	(2.59)	0.8	(0.13)	1.7	(0.77)
Spain (Asturias)	**516**	(6.5)	502	(6.7)	490	(7.7)	**459**	(7.0)	**-20.7**	(2.74)	0.6	(0.11)	4.9	(1.19)
Spain (Balearic Islands)	**477**	(7.3)	465	(5.8)	455	(8.0)	**445**	(6.2)	**-11.5**	(2.57)	0.7	(0.12)	1.5	(0.68)
Spain (Basque Country)	**516**	(3.3)	502	(3.8)	488	(4.1)	**475**	(4.0)	**-17.8**	(1.43)	0.6	(0.05)	3.9	(0.62)
Spain (Canary Islands)	**472**	(6.6)	456	(6.5)	447	(7.5)	**445**	(5.8)	**-11.3**	(3.13)	**0.7**	(0.10)	1.4	(0.81)
Spain (Cantabria)	**509**	(7.7)	496	(5.3)	483	(6.4)	**469**	(4.9)	**-16.2**	(2.79)	0.6	(0.10)	2.9	(1.02)
Spain (Castile and Leon)	**519**	(6.0)	517	(5.3)	500	(6.9)	**483**	(5.9)	**-15.3**	(2.28)	**0.7**	(0.09)	3.1	(0.97)
Spain (Catalonia)	**528**	(5.5)	511	(6.0)	491	(7.7)	**470**	(7.8)	**-24.0**	(2.53)	0.4	(0.07)	7.3	(1.36)
Spain (Ceuta and Melilla)	**457**	(5.8)	435	(6.0)	412	(6.8)	**402**	(6.0)	**-21.4**	(2.85)	0.6	(0.08)	4.6	(1.15)
Spain (Galicia)	**499**	(5.5)	495	(5.4)	484	(5.5)	**468**	(6.0)	**-14.7**	(2.22)	0.8	(0.10)	2.5	(0.76)
Spain (La Rioja)	**535**	(4.7)	504	(6.0)	488	(6.6)	**470**	(5.3)	**-26.5**	(2.41)	0.4	(0.08)	8.5	(1.53)
Spain (Madrid)	**528**	(6.2)	515	(6.8)	504	(5.7)	**481**	(5.6)	**-18.2**	(2.65)	0.5	(0.11)	4.7	(1.35)
Spain (Murcia)	**496**	(6.3)	489	(6.9)	483	(5.7)	**458**	(6.5)	**-15.2**	(2.43)	0.7	(0.14)	3.1	(1.00)
Spain (Navarre)	**512**	(5.3)	505	(6.0)	495	(5.1)	**479**	(5.2)	**-14.8**	(2.42)	0.6	(0.11)	2.7	(0.90)
United Kingdom (Scotland)	**513**	(4.0)	513	(4.1)	500	(4.8)	**485**	(4.5)	**-12.0**	(1.81)	0.8	(0.09)	1.5	(0.45)
Non-adjudicated														
Belgium (French Community)	**511**	(4.8)	518	(5.4)	487	(5.8)	**465**	(6.0)	**-17.7**	(2.02)	**0.8**	(0.07)	3.0	(0.67)
Belgium (German-Speaking Community)	**513**	(6.1)	524	(7.4)	497	(6.8)	**465**	(6.3)	**-20.6**	(3.44)	0.8	(0.14)	4.1	(1.28)
Finland (Finnish Speaking)	**554**	(3.4)	552	(3.7)	535	(3.7)	**512**	(3.5)	**-17.2**	(1.60)	**0.7**	(0.07)	3.9	(0.71)
Finland (Swedish Speaking)	**524**	(5.6)	529	(5.5)	513	(6.5)	**489**	(5.0)	**-15.3**	(3.02)	0.8	(0.11)	2.6	(1.02)
Italy (Provincia Abruzzo)	**500**	(9.6)	496	(7.7)	488	(6.7)	**449**	(6.8)	**-21.3**	(5.14)	0.7	(0.16)	4.9	(2.23)
Italy (Provincia Autonoma di Bolzano)	**506**	(4.4)	506	(5.6)	487	(4.7)	**470**	(6.3)	**-16.1**	(3.09)	0.8	(0.10)	2.5	(0.94)
Italy (Provincia Basilicata)	**497**	(5.7)	487	(5.0)	474	(6.5)	**446**	(8.8)	**-22.1**	(4.18)	0.6	(0.12)	5.3	(1.91)
Italy (Provincia Calabria)	**480**	(7.0)	480	(5.5)	447	(7.2)	**413**	(5.9)	**-27.1**	(2.86)	0.5	(0.09)	9.2	(1.71)
Italy (Provincia Campania)	**474**	(7.1)	475	(6.6)	456	(8.3)	**427**	(9.1)	**-19.8**	(3.87)	0.7	(0.11)	3.9	(1.48)
Italy (Provincia Emilia Romagna)	**520**	(5.3)	518	(5.2)	521	(5.9)	**470**	(7.4)	**-20.5**	(3.24)	0.8	(0.09)	3.3	(0.98)
Italy (Provincia Friuli Venezia Giulia)	**534**	(6.2)	540	(4.9)	517	(6.1)	**471**	(7.5)	**-26.2**	(2.86)	0.6	(0.11)	6.7	(1.32)
Italy (Provincia Lazio)	**513**	(6.0)	506	(6.1)	483	(8.4)	**433**	(8.2)	**-29.9**	(4.22)	0.5	(0.10)	9.7	(2.60)
Italy (Provincia Liguria)	**510**	(8.5)	515	(7.1)	502	(11.2)	**453**	(12.4)	**-22.3**	(4.71)	0.6	(0.10)	4.7	(1.52)
Italy (Provincia Lombardia)	**545**	(6.4)	540	(7.5)	530	(7.6)	**483**	(7.1)	**-24.9**	(3.47)	0.6	(0.11)	6.0	(1.69)
Italy (Provincia Marche)	**526**	(7.6)	515	(7.4)	501	(8.3)	**469**	(10.7)	**-25.3**	(4.27)	0.6	(0.12)	5.9	(1.89)
Italy (Provincia Molise)	**492**	(5.2)	492	(6.3)	470	(6.5)	**435**	(5.2)	**-23.8**	(2.63)	0.5	(0.08)	6.8	(1.41)
Italy (Provincia Piemonte)	**531**	(6.0)	518	(7.8)	491	(9.4)	**456**	(10.3)	**-31.6**	(4.18)	0.4	(0.10)	9.6	(2.37)
Italy (Provincia Puglia)	**509**	(6.2)	509	(6.5)	492	(8.0)	**463**	(7.0)	**-22.4**	(2.70)	0.6	(0.10)	5.7	(1.27)
Italy (Provincia Sardegna)	**495**	(5.9)	495	(6.3)	471	(7.8)	**426**	(7.7)	**-26.8**	(3.34)	0.7	(0.11)	7.9	(1.65)
Italy (Provincia Sicilia)	**490**	(9.2)	480	(8.3)	464	(10.9)	**425**	(8.9)	**-27.1**	(4.26)	0.5	(0.11)	7.0	(1.86)
Italy (Provincia Toscana)	**514**	(5.9)	515	(6.0)	499	(6.4)	**457**	(8.4)	**-24.0**	(3.67)	0.7	(0.10)	5.3	(1.53)
Italy (Provincia Trento)	**527**	(6.6)	526	(6.3)	517	(5.5)	**473**	(5.7)	**-23.8**	(3.01)	0.7	(0.12)	5.2	(1.28)
Italy (Provincia Umbria)	**510**	(6.6)	513	(6.4)	498	(7.2)	**458**	(9.9)	**-22.8**	(4.32)	0.8	(0.12)	4.0	(1.42)
Italy (Provincia Valle d'Aosta)	**528**	(5.6)	532	(7.4)	519	(6.2)	**482**	(5.2)	**-18.8**	(2.87)	0.7	(0.13)	3.5	(1.05)
Italy (Provincia Veneto)	**524**	(6.3)	521	(6.5)	507	(8.9)	**477**	(7.8)	**-21.1**	(3.78)	0.7	(0.10)	4.4	(1.49)
United Kingdom (England)	**510**	(3.9)	511	(3.5)	494	(3.8)	**476**	(4.2)	**-14.8**	(1.80)	0.7	(0.05)	2.3	(0.55)
United Kingdom (Northern Ireland)	**516**	(5.6)	514	(4.8)	500	(6.5)	**478**	(6.8)	**-16.0**	(3.16)	0.8	(0.10)	2.5	(0.97)
United Kingdom (Wales)	**500**	(4.4)	488	(4.5)	476	(3.9)	**452**	(4.6)	**-20.5**	(2.09)	0.6	(0.07)	4.3	(0.85)

Notes: Values that are statistically significant are indicated in bold (see Annex A3). See Table III.2.6 for national data.
StatLink ⫶ http://dx.doi.org/10.1787/888932343304

[Part 1/2]

Index of understanding and remembering and reading performance, by national quarters of this index

Table S.III.o — *Results based on students' self-reports*

| | Index of understanding and remembering | | | | | | | | | | | | | | | |
| | All students | | Males | | Females | | Gender difference (B – G) | | Bottom quarter | | Second quarter | | Third quarter | | Top quarter | |
	Mean index	S.E.	Mean index	S.E.	Mean index	S.E.	Dif.	S.E.	Mean index	S.E.	Mean index	S.E.	Mean index	S.E.	Mean index	S.E.
Adjudicated																
Belgium (Flemish Community)	0.22	(0.02)	0.11	(0.03)	0.32	(0.03)	**-0.21**	(0.05)	**-1.13**	(0.02)	-0.02	(0.01)	0.66	(0.01)	**1.35**	(0.00)
Spain (Andalusia)	0.06	(0.04)	-0.05	(0.05)	0.18	(0.05)	**-0.23**	(0.06)	**-1.28**	(0.02)	-0.13	(0.01)	0.45	(0.01)	**1.20**	(0.01)
Spain (Aragon)	0.15	(0.03)	0.06	(0.04)	0.24	(0.04)	**-0.18**	(0.05)	**-1.09**	(0.03)	-0.04	(0.01)	0.48	(0.01)	**1.24**	(0.01)
Spain (Asturias)	0.05	(0.03)	-0.11	(0.04)	0.22	(0.03)	**-0.33**	(0.04)	**-1.24**	(0.03)	-0.13	(0.01)	0.43	(0.01)	**1.15**	(0.02)
Spain (Balearic Islands)	0.05	(0.04)	-0.01	(0.05)	0.11	(0.05)	**-0.12**	(0.05)	**-1.33**	(0.02)	-0.20	(0.02)	0.47	(0.01)	**1.27**	(0.01)
Spain (Basque Country)	-0.01	(0.02)	-0.10	(0.03)	0.08	(0.03)	**-0.18**	(0.03)	**-1.33**	(0.02)	-0.32	(0.01)	0.42	(0.00)	**1.18**	(0.01)
Spain (Canary Islands)	0.14	(0.03)	0.05	(0.04)	0.23	(0.04)	**-0.18**	(0.05)	**-1.19**	(0.03)	-0.05	(0.02)	0.51	(0.01)	**1.28**	(0.01)
Spain (Cantabria)	0.13	(0.03)	0.06	(0.04)	0.20	(0.04)	**-0.14**	(0.06)	**-1.13**	(0.02)	-0.06	(0.02)	0.49	(0.01)	**1.24**	(0.01)
Spain (Castile and Leon)	0.23	(0.03)	0.10	(0.05)	0.35	(0.03)	**-0.26**	(0.05)	**-1.03**	(0.03)	0.07	(0.01)	0.59	(0.01)	**1.27**	(0.01)
Spain (Catalonia)	0.17	(0.04)	0.05	(0.05)	0.30	(0.04)	**-0.25**	(0.05)	**-1.14**	(0.03)	-0.06	(0.02)	0.58	(0.01)	**1.31**	(0.01)
Spain (Ceuta and Melilla)	-0.03	(0.03)	-0.11	(0.05)	0.05	(0.04)	**-0.16**	(0.06)	**-1.34**	(0.02)	-0.35	(0.02)	0.40	(0.01)	**1.17**	(0.02)
Spain (Galicia)	0.09	(0.04)	0.00	(0.05)	0.18	(0.05)	**-0.18**	(0.06)	**-1.21**	(0.03)	-0.12	(0.01)	0.46	(0.01)	**1.24**	(0.01)
Spain (La Rioja)	0.15	(0.03)	0.01	(0.04)	0.30	(0.04)	**-0.30**	(0.05)	**-1.13**	(0.03)	0.01	(0.02)	0.49	(0.01)	**1.24**	(0.01)
Spain (Madrid)	0.21	(0.04)	0.07	(0.05)	0.34	(0.04)	**-0.28**	(0.04)	**-1.02**	(0.02)	0.06	(0.01)	0.53	(0.01)	**1.25**	(0.01)
Spain (Murcia)	0.14	(0.03)	0.05	(0.04)	0.23	(0.03)	**-0.17**	(0.05)	**-1.12**	(0.03)	-0.04	(0.02)	0.48	(0.01)	**1.24**	(0.01)
Spain (Navarre)	0.08	(0.03)	-0.03	(0.04)	0.19	(0.03)	**-0.22**	(0.05)	**-1.26**	(0.02)	-0.15	(0.02)	0.47	(0.01)	**1.25**	(0.01)
United Kingdom (Scotland)	-0.04	(0.03)	-0.14	(0.04)	0.06	(0.03)	**-0.20**	(0.05)	**-1.33**	(0.02)	-0.41	(0.01)	0.36	(0.01)	**1.21**	(0.01)
Non-adjudicated																
Belgium (French Community)	0.21	(0.03)	0.09	(0.03)	0.34	(0.03)	**-0.24**	(0.04)	**-1.19**	(0.02)	0.01	(0.01)	0.68	(0.01)	**1.36**	(0.00)
Belgium (German-Speaking Community)	0.21	(0.04)	-0.05	(0.05)	0.47	(0.04)	**-0.52**	(0.06)	**-1.23**	(0.03)	-0.09	(0.02)	0.75	(0.02)	**1.42**	(0.00)
Finland (Finnish Speaking)	0.05	(0.02)	-0.23	(0.03)	0.32	(0.02)	**-0.56**	(0.03)	**-1.35**	(0.01)	-0.22	(0.01)	0.50	(0.01)	**0.98**	(0.02)
Finland (Swedish Speaking)	-0.30	(0.03)	-0.59	(0.04)	-0.01	(0.03)	**-0.58**	(0.05)	**-1.57**	(0.02)	-0.71	(0.01)	0.11	(0.02)	**1.31**	(0.01)
Italy (Provincia Abruzzo)	0.26	(0.03)	0.13	(0.04)	0.40	(0.04)	**-0.27**	(0.06)	**-0.99**	(0.02)	0.10	(0.01)	0.62	(0.02)	**1.35**	(0.01)
Italy (Provincia Autonoma di Bolzano)	0.24	(0.03)	0.03	(0.04)	0.45	(0.03)	**-0.42**	(0.05)	**-1.12**	(0.03)	0.04	(0.01)	0.70	(0.02)	**1.35**	(0.01)
Italy (Provincia Basilicata)	0.23	(0.03)	0.13	(0.04)	0.35	(0.05)	**-0.22**	(0.05)	**-0.97**	(0.02)	0.08	(0.01)	0.53	(0.01)	**1.30**	(0.01)
Italy (Provincia Calabria)	0.17	(0.04)	0.02	(0.04)	0.31	(0.05)	**-0.29**	(0.06)	**-1.05**	(0.03)	0.01	(0.01)	0.47	(0.01)	**1.24**	(0.01)
Italy (Provincia Campania)	0.13	(0.03)	0.02	(0.04)	0.26	(0.05)	**-0.24**	(0.06)	**-1.12**	(0.03)	-0.04	(0.01)	0.44	(0.01)	**1.23**	(0.01)
Italy (Provincia Emilia Romagna)	0.35	(0.02)	0.24	(0.04)	0.45	(0.05)	**-0.21**	(0.08)	**-0.91**	(0.02)	0.20	(0.01)	0.73	(0.01)	**1.36**	(0.01)
Italy (Provincia Friuli Venezia Giulia)	0.30	(0.04)	0.12	(0.05)	0.48	(0.04)	**-0.36**	(0.05)	**-0.95**	(0.03)	0.13	(0.01)	0.69	(0.01)	**1.32**	(0.01)
Italy (Provincia Lazio)	0.26	(0.03)	0.10	(0.04)	0.43	(0.04)	**-0.33**	(0.05)	**-1.00**	(0.04)	0.14	(0.01)	0.60	(0.01)	**1.29**	(0.01)
Italy (Provincia Liguria)	0.26	(0.04)	0.13	(0.06)	0.42	(0.03)	**-0.29**	(0.07)	**-0.97**	(0.03)	0.12	(0.01)	0.60	(0.02)	**1.31**	(0.01)
Italy (Provincia Lombardia)	0.34	(0.04)	0.22	(0.04)	0.49	(0.04)	**-0.27**	(0.04)	**-0.82**	(0.02)	0.17	(0.01)	0.68	(0.01)	**1.35**	(0.01)
Italy (Provincia Marche)	0.34	(0.04)	0.20	(0.06)	0.50	(0.03)	**-0.30**	(0.06)	**-0.88**	(0.05)	0.21	(0.01)	0.69	(0.01)	**1.33**	(0.01)
Italy (Provincia Molise)	0.24	(0.03)	0.05	(0.04)	0.44	(0.04)	**-0.40**	(0.05)	**-0.97**	(0.04)	0.05	(0.02)	0.59	(0.02)	**1.29**	(0.01)
Italy (Provincia Piemonte)	0.23	(0.05)	0.13	(0.06)	0.33	(0.05)	**-0.19**	(0.06)	**-0.97**	(0.03)	0.08	(0.02)	0.56	(0.01)	**1.27**	(0.01)
Italy (Provincia Puglia)	0.20	(0.03)	0.07	(0.04)	0.32	(0.04)	**-0.26**	(0.04)	**-1.02**	(0.03)	0.07	(0.01)	0.48	(0.01)	**1.26**	(0.01)
Italy (Provincia Sardegna)	0.15	(0.03)	-0.03	(0.05)	0.31	(0.03)	**-0.35**	(0.06)	**-1.10**	(0.03)	-0.01	(0.02)	0.47	(0.01)	**1.24**	(0.01)
Italy (Provincia Sicilia)	0.20	(0.04)	0.08	(0.05)	0.31	(0.05)	**-0.23**	(0.06)	**-1.08**	(0.04)	0.06	(0.01)	0.53	(0.01)	**1.28**	(0.01)
Italy (Provincia Toscana)	0.32	(0.03)	0.18	(0.05)	0.48	(0.04)	**-0.30**	(0.08)	**-0.91**	(0.02)	0.18	(0.01)	0.69	(0.01)	**1.33**	(0.01)
Italy (Provincia Trento)	0.29	(0.03)	0.12	(0.04)	0.47	(0.04)	**-0.35**	(0.06)	**-0.93**	(0.03)	0.15	(0.01)	0.64	(0.01)	**1.30**	(0.01)
Italy (Provincia Umbria)	0.32	(0.04)	0.20	(0.04)	0.43	(0.05)	**-0.23**	(0.06)	**-0.89**	(0.03)	0.21	(0.01)	0.66	(0.01)	**1.32**	(0.01)
Italy (Provincia Valle d'Aosta)	0.33	(0.03)	0.17	(0.04)	0.48	(0.04)	**-0.31**	(0.05)	**-0.95**	(0.03)	0.17	(0.01)	0.74	(0.02)	**1.36**	(0.01)
Italy (Provincia Veneto)	0.32	(0.04)	0.16	(0.06)	0.46	(0.04)	**-0.29**	(0.08)	**-0.92**	(0.03)	0.18	(0.01)	0.69	(0.01)	**1.31**	(0.01)
United Kingdom (England)	0.10	(0.02)	0.00	(0.03)	0.20	(0.02)	**-0.21**	(0.04)	**-1.21**	(0.02)	-0.14	(0.01)	0.50	(0.01)	**1.27**	(0.01)
United Kingdom (Northern Ireland)	0.13	(0.02)	0.06	(0.04)	0.20	(0.03)	**-0.14**	(0.05)	**-1.13**	(0.02)	-0.11	(0.01)	0.49	(0.01)	**1.28**	(0.01)
United Kingdom (Wales)	0.08	(0.02)	0.00	(0.03)	0.16	(0.03)	**-0.16**	(0.04)	**-1.27**	(0.02)	-0.15	(0.01)	0.48	(0.01)	**1.26**	(0.01)

Notes: Values that are statistically significant are indicated in bold (see Annex A3). See Table III.1.14 for national data.

StatLink ⟨⟩ http://dx.doi.org/10.1787/888932343304

[Part 2/2]
Index of understanding and remembering and reading performance, by national quarters of this index

Table S.III.o *Results based on students' self-reports*

| | Performance on the reading scale, by quarters of this index | | | | | | | | Change in the reading score per unit of this index | | Increased likelihood of students in the bottom quarter of this index scoring in the bottom quarter of the reading performance distribution | | Explained variance in student performance (r-squared x 100) | |
| | Bottom quarter | | Second quarter | | Third quarter | | Top quarter | | | | | | | |
	Mean index	S.E.	Mean index	S.E.	Mean index	S.E.	Mean index	S.E.	Effect	S.E.	Ratio	S.E.	%	S.E.
Adjudicated														
Belgium (Flemish Community)	471	(2.9)	512	(3.3)	541	(3.7)	583	(3.0)	44.2	(1.68)	2.7	(0.19)	23.5	(1.40)
Spain (Andalusia)	420	(7.4)	461	(6.2)	481	(5.0)	492	(5.7)	29.6	(1.89)	2.5	(0.25)	10.6	(1.29)
Spain (Aragon)	463	(7.1)	493	(6.4)	510	(5.6)	521	(4.9)	25.4	(3.31)	2.1	(0.24)	7.5	(1.79)
Spain (Asturias)	447	(6.4)	493	(7.2)	504	(5.4)	523	(6.0)	31.6	(3.45)	2.4	(0.27)	10.2	(1.96)
Spain (Balearic Islands)	425	(6.9)	455	(7.1)	476	(6.7)	493	(8.0)	27.4	(3.74)	2.0	(0.28)	9.7	(2.29)
Spain (Basque Country)	461	(4.7)	490	(3.5)	505	(3.3)	527	(3.1)	26.5	(1.68)	2.0	(0.13)	9.7	(1.09)
Spain (Canary Islands)	405	(6.8)	450	(7.1)	464	(5.7)	487	(5.9)	32.6	(3.06)	2.4	(0.33)	12.1	(2.30)
Spain (Cantabria)	452	(5.3)	484	(6.8)	503	(5.5)	520	(5.3)	29.8	(2.09)	2.1	(0.25)	9.9	(1.32)
Spain (Castile and Leon)	462	(8.2)	505	(6.5)	515	(5.6)	534	(4.6)	31.7	(3.04)	2.4	(0.27)	11.5	(2.25)
Spain (Catalonia)	461	(7.4)	491	(7.1)	514	(5.3)	533	(6.0)	30.4	(3.50)	2.2	(0.31)	12.8	(2.55)
Spain (Ceuta and Melilla)	370	(6.2)	404	(5.6)	440	(5.6)	462	(5.1)	38.0	(2.94)	2.1	(0.23)	13.4	(1.91)
Spain (Galicia)	443	(6.7)	485	(5.5)	503	(6.3)	519	(5.0)	32.3	(2.64)	2.5	(0.30)	12.5	(1.85)
Spain (La Rioja)	446	(6.0)	501	(6.0)	521	(5.6)	526	(4.5)	36.7	(3.00)	2.8	(0.32)	13.8	(2.18)
Spain (Madrid)	469	(7.4)	503	(6.6)	517	(5.1)	532	(5.3)	27.9	(3.53)	2.1	(0.24)	8.8	(1.96)
Spain (Murcia)	451	(7.4)	483	(5.7)	483	(6.4)	511	(5.8)	23.5	(2.93)	2.0	(0.21)	7.6	(1.83)
Spain (Navarre)	461	(6.4)	490	(5.3)	508	(4.8)	534	(4.6)	29.2	(2.65)	2.1	(0.23)	11.5	(1.93)
United Kingdom (Scotland)	463	(4.3)	490	(4.6)	516	(5.0)	547	(4.2)	33.3	(1.99)	2.2	(0.18)	12.9	(1.39)
Non-adjudicated														
Belgium (French Community)	436	(6.4)	490	(4.9)	528	(4.9)	559	(4.3)	49.2	(2.16)	3.3	(0.31)	23.6	(1.58)
Belgium (German-Speaking Community)	438	(6.1)	489	(5.8)	524	(5.7)	558	(5.7)	44.3	(2.82)	3.3	(0.46)	28.2	(2.94)
Finland (Finnish Speaking)	491	(3.6)	528	(3.3)	555	(3.2)	583	(2.5)	35.0	(1.31)	2.5	(0.14)	17.2	(1.08)
Finland (Swedish Speaking)	472	(5.2)	488	(5.5)	527	(4.9)	565	(4.6)	37.0	(2.21)	2.2	(0.22)	18.2	(2.08)
Italy (Provincia Abruzzo)	439	(5.2)	480	(6.8)	501	(6.3)	518	(7.6)	34.5	(2.97)	2.4	(0.30)	12.7	(2.29)
Italy (Provincia Autonoma di Bolzano)	443	(6.2)	485	(5.4)	507	(4.5)	535	(4.0)	36.6	(2.79)	2.6	(0.31)	15.2	(2.02)
Italy (Provincia Basilicata)	430	(5.4)	471	(6.3)	490	(5.4)	513	(6.1)	36.5	(2.46)	2.5	(0.29)	14.1	(1.91)
Italy (Provincia Calabria)	407	(7.5)	444	(6.8)	468	(7.6)	491	(5.2)	37.6	(3.51)	2.3	(0.27)	14.1	(2.11)
Italy (Provincia Campania)	416	(9.1)	442	(7.9)	460	(7.2)	494	(7.4)	33.7	(3.84)	2.0	(0.23)	10.8	(1.70)
Italy (Provincia Emilia Romagna)	456	(6.5)	502	(5.9)	525	(6.0)	547	(5.6)	40.9	(3.73)	2.5	(0.23)	14.7	(2.10)
Italy (Provincia Friuli Venezia Giulia)	460	(8.7)	515	(5.4)	528	(5.5)	555	(5.0)	42.4	(3.57)	2.6	(0.34)	17.3	(2.57)
Italy (Provincia Lazio)	433	(6.0)	481	(5.4)	495	(6.9)	524	(5.4)	37.6	(2.41)	2.5	(0.34)	13.9	(1.74)
Italy (Provincia Liguria)	441	(12.3)	495	(10.3)	507	(7.6)	528	(6.8)	38.4	(4.64)	2.5	(0.31)	13.3	(2.21)
Italy (Provincia Lombardia)	475	(5.8)	516	(7.0)	546	(6.4)	554	(5.8)	38.3	(2.84)	2.4	(0.25)	13.4	(1.65)
Italy (Provincia Marche)	450	(11.5)	498	(7.8)	515	(6.6)	544	(5.2)	43.9	(4.39)	2.6	(0.23)	17.6	(2.58)
Italy (Provincia Molise)	432	(5.8)	458	(5.1)	487	(5.5)	511	(5.1)	36.9	(2.68)	2.1	(0.31)	15.4	(2.02)
Italy (Provincia Piemonte)	445	(7.8)	492	(7.7)	518	(6.4)	534	(5.8)	41.4	(3.78)	2.8	(0.32)	14.6	(2.38)
Italy (Provincia Puglia)	452	(6.0)	488	(6.9)	498	(6.5)	526	(7.6)	32.8	(3.45)	2.1	(0.26)	11.6	(2.06)
Italy (Provincia Sardegna)	432	(7.2)	468	(7.0)	485	(6.5)	511	(4.8)	34.2	(3.95)	2.2	(0.30)	12.1	(2.69)
Italy (Provincia Sicilia)	399	(14.3)	458	(10.8)	472	(9.3)	502	(7.8)	44.1	(6.22)	2.5	(0.33)	16.7	(3.29)
Italy (Provincia Toscana)	437	(7.9)	489	(6.0)	519	(6.3)	537	(5.9)	47.4	(3.41)	2.8	(0.30)	19.6	(2.27)
Italy (Provincia Trento)	465	(5.7)	502	(6.7)	529	(7.3)	549	(5.0)	39.8	(2.83)	2.2	(0.24)	14.5	(2.09)
Italy (Provincia Umbria)	446	(7.8)	487	(7.6)	511	(7.5)	535	(5.8)	41.2	(3.98)	2.4	(0.28)	14.3	(2.35)
Italy (Provincia Valle d'Aosta)	469	(5.9)	512	(5.9)	526	(6.8)	556	(5.5)	36.4	(3.30)	2.4	(0.30)	14.9	(2.62)
Italy (Provincia Veneto)	460	(10.1)	502	(6.6)	524	(5.6)	545	(6.1)	41.0	(4.96)	2.4	(0.33)	16.5	(3.44)
United Kingdom (England)	459	(3.5)	485	(3.8)	515	(4.1)	538	(4.0)	33.7	(1.89)	2.2	(0.17)	12.2	(1.28)
United Kingdom (Northern Ireland)	458	(6.3)	499	(5.7)	517	(3.7)	541	(4.8)	34.9	(2.56)	2.3	(0.19)	11.8	(1.40)
United Kingdom (Wales)	433	(4.0)	475	(4.0)	492	(4.7)	517	(3.9)	33.4	(1.66)	2.4	(0.17)	12.6	(1.14)

Notes: Values that are statistically significant are indicated in bold (see Annex A3). See Table III.1.14 for national data.
StatLink ᵍᵐˢᵖ http://dx.doi.org/10.1787/888932343304

[Part 1/2]

Index of summarising and reading performance, by national quarters of this index

Table S.III.p   *Results based on students' self-reports*

	All students Mean index	S.E.	Males Mean index	S.E.	Females Mean index	S.E.	Gender difference (B – G) Dif.	S.E.	Bottom quarter Mean index	S.E.	Second quarter Mean index	S.E.	Third quarter Mean index	S.E.	Top quarter Mean index	S.E.
Adjudicated																
Belgium (Flemish Community)	0.15	(0.02)	0.01	(0.03)	0.29	(0.03)	**-0.28**	(0.05)	**-1.32**	(0.02)	0.04	(0.01)	0.65	(0.01)	**1.24**	(0.01)
Spain (Andalusia)	0.01	(0.04)	-0.12	(0.04)	0.16	(0.05)	**-0.27**	(0.05)	**-1.22**	(0.04)	-0.16	(0.01)	0.40	(0.01)	**1.03**	(0.02)
Spain (Aragon)	0.07	(0.03)	-0.08	(0.04)	0.21	(0.03)	**-0.29**	(0.04)	**-1.13**	(0.03)	-0.13	(0.01)	0.48	(0.00)	**1.05**	(0.01)
Spain (Asturias)	0.09	(0.04)	-0.03	(0.05)	0.22	(0.04)	**-0.25**	(0.05)	**-1.13**	(0.04)	-0.12	(0.01)	0.48	(0.01)	**1.13**	(0.01)
Spain (Balearic Islands)	-0.09	(0.05)	-0.20	(0.06)	0.01	(0.05)	**-0.21**	(0.07)	**-1.45**	(0.03)	-0.28	(0.01)	0.37	(0.01)	**0.99**	(0.02)
Spain (Basque Country)	-0.04	(0.02)	-0.19	(0.03)	0.12	(0.02)	**-0.31**	(0.03)	**-1.34**	(0.01)	-0.20	(0.01)	0.39	(0.01)	**1.01**	(0.01)
Spain (Canary Islands)	0.06	(0.03)	-0.01	(0.04)	0.13	(0.03)	**-0.14**	(0.04)	**-1.12**	(0.04)	-0.13	(0.01)	0.45	(0.01)	**1.04**	(0.02)
Spain (Cantabria)	0.13	(0.02)	0.01	(0.04)	0.25	(0.03)	**-0.24**	(0.05)	**-0.99**	(0.03)	-0.07	(0.01)	0.46	(0.01)	**1.13**	(0.02)
Spain (Castile and Leon)	0.13	(0.03)	-0.01	(0.05)	0.27	(0.03)	**-0.28**	(0.04)	**-1.06**	(0.04)	-0.08	(0.01)	0.51	(0.00)	**1.15**	(0.01)
Spain (Catalonia)	0.14	(0.04)	-0.02	(0.04)	0.31	(0.04)	**-0.33**	(0.04)	**-1.09**	(0.04)	-0.04	(0.01)	0.53	(0.01)	**1.15**	(0.01)
Spain (Ceuta and Melilla)	-0.12	(0.02)	-0.23	(0.03)	-0.02	(0.03)	**-0.22**	(0.05)	**-1.38**	(0.03)	-0.33	(0.01)	0.32	(0.01)	**0.91**	(0.02)
Spain (Galicia)	0.11	(0.03)	-0.03	(0.04)	0.26	(0.04)	**-0.29**	(0.05)	**-1.13**	(0.03)	-0.07	(0.01)	0.51	(0.00)	**1.15**	(0.01)
Spain (La Rioja)	0.10	(0.03)	-0.07	(0.04)	0.28	(0.03)	**-0.35**	(0.04)	**-1.10**	(0.04)	-0.11	(0.01)	0.47	(0.01)	**1.16**	(0.01)
Spain (Madrid)	0.20	(0.03)	0.01	(0.04)	0.39	(0.04)	**-0.38**	(0.04)	**-0.90**	(0.04)	0.01	(0.01)	0.53	(0.01)	**1.18**	(0.01)
Spain (Murcia)	0.12	(0.04)	-0.03	(0.06)	0.26	(0.04)	**-0.29**	(0.05)	**-1.04**	(0.05)	-0.08	(0.01)	0.50	(0.00)	**1.11**	(0.01)
Spain (Navarre)	0.07	(0.03)	-0.01	(0.04)	0.16	(0.03)	**-0.17**	(0.04)	**-1.15**	(0.04)	-0.13	(0.01)	0.45	(0.01)	**1.11**	(0.01)
United Kingdom (Scotland)	-0.14	(0.03)	-0.23	(0.04)	-0.05	(0.03)	**-0.18**	(0.04)	**-1.56**	(0.02)	-0.40	(0.01)	0.35	(0.01)	**1.03**	(0.01)
Non-adjudicated																
Belgium (French Community)	0.20	(0.03)	0.08	(0.03)	0.31	(0.03)	**-0.22**	(0.03)	**-1.13**	(0.03)	0.04	(0.01)	0.61	(0.01)	**1.26**	(0.01)
Belgium (German-Speaking Community)	0.21	(0.03)	-0.03	(0.05)	0.45	(0.04)	**-0.48**	(0.06)	**-1.20**	(0.04)	0.09	(0.02)	0.66	(0.02)	**1.28**	(0.01)
Finland (Finnish Speaking)	0.10	(0.02)	-0.21	(0.03)	0.40	(0.02)	**-0.60**	(0.03)	**-1.27**	(0.02)	-0.08	(0.01)	0.55	(0.00)	**1.19**	(0.01)
Finland (Swedish Speaking)	-0.11	(0.04)	-0.41	(0.05)	0.18	(0.03)	**-0.58**	(0.06)	**-1.55**	(0.03)	-0.37	(0.02)	0.40	(0.01)	**1.22**	(0.01)
Italy (Provincia Abruzzo)	0.28	(0.03)	0.14	(0.05)	0.43	(0.04)	**-0.29**	(0.05)	**-0.88**	(0.04)	0.16	(0.02)	0.63	(0.01)	**1.27**	(0.01)
Italy (Provincia Autonoma di Bolzano)	0.24	(0.04)	0.04	(0.05)	0.43	(0.04)	**-0.39**	(0.05)	**-1.11**	(0.05)	0.13	(0.02)	0.67	(0.01)	**1.22**	(0.01)
Italy (Provincia Basilicata)	0.24	(0.03)	0.06	(0.04)	0.43	(0.04)	**-0.37**	(0.05)	**-0.97**	(0.03)	0.12	(0.01)	0.60	(0.01)	**1.12**	(0.02)
Italy (Provincia Calabria)	0.11	(0.03)	-0.05	(0.05)	0.26	(0.03)	**-0.32**	(0.07)	**-1.11**	(0.05)	-0.08	(0.01)	0.50	(0.00)	**1.11**	(0.01)
Italy (Provincia Campania)	0.12	(0.04)	0.02	(0.05)	0.26	(0.05)	**-0.24**	(0.06)	**-1.05**	(0.04)	-0.07	(0.01)	0.50	(0.00)	**1.30**	(0.01)
Italy (Provincia Emilia Romagna)	0.38	(0.02)	0.26	(0.04)	0.49	(0.04)	**-0.23**	(0.06)	**-0.85**	(0.04)	0.31	(0.01)	0.74	(0.01)	**1.33**	(0.00)
Italy (Provincia Friuli Venezia Giulia)	0.38	(0.05)	0.20	(0.06)	0.58	(0.05)	**-0.38**	(0.05)	**-0.85**	(0.04)	0.32	(0.01)	0.73	(0.01)	**1.24**	(0.01)
Italy (Provincia Lazio)	0.28	(0.04)	0.13	(0.06)	0.44	(0.04)	**-0.31**	(0.07)	**-0.94**	(0.04)	0.16	(0.02)	0.65	(0.01)	**1.28**	(0.01)
Italy (Provincia Liguria)	0.31	(0.04)	0.15	(0.06)	0.50	(0.03)	**-0.35**	(0.06)	**-0.89**	(0.05)	0.21	(0.02)	0.66	(0.01)	**1.31**	(0.01)
Italy (Provincia Lombardia)	0.41	(0.03)	0.32	(0.05)	0.52	(0.03)	**-0.20**	(0.05)	**-0.72**	(0.02)	0.33	(0.01)	0.74	(0.01)	**1.28**	(0.01)
Italy (Provincia Marche)	0.34	(0.03)	0.21	(0.04)	0.49	(0.04)	**-0.28**	(0.05)	**-0.86**	(0.04)	0.26	(0.01)	0.68	(0.01)	**1.25**	(0.01)
Italy (Provincia Molise)	0.30	(0.03)	0.13	(0.04)	0.48	(0.04)	**-0.35**	(0.06)	**-0.85**	(0.04)	0.17	(0.02)	0.65	(0.01)	**1.29**	(0.01)
Italy (Provincia Piemonte)	0.35	(0.05)	0.23	(0.06)	0.46	(0.05)	**-0.23**	(0.06)	**-0.81**	(0.06)	0.26	(0.01)	0.68	(0.01)	**1.23**	(0.01)
Italy (Provincia Puglia)	0.23	(0.03)	0.10	(0.05)	0.35	(0.03)	**-0.25**	(0.05)	**-0.98**	(0.03)	0.07	(0.01)	0.60	(0.01)	**1.21**	(0.01)
Italy (Provincia Sardegna)	0.21	(0.04)	0.04	(0.07)	0.36	(0.04)	**-0.31**	(0.08)	**-0.97**	(0.04)	0.03	(0.02)	0.56	(0.01)	**1.17**	(0.01)
Italy (Provincia Sicilia)	0.13	(0.04)	0.05	(0.05)	0.21	(0.06)	**-0.16**	(0.06)	**-1.12**	(0.05)	-0.06	(0.01)	0.54	(0.01)	**1.30**	(0.01)
Italy (Provincia Toscana)	0.38	(0.02)	0.21	(0.03)	0.57	(0.03)	**-0.37**	(0.05)	**-0.78**	(0.03)	0.30	(0.01)	0.72	(0.01)	**1.33**	(0.00)
Italy (Provincia Trento)	0.39	(0.03)	0.21	(0.04)	0.59	(0.04)	**-0.38**	(0.06)	**-0.90**	(0.04)	0.36	(0.01)	0.78	(0.01)	**1.32**	(0.01)
Italy (Provincia Umbria)	0.39	(0.04)	0.23	(0.05)	0.53	(0.03)	**-0.30**	(0.05)	**-0.82**	(0.03)	0.33	(0.01)	0.72	(0.01)	**1.28**	(0.01)
Italy (Provincia Valle d'Aosta)	0.37	(0.03)	0.26	(0.04)	0.47	(0.04)	**-0.21**	(0.05)	**-0.81**	(0.03)	0.32	(0.01)	0.68	(0.01)	**1.31**	(0.01)
Italy (Provincia Veneto)	0.40	(0.04)	0.25	(0.07)	0.54	(0.04)	**-0.29**	(0.08)	**-0.79**	(0.04)	0.33	(0.01)	0.75	(0.01)	**1.13**	(0.01)
United Kingdom (England)	-0.04	(0.03)	-0.16	(0.03)	0.07	(0.03)	**-0.23**	(0.04)	**-1.43**	(0.02)	-0.27	(0.01)	0.40	(0.01)	**1.07**	(0.01)
United Kingdom (Northern Ireland)	-0.10	(0.03)	-0.23	(0.05)	0.02	(0.04)	**-0.25**	(0.07)	**-1.48**	(0.02)	-0.34	(0.01)	0.36	(0.01)	**0.99**	(0.01)
United Kingdom (Wales)	-0.16	(0.02)	-0.28	(0.04)	-0.05	(0.03)	**-0.23**	(0.04)	**-1.56**	(0.02)	-0.41	(0.01)	0.34	(0.01)		

Notes: Values that are statistically significant are indicated in bold (see Annex A3). See Table III.1.16 for national data.
StatLink ᴍᴸˢᴸ http://dx.doi.org/10.1787/888932343304

[Part 2/2]

Index of summarising and reading performance, by national quarters of this index

Table S.III.p *Results based on students' self-reports*

| | Performance on the reading scale, by quarters of this index | | | | | | | | Change in the reading score per unit of this index | | Increased likelihood of students in the bottom quarter of this index scoring in the bottom quarter of the reading performance distribution | | Explained variance in student performance (r-squared x 100) | |
| | Bottom quarter | | Second quarter | | Third quarter | | Top quarter | | | | | | | |
	Mean index	S.E.	Mean index	S.E.	Mean index	S.E.	Mean index	S.E.	Effect	S.E.	Ratio	S.E.	%	S.E.
Adjudicated														
Belgium (Flemish Community)	454	(2.7)	519	(3.5)	550	(3.3)	584	(3.5)	48.3	(1.40)	3.8	(0.24)	30.2	(1.27)
Spain (Andalusia)	409	(6.2)	464	(7.6)	479	(6.4)	503	(5.9)	40.2	(2.20)	2.9	(0.32)	17.8	(1.63)
Spain (Aragon)	448	(6.7)	495	(6.0)	513	(4.7)	530	(5.3)	36.5	(3.27)	2.6	(0.30)	14.8	(2.33)
Spain (Asturias)	432	(6.6)	486	(6.4)	517	(4.6)	534	(5.8)	46.4	(2.93)	3.0	(0.30)	20.6	(2.22)
Spain (Balearic Islands)	412	(7.3)	454	(6.9)	480	(8.1)	504	(4.5)	37.2	(3.04)	2.6	(0.31)	16.8	(2.28)
Spain (Basque Country)	443	(4.8)	496	(3.3)	511	(3.7)	533	(2.7)	36.4	(1.81)	2.8	(0.16)	16.5	(1.26)
Spain (Canary Islands)	400	(6.5)	442	(5.4)	476	(5.8)	488	(6.4)	40.3	(2.38)	2.5	(0.30)	15.3	(1.93)
Spain (Cantabria)	437	(5.3)	486	(5.9)	507	(5.7)	530	(4.6)	42.3	(1.96)	2.8	(0.37)	17.3	(1.67)
Spain (Castile and Leon)	455	(6.8)	502	(5.7)	522	(5.2)	537	(4.3)	38.5	(2.50)	2.8	(0.30)	16.6	(2.20)
Spain (Catalonia)	450	(7.1)	495	(6.0)	517	(5.9)	537	(5.0)	39.2	(2.70)	2.8	(0.29)	18.8	(2.10)
Spain (Ceuta and Melilla)	358	(5.2)	410	(5.6)	446	(6.9)	466	(6.7)	45.9	(2.58)	2.6	(0.29)	17.7	(1.87)
Spain (Galicia)	430	(6.9)	483	(5.8)	515	(4.5)	526	(4.8)	43.8	(2.30)	3.1	(0.35)	21.8	(1.88)
Spain (La Rioja)	445	(6.1)	495	(5.8)	516	(5.4)	541	(5.2)	43.3	(2.88)	2.7	(0.30)	18.7	(2.46)
Spain (Madrid)	458	(6.2)	501	(5.3)	520	(6.3)	544	(5.5)	41.6	(2.94)	2.9	(0.28)	18.1	(2.18)
Spain (Murcia)	440	(6.5)	479	(6.3)	499	(5.5)	513	(5.6)	33.1	(2.66)	2.6	(0.36)	13.5	(1.97)
Spain (Navarre)	446	(5.0)	498	(5.5)	515	(5.2)	533	(4.3)	36.7	(2.43)	2.9	(0.36)	15.7	(1.75)
United Kingdom (Scotland)	451	(4.2)	491	(4.6)	519	(3.8)	553	(4.6)	38.5	(1.79)	2.5	(0.24)	18.0	(1.51)
Non-adjudicated														
Belgium (French Community)	427	(6.0)	498	(4.6)	530	(4.2)	560	(3.7)	55.2	(2.41)	3.7	(0.30)	27.4	(1.59)
Belgium (German-Speaking Community)	437	(6.0)	499	(7.3)	520	(7.8)	553	(6.5)	46.3	(2.67)	3.7	(0.54)	27.7	(2.89)
Finland (Finnish Speaking)	476	(3.1)	538	(3.0)	561	(3.3)	582	(2.5)	42.2	(1.29)	3.4	(0.19)	23.3	(1.26)
Finland (Swedish Speaking)	451	(4.9)	506	(5.0)	532	(5.4)	566	(5.2)	42.3	(2.06)	3.1	(0.35)	25.8	(2.59)
Italy (Provincia Abruzzo)	432	(5.2)	483	(7.6)	498	(6.6)	529	(5.2)	45.3	(2.93)	2.8	(0.33)	19.7	(2.08)
Italy (Provincia Autonoma di Bolzano)	428	(6.6)	492	(5.2)	513	(4.2)	541	(4.2)	44.5	(2.64)	3.1	(0.36)	21.9	(2.41)
Italy (Provincia Basilicata)	418	(7.1)	472	(5.6)	492	(6.6)	520	(5.3)	45.7	(2.91)	3.2	(0.42)	22.0	(2.05)
Italy (Provincia Calabria)	397	(9.1)	448	(5.9)	472	(7.7)	492	(5.5)	42.4	(3.82)	2.8	(0.32)	18.4	(2.61)
Italy (Provincia Campania)	402	(9.5)	449	(6.1)	469	(7.6)	496	(7.7)	42.1	(4.49)	2.5	(0.27)	15.7	(2.42)
Italy (Provincia Emilia Romagna)	441	(7.6)	509	(6.0)	524	(7.5)	551	(4.8)	52.2	(3.53)	3.1	(0.29)	22.2	(2.37)
Italy (Provincia Friuli Venezia Giulia)	455	(6.4)	512	(5.8)	537	(5.9)	559	(4.7)	48.5	(3.57)	2.8	(0.36)	21.6	(2.83)
Italy (Provincia Lazio)	426	(5.9)	480	(5.4)	497	(5.2)	528	(5.8)	45.2	(2.84)	3.0	(0.38)	19.2	(2.00)
Italy (Provincia Liguria)	433	(17.6)	493	(8.0)	508	(8.5)	540	(6.3)	49.1	(6.18)	3.0	(0.34)	21.1	(2.83)
Italy (Provincia Lombardia)	469	(6.8)	518	(7.0)	540	(5.9)	565	(6.7)	47.4	(4.14)	2.7	(0.36)	18.5	(2.34)
Italy (Provincia Marche)	450	(10.0)	496	(9.6)	512	(9.0)	546	(5.4)	44.0	(3.51)	2.7	(0.31)	17.2	(1.93)
Italy (Provincia Molise)	421	(5.8)	467	(5.4)	489	(8.1)	513	(4.9)	43.6	(2.70)	2.8	(0.29)	19.5	(2.09)
Italy (Provincia Piemonte)	443	(8.5)	493	(9.5)	516	(6.1)	541	(5.5)	47.5	(3.56)	2.8	(0.41)	18.1	(2.79)
Italy (Provincia Puglia)	449	(7.6)	483	(7.3)	506	(6.6)	527	(5.1)	35.7	(3.37)	2.5	(0.35)	13.6	(2.43)
Italy (Provincia Sardegna)	432	(8.2)	461	(6.6)	494	(5.9)	507	(5.6)	35.7	(4.80)	2.1	(0.32)	12.3	(3.19)
Italy (Provincia Sicilia)	395	(14.6)	454	(8.3)	479	(8.4)	504	(7.7)	46.7	(5.78)	2.9	(0.42)	18.5	(3.30)
Italy (Provincia Toscana)	441	(7.8)	489	(8.3)	514	(6.5)	542	(4.8)	50.2	(3.78)	2.7	(0.42)	20.0	(2.37)
Italy (Provincia Trento)	447	(5.3)	508	(6.9)	531	(5.5)	555	(5.1)	48.6	(2.84)	3.1	(0.30)	22.3	(2.42)
Italy (Provincia Umbria)	435	(7.7)	497	(6.2)	512	(5.7)	539	(5.1)	50.0	(4.23)	2.9	(0.39)	20.6	(2.80)
Italy (Provincia Valle d'Aosta)	465	(6.1)	510	(6.4)	536	(4.9)	549	(5.4)	43.9	(3.30)	2.7	(0.37)	18.3	(2.45)
Italy (Provincia Veneto)	446	(8.2)	514	(6.2)	527	(4.7)	549	(4.7)	48.5	(3.87)	3.5	(0.35)	22.0	(3.13)
United Kingdom (England)	446	(3.9)	488	(4.3)	513	(4.0)	549	(3.8)	39.8	(1.46)	2.5	(0.16)	18.2	(1.32)
United Kingdom (Northern Ireland)	458	(6.8)	490	(6.0)	517	(5.5)	550	(4.1)	34.8	(2.76)	2.1	(0.17)	13.5	(1.64)
United Kingdom (Wales)	427	(4.1)	469	(4.1)	496	(3.9)	524	(4.6)	37.8	(1.31)	2.7	(0.16)	17.1	(1.08)

Notes: Values that are statistically significant are indicated in bold (see Annex A3). See Table III.1.16 for national data.
StatLink ⌐ http://dx.doi.org/10.1787/888932343304

[Part 1/2]
Index of control strategies and performance on the reading scale, by national quarters of this index

Table S.III.q   *Results based on students' self-reports*

	Index of memorisation strategies															
	All students		Males		Females		Gender difference (B – G)		Bottom quarter		Second quarter		Third quarter		Top quarter	
	Mean index	S.E.	Mean index	S.E.	Mean index	S.E.	Dif.	S.E.	Mean index	S.E.	Mean index	S.E.	Mean index	S.E.	Mean index	S.E.
Adjudicated																
Belgium (Flemish Community)	-0.32	(0.02)	-0.38	(0.02)	-0.25	(0.03)	**-0.12**	(0.03)	**-1.48**	(0.02)	-0.53	(0.01)	-0.02	(0.00)	**0.77**	(0.02)
Spain (Andalusia)	0.47	(0.05)	0.42	(0.06)	0.53	(0.05)	-0.11	(0.06)	**-0.95**	(0.04)	0.18	(0.01)	0.78	(0.01)	**1.89**	(0.03)
Spain (Aragon)	0.34	(0.04)	0.24	(0.05)	0.45	(0.04)	**-0.21**	(0.06)	**-1.00**	(0.04)	0.07	(0.01)	0.62	(0.01)	**1.68**	(0.03)
Spain (Asturias)	0.26	(0.03)	0.12	(0.05)	0.42	(0.05)	**-0.30**	(0.08)	**-1.19**	(0.04)	-0.02	(0.01)	0.60	(0.01)	**1.67**	(0.04)
Spain (Balearic Islands)	0.30	(0.04)	0.15	(0.05)	0.45	(0.05)	**-0.30**	(0.05)	**-1.05**	(0.05)	0.05	(0.01)	0.60	(0.01)	**1.59**	(0.04)
Spain (Basque Country)	0.14	(0.03)	0.02	(0.03)	0.28	(0.03)	**-0.26**	(0.04)	**-1.12**	(0.03)	-0.13	(0.01)	0.42	(0.01)	**1.41**	(0.02)
Spain (Canary Islands)	0.43	(0.03)	0.36	(0.04)	0.51	(0.03)	**-0.14**	(0.06)	**-0.96**	(0.04)	0.12	(0.01)	0.76	(0.01)	**1.82**	(0.04)
Spain (Cantabria)	0.34	(0.04)	0.27	(0.05)	0.41	(0.05)	-0.13	(0.05)	**-1.00**	(0.04)	0.08	(0.01)	0.61	(0.01)	**1.67**	(0.03)
Spain (Castile and Leon)	0.33	(0.03)	0.21	(0.05)	0.44	(0.04)	**-0.23**	(0.07)	**-1.00**	(0.05)	0.03	(0.01)	0.63	(0.01)	**1.66**	(0.03)
Spain (Catalonia)	0.16	(0.03)	0.04	(0.04)	0.28	(0.04)	**-0.24**	(0.06)	**-1.15**	(0.04)	-0.07	(0.01)	0.46	(0.01)	**1.40**	(0.04)
Spain (Ceuta and Melilla)	0.68	(0.03)	0.62	(0.04)	0.74	(0.04)	**-0.12**	(0.06)	**-0.69**	(0.03)	0.34	(0.01)	0.95	(0.01)	**2.12**	(0.03)
Spain (Galicia)	0.15	(0.03)	0.01	(0.04)	0.30	(0.05)	**-0.30**	(0.06)	**-1.29**	(0.04)	-0.12	(0.01)	0.48	(0.01)	**1.55**	(0.03)
Spain (La Rioja)	0.31	(0.03)	0.23	(0.05)	0.39	(0.05)	**-0.16**	(0.06)	**-0.96**	(0.05)	0.03	(0.01)	0.56	(0.01)	**1.62**	(0.04)
Spain (Madrid)	0.35	(0.04)	0.28	(0.06)	0.42	(0.04)	-0.14	(0.07)	**-0.98**	(0.06)	0.05	(0.01)	0.63	(0.01)	**1.70**	(0.04)
Spain (Murcia)	0.52	(0.03)	0.42	(0.05)	0.62	(0.04)	**-0.20**	(0.07)	**-0.83**	(0.03)	0.20	(0.01)	0.79	(0.01)	**1.95**	(0.03)
Spain (Navarre)	0.16	(0.04)	0.03	(0.04)	0.31	(0.05)	**-0.28**	(0.05)	**-1.04**	(0.03)	-0.11	(0.01)	0.40	(0.01)	**1.41**	(0.03)
United Kingdom (Scotland)	0.12	(0.02)	0.04	(0.02)	0.19	(0.03)	**-0.15**	(0.03)	**-0.97**	(0.02)	-0.12	(0.01)	0.36	(0.01)	**1.20**	(0.02)
Non-adjudicated																
Belgium (French Community)	0.05	(0.02)	-0.08	(0.03)	0.19	(0.02)	**-0.27**	(0.04)	**-1.15**	(0.03)	-0.20	(0.01)	0.33	(0.01)	**1.23**	(0.02)
Belgium (German-Speaking Community)	0.08	(0.03)	-0.04	(0.04)	0.21	(0.05)	**-0.25**	(0.06)	**-1.05**	(0.05)	-0.12	(0.02)	0.34	(0.01)	**1.17**	(0.05)
Finland (Finnish Speaking)	-0.27	(0.02)	-0.35	(0.02)	-0.18	(0.02)	**-0.17**	(0.03)	**-1.38**	(0.02)	-0.47	(0.00)	0.00	(0.01)	**0.78**	(0.02)
Finland (Swedish Speaking)	0.01	(0.02)	-0.05	(0.04)	0.08	(0.03)	**-0.13**	(0.04)	**-0.99**	(0.03)	-0.21	(0.01)	0.25	(0.01)	**1.00**	(0.03)
Italy (Provincia Abruzzo)	-0.24	(0.02)	-0.33	(0.04)	-0.14	(0.04)	**-0.19**	(0.06)	**-1.42**	(0.04)	-0.43	(0.01)	0.07	(0.01)	**0.82**	(0.02)
Italy (Provincia Autonoma di Bolzano)	0.03	(0.03)	-0.03	(0.03)	0.09	(0.04)	**-0.13**	(0.04)	**-1.11**	(0.03)	-0.20	(0.01)	0.32	(0.01)	**1.11**	(0.03)
Italy (Provincia Basilicata)	-0.18	(0.03)	-0.24	(0.04)	-0.12	(0.05)	**-0.12**	(0.05)	**-1.31**	(0.03)	-0.37	(0.01)	0.10	(0.01)	**0.87**	(0.02)
Italy (Provincia Calabria)	0.01	(0.03)	-0.10	(0.04)	0.13	(0.03)	**-0.23**	(0.05)	**-1.09**	(0.04)	-0.20	(0.01)	0.29	(0.01)	**1.06**	(0.02)
Italy (Provincia Campania)	-0.09	(0.03)	-0.12	(0.05)	-0.03	(0.03)	-0.09	(0.05)	**-1.24**	(0.04)	-0.33	(0.01)	0.22	(0.01)	**1.01**	(0.03)
Italy (Provincia Emilia Romagna)	-0.26	(0.02)	-0.36	(0.04)	-0.16	(0.03)	**-0.20**	(0.05)	**-1.44**	(0.05)	-0.49	(0.01)	0.05	(0.01)	**0.84**	(0.03)
Italy (Provincia Friuli Venezia Giulia)	-0.29	(0.03)	-0.39	(0.05)	-0.18	(0.06)	**-0.21**	(0.08)	**-1.50**	(0.04)	-0.49	(0.01)	0.01	(0.01)	**0.81**	(0.03)
Italy (Provincia Lazio)	-0.17	(0.03)	-0.31	(0.03)	0.01	(0.04)	**-0.32**	(0.05)	**-1.33**	(0.04)	-0.37	(0.01)	0.16	(0.01)	**0.88**	(0.03)
Italy (Provincia Liguria)	-0.19	(0.02)	-0.27	(0.04)	-0.10	(0.03)	**-0.16**	(0.06)	**-1.39**	(0.05)	-0.38	(0.01)	0.13	(0.01)	**0.87**	(0.03)
Italy (Provincia Lombardia)	-0.24	(0.04)	-0.35	(0.04)	-0.13	(0.04)	**-0.22**	(0.04)	**-1.43**	(0.04)	-0.43	(0.01)	0.05	(0.01)	**0.83**	(0.03)
Italy (Provincia Marche)	-0.30	(0.03)	-0.40	(0.05)	-0.18	(0.04)	**-0.22**	(0.07)	**-1.49**	(0.06)	-0.49	(0.01)	0.00	(0.01)	**0.79**	(0.02)
Italy (Provincia Molise)	-0.16	(0.03)	-0.23	(0.05)	-0.08	(0.04)	**-0.16**	(0.06)	**-1.26**	(0.04)	-0.36	(0.01)	0.10	(0.01)	**0.90**	(0.03)
Italy (Provincia Piemonte)	-0.22	(0.03)	-0.39	(0.04)	-0.06	(0.03)	**-0.33**	(0.04)	**-1.49**	(0.05)	-0.39	(0.01)	0.10	(0.01)	**0.89**	(0.03)
Italy (Provincia Puglia)	-0.11	(0.03)	-0.18	(0.04)	-0.05	(0.03)	**-0.13**	(0.06)	**-1.29**	(0.03)	-0.34	(0.01)	0.22	(0.01)	**0.96**	(0.03)
Italy (Provincia Sardegna)	-0.06	(0.04)	-0.11	(0.06)	-0.01	(0.04)	-0.11	(0.06)	**-1.23**	(0.04)	-0.31	(0.01)	0.25	(0.01)	**1.06**	(0.03)
Italy (Provincia Sicilia)	0.01	(0.04)	-0.09	(0.05)	0.09	(0.05)	**-0.18**	(0.07)	**-1.19**	(0.04)	-0.20	(0.01)	0.30	(0.01)	**1.11**	(0.02)
Italy (Provincia Toscana)	-0.22	(0.03)	-0.29	(0.03)	-0.14	(0.04)	**-0.15**	(0.05)	**-1.40**	(0.03)	-0.41	(0.01)	0.11	(0.01)	**0.84**	(0.02)
Italy (Provincia Trento)	-0.20	(0.03)	-0.30	(0.04)	-0.08	(0.04)	**-0.22**	(0.04)	**-1.39**	(0.04)	-0.39	(0.01)	0.13	(0.01)	**0.85**	(0.03)
Italy (Provincia Umbria)	-0.26	(0.02)	-0.35	(0.04)	-0.19	(0.03)	**-0.16**	(0.06)	**-1.48**	(0.03)	-0.47	(0.01)	0.05	(0.01)	**0.85**	(0.03)
Italy (Provincia Valle d'Aosta)	-0.26	(0.03)	-0.37	(0.04)	-0.15	(0.05)	**-0.22**	(0.07)	**-1.48**	(0.05)	-0.48	(0.01)	0.06	(0.01)	**0.87**	(0.04)
Italy (Provincia Veneto)	-0.31	(0.03)	-0.42	(0.04)	-0.20	(0.04)	**-0.22**	(0.05)	**-1.56**	(0.05)	-0.50	(0.01)	0.02	(0.01)	**0.81**	(0.02)
United Kingdom (England)	0.02	(0.02)	-0.04	(0.03)	0.07	(0.02)	**-0.11**	(0.03)	**-1.06**	(0.02)	-0.22	(0.00)	0.27	(0.00)	**1.09**	(0.02)
United Kingdom (Northern Ireland)	0.24	(0.03)	0.12	(0.04)	0.35	(0.03)	**-0.24**	(0.04)	**-0.95**	(0.03)	-0.01	(0.01)	0.52	(0.01)	**1.41**	(0.03)
United Kingdom (Wales)	0.21	(0.02)	0.10	(0.03)	0.32	(0.02)	**-0.22**	(0.03)	**-0.92**	(0.02)	-0.04	(0.01)	0.46	(0.01)	**1.36**	(0.03)

Notes: Values that are statistically significant are indicated in bold (see Annex A3). See Table III.1.18 for national data.
StatLink ᛗᛁᛊ᠊ http://dx.doi.org/10.1787/888932343304

[Part 2/2]

Index of control strategies and performance on the reading scale, by national quarters of this index

Table S.III.q   *Results based on students' self-reports*

| | Performance on the reading scale, by quarters of this index | | | | | | | | Change in the reading score per unit of this index | | Increased likelihood of students in the bottom quarter of this index scoring in the bottom quarter of the reading performance distribution | | Explained variance in student performance (r-squared x 100) | |
| | Bottom quarter | | Second quarter | | Third quarter | | Top quarter | | | | | | | |
	Mean index	S.E.	Mean index	S.E.	Mean index	S.E.	Mean index	S.E.	Effect	S.E.	Ratio	S.E.	%	S.E.
Adjudicated														
Belgium (Flemish Community)	**538**	(3.9)	535	(4.2)	524	(3.2)	**500**	(3.7)	**-13.5**	(1.90)	**0.9**	(0.06)	1.9	(0.52)
Spain (Andalusia)	**442**	(10.5)	470	(6.0)	465	(5.8)	**469**	(6.3)	11.4	(3.38)	1.7	(0.20)	2.3	(1.33)
Spain (Aragon)	483	(9.4)	504	(6.4)	498	(5.9)	498	(4.5)	7.9	(2.88)	1.5	(0.17)	1.1	(0.77)
Spain (Asturias)	484	(6.9)	499	(6.9)	490	(6.5)	491	(5.5)	4.4	(2.85)	1.3	(0.13)	0.3	(0.41)
Spain (Balearic Islands)	**447**	(10.8)	461	(7.6)	462	(6.2)	**468**	(5.0)	8.6	(3.45)	1.4	(0.17)	1.1	(0.91)
Spain (Basque Country)	**485**	(5.2)	498	(3.7)	498	(4.3)	**499**	(2.9)	7.7	(2.14)	1.4	(0.10)	0.9	(0.51)
Spain (Canary Islands)	**436**	(7.2)	454	(5.5)	458	(7.8)	**450**	(5.7)	5.4	(2.92)	1.3	(0.17)	0.5	(0.49)
Spain (Cantabria)	482	(7.2)	491	(6.3)	486	(6.3)	494	(5.4)	4.8	(2.84)	1.3	(0.16)	0.4	(0.44)
Spain (Castile and Leon)	501	(7.4)	504	(6.2)	499	(6.3)	511	(5.5)	4.3	(2.73)	1.3	(0.15)	0.3	(0.42)
Spain (Catalonia)	493	(8.9)	501	(6.7)	500	(6.3)	500	(4.3)	3.8	(2.61)	1.2	(0.14)	0.2	(0.34)
Spain (Ceuta and Melilla)	415	(6.5)	425	(5.9)	412	(5.4)	408	(5.4)	-1.9	(2.98)	1.2	(0.15)	0.0	(0.18)
Spain (Galicia)	476	(7.0)	485	(6.9)	496	(4.9)	488	(5.3)	6.3	(2.60)	1.3	(0.12)	0.7	(0.59)
Spain (La Rioja)	494	(6.2)	498	(5.9)	502	(6.1)	498	(4.7)	4.8	(2.78)	1.3	(0.19)	0.3	(0.36)
Spain (Madrid)	505	(10.2)	508	(6.2)	503	(6.3)	499	(5.7)	-0.3	(4.89)	1.3	(0.18)	0.0	(0.30)
Spain (Murcia)	477	(8.9)	486	(5.0)	485	(6.4)	478	(5.0)	-0.3	(1.96)	1.2	(0.17)	0.0	(0.07)
Spain (Navarre)	493	(7.2)	497	(4.7)	501	(4.8)	499	(6.4)	2.5	(2.62)	1.2	(0.15)	0.1	(0.21)
United Kingdom (Scotland)	500	(5.6)	506	(4.8)	501	(5.5)	500	(4.6)	3.4	(2.75)	1.1	(0.13)	0.1	(0.19)
Non-adjudicated														
Belgium (French Community)	**506**	(5.7)	506	(6.7)	499	(5.9)	**480**	(5.8)	-6.6	(2.76)	0.9	(0.08)	0.4	(0.32)
Belgium (German-Speaking Community)	500	(6.9)	509	(6.9)	503	(6.4)	492	(6.6)	-2.1	(3.69)	1.1	(0.23)	0.1	(0.21)
Finland (Finnish Speaking)	535	(3.5)	540	(3.7)	538	(3.2)	538	(3.5)	2.7	(1.77)	1.1	(0.06)	0.1	(0.10)
Finland (Swedish Speaking)	**495**	(6.8)	506	(5.2)	519	(4.5)	**527**	(4.7)	16.3	(3.17)	1.6	(0.19)	2.4	(0.93)
Italy (Provincia Abruzzo)	**499**	(5.8)	490	(6.2)	470	(8.7)	**473**	(5.8)	-9.1	(2.86)	0.7	(0.10)	0.9	(0.54)
Italy (Provincia Autonoma di Bolzano)	492	(7.3)	497	(6.1)	499	(4.4)	472	(6.5)	-5.4	(3.37)	1.0	(0.20)	0.3	(0.36)
Italy (Provincia Basilicata)	**489**	(5.9)	479	(7.1)	465	(6.8)	**461**	(6.4)	-11.2	(3.73)	0.8	(0.11)	1.4	(0.87)
Italy (Provincia Calabria)	461	(8.3)	456	(7.9)	442	(6.7)	434	(6.3)	-10.1	(4.31)	0.9	(0.19)	1.0	(0.83)
Italy (Provincia Campania)	**475**	(11.3)	461	(7.0)	440	(7.9)	**429**	(9.2)	-17.3	(5.65)	0.7	(0.14)	3.0	(1.84)
Italy (Provincia Emilia Romagna)	**513**	(5.8)	512	(5.8)	505	(6.1)	**484**	(7.3)	-8.6	(3.42)	0.9	(0.10)	0.7	(0.56)
Italy (Provincia Friuli Venezia Giulia)	**520**	(8.6)	518	(6.7)	518	(6.8)	**499**	(6.2)	-2.5	(4.39)	0.9	(0.13)	0.1	(0.31)
Italy (Provincia Lazio)	487	(5.8)	482	(6.4)	487	(6.4)	471	(5.9)	-2.8	(3.35)	1.1	(0.14)	0.1	(0.25)
Italy (Provincia Liguria)	505	(11.9)	499	(10.4)	490	(8.0)	472	(13.0)	-9.5	(4.06)	0.8	(0.13)	0.9	(0.77)
Italy (Provincia Lombardia)	530	(7.8)	531	(7.5)	520	(8.0)	507	(7.4)	-7.6	(4.45)	0.9	(0.12)	0.6	(0.72)
Italy (Provincia Marche)	506	(11.6)	504	(8.9)	501	(6.5)	485	(7.8)	-3.8	(4.79)	1.0	(0.14)	0.2	(0.44)
Italy (Provincia Molise)	476	(6.2)	476	(6.1)	469	(7.1)	461	(6.0)	-3.4	(3.50)	1.0	(0.14)	0.1	(0.31)
Italy (Provincia Piemonte)	507	(7.8)	504	(7.6)	493	(9.1)	482	(7.3)	-3.8	(3.88)	1.0	(0.15)	0.2	(0.36)
Italy (Provincia Puglia)	**502**	(6.6)	496	(6.1)	490	(6.2)	**470**	(6.9)	-10.0	(3.41)	0.9	(0.13)	1.2	(0.71)
Italy (Provincia Sardegna)	475	(6.8)	474	(7.7)	476	(5.0)	458	(8.1)	-2.5	(3.32)	1.1	(0.14)	0.1	(0.28)
Italy (Provincia Sicilia)	**468**	(12.2)	458	(8.3)	457	(9.4)	**440**	(8.8)	-7.5	(4.19)	0.9	(0.15)	0.5	(0.65)
Italy (Provincia Toscana)	**506**	(6.4)	501	(7.4)	490	(5.9)	**479**	(5.1)	-6.6	(3.47)	0.9	(0.10)	0.4	(0.46)
Italy (Provincia Trento)	**519**	(6.2)	513	(5.4)	509	(8.2)	**490**	(5.2)	-7.6	(3.31)	0.9	(0.12)	0.6	(0.50)
Italy (Provincia Umbria)	**504**	(7.3)	498	(8.3)	494	(5.9)	**472**	(7.4)	-10.8	(4.19)	0.9	(0.11)	1.1	(0.88)
Italy (Provincia Valle d'Aosta)	515	(6.8)	526	(5.4)	512	(5.5)	503	(6.1)	-4.4	(3.25)	1.0	(0.16)	0.3	(0.37)
Italy (Provincia Veneto)	**517**	(8.3)	509	(7.1)	507	(5.4)	**491**	(7.2)	-5.5	(3.63)	0.8	(0.12)	0.4	(0.47)
United Kingdom (England)	490	(3.9)	505	(4.2)	506	(4.3)	485	(3.5)	0.3	(1.95)	1.1	(0.09)	0.0	(0.03)
United Kingdom (Northern Ireland)	**485**	(7.1)	509	(5.3)	508	(5.8)	**501**	(5.5)	6.8	(2.46)	1.5	(0.11)	0.5	(0.33)
United Kingdom (Wales)	**460**	(5.8)	478	(4.4)	487	(4.4)	**483**	(3.9)	10.6	(2.27)	1.5	(0.12)	1.2	(0.51)

Notes: Values that are statistically significant are indicated in bold (see Annex A3). See Table III.1.18 for national data.
StatLink ⌐ऽ⌐ http://dx.doi.org/10.1787/888932343304

[Part 1/2]
Index of memorisation strategies and reading performance, by national quarters of this index

Table S.III.r   *Results based on students' self-reports*

	Index of elaboration strategies															
	All students		Males		Females		Gender difference (B – G)		Bottom quarter		Second quarter		Third quarter		Top quarter	
	Mean index	S.E.	Mean index	S.E.	Mean index	S.E.	Dif.	S.E.	Mean index	S.E.	Mean index	S.E.	Mean index	S.E.	Mean index	S.E.
Adjudicated																
Belgium (Flemish Community)	-0.35	(0.02)	-0.28	(0.03)	-0.43	(0.02)	**0.16**	(0.03)	**-1.67**	(0.02)	-0.56	(0.01)	-0.03	(0.01)	**0.84**	(0.02)
Spain (Andalusia)	-0.07	(0.03)	0.00	(0.05)	-0.15	(0.05)	**0.15**	(0.07)	**-1.47**	(0.03)	-0.31	(0.01)	0.30	(0.01)	**1.20**	(0.03)
Spain (Aragon)	-0.10	(0.03)	-0.04	(0.04)	-0.15	(0.04)	0.11	(0.06)	**-1.41**	(0.03)	-0.30	(0.01)	0.25	(0.01)	**1.08**	(0.03)
Spain (Asturias)	-0.12	(0.04)	-0.06	(0.06)	-0.19	(0.04)	**0.13**	(0.06)	**-1.59**	(0.03)	-0.36	(0.01)	0.28	(0.01)	**1.20**	(0.02)
Spain (Balearic Islands)	0.00	(0.03)	0.05	(0.05)	-0.05	(0.04)	0.11	(0.06)	**-1.39**	(0.03)	-0.22	(0.01)	0.38	(0.01)	**1.24**	(0.03)
Spain (Basque Country)	-0.18	(0.02)	-0.14	(0.03)	-0.22	(0.02)	**0.09**	(0.03)	**-1.46**	(0.02)	-0.40	(0.01)	0.16	(0.00)	**0.98**	(0.02)
Spain (Canary Islands)	-0.03	(0.03)	0.00	(0.04)	-0.05	(0.04)	0.04	(0.06)	**-1.37**	(0.04)	-0.30	(0.01)	0.34	(0.01)	**1.24**	(0.04)
Spain (Cantabria)	-0.03	(0.03)	0.01	(0.04)	-0.08	(0.03)	**0.09**	(0.05)	**-1.36**	(0.03)	-0.28	(0.01)	0.33	(0.01)	**1.19**	(0.03)
Spain (Castile and Leon)	0.07	(0.03)	0.10	(0.05)	0.03	(0.04)	0.07	(0.06)	**-1.22**	(0.04)	-0.17	(0.01)	0.38	(0.01)	**1.29**	(0.04)
Spain (Catalonia)	-0.04	(0.04)	0.01	(0.05)	-0.09	(0.04)	0.10	(0.06)	**-1.34**	(0.03)	-0.30	(0.01)	0.31	(0.01)	**1.19**	(0.03)
Spain (Ceuta and Melilla)	0.12	(0.03)	0.16	(0.04)	0.08	(0.05)	0.09	(0.06)	**-1.27**	(0.04)	-0.15	(0.01)	0.47	(0.01)	**1.43**	(0.03)
Spain (Galicia)	-0.07	(0.04)	-0.05	(0.04)	-0.10	(0.05)	0.05	(0.06)	**-1.56**	(0.03)	-0.31	(0.01)	0.32	(0.01)	**1.27**	(0.03)
Spain (La Rioja)	0.02	(0.03)	0.05	(0.04)	-0.01	(0.04)	0.06	(0.05)	**-1.22**	(0.04)	-0.21	(0.01)	0.34	(0.01)	**1.17**	(0.03)
Spain (Madrid)	-0.07	(0.03)	-0.03	(0.05)	-0.11	(0.04)	0.07	(0.07)	**-1.39**	(0.04)	-0.31	(0.01)	0.26	(0.01)	**1.16**	(0.03)
Spain (Murcia)	-0.06	(0.03)	0.05	(0.04)	-0.16	(0.03)	**0.21**	(0.05)	**-1.37**	(0.04)	-0.33	(0.01)	0.29	(0.01)	**1.19**	(0.04)
Spain (Navarre)	-0.15	(0.03)	-0.11	(0.03)	-0.20	(0.04)	0.08	(0.05)	**-1.40**	(0.03)	-0.37	(0.01)	0.17	(0.01)	**0.99**	(0.03)
United Kingdom (Scotland)	-0.02	(0.02)	0.03	(0.02)	-0.08	(0.03)	**0.11**	(0.04)	**-1.25**	(0.02)	-0.25	(0.01)	0.30	(0.01)	**1.12**	(0.02)
Non-adjudicated																
Belgium (French Community)	-0.27	(0.02)	-0.18	(0.03)	-0.36	(0.03)	**0.18**	(0.04)	**-1.56**	(0.02)	-0.50	(0.01)	0.05	(0.01)	**0.90**	(0.02)
Belgium (German-Speaking Community)	-0.18	(0.02)	-0.02	(0.05)	-0.35	(0.04)	**0.33**	(0.06)	**-1.46**	(0.04)	-0.41	(0.01)	0.14	(0.01)	**1.01**	(0.04)
Finland (Finnish Speaking)	-0.14	(0.02)	-0.12	(0.02)	-0.15	(0.02)	0.04	(0.03)	**-1.36**	(0.02)	-0.34	(0.01)	0.18	(0.01)	**0.99**	(0.02)
Finland (Swedish Speaking)	-0.31	(0.03)	-0.24	(0.04)	-0.39	(0.04)	**0.15**	(0.05)	**-1.55**	(0.03)	-0.53	(0.01)	-0.01	(0.01)	**0.84**	(0.03)
Italy (Provincia Abruzzo)	-0.13	(0.03)	-0.11	(0.04)	-0.14	(0.05)	0.03	(0.05)	**-1.43**	(0.04)	-0.35	(0.01)	0.23	(0.01)	**1.05**	(0.02)
Italy (Provincia Autonoma di Bolzano)	0.01	(0.03)	0.10	(0.04)	-0.08	(0.04)	**0.19**	(0.06)	**-1.26**	(0.03)	-0.21	(0.01)	0.32	(0.01)	**1.18**	(0.03)
Italy (Provincia Basilicata)	0.02	(0.02)	0.05	(0.03)	-0.02	(0.04)	0.07	(0.04)	**-1.21**	(0.03)	-0.19	(0.01)	0.37	(0.01)	**1.31**	(0.02)
Italy (Provincia Calabria)	0.20	(0.03)	0.16	(0.05)	0.24	(0.03)	-0.08	(0.05)	**-1.00**	(0.04)	-0.03	(0.01)	0.52	(0.01)	**1.20**	(0.02)
Italy (Provincia Campania)	0.08	(0.03)	0.13	(0.04)	0.01	(0.04)	0.12	(0.06)	**-1.15**	(0.03)	-0.14	(0.01)	0.41	(0.01)	**0.99**	(0.02)
Italy (Provincia Emilia Romagna)	-0.22	(0.03)	-0.18	(0.04)	-0.27	(0.05)	0.09	(0.06)	**-1.62**	(0.02)	-0.45	(0.01)	0.19	(0.01)	**1.06**	(0.03)
Italy (Provincia Friuli Venezia Giulia)	-0.18	(0.03)	-0.16	(0.04)	-0.20	(0.04)	0.04	(0.05)	**-1.54**	(0.03)	-0.42	(0.01)	0.20	(0.01)	**1.08**	(0.03)
Italy (Provincia Lazio)	-0.12	(0.03)	-0.13	(0.04)	-0.10	(0.04)	-0.03	(0.05)	**-1.44**	(0.03)	-0.36	(0.01)	0.25	(0.01)	**1.04**	(0.02)
Italy (Provincia Liguria)	-0.17	(0.03)	-0.14	(0.04)	-0.20	(0.05)	0.05	(0.07)	**-1.52**	(0.05)	-0.39	(0.01)	0.20	(0.01)	**0.94**	(0.03)
Italy (Provincia Lombardia)	-0.21	(0.04)	-0.23	(0.06)	-0.19	(0.04)	-0.04	(0.06)	**-1.47**	(0.03)	-0.44	(0.01)	0.13	(0.01)	**0.97**	(0.03)
Italy (Provincia Marche)	-0.24	(0.03)	-0.21	(0.06)	-0.28	(0.04)	0.07	(0.07)	**-1.58**	(0.04)	-0.48	(0.01)	0.11	(0.01)	**1.17**	(0.04)
Italy (Provincia Molise)	-0.02	(0.03)	0.06	(0.05)	-0.11	(0.04)	**0.18**	(0.07)	**-1.34**	(0.04)	-0.26	(0.02)	0.35	(0.01)	**1.05**	(0.02)
Italy (Provincia Piemonte)	-0.17	(0.04)	-0.18	(0.04)	-0.17	(0.04)	-0.01	(0.05)	**-1.51**	(0.04)	-0.41	(0.01)	0.18	(0.01)	**1.18**	(0.03)
Italy (Provincia Puglia)	0.01	(0.03)	0.04	(0.03)	-0.03	(0.04)	0.07	(0.05)	**-1.30**	(0.03)	-0.23	(0.01)	0.37	(0.01)	**1.27**	(0.04)
Italy (Provincia Sardegna)	-0.04	(0.04)	0.02	(0.07)	-0.09	(0.04)	0.12	(0.07)	**-1.46**	(0.04)	-0.28	(0.01)	0.33	(0.01)	**1.31**	(0.02)
Italy (Provincia Sicilia)	0.20	(0.03)	0.29	(0.04)	0.12	(0.04)	**0.18**	(0.06)	**-1.02**	(0.04)	-0.01	(0.01)	0.52	(0.01)	**1.02**	(0.02)
Italy (Provincia Toscana)	-0.14	(0.03)	-0.09	(0.03)	-0.18	(0.04)	**0.09**	(0.04)	**-1.42**	(0.03)	-0.36	(0.01)	0.21	(0.01)	**1.06**	(0.03)
Italy (Provincia Trento)	-0.12	(0.03)	-0.06	(0.05)	-0.19	(0.04)	**0.13**	(0.06)	**-1.45**	(0.05)	-0.32	(0.01)	0.23	(0.01)	**1.09**	(0.03)
Italy (Provincia Umbria)	-0.08	(0.03)	-0.05	(0.04)	-0.11	(0.03)	0.06	(0.05)	**-1.35**	(0.03)	-0.30	(0.01)	0.20	(0.01)	**1.06**	(0.03)
Italy (Provincia Valle d'Aosta)	-0.17	(0.03)	-0.12	(0.05)	-0.22	(0.05)	0.10	(0.07)	**-1.54**	(0.04)	-0.41	(0.01)	0.17	(0.01)	**1.01**	(0.02)
Italy (Provincia Veneto)	-0.18	(0.02)	-0.20	(0.03)	-0.16	(0.03)	-0.04	(0.05)	**-1.47**	(0.04)	-0.42	(0.01)	0.17	(0.01)	**1.10**	(0.02)
United Kingdom (England)	-0.03	(0.02)	0.04	(0.02)	-0.09	(0.02)	**0.13**	(0.03)	**-1.25**	(0.02)	-0.25	(0.01)	0.29	(0.01)	**1.10**	(0.02)
United Kingdom (Northern Ireland)	-0.18	(0.02)	-0.12	(0.03)	-0.22	(0.03)	**0.10**	(0.04)	**-1.49**	(0.03)	-0.43	(0.01)	0.17	(0.01)	**1.05**	(0.02)
United Kingdom (Wales)	-0.06	(0.02)	0.01	(0.03)	-0.13	(0.02)	**0.14**	(0.03)	**-1.28**	(0.02)	-0.29	(0.01)	0.25	(0.01)	**1.07**	(0.02)

Notes: Values that are statistically significant are indicated in bold (see Annex A3). See Table III.1.20 for national data.
StatLink ⟋⟍⟋ http://dx.doi.org/10.1787/888932343304

[Part 2/2]
Index of memorisation strategies and reading performance, by national quarters of this index

Table S.III.r *Results based on students' self-reports*

| | Performance on the reading scale, by quarters of this index | | | | | | | | Change in the reading score per unit of this index | | Increased likelihood of students in the bottom quarter of this index scoring in the bottom quarter of the reading performance distribution | | Explained variance in student performance (r-squared x 100) | |
| | Bottom quarter | | Second quarter | | Third quarter | | Top quarter | | | | | | | |
	Mean index	S.E.	Mean index	S.E.	Mean index	S.E.	Mean index	S.E.	Effect	S.E.	Ratio	S.E.	%	S.E.
Adjudicated														
Belgium (Flemish Community)	521	(3.4)	525	(3.3)	521	(3.6)	530	(4.9)	**4.6**	(1.92)	1.0	(0.07)	0.3	(0.23)
Spain (Andalusia)	**444**	(6.6)	464	(7.0)	465	(7.1)	**474**	(6.6)	**12.0**	(2.81)	**1.4**	(0.18)	2.1	(1.00)
Spain (Aragon)	**484**	(5.3)	498	(6.4)	498	(5.6)	**503**	(5.6)	**10.0**	(2.22)	1.1	(0.16)	1.4	(0.64)
Spain (Asturias)	470	(6.7)	484	(5.7)	503	(6.5)	509	(7.0)	**14.3**	(2.91)	**1.4**	(0.16)	2.9	(1.14)
Spain (Balearic Islands)	**445**	(7.5)	455	(7.6)	466	(7.3)	**474**	(5.8)	**13.6**	(2.57)	1.2	(0.14)	2.6	(1.01)
Spain (Basque Country)	**488**	(4.6)	491	(3.3)	496	(3.2)	**505**	(3.7)	**7.9**	(1.63)	1.1	(0.09)	0.9	(0.35)
Spain (Canary Islands)	446	(5.9)	448	(6.9)	450	(5.4)	455	(6.4)	4.5	(2.41)	1.0	(0.11)	0.3	(0.31)
Spain (Cantabria)	**474**	(7.0)	481	(6.3)	497	(5.9)	**501**	(6.0)	**11.6**	(2.63)	1.2	(0.15)	1.9	(0.81)
Spain (Castile and Leon)	**489**	(5.7)	502	(6.2)	510	(7.2)	**514**	(6.4)	**11.9**	(2.65)	1.2	(0.15)	2.0	(0.95)
Spain (Catalonia)	478	(7.1)	504	(5.6)	499	(6.1)	514	(8.6)	**13.8**	(2.64)	**1.5**	(0.23)	3.0	(1.16)
Spain (Ceuta and Melilla)	428	(5.1)	410	(5.8)	412	(6.4)	415	(5.5)	-4.2	(2.44)	0.8	(0.13)	0.2	(0.25)
Spain (Galicia)	**469**	(5.9)	488	(5.8)	495	(7.6)	**493**	(7.3)	**8.6**	(2.53)	1.3	(0.15)	1.3	(0.75)
Spain (La Rioja)	**490**	(5.2)	490	(5.8)	504	(5.6)	**511**	(5.4)	**10.3**	(3.11)	1.1	(0.15)	1.2	(0.72)
Spain (Madrid)	492	(9.2)	503	(6.6)	505	(6.0)	516	(6.3)	**11.0**	(3.11)	1.2	(0.14)	1.8	(0.98)
Spain (Murcia)	477	(6.7)	477	(7.2)	484	(5.9)	489	(6.9)	4.5	(2.40)	0.9	(0.12)	0.4	(0.37)
Spain (Navarre)	500	(5.2)	493	(5.1)	499	(5.0)	497	(5.2)	1.1	(2.17)	**0.8**	(0.10)	0.0	(0.08)
United Kingdom (Scotland)	497	(4.6)	498	(5.0)	505	(5.2)	507	(5.4)	**7.5**	(1.98)	1.1	(0.10)	0.6	(0.32)
Non-adjudicated														
Belgium (French Community)	**505**	(5.0)	502	(5.4)	504	(5.4)	**482**	(6.7)	**-5.6**	(2.38)	**0.8**	(0.08)	0.3	(0.24)
Belgium (German-Speaking Community)	505	(6.5)	498	(6.0)	505	(5.9)	496	(6.7)	-0.8	(3.01)	0.9	(0.14)	0.0	(0.12)
Finland (Finnish Speaking)	**526**	(3.2)	530	(3.2)	543	(3.6)	**552**	(3.6)	**12.9**	(1.66)	**1.2**	(0.08)	2.0	(0.52)
Finland (Swedish Speaking)	**506**	(4.8)	501	(7.4)	512	(5.8)	529	(5.7)	**11.8**	(2.42)	1.1	(0.15)	1.7	(0.70)
Italy (Provincia Abruzzo)	**472**	(5.8)	479	(7.1)	485	(6.9)	**495**	(7.3)	**8.2**	(2.64)	1.1	(0.14)	0.9	(0.59)
Italy (Provincia Autonoma di Bolzano)	489	(5.1)	489	(8.9)	493	(4.8)	490	(4.9)	2.5	(2.26)	0.9	(0.12)	0.1	(0.13)
Italy (Provincia Basilicata)	468	(5.9)	471	(4.6)	479	(8.1)	477	(6.2)	**7.6**	(2.49)	1.0	(0.17)	0.7	(0.48)
Italy (Provincia Calabria)	442	(7.7)	449	(7.9)	451	(8.1)	453	(6.3)	**8.1**	(2.85)	1.1	(0.12)	0.7	(0.51)
Italy (Provincia Campania)	448	(8.9)	447	(8.2)	457	(8.9)	456	(7.2)	6.1	(3.13)	1.0	(0.14)	0.4	(0.40)
Italy (Provincia Emilia Romagna)	**487**	(6.2)	492	(5.5)	515	(5.4)	**522**	(7.2)	**14.2**	(2.95)	1.2	(0.12)	2.3	(0.88)
Italy (Provincia Friuli Venezia Giulia)	507	(6.6)	510	(6.3)	520	(6.9)	518	(6.4)	**7.6**	(2.84)	0.9	(0.14)	0.7	(0.54)
Italy (Provincia Lazio)	466	(6.2)	480	(5.9)	488	(6.9)	493	(6.4)	**12.6**	(1.73)	1.2	(0.16)	2.0	(0.55)
Italy (Provincia Liguria)	485	(15.1)	496	(8.3)	491	(8.8)	494	(10.4)	5.3	(4.26)	1.0	(0.21)	0.3	(0.50)
Italy (Provincia Lombardia)	512	(8.5)	527	(6.1)	518	(7.7)	530	(8.4)	6.4	(5.21)	1.1	(0.19)	0.5	(0.79)
Italy (Provincia Marche)	**488**	(10.3)	496	(7.5)	496	(9.2)	**517**	(6.8)	**12.5**	(2.84)	1.2	(0.15)	1.9	(0.78)
Italy (Provincia Molise)	466	(6.3)	466	(5.8)	472	(6.1)	479	(7.0)	6.5	(3.30)	1.2	(0.16)	0.6	(0.59)
Italy (Provincia Piemonte)	486	(6.3)	492	(7.8)	504	(7.9)	505	(11.0)	9.4	(4.29)	1.1	(0.19)	1.0	(1.01)
Italy (Provincia Puglia)	485	(4.9)	487	(7.0)	494	(7.2)	493	(7.1)	5.8	(2.38)	1.0	(0.11)	0.5	(0.39)
Italy (Provincia Sardegna)	**458**	(7.0)	476	(5.3)	470	(6.4)	**480**	(6.4)	**11.8**	(2.30)	**1.3**	(0.13)	2.0	(0.75)
Italy (Provincia Sicilia)	456	(9.2)	453	(10.4)	451	(10.6)	463	(10.3)	6.1	(3.40)	0.9	(0.17)	0.4	(0.40)
Italy (Provincia Toscana)	**485**	(7.4)	494	(7.0)	496	(7.7)	**502**	(5.5)	**8.6**	(2.85)	1.2	(0.15)	0.8	(0.51)
Italy (Provincia Trento)	502	(5.2)	510	(4.4)	509	(6.0)	512	(5.9)	5.6	(2.61)	1.0	(0.13)	0.4	(0.36)
Italy (Provincia Umbria)	483	(7.2)	492	(6.5)	494	(6.7)	499	(8.3)	8.5	(3.05)	1.0	(0.10)	0.7	(0.56)
Italy (Provincia Valle d'Aosta)	505	(6.2)	511	(5.0)	524	(4.7)	518	(6.2)	6.7	(3.10)	1.2	(0.18)	0.7	(0.64)
Italy (Provincia Veneto)	**495**	(6.7)	504	(7.3)	505	(5.7)	**521**	(6.7)	**12.3**	(2.33)	1.1	(0.12)	1.8	(0.68)
United Kingdom (England)	494	(4.3)	492	(4.6)	501	(3.9)	498	(4.0)	**4.2**	(1.69)	1.0	(0.08)	0.2	(0.15)
United Kingdom (Northern Ireland)	503	(4.5)	499	(4.1)	499	(5.5)	501	(9.0)	0.5	(2.58)	0.9	(0.10)	0.0	(0.07)
United Kingdom (Wales)	472	(4.8)	473	(4.5)	480	(4.6)	483	(4.7)	**6.0**	(2.01)	1.1	(0.09)	0.4	(0.25)

Notes: Values that are statistically significant are indicated in bold (see Annex A3). See Table III.1.20 for national data.
StatLink ⬛📊 http://dx.doi.org/10.1787/888932343304

[Part 1/2]

Index of elaboration strategies and reading performance, by national quarters of this index

Table S.III.s *Results based on students' self-reports*

	Index of control strategies															
	All students		Males		Females		Gender difference (B – G)		Bottom quarter		Second quarter		Third quarter		Top quarter	
	Mean index	S.E.	Mean index	S.E.	Mean index	S.E.	Dif.	S.E.	Mean index	S.E.	Mean index	S.E.	Mean index	S.E.	Mean index	S.E.
Adjudicated																
Belgium (Flemish Community)	-0.05	(0.02)	-0.13	(0.03)	0.04	(0.03)	**-0.18**	(0.03)	**-1.11**	(0.02)	-0.27	(0.01)	0.19	(0.01)	**1.01**	(0.02)
Spain (Andalusia)	0.12	(0.04)	0.01	(0.05)	0.24	(0.05)	**-0.23**	(0.07)	**-1.21**	(0.06)	-0.10	(0.01)	0.43	(0.01)	**1.34**	(0.03)
Spain (Aragon)	0.08	(0.04)	-0.06	(0.05)	0.21	(0.05)	**-0.27**	(0.06)	**-1.24**	(0.05)	-0.19	(0.01)	0.38	(0.01)	**1.36**	(0.03)
Spain (Asturias)	0.03	(0.04)	-0.14	(0.06)	0.22	(0.04)	**-0.36**	(0.07)	**-1.35**	(0.04)	-0.25	(0.01)	0.37	(0.01)	**1.36**	(0.02)
Spain (Balearic Islands)	0.07	(0.03)	-0.11	(0.04)	0.26	(0.04)	**-0.37**	(0.05)	**-1.21**	(0.05)	-0.19	(0.01)	0.37	(0.01)	**1.34**	(0.03)
Spain (Basque Country)	-0.04	(0.02)	-0.15	(0.03)	0.08	(0.03)	**-0.23**	(0.04)	**-1.22**	(0.03)	-0.28	(0.01)	0.23	(0.01)	**1.09**	(0.02)
Spain (Canary Islands)	0.11	(0.04)	-0.04	(0.05)	0.28	(0.04)	**-0.32**	(0.06)	**-1.26**	(0.05)	-0.17	(0.01)	0.47	(0.01)	**1.43**	(0.02)
Spain (Cantabria)	0.10	(0.03)	0.00	(0.04)	0.21	(0.04)	**-0.22**	(0.05)	**-1.18**	(0.04)	-0.14	(0.01)	0.40	(0.01)	**1.33**	(0.03)
Spain (Castile and Leon)	0.14	(0.03)	0.01	(0.06)	0.27	(0.03)	**-0.26**	(0.07)	**-1.14**	(0.05)	-0.12	(0.01)	0.46	(0.01)	**1.38**	(0.04)
Spain (Catalonia)	0.14	(0.04)	0.00	(0.04)	0.30	(0.05)	**-0.30**	(0.04)	**-1.07**	(0.04)	-0.09	(0.01)	0.42	(0.01)	**1.32**	(0.03)
Spain (Ceuta and Melilla)	0.32	(0.03)	0.21	(0.04)	0.43	(0.04)	**-0.22**	(0.06)	**-0.97**	(0.03)	0.03	(0.01)	0.60	(0.01)	**1.64**	(0.03)
Spain (Galicia)	-0.02	(0.03)	-0.15	(0.04)	0.12	(0.05)	**-0.27**	(0.05)	**-1.38**	(0.05)	-0.25	(0.01)	0.31	(0.01)	**1.26**	(0.02)
Spain (La Rioja)	0.10	(0.03)	-0.02	(0.05)	0.22	(0.04)	**-0.24**	(0.06)	**-1.13**	(0.04)	-0.18	(0.01)	0.39	(0.01)	**1.32**	(0.03)
Spain (Madrid)	0.14	(0.04)	-0.01	(0.06)	0.29	(0.03)	**-0.30**	(0.07)	**-1.11**	(0.07)	-0.11	(0.01)	0.43	(0.01)	**1.37**	(0.03)
Spain (Murcia)	0.17	(0.04)	0.08	(0.05)	0.26	(0.04)	**-0.18**	(0.05)	**-1.06**	(0.04)	-0.10	(0.01)	0.48	(0.01)	**1.37**	(0.04)
Spain (Navarre)	0.03	(0.03)	-0.13	(0.04)	0.22	(0.04)	**-0.35**	(0.05)	**-1.13**	(0.03)	-0.23	(0.01)	0.31	(0.01)	**1.20**	(0.03)
United Kingdom (Scotland)	0.21	(0.02)	0.12	(0.03)	0.29	(0.03)	**-0.17**	(0.04)	**-0.98**	(0.03)	-0.05	(0.01)	0.46	(0.01)	**1.39**	(0.02)
Non-adjudicated																
Belgium (French Community)	0.17	(0.03)	0.03	(0.04)	0.30	(0.03)	**-0.26**	(0.05)	**-1.10**	(0.03)	-0.07	(0.01)	0.46	(0.01)	**1.37**	(0.02)
Belgium (German-Speaking Community)	0.10	(0.03)	-0.10	(0.04)	0.30	(0.04)	**-0.40**	(0.06)	**-1.06**	(0.05)	-0.15	(0.01)	0.35	(0.01)	**1.25**	(0.03)
Finland (Finnish Speaking)	-0.33	(0.02)	-0.44	(0.03)	-0.21	(0.02)	**-0.23**	(0.03)	**-1.50**	(0.02)	-0.59	(0.01)	-0.05	(0.01)	**0.84**	(0.02)
Finland (Swedish Speaking)	-0.50	(0.03)	-0.63	(0.04)	-0.38	(0.03)	**-0.25**	(0.05)	**-1.60**	(0.03)	-0.74	(0.01)	-0.23	(0.01)	**0.57**	(0.03)
Italy (Provincia Abruzzo)	0.09	(0.03)	-0.10	(0.03)	0.29	(0.04)	**-0.40**	(0.04)	**-1.08**	(0.03)	-0.14	(0.01)	0.37	(0.01)	**1.21**	(0.04)
Italy (Provincia Autonoma di Bolzano)	0.12	(0.03)	-0.04	(0.04)	0.28	(0.04)	**-0.32**	(0.05)	**-1.09**	(0.04)	-0.11	(0.01)	0.40	(0.01)	**1.28**	(0.03)
Italy (Provincia Basilicata)	0.22	(0.02)	0.02	(0.03)	0.44	(0.03)	**-0.41**	(0.05)	**-0.88**	(0.03)	0.00	(0.01)	0.46	(0.01)	**1.31**	(0.02)
Italy (Provincia Calabria)	0.29	(0.04)	0.06	(0.05)	0.53	(0.03)	**-0.47**	(0.05)	**-0.81**	(0.06)	0.07	(0.01)	0.55	(0.01)	**1.37**	(0.03)
Italy (Provincia Campania)	0.25	(0.03)	0.09	(0.04)	0.46	(0.04)	**-0.37**	(0.06)	**-0.79**	(0.04)	0.00	(0.01)	0.46	(0.01)	**1.35**	(0.03)
Italy (Provincia Emilia Romagna)	0.07	(0.03)	-0.08	(0.03)	0.21	(0.04)	**-0.29**	(0.05)	**-1.12**	(0.04)	-0.14	(0.01)	0.36	(0.01)	**1.18**	(0.02)
Italy (Provincia Friuli Venezia Giulia)	0.09	(0.05)	-0.12	(0.05)	0.31	(0.05)	**-0.42**	(0.05)	**-1.10**	(0.06)	-0.13	(0.01)	0.37	(0.01)	**1.21**	(0.02)
Italy (Provincia Lazio)	0.11	(0.03)	-0.16	(0.05)	0.41	(0.04)	**-0.57**	(0.07)	**-1.07**	(0.04)	-0.11	(0.01)	0.36	(0.01)	**1.26**	(0.04)
Italy (Provincia Liguria)	0.10	(0.04)	-0.08	(0.08)	0.31	(0.04)	**-0.39**	(0.10)	**-1.04**	(0.05)	-0.12	(0.01)	0.35	(0.01)	**1.21**	(0.03)
Italy (Provincia Lombardia)	0.09	(0.04)	-0.08	(0.06)	0.28	(0.04)	**-0.36**	(0.07)	**-1.04**	(0.05)	-0.09	(0.01)	0.35	(0.01)	**1.13**	(0.02)
Italy (Provincia Marche)	-0.05	(0.06)	-0.23	(0.10)	0.16	(0.04)	**-0.39**	(0.11)	**-1.27**	(0.07)	-0.23	(0.01)	0.25	(0.01)	**1.06**	(0.04)
Italy (Provincia Molise)	0.12	(0.03)	-0.10	(0.05)	0.35	(0.04)	**-0.45**	(0.06)	**-1.06**	(0.05)	-0.07	(0.01)	0.38	(0.01)	**1.23**	(0.04)
Italy (Provincia Piemonte)	0.04	(0.04)	-0.16	(0.06)	0.22	(0.06)	**-0.38**	(0.08)	**-1.21**	(0.07)	-0.19	(0.01)	0.34	(0.01)	**1.20**	(0.03)
Italy (Provincia Puglia)	0.22	(0.03)	-0.02	(0.03)	0.45	(0.04)	**-0.47**	(0.05)	**-0.86**	(0.03)	0.02	(0.01)	0.47	(0.01)	**1.27**	(0.03)
Italy (Provincia Sardegna)	0.16	(0.04)	-0.04	(0.06)	0.34	(0.04)	**-0.37**	(0.06)	**-1.13**	(0.04)	-0.03	(0.01)	0.46	(0.01)	**1.32**	(0.04)
Italy (Provincia Sicilia)	0.27	(0.03)	0.06	(0.05)	0.47	(0.05)	**-0.41**	(0.06)	**-0.84**	(0.05)	0.05	(0.01)	0.50	(0.01)	**1.37**	(0.03)
Italy (Provincia Toscana)	0.13	(0.03)	-0.09	(0.04)	0.36	(0.04)	**-0.45**	(0.06)	**-1.07**	(0.03)	-0.06	(0.01)	0.41	(0.01)	**1.24**	(0.03)
Italy (Provincia Trento)	0.08	(0.04)	-0.11	(0.05)	0.28	(0.04)	**-0.39**	(0.07)	**-1.04**	(0.04)	-0.16	(0.01)	0.32	(0.01)	**1.19**	(0.03)
Italy (Provincia Umbria)	0.15	(0.03)	-0.03	(0.05)	0.32	(0.03)	**-0.35**	(0.05)	**-0.96**	(0.04)	-0.07	(0.01)	0.37	(0.01)	**1.25**	(0.03)
Italy (Provincia Valle d'Aosta)	0.03	(0.03)	-0.07	(0.04)	0.13	(0.04)	**-0.20**	(0.06)	**-1.15**	(0.04)	-0.20	(0.01)	0.32	(0.01)	**1.15**	(0.04)
Italy (Provincia Veneto)	0.07	(0.04)	-0.19	(0.07)	0.32	(0.04)	**-0.51**	(0.09)	**-1.13**	(0.06)	-0.15	(0.01)	0.36	(0.00)	**1.20**	(0.02)
United Kingdom (England)	0.06	(0.02)	-0.02	(0.02)	0.14	(0.02)	**-0.16**	(0.03)	**-1.09**	(0.02)	-0.18	(0.00)	0.32	(0.00)	**1.19**	(0.02)
United Kingdom (Northern Ireland)	0.12	(0.02)	-0.02	(0.04)	0.25	(0.03)	**-0.27**	(0.05)	**-1.07**	(0.03)	-0.13	(0.01)	0.39	(0.01)	**1.30**	(0.02)
United Kingdom (Wales)	0.08	(0.02)	-0.02	(0.03)	0.18	(0.03)	**-0.21**	(0.04)	**-1.09**	(0.03)	-0.20	(0.01)	0.34	(0.00)	**1.27**	(0.02)

Notes: Values that are statistically significant are indicated in bold (see Annex A3). See Table III.1.22 for national data.
StatLink ⫘ http://dx.doi.org/10.1787/888932343304

[Part 2/2]

Index of elaboration strategies and reading performance, by national quarters of this index

Table S.III.s · *Results based on students' self-reports*

| | Performance on the reading scale, by quarters of this index | | | | | | | | Change in the reading score per unit of this index | | Increased likelihood of students in the bottom quarter of this index scoring in the bottom quarter of the reading performance distribution | | Explained variance in student performance (r-squared x 100) | |
| | Bottom quarter | | Second quarter | | Third quarter | | Top quarter | | | | | | | |
	Mean index	S.E.	Mean index	S.E.	Mean index	S.E.	Mean index	S.E.	Effect	S.E.	Ratio	S.E.	%	S.E.
Adjudicated														
Belgium (Flemish Community)	**482**	(3.4)	521	(4.2)	536	(3.7)	559	(4.4)	**31.7**	(2.11)	**2.0**	(0.13)	9.6	(1.24)
Spain (Andalusia)	**410**	(7.5)	463	(5.8)	479	(6.0)	495	(6.2)	**31.0**	(2.52)	**2.8**	(0.25)	13.9	(2.25)
Spain (Aragon)	**453**	(6.8)	490	(5.1)	509	(4.6)	531	(4.1)	**29.1**	(2.29)	**2.2**	(0.21)	13.7	(2.13)
Spain (Asturias)	**442**	(6.5)	489	(6.1)	509	(6.6)	526	(6.2)	**29.2**	(3.06)	**2.4**	(0.31)	12.2	(2.31)
Spain (Balearic Islands)	**415**	(8.3)	454	(6.6)	476	(5.1)	493	(6.0)	**27.8**	(2.39)	**2.1**	(0.18)	10.7	(1.67)
Spain (Basque Country)	**454**	(4.3)	493	(3.8)	506	(3.4)	527	(2.9)	**29.2**	(1.74)	**2.2**	(0.14)	11.4	(1.33)
Spain (Canary Islands)	**408**	(7.7)	451	(6.4)	464	(5.3)	474	(5.8)	**21.6**	(2.53)	**2.0**	(0.21)	7.0	(1.58)
Spain (Cantabria)	**445**	(5.6)	483	(6.1)	505	(5.8)	521	(7.0)	**27.4**	(2.96)	**2.0**	(0.25)	10.3	(2.18)
Spain (Castile and Leon)	**461**	(7.0)	498	(6.4)	515	(5.0)	541	(5.7)	**29.2**	(1.90)	**2.3**	(0.23)	12.9	(1.62)
Spain (Catalonia)	**456**	(7.0)	492	(6.7)	516	(5.3)	530	(5.8)	**30.3**	(2.86)	**2.2**	(0.29)	13.6	(2.25)
Spain (Ceuta and Melilla)	**389**	(6.8)	408	(5.5)	425	(6.0)	440	(4.9)	**17.4**	(2.84)	**1.5**	(0.16)	3.2	(1.00)
Spain (Galicia)	**442**	(5.3)	477	(5.8)	509	(4.5)	518	(5.7)	**28.8**	(1.93)	**2.3**	(0.25)	13.2	(1.78)
Spain (La Rioja)	**452**	(6.0)	490	(5.9)	513	(6.4)	538	(5.1)	**31.9**	(2.69)	**2.2**	(0.29)	12.3	(1.80)
Spain (Madrid)	**468**	(7.9)	498	(5.6)	516	(6.6)	533	(6.5)	**26.2**	(3.93)	**2.0**	(0.23)	9.9	(2.88)
Spain (Murcia)	**456**	(6.1)	482	(4.7)	490	(6.3)	498	(8.3)	**16.2**	(2.64)	**1.7**	(0.21)	4.2	(1.29)
Spain (Navarre)	**453**	(5.9)	494	(4.8)	513	(4.3)	530	(5.8)	**30.1**	(2.95)	**2.4**	(0.26)	11.7	(2.15)
United Kingdom (Scotland)	**458**	(4.6)	497	(4.2)	511	(5.4)	540	(4.2)	**31.8**	(1.95)	**2.3**	(0.16)	11.0	(1.23)
Non-adjudicated														
Belgium (French Community)	**444**	(6.2)	494	(5.8)	517	(5.2)	536	(5.6)	**32.6**	(2.65)	**2.3**	(0.21)	10.2	(1.52)
Belgium (German-Speaking Community)	**457**	(5.8)	503	(5.2)	510	(5.5)	534	(7.1)	**27.4**	(3.50)	**2.4**	(0.32)	9.1	(2.36)
Finland (Finnish Speaking)	**506**	(3.6)	532	(3.4)	547	(3.2)	566	(3.7)	**25.0**	(1.65)	**1.9**	(0.12)	7.8	(1.03)
Finland (Swedish Speaking)	**474**	(5.1)	505	(6.2)	526	(5.3)	542	(4.4)	**30.9**	(2.37)	**2.1**	(0.23)	10.2	(1.49)
Italy (Provincia Abruzzo)	**447**	(6.7)	476	(8.1)	500	(5.7)	509	(6.0)	**25.3**	(3.65)	**2.1**	(0.24)	7.6	(1.95)
Italy (Provincia Autonoma di Bolzano)	**452**	(7.0)	490	(5.1)	504	(5.1)	515	(4.3)	**23.0**	(2.70)	**1.8**	(0.21)	5.8	(1.22)
Italy (Provincia Basilicata)	**434**	(7.8)	469	(6.0)	486	(5.8)	504	(5.2)	**29.2**	(3.30)	**2.3**	(0.24)	9.4	(1.90)
Italy (Provincia Calabria)	**411**	(8.2)	441	(6.8)	468	(7.7)	474	(5.9)	**28.3**	(3.69)	**2.2**	(0.20)	8.1	(1.99)
Italy (Provincia Campania)	**417**	(7.9)	449	(9.3)	459	(7.9)	482	(7.0)	**25.4**	(2.63)	**1.9**	(0.26)	5.9	(1.21)
Italy (Provincia Emilia Romagna)	**462**	(6.8)	496	(6.2)	520	(5.1)	537	(6.3)	**33.3**	(3.13)	**2.1**	(0.22)	10.5	(2.03)
Italy (Provincia Friuli Venezia Giulia)	**463**	(7.7)	514	(5.3)	528	(5.9)	550	(6.3)	**34.7**	(2.89)	**2.2**	(0.26)	13.6	(2.24)
Italy (Provincia Lazio)	**440**	(5.5)	478	(5.2)	495	(6.4)	514	(6.6)	**28.5**	(3.27)	**2.2**	(0.24)	9.3	(2.06)
Italy (Provincia Liguria)	**447**	(18.6)	483	(9.2)	515	(7.1)	521	(6.1)	**32.0**	(7.41)	**2.2**	(0.27)	10.4	(4.02)
Italy (Provincia Lombardia)	**484**	(8.8)	515	(7.1)	539	(7.3)	549	(9.1)	**30.9**	(5.30)	**1.9**	(0.28)	9.8	(3.28)
Italy (Provincia Marche)	**453**	(13.2)	501	(7.2)	513	(6.5)	530	(6.0)	**31.2**	(5.28)	**2.5**	(0.28)	11.1	(3.56)
Italy (Provincia Molise)	**435**	(6.3)	457	(5.6)	486	(5.4)	505	(5.0)	**29.5**	(2.88)	**1.9**	(0.23)	10.9	(1.87)
Italy (Provincia Piemonte)	**451**	(8.5)	502	(5.7)	512	(9.3)	522	(6.0)	**27.4**	(3.14)	**2.3**	(0.28)	8.5	(2.05)
Italy (Provincia Puglia)	**456**	(7.0)	483	(6.9)	506	(6.4)	515	(6.4)	**26.7**	(2.55)	**2.2**	(0.24)	7.9	(1.53)
Italy (Provincia Sardegna)	**430**	(6.1)	466	(5.1)	486	(6.1)	500	(6.4)	**27.7**	(2.69)	**2.0**	(0.21)	9.7	(1.76)
Italy (Provincia Sicilia)	**409**	(12.1)	447	(10.3)	480	(8.0)	487	(8.1)	**35.5**	(5.08)	**2.2**	(0.29)	11.3	(2.59)
Italy (Provincia Toscana)	**448**	(7.4)	484	(7.5)	515	(6.0)	530	(5.7)	**35.9**	(3.00)	**2.2**	(0.23)	13.1	(2.01)
Italy (Provincia Trento)	**468**	(6.4)	503	(6.3)	527	(6.6)	535	(6.2)	**29.7**	(2.99)	**2.0**	(0.25)	8.7	(1.77)
Italy (Provincia Umbria)	**447**	(8.0)	491	(6.4)	507	(6.2)	523	(7.2)	**32.0**	(3.76)	**2.1**	(0.21)	9.4	(2.22)
Italy (Provincia Valle d'Aosta)	**474**	(6.0)	509	(5.8)	531	(5.6)	543	(5.2)	**28.7**	(3.24)	**2.2**	(0.29)	9.9	(2.16)
Italy (Provincia Veneto)	**466**	(10.4)	499	(6.5)	520	(5.8)	540	(6.0)	**32.3**	(3.60)	**2.1**	(0.35)	12.2	(2.62)
United Kingdom (England)	**456**	(3.7)	495	(3.8)	514	(3.9)	520	(3.9)	**26.7**	(1.71)	**2.0**	(0.13)	7.2	(0.94)
United Kingdom (Northern Ireland)	**463**	(6.7)	496	(4.7)	513	(5.7)	531	(4.6)	**25.5**	(2.53)	**2.0**	(0.18)	6.6	(1.24)
United Kingdom (Wales)	**433**	(4.2)	472	(4.2)	495	(5.1)	509	(4.2)	**28.9**	(2.04)	**2.3**	(0.15)	9.1	(1.11)

Notes: Values that are statistically significant are indicated in bold (see Annex A3). See Table III.1.22 for national data.

StatLink ⟲ http://dx.doi.org/10.1787/888932343304

Annex C

THE DEVELOPMENT AND IMPLEMENTATION OF PISA – A COLLABORATIVE EFFORT

INTRODUCTION

PISA is a collaborative effort, bringing together scientific expertise from the participating countries, steered jointly by their governments on the basis of shared, policy-driven interests.

A PISA Governing Board on which each country is represented determines, in the context of OECD objectives, the policy priorities for PISA and oversees adherence to these priorities during the implementation of the programme. This includes the setting of priorities for the development of indicators, for the establishment of the assessment instruments and for the reporting of the results.

Experts from participating countries also serve on working groups that are charged with linking policy objectives with the best internationally available technical expertise. By participating in these expert groups, countries ensure that the instruments are internationally valid and take into account the cultural and educational contexts in OECD Member countries, the assessment materials have strong measurement properties, and the instruments place an emphasis on authenticity and educational validity.

Through National Project Managers, participating countries implement PISA at the national level subject to the agreed administration procedures. National Project Managers play a vital role in ensuring that the implementation of the survey is of high quality, and verify and evaluate the survey results, analyses, reports and publications.

The design and implementation of the surveys, within the framework established by the PISA Governing Board, is the responsibility of external contractors. For PISA 2009, the questionnaire development was carried out by a consortium led by Cito International in partnership with the University of Twente. The development and implementation of the cognitive assessment and of the international options was carried out by a consortium led by the Australian Council for Educational Research (ACER). Other partners in this consortium include cApStAn Linguistic Quality Control in Belgium, the *Deutsches Institut für Internationale Pädagogische Forschung* (DIPF) in Germany, the National Institute for Educational Policy Research in Japan (NIER), the *Unité d'analyse des systèmes et des pratiques d'enseignement* (aSPe) in Belgium and WESTAT in the United States.

The OECD Secretariat has overall managerial responsibility for the programme, monitors its implementation on a day-to-day basis, acts as the secretariat for the PISA Governing Board, builds consensus among countries and serves as the interlocutor between the PISA Governing Board and the international consortium charged with the implementation of the activities. The OECD Secretariat also produces the indicators and analyses and prepares the international reports and publications in co-operation with the PISA consortium and in close consultation with Member countries both at the policy level (PISA Governing Board) and at the level of implementation (National Project Managers).

The following lists the members of the various PISA bodies and the individual experts and consultants who have contributed to PISA.

Members of the PISA Governing Board
Chair: Lorna Bertrand

OECD countries
Australia: Tony Zanderigo

Austria: Mark Német

Belgium: Christiane Blondin, Isabelle Erauw and Micheline Scheys

Canada: Pierre Brochu, Patrick Bussière and Tomasz Gluszynski

Chile: Leonor Cariola

Czech Republic: Jana Strakova

Denmark: Tine Bak

Estonia: Maie Kitsing

Finland: Jari Rajanen

France: Bruno Trosseille

Germany: Annemarie Klemm, Maximilian Müller-Härlin and Elfriede Ohrnberger

Greece: Panagiotis Kazantzis (1/7/05 – 31/03/10) Vassilia Hatzinikita (from 31/03/10)

Hungary: Benő Csapó

Iceland: Júlíus K. Björnsson

Ireland: Jude Cosgrove

Israel: Michal Beller

Italy: Piero Cipollone

Japan: Ryo Watanabe

Korea: Whan Sik Kim

Luxembourg: Michel Lanners

Mexico: Francisco Ciscomani

Netherlands: Paul van Oijen

New Zealand: Lynne Whitney

Norway: Anne-Berit Kavli

Poland: Stanislaw Drzazdzewski

Portugal: Carlos Pinto Ferreira

Slovak Republic: Julius Hauser, Romana Kanovska and Paulina Korsnakova

Slovenia: Andreja Barle Lakota

Spain: Carme Amorós Basté and Enrique Roca Cobo

Sweden: Anita Wester

Switzerland: Ariane Baechler Söderström and Heinz Rhyn

Turkey: Meral Alkan

United Kingdom: Lorna Bertrand and Mal Cooke

United States: Daniel McGrath and Eugene Owen

Observers
Albania: Ndricim Mehmeti

Argentina: Liliana Pascual

Azerbaijan: Talib Sharifov

Brazil: Joaquim José Soares Neto

Bulgaria: Neda Kristanova

Colombia: Margarita Peña

Croatia: Michelle Braš-Roth

Dubai (United Arab Emirates): Mariam Al Ali

Hong Kong-China: Esther Sui-chu Ho

Indonesia: Mansyur Ramli

Jordan: Khattab Mohammad Abulibdeh

Kazakhstan: Yermekov Nurmukhammed Turlynovich

Kyrgyz Republic: Inna Valkova

Latvia: Andris Kangro

Liechtenstein: Christian Nidegger

Lithuania: Rita Dukynaitė

Macao-China: Kwok-cheung Cheung

Montegegro: Zeljko Jacimovic

Panama: Arturo Rivera

Peru: Liliana Miranda Molina

Qatar: Adel Sayed

Romania: Roxana Mihail

Russian Federation: Galina Kovalyova

Serbia: Dragica Pavlovic Babic

Shanghai-China: Minxuan Zhang

Singapore: Low Khah Gek

Chinese Taipei: Chih-Wei Hue and Fou-Lai Lin

Thailand: Precharn Dechsri

Trinidad and Tobago: Harrilal Seecharan

Tunisia: Kameleddine Gaha

Uruguay: Andrés Peri

PISA 2009 National Project Managers

Albania: Alfonso Harizaj

Argentina: Antonio Gutiérrez

Australia: Sue Thomson

Austria: Ursula Schwantner

Azerbaijan: Emin Meherremov

Belgium: Ariane Baye and Inge De Meyer

Brazil: Sheyla Carvalho Lira

Bulgaria: Svetla Petrova

Canada: Pierre Brochu and Tamara Knighton

Chile: Ema Lagos

Chinese Taipei: Pi-Hsia Hung

Colombia: Francisco Ernesto Reyes

Croatia: Michelle Braš Roth

Czech Republic: Jana Paleckova

Denmark: Niels Egelund

Dubai (United Arab Emirates): Mariam Al Ali

Estonia: Gunda Tire

Finland: Jouni Välijärvi

France: Sylvie Fumel

Germany: Nina Jude and Eckhard Klieme

Greece: Panagiotis Kazantzis (from 1/7/05 to 18/11/08)
Chryssa Sofianopoulou (from 18/11/08)

Hong Kong-China: Esther Sui-chu Ho

Hungary: Ildikó Balázsi

Iceland: Almar Midvik Halldorsson

Indonesia: Burhanuddin Tola

Ireland: Rachel Perkins

Israel: Inbal Ron Kaplan and Joel Rapp

Italy: Laura Palmerio

Japan: Ryo Watanabe

Jordan: Khattab Mohammad Abulibdeh

Kazakhstan: Damitov Bazar Kabdoshevich

Korea: Kyung-Hee Kim

Kyrgyz Republic: Inna Valkova

Latvia: Andris Kangro

Liechtenstein: Christian Nidegger

Lithuania: Jolita Dudaitė

Luxembourg: Bettina Boehm

Macao-China: Kwok-cheung Cheung

Mexico: María-Antonieta Díaz-Gutiérrez

Montenegro: Verica Ivanovic

Netherlands: Erna Gille

New Zealand: Maree Telford

Norway: Marit Kjaernsli

Panama: Zoila Castillo

Peru: Liliana Miranda Molina

Poland: Michal Federowicz

Portugal: Anabela Serrão

Qatar: Asaad Tounakti

Romania: Silviu Cristian Mirescu

Russian Federation: Galina Kovalyova

Serbia: Dragica Pavlovic Babic

Shanghai-China: Jing Lu and MinXuan Zhang

Singapore: Chia Siang Hwa and Poon Chew Leng

Slovak Republic: Paulina Korsnakova

Slovenia: Mojca Straus

Spain: Lis Cercadillo

Sweden: Karl-Göran Karlsson

Switzerland: Christian Nidegger

Thailand: Sunee Klainin

Trinidad and Tobago: Harrilal Seecharan

Tunisia: Kameleddine Gaha

Turkey: Müfide Çaliskan

United Kingdom: Jenny Bradshaw and Mal Cooke

United States: Dana Kelly and Holly Xie

Uruguay: María Sánchez

OECD Secretariat

Andreas Schleicher (Overall co-ordination of PISA and partner country/economy relations)

Marilyn Achiron (Editorial support)

Marika Boiron (Editorial support)

Simone Bloem (Analytic services)

Francesca Borgonovi (Analytic services)

Niccolina Clements (Editorial support)

Michael Davidson (Project management and analytic services)

Juliet Evans (Administration and partner country/economy relations)

Miyako Ikeda (Analytic services)

Maciej Jakubowski (Analytic services)

Guillermo Montt (Analytic services)

Diana Morales (Administrative support)

Soojin Park (Analytic services)

Mebrak Tareke (Editorial support)

Sophie Vayssettes (Analytic services)

Elisabeth Villoutreix (Editorial support)

Karin Zimmer (Project management)

Pablo Zoido (Analytic services)

PISA Expert Groups for PISA 2009

Reading Expert Group

Irwin Kirsch (Education Testing Service, New Jersey, USA)

Sachiko Adachi (Nigata University, Japan)

Charles Alderson (Lancaster University, UK)

John de Jong (Language Testing Services, Netherlands)

John Guthrie (University of Maryland, USA)

Dominique Lafontaine (University of Liège, Belgium)

Minwoo Nam (Korea Institute of Curriculum and Evaluation)

Jean-François Rouet (University of Poitiers, France)

Wolfgang Schnotz (University of Koblenz-Landau, Germany)

Eduardo Vidal-Abarca (University of Valencia, Spain

Mathematics Expert Group

Jan de Lange (Chair) (Utrecht University, Netherlands)

Werner Blum (University of Kassel, Germany)

John Dossey (Illinois State University, USA)

Zbigniew Marciniak (University of Warsaw, Poland)

Mogens Niss (University of Roskilde, Denmark)

Yoshinori Shimizu (University of Tsukuba, Japan)

Science Expert Group

Rodger Bybee (Chair) (BSCS, Colorado Springs, USA)

Peter Fensham (Queensland University of Technology, Australia)

Svein Lie (University of Oslo, Norway)

Yasushi Ogura (National Institute for Educational Policy Research, Japan)

Manfred Prenzel (University of Kiel, Germany)

Andrée Tiberghien (University of Lyon, France)

Questionnaire Expert Group

Jaap Scheerens (Chair) (University of Twente, Netherlands

Pascal Bressoux (Pierre Mendès University, France)

Yin Cheong Cheng (Hong Kong Institute of Education, Hong Kong-China)

David Kaplan (University of Wisconsin – Madison, USA)

Eckhard Klieme (DIPF, Germany)

Henry Levin (Columbia University, USA)

Pirjo Linnakylä (University of Jyväskylä, Finland)

Ludger Wößmann (University of Munich, Germany)

PISA Technical Advisory Group

Keith Rust (Chair) (Westat, USA)

Ray Adams (ACER)

John de Jong (Language Testing Services, Netherlands)

Cees Glas (University of Twente, Netherlands)

Aletta Grisay (Consultant, Saint-Maurice, France)

David Kaplan (University of Wisconsin – Madison, USA)

Christian Monseur (University of Liège, Belgium)

Sophia Rabe-Hesketh (University of California – Berkeley, USA)

Thierry Rocher (Ministry of Education, France)

Norman Verhelst (CITO, Netherlands)

Kentaro Yamamoto (ETS, New Jersey, USA)

Rebecca Zwick (University of California – Santa Barbara, USA)

PISA 2009 Consortium for questionnaire development

Cito International

Johanna Kordes

Hans Kuhlemeier

Astrid Mols

Henk Moelands

José Noijons

University of Twente

Cees Glas

Khurrem Jehangir

Jaap Scheerens

PISA 2009 Consortium for the development and implementation of the cognitive assessment and international options

Australian Council for Educational Research

Ray Adams (Director of the PISA 2009 Consortium)

Susan Bates (Project administration)

Alla Berezner (Data management and analysis)

Yan Bibby (Data processing and analysis)

Esther Brakey (Administrative support)

Wei Buttress (Project administration and quality monitoring)

Renee Chow (Data processing and analysis)

Judith Cosgrove (Data processing and analysis and national centre support)

John Cresswell (Reporting and dissemination)

Alex Daraganov (Data processing and analysis)

Daniel Duckworth (Reading instruments and test development)

Kate Fitzgerald (Data processing and sampling)

Daniel Fullarton (IT services)

Eveline Gebhardt (Data processing and analysis)

Mee-Young Handayani (Data processing and analysis)

Elizabeth Hersbach (Quality assurance)

Sam Haldane (IT services and computer-based assessment)

Karin Hohlfield (Reading instruments and test development)

Jennifer Hong (Data processing and sampling)

Tony Huang (Project administration and IT services)

Madelaine Imber (Reading instruments and administrative support)

Nora Kovarcikova (Survey operations)

Winson Lam (IT services)

Tom Lumley (Print and electronic reading instruments and test development)

Greg Macaskill (Data management and processing and sampling)

Ron Martin (Science instruments and test development)

Barry McCrae (Electronic Reading Assessment manager, science instruments and test development)

Juliette Mendelovits (Print and electronic reading instruments and test development)

Martin Murphy (Field operations and sampling)

Thoa Nguyen (Data processing and analysis)

Penny Pearson (Administrative support)

Anna Plotka (Graphic design)

Alla Routitsky (Data management and processing)

Wolfram Schulz (Management and data analysis)

Dara Searle (Print and electronic reading instruments and test development)

Naoko Tabata (Survey operations)

Ross Turner (Management, mathematics instruments and test development)

Daniel Urbach (Data processing and analysis)

Eva Van de gaer (Data analysis)

Charlotte Waters (Project administration, data processing and analysis)

Maurice Walker (Electronic Reading Assessment and sampling)

Wahyu Wardono (Project administration and IT services)

Louise Wenn (Data processing and analysis)

Yan Wiwecka (IT services)

Westat

Eugene Brown (Weighting)

Fran Cohen (Weighting)

Susan Fuss (Sampling and weighting)

Amita Gopinath (Weighting)

Sheila Krawchuk (Sampling, weighting and quality monitoring)

Thanh Le (Sampling, weighting, and quality monitoring)

Jane Li (Sampling and weighting)

John Lopdell (Sampling and weighting)

Shawn Lu (Weighting)

Keith Rust (Director of the PISA Consortium for sampling and weighting)

William Wall (Weighting)

Erin Wilson (Sampling and weighting)

Marianne Winglee (Weighting)

Sergey Yagodin (Weighting)

The National Institute for Educational Research in Japan

Hidefumi Arimoto (Reading instruments and test development)

Hisashi Kawai (Reading instruments and test development)

cApStAn Linguistic Quality Control

Steve Dept (Translation and verification operations)

Andrea Ferrari (Translation and verification methodology)

Laura Wäyrynen (Verification management)

Unité d'analyse des systèmes et des pratiques d'enseignement (aSPe)

Ariane Baye (Print reading and electronic reading instruments and test development)

Casto Grana-Monteirin (Translation and verification)

Dominique Lafontaine (Member of the Reading Expert Group)

Christian Monseur (Data analysis and member of the TAG)

Anne Matoul (Translation and verification)

Patricia Schillings (Print reading and electronic reading instruments and test development)

Deutsches Institut für Internationale Pädagogische Forschung (DIPF)

Cordula Artelt (University of Bamberg) (Reading instruments and framework development)

Michel Dorochevsky (Softcon) (Software Development)

Frank Goldhammer (Electronic reading instruments and test development)

Dieter Heyer (Softcon) (Software Development)

Nina Jude (Electronic reading instruments and test development)

Eckhard Klieme (Project Co-Director at DIPF)

Holger Martin (Softcon) (Software Development)

Johannes Naumann (Electronic reading instruments and test development)

Jean-Paul Reeff (International Consultant)

Heiko Roelke (Project Co-Director at DIPF)

Wolfgang Schneider (University of Würzburg) (Reading instruments and framework development)

Petra Stanat (Humboldt University, Berlin) (Reading instruments and test development)

Britta Upsing (Electronic reading instruments and test development)

Other experts

Tobias Dörfler, (University of Bamberg) (Reading instrument development)

Tove Stjern Frønes (ILS, University of Oslo) (Reading instrument development)

Béatrice Halleux (Consultant, HallStat SPRL) (Translation/verification referee and French source development)

Øystein Jetne (ILS, University of Oslo) (Print reading and electronic reading instruments and test development)

Kees Lagerwaard (Institute for Educational Measurement of Netherlands) (Math instrument development)

Pirjo Linnakylä (University of Jyväskylä) (Reading instrument development)

Anne-Laure Monnier (Consultant, France) (French source development)

Jan Mejding (Danish Schoool of Education, University of Aarhus) (Print reading and electronic reading development)

Eva Kristin Narvhus (ILS, University of Oslo) (Print reading and electronic reading instruments, test instruments and test development)

Rolf V. Olsen (ILS, University of Oslo) (Science instrument development)

Robert Laurie (New Brunswick Department of Education, Canada) (Science instrument development)

Astrid Roe (ILS, University of Oslo) (Print reading and electronic reading instruments and test development)

Hanako Senuma (University of Tamagawa, Japan) (Math instrument development)

Other contributors to this publication

Fung-Kwan Tam (Layout)

ORGANISATION FOR ECONOMIC CO-OPERATION AND DEVELOPMENT

The OECD is a unique forum where governments work together to address the economic, social and environmental challenges of globalisation. The OECD is also at the forefront of efforts to understand and to help governments respond to new developments and concerns, such as corporate governance, the information economy and the challenges of an ageing population. The Organisation provides a setting where governments can compare policy experiences, seek answers to common problems, identify good practice and work to co-ordinate domestic and international policies.

The OECD member countries are: Australia, Austria, Belgium, Canada, Chile, the Czech Republic, Denmark, Finland, France, Germany, Greece, Hungary, Iceland, Ireland, Israel, Italy, Japan, Korea, Luxembourg, Mexico, the Netherlands, New Zealand, Norway, Poland, Portugal, the Slovak Republic, Slovenia, Spain, Sweden, Switzerland, Turkey, the United Kingdom and the United States. The European Commission takes part in the work of the OECD.

OECD Publishing disseminates widely the results of the Organisation's statistics gathering and research on economic, social and environmental issues, as well as the conventions, guidelines and standards agreed by its members.

OECD PUBLISHING, 2, rue André-Pascal, 75775 PARIS CEDEX 16
(98 2010 09 1 P) ISBN 978-92-64-09147-4 – No. 57729 2010